A HISTORY OF ENGLAND

A HISTORY OF ENGLAND

From the Coming of the English to 1918

BY

KEITH FEILING

BOOK CLUB ASSOCIATES

Printed in Great Britain by
Redwood Burn Limited, Trowbridge & Esher

PREFACE

MORE than one 'History of England' exists of lasting value as an individual interpretation or commentary. The primary purpose of this book is a different one; to tell the story, so far as may be in the space of one volume, in a narrative form, and to lay the emphasis on the period within which Britain became a great Power.

No narrative, perhaps, has ever yet taken the place of John Richard Green's momentous *Short History*, first published by Messrs. Macmillan's in 1874. Since that date, however, a multiplication of sources, a vast amount of research, and a line of great scholars in all countries, have qualified and often reversed Green's conclusions, sometimes on fundamental points, such as the Saxon settlements, the nature of feudalism, or the fifteenth century. Green's pen, moreover, faltered after reaching 1688; his own contribution stopped at 1815, — an epilogue on the nineteenth century being only added by his widow in 1916; and he almost ignored the history of the Empire overseas. On such matters I have tried to indicate the changed outlook of modern scholarship.

The bibliography makes no attempt to tabulate the material, original and secondary, on which this book is based, but merely suggests a short list of books for varied reading in each section. And the tables of dates attached are, as they must be, similarly restricted or arbitrary; yet may serve their purpose, I hope, of reminder or suggestion.

If this book deserved such a dedication, it should be to my pupils, living and dead, at Christ Church, Oxford.

KEITH FEILING

OXFORD,
Christmas, 1948

CONTENTS

BOOK III

IN TRANSITION
1360–1509

BOOK IV

MAKING OF MODERN ENGLAND
1509–1660

BOOK V

EQUILIBRIUM
1660–1760

BOOK VI

INDUSTRY AND EMPIRE
1760–1852

BOOK VII

A GREAT POWER
1852–1918

AFTERMATH
1919–1938

LIST OF MAPS

GENEALOGICAL TABLES

GENEALOGICAL TABLES

SUPREMACY OF NORTHUMBRIA

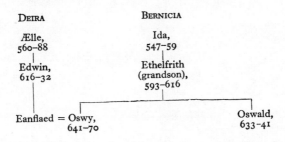

DEIRA

BERNICIA

Ælle,
560–88

Ida,
547–59

Edwin,
616–32

Ethelfrith
(grandson),
593–616

Eanflaed = Oswy,
641–70

Oswald,
633–41

KINGS OF MERCIA

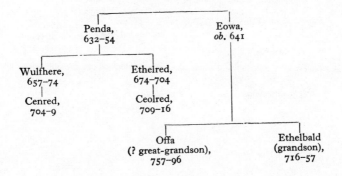

Penda,
632–54

Eowa,
ob. 641

Wulfhere,
657–74

Ethelred,
674–704

Cenred,
704–9

Ceolred,
709–16

Offa
(? great-grandson),
757–96

Ethelbald
(grandson),
716–57

SUPREMACY OF WESSEX

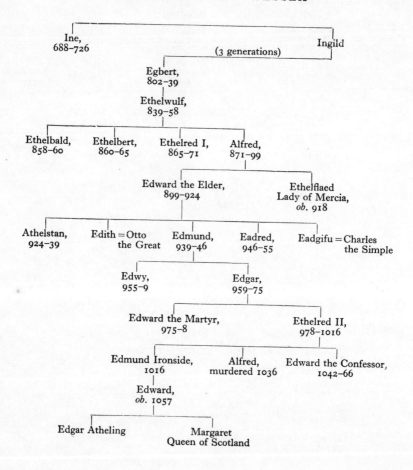

DANES AND NORMANS

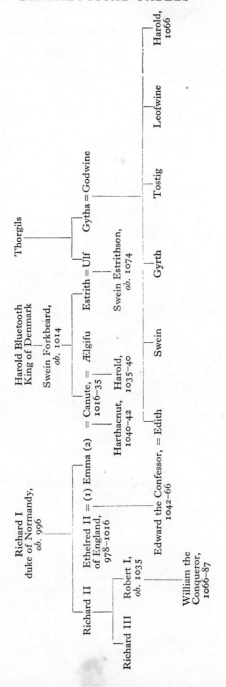

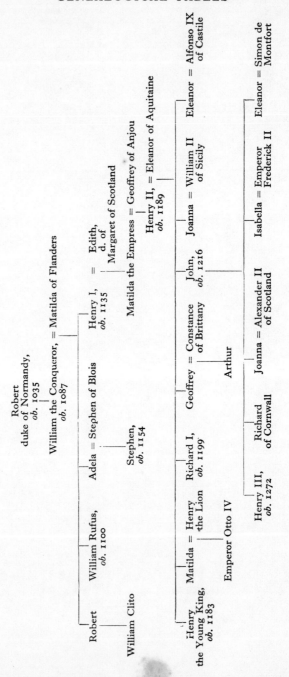

NORMANS AND ANGEVINS

Robert
duke of Normandy,
ob. 1035
|
William the Conqueror, = Matilda of Flanders
ob. 1087

Robert

William Rufus,
ob. 1100

Adela = Stephen of Blois

Stephen,
ob. 1154

Henry I, = Edith,
ob. 1135   d. of
Margaret of Scotland

Matilda the Empress = Geoffrey of Anjou

Henry II, = Eleanor of Aquitaine
ob. 1189

William Clito

Henry
the Young King,
ob. 1183

Matilda = Henry
the Lion

Emperor Otto IV

Richard I,
ob. 1199

Geoffrey = Constance
of Brittany

Arthur

John,
ob. 1216

Joanna = William II
of Sicily

Eleanor = Alfonso IX
of Castile

Henry III,
ob. 1272

Richard
of Cornwall

Joanna = Alexander II
of Scotland

Isabella = Emperor
Frederick II

Eleanor = Simon de
Montfort

CLARE AND GLOUCESTER

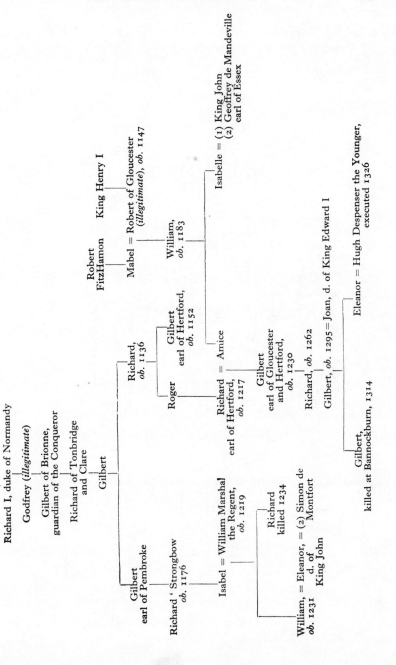

PLANTAGENETS

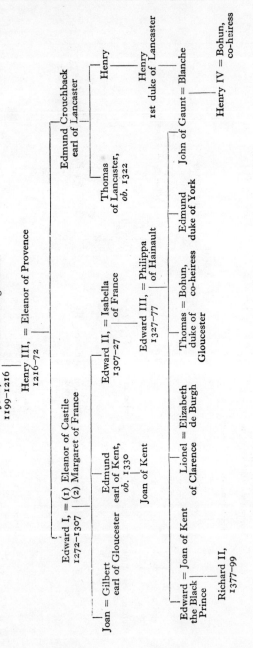

THE CROWN OF SCOTLAND

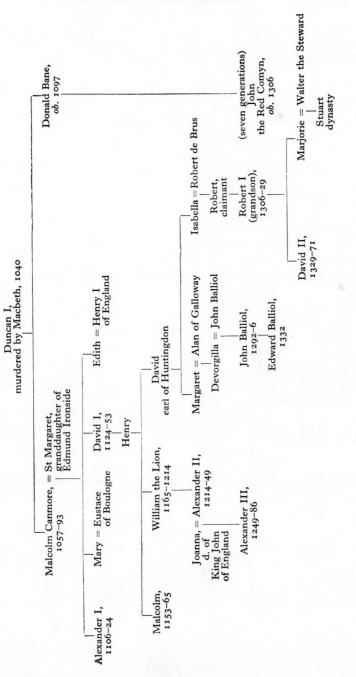

LANCASTER AND YORK

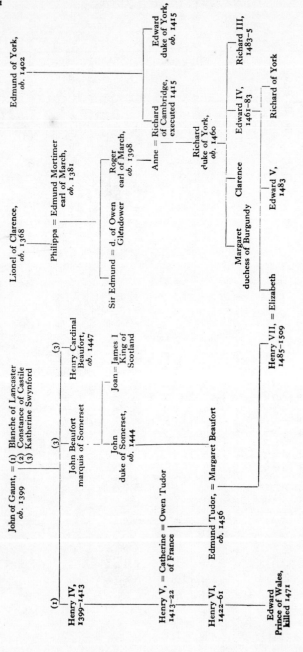

NEVILLE, PERCY, AND MORTIMER

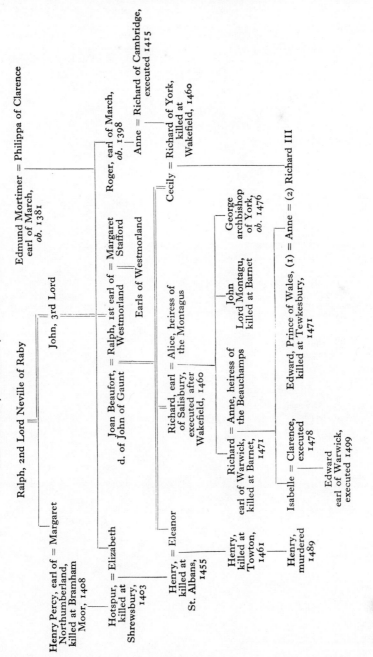

THE RIVAL DYNASTIES:

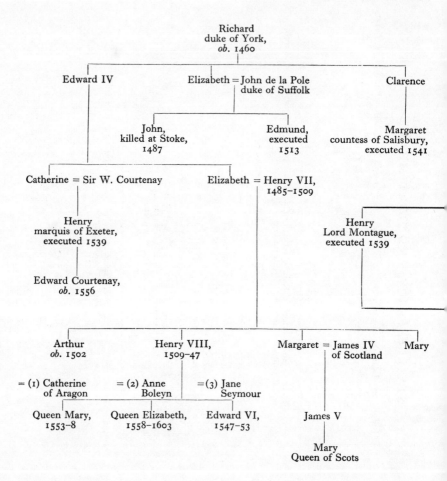

Richard
duke of York,
ob. 1460

Edward IV   Elizabeth = John de la Pole   Clarence
duke of Suffolk

John,   Edmund,   Margaret
killed at Stoke,   executed   countess of Salisbury,
1487   1513   executed 1541

Catherine = Sir W. Courtenay   Elizabeth = Henry VII,
1485-1509

Henry   Henry
marquis of Exeter,   Lord Montague,
executed 1539   executed 1539

Edward Courtenay,
ob. 1556

Arthur   Henry VIII,   Margaret = James IV   Mary
ob. 1502   1509-47   of Scotland

= (1) Catherine   = (2) Anne   =(3) Jane
of Aragon   Boleyn   Seymour

Queen Mary,   Queen Elizabeth,   Edward VI,   James V
1553-8   1558-1603   1547-53

Mary
Queen of Scots

16TH CENTURY

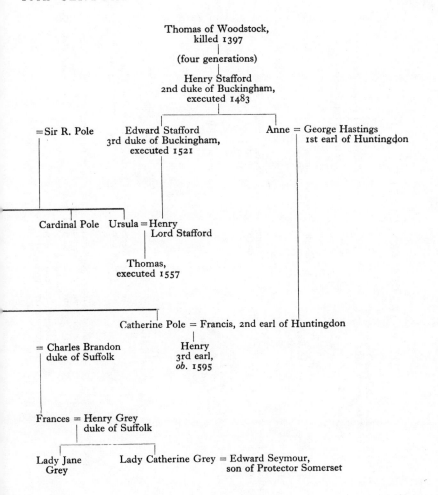

Thomas of Woodstock,
killed 1397

(four generations)

Henry Stafford
2nd duke of Buckingham,
executed 1483

= Sir R. Pole   Edward Stafford   Anne = George Hastings
3rd duke of Buckingham,   1st earl of Huntingdon
executed 1521

Cardinal Pole Ursula = Henry
Lord Stafford

Thomas,
executed 1557

Catherine Pole = Francis, 2nd earl of Huntingdon

= Charles Brandon   Henry
duke of Suffolk   3rd earl,
ob. 1595

Frances = Henry Grey
duke of Suffolk

Lady Jane   Lady Catherine Grey = Edward Seymour,
Grey   son of Protector Somerset

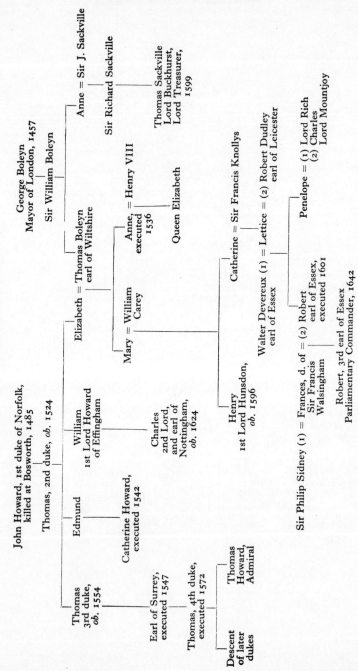

THE ELIZABETHAN CIRCLE

THE HOUSE OF STUART

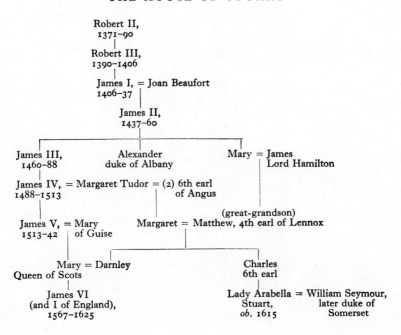

Robert II,
1371–90

Robert III,
1390–1406

James I, = Joan Beaufort
1406–37

James II,
1437–60

James III,   Alexander   Mary = James
1460–88   duke of Albany   Lord Hamilton

James IV, = Margaret Tudor = (2) 6th earl
1488–1513   of Angus

(great-grandson)

James V, = Mary   Margaret = Matthew, 4th earl of Lennox
1513–42   of Guise

Mary = Darnley   Charles
Queen of Scots   6th earl

James VI   Lady Arabella = William Seymour,
(and I of England),   Stuart,   later duke of
1567–1625   ob. 1615   Somerset

THE ROYAL HOUSE, 17TH CENTURY

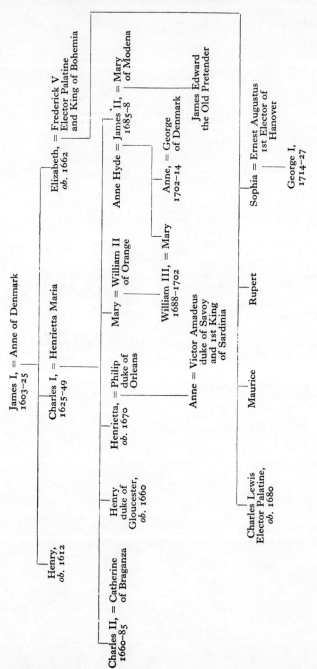

[GENEALOGICAL TABLES *continued overleaf*

THE OPPOSITIO

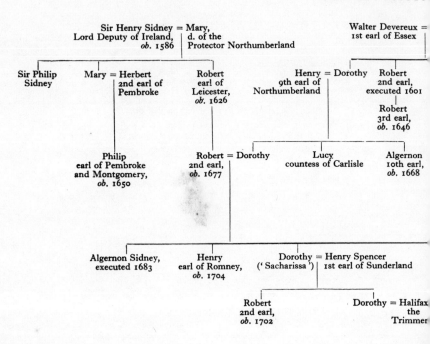

[GENEALOGICAL TABLES *continued overleaf*

THE OPPOSITIO

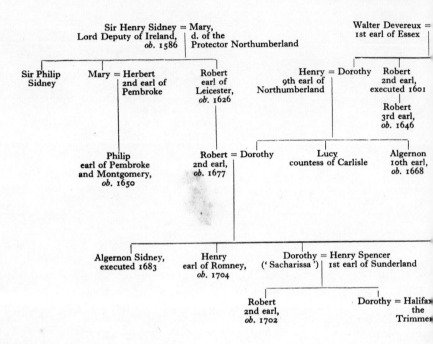

MAGNATES: 17TH CENTURY

Lettice Knollys

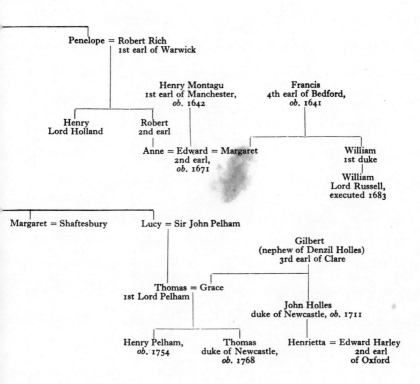

```
Penelope = Robert Rich
           1st earl of Warwick
```

```
                    Henry Montagu                    Francis
                    1st earl of Manchester,          4th earl of Bedford,
                         ob. 1642                         ob. 1641

    Henry            Robert
Lord Holland         2nd earl
              Anne = Edward = Margaret                    William
                     2nd earl,                            1st duke
                     ob. 1671
                                                          William
                                                      Lord Russell,
                                                      executed 1683
```

```
Margaret = Shaftesbury          Lucy = Sir John Pelham
                                                 Gilbert
                                        (nephew of Denzil Holles)
                                           3rd earl of Clare

                          Thomas = Grace
                      1st Lord Pelham       John Holles
                                         duke of Newcastle, ob. 1711

          Henry Pelham,           Thomas          Henrietta = Edward Harley
             ob. 1754         duke of Newcastle,                2nd earl
                                  ob. 1768                      of Oxford
```

ley

THE SPANISH SUCCESSION

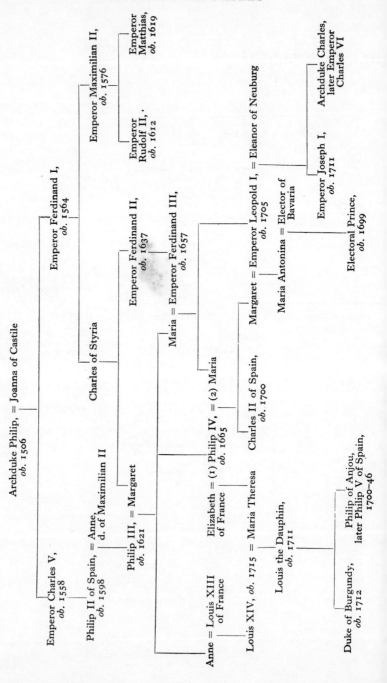

THE HOUSE OF HANOVER

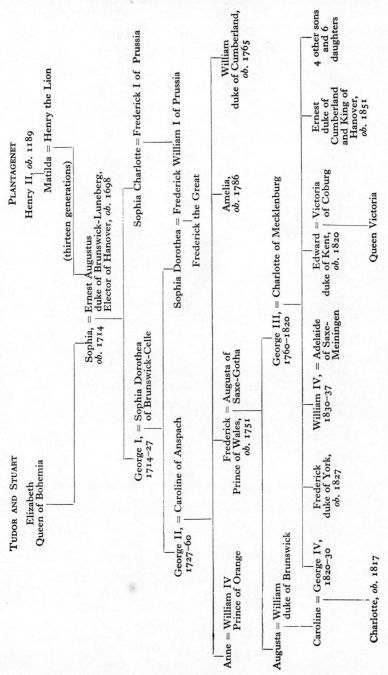

TUDOR AND STUART

PLANTAGENET

Henry II, *ob.* 1189

Matilda = Henry the Lion

Elizabeth
Queen of Bohemia

(thirteen generations)

Sophia, = Ernest Augustus
duke of Brunswick-Luneberg,
Elector of Hanover, *ob.* 1698

Sophia Charlotte = Frederick I of Prussia

George I, = Sophia Dorothea
1714–27   of Brunswick-Celle

Sophia Dorothea = Frederick William I of Prussia

Frederick the Great

George II, = Caroline of Anspach
1727–60

Frederick = Augusta of
Prince of Wales,   Saxe-Gotha
ob. 1751

Amelia,
ob. 1786

William
duke of Cumberland,
ob. 1765

George III, = Charlotte of Mecklenburg
1760–1820

Anne = William IV
Prince of Orange

Augusta = William
duke of Brunswick

Caroline = George IV,
1820–30

Frederick
duke of York,
ob. 1827

William IV, = Adelaide
1830–37   of Saxe-
Meiningen

Edward = Victoria
duke of Kent,   of Coburg
ob. 1820

Ernest
duke of
Cumberland
and King of
Hanover,
ob. 1851

4 other sons
and 6
daughters

Charlotte, *ob.* 1817

Queen Victoria

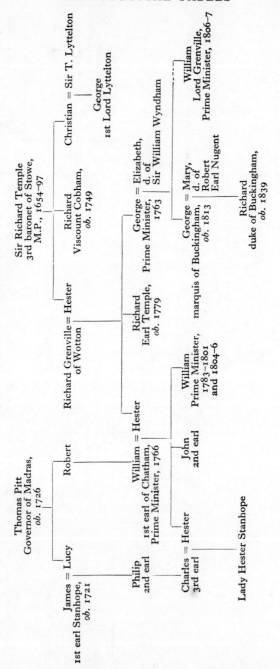

GRENVILLES AND PITTS

PRELUDE

BRITAIN BEFORE THE ROMANS

NATIONAL history only begins when a people is recognizable as a community or group of communities, settled within geographical bounds that can be defined, and distinguished from others by a rule, a livelihood, and arts of its own. If some such boundaries be accepted between history and pre-history, we are not here concerned with the first immense periods that geology records. We cannot speak of ' Britain ' when it was not an island at all, either when it made part of some long-drowned western ' Atlantis ', or when later the Thames was tributary to a Rhine system and the North Sea was a mass of fens and islets. We cannot read its history when, in ages defying exact measurement, it passed through extremes both of heat and cold, which have left behind evidence that sometimes elephant, lion, and rhinoceros, and at others the mammoth, reindeer, and elk disputed life with man. We believe, indeed, that we can prove the existence of human beings through those tracts of time, shaping flint weapons, fighting cave-hyenas and bears, and scratching sketches of the human form in some Derbyshire cave, but we know little more. Even far into historic times, after 2000 B.C., there were profound changes from a warm climate to an air more moist and cold, together with tiltings and submergings of the south-east regions, which covered with fen or peat some areas where men before had lived, and left forests buried beneath the sea. For anything like agreed fact, or contribution to the historic future, our story begins in the age, from 3000 B.C. onwards, of Neolithic man.

When earthquake and volcanic action and glaciers had finished their work, and our rivers had found something like their modern level, laying down their gravel beds or forming swamps fringed by dense scrub and haunted by beavers, we are left with the familiar twofold division of Britain. A line roughly drawn from Durham to Exeter marks the frontier between the north-western hills and the south-east plain, upon which in all ages our inner history has turned. Broken by one gap at the Severn estuary, and another in the damp country leading to the Mersey and Dee, the line passes where the older rock formations raise a barrier, sometimes two thousand feet above sea level, as on Dartmoor, in the Welsh March, and the Pennine chain. South and east are the newer and softer limestones which run from the Cotswolds to the East Riding, the chalk plateau that radiates in all directions from Salisbury

Plain, and then the sands, gravels, and river deposits.

Geology, thus lowering this plain down towards the sea, had also in making North Sea and Channel left like gazing at like over the water; the Rhine, Somme, and Seine looking into the Humber, Wash, and Thames, while the Breton peninsula, the Loire, and capes of Spain pointed to Dover, the harbourages of Southampton Water, and the western voyage round the Lizard. Here lay the inviting routes for invasions which, many times over, seem to have run much the same predestined course. Steering in their dug-out canoes far into the country by easy inlets, and then taking the upland drier tracks, they would conquer or drive before them the previous occupants of those lowlands, imposing on them something new. They would halt at, or skirt with dislike, the Midland forests; finally, they would be arrested by the rock barriers. Here the cultures successively displaced by waves of conquerors could find refuge, and the new world painfully and very slowly fuse with the old, which at its back had rival influences derived from Ireland; out of which fusion would emerge something very different from the pattern triumphant in the coastal plain.

Till the first century before Christ, substantially all invaders seem to have followed much the same objective. Though some would stay to fish and fowl by rivers and estuaries, the mass would seek at all costs to get away from the forests they dreaded, from oak and ash which their weapons could not cut, and from clays and water-logged soils where their beasts would fare ill. They wanted room, dry grazing, and good water. The higher hills they found useful for refuge camps and summer pasture, but in general they made for the higher fringes of the lowland plain, and throughout, therefore, relics of their dwelling-places, their tombs and ornaments, have been found thickest on the Thames gravel terraces, chalk downs of northern Wessex, the porous water-bearing ridges which stretch from the Severn to east Yorkshire, or the East Anglian heaths. In such regions, connected by trackways of unknown antiquity, and above all in the Salisbury Plain centre, lay the heart of the first historic England.

All our efforts to distinguish more nearly either dates or racial movement must be subject to guess-work and historic accident. Our first written evidence is very much later, coming (and then only indirectly) from the Greek Pytheas of Marseilles, who explored these coasts about 325 B.C., and we, therefore, depend on what archaeology can make of camps and hut-circles, metal weapons and ornaments and pottery, or on anthropology's deduction from discovered skeletons and later human types, or the verdict of philology as regards development in speech. How hard it must be to separate evidence of invasion from evidence of trade is obvious, or how difficult to build conclusions on the grave-ornaments of many centuries, during which some settlers inhumed their dead, and others cremated them.   Two general considerations, however, may probably be accepted.   First, that, in geographical conditions immensely more remote and isolated than our own, any particular immigration or culture might affect only one small part of the island, and again, that these early civilizations overlapped, so that clear divisions of time are untenable.   Thus flint arrow-heads persisted for ages after the general use of bronze, and barrow burials continued to the time of the Romans.   In the hill regions, above all Dartmoor or the Yorkshire moors, life went on with little visible change or, if change, in obedience to influences different from those ruling the oft-conquered south.

Yet what we can detect of Neolithic man, in the third millennium before Christ, though little enough, is all-important.   They came to Britain, it seems, from several quarters — one northern element of Baltic origin, some from southern France, and a third dominant stock by way of the Atlantic and Irish Sea which, passing along the Cotswolds, left long burial barrows and clustered thickly over the west, as they did also in Ireland.   A majority were people of a dark, slight, dolichocephalous or long-headed, Mediterranean type.   They worked much in flint and bone, trading far afield with their stone axes ; from deer antlers they fashioned the picks with which they sunk mine-galleries for flint in Sussex and Norfolk.   They had domesticated animals — horses, and dogs, wide-horned cattle, sheep, and pigs.   They sowed a little wheat, and worked some coarse finger-moulded pottery.   Sometimes they protected their villages with a wooden palisade, while on the downs they erected camps and cattle kraals, often defended by rampart and gate.

From the neighbourhood of 1900 to about 1000 B.C. there followed what are styled the Early and Middle Bronze Ages, though where and by what divided is less easy to say.   The so-called ' Beaker folk ', who began this new set of invasions, if originally of Mediterranean stock, seem in their wandering to have absorbed some Nordic strain, their broader heads and sturdier build marking them out from their predecessors.   If some came from Brittany, the mass appear to have moved last from the Rhineland, and they settled in numbers over the whole east, from the Yorkshire wolds down to the Thames entry.   They inhumed their dead in many sorts of round barrows, and may have practised human sacrifice.   If they kept flint for common purposes, bronze, mixed perhaps from Irish copper and Cornish tin, was the material of their chieftains and fighting-men, and a medium of their trade, which embraced a flourishing commerce in Irish gold and much use of Yorkshire jet.   That their organized strength, even their ideas, were larger than anything seen in Britain before may be judged from their religious monuments, for in this Early Bronze Age, it seems, were made the first works at Stonehenge and the circles of Avebury. What power brought giant blue stones from Pembrokeshire to Salisbury Plain, cut ditches fifty feet deep, or morticed lintels into vast shaped uprights?

From about the year 1000 we enter the Late Age of Bronze which shades, by stages and agencies unproven, round 500 B.C. into the Early Iron Age. It must, apparently, be taken first as a period of amalgamation between conquerors and conquered, especially in the north where the conquerors had been few in number; an age, also, of expanding population, spreading pit-dwellings and wattled huts over every upland and in many sheltered ravines, of a people who wove cloth and smelted charcoal. Most marked of all was the increased quantity of their metal working, and an introduction of new types, in socketed and hollow-cast axes, swords with a cutting edge and sickles, wheeled vehicles and cauldrons. It is believed they brought in a rude plough, improving on the hoe and mattock husbandry of primitive days, and from this age we trace the small rectangular fields on the downs, the terraces of which may still be seen, made by the earth ploughed downwards as ages passed.

Their arts and crafts seem to denote new immigrations, of an Alpine element again, and again too a western link with Spain. Yet, though both of these were to recur, from this time on it seems true to conclude that the trend of immigration came predominantly from the North, notably from the Rhineland and the Ardennes. We have, in fact, as bronze very gradually yields to iron, reached the epoch of the Celts, and the beginning of those folk-wanderings which for a thousand years would convulse Europe. Coming from the hive of eastern Europe, the Celts had struck out west and south, and now, ever pushed on by formidable races behind them, German and Illyrian, were moving again. All of which was to bring about their penetration of Spain, their attack on Rome, their drive over the Danube and into Asia Minor.

How precisely they affected the British Isles, and when, is still disputed in every detail. Two different families of Celtic tongues were later developed, respectively called Goidel and Brythonic; Erse and Gaelic in the first, and then Welsh, Breton, and Cornish; but the crux still remains as to when that distinction was made, whether before, or after, reaching these islands. Archaeology, moreover, can only with many doubts distinguish between cultural connection and immigration; can hardly fix the deciding stage between British and Irish imitation of imported luxuries, or the arrival, maybe, of skilled Spaniards to exploit Cornish tin, and that mass import, or making, of essential goods which must denote a fixed settlement. Yet, in one way or the other, it seems to establish a perpetual arrival of many groups, from about 800 to 450 B.C.; from Swiss lake-villages, Champagne, and Brittany, and even more from the northern French and lower Rhine region, where Celt and Teuton had met and mixed. They made their way to the Scarborough headland, into the Fens and the Thames, and the Hampshire harbours; another wave, sailing from Atlantic ports, reached the tin workings which exported through St. Michael's Mount, and by way of the Severn passed into the Midlands.

These tall fair-haired people, who called the natives whom they defeated the ' Pretanni ' or ' painted folk ', were experienced warriors. They brought with them the power of iron, for which later on they used ores of the Sussex Weald and the Forest of Dean; making six-foot ash-hafted spears, chariots with iron-rimmed wheels, and horse harness. They were great builders of fortified camps, which stud many cape promontories and all the southern downs, and of which Maiden Castle in Dorset is a famous type; often with vast ditches and guarded gates. Their pottery and carefully-wrought brooches and artistic bronze work suggest a wide trade and a powerful aristocracy. Between 250 B.C. and about A.D. 100 we have evidence of two further, widely separated settlements, well advanced in culture. One is identified in Yorkshire, coming from the Paris region and spreading by the Fens into East Anglia; who buried their chieftains with horse and chariot and daggers. Far away at Glastonbury other invaders raised over the peat of those marshy meres their lake-dwellings on a log platform; here they worked in iron, bronze, stone, and bone; they had rings of Dorset shale, amber and glass beads, pottery incised in fine lines, and skilfully-carpentered woodwork; they smelted lead and sowed barley, moved by canoe, and killed man or game with pellets from slings.

About 75 B.C. began a final sequence of invasions, which were to bind Britain in a permanent relation with Europe. The Belgae, centred on the Marne and Aisne, and part-German in culture, had already won some footing over these waters, and now, headed by the tribe of the Catuvellauni, appeared in force in Kent, thence spread over the Thames into Essex and Hertfordshire, where at Wheathampstead they began making a fortified capital, and so on to the Midland streams lying between Oxford and Cambridge. Some thirty years later, when Caesar had come and failed and departed, another Belgic tribe, the Atrebates, refugees from Roman power, crossed from Normandy, fixed a capital at Silchester in Berkshire, and ruthlessly attacked the peoples of West Sussex and Somerset. The Belgae brought with them a rude vigour, and some positive improvements. Their power was considerable enough to make sizable States. They struck coins, like the Gauls copying old Macedonian models, from the horse of whose chariots perhaps descends the white horse cut on the Berkshire downs. They made pottery on the wheel. Perhaps introducing a heavier build of plough, which could really turn the sod, they began some clearance of forest lands for settlement.

Ignoring for the moment the episode of Caesar's invasion and the first effects of Romanization, at the opening of the Christian era we find many British kingdoms, but no united Britain nor uniform culture. Outside the two substantial Belgic States mentioned, there survived strong Celtic communities; the Dobuni, extending from the Cotswolds to the Welsh foothills, and with one wing stretched into Dorset; Trinovantes in Essex, Iceni in East Anglia, and the Brigantes in the north. Alike in the north and the Cornish west and Wales, a Bronze Age civilization, or an even ruder life, was perpetuated, ranging from chiefs in hill-forts down to villages of pit-dwellings or stone huts. In the Belgic areas there was growing wealth, much wheat-growing and iron-making, but a finer artistic sense lived on in the Celtic middle west, where pottery retained the bold curves and spirals of an earlier age, and whence derived some magnificent ornament in bronze. Everywhere we seem to stumble on separate units, sometimes wholly disconnected but sometimes at war; whether Breton immigrants who defended Maiden Castle with sling stones, subterranean shelters in Wales, pile-dwellings in Yorkshire, or isolated farms, all alike barely touched by the series of conquerors.

While the Platonic philosophy covered the Middle East, while Christ was born and suffered, and while the Stoics were elevating Rome, no written or archaeological evidence tells of a spiritual life in Britain. The tattooed Britons still offered human sacrifice; Glastonbury, and the Celtic forts outside Winchester and Chichester, seem to have fallen in massacre before those new towns were made by the Belgae. Like the Gauls, the Britons deferred to the Druid caste, with whom lay the secret of their sacred songs, the taking of auspices, the award of punishment, and the dread power of ' taboo ', which made a class of untouchables. Their gods were many and of all sorts, gods of war and thunder, or local deities of some holy well or haunted wood. They feared the Scottish forests as the dwelling-place of demons, and propitiated the unseen by burning victims in wicker cages.

They were now to receive the two destined agents of mediaeval power, the Roman legion and the religion of Christ.

CHAPTER II

ROMAN BRITAIN, 55 B.C.–A.D. 450

IN 55 B.C., when Julius Caesar in his camp on the Rhine was meditating invasion of Britain, the island was divided by war. The
advance guard of the Belgae, the Catuvellauni, had pushed on from
Kent over the Thames, held its north bank almost to the Cotswolds and,
under a strong king, Cassivellaunus, were bidding for a larger kingdom.
In Essex the non-Belgic Trinovantes were ready to appeal to the
Romans against them, while in East Anglia the Iceni were making
camps and dykes to ward them off. With the tribes of earlier immigration, the Yorkshire Brigantes or Silures in south Wales, Caesar was not
concerned; the Belgae alone had given him provocation, and they held
the ports of entrance.

The destiny of Rome, had Caesar never lived, must in any event
have brought her to the Atlantic. She had destroyed Carthage, absorbed Greece, crushed Asia Minor, and carried her frontier to the
Euphrates. Only on the north and north-west she lay exposed to the
barbarians who, since the first Celtic drive three centuries before, had
never rested and whom Marius, only fifty years before Caesar, had
hardly stemmed. In 71 a new swarm of Germans, crossing the Rhine
to fight as mercenaries in Gaul, remained as settlers, proving strong
enough to push the Celts of central France down on the Roman province
between the Alps and the Spanish border, and to ruin the great wealth
of Marseilles and Toulouse.

In this emergency Caesar accepted in 58 a five years' command of
Gaul, and in three campaigns seemed to have rolled the cloud away.
Having shown his power beyond the Rhine, attacked the Belgae from the
Aisne to the Scheldt, and overcome the sea-going Veneti in Brittany, at
midsummer 55 he decided on an exploratory expedition to Britain, as
a preliminary to conquest.

The motives of his two brief expeditions, of August 55 and July 54,
were, of course, in part derived from his personal ambition, though he
might hope to refill his war chest from the much-rumoured British
mineral wealth and the sale of prisoners. But the Channel, he had also
found, was no more a political frontier than we in our day have found
the mountains of Afghanistan. Some of the Belgae in Britain acknowledged a Gaulish suzerain, others sheltered Gaulish exiles. And he was
well aware of its divisions, for no sooner had his plans leaked out than

British deputations reached him with pledges of submission.

He got little out of his expeditions. The first was nothing more than an armed reconnaissance, but in the second he took with him five legions and cavalry, and they proved none too many. He did, of course, fight his way from his landing south of Sandwich, cross the Thames near Brentford, and storm the Catuvellauni stronghold at Wheathampstead, near St. Albans, and came away having proved that Roman troops need not fear the British chariots, and with notes on the plentiful Kentish grain and the best landing-places. But his triumph hardly outlived his presence, and within two years a last great patriot revolt shook Roman Gaul. Once again Gaulish exiles fled to Britain, among them Commius chief of the Atrebates of Arras, who made a kingdom in Wessex; the allies Caesar had patronized were soon crushed by the Catuvellauni, while the tribute he had exacted was unpaid. Except for a steady coming and going of merchants, Britain was not troubled by Rome for near ninety years.

In that interval, during which Caesar killed Pompey and was himself slain, Mark Antony and Augustus fought over the succession, Tiberius reigned and Christ suffered, the British scene saw an important change. For some time past, superiority had been passing away from Salisbury Plain to the south-east, and now the Catuvellauni made themselves supreme. During Cymbeline's long reign from A.D. 5 to after 40, they finally overcame the Trinovantes and set up a capital at Colchester; Kent and Sussex seemingly admitted him as overlord, while the frequency of his coinage all along the Thames testifies that there he could call himself ' Rex Brittonum '. In due course they seem to have overthrown the second Belgic dynasty, seated at Silchester.

What was left of Celtic arts and culture belonged to the middle west and the north, and magnificent some of their bronze and enamel work remained; the outstanding political and economic fact, however, was exactly the contrary, — the Romanization of the south-east well before the Roman conquest. Belgic princes appealed to Augustus and his successors, and in their mints struck gold and silver coins imitating Romano-Gaulish models. A colony of Latin-speaking traders appeared in the towns, and British exports of corn, minerals, and slaves brought back wine, glass, and amber from the Continent; classical statuettes and rich work in silver and enamel are found buried with a Belgic chief. Even the humbler houses of Colchester boasted their flagons and pottery from Italy, France, and the Rhineland.

Only other distractions postponed a Roman occupation of this part-Romanized island, and in A.D. 43 the Emperor Claudius undertook the conquest, pointed to by poets and urged by business interests. He took action, we may suppose, from those motives which have so often driven forward an Imperial frontier against a half-civilized neighbour.

Security, — for Gaul still had gusts of rebellion and was tainted by Druid influence from Britain; profit, — from British mines and grain; opportunity, — when on Cymbeline's death his sons quarrelled and his subject kingdoms were restless. Certainly Rome took this matter seriously, despatching a veteran general with four legions, followed up by the Emperor in person. So began an occupation which was to last for three hundred and sixty years, a span as long as that which now divides us from the coming of the Armada.

To divide this long occupation symmetrically into two, a period of offensive conquest followed by one of a defensive peace, seems to blur the main truth. For if within forty years of the Claudian conquest Roman armies reached the extremities of Wales and Scotland, several times a military disaster or rebellion threatened to end Roman government, even two hundred years before the real end was reached. The story seems, rather, one of a border province, always weakly held, and often with inferior troops, instantly responding to a spell of good governance but in its own character never self-sufficing, and drawing all its energy from the heart of the Empire. When Rome sagged under Nero, or rose in new glory under the Antonines in the second century, was restored in the fourth by Constantine and broke at last before the Goths and Huns, so correspondingly Roman power in Britain faltered, flowed again, and then ran dry. There were years of a forward policy and years of economy, bouts of centralization and experiments in a half-freedom, but the disease of Empire was incurable and we shall find a date after which the loss of Britain became certain.

The first generation of Roman governors made, to all appearance, swift progress. One year's campaign gave them Kent, London, and the kingdom centred on Colchester, whose last ruler, the brave Caractacus, took flight for Wales. By the year 51 he was taken prisoner and sent to Rome; one legion had reached Lincoln, from that point the great frontier road of the Fosse Way had been driven south-west to Cirencester and the Severn, the Watling Street was presumably already pushing to the north-west since other forces had reached Wroxeter, and the Mendip lead mines were producing under Roman control. In the next stage, to 77, when the famous Agricola arrived as governor, the Lincoln legion had moved forward to York, another from Wroxeter to Chester, and a third from Gloucester to Caerleon on Usk; the Ordovices of north Wales were subdued and the Silures of Glamorgan; Verulamium was already a municipality, and the pleasure city of Bath was building. Sword in one hand and spade in the other, the army made its communications as it advanced, a ribbon of hard stone and gravel thus holding together its bivouacs.

Fighting had been severe and constant. Sometimes whole regions were disarmed, sometimes unsatisfying alliances were made with puppet

kings, but the untamed Brigantes beyond York were always raiding
south, Wales was hardly controlled, and southern Britain plainly hated
this foreign rule. Their special grievances were heavy taxation, military
conscription, and the corrupt high-handed officials who directed the
commissariat and Imperial lands; while the money-lenders that batten
on every early Imperialism ruined some leading families. Twice the
Iceni led the whole east in rebellion, and in the second, Boadicea's
famous revolt of 61, they nearly destroyed the Roman power. They
avenged the barbarous treatment of their queen and royal family by a
massacre of Roman civilians, sacked the veteran soldiers' colony at
Colchester, Verulamium, and London, and all but wiped out one
legion. Suppression by fire and sword, and then some years of lenient
government, had restored peace in the south when Agricola, who as a
young staff officer had seen these events, returned as governor.

His son-in-law Tacitus has told us of the governor's belief that his
countrymen had been much to blame and in the virtues of a moderate
policy. So he spent large sums on development in courts of justice,
houses, and temples, and tried to persuade the British chiefs to give
their children a Latin upbringing. But such a scheme must be slow in
its effects, Agricola was here only seven years, and his military achievements opened an age of forward Imperialism. Whether the decision
came from him or his master, the Emperor Vespasian, who also had
served in Britain, its purpose was to make a firm frontier both in the
North and the West.

His first two years passed in completing the work of his predecessors.
In north Wales the Ordovices were at last suppressed and Anglesey
taken; forts were built in the Brecon area and at Carnarvon, at first in
timber but later remodelled in stone, linked up by roads crossing the
mountains and traversing the south coast. North of Trent began the
country of the Brigantes, who had given endless trouble and were
already pinned down by the legionary fortress at York and a camp at
Malton. Here too Agricola seems to have expanded widely the fort
system, at Skipton and Ambleside for instance on the west, Bowes and
Catterick eastwards, together with parallel roads from Manchester to
Carlisle and from York to the Tyne.

From the year 80 he began larger projects. Between Carlisle and
Corbridge on the Tyne he seems to have selected, and part-fortified. the
military road-line later called the Stanegate; and then, in five successive
campaigns, overran most of Scotland, finding the shorter frontier he
sought in the thirty-seven miles between Forth and Clyde. Here again
his temporary forts anticipated the future of the Antonine Wall,
and again he connected them by roads with Corbridge and Carlisle.
An attack on the Picts of Galloway, combined operations with fleet and
army from Fife to the Tay, a great battle at Mons Graupius somewhere

north of Perth, a circumnavigation of the Orkneys and into the Irish Sea — so the time passed before Agricola was recalled in 83 or 84, too soon for his vision of invading Ireland.

Pressures on the Empire elsewhere in the next generation, and the permanent withdrawal of one legion, showed the difficulty of holding his frontiers. Some Lowland forts were lost, continued reconditioning of others in Yorkshire and the Peak country proved danger on the lines of communication, and before the Emperor Trajan died in 117 troops seem to have been retired from Scotland, to stand on the Stanegate. In 121 or 122 his successor Hadrian visited Britain and devised the building of the famous Wall, the Romans' most permanent monument in this country. As carried out after many experiments, it comprised a whole defended system; first the Stanegate, as lately refortified by Trajan; north of it the Vallum, a wide earthwork with seven-foot ditch; north of that, a military road and the Wall itself, running about seventy-three miles from sea to sea, from Wallsend beyond Newcastle to Bowness on the Solway; with turret signal-stations, small forts every mile, and at important points a fortress with quarters for a regiment.

North of the Wall more work was done on forts in Lothian and Dumfriesshire, and twenty years later, under the wise Emperor Antoninus Pius, the Romans made the second Wall, called by his name, between Forth and Clyde. The barrier here was raised only in turf and clay, but nineteen forts were packed in those thirty-seven miles, and a series of fortified posts connected this second frontier with the Tyne.

At this point, a hundred years after Claudius' invasion, the outward structure of Roman Britain seemed complete; when their sentries signalled to each other in the Highlands and the Menai Straits, London's walls had risen, and Roman milestones would soon enter even Cornwall. We must look at the civilization which the structure contained, and its progressive causes for decay.

The girder underpinning it was an army of some 50,000 men. Of the regular troops, the second legion garrisoned Caerleon; the sixth, York; and the twentieth, Chester; though in emergency their detachments went far afield, working parties from all three thus taking a hand in building the Walls. They were supported by some seventy regiments of auxiliaries, recruited from every race of the Empire: Belgians, Spaniards, Germans, Greeks and Moors and Gauls, besides some British levies whom we can trace from Yorkshire, Devon, and other regions of the south. So it is that, on the Clyde or the heights of Snowdon, we find their diplomas of discharge after service, or the altars they raised to the mother goddesses or Mithras the sun-god, or discover at Bath the record of a Spaniard serving in Wales. But during the long centuries of occupation this army underwent a substantial change; ceasing to be

Roman and becoming British, or rather British-Germanic, losing its original recruitment, and absorbing elements which might make it anti-Roman, or at least anti-official.

From bitter experience of such mutinous heterogeneous troops, in Britain as elsewhere, came about the later changes in provincial administration. Soon after 200 the Emperor Severus divided the power hitherto concentrated, making one province of ' Lower Britain ' north of a line drawn from the Mersey to the Wash, and another of ' Upper Britain ' to the south. This process was carried much further, first after 296 by Diocletian, who divided the Roman world, and then again by Constantine, who moved its centre eastward. Britain became a diocese under the prefect of Gaul, while military and civil authority were lodged in separate hands. A ' vicarius ' controlled civil government, and below him four lieutenants for the four provinces into which the island was now re-divided. Balancing these civilians were the military junta : the *Dux Britanniae*, commanding York, the Wall, and thus the bulk of the army ; the Count of the Saxon Shore, in charge of coast defence and the fleet ; and, only perhaps in the last stages, a *Comes Britanniarum* commanding a field army.

Yet no more in Britain than elsewhere was the Empire ruled by the sword alone, or a centralized bureaucracy. There were, indeed, high officials and their clerks, Crown estates, government service in Somerset lead works and Cornish tin-mining, and heavy Imperial taxes. But Roman practical sense, and the necessity of the case, made decentralization the rule. Here, as in Gaul, Imperial civilization turned on the city, though in this backward province only five possessed full civic liberties — the four *coloniae* of Colchester, Lincoln, Gloucester, and York, and the municipality at Verulamium. On a lower scale the same type of government was given to the tribal centres, in the south at least. There was a ' senate ' of the Silures centred on Caerwent, Silchester made a similar capital for the Atrebates, Canterbury and Winchester and Cirencester had tribal cantons grouped round them in the same way.

What were their powers of choosing their magistrates, or raising taxation, is dark to us ; how the countryside was governed, is still more obscure. There were certainly some Imperial estates, and many rich villa properties, both of which probably involved slave labour, and, as in other provinces, there were also a class of *coloni* — farmers paying part of their produce as rent. But of private jurisdiction or legal lordship we have no evidence, and even if we allow for many up-country private estates, it is certain that hundreds of native villages continued their squalid life without change ; sinking pit huts, treasuring some coarse imported pottery, living still in the style of the Age of Bronze, even in civilized Somerset. All this was much more true of the north, in whose land-tenure and customs, unaltered before and after the Romans, we have proof of surviving tribal communities. Romanization was, in fact, both local and transitory.

Yet south of Trent and east of Severn, where perhaps over half of its million-odd population were contained, we find in the third and early fourth centuries a respectable level of civilization. Ploughing up old hill ramparts, Wessex villagers spread their cultivation down to the valleys and made settlements in what before was forest; embankments protected the eastern fens, barges threaded their slow rivers. Many country houses have been discovered, which had held imported comforts and luxuries; some fifty to our knowledge in Kent, over sixty in Somerset, thirty even in cold Northamptonshire; most of all, in the warmer clime of Hampshire and the Isle of Wight. Though, measured by the standard of Gaul, many were humble, single-storied and wooden framed, they were usually warmed by a furnace and radiating pipes, while many could boast of baths, window glass, and mosaic painting.

Naturally this material civilization was strongest in the towns. The smallest of them seem to have bought glass, pottery, and bronzes; even a Mendip village had its miniature amphitheatre; while the legionary and trading centres seemed to promise a long life of Latin culture. At Silchester, with its twenty-foot wall and its *forum* a hundred yards square; Colchester, holding the great temple of Claudius, and with gates for horse and foot passengers; Caerleon, with its gilded tiles and amphitheatre to seat thousands; Bath, approached through many villas and with its medicinal springs, — in such places their people were buying pottery from Gaul and the Rhineland, toilet sets of pewter, purple-glazed New Forest ware, writing tablets, and honey ointment for ophthalmia. London had become the centre of the road system, and an export market for corn and cloth; with its justice hall in Cornhill, its mint, gates, and wharves. On its walls artisans scribbled in Latin their love affairs, their jokes, or their weariness of work, and in such cities men might hear the grammar and poetry of Rome. Rome was all-encompassing here, a clinging pall of cosmopolitan civilization. With rare exceptions the Celtic race seemed to have lost its artistic originality, for building was Roman, mosaics set forth Roman mythology, and heating of Roman type might be found far afield in Dorset huts.

But the other half of Britain told a different tale. On the heavy soils and in the forest belts lay thin tracts of settlement, devoid of any Romanizing influence except the sword. Warwickshire was largely empty, hardly a dozen villas have been found in Norfolk, only a few clustered round the York garrison. In this armed north-west the stone villages persisted of the clans whom a hundred years of fighting had not absorbed, and danger was constantly renewed; no fortification sufficing to stem the flow of Celtic influence from Ireland and the west Highlands.

Long before disaster became irretrievable, we feel that three evils are exhausting this Empire; an extension of frontiers which it had neither the men nor the money to hold, pressure from without, and faction at the centre.

The Forth-Clyde Wall and its outlying posts in Perthshire had hardly been built when they were abandoned, and the Antonine age closed in tribulation. The northern Wall, once recovered, was evacuated for good between 180 and 200. Hadrian's was penetrated and barely held; many of the Welsh forts were dismantled. From 192 to 197 civil war raged for the Imperial succession, marked in Britain by mutiny in the legions, and by a move which might have been fatal: when Albinus, commanding the troops, was put up as Caesar, stripped the Wall of its best regiments, and with them crossed to Gaul. The tribes of the north broke through it, carrying destruction as far south as York and Chester.

His successor Severus, old and crippled but indomitable, once more restored the State, and gave Britain a last long spell of tranquillity. Yet though the Wall was thoroughly restrengthened and forts rebuilt in all directions, when Severus died at York in 211 it must have been in a consciousness of failure. For two years he had taken his troops from Northumberland to the Moray Firth, only to lose half of them by ambush, winter campaigning, or disease, and when he died his sons gave up the northern war.

A third century of occupation wore away, with much peaceful development in country houses of the south, but at its end the same story of anarchy was repeated, when a pretender of a new type claimed the Empire. This was the Belgian Carausius, commanding the squadron based on Boulogne, which was meant to overawe the Frankish and Saxon pirates. He held his own for eight years from 286, appealing to local patriotism in Gaul and Britain, but with his assassination the scheme fell to pieces. In 296 Constantius, the able joint-Emperor in the West, defeated the relics of the rebel troops; and once more Britain enjoyed, as some London coins boasted, the ' *beata tranquillitas* ' of Roman peace.

It lasted till the death of his son the great Constantine, in 337, years which on the whole reveal, outside the towns, a considerable prosperity. New country houses were being built, roads were being repaired, other countries were using the British market. Christianity was winning a foothold, for to this period it seems we must ascribe Alban and the first British martyrs, while British bishops appeared, as at Arles in 314, in Councils of the Church. But within thirty years of Constantine's death new blows were inflicted, heavier than army mutiny and the Pict danger in the north, which proved fatal.

In the west we perceive signs of a strong backwash from the Celts.

Scots from northern Ireland joined the Picts in forays on and beyond the Wall; other Irishry trickled into the gap north of Chester, and even made some settlement on the Welsh coast. Still worse was the prospect eastwards, where the Saxons whom Carausius had kept at bay were swarming in the Channel, carrying Britons off into slavery and imperilling communication with Gaul.

To meet these dangers the military system was once more recast. A new official of Constantine's appointment, the Count of the Saxon Shore, was raised in status, his command being extended to take in all from the Wash to Southampton Water, with fortresses all the way from Brancaster in Norfolk to Carisbrooke, together with the Dover fleet establishment, signal-station, and lighthouse; under him too was the second legion, now moved back from Caerleon. Indeed, the whole scheme looked out to sea. Forts at Cardiff and Carnarvon guarded the Irish entrance, more signal-stations watched the Scarborough coast and the Bristol Channel, seven regiments were crowded in Cumberland and Westmorland.

These new defences had no fair chance of proving their worth. Constantine's dynasty relapsed into civil war, the Rhine frontier buckled, both Rome and Constantinople staved off war only by enlisting one set of barbarians to fight another, and the Empire fell into convulsions; marked by the Goths' victory of 378 at Adrianople, the loss of Gaul to the Germans, and in 410 the sack of Rome by Alaric the Visigoth. Three times in those sixty years a commander in Britain, two of British birth, usurped the Empire, in each case taking off the flower of the garrison to fight in Gaul and Spain. In 367 Picts, Scots, and Saxons joined hands and broke through the Wall, both the *Dux Britanniae* and the Count of the Saxon Shore were killed, fighting and sack and siege stretched to the Midlands and London. Twice a great soldier, the Spanish Theodosius and the Vandal Stilicho, attempted some restoration, but the needs of Britain came last in the Imperial scale, and its administration was starved of troops. By 400, at latest, both the Wall and the Welsh fortresses seem to have been abandoned, in 402 Stilicho took away one of the two remaining legions, and in 407 Constantine, the last usurper, withdrew the mass of troops to the Continent, not to return.

If this was the removal of the official casing, the military and civilian services, the life within seems to have decayed more than a generation before. The urban civilization, which the first two centuries of Roman government had imported, was an artificial growth — alien to the Celtic habit of mind, and demanding expenditure which those petty tribal communities could not afford. Evidence accumulates, in one town after another, of massive buildings never completed and street-planning schemes never filled up; whether from dour passive resistance, overtaxation, or a ruinous inflation, effort and expansion in the towns long ago had stopped. Wroxeter shows very early the signs of this creeping decay, while the people of Verulamium and Silchester were quarrying their best buildings and sinking from mosaic to clay floors. From about 350 this ruin seems to spread to the country houses, with the growth of insecurity and barbarian raids. Villa owners are found burying hoards of plate and coin, some villages went back to trade by barter, there was some refortifying of ancient camps.

We thus picture the last scene, not as one of any sudden fierce destruction but rather as fading out in a slow long-drawn dusk, and may visualize it best at Silchester, the most thoroughly excavated of provincial capitals. From the west we find traces of a Celtic return, with the arts of the Irish, and gradually owners of property began to desert the city. So that one day the priest serving its small Christian church, finding no flock left to minister to, put out the light on the altar for the last time.

CONTEMPORARY DATES

B.C.

51–30	Cleopatra queen of Egypt.
44	Murder of Caesar.
30–A.D. 14	Reign of Augustus.

A.D.

25–30	Pontius Pilate procurator of Judaea.
51, onwards.	Missions of St. Paul.
c. 60	Buddhism introduced into China.
70	Titus destroys Jerusalem.
138–80	The Antonine Emperors.
161	The Institutes of Gaius.
226	The Sassanid dynasty begin in Persia.
230–70	Goth invasions of the Balkans and Asia Minor.
306–37	The reign of Constantine.
320, onwards	The Gupta dynasty master Hindostan.
374	St. Ambrose bishop of Milan.
378	The Emperor Valens killed by the Visigoths.
395	Final partition of the Empire.
396–430	St. Augustine bishop of Hippo.
406	The Franks take Flanders and the Rhineland.
410	Alaric the Visigoth sacks Rome.
416–29	Vandal conquests in Spain and Africa.
432	St. Patrick begins his mission in Ireland.
433–53	Reign of Attila the Hun.

BOOK I

CELTS, SAXONS, AND SCANDINAVIANS
450–1066

CHAPTER I

THE COMING OF THE ENGLISH, 450–613

FOR the better part of a century this darkness covers British history, lighted only at intervals by a momentary gleam from archaeology, which may show us an Anglian war-band cooking in an abandoned villa, or water-fowl nesting in the ruins of Bath. We are thus almost ignorant of every vital detail upon the very turning-point of our destiny, when Britain was conquered by the races which, if not making the majority of its population, have assuredly determined language, structure of society, and national character. This darkness is felt the more, when we consider the evidence at our disposal.

Now and then some writer on the Continent made room for a scrap of rumour about Britain amid their tale of troubles nearer home, the terror of the Huns or the sweep onward of the Franks. A Gaulish chronicle ending in 452, a life written round 480 of St. Germanus bishop of Auxerre, who visited Britain in 429 and again about 447, Byzantine historians writing after 500, of such sort are our nearest written authorities; writing from hearsay, from a distance, unthinking of Britain except by chance. Nor can much of solid weight be gleaned from the first writers of British race. The Celtic monk Gildas wrote his tract little before 550, and then mainly to scourge the vices of Welsh kings. The *Historia Britonnum* of the Welshman Nennius was edited after 800, while the earliest fragment it embodies can hardly be dated before 680; the first Welsh annals come from the tenth century. As for our two fundamental authorities, Bede's *Ecclesiastical History* is the greatest book of the early Middle Ages, but it was written in a Northumbrian monastery and not before 730; the Anglo-Saxon Chronicle, though incorporating some lost earlier originals, in the form we have it was rearranged not before 890, and compiled under King Alfred's eye for the glory of his dynasty. We are thus thrown back upon other types of evidence; on parallels from times before and after, whether the first-century Tacitus or seventh-century Saxon law, on race traditions buried in some royal genealogy or folk-song, on language and place-names, and on all that has been excavated by the spade.

From one famous problem we may judge of the uncertainties in which we are plunged by this piecemeal and often contradictory testimony. Did the West Saxons, as their Chronicle avows, reach England later than the Angles and fight their way north from Southampton

Water ? or did they come very early, as archaeology claims, and by the Thames valley and the Wash ? On one side, we have a chronicle full of duplicate entries, suspiciously symmetrical dates, and heroes who were certainly not all West Saxon ; on the other, an argument from the silence of no early burial-places in Hampshire, and reliance on the witness of grave-ornaments along the upper Thames.   Since doubts almost as great surround many another burning question, — how far the Britons survived, whence Angles and Saxons had sailed, or who were the Jutes, — we can only put forward some broad provisional conclusions by elimination, balance, and compromise.

As in all western Europe, the fall of Rome in Britain did not come about in any single catastrophe.   No province surrendered at a blow, for Rome and barbarian had long been mingled.   As in Gaul, so in Britain there were Romanized provincials, who showed themselves capable of long resistance.   There were some barbarians dazzled by the name of Rome, and ready to use its benefits ; there were also barbarians of the outer fringe, desirous only to destroy.   At such different levels Britain had been left by the Romans, and its unorganized peoples reacted in several different ways.

In west and north we find a revival of tribal warfare and petty royal families.   Elsewhere, there was some contest between pure Celts and a half-Romanized ruling caste, some refortification of Iron Age camps, and new defences thrown up even in the heart of England ; as in the fortified Wansdyke which, faced to the north, runs from the Bristol Channel to Berkshire.   Far to the north the Picts surged about and over the deserted Wall.   One British chief set up a kingdom on the Clyde, another dynasty migrated from the Forth to north Wales, some Christians were in flight for Ireland.

These stages of ruin may be dated more nearly.   In 429, when St. Germanus first came over, southern Britain was holding out, for he assisted the natives to repel a barbarian raid and found St. Alban's shrine still a centre of worship.   By 460, and probably a few years earlier, all had changed ; to that decade points every converging line of testimony, of chronicles, archaeology, and tradition, for the collapse of Britain.   Saxon pirates are found at every point of the compass, ravaging Flanders and Brittany, making settlements in Normandy and the Pas de Calais.   We may well believe too the ancient tradition that Hengist, with the earliest Jute force in Thanet, came as mercenaries, for Germans had long been playing that part in Gaul and the Rhineland ; it is even possible that Cerdic, the Celtic name of the founder of the Wessex royal house, makes part of the history of some similar war-band, taking a princess from the British with whom, or for whom, they fought.

Disunity is stamped on the English invasion.   No great army under a single leader swept, as Gildas' lamentations depict, across the island from sea to sea and, by a process exactly the reverse of that in Carolingian France, Anglo-Saxon history tells the slow welding together of many separate ventures, each of which, from Kent to Northumbria, preserved its own royal house and its own identity. Judging from their ornaments and culture, the invaders came in on every wind, some direct from Schleswig, others from Frisia, and more again from the Rhine.

When a new century dawned after 500, conquest was not complete, and not even certain. The British had offered a long resistance, led by men of mixed descent and sometimes of royal race, though two names alone have come down to us as flesh and blood of that struggle. Aurelius Ambrosianus, descending from men who had worn the purple, held out, it would seem, in the region of Glastonbury, and appears, round about 470, to have brought the Saxons to a standstill. After him we meet the mysterious figure of Arthur, whom every province claims for its own from Lothian to Cornwall, and none of whose twelve great battles can safely be identified on any map. But at some date between 490 and 516 years of fighting ended at some place unknown, called Mount Badon, in a British victory ; their leader being a Christian hero known in the Welsh March, at least by the ninth century, as Arthur of Britain, who was to become a legendary saint of all Celtic Europe, and for whose return Cornish and Bretons waited in expectance. This fighting brought about a lull, lasting the better part of half a century, in the Saxon advance ; there is even evidence making it probable that some of them, in search of land to be more easily won, returned to Germany.

At the end of this first stage of conquest the map would show few firm English settlements. The Jutes, led by Hengist first and then in greater strength by Oisc his son, had occupied Thanet and east Kent ; other Jute bands, probably derived from Kent, were on the way to settle the Isle of Wight and part of eastern Hampshire. Somewhere north of them we must suppose a West Saxon force led by Cerdic, their ally, though not, it seems, in any strength ; separating them from their Kentish kindred was a realm of the South Saxons, almost confined to the coast, whose king Ælle came down in tradition as the spear-head of the English in this early fighting. Wooded south Essex, the Buckinghamshire Chiltern hills, and the north bank of Thames below them, seem occupied only very thinly ; there is a gap in the history of London, and though the Thames basin had many early settlements, the Middle Saxons, with their ' Surrey ' or southern district, never succeeded in making a kingdom. But Saxons in plenty, of the same stock as the West Saxons, had come down very early on the western Thames, probably both by the Icknield Way and by navigation upstream to its source ; they are found in Bedfordshire and Berkshire and past Oxford to the

Cotswolds' edge, and north again from Thames to the Warwickshire Avon and the Cherwell.   In eastern Britain, both place-names and cremated bodies show an early Anglian seizure of Norfolk from the Wash; by the Fens the Middle Angles had pushed into the central Midlands, while it is possible, though not certain, that others coming down from the Humber had laid the foundations of Mercia along the Trent. The East Riding and York itself were in their hands, but further north there are signs enough of raids, without proof of settlement.

From about 550 a second stage opens, seemingly full of migration and war. Even earlier there were movements in the West country, a flight of British Christians from Devon and Cornwall to Brittany, where they carried their speech, their saints, and their traditions, and this perhaps should be connected with the outstanding fact of a new West Saxon advance. For at the mid-century Cerdic's grandson Cynric, and Cynric's son Ceawlin, were warring in Wiltshire, and by 571 appeared in force on the middle Thames where part of their race had settled a century before; conquering everything between Oxford and the Chilterns, where British elements had taken refuge, they passed into country barely touched and reached the Anglian sphere on the Nene and the Bedford Ouse. In 577 they consolidated their hold on the middle west by a great victory at Dyrham, near Bath; the lower Severn valley lay open before them, and soon the Hwicce, of mixed Saxon and Anglian blood, gave their name to Wychwood Forest.

But here the early expansion of Wessex ended. In 584 they were heavily beaten by the Britons in the Midland forest, and lapsed into civil war in which Ceawlin perished. In the rich south country the conquerors were beginning to quarrel among themselves; twice in this century, once over possession of the Isle of Wight and once for Surrey, we find West Saxons and Jutes at each other's throats, while along the watersheds of the Midland rivers Saxons and Angles must collide. But the Jutes were soon avenged. On Ceawlin's death the predominance over the south and Midlands passed, Bede tells us, to that Ethelbert of Kent whom St. Augustine came to convert; his power was certainly enough to smooth Augustine's way to the Welsh border and to expand Kentish trade all over Wessex.

In the Midlands, by a process dark to us, a mosaic of little States was being put together. Staffordshire was already under the dynasty of Penda, which was to make its greatness in the next century, and the Middle Angles had reached Leicester and Warwick. Essex had its own ruling house, before 600 London seems reckoned as an East Saxon city. Beyond their northern frontier, the river Stour, East Anglia was protected by the Fens and made a powerful unit under an early dynasty. But how rich, and how close-knit to the Continent by trade, was only fully revealed in 1932, by the discovery of one of its royalty at Sutton

Hoo, near Woodbridge, buried with his ship, silver bowls, chain mail, and ornaments in gold, enamel, and garnet. There are signs of long Celtic survival at Lincoln, but Anglians had occupied most of the shire. A great belt of Middle England, with wide forests, communicating rivers, and a frontier open to Wales, made a land pre-eminent for war and adventure, and so, for instance, we can prove the presence in later Saxon Worcestershire of warriors who had come from Lincoln and Kent.

In the distant north the Celtic world had disintegrated. One British Christian kingdom was centred on the Clyde at Dumbarton, there was a Pict principality in Galloway, a third held the Cumbrian border, another stretched away through Elmet in the West Riding to the Welsh mountains. Scots from Ulster had made a kingdom of Dalriada in Argyllshire. But meantime the fifth-century Anglian bands in eastern Yorkshire had pushed on to the Tees, and from about 550 we can discern the formation of two Northumbrian kingdoms; one under the house of Ida in Bernicia, with a capital at Bamborough, and the other under Ælle in Deira, centred at York. Then fierce fighting opened with the Celts, of which dim accounts reach us in the annals of both races; of Arthur's kinsmen, sieges of Holy Island, murderous battles on the sands, and in the result a steady pushing of the Celts backwards towards the Irish Sea. From 588 these two Angle states were joined under one ruler, and found in Ethelfrith a ruthless unwearying leader. The very name transplanted in this age by the Cymry from Cumberland to Wales shows the racial sense burning in the defeated, and from this reign we must date the real Anglian settlement of the eastern Lowlands, Lothian, and inland Northumberland. A stronger foe came forward in Aedan, the Scots Christian king of Dalriada, with his Ulster allies. But in 603 Ethelfrith disposed of him at Dawston in Liddesdale, since which time, wrote the Anglian Bede proudly, no Scot king ' has dared ' to battle with the English. Ten years later Ethelfrith struck at the north Welsh. Their lands reached north to the Ribble, but their power was disputed among many petty tyrants, whose crimes were groaned over by Christian teachers and whose wars were sung by many minstrels. Outside Chester the Northumbrian annihilated their army also, together with their attendant monks from the famous school of Bangor.

So, in 613, ended the course of English conquest on the grand scale; their rule, in many different hands, stretched from Kent to the Clyde and from the Severn to the Wash, and outside Wales no substantial Celtic power survived.

What judgment are we to pass upon this process? had it been a war of extirpation, had Celtic Britain disappeared, or had it, on the contrary, left things behind which to this day affect the nation's temper and institutions? In this controversy we cannot safely generalize from particular instance; from the South Saxons' massacre of those defending

Pevensey, or burials in Berkshire of beheaded bodies. Yet, though the end may not have come about by such slaughter, come it did and, however we qualify it, made an undoubted revolution; the replacement of Celt by Teuton, Christian by heathen, a western culture by one mainly northern, an old scheme of agriculture by a new.

Remembering that our first stage of conquest seems to have been one of penetration by small groups, there was, it seems assured, some more or less peaceful amalgamation. We have early proof on the upper Thames of conquerors and conquered mingling without violence. Saxons and Romano-Britons are found to have used the same cemeteries, within a stone's throw of Cirencester, still in British hands; without bloodshed, our evidence suggests, a British village could change into one predominantly heathen, and then back to Christianity once more. Yet the crucial matter of intermarriage receives from archaeology little or no support.

In the next stage, during the sixth century, our first sensation is of many empty spaces. Colonization and conquest were gradual. The settlers clung to the rivers, good water, and dry soil, and were slow to occupy the woods and marsh of Essex, or the precipitous scrub-covered Chilterns; Devon and Cornwall were thinly populated, even by the Celts. There was room then, even in the south, for British communities to survive, and we find them in all parts. Names like Walton or Bretby mark where Saxon and Dane noted a Welsh or British village; even in the eighth century Britons in the Wiltshire downs were struggling against Wessex.

We are left with an impression that for a time at least two civilizations co-existed, the new more vigorous than the old, yet side by side, and with more evidence of decay than of fire and sword. At York, Roman coffins and Anglian urns are found together; a Jutish suburb flanked a half-empty Roman Canterbury; Lincoln kept its Roman name and fortifications; London a hundred years later was important enough in Roman eyes for Pope Gregory to choose it as a metropolitan see. None the less, outside the hill regions, our dominant view must be of a beginning altogether new. Farmers, fishermen, and woodcutters, often in a numerical minority, in general the conquerors avoided settlement along the Roman roads, or in Romano-British towns and villas. Unless it be in Kent, we cannot trace any continuity from Celtic township to English borough, while, except in the north and far west and Wales, none whatever seems to exist between Celtic estates and the first appearances of an Anglo-Saxon manorial system. Many Celtic fields on the downs went back to their native turf; essentially, ploughing methods and field tenures and local government in Wessex and the Midlands are all new, and by origin Teutonic.

British place-names, of rivers especially, survive in plenty, yet towards determining the elements of population they give no final guidance; Teutonic names thus making the great majority in Devon and Cornwall, the one region where Britons and their language undoubtedly remained in strength. Christian evidence helps almost as little. In the greater part of Britain it was no doubt obliterated, for no vestige of it was alleged either by Gregory's Roman mission or the Scottish-Irish monks working from the north. Yet British Christianity had been a late superficial growth, and its lapse cannot imply racial extermination. Our picture of the English world round about 600 must be a mosaic, assembled from innumerable fragmentary details.

To the west of a line drawn from Carlisle to Leeds, and thence prolonged to Bristol and Exeter, a part-Celtic-Roman world lived on, with strong spiritual traditions and race consciousness, older than and overlapping the Saxon invasion. Before the Roman officials departed, Ninian, a north Briton trained at Rome, saw the work of St. Martin at Tours, and about 397 founded his church at Whithorn in Galloway. His evangelizing spread over Cumbria and the region of the Wall, and monasticism inspired by him probably reached Ireland before St. Patrick took up the task. A little later St. Germanus, whose two missions to Britain to fight heresy are on record, had as one of his disciples at Auxerre Illtud, from whose example Welsh monasticism was derived, and who seems to have been teacher in his turn both of Gildas and of St. Samson, founder of Dol in Brittany. That carries us well into the sixth century and the age of St. David, to whom churches were soon dedicated in Cornwall, Ireland, and Brittany, besides his own land, and if David himself did not come of north-British stock, as some authority indicates, in the fifth century there had certainly been migration from Celtic Scotland to Wales. About 520 St. Columba was born, through whom Irish monasticism, thus inspired from Rome and Gaul, Wales and Scotland, returned to England; from whose age begins the glorious line of Irish saints and scholars who evangelized and civilized half western Europe, and some of whose last products were Dunstan's teachers at Glastonbury in the tenth century. All that survived of Roman-Celtic influence had, it must never be forgotten, this enduring, racial, and powerful background.

Within England Celtic place-names lie thick on the map from the Lakes to Lancashire, and again in the west country tors and combes; not till 617 did the Anglians absorb the West Riding, nor Wessex reach Exeter till about 690. Along the Marches no British priest would communicate with Augustine, no Celt act as a guide, or as much as use a cooking-pot soiled by the Saxon. For the other extreme we may go to Buckingham or East Anglia, where hardly a Celtic name can be found. Generally, however, a racial map would not show this black or white shading, but an endlessly variable pattern between the two.

Some areas there were, indeed, where we may be sure of Celtic and Roman survival. It was present in the high civilization of Kent, whose wheel-turned pottery continued, and whose art was full of classic design. Western Mercia ruled over many British subjects, from whom its bronze and jewel work borrowed much Celtic influence. The Wessex laws round about 700 deal specially with British landholders, some of them men of substance who were enlisted in the King's warriors. ' Black-tressed ' British slave-girls meet us in Northumbrian poetry, carrying the pitcher to the well; Celtic and Irish models stimulated the superb stone carving of the North; indeed, it is hardly possible to explain the ' feudal ' North so late as the Norman conquest, if we do not assume the continuance of Celtic subject villages. Finally, nature herself, in impenetrable forest and granite rock, or in the form of many British women, must have prevented a war of extirpation. The defeated sank to be auxiliary allies, or more often to be hewers of wood and drawers of water, but their arts and crafts, their names and some of their blood, the very fact that they provided servile labour, influenced the community set up by the conquerors.

These invaders had come over, in the later stages at least, with their wives and cattle, their ancient songs and their own way of tilling the soil, and had come in whole clans at a time, leaving their Baltic homes in some places swept and empty. Taking from their captives the old names of towns or rivers, and accepting the services rendered to Celtic lords before them, they imposed on the land a new structure of society. They called their new homes after their military leaders, or their gods like Woden, or sometimes from the winding stream, the birch wood, or the heron's ford. Their earliest records tell us the boundaries they set to their habitations, the maple or the pear tree, the Roman road, or the burying-place of the heathen. They had taken the land into their possession and, looking round, they found it very good.

CONTEMPORARY DATES

451	The Monophysite heresy strikes the Eastern Church.
476	Deposition of Romulus Augustulus.
487, onwards.	Theodoric the Ostrogoth begins his conquest of Italy.
496	Baptism of Clovis, King of the Franks.
523	Execution of Boethius.
527–65	Reign of Justinian.
529	Benedict of Nursia founds Montecassino.
568	Lombards invade Italy.
575–613	Brunhild, regent of the East Franks.
580	Slavs overrun the Balkans.
590–604	Pope Gregory the Great.
613	Foundation of monastery of St. Gall.

CHAPTER II

THE LAND AND THE CONQUERORS

I T was, indeed, a good country, cut by silver rivers in which the British bards delighted, clothed with forest, abundant in pasture, rich in the Romans' roads, mines, and walled cities.

But it was not the England that we know, and to understand the slow growth of the Saxons, their civil wars, and weakness, we must transport ourselves to an older physical world; one more like the thousand miles of heath and sand-dunes between Jutland and Frisia, from which they had sailed, or the Baltic forests that made the background of their songs. The very atmosphere was different, and an indescribable feeling of cold storm chills the earliest English poetry. The trees are blasted and bent by the sea wind; lashing hails and frost, ice floes breaking, the sea-mew crying, ' winter wretchedness ', high stony cliffs on whose ledges the ravens nest, — such is its refrain, and it makes natural the paean with which it always salutes the sun, ' the noble creature ', ' heaven's candle ', ' brightest of beacons '. Beast and bird of the north lingered on. Brown bears, wild cattle, and beavers roamed Northumbria and Wales. The wolf, ' grey ganger of the heath ', haunted the Midlands, tenth-century shepherds still guarding their flocks against his spring. Wild boars were hunted within ten miles of London. Golden and white-tailed eagles sailed over cape and fen.

The island seemed to float on a waste of water. Its rivers, undrained and unchecked, opened into brackish estuaries as they neared the sea. A great marsh, in which Roman infantry had sunk, spread from London and the Lea along the Thames. The Wash flowed into middle England, making a Fen of 1300 square miles, reaching inland to Stamford and Huntingdon ; where, even in the latter Middle Ages, cattle had to be rounded up by boat. Another swamp marked the junction of Trent and Humber ; peats and mosses made half of Staffordshire uninhabitable, and blocked the openings of Solway, Dee, and Severn. In Somerset the Tone and Parrett marsh made a no-man's-land from Athelney to Glastonbury, where broken men took refuge all down the ages, from Roman coin forgers to the hero King Alfred, and from which the pelican and bittern had not disappeared. Land and sea melted into one another by lagoons where the salt workers drove their trade, and our present coast-line has only come about through centuries of loss to the sea by cliff erosion, and gain to the land by embankment. The Jutes sailed on salt water from Sandwich into mid-Kent, and the South Saxons up to Lewes and Pulborough. Holy Island was a peninsula, and Thanet an island; it was on points of vantage like these that the conquerors seized.

But the silence of Thames, Fen, or Trent was broken now by cries other than the marsh birds'; there is the plash of the thirty-oared boat, curved in prow and stem, rounding the river bends. Halting where firm gravel would hold their anchor stones, the invaders seem generally to have made their way direct to the nearest dry uplands. There ridgeway tracks ran into country unknown, all about them were the Britons' fields, and huts where the embers were hardly cold. Below and beyond they could see nothing for trees; they could hear the call of innumerable birds, catch sight here and there of a column of smoke, but a dense belt of woods hid their enemies, and shortened every horizon.

In the damp undrained bottoms a thick jungle of holly and thorn, briar and bramble, underlay oak and ash trees, — you may know the cattle thief, said a Saxon doom, by the bramble-tear on his face; ash, birch, and yew clothed the slopes of chalk and limestone, together with a scrub of box and juniper, while the higher they went the denser grew the beeches. Axe in hand the pioneers battled with the woods, from which most of our trim villages have been rescued, and which decided the fate of kingdoms. For thus the Andredsweald, 120 miles of impass-able timber, isolated the South Saxons, leaving them a backward tribe on a ribbon of the coast, and making Surrey a prize to be scrambled for by peoples from the north. On the clays north of Thames dense woods hemmed in London and kept empty south Essex and eastern Herts, two counties which, even in Domesday Book, were reckoned as having feeding-ground for 120,000 swine. The West Saxons, pulled up by the Andredsweald to the east and the New Forest scrub on the south, had little better fortune in the west, where they must first pass the barrier of which one fragment survives in Cranborne Chase, and the solid mass of Selwood and Braden which protected Glastonbury and Frome. If proceeding north-westwards they passed through Braden at Malmes-bury, they found any advance across the Severn blocked in its lower reaches by the Forest of Dean, and further north by that of Wyre, depth so impenetrable that King Offa thought it needless, two hundred years later, there to prolong his famous Dyke. If, on the contrary, they passed through the Oxfordshire Wychwood, their pace slackened and finally stopped at the entrance of Arden.

Here they touched the southern fringe of forests with which the Angles were wrestling, and which in themselves are enough to explain the fragments, — Middle Angles, South Angles, and Mercians, — out of which the State of Mercia had to be fashioned. Forest and heath, continuously from Hertford to Norfolk, checked every movement from the Fens; the South Angles, who had ascended the Nene valley, were held in, north and east, by the forest of Rockingham, while west of them everything between Avon and Severn was guarded by Arden. Their brothers to the north, Middle Angles and Mercians, who had passed up the Trent and its tributaries, had on their left Charnwood and on the right the mass of Sherwood, which covered to the fourteenth century a quarter of Nottinghamshire. And when the Mercians had struggled upstream to Repton and Tamworth, only a single narrow valley forced its way between Needwood, under the Peak, and Cannock Chase; if they passed through, and stood on that watershed between Trent and Severn, their road to Dee, Mersey, and the sea was barred by the dense Cheshire woods, growing in thirty miles' breadth of boulder clay. Between Mercia, again, and the Angles of Northumbria lay Hatfield Chase, filling the valleys by which Ouse, Aire, and Wharfe reach the Humber. York and its rich vale had barely room to breathe, shut in by wild western moors and to the north by the trackless wood of Galtres. North once more, the Bernician kingdom lay on the coast strip from Bamborough to the Forth and then inland to Edinburgh, but here the roads for a new advance, the valleys of Tweed, Esk, or Ettrick, were arrested in the forest of Selkirk.

Such were the forests, master for the time being of the Anglo-Saxon, and of his mind. In those sunless distances lived his foes, — the wolf, the outlaw or wolf-man, and bands of robbers; you must sound your horn, the Wessex law said, if you leave the path leading from forest to village. On its edge would stand the wooden temple of Woden or Frea, or the sacred tree, defending the home from evil spirits that lurked in shrouded places. But from the forest came also everything that made their home: oak planks for their houses, ash for the spear shaft, wild honey for the feast, beech-mast for their pigs. On wood they carved poetry in runes, and in wood first conceived the forms and ideas which later they put into pottery and stone. With stags' antlers they rounded off the gables of their hall, and from wild cattle horns fashioned and set in silver their deep drinking-cups.

So, as a thousand village names tell us, ' leys ' or ' dens ' or ' holts ', year by year the settlers broke into the woodland, here a colony of thegns seeking the Severn, there a few squatters allowed by their lord a free corner where they might fish and hawk. Their poets show them to us as the smoke curls up from the new chalets, where

> *silent in their dwelling*
> *they are sitting, leaning forwards,*

listening to ' the evening singer old ', the nightingale.

The people came from three Teutonic races, belonging to the same main stock as Goths, Germans, or Lombards, and the other conquerors of the Roman Empire. But our particular ancestors were originally seated in the North, the Jutes in Jutland and the Anglo-Saxons in Schleswig-Holstein; the Angles, dominant among the three, belonged emphatically to the Baltic, some of whose islands they had ruled, and in Angeln on the Baltic can still be seen their ancient home.

By the time of their invasion of Britain they had wandered far. Angles and Saxons had overlapped along Elbe and Weser into Hanover and Westphalia, Saxons had spread south into the long sands of Frisia, while some of the Jutes had reached the Rhine. Testimony to this effect comes from the closeness of Frisian and English speech, the likeness of our Jute settlers' arts and agriculture to those of the Franks, and the Saxons' close contact, as allies or foes, with the Roman Empire. The distribution of races in England makes it likely that the Jutes came to Thanet from ports far south of Jutland, nor is it probable that the Anglian undecked boats sailed direct from the Baltic.

Two hundred years of civil war were now to divide them. They had royal dynasties competing for supremacy, there were prizes at stake like London, or the ridges separating rich valleys, and their new settlements, cut off by wood and fen, deepened original variety of language. In sharp distinction of race the Jutes stood alone, and well into the Middle Ages the men of Kent prided themselves on their almost nationality. Their speech was different, their ' wergilds ' or life-values at law seem those of a superior race, they had different coinage and tenures of land, and in the sixth century developed an art much in advance of that of Anglo-Saxondom. The graves they have left, at Faversham or Sarre or by the Medway, were filled with enamelled jewels and garnet brooches which they had acquired with the Franks, vessels of blue and jade-green glass, crystal balls, ivory combs, and beads of amethyst; instructed, perhaps, by a subject Romanized people, they made pottery on the wheel, their designs came under the influence of Lombard Italy, and they imported Indian stones, Byzantine bronzes, and bowls from Egypt. Distant parts of Britain prized what they made; St. Cuthbert thus wearing a cross from the Kentish workshops.

As between Angle and Saxon the differences were originally less, and more obscure, though a line drawn from Bedford through Stratford-on-Avon to the Severn may serve to mark the zone where the two races met. The further north of that line we go, the coarser are the heavy-headed and cruciform brooches, which seem to breathe of the Goths and far-off wanderings in the Crimea, or Oriental caravanserais; the more garish is the early metal-work, in girdle hangers, or twisted torques and rings of light-coloured gold; to the Wessex area belong the neat round brooches, and the contacts south of Salisbury Plain established with the Jute arts in Hampshire. As time went on, and under Celtic influence, such differences increased between the arts of the North,

— the great stone crosses, for instance, of Lancashire and the Lakes, incised in curves and runes, — and the Rhineland or Latin models that stamped themselves on the South.

North and South were, indeed, to have a different history for a thousand years, yet, politically, such distinctions of race or culture as existed at the conquest were insignificant. At heart they felt themselves to be one. Their systems of rank and classes were much the same. West Saxon kings claimed descent from the same ancestors as those of Anglian Deira; Bede in the eighth century applies ' Saxon ' or ' Angle ', indiscriminately, to the whole race; Mercian kings of that age styled themselves ' Rex Brittonum ', and a century later Alfred used ' England ' (' Angelcynes lond ') to cover his native Wessex. The *imperium*, Bede tells us, or the power of ' Bretwalda ', passed in succession from Ælle of Sussex, Ceawlin of Wessex, Ethelbert of Kent, and then to East Anglia, before it reached seventh-century Northumbria; with an unconsciousness of any racial division, soon to be immensely strengthened by their common Christianity, which made it possible for Bede to get his knowledge of Wessex from the bishop of Winchester, or for the Northumbrian Cuthbert to become patron saint of Wells. English nationality broke out in English literature. Bede had all the north-countryman's suspicion of the Scot, while Alfred's Chronicle boasts in its finest ballad of ' the proud warsmiths ' who had laid low the Welsh.

They had won England together, but they had also a common background, and the same northern spirit breathes in Tacitus' sketch of first-century Germany, Gaulish histories of the fourth, English epic of the eighth, and Saxon law of the tenth. It was of Offa, the fourth-century hero of Angel, that our first poets sang in ' Widsith ' and ' Beowulf ' three hundred years later, — of Offa and kings of the Goths and Vandals, of Sceaf, the legendary founder of their race, the mystic child who had been thrown on their shores in a boat alone, of Weland the smith, welder of swords, whose smithy West Saxons pointed to in Berkshire downs, of Loki the crafty who is carved on Cumberland stones, and of battles with the Huns ' all about the Vistula wood '. In Northumbrian monasteries the monks sang Scandinavian folk-songs, while English missionaries desired especially to convert ' their own kin ' in Saxony overseas.

Their annals breathe not the atmosphere of a democratic and peaceful peasantry, but the passions and virtues of fighting-men. Down to the fifth century the Latins accused the Saxons of human sacrifice, while the charge of cruelty is borne out only too well by the English Chronicle and early law. From these we find that the thieving slave was scourged or scalped, that the witch was slung over London Bridge, or that the adulterous woman lost her nose and ears. Murder stalks through the royal chronicle. Kings were forcibly tonsured or burned alive; of fifteen who reigned in eighth-century Northumbria, five were murdered and another five deposed; queens were killed in palace revolutions; ambassadors were assassinated. The short knife, or scaex, was in every man's hand, and may be found in almost every grave.

As were their annals, so were their songs at night in the mead-hall, ' when loud to the harp the lilt made melody ', and horses stamped in the cold courtyard. They sang of war, of boar-crested helmets, of nights when the swords flashed ' as if all Finsburg were on fire ', of the linden shield shattered by the ash spear, arrows sleeting like hail, booty and women, of the eagle, wolf, and raven shiftily watching dying men. They sang of heroic kings, givers of bracelets and ringed mail and swords cut with runes, in whose hall warriors slept on the table, arms beside them, lest the moor-stalker, the evil Thing, surprise them, and of excellent *eorls* dead and gone, such as those whom Beowulf hoped to join. They sang of far venture, of their dragon-prowed ship, ' foam crester ' or ' wide-bosomed ', of voyages over ' the whale road ' or in fiords where the wild swans fly; of a longing for the sea, passing the love of women or the harp, of voyages like those of Othere, the Norse captain who told King Alfred of walrus and reindeer in the Arctic, or those of the English pioneers when, ' over the bulwarks their bright targets ' and their ship's hold full of horses, armour, and longhorned cattle, they first grounded on the Sussex shingle. ' Come south to me, beloved,' says one such song, ' I am in a rich land.'

Mercy and mildness made no part of this northern faith. Their gods, Woden or Tiu or Thor, were by this time merely heroes writ large, or forefathers of their kings; strong enough to stamp themselves on times and places, on the days of the week or on some Woden's burh (or Wednesbury), but not to govern the heart. Behind and overruling them the Saxon saw a god or demon in every manifestation of nature; Valkyrie women who rained spears from heaven, elves of the wood, monsters of the misty hills, and, strongest of all, Weird, the force of fate, to whom both gods and heroes bow. Older still was their folk-worship; of Eostra, symbol of fertile spring triumphing over buried winter, whom Christians transmuted into the resurrection feast, and again of Mother Earth, whom the primitive Baltic Anglians had adored.

Relics of these superstitions long lived on. St. Augustine found the men of Kent sacrificing oxen and horses at their festivals, with warriors masked in the skins and horns of bull and deer. In the eleventh century Canute had to denounce the worship of trees, weather prophets, and wizards, and a mass of charms accompanied the tracking of stolen cattle or sowing the seed :

Hail be thou Earth, mother of men,
In the lap of the god be thou a-growing.

Nor did Christianity change, for many centuries, the heroic temper. Christ seemed an Etheling who wins peace after his ' war play ', St. Andrew is ' the hero hard in war ', Cædmon styled the apostles ' thegns of God ', while the favourite English story of the merciful Saviour was His ' Harrowing of Hell ', a combat in dark places like Beowulf's with the fiend Grendel.

Their scale of virtues was older than Christianity's. Nothing in this life, or life to come, was certain except the doom of Weird : mighty kings who had ruled fifty winters, honourable and chaste women who rewarded them with mead and bracelet in hall and urged them to battle, whose embroideries and needle-boxes are found buried with them, — all must perish ; was not the life of man, asked the thegn when the Northumbrian King was considering baptism, only that of the bird flying from the cold into the lighted hall, and out into cold again ?

> *Where is gone the horse ? where is gone the hero ?*
> *where is gone the giver of treasures ?*

But the brave man must fight on, must never desert his lord or abandon steadfastness, his bosom's treasure. Did not Weland himself ' know exile, sorrow and longing he had to as fellow, winter-cold wretchedness ' ? But ' that ancient woe was endured, and so may mine·'.

Fortitude in life, fame after death, was the fighting-man's faith ; on a high barrow, in sight of sea-wayfarers, Beowulf asked to lie, a life of action ending in the blaze of the pyre, round which the thegns ride singing the praise of the dead. While Saxon England lived, her best sons held the same thoughts, and never were they more superbly expressed than in the ' Song of Maldon ', written of that battle with the Danes in 991 when Ethelred the Unready was destroying his country. Once more we have the hero ' grey in war ' Byrhtnoth ealdorman of Essex, who promises the enemy ' grim war-play ' and dies thanking the ' ruler of nations ' for the joy of earth ; once more, the true companions of his hearth, who swear to make good in the fray what they promised in the mead-hall. ' Never shall the steadfast men round Stourmere reproach me that I journey lordless home.' With their lord they fight and die, whatever the odds ; for

> *thought shall be the harder, heart the keener,*
> *mood shall be the more, as our might lessens.*

Such were our fathers and, deep though is our ignorance of their first institutions on English soil, we can hardly suppose that they differed widely from the picture in their songs. We shall be safe, perhaps, in remembering that we deal with the effects of two contrasted historical forces ; on one hand an old civilization, proud of its heroic legend, delighting in the arts of war, adept in ornate romantic language and, on the other, a conquered country, in extent almost limitless if compared with the number of its conquerors, severed by natural barriers, fringed by unconquered tribes.

Certainly we find royalty, aristocracy, and war on every page of our earliest history. The might of a stronger heir could rise superior to hereditary right, Alfred thus taking precedence of his nephews, but no king reigned at all who could not claim the half-divine blood royal. Even if we knew nothing of the English before they reached England, what we find in England proves that the conquest was made by royal families, whose younger sons swarmed off to found new dynasties as the conquest spread inland. In the seventh century three co-heirs simultaneously ruled Essex, thirty princes followed Penda of Mercia, five kings are found at once in early Wessex. A dozen principalities fought for supremacy, as larger kingdoms rose on the forcible suppression of the small. Warriors from all provinces would take service with any King who could give them war and land, and when a tenth-century noble's will bequeathes spear, horse, or deerhounds to his ' royal lord ', it is a survival of ruder days when his ancestor had received a sword or bracelet from his prince.

From such men came the retinue of the king, his court, and the sinews of his war; *ministri* or *milites*, as Bede wrote, ' thegns ' and ' gesiths ' in the native tongue, of all grades from the noble down to the humble companion, or ' huscarle '. Keeping of the peace in his *burh* or enclosed homestead was the right of every freeman, and how much more of the King! Kentish laws, before 616, assign double penalties for an attack on the court, while those of Wessex, eighty years later, threaten the guilty with death. Ine, maker of these last, ruled a fully-fledged monarchy; with Welsh horse vassals, *villae regales* or crown estates administered by royal reeves, a thegn class bound under forfeit of their land to serve in war, and a fixed revenue.

In a heroic age it is vain to expect constitutional rules; the early King reigned because he was strong, and not in virtue of a constitution. His council, the ' moot ' of the Witan or wise men, seem generally to have been his kinsmen or his nominees; Ine named and removed reeves of estates and ealdormen of shires, Penda handed over the Middle Angles to his son, and we know of no clear case, apart from civil war, where the Witan deposed or elected a King. But deposition would certainly await the despot, if only because despotism implies a power that could not exist in these scattered forest clearings, while the balance of that rude society would act automatically, since the King led warriors without whose good will he must perish. As Beowulf put it :

> *Here is every earl by the others trusted,*
> *mild of mind, to the master loyal,*
> *the thegns are kindly, the commons submissive.*

Our village place-names, generally taken from a man or family, remind us of two basic things : the clan bound together by blood, and a hereditary class system. Trying to pierce beneath the map surface, we see the first conquerors settling down in kindred groups, Barkings or Hastings or those ' Waeclingas ' from whom Watling Street was named ; we find large areas splitting into many sections of the clan, like the eight Rodings in Essex, or parishes intertwined with others, all tending to show that our early settlement names are not so much those of places as of groups. Land was family land, and from the family it could not be left away, held as it was on an unwritten tenure of ' folkright ', more binding than documents. In Kent this clan system lived on for centuries under the name of gavel-kind, and Domesday Book is full of thegns who share their land on a family basis. The unit for land measurement or royal taxes was the hide, or family holding ; so many ' families ' was Bede's way of measuring Mercia or the Isle of Wight.

A society of fighting-men divided into clans must, if unchecked, mean war without end ; ' buy off the spear, or bear it ', said their proverb. Hence arose the custom, universal among Germanic peoples, of the ' wergild ', an instrument designed to stop the blood feud by giving money compensation ; so that all men and all things in our early laws had their price, from 100s. for murder of a king's courier down to 30 copper pieces for loss of the big toe-nail. In all this the first responsibility rested on the clan. They must produce their kinsman in court, they will share in compensation for his death, they must ride in to act as ' oath-helpers ' to swear his innocence ; it was for them, in this rough justice, to decide if the wrongdoer should be abandoned by his folk, to die at his enemy's hand. In early days such oaths were measured in numbers of hides, as if so many family groups, more or less, must purge the guilt away.

But the wergild itself is our best ground for saying that aristocracy was even more potent than the blood tie. By 700 the population was divided into ' twelhynde ', ' sixhynde ', or ' twyhynde ', — the King's principal thegns, that is, having wergilds of 1200s., a middle class at 600s., and the ceorls or yeomen at only 200s. Measured in oxen, as perhaps they originally were, the three classes stood respectively at the value of 200 cattle, 100, or 33.

What made the origin of this aristocracy? Whether it sprang first from nobility of blood or the service of kings? To such questions there seems to be no decisive answer. Saxon law, at least, proves that the wergilds were inheritable ; that wergilds on a lower scale existed for the defeated Welsh, who were generally rated at roughly half the value of Saxons ; and that most men were assumed to be under some lord's control. ' Happy days ', says an eighth-century poem, ' when I laid head and hands on my lord's knee.' We can hardly suppose a greater degree of democracy existed during the wild centuries of conquest, from which came the treasures found in great men's tombs like that of the chief buried at Taplow, with his weapons, gilt clasps, bronze bowls and glass cups, draughtsmen and drinking-horns, or that other found in the Peak with boar helmet and chain mail.

This society, moreover, was to a great extent based upon slavery; for to capture slaves was an essential object in primitive war. In fifth-century Britain, in the Severn valley, slaves belonged to the Roman citizen whose son was St. Patrick; all through the sixth, British slaves were selling in Gaul and Rome, winning, as all know, the pity of Pope Gregory; five centuries later, Domesday Book called ' slaves ' some 16 per cent of the people in the western shires. In all ages pious Churchmen, from Aidan and Wilfrid downwards, taught the duty of setting the slave free. Laws and literature tell us of British slave-girls who carried water in yoked buckets or ground at the mill, and of English ' theows ' reduced to slavery by poverty or crime. They formed, of course, a sort of property and, as such, fines protected them from murder. But they were chattels : if they ran away, they were liable to the gallows; only by payment could they escape the lash for many offences; they could be tendered with other cattle in payment of a wergild, stoned or burned for theft. Worst of all, this servitude descended to their children.

So far we have been on fairly safe ground, building on evidence coming from the first two centuries. But if we enquire as to the general frame of this society, how they settled on the land, how they divided it and ruled themselves every day, we run the danger of reading forward from Tacitus' picture of Germany, or backwards from the eleventh-century Domesday Book.

It was, however, clearly a land of endless variety, a network of small principalities compelled by physical reasons to develop on many different lines. We cannot, therefore, frame rules that will be equally true alike for the fens and Essex marshes, where shepherds of scattered hamlets fought against ague for existence, for the Mercian-Welsh or North-umbrian border, each full of Celtic slaves and tributary villages, for cosmopolitan Kent, and the rich Thames valley. Yet two or three broad conclusions apply more or less to all.

Though ruled by kings and divided by class, the body of the conquerors were free men. The ' twyhynde ' ceorl could himself own slaves; he could rise to become a thegn; his family was presumed to own a hide of land. He paid ' gafol ' or taxation, and was bound to serve in the ' fyrd ', or army, when summoned; his homestead was protected by law, as was every part of his anatomy, from his long hair downwards which no enemy might cut. And above all, the village community testified to a hard core of Saxon liberty.

It was a land of villages; for, though life was flowing back to Roman York or London, the English had come from open country or from water, and they cleaved to them; using a Roman road often enough to make a boundary, but ever going deeper on to the wood and clay lands which earlier races had shunned. So, while kings fought and Christians preached, villages of all types sprang up, with thatched roofs and daub and wattle walls. Kent, as ever, had its own system, Norfolk its peculiar compact holdings, and the western moors their scattered pastoral farms. But even there, and much more in the concentrated villages and open-field farming of Wessex and the Midlands, everything about the normal village, or the manor as it became afterwards, suggests that it was first and always a community, to meet the needs of men who required each other's help, and who meant to have a fair deal, though not equality. Their arable land lay usually in two or three huge unhedged fields, which, turn by turn, went down to wheat, to barley or oats, or lay fallow, and in those fields, running over good and bad soil alike, were the separate family strips, a furlong long and up to twenty yards wide. Each family's portion lay scattered, often with many strips in each field, so minutely divided that we find villages in Norman England with 2000 separate holdings. With each arable allotment went a share in the common meadow, the waste, and the woodland, where they could get rough pasture, fuel, and food for their pigs. In the wilder countries of fen and moor these were often controlled jointly by several villages, who 'intercommoned' in the summer pastures, sheep-walks, or fisheries.

By the year 700 inequality had gone far. There were thegns and even yeomen with five hides, some with the traditional one hide, but the majority perhaps with a quarter-hide, or 'yardland'. Yet, even on the evidence of this later age, we cannot doubt that equitable co-partner-ship had been the original ideal. Land measurements in some areas were based upon the ploughing capacity of the team of eight oxen, which several neighbours would have to supply; taking of lots, to very late times, often regulated the share-out of the meadows; a ceorl was fined whose uncleaned ditches or unfenced pasture damaged the common interest.

Moreover, though every village had a sort of colonial expansion into the backwoods, it was usually the old original holdings which monopolized rights over the commons, while for big operations, like threshing, the hides often for centuries worked as units. It was upon the village and its hides, not on later manorial holdings, that the State assessed taxes; on what had, in short, once been a real unit, tied to-gether by kindred and economic partnership. But this unity was already cut into by lordship, and exploited by kings.

By 650 there were in existence kingdoms of fair size, sometimes ruling six or more of our modern counties, and systems of government above the village co-existed with them. Of their form and function we know next to nothing. The shire court is old, but cannot be traced before Alfred's day; its subdivision, the hundred, cannot be proved as a governmental area till the time of Alfred's children; finally, if the village elders met to govern their own concerns, they have left no record of it. We have to guess, to read back, to piece together, our first germs of self-government.

Seventh-century England seems, however, to have been divided into *regiones*, of so many hundred, or thousand, ' families ' or hides; 1200 in the Isle of Wight, 1200 to the Peak dwellers, such was Bede's way of computation, which the eighth-century Mercian list, the ' Tribal Hidage ', confirms. Within the bounds of each such group were royal tuns, or ' *villae regales* ', centres not only for the King's estate but for the government of areas round them. Directed by officials called the king's reeves, they had to feed King and Court, to entertain his servants, provide him with guides through the forest, or keep up the walls of his fortress. For these purposes they were assessed in groups of hides; every 10 hides, Ine's laws say, must produce 10 vats of honey, 300 loaves, and so on; a century later, Mercian monasteries had to entertain envoys from the north or from Wessex, not to mention their own sovereign's huntsmen, hawks, and hounds. Such was the ' feorm ', our first rough system of revenue, whereby the King and his Court ate the taxes as they moved; the ' firm of one night ', or more nights, in the pages of Domesday, which time the progresses of the earliest kings. 3000 loaves from Cirencester, ' half a day of honey ' from some Suffolk village, — these crude payments survived from days when the Court rode in to claim its dues. For only from such exploiting of the soil could come the King's power; his rents and taxes were still one and the same, his ' reeves ' were estate bailiffs in one sense but public officials in another.

An unknown and perhaps unascertainable descent separates the shires and hundreds, as rearranged in the tenth century, from the original folk-groups, whether the Kentish lathes, the small shires of the north like Hallamshire, or the Sunningas (Sonning) territory in Berkshire. We move from the conception of a folk-group to one of an area, from the Wilsaetan who dwelt by the Wylye river, for instance, to ' Wiltshire ', ruled from a centre at Wilton. But it seems clear that the system was first, and most, elaborated in Wessex and southern Mercia, whereby old *regiones* were arranged in hundred-hide districts and five-hide (' Fyfield ') villages for assessment to the feorm, and held responsible to the local meeting-place for the King's estates.

Public duties at any rate were laid upon these hide groups, of service in war, upkeep of the royal ' tuns ', and repair of bridges and roads, and in all this the citizen *par excellence* seems originally to have been the substantial peasant; the owner of a hide (or more) with full privileges in the village fields, a payer of land revenue, the man called ' moot-worthy, foldworthy, fyrdworthy ' — with rights and duties, that is, in the court, the sheepfold, and the army. His civic duties were larger than the agricultural routine of his village, where he helped in the apportionment of the commons, or in fixing the date at which fields should be unfenced after harvest; in the tenth century all substantial tenants of the manor attended the hundred court, and so their predecessors had gone, we must assume, to whatever local court preceded it.

But the life of this English village, so far as history can see back, was controlled by royal agents, graded for royal service, and was rather communal than free. We cannot believe that its consent was asked to a royal ' feorm ', or to forced labour on the royal ' burhs ', and, more-over, grants to royal servants, together with an inevitable growth of inequality in a conquered country, were sapping this community away. These grants to thegns and churches, whether for one life only or for ever, gave away, as it were, a slice of the King's regality; the same ten or five hides were still charged with the same taxation, but now it must be paid, in the first instance, to the lord. It was for him to answer for the keeping of the peace, to make good thefts committed by his men, and to see to the discharge of public service in law court or ' fyrd '; if his tenants ran away, he was legally empowered to bring them back. Inequalities were coming, too, in other ways. The thegn was more than a courtier or a warrior; he was a small capitalist, a cog in a rude economic machine. The Wessex laws thus insisted that he must leave his holding in proper cultivation; on the other hand, they recognized his right to take labour services from humbler men, to whom he had leased house or land. Whether he paid rent to a king or a lord, the peasant was in either case a payer of tribute. The full-fledged manor, with a demesne or home farm worked by serfs, had not yet arrived, for the peasant's tribute still rather took the form of food rents, defence, and public service. But public rights in private hands must, sooner or later, become feudal privilege.

Already, then, there existed in this small country the system of ' removable inequalities ' which has always been the character of its society. There was a monarchy, able to enforce political action upon, and to tax, the whole soil. There was a landed aristocracy, rapidly losing all signs of a closed caste, and composed of men rewarded as royal servants, stimulated as landlords, thriving to thegnhood by energy and prowess. There was still a mass of yeomen descending from the first pioneers. Some were ascending the ladder, in the ceorls whom we find winning five hides and thegnhood, or Welshmen acquiring hides and wergilds; but others were coming down, sinking into servitude through crime or war, renting land from a rich neighbour, or reduced to the condition of landless men whom the law did not admit as full citizens. The family-holding was often still intact, but it was buffeted by royal exactions, by the subdivision coming with a larger population, and by human inequality working itself out, by a hundred channels, on unequal soils.

In the fullness of time the village self-governing unit was to find itself again ; it would return from the sheer necessity of mutual arrangements for land cultivation, while its political life would range upwards from the cleaning of ditches, or the punishment of cattle theft, to meet larger demands in hundred and shire. But this village-bred, long-enduring liberty had much to suffer before it became a pillar of the State ; and not least from the return of Roman power, in the form of landowning Christian churches.

CHAPTER III

CONSOLIDATION OF THE CHURCH

WHILE the Anglo-Saxons were settling into their frontiers, two new elements entered into the making of English civilization. In 563 the Irishman Columba brought Christianity to Iona, an island off the west Highland coast, while in 597 Augustine landed in Kent with a mission from Rome. Within a hundred years England was organized into bishoprics and churches; Saxon kings were competing for relics of the martyrs; and the whole race were united, not under a king but under an English-born archbishop of Canterbury.

Such Christianity as Rome had left behind was established most solidly in Wales. Thither had fled many British Christians, while there was a constant interchange of saints and missioners between Wales, Cornwall, Strathclyde, and Brittany, and from Wales we might have expected efforts to proceed for the conversion of England. But the Welsh Church, entrenched most strongly in the south and by the western sea, refused contact with the barbarian. An intense tribalism coloured its life. Monks had taken the place of the tribal Druids, and within each clan sprang up a monastery, with hereditary abbots ruling a sub-tribe of religion. ' Bishops ' were only preachers in the abbot's obedience or, like St. David himself, rather the priest of a clan than a territorial official; settlements of married priests ministered to tribes, not parishes, nor was there any regular system of Orders.

The refoundation of English Christianity thus came not from Wales but from overseas, and ultimately from Rome. St. Patrick set in motion the first impetus. Springing from a family on the Welsh March who had for three generations been Christian and Roman citizens, he had been taken to Ireland by slave-raiders and after his escape still heard the cry of the unbaptized Irish children. Receiving his inspiration from Gaul and Rome when in 432 he returned to Ireland as bishop, he took those churches as his model, and the Latin tongue as his medium. He died in 461.

> Patrick's soul from his body after labours was severed,
> God's angels the first night kept watch thereon unceasingly.

The devout learning of Ireland attracted students from all nations; thence went Columba the apostle of the Scots, and Columban whose life-work resulted in more than a hundred monasteries, some of immortal fame like the Swiss St. Gall or Bobbio in Italy; there studied the best Englishmen of those centuries, Chad the saint of Lichfield and Willibrord the Yorkshireman who evangelized Frisia ; from Ireland came the inspiration of the manuscripts, metal-work, and sculpture, which marked the golden age of northern England.

But the century following St. Patrick's death was a dark one. Italy and Gaul were scourged by barbarians, the Eastern Empire under Justinian recovered for a space some of its hold on the West, and finally the Lombards, most savage of the conquerors, encamped round Rome. Cut off from its sources by these events and the Saxon invasions, Irish-Roman Christianity sank into a native cult, with standards of its own in the matters most vital to the faith. It abandoned the Roman tonsure, adopting from the Druids the crown shaven in front from ear to ear, and clung to a reckoning of Easter which Rome had altered. As in Wales, the Church lived by compromising with the morals of a primitive people, who lived in undivided pastures and with no walled towns, — a land where war was the sport of kings, where women fought like Amazons, where the marriage tie was unobserved, and the mental air was full of sun-worship, holy wells, and evil spirits. The priest became a superior medicine-man, from whom miracles were expected and were duly forthcoming, and whose life reproduced the wildest practices of Christian origins in the East. Anchorites and fakirs set up huts on mountain tops, or lived in caves like wild beasts. Heaven was far, — they would storm it by going into the desert ; the flesh was too near, — they would mortify it by suffering, like the Scottish monk we find later who stood many hours reciting his psalms in the icy Tweed.

The kingdom of God, thus sought by escape to nature, could not produce the organization which makes a Church militant here on earth. Each community sought out a tribe from whom it received land, whose children it trained for the priesthood, and within which it formed, as it were, an inner circle, — the sub-tribe of the saint. Its organization took the form of hereditary holy men ; there were bishops and priests to ordain and minister the sacraments, but they were recruited and directed by the head of their group, abbot or abbess as the case might be. Of this sort was the community under the abbot of Louth :

> *Not poor was the family of Mochta ;*
> *three hundred priests and a hundred bishops,*
> *sixty singing men ;*
> *They ploughed not, they reaped not, they dried not corn,*
> *they laboured not, save at learning only.*[1]

Such a body Columba planted in Iona. Coming from the Hy Neill royal house, he was devoted to his race, its songs and learning, and had already achieved fame in founding of monasteries and tribal war, when

---

[1] Helen Waddell, *The Wandering Scholars.*

he went out to help an Irish Christian race, the Scots of Dalriada, who were fighting for existence against the Picts. In Iona his company set up their wooden church and their chain of cells, and there nine successive abbots of his clan ruled the missioners who made Scotland and two-thirds of England Christian, and so produced the great saints of the north, Aidan, Hilda, and Cuthbert. He himself converted the Picts, sent his monks even to the Orkneys, and founded houses, as at Melrose and Dunkeld, to hold what he had won. He was plainly a prince among men, poet and ruler both, with an organ voice and splendid presence, and the heart of a St. Francis; he died in 597, blessing the grain and the white horse that worked the monks' dairy. A month or two before, a ship from Gaul had reached Thanet, bringing forty monks from Rome.

Very different was the new agent of Providence. Pope Gregory the Great, a Roman noble, saw that the Papacy could seize the place left vacant by the Empire; but to do so it must use the barbarians, turning a blind eye to their crimes, if they accepted the faith. For Britain his scheme was of grand design. He planned a Church ruled by two co-equal metropolitans in the Roman cities of London and York, each with twelve dependent bishops, and equipped the mission with every privilege and ornament which could impress the grandeur of Rome. Augustine, its leader, received the pallium that marked a favoured son of the Church; he was provided with Frankish interpreters, relics and manuscripts, painted banners, and silver crosses. The Pope himself, in fact, was the heart of this mission. He drove Augustine on when his heart quailed; reinforced him with recruits, bade him become all things to all men, — to allow differences of ritual, to use and not destroy the heathen temples, and to win the Kentishmen even through their feasts and animal sacrifice.

He knew, presumably, that his mission would be allowed to enter England; for a hundred years had passed since the conversion of the Franks, and he counted on the good offices of a Frankish princess, Bertha, who had left Paris to wed Ethelbert of Kent, now the strongest of English princes. Ethelbert had long allowed liberty of worship to his wife and her bishop, and was himself baptized, with thousands of his subjects, within a month or two of Augustine's arrival, so that it would seem that, like the Franks before him, he saw the advantage of belonging to a Church which provided obedient subjects and educated administrators. In any case, it was a vitally important fact that the English conversion came so late in the day. For it received a faith orthodox, no longer tainted by the heresies which had torn the Goths in pieces, and not through slow penetration or suffering but direct from Rome, and at the hands of kings. It came when all zeal had departed from heathendom; if there was natural suspicion of the new God, we hear of no English Christian martyr.

These very facts perhaps explain the comparative failure of Augustine. He won over Ethelbert and his nephew the King of Essex, and set up bishops at Rochester and London, but the Christian hold vanished with the death of these sovereigns, the mission was within an ace of being abandoned, and four Roman archbishops worked thirty years almost in vain. All attempts failed at reunion with the Welsh and Irish Churches, who clung to their peculiar observance and refused to join in the work of conversion. The English rulers, on the other hand, simply used the name of Christ for political prestige, or set Him among their idols. His religion, said one East Saxon who slew his king on that account, made men too mild. Warriors combined on their helmets the cross and Woden's tusked boar. The young kings of Essex refused baptism, but demanded ' the white bread ' which they had seen comfort their father.

But one wider triumph did proceed from Canterbury. A new power arose in the north in Edwin of Deira who, by slaying Ethelfrith the slayer of the Welsh monks, made himself master of all Northumbria. In 625 he took to wife a Kentish princess, with whom went Paulinus, a last survivor of those sent by Gregory. The King and his house were converted and in all his territories, from the Tweed to Lincolnshire, we hear of Paulinus at work, — baptizing multitudes in the Trent, setting up stone churches, introducing the Gregorian chant. In 632 all this too seemed to be swept away; Edwin was slain in battle by Mercians and Welsh, his widow and Paulinus fled to the south, Northumbria fell into heathen hands.

Yet from about this date the tide turned. A new and wonderful current set in from the Scots, and another from Europe, especially Gaul, the joint effects of which prepared England for the final victory of religion. Even the deadly hatred between Mercia and Northumbria contributed; for the Mercian Penda's savage heathendom, allied with an equally savage Christianity in Wales, cemented Christian Northumbria in suffering, while, when Mercia itself became Christian, it tried to outbid its rival in the Church's favour.

When Ethelfrith's children had fled before Edwin, they found refuge at Iona, and when in due course they returned, they brought Iona's religion with them, and in St. Aidan almost her purest saint. It was a century of Northumbrian supremacy, and political motives entered even here; when St. Oswald, for instance, married a princess of Wessex, his wedding was combined with the baptism of his wife's father. But in the main this age was the most spiritual in the thousand years of Saxon Christianity, and a deep seed-plot of English civilization. For seven short years, till Oswald also fell in battle before Penda, the King and Aidan showed the perfection of the Christian life on the large stage of power. The saint, indeed, true to the Celtic spirit, spent most of his life in retreat on Lindisfarne or the more remote Farne islets, but monasteries sprang up in disused Roman camps or in thorn-hedge circles, the thegnhood gave their land, schools began to train boys for the priesthood, and the missioners, setting up a wooden cross by the roadside, brought their tidings to distant sheep-farms.

This holy living and dying of the northern saints evoked a literature of legend, miracle, and salvation, which stamped Christianity on the soul of the people. Alfred was preceded in their folk-stories by Oswald; how he was upheld in battle by the arm of Columba, or how the grass grows more green at Oswestry where Penda killed him, with the memory of his last thought for his army, ' " God have mercy on their souls," said Oswald, falling to the ground '. His right hand, which had given his substance to the poor, was kept, uncorrupt, at Bamborough; his head was buried, at last, in St. Cuthbert's coffin; his old enemies of Mercia tried to save his body from the Danes. Heaven and earth seemed very near together in this age of the North. In 651 the farmer's son Cuthbert, watching his sheep in the Lammermoor hills, saw angels bearing Aidan's soul to heaven, and entered the monastery at Melrose; it was he who preserved Aidan's tradition for thirty years more, sometimes in utter solitariness on the islands and sometimes in long tours of preaching, dying as bishop in Northumbria's evil days, yet having amassed round his name such a treasury of devotion that his shrine became the fortress, and his banner the battle-cry, of all the north as long as the Catholic north lasted.

The housetops shone, too, with light at the death of St. Hilda, whose life was the most continuous and characteristic in Northumbrian Christianity. Baptized by the Roman Paulinus, she was given her task by the Scot Aidan; Northumbria was torn between rival princes, but she, a princess of Deira, was styled mother of them all. At Whitby she founded the most famous of those mixed monasteries, men and women, which flourished in the Celtic world, — a house which became a nursery of bishops, a centre of unity, a school of literature. In her stable there worked Cædmon, the first recorded English Christian poet, whom a vision bade sing of the Creation; his songs, of ' the Father of Glory ', who made for men ' heaven for their roof and then the earth ', opened the volume of northern poetry which, beginning with the voice of the harper or runes on stone crosses, was borrowed later by Wessex and in that dialect written for preservation. Two masterpieces have come down to us of that mingled Christian and northern art. Carved on the whalebone-box known as the Franks casket are the sack of Jerusalem, Romulus and Remus, the Adoration of the Magi, together with the German legends of Weland and Siegfried. And in ' the Dream of the Rood ' a Northumbrian poet told of a tree more holy than any in their forests, — ' the Healer's tree ', on to which stepped Christ ' the young hero ', ' the lord of the folk kin ', — of the tree's agony, pierced with nails, and the moment when, as darkness covered the earth, soldiers lifted down the King and left the Tree all with blood streaming.

This fire of Northumbrian religion caught all England. Its missioners reconverted Essex; Irish monks worked in Wiltshire, in East Anglia, and the creeks of Chichester harbour, and finally Northumbrians took Christianity to Mercia,. the rising State. There Chad and Wilfrid were made welcome; children and grandchildren of the heathen Penda became Christians, fervent in zeal, imposing the faith on subject princes and endowing famous shrines of the future at Peterborough and Crowland, Chester and Worcester.

Meantime, not so much disconnected with Canterbury as growing by its own weight, the faith impressed itself on large districts of the south. Soon after 630 an East Anglian King, converted in Gaul, took Felix, a Burgundian, as his bishop, and the piety of that dynasty became proverbial; its daughters went to the great Frankish nunneries, while two of them, queens in their turn of Northumbria and Mercia, ruled the family foundation of Ely. Round 650 Cedd, trained in the north, restored the faith among the East Saxons. Wessex was a more slow and difficult ground. Here the first leader was the foreign Birinus, to whom was given Dorchester, on the Mercian Thames border, as his centre, but about 660 an English successor, trained in Gaul, moved to Winchester, the capital of Wessex in church and state. By that time only the little princedoms of Sussex and the Isle of Wight remained heathen. The barriers were breaking down that kept churches and provinces apart. Southern Ireland had accepted the Roman ruling as to Easter. Bishops trained in France and Ireland worked alongside Scottish monks in southern England. St. Chad, Aidan's pupil, was consecrated bishop by a prelate from Gaul and by others from the Britons of Devon and Cornwall.

Two Northumbrians did most to subordinate Northumbrian religion to the supremacy of Rome. Both belonged to the thegn class; both broke away from their native training to visit monasteries abroad, and to study religion as it was practised at the source. Benedict Biscop's work was, perhaps, the more enduring. The first of his six visits to Rome was in 653; from them all he returned with manuscripts, relics, and vestments, and brought to the north stone-masons and glass-makers from France, music from the Pope's chapel, and the Benedictine rule for the monks. He founded the ever-memorable houses of Wearmouth and Jarrow, which produced Bede and the school of York, from which in turn came Boniface the apostle of Germany, and Alcuin the adviser of Charlemagne. Winter froze his monks' hands so that they could not write, plague decimated them; Scots, Mercians, and then Danes preyed on the north; but for one hundred and fifty years the reading and copying went on; till the monk died in dictating a last word.

Benedict's first fellow-traveller was the high-mettled Wilfrid, whose vision was of a Church overstepping all kingdoms; Wilfrid, builder of great churches at Ripon and Hexham (where his crypt survives), restorer of York, and apostle to the South Saxons. With a knightly train, like Becket or Wolsey later, he moved from one Court to another, making kings the pawns in his game. Northumbria exiled him, two archbishops of Canterbury found him impossible, St. Hilda resisted him, but for fifty years his iron frame, energy, and wealth were dedicated to one object, the bringing together of England and Rome, with the north in his own command.

Fired by experience in Italy, and antagonized by the Celtic church-men, it was he who spoke of Rome at the meeting called by Oswy of Northumbria to Whitby, probably in 663, at which the old differences were extinguished. Rome, Gaul, ' all Christendom ' agreed, he said, except these two small islands. The new generation of princes was on his side, so were Wessex and Kent, and Oswy's Kentish queen. The King was clear that it was best to be on the side of the big battalions, for St. Peter was the door-keeper of heaven and not St. Columba, and Chad, Hilda, and Cuthbert, the flower of the northern Church, loyally accepted his ruling.

The decision was irrevocable and inevitable; the Church's influence would be doubled by national unity and an agreement with Latin Europe, while Oswy would achieve peace in his own Court and weld new links with Kent and Essex against Mercia. But the old fire long smouldered; it was fanned by Wilfrid, now bishop in Northumbria, who showed his cosmopolitan contempt by seeking consecration abroad and long absence, and who, when he was consequently deprived, made incessant appeal to Rome. To make the unity of Whitby a real one, and to build the Church on a basis independent of kingly feud, ambitious bishops, and provincial hatred, was the task left to a master-builder, Theodore of Tarsus. Every circumstance of his appointment marked the power of Rome, for Northumbria and Kent (perhaps other States) had left the choice of an archbishop to the Pope, who selected this Greek monk, with the African abbot Hadrian as his right hand, and Benedict Biscop as his English adviser.

When in 669 Theodore reached England, he was a man of nearly seventy, but for twenty-one years, resolute, peace-loving, and systematic, he lived on and laboured. Journeying all over the country, he brought Canterbury out of Kent and made it metropolitan, and by 672 was able to call a Council of the whole Church in England. His detachment from English prejudice allowed him to arbitrate between Mercia and Northumbria, nor did he distinguish between men of Celtic and Latin training for the episcopate, if they gave canonical obedience. His task was to make a Church corporate out of fragmentary missions, to map out its officers in fixed areas, and his first synod thus forbade bishops to invade each other's territory, monks to wander from one house to another, and priests to leave their diocese at will.

His greatest work, and the condition of all else, was an increase in the episcopate; here he had to fight spiritual pride in Wilfrid, political jealousy in kings, and a conflict of Celtic and Latin orders. Keeping Canterbury and Rochester for Kent, and London for Essex, he divided the East Anglians between Elmham and Dunwich, while, despite Wilfrid's repeated visits to Rome, the north was distributed between York, Lindisfarne, and Hexham; yet another see was allotted to Lindsey, the province always contested between the north and Mercia. It was, in fact, one of Theodore's best achievements to make Mercia an instrument in his work. Lichfield became the bishopric for the core of it, Leicester for south Mercia, Dorchester for its new-won Chiltern lands, Hereford for its gains from the Welsh, and Worcester for its vassal, the Hwiccas.

Before his death Theodore had thus carried out the first essential, — a unified and properly distributed higher command; the parish organization below, with its endowment, must be the work of time, and for another century at least there were not clergy enough to man it. In this first stage they were grouped in the minsters, or mother-churches of vast ' parishes ', like those that have survived in the north, from which priests went out periodically to visit distant or new settlements, where a graveyard, and a shack for the priest and his horse, made up all their organization. Gradually the thegnhood gave land for the building of churches, like those we still see at Brixworth or Bradford-on-Avon, — rough-rubbled, fortified, with narrow slit windows and rude-angled western towers, adorned within by wall-painting to let the people see the Saviour and His saints.

When a hundred years had gone by, English law testified how deep Christianity had sunk into the national life. Bishops' and abbots' houses were made as inviolate as those of royalty; their owners sat in Witan with the kings. Heavy fines protected the humblest priest. A communicant's oath at law was held superior to all others'. A church's sanctuary saved the criminal, even the murderer. Severe penalties forbade Sunday labour, and held each lord responsible for enforcing this on his tenants. And though tithe did not become a system till the reign of Edgar, the State insisted on regular payment of ' church scot ', or offerings in kind, to the clergy.

Two impressions especially are borne in upon us, if we leave the history of this early Church with Bede's death in 735 as our terminus: the zeal for religion which had seized the country, and the immensity of its effect on Saxon civilization. Working first on princesses of the much-intermarried royal families, the Church ended by capturing a ruthless savage like Cædwalla of Wessex, or Ine his most politic successor, both of whom abdicated to die within sight of St. Peter's; countless kings took the monk's tonsure, followed by their fighting-men like the Mercians' favourite St. Guthlac, who turned hermit after wars against the Welsh, and by solitariness in the marshes of Crowland drove out the foul fiend. Monasteries followed, or preceded, the conqueror and pioneer; these were the days when sprang up Malmesbury and Exeter on the Welsh border, and Evesham on the dark edge of Arden. From Theodore's arrival Englishmen in plenty held bishoprics and abbeys, while the people heard the Lord's prayer, the Creed, and homilies in their mother tongue. Hardly anything in contemporary Europe could match the learning of Canterbury and Malmesbury, York and Jarrow. The Kent school taught Greek and Latin, music, astronomy, and medicine, and from its pupil Aldhelm we might illustrate this renaissance in the south. By birth belonging to the blood royal of Wessex, he received the learning of east and west at Canterbury, and then from the Irish monks at Malmesbury, where he became abbot in 675; thirty years later he was first bishop of Sherborne. His nature and his activities were both universal. To him were due the great churches in the West country, at Sherborne, Bradford-on-Avon, and Frome. He sent his Latin verses to a king of Northumbria, a Latin 'Praise of Virginity' to the nuns of Barking, and a tract on schism to Geraint, the British prince of Devon. He was in touch with Ireland, he was asked to Rome, while he wrote ballads in English to catch loafers outside the churches, which were valued by Alfred and still sung after the Norman Conquest.

But it is to the north that we look for the flower of early English learning, to Bede, especially in this part of our history, which owes all to him. Here was the pure Northumbrian, placed as a boy with Benedict Biscop and settled at Jarrow for half a century; which was not too long for his labour. He was master of the Latin fathers, quotes Pliny and Vergil, and acquired some Greek. He wrote on metre, penmanship, and chronology, a long series of commentaries on the Old Testament and the New, a biography of St. Cuthbert, and above all the great *Ecclesiastical History of the English Nation*; on the day he died, he was dictating a translation of St. John's Gospel. He loved his country and the truth in equal perfection; though an orthodox son of Rome, he venerated the Celtic saints of the north, and while he gloried in the greatness of Northumbria denounced, in writing and to their face, the vices of her kings. His *History* is in itself an epitome of what England had been, and had now become. He had ranged for his facts to Gildas and Gaulish chronicles, the archives of Rome, the memories of Wilfrid, or the surviving followers of Cuthbert; his fame made English learning reputed in Europe; within ten years of his death bishops in Germany were asking for his works. Once, his biographer tells us, when old and half-blind, he was preaching to a completely empty church, but when he ended his sermon with the invocation ' this may God deign to grant to us ', invisible angels answered ' Amen, very venerable Bede '; which all may echo, who breathe the air of his *History*.

Armed with such men, and now part and parcel of Christendom, the English Church gave back to Europe what Europe had brought. English religious energy was carried far overseas. Willibrord, a Northumbrian of Wilfrid's school, created the diocese of Utrecht; Boniface, a priest trained in Devon and Hampshire, passed from Frisia on into Germany, set up the monasteries and bishoprics of Thuringia, Hesse, and Bavaria, ruled the Empire as Papal legate to all the Franks, and died a martyr in 754 by the Zuider Zee. English missionaries had gone with him, and the English Church assembled in Council gloried in his fame; another Englishman succeeded him as archbishop of Mainz: yet another was first bishop of Bremen.

We pursue, then, the development of England, conscious of a new influence of boundless possibilities. Beside the King and his thegns we have henceforward to reckon with the all-accomplished structure of the Church, a unit far in advance of the State, with its leaders meeting in regular council, and with bonds stronger than Mercian or West Saxon allegiance. It was attached to Rome, capital of the civilized world, by ties that no king could put asunder. It belonged to another world, yet it claimed endowments in this, which would make it a landlord on a mighty scale and set it in the seat of princes. Its officers were an educated class, who could teach kings their business and the drafting of their first charters. All this, and more, was the Church. It would work through the big forces, and support the strong ruler against the weak; it would break through the clan system and the grades of the wergild, and assess its values by the individual soul; it would put the State before race, and the Church before either.

Time was to show the weakness that its flesh was heir to, or the danger of spiritual pride; the tribal survivals of a married clergy and hereditary priests, the land grants and riches, rents and labour services from an oppressed peasantry. It might sink to become the tool of one king against another, or the instrument of Rome against its native country, and as Bede's tireless pen fell from his hand, it betrayed such forebodings. But its first century and a half was glorious indeed. It had restored England to the circle of civilization, it had set up intelligence in place of brute force, and made mercy and justice, instead of bloody war, the duty of kings.

CHAPTER IV

ANARCHY, COLLAPSE, AND RECOVERY
613-899

GENERATIONS were to pass before any solid result appeared of the Church's moral teaching, or the national unity which it fostered. Two hundred and twenty years stretch from the Northumbrians' victories over the Celts, between 603 and 613, to the beginning of Danish invasion; years of battle, murder, and sudden death. Despite many high-sounding claims, no king made himself master of England. Petty dynasties continued in East Anglia, Kent, and Sussex, and though three States, of Northumbria, Mercia, and Wessex, stood out above others, each was continuously fighting, whether with Welsh, Picts, or Scots, and each was troubled within by nobles claiming royal blood. In this confusion the first strand of unity was the growing supremacy of Mercia.

Penda (632-54) was its real founder. He it was, apparently, who took the Hwiccan district and the lower Severn valley from Wessex; three kings of East Anglia fell in battle before him; he slew two successive Northumbrian kings, Edwin the patron of Paulinus, and Oswald the friend of Aidan. He perished himself at last in the ·battle of the Winwæd river in Yorkshire, at the hand of Oswald's brother Oswy, the arbiter at the synod of Whitby. But though this battle made Oswy overlord, or ' Bretwalda ' as Bede called it, of most of England, his reign did not for long arrest Mercian progress. The officials he sent to rule there were expelled, and two sons of Penda, Wulfhere (657-74) and Ethelred (674-704), steadily pursued the path of their father. From the Welsh they took what became the diocese of Hereford, and from Northumbria they permanently annexed Lindsey. They appointed ealdormen in Surrey and bishops for London and Dorchester, pushed their frontier through former Wessex country to the Thames, and sometimes treated Kent and Sussex as vassals.

This advance was the easier, because Northumbria had collapsed. Stretching from Humber and Ribble north to the Forth and Aberdeen, it was exposed to the strongest surviving Celts. Oswald had, indeed, ended any immediate danger from a Welsh State by overthrowing Cadwallon king of Gwynedd, the Britons of Strathclyde were nominally Northumbrian subjects, and before Oswy died in 670 he annexed much of what now is Scotland. But trouble unceasing came from the Highland Picts and the Scots of Argyllshire, with Ireland at their back. In 685 his son Ecgfrith and his army were wiped out at Nectansmere, near Forfar. All power was lost beyond the Forth, in Lothian the Abercorn bishopric disappeared, while Strathclyde revolted, never really again to return to English rule.

For another century the arts, libraries, and learning of Northumbria endured, rising indeed to their greatest glory. The eighth century gives not only the supreme name of Bede, but the figure sculpture of the stone crosses, the Codex Amiatinus taken from Jarrow to Rome soon after 716, and the illuminated Lindisfarne Gospels preserved at Durham. It closed with the career of Alcuin, scholar and head of the school of York, from 782 chief religious adviser of the Emperor Charlemagne, abbot of St. Martin's at Tours, a chief link between his native land and the Carolingian renaissance, and, by his part in revision of the Vulgate and making of the Roman missal, a doctor of the mediaeval Church. But in general a series of failures filled the throne, — savages who seized nuns and drowned infant rivals, weak men who fled to monasteries, lawless adventurers, — making a scene of decadence vainly denounced by Bede, Charlemagne, and Alcuin.

Broadly speaking, the Mercians were content to leave this anarchy to devour itself, concentrating on the two greater dangers of the Welsh and the West Saxons. Since its first conquests, Wessex had been plagued by civil war and had lost much ground. It was driven back from the Severn, the Thames, and finally even from Southampton Water; its solitary success lay in some conquests from the west Welsh, though in 660 it had only reached eastern Somerset. Then, for a short forty years, Wessex suddenly revived under two strong men. In 685 Cædwalla, one of Ceawlin's line, having formed a war-band in the depths of the Weald, sprang like a tiger on Sussex, seized the Wessex throne, carried conquest and massacre over the Isle of Wight, and set up his brother in Kent. Before he was thirty he threw down his murdering arms, abdicated, and died at Rome, but his successor Ine, in a long reign (688–726), raised Wessex to equality with Mercia. Steady campaigning against the Welsh brought him to Taunton, then to Exeter, — conquests marked out by fortresses, a bishopric at Sherborne, and fixed revenues taken from British subjects. He was so far master of London that he could speak of its bishop as his own, and Sussex became a sub-kingdom.

Yet his power proved as fleeting as all before him; his last years were cursed by rebels of his own house, and when he died Wessex died away again. It was now, under two remarkable rulers, Ethelbald (716–757) and Offa (757–96), that Mercia came nearer to supremacy than anything England had seen. Both were ruthless despots; the dissolute Ethelbald was killed by his own guards; Offa began his reign by assassinating another claimant, and ended it by kidnapping and slaying a king of East Anglia. But there is no doubt of their general acceptance as overlords, which Bede admits for all England south of Humber, while in Papal letters and Kentish charters Offa was styled ' Rex Anglorum '. They had a palace at London, where they levied tolls on Frisian and Frankish merchants ; Essex and East Anglia were annexed, Wessex and Kent became unwilling vassals. Their original middle kingdom had long been assessed in ' hides ' for land revenue ; Offa issued a code of laws, struck gold coins copying those of the Caliphs of Baghdad, and centralized power by setting up his kindred as earls over annexed provinces.

And the Mercian kings well knew what was their greatest asset. Lavish in new foundations like the abbey of St. Albans, they raised the feudal power of the Church to heights as yet unknown, by decreeing that tenants on Church estates should pay the land revenue and other dues (except service in war and borough wall-duty) to the Church instead of the Crown. Just as Northumbria fifty years before had induced the Papacy to recognize York as an archbishop's see, so Offa in 786 made Lichfield another. For the first time since Augustine's mission Papal legates came to England, several bishoprics were severed from Canterbury, while in return Offa accepted some important canons regulating doctrine and morals, and promised an annual payment to the Holy See. His position was now great enough to rouse some displeasure in Charlemagne, whose Court was besieged by English exiles, and who held Offa responsible for misconduct in English merchants and pilgrims ; English cloth was selling in the Frank realms.

Offa died in 796, and his only son a few months later ; the blood he had shed, wrote Alcuin, would fall on his innocent descendants. In fact, he had bequeathed three dangers which, even had the Vikings never come, might well have ruined Mercia, — inextinguishable hatreds in the kingdoms he had oppressed, overmighty power of the Church, and the Welsh frontier. The last was a slow smouldering fire. His predecessors, who had made the Welsh useful in ravaging Northumbria, found them stubborn in their opposition to the Mercian westward advance from the Chester gap towards the Conway and from the Severn to the Wye. Twice Offa devastated south Wales ; finally, late in his life, he set up the dyke still called by his name which, facing the west, runs northwards for some hundred and twenty miles from Chepstow, over the hills of Radnor and Montgomery, sometimes a thousand feet above sea level, till it ends at the mouth of the Dee. Yet his last years were complicated by revolt on the Marches, nor did his successors achieve a defensible frontier.

Their real danger lay elsewhere. On Offa's death Kent, which had long been simmering, broke out in revolt ; to meet it the Mercians bid for the all-important help of the Church by surrendering the new arch-bishopric of Lichfield. Canterbury resented this alien control, struggled for great manors like the prince-bishops of the Continent, and intrigued to raise a pretender to the Mercian throne. These troubles, rising to a climax in 823, gave his opportunity to Egbert of Wessex.

Yet we have no reason to think that Wessex was predestined to supremacy, or that a Mercian revival was impossible. The founder of Alfred's line was a capable man, but not a Bonaparte. He had been exiled through Offa's power, and for twenty years after his accession in 802 he was deferential to Mercia, not even daring to move on Kent, where his father had been under-king. His Cornish victories did not stop the defeated Welsh from joining the Danes later, and though in 825 he won a great battle over a weakened Mercia and struck coins in London, and though Kent and Essex acknowledged him, Northumbria really went its own way, while independent dynasties continued in East Anglia. The great churches of Canterbury and Winchester had to be wooed by regular alliances, while to hold Cornwall the bishop of Sherborne was endowed with a rich slice of territory. All the old and the new enemies of unity, in half-subdued kingdoms and feudal growths, still menaced the country when Egbert died in 839; that unity was only to be made real by Danish invasion.

Long before Egbert died, two blows from the Vikings open for us a window on to that defenceless England. One day round about 800 the King's reeve at Dorchester heard that unknown merchants had landed at Portland, but when he rode to order them to pay customs, the Norsemen, for such they were, slew him and his company. And at midsummer 793 pirates seized Lindisfarne, drowned some monks, took the novices as slaves, and stole the relics. Alcuin voiced the horror of Christendom, — their sins had found them out, St. Cuthbert could not defend his shrine, the heathen were jeering ' where is now their God ? '

For two hundred years the storm, of which this was the first spray, was to beat upon the English, destroy half their civilization and all but one of their kingdoms, and not to cease until Northmen from Normandy had levelled England to the ground. Against the immediate destruction wrought by the Vikings, whose sword cut clean through the mesh of all things, good and bad, we have to balance some lasting benefits. The once glorious religion of Northumbria was wiped out. A new and much more dangerous middle England destroyed all hope of national unity. The Picts, ground between Norsemen and Scots, disappeared as an independent force, while a new Scotland pushed the English back to the Tweed. Ireland, once the brother-in-arms of English religion and learning, was sharpened by bloody war with the Norse into a self-conscious, hostile, and anarchic race. Ravage and campaigning pressed the English peasantry down into serfdom.

On the other hand, a stock of fighting-men, seamen, and farmers poured into northern and middle England, bringing with them a will for self-government, activity in trade, and capacity for arms. Through their virtues, or in resistance to their prowess, a fresh life filled the channels of the State. The Kingship became, at least in name, undisputed and political, and not merely the sway of a tribal patriarch, clear divisions of government appeared in hundred, borough, and shire, while an administrative caste and a military aristocracy tied the soil to the King in bonds of service. All that in later days became the headstones of the corner, — law, liberty, and sea power, — bear on them, rough-hewed, the axe mark of the Vikings.

What they brought was not so much new as a vitality added to the old, for like the Angles they came from the Baltic, and their gods and heroes were those of whom an English poet had lately sung in ' Beowulf '. They had not yet received the white Christ; it was Odin and the hammer-god Thor whom they carved on the stone crosses of Cumberland. They buried their leaders with horses and hounds, and sometimes in their ships; heaven itself, they thought, was waiting for the fighting-man, and the Saga tells how there was thundering at the door of Valhalla when Eric Bloodaxe, king of York, came to rest with his peers. Their qualities, in fact, were those of the fifth-century Saxon, enlarged. Their cruelty was fearful; they practised human sacrifice, wives perished on the funeral pyre, children were thrown from pike to pike, and prisoners had ' the blood eagle ' cut in their back and ribs. Wine, women, and fine clothes were their desire; their ships had dragon bows in gold and many-coloured sails, while their crews, with hair carefully combed, and hung with brooches and bracelets, went out in ' bearsark ' lust to kill. Their bards, who in Canute's time travelled from Oslo to Winchester, glorified their war, — singing of ships locked together, of the twanging bow, and of sword-cut bodies, with sand in their mouths, drifting ashore.

It must always remain a marvel, — just as centuries later with the Sweden of Gustavus Adolphus, — what great things were done by these few thousand men from a barren land. Between 830 and 900 they sacked London and Paris, Hamburg and Antwerp, Bordeaux and Seville, Morocco and the Rhône; they founded Russia in Novgorod and Kieff, besieged Constantinople, and reached the Caspian. Before 1016 they had won Normandy and Iceland, discovered Greenland and America, and united England to Denmark. Moorish slaves were seen in the streets of Dublin, and hoards of English coins reached Russia.

Their ships, clinker-built in oak, were of many designs, but the typical warship was an open boat of thirty or forty tons, with one square sail, sheer-keeled, and low in the water amidships, where the warriors, whose shields hung on the bulwarks, tugged at the oar. In such craft, carrying sixty or seventy men and sometimes horses, they crossed the North Sea. Once ashore, their superiority to the English was as great as afloat; time and time again they rode across ten counties, they were masters both of the bow and battle-axe, while their leaders had coats of ringed mail. They broke the rules of gentlemanly war by attacking in winter, even at Christmas, fearing neither God nor man, nor the rigour of cold.

Neither Denmark nor Norway was yet a settled kingdom, and till Alfred's death the Vikings broke on Europe in many independent bands. Charlemagne's Saxon and Frisian wars had first unsettled them, so that when his Empire began to crack on the death (839) of his son Lewis, they took their opportunity. Some among them were exiles cast out by civil war, some were younger sons, but most, in the last stage, were sober emigrants, farmers squeezed out from the narrow cultivated strips above the fiords, or traders attracted by Irish gold and French wine. Many left the North when a centralized kingship cramped their wild freedom, just as some moved later from Britain to more lawless liberty in Iceland.

Though we call them Danes, the earliest Vikings, and a majority perhaps throughout, were Norwegians, for southern Norway was still ruled from Denmark and chiefs of one race often led armies of the other. Generally, however, the two peoples penetrated Britain by different routes and settled in separate areas. The Norsemen, sailing due west, conquered the Orkneys and Shetland, which they held till 1460, together with the Sodor or 'southern' Hebrides and the Isle of Man (held till 1266), and northern Ireland; from these they poured men into the Highlands, Galloway, the Lake district, Lancashire, and south Wales. After twenty years' concentrated fighting the Danes, coasting the Channel, set up the Danelaw in East Anglia and the Midlands, and another kingdom in Yorkshire and Durham.

For the greater part of Egbert's reign the terror centred in the Irish Sea. Iona was destroyed, the Welsh coast pillaged, while Ireland was completely encircled, its loughs and rivers sheltering nests of pirates who, reinforced by renegade Irish, issued forth to loot England and France. From 834 onwards Norse kings, fighting for the supremacy of Ireland, founded the 'Ostmen' cities of Dublin, Waterford, Wexford, and Limerick. Simultaneously Danish squadrons fell upon England; Egbert beat them, with their Cornish allies, at Hingston in 838, his son Ethelwulf slaughtered them in 851, but nothing stopped them long. Between those years Mercian London was twice ravaged, a king of Northumbria was killed in battle, and all round the coast we hear of raids, in which some ealdormen were killed and the peasant soldiers fled.

As with the Turks of later days, it was proved many times that staunch united resistance could wear the Vikings down, but in the ninth century Charlemagne's grandsons were tearing his Empire to pieces, and in England Egbert's supremacy was still a shadow. Ethelwulf, who succeeded him, was full of good works, so much so that while the Danes wintered in England he was on pilgrimage at Rome, but his eastern provinces of Kent and Essex bickered with Wessex, and his heir conspired with ealdormen and bishops. Mercia, beset by dynastic dispute, was also attacked by Rhodri Mawr king of Gwynedd who, by capturing Powys, had laid the base of a kingdom of Wales. Northumbria was in its usual chaos, with two kings contesting a phantom throne. Ethelwulf's sons were shortlived and delicate ; two short reigns slipped by with no serious disaster, except the sack of Winchester, but just as Ethelred, his third son, came to the throne in 865, the full Viking force was turned against England.

We thus reach the age of Alfred, who had made an agreement with Ethelred that, if the heathen swept one of them away, the survivor should protect the other's interests and the children of their house ; and in 871, after five years' comradeship, Ethelred died. But one continuous war ran on till the peace of 878 ; these thirteen years were also the most decisive, because the Vikings had set out to conquer England, and failed.

This first stroke was dealt by a family famous in legend, the sons of Ragnar Lodbrok, who had himself entered Paris and ruled the Orkneys. His children had fought the Moors and held the Bay of Genoa, had designs on the Danish crown, and were to be kings in Dublin and York ; Halfdan, Ubbi, Ivar the Boneless, names of terror, for whom their sisters had woven the raven banner, whereon the wings flapped in the hour of victory.

They did terrible work in the first five years of their onslaught. York was taken in 866, and the Northumbrian kings slain. Alfred's brother-in-law, Burgred of Mercia, bought a truce, but east Mercia was destroyed with the civilization of its famous churches. In 869 Edmund of East Anglia, the future saint of Bury, was barbarously murdered, his kingdom taken, and Essex also. In the winter of 870–71 it was the turn of Wessex. Nine battles were fought by the end of May ; the English won a great victory at Ashdown in the west Berkshire downs, but the campaign as a whole was a defeat. From their base at Reading, to which reinforcements came by the Thames, the Danes pushed the English back to Hampshire, Savernake Forest, and then to Salisbury Plain, and when at last they withdrew, it was only because Alfred bought them off.

That sealed the fate of Mercia, which by 874 was annihilated. From the Peak of Derby and the Wash down to Northamptonshire and the Welland, the soil of east Mercia was divided among the Danish warriors.

Halfdan did the same between Humber and Tyne; only Bernicia and west Mercia were left under English vassals. Thus heathendom was solidly entrenched. The bishoprics of Lindisfarne, Lincoln, and Dunwich disappeared, while even south of Thames men were burying their money, and the priest his silver chalice. All England, Alfred wrote later, was ' harried and burned '.

In 876 the blow, which he had once bought off, fell again, and for two years it looked as if Wessex, and with it what was left of England, must perish. True to their vulture instinct, the Vikings flocked from all quarters, — Norse from Ireland and Danes from France coming to join Guthrum and the settlers of East Anglia. By Easter 878 Alfred had been driven back to the Somerset marshes, where he stockaded himself at Athelney, leading (though, in fact, only for three months) the hunted life round which grew the legends of his fame : some Englishmen were fleeing to France. But though surprise and treachery had carried the Danes thus far, they had not beaten Alfred in the field. The fyrds of Wessex stood firm ; Norsemen coming from Wales were crushed in Devon, and in May Alfred came out again to rout the enemy at Edington. Forced to surrender at Chippenham, Guthrum swore to evacuate Wessex and to be baptized, and kept his word.

But this treaty of Wedmore (so called from the village where the baptismal ceremonies were completed) was not a final victory. Though Wessex was saved, and though west Mercia submitted to it, two-thirds of England was lost ; three Scandinavian kingdoms covered the country between the Scottish border and the Thames, — the one planted by Halfdan in Deira, a confederacy settled round the five boroughs of Lincoln, Derby, Stamford, Nottingham, Leicester, and Guthrum's eastern kingdom, which included London and reached the Chilterns. Alfred's life was not to be long enough to undo these losses.

For some years the Viking energy ebbed back to France and the Netherlands, but Guthrum, though Christian enough to strike coins in honour of St. Edmund whom his comrades had butchered, could not resist the temptation to intrigue with any wandering squadron, so giving Alfred an opportunity to use his new fleet and his remodelled army. Hence came about (886) ' Alfred and Guthrum's peace ', which pushed the Danish frontier back from London and Buckinghamshire to the Lea, Bedford, and Watling Street. A final crisis was reached in 892, when 800 ships of Vikings, driven out of Germany, seized the Thames estuary and Romney Marsh, bringing wives, children, and horses with them. One of their leaders, Haesten, had made his name a terror on the Loire and the Somme, and now he was at Milton-on-Swale, in easy reach of Canterbury and London. Now too was shown, not for the last time, what the presence of a Danish colony meant in England, for the settlers of Northumbria and East Anglia, breaking their oath, put out to sea and reached Exeter. Covered by these friends in the Danelaw, Haesten's men were three times able to ride the breadth of England to the Welsh March; nearly four years ensued of fierce open war, of which we can catch a few vivid glimpses, — of the English searching the Andredsweald by night, of the London army guarding those cutting the harvest, of the Danes blockaded in Chester, or eating their horses. But Alfred's new fortified towns beat off attack, Wessex and Mercia acted together, and even the Welsh, tired of Viking foray, offered their help. In 896, then, the raiders returned to pillage the Franks, the Danelaw settlers went back to their holdings, and for the last three years of his life Alfred had peace.

'England's Darling', the people called him after the Norman Conquest; 'the immovable pillar of the West Saxons', wrote one of his own family. The legends which surround great men are sometimes (as with Napoleon) a work of art, but for Alfred it is enough to study the facts. He began to reign, an ailing young man of twenty-three, when a few thousand farmers stood between the Danes and the downfall of Britain; when the strong were taking the law into their own hands and seizing their neighbours' land; when Canterbury had not monks enough to do duty, and when not a priest south of Thames could read Latin. For sixteen years, in a reign of twenty-eight, he was at war; he died at the age of fifty-one, having saved Wessex by his sword, created the machinery of an English State or restored it, given the Church new life, and founded the tradition of a nation. 'Thanks be to God', his Chronicle wrote for the crowning mercy of 896, 'the army had not utterly broken down the English nation.' But what if Alfred had been killed twenty-five years before, in his charge 'like a wild boar' up the hill at Ashdown?

In extent the kingdom he bequeathed was little larger, now that Essex and East Anglia were Danish, than that over which Egbert had claimed suzerainty, but in compactness and reality had far advanced. Helped, perhaps, by his marriage to a Mercian ealdorman's daughter, he had tight hold over the Mercian districts not in the Danes' hands, — the tract having Watling Street and the Peak as its north-eastern points, and in the west the Severn and Dee; its last sub-king, Ethelred, married his daughter Ethelflaed, whose fame as 'the lady of Mercia' filled the next age. In this reign the Mercian Witan acted with Alfred's permission, and though Ethelred's loyalty was rewarded by a grant, for life, of the London-Thames area taken from Guthrum, he was nothing more than the greatest of Alfred's vassals. And this brought Wessex, in a new sense, to the Marches of Wales. Rhodri Mawr of Gwynedd was killed in 878; his sons, weary of the Danes as allies, visited Alfred's Court and did homage, — their trembling rivals in south Wales followed suit, — so that a Welsh Churchman like Alfred's biographer, Asser, thought he could best serve his native St. David's by serving the English King. But centuries were to pass before this overlordship became sovereignty.

His work was done in time of war, and that set a mark on it. Some measures were simply common sense, or temporary reforms, driven through to meet emergency. Such was the division of the army into two halves, for alternate spells of duty; a rota system for his thegns, of one month's attendance at court in every three; the building of ships, longer and faster than the Danes', and manning them with Frisians. But there were others, of more lasting import.

For twenty years England had been overrun by mobile, professional, and heavily armed soldiers; to meet them Alfred organized a force of mounted thegns and a network of fortified boroughs. A king, he wrote, must have ' men of prayer, men of war, and men of work '; his men of war could come only from the landed aristocracy, for no other class could keep the field through seed-time and harvest, or afford a suit of armour which was reckoned the equivalent of twenty oxen. From his predecessors and his Jutish mother he had inherited many estates, from hunting lodges in Cornwall to the Sussex coast, whence he drew serf labour and paid warriors, and his laws and charters show a rapid extension of similar powers to the thegns. Henceforward no tie of blood was to excuse treason to one's lord. A king's thegn was given a wergild six times the value of the peasant's, while failure in his military service would entail forfeiture of his estate. Alfred and his sons, in making land grants to bishops, monasteries, and nobles, privileged these ' booklands ' with the right of taking fines for offences against the peace, — that is, with private jurisdiction, — and, in insisting that every five hides must provide one fighting-man, flung their net over the middle class.

On this class fell, too, the defence of the new boroughs, copied perhaps from the Danes, which were to bear the brunt for the rest of Saxon history. London was naturally the greatest, but twenty-five more at least covered the south from Sussex to Exeter, and back again from Barnstaple to Southwark, each with its apportionment of surrounding hides and its garrison from the country round. Relics of this borough duty may be found in Domesday, as at Lewes, where 35 manors of the county kept up between them 258 houses in the town.

Continuous war favours the Crown, and Alfred, though personally a man of extraordinary humility, ruled as an autocrat. Half of his laws deal with armed violence and, compared with earlier codes, greatly sharpen the conception of the State. The King has become the Lord's anointed; double penalties punish any disturbance of his courts or desertion of his army; for harbouring outlaws, or plotting against the King's life, death is decreed. Alfred was accustomed to arbitrate in difficult cases of justice, he appointed ealdormen and made land grants at will, while the history of both Witan and Church councils in his age is almost a blank. Sole survivor of many royal houses, he nationalized English law by incorporating those of Kent and Mercia with the custom of Wessex; in virtue of his character and achievement, the King's peace was tending to become, what it had not been in the tribal age, the sole source of justice.

But in Alfred's case his person, rather than his power, explains his hold both on his subjects and on posterity. ' What is rule and authority but the soul's tempest ? ' he asked late in life; twenty years' struggle had deepened the qualities received from nature, and that ardent curiosity, that breadth of sympathy, can scarcely be ascribed to parents who died before he was ten, or to visits to Rome in childhood. It was his glory to be able to see that his duty was not only to win wars, but to restore a civilization. He called to mind what he had heard and seen, — when kings ruled well, and counsellors were wise, and the churches were full of learning, so that strangers came here to get wisdom; he would ' follow the track ', and bring back that happiness.

For assistance he must look outside his burned and ruined Wessex. A good many helpers came from western Mercia, which the Danes had hardly damaged; Asser from Wales; others from the Continent. With their assistance he put into English Bede's *History*, Orosius' *History of the World*, and two other books which all down the Middle Ages had a deep spiritual influence, Gregory the Great's *Pastoral Care* and Boethius' *Consolations of Philosophy*. In those translations he inserted stories that interested him, like those told by Othere, his Norse sea captain, of Jutland ' where dwelt the English before they came into this land '; with metaphors that show the poet in him, and stray reflections from his own experience; as that the golden age knew no pirates, or that a soft life was a poor thing.

He had, in full, the gifts of action, — ardour in hunting, gay endurance in war, interest in all human doing, simple broad strokes of policy, — but to them added, what are rarely so combined, the artist's eye and a dedicated purpose. One side of him turned to planning war-ships or lamps, to setting craftsmen to work in gold and enamel, — like the jewel which he dropped in dark days at Athelney, and which was found there in William III's time, — or to collecting English ballads; another, to correspondence with the churches of Jerusalem or India, and his own new foundation at Winchester. But all roads in his mind led back to England. To raise up a governing class he created a court school, where his thegns' sons should learn the Psalms and English poetry before they learned to hunt; his clergy must know Latin, his reeves must be able to read their mother tongue. Of these ideals the most imperishable monument is the Chronicle, the original of which, up to 892, was compiled by his order, — from Bede, Wessex traditions preserved at Sherborne, Northumbrian records and Canterbury archives, and of which copies were sent to Midland churches like Worcester or Peterborough.   And the Chronicle was much more than the beginning of English prose ; telling one story, the glory of Wessex and how it had saved England from the heathen, it marched on just as much as English law, as a rallying force for national feeling.

So working, as his chaplain tells us, day and night, Alfred filled his few intervals of peace. He died on the 26th October 899. From his birthplace at Wantage, fifty miles each way take us to Athelney his city of refuge, to London his new capital, and Winchester his burying-place ; a petty kingdom, but he had inspired ' that little body with a mighty heart '.

CONTEMPORARY DATES

622	The Hegira of Mohammed.
629	Heraclius recovers Jerusalem from the Persians.
634–93	Arab conquest of Syria, Iraq, Persia, and north Africa.
653	Final compilation of the Koran.
711	Arab invasion of Spain.
732	Charles Martel defeats the Arabs at Poitiers.
768–814	Reign of Charlemagne.
780–802	The Empress Irene in power at Constantinople.
786–809	The Caliph Harun-al-Rashid rules at Baghdad.
800	Charlemagne crowned at Rome.
800, onwards.	Rajput kingdoms rise in central India.
843	By the treaty of Verdun, Charlemagne's grandsons partition the Empire.
845	Vikings sack Paris.
862	Vikings under Ruric occupy Kieff and Novgorod.
867–86	Basil I, first Emperor of the Macedonian dynasty ; southern Italy recovered from the Arabs.

CHAPTER V

THE HEIGHT AND FALL OF SAXON
ENGLAND, 899-1017

FIFTY years on from Alfred's death, his dynasty appeared in arms as overlords from Brecon to Aberdeen; another fifty, and both dynasty and England had fallen to foreign conquerors. Deeper causes than the wisdom or folly of kings must explain this swift rise and inglorious fall. Much no doubt must be put down to the ability of Alfred's children, Edward the Elder, and Ethelflaed his sister, of his grand-children, the three successive kings, Athelstan, Edmund, and Eadred, and of Edmund's son Edgar. But Providence doomed this resolute family to short lives, and none after Edward reached the age of fifty.

Alfred was hardly in his grave when all his work was put to the test. Of his elder brother Ethelred's sons, now grown men, who had been passed over in favour of their cousin Edward, one fled to the Danes, and with them ravaged the country as far as Wiltshire. It took three years of fighting to end this, but worse was to come. The Viking world, which turned on so many poles, was quivering again. Harold ' Fairhair ', the first real king of a united Norway, was harrying his pirate subjects into exile. Fierce jarls of the Orkneys were plunder-ing Scotland and the Isle of Man. The French king was compelled to let the Norseman Rollo settle down in Normandy. Most active of all were the descendants of that Viking family which had nearly over-whelmed Alfred, the sons and grandsons of Ivar the Boneless, already lords of Dublin and with inherited claims upon York. All down the western shore the Irish Norse were oozing in, making a new Cumbria round the Solway, lodging themselves in the Lakes and the Lancashire coast, till they reached the West Riding, and another section planted themselves in Durham. What these forays meant we can guess from one treasure chest buried in Lancashire, filled with ten thousand coins, lumps of silver, and bracelets.

The Scandinavian danger thus confronted Edward, fold behind fold. For if East Anglia, with its Christianity and thin Danish popula-tion, might be overcome, beyond it lay the crowded and pure Danish Five Boroughs, with a straggling artificial frontier which English thegns were already breaking down; beyond that again was Northumbria, contested between Dane and Norse, and the sport of any Viking. And as all their settlements were armies rather than kingdoms, one spark would set the whole heather alight.

In 910 an attack from the north on Mercia gave Edward his opportunity. For Mercia was his to direct as much as Wessex; when his brother-in-law died he took over the London-Oxford district, and when Ethelflaed died herself in 918, he sent her daughter into a convent and annexed Mercia outright. But, until that happened, brother and sister worked together, pressing in upon Danish England by converging lines. Fending off Welsh attacks on the flank, the Mercians fortified boroughs at Chester, Bridgnorth, Shrewsbury, and Warwick, while Edward set up his at Hertford, Witham in Essex, and Bedford; in 917–18 Ethelflaed seized Derby and Leicester, while Edward took Colchester, Northampton, Nottingham, and Lincoln. Before he died in 924, he fortified the Peak, and prolonged the Mercian defences as far as Manchester; receiving the nominal homage of the Norse at York, and of Welsh and Scottish kings. South of Humber, at least, all seemed subdued. English and friendly Danes were brought in to hold important fortresses. A new Midland administration was carved out round each conquered capital like Cambridge or Derby, several shires being grouped for defence under one earl.

There remained the north, where no king of Wessex had ever ruled, with its ramified divisions. Ivar's Norse-Irish kindred had captured the old Danish kingdom of York. Bernicia was under ' high reeves ' of English race. A Norse colony held the Lakes, and what they had left of Strathclyde was under a Scottish prince. Finally, Constantine III, King of the Scots and Picts, was hemmed in between Norse-Irish in Argyll and the Isles, and Norse jarls from the Orkneys overrunning the Highlands.

It seems to have been the first idea of Athelstan, Edward's successor, to set up a friendly Scandinavian ruler at York; only when that broke down, through the Viking feuds, did he take over Northumbria himself. That step roused two deadly enemies, the Scot Constantine, who feared for the Border, and Olaf Guthfrithson of Dublin, whose kinsmen had reigned at York. Hence came about, in 937, perhaps just north of the Solway, the great fight of Brunanburh, where Athelstan defeated a league of Scots, Irish, Norse, and Welsh; a battle sung in the Chronicle's ballad of the Englishmen's ' hard handplay ' to guard ' land, hearth, and home ', telling how Constantine ' crept home again ', while the Norse ' shamed in their soul ' sailed for Dublin. But Athelstan's brothers, Edmund and Eadred, had worse to face, for Olaf of Dublin broke out again. By the end of 939, the year of Athelstan's death, York was in his hands, with the connivance of its archbishop; the Five Boroughs, long terrorized, opened their gates, all was lost southwards to Northampton, and Edmund had to swallow the shame of surrendering all east of Watling Street, and north of the Welland. Even when he recovered the Five Boroughs in 942, anarchy raged beyond the Humber. Norsemen under Eric Bloodaxe, Harold Fairhair's son, fought against Norse from Ireland, while the archbishop, despite huge

land grants from Eadred, again joined the heathen. Not till 954 was
Yorkshire subdued. The rest of Northumbria was placed under a
Bernician earl, while Cumbria was abandoned to the Scots, in the vain
hope, maybe, of checking their attacks on Edinburgh and Lothian.

Yet at last, in outward form, England was one. The royal style
rose from Alfred's ' King of the West Saxons ' to ' Emperor of Britain ',
or ' Lord of all Albion '. Separate Witans ceased to meet in Mercia
and Northumbria, Welsh vassals and Midland Danes witnessed Athelstan's charters. Edmund gave the archbishopric of Canterbury to the
Dane Oda, whose nephew St. Oswald was Edgar's archbishop of York.
In 973 Edgar was crowned at Bath with the coronation order devised
by Dunstan; led to the altar by two archbishops, the choir singing the
while ' righteousness and judgement are the habitation of thy seat ', he
took his oaths and his anointing, received crown, ring, and sceptre, and
girded on the sword; then, at Chester, the kings of Wales and Scotland, Man, and Strathclyde, did him homage. The new monarchy
stood also for prestige and security abroad. Athelstan's sisters were
married to Charles the Simple of France, Otto I the great Saxon
Emperor, Hugh Capet of Paris, and Louis of Provence. The son of the
first, Louis IV, and Alan of Brittany took refuge at his Court from the
Normans, who in their turn sheltered refugees from the Danelaw.

If we anticipate so far as to include the reigns of Edwy and Edgar,
who followed their gallant uncle Eadred, we find that the tenth century
much advanced the structure of the State. Hitherto each ancient
community, Kent or Mercia, had kept its own Witan and ealdormen;
revenue had come only from a mass of estates farmed by royal reeves;
the public peace was broken by strong kindreds, who claimed a right
of private war. London was beset by bands of robbers; Edmund had
been murdered by an outlaw in his own hall. But now the kingdom was
large, foreign elements had been absorbed in Cornwall and East Anglia,
incessant war demanded a larger revenue, everything called for uniformity and reorganized areas.

Throughout the war period Alfred's plan of fortified boroughs
remained a necessary part of local government. We find in such
boroughs a market, a mint, and sometimes a local court; often thegns
of the neighbouring countryside provided a garrison and maintained
their walls. The needs of war, presumably, also led to reassessment for
revenue purposes. Instead of vague totals of ' families ' traditionally
assigned to tribal settlements, south and middle England appear as
rearranged in symmetrical blocks, sometimes corresponding to a new
earldom, and each being given a round, that is, an artificial, number of
hides. So Oxfordshire was put at 2400 hides alike in Athelstan's reign
and over a century later in Domesday Book, while the east Midlands
were assessed at 12,000 as a whole.

Another step, it seems, was to systematize the ancient scheme of ' hundreds ' of hides, used for the food revenues of the dark ages, into fixed areas and local courts, which for many centuries made the hundred the lowest rung in the State's jurisdiction. Here each month the substantial villagers, in person or by small delegations of six or four with their reeve, met the royal officers ; here priests conducted the ordeal, oath-helpers testified to character, and witnesses ratified sales. What had been the precise line of descent from the original courts of the royal reeves to these historic hundred courts, remains dark, though we may conjecture that a royal estate machinery had been adapted for public purposes ; a process suggested, for example, by the fact that all twelve Lancashire hundreds of the eleventh century, and nineteen out of twenty-two in Oxfordshire, were centred round royal demesne manors.

By the end of Edgar's reign, the shire system had been extended from the south over all England, except for the distant and half-independent regions which were later to make Lancashire, Cumberland, Westmorland, and Northumberland. In Wessex this division had taken root, it seems, before Alfred's death ; some were old kingdoms like Kent, some like Berkshire the endowment of a royal prince, others a conquered land like Devon. But north of Thames the work done piece-meal was new, Bedford or Northampton or Cambridge thus representing an area settled by a particular Danish host, — Worcester or Cheshire, the borough centres of Edward and Ethelflaed. By the year 1000 our familiar counties were all in sight, as far north as Humber and Mersey. In each a royal shire-reeve was appointed to collect the revenue, lead the militia, supervise the hundred courts, and get in the dues of the Church. Twice a year the shire court, thegns and their reeves and village deputations, met the sheriff and the bishop.

A primitive machine had thus been manipulated to meet the needs of a territorial kingdom. The conception of the King's peace, of offences against the State, was more dominant. His court and its dignity, desertion of his army, lands given by his charter, such high matters were reserved to him alone. But there were sharp limits to his power, and the land was cumbered with debris of older systems. Wandering bands broke the peace, the kindred group — powerless now for good — refused to produce their guilty members, strange cattle were smuggled into village pastures. Ancient law was soaked in the notion of self-help ; justice was impeded by venerable appeals to heaven, — to ordeal by holding the bar heated in fire, or ordeal by sink or swim in the water, or solemn ritual oath. Slaves could hardly hope for legal remedy. Immemorial custom, in which the King's court had no part, regulated the tenure of most land.

Tenth-century law showed, however, a steady encroachment by the State. Athelstan transported criminals to any part of his kingdom.

Edmund freed the kindred from the blood feud, if they refused to pay
a criminal's wergild, and forbade them to take vengeance from any
save the wrongdoer himself. Edgar fined those refusing to arrest men
who defied the hundred. From his time onwards every man must have
a standing surety, whether his lord or another; every free man must be
enrolled in a group of ten, — a village police association, which under the
name of ' tithing ' endured for many centuries. But resort to the King
himself was forbidden, until hundred and shire court had been appealed
to and failed, and all depended on the thegnhood. It was to them in
shire court that bishops looked to ratify their endowments, serfs to
make them free, or children to enforce the last testament of their father.

There was nothing new in a landed aristocracy, and it was not
democracy in decline that ruined Saxon England. Nothing was more
inevitable in a war period than the growth of feudalism, — the attach-
ment of rights and duties to property in the soil. No King, from
Winchester, could ensure that right was done on the Welsh March. If
the coast were to be defended, if trade was to grow, if the Church was
to receive benefactions, public duties must be harnessed to private
property. Such ' feudalism ' was, in fact, the primitive State's way of
getting things done. If Alfred wanted London wall rebuilt, he granted
land and wharves on the Thames to the see of Canterbury; if a
monastery was to be founded and flourish, or a country thegn to help
in the upkeep of a borough, they would receive some privileged grant
of land. From the days of Offa onwards we find kings making such
grants by ' book ' or charter, at first usually to Churchmen but increasingly to thegns, and discover in Alfred's age that such an estate of
' bocland ' is distinguished from ' folkland ', or land in general. ' Bocland ' was, as it were, a segment cut out of the ancient obligations of public
revenue and service, which occupiers of folkland must fulfil; the ' book '
transfers such services henceforward to the new lord who, as charters
testify of the tenth century and we can hardly doubt still earlier, was
given over the occupiers that jurisdiction which the English called ' sake
and soke '. And that jurisdiction, if we may read from the Confessor's
reign backwards, included suit to his court, a toll on sales, a warranty
of transactions by witnesses, and hanging of the thief taken redhanded.

By Alfred's death a lordless man was becoming a rare phenomenon;
to be ' free ' meant, rather, a freedom of choice what lord you would
have. The thegn had to answer as surety for his tenants; he could take
life for refusal of his rents. He was responsible for payment of tithe,
and for his lesser tenants' taxes. At the head of this aristocracy were the
King's thegns, with a seat in his hall, and liable only to his jurisdiction.
At death what (in theory) they had received from the King, — horses,
swords, or coat of mail, — must return to him as a ' heriot '.

Economic pressure had contributed to this growth as much as

royal policy. Reduction to slavery, captivity in war, or hunger, might drive a poor man to ' commend himself ' to a rich, in order to win protection, to get bread and board, to have someone who could ' warrant ' him in the King's court. In all early agricultural communities the moneylender also plays a part, and loans in Saxon England must come from the thegns or the monasteries. And as nine men out of ten lived by the land, land was the commonest loan, ' laen land ' or leases for lives. To a peasant whose harvest had been looted the thegn could supply stock, seed, and implements; while a gift of land to the Church would get a life tenancy, a grave in holy places, and wax candles perpetually commemorating the donor in many Masses.

So, by a thousand individual histories, a crude feudalism grew, making the network of service and tenure that we meet with in Domesday Book. It had begun long before. What was new in the tenth century was the blending of this feudalism with public machinery, — in ' sokes ', or private courts, which removed the tenant from the hundred court, or (in a last stage) transferred the hundreds themselves to private hands. Thus Edwy gave the archbishop of York twelve villages near Southwell, or Edgar gave eight Northamptonshire hundreds to the reformed abbey of Peterborough. A careful type of these new lords, like St. Oswald at Worcester, would set about elaborating his powers, giving leases to his thegns and carefully recording their duties, to provide him with armed escort, or pasture rents, and to organize his hunting. Local services so worked downwards, till they reached the peasant; add a new burden like Danegeld, and he would topple into the mire.

The political force which crowned this new society was the earldom. Besides the practical reasons we have seen for delegating power, Edward the Elder seems to have thought that he could break up Mercia and the Danelaw by regrouping them under magnates of his own house. By the middle of the century, only eight men ruled the Midlands (outside the Danelaw proper) and England south of Thames. Their origin, their size, their power, all made them a threat to the Crown. Athelstan ' the half-king ', raised up by his namesake and kinsman, combined East Anglia, Cambridge, and Northampton; King Edgar, his foster-son, married his daughter-in-law, and his own son was all-powerful with Ethelred. For nearly forty years Essex, Buckingham, and Oxford were under Edmund's brother-in-law Byrhtnoth; west Mercia fell to another royal kinsman Ælfhere, whose brother ruled mid-Wessex. Their wealth allowed them to win the Church by endowing monasteries, as the East Anglian line founded Ramsey, and to patronize scores of ' commended ' vassals. The earl presided in the court of his shire and led its fyrd; he was the King's deputy in correcting his reeves and enforcing the law. He usually received a third part of the profits of the court pleas; both official and landowner, with private hundred courts, official estates, and social privilege, the earl had the best of both worlds.

Neither their power nor the King's depended upon the Witan, which in name and fact was vague and shifting. In practice the citizens of London, or Winchester, or wherever the Court chanced to be, could be found cheering or receiving the magnates' decisions. But the Witan never had a representative character : all those who attended it were the King's nominees or servants, one of Edgar's thus being attended by the King and his mother, nine ecclesiastics, five earls, and fifteen thegns ; more than half of its recorded meetings took place at great feasts of the Church, when the King gathered his Court and friends round him. Nor did the Witan ever use the powers so freely claimed for it in after-days. Till the need arose for Danegeld, there was no taxation. Till Swein was undisputed military master, they dare not depose Ethelred. To act with the advice of his chief men was the part of a wise King, both in the tribal and the feudal stage, but beyond that we cannot go, and no formed body existed which was authorized to check the King by legal process. The Witan, finally, was no sovereign body, for shire courts existed, full of thegns, to whom copies of its decrees were sent ; on their co-operation, or on pledges taken from the sheriffs, the Witan must depend for execution of the law.

While the King's England was shared with this aristocracy, in the Danelaw was entrenched another aristocracy, of foreign race. Of racial hatred there is not, indeed, much sign. The southern Danes had accepted Christianity freely, as London churches show like St. Clement Danes, while Danish earls often loyally served the King, and East Anglia had been annexed to English earldoms. But in the Five Boroughs and Northumbria, — a country as big as Normandy and almost as much separated from England, — Scandinavian speech lingered, and indeed developed, up to the twelfth century, and the King did not dare raise his revenue. Here their jarls had settled fighting-men on estates round their halls. They built up great sokes from the Wash to the North Riding, in which a central court controlled a mass of free yeomen : their towns, each under twelve hereditary magistrates, were grouped in a general assembly, while a coinage of their own testified to the trade which they exchanged with their original home. They had never been conquered, but only held at bay ; they had extorted from Alfred a system of wergilds, which equalized their yeoman with the Wessex thegn ; Edgar expressly admitted their right to keep their old customs and fix their own legal penalties. Here and there a royal manor formed a small oasis, but broadly speaking it was a foreign land. Armies they had been, and armies they remained : to Earl Oslac ' and all the army which dwells in his earldom ', ran Edgar's writ. Place-names and language show that they had almost driven out

English-speaking people in parts of Lincolnshire and Yorkshire. But the map shows, over a much wider area, places where their ' thing ' or court met, their cattle shielings, and their tofts or small-holdings ; their land divisions, of carucates instead of hides, oxgangs instead of virgates, — their governmental areas, wapontakes instead of hundreds, — stretched from the far north to Northamptonshire, while outlying bodies of Danish landowners brought their customs even to the Chilterns and the Bedford Ouse.

The last great battle with the Yorkshire Norsemen had been in 954 : in 980 a new period began of Viking raids. Twenty-six years ; all too short in which to direct from one centre, under new machinery, provinces none of which had been under one government for as much as a century. Yet an English nationality was growing, and an English civilization. In York Cathedral the bidding prayer asked blessings on the King, archbishop, and ealdorman : the Wessex dialect was rapidly becoming a national language, both for learned men and for government business. Even a formal unity makes a habit of obedience, and it was something that the Five Boroughs accepted Ethelred's police regulations and his silver pennies. English literature showed a new life. Copies of the Chronicle, embodying information which passed from one monastery to another, and now and then a splendid poem, were being maintained at Canterbury and Abingdon, Ripon or Evesham. It was even more important that English prose was being made for every purpose ; in homilies and sermons, translations of foreign romances, lives of the Saints, and rules for the monks. The great Churchmen used English to reach their people : Wulfstan of York, to attack the sins which had exposed the country to the Danes, — Abbot Ælfric of Eynsham, to translate parts of the Bible into free-flowing prose. Latin scholarship, the loss of which Alfred had deplored, partly returned ; Ethelweard, an ealdorman of the royal kindred, wrote during Edgar's reign a chronicle of his family, and nearly contemporary lives were written of the Church leaders, Dunstan and Oswald. In some arts and crafts the English showed high ability. Their embroidery, the vigorous drawing in their illuminated manuscripts, their goldsmiths' work, were the best in Europe, and though architecture was still rude, their parish churches, full of carving, painted stucco, and bells, were binding together all England south of Trent by a common inheritance.

In these arts, as in all else, England was showing her dual nature : a child of the Roman Empire and an island of the North. The German Rhineland provided models for many of our churches : Scandinavian and Irish influences sent the carving and the stone crosses of the north country, while a vigorous commerce proved the enlargement of English wealth. Tenth-century laws showed this by their emphasis upon one coinage, on one standard of weights and measures, — those in use at London and Winchester — and their precautions for honest trading : in London a false coiner was to lose one hand, and that was to be nailed up outside the mint. Already trade was drawing together the isolated villages, with all the vast consequences of a circulation of cash. Oxford-shire manors kept depots at Droitwich where they might get salt : the monks of Ely had houses at Dunwich so that they might be sure of their herrings : there was much buying and selling of land in the Danelaw.

For the Danish settlers brought with them the trading instinct and trading connections. Scandinavian merchants were making York a considerable city, as Norse-Irish trade was making Chester, and Danish merchants stamped their language on the ' husting ' court, or governing body of London. For the first time England had a capital. Meetings of the Witan in London or its near neighbourhood became the common rule, and though the city was still a military outpost, garri-soned by a gild of knights, the growth of its traders and cosmopolitan spirit was to make it the nucleus of resistance in the black years coming. Once-empty spaces between St. Paul's and the Eastcheap market near London Bridge were rapidly filling up, with sokes granted to bishops and knights and small streets of merchants' stalls. The wharves which Alfred had begun were humming now from Queenhythe to Billingsgate ; Rouen wine and fish merchants were in the Vintry ; the Cologne men in Dowgate, who brought Rhine wine and cloths ; the men of Ghent and Ponthieu off Eastcheap. A rich revenue in tolls made London vital to the Crown ; the government of its teeming inhabitants, with the sheriffdom of Middlesex, was centralized under a royal port-reeve, who presided both in the folk-moot meeting in the open air, summoned by the bell of St. Paul's, and the weekly ' husting ' of the merchants and reeves of the sokes.

So in many fragmentary annals we piece together a picture of a small people, struggling up into prosperity : salmon-fishers by the weirs of the Wye, woodmen in the Weald, the women who brought butter and cheese to London, or pioneers in the long history of English wool. Whether the character or the unity existed, which could form these small cells into a State, was a question depending on other matters than this growth of commerce. It would depend, not least, on the morale of the Church.

Since the great age ending with Bede the Church in England had lost much of its inspiration. In part this was due to the weakness of Rome, which was beset with political danger and reduced to moral degradation ; in part it suffered from an inevitable stage in religious history, when its organization was exploited by rival kings and was becoming part of a feudal system. Most of all, however, it followed upon the enormous destruction wrought by the Danes. When Alfred died, the Church was teeming with abuses ; abbeys were bought and sold, monasticism was nearly dead ; both in cathedrals and monasteries vested interests had sprung up of married canons, while country parishes, especially in the north, descended placidly from father to son. Alfred's personal piety was, indeed, inherited by his successors. Edward the Elder founded new bishoprics at Wells, Ramsbury, and Crediton ; Athelstan was a zealous collector of relics, and gave lavish gifts to Swiss and German churches ; the personal friendship of Eadred brought Dunstan into power.

But ultimately reform could not come from kings nor, in its present state, from the Papacy, but only from the body of the Church. In the early tenth century one of those revivals began which so often saved mediaeval Christendom : starting from Cluny in Burgundy and from Fleury on the Loire, it gradually seized all western Europe. Simultaneously reform was taken up in England by two remarkable groups of men, — by Oda the Danish archbishop of Canterbury with his nephew St. Oswald, and by a Wells-Winchester group, kinsmen of the royal family, of whom Dunstan was youngest and chief.

Glastonbury, of which he was abbot, was the first reformed centre ; under his pupil Ethelwold, Glastonbury monks went to revive Abingdon, and had the greatest part in restoring the East Anglian abbeys ruined by the Danes. Their joint influence rose to its height in Edgar's reign, when Dunstan was the King's chief minister and archbishop of Canterbury, Oswald archbishop of York, and Ethelwold bishop of Winchester ; the politic Dunstan, who left the married canons alone and concentrated on moral reform, — Oswald, who by patience succeeded in bringing monks to Worcester, — and the bitter Ethelwold, who would welcome even a murderer if he had slain a spoiler of the Church. But on one thing they agreed ; on the making of a reformed Benedictine rule for all England, with the enforcement of celibacy and a real community life, as the only means of keeping their clergy unspotted from the world.

Their work was reflected in the laws of Church and State, in a severe enforcement of tithe and Peter's pence, strict observance of Sunday and feast days, rights of sanctuary, or the prominence given to bishops in the shire court. Here and there, no doubt, the religious temper really improved. Gilds and fraternities sprang up in towns and villages, for charity among their living members, and to say Masses ' for those who have fared forth '. Benefactors like the East Anglian earls were met by the monks in procession with books and relics, good Churchmen's wills left more and more property to the priests, and while Northumbria swam in civil war, priests of the North Riding can be found peaceably putting up their parish sundial.

ENGLAND IN THE
10TH CENTURY

English Miles

0 10 20   40   60   80   100

English
Scandinavian

GODWINE Principal Earldoms
— c. 1050

SCOTLAND

Tay

Forth

Firth of Forth

Clyde

STRATHCLYDE

Firth of Clyde

GALLOWAY

Edinburgh

Tweed

Lindisfarne

Bamborough

Carlisle

Dacre

CUMBRIA

Eden

Hexham

Tyne

Jarrow

Durham

WESTMORLAND

Whitby

Man

NORTH

SEA

IRISH SEA

KINGDOM OF YORK

York

Stamford Bridge

Beverley

Ribble

Ouse

Aire

Trent

Humber

Anglesey

GWYNEDD

Manchester

Mersey

Runcorn

Eddisbury

Chester

Bakewell

Derby

Repton

Nottingham

DANISH

MERCIA

Torksey

Lincoln

The Wash

Elmham

Norwich

POWYS

Severn

Stafford

Shrewsbury

Lichfield

Tamworth

Stamford

Leicester

Croyland

Peterborough

Ely

Thetford

Dunwich

Bridgnorth

Brixworth

Northampton

Bury

St. Edmunds

Tempsford

KINGDOM OF

EAST ANGLIA

Warwick

Worcester

Towcester

Bedford

Hereford

Wye

Gloucester

Oxford

Berkhampstead

Hertford

Witham

Colchester

Brecon

Usk

Cirencester

Maldon

Malmesbury

Ashdown

MERCIA

London

Benfleet

I. of

Thanet

Bristol

Chippenham

Kennet

Reading

Southwark

Kingston

Rochester

Canterbury

Dover

Appledore

Wedmore

Bradford

Ethandun

Basing

Farnham

Watchet

Glastonbury

WESSEX

Winchester

Wilton

Chichester

Pevensey

Athelney

Taunton

Crediton

Sherborne

Selsey

Frome

Exeter

Dorchester

I. of Wight

CORNWALL

Swanage

Wareham

ENGLISH CHANNEL

West from 2 Greenwich

Copyright 1948, Edward Stanford, Ltd.

But there was a different side. Forcible eviction of the canons was answered by forcible attacks on the monks. The Church did not gain by the absorption of its bishops in politics, and the Witan practically took the place of Church councils. In their immediate object the reformers achieved but small success. Canons held on to the cathedrals at Canterbury and York, London and Wells, down to the Norman Conquest; no monasteries reached the north; a married parish clergy continued as a rule. It was more serious that the Church had not made a moral or loyal people. The annals of the royal family and the earls were full of assassination, treachery, and land-grabbing. And by the evidence of the State's laws and Churchmen's sermons, round about the year 1000, when superstitious souls dreaded the end of the world, the English were still as drunken as Alcuin had said two hundred years before, serfs were still flogged or branded, men still worshipped idols, and Englishmen were still selling English slaves into foreign lands. At any rate, innocent and guilty alike were now to suffer; ' thus saith the Lord of Hosts, because ye have not heard my word, I will send all the families of the north against this nation ', quoted St. Oswald's biographer, ' and will make it a perpetual desolation '.

A first foretaste came upon Eadred's death in 955. The royal house was divided : the East Anglian nobles, who had held power for the last two reigns, quarrelling with the Wessex leaders, civil war was only prevented by a partition of the realm between Edmund's sons, Edwy and Edgar. But Edwy's early death remedied this, so that until Edgar's death in 975 there was superficial peace. The King was able, active in journeys and hunting, ardent for Church reform, and with Dunstan's conciliating influence continued reorganization in hundred and shire. His ability mainly consisted, perhaps, in ignoring disagreeable facts. The Danelaw, as we have seen, was left to rule itself, though individual Danes served in his Household and the Church. Oslac ruled Northumbria like a king. Edinburgh was abandoned to the Scots. As between the great earls a delicate balance lasted all his time, though the King leaned on the East Anglians as against Ælfhere of Mercia. The outward peace which he secured was a gift of fortune; for Harold Bluetooth of Denmark was involved in war with the Saxon emperors, while Normandy was first torn by civil strife, and then entangled in the feud between the Carolingian kings of France and the Dukes of Paris.

But the peace which only a king could keep was destroyed when Edgar died, leaving two young boys, sons of different mothers. Though the elder, Edward the Martyr, was crowned by the archbishops, his stepmother would not submit; the quarrel revived between her East Anglian kinsmen and Ælfhere of Mercia, who took as his pretext the cause of the evicted canons. After three years' chaos, on one March evening of 978 Edward came in after hunting to Corfe Castle ; his step-mother's thegns gathered to meet him. We have only a hint of that murderous scene, — ' what do ye, breaking my right arm ? ' called out the King, caught up while the others stabbed him : ' worse deed was never done among the English ', wrote the Mercian scribes on their copy of the Chronicle. And with that began the thirty-eight years' ignominy of Ethelred the Unready.

He was only a child of ten when, from inside the walls of Corfe, he heard his brother crash from his horse, but when he grew up, his character was fatal. He was soft, luxurious, and unfaithful, fearful of conspiracy, and disgraced his reign by cruel punishment. He vacillated from man to man, from policy to policy ; if he followed any steadily, it was his purpose of overthrowing the great earls, to replace them by new men of his own. So he drove into exile the heirs of Mercia, granting most of its territory to his favourite, and son-in-law, Eadric Streona, the most grasping and perjured man of a bad generation. Something like an earlier edition of Richard II, with the same liking for imperial language and for creating new offices, Ethelred suffered the same fate in the detestation of his new ministers. When Dunstan died in 988 and all Edgar's advisers disappeared a year or two later, the Court became a nest of traitors. On this one contemptible king of a great family, and this factious country, broke the second storm of Danish warfare.

It falls into three stages, — one of pure piracy from 980 to 991, then a long straggling war with Norse and Danes up to 1013, and last a furious, concentrated, and successful fight to seize England for the Danish Crown. Just as a hundred years earlier, the North broke out again through its own anarchy. Harold Bluetooth had made Denmark overlord of southern Norway, and the seas were full of Norse exiles : before he died in 986, his son Swein had rebelled, cast off Christianity, and identified himself with the fiercest Vikings. From the Oder sailed out the Vikings of Jomsburg, a community sworn, almost like a knightly order, to war and piracy. At the same time the Irish Norse, pressed hard by the rising power of the Irish hero Brian Boru, fell on the shores of western England and Wales. Revolt in Norway and Sweden drove Swein to go ' Viking ' himself, so postponing the day when, as master of the North, he could devote himself to the conquest of England.

Even in the first stage, the English weakness was appalling. Pirates descended with impunity on every harbour from Chester to South-ampton, took up permanent winter quarters, and sold their spoil in Normandy. And when in 991 the first real test came, and Byrhtnoth the Essex earl fought his immortal fight at Maldon against the crews of ninety-three ships, he was left to fight alone. The money which he had indignantly refused was given by the Witan, who had no better plan than to bribe these wolves to act as sheep dogs against the next contingent.

For over twenty years this slithering process continued. The King turned desperately from hiring Danes as his bodyguard, to hiring Joms-burg Vikings : payments of Danegeld, larger at each transaction, and amounting in all to half a million of our money, thrust thousands of the peasant class down into slavery. Sometimes Ethelred dealt short-lived savage blows at his enemy. Once he devastated Cumbria and the Isle of Man, and in 1002 organized a treacherous massacre of the Danes in his service, with Swein's sister among them. The same year he married Emma, daughter of the Duke of Normandy, hoping no doubt to close that refuge to the pirates.

Saxon England, built up with such heroism, fell into ruin. Under Welsh and Scottish raids the frontiers began to crumble, Northumbria once more relapsed to civil war, thegns of the Danelaw were suspected of welcoming the enemy. London, the Viking's special objective, beat off every attack, but the coast shires, desperate and unprotected, began to offer local Danegelds, serfs joined the invader, treachery opened the gates of Canterbury. A long list of burnt and ruined towns, — Oxford, Exeter, Norwich, Northampton, Bamborough, — gives us some idea of the universal weakness. Danish bands horsed themselves as of old, harried inland from the Berkshire to the Sussex downs, and calmly drove their captives to their ships. The archbishop of Canterbury was held prisoner for six months, before he was pelted to death by drunken soldiers. In vain the King, much unlike his ancestors, continually called together his Witan ; in vain they planned national fasts on water and raw herbs, with a special Mass ' against the heathen ' ; in vain raised a Navy by new taxation ; in vain the King, late in the day, admitted the holiness of his murdered brother.

His vacillation destroyed the spirit of resistance. Defence had always rested entirely upon the south, which again depended on a strong king and earls in harmony with each other. Neither of these conditions existed. The earl of mid-Wessex had been one of King Edward's murderers, the earl of Essex murdered the head of Ethelred's household ; Eadric Streona, now earl of Mercia, murdered the sup-porters of the old Mercian family ; the chief thegn of Sussex turned pirate. These men of new family had no influence except what they derived from the Crown, and great was the contrast from the days of Athelstan, in the delays of the fleet, bickering in the fyrds, a general flight for self-preservation. It cannot be explained except by lack of good will in the landowning class.

The end began in 1013. Swein Forkbeard himself returned to England, for the first time since 1006 ; free now from his Norse and Swedish rivals, and perhaps jealous of the great position won by Thorkill the Tall of Jomsburg, whom the miserable Ethelred had taken into his pay. All northern and Danish England submitted. Ethelred fled to Normandy, and though he returned after Swein's death in 1014, he died himself within two years after, leaving the essential position unchanged. For Swein's son Canute had recruited the flower of Viking Europe, and Ethelred's brave son Edmund Ironside could not remake England. In four great battles he revived some of the old Wessex loyalty, but Thorkill, offended by Ethelred's double-dealing, joined Canute, and the double traitor Eadric Streona likewise — who was pardoned, but only to ruin Edmund again by deserting him in the last battle at Ashingdon in 1016. The earl of Northumbria, and the Dane-law, outraged and betrayed by Streona, would not pit themselves against the invader alone. Even the west Wessex shires waited until Edmund showed his power to defend them, and the Witan, some in London and some outside it, voted for different kings.

A truce, arranged in the autumn, reflected the facts of the situation, grim as they were : Edmund kept Wessex and part of Mercia, Canute was given the north and the Danelaw, and was able to extract Danegeld and a harbour for his ships from the city of London. Edmund was only twenty-two years old, Canute perhaps a year younger, and it is hard to believe that this truce could have lasted. But Canute's enemies had the habit of speedy death ; six weeks after the truce was signed Edmund Ironside died, leaving only infant children, and at mid-winter 1016-17 the Witan acclaimed Canute as King of all England.

CONTEMPORARY DATES

910	Foundation of the abbey of Cluny.
912	Rollo granted Normandy by Charles the Simple.
900, onwards.	Gorm and Harold Fairhair establish the kingdoms of Denmark and Norway, respectively.
c. 918-50	Hywel the Good reigns in Wales.
920-60	The Omayyad caliphate of Cordoba at its height.
c. 930	The Saxon church at Bradford-on-Avon.
936-73	Reign of Otto I the Great in the Empire.
971	The Blickling Homilies.
980, onwards.	St. Vladimir in Russia accepts Christianity from Constantinople.
985	Norse settlement in Greenland.
987	Hugh Capet becomes King of France, and Fulk the Black Count of Anjou.
997	Accession of St. Stephen in Hungary.
997	Mahmud of Ghazni begins reign of Mohammedan conquest in India.
999	Sylvester II (Gerbert of Rheims) initiates Papal reform.
1000	Swein of Denmark slays Olaf Trygvason of Norway.
1014	Brian, King of Munster, defeats the Norse at Clontarf.

CHAPTER VI

DANISH RULE AND NORMAN CONQUEST
1017–1066

IN 1017, one of two things seemed probable: either Canute would consolidate his government in partnership with Scandinavia, or there would be an English insular revival. An extraordinary series of events decided that neither of these should endure, but a third; a new and final conquest of England, which bound her for four hundred years to the political system of France.

It was a period unpleasant for English pride. On the eve of the Norman Conquest the country showed the same feuds between earls and provinces, the same religious stagnation, the same anarchy in its institutions. Yet while for eighteen years it obeyed Canute without serious revolt, it stoutly resisted the Normans, showing that, however ill-led and unorganized, it had become more of a nation.

Canute's time of peace came partly from the English exhaustion, partly from his own calculating ability. Unlike the Conqueror, he had no organized State at his disposal overseas, for he did not obtain the Danish Crown until 1019, while Norway was not conquered, and then most superficially, before 1028. He began only with his housecarles, three or four thousand veteran soldiers, and with what support he could get from England.

His aim seems to have been, — and it would win much English sympathy, — to obliterate the England of Ethelred by all means in his power. Till 1021 Thorkill the Tall, who had been in England so long, was second to the King, and earl of East Anglia. The English earl of Northumbria was given up to assassination by his private enemies, and his province was handed over to Canute's Norse brother-in-law, Eric of Hlathir. Eadric Streona, who had betrayed Edmund and seemed likely to betray Canute, was promptly executed, Worcester and Hereford being detached from his territories to make earldoms for Eric's son and for another Viking, while most of Mercia was given to Leofwine, a thegn of mixed English-Danish blood. In Wessex, by 1018, we hear of the famous Earl Godwine, destined to be, after Canute had gone, the real ruler of England and father of the last English king. But in Canute's time Godwine played a very different part. His father had been that Sussex thegn who had broken up Ethelred's fleet by his piracy; he himself was married by Canute to Gytha, sister of Ulf, husband of

80

the King's sister Estrith. Such, even up to the end of the reign, was the preponderance among the earls of Scandinavian connection.

The English royal house fared no better. Edmund Ironside's infant sons were sent off to Canute's uncle in Poland, with a hint that they had better disappear, while his sole surviving brother was hunted down and killed. But there remained his stepmother, Ethelred's widow Emma who, with her sons, had taken refuge in Normandy. By one of the most cynical transactions in history, Canute suppressed the sons' claim by marrying their mother. He was himself already united to one Ælgifu of Northampton, of an old family ill-treated by Ethelred, and by her had two sons, Harold Harefoot and Swein, but the Church had not recognized their union as marriage and he now agreed to put her away. Emma had no reason to respect the memory of Ethelred, but her forgetfulness extended to his children also; she left them in her brother's charge in Normandy, never saw them again until Edward the Confessor arrived in England twenty years later, and used the wealth which Canute heaped upon her to build up a party for her son by him, Harthacnut. In the Norman background were these two boys, dimly representing the blood of Alfred.

Meanwhile, they were forgotten and overshadowed by the growth of their stepfather Canute, the best King of England since Alfred. There seems no reason to argue a great moral change in order to explain his career, or that he loved England above his other kingdoms. His Court to the end remained cosmopolitan : as he took Englishmen to his Baltic wars and used English bishops in the Norwegian Church, so Norsemen guarded him and witnessed his charters in England. He committed the protection of London, with great estates in the home counties, to trusted Danish officials, and to him, as in after-days to the Dutch William III, England must be a secondary interest. From 1019 to 1030 he was wrestling with the settlement of Denmark, conquering Norway, and building up alliances. While the Scots occupied Lothian, he was winning Schleswig for Denmark by diplomacy with the Emperor Conrad, and his famous pilgrimage to Rome was designed to win Papal support against St. Olaf of Norway. By 1030 he ruled a northern empire : his son Swein with his English mother was governing Norway, Emma's son Harthacnut held Denmark, and he was obeyed by Viking settlements from the Vistula to the Hebrides.

His English government, which had begun with so much bloodshed, continued as a policy of wise self-interest. Proclaiming at once his intention to keep Edgar's law, he made no change in the structure of government. His laws recognized the separate customs of the Danelaw, and stereotyped the nobility's power over their tenants. Insisting on the rights of the State, he organized the heriots due from different ranks of the thegnhood, strengthened the hundred, and defined those pleas

of the Crown which he would not surrender to any private court, —
that is, violation of a protection given by the King, armed assault,
forcible attack on houses, and desertion of the army. But, in fact, he
gave even these privileges away in several cases; to the archbishop of
Canterbury for all his lands, and to his Queen over her Suffolk estates:
ordinary grants of jurisdiction were probably plentiful, and the magnates
were seizing a good deal of Church property.

His proclamations to his people, particularly that from Rome in
1027, were lofty in tone and individual; the King has been working
for his people, he admits God's goodness in shielding him from danger,
he means to make amends for the negligence of his youth, ' I have
never spared, nor will I in the future spare, to devote myself to the well-
being of my people '. The hearts of kings are inscrutable; six months
before writing these words Canute had murdered Ulf, his brother-in-
law. But, whatever lay in his heart, his mind saw clearly that both at
home and abroad he must have the Church's support, most of all for
the conciliation of England. From such mixed motives came a remarkable set of measures, calculated to wipe out the injuries most wounding
to English feeling: his endowment of a church on the battlefield of
Ashingdon, fixing feast-days in honour of Edward the Martyr and
Dunstan, translation of the murdered archbishop Alphege's body from
London to Canterbury, and the refoundation of Bury St. Edmunds.
The English Church which he thus honoured provided his administration; his chaplains were laying the foundations of the Chancery,
while his bishops led the shire courts.

It was the same abroad; splendid English manuscripts went to foreign
shrines, while the King's journeys were marked by pious pilgrimage. But
he was a heathen born, and he was enlisting the heathen part of Norway
against St. Olaf. Pure religion did not dictate his visit to Rome; he
did much useful business with the Emperor, arranged lower tariffs for
English merchants, and returned to attack his Christian rival in Norway.

The Lord of London, as the Norse called him, so remained in some
respects a Viking to the end. English bishops were jostled in the court
by wandering poets from Iceland: his laws on behalf of nuns, or
widows, or tithe, contained also barbarous punishments of mutilation.
He watched English opinion but called few meetings of the Witan,
and was surrounded by armed men; the *corps d'élite* of the housecarles,
who held important garrisons together with many estates, manned his
ships, and were richly paid from a Danegeld levied on all unprivileged
land. With them he lived, like Frederick the Great, on terms of
military equality, and on a ceremonial occasion could be found himself
steering the royal ship on the Thames. Defence and police in his reign
was of a garrison type; the thegns' duties were being worked out on
great Church properties, but there was not as yet anything like a system of

fiefs; we hear rather of grouped bodies, such as the knights' gild who held Portsoken Ward in London, or a thegns' gild at Cambridge.

Time, indeed, might have made a Christian king out of Canute, but in November 1035 he died, not yet forty years old, and was buried at Winchester with the English kings, where his body, still crowned, was found centuries later. The joint realm, which he had planned for Emma's son Harthacnut, fell to pieces. Olaf of Norway had been killed in battle in 1030, but before Canute's death Olaf was being worshipped as a saint, and his son Magnus expelled the Danish government. So that for two years after his father's death Harthacnut was detained in Denmark.

In any case this drunken vindictive young man could not have saved his father's throne. English parties, forcibly held under for twenty years, broke out again, and were equally matched, representing two stages in Canute's career and two halves of England. Mercia, the Danelaw, the London housecarles, and the north all championed the cause of Harold Harefoot, and it was agreed that he should administer the realm, though Wessex should be ruled by Emma and Godwine. But in 1036 another turn of the wheel fixed Harold on the throne.

Emma had other children than Harthacnut, in Ethelred's two sons left in Normandy. Once already England had been reminded of their existence. Her nephew Robert ' the Devil ', Duke of Normandy, had not shown his father's peaceful temper : he had married and then had repudiated Canute's sister Estrith, just about the time when his long-cherished mistress at Falaise bore him the son who was to be the Conqueror. And about 1030 he had taken up the cause of his cousins, though a storm at sea wrecked his fleet and their hopes. Meantime, Robert was dead, but then Canute was dead also, and Harthacnut lingered in Denmark.

In 1036 the younger of the two Athelings, Alfred, landed with a few knights, intending to see his mother at Winchester. He was welcomed by Godwine, who diverted him to Guildford; there the housecarles seized him, killed and broke up his company, and handed him over to Harold, by whose orders he was blinded and sent to die as a monk at Ely. Harold was recognized now as sole king. Emma, abandoned by Godwine, fled to Flanders. The Earl's treachery was generally taken for granted at the time, it was charged against him in a Witan of the next reign, and was made a pretext for invasion by William the Conqueror.

King Harold died in March 1040 : an attack had long been expected from Harthacnut, who now took the crown without opposition. Mercifully his reign only lasted two years, marked as it was by heavy Danegelds, local riots, and Court faction. He had dug up his brother Harold's body and cast it into the Thames; his own end was worse, by the Thames also, for ' he died as he stood at his drink ' at Lambeth, at a wedding feast of his Danish officers in June 1042. So ingloriously ended the house of Canute, but not the entanglements in which Canute and Emma had left England.

When Harthacnut returned, his half-brother Edward (Emma's last surviving son by Ethelred) had returned also, and was, it seems, formally recognized as the heir. In 1042 both honour and pity for Alfred's murder had caused a new feeling for the old family, while Canute's sons had lost the Church's favour and their housecarles had angered the nation. There were, of course, other claimants. Swein Estrithson, nephew both to Canute and to Godwine, came to urge his right, but all he got was an earldom for his brother Beorn. And Magnus of Norway, who was defeating Swein in Denmark, claimed Harthacnut's promise that the survivor of the two should succeed in all the other's kingdoms. More was to be heard of these threats later, but for the next few years Swein and Magnus neutralized each other, while Edward was on the spot and was supported by the strongest partisans of Canute's family, Godwine and the Danelaw.

If the dynasty was to endure, Edward must have a son, or one of Edmund Ironside's children be brought back from the East; while for domestic peace the balance of power must be restored, which in Edgar's time had existed between the Crown and the great ruling families. These were now reduced to three. Far off the seat of government was Northumbria, so long a scene of confused bloodshed. When Earl Eric and his line had passed away, Canute had given Deira to another Dane of the royal family, Siward the Strong, who in course of time reconquered Cumbrian lands held by the Kings of Strathclyde and established authority over all Northumbria. He had married a kinswoman to Duncan king of Scotland, and when, in 1040, that prince was murdered by Macbeth, his son Malcolm Canmore was taken to Siward's Court and nursed up for revenge. The old Viking's ambition thus looked mainly northward, but in English politics he usually acted with the Mercian earls against the south. The Mercians, unlike the new men raised by Canute, had held their earldom half a century, and nothing, till Norman days, shook their power over the west Midlands. The present earl, Leofric, had served Canute, his power had been shown in the adoption of Harold Harefoot, he was popular, and with his wife Godiva a princely benefactor to the Church. Last came Godwine of Wessex; whose eloquent tongue and great wealth had carried him round so many awkward corners; who had abandoned Harthacnut for Harold, had helped to kill Alfred, had won back Harthacnut by bribes, and now forced himself on Edward also.

For six years the King showed no overt sign of wishing to resist Godwine's influence. King and Earl joined in stripping the queen-mother of her estates; most of England fell to Godwine's house. His

eldest son Swein had an earldom reaching from Oxford to Somerset;
his second, Harold, had East Anglia; his nephew Beorn came next to
Harold between Hertford and Oxford; his daughter Edith became
Edward's queen. When Swein was outlawed in 1046, his earldom was
divided between Harold and Beorn, only Hereford going to the King's
nephew Ralph; when Swein returned from exile and assassinated Beorn,
again he was pardoned. All this took place before the middle of 1050.

The Confessor King's personality was a curious one. His rosy face,
and prematurely white hair and thin hands, like his usual debonair
manner and his petulance when contradicted, showed the frail man who
would be King but had not the physical vitality to rule. His tastes,
like his friends, were French, yet it cannot be said that he pursued a
settled policy of Normanization. Two Normans, — one his intimate
adviser Robert, abbot of Jumièges, — received bishoprics : a few fiefs
went to Frenchmen and Bretons, who began to build castles : a few
Sussex manors to a Norman abbey. But beyond that he did not go.
No king held more regular meetings of his Witan, and it was not a
Norman despotism which destroyed England but the fateful division
among Englishmen.

For this the heaviest responsibility rested on the house of Godwine.
By 1050 they held all England, except Northumbria and a Mercia which
they had cooped in on every side. Godwine's adaptability carried him
through all inconsistencies. He had tried to make Edward support his
own nephew Swein Estrithson against Norway, but did not resist the
exile of prominent English Danes. He had abandoned Emma but
enlisted her adviser Stigand, whom he raised to the bishopric of Winchester. His activity roamed to the Continent. Watching with anxiety
the rise of Normandy, he countered it by marrying his son Tostig to
Judith, a near relative to Baldwin count of Flanders, who had sheltered
Swein in exile, and was careful to keep on good terms with another
enemy of Normandy, the king of France. But the family power rested
upon more than the prestige of thirty years' high office, or resistance to
foreigners in which all England sympathized. Years later the juries
whose oaths were recorded in Domesday Book accused Godwine and
Harold of land-grabbing far and wide. Here they had suppressed a
monastery, here had reduced the geld on their own lands, or there had
added acre to acre.

This overweening ambition, and Godwine's shielding of Swein,
produced the crisis of 1050–52. It began with the King's insistence
that Robert of Jumièges should be archbishop of Canterbury : next
year came Tostig's marriage, and the visit to England of the King's
brother-in-law, Eustace of Boulogne. The burghers of Dover, in
Godwine's earldom, killed some of Eustace's followers, and the earl
refused to obey a royal order for their punishment. Possibly the

Norman party round the King induced him to use this pretext; what
is more significant is that, when Godwine was summoned to the Witan
at Gloucester, he answered by calling out his armed men, and that the
earls of Mercia and Northumbria responded to the King's appeal. The
Witan, adjourning to London, took drastic measures : Swein was again
outlawed, Godwine and Harold were ordered to hand over the ' commended ' men in their earldoms, and rather than meet the Witan without
guarantees they fled the country.

Their return in the autumn of 1052, marred by barbarous piracy on
Harold's part, was a triumph rather for the country than for themselves.
A real sense of nationality appears in the chronicles, with a sense of
shame that English should fight against English. The foreigners had
sent the queen to a nunnery ; William of Normandy had visited Edward
who, it was said, had promised to do his utmost to make him his heir.
At any rate, the northern earls, who had stood by the King in 1051, did
not oppose Godwine's return ; Wessex, of course, was hot on his side,
and Londoners rabbled the Norman bishops.

After Godwine's death in 1053 the crisis accelerated. Harold was
indeed more congenial to the ageing King, nor did the murdered
Alfred's blood flow between them, but the house of Godwine had
learned nothing and forgotten nothing. Without asking the Holy See,
Robert of Jumièges was declared to have forfeited his archbishopric,
which was assigned to Stigand. In 1055, when old Siward died, the
claims both of his son Waltheof and those of the Bernician line were
passed over, and Northumbria was given to Tostig. After Leofric's
death in 1057 East Anglia went to another brother Gyrth, while Harold
himself replaced the Frenchman Ralph in Hereford. At last the work
seemed to be done : except for a much-reduced Mercia left to Leofric's
son Ælfgar, all England was governed by the grandsons of the Sussex
pirate. And an event of the same year brought grander visions. Soon
after Godwine's death King Edward planned the recall from Hungary
of Edward, son of his half-brother, Edmund Ironside. In due course the
exile reached England, but he died within a few weeks, and his son, Edgar
the Atheling, was a boy. Who then should be next King of England ?

Harold Godwinson, who made himself King in 1066, endeared
himself to the national memory by dying in England's defence; ' a
little man ', the Norwegian Saga said, ' and he sat proudly in his stir-
rups '. But his seat in the saddle of power was never secure, and even
if no foreign claimant had contested the succession, if Magnus' successor
in Norway, the famous warrior Harold Hardrada, and if William the
Norman had left him in peace, he had enemies to meet within the
realm, — the same enemies which previous Kings had found so perilous, — Mercia, Northumbria, Wales, and the Church. Politically his
government from 1053 onwards was not a triumph, but a steady retreat.

His effort to destroy Mercia not only failed, but drove Mercia to a dangerous alliance with Wales. When Welsh princes had appeared in the Court of Alfred's children, the whole power of their country had been momentarily united under Hywel, the Good and the legislator; since his death in 950 the north (Gwynedd and Powys) had fallen into war with the kingdom of Deheubarth, the State built upon the ruins of petty principalities in the south, while Glamorgan and Gwent in the southern angle nearest England pursued an anarchy of their own. Ceaseless Norse and Irish pressure from the sea was pushing the Welsh fighting-men towards the Mercian frontier. Villages with English names east of Offa's Dyke were becoming Welsh again, and Canute and his successors set up earldoms along the Severn. From 1039 onwards Gruffyd ap Llewelyn of Deheubarth began to weld together a Welsh kingdom, and took the offensive against Mercia, raiding all Hereford-shire despite Earl Ralph's new castles.

This was the man to whom Ælfgar of Mercia had turned, even in 1055, when the Welsh tenantry of Hereford collapsed, the cathedral was burned, and the clergy killed. The English government gave way; Ælfgar was restored and married his daughter to Gruffyd, who killed the bishop of Hereford in a raid of 1056. Not until after Ælfgar's death did Harold take the field in Wales again, and was relieved by the assassination of Gruffyd in 1063. But Wales was not subdued, and Harold had to repel more attacks in the year before Hastings; even though the English border was restored and advanced to the Usk, for many a year it lay desolate. Most important of all, Harold had been compelled to a very different treatment of Mercia. For if he was to win the Crown, Mercia and Wales with it must not be hostile; no further attempt, then, was made to upset Ælfgar, or his son and successor Edwin.

Whether we call this weakness or policy, it came out even more clearly in Northumbria. There ambition had overreached itself; a southerner and an absentee could not rule the north. Tostig was ambitious, like Harold, but had none of his patriotism; he had abandoned Northumbria to Scottish forays, taxed it to the bone, and assassinated thegns of the old ruling house. In the autumn of 1065 the nobility, Scandinavian and English, seized York, offered their earldom to Morcar, Edwin's brother, and with reinforcements from the Danelaw marched south. At Northampton Edwin with Mercian and Welsh troops joined them and, ravaging as they went, they approached Oxford. Once more, as in 1055, the government capitulated. Tostig, swearing that Harold had engineered his fall, was sent into exile, Morcar was admitted as Earl, the young Waltheof, Siward's son, was given North-ampton and Huntingdon, and the Witan confirmed Canute's law which admitted the self-government of Scandinavian England.

Mercia and Northumbria, therefore, only obeyed the King on their own terms; Wales remained unconquered: the Scottish frontier was falling in. Since Malcolm's defeat of the Northumbrians at Carham in or about 1016, Canute had recognized the final loss of Lothian; the Scots had the Tweed line, and were for ever raiding Durham. Siward had turned out the Highland usurper Macbeth, and crowned his own protégé Malcolm Canmore, but if gratitude existed on the Border, it perished with Siward's death.

Such was the state of England after twenty years of weakness from King Edward, and the ambitions of Godwine's family. Administratively, it was a time of stagnation. There were, indeed, one or two advances in technique. Royal clerks were devising writs whereby the King's orders might be accurately carried out, while the Danegeld called forth an organized treasury at Winchester. But in all essentials government was nerveless. There were no new laws. The last of Canute's seamen were paid off, and though Harold improvised a naval force for his last Welsh war, we hear of no effort at sea in 1066 to intercept the Normans, while pirates so dogged the coast that the Devonshire bishopric was moved from Crediton to Exeter.

While the rulers of England proved themselves devoid of resource, their relation to the Church showed a dangerous ignorance of Europe. Danish war and the feudalizing process between them had largely destroyed the independence and spirituality of the English Church. There were still, of course, good bishops like Wulfstan who held Worcester till after the Conquest; there were learned bishops like him who left to Exeter a great library, including a volume of old English poetry, and there was considerable church-building by thegns and monks. But the Church had become dependent on the State, with dire results. In the south it was over-endowed; Canterbury, for instance, owned nearly one thousand hides, the Church held two-thirds of Wiltshire, and its leaders became politicians. In Danish England its property was small, but the archbishopric of York was attached to the south by being linked with Worcester. Vested and hereditary interests cramped church life, and of all this archbishop Stigand was an unhappy type. Having made his peace with Godwine by deserting Emma, he combined Canterbury with the rich bishopric of Winchester, with several canonries and private estates. The line between Church and State was hopelessly blurred. Church councils ceased to meet. Bishops owed their appointment solely to the King or his magnates. Clerical offences were tried in hundred and shire courts, like those of the laity.

Any impulse towards reform must therefore come from outside. As against the King, Godwine's family followed Canute in appointing Germans, who pressed on their unwilling chapters a more austere common life, — just as Harold, in endowing what was to be his burial place at Waltham Abbey, filled it with canons under a scholar from Liége. But if the Church looked abroad, it would find a spirit which must condemn its present character. With the German Popes appointed by orthodox emperors had begun the Papal reform which was one day to destroy the Empire. Hildebrand, who as Pope Gregory VII was to crown this policy, was in power at Rome by the middle of the century; ardent proselytes, from reformed centres like Cluny, brought a new tone into Normandy. They taught the separation of the clergy as a sacred caste; lay interference in Church appointments must be stopped, clerical marriage must be prohibited, and the clergy be judged in their own courts by Canon law. When this new atmosphere reached England, it found a rock of offence in Stigand, who had usurped the seat of a lawful predecessor and received his pallium from a usurping Pope. English bishops refused consecration at his hands; Robert of Jumièges had taken his grievances to Rome. The danger was real, since the Church's champion, and King Edward's heir and cousin, were one and the same, the Duke of Normandy.

Each century of European history brings a new force to the surface, and the eleventh was the century of the Normans. Throwing their weight, first into the duel between the Carolingian kings and the Dukes of Paris, then between those dukes now become Kings of France and the vassals who hemmed Paris in, the Norman settlers had become a formidable power. The Dukes had kept together the two wings of their territory, Scandinavian districts round Bayeux and the Cotentin and the French regions round Rouen, and had absorbed all that France could give them of religion and law. Over Brittany they had a suzerainty, and over the French Vexin also, which brought them within fifty miles of Paris. Norman nobles, deprived of blood-letting at home, betook themselves to Moorish crusades in Spain, or plunged into Italy where, before William conquered England, they founded kingdoms in Sicily and Naples. One thing above all they had done, vital to the later history of England: in a small territory they had set up a centralized feudal State, with clear-cut institutions.

All land was held of the Duke, in baronies of fairly even size, by nobles, bishops, and monasteries, and of them again by knightly sub-tenants, from whose fiefs, grouped on a five-knight basis, the Duke drew his army. He had further the rights of wardship over, and of giving in marriage, his vassals' heirs, money aids on fixed occasion, and a ' relief ' or payment by the heir on his succession. And as service was fixed in units of the soil, so too was jurisdiction; the lord of the fief, in virtue of that fact, held a court for his tenants. But the ducal sovereignty was all-superior. There were some pleas, offences in time of war for instance, which he always kept for himself; there were other ' pleas of the sword ', which he would only rarely allow a baronial franchise to hold. His law sharply restricted any private war. Castles could only be built with his permission, and he could claim to garrison them. His officials, the vicomtes, farmed the revenues, held local courts, and could call out a general levy to resist invasion. By setting definite penalties, his justice had done away with the arbitrariness of the wergild. Over the Church he was supreme, — appointing bishops, calling councils, and regulating the spiritual courts. Of his ' Curia ', or high court, with whose aid he ruled and judged, he seems to have been entirely master, its composition varying at his will. Such was the machine, logical and singly controlled, which was to destroy the ramshackle half-feudalism of England.

It needed a strong man to direct it, but out of the sheer ruin of his childhood William drew his lessons and rebuilt the ducal power. When his father Robert died on his way back from Jerusalem in 1035, this child of seven years, the illegitimate son of Arlette, a tanner's daughter at Falaise, was left to struggle for dear life with the most war-like baronage in Christendom. One of his guardians was poisoned, a second was knifed in his bedchamber ; he had been forced to hide in poor men's cottages. His uncles and cousins raised rebellion against the bastard, and he had to bring in his overlord, the French king, to crush them. Among these murderers he learned the barbarous punishments which he later practised, though he found, too, the loyal companions, William fitzOsbern or the house of Clare, on whom he heaped power in England. He grew up a tall forbidding figure, a tireless horseman, wielding a bow which others could not bend, with a fiercesome voice, swearing oaths of vengeance ' by the splendour of God ' which struck terror, because he kept them.

Always charging straight at the immediate danger, as he did in battle, by 1060 William had made himself a considerable power. He had crushed his kinsmen, raising up his own half-brothers, Odo as bishop of Bayeux and Robert as Count of Mortain. He had twice beaten off French invasion and had taken fortresses southwards, which showed his plan to wrest Maine from the rival power of Anjou. He had married the woman he had meant to, Matilda, daughter of Baldwin of Flanders, in spite of the Pope's objection. He had made the Count of Ponthieu his vassal, so securing the river Somme. And that year, 1060, was the turning-point, for his two deadly enemies died, Henry I of France and Geoffrey Martel of Anjou, — the first leaving a child of seven, and the other no son at all, but a civil war — and William was consequently able to declare himself Count of Maine. By his own greatness he had out-ridden every storm, and taken every gift of fortune ; in 1064 another memorable one came in the unexpected arrival of the English Earl Harold at the Court of Rouen.

A dark veil hangs over their meeting ; indeed, over every step in their contest for the throne. The Duke had visited England in 1051-2 during Harold's exile, but if King Edward held out hopes then, he changed his mind later, when he recalled Edward the Atheling from Hungary. Only with the Atheling's death did the real struggle begin; in accordance with English custom the decision would rest upon a recommendation from the reigning King, and the acceptance of that recommendation by the magnates. We can hardly believe that Harold waited with folded hands. He had visited France about 1058, and could not be blind to William's character. He had ground for jealousy of his brother Tostig's favour with the King and Queen. Might it not be easier to secure himself by agreement with the Mercian Earls, and a direct approach to his Norman rival?

However this may be, two things are certain: that sometime, probably in the summer of 1064, Harold was in Normandy and took some oath to William, and that in January 1066 he was crowned King of England, on the day following Edward's death, with all the haste of a *coup d'état*. Whatever the form of his oath, willing or unwilling, on the saints' relics or not, it included a promise to marry one of William's daughters; by taking knighthood at William's hands he became his man, went off with him on a Breton war, and when he returned to England left one of his brothers as a hostage. Normans asserted that he promised to help William to the Crown, and Englishmen were aware that some sort of oath had been taken. In any case Harold had given some undertaking which he did not fulfil.

Since the expulsion of his favourite Tostig, King Edward had taken to his bed: in December 1065 he was too ill to see the great achievement of his life, the opening of his rebuilt abbey at Westminster. On the 5th January he died, and next day Harold wore the crown. It was the first time that a man not of the blood royal had worn it, and only the few present at the old King's deathbed could know the gist of his last words. Public opinion was divided. Edgar the Atheling, son of him who had died so suddenly in 1057, was now of fighting age. The north, under its powerful earls, was resentful, and among Harold's first steps was a rapid journey to York and his marriage to those earls' sister, widow of Gruffyd of Wales. Desperately he strove to energize resistance, appealing to the Church, coining money, and collecting a London fleet; but he could not improvise a nation. England did not fight with him at Hastings, but only his bodyguard, the thegnhood of his brothers' earldoms south of Trent, and the Churchmen of Wessex. His own house was divided, the Confessor's widow being one of the first to submit to the Conqueror, while Tostig brought together two enemies from abroad.

For the English Crown, though claimed by William in hereditary right, by Edward's bequest, and Harold's oath, was claimed also by St. Olaf's half-brother, Harold Hardrada the last great Viking, who had fought all over Europe, and at length fought his way to the Norwegian throne. And Harold of England was isolated in Europe. William's claims were laid before the Holy See and approved : a consecrated banner was sent to bless the war against a usurper, who had broken his vow and defended the usurping Stigand. France was under the guardianship of William's father-in-law, Anjou was distracted, Eustace of Boulogne was enthusiastic in William's cause. Swein Estrithson of Denmark had claims of his own, but would certainly make no move till he saw what success waited his rival of Norway. In the face of these appalling dangers the old military weakness of England was revealed. Before Harold's fleet was equipped, Tostig with his Flemish mercenaries was able to pillage the Isle of Wight and seize royal ships at Sandwich : from June onwards Harold continued watching the south coast, but early in September the provision of food failed, the fyrd began to desert, and his fleet dispersed.

That month Tostig's intrigues bore fruit. Harold Hardrada, with the jarls of the Orkneys, reached the Tyne, where he met Tostig and more auxiliaries from Scotland. Almost unopposed they sailed into the Humber, and so up the Ouse : there leaving their ships, they marched on York, crushed the stiff resistance of Edwin and Morcar at Fulford, and entered the city on the 24th September. Tostig's sympathizers began to come in, and the Norsemen, leaving their armour and many of their men with the ships, met next day, a few miles east of York at Stamford Bridge, to discuss the division of the conquered territory.

Early that morning (25th September) Harold of England entered York from the west, marched across it, and caught the enemy army in confusion, with one section ten miles away and the main body divided by the Derwent. Out of the morning haze, their Saga tells us, they saw the sun fall on the English armour like glistening ice. The battle went on till evening; at its end the King of Norway and Tostig lay dead, with nearly their whole force round them.

But the stars in their courses fought against Harold. The south wind, which he had hoped for, blew this week for the first time in many months; so it happened that he was at York when word reached him that, on the 28th September, the Normans had landed at Pevensey. That this blow would fall he had long known, for fierce messages had come from William to denounce his perjury; but the superiority of William to Harold lay essentially in this, that the Normans seized and kept the initiative. Harold waited, but they struck: no English fleet or English ally intercepted them.

A holy war blessed by the Church, the spoils of England, the prospect of fighting under a great captain, all this allowed William to create within six months a fleet of 800 ships and an army of, perhaps, 12,000 men. His baronage were not obliged to fight overseas, so that he appealed to them as individuals. Broadly speaking, his strength came from three sources : the ducal house represented by his half-brothers, his personal friends among the baronage, and adventurous knights from beyond his realm. Alan of Brittany brought a large contingent, and Walter Tirel came from Ponthieu; others came from Flanders, Poitou, and even Spain. This heterogeneous army had to be fed, disciplined, transported, and to wait for weeks on a favourable wind. But William's discipline was hard and his staff work perfect, and on the 12th September the expedition moved from its first base, on the Dives, to St. Valéry at the mouth of the Somme.

At last the wind changed : at nine in the morning on the 28th the ships began to disembark at Pevensey, knights and archers, monks, William's Spanish charger, pioneers and camp followers. Leaving the ships protected by rough fortifications, the army marched on to Hastings unopposed, where it was better placed on the London road, and in a rich country for supplies. William would not lose touch with his ships : Harold on his part could not afford to wait. By one stupendous effort he had so far held the north, but only speedy victory would keep Edwin and Morcar to their word. If he hoped that Stamford Bridge would frighten William he was soon disillusioned, and the envoys he sent to Hastings returned with scornful replies.

Those who fought with him at the end were but a fragment of England; thegns who, making a last gift of land to the Church, came from Worcestershire or Huntingdon, Winchester monks who were found dead with robes under their armour, or the sheriff and thegns of Berkshire who were wiped out almost to a man. They came on a furious summons, for Harold was back in London within ten days of Stamford Bridge, and after a bare week there marched on the 12th October to force a battle. Waving aside advice to starve William out, he marched with his surviving housecarles and hasty levies, came out of the Sussex forest on the 13th, and where the London road entered it seized a position of great strength, north-west of Hastings. At nine the next morning William attacked him, before the English were deployed.

All day long the noise of battle rolled, as the Normans, first foot and then horse, pressed up the bare uncultivated hill : at three in the afternoon it was still undecided. Protected in flank and rear by sharp-falling ground, if the English shield-wall held firm, it could go on killing the enemy and still survive. The Bretons broke : William himself had three horses killed that day : Taillifer the minstrel, singing the Latin songs of Charlemagne and Roland, throwing his sword in the air and catching it as he rode, perished with the first charge. ' Holy Cross ', ' out, out ', came the English cries, as the housecarles wielded their two-handed axes.

But the English had few archers and fought entirely on foot, and it was the Norman archers and cavalry, together with better discipline, which wore the defence away. Twice Harold's troops, galled beyond endurance by arrows and deceived by feinted flight, broke rank, poured down hill in pursuit, and were cut to pieces by the horsemen. They began to be too few to hold the ridge, and finally the Norman archers, shooting high, sent that hail of arrows to which there was no reply, — one of which blinded Harold. As twilight came on, a last charge broke the line : Harold was killed, — and darkness fell on the woods, through which the remnant of the English fled away. That night William slept on the field ; next day Harold's mangled body was buried on the shore at Hastings.

There was no England left : if there had been, resistance could have been organized during the next month, when William lay ill near Canterbury. But Winchester and Dover surrendered : London proclaimed Edgar the Atheling King but, though they accepted him, Edwin and Morcar moved their troops back to the north ; a third party determined that submission was the only course, and approaches from London officials and archbishop Stigand showed William that the prize was won. It would be all the better if he could avoid fighting for his inheritance. He therefore encircled the London area by a long march, ravaging as he went, from Southwark to Wallingford, where he crossed the Thames, and so back through the Chilterns to Berkhamstead. There he received an offer of the crown, from his rival the Atheling, the Church leaders, and London : on Christmas Day he was crowned in the Abbey, and within a few weeks submissions began to come in from the north. By March 1067 he had arranged a temporary government under his brother Odo and fitzOsbern, erected castles at danger-points, not least in beginning the Tower of London, and distributed much land to his barons ; that month he sailed to Normandy, and in his entry into Rouen the citizens saw, with triumph or curiosity, Edwin and Morcar, Siward's son Waltheof, and Stigand.

CONTEMPORARY DATES

1027   Conrad, the first Franconian Emperor, crowned at Rome in presence of Canute.

1034, onwards.   The House of Hauteville and other Normans conquer southern Italy.

1040   Macbeth, King in Scotland.

1052   Beginning of the Confessor's abbey at Westminster.

1054   Godfrey of Lorraine marries Matilda of Tuscany.

1059   Papal elections vested in the college of Cardinals.

1060   Death of Henry I of France, and Geoffrey Martel of Anjou. William the Conqueror occupies Maine.

1062, onwards.   Seljuk Turks invade Syria and Asia Minor.

BOOK II

MEDIAEVAL ENGLAND
1066-1360

CHAPTER I

THE TRANSFORMATION OF ENGLAND
1066-1154

THE second, and much the greatest, revolution in English history was accomplished. Since 1066 the country has undergone civil war, invasion, and change of dynasty, but never again a change like that wrought by the Normans; in a reshaping of society, remodelling of Church and State, a new ruling culture, and a new relation to Europe. This feudal, French-influenced, England may be said to have lasted till 1215. But feudalism was never wholly triumphant, and was swiftly undermined both by old English custom and new economic necessity.

Moreover, the Normans were few in number, not more than five thousand knights perhaps followed William's host, and if we add to them merchants, priests, women, and servants, the one and a half million English did not, probably, submit to more than one hundred thousand persons of foreign blood. Such a conquest must inevitably result in amalgamation. Even some leading barons, Robert d'Oilly the new lord of Oxford for instance, married English heiresses, and intermarriage gradually blended together the middle class of both races. Foreign soldiers and churches did, indeed, give their names to many hundred villages and homes. Weedon Pinkney speaks of a Picquigny baron in Northamptonshire, Willingale Spains of a Spanish venturer in Essex, Tooting Bec of a church given to Lanfranc's abbey, and Montgomery of the powerful lords who brought that name from Lisieux to the Welsh hills. Yet the newcomers, who rearranged the native life, could not destroy it.

What this ' feudalism ' meant is best found by looking to its roots in the manor, for nine-tenths perhaps of the people lived on the soil, upon which a true feudal system must logically base all rules of government, class gradations, finance, and military service. In 1086, facing the possibility of a Danish invasion which called for costly defensive measures, and many arrears of claims and counterclaims to property, the King sent out four circuits of his leading magnates, to traverse all England south of Tyne. Their instructions were to receive, from every hundred and shire, the sworn reports of witnesses, half-English and half-Norman, on the relevant facts; the area of soil cultivated, names of landowners, rights of lords and tenants, cash outgoings to lords and sheriffs, the local structure of courts, values of mills, fish-ponds, and cattle. These reports were speedily rearranged by each regional enquiry in a true Norman grouping, under tenants-in-chief and baronial fiefs, and finally, probably before 1090, compiled by the Treasury clerks at Winchester into what has ever since been known as Domesday Book. Their form was that of a double picture, of the English soil as in King Edward's day and, again, twenty years after.

Though Saxon society had never been of one and far less of one democratic pattern, and though lordship had grown rapidly since the Danish wars, in Norman eyes the Edwardian picture offended every feudal principle. Personal rank, delegated royal authority, and land-lord's rights, were all confused. Rules of tenure and inheritance varied widely from one shire, even one village, to another. It was left vague whether military service lay on the individual, or on some grouping of hides. Jurisdiction was a chaos. Lords might have ' sake and soke ' over all their tenants, or over a part of them, or over none. There were manors where tenants with thirty acres or more attended a royal court, but the smaller men went to the lord's ' hallimote '. There were sokemen who could sell their land freely, by such sale transferring the soke from the old owner to the new. There were many more ' commended ' by a loose tie to one lord, but owing suit to another lord's court. A ' manor ' might mean a large territory like the bishop of Winchester's at Taunton, with land for 120 plough teams, or some strips worth a few shillings annually and farmed by peasants.

Conquest and then English revolt gave the Normans an opportunity to clear this jungle, and by 1086 scarcely 1 per cent of the Saxon land-owners, though innumerable Saxon tenants, remained. Gradually certain primary rules were imposed from above. All land is held of the King, and of his tenants-in-chief under him. The military fief is a unit : it belongs to one man, it cannot be alienated, the heir is the elder son : by its own rules it must keep together the unity of its dependent holdings. Service is specialized service ; war for a knight — prayer for a priest, — money rent for a yeoman or a trader. Tenure is a legal definite thing : the rights on either side can be put in black and white, and it is either free or unfree. Finally, with tenure goes the court; ' suit of court ' is every tenant's duty.

Even in Domesday Book many a peasant, we can see, has felt the downward pressure of these rules. The free villages of East Anglia were subjected now to Norman lords. In Cambridgeshire the sokemen have sunk from 900 to 200, in Yorkshire they are being pieced together to make manors for Norman knights. What had once been rare, a village manor-court, rapidly became almost universal, and with it a levelling out of labour services, so that within fifty years, on any average manor in southern England, every villein would be found doing much the same work. Domesday, again, had recorded some 25,000 Saxon slaves, particularly dense in the west country, but slavery was not reconcilable with the Normans' Christian notions, nor fitted to their manorial method. Within a generation of the Conquest we find in one half-servile mould not these slaves only, now elevated into freedom, but all those once partly-free peasants whom the Norman clerks lumped together as ' villani ', the folk of the villages.

Angevin lawyers later attempted to lay down some tests separating the two broad categories of free men and villeins. The mere fact of labour service hardly met the case, for thegns and sokemen often ploughed and cut the harvest. ' Merchet ', the proof of base blood, a payment made when a villein's daughter married with the lord's assent, was more a symptom than a test. The essence of villein tenure lay, rather, in the character of its service ; of fixed weekly days of work on the lord's demesne, together with a variation of each day of work (reaping, hedging, or carting, as it might be) at the discretion of the lord's reeve. Their lot became harder during the next two hundred years ; even by Henry I's time the abbot of Peterborough's villeins worked three days a week on his demesne, in addition to money rents, ploughing duties, quantities of hens and eggs, and payment for grinding their corn at the lord's mill. His demesne, and the ' works ' maintaining it, made the core of the manor. Instead of a loosely-knit body of villagers, attached to the lord by ties of varying freedom, the villeins became a caste, marked out by servile work, so much so that a royal court recognized no right to property in a villein's son.

The free tenures gradually fell into three groups. Frankalmoign, the ' free alms ' by which spiritual men held land free of any earthly duty, was confined to specially favoured monasteries and the glebe of the parish churches. ' Socage ' (or in towns ' burgage ') was the tenure by money payment for most non-military lay property. More far-reaching politically, and more new to England, was the third group : the military tenures of barony, knight service, and sergeantry, by which the great bulk of the soil was held in chief of the Crown. Here lay the essence of the change forced on England.

The feudal tie was a contract, whether between the King and his tenants-in-chief, or between those tenants and their sub-tenants. In either case, between lord and man lay a moral obligation, the sacred tie of homage and fealty, which only death or a solemn repudiation could snap. Unarmed the vassal knelt on both knees and, putting his hands between those of his lord, swore, ' I become your man of the tenement that I hold of you, and faith to you will bear of life and limb and earthly worship, and faith to you shall bear against all folk who can live and die '. Thus sworn, he must fight for his lord and attend his court : when he died a ' relief ' was due, — if without heirs, the land itself

' escheated ', — to the lord, in token that from him it had come. The lord had wardship of his tenant's children if under age, and marriage rights over his heir or heiress. Aids in money were the lord's right, for his own ransom, the knighting of his eldest son, or the marriage of his daughter. All of this structure was knit together by the feudal courts. For his freemen the lord held a ' curia baronum ' ; as owner of a manor, his court had to determine the customs of husbandry, with the daily routine of ploughing or pasturage ; if he had inherited a Saxon ' halli-mote ' with sake and soke, or if the Norman king granted him a hundred, he wielded also some police powers of the State. In time to come the greater lords developed a whole tier of courts for different purposes. A great Honour like that of Clare in Suffolk, — and over a hundred fiefs were styled Honours, — could demand attendance from vassals in three or four counties, its central court keeping an eye on its subordi-nate manors and apportioning between them the military service due from the whole ; its principal vassals, though sub-tenants, might be reckoned as ' barons ' of the realm. Infinite in variety, the privileges of these private courts depended on history, or power, more than rules of law. The abbots of Ramsey were exempted, for instance, from hundred and shire : by Edward I's time 358 out of 628 hundreds in England were in private hands. Finally, we reach potentates like the palatine earls of Durham and Chester, who appointed justices of their own, coined their own coins, and controlled even pleas of the Crown. But the commonest type was the court of a single village, or part of one, with full power over its villeins, and the right by royal grant, or by encroachment, of policing all its tenants in a ' view of frank-pledge ', which had grown out of the English tithing system.

Such was the logic of feudalism, which would leave the King only the highest lord among many, and by which he was limited to dealing direct with tenants-in-chief alone : if the Duke of Normandy might raise his vassals against the French King, so might those vassals in turn, on feudal theory, call out their men against him. The practice fortun-ately was different ; the Dukes had checked private war in Normandy, and as Kings would curb the feudal principle in England. But that principle was the very root of their government, and it is vital not to read English mediaeval history as a perpetual struggle of King against barons. Generally speaking, there was no serious baronial rebellion which was not stirred up by the King's kinsmen, or unconnected with the succession to the throne. How could the Norman King dispense with the help of the military leaders who had conquered England, or how, if that class were hostile, could he hope to resist France ?

By the middle of his reign the Conqueror had divided England between some six hundred tenants-in-chief, assigning the greater part in knight service to his magnates and fixing upon each a quota, on the plan long used in Normandy. The numbers varied according to circumstance; from the archbishop of Canterbury he asked sixty knights, but from Durham, burdened with the defence of the frontier, only ten; fifty from the Yorkshire Honour of Richmond, while petty barons of the north were liable for five. He had introduced a principle new to England, the knight's fee as an individual military liability; totally different from that of the Saxon thegns, who had supervised a duty owed by some rustic community or group of hides. and whose service had been mixed up with escort duty or the royal hunting. Nor did the Conqueror ask how knights were actually provided; the abbot of Westminster kept his twenty-five in hand as a personal escort, others hired knights when the King's call came, others again built up in their manor-houses a small private army. From this source came the heavy armed cavalry which made the strength of a feudal host; for light horsemen the King looked to the sergeantries, which provided for his body servants, huntsmen, falconers, and the whole staff of the Court.

In this age feudalism was not the elaborate ladder of tenures and sub-tenures which it became by Henry II's time. Instant readiness for war was the Normans' need. The King demanded castle-guard from his vassals, the knights of Abingdon Abbey, for example, forming a garrison at Windsor Castle; his barons, in their turn, especially on the dangerous Welsh Marches, grouped tenants round their castles, or kept trains of knights in their households. Yet we find present from the first those hard economic facts, which were to make English feudalism not so much a military scheme as a social arrangement. Even before 1100 the King sometimes took scutage, a money payment in replacement of service in war; while in the process of ' enfeoffment ', the carving out of estates, we meet knights' fees of many different values and sizes, adjusted to different sorts of country, varying estate requirements, and countless family plans. As population grew and cultivation extended and the royal revenue became more exacting, six or more tenancies might by sub-infeudation be intercepted between the King and the actual occupier; before 1135 knights' fees are found partitioned into such small fractions, that plainly only a cash payment could represent the equivalent of their share of service due.

Facing a hostile England, King and baronage depended on each other. True, the manors which the Conqueror gave to his great men were usually scattered, but the conquest was, after all, a slow one, while Saxon England had been full of landowners with estates in several shires, which passed (as a block of Harold's, for example, went to Battle Abbey) to some individual Norman. There were, moreover, many solid holdings, where one magnate was not only chief landowner but sole administrator. Thus Roger Montgomery held four-fifths of Shropshire, seven hundreds were attached to his manors, he appointed the sheriff; and there were many smaller men holding forty or fifty manors in one district. William's sheriffs were almost invariably large owners in their counties; several made their office hereditary, like the de Mandevilles who claimed the custody of the Tower and sheriffdom of London, or the Worcestershire Beauchamps. This reality of feudalism lasted for a hundred years. Henry I, strong and extortionate though he was, would not sap the foundation of his power. His castles were garrisoned by baronial knights. He relieved lords' demesnes from taxation. To loyal servants he freely distributed new fiefs; his court in all ordinary cases respected the baron's right to try his own vassals, and great men are found delegating powers of jurisdiction, even of capital punishment, to their sub-tenants.

But though the Norman kings could not override their baronage, they would not tolerate the weakness which had wrecked Saxon England. At the end of the Conqueror's reign there were only four earldoms, and five only in 1135, in the hands of non-royal barons. For the same reason that William had promised to preserve the law of Edward or the customs of London, he kept up the ancient courts of hundred, borough, and shire, while over against the feudal army he maintained the fyrd. From the first, then, these Kings were not lords only, but overlords. Heavy taxation was taken, based upon the English townships and hides. A growing list of pleas (armed violence, or offences against the coinage, for instance) were reserved for the King's Court. Military service was primarily due to the King: building of castles needed his leave, and private war was illegal. Oaths of allegiance, which in 1086 the Conqueror exacted from all large landowners in a solemn assembly at Salisbury, were declared to override a man's fealty to his immediate lord, and twice a year, in his ' tourn ' of the hundred courts, each sheriff took this oath from the whole male population over twelve years of age, when he inspected the tithings. Even the private hundred kept its original character of a royal court, for the sheriff had a right of entry and shared the proceeds.

As for the shire court, it was not only an instrument for taxation or judging pleas of the Crown; it was the chief link between King and people where, for example, Henry I's coronation charter was read aloud; it was also the court where a baron would get his privileges recognized, or his land transactions registered. To check the aggression of Bishop Odo on the see of Canterbury, or those of the ravening sheriff of Cambridgeshire, or to report conflicting claims to the Domesday commissioners, for all this and from the first months of the Conqueror's reign, the shire court was called on to state the English law and apply it. An important edict of Henry I ordered that it should meet as of old, — usually two ' great courts ' a year, in addition to a routine monthly meeting, — and provided that cases affecting tenants of two lords must come to the shire. Its very composition testified to something older than feudalism. As time went on much of the ' suit of court ' was, indeed, feudalized, in the sense that particular acres or holdings, whoever held them, were obliged to provide a suitor. But in the lord's absence, and absent he usually was, four men and the reeve represented each village : both this, and the regular attendance of village tithings in the hundred court, brought these old communities face to face with servants of the Crown.

Domesday, and the method of its compilation, showed in germ the links whereby local government was tied to the central power; by the royal writ, the sworn enquiry, the itinerant royal justice, and the concentration of responsibility in the sheriff, all of which were to be perfected under Henry II. As yet, this procedure was abrupt and ill-defined. Judicial writs to the sheriff, to do right to some monastery for instance, were hardly distinguishable from executive commands : juries were sworn, but usually only to testify to the Crown's rights, or those of some favoured church. Yet by Henry I's death the occasional appointment of a local royal justice, or visit of a royal official, had become systematized, so that members of the ' Curia regis ', justices in eyre as they were called later, visited the shire courts, charged not only to collect revenue but to do justice. Here they would take the verdict of an ' inquest ', the system borrowed by the Normans from the Franks, the neighbours put on oath to testify to the facts, whether it were the boundaries of some royal forest, or a controversy touching a landowner to whom the King had extended this privilege. This steady encroachment from the centre Henry I exercised through his sheriffs. The earldom had become a mere title ; the bishop, as we shall see, had left the shire court, so that the sheriff was supreme. In him were concentrated control of royal estates, leadership of the fyrd, farming of revenues in shire and borough, all initiative and action. Henry not only removed many of baronial family, but increasingly chose his sheriffs from the inner ring of officials. In 1110 six members of his Household held sixteen sheriffdoms between them ; in 1130 one of his chamberlains acted as justice in seventeen shires.

In the Curia Regis lay the mainspring of Norman government, and the greatest boon which it brought to England. In character this court was universal ; in one sense a collection of the King's household officers, in another a feudal court where he took his vassals' advice and judged their controversies, in a third a national Council with all powers. Unlike the Witan it was feudal in composition, for all who attended it, bishops and abbots included, were tenants-in-chief, but its composition on any one occasion, like its power, flowed from the royal will. On the three great festivals when the King wore his crown, — Easter at

Winchester, Whitsun at London, and Christmas at Gloucester, — or in great meetings like the council when Rufus tried to crush archbishop Anselm, it would become a council of all chief vassals ; barons would attend the presence in robes of state, and to be absent was to incur the King's displeasure. But usually it shrunk to a handful of officials, a few ecclesiastics, and one or two barons distinguished, like the first Hugh of Chester, by experience or loyalty : its meetings circled round the King, who might be hunting from his palace at Woodstock, or making war from Rouen. Yet whether the meeting was large or small, it remained one and the same court with the same powers, holding within it all the seeds of the constitution.

Edward the Confessor had maintained some rude government departments. The seal used for his writs had been held by a chancellor, the head of his chapel clerks, and his Treasury was staffed by chamberlains, who were capable enough to fix money contributions in replacement of the ancient revenue in kind, and to enforce a scientific assay of the coin tendered. After the Conquest there was more rapid development. So long as the King was constantly abroad, some trusted servant had to control England ; a sort of vice-royalty, which the Conqueror tested in Lanfranc, which Rufus carried further in his evil minister Ranulf Flambard, and which under Henry I crystallized into the office of Justiciar. The Treasury, fixed at Winchester Castle till about 1200, became an administrative machine, with Domesday Book among its records, and gradually the chamberlains, who marked its origin in the Household, were limited to the privy purse ; simultaneously another Treasury for Normandy was based upon Rouen. With the growth of royal writs the Chancellor's importance grew also, his office becoming the government secretariat. The master maker was bishop Roger of Salisbury, and the official family which he founded : in 1135 he was himself justiciar, his son chancellor, his nephew treasurer, and it was that nephew's son, Richard FitzNeal, treasurer from about 1160 to 1198, who wrote the *Dialogue on the Exchequer*, the classic account of Angevin administration.

The creation of the Exchequer was their greatest achievement. A rigorous system, introduced from France, made possible a swift and accurate render of accounts, and henceforward the Treasury went back to its first uses as a storehouse. Ultimate financial control was kept for the Curia Regis itself, the ' barons ' of the Exchequer being drawn from the central court and continuing to act as judges at headquarters, or in the provinces. As part of the King's Court the Exchequer at first followed his person, though practical reasons naturally soon fixed it at Westminster. Twice a year it exacted the presence of all chargeable to the Crown, — sheriffs, bailiffs of honours, or royal debtors, — and passed in review the ferms of the shires, the profits of the judges,

Danegeld, feudal dues, and forest fines; an elaborate system of rolls and records checking the balance in the sheriff's account and protecting the subject against oppression. Of this early school of government servants we may still be reminded by the Prime Minister's official house at 'Chequers', which once belonged to the Angevin family 'de Scaccario'.

This centralized government rendered another service of inestimable price, the beginning of a Common Law. It had against it a mass of local custom, Danish, Mercian, or West Saxon, with the venerable apparatus of 'wer' and 'wite' assessed by local doomsmen, and a new mushroom growth of baronial courts. Normandy had produced no legal code, while those of Edgar and Canute could not meet feudal requirements. Such common law as the King's Court evolved came, therefore, from hand-to-mouth action, rather than from legal theory or any deliberate blending of English and Norman. As St. Edward's successor the King had promised to maintain his law, while his barons inherited the rights of English thegns, all of which meant constant recourse to English custom, sworn to by juries of Englishmen. But the King had also inherited Edward's prerogatives, and a growing list of Crown pleas was savagely enforced. The criss-cross pattern of feudalism brought much conflict of courts, and made it worth while to buy royal justice, in the shape of those curt writs which bade justice be done, or the King would do it himself. For important persons his Court thus became a court of appeal; it began also to protect 'seisin', or possession of property, and to use an overlord's admitted power to intervene where the vassal's court had failed to do justice. Constant re-employment of the same men as judges was building up, within the Council, a true law court; their judgments were still arbitrary, but repeated use of the same rules by 'eyres' in every county was outlining the fabric of a Common Law, already centred in Rufus' new-built Westminster Hall.

What would be the outcome between these two Norman creations of feudal society and centralized government? In the early twelfth century it was uncertain, nor did all England move at the same pace. But it can truthfully be said that feudalism was superimposed on England too late for a feudal triumph. Through the feudal over-casing we catch glimpses of the older substance of township and village, or even of Celtic clans. No neat manor-house system covered the wild north, where scattered groups of incalculable age rendered military service or suit to baronial centres. In the old Danelaw humble villagers freely used charters to buy and sell land, and here at least manor and township hardly ever coincided. A deeper unit of life than the manor was the parish church, where charters were read aloud, where maiden knights laid their swords on the altar, and where the priest taught

children in his room over the porch. Even the customs of the manor
court were those of a community ; for judgment was given by the court,
not by the lord's steward, and by their sworn testimony the lord would
abide.

A King of genius would surely cut through the sheath to this native
metal below.

But the conflict would come in an England transformed, for the
Conquest had brought her out of isolation into the Latin world. English
religion was redoubled by the sweep of reform, and the Church became
Catholic in a sense unknown to Dunstan. Here, as in Normandy, the
Conqueror made it clear that reformed his Church should be, but always
royal. The great Hildebrand had done more than any man to get the
Church's blessing bestowed on William's invasion, but when as Pope
Gregory VII he asked that William should do homage to the Holy See,
he was rebuffed. The King's rule, and his sons maintained it, was that
no Pope should be recognized, that no royal servant should be excommunicated, that no Church synod should make canons, without his
leave. Most prelates of his appointment were thoroughly competent
but, defying the reformers' ideal, he named them himself and invested
them with the spiritual staff and ring.

He chose a perfect instrument in Lanfranc, by birth a Lombard, by
training a lawyer, by temper a politician, who only in middle life had
taken orders and become abbot of the model Norman monastery of Bec.
It was the nature both of King and archbishop to carry out reform
without attention to principle. They deposed Stigand and gradually
filled up bishoprics and abbeys with well-qualified Normans, but St.
Wulfstan was left at Worcester and the English clergy were guided, not
coerced. Those already married might keep their wives, but no more
married men would be ordained. Lanfranc was never ready to tolerate
rebellion masquerading as clerical liberty : he arrested Odo of Bayeux,
the Conqueror's brother, for his crimes as Earl of Kent. He was not
prepared to be more than neutral between Gregory VII and an anti-
Pope, and monasticism was to him rather a means than an end. But the
Church must be brought to order. Bishops were moved from obscure
villages to growing centres, like Chichester or Norwich. A decree of
1076 ended the chaos between lay and spiritual justice : cases affecting
' the care of souls ' were henceforth to be tried by the bishop. Church
councils, which had lapsed for almost a century, were revived to meet
under the King's eye. Copies of the Decretals were distributed to
cathedrals. And Lanfranc's bishops began to build the great churches
which still embody the Norman strength, as at Canterbury, Rochester,
or Exeter, followed in a few years by the daring beauty of Durham, and
by 1107 fifteen cathedrals had been either rebuilt or built from the
beginning. What could not be had at once was won by delay : during

William's lifetime the Papacy agreed not to demand investiture of the clergy, while for Lanfranc's the supremacy of Canterbury was conceded over York.

This was the first stage; a restoration of order and learning, and a new contact with the best European churches, all under the direction of the Crown. Very different was the next half-century, in which all Europe and England were caught up in a spiritual whirlwind. Mediaeval Christianity was freed at last from the ruin wrought in the last two centuries: Saracens, Magyars, and Vikings had been beaten back or absorbed. The ideal of one Crown and one Christ, first set on high by Charlemagne, leaped forward in a Christian renaissance, in which German reforming Emperors and French monks from Cluny played the great part; a passion for learning swept over Europe, passing from monasteries where the torch had been kept lighted when all was dark, to cathedral schools and capital towns, and gathering round great teachers the elements of universities at Bologna, Paris, and Oxford. Forced by the warfare of Empire and Papacy to come down to first principles, and enabled at last to reap the harvest of ancient learning, the Italians constructed codes of law, while north of the Alps scholars began to buttress their faith by the scholastic philosophy. Interlocked with this, as cause and effect, were the new wealth of Italian cities, and the fighting energy flowing out to conquer new worlds. Mohammedanism had nearly wrecked the Eastern Empire and threatened Rome: Jerusalem and Antioch both fell to the Turks in the Conqueror's reign. But then the tide turned. In 1085 the Christians won Toledo and northern Spain, by 1091 Sicily was Norman; each must involve a clash with Islam, and in 1095 Urban II proclaimed the first Crusade.

Rome was leading the world again. Preaching a rule of righteousness on earth, a line of great Popes attacked the corruption in which feudal kingdoms had sunk their clergy. They condemned the sale of spiritual office, excommunicated the laymen who ' invested ' the priesthood, and declared invalid the Masses sung by married priests. They had humbled the fierce bishops of Germany and France, and had not feared to proclaim that the Fisherman, *servus servorum Dei*, could uncrown kings and take away kingdoms. The pallium, originally a token of honour for archbishops, was now taken as the mark of Papal consent to their appointment. Their court was becoming a high court of appeal, and for a century past their best heads had been building up, from sources good and bad, from Roman law, Celtic penitentials, or local bishops' rulings, a uniform Canon law. Appeals to the Pope had already gone from Norman England, before the monk Gratian of Bologna produced in 1140 a permanent text-book in his *Decretum*. Henceforward the humblest English archdeacon punished the fleshy frailty of his flock, or claimed from the sheriff the body of a criminal clerk, in virtue of a universal law, and sitting as a delegate of courts which ruled Christians from the Atlantic to the Syrian Sea, and which could burn the body and doom the soul.

While the canonists built the system, the monks revived the spirit of reform. The Normans were devoted to them. Domesday Book tabulated the wealth heaped on the now few surviving Benedictine houses, as at Glastonbury or Westminster, surpassing all but the greatest bishoprics. Battle Abbey represented the Conqueror's vow in victory, as Lewes fulfilled the devotion of his loyal follower Warenne; the Cluniac order owed much both to Henry I, founder of Reading, and to the long-lived powerful brother of Stephen, Henry bishop of Winchester, who had himself begun as a Cluniac monk. The full tide of new and reformed foundations flowed after 1100. First came an extraordinary growth of the regular or Austin canons, with fifty foundations in Henry's reign, St. Bartholomew's in London and St. Frideswide's, Oxford, among them, and rather later the Cistercians. For this, till his death in 1153, was the age of St. Bernard, abbot of Clairvaux. In Henry's reign the white monks planted their first settlements at Waverley, Tintern, Whitland, Rievaulx, and Fountains, from those mother houses spreading throughout the island; in Stephen's their growth was still faster, while in 1147 they absorbed the originally distinct Norman order of Savigny, which had begun work in England at Furness. Meanwhile a Lincolnshire priest, Gilbert of Sempringham, founded his mixed order for double houses of canons and nuns, and the white canons of the Premonstratensian order appeared both in Scotland and England, though their prime came later; altogether, at least 120 new houses of all sorts were made in this reign, and great estates were given to the soldier monks of the holy city, Templars and Knights of St. John.

Never again was monasticism so powerful, or its roots so deep. Great figures were at the head of the principal houses; of the stature of Ailred abbot of Rievaulx, whose English blood and hereditary religion linked this age to the Saxon Christianity of Hexham, or de Lucy of Battle, the justiciar's brother and a mighty man at law, or Samson of Bury St. Edmunds, whose personality is made real to us in Jocelin of Brakelond's chronicle. As many other chronicles show, written at Battle or Peterborough or elsewhere, this was a great age of monastic learning, yet two other sides of their new activity were at least as important. The one, seen in the Cistercians especially, took the form of some reaction against incessant liturgical service and some return to the manual labour of monasticism's first days, and the other, which Gilbert of Sempringham practised also, was the attention given to lay brothers. Taken as a whole, the monks were the Papal vanguard, the Cistercians and some great houses of other orders, like the Benedictines of St. Albans, being exempt from the bishops' jurisdiction and immediately subject to Rome. They had kept besides a strong hold on the normal system of the Church. In Henry's reign Ely and Carlisle completed the seventeen bishoprics which thenceforth stood unchanged till the Reformation, and ten of them were ruled by monks or regular canons.[1]

England thus entered into the full Roman heritage; Stephen Harding, second head of the Cistercians, was an Englishman, in Stephen's reign we get the first English cardinal, and in 1154 a Hertfordshire man, Nicholas Breakespeare, became as Adrian IV the first and last English Pope. Latin civilization entered to mingle with, — it might be to supplant, — the Teutonic and Scandinavian in our blood. English speech continued as the tongue of the people, it was written by Peterborough monks in the last chapters of the Chronicle, but seemed likely to break into many provincial *patois*; while Latin became the vehicle of law and learning. French was not only the speech of society but provided, in the epics of Charlemagne or Arthur or Roland, and in Provençal songs, the models both for courtly verse and the people's ballads.

Henceforward the paramount influences on the English mind were the Latin Church and a Latin-French revival of learning. Barons and merchants went on crusade, or on pilgrimage to Rome and Compostella. Scholars sought the masters of knowledge at Laon, Chartres, or Paris, medicine at Salerno, law at Bologna, and from Spain and Sicily derived, through Arab pundits, versions of Greek philosophy and mathematics. There were schools attached to London churches like St. Martin's or the Waltham canons, and schools in cathedral cities; there was teaching before 1150 at Canterbury and Oxford, each of which might grow into a university; the Bury monks had a hostel for poor children; village priests taught the Scriptures and elementary Latin. English history was kept alive by monks, like William of Malmesbury, of mixed Anglo-Norman blood, whose learning was due to Norman abbots, who wrote in Latin, and whose eyes were fixed on Rome.

It is not unimportant that England received this humanism as a direct consequence of the Conquest, which taught her the meaning of law, political ideas, and public opinion, and raised up men competent to execute Henry II's legislation, resist Rome, and frame Magna Carta. Stephen's weakness might dissolve government into temporary anarchy, but the leading figures of his reign show that civilization was saved. Archbishop Theobald, the third abbot who came from Bec to rule Canterbury, introduced the Italian Vacarius to teach Roman law; his secretary was the greatest scholar of the age, John of Salisbury, who

[1] Canterbury, Winchester, Worcester, Durham, Rochester, Norwich, Ely, Carlisle, Bath, and Coventry; though the two last had a peculiar double government.

had learned from Abelard himself, and who for thirty years conducted negotiations between England and Rome ; another member of his household was Thomas Becket, a London citizen's son, who had read at Paris and Bologna. Stephen's brother, Henry bishop of Winchester, was a magnificent builder at Farnham and St. Cross, and a great patron of the arts. Leading the other side in politics was Henry I's natural son, Robert earl of Gloucester, who encouraged William of Malmesbury to write, and to whom Geoffrey of Monmouth dedicated his mythological history of Arthur. Through the hands of Englishmen passed all the learning and administration of the new age. A layman, Adelard of Bath, who had seen the whole Mediterranean world and translated Euclid from Arabic into Latin, was employed to teach the future Henry II ; English officials went to and fro between the Norman states in France, Italy, and Britain.

A feudal frame of society, a central government, and the Catholic mind ; such were the Norman gifts to England. We must turn to the men who wielded these forces in the living world.

CHAPTER II

THE CROWN AND ITS RIVALS, 1066–1154

HASTINGS had ended the English resistance as a nation. From 1067 to 1071 there was, indeed, constant fighting, but it was war of a sort to which every earlier King of England was accustomed, barbarous and unconnected. Exeter refused to admit Norman troops and gave refuge to Harold's mother; his sons, true to type, ravaged the Bristol Channel with Irish help; thegns of the Welsh March, backed by princes of Gwynedd and Powys, attacked the new castles at Hereford and Shrewsbury. All failed; it is more remarkable that, within two years of Hastings, English thegns and peasants were fighting for the government.

Nor was racial resistance seriously involved in the dangerous rising of the north. Neither Mercia nor Northumbria had ever really submitted to Wessex, nor was Malcolm Canmore of Scotland willing to see English rule become a reality on the Border. Edwin and Morcar, Siward's son Waltheof, Edgar Atheling, whose sister Margaret married the Scottish King, and the Bernician earls whom William had provisionally left alone, — this league represented many old elements of anarchy, but hardly a trace of national feeling. The addition of Swein Estrithson of Denmark might have been predicted, for as Canute's nephew he had claimed the crown against the Confessor, his Norwegian rival was dead, and he might hope to raise the Danelaw.

1069 was the crisis. At Durham 500 Norman knights were surprised and murdered. York and its minster were burnt. A Danish fleet held both sides of the Humber, and sent detachments up the Ely fens. All the March from Stafford to Chester was getting under arms. But the captain who had crushed France was equal to this alliance of fragments; leniency and cruelty, bribery and lightning speed, all were employed to frighten the Mercians, to keep Scotland neutral, and buy off the Danes. By 1072 danger was over. Hereward the Wake, a tenant of Peterborough Abbey who held out last in the Fens, had to surrender : Edwin was killed by his own men, Waltheof married William's niece and became Earl of Northumbria, King Malcolm did homage, and Edgar the Atheling was a Norman pensioner.

If England was ever to be made, an end had to be put to provincial anarchy, and it was done at a fearful price of suffering. Between York and Durham William left a desert, burning villages and towns, crops and cattle, so that Domesday Book seventeen years later writes the blackened legend ' waste ' over several hundred manors, and historians of Stephen's time tell of weed-grown ruins and fields fallen into prairie. Much the same was done between Chester and Shrewsbury. Famine followed the sword and fire, the strong men taking to the hills as out-laws, while the weak begged bread from monasteries and died as they begged. At every point of vantage rose a new castle, at Exeter or Lincoln or Cambridge, built by forced labour and often making a great destruc-tion of houses. English women fled to nunneries for safety, and English exiles could be found even in the Imperial Guard at Constantin-ople. Heavy Danegeld and increased ferms fell, in the last resort, on the shoulders of the peasant at the plough.

Oppression did not stop with the years of Conquest. To save the lives of his scattered Norman setttlers, William devised the *murdrum* fine, whereby the whole hundred lay ' at mercy ' unless the dead could be proved a mere Englishman. Power rode roughshod over the defence-less ; power in the sheriffs, in and out of court, to extort money or land, or power seen in the looting of the countryside by Rufus' courtiers. But probably the worst suffering came from the forest law. The New Forest, where the Conqueror destroyed villages to make room for his game and where Rufus met his death, was a mere fraction ; Sherwood, Rockingham, Clarendon, some seventy forests in all, ranged from Northumberland to Cornwall, in Essex covering the whole shire. The Kings had brought from Normandy not only a love of hunting, but a forest organization. A royal ' forest ', not merely the area of woodland but all the villages and fields within it, was a legal area, in which the King had sole privileges ; ' venison and vert ' were his, not only the red or fallow or roe deer and the boar, but the trees under which they grazed. No part of Norman government was more hateful. An array of foresters and special courts defended this monument of oppression, while a triennial enquiry reported any waste of the royal rights. It was forbidden to have bows and arrows in a forest, or to keep greyhounds ; indeed, to keep a dog at all, unless three claws were cut from its fore-foot. A battery of fines punished the making of a hedge or cutting of firewood, while blinding or ghastly mutilation struck those who poached the deer. Before the forest law even the clergy's liberty gave way.

Yet from the first the Kings could count on the thegns, the sub-stantial yeomen, and walled towns, — the only English, in fact, whose voice could be heard ; for the mass of the people were still primitive peasants, huddled together in wattle and daub huts, tied down by routine to their fields, brutalized and superstitious, obedient to any strong man. English soldiers fought for the King against his barons, and we are told how they cried out for more severe punishment, ' lord King, do not trust the traitors '. They fought for the Conqueror in

Maine, and for Henry in 1106 when he finally defeated the Norman baronage at Tenchebrai; just as the northern peasants rallied against the Scots in 1138, under the leadership of Norman barons but under the standard of Saxon saints, Cuthbert and Wilfrid.

So the Conquest meant the addition of a ruling class, not the obliteration of a people. Though confiscation after 1070 left few English tenants-in-chief, as sub-tenants they held their ground. Stark man the Conqueror was, but not cruel for cruelty's sake, and if he destroyed the north, it had risen three times in two years and massacred his garrisons. Waltheof, who had once been pardoned and given royal honours, dabbled in conspiracy again and was executed; his fine stature and mighty deeds with the battle-axe, with his piety at death, exalted him into a popular hero, though he had shown himself as revengeful and treacherous as all Northumbrian earls. The Exeter rebels and even the outlaw Hereward were freely pardoned. And except for the *murdrum*, which soon became simply a means of raising money, there was no racial legislation; English courts were not backward in denouncing Norman sheriffs to the royal judges, and marriage soon mingled all classes except the high nobility. Henry I's reign marked a further stage in the Crown's relation to its subjects. He had been born in England and knew the English language and law; as his wife he chose Edith, daughter of Malcolm of Scotland and St. Margaret, of the royal English blood. To her the King was grossly unfaithful, but not to the ideal which their marriage might be said to represent, — the equality of English and Norman before the law.

In this work of political fusion, which the Normans had done once in France and were repeating in Sicily, it was to the Kings themselves that their English subjects looked, not in vain. The Conqueror's wrath vented itself in slaughter, and he loved money as he loved the tall deer, but he could be true to a high standard; he heard Mass daily, he was unswervingly loyal to wife and councillors, and could recognize a saint like Anselm. Henry I had no bowels of mercy, but showed the moderation of an experienced man who saw the limits of physical force and the power of opinion. He appreciated the growing strength of the towns; his charters gave London the right to choose its sheriff, or Lincoln to collect its own revenue, and if his justice degenerated into money-making, it was the same for all. The brutal Rufus, who wallowed in vice, who derided the keeping of his word, and as he showered oaths ' by the Holy Face of Lucca ', mocked at God and the saints, was still devoted to his father's memory, and had the strength which the English admired in that father, ' the good peace he kept in the land '. How much strength was needed was seen on the succession of Stephen, an ordinary, good-natured man-at-arms.

Their success in making an Anglo-Norman State was endangered,

however, by problems from without; from the never-absorbed neighbours in Scotland and Wales, from a cosmopolitan aggressive Church,
and most of all from Normandy, which was dependent on a half-tamed
baronage and beset by foreign enemies. While the Conqueror proceeded
in the task of reorganizing England, he had only been able to keep these
problems at bay. Assisted by Lanfranc, he had staved off demands from
the Papacy. The one baronial rebellion in England, of 1075, was easily
crushed, while his ambitious brother Odo was stripped of his estates
and imprisoned, but released at the King's death. Malcolm of Scotland
had to do homage, and Newcastle was fortified against him; but the
Scots still held Cumbria down to Morecambe Bay, and cruel raids, the
murder of a bishop of Durham, close contact between Northumbrian
nobles and the Scottish kings, all showed that the northern nettle must
one day be grasped. On the Welsh side the King, taking some risk for
the future, set up three earldoms in Chester, Shrewsbury, and Hereford,
allowing them to conquer and to build castles; in Gwynedd they
reached the Conway, in Powys they fortified Montgomery, southward
an advance post was held at Cardiff.

But his energy was really exhausted by France. With the death of
his father-in-law Baldwin, the peace of Flanders and its English alliance
ended. Maine, which he had held in right of his son Robert since 1062,
was never reconciled, its barons were more Angevin than Norman, and
its capital Le Mans had a fierce love of liberty. After two wars William
died still in possession, but Robert had to recognize Anjou as overlord
and the baronage were not conquered. Here, as in his attempt to master
Brittany, William met with the undying enmity of France, with whom he
had another more immediate feud. The Vexin, between Oise and Epte,
held the western roads to Paris; disputed for half a century past, it was
annexed in 1077 to the French royal demesne and made the spearhead
against the Norman frontier. Here ten years later the Conqueror fought
his last war, and in the burning town of Mantes received, as his horse
stumbled on hot ashes, the blow that killed him. As he lingered in
agony six weeks, his mind was troubled by the problem he found
inevitable and whose evil effects he foresaw, — the division of his
realm. He expressly named Rufus, his second son, as successor in
England, but Robert the first-born must have Normandy.

Round this double succession sprang up at once every peril. There
was the wolfish element in the Norman baronage, which seized on the
removal of a strong man; some of them mere brigands, who lived by
plunder and gouged out the eyes of their hostages, ' enemies to God,
to pity, and to mercy '. There were fierce Marchers on the borders of
Scotland, Wales, and Maine. There were princes of the ducal blood,
Odo with his hatred of Lanfranc, and the counts of Eu, Warenne, and
Mortain. There was Norman jealousy of English counsels. And there

was a very real dilemma for barons owning lands on each side of the Channel, who might find themselves involved in a clash between English and Norman overlords. All this was made a hundredfold worse by Robert's character. Always his mother's spoiled darling, he was a gallant knight who cared for nothing but hawk and hound, and parted with all his money to courtiers. His father having never allowed him any responsibility, they had quarrelled violently, and Robert took refuge in France. The baronage had taken his measure, and within a year of William's death turned out his garrisons, while Maine became a mass of private war.

So long as Robert ruled, the King of England could have no peace, and the barons' risings between 1088 and 1102 led to the determination, first of Rufus and then of Henry, to reunite Duchy and Kingdom. Invariably Robert, or some other member of the royal house, was put forward as King; in each case the Marcher lords took the lead, Mowbray of Northumberland, rising families like the Mortimers of Wigmore, and above all the great Montgomery house, with their Welsh allies. With a true instinct England hailed the expulsion of Robert of Montgomery and Bellême in 1102 as marking the time when Henry could call himself a real king. He had been Duke Robert's evil genius and now, pardoned by Rufus, he was Earl of Shrewsbury and lord of Arundel, besides great fiefs in Normandy and Maine, and Ponthieu on the Flemish frontier. His eloquence, leadership in war, skill in engineering, were matched by a falseness unparalleled and the desperation of a wild beast; he was said to delight as much in watching his prisoners starve or burn, as in the Spanish horses which he brought to Wales. His brothers had the great lordships of Lancaster and Pembroke, and behind them were the Welsh princes.

The downfall of the greatest baronies in England, Montgomery and Mortain, Lacy and Grantmesnil, was the work of Rufus and Henry, but the disinherited carried their hopes of revenge to Normandy, the weakness of which produced in turn a perpetual revolt in Maine. Here an heroic leader, Helias de la Flèche, made the province independent, and bequeathed his claim to the counts of Anjou.

Yet in his own wild way Rufus had done well. By dint of intrigues against both his brothers he mastered most of Normandy, and held the whole on mortgage when Robert left for the Crusade. He ravaged the French Vexin and twice occupied Le Mans. In north Wales, in spite of three campaigns, the Norman knights could not reach the high hills, but southwards they made great strides, mastering Brecknock and Glamorgan, Radnor and Pembroke. Against Scotland Rufus was even more successful. Cumbria had been in Scottish hands for over a century, but English priests and settlers had made their way into it and in 1092 Rufus seized Carlisle. The next year died Malcolm and his wife Margaret, and this opened up a ten-year struggle between their Anglicizing Lowland party and the Celtic Highlands, during which Rufus was enabled to crown one of Malcolm's younger sons, who had neither time nor inclination to trouble England.

Providence or conspiracy ordained that, while Robert loitered on his way home from the Crusade, in August 1100 the Red King met his death in the New Forest; before his body was brought on a forester's cart and huddled into a grave at Winchester, his brother Henry seized the Treasury there and induced the baronage at court to make him King. That autumn he married his English queen, and sent Rufus' extortionate servant, Ranulf Flambard, to the Tower; a charter promised a return to St. Edward's law, a good coinage, and a firm peace, and made large concessions to the landowning-class in regard to fines, reliefs, and wardships. Not least important was a promise to respect the liberties of the Church, with whom Rufus had left a quarrel most damaging to national peace.

The King had treated the Church like a criminal vassal. Bishoprics and abbeys were kept vacant, till both the new prelate and his under-tenants had paid enormous sums; for nearly four years the Church was left headless, Canterbury revenues were swallowed by the Treasury, and when Rufus died he still held eleven abbeys. But it had been a quarrel of persons as well as of principle.

In 1093 terror and remorse in serious illness induced Rufus to appoint Anselm to Canterbury, a monk who had been for thirty years at Bec, a man of simple and unbending righteousness. He at least would not be disobedient to the vision, which he had first sighted in his Aosta hills, and which he had fortified by years of philosophy. His faith was absolute, — credo ut intelligam was his principle, — a faith prior to knowledge and reason, and an avenue to them. There was still a schism in the Papacy, but Bec had given obedience to Urban II, and this obedience Anselm would follow, wherever it might lead him. Over the restoration of the Canterbury estates, the moral reform of Rufus' vile court, or on demands of money for war, Anselm steadfastly resisted, but what drove him into exile and imperilled the kingdom were much graver things, his obedience to Rome and the investiture of the clergy. For while he made it clear that his recognition of a Pope must depend on the voice of the Church Catholic and not on that of the Curia Regis, Pope Urban's demand over investitures challenged the Conqueror's whole system.

Yet the archbishop's patriotism was never lost; he stood between Rufus and excommunication, and gave Henry valuable help in resisting baronial faction. He was not fighting for a formula, but for the right of appeal to Rome and the Church's liberty. And fortunately both the Papacy, now at the height of its contest with the Empire, and Henry, who was deeply engaged in France, were ready for peace. The terms reached at last in 1107 were in the long run a victory for the State, for prelates were to be elected in the King's presence and to do homage for their baronies before consecration. Yet by appeal to Rome the reformers had forced the King to renounce investiture, and in theory elections would be free.

Whatever the future held for this never-ending argument, peace for his time was all that Henry asked ; he had more immediate dangers to face. To deal with the loquacious, spendthrift, and chivalrous Robert was not difficult, for he always threw away the cards. He invaded England a year after Rufus' death and was bribed to leave it by a pension ; while in Normandy he was too weak to restrain Robert of Bellême and his associates, and so gave Henry good ground for intervention. On 28th September 1106, forty years to a day after Hastings, Henry with an army largely English crushed the Duke of Normandy, who remained a prisoner in English castles, as did Robert of Bellême a few years later, till his death a weary time after. Normandy was taken in hand and organized like England ; though baronial rebellion still reappeared, the King's peace grew, castles were demolished, the Rouen exchequer centralized revenue and justice. But Robert had left an infant son, William the Clito, who was taken by his guardians to the Court of France.

Fate dealt mercilessly with the hard heart of Henry I. His affections, like his foreign policy, were centred in his only son William ; both were cut in half by the tragedy of November 1120, when that son was drowned in the wreck of the ' White Ship ' on a reef within sight of Barfleur. ' Jacob did not grieve more bitterly for Joseph.' Essentially, however, his policy remained the same ; to keep intact all his father's claims and dominions, and to transmit them to one heir. By breaking the English rebels and separating their English from their Norman fiefs, he had partly eliminated the danger of Norman war leading to English rebellion, but in itself the Norman situation was terrible, and in a reign of thirty-five years there were only ten in which he did not cross the Channel. Along the border warlike French baronies like the Montforts raided Normandy, with the backing of Louis VI and the sympathy of all who favoured the Clito. Henry, of course, could play that game too. The territory of Blois, conveniently near Paris, was ruled by his nephews, and on the younger, Stephen, he heaped the great honours of Mortain, Boulogne, and Lancaster. Through his daughter Matilda's marriage to the Emperor, and his own second marriage to a Lorraine princess, he kept alive the threat of a German invasion into France. By such means he wore down French and Norman opposition, especially as the baronage were divided by their jealousies and no French support could make much of the Clito, who grew up as unwise as his father Robert. Meanwhile, the internal feuds of Flanders shattered its power, and Brittany was won over by subsidies. There remained, then, the twin danger of Anjou and Maine. For over a century now the Angevins had threatened all their neighbours; seated firmly on the Loire they connected, and hoped to control, the policies of northern and southern France. They had absorbed Touraine, since 1109 they controlled Maine also, they had ambitions on western Brittany. 'From the devil we came', said Cœur de Lion their descendant, but with all their diabolical crimes and passion no family produced a longer array of audacious ability. Though Fulk V was a better Churchman than most of his house and was to die King of Jerusalem, he was determined to keep Maine by fair means or foul, and to be on the winning side between Henry and the Clito. The end of one stage was marked in 1119 by his daughter's marriage to Henry's heir William, but this basis was destroyed in the 'White Ship', and the Clito's star rose to its highest. Henry's diplomacy, however, won the help both of Empire and Papacy, and when in 1125 his surviving child the Empress was left a widow, he recovered his best political asset. Two years later he remarried her to Fulk's son Geoffrey, called (after his arms) Plantagenet; the vision of Normandy, Maine, Anjou, and England united in their grandson would satisfy both Henry's fear and Fulk's ambition.

In Normandy this marriage with the historical rival was most unpopular, and Geoffrey, much younger than his wife, did not hide his wish to control Normandy here and now. But Heaven at last seemed to smile on Henry I. By the end of 1134 both the Clito and his unhappy father Robert were dead, while the future Henry II was a year old. The King's plan — to pass all his realms to a woman, with a consort of a foreign dynasty, — was bold and unprecedented, but he buttressed it by every means in his power. Once before, and twice after, Matilda's second marriage he forced the English baronage to swear homage to her. He showered fiefs on loyal supporters, like the Beaumonts of Leicester or his Breton friends. The ablest of his children, his natural son Robert, he made lord of Gloucester and Glamorgan, together with the vital spots of Dover and Canterbury.

At other danger-points Henry had walked with his usual caution. He might well hope that Scotland was secure, for his two brothers-in-law, Alexander and David, ranked almost as English vassals, appearing at his Court, fighting in his wars, and planting new abbeys with English monks. But Henry's fortification of the Tweed showed the hollowness of this good will; David's wife, who brought him two English earldoms, was Waltheof's daughter, and the Norman adventurers who entered his service, — Bruces, Lindsays, or FitzAlans, — might just as easily mean the loss of the English Border as the Anglicizing of the Lowlands.

In Wales there was broken peace, with a good deal of English penetration. The house of Clare set themselves up in Ceredegion; a Fleming colony appeared in Pembroke; the see of Canterbury was acknowledged, and a line of Anglo-Norman bishops began in Bangor, Llandaff, and St. David's. In Gwynedd the veteran Gruffyd ap Cynan, who had given Rufus so much trouble, kept aloof from the broils of his neighbours.

Since the healing of the breach with Anselm, the King trod warily in dealing with the Church, whose diplomacy he found invaluable abroad, and which was on its flood-tide of reforming enthusiasm. When he could, he diverted her aggression, avoiding, for instance, the claims of Papal legates by getting a legateship for the archbishop of Canterbury. Appeals to Rome rapidly increased, however, with correspondingly high claims for the English Church courts, and the power of a Church reformed, armed with the new-made Canon law and directed by the zeal of St. Bernard, would play a decisive part in the acceptance of Henry's successor.

In 1135 the King died; he was sixty-seven years old, and had known exile and imprisonment and what it is to sleep with sword in hand. He had spent himself in crushing rebels and pardoning self-seekers, he had worked well, but only his own will had 'forced the kingdoms old into another mould'. And now his centralized government, his delicate succession scheme, the frontiers so weakly held, his new aristocracy, the balance of Church and State, — all were flung into the fire of civil war.

Within a fortnight of his death his favoured nephew, Stephen of Blois, son of the Conqueror's youngest daughter, crossed to England, and was promptly accepted as King by the Church, the city of London, and the high officials. His usurpation was not in its origin a baronial revolution. The ground had been prepared by his brother Henry bishop of Winchester, but men needed little argument to make them repudiate the solemn oaths taken to Matilda. Had her son been older they might have kept them, but no Norman would accept the hated Angevin Geoffrey, and any hesitation was removed by the savagery of his troops who invaded Normandy; between Blois and Anjou there was also a vendetta of old standing. What weighed with Englishmen was first, perhaps, that no woman had ever reigned in England; that since her childhood Matilda had been only two years here, and was absent now; she was said to be proud, and had sided with her husband against her father in their last quarrel. Stephen was well known and popular, and his wife came of English royal blood; above all, he was on the spot. Only prompt action could save the public peace; already villagers were pillaging the royal forests.

Some baronial reaction, however, was certain, for Henry I had driven them hard with fines and forest laws, broken up and redistributed their fiefs, and given to his officials the castles and boroughs which great barons liked to think were hereditary possessions. The Church, too, was in an aggressive mood. A long list of concessions showed that Stephen saw the razor edge on which he walked. The Londoners should have their liberties; Henry I's new forests should be surrendered; the Church was promised free elections, free synods, and sole jurisdiction over clerks. But concession without strength to refuse must ruin any government, and within three years Stephen showed his unfitness to rule.

Wales, always a test of English weakness, began to stir within a month of his coronation. Cardigan and Carmarthen were destroyed; the Fleming colony in Pembroke was nearly wiped out; and all security was lost up to the Wye. And the King, after one failure, left them to their fate.

Scotland was infinitely more serious, for David was the Empress's uncle and determined, if he could not crown her, at least to win much for himself. One raid extorted from Stephen the grant of Cumberland and Westmorland. In 1138, aided by Angevin supporters in northern England, he ravaged Durham and Yorkshire; in August the Yorkshire barons and fyrd, roused to action by archbishop Thurstan, defeated him at Northallerton, but the battle won for David what he wanted, the earldom of Northumbria. And so Scotland and Wales both saw Englishwomen dragged in ropes into captivity.

If Stephen could not defend England, one visit proved that he could never keep Normandy. Its southern frontier was torn between Norman and Angevin parties. His confidence in Flemish mercenaries mortally offended the baronage, and gave a handle to the most dangerous Angevin leader, Matilda's half-brother Robert of Gloucester, and at the end of 1137 he left Normandy for good, signing a truce which was at once violated. 'A mild man,' wrote the Peterborough chronicler, 'soft and good, and did no justice'; it was this steady exposure of his weakness, and not a long planned conspiracy, which caused civil war.

At the height of the Scottish troubles Robert of Gloucester repudiated his homage; his supporters in the west fortified themselves in strongholds like Bristol, Dunster, and Shrewsbury, and as Stephen failed to bring these rebels to book, every official began to waver. Hitherto the King had been served faithfully by the dynasty who had made a fortune in Henry's administration, — Roger of Salisbury, his son the Chancellor, his nephews Nigel bishop of Ely and Alexander of Lincoln, — but now in self-defence they began to arm. In 1139 Stephen offended all Churchmen by besieging the bishops' castles and arresting them in person; that autumn the Empress with Robert of Gloucester landed in England.

In this most desultory of civil wars, all hard fighting was concentrated in the first two years. Matilda got her opportunity when Stephen was captured in a battle at Lincoln in February 1141, and hopelessly she misused it. She proved her vindictiveness by proposing to make Stephen a prisoner for life, and her lack of sense by offending London. Driven out by a riot, she then proceeded to attack Stephen's brother at Winchester, near which she was defeated with the loss of her own indispensable brother Robert as a prisoner; before the end of this kaleidoscopic year King and Earl were both released by an exchange, and Stephen, whom the clergy had once declared deposed, was crowned again. For another year Matilda was beleaguered at Oxford : at Christmas 1142, just before the castle fell, dressed in white robes she dropped by a rope on to the snow, and by her escape prolonged the anarchy.

London, the south-east, and east Midlands generally obeyed Stephen; here his revenue system still functioned, and the courts could sit to do justice. Except for an advance post at Wallingford, Matilda's power did not extend east of Wiltshire, having for its heart Bristol and the Welsh March. Great tracts obeyed neither sovereign but their own great lords, who were determined to wait for the day of decision. The worst horrors came outside such areas, — on the frontiers where factions were equally divided, and where soldiers of fortune fought for plunder. Mushroom castles sprang up, filled (the monks wrote) ' with devils and evil men ', where with ' unspeakable torture ' they put men and women to ransom, by the slow fire, the knotted cord, or crushing irons. No man's cattle was safe; the mere sight of horsemen sent peasants flying to the forests. Harvests rotted because their reapers had taken sanctuary or were dead of famine; the ruin wrought was so great that taxation was still being remitted under Henry II. ' Men said openly that Christ slept and His saints; such things, and more than we can say, did we endure nineteen winters for our sins.'

This barbarism, not confined to one side, more often than not was the work of foreign mercenaries. But in one famous case it was combined with the purest Norman blood and feudal ambition. Domesday Book shows us the first de Mandeville with estates in eleven counties; the Conqueror had made him sheriff of London and Middlesex, Essex and Hertford, and his son became constable of the Tower. It was to recover these honours that the grandson, of Stephen's time, made his name infamous. Four times he changed sides, the impregnable fortress of the Tower enabling him to bid King against Empress ; until he had the Tower with freedom to fortify it as he would, the hereditary sheriffdoms and justiciarships of London and three counties, the earldom of Essex, large grants of land in England and Normandy for all his kin. He aimed at last at a principality into which no royal justice should enter. When Stephen plucked up courage to defy him, de Mandeville,

seizing Ely, set up a reign of terror in the Fens ; at night his mercenaries took the villagers from their beds ; churches, towns as big as
Cambridge, and plough-teams, all were harried and destroyed. At last
a chance arrow, on a hot day, caught the brigand with his helmet off,
and killed him.

So, on all sides, big men and small seized their chance to recover
lost power, to gain new, or to make themselves safe. On the big scale
we have the palatine earl of Chester, whose ambition had brought
Stephen into captivity, and was only satisfied when he was promised the
honour of Lancaster, together with Tickhill, Belvoir, and all the key
fortresses of the Midlands. When Stephen created nine earldoms and
Matilda five, these titles merely capped a reality of power in estates and
castles, which the greatest families of the realm, Beaumonts, Clares, or
de Veres, extracted from a disputed Crown.

But indictments of a whole class are always untrue, and the average
baron had not the guilt of de Mandeville. If the King's peace failed, a
peace enforced by the barons was the only alternative, so that when we
find two earls agreeing to allow no more castle-building, it meant the
creation of a neutral zone. Nor was all faith and decency lost in the
baronial class. Many loyally served King or Empress, many endowed
monasteries, and indeed the anarchic side of Stephen's reign has been
exaggerated. It was an age of new learning, benefaction, and grand
building : when the bishop was building St. Cross at Winchester, when
barons and Londoners volunteered for the second Crusade and fought
the Moors in Portugal, when Fountains and Norwich and Romsey were
making the churches which we still see.

Yet war went on. The Empress, indeed, was beaten, and after her
brother Robert died she herself went back to Normandy. The perils to
peace were the great houses who would not lose their hard-won power
by staking their all. New forces had to end this deadlock ; the power of
the Church, the Angevin conquest of Normandy, and the growth to
manhood of the Empress's son. The Papacy had been a good friend to
Stephen ; against Angevin protest it had recognized his usurpation, and
when in 1138 a new archbishop of Canterbury was found in Theobald
of Bec, not the archbishop but the King's brother Henry became Papal
legate. The legate's claims for the Church were high, but his own
ambitions higher, and his rapid changes during 1141, from declaring
Stephen deposed to deposing Matilda, destroyed his influence. But
Stephen had publicly admitted his obligation to Rome, in England he
had found what an attack on the bishops cost him, while in Normandy
the Church was his only staunch supporter. With extraordinary folly
he made a new quarrel. His candidate for the see of York was refused,
the Cistercian abbot of Fountains, supported by Theobald, was declared
elected by a new Cistercian Pope, the King seized his estates, and

refused leave to his bishops to attend the Papal court. Meantime Henry of Blois had ceased to be legate, and Church leadership passed to the more pure persistent hands of Theobald, round whom gathered the men of the future, young Becket and his rivals; and this strong circle was now pledged to the Angevins.

Even in the depths of his wife's misfortunes Geoffrey Plantagenet had refused to leave Normandy, which he was bent on adding to Anjou. His fierce energy won his object in three campaigns: in 1144 he entered Rouen, and the French recognized him as Duke. Normandy, moreover, was not only won, but conciliated, for Geoffrey ruled through Normans and by Norman institutions, and carefully respected the right of his son, to whom in 1150 he handed over the duchy. A year later, not yet forty years of age, he died. Now that undisputed possession of Normandy, Maine, and Anjou made the young Henry a much more formidable candidate than his mother, every English baron with Norman lands moved a pace nearer to the rising sun.

But the greatest men still hesitated, and Henry returned from one English visit with empty hands. Moreover, he had to face the power of France. Louis VII had wasted his youth in quarrels with the house of Blois and the Church, and had spent years, precious to France, on the second Crusade. At last he awoke to the new enemy; his sister Constance was married to Stephen's heir Eustace, and the kinsmen attacked Normandy, forcing Henry to surrender the Norman Vexin. But then Louis finally destroyed his own chances. Early in 1152 he divorced his wife, the turbulent and remarkable Eleanor, in her own right Duchess of Aquitaine, and within two months she married Henry, who thus ruled all western France from Flanders to Spain. Simultaneously Stephen's quarrel with the Church reached a climax; the Pope forbade English bishops to crown Eustace as heir-apparent, while Theobald fled overseas. With extraordinary blindness the French next year allowed Henry to reach England, and he was successfully clearing the Midlands of Stephen's garrisons when, in August, Eustace died. Finally Providence, weary of this generation, in one year swept away those who blocked the path to peace, for before the end of 1153 not only Stephen's queen and son, but David of Scotland, St. Bernard, Ranulf of Chester, and five other great earls, all passed away.

The King himself was now over sixty; his brother the bishop was not ready to defy a united Church. It was agreed, then, that Stephen should keep the crown for life, but that Henry should succeed him and meantime share in the government; King and Duke would co-operate in getting rid of the mercenary soldiers, and in pulling down the unlicensed castles built during the war. This was November 1153; an atmosphere of distrust made the compromise uneasy, and Henry retired to resist a new menace from France. In the next October, however, Stephen died, and before Christmas 1154 the rightful heir, long awaited by people and prophecy, received the crown which his grandfather had meant him to inherit. But its lustre was dimmed by nineteen years of misgovernment.

CONTEMPORARY DATES

1071	The Turks capture Jerusalem and defeat the Eastern Empire at Manzikert.
1073-85	Pope Gregory VII (Hildebrand).
1077	The Emperor Henry IV at Canossa.
1081	Building of the Tower begun.
1086	Foundation of the Carthusian Order.
1081-1118	Reign of Alexius Comnenus in the Eastern Empire.
1093	Building begun of Durham Cathedral.
1096	Urban II summons the First Crusade.
1098	The first house of the Cistercian Order.
1099	Opening of Westminster Hall.
	Death of the Cid Campeador.
1100, onwards.	Revival of Roman law in the school of Bologna.
1113	Abelard takes the lead in the schools of Paris.
1115	St. Bernard becomes first abbot of Clairvaux.
1118	Foundation of the Order of Templars.
1122	In the Concordat of Worms the Emperor Henry V reaches agreement with the Papacy over investitures.
1137-80	Reign of Louis VII in France.
1137, onwards.	The abbot Suger builds the Church of St. Denis.
1138	Accession of Conrad, the first Swabian Emperor.
c. 1142	The Decretum of Gratian.
1147	The Second Crusade.
1150	Albert the Bear inherits Brandenburg.
	Foundation of Fountains Abbey.
1152-90	Reign of the Emperor Frederick Barbarossa.
1154	Accession of Adrian IV, the English Pope.
	The Turks capture Damascus.

CHAPTER III

THE ANGEVINS, 1154–1213

A FEUDAL society, a strong under-life of English custom, central government, a French culture, had marked the age of conquest; at the end of Henry II's thirty-five years of rule they were flowing towards a nationality. But their final character was achieved in a new setting, in that England formed part of a European State. Good and evil came of this. Norman and Saxon, both subordinate now in a realm which reached the Pyrenees, were compounded into Englishmen. Henry's needs forced him to work through local liberties. Domestic peace and foreign connections increased English wealth, simultaneously enriching things of the spirit. On the other hand, this realm was built upon, and perpetuated, war; a war inevitable while England held Rouen and Bordeaux, and one which encouraged the insularity of strong barons and the faction of Scottish and Welsh Marches.

Twelfth-century Europe was not one of centralized States. Beneath the formal ideal of unity in Empire and Papacy, the feudal bond had split up natural geographical units, and restoration of a larger unity could only come about through the force of individual rulers. On the character of Henry and his family must depend the destiny of his dominions.

There were higher characters and greater politicians than Henry II among his contemporaries — Innocent III, the Emperor Frederick Barbarossa, and the French Philip Augustus — and there have been better rulers of England; but none of more individual genius, and few to whom the nation owes such a lasting debt. The impression which he made on those who served or loved or hated him was so vivid that, after seven hundred years, his figure still stands outlined against an angry sky. That stocky, bandy-legged figure, with lion face, bloodshot grey eyes, and cropped reddish-grey hair, never seated a minute, hating ceremony, careless of time and meals and comfort, was the might and passion of the flesh rather than a lofty mind or fine spirit. What he loved he kept, what he wanted he took, and he reaped the harvest, of those who make themselves the centre and others merely pawns. For those nearest and dearest to him became his deadliest enemies.

His wife Eleanor, his equal in vitality, lived to do great service to the State in the reigns of her sons. But Henry made her a rebel, for years keeping her a prisoner, and wronged her deeply; for no woman was too high or low for his lust, neither a girl betrothed to his son nor a ward committed to his care. Of his sons, Henry ' the young king ' was a light, fickle, and attractive knight; Geoffrey was ill-conditioned and crafty; Richard had greatness, rarely given to a great purpose; John was clever, false, and jeering. All four grew up like a wolf-pack, ready to tear the old leader down, and to combine against his heir or his favourite, and ultimately Henry's indulgence to John drove Richard to desperation. Of natures like these Henry asked an impossibility: to bear the title and the burden in Normandy, Brittany, or Aquitaine, but to leave all power to his arbitrary will.

But though these strains wrecked his peace and his kingdoms, he was a great ruler; alert and decisive, thrifty in managing his estates, tireless in the saddle and in council, genial in negotiation, a judge of men, as loyal to his servants as unrelenting to his foes. Hawks and hounds, his real passion, moved with his ever-moving Court, and the forest law was his one severity, but he was neither irreligious nor unintellectual. He would talk or scribble during Mass, but chose administrator-bishops of decent character and befriended the saintly Hugh of Lincoln; his mind was always working, though he took more pleasure in conversation than in books. For administration he had both a taste and a genius; never losing sight of main principles, he perpetually experimented in detail, and was himself well skilled in criticizing a charter or drafting a clause. With rare exceptions he was merciful and magnanimous. A sort of politic restraint, supplying the place of justice, kept him from aggression abroad or tyranny at home, and since action itself was what he lived for, he preferred the next, or the best possible step, to fine-spun theory or deep design.

It was task enough for any ability to hold his lands together in the feudal world. Outside England, with its Welsh fringe and its half-vassal of Scotland, he inherited three different dominions: his father's new conquest of Normandy, with claims over Brittany and Maine, his native Anjou and Touraine, and his wife's great dowry, the Duchy of Aquitaine. Not only was he for every acre abroad the vassal of France, but his power varied from province to province through every shade of historical, racial, and feudal resistance. Aquitaine, which was his only by marriage, had itself no unity. Old rivalries divided Poitou from Auvergne, and while the northern speech, the *langue d'oil*, reached down to Poitou, south of the Garonne Gascony shared the *langue d'oc* with its bitter enemy in Toulouse.

Of this complex the strategical centre was the Loire valley, with its key at Tours, from which radiated easy roads northwards to Rouen, and southward to Spain. Pilgrim and trade routes kept contact between its northern and southern provinces, while cold trackless hills and peat-hags separated Paris from Berri and Auvergne.

But there were weak spots on Henry's frontiers. There were jagged points in the south, where Quercy ran into Toulouse, or where mountain lordships like Béarn looked down defiantly from the Pyrenees. Against France the Norman frontier was merely an artificial line, crossing rivers, shot through by baronies, and buttressed by fortresses. Sentiment, in the Church especially, beckoned Frenchmen towards the

Where Henry II kept his Christmas Court

1154	Bermondsey	1172	Chinon
1155	Westminster	1173	Caen
1156	Bordeaux	1174	Argentan
1157	Lincoln	1175	Windsor
1158	Cherbourg	1176	Nottingham
1159	Falaise	1177	Angers
1160	Le Mans	1178	Winchester
1161	Bayeux	1179	Nottingham
1162	Cherbourg	1180	Le Mans
1163	Berkhamsted	1181	Winchester
1164	Marlborough	1182	Caen
1165	Woodstock	1183	Le Mans
1166	Poitiers	1184	Windsor
1167	Argentan	1185	Domfront
1168	Argentan	1186	Guildford
1169	Nantes	1187	Caen
1170	Bures	1188	Saumur
1171	Dublin		

Note.—Correction of these dates (as given in Eyton's *Itinerary*) in detail leaves their historical importance unaffected.

French Crown, while an appeal to the overlord at Paris was an obvious game for every robber baron in the south.

In this inheritance, where separate provincial custom ruled everyday life, unity could be found only in the King's court. Writs from his single Chancery ran alike in the Welsh hills and the scattered farmsteads of south-western France; identical measures — an assize of arms or an enquiry into tenures — were applied to England and Normandy. But even Henry could not be in all places at once, and administration must depend on his baronage and his sons.

In England for twenty years he was wholly successful. The baronage of both parties were made to surrender their castles. Important reforms regulated the system of justice, baronial courts, and the sheriffs' powers. There were new taxes and a new coinage. Geoffrey de Mandeville's sons became the loyalest of subjects, and one of Stephen's court, Richard de Lucy, was now justiciar.

With Scotland there was a short, sharp reckoning. Henry's uncle, the pious and canny David, had left the seeds of greater strength than Scotland yet had known — in feudal institutions, chartered boroughs, and a strong Church. But as his throne came next to a grandson of twelve, Malcolm the Maiden, and the Gaelic folk were rousing against the Norman nobles, Henry promptly seized his opportunity. Northumberland, Westmorland, and Cumberland, were returned to England, and as Henry's vassal for the earldom of Huntingdon Malcolm served in his French wars. To recover these losses must be the ambition of Malcolm's successor, William the Lion, who cast his eyes for help to France, but for many years he was at the mercy of Highland and Norse rebels.

Infinitely more serious was the dual problem of Wales and Ireland, where the alternatives seemed to be perpetual war or an over-mighty baronage. Since 1066 English advance in Wales had moved along three separate lines — from the Dee against Gwynedd, up Severn and Wye into Powys, and a seaborne attack along the coast against Deheubarth. Fortune had varied, in accordance with the energy of individual Marchers and Welsh feuds, nor had raids by royal armies altered the balance, for on any relaxation the Welsh sprang forth again from three never-mastered sources — the Snowdon mountain range, the trackless woods of the south centre, and Ireland and the Irish Sea, where Welsh princes found their allies. During the anarchy of Stephen, they retook a whole circle of English castles, from Rhuddlan in the north to Caerleon and Carmarthen.

With the ending of English civil war, however, the permanent advantages of the stronger civilization asserted themselves. The Clares, Cliffords, and FitzAlans began to recapture their castles, while Canterbury tightened its hold on the Welsh bishoprics. Yet the decisive action which could only spring from the Crown was not forthcoming, for Henry II had no time to drive home his three brief expeditions. Though the Kings of Gwynedd and Deheubarth became nominal vassals, some great fortresses were lost again, and from 1170 Henry dropped the method of war. Under the title of justice of south Wales, Rhys ap Gruffyd was allowed a practical independence in the strong places from Cardigan to the outskirts of Chester.

Indeed, the Welsh problem was altering in character. Except in the inaccessible Gwynedd the Marchers were creating a new formidable society, the blend of a feudal and a tribal system, Norman and Welsh rather than English. Welsh princes enhanced their own power by imitating Norman customs and churches; the Normans protected themselves by alliance and intermarriage, a famous case of which was the Welsh princess Nest, mother of two famous warrior families, the Fitz-

Geralds and FitzStephens, whose swords, first fleshed in Pembroke and Cardigan, conquered Ireland. And at Henry's death the mightiest figure on the March was William de Braose, lord of Radnor, Brecknock, and Abergavenny, whose power was cemented by his children's marriages to Welsh royalty, and brutalized by an unceasing war of ambush and massacre. Against such men an English ruler might well consider using the Welsh princes, many of whom were eager to win English fiefs and able to produce good mercenaries. Henry ceased, then, to waste his resources on a country where success might be as dangerous as failure; for his time, he would trust to the work of the Church and to a delicate balance between Marchers and natives.

To such a view he was partly led by the Marchers' invasion of Ireland, an epoch-making event as it turned out, for it brought the conquest of a kingdom, but at the moment only a new embarrassment to an overloaded King. Here, in a more unknown field, he pursued much the same policy, to claim for the Crown what would otherwise be usurped by subjects, but to postpone, to balance, to let things cancel out.

In the first year of his reign, when he was still ardent for the Church's friendship, he approached Pope Adrian IV, whose Bull warmly approved his pious project of reducing a vicious Church and people to subjection. Tasks in England and France, however, prevented further action, and in 1166 it proceeded from the initiative of others. In that year Dermot, King of southern Leinster, was expelled by his enemies and fled to Bristol. In character a bestial savage, with a voice hoarse from perpetual shouting in battle, he was determined enough to seek out Henry in Aquitaine and get his leave to enlist any assistance he could find. His natural choice was in Wales, with which Irish chiefs had old contacts; he came at a time, moreover, when the southern Marchers wanted just such an opening, for the King's policy of alliance with Rhys had left them in the air. None had suffered more than the house of Clare, once the conquerors of Pembroke; at this moment Richard, called Strongbow, was earl only in name, and as an old adherent of Stephen was out of favour. The bargain was struck; Strongbow received a promise of Dermot's daughter in marriage, and of the succession to his kingdom. In 1169 Nest's children, the half-brothers Robert FitzStephen and Maurice FitzGerald, reached Ireland, with Pembrokeshire Flemings, knights, and archers; in 1170 Strongbow himself, seizing on a vague permission from the King, used his credit with the Jews and reinforced them. In two campaigns they took the Ostmen towns of Wexford, Waterford, and Dublin, and mastered Leinster; with their battle-cry ' St. David ' this handful of adventurers put to flight hordes of Irish and Norsemen, hacked their way through tree palisades or over swinging wicker bridges, and escaladed walled cities. In 1171 Dermot died, and Strongbow claimed an Irish kingdom.

Henry, having already taken the alarm and ordered the return of these bold subjects, now determined to seize the Irish situation for himself and, incidentally, to find a hiding place from the tempest which had broken on his head with the murder of Becket. Reaching Ireland in October 1171 with some four thousand troops, in six months he put up the scaffolding of a royal dominion. The native kings flocked to do him homage. At Cashel a church council promised to conform in all things to the Church of England, providing Henry with a reforming programme which he could submit to Rome in testimony of character. Ample measures were taken to assert the Crown's power against the Marchers. The garrisons of the Ostmen towns were left in the hands of royal officials, one of whom, Hugh de Lacy, became justiciar and lord of Meath; the holdings of Strongbow and the Geraldines were reduced and separated; a charter gave trading privileges in Dublin to the merchants of Bristol.

In Ireland, as in Wales, he thus made a temporary solution. Within a few years the Papacy sanctioned his conquest, immigration from all England began to fill Dublin, and a treaty recognized Rory O'Connor of Connaught as overlord of Ireland under Henry, outside what we may already call the English ' Pale '. But while Irish chiefs and English soldiers defied this balance, Henry's action was demanded nearer home.

Transcending all else in the first half of his reign was the struggle with Becket and the Church, on whose support his throne originally rested. The Papacy of St. Bernard was rising to the climax of its history. It had crushed heresy in Arnold of Brescia and rationalism in Abelard, and was beginning its duel with the Empire for the control of the Christian world. Appeals from all Europe filled its court; its legates made law alike in Norway and Ireland. Within the next century the Gothic cathedrals cut in stone the whole scheme of salvation, the friars added a new spirit to this great engine of power, a line of masterful Popes claimed the sword not only of the spirit but of empire, deposed Henry's son John and again set him up, protected his grandson Henry III and in so doing destroyed his crown.

Far and undreamed of was this when Henry II, as part of his debt to the Church, took Theobald's favourite archdeacon Thomas Becket as his chancellor, or when in 1162 he made Thomas succeed Theobald at Canterbury. All, and more than all, that Wolsey meant to Henry VIII, was Becket to Henry II. Though neither scholar nor divine, he was diplomat, war minister, and the King's bosom friend, who as chancellor and archbishop must share with Henry the burden of Church and State.

The archbishop had made much of this world, surrounding himself with clerks and knights, and delighting in fine raiment and care of his person. But, with his restless eyes and white hands, and self-conscious power of winning younger men, he was a more sensitive creature than the King, being one in whom a wound to his spirit rankled like a stab, and whose conscience lived not far from his pride. He threw up his chancellorship, adopted a monk's habit and a hair shirt, submitted himself to the scourge, and in the dawn hours secretly washed the feet of the poor. Leaping to the glory of his new rôle, he immediately demanded the canonization of Anselm, and pressed the extremest claims of Canterbury to patronage and land ; at once, too, he used freely his supreme penalty of excommunication.

His violence brought to the top of Henry's mind something which had smouldered there some time — a resentment at the clergy's incessant appeals to Rome, and at the growing claims of their courts in England and Normandy. Stephen's weakness had given them a licence which the Conqueror had never contemplated. Not merely were they stretching out ' spiritual causes ' to include cases of contract and frankalmoign tenure, but their extremists claimed that no clerk could be tried by the laity, for however foul a crime. With the result that clerks had committed at least one hundred murders with impunity in the last ten years ; or so argued the royal judges, who had no good opinion of the trivial punishments ordered by the bishops.

But Becket would not hear of laymen sitting in judgment on priests, by whose hands the bread and wine became the very Body and Blood of Christ, and the King, therefore, bade his officials draw up the customs governing Church and State in his grandfather's time. These ' constitutions ', presented at a Council at Clarendon in 1164, he published. Some concerned points on which earlier Kings had stood firm, and which Henry now linked to his scheme of common law ; such were his court's control of advowsons, since they involved land, the sending to a jury (the assize *Utrum*) the question ' whether ' land were a lay or a spiritual fief, or the proviso that the King must be associated with the chapter in choosing a bishop. But two particular clauses, though in agreement with Norman precedent, antagonized the reforming clerical world. One forbade appeals to Rome without royal licence ; by the other, criminous clerks were to receive a preliminary hearing in a royal court, their trial would then take place in a Church court but in the presence of a royal official, and if found guilty they would be degraded and handed over to a lay court for sentence. To justify this claim the King could show some rulings of Canon law but Becket, apart from any higher view, steadily argued that one offence ought not to involve two punishments.

A majority of the bishops bowed to the storm, the Cardinals were divided, Pope Alexander III was in exile in France and dared not drive the Angevins into the open arms of the Emperor. For a moment even

Becket blenched but then, suspending himself from celebrating Mass in shame for his weakness, he flamed out defiant. Though persecuted by Henry with litigation and mean demands for his arrears of accounts as chancellor, and though pressed by the bishops to resign, in the decisive council of this year at Northampton he swept in, carrying his own cross in sign of combat, and in November fled to the Low Countries.

Five years passed; without sign of commotion in England, or of yielding from Becket. On each side the original quarrel was lost in savage temper, in Henry's oppression of Becket's family, and in Becket's shower of excommunications. Each side appealed to Rome, yet neither would sincerely accept Papal arbitration. The Pope and wise English Churchmen, like John of Salisbury, deplored Becket's violence, but could not abandon him : English opinion would not stomach alliance with the anti-Pope and Barbarossa.

But the strain was becoming dangerous. By taking refuge finally in France, Becket put an instrument in hands hostile to England. De Lucy the Justiciar was excommunicated; another sentence was served on Becket's ablest enemy, Foliot bishop of London, during service at St. Paul's; the clergy began to fear an interdict. In June 1170, by having his son the young Henry crowned by the archbishop of York, Henry gave Becket a real grievance, and Rome good ground for resolute action; at all costs he must get Becket out of France. A truce was patched up and, with no pledge as to the Constitutions, no guarantee for his revenues, and without the royal kiss of peace, the archbishop was restored to his office, and early in December reached England.

But, before sailing, he sent ahead Papal letters to suspend the bishops who had crowned young Henry; on Christmas Day from his pulpit at Canterbury, taking for his text ' peace on earth to men of goodwill ', again he cursed them and those who had pillaged his manors, ' may their memory be blotted out from the company of the saints '. Time was getting short; his actions were even now being reported in the King's Christmas Court near Bayeux, and Henry's furious question, ' why no one would rid him of this low-born priest ', was answered. On the 29th December four knights, who had just crossed from Normandy, threatened the archbishop in his palace and on his defiance followed him, with cries of ' King's men ', into the cathedral, and there at vespers, after an effort to drag him from the church, killed him with their swords. That day the most popular of English saints was made, whom the Pope canonized three years later. Miracles began within a week; a shrine blazing with gems and surrounded by the crutches of the halt and maimed, leaden bottles of Canterbury water, and boxes with mirrors for the more worldly, a beaten pilgrims' road of hostelries, — all that was soon to come.

His political instinct, and perhaps his heart, drove Henry to a public penance and a part-surrender. He declined to give up the Constitutions by name, and his judges kept hold of all cases touching property, nor did he cease to get bishops named as he desired. But on two fundamental points he gave way: appeals to Rome should be allowed, and only a Church court should have the disposal of a criminous clerk. Such was the real offering which Henry made to the martyr when, in a dark hour of his fortune in 1174, he walked barefoot to the shrine, there to be scourged by the monks, and to kneel fasting all one night.

The power of the Papacy, so hesitatingly used for Becket, was to play a larger part in England, but for the moment it was overborne by the Hohenstaufen, and the real peril for Henry II came from France and his own sons. Nothing in his policy showed a wish to shake off his French overlord; on the contrary, he was careful to avoid attacking Louis VII in person and helped his son Philip Augustus against powerful vassals. His aims were entirely conservative: to assert the just claims of his house and to settle his territories before his death. His father, for instance, had been forced to surrender the Norman Vexin; Henry recovered it as the marriage portion which Louis' daughter Margaret brought to the young Henry. Upon Brittany he inherited claims, both from Anjou and Normandy, and ruthlessly he pursued them, until he had won the heiress Constance for his son Geoffrey. On Toulouse the Dukes of Aquitaine had pressed their rights for a hundred years, and in any case there were Naboth's vineyards on the border. By war and by alliance with the southern neighbours of Toulouse, like Aragon, pressure was kept up until in 1173 Raymond V did homage. As time went on, his interests expanded. The Becket business, drawing him nearer to Frederick Barbarossa, led to his daughter Matilda's marriage to Henry the Lion of Saxony, and to the making of friendships southwards, which might restrain Rome and protect Aquitaine; to Joanna's marriage with the last Norman king of Sicily, to Eleanor's with Alfonso of Castile, and to John's betrothal to a princess of Savoy. His activity, his kinship with most crowned heads, his wealth and fame, put him higher in Europe than any earlier English king; rival princes invited his arbitration, while Templars and Patriarchs begged him to save Jerusalem from the Turk.

His stakes were too many to allow him to wish war, but they were so relentlessly held that any French king must resent them, while his titles were so diverse that pretexts for war were innumerable. But Louis VII, his unsuccessful rival in love, who lived on till 1180, willing to wound but afraid to strike, always ended by giving way, and it was from within its own circle that the house of Anjou was destroyed.

Three great rebellions shook Henry's power, the third of which killed him, and each was the work of his children. The ' young king ', who was refused any real power, and angry at a strip of Anjou being given to John, fled in 1173 to his French father-in-law. Richard, who was just installed as Duke of Aquitaine, and Geoffrey joined him, while their mother Eleanor was arrested in a man's dress on her way to Poitou. Every enemy of England, with every element threatened by Henry's centralized government, joined the princes; William of Scotland, Breton nationalists, and the older Norman houses of the baronage — Chester, Ferrers, Bigod, and Beaumont of Leicester. The King was saved by the loyalty of half the baronage, his officials, the Church, and the English people, by the steadiness of Normandy, the lucky capture of the Scottish king in a skirmish at Alnwick, and most of all by his own courage and foresight. At the end of 1174, his power seemed greater than ever. Eleanor was kept a prisoner, William did homage for all Scotland and received an English garrison in Edinburgh, while Richard was given real authority and did doughty deeds against the anarchy of Aquitaine.

A new world began with the accession of Philip Augustus, a great sovereign, to whom honour and mercy were only words, and one who knew how to make his rights as suzerain a reality and to turn the Angevins' sword against themselves. The homage which Henry demanded from Richard to the young king, that young king's death and the French claim to his widow's portion, the death of Geoffrey of Brittany, the rights of his infant son Arthur, fiefs in the disputed provinces of Berri and Auvergne, — in such questions Philip's strategic eye found a perfect field. Henry's relation to his sons did the rest. Young Henry, whom he loved, died at war for the second time with his father, because he would not suffer Richard to rule Aquitaine; Richard in 1188 joined his army to the French because he would not endure a partition with John; while John, basest of all, turned against the father who for his sake had offended Richard. The curtain fell on Henry II, blaspheming at misfortune which he felt undeserved — ' why should I worship Christ who takes away my honours and lets a boy put me to shame? ' At the age of fifty-six he was worn out, abandoned, and defeated. Tours was in French hands, Le Mans his birthplace was in flames, and his beloved John a traitor. On 6th July 1189 he died at Chinon, crying ' shame on a conquered king ', and was buried in borrowed robes by the nuns of Fontevrault.

The short reign of Cœur de Lion showed very clearly both what his father had done, and had left undone. In most ways Richard was a calamitous king. He bled the country white by taxation, and sold every office; for nearly four years he was absent, first on the Crusade and then in captivity. The Norman William Longchamp, whom he left in charge of England, was a loyal servant, but a bad appointment; inexperienced, grasping for his kindred, and unlikable, for he was accused of being openly anti-English, and rode, the baronage said, like a monkey on horseback. And while Richard's absence encouraged the Welsh to attack the Marches, William the Lion received back his castles in return for £10,000.

In fact, Richard was a knight of Aquitaine, not an English sovereign. He was used to countries where war and the mimic war of tournaments filled a knightly year; where war was provoked by a song and ended by mercenaries, and loyal vassals followed a warrior Duke. This helps to explain his mistaken generosity to John, to whom he gave Ireland in full lordship, six English counties exempt from royal judges and the Exchequer, and the Gloucester honour with its heiress Isabelle. Another dangerous man who profited by this policy was Hugh Puiset bishop of Durham, a former rebel of 1173, now given the earldom of Northumberland.

While Richard was on his way to Palestine, England broke out in disorder. The magnates' dislike of Longchamp was inflamed by John, who knew that Richard meant their nephew Arthur to succeed him, and this coalition during 1191 resulted in the expulsion of Longchamp from England, the acceptance of John as the heir, and recognition of London as a free commune. Late that year Philip Augustus returned from Palestine to stir up trouble, and in 1192 Richard was captured on his way home by the Austrians and flung into prison. At this news John broke all bounds, offered the Vexin and half Touraine to the French, and demanded fealty from England and Normandy; and Philip, offering vast sums to the Emperor Henry VI that Richard might be kept captive, laid siege to Rouen.

But England and Normandy stood firm, loyally repelling John's treachery and paying up a great ransom for Richard, while neither treason nor captivity weakened the administration, or the sense of law which Henry II had inspired. When in 1194 Richard's release brought war with France and again he left England, this time for ever, the country moved steadily forward under Hubert Walter, justiciar and archbishop. John's palatine powers were reduced, royal garrisons held the vital castles, and all Richard's exorbitant demands for men and money were supplied. The Justiciar, devoted to power, wealth, and the law, had little regard for spiritual learning or monastic zeal. But he was the true successor of Henry II in grasping the well-being of the State, in leaning on the knightly class as his best support, in organized finance, and the grant of borough charters.

Just as in England, so on the Crusade, Richard's reckless impulses made his own difficulties. His exploits in Sicily, Cyprus, and the Holy Land made mortal enemies of Leopold of Austria, who took him captive as he returned overland, of the Emperor who traded his alliance against a ransom, and of Philip Augustus. Yet he left prison with his power and fame enhanced, a European hero. He had found the Crusaders a mass of jealous princes. The French had left him in the lurch; Conrad of Montferrat, ablest of the men on the spot, for ever stabbed him in the back; Saladin's emissaries divided the Christians by adroit negotiation. But Richard endured all. In hot marches through the sands, in the autumn rains, in the harsh limestone hills round Jerusalem, racked by ague himself, and leading men of all nations who had often no water and no food but horseflesh, he had saved Acre and the coast, and though the Holy City was denied him, gave the kingdom of Jerusalem another half-century of life.

He had a wonderful welcome back to Normandy, and the peace signed in 1196 undid much of the damage. Richard recovered all north of the Seine except the Vexin, and established an impregnable fortress beyond it at Château-Gaillard. He began to build up a circle of allies. The Count of Navarre was his brother-in-law, Raymond VI of Toulouse became another. Philip Augustus was quarrelling with the Papacy, German sentiment was reaching out to the Rhine and the Rhône, Flanders and Brabant were Richard's pensioners. On the death of the overweening Henry VI in 1196 the Imperial succession was contested, the northern Germans choosing Richard's favourite nephew Otto of Saxony, and the prospect opened of a coalition against France. But in April 1199, fighting over an alleged treasure near Limoges, a chance shot from a crossbow mortally wounded Cœur de Lion.

His nomination of John to succeed him was inevitable, for Arthur of Brittany was only twelve and his mother Constance was in the French interest, but it was accepted with gloomy misgivings. His reign was, in truth, to open a new chapter during which two-thirds of the Angevin realm was lost, with the result that the King was thrown back on English support, while simultaneously his tyranny drove together the baronage, Church, and middle class to form a public opinion. Here began an English people with a life of its own, no longer at the whim of foreign kings.

Bretons and Angevins, loath as they were to accept John, were not yet ready for French rule and, by the terms of the peace of le Goulet of 1200, Philip recognized John as lord of all his father's territories. But this acceptance of a judgment by Philip's court, with the payment of a large relief to him, made a dangerous precedent, as was proved within two years. John, repudiating his wife Isabelle of Gloucester, fell in love with a girl of fourteen, Isabelle of Angoulême; this meant conflict with the rival of Angoulême, the house of Lusignan, to one of whom Isabelle was betrothed, and who promptly appealed against John's seizure of their fiefs to the overlord at Paris. In 1202 Philip's court declared John's French provinces forfeit; the King himself invaded Normandy, sending Arthur to lead the rebels further south.

Twenty years of French activity had seriously weakened Angevin rule. The towns were weary of war, and for some years now the English exchequer had had to subsidize Normandy. The knightly class, who would always follow Richard, had begun to desert, Rouen was nearly surrounded by French territory, while Norman Churchmen were steadily drawn towards St. Denis and the rich religious tradition of France. In short, the Duchy had lost its native life and was little more than a militarized frontier. Still the fall might have been postponed, but for the conduct of John. When Arthur was captured in Poitou, he still held the winning cards; he threw them away by cruelty to his prisoners, the ravages of his mercenaries, long bouts of luxurious idleness, and finally by a monstrous crime. Arthur, who had first been kept loaded with chains at Falaise, was taken to Rouen where, about April 1203, he was murdered. That meant the loss not only of Brittany but of Anjou, which made the vital link between north and south, and opened up the Norman frontier. At the end of the year John abandoned his Duchy; by midsummer 1204 its capital towns, Rouen, Falaise, and Caen had fallen; Touraine, holding out longest under Hubert de Burgh, was lost in 1205.

At the height of these disasters Eleanor of Aquitaine died, and her Duchy seemed likely to follow the north. But the very anarchy of Aquitaine meant that there would always be some English partisans; while the Gascon cities lived by the English wine trade, and preferred an absent King to a Paris despot. In 1206, therefore, John was able to save Gascony and most of Poitou, so preserving English dominion in France for another two hundred years. Philip, busy absorbing his conquests, meant to strike next at the Netherlands and England itself, but a decisive reckoning was postponed. For both England and France were caught up in the policies of the outstanding figure of the age, Pope Innocent III.

His ambition was to make the Holy See the standard and arbiter of public righteousness, against which Philip had been an arch-offender. He had defied the Church by repudiating his wife and rejected its mediation for peace with England; even in the crusade, which the Church was stirring against the Albigensian sects of Toulouse, little help was given by the French king. For a long time, too, French and Papal policies had disagreed as to the Empire. Determined to avoid any union between Germany and Sicily or a revival of Hohenstaufen lordship, the Pope had raised up Otto of Saxony, the natural enemy of France.

So long as Otto prospered, and while Innocent was antagonized by France, John might hope to resist invasion, or even to recapture the lost provinces, but both these conditions ceased to be true through the events of the years 1207–10. No Emperor could put up with the Papacy's claim to transfer empire from one dynasty to another, to rule all central Italy, and to destroy the notion of national churches, but the crude dour Otto was hopelessly incapable of wrestling with a master like Innocent, or of holding Germany together. From different reasons the Pope and Philip agreed, therefore, to raise up the youthful son of Henry VI, the future mighty Frederick II, while Otto looked for support to England, which was itself in conflict with Rome.

When Hubert Walter died in 1205 John determined to have a complacent archbishop, to which end he made the Canterbury monks nominate John de Gray, bishop of Norwich. But the younger monks, always anxious to stop interference from outside, had already rushed through the election of their sub-prior. Two candidates thus appealed to Innocent III. His right to hear the appeal could not be denied, and the King, confident in a secret promise from the monks, made the mistake of agreeing that the election should take place at Rome. Whereupon Innocent, passing over both candidates, persuaded the monks to elect the English cardinal Stephen Langton, whom he consecrated without the King's assent. It was not a step which Henry II would have endured, and when John appealed to national custom, he rallied round him considerable patriotic feeling. In 1208 England was put under an interdict. For the next five years Mass could only be heard once a week outside the church, while the churchyard and the priest's office were refused to the dead, church bells were silent, and gloom settled on a religious people. In 1209 John himself was excommunicated. But the administration held on its way, and though all the bishops left England except the King's servants, de Gray and Peter des Roches, the mass of the clergy were obedient. All Church property was taken into the custody of the Crown, which appointed parishioners to dole out a pittance to their priests.

All this time John was active, vigilant, and successful. William the Lion of Scotland was now ageing, and faced by Celtic revolt, so that John was able to stop the encroachments on the Border, and to secure the right of marrying William's heir, Alexander. Serving in the army which forced these terms upon Scotland was Llewelyn of Gwynedd, who married one of John's illegitimate children, and whose ambitions had to be humoured or suppressed. Princes of Powys were balanced against him, and two expeditions in 1211 seemed to have brought him to his knees.

And it was not only against the native Welsh that John proved his power, but against the Marcher lords of Wales and Ireland. Henry II's Irish settlement had long ago crumbled, and a fleeting invasion by John in 1185 had only shown the Marchers to be indispensable. John de Courcy in Ulster, the Lacies in Meath, William Marshall (Strongbow's son-in-law) in Leinster, and the Braoses at Limerick, had made themselves petty kings, allied in marriage and war with the princes of Ireland and Man.

Early in his reign John granted great principalities to Braose and the Lacies, but they quarrelled with the royal justiciar and their power was overweening, for Braose also held half the Welsh March, as the Lacies held Ludlow; it seems also that Braose knew the secret of Arthur's murder, and did not keep it to himself. In 1210 the King seized their estates in both kingdoms, dashed over to Ireland, and drove them into exile; William Marshall in Leinster was the only great Marcher left, English law and the shire system were enforced on Ireland, while Braose's wife and heir were starved to death in Windsor Castle.

Abroad, John was knitting up alliance with all those whom Rome or France had affronted; with Toulouse, the Emperor Otto, Flanders, and Boulogne. He had increased his revenue, raised a great army of mercenaries, and got control of English shipping. But in 1212 it was proved that this active power was only a machine, that the baronage were intriguing with the enemy, and that no one in England would stand by the King.

However solid the grievances against him, there remains something mysterious about the hatred of John. His father, too, had been lustful, Richard also had flayed his subjects for money, but ordinary beings felt a repulsion for John, as for something inhuman, distorted, and cold to the touch. He combined the softness of a luxurious man, who loved jewels and long hours in bed, with the ferocity of a snake. He liked to trap men by encouraging them to speak out, and to torture their feelings by oppression of their young children. His cackling laugh jeered at religion or ill-fortune, but at the end he grovelled to God, as he had grovelled to Richard, whom also he had betrayed. When Hubert Walter died who had won him the Crown, he rejoiced, and when in 1213 Fitz-Peter the Justiciar died, who for four years had kept the barons loyal, John hoped he might join Walter in hell, for ' now by God's feet I am at last King of England '. Yet while boasting so of his strength, he felt terror in every wind rustling the arras.

War and interdict lay heavy on the country. Scutage, which Henry II took only five times in thirty-five years, John took every year till 1206 and again from 1209 onwards, sometimes on top of personal service. The ferms of the shires and royal rents were both enormously increased, heavy tallages fell on the boroughs, and the Church was bled of at least £100,000 during the interdict. The monastic orders were so robbed that some monasteries closed their doors, the Cinque Ports' shipping was conscripted, and the King threatened a new Domesday enquiry into all estates. The bridges between the nation and the executive were broken down. More and more John depended on his mercenaries, some of the worst of whom he set up as sheriffs, the Tourainer Engelard de Cigoné in Gloucestershire and Fawkes de Breauté the Norman in

Glamorgan. The Poitevin bishop of Winchester, Peter des Roches, had begun his long and sinister career. The King was strengthening his Household, using a privy seal to counteract his great officials, and developing his Wardrobe into a war office.

Some great barons John had injured personally; while towards the mass of them his attitude was suspicious and severe. The Clares, for instance, were robbed of the Gloucester inheritance when John divorced Isabelle; and the Braose connections included the Mortimers and de Montforts. Many families had been forced to give up a child as a hostage, for whose fate they might well shudder. Wardship and marriage had been cruelly abused. And there were worse stories; as that John himself had ruined the homes of the younger FitzPeter and Eustace de Vesci.

But the quarrel of the political classes was not merely with a single tyrant. In Richard's time they had shown that they would resist any arrangements for a long-service army, or a new land tax, and resented the never-ceasing interference with their vassals. Most of them had long ago lost their Norman fiefs, and took no interest in Poitou; contrary to the facts, some were arguing that they were not liable for foreign service. They shared other grievances with the whole free class; such as the forests, which John had extended and where they could not safely pasture a pig; capricious fines, or arrests without trial. Against these things they determined to assert what Henry II had taught them — a rule of law.

In 1212 the winds, near which John had sailed so successfully, blew up into a storm. It was believed that the Pope had released Englishmen from their oaths of allegiance. The people were excited by the prophecy of a Yorkshire hermit, that John would die before the next summer. The Welsh, well aware of his unpopularity, encouraged by the Church and in touch with France, rose in all parts from Aberystwyth to Swansea. New reports that the barons were plotting to dethrone the King were followed by flights to the Continent; notably of Robert FitzWalter, grandson of de Lucy, kinsman of the Clares, and hereditary captain of the London militia. Abandoning his projected Welsh war, John raised more troops and looked to his foreign allies, but there he found a despairing outlook. His nephew, the Emperor Otto, had been driven to a corner in Brunswick, and French crusaders, under the elder Simon de Montfort, were encircling Toulouse.

Against the enemies of the faith and of the French monarchy — Otto, John, and Raymond — Innocent III and Philip Augustus had, for the time at least, a common interest. Exiled Englishmen were working at Paris, and in January 1213 archbishop Langton and the legate Pandulf arrived with the Pope's order — let the most Christian king gird up his loins, and deprive John of his crown. In Holy Week

Philip, in counsel with his vassals, accepted the task, and a great army and navy gathered at Boulogne for the conquest of England.

CONTEMPORARY DATES

1155	Execution of Arnold of Brescia at Rome.
1159	John of Salisbury's *Policraticus*.
1163	Building begun of Notre-Dame.
1167	First germs of the University of Oxford.
1169–93	Saladin rules at Baghdad and Damascus; conquers Egypt in 1171.
1169	The towns of Castile win representation in the Cortes.
1176	Barbarossa defeated by the Lombards at Legnano.
	Building begun in stone of London Bridge.
1180	War between Barbarossa and Henry the Lion of Saxony.
1185	Building begun of Lincoln Cathedral.
1186	Henry VI, Barbarossa's son, married to Constance, heiress to Norman kingdom of Sicily.
1187	Saladin takes Jerusalem.
1189	The Third Crusade.
1190	Foundation of the Knights of the Teutonic Order.
1193	Mohammedan conquerors occupy Delhi.
1198–1216	Pontificate of Innocent III.
1202–4	The Fourth Crusade.
1204	Philip Augustus of France conquers the Angevin dominions.
1206–27	Mongols under Jenghiz Khan invade China, Persia, and India.
1209	St. Francis of Assisi creates his Order.
	A crusade launched against the Albigensians in southern France.
1210	The Papacy declares for the young Emperor Frederick II.
	New buildings at Chartres Cathedral.
1212	The Arabs defeated by the Spanish forces at Navas da Tolosa.

CHAPTER IV

PREPARATION FOR NATIONALITY

FROM 1212 there followed sixty years of revolution, closing with the accession of Edward I; in whose reign mediaeval England reached equilibrium, completed its governmental fabric, and established long-enduring relations with foreign States. But to understand the national temper, or the forces behind Magna Carta and de Montfort, we must look back to the constructive work of Henry II, and the influences moulding the mind of the people whom he united.

At first sight his rule seems a despotism. Though he took his barons' advice on great questions like the treatment of Becket, his will prevailed even over his most trusted ministers. He exacted military service from the baronage in whatever form he chose, whether in person, or by way of scutage (a money commutation at a fixed rate for each knight's fee), or by a heavy fine reached in individual bargains; he held searching scrutinies into their fiefs, and tried to increase their military liability. For Danegeld he substituted a heavier taxation, 'aids' on the shires and tallage on the towns. He screwed up the sheriff's ferms to new heights. He took more money from London, yet cut down its self-government. The forest law and extortion from the Jews were employed at the expense, direct or indirect, of all landowners. Mercenary soldiers, from Brabant, Wales, or Galloway, marched in every province of his realms. And if he tried his subjects with lashes of the whip, his sons whipped them with scorpions. Yet what Napoleon did for Italy, Henry did for England, for he created the consciousness of the people whose customs he harnessed to his purpose.

The nation's fortune and character have been largely due to its government, the essence of which is the rule of law, one and the same law for north and south, rich and poor, Church and lay — a rule not framed in written rights, but in the body of remedies for wrong which will be enforced by the King's courts. Steadily the law grew so strong that it became superior even to the King; so giving a second characteristic of English government, that the final checks upon it are automatic, not inspired from outside by some rival body but by the very high court of the King. Far distant, but in logical sequence from the Angevin Curia Regis, we therefore see 'the High Court of Parliament at this time assembled': towards this unique, and hitherto indestructible, constitution the longest single stride was taken by Henry II and his servants.

They weighed carefully each step they were taking, but took them one by one, for the King was a practical politician, not a theorist, who built on Henry I's foundations to meet proved necessity and present need. Royal justice must be made more available; Henry began by appointing local justiciars, but from 1166 the justices in eyre became a regular routine. The Assize of Clarendon that year, strengthened by the Assize of Northampton ten years later, gave the royal judges sole jurisdiction over murder, robbery, arson, and forgery; sheriffs were empowered to hold the preliminary hearing in their tourns and to arrest those accused in any lordship, however great. Goods of those convicted went to the Crown, and a gaol was set up in every county.

The next step, to give security to the occupiers of land, would touch feudalism in its tenderest spot. His predecessors had used ' writs of right ', bidding the baronial court do justice in cases of *Disseisin*, or the King would act himself; Henry pushed this further in the writ *Praecipe* which evoked cases of ownership to his own court, and ordered his judges to protect seisin, or the man in possession, against eviction without legal process. But the peculiar merit of his laws lay in converting such occasional royal action into universal remedies. His ' grand assize ' allowed any defendant whose title to land was attacked to claim a hearing in a royal court, with the judgment of a sworn jury instead of trial by battle. By the petty assizes of *Novel disseisin* and *Mort d'ancestor*, the actual occupant, or the heir of the occupant deceased, if turned out without trial, could claim a royal writ, giving him a jury in the King's court to decide this single point; a favourable verdict would simply protect his present possession, leaving the matter of final ownership to a trial in his lord's court, with the possibility of a grand assize in the last resort. The assize of *Darrein presentment* applied the same principle to church livings, while the assize *Utrum* similarly left to a jury the question whether a particular piece of land were a clerical or a lay fief. By the end of his reign, the judges claimed that even to begin an action in a manor court touching a free tenement required a royal writ.

The King, then, sometimes by compulsory process but more often by offering a quicker alternative, undermined the power of all courts save his own. To all free men he offered a wide choice of writs from his Chancery, which not merely set the wheels of the law turning, but by rigid formulas to suit each class of action made a system of law, tough enough to resist all onslaughts. A Common Law was thus created, before Roman or Canon law could arm the Crown with maxims dangerous to liberty.

Just as important as the law was the method of trial which it employed. By the grand assize four knights of the shire chose, in the presence of the judge, twelve other knights to make a verdict; for the criminal assizes, or the eyre, the sheriff summoned twelve freeholders of each hundred and four men from each village, and twelve also for the petty assizes. From the point of view of justice and human happiness, what a change ! Title to property was now decided by a man's neighbours, and not by the cruel gamble of trial by battle — a Norman innovation which the English hated, and which was abused by hiring professional champions — while the old absurdity of compurgation gave way to a verdict on the facts. True, in Henry's time the jury's verdict was final only in the case of his land assizes ; his grand jury merely presented an indictment, final proof being still left to ordeal by water, and where an individual launched a criminal charge by an ' appeal ', the case still ended in battle. But all the judges' weight was cast on the side of the jury, and this most elastic system speedily grew. In any civil case not covered by the assizes a jury might be empanelled by consent of the two parties, while in criminal suits individuals began to ' put themselves on their country ', and ask for a jury. Meantime, in cases begun by a grand jury, the situation changed radically in 1215 when the Papacy forbade the priesthood to take part in the ordeal ; some substitute had to be found to provide the final verdict, which by slow degrees passed to a second, or petty jury, to traverse the indictment of the first.

The jury system survived in England, first because, though called to testify to facts, it represented not witness only but the public opinion of a neighbourhood ; and second, because in England it got a strong start in the petty assizes before it could be turned, under Canon-law influence, from an inquest into an inquisition. Even more fundamental was it that Henry built his jury on the ancient courts, where time out of mind villagers had given judgment and village tithings had presented the guilty. This royal instrument was thus warped into the oldest stuff of popular custom, and from this time on was employed for every need of government ; for assessing taxes, or viewing arms and armour, even to safeguard the hated forests — for these and much more were sworn bodies of Englishmen in incessant employment.

This self-rule, which the Crown forced on unwilling subjects, and this confidence which is the test of strong government, were shown in the royal alliance with the gentry against both barons and officials. In 1170 the Inquest of Sheriffs put knights and freeholders on oath to reveal not only the sheriffs' misdeeds — in consequence of which nearly all existing sheriffs were removed — but those of the barons' officials also. In 1181 the Assize of Arms assessed, by the oath of knights, the whole free population for military service, on the basis not of tenure but of wealth. By 1194 coroners were established, elected in county court, to prepare pleas of the Crown for the judges, while sheriffs were forbidden to hold such pleas in their own county : the next year knights were assigned to keep felons in custody.

All later history testifies to the effect of this nationalizing of the law. The palatinate court of Durham copied the royal assizes. In their court leets the baronage formed their villeins into sworn juries. Monasteries found it wise to own copies of Chancery writs, and books of legal forms. Knights carrying the record of a plea, or whole juries, could be seen riding to Westminster, to defend their verdict before the very makers of the law. And at the great Eyre the royal judge was met by a thousand or more apprehensive countrymen — juries and witnesses, litigants and compurgators, tithings and hundred bailiffs, and the swarm of those whom the law insisted must stand as pledges for the appearance of the accused. Anti-feudal the long effect must plainly be, but it is a mistake to exaggerate the rivalry of King and baronage. Except in criminal cases he had not robbed baronial courts but rather outflanked them, by offering alternatives and by using their vassals in his own service. The shell of feudalism was left intact. Henry would send a judge to take Crown pleas in great ' liberties ', but in the archbishop of York's court, for instance, he would leave the profits to the lord, just as at Dunstable the Prior sat alongside, and judged with, the royal agents. Anarchy was out of date ; the makers of Magna Carta cordially approved the petty assizes, and only asked that the writ giving a jury in cases of murder should be given freely. And lastly, of three-quarters of the population neither Henry nor the baronage thought at all ; as his reforms were for free men only, so in the Charter they made it clear that their villeins were their own.

This immense growth of business brought about great changes in the central machinery. It was, indeed, one and the same court, revolving round the King, whose Household servants shared power with high officials, and whose will alone determined what should go to each department. For all were branches of his court, the same men acting alternatively at the Exchequer or on assize, and for another hundred years all elements of the Council might be reassembled in a solemn meeting. Yet the stress of business necessarily brought about routine, record, and specialization. The King's frequent absence raised the Justiciarship to a viceroyalty, while the Chancellor was creating writs and controlling the secretariat of an empire. The Exchequer, losing the services of these magnates, thus acquired its own personnel ; though it still heard pleas, and landowners were glad to get their deeds enrolled there, it became mainly a financial department and by 1200 absorbed the Winchester treasury. In 1178 Henry II began experiments which ended in something like a permanent law court, when five judges were ordered not to leave the King's person ; a process which went on, through many fluctuations and royal absence abroad, till we find two tribunals, the ' Bench ' or Court of Common Pleas, and the Court *Coram rege* or King's Bench, each with its own rolls and each just distinguishable from the main *curia*. The especial creators of this machinery were Ranulf Glanville, the Essex baron who was justiciar when Henry died, and his nephew Hubert Walter, who was Richard's justiciar and John's chancellor. By one or the other was compiled the *Tractatus de Legibus* which tells us the law of Henry's day; Walter, who in the last three months of 1196 is on record as hearing pleas on twenty-nine days, also began the great rolls of the royal court and the Chancery, showing us how that law was made to prevail. Not the least important legacy of the Angevins was this professional pride, the creation of a service which lived by rule — a memorable type of which was the still-continuing clan of Roger of Salisbury, whose great-nephew held the Treasury till 1198, and passed it on to a kinsman who prolonged the family tenure till the time of Henry III.

Law is devised to protect property. A great increase of revenue, the astonishing demand for the assize of novel disseisin, and magnificent building, showed that English society was attaining a new level, and that capitalism, the first essential for any division of labour and civilization, was coming to life. As yet, it was on a petty scale. The country was almost entirely rural, its population barely over two millions, its staple exports were raw wool, hides, and coarse cloth. No English town could be compared to the ancient cities of Italy or Germany or France, proudly independent of rustic feudalism, seated on the arterial roads of Europe, with Roman traditions and famous bishoprics. In this small country the Crown always asserted equal power over town and village alike, and to the end our boroughs formed no separate Estate like Spanish communes, or French *Tiers État*. Their court was like a walled hundred, their cattle grazed on common fields outside, and in the heyday of East Anglian prosperity Norwich still suspended its cloth-making during the harvest.

Their origin and their population were both heterogeneous. Some were natural trading centres like London or Chester, some were military posts of Danish days like Derby, some rose round shrines, as at Canterbury or Beverley. The tenth and eleventh centuries had overlaid them with a network of feudalism, of ' sokes ' and exempt areas and privileged vassals. Wallingford had some of Harold's housecarles planted in it; Canterbury monks took the tolls of Sandwich; the bishop contested Winchester with the King. Since the Conquest some boroughs had been deliberately planned, sometimes with fixed building laws and equal plots of land, like the group to whom William fitzOsbern gave the customs of Breteuil from his native land — Hereford, Ludlow, and other March towns, who passed these customs on to Ireland; or the little borough of Egremont in Cumberland, bound to fight and to plough for its lord. There were important towns which remained

feudal till the Middle Ages ended. Leicester could not escape its earls ;
at Reading the abbot controlled even the gild.

But, infinite though was their variety, a majority had no one lord
but the King, whose charters compelled private lords to imitate him,
and since to become a *liber burgus* was the passion of them all, with
customs as free as those of York or Oxford, the growth of municipal
liberty followed a fairly uniform pattern. Royal charters, for which the
citizens gave hard cash, were sparingly conceded by Henry II, but
Richard and John sold them freely — John alone issuing over seventy.

Their dearest wish was to exclude the sheriff, his clerks and his
horsemen, the *scotales* when he forced them to pay extortionately for
beer, and the fees he took at every court. Even in Domesday some
towns had paid a fixed sum in lieu of ancient dues of honey, bread, or
hunting dogs, and this extended till they won the right to pay a *firma
burgi* direct to the Exchequer, commuting for a lump sum all they owed
the Crown for house rents, market tolls, and court fees. When this was
stabilized, they claimed to be holding in ' fee farm '. They bought other
rights too, that the sheriff's jurisdiction over them should cease, and
that no citizen should have to plead outside the walls ; save in pleas of
the Crown before a justice in eyre, and then twelve burgesses should
represent them all. They won the election of their reeves and coroners ;
the holding of a market ; freedom for a citizen to dispose of his land and
goods as he pleased ; freedom of the borough for villeins who had lived
there over a year ; and a burgage tenure by which a money payment
would compound for all services.

In their fight against feudalism the Crown helped by insisting that
all townsmen, whosoever tenants they were, should share alike in paying
tallage, — the forced levy which the King could take of his boroughs and
demesnes. All over England they were squeezing concessions out of
their lords ; paying cash to Bury St. Edmunds abbey instead of harvesting, or getting leave from the Balliols of Castle Barnard for each man to
bake in his own oven. Before the mid-thirteenth century they were
copying London in electing a mayor ; town councils were making bye-
laws regarding usury or building leases, under their common seal, which
marked something new in the feudal scheme ; raised out of vassalage to
almost an organism with a general will.

Their corporateness owed much to an institution which began
independently of the borough court, but became almost the borough in
another capacity : the merchant gild. When a fraudulent baker taking
refuge in a feudal manor, a crushing tallage, or a debt contracted by a
single townsman, might bring reprisals on them all, the mediaeval town
could only survive by becoming a band of brothers. All their traders
must form a gild, then, to share alike. All gildsmen could claim a share
in purchases made by any one of them, at the original price; they expected

a first option on imported goods, hoping by a fair distribution of the
' common bargains ' to check a monopoly by the rich. The gild kept
festival for its brethren on their patronal saint's day, fined them for
a breach of rules, sent them bread and wine in sickness, and sang
Masses when they died. Against non-gildsmen they waged relentless
war. Such persons might carry on no retail trade; even in wholesale
transactions they must sell to gildsmen only, must pay tolls (which the
gildsmen did not), and must not deal in staple trades, like corn or wool,
at all. Equally jealous was their care to fix prices and wages; to insist
on the exact measure of cloth, or decent quality of beer; to crush the
middleman and independent craftsman. For the merchant gild aspired
to control the town's trade in all its bearings. The day of the specialized
craft gild had not arrived; its first efforts, of the weavers particularly,
were suppressed, as an attempt to win private privilege without sharing
in the common burdens.

So, in its early form of exclusive rights, civic liberty bore fruit. It
was growing in mean streets. Except for the Jews' stone houses, the
town was a mass of thatched hovels, causing endless fires. Pigs
scavenged its undrained unpaved alleys, where all was dark when the
taverns closed at curfew; except near London and large towns the
roads were mere cart-tracks, soon disappearing into forest. But these
isolated settlements were ruling themselves, and others. They were
meeting in their churchyard to approve a new charter, and electing
aldermen, coroners, or bridge-wardens. Sworn jurors were dividing
the town meadows in Romney Marsh; the Cinque Ports made something
like a federation; night watchmen with their lanterns patrolled Bury
St. Edmunds.

Head and crown of this civic life was London, in whom John was
to find a mighty enemy. Its chartered liberties of 1130 had suffered
much at the hands of Henry II, not unmindful of his mother's wrongs,
for he took away the City's choice of sheriffs and increased its ' ferm '.
It was gripped between a royal garrison at the Tower and the Essex
knights who held Baynard's Castle. Sokes and privileged areas — the
Priory at Aldgate, the Jewry off Cheapside, or the Templars' new home
on the river bank — and baronial estates broke up its jurisdiction. Its
machinery of self-government was limited to the ancient moots of the
twenty-four Wards, to the Monday husting court at the Guildhall where
Ward aldermen did justice, and the thrice-yearly folk-moot in St. Paul's
churchyard. But a pulsing life was straining these old forms.

Shut in on the north by the Moorfields marsh, where the citizens
skated in hard winters, surrounded beyond that by pasture and water-
mills and the woods of Highgate and Hampstead, London itself was
enclosed between Ludgate and Aldgate, Cripplegate and the Thames, a
small walled city of gardens, orchards, and wide frontages. Population,

however, was growing fast. By Henry II's death there were a hundred churches within and just without the wall, while soon St. Brides and St. Clement Danes rose in the suburb linking London to royal Westminster. The Southwark side was already embanked, and in 1176 a new London Bridge was begun in stone. Normans, Flemings, and Italians had followed on older immigrants; down by the river, in cookshops and wine cellars, jostled the traders of all nations. This city life, so mobile and abounding, could not be tied up in feudal custom or clerical ideal. It produced financiers, like the Fleming William Cade, whose loans were indispensable to the King. Property changed hands so fast that all notion of tenure perished. Monasteries were growing rich on ground-rents.

Standing on a tidal stream, facing the rivers of the Low Countries whence ran trade routes even to Constantinople, and at the junction of the main English roads, London lived by business. Upon it concentrated the home trade of the south: East Anglian corn dealers and Yarmouth herring fishers and the graziers who marketed at Smithfield; by road and river, from England and abroad, imports flowed in to satisfy the capital of trade, fashion, and government. Through Lorraine and Utrecht, luxury goods of the East streamed to the Cologne wharfe below Thames Street: pepper and precious stones, armour and fine linen. The Rouen men at Dowgate were free of all tolls, except on wine. Flemings, Danes, Riga timber-men, and Amiens traders in woad and onions, had all to be housed, fed, and policed. Londoners were proud of their city. Intense local patriotism filled the parishioners who with their church crosses marched to beat the bounds, or to meet their aldermen with pennons flying; the gilds who competed at football, and held wrestling matches against Westminster; the sober citizens who scanned the records to see what country towns were free from toll, or who left legacies to their hospital of St. Bartholomew. They were passing bye-laws for a growing city, for safe building, sanitation, and protection against fire; their interests were united and insistent, pressing towards a new government to express them adequately.

They found their chance in the feud of 1190 — between Richard's justiciar and Richard's brother John. From the one they extorted the choice of their sheriffs, and from the other a grant of a Commune, with the appointment of a mayor. This extreme claim for complete self-government disappeared, however, when Richard came home from his Crusade. They could not escape the Crown's tallages, while their own quarrels and class conflict more than once encouraged the King to appoint committees of reform. But their essential government held its own, under the mayor and the Ward aldermen.

London held no monopoly in the expansion of trade. Sussex could take a royal order for 50,000 horse shoes; Yarmouth herrings supplied the whole south; the Cornish tin miners were already on a capitalist basis. Nor was the London customs revenue much larger than that of Southampton, the headquarters for Italian merchants, or of Lynn, where Baltic shippers had a strong colony. Tyneside coal already went to the Low Countries, while cloth from eastern England and wool from Yorkshire monasteries went to all Europe. English consumers and foreign importers were linked together by the great fairs, the most famous of which were St. Bartholomew's at Smithfield, St. Giles' at Winchester, St. Ives on the Ouse, and, above all, Stourbridge near Cambridge. Here, sometimes for a month together, sprang up streets of booths and stalls, where English towns and foreign firms had the same ' pitch ' year after year; so important for the season's spices or salt herrings, that boroughs would suspend their court meetings in fair-time; so lucrative that magnates and monasteries treasured the right of holding a fair on their land; so crowded and heated that they needed a private police, and developed an international law. A special court of ' pie-powder ' (*pieds poudrés*), with foreign merchants as assessors, kept the peace and held men to their bargains, and we find villeins of Ramsey abbey bound to do night guard-duty at St. Ives.

The State's interest in this growing wealth was impressed on Angevin policy. In 1197 an assize standardized measures and weights for corn and cloth, which elected officers had to supervise in every borough; John appointed customs officers at each principal port. Our cloth was already a weapon in diplomacy, and only the Crown could enforce decent treatment of foreigners by the jealous natives. One other economic instrument the Crown had always in its hand, the Jews; who, being excluded by the Church's teaching from the rights of men, and from holding property by the law, could only flourish as royal creatures. The King would enforce debts due to those whose chattels were legally his own, and whose property must escheat to him, and on these precarious terms their ghettoes and synagogues sprang up wherever wealth was growing, London or York or Lynn. Their extortionate loans financed Strongbow's conquest of Ireland, and even built monasteries, while a special branch of the Exchequer registered their dealings. But barbarous attacks on them by indebted crusaders and wild stories of their crucifying Christian children showed the popular hatred, and though John wrung huge tallages from them, they could not help him in the day of trouble.

An immense contribution to this age of activity was made by the Church. Papal concentration of power, monastic wealth, and the clergy's political influence had, indeed, not only created new grievances but damaged Christianity. English Churchmen were being driven to face a dilemma, whether they would stand with Papal sovereignty, or with the law and opinion of their own land. Savage remarks from Henry II, and the satire of his chaplain Walter de Map, denounced political

prelates and the fat ease of many monks. Parish churches, whom pious
laymen had robbed of endowment by ' appropriating ' tithe to monasteries, were too often held by illiterate peasants or courtly non-residents.

But, as the twelfth century went on, the Church was swept by one
of those reforming waves which have so often saved it. To rend the
seamless robe, to leave the one ark of salvation, entered no man's mind,
but there were men in plenty who would stand up for the rights of the
State, strive to reconcile faith with reason, or struggle to recall the spirit
of Christ. John's advisers were as ready to defend the theory of the
two swords, and argue that Christ's kingdom had nothing to do with
temporal power, as were the Hohenstaufens' lawyers, and the greatest
legal writer in the English midde ages, Henry Bracton, himself a
Devonshire rector as well as a royal justice, sturdily championed his
common law against Rome.

Much more vital was the revolt of the European conscience, which
from radicalism might grow into heresy. Its first leader, Arnold of
Brescia, had been burned at Rome while Henry II was settling into his
kingdom ; since that day new movements had raised their heads in
every corner — Waldenses or Vaudois in central Europe, Cathari in
northern Italy, Beguin fraternities among the Flemish artisans suffering
from a crude capitalism, in Calabria the mystic Joachim de Fiora preaching a reign of love, and in southern France the fierce Albigenses.

In some the reforming spirit sank to ugly fanaticism, to a hatred of
the body, or to repudiation of war, marriage, law, and property, but
all professed that Christ could only be found by those willing to live
like Him and His first disciples. Their programme, as gradually un-
folded, took the same course as those of much later reformers. From
attacking the sins of the priesthood they advanced to attack the sacrament which gave the priesthood its power, and ended by setting themselves up as a church of the elect.

The great Pope who excommunicated John was not blind to this
crisis in the faith. Against the Albigenses he let the laity draw the
sword, but his last constructive work was the Lateran Council of 1215,
which affirmed the Church's dogmas, and transubstantiation in particular, took steps to educate the clergy, ordered annual provincial
councils and triennial chapters of the monastic orders, and bade every
Christian confess yearly to his parish priest. Innocent saw too that, if
Europe was to be saved from heresy, the Church must recapture the
heretics' virtues, and saved her by enlisting on her side the Castilian
Dominic and Francis of Assisi.

St. Dominic's preachers arrived in England in 1221, and built forty
houses in the next half century ; the Franciscans came three years later,
had twelve hundred brethren in England before 1250, and finally some
fifty-eight houses, divided between seven ' custodies ' ranging from

Bodmin to Dumfries. Differing widely in the spirit of their founders and their constitution, in this first golden age both Orders lived as few Christians had for centuries, true to the injunction of both Francis and Dominic that their only duty was to save souls. Instead of the monks' cloister they lived in the world, in business cities and universities. And yet they would eschew the world; carrying neither purse nor script, they would refuse endowments, would walk barefoot in shine or snow, their heads should not lie on pillows, they would wed Poverty and go singing to sister Death as had St. Francis, and trust for bread to Him who fed the sparrows.

Some of the joyousness of Assisi threw a beam of light on thirteenth-century England, whose people welcomed men so different from landed abbots and tavern-haunting priests. As the friars would not hold property, citizens gave land and houses for them in trust to borough councils, men of knightly rank and the pick of the universities joined them, Henry III and most of the bishops were unwavering supporters. Public opinion was behind them in their inevitable struggle with the monks, and when the crisis came in the Franciscan Order between the strict and the more lax schools, the English province was one of the firmest for utter poverty. Each Order had gifts of its own. The Dominicans gave confessors to kings, their democratically-elected chapters were a model in government, and their scholarship, amalgamating Aristotle with theology, culminated in the final work of St. Thomas Aquinas. The Franciscans were the brothers of the poor, lepers, and outcasts, brought doctors and water supplies to common streets and slums, and won the heart of London merchants.

But their joint contribution to English civilization was fundamental — holiness, public spirit, and learning, for a short space joined together. To the Church they gave a centralized staff, and a new mobility; for unlike monks they were not tied to one house, they were exempt from bishops' jurisdiction and responsible directly to Rome, while constant change of men and free election kept the channel free and flowing. They almost re-created confession and preaching; the sermons in their large churches were on common themes, on gluttony and money-getting and repentance, driven home by familiar instance of harvest or law courts or market-place, or by rude humour of tavern and ballad. Like the Jesuits later, they took education as their own. The Oxford Franciscans chose as their first lecturer Robert Grosseteste, the most learned man of his age, who with his successor Adam Marsh set the tradition later glorified by Roger Bacon, Duns Scotus, and William of Occam. Greek and Hebrew, physics and natural science, were brought to reinforce theology, systematic teaching and libraries sent up a stream of novices to the university, and every principal city had its school.

This hunger and thirst after righteousness could not be circumscribed, and the English friars touched the whole public action of the age. There were individual friars reverenced by whole counties, even when they went against popular prejudice in protecting the Jews. Franciscans inspired de Montfort's reforms; one warden of their Oxford house fell on crusade at Tripoli; they had a hand in founding the first colleges. Under their influence fraternities of laymen sprang up to tend the sick, or to rescue the victims of moneylenders.

Later on, under Papal injunctions, the Mendicants departed from the testament of St. Francis. In their dependence on house-to-house begging, which to the end was their chief resource, there was obvious danger. They had privileges of preaching and hearing confessions which offended the village priesthood, and there were extremists among them who were very near heresy. But all this had not, before 1272, prejudiced the great work which they were doing for England. Yet it made but one part of a spiritual revival in the normal life of the English Church. The best of its leaders in the thirteenth century were characters of real nobility, sanctity, and learning; as the two archbishops Stephen Langton and Edmund Rich, Richard le Poor who began the building of Salisbury cathedral, Grosseteste of Lincoln, or Thomas Cantelupe, de Montford's ally, bishop of Hereford and canonized saint. Though the Church was full of misused endowments and was exploited both by Rome and the laity, in the development of its machinery and legislation, and in the regularity of bishops' visitations, this was a creative age.

Through the Church also originally flowed another source of intellectual and political advance. Oxford had imperceptibly become a university, and one of unusually independent type. Its early schools doubled in importance after 1167, when Henry II recalled English clerks from France and the dangerous infection of Becket, and by John's time it was a cosmopolitan university town. Made by this Paris migration, it grew up on the Paris model of a self-governing body of teachers, though unlike Paris was free from the pressures of a Court or a capital, nor was it overshadowed by a cathedral, for Oxford then had none and lay on the outskirts of the diocese of Lincoln. The chancellor who ruled this body of teaching clerks became, in fact, rather their elected representative than the bishop of Lincoln's official, while royal charters gave him wide powers over town and gown.

A mediaeval university was not formed by buildings and examinations, but by the attraction of great teachers for wandering students, equally at home at Paris, Oxford, or Bologna. For Latin was the universal tongue of learning, Christian learning was the same all the world over, and like *Imperium* and *Sacerdotium* the *Studium* made part of a world order. It ebbed and flowed with movements inside the Church, for whose service most of its youth was trained, or with the fame of individual teachers. Troubles of the Interdict thus dispersed

the Oxford scholars in 1209, in large part to Cambridge, which from
this time slowly evolved a university of its own; riots against a Papal
legate in 1238, a royal order of 1263 against sympathizers with de
Montfort, caused more migrations to temporary 'universities' at
Northampton and Salisbury.

Movement and spiritual energy, a torrential tributary breaking
into a sluggish stream, came from this early Oxford, where two or
three thousand boys, between fourteen and twenty-one years of age,
chose their own masters, ruled their own hostels, roamed the streets
with bows and arrows to attack townsmen and Jews, sank to animal
depths in the taverns, soared to the highest themes of philosophy and
salvation. Here the 'nations' into which they were divided, England
beyond Trent and Scotland ranking as the north, southern England with
Wales and Ireland as the south, learned the ways of arbitration and
union. Four out of every five students, perhaps, became secular priests,
the others doctors or lawyers or monks, and though such things cannot
be measured it was impossible that public life should not feel the
thrust of these oncoming generations; trained by Grosseteste and his
disciples in Aristotelian thought, in the difference between tyranny and
rule by law, or the prerogative of the mind to follow reason.

The wandering scholar still went to Paris or further afield, nor
must we picture a high proportion of trained graduates, for the
great majority did not complete the seven years required for a master-
ship in arts. But Oxford, and soon Cambridge, became fixed homes
of the English mind, where good men left money for poor students,
and whence eager idealists went to fight for de Montfort, or young
men took back to middle-class homes up and down England an
argument against Papal extortion, a political ballad, or something of the
divine discontent of the Friars. A bishop's pastoral staff might be in
the wallet of the most ragged student; a far horizon for the talents
stretched away over Europe. In the high privileges given by royal
charter, in the support of Rome and Canterbury against the local clergy
or the town, we see the importance attached to the University, last and
not least powerful of mediaeval corporations.

Other channels for public opinion were being cut by new currents
of government and wealth. The King's judges were becoming a professional lay class, drawn from pleaders who practised in royal and
manorial courts, or clerks of Chancery and Household. They administered a native law, and thus Bracton noted some two thousand
cases from the rolls, from which he built, before 1260, his *Treatise on
the Laws of England*. Grammar schools and singing schools, not only
round cathedrals and monasteries, but attached to parish churches,
were sinking shafts into the illiteracy of the masses, and there were
villeins' sons only anxious to learn.

However taught, in the century from Henry II's accession English civilization achieved glorious things. The third generation of Normans were bilingual, for not only learned men spoke English, like the historian Giraldus Cambrensis, but barons and their wives; town schools had French word-books for English boys, while a great abbot of Bury St. Edmunds held his influence by preaching in the Norfolk dialect. And though Latin dominated learning, and French was the tongue of the Court and the City records, a strong English tradition, particularly in the secluded middle-west, survived both in literature and art. Just after 1200 Layamon, priest of Ernley on Severn, wrote his *Brut*, describing in English verse, though from French material, the noble deeds of Britain from Brutus to Caedwallader. Somewhere in Worcestershire a priest could not get out of his head the English refrain he heard from his churchyard, ' Sweetheart, have pity '. Not far off, Orm, an Austin canon in the Midlands, paraphrased in verse the gospels of the Church year, while rich carvings on pillars and porches kept alive the spirals, the grim beasts, and all the motives of Celtic and Scandinavian art. Meantime English speech lived on in a literature of religion, which bridged the apparent gulf from the Chronicle's end in 1154 to the outburst of fourteenth-century prose. Not later than 1200 was written the *Ancren Riule*, a book of devotion for women which kept its popularity almost to the Reformation; sermon collections, satirical poems against Papal taxes or dishonest bakers, reproductions of Ælfric's two-hundred-year-old homilies, and a new French mysticism, all these survive to show what English-speaking folk asked, and the sources of their thought.

For the literature of mediaeval England was not one of two races, English and Norman, but the transformation into English speech of the whole inheritance which both peoples had received. There was, of course, an efficient literature of Court and Church in the Latin vehicle of Angevin civilization. Contact between literature and politics was not closer in the age of Anne than in that of Henry II, whose highest officials described their manner of working for their successors, and whose every move was watched by men of letters. Walter de Map, justice in eyre and royal chaplain, in his *De Nugis curialium* painted not only the light side, but the anti-clericalism of the Court, the force and corruption of its servants. Brilliant narrative and biographical sketches from Giraldus Cambrensis, historian of his kinsmen-Marcher in Wales and their Irish conquest; letters, as studied as those of Pope, from the diplomat Peter of Blois; chronicle and official documents from the Yorkshire canon William of Newburgh, the justiciar Hoveden, or Diceto dean of St. Paul's; blast and counter-blast from all who had known Becket at London and Canterbury, such heat was generated from Henry's central flame. Chronicles were being written in every great abbey, from Battle to Melrose, crowned in the line of historians officially appointed at St. Albans. Its greatest figure was Matthew Paris, historian, artist, intimate of the court, whose chronicle for the years 1235–59 is a contemporary authority, written with all a monk's prejudice but with a robust hatred of Papal extortion or royal incompetence.

But the Latin chronicle would not touch the people, and the literature of the future was inspired from France. Thence came the romances, first sung by minstrels on the pilgrimage roads to Rome or Compostella, which produced the English heroes Guy of Warwick or Bevis of Southampton, while in the south, the troubadours' land where Richard ' Yea and Nay ' had fought and died, sprang up a vernacular poetry, the lyric of love and nature. Even old English Vikings were re-borrowed in a French dress, while in western England particularly a mystical poetry transformed Provençal passion into adoration of Christ crucified and the beauties of Mary. Nothing better illustrates this migration of ideas than the cycle built up round Arthur of Britain, whose body, of huge size and covered with wounds, was found, so men believed, at Glastonbury under Henry II. From its origin by Stephen's subject Geoffrey of Monmouth, through French translation and Layamon's addition to the French, enriched in each flight over the sea by new glories — Gawain, Lancelot, Sir Perceval, and the mystery of the Holy Grail — the seed sown in the ninth century had by the thirteenth grown into a giant of the forest, whose branches carried all the chivalry and folk-lore of Celtic Europe. In the people's revolt against John, alongside his nephew and victim Arthur of Brittany stood the heroic wraith of Arthur of Britain, founder of the Table Round of perfect knighthood, a King who ruled by law.

A mass of new themes and new metres, a sensitive love of form, spiritual revolt and criticism, all this was breaking on the England of King John. From the Franciscan Order alone we might tell it. While one friar composed a solemn Latin ode, ' The Song of Lewes ', in vindication of de Montfort, another from Gloucestershire was singing the fleetingness of power and beauty :

> *Where is Paris and Heleyne,*
> *That were so bright and fair of blee?*

Tristan and Iseult, Hector and Caesar, are all gone like corn from the hillside. *Sumer is icumen in :*

in the Berkshire downs a song already said so, in words already set to English music.

In the arts there had been the same story of loss, but of much more gain. As literature had lost the northern epic spirit, so the delicate illumination, fine coinage, and metal-work of late Saxon England had disappeared. But their form and beauty were caught up in the magnificence of architecture, which between 1150 and 1250 rose to the climax of Gothic. A tide of new influence transformed English Romanesque and the heavy early Norman, into something English but also European. Monasticism with sister-houses in all countries, not the Île de France only, but Poitou, Toulouse, and Spain, not the Burgundian Cistercians only, but all Orders, all the Catholic world and all the Angevin Empire, sent models and craftsmen to England. An immense growth of structural skill, from the flat roof to the round barrel vault and so to the groined and ribbed vaulting springing from the more pointed arch, the counteraction of the vault's thrust by pinnacles and flying buttress, mingled with architectural effects of ritual and the needs of worship; with the substitution of towering piers for heavy wall support, and the glory of great windows, an elongation of the choir to hold a saint's shrine, or an ambulatory round the high altar to take the procession of worshippers, the piercing of old arches to form aisles, and a piling of chapel on chapel, altar on altar, to house relics and pilgrims and gilds.

This work was done by the Church and the propertied class in every part of England, and by master craftsmen in every local stone, owing nothing to any King, until Henry III rebuilt Westminster Abbey on a French model. Between 1154 and 1250 the abbeys of the north were built at Fountains and Bolton, Jervaulx and Lanercost: Buildwas and Wenlock rose in the Marches, Malmesbury and Glastonbury in the south. Perpetual rebuilding in the cathedrals gave what we see in the choirs of Canterbury, Lincoln, and Oxford, the main fabrics of Wells and Southwark, St. David's and Salisbury, the Galilee at Durham, the east arm at Ely, and the transepts at York. Colleges of canons, Orders, and parishes built or refashioned the churches which are still the glory of England.

For the parish gave all the colour and warmth of life to the countryman. To its boundaries he would march in procession on Rogation days, and there take leave of friends going on pilgrimage; its church porch was a business centre in wet weather, in its churchyard took place fairs and mystery plays and the sheriffs' proclamations; its Sanctus bell reached the peasant working in the fields; on the church walls were painted the miracles of the saints or the harrowing of hell, while aloft hung the shields of good knights gone to dust.

Among the makers of England we may, therefore, salute Elias de Dereham, archbishop Langton's steward and rebel to John, who supervised the building of Salisbury and Wells, and all the others, by name unknown, who were working in stone these masterpieces of harmony and strength; in an England united in blood, acclimatized to law, enriched by the wealth and civilization of the western world.

The first test of this new nationality came in contest with King John.

CHAPTER V

REVOLUTION AND REFORM, 1213–1272

IN May 1213 John resolved to make his peace with Rome, play off the Church against his subjects, and complete his foreign alliances. It was a game typical of this shallow, clever despot, who misjudged the three big pieces on the board : the extent to which Innocent III could drive English opinion, the passion for internal reform, and the strength of France. For the moment, however, it seemed to work. The King received absolution, on his own initiative agreeing to hold England and Ireland as Papal fiefs on a yearly tribute of 1000 marks. But the next two years showed that the English people had a formed public opinion, able to distinguish between reform and anarchy, or a king and a tyrant.

Though there was a baronial left-wing as violent as John, ready to call in the French, the majority were consistently moderate, and it was their programme which evolved into Magna Carta. In archbishop Langton they found an ideal leader, a sober Lincolnshire gentleman, scholarly, high-minded, conservative. Churchmanship and patriotism to him were both part of a legal order, the righteous government of the world, and he regretted John's surrender to Rome. From his first arrival in England he associated himself with the unorganized moderate group, the justiciar FitzPeter, a few barons, and the Londoners, who were determined to stop John's evil ways ; even in 1213 they were pressing reform on the lines of Henry I's charter, for no imprisonment without legal trial, and for restriction on scutage and service abroad. For a year they restrained both the King and the extreme barons. The King promised freedom of election to the Church and checked his extortionate sheriffs and foresters, while most of the barons sent their contingents to his invasion of France.

On this turned the immediate fate both of England and Europe. One army was to pierce France from the north, under Otto the Emperor and John's subsidized allies from Lorraine to Flanders, while the King himself would strike from Poitou to the Loire, and so to Brittany. Victory might have ended both Hohenstaufens and Capets, and must certainly have postponed English reform. But both ventures collapsed. The Poitevins, however ready to exploit England for their independence, would not face a French army, while on the 27th July 1214 at Bouvines, between Lille and Tournai, Philip Augustus crushed Otto and the Netherlanders.

Compelled to ask a truce, John came home to revenge himself on those who had opposed the war. On FitzPeter's death the alien Peter des Roches became justiciar; mercenaries were brought in from abroad; a heavy scutage was demanded from all who had not served in Poitou; the shire courts were tuned to put the royal case against the barons. All of which strengthened the hand of those who had always argued that John was incorrigible.

Simultaneously the Holy See destroyed the mediating position of Langton. Its eyes were fixed not on the minute grievances of England but on the forthcoming Lateran Council, which might settle the whole future of the Church, and for which peace between France and England was urgently required. Not only did John get his nominees appointed to bishoprics, not only did he escape lightly for the ruin he had inflicted during the Interdict, but the Pope denounced the barons, and in 1215 declared the Charter null and void, and suspended Langton. That John became a crusader and the archbishop an exile, is a sufficient condemnation of Papal policy.

The lead thus came to men determined to force John to his knees. They included remote northerners who had refused scutage and were in touch with the Scots, young men whom John had fleeced by reliefs and fines, and the injured kinsmen of Braose. Most concentrated and resolute were an eastern group — FitzWalter of Dunmow and Baynard's Castle in London, young FitzPeter earl of Essex, Bigod of Norfolk, and de Vere of Oxford. In November 1214 at Bury St. Edmunds this party vowed to compel John to honour the oaths he had forsworn, and at Easter 1215, distrustful of mediation, met at Stamford under arms.

For the first time since the Conquest the mass of the people were deaf to the Crown's appeal, and when in May the barons marched on London, the City gladly opened its gates. Risings broke out in north and south, Llewelyn of Gwynedd captured Shrewsbury, the revenue failed, and the best heads in England begged John to give way, not Langton only with the mass of the bishops but the loyalest of the loyal, William Marshall earl of Pembroke, Hubert de Burgh, Ranulf earl of Chester, and the administrators. For only compromise could avert a desperate war between the King's foreign mercenaries and the extremists who were already in touch with France. In fact, both came true. Magna Carta represented the compromise, the extremists on both sides made the civil war of 1215-17, and only John's death enabled the moderates to combine resistance to French invasion with acceptance of the Charter.

In dealing with the Charter, which was signed at Runnymede near Windsor on the 17th June, we have to distinguish reforms, which the moderates had long discussed and carefully drafted, from political safeguards aimed against John or temporary clauses meant to please the

barons' friends, and to distinguish both of these from the high-sounding
claims, for trial by jury or Parliament, which later Englishmen loved to
read back to Runnymede. Its real essence lay in the ideal of the governing class of 1215, barons and knights and freeholders, who had served
a long apprenticeship in Henry II's law.

Of the Charter's sixty-two clauses, over half dealt with practical
feudal grievances. Such clauses fixed precise payment for reliefs,
protected estates under wardship, granted the widow her dower, saved
children from ruin on account of their father's debts to the Jews, and
forbade use of the writ *Praecipe* which summarily removed cases from
feudal courts. Not a line gave any protection to the villein, whose lord,
be he King or baron, was left free to tallage him or increase his service,
while except for a vague clause on behalf of London the towns too
were left exposed to tallage. And when the barons demanded that
the taxes affecting themselves, scutages and aids, should be levied ' by
common consent ', they defined that consent as the full meeting of
tenants-in-chief in the Curia Regis, to which greater barons had long
been summoned personally, and lesser men through the sheriff. They
meant, in short, to stand upon the ancient ways, for if they asked their
own rights, they left to the King his demesnes, boroughs, and wardships.

Yet, though their programme was conservative, it was not ignobly
self-seeking, and the clerks who on those June days hastily transcribed
copies for distribution to sheriffs and bishops were laying some corner-
stones of English liberty. There were some clauses, simply re-enacting
what Angevin administrators had ruled ; as that foreign merchants
should freely come and go on paying customs, or that there should be
one standard of weights and measures. But others accepted the limits
Henry II had put to baronial power, or extended to all free landowners
the feudal rules of justice. Clause I, repeating John's charter of 1214,
promised the Church entire freedom of election. Common pleas were
not to follow the court, but to be heard at Westminster. Petty assizes
should be held in each shire at regular intervals. No sheriff must try
pleas of the Crown. In a case of murder a defendant might claim,
freely, the writ *De odio*, giving him a jury. A whole array of clauses
attacked the hated forests, those created by John being disafforested
and juries being set up to report on abuses. A jury, again, was to assess
judicial fines, which were never to stretch to depriving a landowner of
his holding, or a merchant of his stock-in-trade. And, lastly, no free
man was to suffer arrest, disseisin, or imprisonment, except by a legal
process or the verdict of his feudal equals. Such were the fundamentals
of what, within ten years, was called ' the great Charter ', issued in the
form of inheritable liberties to all free men.

But how was it to be enforced upon an unwilling King ? Its
executive clauses not only ordered the removal of foreign sheriffs and

the sending away of foreign mercenaries, but set up a body of twenty-five barons empowered, without any time-limit, to make war on the King if he broke his word. The misgivings of the moderates were quickly realized. John's most bitter enemies packed the twenty-five, heaped insult on the King, and ejected his sheriffs. In the north the extremists repudiated the Charter; while all over England men were fortifying castles and looting royal estates. So a constitutional reform turned, in part through the fault of extreme reformers, into civil war. Moderates like the Marshall or Ranulf of Chester came back to the side of John, behind whom stood his Papal overlord and a horde of new mercenaries.

Philip Augustus would not again defy Innocent III, but allowed his son to claim the English throne: whose remarkable wife, Blanche of Castile, was, indeed, a granddaughter of Henry II. When in May 1216 Louis reached Thanet, he found the barons and the first French contingent cooped up in London, while John, who held the south-west firmly, had broken like a whirlwind into the eastern shires and ravaged them from Bury St. Edmunds to Berwick. The baronage, in fact, had neither a plan nor a leader. Some did homage to Alexander of Scotland, but John chased that ' sandy fox cub ', as he called him, back from the Border. And those who did homage to Louis were indignant at his grants of land to Frenchmen. Londoners mobbed his soldiers, others were ambushed in the Hampshire and Sussex woods, while old hatred of the French made the Cinque Ports loyal to the King.

The worst suffering fell on the home counties and the northern roads, where the French raided for tribute and where John's captains, led by the fierce little Norman, de Breauté, robbed churches and fired the harvest. And though there was much loyalty, though even in the far north the Balliols were staunch, and though the new justiciar de Burgh held Dover against all attack, no decision could come while the greatest barons wavered, and while the London clergy defied the Pope's interdict in the name of the Charter.

But death, ' eloquent, just, and mighty death ', cut the knot. In September 1216 John, from loyal Lincoln, began to harry the fens; in October he fell ill of dysentery, and amid his feasting granted land to found a religious house in memory of the Braoses, whom he had done to death; on the 12th, as he crossed the Wash quicksands, he lost his treasure; on the 19th he died at Newark, asking to be buried in a monk's habit and commending his son to the Papacy.

Henry III was a child of nine years, his mother was an unpopular foreigner, and power would go to the hands that could take it. To the credit of the country it rallied to the child King as a symbol of reconciliation. John had begged William the Marshall to protect Henry, and now this eighty-year-old warrior, who had fought loyally for so many lords from 'the young King' in 1180 onwards, swore to his new sovereign. 'Fair Sir,' he said weeping, 'I tell you loyally, as I trust my soul to God, I will be in good fealty to you and never forget you.' Guala the Papal legate, Peter des Roches, Ranulf of Chester, John's mercenaries, accepted the Marshall as Regent, and by a master-stroke this small band, when they crowned the little King, reissued the Charter. Against Frenchmen and rebels they thus reunited two great forces, the Pope's anathema and English law.

This, perhaps even more than the Regent's high character, brought bishops and barons steadily over to the government. In May 1217 the Regent defeated the French in a desperate battle at Lincoln, in which eight of the twenty-five were captured. In August a convoy, bringing large French reinforcements, sailed from Calais under a noble free-booter, Eustace the Monk; it was destroyed in the Thames estuary by the Cinque Ports' and Channel Islands' ships under de Burgh, and while Eustace's head, on a pike, was paraded through Kent, the Regent began to blockade London. The French could hold out no longer. In September, on a promised payment of 10,000 marks, Louis left England, an amnesty covered his English supporters, the city of London was confirmed in its liberties. A second reissue of the Charter was accompanied by a Forest charter which threw open all forests created since 1154, and abolished, in forest law, penalties of death and mutila-tion. Only the fines and deprivations inflicted by the legate on rebel clergy suggested that the Church in England might, one day, have to choose between national liberties and obedience to Rome.

Half a century divided this victory of moderation from its next triumph in the *Dictum* de Kenilworth of 1266, which, in fact, ended the long inglorious government, though not the life, of Henry III. They were years of permanent decision — between personal and constitu-tional government, an Angevin and an insular foreign policy, Papal supremacy and religious compromise — conflicts out of which came nationality. For the moment England suffered two particular evils, the minority of an infant King and the demoralization left by civil war. There were claimants two deep to every estate, feudatories who had been loyal to the Charter, or professional soldiers who had been loyal to John. Constant tournaments and disobedience to the King's writ showed how war had got into the blood, and the Regent's death in 1219 removed the one force above parties. For though the Papacy did great service in securing peace with Scotland, and a truce with France till Philip Augustus' death in 1223, and though its legates Guala and Pandulf were moderate and single-minded, their power jarred on the English bishops.

Langton's voice was always for peace, but his appeal to the Charters did not meet the immediate danger, which was the connivance of the

King's best supporters at illegality and violence. Fawkes de Breauté, whose disciplined mercenaries put down feudal castles and London riot, was himself a danger to the State. Ranulf, last palatine earl of Chester, though not a bad public servant, depended for the peace of his wide territory on good relations with Wales and Scotland. De Burgh, the Justiciar, though anti-clerical and anti-French, was greedy for riches, and led a bureaucracy that cared much more about strong government than the Charter. Against him stood Peter des Roches, the King's tutor, a good financial administrator, who could certainly count on many nobles and captains for help in overthrowing the Justiciar. But all alike, patriots and partisans, agreed on ending the minority at the first possible date, and in 1227 Henry declared his intention to rule.

From 1219 till 1232 de Burgh dominated the State, triumphing by doggedness more than character, by a divided opposition rather than by a united government. He recovered royal castles and demesnes. He drove de Breauté into exile. He utilized the royal house in the cause of peace, marrying one of Henry's sisters to Alexander of Scotland and another to the ambitious William Marshall the younger. The Council resisted Papal pressure for a permanent revenue for the Holy See, steadily proclaimed the rules of common law, and step by step restored normality. And since poverty led to constant full meetings of the Council, the self-government which Henry II had adapted to his own purpose was tending to become a principle. Knights, elected and paid by their counties, were summoned to London to report breaches of the Charters, barons and shires declared consent was necessary to taxation, while in 1226 Langton called the first representative meeting of clergy to discuss, and to reject, the Pope's exactions.

The malice of Peter des Roches could easily assemble enemies against the Justiciar: the King, whom he had kept in leading strings and whom he offended by offending the Church; London, where he had ruthlessly enforced order; and most of all the magnates, outraged by his greed and justly indignant with his policy. Wales showed most glaringly the worst both of de Burgh and his rivals. No one had reaped more from the troubles than Llewelyn, whom the peace of 1218 had left in possession of every key of south Wales, with Montgomery in the middle March and Rhuddlan on the north. He had set himself to foment English quarrels, showing sympathy with de Breauté, marrying his daughters into Marcher houses, stirring those houses against the Marshalls, and finally encouraging the Marshalls to break with the Crown. De Burgh's policy was to protect English interests by binding them up with his own; he took under his administration Cardigan and Carmarthen, Montgomery, Gower, and the wardship of the whole Gloucester fief. Where would his ambition stop? He was, besides this, earl of Kent, husband of a Scottish princess, and Justiciar

of Ireland. Yet all this power did not prevent Llewelyn in 1231 sweeping the English out of Cardigan again, and raiding Herefordshire.

But Hubert's fall, like that of his old master John, proceeded from
France. Louis VIII died in 1226, before he had taken more of Poitou
than La Rochelle, but Poitevin nobles changed sides at the approach of
any army or the offer of any bribe, while a new embarrassment arose
from the marriage of Henry's foolish mother Isabelle to the most grasping among them, Hugh de Lusignan. Gascony, bankrupt and torn by the
feuds of nobles and communes, was the grave of the reputation of any
Englishman unhappy enough to be appointed seneschal. Yet in 1230,
against Hubert's instinct, buoyed up by false visions of a Breton alliance
and boasting he would reconquer Normandy, Henry marched from
Brittany to Bordeaux, and back again, with no result but ruin to his
revenue. The baronage, refusing further taxes, and making common
cause with the Pope and des Roches, vented their wrath on the Justiciar,
whose dismissal in 1232 opened the personal rule of Henry III.

Powerful forces were working for the thirteenth-century Crown.
There was a deepened sentiment for the blood royal, a new consciousness of the State, a recognition that only the King stood between the
realm and anarchy. His government, loaded with business, had to form
new departments which only experts could direct, to expand its revenue,
to wield an active executive. John had developed his Household
servants of Chamber and Wardrobe into a war office and a private
exchequer, his privy seal translating their decisions into action. An
age of constitutional definition was overdue, to relate these new needs
and engines of State to the public opinion, the representative bodies,
the legal principles, of Henry II and the Charter.

In the character, as in the councils, of a mediaeval king there could
be no division of private and public, and Henry III's had at least the
merit of forcing issues to a head. This artistic child never grew up.
His energy and treasure went into fine building — the Abbey, St.
Stephen's Chapel, or Windsor — into the curve of an arch or the colour
of a curtain, ruby rings and rich furs, but he never grasped the ingredients of public life, men and money, method and the human heart.
His fickleness was childish, carried hither and thither by affection, by a
large comforting idea, or by the last speaker. What had been terrifying
in the Angevins in him descended to petulance. He liked counsellors
who told him what he wanted to hear, or were amusing company ; a
favourite clerk might pelt him with apples, but he would attack de
Burgh with drawn sword and scream ' traitor ' at de Montfort. And
though he was deaf to argument and blind to national feeling, his nerves
always retreated before a threat of force, an armed magnate, or fear of
excommunication. His foreign policy was an inconsistent bundle of
huge designs, ignorance, and piety, good will to the Emperor and defer-

ence to the Papacy, ever taking at its face value any plan optimistically presented.

Marriage to Eleanor of Provence put by his side another spend-thrift, zealous for her kinsmen and used to the pure monarchy of France. His brother Richard of Cornwall, through his first marriage to a Marshall, had some sympathy with the baronage and was as thrifty as Henry was the reverse, but when the glass blew to storm he stood by his brother, and at the crisis of the reign was pursuing his claim on the Empire, to which northern Germany called him on the death of Frederick II. So Henry stood alone, to meet the whirlwinds in the middle of the century.

He received a first sharp lesson in the two years following the fall of de Burgh. His new minister was Peter des Riveaux, a Poitevin like his uncle des Roches, but an able and experienced administrator, in whose hands he concentrated the Exchequer, Wardrobe, forests, and sea-ports; de Burgh was imprisoned and foreign mercenaries held the great castles. The royal advisers aimed high, at Richard Marshall the new earl of Pembroke, the equal of his father the Regent in character and popularity. Driving him into revolt and refusing him a trial by his peers, they finally entrapped him in Ireland and killed him by the arm of the Lacies. While the barons refused to attend Council and Richard's Welsh allies sacked the March, the Church protested by the voice of archbishop Rich and the leading friars, and in 1234 Henry dismissed the two Peters. But though his method henceforward was less uncon-cealed, his aim was unchanged.

Appointing mere clerks to the high offices of justiciar, treasurer, and chancellor, he entrenched his Household with foreigners whom he loaded with estates. The earliest, and the best, group were the Queen's kinsmen from Savoy, among whom her uncle Boniface succeeded Rich at Canterbury. Much worse were Henry's Lusignan half-brothers, who fled to England after the French conquest of Poitou; the vicious Aymar, whom Henry forced on the see of Winchester, and William de Valence, who took the Marshalls' title of Pembroke. Marriages into great houses like Warenne and Ferrers, and the grant of earldoms — Leicester to a Frenchman, Warwick to a Poitevin, Richmond to a Savoyard — built up a foreign royalist party.

From their stronghold in the Wardrobe the aliens were handling sums which in wartime rose to £30,000 a year, while as councillors they encouraged Henry to wage the wars. Since his folly in 1230 he had flirted with an anti-French policy, marrying his sister to the Emperor and betrothing his son Edward to Eleanor of Castile. His single and most ignominious excursion into war, in 1242, came from the instigation of the Lusignans. His army was routed, the French occupied Poitou, Auvergne, and Saintonge, and within a few years acquired, by marriage alliance, both Toulouse and Provence. Our territory thus shrank to a coast strip of Gascony, dependent for existence on the forbearance of Henry's brother-in-law, the great St. Louis.

During these years of failure, the royal financial demands were persistent rather than crushing. In the twenty-eight years preceding the crisis of 1258, there were only eight scutages or feudal aids, one grant of one-fortieth on movables and one of one-thirtieth, besides tallages on London and the Jews. The engineer of revolution was, in fact, not so much Henry as the Holy See.

The Church had done much for England during the minority. It was an age of passionate faith, given new life by the Lateran Council of 1215, transmitted from the heart at Rome through the close-knit society of Catholic Europe; and in England through Langton's new Church councils, active diocesan synods, and the newly founded chapters of monks and friars. This abundant legislation insisted on regular confession, the clergy's celibacy and residence, fixed the intricate relation of the monks to the parish churches which they had appropriated, or urged instruction of the people in their mother tongue. Franciscans and Dominicans multiplied this zeal, and never before had English devotion proved itself in such sublime building to embody the beauty of holiness. St. Thomas of Canterbury, in his new shrine, was drawing all English pilgrims.

There was another side, revealed in grumblings from common lawyers against the Church courts and in a general feeling that monks had too much land. England revolted, however, not through anti-clericalism or heresy, but in indignation at the political demands of the centralized Papacy. Its masterfulness was shown in constant appointment of Papal commissioners to investigate disputes, in some thirty cases of episcopal elections referred to Rome, or in the rejection, in 1232–3, of three successive candidates put forward for Canterbury. Finally, the pontificates of Gregory IX and Innocent IV (1227–54) wore away English loyalty, along with other things; if they succeeded in ruining the Empire, they paid for it dearly in the destruction of spiritual integrity, and the awakening, in self-defence, of every national government.

Their enemy was the unique genius Frederick II who, having by punishments and codes worthy of Bonaparte created bureaucratic despotism in Sicily, aspired to unite Italy. Though they branded him as a heretic, he was something much more dangerous, — the incarnation of the future, irreligious, all-embracing State. To crush him they would drain the Christian world dry. They began in England in 1229 by demanding one-tenth from the clergy; from 1237–41 a cardinal legate was in charge of the requisitions, which rose to one-fifth; in 1245 Innocent, driven into exile at Lyons, asked a ' crusading ' twentieth, with a tariff on benefices rising to 50 per cent.

More abominable and injurious was the misuse of patronage. Disregarding alike parishioners' needs and patrons' rights, they financed themselves by ' providing ' (that is, claiming to appoint immediately or at the next vacancy) to English benefices many hundred Italians, usually absentee and sometimes illiterate ; a demand of this sort, for the next 300 vacant livings, broke the heart of Edmund Rich. Threats of interdict, with Italian usurers to advance the money, accompanied the process. From that day we see a new organization of public opinion ; Berkshire rectors meeting in protest, Oxford students mobbing the Legate, a league of knights to terrorize Italians, a solemn national remonstrance to the Council of Lyons. In vain ; the logic of the Church combined with the policy of the King to betray them.

The leadership which dropped from the outworn hands of St. Edmund Rich was taken up by the virile omniscient Grosseteste, bishop of Lincoln, guide of the Oxford Franciscans, friend of the Marshalls and de Montfort. Intellectually convinced against despotism and the champion of union between clergy and laity, he carried to the presence of Innocent IV his protest against the killing of English faith and the degradation of powers given to St. Peter for good, and not for destruction. But beyond protest he, like Langton, could not go, holding a view of the Church's mission, union, and independence, which forbade disobedience to the vicar of Christ.

Henry III also put the Papacy above his kingdom. All that France was later to Charles II, Rome was to him, the friend of his childhood, inspiring model, refuge in distress, and he himself forged the link between resistance to Rome and opposition to the Crown. More than a shield against France, or an ally in choosing docile bishops, he found in her a buttress against his barons, and therefore asked for the sending of the legate Otto in 1237, empowered to absolve him from his oath to the Charter. Innocent IV gave him one-tenth of Church revenues for three years, agreeing likewise to foist Aymar de Lusignan on the see of Winchester.

In 1250 the death of Frederick II inspired the Papacy to destroy his heirs, and to raise up client princes in Italy and the Empire. Though ruined already by a Gascon campaign, Henry accepted the Sicilian crown for his son Edmund, with a pledge to repay Papal expenses ; in 1257 he demanded the revenues of vacant benefices for five years, and produced Edmund, all ready in Apulian dress, before his Council. The same year his brother Richard went off to battle for the Empire. But the opposition, which Richard thus abandoned, had at last found a leader.

Their quarrel was not with the structure of the State or the Angevin creations ; improved as they had been by Henry's ministers in a reformed Exchequer, a closer control by enquiries of *Quo warranto* over prerogative

rights and feudal revenue, a departmental Chancery, a permanent
Council, and separate courts of King's Bench and Common Pleas. To
the man in the street justice had never been so accessible. Skilled
judges manned the Bench, new writs incessantly offered new remedies.
Though the taxation clause of Magna Carta had been repealed, Henry
had kept to its principle of baronial consent. Knights and merchants,
regularly used to assess and collect taxes, were for ever being summoned
to Westminster, to present a county court verdict or forest grievance.
Boroughs were allowed to execute royal writs themselves, and were
wringing charters freely from private lords. There was, indeed, a new
society breaking out of feudal grooves, which resented the sheriffs' petty
oppressions and the baronial courts. But essentially the opposition was
political, bent against the weakness of government and its faults of
policy.

By 1258 the facts were clear and portentous. Henry was bankrupt,
living on moneys scraped up from Ireland or monasteries, or Italian
loans. With France there was neither war nor peace, nor any feudal
tie. A new Llewelyn had won all the upper Severn and Wye, whose
alliance was sought by an anti-English party in Scotland. Aliens held
the best things in Church and State. An irresponsible Household
government stood behind a King who had broken every oath, and
repudiated every public adviser.

Yet many times the Charter had been confirmed, and last in 1253,
when bishops and barons dashed their candles on the ground in token
that its violators should smoke in hell. Daily, fed from many rivulets, the
ideal gained ground that consent was the essence of government, and
that what touches all must be approved by all; in academic teaching
from Grosseteste and friars, representative chapters of Dominicans and
Austin Canons, or Bracton's doctrine of the common law. But the
Charter, which the barons were long content to reiterate, was concerned
with legal rights, not political control.

By 1238 they had already moved far forward, asking in that year, or
soon after, for the election of a standing Council, restraints on expenditure, and amendment of the Charter. For the next fifteen years,
returning to the practice of the King's minority, they made the public
appointment of officials their minimum demand. From the Gascon
campaign of 1253 onwards they refused money grants, the knights
summoned next year followed suit, even the Church would not be bled
further.

To see in this crisis only an insular hatred of aliens misinterprets a
civilization in which the Marshalls still held French fiefs, English
barons invited arbitration from St. Louis, and the same man was mayor
successively of London and Bordeaux; in which, finally, revolution
found its Robespierre in Simon de Montfort, who had come to England,

ignorant of the English tongue, only twenty years before. His father, the brutal conqueror of the Albigenses, was co-heir to the Beaumont earls of Leicester; Simon, his second son, being granted the title in 1231, had found the rich marriage he desired in Henry's sister Eleanor; his reputation was that of yet another foreign adventurer who, as late as the fierce debates of 1238, showed his royalist sympathy. In temper severe and assertive, he ruled his borough of Leicester harshly, he spent much and was always pressing his financial claims, though the King was a generous brother who gave him, with much else, two great castles in Kenilworth and Odiham. Simon did not conceal his contempt for this unstable nature; the King, he was heard to say, ought to be confined at Windsor as an imbecile. Like all his house a warrior, with a great name in the wars of Palestine and Poitou, he had also their stern orthodoxy, which made him a persecutor of Jews and a devout churchgoer, and their high standard of education. This brought him into close touch with the Franciscans, their Oxford leader Adam Marsh, and bishop Grosseteste.

His turning-point came in 1248 when Henry committed to him for seven years, with sovereign powers, the government of Gascony, where law and order had not been known for a century. Within a year he seemed to have triumphed. He renewed the truce with France, conciliated Navarre, stormed and refortified strategic castles, crushed city factions, and broke up the bandit-gangs who pillaged by night and destroyed trade. But he used fire and sword. He imprisoned nobles without trial, extorted unprecedented military service and ransoms, imposed the rule of his own partisans. A torrent of complaint reached England, and after many waverings Henry ordered a hearing in his court. Here King and Earl quarrelled finally, shouting at each other 'traitor', 'unChristian', 'liar'. Against the will of the baronage Henry removed Simon from office, with an ill grace repaid his expenses, and in 1253 went to Gascony himself. Next year the young Prince Edward married Eleanor of Castile and took the province over, ruling it with a success which is perhaps the best condemnation of Simon's severity. The Earl, despite occasional appearances in royal service and more grants from the Crown, was a declared enemy, as he showed when in the Parliament of 1254 he opposed Henry's demand for subsidies.

In April 1258 a small body, with Leicester, Gloucester, and Norfolk at their head, forced Henry to promise execution of the reforms advised by a committee of twenty-four, half chosen by his Council and half by the baronage. In June, at the Dominican convent at Oxford, a city like an armed camp, the committee presented its programme. Just as in the first year of the Long Parliament of 1641, all England except a few courtiers agreed on fundamentals. The twenty-four chose a standing Council of fifteen, by whose advice Henry must act.

Each year there must be three ' Parliaments ', at which twelve chosen by the baronage for the ' community ' would meet Council, while a third committee would discuss taxation. The new government named a chancellor, treasurer, exchequer staff, and chief justice, all to hold office for a year. Chancery must issue no writs ' out of course ', save by leave of the Council. All revenues must come into the Exchequer. The Household should be reformed. Sheriffs must be landowners of their shire, and hold office only a year. In each county court four knights should hear complaints, especially against sheriffs, and prepare hearings for the chief justice.

In the turbulence of the next seven years, which decided the fate of these reforms, we can see six principal political groupings. The King was the weakest, with no personal following except a few faithful clerks, now that the barons had expelled his Poitevin brethren. But there were still royal prerogatives to be recaptured, Papal influence to be used, and old sentiment for the Crown. His brother Richard, who was now an Emperor without an Empire, though amiably striving for peace, fought for the King when it came to civil war.

A much more vital figure was Edward, the heir-apparent. He was now nineteen years old, six feet two, and the picture of a prince, devoted to tournaments, the idol of all young knights. He was bitterly opposed to the reformers, if not to the reforms, tried to save his Lusignan uncles from banishment, and conceived an undying hatred of the Londoners, who had mobbed his mother with stones and obscene abuse. But his two principalities, Chester and Gascony, gave him new responsibilities and contacts, he was learning to wait till the tide turned, and to help it to turn, until at length he emerged as the subtlest politician of them all.

Against his youth rose the mature hardened strength of de Montfort, fifty years old, deep-graved with earthly and spiritual strife, bent on the one purpose of ending the rule of the King. At close quarters few Englishmen could work with him long as an equal, nor was his personal following numerous in the lesser baronage. But he had friends, like Walter Cantelupe bishop of Worcester, or Hugh Despenser, who would die for him, together with the unwavering sympathy of most of the clergy and the mass of the people of London.

Scrutinizing and manipulating these English factions stood Llewelyn of Wales, while midway hovered the Marcher barons, Bohuns and Mortimers and Cliffords, fearful alike of Llewelyn and of Edward, the greatest Marcher of them all. And here, linking the March to the heart of England, was the house of Clare, earls of Gloucester, lords of Glamorgan, with five hundred knights' fees, whose present head was Richard, great-grandson of Strongbow, grandson of Marshall the Regent, son of one of the twenty-five of 1215, and stepson of Richard of

Cornwall. Since the Gascony scandal of 1252 he with de Montfort had led the opposition; whose downfall was to come when they parted company.

Gloucester stood nearer not to the Marchers only, but to the average baron, who wished to shackle the King without a civil war, and who was proud of his rank and antagonistic to radical reform. The first effect of war was a drift towards the Crown; the Bohuns were divided, and among those who left de Montfort were men as enlightened as Hugh Bigod, the first justiciar appointed in 1258. But the deciding force would be the middle class, the knights, gentry, and merchants, most trained in government and the first to suffer from bad administration; whose grievances, treasure, and sympathies would settle this clash of ambitions and ideals.

The constructive achievement of revolution was crowded into this single year 1258–9. The new Council ejected the hated Poitevins, stopped the drain of money to Sicily, and made a settlement in Scotland. A year's negotiation ended in the peace of Paris by which, in return for the surrender of English claims upon Normandy, Maine, Anjou, and Poitou, Louis IX gave up his rights in Limousin, Quercy, and Périgord. Meantime regular ' parliaments ' met, the Exchequer again controlled the Household, Hugh Bigod, armed with summary powers, went on circuit to hear the grievances presented by elected knights, and the Council chose sheriffs from names submitted by the county courts.

Harmony came to an end over the question of wider reform. Some matters touched all landowners: sheriffs' fines, abuse of feudal ' incidents ', or violations of the Forest charter. Smaller men complained that great men's courts had demanded increased services, and produced before Bigod's circuit cases of oppression, even of torture and murder, against the magnates' stewards, not excluding Gloucester. In 1259, accepting the principle that what the King gave them they would give to their under-tenants, the Council after angry debate conceded the edicts known as the Provisions of Westminster.

Their legal clauses, which became part of the permanent law, curbed the power of local officials, and killed the already dying hold of feudal courts over free tenants. By the far more drastic and controversial administrative clauses, elected county knights were to nominate the sheriffs and take oaths from every manorial bailiff, and between the visits of itinerant justices would form a standing judicial committee. Powers at the centre were concentrated in the same way. Six circuits of councillors were to hold a special eyre, barons were to sit with the judges of Common Pleas and no unofficial baron must attend a parliament without summons. Councillors, changed each session, were always to attend the King, whose Household and Exchequer were to be reformed by baronial committees.

It was not to be expected that all the Council would approve this destruction both of royal prerogative and feudal independence; lawyers and conservatives complained that even cases of freehold were being polished off by summary process, without indictment or writ. A bitter quarrel soon raged over the whole arena. Simon accused Gloucester of apostasy, Gloucester accused Simon of obstructing the peace of Paris by his personal grievances, and both charges were half-true. And when a child could have divided these two leaders, it was easy for Prince Edward.

By 1261 civil war seemed certain. Henry appealed to the baronage at large against a small junto who made him their servant, enforced arbitrary law, deprived him of his seals and wardships. He got the Pope to dispense him from his oaths. He seized the fortresses. Royal and baronial sheriffs contested the counties, each side summoning knights to their own ' parliaments '. But there were still enough moderate men to make a compromise, on the basis of keeping but amending the Provisions. Though they would let some questions like the choice of sheriffs go to arbitration, they would not swallow Henry's denunciation of de Montfort, and the legal reforms of 1259 were put in force.

Only de Montfort, without ceasing, preached no compromise. A Parliament, he argued, must meet whether Henry was present or not, and only full control of power would fulfil their pledges to the community. Rather than acquiesce in concession, in September 1261 he left this ' coward ' country, as he called it, for France; events of the next year induced him to strike. His enemy Gloucester died, leaving a son Gilbert, who was an ardent reformer; and the last few years' excitement had brought new classes into politics. In London especially, under a democratic mayor, they were asserting themselves against the aldermen; movements of ' bachelors ' and ' leagues of youth ' appeared in other cities. All these, with the Oxford students and many young knights, looked to the great reformer, whom their ballads urged to stand firm, and to show himself (as his name tokened) a strong rock in a faithless land. And there was another urgent motive for action. Prince Edward was forming a party, particularly among the Marchers who were heavily pressed by the Welsh, and including Bohun and Mortimer, two of the original fifteen.

Early in 1263 de Montfort, announcing that, while he believed the King's good intentions, some of his Council were incorrigible, returned to England, and began war against those who would not keep the Provisions in full. In concert with Llewelyn, his friends pillaged the middle west. Boniface and Peter of Savoy, most moderate of the aliens, were expelled, while the most hated of them, the bishop of Hereford, was assassinated at his cathedral altar. The London mob massacred the Jews and looted. There were fierce attacks on any who could not speak

English, with many assaults and confiscations. By the autumn English opinion, outside London and the Cinque Ports, though loyal to the Provisions, was antagonized by de Montfort and his violent allies; in December both sides accepted the arbitration of St. Louis which, in January 1264, while safeguarding all previous liberties, declared the Provisions null and void, upholding Henry's right of appointing to office whomever he liked, native or alien. De Montfort at once repudiated his word and renewed war.

Thus opened the last act of revolution; when a spirit of revenge almost crushed those who wished for peace, and idealists had so far become partisans that they had adopted dictatorship and class war.

No magnates of the first rank fought for de Montfort except Gloucester and Norfolk, and the north in particular was hostile, Bruces and Balliols fighting in the royal army; while against the archers of his Welsh allies must be set the Marchers. His cause really depended on what, like Cromwell, he might have called the ' poor godly people ', the lesser landowners, the townsmen or the Oxford novices who had already taken up arms, and its heart was London. Making the city's defence his military objective, he drew the royalists southwards into Sussex, whence they hoped to blockade the capital and make connection with France. Hence came about, on the 14th May 1264, the battle of Lewes, where Simon's admirable tactics crushed the over-confident royalists; King and prince, London and the south, were all in his hands. The Mise of Lewes, signed after the battle, agreed to refer a permanent peace to French arbitration; Edward and his cousin Henry of Almaine being surrendered to Simon as hostages. But a month later the Earl submitted to a Parliament, including knights of the shire, a drastic ' provisional ' scheme. This named three electors, — de Montfort, his friend the bishop of Chichester, and Gloucester, — to choose a Council of nine, who would have been not only the King's advisers but a Council of regency; without them Henry might do nothing, but by a majority they could act in his absence. This constitution was to continue until the Mise was fully executed.

In short, if Simon had ever meant to compromise, he had changed his mind. Negotiations proceeded just enough to appease the moderates and keep France quiet, but in August the new scheme, with the Provisions of Westminster, was declared valid until the end of Henry's life. Though for another month or two moderates went on struggling for a return to the Mise, their efforts broke upon Simon's firmness and the hostility of the Papacy. The legate who ordered the bishops to excommunicate Simon was refused admission to England and his bulls were thrown into the sea, while those Churchmen who followed de Montfort appealed to a general Council. The provisional government, therefore, continued, though only ruthless force could save it, and was solemnly confirmed in the unusually full Parliament of January 1265. New keepers were appointed to the shires, government took a tithe from the clergy, and commandeered the wool supply. Simon himself took charge of the castles of Bristol and the Peak, Corfe and Bamborough, at the same time receiving all Edward's Welsh and Cheshire territory, while his sons governed Devon and Cornwall, Norfolk, Surrey, and Dover.

Danger came to this government not from abroad, for St. Louis had no aggressive purpose, but from the fact that it only stood for a little minority in England. We see that best from the composition of the famous Parliament just mentioned, with its short list of 23 barons, the portentous number of 120 clerics, and the direct summons to carefully selected boroughs to send representatives. Adapting the growing customs of the King's Court, he thus summoned classes and districts on which he could depend, but it was not a body which could speak for the country. And the very lawlessness of his supporters showed his weakness. All over England there was organized robbery of prominent royalists, especially judges and former sheriffs, armed bands seizing their manors or cutting down their woods, while a lucrative trade flourished in stolen goods. His own son Simon was a notorious law-breaker, hot in pursuit of heiresses and forcibly disturbing manor courts.

Meantime, within fifty miles of London, a royal garrison continuously held Pevensey, and the Marchers, though ordered into exile, had never laid down their arms. Against them Simon used a desperate remedy, making himself Earl of Chester and repaying Llewelyn's military assistance by promising to confirm all his conquests. This threat finally alienated his only Marcher friend, the young Gloucester, whose quarrel sprang, however, from more things than the March. His whole later life proved loyalty to the Provisions, but like his father he would not bow to de Montfort's autocracy, for Simon after all had evaded the Mise of Lewes and kept the King a prisoner, broken the agreement with Edward over Chester, given his own sons the keys of the kingdom, packed the Council with his creatures, and filled fortresses with foreign mercenaries.

The game was up. Early in 1265 Gloucester took shelter in south Wales, where Mortimer joined him; in May Simon with his royal captives reached Hereford, and each side struck its blow. Edward was now so far free as to be allowed some hunting with his guards; with whose connivance he escaped, joined Gloucester's party, and swore that his father should rule henceforward through the good laws and a council of Englishmen. All the middle west fell into his hands, his allies barring de Montfort from England at each crossing of the Severn. De Montfort's counterstroke was desperate, to recognize Llewelyn as overlord of Wales and to promise him more lordships even on English soil; and not desperate only but unsuccessful, for the Welsh chieftains would not leave their hills. After an effort to cross the Bristol Channel and a long detour through Wales, at the end of July he was back again at Hereford. All this time no real help had reached him from south-eastern England, where even London was beginning to conspire. At last his son Simon made his way to Kenilworth, and since Edward marched off to confront him, the Earl was able to cross the Severn. On the morning of 2nd August Edward and Gloucester, having routed young Simon's army, got back to Worcester and on the same night Simon, knowing nothing of this, entered Evesham. Here early next morning the enemy fell upon him, in the narrow isthmus made by the Avon as it loops round the town, with no chance of retreat since Mortimer had seized the only bridge, and with inferior numbers. He saw that the time was come to die ' for God and the just cause '; while his Welsh followers fled through the orchards and a thunderstorm made the morning dark as night, the Earl and the few left faithful (Justiciar Hugh Despenser among them) met their end.

The Marchers' troops savagely mutilated his body, sending his head on a pike to the wife of Mortimer. But there were those in Church and people who would not be robbed of one who, they felt, was a martyr; the righteous Earl was soon said to be working miracles, and faithful Franciscans composed liturgies in his praise. A people's instinct may be accepted as some certificate of character, and if we knew nothing more of Earl Simon, we could be sure of his religious sincerity, undying courage, and power of inspiring men. But this does not mean that his opponents were all selfish or class-conscious, nor can history allow him a vision of democracy. He was neither the first nor the last great man to seek power remorselessly for righteous ends, to antagonize friends by his temper, or to destroy the distant good by a short-cut way of force.

The first evil effect of his fall was the fate of his supporters. While the King distributed their estates, his partisans evicted Montfortians, declaring null and void the sales and contracts of the last two years. As part of the reprisals London lost its liberties and was ruled by a royal keeper, while the Pope suspended four bishops.

Refusing a tame submission, the ' disinherited ' flew to arms. Young Simon's men held the impregnable keep of Kenilworth, his mother held Dover, others set up armed camps in the Fens, the Cinque Ports took to piracy, while riots prevented recovery of the revenue. Edward, now the real head of the State, realized that to stamp out one ember after another would not extinguish the flame, or save the country from a worse danger, a civil war in which Gloucester, assisted by the Welsh, would resist the extreme reactionaries led by Mortimer. Hence, the moderate counsels of the Pope and St. Louis assisting, came about the Dictum of Kenilworth (October 1266), with redemption of property as its principle instead of confiscation. All who had taken sides with de Montfort could recover their lands on paying a fine varying with the offence, from the five years' value paid by the most guilty down to the one year's taken from those who had been compelled to serve.

But the Dictum annulled the Provisions of Oxford, legal restoration was difficult, and Mortimer's faction was trying to make it harder. In April 1267 Gloucester marchèd on London, with the disinherited from all quarters, and this armed protest brought the government to pardon the last rebels at Ely, and to put a new spirit into the settlement. Before the year ended a special eyre began its long task of deciding equitably on hundreds of disputed properties, while the Statute of Marlborough confirmed the legal victory which the middle class had won in 1259.

For the rest of Henry's reign the judges were still working out this compromise, though once or twice the flames flickered up again, as in 1271 at Viterbo, when Simon and Guy de Montfort murdered Henry of Almaine while hearing Mass. Necessity forced a peace with Wales, admitting Llewelyn as prince and overlord, and leaving him nearly all he had won from de Montfort. The good legate Ottobon, who had done much for peace, issued canons to reform the shattered Church, money from the clergy also enabling more of the disinherited to redeem their homes. The Londoners recovered their right of electing a mayor. The King busied himself with the opening of his new Westminster Abbey, and by 1270 normality was so far restored that Edward could leave the country on a crusade.

In 1268 died Henry Bracton, of late sitting as a judge on the claims of the disinherited; whose book was at once accepted as a classic. English law, he taught, must be found in formal assizes and writs; judgment depended upon previous decisions of the court, whose solemn rulings no royal writ might supersede, and by which even the King himself was bound. This, perhaps, was the true conclusion to the thirty years' troubles.

CONTEMPORARY DATES

1213　Pedro II of Aragon, fighting for the Albigenses, killed at Muret.

1214　Battle of Bouvines.

1215　The Lateran Council.

1216　Honorius III approves the Dominican Order.

1218　Amiens Cathedral begun.

1220, onwards.　Building of Salisbury Cathedral.

1225　Guillaume de Loris' *Roman de la Rose*.

1226–70　Reign of Louis IX (St. Louis).

1233   Founding of the Papal Inquisition.
1238   Mongols take Moscow.
1240   Gregory IX proclaims a crusade against Frederick II.
1241   Origins of the Hanseatic League.
1243–54 Pope Innocent IV.
1245   Council of Lyons.
1249–50 St. Louis in Egypt.
1250   Death of Frederick II.
1251   Ottokar of Bohemia takes Austria.
1252–82 Alfonso X (the Wise) rules in Castile.
1260   Kubla Khan establishes Mongol dynasty (–1368) in
        China.
1261   Michael Palaeologus destroys the Latin Empire at
        Constantinople.
1264   Founding of Merton College, Oxford.
1265   Birth of Dante.
1266   Charles of Anjou kills Manfred at Benevento.
c. 1270   Thomas Aquinas completes his *Summa Theologiae*.
1271, onwards.   The Venetian Marco Polo journeys in Asia.

CHAPTER VI

EDWARD I, 1272–1307

IN 1300 the mediaeval life of Europe was old and, before another century passed, new stresses brought it to an end. The Papacy was driven into a seventy years' exile, while heresy and schism rent the seamless robe. The Empire sank to a German princedom. Ottoman Turks attacked the Mediterranean, on which had turned Italian wealth and all principal trade routes. Feudal and municipal government proved incapable of satisfying larger and more unified populations. International trade brought division of labour, riches and poverty, glut and scarcity. A money system replaced labour services, undermining the customs of manor and gild. Such political and economic change demanded a central authority in the State. From the conflict and bloodshed which these things entailed upon Europe, fortunate England escaped with a minimum of upheaval, having attained, in the century before they reached a climax, a government and economic system strong and self-developing enough to take her through them.

Thus the three Edwards' reigns (and Edward III's leadership ended about 1360) form a single epoch, though divided by stages which were due in large part to causes outside England, — French nationality or a decadent Papacy, Scottish revolt or economic strain. But though Bannockburn was not all the fault of Edward II nor the glories of Crécy all due to his son, in a mediaeval State we have first to reckon with the King.

Later generations made unreal claims for Edward I, as the conscious founder of Parliament, or de Montfort's heir. He was, indeed, a high type of prince, a pattern of most things which the Middle Ages admired. His towering figure, straight as a dart, even when his thick hair was white, was that of a knight hardened by self-discipline, of the stag-hunter or the lover of tournaments who held feasts modelled on Arthur's Round Table ; ready to share, when besieged in Conway or bivouacking under Scottish rain, the last crust with his soldiers. He was hard, chaste, and devout, his wife was the same, to whom he was ever faithful, and whom he commemorated by the Eleanor crosses that mark her body's resting-places from Lincoln to Charing Cross. He had every gift of political efficiency, was determined to rule, and to make law prevail. His will and endurance were of iron. His mastery of detail was admirable. He created and kept loyal servants. Believing in the righteousness of his aims, he was ready to make them public and expectantly invited the co-operation of his subjects.

There was another side, however, to the knightly shield. He had some rough ways of the camp, would box the ears of his grown-up children, and tear the lead off a church to make ammunition. With a fixed principle of giving all men their rights, he would especially keep his own, and for this would break his vows. He had a limited amount of compassion or sympathy, and when he was crossed threw restraint to the wind. After many years he ended by laying upon England an intolerable burden: of simultaneous war with France, Scotland, and Wales, baronage and Church discontented, and finances in collapse.

It is proof of a great man to harness all the talents in his service, and Edward's agents were of every type. Like his ancestors, his chief confidence went to Churchmen trained in his Household, pre-eminently to the genial, grasping, and worldly Shropshireman Burnell, chancellor until his death in 1292, and thereafter to the more crooked bishop Walter Langton, but he received devoted service also from Lacy earl of Lincoln, the Italian lawyer Accursi, Valence earl of Pembroke, and his chief justice Hengham. Throughout he continued the practice, common since 1254, of calling knights and townsmen to the ' parliaments ' or full sessions of Council. But just as he summoned knights learned in the law to consider his statutes, or merchants to examine his customs duties, so he always selected any ingredients for a Parliament as he wished; at one moment knights only, at another merchants, at a third councillors and barons, but now and then used all together and the clergy also. Though the heart of government was in its old place, namely, the small council of officials and Household servants, the great works of his prime, the recasting of the law or the conquest of Wales, were managed in the light of day, at the bar of public opinion.

His greatest claim on our gratitude is doubtless the mass of legal reform, accomplished mostly before 1290, in volume greater than any save that of Henry VIII, and in its effect as enduring. Its character was conservative, setting out from Henry II's principles, but it absorbed the remedies found out by lawyers and administrators of the intervening generations, and readjusted an old feudal framework to a changing society.

Many royal rights and old landmarks had gone by the board in the revolutionary years, and Edward's first step was a searching enquiry. This Eyre of 1274 resulted in something like another Domesday Book and another inquest of sheriffs. Juries reported on the King's rights and estates, the encroachment upon them, the conduct of his officers, and all things that impeded justice; from which, and other later enquiries, we derive the information known as the Hundred Rolls. His action upon them went beyond parliamentary statutes, which were hardly as important as his administrative writs, or his judges' rulings, nor is it possible at this date to distinguish the sources of legislation. It is best to take these reforms *en masse*, grouped rather under broad effect than by official origin.

Much was done, in the first place, to bring the law up to date. To this age we owe the definition of our legal actions; necessary distinctions between crime and misdemeanour, notions of trespass and larceny, the first law of conspiracy. The whole scheme of land tenure, now riddled by alienation and subdivision, had to be overhauled; Henry II's summary protection of seisin was amended to give fair treatment to tenants, trustees, distant heirs, and to all other interests which spring up in an advanced civilization.

A second class of reform dealt with the offences of royal servants; forbade the corrupt ' maintenance ' of lawsuits by judges or sheriffs, ordered freedom in local elections, or admitted a scheme of royal writs, elastic without becoming arbitrary.

A third rearranged the courts of law. The Statute of Westminster II (1285), for instance, fixed thrice-yearly assizes, and began the *nisi prius* system, whereby most civil actions would be heard ' previously ' by assize judges, and parties and jurors were saved weary journeys to London. Another statute of 1278 was so interpreted as to confine the county courts to actions not involving over 40s. And the King's Bench was becoming a professional court, separate from the Council.

Another series of measures was designed to stop the lawlessness and corruption which marked the reign of this great lawgiver. More than once Edward replaced the whole set of sheriffs, while in 1289, after three years' absence abroad, he found his highest courts badly tainted. The Chamberlain of the Exchequer (whose salary was 8d. a day) had made a fortune of £50,000, the King removed six out of eight judges from the Bench, and nearly eight hundred officials were accused. Experiments showed that he was feeling his way towards the justice of the peace, to supersede the sheriff. At the end of the reign, to break up gangs of discharged soldiers and ' clubmen ' who were robbing travellers, he set up temporary judges of ' trailbaston '.

The Statute of Winchester (1285), which codified the system of police and defence, illustrated his determination to use all resources, quite regardless of feudal tenure. Juries had failed to suppress crime, neighbours would not convict each other, or were afraid to accuse a powerful owner. The act, therefore, made every village, hundred, and franchise liable in damages for felony; both hundreds and private franchises were to choose constables who must hold a twice-yearly view of arms, preparing the muster-rolls for the King's wars. Property owners must clear the main roads, so that for two hundred feet on each side no ditch or underwood could conceal bandits. Every man under sixty must have arms according to his wealth, from the full-armed horseman down to the poorest with his bow and arrows. Constables must report offences to knights specially assigned, who in their turn must answer to the King in Parliament.

Every measure showed Edward's purpose, not to break up old forms but fit them into a wider scheme. For feudal taxation and service were increasingly unsatisfactory. The baronage wrangled over their liability to scutage, or the number of fiefs on which it fell, would not serve over forty days, and objected to service abroad. London, like all towns, hated tallage: the arbitrary tax which treated them like serfs on the royal farms. More and more Edward had recourse to general property taxes agreed in Parliament, which under the name of ' a tenth and fifteenth ' became the standard for the next two hundred years. He constantly compelled all those, whose-ever tenants, who held land worth £20 a year to take up knighthood or pay a fine, and though in war he could not dispense with the great lords, used their men as part of a professional army. The old quotas were scaled down, the great Lancaster fief, for instance, which in old days had sent over 250 knights, now producing about 50. On the other hand, Edward expected a continuous service for which, after the customary forty days had expired, he would pay, and brigaded the contingents as he wished.

In so far as feudalism was simply a form of property, Edward not only admitted but supported it. If his assizes heard tenants in protest against increased service, they equally protected lordly rights on prickly questions like the use of commons, while on the deepest influence upon a nation, the way in which its land is held, his law determined English society for six centuries. As chief landowner he shared his barons' interest in preserving escheats, marriages, and all feudal rights, the loss of which, through sub-infeudation, had been a grievance since Magna Carta. Now there were two conflicting tendencies at work ; a steady support from the lawyers for free distribution of land, as against the royal and feudal feeling which disliked the splitting up of fiefs. These last so far triumphed that no land until Henry VIII's reign might be dealt with by the owner's last will, but Edward's laws reached a compromise on the question of disposal during the owner's lifetime. The Act *De Donis* (1285) protected entail and family settlement, a far-reaching principle which, not always for good, kept blocks of land in the hands of large owners despite treason and revolution. *Quia Emptores* (1290), on the contrary, fixed for ever a freedom of alienation *inter vivos*. Henceforward, if B. for example, a sub-tenant broken by debt, wished to dispose of land to C., he must sell it outright, and not create a new sub-tenure ; C. would thus step into B.'s place as regards A., the chief lord ; in other words, no new manor in fee simple could henceforth be created. In the end, the King as chief landowner must benefit ; as families died out, the feudal ladder, unable now to push new rungs downwards, must move towards him, more freeholders must become his immediate tenants, and, moreover, the freedom of alienation, which he thus encouraged lower down, he entirely forbade to his tenants-in-chief.

As one form of landed estate, or a means of getting public work done without royal expense, Edward gave feudal tenures a new lease of life, but destroyed their power of growth and attacked their political privilege. Following upon the Eyre, he issued as a universal scheme, what previous sovereigns had occasionally used, writs of *Quo warranto*, demanding by what right each tenant-in-chief held courts or services. His judges ruled, and a statute of 1290 confirmed them, that court leets, views of frankpledge, and private hundreds were ' regalities ', whose existence must be justified either by charter or by a tenure time out of mind, — Richard I's coronation being taken as the deciding date of legal memory.

Such enquiries, and Edward's attack on Marcher privilege, estranged him from the mightiest earls of his early years. He resolved to absorb them into the royal family. He made Gloucester marry his daughter Joan, tying up his lands upon her heirs ; the younger Hereford married another daughter on the same terms. The Bigod fiefs lapsed to the Crown, Cornwall had fallen in too, Edward's nephew Thomas of Lancaster married the last Lacy heiress of Lincoln. In due course we shall see the fatality of this scheme, which encircled the King within a narrow ring of potentate-kinsmen.

Against the feudatories a mere tactician might have leaned for support upon the towns and clergy. But not so Edward I. He was indeed aware of the importance of trade. In 1275 he got from Parliament a permanent duty on wool, later known as the ' great customs ' ; in 1303 by agreement with foreign traders he took additional duties, especially on wine and cloth. He legislated for the better recovery of merchants' debts. He built and privileged many ' bastides ', or walled boroughs, in Gascony and Wales. But he was on bad terms with London, which for thirteen years he deprived of its mayor, partly, no doubt, because he insisted on better terms for alien merchants. Nor was he a thrifty or economically-minded king. His taxes and seizures of raw material in wartime were outrageous. His religious orthodoxy led him first to persecute the Jews, and then to turn them out of England and Aquitaine and, though this was popular, he financed himself later through Christian usurers, at least as grasping. And though townsmen were called so often to his parliaments, they were called to pay taxes and kept in the background.

The double rôle of the Church in regard to Rome and English opinion was severely tested in his reign. Triumphant over the Empire,

the Papacy was intoxicated with power ; its organization pressed heavily
on the growing nations, and embarrassed its most devoted sons. Two
friars in succession received the archbishopric of Canterbury against
Edward's desire, and one of them, the learned and controversial Franciscan Pecham, challenged the very character of the State. Church
councils ordered excommunication of those who procured common-law
writs to prohibit Church courts' proceedings, and claimed sole jurisdiction over patronage and the clergy's goods ; a new copy of Magna
Carta must be posted every year on the church doors. The archbishop
thrust himself forward as arbitrator between England and Wales, and
warned Edward that his soul was in danger if he preferred his own law
to that of the universal Church.

A first answer came in the statute of Mortmain, which forbade all
men without royal licence to give, or bequeath, land to the ' dead hand '
of a religious body. Edward's judges prosecuted clerics who had drawn
borderline questions, such as debts or contracts, into the Church courts.
Finally, in 1286 a writ (*Circumspecte agatis*), making some concession,
defined the province which was left to those courts up to the Reformation ; that is, moral sins, neglected churches and churchyards,
mortuaries, tithes up to a fixed proportion, wills and marriages, and
some cases of slander.

Yet even if the laity had been willing to observe this difficult frontier,
larger questions remained. Edward was a hard taskmaster. His
officials encouraged pluralism, chief justice Hengham alone holding
fourteen benefices. His demands for money were crushing. In 1291
Nicholas IV allowed him one-tenth of clerical wealth for six years, for
which purpose a new and permanent assessment was taken by Papal
commissioners. Three years later Edward asked half the clergy's income
under threat of outlawry, at the same time commandeering their wool.

That year two new personalities entered the field, Pope Boniface
VIII and archbishop Winchelsey. The Church was now reaping the
harvest of the past century. French princes whom she had called in
against the Emperors were mastering Italy, while a dire conflict between
these Angevins and Aragon raged for Naples and Sicily. A ruthless
French king, Philip the Fair, was threatening the French Church, as
Edward was the English. Murderous Guelf-Ghibelline vendettas made
a horror of Tuscany, Dante cherishing hopes of a new Emperor to
cleanse the abominations of Rome. Permanent Papal tax-gatherers
battened on each national church ; had not an abbot of St. Albans spent
10,000 florins to ratify his election ? A deep loathing of the priesthood
was arising from Papal centralization and its hunt for gold. The Franciscan left-wing was turning rebel, and various interests had this very
year raised up a hermit saint as Pope Celestine V. But Rome recovered
this lapse, the hermit abdicated, and Boniface VIII, a canonist, a noble,

of biting tongue and clear ambition, reigned in his stead; bent upon making his family an Italian power, and the Pope a true sovereign. Determined to protect the clergy from the State's extortion, in 1296 he issued the bull *Clericis Laicos*, which forbade the Church to pay taxes without Papal assent. The new archbishop Winchelsey was the free choice of the Canterbury chapter, a secular priest learned enough to have been Rector of the University of Paris, and a great preacher. He was to show himself neither non-patriotic nor non-conciliatory, but he put Rome before his country, and though a Franco-Scottish alliance was menacing, obeyed the bull and refused taxation. Edward thereupon declared the clergy outlaw. So began his last ten years, of storm without ceasing, with strain of his people's loyalty and his own character. He had lost his wife and Burnell; his son was to disappoint him.

The storm blew hardest from France, fast growing now from the foundations laid by Philip Augustus. Before Philip III died he had taken over the direct government of Poitou and Toulouse, and married his successor to the heiress of Navarre. His overweening uncle, Charles of Anjou and Naples, pursued schemes for the conquest of Aragon, and even of the Empire, while the Count of Flanders was a French vassal, who might be supported against his wealthy cities. As in the age of Louis XIV, Frenchmen saw visions of France controlling Europe.

For twenty years Edward faced these stretching ambitions. He had seen the Sicilian Vespers wipe out the French hold on Sicily, and Philip III die in a crusade against Aragon. Under his influence loomed up our future alliance-system against France; Castile and Aragon, the German states, and any Netherland princes who could be bought. He had used French misfortunes to win his wife's inheritance, — Ponthieu on the Somme. More important, he made real progress in solving the intricacies left by the Paris treaty of 1259. While he yielded his claims on Limousin, Périgord, and Quercy, the French in return handed over southern Saintonge, which prolonged his Gascon coastline north of the Garonne, and Agenais which commanded that river's upper water.

But since Frenchmen must covet the whole soil of France, their attitude to Gascony depended not on treaty but circumstances, and these pointed to war. Germany was in weak hands. Wales and Scotland crippled English striking power. Philip the Fair's advisers, mostly southerners from the regions of Roman law, were preaching a centralized State; as for pretexts, they grew on every bush, whether fiefs on the Gascon frontier or fighting between Gascon and Norman sailors. In 1294 Philip summoned his vassal to his Court; Edward, his hands already full at home, agreed to marry Philip's sister and surrendered fortresses as security, but the French, with extreme ill-faith, invaded Gascony in force.

With great resolution Edward set himself to eliminate his enemies. The Welsh revolt of 1294 took a year to suppress, but his heart was set on crushing Scotland, and for this he would compromise with France and Rome. Fortune favoured him. The Flemish cities rose against France and at Courtrai in 1302 showed that they could destroy the French chivalry. And then France and the Papacy attacked each other. Boniface VIII's wild temper rose after the Jubilee of 1300 almost to insanity; he answered Philip's brutal treatment of the French Church by a series of bulls, culminating in *Unam Sanctam*, which declared there was but one fold and one shepherd, and one moral order of which the Pope was judge. The response was the creation of the Estates-General, the seizure of the Pope by French officers, and his death; in 1305 a Gascon Pope took up residence in France, thus beginning a seventy years' captivity at Avignon and ending the mediaeval Church. Meantime Boniface's declaration that Scotland was a Papal fief roused English patriotism into the parliamentary protest of 1301. From this course of events Edward was able to win first a truce, then his own French marriage, and another for his son Edward with Philip's daughter. The truce of 1303 restored Gascony, and the same year saw an apparent end of resistance in Scotland. But all this had taken him nine years, for the reason that England itself had turned against him.

His ceaseless inquisitions had offended the magnates, his writs and taxes tried the Church, and in this war period he drove all England together by tyranny; if tyranny it is to pursue one end, at whatever cost to the governed. Merchants' wool was seized and only released for enormous ransom, criminals were conscripted to fight in France; the poorest nunneries and starving benefices were brought into the tax collectors' net. In 1294 the landed classes gave a tenth of their movables, an eleventh and a twelfth in the two next years. Towns and clergy had to disgorge much more. The royal commissariat seized wheat and meat for the army; Yorkshire clergy, for instance, had seen their cattle driven off to Scotland. And all, it seemed, to no purpose. For in 1297 our forces were everywhere defeated. The French held Bordeaux, Wallace held Scotland, Edward's Netherland alliances failed, and he was cooped up in Ghent with a mutinous army.

He had taken a great risk in leaving England at all. With his invariable assurance he put his difficulties before Parliament, protesting he made war not out of vainglory but in their defence; while in moving speeches and circulars he asked forgiveness for the heavy burden put on his people. In vain. In 1297 a more serious opposition than that of the divided clergy rose from the baronage, led by the great Marchers, Bohun the Constable and Bigod the Earl Marshal, whose fathers had championed the Provisions of Oxford. They declared that the law had been broken, that they were being arbitrarily taxed as if they were villeins,

and that no feudal duty bound them to serve in Flanders. Edward
defied them by negotiation with the smaller barons, on whose authority
he levied still more taxes, and ordered out all landowners for service
overseas. The magnates replied by stopping his officials taking war
supplies, the day he sailed for Flanders London welcomed their forces,
and they held armed gatherings in the Midlands.

Their pressure and Winchelsey's mediation had already wrung
from Edward a vague promise to confirm the charters, but they asked
much more. In future the King must not impose taxes at will without
due assent, he must stop forcible seizures, twice a year the clergy should
read this new charter in every parish church. The regency yielded;
omitting mention of tallage, and with a clause saving ' the ancient aids ',
they accepted the *Confirmatio Cartarum*, which in November was
ratified by the King. But the struggle was only beginning.

Prompt grants of supply from barons and clergy showed that, if
assured of Edward's good faith, they would assist his resistance to
France, but their weariness of the Scottish war embittered the King, who
for his part was quibbling over his promises. There were forests,
Exmoor in particular, which he was determined to keep. For years
past dispute had raged over the Forest charter of 1217; did the proviso,
to disafforest all those made since 1154, include woods which Stephen
had let go but which Henry II had regained? Edward persisted with
his reservations and, though forced to accept an enquiry by sworn jurors,
disregarded their verdict. In every parliament opposition grew more
determined. In 1300 *Articuli super Cartas* attacked the arbitrary courts
of the Household and the issue of writs under privy seal. In 1301 a
memorable parliament at Lincoln accused his minister Langton,
demanded clear powers for county knights to protect the charters, and
declared the principle that redress of grievances must precede supply.
Edward sent to the Tower the Lancashire knight who moved this
petition, and seized the estates of his old friend bishop Bek of Durham,
who had joined the opposition.

The King, in fact, died desperate. He financed his policy through
Italians, leasing to one syndicate all the customs. When freed from
French war and relieved by death of his old enemies like Bohun, he
broke the pact of 1297 by taking tallage and finally, like his father,
called Rome to his aid. The Gascon Clement V obliged him by suspending Winchelsey and declaring void all concessions since 1297. The
King was ready to reward this useful assistance, and when his last
Parliament launched out against Papal collectors and provisors, he
ignored them, empowering the nuncio to begin the long-lived Papal tax
known as annates.

On the 6th July of that year, 1307, his iron will dragged him out of
bed for the last time to mount his horse, to attack Robert Bruce. The

next day, at Burgh-on-Sands, he died, firm in the belief that now as always he had done right. Had he not once told Winchelsey ' by God's blood neither Mount Zion nor the walls of Jerusalem shall keep me from defending my rights '? And now Winchelsey was in exile; so was Peter Gaveston, his son's favourite; half the earldoms were in the Crown's power; Wales was conquered; Gascony restored. Surely a little effort would have finished the perjured Scots?

CONTEMPORARY DATES

1273	Rudolf, the first Hapsburg Emperor.
1278	Ottokar of Bohemia killed at battle of the Marchfield;
	the Hapsburgs win Austria and Styria.
	Beginning of S. Maria Novella, Florence.
1282	The Sicilian Vespers.
1285–1314	Reign of Philip the Fair.
1291	The Mamelukes take Acre.
	First beginnings of the Swiss Confederation.
1293	The Ordinances of Justice at Florence.
1294–1303	Pope Boniface VIII.
1294, onwards.	Arnolfo de Cambio building at Florence.
1297	Closing of the Great Council at Venice.
1301	Angevins succeed the Arpad dynasty in Hungary.
1302	First meeting of the French Estates-General.
	Dante exiled from Florence.
1303	The Catalan Company serving at Constantinople.
1305	Clement V begins the Captivity at Avignon.
1306	End of the Premysls dynasty in Bohemia.

CHAPTER VII

THE CONQUEST OF WALES

THE making of Britain necessitated a settlement with Wales, which constituted a double danger on the flank of the State made by the Normans. For there was an unconquered race which assisted every English rebel, and on the Marches a chronic feudal disease.

Since the golden age of Hywel Dda in the tenth century or the struggle of Gruffydd against Harold in the eleventh, Wales had very rarely acted for long as a political unit. For the country was full of princes claiming royal descent, who would employ the dissolvent forces of every generation, whether Danish pirates or Irish mercenaries, to make good their claim. Periodically some great personality of the South, like Rhys ap Tewdwr who stood up to the first wave of Normans, or that other Rhys whom Henry II had made an ally, contrived to hold his ground. Yet both geography and enduring tradition made more usual the supremacy of Gwynedd, which was centred on Anglesey, the nest of Welsh royalty, and could from its mountain massif strike down every valley of strategic importance.

An evil, ever-repeated, rhythm ran through Anglo-Welsh relations. Till 1135 the Norman adventurers advanced, even to Anglesey and Cardigan; from 1135 to 1199 there was a Welsh recovery which Henry II had left almost undisturbed; John divided Wales against itself, but it was reunited by Llewelyn ap Iorwerth of Gwynedd. Before Llewelyn died in 1240 he almost obliterated the English power. Northwards he reconquered all between Conway and Dee, in the centre held the Braose fief of Builth and hanged its owner, Cardigan was his too. No sooner was he dead than jealousies between his descendants enabled the English to win back half of their losses; but then his youngest grandson, Llewelyn ap Gruffydd, in the next twenty years extended Welsh power to its greatest, and by his defiance brought about the destruction of independent Wales. That downfall was in part due to new circumstance, but deeper causes account for this long vacillating history of recovery and defeat.

Nature gave Wales no defensive advantage except the mountain range of Snowdon, and history cursed her with a dreadful weakness. Society was still in a pastoral and tribal stage, tillage for corn was rare outside Anglesey, their fighting-men were scattered over mountain pastures, or ranged river valleys for fish and game. Town life was in effect unknown, they had to import iron for their arms, no commerce filled their war chest. Despite the victories of Gwynedd under the two Llewelyns there were still royal families in Powys and south Wales who held their own by loyal clansmen or English intrigue, so that though a hero might temporarily unite all Welshmen, their permanent loyalties were hereditary and local. The foundations of life were vague and primitive, there was an easy attitude towards marriage and legitimacy, with a land system under which kinsmen held the land in common to the fourth generation. While Henry II's clerks were drawing up the *Dialogus de Scaccario* and scientific writs, the Welsh King still legislated for his own wergild, of ' a hundred cows from each cantref, and a white bull with red ears to each hundred cows, and a plate of gold as broad as his face '.

A spirit which the Saxon could never share breathed in the mountainous watershed where sprang the rivers, Severn and Wye and Usk, Towy and Teifi, that flowed some to peaceful England and some to the Irish Sea ; conquest would not crush, but only concentrate, its savour. In the Welsh songs and legends are the fruits of their history, their early but individual Christianity, their passion for liberty, and an imagination in which remembrance takes the place of deeds. Hereditary harpers sang in elaborated verse of the kings who gave them mead in blue buffalo-horns, their golden torques and white horses. All their glory was war, ' to play ball with Saxons' heads ' ; the last Llewelyn was ' the war wolf ', or ' the Eagle of Snowdon '. Here lay the honour of manhood :

> *Four and twenty sons have been to me,*
> *Wearers of gold chains, leaders of arms ;*

by war for his chieftain a man was judged :

> *The grave will be better than the life of him who sighs,*
> *When the horns call men to the squares of conflict.*

A great sadness attuned their songs of this life, so violently cut short and so dogged by conflict. They breathe perpetual lament for the young men, straight as hazel saplings, — ' short were their lives, long is the grief of those that loved them ' — whose blue blades are rusted, and whose homes are desolate :

> *The hall of Cyndylan pierces me,*
> *To see it without roof, without fire ;*
> *Dead is my chief, myself alive.*

They fed their sorrow on the beauties of nature, drawing metaphors from earth, sky, and sea, and painting in the direct colouring of pure poetry the small white towns, the golden grass, crimson spears, green dawn, and war with shining wing. On this tapestry they made their old leaders once more move and conquer. Cædwalla and Arthur,

Geraint and Kay with Tristan, would come again; the Cymri would drive the Saxons in front of them:

> *When there shall be a bridge on the Taw and another on the Towy,*
> *There will be an end of war.*

Causes inside Wales began to transform, as previously in England, this ancient system. The kings developed a sort of central justice, war and expenditure produced commendation and clientship, the feudal lord and his court. But Wales was not left to its own development, after the English Marchers had warped their politics and diluted their nationality. Round their castles they set up manors, in general divided between the English tenants in the valleys and an outer belt on the hills of Welsh tribute-payers. Their ambitions kept alive Llewelyn's rivals; princes of Powys intermarried with the English Audleys, Corbetts, or Charltons.

And if such conditions help to explain the ups and downs in Welsh politics, much had happened lately to make war inevitable. The extinction of Braose and the Marshalls raised up on the March the power of Mortimer and Bohun, while increasing that of Bigod and Clare. Greater still was the expansion of the Crown. Henry III gave to his son Edward the palatinate of Chester, with Cardigan, Carmarthen, Montgomery, and the chief castles between Usk and Wye, and it was the activity of Edward's officials in forcing tenants to their shire courts, which set Llewelyn off on his warfare.

By the treaty of 1267 he had triumphantly concluded his balancings between the Crown, de Montfort, and the Marchers. Recognized as overlord of all Welsh barons and hereditary Prince of Wales, his territory reached the Dee, touched the Severn at Montgomery, robbed the Mortimers of their lands on the Upper Wye, and included all Brecon. He had, in fact, all Wales, save the struggling new shires and the southern coast which the Normans had never lost.

Though there is nothing surprising in the short life of such a peace, there is much in the completeness of Llewelyn's fall. As in all feudal treaties, there were many properties left over to arbitration, while at Caerphilly, in Glamorgan, Gilbert of Gloucester was building a superb lake fortress which Llewelyn vainly tried to destroy. But Edward was out of England till 1274, and the occasion of war came essentially from the Welsh side. Llewelyn, who was in arrears with his war indemnity, also evaded doing homage; in 1274 his brother David, with the prince of Powys, conspired against him and fled to England. Llewelyn then sent to France for Eleanor de Montfort, whose hand her father, Earl Simon, had promised him ten years before, but her ship was intercepted and she fell into Edward's power. Inflamed by his bards, the Prince thought that he could revive a de Montfort party, at the same time negotiating with Rome that he might be as independent of Canterbury as he was of Westminster.

The war of 1277 showed his weakness and the strength of England, if it were well led. South Wales and Powys abandoned him. Two lines of advance pierced central Wales from Worcester and Carmarthen, a third led by the King moved systematically from Chester, making roads and base camps at each stage, while the fleet cut Llewelyn off from his granary in Anglesey. All roads northwards were full of Cheshire and Gwent archers, carpenters, wood-cutters, miners, crossbowmen from Gascony, and carts with the army's pay. Gwynedd was thus isolated and starved out, and by the treaty of Conway Llewelyn lost all that Wales had won since John's time. The Crown recaptured all the lands between Dee and Conway, setting up David in part of them as a vassal, together with the upper Severn and Wye; Bohun and Mortimer leaped upon their lost fiefs, and south Powys became another English dependant.

It seems that Edward meant to treat Llewelyn henceforward as a friend, for he allowed him to marry Eleanor and remitted his indemnity. But no good will could yoke together Celtic and English civilizations, or clear the disputed ground between Edward's admitted overlordship and the power Llewelyn claimed over some English tenants-in-chief. The treaty promised to the Welsh their old customs, but it was easy even for honourable officials to read English law into those customs, or to argue that Welsh law had become unworkable. And if Welsh chieftains loathed the shire courts, or an appeal to the justiciars that weakened their hold on their tenants, Marchers and Welsh alike selected the brand of law, Welsh or English, most likely to satisfy their particular case. Trial by jury broke up the clan customs, dwellers by the sea were stopped wrecking and plundering ships, new roads and castles hemmed in outlaws of the valleys, while an army of new officials, some of them renegade Welshmen, were in Saxon pay.

In 1282 David appealed to his brother Llewelyn, and they were joined by the surviving princes of the south, which made this, unlike that of 1277, a national war. For over a year Edward concentrated his whole State against Wales, those enemies, as he proclaimed, who had sworn to exterminate the English tongue. Exchequer, King's Bench, and Parliament, all met at Shrewsbury; his army included the greatest names of Gascony, with whom he chased David from the Conway to Cader Idris. But the end was inevitable. In December Llewelyn was killed while attacking the Mortimers; his own countrymen betrayed David who in 1283, after a trial in Parliament, was executed. Llewelyn's head was put on the Tower of London, his only child lived long as an English nun, and Edward undertook to reorganize the conquered country.

The Statute of Wales (1284) was not a union of lands, legislatures, or laws, a task which was reserved for the Welsh house of Tudor. What it did was to stabilize under a new control the existing threefold division of Principality, Welsh princes, and Marcher lordships, though the second division was now confined to the insignificant Powys house round Welshpool, and a small southern dynasty on the Towy. In fact, the one area directly dealt with in the Statute was the Principality, based upon the six counties centred round Chester, Carnarvon, and Cardigan, and cemented by the creation in 1301 of Edward's heir as Prince of Wales.

In these shires the Statute, in effect, created a royal March in applying a mixed law, English in its courts and feudal tenures, yet retaining Welsh tribal areas and limiting trial by jury to cases affecting land. Strong castles at Conway, Carnarvon, and Harlech were its ligaments, while new chartered boroughs colonized with English were meant to fill its arteries with trade.

Last came the Marchers, whose title dated back to the Norman Conquest, whom even Edward could not displace, and whose help, in fact, had been so necessary to his conquest that he rewarded them with new Marcherships — Grey of Ruthin, Lacy, Mortimer of Chirk. Their numbers through subdivision and marriage rose later to over one hundred and thirty, but it was in the great examples, Mortimer of Wigmore, Clare of Gloucester, Bohun of Brecon, Valence of Pembroke, that the political problem consisted, and none in English history has been more dangerous. Claiming to hold by conquest, the Marcher aspired to be a sovereign. No royal writ ran on his land, and no appeal lay from his court to the King's. By the custom of the March he had a right of private war, claiming, too, that arbitration should settle disputes between Marchers.

Of the two dangers, Welsh nationality was much the least. Incessant taxation and conscription caused a serious revolt in 1294, while now and then in the Hundred Years' War we find Welsh knights in the French armies, or French troops landing in Wales. But Wales had neither unity nor resources enough to give much trouble, the Church and commerce diffused English contacts, 10,000 Welsh troops served in Edward's Falkirk campaign, while insistence on ' escheat ' as the penalty of rebellion sapped the clan system. The liberties of the March, on the other hand, were promptly attacked by Edward I, whose acts of Parliament declared him ' sovereign lord '. He taxed the Marchers, imprisoning Clare and Bohun for private war, while on any favourable opportunity the Crown enforced strict feudal rules and offered its protection to under-tenants. Throughout the next century prerogative and the King's peace were declared to override custom, and the Marchers' strength lay now not so much in their peculiar privilege as in their mighty territories in Wales and England. This it was which kept intact the bitter resistance of which we still see the ruins, whether in Mortimer's eyrie at Wigmore or his magnificent palace at Ludlow, or the moated four-square red Valence castle at Goodrich. Only when that power faded would the March fade, and meanwhile it continued to transmit a poison of lawlessness over the Border.

CHAPTER VIII

EDWARD II AND EDWARD III, 1307 TO 1360

IN fifty years humanity revenged itself on the disproportions in Edward's policy. Only a block of sandstone in the Abbey remained of his Scottish imperialism. Unceasing war exposed the weakness of Gascony, protected only by paper guarantees. In England his centralization caused revolution. But salvation was found in three things which he had made his instruments : the royal administrators, the common law, and Parliament.

Unless we banish morals from history, some connection must exist between national fortunes and national character, though to distinguish cause and effect is more hazardous. Lack of character brings about a Bannockburn, and a Bannockburn weakens character yet further. But we cannot fail to be impressed by the dearth of heroic, or even ordinarily honest, men at the head of fourteenth-century England; the good qualities in the country had to fight their way to the upper air.

Character was needed, for the old King left behind a tangle of trouble; arrears of scutage going back twenty years, deficits on the sheriffs' accounts, debts to Italian bankers, constitutional dispute, and war. There were patches of pure despotism in the forests, where foresters could shoot poachers at sight, and where the royal hunting ruined neighbouring farms. The Welsh March was eaten up by hereditary feuds; in the north, burned villages and blank revenues showed the handiwork of the Scots. Edward's legal machine was, indeed, slowly spreading the common law, but it needed constant vigilance to prevent it becoming an engine of oppression, whereby every underling eked out his salary. Coroners asked money for viewing the dead, the sheriff took bribes to release men from jury service, the manorial bailiff had his palm greased by the yeoman who wished to avoid becoming a reeve. Every record tells us of cruelty and suffering : of deep pits where sheriffs threw their prisoners, fines extorted from an illiterate peasantry, and countless murders unpunished.

There were other evils more fundamental. Avignon was sapping the character of the Church. Not only was the Papacy a tool of France but, having lost its Italian revenues, tried to replace them by elaborating the fees, annates, and ' provisions ' which drove to fury every national government and clergy. Its spiritual inspiration ceased. Gone were the days of Edmund Rich and the early Franciscans. In 1312 Philip the Fair forced on the Church the suppression of the Templars, their extermination by torture and burning, and confiscation of their wealth, an iniquity in which Edward II and his bishops meekly followed suit. Yet the defence of liberty against despotism, a struggle in which the Church was becoming unfitted to engage, was the burning question under Edward and his son. Royal judges were arguing that the King was ' prerogative ', the sole source of law; who else should control the administration which the Angevins had raised? Failing the Church, the brunt of resistance fell on the baronage. Brutal and self-seeking many of them were, but the truth remains that they alone were strong enough to make sure that government by consent should not perish from the earth.

Their action was revolutionary, yet like most revolutions began in self-defence. The new King was good-looking, large, and lazy, liked lying late, drank heavily, and delighted in his creature comforts. He had little of his father's religion, and knew no Latin; was proud of his Sussex horses, yet liked even better odd amusements and queer company, thatching or blacksmith work, and associated with minstrels, grooms, and watermen. Temper might drive him into revenge; other serious purpose he had none. Nor was he the only man to breathe again when old Edward died; there were returned exiles like Winchelsey, and new ministers who replaced Walter Langton and the old advisers. The exiles included Peter of Gaveston, who had been brought up with Edward and won his affection.

A foreign favourite had always much to live down, and Gaveston was nothing but an average Gascon knight, courageous, boastful, greedy. The King made him Earl of Cornwall, regent while he went to meet his French wife Isabella, and finally Lieutenant of Ireland when the Council, true to Edward I's wishes, first renewed his exile. He allowed this upstart to carry St. Edward's crown at his coronation, and married him to his own niece. Gaveston paraded the royal affection ostentatiously, using it to enrich his Bordeaux kinsmen in Cornish tin mines or posts in France. He was so foolish as to challenge the magnates to tournaments and jeer at them with nicknames; at Lancaster as ' the play actor ', Pembroke ' Joseph the Jew ', or the fierce Warwick, ' the black dog of Arden '. Three years went by, while Exchequer and Wardrobe rolled up deficits, and Bruce steadily won Scotland; Gaveston was recalled from exile, unchanged. After several warnings the magnates took action in 1310, attended Parliament with armed vassals, and appointed a committee to draw up reforming ordinances. Thus began a period which with many fluctuations lasted till 1322, much like the days of de Montfort, during which a baronial council put the Crown under close control.

The Lords Ordainers failed ultimately through their own short-comings. But their first measures were approved by a parliament including knights and burgesses; London opinion looked up to the magnates, and they showed no wish to uproot Edward I's reforms. Their twenty-one members included not merely bitter aristocrats like Warwick, but moderates like the Valence earl of Pembroke and old servants of the Crown like Winchelsey, while their work, completed after a year of consultation, went far beyond a third sentence upon Gaveston, and amounted to a vote of censure on all the government's recent tendencies. The forests, whose bounds were still extending; alien bankers; the extra customs duties of 1303; the courts of the Steward and Marshal which encroached on the common law, privy seal writs — these had already been represented to Edward I. But other clauses, new and searching, struck at the root of the government, the royal Household. Here lay the inner ring of officials and the separate treasury, which overrode the public departments. The Crown was a corporation, but the King was a man; the Ordainers, separating these two capacities, declared that obedience was due not to the King but to the Crown, whose powers and advisers must be known to the law. The Exchequer must not be checked by the Wardrobe, nor the great seal by private seals. They demanded the public appointment not only of high officials and judges, but of the principal Household staff, asked for regular annual Parliaments, which should appoint a standing committee of magnates, and put officials on their oath to keep the Ordinances.

But Edward II, like Charles I, kept no promise given under compulsion; he swore he would not have his servants chosen for him like a lunatic, raised an army in the north, and again recalled Gaveston. In May 1312 the Ordainers captured the favourite in Scarborough Castle; in June Warwick, breaking a solemn safe-conduct, bore him off to his own Kenilworth and executed him in the presence of Lancaster, Hereford, and Arundel. This lynch law broke their party; Pembroke led a moderate wing, who for ten years attempted to work the Ordinances by agreement with the King.

This patriotic group was ground between the millstones of two crude personalities. So far as he dared, Edward ignored the Ordinances, appealed to the Pope, and fought every official appointment. He had exchanged the kiss of peace, but had war in his heart against those who had killed his friend. At their head was his first cousin, Thomas of Lancaster, Derby, and Leicester, Earl by marriage also of Salisbury and Lincoln; with de Montfort's earldom he held something like his position, especially in the support of the clergy, while both his safety and his prestige were wrapped up in the Ordinances, which he had commemorated by a tablet in St. Paul's. This proud and obstinate man refused to budge; Edinburgh fell to the Scots, Stirling was besieged, but unless Edward would keep the Ordinances Lancaster would not fight.

He and his friends, though they sent contingents, were absent, then, when, in June 1314, at Bannockburn Bruce annihilated the English army and so delivered Edward into the Ordainers' hands. Lancaster was able to appoint new officials, take command of the army, and strip Edward's servants of their estates, while Parliament empowered him to direct the royal actions as ' chief councillor '.

But the Earl was dour, incompetent, a master who won no loyalties. He would not use the only real means of reform, a regular attendance in Council and Parliament, and moved gloomily about the north with an armed camp, declaring his life was not safe at London. It was noticed also that the Scots raiders spared his lands. Gradually a paralysis crept over the government, torn between an unwilling king and a passive chief councillor. Private war broke out, in Wales especially, and class-war in populous towns like Bristol. Northumberland brigands robbed two Papal legates and held the bishop of Durham to ransom. The Bruces invaded Ireland in 1316, while French agents overran Gascony.

From a mixture of public and personal motives, good men and bad, a movement and a party arose to end this chaos. There were personal friends of Lancaster's Lacy wife, who eloped from him; with barons jealous of his supremacy in Yorkshire or his greed of power. Serious officials and ambitious courtiers joined them. Royal blood and some patriotism drew in Hereford, once a leading Ordainer. There were other Marchers with mixed motives, not least a wish to share the inheritance of the last Clare earl of Gloucester, killed at Bannockburn. The centre of this party was Pembroke, who for three years (1318–21) succeeded in his moderate policy. A standing council, on which Lancaster was represented, controlled all sovereign acts, supported the Ordinances, and purged the Household. After many defeats they patched up a truce with Scotland. Both in Parliament and in conference with the merchants the new government attempted reorganization of the cloth trade. Their attitude to the King was firm but respectful, leaving his personal freedom intact over grants of land and minor office.

Their work did not wholly perish, but the factions soon broke apart again. The arch-offender was the King's new favourite, Hugh Despenser the younger, a much more dangerous man than the butterfly Gaveston. His grandfather was that chief justice who fell with de Montfort, his father a sober loyal official, while the son had been made king's chamberlain by the Pembroke government, and soon captivated Edward's weak nature. From his position in the Household he began to influence all appointments, and add to the share he had by marriage in the Gloucester inheritance. This offended the Marchers, to whom their own custom was more sacred than any royal grant; especially

Hereford and Roger Mortimer, who had made a name fighting in Ireland.

1321 was a year of violent revolution. The Marchers rose and Lancaster called on the northern barons and clergy, clamouring for the Ordinances and nothing but the Ordinances, while a parliament exiled the Despensers. Yet within three months of this triumph all was swept away in a reaction, which left the Crown higher than at any date since 1307.

Accident gave the King his opportunity, in a blunder made by one of the trimmers, Lord Badlesmere, whose wife refused the Queen the hospitality of Leeds Castle, but no accident determined Edward's success or its duration. Fifteen years' anarchy had convinced moderate men that no reform could last in defiance of the Crown, nor were they yet agreed that Edward was incorrigible. Meanwhile, the factions which split Pembroke's ministry had equally divided the Opposition. While Edward marched against Badlesmere in Kent, Lancaster made no move; Welsh loyalists threatened the Marchers; each group acted separately and was conquered in detail. In March 1322 the King's southern army and his Border levies closed in upon Lancaster, who was captured at Boroughbridge and executed without trial in his own castle. Hereford died in the battle, Badlesmere was hanged, the Mortimers were in the Tower. So Gaveston was avenged.

But though northern parish churches prayed for Lancaster as a martyr, the essentials of the Ordinances were caught up in a reformed administration. Despenser was an experienced man, well aware of the power of opinion. A representative Parliament, meeting at York after Boroughbridge, though it repealed the Ordinances, declared that great matters affecting King and kingdom must receive the royal assent in Parliament by the counsel of clergy, barons, and the ' Commonalty '. For the rest of the reign the Commons were regularly summoned. New statutes provided for some long-desired reform in the forests and the appointment of substantial landowners as sheriffs, and even after Pembroke's death in 1324 there were civil servants, like bishop Stapledon of Exeter, who protected orderly government against the King. Exchequer reform cleared off the debt of two reigns. Chancellor and Treasurer were strong enough to restrain the Household. It was not despotism, in fact, which brought about revolution in 1327, but the King's incompetence, his advisers' greed, and bitter memories of bloodshed. That revolution, therefore, involved not so much a change of measures as of men.

The Scottish humiliation was a first charge against the government. In 1322 their raiders nearly captured the King; next year the hero of Boroughbridge, Harclay Warden of the Marches, was executed for treasonable correspondence with Bruce, and Edward, though refusing to admit the Scottish independence which Harclay thought inevitable,

signed a long truce. In the same year came about the inevitable breach
with France, the occasion arising from that interlacement of feudal
estates on a jagged frontier, which the treaty of Paris (1259) had left
as arguable as ever. Repeating the game of 1303, the French invaded
Gascony, drove the English to the coast, and then announced they
would surrender the Duchy in return for homage, excepting some
territories on which there should be arbitration. Only national union
could save Gascony, and this had been destroyed by Despenser. He
had seized the whole Clare heritage and that of Bigod, with the custody
of Pembroke's and Lacy's, so that Wales was in his hands. He divided
the King from the Queen and from his half-brothers. A new Lancaster,
Henry, pious and moderate, had succeeded Earl Thomas, and he too
was driven into opposition. Then fortune or design threw together
two more dangerous enemies, Roger Mortimer who escaped from the
Tower, and the Queen, whom Edward unwillingly allowed to go overseas to seek a settlement with France ; to whom Edward himself gave
their trump card, by sending his son to France to do homage in his
stead. By the spring of 1326 the Queen and Mortimer, now living
together in adultery, were assembling an army in the Netherlands,
paying for it by a betrothal between the young Edward and Philippa
of Hainault. In September they crossed to Suffolk, by November they
held the King a prisoner.

Destruction, the first stage of revolution, was easy ; Edward's fall
was instant, unanimous, complete. His half-brothers Kent and Norfolk,
the Lancastrian north, the native Welsh, Marchers, bishops and civil
servants, were all so far united. A London mob lynched bishop Stapledon in Cheapside. Bristol forced the elder Despenser to surrender,
Welshmen betrayed the younger, and both were hanged. But on the
second stage, reconstruction, the victors of 1314, 1318, and 1322 had
all alike failed ; could it come from the squalid hands of Mortimer
and the Queen ?

Since experience showed that to wield government against the King
was impossible, the conspirators must have a new King. In January
1327 a full Parliament resolved that Edward was incompetent, and he
was induced to resign in favour of his son. But while he lived, the
faction never felt safe, and one attempt at his escape convinced them
that ' stone dead hath no fellow '. And as slow starvation failed, in
September he was murdered at Berkeley Castle. His murderers had
now to face the Commons, who had asked for the canonization of Earl
Thomas and Winchelsey ; they had also to deal with Scotland, Gascony,
finance, and the factions, on which all their predecessors had shipwrecked. The King was dead, but only a King could work the King's
government ; such was the moral once more of the three years when
Mortimer exploited Edward III.

English pride felt 'the shameful peace' of 1328 with Scotland, which meant that Edward I had fought in vain, and the peace made with France, which surrendered a good third of all he had held. And nothing like Mortimer's rule had been seen since Earl Godwine. He had Wigmore and Chirk by inheritance, Ludlow and half Meath by marriage, he made himself Earl of the March and justiciar of Wales for life, he held the forfeited estates of Despenser and Arundel. He married his daughters to the greatest houses in England. He assigned large blocks of Crown lands to the Queen. His partisans held every principal office, the Treasurer being his tame bishop — the repulsive Orlton of Hereford, who had drilled the London mob to shout for the deposition of Edward II.

There was nothing in common between this ravening wolf, head of a house which had opposed de Montfort and the Clares, and the Lancastrian or moderate groups who stood for the Ordinances and the power of a constitutional baronage. The Church was divided, since many successive factions had appointed bishops, but some of the strongest, led by Stratford of Winchester, were Lancastrian, many were royal servants by training whose feeling was for a decent government. From London meetings the opposition passed to raising armed men, but their hesitating divisions destroyed them, and Mortimer entrapped the Earl of Kent into a traitor's death.

At last the conspirators awoke to the one person who could save them. When his uncle Kent was executed, Edward III was nearly eighteen; it was three months since his wife Philippa had given birth to the future Black Prince. He was resolved to rule, and listened to the advice of Lancaster. In October 1330, at Nottingham Castle, he engineered a plot; his closest friend, William Montague, arrested Mortimer in the bedroom next to the queen-mother's. The wretched woman's cry 'fair son, have pity on the gentle Mortimer', woke no pity for the pitiless. The Earl of March was hanged at Tyburn on the thieves' gallows, and the King not only reigned but ruled.

Edward III's monarchy, thus restored, was not the autocracy of his grandfather. Scaffold and battlefield, which had destroyed competitors for power, had not stopped the annual round of the judges on assize, or the wheels of the common law. Year by year riches filtered down to new hands. International capitalism, with nerve centres at Bruges, Rome, and Florence, called out new demand or supply, in Cotswold sheep-farms or clothing towns of Norfolk; London merchants impressed their will even on the Despensers. Each successive ministry deferred to this middle-class opinion and, exploited though it might be, Edward III's Parliament had the last word in a sense undreamed of by Edward I.

It worked in, as it helped to form, a new atmosphere of nationality.

Not that this yet meant the racial pride or deliberate policy which came with the Hundred Years' War, for Edward's court spoke and thought in French, while some of his best generals came from Hainault or Gascony. Yet the breaking of the world unity once centred in the Papacy, a new wealth, and lay-learning, were making national civilizations. Obedience to the Holy See was not so unquestioning, now that the Popes lived in what the Commons called ' the sinful city of Avignon '. Monasticism had seen its best days. Secular priests and London citizens were out-writing the chronicler-monks of St. Albans, while royal officials, Merton or Stapledon or de Brome, founded their Oxford colleges neither for monks nor friars.

One proof of such new conditions was the sweeping progress of English speech. For the Romance epics derived from France there was always a certain audience but, a full generation before Chaucer wrote, English poetry and prose reached maturity. Poems like ' Sir Gawain ', in the old alliterative metre, passed on the spirit of the Arthur legends to Spenser. While Gaveston struggled, a Herefordshire man was collecting songs of earthly beauty ;

right lovesome thou art in May, thou wide wide earth.

From the north came a group of poems, the most famous of which was ' Pearl ', full of admirable word-painting ; the ' Cursor Mundi ' also, which set out to tell to common people the spiritual history of the world, and the religious writings of the Yorkshire hermit Richard Rolle, whose prose reached far more readers than Chaucer's verse, and both in time and merit preceded Wyclif. Mediaeval still in its choice of subjects, this literature was modern in spirit and form. Sermons, poetry, and legend, whether from Lincoln or Gloucester, borrowed colour and metaphor from the common life about them, — taverns and usurers, tournaments or the peasant in all weathers in the field, — tran-scending all the bounds of the orthodox Church.

Their vocabulary was compounded of the three tongues, English, French, and Scandinavian, which had made the race, and had already nearly achieved a standard English; other dialects were giving way before that of the East Midlands, the patois of London and Oxford, Cambridge and Stratford-on-Avon. Though legal conservatism kept French for another two hundred years as a professional language, a statute of 1362 ordered that in all law courts men should plead in their mother tongue, while the Chancellor kept the records of his court in English. And as nationality had made this language, so the language deepened national-ity, in fierce songs against the Scots or French, and glorification of English bowmen. The French have done their worst, boasted the Midlander Lawrence Minot,

and yet is England as it was.

In England as elsewhere nationalism made for new economic groupings, wider than the market town and feudal village, and, though in this respect England lagged behind Flemings or Florentines, its business grew to a larger scale. Both the wool trade and the customs revenue demanded central control, whether by merchants or the Crown. Centralized wealth was making London a capital with a stationary government, independent of the royal presence. Many weary journeys the departments of State made to York or Shrewsbury, but after 1340 the King was sometimes abroad for a year on end, while the administration acquired its fixed seat at Westminster. It was, in short, an age of increasing revolution, and though its changes had far-back origins, three interlocked circumstances decided the shape and stages of progress; the Black Death, the Hundred Years' War, and the character of Edward III.

He was in many ways the man of his people. No king since Cœur de Lion had so won the baronage, in whose zeal for tournaments he shared. He loved to hold the lists, to show himself in a new device, with a gallant motto on his shield :

> Hey, hey, the White Swan,
> By God's soul I am thy man.

To restore the chivalry of Arthur he founded the Order of the Garter, with the Round Tower at Windsor as its hall. But he was not a carpet knight; he was wounded in the sea-fight of Sluys, his doggedness in a winter siege won Calais.

Of political gifts he had a royal share. His easy good humour and gifts conciliated, where Edward I had given offence. He could speak English to the Londoners, and their wives, whom he asked to his festivals; like them he was a devout pilgrim to English shrines and firm against Roman interference. And if later in life he grew lazy, this temper had its political advantage. He disliked business, avoided living in London, and would give up power to Parliament and the magnates, if they left him its dignity. He was much too anxious for money to resist attack, and open-minded enough to let the Commons have what they wanted, if they would finance his wars. There were crises in his long reign but he eluded them, not only by postponement but by a genuine gift for peace. He pardoned Mortimer's friends, nor did he show any rancour to the ministers whom he so freely dismissed.

The French war determined the character of his reign and its every epoch. Its glories made his early popularity. Its opportunities enabled the military magnates to stand out for their hereditary privileges. Its perpetual call for money created the House of Commons. The need of a Flemish alliance enabled English wool merchants to call the tune, and from the Flemings' insistence came Edward's decision to claim the

French Crown, while Papal mediation to stop the war caused half the hatred of Avignon. On English society its effects were still deeper. Our army was recruited by 'indentures' between the Crown and individual barons or knights, who would raise so many men for a fixed wage; a new monied and military feudalism which was to cause great ills. The intoxicating draught of victory created national pride. War prices and booty, with the Black Death and incessant spending, transformed English landholding. Property continuously passed to the sons of yeomen archers, who had burned France to the gates of Paris or sacked Spanish convents, to clothiers whose industry grew by war, or to Cinque Ports' sailors who had bound together patriotism, piracy, and profit.

Looking back at the ghastly duration of a hundred and twenty years of war, from the ruin of defeat and the Wars of the Roses, we are perhaps too apt to see in it a criminal purpose, a monument of bad statesmanship, or sheer national loss. To prolong or renew this war did, indeed, tempt governments who were anxious to avoid internal trouble, while our final defeat also was certain if once France, with her eighteen million people, organized herself against the English three or four.

But neither statistics nor a long-range policy govern humanity, as it moves from one setting to another. In a real sense France had taken the aggressive against all that the Middle Ages prized. Its ambitious centralized sovereignty attacked alike the neutrality of the Pope, the independence of Flemish cities, and ancient English rights in Gascony; it challenged the existence of the Empire; its princes ruled Naples; its clients claimed Castile. Though Edward III, then, was technically the aggressor, he was defending an old order, impossible perhaps but inherited, nor did he set out with a vision of making himself King of France.

He was bent, however, from the first on claiming all his grandfather held and wiping off the shame of Mortimer. Every year till 1336 he went forth against Scotland, refortifying castles and marching as far as Perth. There he found Papal and French diplomacy combining in demands for a truce, and in the refuge given, at Château-Gaillard of all places, to the young David Bruce. French influence was damaging our trade with the clothiers of Bruges and Ghent, while Robert count of Artois, dispossessed by the French, was in London urging him to war.

If war were desired, there was one pretext better than all these. Between 1316 and 1328, while England was distracted, three Kings of France died, sons of Philip the Fair. None left a son nor, as yet, had their daughters borne sons, while at each vacancy the French treated the throne as an office for a man, passing over the dead man's daughter. But in 1329 all Philip's sons were dead; could his daughter Isabella pass on her claim to her son Edward III? French lawyers had not yet invented an imaginary Salic law, forbidding succession through a female; the nobles acted on a simpler theme, of a Frenchman for France, and crowned Philip VI, son of Charles of Valois, brother of Philip the Fair. Even in 1328 the men of Bruges proposed to recognize Edward as King, but Mortimer's government was too weak for war and Edward did homage, making no claim to the throne till other causes brought war indeed.

The ultimate cause was Gascony, which England had ruled for two hundred years but which France was resolved to conquer. Its status depended on the peace of 1259, as amended by the treaties of 1303 and 1327; none of which had been carried out. Edward I's acquisitions, Agenais and southern Saintonge, were full of feudal islands, the property of privileged barons whom the peace of Paris had excepted from surrender of territory. Philip the Fair, again, had never honourably restored Gascony, while the French kept tight hold of the lands conquered from Edward II. Indeed, Mortimer's peace planted every seed of war. The new frontier ran athwart the big rivers from the Gironde to the Adour; east of the sand-dunes and marshes between Bordeaux and Bayonne, English outlying fortresses were intermingled with the French; there were claims and counter-claims for a war indemnity. Meantime Edward I's careful supervision was over; Gascon finances were mortgaged to Italians, and the bankrupt Edward II tried to pawn them to the Pope.

It was a difficult province at the best of times. From the lighthouse in the Gironde to the Pyrenees, it stretched like a snake in the sun; a long string of seigneurs who took toll on every river and rents from a swarm of peasants, and of towns with jealously guarded liberties. Yet it was a land worth saving. Wines of Bordeaux and the Médoc, salt and armour, exchanged for English cloth and corn. The Seneschal's jurisdiction made a royal common law; mayors named by the Crown had restored some order in the towns. Gascon nobles fought well in Scotland and Wales, and though London was jealous of the Gascons' marketing privileges, it could not dispense with their wine.

In 1336, since France would neither yield the Agenais nor abandon the Bruces, Edward began to make alliances. The first phase of war, lasting till 1341, was centred on the Netherlands and the Rhine. The Flemings, forced to a decision by prohibition of the export of our wool, sunk for the time being their jealousies and class feuds, and found a determined leader in James van Artevelde, a clothier of Ghent. Edward offered a wool-staple at Bruges, with a free English market for their cloth, and at their request took the title ' King of France '. Beginning with his Hainault kinsmen he simultaneously made a coalition of Netherland princes, which in turn connected him with Germany, for the Emperor Lewis was married to Queen Philippa's sister. For twenty years now the Emperor had waged war with Rome, having behind him, if he could wield them, a new German national feeling, a theory of empire, and an evangelical religious movement. Against the French Popes he welcomed an English alliance. In 1338 the brothers-in-law met in great pomp at Coblenz, where the Emperor declared France forfeit and appointed Edward his Vicar-general on the Rhine.

One success only rewarded Edward's efforts, when in 1340 at Sluys he completely destroyed a French fleet. His allies were faithless, the Emperor's family ambition demanded peace, and nothing resulted but the ravaging of the plains from the Scheldt to the Aisne, and the burning of English villages by French landing parties. In September Edward signed a truce, compelled by the two good reasons, that he was bankrupt and that Parliament was threatening revolt.

When his own rule began in 1330, internal peace depended on a balance of two forces : the Lancastrians who represented the Ordainers, and the royalist circle, half made up of Edward's friends like Montague and half of officials. For nearly ten years this harmony lasted. Stratford, the Lancastrians' ablest man, was both archbishop and chief minister, earldoms were given to both parties, parliaments were summoned more often than ever before, Edward's case against France was submitted to the Commons and circulated to the county courts.

But war, which showed up the King's character, brought out the conflict of principle in this government. From the Scottish campaign of 1333 onwards, his demands for money were enormous. Year by year the counties gave him one-fifteenth, the boroughs and clergy one-tenth, and on top of that he requisitioned the wool supply. He sounded separate assemblies of merchants, shire courts, and Churchmen. Into this endless sink he poured anything he could scrape together, church plate and Cornish tin, his judges' salaries and Papal dues. Even his own crown was pawned in Germany. His expenses rose to £250,000 a year. Every tax was mortgaged in advance to anyone who obliged him with cash or war material, to German princes, wool merchants, or Italian bankers, and it was, for example, by lending the King £76,000 in a year, that William de la Pole of Hull originated the precarious fortunes of a famous family.

This manner of government was highly unpopular. Each year the Commons growled a little louder ; they must ask their constituents, tallage was illegal, tampering with the wool supply must stop, the peers advised making a peace. By 1340 there was open strife between the regency at London, directed by Stratford, and Edward's Council at Antwerp. Like his grandfather, he used his Household as a war department. He tried to submit Chancery and Exchequer to a rigid control, authorized under his privy seal and checked by his Chamber.

This wild finance, this small clique under the influence of grasping allies and contractors, called out immediate resistance. The magnates meant to be the King's councillors. Stratford loathed the war policy and the humiliation of high officials and, shrewd politician that he was, began to preach that the clergy were victimized and reminded them of Becket's martyrdom. To get money for the next campaign Edward had to make a great surrender, accepting statutes which forbade taxation without parliamentary assent, restricted purveyance, and protected the clergy against exactions. The crisis came after the campaign of 1340–41, when want of money forced Edward to another truce. Slinking away from his creditors in Flanders, he dismissed the ministers who had failed him, and arrested judges and officials.

Now for the first time was seen the developed strength of Parliament, and a new civilian feeling against militarism. The King wished to try Stratford by special commission, and Household knights turned him back from the door of Parliament. Pamphlets on both sides showed the existence of a public opinion. Warenne, an earl of ancient and royal blood, attacked the ' menials ' of the Household; ' Parliaments of old ', he said, ' were not like this.' The magnates, demanding their rights as hereditary councillors, declared that the archbishop, like all ' peers ', could only be judged in Parliament. Lords and Commons jointly petitioned Edward to accept parliamentary audit of his war taxes, together with the far-reaching principle that ministers must be chosen by, and be responsible to, Parliament.

Within a few months Edward declared these two statutes void, as put upon him by force and as against the custom of the realm. But, in fact, he admitted defeat. For the next twenty years he returned to government of a normal type, through the administrative bishops and the magnates with whom they were allied. He took their advice in great councils and used them in war. Gascony was re-won in 1345–6 by the second Henry of Lancaster, whom Edward made duke with palatine powers. Bohun, earl of Northampton, was the hero of Brittany; he and Beauchamp of Warwick, son of the ' black dog of Arden ', led the two wings at Crécy. Sheriffdoms for life rewarded their loyalty; marriages united their heiresses to the King's sons.

Save for the universal horror of the Black Death, England went its way in peace. Parliament asserted entire control of taxation, including the wool trade. It attacked the commissions of array, by which Edward conscripted troops for foreign service. Its pressure drew a line between administrative routine and those matters of importance which must take shape in statute, while new laws testified to the matters which it had most at heart. The statute of Provisors (1351) tried to end one old grievance; all who got patronage from Rome would be imprisoned, and their livings lapse to the Crown. In 1353 the statute of Praemunire outlawed all who sued in foreign courts. The Treasons Act of 1352 checked arbitrary law and arrest; treason was limited to attack on the sovereign, levying war or adhering to his enemies, tampering with his coinage, or killing his high officers, while conviction would require the verdict of a jury, or of the lords in Parliament. Finally, local government was committed to the very class which made up the House of Commons. After many experiments, especially a commission to regulate wages during the Black Death, an Act of 1361 determined the office of justice of the peace, with powers to arrest and imprison, and to try felonies and trespass.

But the war went on. Edward was not the man to sit down under his humiliation, and the French had taken the suburbs of Bordeaux. In 1341 a contested succession to the Duchy of Brittany gave him a new base, and a new glorious stage of war lasted till 1347. For the first time the country responded to his ardour. Parliament repeatedly voted taxes for three years at a time, arguing that either war or peace was preferable to desultory truces, or insincere Papal mediation.

For fifteen years victory shone on this national effort. While our fleet swept the Channel, small armies won pitched battles against much greater numbers, using the tactics and weapons painfully learned in Scotland and Wales. The armoured troopers were now usually dismounted to fight in deep lines, having on the wings, or écheloned in advance, archers whose fire broke up every attack. They used the longbow, first employed by the south Welsh against the Angevins; six feet long in elm or yew, drawn back to the ear, and sending that sleet of arrows which outranged any crossbow-bolts. As time passed, they became more often a mounted infantry, fighting on foot but equipped to win tactical superiority by speed of movement. Army recruitment had long ceased to be feudal and was built now on two different elements: conscription and professional mercenaries. The sheriffs conscripted forces under commission of array; so in the Crécy campaign the Principality of Wales was asked for 3500 infantry, Sussex for 200 archers, Norwich for 60 mounted spearmen. Increasing numbers, however, were raised by contracts with professional soldiers, nobles, or landowners, who guaranteed to serve or maintain a garrison, at fixed rates of pay. Under this system rose great captains, — John Chandos the right arm of the Black Prince, or the Cheshire squires Knollys and Calverley, whose companies became the terror of France, and whose spoil founded many a yeoman family.

In 1345-7 two such armies swept all before them. Henry of Lancaster, after relieving Gascony, captured Agenais and Périgord and then penetrated to Poitou, where Englishmen had not fought since John's time. In July 1346 Edward himself landed in Normandy with the Black Prince, his greatest barons, and some 12,000 men. His first aim seems to have been merely loot and demonstration, but when after

storming Caen he struck at Rouen, he found the bridges cut over the
Seine. He therefore marched up its left bank, hoping for a crossing,
and a retreat upon friendly Flanders. The smoke of burning villages
could be seen round Paris, in mid-August he crossed the river at
Poissy, and the French were hard in pursuit, threatening to coop him
up between Amiens and the sea. But on the 24th he saved himself by
finding an undefended ford on the Somme, where it nears the sea
below Abbeville; his men waded over with water to their knees, and
the tide rose behind them to stop the French advance guard. He now
could fight in a position of his choice, which he found just north of the
forest of Crécy. Protected by woodland in their rear and right, the
English entrenched themselves on a rolling down; a frontal attack
would have to climb out of the valley beneath, along one road. The
King meant this day to be his son's baptism of fire; after taking the
sacrament together, he posted him in the place of honour on the right,
Northampton on the left, and himself took the reserve. All three
'battles' were dismounted; on the wings of both front divisions,
archers were thrown forward.

It was not till about four o'clock on the 26th August that the French
appeared on the opposite ridge. They had lost touch and wasted a day
in cross-country marching; if King Philip had had the courage of his
opinion, they would have halted this night, and encircled the English
left, for they had received reinforcements from their Gascon army,
and had quite 30,000 men to the English 12,000. But the nobility
overpersuaded him to fight at once. While a thunderstorm soaked
both armies, they despatched against the English right their Genoese
crossbow-men who, under a blazing evening sun, painfully crossed
the valley. Exhausted by their march, and outranged by a whirlwind
of arrows, they broke and fled; the French knights hacked their way
through them and streamed, wave after wave, at the Black Prince's
men at arms. They never reached them; fifteen charges in turn were
annihilated by his archers. At dusk Northampton's division advanced
to take this demoralized mass in flank, and all was over, the Welsh
archers with their knives pursuing broken parties in the darkness.
Even in the mists of the next morning scattered French detachments
came up and were shot down; fields and hedges were full of their
dead. The English heralds counted over 1500 knights alone, and
among them Philip's brother Alençon, the Count of Flanders, the Duke
of Lorraine, and John the blind King of Bohemia, whose ostrich-
feather crest the Black Prince took for his own.

For the first time England impressed itself on Europe by a great
victory. Before the new year, mounted archers destroyed the Scots at
Neville's Cross outside Durham, taking King David prisoner. From
September Edward himself was blockading Calais, housing his army

and administration in a city of tents and huts. But only starvation could take the fortress, girdled in by marsh and salt water, and it was not until August 1347 that its brave garrison surrendered, having long ago eaten their dogs and horses. Meantime an English captain in Brittany captured Charles of Blois, the French claimant.

With the truce of September this stage of war ended, not to be reopened on a big scale until both countries had passed through the Death, though in Brittany, Gascony, and on the high seas both fought on to keep their advantage; in Brittany especially the war took on an atrocious character, our mercenary captains living on the countryside and ' farming ' the profits of war from the King. But the plague had ruined most landowners, the Commons were weary of taxes, impressment of shipping, and conscription, and shouted ' yea, yea ' when asked if they wished for peace. The accession of the new French King John made peace more possible, but the negotiation of 1354 broke down, for if Edward abandoned his claim to the Crown, he asked in return a full sovereignty over Gascony, Ponthieu, and Artois. War to a finish became certain when anarchy divided France. Its evil genius was the King's cousin Charles of Navarre, who would move heaven and earth for his ambition, and whose Norman lands made a base for the English. The Paris merchants became one of his instruments, and a constitutional revolt of the States-General threatened the Crown.

In 1355 fighting broke out again from Scotland to Gascony. After local forays innumerable, in 1356 the English attempted a combined strategy; the Black Prince, having made Gascony safe, would strike north to the Loire, to join hands with Lancaster coming from Normandy. Lancaster was driven back, yet the prince marched in August, bent upon plunder, with only vague hopes of cutting his way to the north.

By the first week of September he had ravaged all up to the Loire, but found the river in flood and the bridges broken. He determined to retreat; the French outmarched him, and by the 15th stood between him and the south. It was urgent to fight quickly, if at all, for French reinforcements were arriving, while he had only 6000 men at most, cumbered with spoil and prisoners. Two cardinals from Avignon were pressing him for a truce, and if the French had offered a truce with honour, he must have accepted it. In fact, however, King John would take nothing but surrender, and on the 19th, as Edward was preparing a further retreat, issued from Poitiers to attack.

The battle was much more obstinate than Crécy, for the mass of the French knights fought on foot, without spurs and with lances cut down, while Edward had only time to take the first defensible slope he could find among the vineyards. Fighting lasted from about eight in the morning until vespers; a soldiers' battle, ending hand-to-hand with sword and knife, when our archers were using any arrows they could pull from the dead bodies. Edward was saved partly by the folly of the French horse who, far ahead of their main body, charged down the one cart-track which broke the hedgerows, and were shot down by archers on either side. But victory came much more from the skill of the English, hardened by a year's fighting and led by their best officers, — the Prince and Chandos, Warwick and Salisbury, Suffolk and Oxford, Audley, Felton, Loring, and the Gascon Captal de Buch. None but great captains and good troops could have had the morale, after beating off six hours' attacks of greater numbers, to take the offensive in line against dense columns, hold them until a troop of horse took them in flank, and drive them in confusion. So with kettledrums, bagpipes, and trumpets blowing, and shouts of ' St. George ', they encircled the last French division. Among their 2000 prisoners was King John ; the next spring the citizens of London saw a captive King of France, led in procession to the palace of the Savoy.

Such was the keynote of this stage ; English generals who showed no sign of strategy, but English captains who could handle any tactics, and troops who could beat twice their numbers. But this glorious and fortunate victory did not end war. France found better men than her King, in the Dauphin Charles and in the magnificent Breton general du Guescelin, round whom gathered a national revival, which slowly got rid of the ruin left by the treachery of Navarre and the peasants' rising known as the Jacquerie. Dauphin and people indignantly rejected a treaty signed by the captive John, which would have given England all the old Angevin provinces.

The very fact that the Pope worked so earnestly for peace made war more popular, and in November 1359 Edward moved out of Calais with the intention of being crowned at Rheims. But the fortified towns shut their gates, the country was swept bare of food, and his circular march by Rheims and Burgundy had brought him at Easter 1360 within sight of Paris, with nothing to show. His continued absence might imperil the peace just made with Scotland; while Norman sailors had burned Winchelsea. In May, therefore, at Brétigny near Chartres, where he had retreated to rest his troops, he signed the peace preliminaries which in October King John, released for that purpose, accepted as the peace of Calais. By it Edward and his heirs received, ' as the kings of France ' had held them, Calais, Guines, and Ponthieu, and in the south Poitou, Saintonge, Périgord, Limousin, Quercy, Rouergue, Bigorre, in addition to his Gascon domain; his frontier would stretch almost to Nantes north-west, and southwards nearly to Toulouse. France would pay a ransom of £500,000 for John and renounce her Scottish alliance. Further negotiations were to settle the Breton succession, and to make good Edward's renuncia-tion of the French crown, with John's corresponding renunciation of lordship over the surrendered provinces.

So, though in ways he had not foreseen or desired, Edward I's England might seem to have reached stability; with half France mastered, Scotland in the toils of a ransom and a puppet king, trade expanding, and a government dependent on public opinion.

But while Chandos wrestled with Poitevins unwilling to become English, and du Guescelin with English adventurers who refused to give up castles, the Black Death in 1362 visited England for the second time. Below the surface of Edwardian forms a new society fermented.

CONTEMPORARY DATES

1307 Philip the Fair begins prosecution of the Templars.

1308 Death of Duns Scotus.

1310 Formation of the Council of Ten at Venice.
        The Knights Hospitallers establish themselves in Rhodes.

1312 Can Grande della Scala becomes lord of Verona.

1313 Death in Italy of the first Luxemburg Emperor, Henry
        VII : succeeded by the Wittelsbach, Lewis of Bavaria.

1315 Swiss victory over the Hapsburgs at Morgaten.

1316-34 Pope John XXII.

1321 Death of Dante at Ravenna.
        Beginning of Moslem Tuglak dynasty at Delhi.

1328 Death of the last Capet King of France ; succeeded
        by Philip VI (Valois).
        Ivan Kalita begins consolidation of the supremacy
        of Moscow.

1331, onwards. Stephen Dushan makes Serbian predominance
        in the Balkans.

1336 James van Artevelde leads revolt against the Count
        of Flanders.
        Resistance to Moslem supremacy in India by the Hindu
        empire of Vijayanagar.

1338 At Rense the German Electors declare against Papal
        interference.

1341 Petrarch crowned poet at Rome.

1342-82 Louis the Great (Angevin) of Hungary.

1345 Luxemburg princes set up in Holland and Hainault.

1346-78 The Emperor Charles IV.

1347 Cola di Rienzo in power at Rome.

1349 Dauphiné annexed to the French Crown.

1348, onwards. Boccaccio's *Decameron.*

1354 The Ottoman Turks take Gallipoli.

1355 Execution of the Doge Falieri.
        Étienne Marcel leading in the Estates-General.

1358 The Jacquerie in France.

CHAPTER IX

ENGLAND AND SCOTLAND, TO 1369

SINCE the days when Romans held the forts of Perthshire, no single power ruled over this island till a Scottish King ascended the English throne in 1603. This division was not all loss; for if it contributed to make mediaeval England only a second-class power, from it came also the individuality of Scotland. The turning-point came when Edward I, fresh from his conquest of Wales, tried to conquer Scotland also, a country twice as far distant from the English capital and with much greater political strength.

Scottish nationality had reached its first stage in the tenth century, in a union under one crown of Scots, Picts, and Strathclyde. Norwegian attack hardened it. The winning of Lothian doubled its strength, and began a process of Anglicization which Malcolm Canmore's marriage with St. Margaret cemented. From the twelfth century, therefore, England faced a new Scotland like unto itself, built not on the Celtic north but the Lowlands, with a feudal royalty, a strong church, and a Norman baronage.

A clean frontier and feudalism could never co-exist. Thus the Balliols, lords of Castle Barnard in Durham, held fiefs in Galloway, while the Bruces' lay both in Yorkshire and Annandale. Geography interposed no barrier, for several river valleys penetrate the Cheviots, whose middle heights, moreover, bulge out southwards so as to out-flank Northumberland. History and geography, language and blood, together made the Border a debatable land, and we have seen the Scots' incessant attempts to conquer Cumberland and Northumberland by the easy passes of the Tweed valley and the Carlisle gap.

From the time of Edward the Elder, and bound up with the English surrender of Strathclyde and Lothian, Scottish kings admitted a general supremacy in the English Crown. In Stephen's time they became vassals for the Honour of Huntingdon. Kings of Scotland served in Henry II's army. This homage was clearly defined as for the whole realm of Scotland in the treaty of Falaise, when Henry held William the Lion captive, but Cœur de Lion cancelled it in return for money, and the question slipped back to its old vagueness.

To make it binding was the aim of England long before Edward I. John compelled William the Lion to give up his children's marriages to English arrangement. Henry III tried through the Papacy to wring an

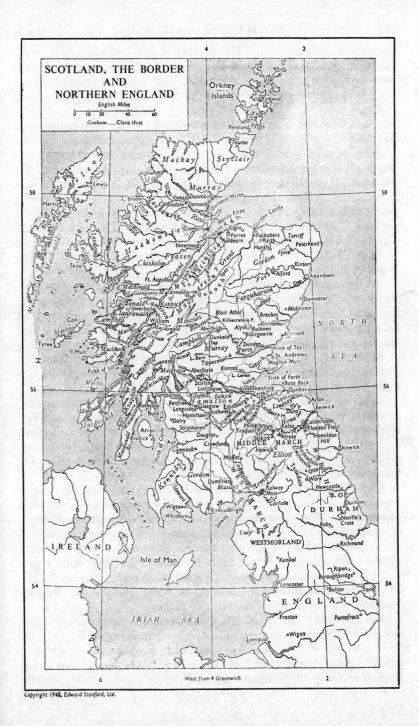

SCOTLAND, THE BORDER AND NORTHERN ENGLAND

English Miles

0 10 20   40   60

Graham .....Clans thus

unreserved homage from his brother-in-law, Alexander II.   He used the minority of his son-in-law, Alexander III, to form an English party and pack the Scottish council, and it was the overthrow of his nominees by Scottish revolt which first faintly marked a national feeling.

Uneasy lay the head that wore a Scottish crown ; how many kings had perished already, ' without bell, without communion, in the evening, in a dangerous pass ! ' In the thirteenth century any concession to the English King or Norman barons at once offended the untamed Highlanders.   In Moray Lady Macbeth's descendants still resisted ; savage half-Norwegians held the far north in Caithness, whose people (when Langton ruled at Canterbury) roasted their bishop on his own fire.   Thanes of Ross called in Irish pirates.   The Hebrides and Western Isles, when they obeyed anyone, obeyed the King of Norway. In short, freedom of action against England could come only when Scotland had mastered itself.

Its government, however, took a great impetus from David I. Royal officials replaced the Celtic chiefs : the FitzAlans, for instance, becoming hereditary stewards and so founders of the Stewart line.   A feudal council granted the taxes.   Royal charters feudalized tribal tenures, and privileged the royal burghs, — Edinburgh, Stirling, Berwick, or Roxburgh, — with the trading monopolies which their brethren in England had won.   Sheriffdoms reduced the feudal ' regalities ' to some order and garrisoned the castles, while trial by jury and Glanvill's teaching were absorbed in Scottish law books.   In this new nation, moreover, rose a rich national church, defiant of old claims of supremacy from Canterbury or York, and devoted in its own interest to Scottish independence.   Abbeys of great magnificence, — Holyrood, Newbattle, or Melrose, — were founded by David, who more than doubled the bishoprics and enforced tithe.

The reigns of the two Alexanders (1214–86) were long and comparatively prosperous.   They subdued Argyll and crushed the last pretenders in Moray, intermarriage with Normans divided the strength of Galloway, in 1266 the Norwegians abandoned all claim to Man and the Western Islands.   A growing defiance showed that Scotland could dispense with English help.   Each Alexander, provided with a first wife by England, took a Frenchwoman for his second.   Alexander III's council signed alliance with Llewelyn of Wales, his son married into Flanders, and his daughter the King of Norway.

But all hung on the King's life, and by 1284 all Alexander's children were dead ; at last, on a stormy March night in 1286, he rode his horse over the cliffs on the Firth of Forth, leaving no heir except a granddaughter Margaret, far off in Norway.   The nobles saw in an English marriage for Margaret the only chance of peace, with security for their own English estates, and the treaty signed in August 1290 guaranteed Scottish independence in church and state. That autumn the Maid of Norway died, on her voyage to Scotland.

Edward I was not unready. Even in the marriage negotiations he had reserved his own claim as lord paramount, with custody of the chief castles, and now the Scottish magnates played into his hand. Some native feeling supported the Comyns of Badenoch, who claimed descent from a royalty older than St. Margaret. But the best hereditary right and the strongest following were divided between Robert Bruce (grandfather of the future King) and John Balliol.

The whole line of William the Lion and the male line of his brother David both being extinct, those nearest the Crown were descended from David's daughters; Balliol, grandson of the eldest, and Bruce the son of the second. If primogeniture prevailed, Balliol had the better title; but Bruce, if the rule were nearness to the source. Apart from this, the claimants were much alike. Both were English vassals for English fiefs, both were based on south-west Scotland, both now armed their followers, and both approached Edward. But the veteran Bruce was the more dangerous man. Fifty years earlier Alexander II, then childless, had recognized him as heir. He had fought for Henry III, had been chief justice of England, the Stewarts backed him.

In 1291 Edward with an army behind him met the Scottish nobles, and forced an unwilling admission of his ' sovereign lordship ', on the strength of which he took over the provisional government. Through the whole summer and autumn of 1292 his advisers heard the claims at Berwick; their judgment was that Scotland was an impartible kingdom, ruled by primogeniture, and that Balliol was the heir.

By means satisfying his legal sense, Edward had acquired an over-lordship, which he did not mean to lose. He insisted that the guarantees given to Scotland in 1290 should be cancelled, declared his right of hearing appeals, and forced the new King to plead in person at Westminster. The fierce families, who had accepted the weak Balliol with scorn, found their opportunity when all the nationalities which Edward exasperated got out of control; when in 1294 he was confronted in Wales by the rebellion of Madog, and was himself summoned to appear before the parlement of Paris. Setting up a committee to rule their own King, the Scottish magnates drove Englishmen from court, transferred the Bruce estates to a Comyn, and formed an alliance with France.

In 1296 Edward took the field, massacred the men and women of Berwick, and deposed Balliol, marching without difficulty as far as Elgin. He made no further pretence of giving Scotland another king, but after five months left her apparently conquered, in the hands of English garrisons and of an English council, under the Earl of Surrey.

He took Balliol south with him, together with the ' stone of destiny '
on which Scottish kings were crowned, which was removed from Scone
to Westminster Abbey. Scottish landowners took the oath of fealty in
hundreds and Edward imagined he was free of the problem; ' a good
business to get rid of dirt ', he said when he gave Surrey the seal.

Revolt broke out among humble men and from ordinary causes.
Surrey was an incompetent absentee, while the real English ruler, the
treasurer Cressingham, was a fat Exchequer clerk whose greed drove
Scotland to frenzy. Bands of outlaws held the hills, finding at last one
heroic leader in William Wallace, from an English knightly family in
Clydesdale. While Bruces and Comyns now counselled resistance and
now submitted, Wallace and the Highlander Andrew of Moray acted
without hesitation. In May 1297 we get a first authentic glimpse of
Wallace in action; a dark night at Lanark, houses on fire, the English
sheriff hewed in pieces. All English government perished north of the
Forth, even English priests were murdered. In September, at the bridge
of Stirling, the gate of the Highlands, Wallace destroyed Surrey's army.
Cressingham's skin was tanned into sword-belts, only two isolated
garrisons held out at Roxburgh and Berwick, while the Scots ravaged
the Border from Hexham to Carlisle.

Edward's counter-blow was swift and tremendous. Collecting the
greatest army which had ever yet left England, in July 1298 he marched
through a wasted country to Edinburgh and on the 22nd routed
Wallace's pikemen at Falkirk, his archers proving the skill learned from
the wars of Wales.

The Wallace episode was over, but the resistance which he inspired
lived on, though in a new guise. Seventy years of conflict followed;
divided into a stage of preparation (1298–1306), the winning of independence under Bruce (1306–28), and a new English aggression ending
in compromise (1328–70).

In the conditions of the thirteenth century only the great lords could
save Scotland, not a small Clydesdale laird, and the regents, who after
Falkirk took over power from Wallace, waited warily on events. While
Edward was immersed in French war and quarrelling with his barons,
they kept up resistance. But from 1302 he doggedly devoted himself to
beating Scotland to her knees ; having won peace by his French marriage
and overcome domestic opposition. Year after year, though old and
ill, though barons obstructed and troops deserted, he fought on, till he
died in 1307 beyond the Border.

Before this fierce purpose the Scottish regents might well blench,
especially as both France and the Papacy had failed them. Moreover,
Edward offered them peace, with honour and estates. The elder Bruce,
son of the original competitor, had long stayed aside ; his son Robert
joined Edward in 1303, Comyn did homage next year when Stirling fell,

and only Wallace was left defiant. But he was taken in 1305, and while his head decked London Bridge, a joint assembly of English-Scottish nobles drew up a government for Scotland. Her own parliament and council were to continue, and many Scots were appointed sheriffs, but English officials, controlling the castles, were to remodel Scottish law, Highland customs were abolished, offenders against the peace would be deported. Among the Scotsmen who, that October, swore homage at Richmond was Robert Bruce, who in the following March crowned himself King.

He was now head of his house, with sworn friends among the bishops, but between him and power stood the Red Comyn, Balliol's nephew, whose resistance to Edward had been stauncher than his own. The King's lieutenant had not yet reached Scotland, and the King, Bruce himself had seen, was ailing. Could he win Comyn to support his own claim ? In February 1306 the rivals met in the Franciscan church at Dumfries ; we do not know what passed, what temptations, reproaches, charges of treachery ; only that Bruce came out saying, ' I doubt I ha' slain the Red Comyn ', and that his squires finished the Comyn off. The crown which he desired was now his only means of escape, though between it and him lay murder and sacrilege, besides incarnate vengeance in Edward I.

But a people pardons crime in men who make their destiny. Vainly Edward added terror to force. He deported Bruce's wife, hanged his brothers, distributed the rebels' lands, imprisoned women in cages. Within a year Bruce was mastering the south-west, and with Edward all the English energy died away. The Scottish victory was won by a few determined men, — Bruce and his brother Edward, Sir James Douglas, Thomas Randolph, — who for some years depended even for food on nothing but their own strong heads and hands. They were beset by Highlanders, tracked by bloodhounds, starved with the cold lying in the heather and in long nights of waking. Except the Stewarts, hardly a great family joined them, while the fighting-class changed from one side to another.

Bruce's personal gifts, his tireless strength, gallantry, genial irony, were in themselves an army, and the Church declared for his cause. His first task was to overcome his Comyn and Balliol rivals ; that done, he besieged the garrisons which England left unaided. By the spring of 1314 he held Perth, Aberdeen, Linlithgow, Edinburgh, and Roxburgh ; the castellan of Stirling swore to surrender, if not relieved by the 24th June.

This it was which brought Edward II north again, for Stirling was his father's proudest conquest, and on the 23rd June the English army drew near, numerically twice the strength of the Scots. But half the great earls had refused service, the Welsh and Irish levies were of doubtful value, while forced marching, an enormous baggage train, and bad supplies brought the army to the field tired and shaky.

To the English, approaching from Falkirk, the direct roads to Stirling led over the Bannock burn and through a densely wooded park, of which the Scots held every entrance. In the first day's fighting the English vanguard failed to master these roads; the mass of the army was compelled to cross the Bannock lower down, where it turns sharp north to the Forth. Here, still crossing in detachments, they spent a miserable night, dispirited and with horses unbitted; in broken, swampy ground where, if defeated, they must be driven either into the burn or the sea.

On the early morning of the 24th Bruce, inspired by his first success, left his prepared position and advanced eastward to attack; his knights were dismounted, and his spearmen in solid, impenetrable squares. The English gave themselves into his hand, through bad leadership and rotten morale. As the Scots moved from the wood to the upper strip west of the burn, they knelt to say a paternoster. 'Yon folk kneel to ask mercy,' said Edward; 'they ask mercy,' his knight Umphraville replied, 'but not of you.' His army was crowded on a narrow front, where he could not deploy their numbers; one undisciplined charge after another failed, and when Bruce counter-charged they broke in panic. With great difficulty, and by a circular march, Edward himself escaped to take ship at Dunbar; of his earls, Gloucester was killed, Hereford made prisoner, while Pembroke retreated on foot with his Welshmen. In fact, the army was annihilated; the Scots captured Edward's wardrobe and his privy seal, a rich spoil of vestments decorated the Scottish churches, a flood of ransom money for captured knights enriched Bruce's men. Scottish independence had yet sterner trials to meet, but Bannockburn meant safety so long as Edward II reigned, and year by year Bruce avenged all that Scotland had suffered from Edward I. His troops after taking Berwick twice reached the gates of York, northern England was so ravaged that it had to be exempted from taxation, and so demoralized that whole counties paid ransom and the Warden of the Marches conspired with the Scots. Edward Bruce temporarily conquered Ulster, Scottish intrigue occupied the Marchers in Wales, France renewed her Scottish alliance, the Papacy accepted Bruce as a sovereign king. Spasmodic English expeditions never got near his armies, who, by tethering their ponies, could turn themselves into infantry, whose baggage was a frying-pan and a bag of oatmeal, who struck swiftly and faded into mist. At last the Mortimer group who deposed Edward II agreed to the outright surrender which Edward had refused. The peace of Northampton in 1328 admitted Scottish independence, Bruce's son David was to marry an English princess, and the enemies whom Bruce had disinherited were left without remedy.

Next year Robert Bruce died of leprosy, still under sixty; he had ordered a gorgeous tomb from France, but his heart he left to James Douglas, who took it on crusade against the Moors in Spain. Like Joshua or Maccabeus, his parliament wrote to the Pope, he had endured all to save his people. He had reconquered the Western Isles, armed all men of fighting age, built ships, called burghers to his parliament, and laid down the line of succession to the throne. But he had made many stark enemies, whom he left to his son David, a child of six. David was to reign forty-two years, seven of them in French exile, eleven as an English prisoner, and his insignificance threw Scotland back into civil strife, which blended with the larger pattern of the Hundred Years' War.

Bruce had made his Scotland by force; had been good to his friends but hard on his foes, and dealt lavishly in confiscated land. 'The Disinherited' would be formidable in any case, but doubly so because, like Bruce himself of old, their leaders were men without a country, who combined Scottish ambition with English estates. The Comyn claims had passed by marriage to Englishmen; John Balliol's to his son Edward, who lived only in England or France. Their chance came when in 1330 real power in England went to Edward III, who longed to undo the ignominies of Mortimer. With his connivance the disinherited landed in Fife in 1332, defeated the Scots' army at Dupplin near Perth by their archers, and crowned Balliol King. This foreign invasion awoke Scotland and soon Edward had to rescue his client; at Halidon Hill, outside Berwick, the Scots' mad attack was routed by a superior army, holding a position of its own choice. The wretched Balliol did homage, surrendering to England Berwick, Edinburgh and Lothian, Haddington and Peebles, Roxburgh and Selkirk. David Bruce was sent to France; on paper, England held everything vital south of the Forth.

From this annihilation Scotland was saved by the French war and the disunity of the disinherited, but most of all by the passion of her people. All over Scotland scattered loyalists held out, sending money from their plunderings to maintain their young King in Normandy. And though it was a meaner generation, a new Douglas, a new Stewart, and a new Moray saved Scotland in fighting to save their own broad acres. While Edward was invading France they recaptured Stirling and Edinburgh, and in 1341 recalled David.

Feud, plague, treason, had left little of Scotland, and what was left was nearly lost in one defeat. In the year of Crécy, urged by the French, David invaded England and reached the hills just west of Durham. There the feudal levy of the York churches, with the Percies and Nevilles, broke his army in a hand-to-hand fight at Neville's Cross. For eleven years David was kept prisoner, and became a prisoner in spirit. He was only twenty-two when captured, fearful of ruling stronger men, impressed by his magnificent brother-in-law Edward III, and jealous of his own heir, the Stewart. What price would he not pay to be safe and free ?

Edward had now both Bruce and Balliol in his hands, and soon added to his captives the King of France. He played on these weak instruments what note he pleased, chose finally the cheapest way, sent Balliol to his Yorkshire lands, and sold David's liberty for the crushing ransom of 100,000 marks. It proved an impossible burden and the Scots revolted ; weary of the struggle, David agreed that, if the remaining money were waived, Edward or one of his sons should succeed him. Inflamed by the Stewart, a constitutional opposition sprang up and fettered the last Bruce ; revoked his grants, removed his officers, declared the common law above orders under his seal, and hedged him in with noble committees.

David died in 1371, by which time England was plunged in black disaster in France. Two hundred years of English aggression and of feudalism had left Scotland distraught, while the Celtic north was still unsubdued. Yet her territory was nearly intact, and she had made the hard core of a nation. Even in this most wretched reign Barbour arch-deacon of Aberdeen was collecting material for his epic poem of the ' Brus ', with the motto :

> *Freedom all solace to man gives ;*
> *He lives at ease that freely lives.*

Between Scotland and England lay memories of Bannockburn, of naked prisoners and black, ruined farms, and all the breadth of a Border for ever under the shadow of war.

CHAPTER X

GROWTH OF THE CONSTITUTION, 1215–1377

THE uniqueness of the English constitution consisted in this, that it alone carried into the modern world the mediaeval ideal. Until the nineteenth century it rested, as to some extent it still rests, on three corner-stones : one common law which binds even the government, a concentration of government in one high court, and the incorporation in that court of local communities with inherited customs. Many other countries in 1300 had parliaments or estates, but in England alone Parliament survived, for the reason that these ingredients were built into its structure from the beginning.

Unity of our institutions began with the Normans' conquest, at one blow, of a country without serious difference of race, and small enough to be ruled from one centre. That centre was the King and his court ; Household, great officers, tenants-in-chief, and prelates. Within this court an increasing business called for specialized branches. The Exchequer had rooms and barons of its own by 1120, a bench of judges for common pleas began about 1178, and a King's Bench for more important cases kept its own roll by 1234. All this went on into the fourteenth century, sometimes because the baronage demanded public departments working in the light of day, but inevitably also from the needs of a growing State.

The King, for instance, had to seal thousands of orders a year, which set each wheel of government turning ; for that he must have his privy seal, to use when he was separated from his Chancellor. But when pressure of business and the Ordainers' attack set up a special Keeper of that seal, it became detached from the Household ; ' gone out of court ', as Exchequer had before it. In Edward III's time the Chancellor's jurisdiction broke off likewise from Council, for there was urgent need for such an equity court, elastic enough to deal with intricacies of law and conscience, trusts, for example, or contracts, which the stiff rules of common law could not cover.

But this elaboration had not destroyed the original of power in the central court. Government was still a domestic thing. If the King's treasure was no longer, like Edward the Confessor's, kept in his bedroom, his Chamber still had to clothe his servants ; his Wardrobe held not only robes and jewels, but engines of war. Edward III's Chancellor would dine with him, Exchequer clerks slept in the palace of Westminster, and the royal doctor in the Wardrobe. Outside his Household there were no trained officials, and in the emergency of war the Household instantly took the front place. Like Louis XIV's *Maison du Roi*, it provided the core of the army ; it alone had the speed and unified power which could make an army move. hire mercenaries, commandeer oats or bacon, draw upon foreign bankers.

From their private servants the Edwards thus recruited public officials, nor did the special departments limit the parent Council's power. At will it would call up a case from the Benches, refer petitions to the Chancellor, or sit as a whole in the Exchequer. The King occasionally sat in person to correct the law ; ' by God's blood,' we hear Edward I harangue his judges, ' you shall give me a good writ before you go hence '. His judges still drafted statutes. ' Do not gloss the statute,' said a chief justice in 1305 to counsel, ' we know it, because we made it.'

While government remained so fluid, despotism was never far away, and the crises from 1215 to 1341 were all landmarks in a struggle to make it impossible. It was vital for our history that the political classes concentrated upon mastering the King's court, and making the law of that court prevail over the King. And though in Magna Carta they safeguarded many privileges of their own, they did so by getting them recognized by the King's court, which, they insisted, must for great purposes represent themselves.

Thus in one sense feudalism was the root of the constitution, which survived because the King's vassals claimed to be his councillors and to give taxation only by consent. Of Henry III they demanded from 1238 onwards the nomination of a select council, while from Edward II they asked the choice not only of high officials but the heads of his Household.

So, though they fought for their own franchise, like the Church that often supported them, with all their shortcomings they championed the ideal that law was not the ruler's mere will but a rule of righteousness. ' Take away justice ', cried St. Augustine, ' and what are kingdoms but dens of thieves ? ' The notion of a sovereign State could not co-exist with the universal Church and was inconsistent also with mediaeval thought, to which law was something sacred and unalterable, and the ruler's business not to change but to declare it. Different minds would put this with different emphasis ; Churchmen might make law the voice of God, the new students of Aristotle might call it the law of reason, lawyers would defend it on ground of custom and antiquity ; statutes against the Charter, said Parliament in 1368, ' shall be holden for none '. But the whole age agreed that law was a righteous rule, obedience to which was the very definition of a king in contrast with a tyrant.

If such ideals assisted, they did not create in English government its unique strength, which came from the steady enforcement since

1154 of one law by the King's court. It was ' common ' law, and first because it covered the whole country outside the Marches. It was ' common ' also because the royal judges bent all privileges to its rules, constricting feudal, borough, and Church courts within shrinking limits. This law was strong because it was both positive and professional. It gave remedies by definite writs, framed in Chancery to meet problems as they arose, and so multiplied that the 39 writs available in Glanville's time were 121 by 1260, and over 400 by 1307. Such law was judge-made law, for Bracton's book was built on previous decisions in the King's court, and it was also insular, borrowing from Roman law little but a more polished form. Its character demanded professional inter-pretation. By Edward I's day most of his judges were laymen, while the same leading counsel argued over the same writs before the same judges from Canterbury to Bodmin. Before the King died a formal education had been arranged for legal apprentices; from 1292 French year-books were being written to teach the practice of the courts; by the year of Crécy young barristers were housed in the Temple.

This strong law hardened English liberties for the very reason that, when it began, feudalism and old communities were living things. An Angevin King could make no frontal attack on his baronage, nor dispense with the loyalty of shires and towns. His law did not destroy their life, but caught it up in its own, treating court-leets and views of frankpledge as royal courts, and tenures as part of the King's law. Barons were forced to judgment in his court, where they learned, in *Novel disseisin* for instance, to appreciate a swift remedy. In a hundred instances their officials worked hand in hand with the sheriff, while at the eyre their bailiffs shared responsibility for producing wrong-doers. We have seen the method, too, whereby government assigned land title, tested borough custom, fined villages who sheltered the guilty — by the universal method of the sworn jury. Royal law, then, was partly made by the people themselves, who, year in, year out, were giving thousands of verdicts on facts within their own knowledge, but on principles put to them by royal judges. So the common law and representative government grew, as they must endure, together.

The Curia Regis whence this law came kept its original character till the reign of John. True, on a great occasion like Becket's trial it would expand to something like the shape provided in Magna Carta for a grant of scutage, a meeting of all the King's barons. But for most of Henry II's reign it was still the same varying assembly; thus only the presence of magnates, as distinct from the professional judges, drew a faint line between the court we call King's Bench and the Council. From about 1200, however, political reasons brought about a change.

Its full meetings began to embrace others than tenants-in-chief. The loss of the French provinces, with John's expenditure, demanded new taxation, which could be most easily raised through the whole land-owning class. Knights had long been coming to Council with the record of some suit, they had been commissioned to clear a gaol, or to act with a justice of assize : apart from their administrative value, they meant a body of opinion to which both King and barons appealed. We find, therefore, an ever-increasing summons of knights to the Council. In 1213 John ordered four from each shire ; in 1227 elected knights reported on the bounds of the forest. From the use of them to assess taxes and hand the proceeds over, it was not a long step to assemble them for the same purpose in Council, which was done (for the first time on our present knowledge) in 1254. That year each sheriff had to explain to his county court the King's need of money, and how the barons had promised to serve in person, and ask them to elect two knights, fully empowered to treat with the Council. In 1261 de Mont-fort's party and the King rivalled each other in summoning knights to support them ; in 1265 the Earl called representatives from selected boroughs ; in 1268 Henry did the same.

It was, moreover, impossible to isolate the idea of government by consent. A carucage in 1220 was resisted in the Yorkshire shire court by baronial stewards, who said their lords had not been consulted. Royal and Papal taxation of spiritualities drove the clergy to demand representation in their synods ; after many experiments, by 1283 the Canterbury province obtained its Convocation, including, in addition to bishops, deans, archdeacons, and the heads of monasteries, one delegate from each cathedral and two for the parish clergy of each diocese.

Such pressure, and this enlargement of Council, carried two natural consequences : a demand for annual meetings of this enlarged body, and a clearer distinction between it and the small continuous Council. ' Parliament ', which in twelfth-century poets meant a ' parley ' any-where, between kings or lovers, could be applied by William Marshall to his Welsh honour court. But in 1242 we find it officially used by Henry III of his Council, and when the Provisions of Oxford asked three ' parliaments ' a year, the baronage were asking not a new thing nor popular representation, but regular sessions of the full Council, to which they were accustomed since the crown-wearing days of Norman kings.

Such, and no more, was the primary meaning of ' Parliament ' to the death of Edward I. It was a meeting of the King's court, in par-ticular to do justice ; for cases in the benches were adjourned ' till the next parliament ', with which the judges were reunited. It was a solemn meeting at fixed dates ; none might come to it wearing arms ; no member of it might be prosecuted by a lesser court during its session. The King's presence made it, so that holding a Parliament in his absence was made a charge by Henry III against de Montfort. How any particular meeting was composed, and its programme, depended on the King's intimate advisers; it was for them also to assign business; to despatch this petition to the Exchequer, that to the royal Lieutenant in Scotland, or to reserve some for the King's own eye.

It took a hundred years to become 'Parliament' in our meaning; no contemporary suggested that something new had come into being, and nothing had. None mentioned the point of who had a vote; for knights and townsmen represented not so many individuals, but came as delegates from communities with a continuous life of centuries. None spoke yet of separate 'houses', for Parliament was only the King's administration, writ large.

There was, then, no 'model' Parliament in Edward I's time. He summoned knights and burgesses in 1275 as he did in 1295, and in the latter year proctors of the clergy also. But in 1283 he called a northern Council at York, a southern at Southampton. In 1303 he demanded new customs duties from an assembly of merchants, just as in 1301 he ordered a special number of lawyers up from the universities, and in 1305 summoned his favourite friars. His grandson did much the same. In 1360 four 'parliaments' simultaneously granted taxes, at London, Worcester, Taunton, and Lincoln; in 1371 commoners nominated by the Crown voted a grant.

The essence of Parliament was, in fact, the King with his councillors, and the regular session of the Council (twice a year normally under Edward I) was called 'Parliament', fairly irrespective of who were present. Thus at Easter 1305 Edward called up knights and burgesses and dealt with their petitions, but 'Parliament' proceeded, weeks after they were dismissed, to important questions like the government of Scotland. And at Michaelmas that year he summoned only thirty-seven councillors; yet that meeting was also a 'Parliament'.

To a much later date all sorts of anomalies showed that it was rather a way of getting the King's business done than a body with definite powers, or an obligation rather than a right. Colchester was exempted from sending members by Richard II, because it was rebuilding its walls; villeins begged they need not pay taxes, because their lord had done service in Parliament; abbots and towns made desperate efforts to escape attendance. Nevertheless, we find by 1360 that the King's Council has broken into a Council, a Peerage, and a 'House' of Commons, with powers joint and several which can be distinguished.

1. After the baronial appointment of a Council in 1258, a distinction grew steadily between the Council *per se* and the Council in Parliament. The smaller body was put on oath, some of them were salaried, by Crécy it was a definite enough body to have its own rooms in the Star Chamber on the river front at Westminster; not that we must exaggerate this definition, for Edward III's Council was still very vague. But the

Council in Parliament kept its old character of a vassal court, where homage was done and where the King announced his daughters' marriages. In 1327 Sir Thomas Berkeley was tried in Parliament for the murder of Edward II, and acquitted by twelve knights, his peers.

2. From this inherited character, and even more from their struggle against the Crown, the Council in Parliament slowly turned into the Lords. Their original title was not in the least hereditary. Edward I summoned 43 in 1296, 110 in 1300, and the barony of his time was barony by writ. Yet the idea of tenure was older, for all those summoned were tenants-in-chief, and it was more fundamental, since from it the barons got the idea of peerage. 'There are no peers in England', Peter des Roches scornfully told them at the Marshall's trial in 1234. In one sense he was right, and few things have been more important in English history than this; that English peerage has never been a nobility of blood, but an official distinction. Nobility belonged to the official representative of the family alone, his sons were commoners with no more privilege than a yeoman. It was thus on official grounds that Magna Carta distinguished greater and lesser barons; there were earldoms and baronies so ancient or privileged that their holders had a right to an individual summons to Council.

In this vague sense they entitled themselves ' peers of the realm ' when they put conditions on Edward II, and in 1341 compelled Edward III to admit that a lord was responsible only to his peers. Gradually they insisted that once summoned, always summoned, — making a peerage an inheritable expectancy. But at least till the fifteenth century original motions of tenure persisted; whoever actually held a barony, the husband of the heiress or the stepfather of the youthful heir, would receive a writ. At last in 1387 the first creation of a hereditary peerage, by letters patent, began the closing of the ranks.

Edward III's dependence on his baronage showed itself also in frequent ' great councils ', of bishops and barons alone, which helped further to distinguish them from the sworn permanent Council. By the middle of the reign the Lords had made good their claim to represent the superior part of the Curia Regis, and the judges took a definitely inferior place, attending Parliament now only as advisers. As the King's highest court the Lords heard the Commons' petitions, and specially claimed it as their right to vindicate the common law; earlier, perhaps, than we realize, the rule was accepted that a true Parliament must include the magnates. Council, on the other hand, handled the vague powers left to the Crown, kept no rolls, acted on secret information, and arrested men on writs of *sub poena* under privy seal, without an indictment. So the two oldest parts of the King's court, the baronage and the councillors, gradually became separate bodies, standing for rival principles.

3. Nothing at the end of Edward I's reign indicated the great place destined for the third element in his court, — the Commons. In the *Confirmatio Cartarum* of 1297 he did not explicitly accept the view that ' the Community ' necessarily included knights and townsmen, and excluded ' the ancient aids ' from the Community's control of taxation. Their presence was still haphazard, their rôle in making law was confined to petition, they never claimed to take part in judgments.

Their history, indeed, depends essentially on one fact, that they were fitted into the central structure by steps so gradual that their position grew impregnable by stealth.   To make local representative verdicts assist his justice, to see face to face knights who would assist the smooth collection of taxes, to assert his court's power to hear all his subjects irrespective of tenure, for all this Edward I created an outer fringe of his court.   But by Edward II's death this custom of using the Commons had turned into a claim, through the knights' usefulness to all factions and the Crown's need of money.

Between 1307 and 1340 a more vital thing had taken place ; knights and burgesses were spoken of in particular as ' the Community ', and acted together.   To this all-important fact many converging forces had contributed.   Primogeniture threw the barons' younger sons into the world as commoners.   For two centuries knights led, and burgesses attended, the county court and made up juries.   Edward I ignored all social differences in his taxes, except the scale of wealth.   And in England the deepest social line was drawn between the magnates, — so near to the King in blood, marked out by the idea of peerage, with elaborate households and London houses, — and the country knights or merchants.   Not only so ; the knight and townsman represented more than himself or his pride of family, — a community and not a class. It was for that reason that Edward summoned them, taking pains to compel their presence by binding them in sureties, and requiring them to pledge their communities.

From immemorial local training their consciousness matured with astonishing speed.   Their earliest interest in Parliament was in its rôle as a court of justice, for which reason they demanded annual meetings, but under Edward II they organized collective petitions or ' bills ', asking a remedy against the drain of money to Rome or the corruption of juries.   A habit grew up of knights and burgesses retiring from the Palace of Westminster for private consultation in the Chapter House, while by the middle of the century they appointed their own clerk, and their own ' orator ', or Speaker, to represent them when they rejoined the magnates.   In the shires something like 40 per cent of these members sat in more than one Parliament, while Oxford and Colchester, under the first two Edwards, each re-elected a member twelve times.   It is not surprising to find such a body aggressive. They protested against the choice of sheriffs as members. The Council itself was deferential to them, supplying them, for instance, with copies of projected laws and asking their written amendments. By 1354 they were emphatic that an ordinance made in Council had not the legal weight of a statute made in Parliament.

At that date, therefore, we may say that a Parliament had arisen out of Edward I's Council, of which he had never dreamed; two houses, one of Lords spiritual and temporal, one of Commons, claiming between them the largest powers which that Council had ever employed. It had taken this particular shape, largely because the third element whom Edward had summoned, representative of the lower clergy, had disappeared. Having their own spiritual courts and the Canon law, and their officials being technically Papal officers, they had little interest in the judicial side of Parliament, and though they could no longer resist taxation on their spiritual wealth, they kept the shadow of independence by voting such taxes in Convocation. From Edward II's time they disregarded the *praemunientes* clause in the writs summoning the archbishops; when the laity voted a fifteenth and a tenth, the clergy habitually voted a tenth as ' a free gift ', and only the occasional presence of a few proctors for the clergy in Parliament, holding a watching brief for their interests, kept up the memory of Edward I's design of one court for all estates of his realm.

The period of rapid growth was in the years after 1340, flowing directly from the stress of war finance. From the Bardi and the Peruzzi of Florence alone Edward borrowed over £350,000, and in 1335 this great firm went bankrupt. To get ready money he tried every device in the Crown's power, and every dodge of a bad debtor. He sometimes seized the whole wool supply at a fixed low price and sold it high; levied maltolts, or export duties far above the statutory scale; gave a monopoly of export to London rings, provincial firms, or foreigners. But all such schemes broke down, not only on a conflict between wool-growers and big exporters who wanted a single Staple, and local exporters who wanted many, but on the hard fact that they killed the goose with the golden eggs, and that this government speculation destroyed the yield of ordinary taxation.

With admirable persistence Parliament used their power to stop this rake's progress. Rather than admit defeat in principle, they would ratify by a subsequent vote what they considered illegal. Thus in 1340 they voted the extra wool duty for three years, but accompanied it with a statute which abolished tallage and all other taxes without assent. In 1341 they demanded an audit of taxes, beginning also to appropriate or earmark their grants for the specific purpose of the war. For twenty years Edward juggled with merchants outside Parliament, and for twenty years Parliament followed his every step. In 1353–4 statutes of the Staple broke the worse monopolies, in 1362 another forbade any extra-parliamentary wool subsidy, a third in 1373 made statutory the irregular customs taken since 1303 as tonnage and poundage.

We can, indeed, say that Parliament was fully recognized as the King's highest court. Even the royalist bishop Stapledon had urged that the Despensers, if exiled by Parliament, only by Parliament could be restored. Their legislative action slowly disentangled the notion of a statute, and though from Edward I's time we have a separate statute roll, it was more decisive when Parliament, from about 1350, argued that a statute could only originate in their petition, not in any separate request from clergy or merchants, and, further, that statutes must embody their petition's words. The judges placed orders of Council below statute, and impugned writs which conflicted with them. Experience convinced the opportunist Edward III that parliamentary money was the only money that came in, and he allowed his Chamber to slide under Exchequer control. The Lords insisted that it was for them, and not for Council, finally to adjudicate on petitions. As to the choice of ministers, Parliament failed, it is true, to keep direct nomination, but ministers had to act with Parliament, and after the crisis of 1341 Edward never opposed a clique of Household officials to the officers of State. Finally, Parliament was linked by hoops of steel to the common law and common lawyers. Like them, it stood for certainty and unity of law; like them, it was at war with the discretionary, vague jurisdiction of Council. Its leading members were often lawyers, while its very way of doing business was by petition and bill on single points, as in the law courts.

Local government, again, illustrates the truth that Parliament created no new principle, but continued the work which Angevin rules had begun. Its statutes hedged in the sheriff's tourn, while a mass of private bills made it, as it still is, the ultimate director of local government. It captured also the justices of the peace, from 1327 onwards by statutes enlarging their powers, and though these justices were royal nominees, they invariably included local magnates. Beginning as police officials, more and more they became judges, using the procedure of the common law, — the jury and presentment on oath.

Yet it is a far cry from Edward III's Parliament to parliamentary supremacy. The old unity of government, though it indued Parliament with half its strength and distinguished it from Continental systems of estates, meant that Parliament was both more and less than a legislature. It was still the highest court to which, for instance, difficult cases were reserved by the Treason Act of 1352. Its 'triers' would remit petitions to lower courts, and it was still the temporary concentration of all government departments. In the Parliament of 1305 the King legislated to stop the monks' money going to the Pope; but he also gave ten oaks from Inglewood Forest to a hospital burned by the Scots, heard an Oxford University petition for a separate prison for women, and bade his Exchequer deal with a squabble between Dunwich and Warbleswick as to the silting up of their harbour. Well after 1360 this confusion of function, or work shared in common between those who were only different aspects of one court, continued. The same case might be adjourned from a hearing by the Lords to a hearing in Council. The Chancellor still presided in Parliament, which he summoned through his clerks, just as he issued writs to lower courts. And one of Edward's favourite knights, his chamberlain Burghersh, sat alike with Council in Star Chamber and with the judges in King's Bench.

Again, the very meaning of law in that age barred the development of a true legislature, for by law they meant a reaffirmation of the charters and the giving to all of their customary rights. His coronation oath bound the King to accept not new law, but ' the laws and righteous customs which the community of your realm shall have chosen '. His ' prerogative ' was his right, his regalities as overlord. He could cancel a statute, as did Edward in 1341 because his councillors told him it infringed his regalities; he could pardon crime; he must execute the law. To that end he issued commissions, as to the justices of Labourers, for example, after the Black Death. He had functions with which his English high court could hardly interfere: he was Lord of Ireland, overlord of Lords Marchers, in a sense head of the Church. He had great estates which were his own, and from which he drew wheat or rents or armed men. Like other lords he was expected to live on his own revenue, except in extraordinary cases when he must ask an aid. And as no lord could be sued in his own court, so there was no legal remedy against the King, and hence two steps were taken to depose Edward II: his own resignation and a repudiation of homage by his court.

What then was the position of Parliament by 1360? It claimed to be master of the chief sources of taxation. It was the chief tribunal. It made the common law predominant. It was an arena within which the King's ministers had to work, assembling the classes which controlled local government, and having a publicity and financial strength which made perilous any alternative scheme of government through the Household.

Yet its powers were negative rather than positive, it could prevent rather than initiate. Its sessions were not long enough to acquire tradition, nor did it aspire to control all functions. The Commons repeatedly washed their hands of foreign affairs; ' let the Cinque Ports ', they said, ' carry out their feudal duty of defending the seas '. They were very deferential to the magnates, whose seals they sometimes attached to copies of laws sent to the county courts. And as there were subjects like religion in which no mediaeval Parliament would go far, so, too, there were areas surviving from a feudal world, and no members had yet appeared from the palatinates of Chester and Durham.

From 1362, indeed, the King could raise no general tax without their sanction. But he had an independent revenue of about £60,000; from feudal sources, farms of the shires, justice, and customs duties. Despite statute, his courtiers still seized supplies by purveyance, and his commissioners conscripted soldiers. The nobles, full of war enthusiasm, would readily grant a tax in a great council, while his inner Council freely negotiated loans from boroughs and merchants. As to the making of law, statute and ordinance had been indistinguishable under Edward I, and still differed only in degree, even though now the mass of petitions nominally originated in the Commons. Both came from the royal Council, each was law, and the difference between them lay rather in the time period for which each was designed than in their authorship; for a statute was supposed to incorporate some permanent addition to law, and was solemnly proclaimed in the shires. But when at the end of a session Parliament sifted the petitions, the decision which should be enrolled as statutes was left to the Council and judges, who might so draft statutes as to evade the Commons' intention. The utmost we can say is that the Commons' assent was necessary to pass a statute; the King alone could enforce it, he could obstruct it, and in ordinances possessed a rival method of making law.

Till Richard II's reign one Roll held the proceedings alike of Council and Parliament, and both history and practical fact gave the Council a dangerous power. Parliament might protest that it must not meddle with common-law rights such as freehold, but someone, after all, must deal with illegality in the intervals of Parliament, and as the Lords proved themselves unable to cope, the mass of private petitions, therefore, drifted to Council or Chancery. For the weakness of mediaeval government was not absence of law, but its non-execution, which only the continuous Council could correct, with its swift procedure, its trained staff, and its hold over the sheriffs. Every step in social progress made, moreover, for more specialized government; the intricacies of the Law Merchant, equity which only the Chancellor could give, anarchy on distant Marches, — all these demanded speed and subtlety, not to be got from the fourteenth-century Parliament.

Council, the original heart of government, was thus still its keypoint. Before Parliament could meet the needs of a growing State, there would have to be a revolution, not so much in law as in society.

BOOK III

IN TRANSITION
1360–1509

CHAPTER I

THE END OF THE MIDDLE AGES, 1361-1376

IN 1348 the Black Death, the bubonic plague which for a thousand years has dogged Asia, was carried from Genoese factories in the Crimea to Italy, struck down the gay life of Florence, passed on to France, and in August reached Weymouth. After devastating Bristol, early next year the pestilence broke on London and East Anglia, crept to the north, and was still scourging Scotland and Ireland in 1350.

No statistics exist accurately to measure its horror. Three archbishops of Canterbury, 800 Norwich diocese priests, half the monks of Westminster, died in a year. Manor-rolls speak of villages where the corn was uncut, cattle wandering, women ploughing, and children abandoned for whom the court found guardians; of empty fish-ponds, or manorial mills stopped because the grinders were few. Parliament and law courts were suspended. The dead townsmen were shovelled two-deep into plague pits, while village churchyards had to take in another field. It bore hardest, no doubt, on the poor, and on monks in their cloisters, but it spared none, from the King's daughter down to the poet-anchorite Richard Rolle.

The death, which carried off perhaps one-third of the English people, was cruel and sudden : hard tumours, burning fever, livid patches on the body, bleeding from the lungs, and within three days the end. In calamity on such a scale human nature recovers its balance more easily in material than in moral things; the Black Death did not destroy manor or gild, but it shook religion and plunged a sword of discontent into society. A spiritual feverishness showed that men were unhappy. Wandering fanatics, scourging each other till the blood ran, passed through London. Monks broke from their cloisters, villeins ran off from their manors. Never was life more luxurious or dress more fantastic among the rich. All classes asked more wealth, higher wages, or profitable war ; walking in a spiritual desert, finding no peace. In 1361-2 plague reappeared, this time called especially the plague of children, and accompanied by a murrain among cattle.

Meantime, despite the peace of Brétigny, the great war went on. Poitevin cities and Pyrenean nobles accepted English overlordship sullenly; north of the Loire English captains refused to surrender their castles. Bands of discharged mercenaries, under high-sounding names like 'the great company', ravaged France, living by torture and ransom, and offering their sword to the highest bidder. In the separate war proceeding in Brittany the English claimant Montfort triumphed in 1364 with the help of the best English generals, but the Duchy remained French at heart. Most decisive of all would be Aquitaine, the huge domain stretching from the Loire to the Spanish mountains. To conciliate his French subjects Edward III granted it for life to the Black Prince, who set up a costly Court at Bordeaux. But the Gascons were proud of being immediately under the Crown, nobles saw with anger an Englishman in every high office, while the clergy demanded benefices for Gascons alone.

Two remarkable men watched and guided a revived French patriotism; Charles V, frail in health, lover of books, subtle and far-sighted, and his general du Guescelin, a soldier of infinite patience and courage. Within ten years they organized a paid army, equipped with archers and artillery, and trained in the tactics of du Guescelin's experience. While Edward was content to borrow merchant ships, the French built a royal fleet. Their diplomacy won the heiress of Flanders for Charles' brother Philip of Burgundy; friendly dynasties were established in Hainault and Brabant, and the Netherlands were lost to England as a base.

Actually the immediate crisis came from Spain. In 1366 Pedro the Cruel of Castile, whose ability had outraged his nobles and Churchmen, was deposed by his bastard brother Henry of Trastamare, and appealed in the name of chivalry and kinship to the Black Prince. Henry, who had come from France, would certainly threaten Aquitaine. But the English decision turned out to be fatal, for it divided, as the wise Chandos prophesied, their energies in men and money. One more famous victory came to the heroes of so many fields, the Black Prince and Chandos, the Captal de Buch, and English archers; striking out for Burgos, in April 1367 they crushed the Spaniards and French at Najera. But it was their last. Dysentery struck down the Prince's army, while he himself began the dropsy which soon rendered him unable to sit a horse. In 1369 Pedro, once more deposed, was murdered by his brother's hand, leaving to the English three deadly inheritances: dishonoured debts which involved heavy taxation and hence rebellion in Aquitaine — two daughters, soon respectively married to Edward III's sons John of Gaunt and Edmund of York, who were thereby pledged to prefer Spain as the theatre of war — and Castile committed to the French friendship.

The opportunity of France and the Gascon nobles had arrived. By the end of 1372 Poitou and all north of Gascony was lost, Brittany went the next year. One English expedition was wiped out by the Castilian fleet off La Rochelle. The armies of Gaunt and Knolles

vainly marched from Calais into the heart of France, and on in wide
circles to Bordeaux; stealthily avoiding battle, cutting off stragglers,
the French allowed men and horses to perish of exhaustion. In 1375
a truce was signed, gradually extended to 1377, and outside Calais and
Brest, Bordeaux and Bayonne, hardly anything was left of the English
occupation. So swift were the effects of a France reorganized and the
loss of sea-power.

On the English side this was not a people's war, but one waged by
military nobility in the Crown's pay; and the Crown was now enfeebled. Edward III had aged quickly under the influence of his
mercenary mistress Alice Perrers, and a corrupt group of courtiers.
Disease drove the Black Prince into retirement. His next brother,
Lionel of Clarence, had died, leaving only a daughter married to the
young Earl of March. John of Gaunt showed no soldierly qualities
except courage, and with his own ambitions upon Spain was not
anxious to risk fortune and fame in Gascony. Half of the famous
captains, Chandos and Audley for instance, were dead, and except from
pardoned criminals it was becoming difficult to raise recruits. There
was another more fatal evil, that those who should have united against
France were manœuvring for power at home; for while the King was
surrounded by doctors, Gaunt attacked the idea of a succession to the
Crown through a woman, that is, through Lionel's daughter, and his
enormous estates, his retained knights, were feared by all friends of the
dying Black Prince and his son.

This disenchanted society and divided Court could get no leading
from the Church. Politically, what Boniface VIII had begun, the
captivity at Avignon completed, the English government no longer
fearing Rome and regarding it with a blend of bargaining indifference.
Loss of their Italian lands compelled the Popes to tighten financial
pressure on northern Europe, while if they tried sincerely to end the
war, the English suspected mediators who lived on French soil. Peter's
pence fell into arrears, Parliament angrily rejected a claim for John's
tribute, and spoke of the sinful city of Avignon where all was bought and
sold.

Patronage, that is, the choice of clergy and their means of support,
was a burning question, involving every property-holder from the
King downwards. On this a struggle had never ceased since early
feudal days, between property-owners and native churches on one side,
and Rome on the other. From the thirteenth century the Pope had
claimed a right of overriding the local patron, to 'provide' a benefice
with a priest, nor was the practice entirely bad, for it stopped the
appointment of candidates of local factions, and provided for university
graduates. But it had become monstrously abused, especially since the
bankrupt Popes at Avignon laid hold on it as a means of paying their

staff. A custom grew up of ' reservation ', at first in special cases like the benefices of those who died at the Papal court, but rapidly extending to almost all patronage except that belonging to laymen. The cardinals were the worst offenders; spiritual interests of parishes were lost sight of, a benefice becoming a mere legal right to be scrambled for by claimants four or five deep. A centralized Papacy thus disintegrated the Church by making every benefice precarious, and by encouraging the worst evils of pluralism and an absentee clergy. The universal outcry in Europe, though not all rising from the purest motives, was at least grounded on a solid grievance. In England since Henry II's time the King's court claimed to control a parsonage as a freehold, and now the statutes of Provisors (1351 and 1365) forbade all further ' provision '; with one apparent effect, that henceforward the Popes generally ceased to appoint aliens. Nevertheless, provisions went on, for spiritual bodies could not defy the Pope, while the King found it an easy way of rewarding his servants. Nor did the Acts of Praemunire (1353 and 1365) much affect the position; for in threatening outlawry against those who pleaded at Rome matters cognizable in royal courts, they only restated a claim made of old by Norman kings. No effort was made to cut down the sphere allotted to English spiritual courts, from which appeals continued to Rome. Had not the Commons themselves called the Pope ' sovereign governor of holy church on earth ' ?

Yet English religion was definitely more insular by the end of the century. War and Avignon snapped many links, for Papal diplomacy obstructed our policy in Germany and the Netherlands, and taxes on aliens drove many priories to break their connection with foreign monasteries. This cleavage was immensely deepened after 1377 by the great Schism, when for forty years England and northern Europe obeyed a Pope at Rome, while France, Scotland, and Spain obeyed his rival at Avignon. Monasticism especially felt the strain, for what obedience could English Cluniacs give when their mother-house obeyed an enemy Pope? In every direction the Crown was tightening its hold. Criminals were compelled more sternly now to prove their clerkship in a lay court; there was constant interference to reform the monasteries in royal patronage.

The face of England, particularly the rich eastern Midlands, was covered by monasteries and nunneries; comprising nearly twelve hundred separate foundations and containing perhaps nine thousand persons fully professed. There were still holy and learned men among them, historians at St. Albans, mystical writers, illuminators and librarians, men who served their neighbours as doctors, preachers, and administrators. But the great day of monasticism had passed. Less than twenty houses were founded in the fourteenth century; colleges at Oxford and Cambridge, built after the Black Death, were meant to fill up the wastage of secular priests, and the Oxford Benedictine students numbered hardly a hundred. Cut off by war and schism from Papal supervision, the Orders lost discipline and unity, their triennial chapters often showing lists of houses who sent no representative. Yet only regular visitation could have healed the damage done by the Black Death, the bad financial system of water-tight compartments (prior, cellarer, or sacrist, each with his separate endowments), or the power of one bad abbot to cripple a house with debt for a generation. Moral scandals were not worse than might have been expected in this large body. The outstanding impression from the bishops' registers and their own visitations is different, though decisive : that the cloistered life was melting into the common world. Just as the monks said their confessions in English, so many lived the lives of English laymen. The abbot of Glastonbury had his choice of many country houses, the abbot of Bury boasted his outriders and silver plate, the canons of St. Frideswide, Oxford, kept their pack of hounds. Monks had to be forbidden to take part in archery, attend dances, sing songs at taverns, occupy separate bedrooms, entertain their relations in the house, or keep hawks. At every point of contact with their neighbours, they did some harm. Their appropriation of parish churches (Glastonbury alone had twenty-one in Somerset) was a scandal, for they took the mass of tithe for themselves and served the church through an ill-paid vicar. To get money they offered corrodies, or allowances in board and lodging, to their neighbours. Their charities were sometimes embezzled, even their hospices for guests were sometimes leased out as inns. Though not harsher probably than other landlords, they were more conservative and more unpopular ; on the 250 manors of Bury or on the St. Albans' estates there were perpetual riots, refusal to do services, and armed risings in the towns at their gates against grinding at their mill or court fines. The bitter Wyclif speaks of ' the religion of fat cows '; the layman Chaucer voices another growing feeling, on the anomaly of robust men who had given up manual labour and professed an ascetic ideal which they did not observe.

Much more devotion even in these later days flowed out to the Friars, from whom Kings chose their confessors, and whose best preachers were masters of vigorous English. To die in a friar's habit was still the death of the pious. Before Edward III died a reform movement among the Franciscans founded the Observantines, whose houses were the best in England till Tudor days. Many friars showed themselves well able to cross literary swords with Wyclif ; many had a radical strain, which led them to encourage the peasants against monkish landlords ; many protested against superfluous riches and Papal taxation. But they had deadly enemies. Great numbers were licensed to hear confessions, and with their portable altars attracted offerings away from parish churches. They had a standing quarrel with the universities, who grudged their exemption from the usual course in Arts before taking a degree. They were accused of captivating children, and, unless they were greatly maligned, had lost much of their morale. Popular ballads and official reports agree with the men of letters, whether the conservative Gower, the mystic Langland, or Chaucer; how the friar loved good living and intrigued with women, how his cape was full of pins for the peasants, or how they got subscriptions for their church's painted window from anyone who liked to see his name inscribed. Having few endowments, they depended more than ever upon begging, which had become a system whereby districts were farmed to individual friars to make their profit.

The parish church was the heart of popular religion. Round it clustered a primitive machinery of churchwardens and poor rates; parishioners took turns to tend the altar lights, or to provide sacramental bread. They took pride in covering its walls with paintings of miracles, of Christ in majesty, St. George and the popular saints. There were parish priests — Chaucer has told us of one — who were true shepherds of their flocks, though peasants themselves and sometimes of villein birth, and the standard set forth in their devotional books was a high one. But of the eight or nine thousand livings perhaps half were annexed to monasteries, colleges, or cathedrals, and the maximum salary officially fixed for their vicars was eight marks a year, hardly more than an agricultural labourer earned; in the rich Norwich diocese over a hundred livings had under six marks. No wonder there was a constant exchange of livings, or a rush to take easy work in the towns; bishops' registers show that the monks let church chancels go to ruin, that windows were broken and service-books torn, while the vicar hunted the hare or played chess in the parish inn. In more remote districts many priests broke their vow of celibacy, and the document often reveals a tragedy, for the accused had lived with the same woman over many years. And systems imposed from above injured parish life. Many young clergy were given leave of absence to study at a university or act as chaplain to some baron; children held livings, if they were sons of a great person, and the cardinals themselves set a scandalous example of pluralism.

Perhaps the Church's most radical fault was simply that there were too many clergy. At one ordination in 1349 the bishop of Hereford ordained 52 acolytes, 73 sub-deacons, 52 deacons, 44 priests. William of Wykeham in his thirty-seven years at Winchester ordained 1273 priests, and there were possibly 10,000 clergy without cure of souls. Much of this came from the piety of middle-class Englishmen whose wealth, as monasteries went out of fashion, flowed in the endowment of chantry chapels, which would provide resident priests instead of absentees, and commemorate the donors for ever. In such chapels, whether in lonely places or crowded into large town churches, late mediaeval religion found expression; the type might be the little chantry set up at Reculver, with Masses sung 'for the good estate of the King, the peace and tranquillity of England, for the soul of the King and for the souls of those who have died in his wars'; or the gild of Our Lady at Burford which maintained a chaplain and kept up bridges; countless chapels in trading towns like Coventry, often attached to gilds of mercers, tanners, or drapers; or large deliberately-planned collegiate churches, like Fotheringay, with a full establishment of choir and chaplains. But the disciplinary effects were pernicious. The towns were full of young men (St. Paul's Cathedral had over seventy chantry priests) only half employed, while cathedrals had another problem of the same sort in the vicars appointed by absentee canons.

The deep hold of religion is shown by the last wills and testaments of all classes, by villeins' legacies to their parish church, London fraternities with early Masses for working men, or rich men's gifts for lights and service-books. A knowledge of religion in their own tongue was not first brought to Englishmen by Wyclif or Protestant reformers. True, the official order might not be carried out, that several times in the year a parson must instruct his flock in English in the Creed, the Commandments, and the Lord's Prayer, but archbishop Thoresby of York issued a catechism which was put into English verse, innumerable families had English versions of the Psalms, and there were many rhymed versions of parts of the Gospels. A good many village schools taught reading, writing, plain-song, and easy Latin, and though the really poor may have been little touched, the mystery plays which any peasant could see, the paintings in his church, the sermons he heard, all meant familiarity with the fundamentals, or at least with the drama, of the faith.

Yet that faith was entering on a new development, challenging the formulas so far found satisfying. There was some decline of church-going and refusal to stop work on Saints' days; there were protests against the archdeacons' officials, church wealth, and immoral priests, or the use of excommunication to enforce tithe. But spiritual restless-ness touched much deeper questions. The thirteenth-century Papacy had demanded a unity of power; Thomas Aquinas had put the crown on one great system of religion and reason, tradition and Aristotle. Now, however, a deep discontent drove the left-wing Franciscans to re-declare the doctrine of utter poverty; their leaders, like the English William of Occam, exalted Christ's kingdom as not of this world, found the will of the Church in the whole company of Christian people, and declared a Council to be above the Pope. Here they joined hands

with the radical thinker Marsilio of Padua, and others who supported
Edward III's brother-in-law, the Emperor Lewis, against Pope John
XXII, and invoked the State to reform a corrupted Church.

From the first half of the century a conflict of faith and reason,
swelling towards Reformation, troubled the mind of Europe. Though it
took many forms, its general tendency was to diminish the weight of
reason in religion, and to emphasize the individual soul. Two great
British Franciscans, Duns Scotus and Occam, abandoned the unity
which St. Thomas had taught and, finding mysteries which were
insoluble to reason, reserved to religion a field in which men must
give utter obedience. Their questioning did not leave untouched the
central doctrine of the Mass; on the manner of Christ's presence, the
annihilation of bread and wine by the miracle of transubstantiation,
or a consubstantiation whereby both bread and Body were present
— their rationalizing was making these mysteries a matter of debate.
Such teaching stressed the individuality of each human will, their God
moved in a mysterious way, salvation lay in obedience, or in a mystical
union with the divine. Against them Bradwardine, who died archbishop of Canterbury in 1349, returned to St. Augustine, to the necessity
of grace as the sole means of salvation, predestination and a Church of
the elect. There was much revival of the Puritanism which had often
broken out in the Church, just as the early friars and heretics had
taught that only those who live like Christ are Christians, that He had
ordained no hierarchy, or that an evil priest could not celebrate the
sacrament. In western Europe there was a mystical revival, a belief in
direct vision and a devotion to the name of Jesus; illustrated in England
by the Nottinghamshire canon Walter of Hilton, whose *Ladder of
Perfection* guided hundreds of homes, or in East Anglian groups
influenced by the Flemish movement, which was soon to produce
Thomas à Kempis.

All these controversies touched England before Wyclif appeared.
Heretics in Devon attacked the Mass; the archbishop of Armagh,
preaching in English at Paul's Cross, criticized the friars' doctrine of
poverty and the harm they did in parish life. A generation who had
seen the innocent slain in thousands by the Black Death began to
ponder the penalty of sin, and justification by faith in Christ. A new
demand for sermons, a preference for prayer to ceremonial, the setting
up of countless chantries, all showed the growth of a more individual
faith.

It was thus the work of John Wyclif not to create these doubts but
to carry them a stage further: national feeling, moral revolt, intellectual
unrest. He was born just before 1330 of good Yorkshire family, which
was the origin of a life-long connection with his local overlord, John
of Gaunt, and for most of his life nothing distinguished him from the

average secular Oxford clergy.   He was Master of Balliol, and then for
a time Warden of Canterbury College, as part of a scheme for making
it over from monks to secular priests.   He received patronage by Papal
provision, he was a pluralist, and an absentee.   His first approach to
controversy came entirely through scholastic philosophy, in which he
followed Plato instead of Aristotle, Augustine and not Occam, Bradwardine and not free will.   He was always an intellectual rather than an
evangelist, seeking Christ indeed with his whole heart and His law as
shown in Scripture, but not like Luther possessed with the enormous
existence of evil, and never a Protestant in the sense that justification by
faith, a blazing individual experience, formed the heart of his creed.

He was already known for his learning, and in some dispute with
Rome over benefices, when in 1374 the Crown presented him to the
rectory of Lutterworth ;   followed by his nomination as one of an embassy to Bruges, to discuss the Pope's claim to tribute and other
questions in controversy.   That mission achieved nothing, the matter
ending temporarily in some verbal promises from the Pope and the
grant of a subsidy by the English Church.   In the interval Wyclif
issued several works on ' dominion ', which marked him as a radical.
Following archbishop FitzRalph and the early Fathers, he declared
that the world belonged to God, the ' capital lord ' ;   that only righteousness could justify property ;   and that though in this world ' God must
obey the devil ', and there must be obedience even to sinful lords, the
Church's rights depended on the moral use she made of them, and if
they were abused, the State must take her endowments away.

These views, his fame as a preacher, his Bruges experience, threw
him into the factions struggling for power.   William of Wykeham's long
administration ended in 1371 in a parliamentary explosion against the
failure in France, and in the dismissal of clerical ministers, while
government took up the cry for heavier taxation of the clergy.   In 1377
the bishops, led by the young fiery Courtenay of London, struck back,
summoning Wyclif to an examination which resulted only in the Londoners rioting against Gaunt ;   then the Pope issued bulls, ordering
Wyclif's arrest, condemning his teaching on dominion, grace, and
excommunication, and declaring his views on disendowment and the
power of the laity as bad as those of Marsilio ' of damned memory '.
Yet Occam and many other radicals had been condemned by Rome
without splitting the Church, nor had Wyclif yet attacked the dogmas
of faith.   Before the bulls reached England, Edward III died.   The
great Schism crippled the Papacy.   Social revolution shook town
and country.   In all of which reactions Wyclif's intellectual protest was
caught up, twisted, and intensified.

Four-fifths of the people lived on the soil, in village units which
could feed and clothe themselves, though for some necessities like iron

or salt they must go outside, and for their small luxuries to the neighbouring fairs. With infinite local variation — the scattered hamlets of
Devonshire or northern moors, Kentish villages with immemorial
communal courts to manage marsh and pasture, small-plot individualism
in the Danish East, large-scale landlordism in the mixed farming of the
Midlands — the general scheme was in essentials the same; of village
communities reorganized into a frame of feudal lordship, maintained
not by free contracts but by labour services enforceable at law. The
labouring population was legally a caste. A villein who left the manor
could be dragged back again, his livelihood and rights flowed not from
rights of a citizen but the custom of the manor. Without special leave
his son could not become a priest, or join a craft. In this servile mould
millions lived in Europe till 1789, and in Russia even later, but in
England the social revolution which broke it was accomplished in the
fourteenth and fifteenth centuries. To make the modern world, both
land and land-workers had to achieve mobility; money would replace
labour services and payments in kind, competitive rents and wages
would replace fixity, there would be contracts instead of inherited
status, and individuals instead of village co-operation.

Since the Conquest many landed generations had made a very
uniform system in the central region between Humber, Severn, and the
southern sea. Regular visits from the lord's steward stereotyped custom
on his manors, so that a large owner like Battle Abbey treated its estates
as a whole, moving cattle and sheep between Essex and Berkshire. If
we ignore variation in detail, the average villein between 1200 and 1350
might hold thirty acres; he must work two or three days a week on his
lord's demesne; his whole family (the wife and shepherd excepted)
must do extra ' boon-days ' at harvest; he had ploughing duties,
scything (when he might carry off for himself as much grass as would not
break his scythe-handle), and harrowing; his team must carry the
lord's crops to market — though if, for instance, Worcester Priory
tenants were kept the night at Worcester, the lord had to provide
forage, firing, and beer. He paid a small fixed money rent, with perhaps
some ancient dues like fish silver or malt silver; there were hens due
at Christmas and eggs at Easter. He must pay for his corn to be
ground at the lord's mill; confiscated millstones were kept in St.
Albans' cloister as a reminder. Every yard of the soil was earmarked in
detail, for the performance not only of every service which the lord's
budget required but of every common need; there were holdings
which must cut down trees, holdings which must take water to the hay-
makers, holdings assigned to do court-duty to the hundred, holdings
for the servants and the shepherd, or holdings to produce bell-ropes
for the parish church.

For it was a community. Intermixed strips in the open fields, the throwing down of fences after harvest, the number of cattle that each might graze on the common, annual allotment of water-meadows, all meant work in common. Hard facts of agricultural life softened the theory of lordship. A Northamptonshire village, shared between six lords, had thus to plan its arrangements as a whole. Isolated hamlets, for the lord's convenience, sometimes paid a lump rent in lieu of all labour; villeins would bargain with him for an exchange of common or woodland.

Their working day was long, from sunrise to sunset, but their life was not unprotected or abject. Villeins' petitions occasionally reached Parliament. The reeve who organized their service was one of themselves, often elected in their court and holding office many years. On most big estates they had a fortnight's holiday at Christmas, a week at Easter, and again at Whitsun, and if a peasant fell gravely ill, for a year he would not be ejected so long as he got his ploughing done by deputy. Then, as now, there were good employers as well as bad. We find instances of service remitted in hard times, special arrangements for widows, court fines handed to the sick, a lord leaving a legacy to his bondmen. They had their wrestling matches and ball games, Yuletide and harvest suppers for which the lord paid. But life, like that of the Indian peasant till lately, was dependent on the caprice of nature and man. Since they had no modern root crops, most of their beasts had to be killed every winter, a harvest failure brought them near starvation, winds and heavy rain demolished their flimsy shacks, and waterlogged their undrained ploughlands. They could be forced to take up holdings against their will, and to distribute week-work as the reeve ordered; there were still cases, though now more rarely, of families being sold with the land and cattle.

There had always been districts which had never known the essence of the manor, the demesne worked by compulsory labour from the village strips intermixed with it, which could not arise in the forest clearings, the northern cattle pastures, or small plots of Lincolnshire. In the thirteenth century, indeed, services had often been stiffened and there had been a boom in demesne farming towards its close. But, taking the country as a whole, it now showed progressive signs of decline. With an increase of population and money, the manor more and more became a business proposition; so Bedfordshire Cistercians sold their famous Warden pears, while the great Berkeleys sold apples in Bristol. Many villages increased the food supply by turning their two open fields into three. Sale of grain and stock brought large profits. Treatises were written on farm management, or the duties of a reeve. Demand and supply in money-terms spread from Edward I's taxes, town markets, and international trade, nor could the manor stand aloof. On its rolls the bailiff now carefully noted the money equivalent of each day's labour, harrowing, reaping, or tribute in eggs.

Landowners increasingly commuted labour for money, by slow experiment devised in their own interest. They built up a staff of skilled men by commuting all other work from ploughmen and shepherds. They would farm out the manor pigsties. More especially, they would commute services which involved food at their expense, like the harvest days when they provided beer, bacon, herrings, and barley bread; for food prices were rising. Here and there they leased out blocks of their demesne.

In other ways, too, money, with the individualism which it means, was breaking up the village. The Crown itself, always wanting money, sold freedom to its villeins for £15 a family. There were village moneylenders, and poor villeins who rented some of their land to others more prosperous. A class of labourer had grown up, either landless or with such small plots that they must seek other earnings; cottiers with gardens, squatters outside growing villages, villeins who had fled to the town.

By the Black Death all this had become common, and on many manors about half the services were commuted in an ordinary year. But there was no permanence and no system, the lord arranging his services from year to year as he liked. If he wanted skilled work done, if he could get cheap wandering harvesters from Wales, or if food were dear, he would commute. He arranged commutation at rates against which many labourers protested, and had usually more labour services on his time-table than he could ever use, for which he took commutation as a sort of extra rent. But wages were already rising, he must watch the market; the number of works 'sold' or performed went up and down, year by year, on a wavy line.

This arbitrary unevenness made for trouble before 1348. Edward II's reign saw a run of bad harvests; there were riots against the great abbeys, Abingdon and St. Albans, Bury and Vale Royal. Upon each restless village in transition fell the Black Death, which within a year halved its population.

Nothing is more difficult than to generalize about its effects. Broadly speaking, both government and landowners wanted to keep the old system, but both legs on which that system stood had collapsed. Labour services could no longer supply the demesne; Berkshire women threw up their holdings as a bad job, 'being without help to do the services', while if surviving villeins were told off for extra work, they would run away. Very unwillingly, therefore, the lords surrendered, making leases for money, which they took care should be short, hoping to return to labour service in better days.

Their alternative, however, of hiring labour, was just as desperate; at one stroke all wages rose nearly 50 per cent, harvesting, for instance, from an average 3d. to 6d. a day. For the first time the central government, therefore, attempted social legislation. In the Council ordinance of 1349, which was followed by many statutes, it detailed the wage-rates which all without means of support must accept; ordered that the price of food be reasonable; forbade alms to the able-bodied, and forbade labourers to wander in search of a higher wage. Special justices of labourers, drawn from the landowning class, and soon blended with the justices of the peace, were to enforce the statutes. The fines collected were first added to the subsidy, but later were returned to the lords of franchises, so making it their interest to carry out the law. In a sense the whole labour supply was pooled, for justices assigned men to whom they pleased, and farm servants had to stand in market towns to be hired. Every labourer was put on oath to obey the statutes, while the royal courts dealt with breaches of contract, trying 9000 such cases before the death of Edward III.

These batteries of the law kept down wages for a time, as the bloody vengeance taken in 1381 proves. But as a policy they entirely failed. Landowners competed for labour, artisans' wages rose sharply, and while other prices rose, partly owing to a depreciated coinage, food prices (which would have helped the landlords) were almost stationary. Labourers formed unions to extort wages above the statute level. Gangs broke the stocks in which defaulters were confined. The Middlesex justices were once stormed out of Tottenham. A mass of petty prosecutions irritated small retailers of beer or coal.

And what happened to the wage-earning labourer directly touched the villein. The rise of wages, for he too was sometimes an employer, affected him, or alternatively tempted him to run off to a better-paid life. Empty holdings became the common outcry; ' run off by night ' with horse and family, we hear — sometimes to the cloth trade, sometimes to a landlord who would pay better. Every step the lords took to patch up their rent-rolls made the villeins more desperate; efforts to cancel short leases and restore labour, or to fill up their deficit by steep fines. In the long run they could only keep men on the land by lightening services or commuting them entirely, but if they did the last, the fixed payments were not usually enough to pay their labour bill. The logic of a money system gradually undermined the whole structure, and we see a double process growing, a growth of leases to villeins and a lease of the demesne itself to farmers, often ending in a lease of the whole manor to one man. If some, like the conservative monks, kept up some demesne, they used it now more for sheep-farming, with fewer hands.

Taken as a whole, then, the worker on the soil had made progress by 1377; their wages were higher, while food prices were reasonable and sinking. But they were exasperated, for progress was only won by everlasting conflict with the law; and though their tenure was dying fast, their personal disabilities lingered on. Inequalities divided their class, and every estate from its neighbour. Beside the labourer with his new standards, his demand for fresh meat and hot fish, and his freedom, stood the villein still liable to game laws, heriots, and the lord's mill; alongside the Berkeleys' leased-out demesne lay estates of Battle and Ramsey Abbeys, where labour was enforced.

After the Black Death, when the old reeves and the families rooted in villeinage had died, we hear all England over of refusals to do service, of villeins put in irons, or of appeals to Domesday Book to prove that their forefathers had been free. Villeinage was dead, and nothing shows it better than the cases tried under the new legislation; for we find lords so anxious for men that they tried desperately to prove a particular ploughman or carter to be a free man, and villeins suing lords for causing them, by demands for service, to break their contracts with others. The judges recognized a new relationship, for they refused to hold servants to contracts when their masters had beaten them or refused adequate food.

Meantime industrial England was being born. A larger population was produced by the wealth which struck out from the towns. Our trade was, indeed, still dominated by foreigners; the Hanseatic League, now at the height of their power, who made almost a self-governing colony of their fortified Steelyard in Cannon Street and who, helped by preferential tariffs, controlled trade with north Germany and the Baltic, or the Venetians who brought Oriental and Mediterranean goods to Southampton. Yet trade was not only increasing fast, but changing in character. Exports of raw wool began to decline; cloth on the contrary rose by leaps and bounds, from about 7000 pieces annually to 50,000 by 1395. The customs revenue averaged nearly £70,000 a year, and Edward III's new gold and silver coinage was meant to meet the demands of foreign exchange.

Primitive trade machinery had broken down. The chartered borough, serving a local market, was merged into a more fluid one, which called for elastic supplies of capital and labour, and faced international fluctuation. Marketing was more centralized. London fishmongers had depots all over the Midlands, London butchers bought as far afield as Nottingham, even the western cloth trade poured out through the port of London. Solemn agreements established free-trade areas between many boroughs, while natural advantages formed some definite industrial areas; the middle west for cloth with Salisbury as its centre, Coventry in the Midlands, or East Anglia with its worsted trade and cheap kerseys, which sold in the Baltic. The new system asked for more hands, besides access to raw material and water; domestic industry began in scores of villages, Lavenham and Coggeshall, Norton St. Philip and Ilchester, whose products, spun and woven by country folk in their homes, passed into the great world through complicated agencies and middlemen.

The great day of this system was yet to come, and the craft gilds still directed industry; drapers and grocers, mercers and tanners and spicers, who by an inevitable specialization had generally replaced the single gild-merchant. Their regulations embodied many fair ideals, a high standard of craftsmanship, a fair price, a training for apprentices, and equality for their members. They fixed the number of apprentices that one master might take, and wage-rates for apprentices who passed on to be journeymen : their wardens inspected shops for bad quality and stopped night work, awarded sick payment, and fined the fraudulent. Such exclusive powers were open to abuse, which brought them into collision with their fellow-townsmen. Town councils intervened to stop gilds forcing up prices and jealously watched their bye-laws, and new developments, within their ranks and without, heralded the capitalist industry which was to leave the gilds high and dry. It was no accident that the peasants' rising was most savage in the industrial areas of London and the east.

For the fair dealing and customary regulations between craft-masters and a few apprentices were giving way to the antagonism of employers and employed. The old avenues became choked. Journeymen or yeomen formed unions, the London shoemakers for instance, even before the Black Death. The price crisis which it caused compelled London, in advance of the government, to tackle wages, for weavers were asking treble the old rate. Clamour broke out of labour displaced by fluctuations ; an outcry against cheap labour in the suburbs, against Flemish weavers who were said to sweat female labour, or fulling machinery which threw honest Englishmen out of work. These local conflicts were made worse by the new powers given to boroughs by the State, of police or markets or admiralty ; while large towns now controlled many interests, issuing loans to merchants, managing almshouses, or constructing water supplies. In East Anglia a particularly angry struggle began, of lesser gilds and the general body of citizens against vested interests.

In London this economic war affected national politics throughout Richard II's reign and helped to deliver the capital to the peasants in 1381. In Edward II's time the crafts had superseded the old ruling families, and superficially the struggle now raged between craft and craft, but its bitterness was due to the very fact that London's trade defied craft restriction. Freedom was the essence of its open-air markets in Cornhill and Cheapside, and the City needed a score of economic types, — the small retailers who hawked charcoal or bread from house to house, the country drovers, or the suburban butchers from Stepney. There were substantial country merchants, Grevilles of Chipping Campden or Cannings of Bristol, who became freemen of London to safeguard their interests, besides the middlemen like the ' bladers ' who sold corn. On the other hand, London trades set up large associations like the grocers, who imported from all Europe, sold wholesale to country fairs, and ran accounts through provincial branches. A statute of 1363 tried to restrict traders to membership of one craft, but it was promptly repealed. Municipal government turned upon economic questions, the clash of traders like the mercers with industrialists, monopoly against free trade, the right of aliens to trade retail, or the mayor's power over the crafts. Now were born the great Livery companies, with membership limited by high entrance fees, with banquets and hoods for full members, and corporate funds reinvested in trade, led by the grocers, mercers, and fishmongers, whose members filled year after year the chairs of mayor and aldermen. By 1380 these interests were arrayed in two factions, the victualling interests of fishmongers and grocers against the rest, and each having a determined leader, Nicholas Brember the grocer against the draper John of Northampton. Their feuds were soon mixed up with larger quarrels ; for Northampton's party championed Wyclif, looked to John of Gaunt, and took their demands for freer trade to Parliament, while Brember invoked the support of the Crown ; Northampton's party bid for popularity by low bread prices, and Brember's by attacking aliens. London government was bandied to and fro. The reformers transferred election of the Common Council from the Wards to the crafts, or forbade aldermen to hold office over a year, while Brember's group after 1384 swung back to the Wards and to aldermen for life.

Ingredients of rebellion thus stirred England in Edward III's last days, when Alice Perrers decked out in many pearls held his tournaments. There was much pure barbarism ; murders innumerable, brutal assaults on priests, attacks led by knights on tax-collectors. But it took a form very different from that of older days, for now it turned on economic matters, was more concerned with the activities of the State, and reflected social movement from below. These unsettled units in society rallied to any strong interest, or any appeal which promised them a better time. In the great Oxford riot of 1355 thousands of peasants under a black flag appeared, with cries of ' havoc, havoc ', to sack the University. Fighting classes took the livery of great men, the Percy crescent or the horse of Arundel, and traders wore the hoods of rival companies. A mantle of religion was thrown over this new radicalism. Franciscan attacks on wealth had sunk deep, some preached that all property should be in common. For many years in the home counties a priest, John Ball, had been speaking in church-yard or market, advising peasants not to pay tithe ; foretelling a time when there should be no more lordship, when peasants would no longer have to face the wind and the rain, when ' the King's Son of heaven should pay for all ', and all be equal as ' when Adam delved and Eve span '. And when revolution came he spoke in the name of ' Piers Plowman ', the idealized man of the soil, who within a few years began to figure in village church windows as Christ the carpenter.

To such a rendering of the Gospel a popular discontent always ran in the Middle Ages; what was new was this rapid tide of opinion, expressed in the English language, which since the Death was rapidly replacing French in the grammar schools and taking its symbol from a widely-circulated English poem. *Piers Plowman* was first written about 1362 and revised about 1377; its author, William Langland, came from the middle west where old English letters and ideals most strongly survived, but passed his life in London in poverty, as a chantry singing-clerk. He had read much in English and Latin, but his fierce loneliness made him a figure of the past rather than the future, and his work was written in that alliterative unrhymed fashion which only remoter shires preserved. His vision was of a world out of joint; where ' Mede ' (or corruption) ruled Court, Church, and law; friars glossing the Gospel and preaching for their bellies' sake; false pilgrims with their wenches, a-foot for the holy land of Walsingham; parish priests who knew Robin Hood better than their Mass-book; drapers who fraudulently stretched their cloth; lords who maintained riotous men at arms; monks who had chastity without charity. Fierce were his denunciations, sparing no class, and dire his prophecies. Hunger one day would force idle labourers to work. A hypocritical Church, this ' dunghill covered in snow ', could not endure.

> *And then shall the Abbot of Abingdon and all his issue for ever*
> *Have a knock of a king, and incurable the blow.*

Antichrist would reign on earth, and the friars would join him.

Yet he has no new scheme for these multitudes crying, ' Upward to Christ and His clean mother '. Though he mentions communism, his ideals were of older days. Let kings do justice, knights defend peasants from outrage, merchants build hospitals and bridges, women spin, preachers denounce the seven sins, and men marry, not for pelf as they had done since the Death, but for love. Christian love was his religion undefiled, and his road to democracy. Without it law and learning are nothing, and ' common labourers ' may storm heaven while the witty and wise lie in hell. For the poor have their purgatory on earth, and how hardly shall the rich man enter heaven.

> *Jesus Christ of heaven*
> *In a poor man's apparel pursueth us ever ;*

and as the vision rises to its mystical end, the risen Christ wears the coat-armour of Piers Plowman. Langland's message was, then, the same as that of St. Francis, and neither more nor less hostile than his to a worldly Church.

The new lay society into which he survived was making its own literature, far different in temper and inspiration. John Gower, the Kentish landowner, wrote less in English than in French and Latin; he drew upon Ovid, the French romances, and Boccaccio, and though he died in Southwark Priory, the form of his English poem was the classical allegory with love as its theme. For him Catholic observance was enough; better be a hedger and ditcher, he wrote, than know all Scripture and err with the Lollards. But like Wyclif he attacked the sloth of prelates and the sin of Avignon; and, like Langland, the war of classes and decline of charity.

His friend and rival Geoffrey Chaucer was better fitted to paint the age. He was born about 1343 from a vintner family in the City, long connected with the royal customs. Beginning as page to Lionel the King's son, he became a squire in Edward's own Household, fought in his wars and was taken prisoner just before the peace of 1360, did diplomatic work in Italy and Flanders, and rose to be customs controller in the port of London, member of Parliament for Kent, and clerk of the King's works. His wife was sister to Katherine Swynford, mistress to John of Gaunt, and mother of the Beauforts; he kept the favour of three sovereigns, and his son was Speaker of the Commons.

To a disposition for public life, to a knowledge of English ballad and religious literature, he added a wide reading in Latin and the Romance tongues. He translated much from French, borrowed from Boccaccio, reverenced Petrarch as he did Virgil. He had none of Langland's passion nor, like Gower, did he profess to be a moralist. Careless in life and money, he was first and foremost a literary craftsman, for ever learning and experimenting. But in setting down life as he saw it, etching in over many years the portraits of his *Canterbury Tales*, he revealed England in its weakness and strength, full of new life, turbulent, and precarious.

He was a modern man, mocking at outworn chivalry as in his parody of Sir Thopas, scornful of the old alliterative songs, disillusioned, but full of curiosity for nature in all aspects, humanity, science, or astronomy. His mind was sceptical rather than speculative, and without sympathy for the ' precious ', Lollards or Utopians. Kings must not act ' like tyrants in Lombardy ', yet kings are natural rulers, lords are ' half gods in this world born ', an order apart. Boethius and the morals which had done duty so long were enough for him, and he disliked this new talk of predestination. The ' courteous love ', out of which he made a masterpiece in *Troilus and Criseyde*, was not blessed by the Church. Human beings were as God had made them, sensual, mean, or magnificent; it was not given to us all to be perfect and, like his most human Wife of Bath, Chaucer's heart rejoices ' that I have had my world as in my time '.

From a man of this type condemnation comes with great force. How atrocious are the figures of most Churchmen who cross his page ! Here is the sinister pardoner, with ' a jolly wench in every town ' and a sack full of false relics; wanton Friar Hubbard, with twinkling eyes and the village women's secrets; the archdeacon's red-faced summoner, who yet

> *would suffer for a quart of wine*
> *a good fellow to have his concubine ;*

Madame Eglantyne the prioress, with her lapdogs, her brooch engraved ' amor vincit omnia ', her devotion to the Virgin and hatred of Jews; and the monks, with horses and greyhounds, full of every appetite except for righteousness.

His writing years, from about 1370 till his death in 1400, were a black time in public life, and in one late poem he entreats Richard II to ' wed thy folk again to steadfastness '. Among his Canterbury pilgrims he put those who did the everyday work of England; the village parson who was ' a shepherd and not a mercenary '; the Franklin who was justice of the peace and knight of the shire; the ' perfect gentle knight ' who had fought all over Europe; the merchant who wishes the sea made safe between Suffolk and Holland; the Dartmouth shipman who, a brigand but ' a good fellow ', knew every creek between Sweden and Finisterre; the reeve of the manor who lived on a Norfolk village green; the lawyer who knew the statutes by heart; the forester who in his hands ' bare a mighty bow '; the good ploughman who lived ' in peace and perfect charity '. All these in his active life Chaucer had seen, and found that, virtue being independent of social degree, ' pity runneth soon in gentle heart '; ' humble folk be Christ's friends ', he makes his parson say. Finding such, he could leave a teaching for England which defied the slings and arrows of fortune, doubt, and division :

> *Forth, pilgrim, forth !   Up beast, out of thy stall,*
> *Know thy country, look up, thank God of all ;*
> *Hold the highway, and let thy ghost thee lead ;*
> *And truth thee shall deliver, it is no dread.*

The late fourteenth century was a dark day, but all Englishmen did not despair. Trevisa, the Berkeleys' chaplain, was writing in the same decade of England, ' full of mirth and game . . . free men of heart and with tongue '.

CONTEMPORARY DATES

1361	Reappearance of the Black Death.
	Froissart begins a stay of some years in England.
1362	The first rendering of Langland's *Piers Plowman*.
1363	Philip the Bold, son of John, King of France, becomes Duke of Burgundy.
1364–80	Reign of Charles V of France.
1366	Pedro the Cruel of Castile deposed.
1368	Overthrow of the Mongol dynasty in China ; the Ming dynasty reign till 1644.
1369–1405	Tamerlane's reign ; Mongol conquest carried to Baghdad and Delhi.
1374	Death of Petrarch.
	Wyclif becomes rector of Lutterworth.

CHAPTER II

REVOLUTION, 1376–1399

THE Parliament called after three years' interval in 1376, — ' the good Parliament ', — opened a new stage. The Commons were, of course, still much directed by the magnates. As their Speaker they chose Peter de la Mare, steward to the Earl of March who, with the Black Prince, spurred them to attack the courtiers whom Gaunt had taken under his wing, and whose conduct of the war was corrupt and inglorious ; when the Prince died, Gaunt packed the next Parliament and in his turn took a Speaker from the ranks of his Household. Yet this very competition in pressure proved the Commons' new power. Knights of the shire could count on the support of many nobles, besides the Church leaders Courtenay and Wykeham, and through all vicissitudes we trace a persistent constitutional programme.

Taking oaths to stand by each other, the Commons of 1376 went beyond the old treason law, devising a new drastic process for impeachment of the arch-offenders before the Lords ; the Londoner Richard Lyons, besides Latimer and Neville, respectively Chamberlain and Steward of the Household, all of whom had made their profit out of loans, customs duties, and royal debts. De la Mare, whom Gaunt imprisoned when the session ended, was the first great commoner of parliamentary history whose fame we can recognize : we find him refusing to speak until all the Commons were admitted to the full Parliament, brandishing a statute book, the hero of London and ballad poetry. For four months it rained petitions, demanding annual Parliaments and parliamentary nomination of justices of the peace, or asking Edward to mark his jubilee by reforming the Church. On social questions their touch was conservative and confused, indiscriminately denouncing Lombard brokers and aliens, high wages and gilds. But Edward had long been senile, and his death in 1377 removed the mask behind which Gaunt had worked ; loyalty to a young King, the good sense of Richard's mother, and London riots against the Duke, all compelled some reconciliation.

For the last ten years Gaunt had been much abroad and could not take the whole blame for national danger, nor is there reason to think that he ever meant to supplant Richard. But he was a conventional soldier who resented criticism, while the Black Prince's death made him a partisan. His hope now was to hold power through the Crown, to whose service he transferred his own servants Scrope and Michael de la Pole, but there was a strong constitutional party among the peers, and till 1382 the Commons won support for their programme for the nomination of paid councils and high officials by Parliament. Government admitted that what one Parliament had done, only another Parliament could undo, and allowed parliamentary control of the war taxes.

For Edward's death coincided with the end of the truce, and within three months the French sacked Rye, Portsmouth, and Plymouth. A Castilian squadron joined them; the Scottish Border, Calais, and Bordeaux were all threatened. Fears of invasion harried Parliament, who suspected spies in every alien priory; London was put in a state of defence, with beacons at Tilbury and Shoeburyness. But Gaunt, his youngest brother Thomas of Woodstock, and their followers, again exposed their incapacity; though we held Brest and Cherbourg, the Bretons made terms with France, every expedition sailed too late in the year, every diplomatic move was anticipated.

Finding that the French would make no peace without Aquitaine in sovereignty, the English accepted a scheme put forward by the Roman Pope in order to crush his French rival; for the King's marriage to Anne, sister of Wenzel, Holy Roman Emperor and King of Bohemia. It brought Richard in 1382 a loyal companion, though an extravagant influence, but no real political assistance.

Having agreed to carry on the war, the royal advisers disagreed on where to fight it. Gaunt was clear that a truce should be made with France, while we assisted Portugal against Castile, and enforced a truce on Scotland which temporarily ended their Border forays and piracy in the Channel. Charles V and du Guescelin being both dead, there seemed better hope of peace with a young King. But powerful interests in England, the Percies especially, wanted war, so did the Scottish nobles, and the Commons advised the King to attack France by way of Flanders.

Civil war between Flemish towns and their Count, which forty years before had given England an opening, had broken out again, and was damaging our wool trade from Calais. While the Count asked French assistance, a second Artevelde, son of Edward's old ally, begged an English army, and Rome announced a crusade against Flemish supporters of Avignon. But hesitation all through 1382 destroyed the English opportunity, for in November the French won a great victory over the Flemings at Roosebeke, near Bruges.

The 'crusade' of 1383 was thus doomed in advance. Upon the Commons lay the chief responsibility, for they argued that religious excitement would mean volunteers and a cheap war. Against the advice of leading lords and soldiers, but amid great popular enthusiasm, the expedition was launched; women poured out their jewels and household silver, while the shadiest adventurers took the red cross under the Pope's nominee, bishop Despenser of Norwich, whose only military experience had been the butchery of a few peasants. In three months the fiasco was over. After attacking harmless Flemings with abominable cruelty, the ' crusaders ' were beaten off from Ypres by a French army, driven back on Calais, and forced or bribed to evacuate all they had won.

Reluctantly Parliament agreed to the King's policy of peace, even at the price of doing homage for Calais. But the French would grant no more than a truce, the Scottish nobles asked their alliance, and the Portuguese had envoys in London. In 1385 war broke out on all frontiers; French troops appearing in Scotland, Richard himself led an army which burned Edinburgh, but never saw the enemy; Ghent, last outpost of Flemish independence, fell to the French, who began preparations to invade England. Only a sweeping Portuguese victory at Aljubarotta over the Castilians gave us hope, and to Portugal Gaunt was despatched with an army at midsummer 1386, with the good will both of the Pope and of Parliament. Most of all, Richard wanted him gone. For much had come to pass in England during the wars; the peasants' rising, a threat of Lollardy, and the maturity of Richard II.

Before Richard's fight came with his aristocracy, they fought together against the first English social revolution, the signs and portents of which we have seen. Since 1375 harvests had been good and prices low, artisans were struggling to keep their new standards, while those hitherto oppressed aspired to an equal freedom. About 1379 Wyclif sent out from Oxford his missionary priests who, going beyond their master, began to join agitators like Ball in advising peasants to refuse tithe and labour services.

It was the government, however, that set fire to the fuel. Twelve years had gone by since war had broken out again, and England was more humiliated than ever. Fighting four enemy countries, we had lost both alliances and trade. High customs duties, tenths and fifteenths, loans from London, purveyance, strained the middle class, at whose instance the ministers introduced poll-taxes on all classes alike. By the first two of these the peasant paid only 4d., but the third, collected in the winter of 1380–81, put on each village an average sum of 1s. a head, so that in places without large owners this was demanded from every soul over the age of fifteen. Payment was evaded on a huge scale, but despite warnings of resistance the government persisted, superseding local collectors by sergeants-at-arms from the Household, who began a house-to-house census. Wild rumours and riots followed at once; on the 2nd of June a mob at Brentwood in Essex killed six jurors and clerks, and on the same day riots began in Kent. Stirred up by

Londoners, the rebels of both shires acted together across the Thames.

Like a prairie fire the rising spread eastward to Colchester, and westward to Romney Marsh. John Ball, rescued from prison at Maidstone, sent broadcast his messages, — 'he hath rungen your bell', 'stand together', 'make a good end of what hath been begun'. On both sides of the river there were the same signs; breaking of prisons, bonfires of manor documents, and attacks on tax-collectors, members of Parliament, justices of the peace, and anyone connected with Gaunt; fierce threats, above all, against the heads of the administration, archbishop Sudbury and the Treasurer Robert Hales. On the 11th June both forces moved towards London; Kent led by Wat Tyler, an old adventurer of the wars, and Essex by a Londoner of good family, Thomas Faringdon. Marching with wonderful determination, by the night of the 12th the first were camped at Blackheath and the second at Mile End, while both King and ministers were blockaded in the Tower.

Fearful was the exposure of a weak government and a divided society. Castles like Rochester were tamely surrendered, boroughs like Canterbury took oaths to the 'commons', for ten days Council, Tower garrison, and nobles had done nothing. And on the 13th June some London aldermen, members of the victualling gilds, who were not sorry to avenge themselves alike on Gaunt, alien merchants, and their democratic rivals, opened London Bridge to the men of Kent, and Aldgate to those from Essex. Nothing but London, with its food supply and its political contents, could have kept the rebels together, and conflagration was immediately redoubled. Revolutionary sympathizers went off to East Anglia, Cambridge, and Surrey, while Wat Tyler's advice was requested at St. Albans. Dimly we discern what filled the minds of those thousands trampling towards London, as they slept in the cornfields, while the fire of burning houses lighted Kent hills and Essex woodlands, or as they shambled over London Bridge with old bows and axes, and for the first time looked on Westminster or the Tower. 'King Richard and the Commons' was their watchword; 'they would have no king called John' was their declaration against Gaunt; the King, it was put about, was on their side. For a time they forbade all robbery, massacred none of the squires whom they captured, even thought of leaving coast guards against the French. Spontaneously the same ideas, the same enemies, were declared in all quarters; to destroy traitors and petty oppressors of the law, and to be free. Richard Lyons, whom the Good Parliament had impeached, had his house in Suffolk destroyed two days before he was beheaded in London, Flemings were killed at Colchester and Lynn, labour services were forbidden from Thanet to the Wash. There was even a certain sympathy from other classes, seen in the moderation of Kent country gentry or Hertfordshire juries who were unwilling to convict, nor probably were all the East Anglian priests and squires, who took part in attacking monks and tax-collectors, simply out for the spoil. But the peasant armies had broken the frame of society and, as they went on, villainy and revenge attached itself to their cause; murder, blackmail, theft, cattle-driving, forcible refusal of debt, all this was done under their rudely-painted banners of the royal arms or St. George.

For two days, while the Council hesitated between negotiation and force, the rebels held London. In vain the King from a turret of the Tower begged them to disperse, or processions of clergy prayed for peace. They were allowed to open the prisons, to destroy Gaunt's palace at the Savoy, to sack the Inns of Court; the garrison let them into the Tower, where they dragged the archbishop and Treasurer from the chapel to summary execution. Cheering mobs hunted the unhappy Flemings, other detachments fired suburban manor houses, the block was kept busy in Cheapside, and Faringdon was compiling a list of those marked down for death. In a first conference the King agreed to their demand for the abolition of serfdom, rents of 4d. an acre, and free markets, and issued charters of enfranchisement, armed with which a good many villagers began to drift home. But Tyler and the main body held firm, putting forward a larger programme in a second conference at Smithfield, for a confiscation of Church lands, an end of lordship, and abolition of the game laws. While Tyler bargained insolently with the King and tried to arrest one of his following, he was stabbed, and then, while thousands of peasants bent their bows, Richard saved himself and his capital; riding out alone and crying, ' sirs, will you shoot your King? I will be your captain ', he led them into the growing corn at Clerkenwell. The tension was broken. Walworth, Lord Mayor, and the old general Robert Knolles at last called out the forces which could have been mobilized long ago, and replaced the archbishop's head on London Bridge by that of Tyler.

Outside London, however, the rebellion had only just begun. It showed the same mixed motives and leadership, and the same weakness, only redeemed by individual action. In Suffolk the leader was a robber priest, in Norfolk a dyer and a knight. In Suffolk they killed the Chief Justice and the prior of Bury, the Norfolk men seized Norwich and looted Yarmouth. There was much pillage of members of the Parliament who had voted the poll-tax. Gaunt's wife was refused entrance to his castles, he himself retreated to Scotland, and the Cambridge college of Lancastrian foundation, Corpus Christi, was fired. Every old feud was exploited. St. Albans and Bury extorted new charters from the monks, parish priests led mobs against the monasteries and advised villeins to claim their rights, small craftsmen of Scarborough seized their chance to attack the rich. Yet a few examples showed that all that was needed was courage. The townsmen of Huntingdon and Leicester stoutly defended themselves. Bishop Despenser with a handful of soldiers put down the Cambridge riot, saved Peterborough Abbey, and rode down the Norfolk rebels at North Walsham.

On Tyler's fall the government declared the charters it had given were null and void, as extorted by force, and though it needed a pitched battle to break the rebels stockaded in the Essex woods near Billericay, and though even in September Maidstone was again in their hands, on the whole the repression was easy and lenient. The total executions seem to have been less than two hundred, and most of them, even that of John Ball, after trial by jury. Parliament, declaring official maladministration chiefly responsible, approved a general pardon, from which less than three hundred persons, half of whom were Londoners, were excepted.

So the social revolution passed over, to be accomplished by a different and more gradual process. A drift set in towards reduction of labour services, an increase of rents, and long leases of demesne. But villeinage was still the legal form, labour services continued commonly and especially on church estates, the Statute of Labourers continued to cause friction, though henceforth the magistrates fixed wages locally. We continue to hear of peasant leagues, burning of records, a passing of countersigns naming ' the true commons ' or ' Piers Plowman ', while bitter feelings were left in London and among Midland artisans, many of whom turned to religion as a solace for their hopes.

Wyclif had reached the height of his influence in 1378, when he was invited to address the Commons ; when the bishops, on instructions from Rome, again investigated his teaching, the government forbade them to proceed, while his University and some leading friars stood by him. But thenceforward the logic of events, with his own combativeness and sincerity, gradually separated him from his allies. For the schism in the Papacy, which began in 1378 and was destined to last forty years, drove him to despair of the old order and to develop, as he met opposition, his original radical principles. By 1380, amid many inconsistencies, we find the harsh structure of his thought fully established. He divided mankind between ' the elect ', the invisible sect of God, existing from all time by omnipotent decree, and the visible sect of antichrist, ' fore-known ' to damnation, whose leader he now identified with Rome. Though for order's sake there must be a priesthood, in one sense all the elect were priests, and could not be divided by orders of monks or vows. And since no hierarchy could stand between man and his God, the power of Pope or priest could only rest on their possession of ' grace '. Absolution and indulgences could not remit sin, neither could excommunication prove it. In worshipping saints, men might be worshipping one of the ' rejected '; all, even Popes, were but ' naked servants of God '; endowments must be replaced by poverty. Against the Bible, the charter by which every man held ' dominion ' from God, neither tradition nor Church councils could prevail, and all men had the right of reading that charter in their native tongue.

Finally, he returned to his early doubts on the Mass. Though he believed that the substance of bread continued, he held that the Body of Christ was also mystically present, not in a material form which would lead to idolatry, but a ' sacramental ' presence, ' the presence of Christ in the soul '.

This great man of action deduced from his theology the two measures which would perpetuate his teaching. His Oxford followers began preaching tours, dressed in woollen robes, living on charity and defying the bishops' licence for preaching, for whom he wrote tracts and sermons in Latin and English. Between 1380 and 1384 they also prepared, under his guidance, the first complete English translation of the Bible since the Conquest, which remained indeed, though there were orthodox translations of parts of the New Testament, the one translation of the whole Bible till the Reformation. By 1396 his secretary, John Purvey of Bedfordshire, had finished another version, more accurate and in finer English, which became a prized possession in many homes.

All this defiant thought and action, together with the peasants' revolt which his preachers were accused of fomenting, drove Wyclif into the wilderness. To stop his attack on the sacraments Gaunt came to Oxford, which itself was bitterly divided. And while the friars abandoned him, and monks christened his followers ' Lollards ' (meaning Flemish heretics), he appealed to Parliament in an English tract to end obedience to Rome. In 1382 Courtenay, the forcible archbishop who succeeded the murdered Sudbury, purged the University and called a synod to condemn heresies. A Council ordinance ordered the sheriffs to arrest Lollard preachers on a bishop's certificate. Many fled or recanted; one, indeed, Repingdon, later became bishop of Lincoln. The master retired to his Lutterworth rectory, forbidden to preach at Oxford but shielded by Gaunt's old friendship and the anti-clericalism of Parliament. Though worn-out and half-paralysed after his toils, his mind was vigorous, and ever more violent. The Pope had now become ' a limb of Lucifer ', the friars ' ravening wolves '; the great scholar called for disendowment of the universities, argued for a married clergy, or that laymen could celebrate the sacrament. In December 1384 he died.

Like many Catholics he was a Puritan, but cannot accurately be called a Protestant, for if he reached some Protestant conclusions, it was by a very different route. He did not so much found his views upon Scripture, as take Scripture to confirm them; he never held the Lutheran doctrine of justification by faith; least of all, did he breathe any toleration. Though a powerful reflector of his age, he was too much the schoolman to capture the masses, and left unsolved the most burning questions, — the relation of Church and State, the proof of the individual's claim to be in grace, and the doctrine of the sacrament. All in all, his teaching rather broke the ground than provided the main root of the English Reformation.

For the rest of Richard's reign Lollardy grew in influence, though the King himself was orthodox and took his religion much from friars, and though no man of political weight joined the heretics. Wyclif's disciples went to extreme conclusions. No learning was necessary, no university graduates, no priesthood, to the ' elect '; ' though you have never bill of pardon nor letter of fraternity, nor chantry after thy death ', salvation was assured ' by grant of Christ's gospel, sealed with His precious blood '. They taught the equality of all ' wretched sinners ', and the greater merit of charity than many Masses, for ' Christ came of poor folk '. They developed a Puritanism before its time, fiercely inveighing against decorated churches, mystery plays, and bearing of arms. Their propaganda, very successful in middle England from London to Leicester and westward to Herefordshire, used broadsheet petitions to Parliament, re-edited devout books with Lollard commentary, and clamoured for more translations, — ' O Christ, Thy law is hid,' wrote Purvey, ' when wilt Thou send Thy angel to remove the stone ? ' Its efficacy depended on individual preachers who, Bible in hand, wandered from squire's house to peasant's cottage, especially in the vast half-disciplined dioceses of the Welsh March, and who were caught, recanted, and appeared again. They were now ' ordaining ' their successors, sometimes a monk broke his vows in order to join them, Midland artisans were smashing images. Gaunt defended liberty of translation and in 1395 both Lollards and their opponents put out pamphlets, the first petitioning Parliament against celibacy of priests, confession, pilgrimages, dancing, and offerings to ' blind roods and deaf images '.

The King's anger was as great as his zeal ; so was that of Courtenay's successor, archbishop Arundel. But the suppression of Lollardy and the question of the English Bible were postponed, for King and archbishop were deep, on opposite sides, in matters more urgent.

The boy, who at fourteen had dominated the peasants, grew up with the Plantagenet yellow hair, good looks, stammering speech, and ungovernable temper. But he had none of their taste for war, or hunger for government. His courage was drawn from his nerves, he was moody, imaginative, abnormal, loved costly jewels and raiment, patronized painters, and encouraged Gower to write. He liked the company of women, but women older than himself, seemed unable to deal with grown men, and confined his affections to a small circle, his governor Simon Burley, his half-brothers the Hollands, and the friend of his own choice Robert de Vere, earl of Oxford. In the long run his temper became uncontrolled. We find him drawing his sword against one counsellor, striking another in the face, pulling down the palace in which his queen had died. And he ended as a typical Renaissance despot, grandiloquent and non-moral and treacherous.

Of the uncles round the throne, York was an easy-going sportsman ; Gloucester was bitter, sharp-tongued, connected by marriage with the opposition baronage, eager for the war. Gaunt could still tilt the scales ; champion of prerogative but contemptuous of his nephew and his ' young men of yesterday ', with European ambitions of his own, and owning vast estates which estranged the peers.

There were four types of opposition. First the magnates, of whom Arundel was an aggressive leader ; distrustful of ministers, insistent on their rôle of hereditary advisers, ardent for honourable war, and linked with prelates of their own blood, like Courtenay and the other Arundel. There were officials such as the experienced Wykeham, poised between deference for the Crown and zeal for ordered government. There was the City, much divided itself but always against courtiers and taxation. Lastly, there were the knights in the Commons, accustomed to follow the magnates in whose household they so often served, with new wealth which they were using to capture borough seats as well as the shires, familiar with the actual effects of misgovernment, and, since the Good Parliament, bitten with an appetite for power. Though their grants to Richard averaged those they had given his grandfather, he resented criticism and their apparent purpose to keep him on the curb. For the Parliaments of 1381–5 attacked his costly Household, blamed his debts, put taxes under treasurers of their own, and demanded that the Lords should name ministers.

Richard showed his teeth, refused to produce accounts, and dismissed the chancellor Scrope. Perfectly honest men might feel that the best way to reform was to reassert the royal authority ; one such being Michael de la Pole, son of Edward III's financier, an old follower of Gaunt like his brother-in-law Scrope, with a good record in war and Parliament, who in 1383 became chancellor. Courtiers steadily filled other places ; a new minister, the King's secretary, began to supersede the Privy Seal.

Unhappily Richard's circle, and their methods, went far beyond a legitimate stand for the Crown. His brother John Holland was a murderous ruffian. Wild accusations of plots drove Gaunt from Court.

Power and titles were heaped on the King's intimates, — Windsor and Dover castles to Burley, the earldom of Suffolk for de la Pole, while de Vere became marquis of Ireland with palatine rights over the Pale. Richard plunged as a partisan into London factions, supporting Brember against Gaunt's friend, the Lollard sympathizer John of Northampton, who was arbitrarily imprisoned in Corfe Castle.

Then Gaunt's departure for Portugal in 1386 removed the buffer between Court and opposition. Both Scottish war and French negotiation had failed. Ghent had fallen. Unpaid troops plundered the home counties. A small circle of magnates drew together, bound by marriage ties, with mighty lands and traditions; Thomas of Gloucester and Gaunt's heir Henry of Derby, Arundel with his FitzAlan castles on the March and Warenne fiefs in Sussex, Mowbray earl of Nottingham with ancient power in Northumberland, Braose fiefs, and the Bigod inheritance in Norfolk, and Warwick, head of the Beauchamps. The greatest prelates, Arundel, Courtenay, and Wykeham, supported them. The Commons asked the dismissal of ministers, and when Richard threatened to bring in help from France, Gloucester reminded him of the deposition of Edward II. Suffolk was made the scapegoat and impeached, but the opposition stopped with the appointment of a committee to control administration for a year, half composed of moderate men like Wykeham.

It was Richard who made civil war inevitable. He dismissed Parliament with a declaration of his prerogative, released Suffolk, made de Vere a duke. All through 1387 he moved restlessly about the Midlands, trying to raise the north and troops from his Welsh and Cheshire palatinates, and instructing the sheriffs to stop the election of hostile knights of the shire. He forced the judges to declare that the appointed committee infringed his prerogative, that the King alone could initiate discussion in Parliament, and that impeachment could only be with his consent. Making a new precedent, he created his Household steward a hereditary baron.

Alarmed at the menace of new stretches of the treason law, the opposition decided to strike first. Arundel, a popular hero through his capture of the La Rochelle wine fleet, joined his armed forces with those of Gloucester and Warwick, who with him ' appealed ' of treason de Vere, Suffolk, Brember, and the chief justice Tressilian. Moderate councillors were still on their side. Though Richard agreed to call Parliament, he attempted to pack it and sounded the City about raising troops; Suffolk fled the country, but de Vere marched south with the Cheshire levies. This brought into the field the more moderate Derby and Mowbray, who headed him off the London roads and in December scattered his army at Radcot Bridge in Oxfordshire, de Vere escaping by swimming the Thames and finally by flight to France.

London and the officials showed they were on the Appellants' side. Though they would not go so far, with Gloucester and Arundel, as to depose the King, the threat was used to compel his surrender, and in February 1388 the ' Merciless ' Parliament began a five months' session. Arm in arm, the five appellants came in with their charges ; evil coun- sellors had withdrawn the King from his magnates, defied Parliament, impoverished the Crown, plotted to betray Calais. To the royal argu- ment that the appeal was against law, the lords made a memorable reply that Parliament was the highest source of law, and that of such high cases, determined by the law of Parliament, the peers were the judges. As a sovereign court they proceeded to execute Burley, Brember, and Tressilian, and to exile the judges to Ireland. Parliament took oaths to prevent any reversal of its judgment and repaid the Appellants' expenses. Yet it recognized that the commission of 1386 had acted in ' great necessity ', and provided that its actions should not be taken as a precedent.

For a year the Appellants held all power. Arundel ravaged the French coast, but negotiations for a truce were checked by Scottish invasion, ending in the famous Border moonlight battle of Chevy Chase, where Percy's son Hotspur was taken prisoner. Council stopped writs issuing under the signet of the King's secretary, and reformed Chancery. An active Parliament enforced holding of quarter sessions, fixed wage- rates, and legislated against wandering beggars.

But Gloucester's violence had shocked moderate men, his ambition offended the house of Lancaster, and in May 1389, with the assent of Derby and Mowbray, Richard dismissed the Arundels, appointed a moderate ministry under Wykeham, and recalled Gaunt from the Peninsula, granting him also the government of Gascony for life. For seven years England enjoyed peace and prosperity. If Richard had learned the rôle of an English King, all might still be well. Parliament allowed he had the right of naming ministers and, though firm that Council must not override the common law, admitted that recent events had not impaired his ' regality '. On the dangerous matter of the armed followers who took the ' livery ' of great men, and received their ' maintenance ' in the law courts, the Commons felt with the King.

But Richard was unchanged, nor are his actions consistent with the view that he had forgiven the past. He vainly tried to recall the exiles. He put de Vere's friends high in Ireland, and when his loved friend died, brought back his body to be buried in state. When the City refused a loan, he suspended its government. He recruited archers for a House- hold reserve, giving them a retaining fee with his own livery of the white hart, and conniving at attacks by his Cheshiremen on Glou- cester's estates. He won over some leading knights, one of whom, Bushy, was several times Speaker.

Gradually he isolated Gloucester and Arundel. Gaunt's foreign ambitions were satisfied, for his daughters were Queens of Castile and Portugal; at home Richard gave him the first place in council, and when he married his mistress Katherine Swynford, their children the Beauforts were legitimized and given honours. Richard being childless, the succession further divided the Appellants, for the Lancastrians were at daggers drawn with Arundel, who had married a sister of the young March. Mowbray, quarrelling over fiefs with Warwick, was high in favour. The King had made a new friend in York's son, the particularly base Rutland, together with some men of courtier families, the highly cultivated Montagu earl of Salisbury, Despensers, and Scropes. And he looked outside England for further support.

When Anne of Bohemia died in 1394, he went to Ireland to strengthen the government there, and during his visit planned a second marriage with a French princess. If it could not bring a full peace owing to the thorny point of sovereignty, at least he might get a long truce, and something more. For the terms at last concluded brought him not only some money down but a defensive alliance, with an understanding of French help against rebel subjects.

He looked also to Rome. English opinion would have liked to make permanent the concordat arranged in 1375, and Parliament tightened up the acts of praemunire and provisors. The King, however, was orthodoxy itself. He wanted Roman help in getting a bench of loyal bishops, asked the Holy See to canonize his predecessor Edward II, and gave Rome a first claim on all benefices in royal patronage, the Pope allowing him in return to take an oath of special obedience from the clergy.

Peace with France, always unpopular, was the more so as it involved our surrender of Brest; the King, grumbled Gloucester, would sell Calais next; he had even suppressed the title 'King of France' on his coinage; his marriage to an eight-year-old child endangered the succession. But Richard seemed possessed. He promised an English army to help the French in Italy, seriously thought of making himself Emperor, and began to use imperial language, styling himself 'sole emperor of the realm'. In the first Parliament of 1397 skilful management by his placemen allowed him to recall the exiled judges, while the lords condemned an attack on the Household as treason to his regality; the Commons, however, refused taxes for his Italian policy, and Gloucester and Arundel withdrew from Council. This opposition drove the King to a desperation, which within two years brought about revolution.

Assured of support from Mowbray, Rutland, and the Beauforts, in July he treacherously arrested Arundel and Warwick, marched on Gloucester's castle at Pleshey, and sent him as a prisoner to Mowbray's captaincy at Calais. In September Parliament met to enforce a revenge modelled, step for step, on the mercilessness of 1388. The King's friends ' appealed ' the Appellants. Arundel was executed, his brother the bishop and Warwick were exiled; Gloucester, it was announced, had ' died ' at Calais, though actually he had been murdered after a confession had been extracted. Parliament, packed by the sheriffs and overawed by the Cheshire guards, repealed the Acts of 1386. Arundel's lands were added to the Cheshire palatinate, and the renegades took their reward in lands and titles, — a dukedom of Hereford for Henry of Derby and one of Norfolk for Mowbray.

Though there were signs of unrest, such as ' miracles ' at Arundel's tomb, Richard pressed on. Parliament, adjourned in January 1398 to Shrewsbury, repealed the acts of 1388 as against prerogative, declared it treason to reverse any of their present measures, and gave the King the customs for his life. Since the victors were already betraying each other, and Hereford was accusing Norfolk of Gloucester's death, its last measure was to appoint a packed committee to deal with this question and others left over. Thus freed by the division of his enemies, Richard acted in Imperial style, held a court of chivalry to organize a duel between the two dukes, and in the lists at Coventry threw down his warder and exiled both, Norfolk for life and Henry for ten years. He had just heard that March, his heir, had been killed in an Irish skirmish; if Henry were well away, he could model the future as he pleased.

Norfolk's lands were confiscated, and in February 1399 Richard took an irremediable step on the death of John of Gaunt. Tampering with the Parliament roll in order to stretch the powers of his committee, he seized the lands of Henry of Lancaster and extended his exile also to life. He swore both Parliament and clergy to observe his acts; he filled the sheriffdoms with Household servants. He sent agents out for forced loans, compelled men to sign charters which the Council would fill up with heavy fines if they gave offence, held threats of outlawry over seventeen counties. His Council was small and centralized, and he had taken many Lancastrian knights into his pay.

Triumph had gone to his head. Both to foreign princes and at home he used high and mighty words, how the laws were in his breast, sitting long hours on his throne to receive servile deference. His Garter feasts were filled with ladies and new-made peers; from whom he would not hear the views of the old nobility, or the people's ballads against his managers in the Commons, — Bushy, Bagot, and Green;

> *there is a Bush that is foregrown,*
> *Crop it well, and hold it low ;*

. . . . .

> *the long grass that is so Green,*
> *It must be mown and raked clean.*

He was playing a lone desperate hand. He was childless, and March had left only children under ten years of age. He had made the Lancastrians enemies. He was allied to France, the old enemy. He had estranged the middle class by arbitrary loans. Avoiding the settled south, he moved about with his wild Marchers. Men thought of him as a petulant child; already the shrewd poet Gower had turned to Henry of Lancaster, whose warfare in Tunis, Hungary, and Prussia at least proved him a man. Permanent officials, Churchmen, and houses like the Percies waited their opportunity, which the King presented to them, when in May 1399 he took his best troops to Ireland.

While his army, half-starved, struggled towards Dublin, at Paris Henry with archbishop Arundel prepared revolution. Sailing with a handful of men from Boulogne, in early July he reached the Humber, where the north under Percies and Nevilles rallied to him. At Doncaster he took solemn oath that he sought only a reformed government and his own rights, and then, assured of sympathy in London, marched to the Severn to get between Richard and his friends. The regent York submitted, at Bristol first blood was drawn by the summary execution of Bushy, Scrope, and Green. On hearing that Richard had landed in Pembrokeshire and Salisbury in north Wales, with excellent judgment Henry anticipated the next move by advancing on Chester.

Finding no response in south Wales, Richard rode hard northwards, only to find that rumours of his death had dispersed the Welsh, and that Salisbury was cooped up in Conway Castle. Half his friends of 1397 had deserted him, his brother John Holland, Duke of Exeter, Rutland, and the Beauforts, and though he could still escape by sea, here Henry's craft came into play. His envoys swore that he asked only restoration of his lands, trial of the guilty, and a free Parliament, on which assurances Richard came to Flint to parley, and was at once treated as a prisoner. Henry had gone too far for a peaceful settlement with a man like the King, whose nearest friends he had executed, and whose loyal Cheshire he had pillaged. White with rage, Richard had sworn aloud he would yet give Henry a death which would 'make a noise even in Turkey' and as they rode towards London his Welsh allies attacked the convoy.

Despite the pledges given at Conway, in September Richard was lodged in the Tower. On the 29th an informal committee, instructed to look into precedents, compelled him to declare his resignation of the Crown, which next day was announced to Parliament, who brushed aside the cry of a small minority that it was given under constraint. A list of charges was produced, covering the whole reign, after which Henry, avoiding the claims made for Parliament by some of his supporters, claimed the throne in an English speech, both by inheritance as the rightful heir and by God's approval of his conquest. A mob of the

Londoners, who showed their hatred of Richard throughout, invaded Westminster Hall, amid which tumult Parliament acclaimed the new King, receiving from him new writs to revive the legality shaken by the abdication.

There was not room for two Kings in England. Parliament asked that Richard be kept prisoner for life, but he had hardly been moved to Henry's castle of Pontefract before a conspiracy of his friends destroyed him. Mortal hatred raged between the Appellants of 1388 and the base men at whose actions Henry had connived in 1397, who exiled him in 1398 but abandoned Richard a year after; York's son the ever-treacherous Rutland, Despenser earl of Gloucester, Montagu earl of Salisbury, and the Hollands. When Henry reduced them now in title and estates but spared their lives, they repaid him at the new year of 1400 by plotting his assassination. Their wild scheme was betrayed. Salisbury and Surrey, the younger Holland, were torn out of Cirencester Abbey and lynched; Gloucester killed by the city council of Bristol, and Exeter by an Essex mob. Before February went out it was announced that King Richard, who was in the custody of Henry's kinsman Swynford, had starved himself to death.

Thus ended, in a despotic King and a treacherous revolution, the direct line of Plantagenet. Would its feuds and their aftermath damage the cause for which men said they had revolted, the law and constitution as the Edwards had left them? Would the problems, religious and foreign and economic, with which government had failed to cope, bring government to the ground? Such were the mediaeval legacies to the new dynasty, while Henry IV heard Mass over Richard's body in St. Paul's.

CONTEMPORARY DATES

CHAPTER III

THE FIFTEENTH CENTURY

CHAUCER died in 1400; between 1446 and 1483 Columbus and Machiavelli, Erasmus and Luther, Wolsey and Henry VIII were born. Before the youngest of these men died a new world had come into existence, with a greater part for Britain. Her mediaeval life ended. Her religious and intellectual outlook grew away from the universal Church. A capitalist structure replaced an agrarian local feudalism. The ancient links by which the Normans had fettered her to France being forcibly severed, for the first time since the Conquest she became politically an island, dependent for life on the open sea. Nature, which gave her that opportunity, thereby allowed her to develop her borrowings from abroad in peace; to work the new into the mediaeval frame without serious revolution; in short, to keep (using the words in their widest sense) a catholic civilization in a protestant policy.

This new life rose painfully out of national agony, for the last age had bequeathed two deadly perils: a revolution which in shaking the title to the throne shook all securities, and a hundred years' war of which only sixty had gone. How dangerous was the first was proved by Henry IV's weary struggle with treason, and how enormous the second by Henry V's ambition, which committed the nation to a fight to the last breath for Normandy. Even so, good fortune might have saved the dynasty, even if it had to lose France, but fortune was unkind. The hero Henry V died at thirty-five, to be succeeded by an infant, who grew up a weakling best fitted to be a monk, and ended as a semi-imbecile. The strong men of the rival house, who combined the claims of York and Mortimer, were pushed up as much by national despair as by their own desires, and Normandy and Gascony had hardly been lost before the Wars of the Roses doomed the country.

Yet English civilization in this age was progressive, and in some ways magnificent. It is impossible to think decadent or barbarous those who built the Divinity School or Magdalen at Oxford, Queens' College at Cambridge, Eton and St. George's Chapel at Windsor. Nor were such achievements and benefactions limited to the Court or a few areas; in one decade York Minster received its great east window, and Whittington, thrice Mayor of London, began the Guildhall. Nobles planned life in superb houses like Tattershall in Lincolnshire, and commemoration in death by memorials as fair as the Beauchamp chapel at Warwick. In the richer parts of England rose a strong native architecture in Perpendicular churches, with tall windows full of glowing glass, vaulting branched into fan tracery, wonderful hammer-beam roofs and carved stalls. Seafaring Bristol showed its wealth in St. Mary Redcliffe, industrial East Anglia in churches rich in Flemish arts, the West Country graziers and clothiers in Cotswold building and Somerset church towers. A native craft, untouched by the foreign Renaissance, continued in the alabaster effigies made at Nottingham and London. Wall-paintings everywhere depicted the people's faith and tradition, from the St. Christopher or St. George, or Piers Plowman with the carpenter's tools, in village churches, to the moral frescoes of Eton or the heroic paintings which till Tudor days caught the Commons' eyes in St. Stephen's Chapel.

No man of letters of Chaucer's stature marked the last mediaeval age. There is not a flash in the Bury monk Lydgate, the versifying civil servant Occleve, or the Augustinian friar Capgrave who wrote annals for Edward IV. Even so, there were memorable things done in fifteenth-century English; versions of the legendary travels of Sir John Mandeville, the great *Morte d'Arthur* written by the Lancastrian member for Warwickshire, Malory; the morality play *Everyman*; Judge Fortescue's tract on *The Governance of England*; the ballad of ' The Nut-Brown Maid '.

These are specimens of the best, but the age had much more, gone from our mind. Neither Chaucer nor Wyclif were half so widely read as the devotional books of the faith, to which women made a notable contribution, and among them Henry VII's mother, who translated part of *The Imitation of Christ*. Religion was also the fount of the mystery plays, the true literature of the man in the street. At York, Chester, Wakefield, and smaller towns innumerable, on Corpus Christi day in early summer mornings the waggons moved the stage from point to point of the narrow streets; each craft being responsible, year after year, for the production of one series: the York fishermen for ' the Flood ', the Norwich grocers representing ' Paradise ', others the ' Harrowing of Hell ' or Pilate sitting high in his ' parliament ', while neighbours laughed at the local humours brought in of Noah's mulish wife, or the sheep-stealers among the shepherds who watched the strange star over Bethlehem. If the action was crude and much of the writing stilted, now and then some mute inglorious monk added a touch of purest poetry, and English drama was exercising its dialogue and humour. There were players in the villages of Romney Marsh, or Christmas plays in homes of Chiltern squires, and private companies who acted interludes under the patronage of great nobles. But the London stationers' gild and the scriveners of Paternoster Row handled many more than religious books; old heroic epics were popular as ever, the *Gesta Romanorum* or *Guy of Warwick*; there were new-translated prose romances, ballads of Robin Hood and the greenwood, with a harvest of songs and carols in an age that loved music.

What is called the Renaissance did not break suddenly but flowed in like a tide, and in three vital ways the English mind changed from mediaeval into modern before the Tudors. Its instrument was now the English tongue, the speech of Parliament, law courts, and common life, though French continued as the language of legal lore. In English were written the Lollard propaganda posted up in country inns, it was in English that City companies regulated their members or Henry V wrote his letters, while Oxford now taught French as a foreign tongue. This English writing was universal, over a hundred manuscripts surviving of one chronicle alone. Here and there a monastery kept up its school of history, but one new mark of the age was the making of many town records, by London citizens, or the men of Lynn, or the town clerk of Bristol. Songs on Agincourt or the defence of Calais, political poems pleading for strong measures to defend trade, savage satire on the bishops and manifestos by the house of York, testify to a public opinion which must be courted in the English tongue.

But English learning had already gone to the fountain-head in the Mediterranean. Lincoln College, Oxford, founded in 1427 as a bulwark against Lollardy, received manuscripts brought from Italy by the founder's kinsmen. Unhappy bishop Moleyns, whom the sailors lynched in 1450, he too had been there and sent manuscripts to Oxford, where an Italian was lecturing on Greek before the Wars of the Roses ended. There was a Balliol group, and some Canterbury monks too, who had studied the new learning at Florence. Princes and nobles took pride in patronizing the scholars; not least Henry V's brother Humphrey, whose gifts were the germ of the Bodleian. Edward IV's constable Tiptoft was accused of learning both his scholarship and his atrocious cruelty at Padua; the King's brother-in-law Anthony Woodville made translations from the French, which Caxton printed; archbishop Neville, the King-maker's brother, kept his Greek scribes. Before 1476, then, when Caxton set up his Westminster press, which was soon followed by others at Oxford and St. Albans, the English Renaissance, which included the renaissance of English, had begun.

It found a people whose education was rapidly widening, and anxious to learn. Cathedral and monastery schools were now reinforced by new foundations, often attached to a chantry or collegiate church, but as often endowed by merchants, who put them under trustees or a City company, and with laymen as masters. London was ardent; one new school in Threadneedle Street taught both Colet and More. At Stratford-on-Avon the gild of Holy Cross built a new school, which a century later was to educate Shakespeare. Wykeham's scholars entered their first buildings at Winchester in 1394, and on his model Henry VI planned Eton, whose building began and paused as the country fell into civil war; the age saw the first germs of Manchester grammar school, and all over England new endowments. Christ's College, Cambridge, was planned expressly to increase the number of good schoolmasters. Archbishop Chichele, who founded All Souls College, Oxford, to commemorate the dead of the French wars, founded a grammar school also; so did Waynflete, founder of Magdalen, and as headmaster of that school Wolsey himself began. Many such schools taught all classes without fees, though country gentlemen often boarded their children with private masters; while one of the Norfolk Pastons, whose family letters tell us so much, went to a young and struggling Eton.

This spiritual development was made possible by a new wealth, flowing from the changes we have seen in the fourteenth century; an early capitalism, the degree and form of which were still undecided. Men, money, and intelligence were forcing out new channels. Regular carriers traversed the country by road and river. Landowners had spare moneys invested with London merchants, who distributed goods through travellers and chapmen, and dealt in foreign transactions by bills of exchange. Both Autolycus and Dick Whittington were making a career of their different talents, and old barriers fell down. Gascon traders like the Russells, London mayors like Boleyn and Wotton, were founding county families. Instead of local gild markets, industry was grouping into provinces, the cloth of the West and Midlands thus coming to London to be shipped for Calais, while Norwich, second city of the realm, controlled export from dozens of the villages, Kersey or Linsey, Coggeshall, Lavenham, or Worstead, which gave their humble names to cloths which would sell in Novgorod or Aleppo, and whose wealth flowered in tall churches and solid houses, often in the red brick new-learned from the Flemings.

The land, still the national backbone, was changing in social structure. Those economic causes which had begun before the Peasants' Revolt acted more decisively after it in ending labour services, and two others were added: the long pressure of the war on land-owners who had to provide both men and money, and the effects of the growing cloth trade on the level of wages. Weary of inelastic and grumbling labour, and unable to get enough income from fixed manorial dues, owners steadily turned to wider plans — whether a lease of their home farms or of peasant holdings for terms of years, or putting land down to pasture with a certainty of profit from the clothiers. Indeed industry sought out the land; so the Tames, the family of graziers who built Fairford church, handled the wool in their Cirencester factory hard by. The State, which had taught the notion of competition by its Statute of Labourers, further assisted this revolution. Its courts began to protect the villeins' legal title in their holdings, and devised ways to circumvent the entailing of property under Edward I's Act of *De Donis*.

Freed, then, from the compulsion of the manor, the peasants hungrily flung themselves on the soil. Continuing for the most part as ' copyholders ' — holding, that is, their old acres in right of a copy of the manor court-roll, in return for some fixed dues and a ' fine ' when a new tenant entered — but often taking a lease for years or several lives, the villeins turned into the yeomen, who for another three hundred years made the heart of England. The question now raised, for the first time, of who should have a parliamentary vote, proved the rise of this new class, from whom came the flower of Henry V's army in the mounted archers. Rejoicing in their new liberty — for we read of a village feast when a neighbour had bought his freedom from the lord — their last wills and testaments, their bequests of feather-beds and silver, and legacies to their parish church, showed how they used it. The prosperous among them were anxious, like their lords, to enclose their land in continuous blocks, free from a neighbour's wandering cattle or weeds and from fixed rotations of husbandry, and by agreement, sale, or exchange began a process the end of which we see in Elizabethan estate maps. It meant not a sudden end of the open fields, which continued in the Midlands at least for generations more, but their persistent replacement by enclosed and hedged fields, the formation of a yeoman class with holdings of all sizes, and the establishment on a money basis of the threefold division of landlord, farmer, and wage-labourer.

So the land, venerable mother, was being compelled to accommodate herself to the lusty infant of industrial England. Lancastrian parliaments wrestled between consumer and producer; by acts, for instance, regulating corn exports in accord with home prices, or holding the ring, in what was to be a long struggle, between wool-growers who wanted free export and clothiers who demanded cheap wool.

This century and a half after the fall of Richard II decided all the future economic foundations and that, in essentials, before the discovery of America. Nature had given Britain a position of vantage as carrier and trader, but it was only in the late fifteenth and early sixteenth centuries that this bounty could be fully used; when the end of French wars stopped the drain of men and money into a blind channel; when the Turkish threat to Italian commerce, the decline of the Hanse, and a long depression in the Netherlands, crippled our rivals and gave us new markets.

In free societies, and the more so before the uniformity of modern days, the stages of industry overlap; old survivals continuing beside the new, or combining with them in transition forms. Broadly speaking, however, in this century the craft-gild ceased to be the main wheel, yielding gradually to another which, under the name of ' the domestic system ', covered most of industry till it was overtaken by the modern factory. For the craft, serving a local market and aiming at equality, could not survive the new specialization or adapt itself to large-scale trade. Money-power asked freedom ; capital began to migrate to suburbs, or to villages where it could own its raw material, control fuel or water-power, and make its labour supply. This migration filled Parliament with complaint from older towns, that they are decayed, that grass grows in Winchester streets, or that undergraduates are declining in numbers at Oxford. The Edwardian tax of the tenth and fifteenth, based on a fixed assessment, dropped sharply in yield. East Anglia began to fall away before the western clothing districts and Yorkshire.

This petty capitalism was one of small masters, some working on their own account, and others to the order of bigger men. It was domestic in two senses : first, that it continued the craft plan of apprentices, housed and disciplined by their masters, but also because the lower stages were handled by home workers, whether working for themselves or for others ; weavers, for example, often with looms owned by large employers, and spinners working in their cottages for clothiers. So a new superstructure gradually replaced the craft, varying in form but in type much the same ; a livery company, or merchant-gild of a new pattern. Sometimes it arose by a deliberate amalgamation of crafts, sometimes by control coming naturally to the branch which handled the final process — the drapers thus winning supremacy over the weavers and fullers. Increased trade implied large firms who traded independently of the crafts, like the grocers and mercers who distributed direct from London and Southampton to country agencies ; it meant also that power went to those who could afford large capital and large risks, and involved an aristocracy of capitalist ' liveries ', marked by restricted elections and high entrance-fees.

London was the centre and climax of the new structure. Its twelve great companies received charters of incorporation from the Lancastrians, Edward IV gave them a direct share in the election of the Lord Mayor, and out of eighty-eight mayors in this century sixty-one belonged either to the pure merchant class of mercers and grocers, or to the drapers who were part-traders too. It was a spirited age in the City when its leaders built the Guildhall, Newgate prison, the Leadenhall granary, and the cloth-mart at Blackwell Hall, when the Moorfields were drained, when fifty churches were new-built or reconditioned, and merchant palaces like Crosby Place. Henry V's campaigns turned upon City loans, and government itself on the opinion of the citizens, who in red and white gala cloaks met Kings and Cardinals, whose watch and ward stopped the affrays of armed nobles, and whose silver-plate astonished the rich Florentines and Venetians.

This new economy called forth a new activity of the State. Parliament intervened to stabilize the labour market, so forbidding peasants to enter the crafts. An act of 1437 referred gild ordinances to justices of the peace, while another of 1504 centralized still more by submitting them to judges of assize. While the Crown freely remodelled company and town charters, concentrating authority in the master class, the central government took over many functions of gilds and local authorities; settling the standard of cloth, fixing wages and sometimes prices, or passing Acts of ' diet and apparel ' which tried to grade the standard of living. Foreign trade also forced on the development of the law and department of Admiralty, bringing into Parliament questions like reprisals and prize at sea.

This regulation was the more necessary because the whole character of our trade was changing. In the Edwards' heyday England exported 30,000 sacks of wool a year, which by Henry VI's time had fallen to about 8000, and the French war annihilated a third of the Gascon wine trade. But new markets made the loss good, finished goods and cloth replaced the export of raw material, and our miscellaneous trade more than doubled. A walk along the quays of London and Southampton would show on what distant poles our commerce turned, the fierceness of competition, and the interlocking of export and import; as the eye passed from casks of blue French woad, our clothiers' dye, or Prussian canvas in which the wool was packed, to Baltic herrings and timber, codfish from Iceland, Spanish iron and salt, or from the luxury silks of Genoa to the apprentices' cheap German caps.

Yet this swelling commerce still flowed in a mediaeval tideway. The Staple controlled the wool export, even in decline a mighty industry; for if it stopped, the streets of Ghent and Florence would be turbulent with unemployed. Most wool, especially the finest coming from the Cotswolds, went through London to Calais, which facilitated tax-collection and enabled government to regulate the flow of bullion. Under the Yorkists, indeed, the Staple became essentially a department of state for the upkeep of Calais.

Outside this special case, commercial supremacy was contested between one English and two ancient foreign agencies. Out of several groups chartered by Henry IV, the Merchant Adventurers trading to the Low Countries emerged as the predominant partner, based in particular on Antwerp and Bruges. Though there were rifts and jealousies between London companies and provincial bodies like the Bristol Venturers, the Adventurers steadily increased their proportion, their fleets carrying the bulk both of exported cloth and imported wine ; till by 1480 they controlled about 80 per cent of the trade handled by English subjects.

Since the Italian traders, making longer voyages with luxury goods and much affected by troubles in Italy and a sea menaced by the Turks, relatively lost ground, the Hanseatic League was now our most serious rival. Masters of the quadrilateral between London and Bruges, Bergen and Novgorod, and seated at Lubeck and Cologne astride both north-south and east-west trade routes, they held the sources of many vital materials and carried goods for all Europe. In England their privileges, dating from Angevin days, were enormous ; unlike other aliens, they could sell retail ; they were exempt from poundage, the duty on miscellaneous goods, while on cloth exports they paid a lower rate than the English themselves. Together with a natural jealousy of this entrenched power, incessant strife raged over the English claim for equal treatment in Prussia, and all the other questions which must spring from foreign factories in enemy lands. After forty years of commercial war, Yorkist England had to admit defeat, and though their share of English trade had slightly fallen, the Hanse still held the Baltic, with its important naval stores, as in a vice.

An outcry for action, furious riots against aliens, filled fifteenth-century England. Acts were passed to regulate the aliens' sales and credits, to check their retail rights, to levy special taxes ; London women, workers in silks and ribbons, demonstrated against the Italians. Bristol ships sailed through the Straits to the Levant, tried to develop Ireland, or joined the fishermen of Hull and Lynn in exploiting Iceland. When lawful channels failed, our seamen took to universal piracy, in which every port of the West Country, their best blood and their magistrates, took a hand. The nobles, the King-maker and Howards and de la Poles included, invested their rents in trading cargoes ; parliamentary petitions and a new literature asked protection for ' the Navy and merchandise '.

A famous book, *The Libelle of English Policye*, written by someone high in political circles before 1440, took as its motto ' keep the Admiralty ' — the supremacy which Henry V's ships had won. It argued that Flanders could only feed itself for a month, and that with the keys of Dover and Calais England could lock the Channel, cut off Italian luxuries, ship her own cloth, and bring the hated Hanse to terms. ' The commonweal of England ', said another pamphlet, ' must rise out of the work of the common people.' Such teaching, that in sea-borne trade lay our strength, coincided with a mass of new shipbuilding, all round the coast from Dartmouth to Hull. William Cannynges of Bristol owned a fleet of ten ships, some of 500 tons, before he abandoned business to become a priest.

To a degree unknown since Viking days the English were taking to their ships, and henceforth the sound of the sea was ever in their mind. We can almost hear the Bristol clerk humming who, in Henry VII's time, scribbled in his court records a sailors' song:

> *Haule and howe rumbelowe,*
> *Stir well the good ship, and let the wynde blow.*

CHAPTER IV

LANCASTRIAN ENGLAND, 1399–1413

HENRY IV was to die at forty-six, worn out, and his reign was unhappy both for England and himself. Two things in particular made it so; the immediate effects of an ugly revolution, and an accumulation of problems long postponed; conflict with France, commercial rivalries, unsettled war with Scotland, a farcical government in Ireland, a restless Wales, and the undimmed anger of the Lollards. Economically it was a time of gloom, with some bad harvests and a sag in the cloth trade of nearly 50 per cent from Richard's best year. And the lawlessness which his reign had let loose had bitten deep.

All this disappointed many patriotic men who had hoped much of the revolution, and though bad health half-crippled Henry from 1405 onwards, some of the failure lay in his character. For ever on the move, argumentative in word and sometimes brutal in deed, his energy was neither continuous nor confident. His expenditure, especially after the advent of his second wife Johanna of Brittany, was extravagant. And whether it came from his health or no, his course seems to be set not by himself but by the last group, or individual, who gained his ear.

Regrets for Richard were few, though as discontent increased his name was used and rumour insisted he was alive. But Henry stood between more dangerous parties. Though March, the legitimate heir, was a boy and a prisoner, the name of Mortimer could conjure up a following; moreover, the King might have to choose between the first and the second phase of the revolution. To the 'new appellants' of 1397, who had lately attempted his life, he was bound by many ties; to his own half-brothers the Beauforts, but also to Richard's, the passionate Hollands, who were linked by marriage to the house of York, whose present leader Rutland was a monument of treachery; and to the young Mowbray of Norfolk, son of Henry's old fellow-conspirator and rival. Arrayed against these were all who looked back to the first appellants of 1388, accused Rutland of murdering the good Thomas of Gloucester, and clamoured for reprisals. Now, though the King refused to keep up this vendetta and continued some of Richard's officials in place, to two members of this right wing he owed an overwhelming debt. Archbishop Arundel, his right arm in exile, represented also the support of the Church and the conservative aristocracy, while to Northumberland, once Gaunt's ally against the Good Parliament, he owed half the success of 1399. Amply he rewarded the Percies. The earl was Constable, and had the West March and the profits of the Mortimer estates; his brother, Worcester, was Lord Steward; his son, the famous Hotspur, who had married a Mortimer, was given the East March and the castles of north Wales.

It would need strength to balance these factions, but the Crown was weak, because it was poor. On his way to the throne Henry had lavished promises of lower taxes, and so liberally rewarded friends, or bribed enemies, that his first House of Commons protested. And seeing that the Commons would not grant him taxes for life, that his revenue independent of them was hardly £60,000 and that he was spending £20,000 a year on his Household alone, he began and ended with a deficit. He dare not resume Richard's grants, and could not pay off Richard's debts. Bankrupt Ireland took English money. Calais averaged nearly £30,000 a year, but even so its garrison was often mutinous for lack of pay, like those of Berwick and Wales. His finances thus revolved in a vicious circle of loans and taxes mortgaged to meet arrears, local revenues pre-charged with grants to his supporters, and unhappy London creditors paid in tallies chargeable on non-existent customs duties.

From this weakness branched off another more fiery circle, of weakness, therefore rebellion, and hence poverty redoubled. The revolution invited attack from old enemies The Scots at once raided Northumberland; not that this was needed to inflame English hatred, which the friars' sermons showed to be a rooted national feeling. While Henry's claims and ' annexation ' of all south of the Tweed came to nothing through lack of resources, he was saved by the feuds among the Scots and by two gifts of fortune. In 1402 the Percy archers crushed a Scots army at Homildon Hill near Wooler, taking prisoner the son of Albany the Regent, and the head of the Douglas clan. And in 1406, James, heir to the throne, was captured at sea on his way to France, and came to spend eighteen years in captivity, which gave him time to become a poet and a scholar. So though the Scots continued to help every enemy of England, self-interest and faction forbade them to go far.

Their allies the French (and French knights fought at Homildon) had much the same difficulty. The Court was sore at the fall of Richard their friend, and refused Henry's talk of a marriage alliance; French troops picked up some towns on the Aquitaine border and encouraged sedition in Bordeaux; pirates from Brittany fought the men of Devon, Burgundians attacked the outlying forts of Calais. But the Flemings disliked the notion of a complete break with English markets, in spite of all frays the truce was intermittently renewed, and in 1407 the murder of Louis of Orleans by Burgundian partisans began the civil war which was to cripple France for thirty years.

These half-wars were most formidable, in fact, because of the lawlessness of England. Piracy redoubled at once under this weak government, which left merchant ships to protect themselves, or gave letters of marque to privateers as a cheap defence. The merchant marine of the time, sometimes in royal pay and sometimes pirates, embroiled us with every seafaring country in Europe. If the Hanse carrying trade escaped the rovers of Scarborough and Norfolk, it ran into the west-countrymen; there were pitched battles among the wooden huts on the Baltic shores, where each summer fishermen of all nations came to catch and salt the herrings; so that at last the League put an embargo on English trade. Spanish ships bringing wine and fruit, Flemings and Dutchmen, fell victims too. In this war of reprisals the Bretons burned Plymouth, while the English ravaged Brest; Henry Pay of Poole, the Drake of the age and the terror of Biscay, cut out his prizes far up the Seine. Spanish and French galleys joined hands; there was fierce fighting in Poole harbour to cries of ' St. Jago ', and landing-parties in the Isle of Wight. And this wasting ruin of trade was doubly serious, because the government were facing a revolt which concentrated every danger.

Though Welsh nationalism had not died with the Edwardian conquest, Wales was penetrated by English garrisons and merchants, landowning families of each race intermarried, and commutation was breaking up the clan system. Owen Glendower's revolt in 1400 did not begin in any other way than dozens of similar incidents in Ireland, in the lawlessness of a weak government where two races clashed. Of all this Glendower was a typical product, a descendant of the princes of Powys, still holding their moated house in the Dee valley, through his mother a prince of south Wales too, and like his ancestors a great patron of the native bards. But his wife was English, so were his daughters' husbands, he had read English law, and served in the Scots wars. His feud with English Marchers only turned to revolt when his lands were confiscated, and when Parliament took up a racial policy in forbidding Welshmen to hold office or settle in March towns. Three expeditions led by the King himself did nothing but ravage; Owen took to the hills, there were risings from Anglesey to Welshpool and up the Towy to Cardigan, Welsh students at Oxford and Welsh harvesters went home to fight. The standard of the golden dragon was raised, when Owen appealed to the Scots King and Irish chiefs against the Saxon.

In 1402 he defeated and took prisoner both his original enemy Grey of Ruthin and Edmund Mortimer, uncle of the well-guarded Earl of March; no Welsh troops could be trusted against him. Rumours were spread, especially by the friars, that Richard was alive; the heads of the Dominicans at Winchester and Cambridge were arrested, the Warden of the Leicester Franciscans with others of his order was hanged. Since the King took no steps to ransom him, Mortimer threw in his lot with Glendower, whose daughter he married, and with whom he declared he would either restore Richard or, if he were dead, crown the Earl of March.

By 1403 the Percies also had taken their decision. They found power slipping away to the King's sons and to their neighbours the Nevilles, Hotspur was Mortimer's brother-in-law and had advised the conciliation of Glendower; the King refused to let them take profitable ransoms from the captured Scottish nobles. Parliament itself had admitted their brilliant services, and they held letters from half the baronage, to whom, however, they did not confide their dream that a Percy would make as good a King as a Mortimer. In July they took the field, charging Henry with breaking the pledges he had given them in 1399, with starving Richard, and packing Parliament. Hotspur appeared in Richard's own county of Chester, where distributions of the white hart badge roused the country clergy and their flocks, and marched south to join Glendower, who was sweeping up castles of south Wales. ' For God's love, my liege lord,' word reached the King, ' think on yourself and your estate, or all is lost.'

Before his enemies could join hands, by hard marching Henry reached Shrewsbury and brought them to battle north of the town, where later he raised Battlefield church for the souls of the slain; in hand-to-hand fighting the Prince of Wales was wounded, but Hotspur was killed and his uncle Worcester taken prisoner and executed.

Yet how weak and unpopular was the King was shown by the fact that Parliament continued to plead for Northumberland, to whom his estates were speedily restored. In 1405 Glendower rose to the height of his power, taking the castles of Harlech and Aberystwyth and burning Cardiff; the bishops of St. Asaph and Bangor joined him, the March was all harried, the suburbs of Shrewsbury burned, the Pembroke county court had to buy a truce. Meantime, under French influence, half the great abbeys of eastern England were conspiring, and Glendower's envoys signed a treaty at Paris.

In 1405, before this took effect, a second English rebellion was attempted. The young Mortimers were smuggled out of Windsor Castle and caught on the road to Wales, the plotters being the Duke of York and his sister, widow of Richard II's murdered favourite, Despenser. This failure, and some sharp defeats of Glendower, brought Northumberland out again. He sealed an agreement for the division of England between Percy and Mortimer, giving Wales and four English shires to Glendower; young Mowbray of Norfolk, married to a Holland, joined him to avenge his father's wrongs, together with Bardolf, a

member of the royal Council; more important still, the piety of the
north was represented by the bishop of Durham and the archbishop
of York. The archbishop was one of the fighting Scropes, whose *bend
or* badge had been shown in Prussia and Egypt, and who was bound
to the Percies by many ties. Manifestos dwelling on the King's
broken pledges, his taxation and lack of governance and packed
parliaments, were set forth in English, and preached in York Minster
by the archbishop and by his clergy in neighbouring towns, while
knights and priests collected peasants under a banner of the Sacred
Wounds.

Westmorland, married to a Beaufort and the Percies' sworn foe,
saved the King by crushing this Yorkshire rising before Northumberland
could join them. By treacherous pretences of sympathy he got the
archbishop and Mowbray into his hands, both of whom, against the
protest of archbishop Arundel, the King tried by special commission
and executed. Within a few months worship and alleged miracles began
at the archbishop's tomb, within a few years the new saint of the north
appeared in stained-glass and missals, while men said that Henry was
smitten with leprosy for his crime.

But counter-revolution had failed, in part because it came from
such scattered elements. The flight of Northumberland and Bardolf
over the Scottish Border, the fall of the Percy castles before the
King's artillery, executions which set heads on the gates of many
Yorkshire and Durham villages, all this was over before French troops
landed at Milford Haven. From Pembrokeshire they advanced with
Glendower to within ten miles of Worcester, but they lost command of
the sea, their supplies failed, and early in 1406 they went home. Though
placards were still sometimes fixed on St. Paul's declaring that Richard
was alive, in fact Henry's throne was at last reaching security.

France was occupied with her own troubles. A temporary peace
was patched up with the Hanse, which was much divided in its interests,
Henry declaring himself ' a child of Prussia ', with reference to his old
crusades with the Teutonic Knights who were now being hard pressed
by the Poles. The rulers of Scotland were ready to bargain over the
head of their captive King; they would not shield Northumberland
and Bardolf who, after many wanderings, made a last fling in invading
Yorkshire in 1408, and were killed by the county forces on Bramham
Moor. Only Glendower struggled on, with appeals to the Avignon
Pope to set up a Church of Wales, and ravaged indomitably until he
died, still at large and free, after Agincourt. But his countrymen began
to fall away. The resources of England and Ireland, overwhelming if
well used, were at last systematically employed under the Prince of
Wales, after a long siege Harlech fell in 1409, and the end became
certain.

Nearly ten years, however, had gone by since Henry of Lancaster had seized the throne, and the country was full of resentment and despair. Social discontent and severe punishment combined to keep Lollardy alive in a revolutionary form. The alliance of King and archbishop bore its fruits in the Statute *De heretico comburendo* of 1401, which gave the Church power to destroy heretical books and to hand over convicted heretics to be burned by the State. Purvey, the translator of the Bible, recanted, but a London priest, Sawtre, perished, the first martyr at Smithfield for views on the sacrament. Powerful men protected the preachers; especially John Oldcastle, one of the Prince's best captains in Wales and member for Herefordshire. Disquieted by the schism in the Papacy, and jealous of the clergy's wealth, the Commons proposed disendowment, asked that no one under age be allowed to become a friar, and attacked the bishops' infringement of praemunire. Oxford was debating the lawfulness of Bible translations, students came from Bohemia to translate Wyclif's works, and the University claimed exemption from the archbishop's visitation. At this Arundel took forcible action; forbade translations of Scripture if not officially approved, unlicensed preaching, or teaching on the sacraments; and got Parliament to affirm his rights. But while this was proceeding, a tract by Purvey was presented in 1410 to the Commons by knights who shared the Lollards' anti-clericalism, asking the King to seize the wealth, ' wasted so proudly ', which might enrich the Treasury and endow knights, almshouses, and universities. They were silenced, and the independence of Oxford was crushed, yet Lollardy worked underground and sometimes came to the surface. Excited fanatics distributed doggerel verses against the bishops and preached against marriage and baptism; Oldcastle, who sheltered some of them on his estates, corresponded with Bohemia; London scriveners were copying tracts which proclaimed the rule of Christ against the friars, and which spread from Bristol into Somerset.

All through the disastrous first half of the reign the tone of Parliament was aggressive and patriotic. The Commons were jealous against Council, and resisted the impressment of soldiers and ships. Though they deferred to the Lords, they legislated against their maintenance of liveried retainers, and successfully claimed that taxes, when agreed to by both Houses, must be given through their Speaker. Their hatred of aliens extended to the Breton servants of Henry's queen, whose costly Household they reduced. Critical from the first of the King's grants, in 1404 they insisted he must live on his own revenues, and demanded a sweeping resumption of royal lands granted away. More than once they compelled him to administer the taxes, doled out so jealously, through treasurers of their own choice, and to submit his accounts; an incessant pressure which brought down expenditure in the second half of the reign by nearly 50 per cent.

Their action reached high-water mark in the Parliament of 1406. Advancing from the principle throughout asserted that the names of the Council should be announced in Parliament (and leading Commoners were included), they tightened this by making the Council swear to guarantees; which would stop gifts, put the Household on an allowance, and make Council the only channel of royal action. Their resolutions encroached on every sphere of government, thus demanding that the Prince of Wales should live on the Welsh frontier, or that tonnage and poundage be paid over to merchants who should take on themselves the defence of the Channel.

Henry IV, stoutly resisting any loss of Richard's prerogative, only yielded inch by inch. He packed Parliament, extended the practice of holding it far from London, and once, in the ' unlearned' Parliament of 1404, excluded lawyers. When loans from monied men or foreign merchants allowed him to dispense with it, he did so, and when the pressure grew less, tried to break the leading-strings and get a revenue for life. And he sharply told his last Parliament that he would remain ' as free in his prerogative as any of his predecessors '.

Parliament had thriven on years of discontent, but in better times would reduce its pressure, and the opposition to Henry changed in character. The Prince of Wales stepped to the front of the stage, a shining and vital figure, with superabundant energy which found vent in riotous living, with warlike tastes and friends of his own choosing. He allied himself with his uncles the Beauforts, the brain of whom was Henry bishop of Winchester, who led an aristocratic opposition; the King leaned on his second son, Thomas of Clarence, and even more on his old friend archbishop Arundel, with whom he would stay at Lambeth, and who opposed the Commons' aggression and detested their Lollard sympathies. By a royal patent the King cut the Beauforts out of the succession to the Crown; and from 1407–9 Arundel was chief councillor. But the King's health went from bad to worse, in spite of public prayers and a Jewish doctor, and during 1410–11 the Prince and his group won more authority; which they used to send English troops to assist the Burgundian faction at Paris. Cultivating power and popularity by armed progresses, the Prince tried to drive his father to abdicate, which brought about yet another reaction, the exclusion of the Prince and the Beauforts from Council, and a rival expedition of Clarence to Normandy in alliance with the rival French faction of Orleans. The last month of Henry IV closed amid recrimination between his eldest son and his closest adviser Arundel, and with London full of armed men, brought up to support the Prince's cause. In March 1413 this most lonely revolutionary died.

CONTEMPORARY DATES

1400	Death of Chaucer.
	Rupert of the Palatinate elected Emperor against Wenzel.
1402	Tamerlane defeats the Turks at Ankara.
1404–19	John the Fearless rules as Duke of Burgundy.
1406	The Florentines conquer Pisa.
1407	Murder of Louis duke of Orleans.
1409	The Council of Pisa elects a third Pope.
1410	John Huss excommunicated at Prague.
	The Poles defeat the Teutonic Knights at Tannenberg.
1411–37	Reign of the Emperor Sigismund.
	Building begins of the London Guildhall.
1412–47	Filippo Maria Visconti rules Milan.
	Founding of University of St. Andrews.

CHAPTER V

HENRY V, 1413–1422

THE English middle ages and the Plantagenet line produced a last great man in Henry V, and in so doing bequeathed a nation. Traditions of his speech to the archers at Agincourt and his care for English sea-power passed on through old soldiers and London chronicles, deepening the patriotism which the Tudors invigorated, and on which Shakespeare set a crown. But the greater the man, the greater the misdirection he can impart, and Henry committed himself and his country to a hopeless quest of conquering France. In this tragedy mediaeval England died, though not bankrupt of ideals and not without glory.

The King was a leader of men. That discipline which he expected of others he imposed also on himself, throwing off at his accession his old companions of the City taverns. He took infinite pains with business and petitions, wrote good English letters, liked to read chronicles and history, and to have tapestries round him of heroic legends. Curt in voice and unbending in decision, under the stress of war his severity became cruel, so that he hung enemy gunners who fired too accurately at his tent, or an unfortunate trumpeter who had sounded defiance. He made himself a man of one purpose; splendid armour, constant Masses, visits to shrines and anchorites, human feelings, all went into the crucible of a holy war. His army, he told the doubters at Agincourt who sighed for reinforcements, were ' a people of God '; he convinced himself, and almost convinced the French, that his cause was just. He would lead his two kingdoms against the Turks, called for a report on the harbours of Syria and Egypt, and had by him in his last illness a history of the first Crusade.

His immediate dismissal of Arundel, like his severity to his stepmother, proved him both masterful and unforgetting, while money grants from Parliament, at first for four years and then for life, marked the national confidence. Unentangled in his father's past, he attempted reconciliation in the national interest. He brought King Richard's body to lie honourably in the Abbey, set free the young Earl of March, restored Hotspur's son and the heirs of Mowbray and Holland. But, even while he did so, two conspiracies showed that the past could not be so easily buried.

Lollardy must be dealt with, if only because Convocation and loud sermons from the friars insisted that it must be, and the King's

Churchmanship was quickly shown in the founding of new monasteries and taking notorious anti-Lollards as his confessors. After a vain private remonstrance he arrested his old companion-in-arms Oldcastle, who under examination stood firm on the sacrament and flamed out against the Pope as antichrist. His escape from the Tower was a signal for the outbreak in January 1414 of a wild plot to seize the King, which was betrayed and broken up after a skirmish in St. Giles' Fields, north of Charing Cross. Over forty executions among all classes, from Shropshire knights to priests, London and Midland tradesmen, and enquiry in twenty counties, showed how widely scattered was the seed. Again Oldcastle escaped and appeared in Worcestershire under the banner of the chalice, and not till 1417 was he caught, desperately wounded, in a raid on the Welsh border, and burned in St. Giles' Fields where (a London chronicler notes) ' he made an end of his cursed life '. An Act of 1414 extended the State's power over heresy, giving initiative to the justices of the peace. But placards, open-air sermons in the Surrey hills, burnings, arrests, and another bill in Parliament for confiscation of Church wealth, showed Lollardy to be unextinguished.

Oldcastle's sympathisers made contact also with a Mortimer plot, discovered at Southampton on the eve of Henry's departure for France. Would no leniency subdue these men ? The two chief conspirators were the Duke of York's brother Richard of Cambridge, whose two marriages had linked him to Mortimer and Percy, and another Scrope, nephew of the martyred archbishop and husband of a Holland, the very families so often pardoned and so entirely false. Once more then the scaffold; but the four-year-old son of Cambridge lived on, to become heir to all the oppositions and to be known as Richard of York.

From the first Henry was determined to force a settlement with France, though not necessarily by war. It was impossible to drift any longer on the basis of the truce of 1396, for old disputes descending from King John's ransom after Crécy still clouded the air, and all Aquitaine was in chaos, its factious barons and towns swinging alternately from French to English allegiance. And if to intervene was necessary, the temptation to do so was overwhelming. Henry inherited both a state of war and a good pretext. In 1412 the Armagnacs, in return for assistance taken to them by Clarence, had promised to surrender Aquitaine and Normandy, but retreated from their promise and paid only a fraction of the compensation agreed; even now English troops were pushing up into Périgord and towards La Rochelle, while on rumours of French invasion English sailors raided Dieppe and the Norman coast. Simultaneously hideous massacres in Paris finally divided France, by September 1413 the Duke of Burgundy had fled to his own Low Countries, the Armagnacs had possession of the King, and each side approached the English.

Henry was ready to employ either, and the uncertainty of French politics delayed his decision. He had, moreover, to convert his own people, who were more interested in commerce than in French provinces, and both Council and Parliament urged him not to press his full rights. Again, if he had war in France, he must have peace at sea, and an end of the piracy on which the English seafaring classes existed. He pressed on with his preparations; a severe statute against piracy, truce with Flanders and other maritime States, and incessant armaments. He put an embargo on the export of arms, had guns making at the Tower and at Bristol, and a flagship of 500 tons building at Greenwich. Meantime he tested the diplomatic instruments put into his hands. While he secretly agreed with Burgundy for an offensive alliance, repeated embassies took his terms to the French, and he also sounded the Emperor Sigismund, whose alliance would involve a challenge to Burgundian supremacy in the Netherlands.

This hard bargaining continued through 1414. Henry dropped his first monstrous claim for territories which England had never held, like Provence, or which had been lost two centuries ago, like Brittany, and agreed to accept the hand of Princess Katharine with 850,000 crowns. The French having offered all Aquitaine south of Poitou, in February 1415 he decided on war if they did not offer more; his ultimatum in July was that he must hold all ceded territories in full sovereignty, and when the French refused he harked back to demand the whole empire of the Angevins. So war began; by this time England was convinced that France had derisively refused the King his rights, the military classes were engaged by an advance of pay, merchants and clergy were making loans on the security of taxes or royal plate. In August, passing through the swans on Southampton Water, 1500 ships carrying nearly 10,000 men set out for the Seine.

Henry was now in his own sphere; for he was a master of detail, from army surgeons down to placing sentries, or the prevention of profiteering in the price of armour. Pawning even his own crowns, he scoured Europe for military talent. He had good Welsh archers, and some undisciplined Irish troops; sixpence a day and a chance of ransom money brought him the English yeomen with their horses; he recruited German gunners, miners from Liége, ships from Holland and Portugal.

At first it was a popular war; there was pride, as the ballads showed, in holding Calais and fortresses overseas;

> *God, let them never scattered be,*
> *And save the King and keep the crown.*

Glory and spoil pulled together the political class. The King's cousin York died at Agincourt; two earls of Suffolk, an Arundel, a Warwick, a Somerset, and a Salisbury, died on service before 1430. Yet from the outset the war was fated to fail. English finance could not carry it through; before Henry died every department was in debt, arrears of wages sapped discipline, and as the flush of the first years, when booty was selling all over England, died away, desertion grew and Council reported they could not find reinforcements. One smashing defeat in 1421 showed how far England was still from victory, while a flow of Scottish mercenaries and Spanish ships towards France made a war on several fronts.

It was, then, in a sense a fatal misfortune that the year 1415 deceived the nation into a dream of victory. Within six weeks Henry's guns battered Harfleur into surrender, whither he invited English settlers in the hope of making a new Calais. But what to do next? He could not attack the large French army at Rouen, for dysentery had killed 2000 of his men and invalided more, so that he had only some 6000 fit men left after garrisoning Harfleur. Winter was coming on, and his Council advised him to be content for that year. His political and religious sense decided otherwise; that he would make for Calais. He would not tamely abandon his rights, northern France might rise for him, and he informed the Dauphin that he must at least be admitted as heir to the throne. With food for a week he set out on the 150 miles' march to Calais, found the lower fords of the Somme guarded, and had to make a long loop to cross far above Amiens; supplies ran short and, after marching over a fortnight, on 24th October they found themselves in a woody country fifty miles from Calais, and across their road a French army five times theirs in strength. Exhausted, short even of water, the English lay that rainy night in the fields, and the position was so desperate that Henry parleyed for a free passage. So 25th October, St. Crispin's Day, dawned, with the fate of the war and the dynasty hanging on what would happen at this village of Agincourt.

It was now that the King's person proved worth many battalions and created an immortal tradition, as he swore he would cut through or die, fired his archers with his own religious faith, and at prime, when ' all England prayeth for us ', ordered ' forward banner ' in the name of Mary and St. George. He appealed to memories of Crécy, and happily for him the French acted Crécy over again. Instead of waiting attack, thousands of dismounted heavily-armed knights, packed on a narrow front many rows deep, charged through the mud; their few cavalry squadrons were shot to bits as they came over sodden cornfields, while their despised archers and crossbow-men were kept in the rear, almost unused. Inside two or three hours the English archers surrounded and destroyed the two first divisions of men-at-arms; the rearguard fled, and the last panic at a French rally was stopped by Henry's instant order to kill the prisoners. At the end of this mêlée there were hardly a hundred English dead, but on the French side thousands, including half their greatest nobles in Albret, Alençon, and two brothers of Burgundy, while more were made prisoners, headed by the Dukes of Orleans and Bourbon.

So all the bells of England were set to ringing, and a month later, followed by his prisoners, the King rode to give thanks at St. Paul's, with set and pondering face. For the war had only begun. French nationalism was rising. Only a desperate sea-battle broke their blockade of Harfleur. Only new armaments or aggressive diplomacy would win the fruits of Agincourt.

Diplomacy achieved little, though Henry worked incessantly to encircle France, as both Edward I and Edward III had tried to do, by German and Spanish alliances. While he fought Agincourt, the Council of Constance under the Emperor Sigismund had some triumphs; it deposed one Pope, forced another to resign, and burned the Bohemian heretic, John Huss. But to end the schism there must be peace in Europe, for France and Spain still supported the Avignon anti-Pope, and in 1416 the Emperor came to England. On paper Henry's diplomacy was highly successful. Since the Armagnac government at Paris, far from surrendering, actually sent ships to ravage the Isle of Wight, he persuaded both Sigismund and Burgundy to recognize his rights. But nothing solid came of it. Sigismund was poverty-stricken, shifty, and soon occupied in the troubles of Bohemia, nor did he look with favour on the Burgundian hope of swallowing Imperial territories, so that, although Henry paid subsidies to various princes, he got no real help from Germany. As for Burgundy, in spite of treaties the Duke still held the English at arm's length. His first purpose was to master Paris, and when this, after plot and massacre, was at last achieved, he found even French faction not ready to swallow Henry's huge demands.

It was thus by the sword alone that Henry V won his campaigns. War-fever for the time held England. The Commons, once sitting under a Speaker who had fought at Agincourt, were generous. Rapidly building ships and sweeping together loans from the City, monasteries, and country towns, in 1417 Henry again sailed to the conquest of Normandy. Landing this time south of the Seine, he swiftly captured the central towns, Caen, Bayeux, and Falaise; thence thrust out one wing south towards Maine, and a westward wing which seized the coast from Cherbourg to the Breton border; at mid-summer 1418, having cut its communications with Paris, he laid siege to Rouen. It was in his hands by January 1419, after atrocious suffering; through survivors who had lived on horses' flesh and dogs, and through women holding dead children in their arms, Henry rode in to his usual religious devotions. Within a few months this triumph brought the surrender of many key points, from Dieppe in the north to the neighbourhood of Chartres southwards; Brittany was frightened into neutrality;

Mantes gave him the upper Seine, the storming of Pontoise severed Paris from the north. And this triumph had its echo in Aquitaine, where rival factions surrendered to the English rather than submit to each other.

These two years' achievement afforded impressive testimony of Henry and his war machine. He played with precision on the motives that move men. Though his discipline was iron, his care for the soldiers and their commissariat was boundless. Two-thirds of his force were archers, who fought on foot but were mobile because they had horses, and their adaptability was wonderful, whether in systematic siege operations of entrenchment and mining, winter campaigns in turf-roofed wooden huts, or night marches ending in heroic assault. The eyes of the King and his Council at home looked to every need; to a flow of supply by sea, pontoons for bridging, sharpened stakes with which the archers fended off cavalry, or the faggots on which they crossed a deep moat. Their activity reached to infinite detail, as when it forbade the use of ashwood for making the peasants' wooden clogs, which might check the supply of arrows. On every village green the geese were cackling, for one million arrow feathers were ordered in 1418 alone.

Henry's negotiations showed his confidence that he could force one of the French factions to his terms, and he asked of each the same: Aquitaine as left by the peace of Brétigny, together with his conquest of Normandy. After Rouen even this was not enough, his claim was rising now to Flanders, even to hints of Touraine and Anjou, and his exorbitance drove Burgundians and Armagnacs into unwilling alliance. But a crime rescued him. In September 1419 the Dauphin's followers assassinated John of Burgundy, and the new Duke Philip, with the French Court in his power and Paris starving, flung himself into the conqueror's arms. So came about in 1420 the treaty of Troyes, which provided that Charles VI should keep the Crown for life, but that Henry should marry his daughter Katharine and become heir, and meantime Regent, of France. His task seemed accomplished by the hand of Providence. English garrisons held the Bastille and the Louvre. The captive King of Scots and the imbecile King of France moved about in his train; he presided over a meeting of the Estates-General. His stiff ceremonial, his troops' discipline, and his reputation for justice to the poor, inspired fear, admiration, unwilling respect. In 1421 after three and a half years' absence he brought Katharine to England, where in December his son was born, hailed by English poets as 'blood of St. Edward and St. Louis'.

He at least knew his work was not done, and on progress from one shrine to another collected loans for the next campaign. In March a sharp reminder came that France was much more than a few Armagnac remnants. The defeat at Baugé was in itself an accident, brought about by the folly of his brother Clarence who, finding the French and Scots across his line of retreat from a raid into Anjou, charged them before his archers could come up, and was killed with a thousand more. Yet this chance exposed a permanent weakness, that the English had no southern frontier short of the Loire, while even in the conquered area the conquest was merely superficial. To rule France from England was not possible, nor, indeed, Henry's purpose. True, he induced a few Englishmen to settle at Caen or Cherbourg, his captains held the important garrisons and upper administration of Normandy, but he employed French councillors at Paris and many Normans in the lower ranks at Rouen, summoned the Norman Estates, and restored their property to all who would swear allegiance. Yet even Normandy was unsafe. Few principal landowners submitted, soldiers had to be used to collect rents, brigands abounded, and informers against them were paid so much a head. So England still bore the brunt of defence, having at least four thousand men scattered about in petty garrisons, while the Somme valley and Paris itself held many enemy sympathizers. It was more serious that the Burgundian alliance, which always jarred over military and commercial jealousy, was strained by a new political difference. In 1421 Jacqueline, Countess of Hainault and Holland, fled from the husband to whom she had been married in the interest of Burgundy, and was welcomed in England, where there was soon talk of her re-marriage to Henry's brother Humphrey.

The King's last campaign, though marked by his old skill and resolution, left these difficulties unsolved. Council used great pressure to raise forced loans, and there was considerable desertion. Siege operations in the Marne valley took up seven precious months, while a march southward to the outskirts of Orleans ended in a breakdown of supply and disastrous disease. Everything north of Chartres was tolerably clear, but the French held the Loire line and were raiding Normandy. Foreign alliances had not helped Henry, though his agents were trying to disentangle Sigismund's difficulties in Bohemia, and seeking soldiers in Germany and Portugal.

There are signs that he was facing the possibility he would have to compromise his claim, when death carried him off; he was ailing all through 1422, since the bitter winter siege of Meaux, and died of dysentery in August. His mind was clear as to the future; Bedford must take his place in France, where they must at all costs keep the Burgundian alliance, and never yield Normandy. And his conscience was clear on the past; for the last words which the priests caught were, ' Thou liest, thou liest, my portion is with the Lord Jesus Christ '. Through conquered Rouen, within hail of Crécy and Agincourt, his body made its way with immense pomp, to be buried in the Abbey,

where helmet and saddle still crown his tomb, and Council records and
chroniclers sorrowfully wrote down the end of ' the Christian champion,
invincible King, flower of all chivalry '.

CONTEMPORARY DATES

1414   Sigismund compels John XXIII to summon the Council
       of Constance.
1415   The first Hohenzollern Elector of Brandenburg.
       Huss executed at Constance.
       Thomas à Kempis, *Imitation of Christ*.
1416   Alfonso V reigns in Aragon and Sicily (and from 1435
       in Naples) till 1458.
       Donatello's ' St. George '.
1417   End of the Schism ; the Council elect Pope Martin V.
1419   Murder of John duke of Burgundy.
       Beginning of Hussite wars in Bohemia.
1420, onwards, Brunelleschi working at Florence.
1422–61 Reign of Charles VII of France.
1423   The Wettin line become Electors of Saxony.

CHAPTER VI

NATIONAL COLLAPSE, 1422–1485

THERE was nothing inevitable about the disease which fastened on England for the next sixty years. For governments are made by men, and no wisdom could have foretold the assemblage of impotence and crime in Henry VI and his wife, Humphrey of Gloucester and Richard III, set against the inspiration of Joan of Arc and the patient craft of Louis XI.

The first supreme misfortune was the fifteen years' minority of the King, which allowed the hardening of two factions in government; the second, the absence abroad of Bedford, the one man of prestige and unselfish wisdom. As it was, Humphrey of Gloucester, the next prince of the blood, was formally head of the government, and no one could have been more deadly. This extravagant jealous sensualist, with his *flair* for books, his Italian secretary and doctor, his fluent pen, had none of the decisive gifts which could help the country, but was for ever negative and critical. Neither politicians nor the best soldiers could abide him. Parliament sharply refused his repeated claim that he was regent by Henry V's will and right of birth, while Council claimed all substantial power and only admitted him as their president. The leader of this opposition was his uncle, bishop Henry Beaufort, the best head in the royal family, whose experience made him the natural leader of the officials, and whose wealth was so great that in twenty years he lent the government many million pounds in our present values.

Though the harm Gloucester could do was limited so long as Bedford lived, it was serious enough. Once he tried to get hold of the King and the Tower by force, stirring up against Beaufort every sort of opinion, whether merchants against aliens, or the Inns of Court, or labourers dissatisfied with their wages; a pitched battle was barely avoided on London Bridge between his partisans and the Cheshire soldiers who held Southwark for the bishop. This feud twice recalled Bedford from the front, while Gloucester damaged the war prospects even more by his scandalous marriage with Jacqueline of Hainault; which, in turn, infuriated Burgundy, who was hardly prevented by bribes of territory from joining the French and forcibly resisted Gloucester's expedition to seize his wife's lands. However, Bedford's energy and Parliament's refusal to support this folly stopped it, the unhappy Jacqueline was left a Burgundian prisoner, while Gloucester solaced himself with her lady-in-waiting. Despite this disgrace, he did not lose his evil influence. When Beaufort became a Cardinal, the Duke played on anti-Roman feeling and tried to exclude him from Council; he was able to unseat hard-working ministers and to get large salaries voted to himself, and as the war turned to disaster his criticism touched even Bedford.

War had entered a new stage, for the mad Charles VI died the same year as his son-in-law Henry V. The new French King Charles VII had never accepted the treaty of Troyes; the new King of England was an infant, who for years could not be crowned. Gradually, therefore, what had begun as a contest between French parties changed into one between rival nations. Bedford himself, indeed, was more popular in Paris than Henry had ever been, he ruled through Normans and Burgundians; Frenchmen served in his police to put down brigandage. But Normandy was the only country of real obedience, and the financial strain was too great for it to bear alone. All reasons, therefore, financial and military, advised an advance and, in spite of difficulties at home, for some years the English superiority was proved. Bedford's marriage to the Duke's sister helped to keep Burgundian friendship, while the release of James I from his long imprisonment checked Scottish reinforcements for France. In 1424 Bedford crushed the French and Scots with great slaughter at Verneuil, a battle which saved Normandy for many years. The last Montacute earl of Salisbury proved a considerable soldier; our troops cleared the French garrisons east of Paris, and held Maine. Our outposts reached the Loire at either end, and in 1428 it was decided to flatten out the salient where it curves north to Orleans. The next six years decided the fate of the war.

The siege of Orleans began in October 1428, and though within a few days Salisbury was killed, the garrison seemed abandoned by the French Court. But as the English had not numbers enough for a complete blockade, operations dragged on till April 1429, when a miracle came to save France. Already the English government at Paris had arrested Churchmen who were preaching a moral revival, and inciting patriotism as a crusade. In this growing excitement Joan of Arc appeared, a peasant girl of eighteen from the Lorraine border, who claimed that divine visions bade her assure Charles VII that he was a legitimate King and lead him to be crowned at Rheims. St. Louis and Charlemagne were on their knees for pity of France; an inner commandment rang in her like a clarion, 'daughter of God, on, on'. For English history, it is enough to note Bedford's admission that belief in her supernatural powers demoralized his army; that within three months the French raised the siege of Orleans, captured Rheims where Charles was duly crowned, swept on to Soissons and Laon, thereby threatened Paris on the north, and cut its western communications with Rouen.

From this summer the initiative passed to the French. It made no final difference that Joan failed in an assault on Paris, that in 1430 she was taken prisoner, and that in May 1431 the English government and Norman clergy burnt her at Rouen; or that the boy Henry was hurried over to be crowned at Paris. Not only did the French still hang on to Champagne and recover Chartres, but continual peasant risings in Normandy itself showed the very foundations were sapped. What the course of war began was completed by the death of Bedford's Burgundian wife, and the triumph of a patriotic party at the French Court, which determined Philip of Burgundy, always a grasping ally and now threatened by a hostile Germany, to abandon England. In 1431 Parliament, declaring no more money could be raised, hinted at peace, for which the Papacy also was using its influence. In 1435, at the Congress of Arras, a French ultimatum offered Normandy and all the English held in Gascony, with the hand of a French princess, agreeing that Henry's renunciation of the throne should wait till he came of age. But the least which the English would accept was the *status quo*, which meant they would keep both Paris and Maine; a renunciation of the throne, urged the war veterans, would be to admit that Henry V's rule had been an unrighteous tyranny, and that our best blood had been shed in vain.

It was the end of an epoch. Burgundy rapidly made his peace with France. Bedford died exhausted, before the year ended. In 1436 Paris opened its gates, the people hooting ' au renard ' as they saw the last English troops leaving and the last of Henry V's badge of the fox's brush. English anger demanded war against Burgundy, perjured ally and commercial rival, and there was genuine enthusiasm when a Burgundian army was beaten off from Calais. For another eight years the war surged to and fro, fortresses like Harfleur and Pontoise often changing hands, partly because the French princes' jealousies obstructed the national revival. But the whole Paris region was steadily recaptured, and a slow advance in Gascony detached English reinforcements. All this created a peace party, led by the two cardinals, Beaufort and Kemp archbishop of York, and by the Earl of Suffolk who, in 1439, made a truce with Burgundy. But since Gloucester and his group refused to hear of the French demand that Henry should surrender Maine and do homage for what was left, peace or war was bound up with this faction fight at home.

Local lawlessness, — the disease of mediaeval government, — which had sunk deep into England since Richard's reign, did not cease under Henry V. Anarchy spread backwards from the Marches. There were acts of Parliament against the brigands of Tynedale, private war was constant between Percies and Nevilles. Armed robbery covered the Welsh frontier, and a long blood feud began when the wife of Talbot, the last great hero of the war, seized some of the Berkeleys in their beds, avenged years afterwards when the Berkeleys killed the Talbot heir in pitched battle. And though the Commons ceaselessly complained of the magnates and their liveried followers, the evil touched the whole political class; the Shropshire members, for instance, themselves organizing armed resistance to the collection of a tax they had voted in Parliament. Occasionally older battle-cries were heard; once a Mortimer was executed, and in 1431 a Lollard conspiracy was put down in blood. There were Lollard pacifists who denounced the crusade against the Bohemian Hussites, occasional burnings of priests and laymen, and even worship on Tower Hill of one of the victims as a saint. But the supreme evil was another, much more dangerous. It was the binding together of this local disorder with great factions through the strongest instruments of the new England, the law and moneyed wealth.

This fifteenth-century aristocracy differed much from the mediaeval baronage whose blood, feuds, and fiefs they inherited. Though a Percy could still bring out the north, the power of the average magnate rested rather on the rents derived from scattered estates and administered through an organized council; and on the influence he had at the heart of government, or with the knightly class whose wealth, collectively, was now greater than the peers'. From Cardinal Beaufort downwards the nobles were shipping wool and investing in trade; Duke Humphrey had his great Inn on the Thames called Baynards Castle, humbler lords of the March had theirs in the Holborn suburbs. Here they kept arms, and here also they cemented the connection between local power and parliamentary influence. It was in consequence of violent elections that in 1430 Parliament passed an act restricting the county vote to 40s. freeholders, and it was the nobles' object in all ways, not only by parliamentary seats, to develop their local power. Moneyed wealth had melted down the mediaeval barriers; county families took pains to make themselves all-powerful in their county towns, as the Stanleys were doing at Liverpool; to make their friends sheriffs or customs officers, so that they might adjourn an election, pack a jury, or reward clients with pickings of office; to get royal letters which would put pressure on a judge, and to buy up and press home, either by legal writ or armed force, claims to property which would sustain their faction. This poison was conveyed through the whole legal system, the subtlety and delays of which were used to cripple justice.

There was great abuse of trusts and concealed conveyance of land, abuse of writs, excommunications, or claims that one's rival had villein blood; even royal judges, whose salaries were constantly in arrears, flinched, while the Bar dared not plead against a rich man. 'Get you lordship,' concluded the Pastons' correspondent, 'thereon hangs all the law and the prophets.' Such was the custom, even in peaceful industrial areas, of the Duke of Norfolk, or the Earl of Oxford. It was in full time of peace that Lord Moleyns mustered a thousand men with guns and bows to seize the Pastons' manor of Gresham, or that the very heads of the administration used private armies, as Cardinal Kemp brought down Borderers to protect his Yorkshire property against the foresters of Knaresborough. Upwards and downwards this contagion passed. Since accident and policy had made half a dozen great families the King's near kinsmen, a local Welsh feud ascended into the royal presence; on the other hand, some favour at Court could upset the balance in the Norwich gilds.

At this dangerous hour in our political society Henry VI grew to manhood. He was not yet the royal saint, happy only in his chapel or telling his Eton foundationers to be good boys, but a high-strung boy himself, strained by being brought too early into business, petulant, and lavish in giving. Of political understanding he was devoid; he had not the harsh Lancastrian sense, his own interests looked to the Church, to a healing of the war between Pope and Council or the canonization of King Alfred; his private taste was the reading of chronicles, he thought hunting cruel and had a horror of war. Power would go to those who won his affection and kept his ear, for through his bad health he had to live much out of London, and foreign envoys noted he was 'watched over like a Carthusian'.

Not unnaturally he surrendered himself to the Beauforts; first the old cardinal and then his nephews, John (who died in 1444 leaving an heiress, the Lady Margaret) and Edmund, successively dukes of Somerset. Soon they built round the King a closed circle; their kinsman Suffolk the Lord Steward, bishop Moleyns the royal secretary, and the first Lord Saye and Sele. At first they had with them other councillors, of good character and sense, while their peace policy won some success in a settlement with the Hanse and a truce with Burgundy. But, as years went on, they developed the vices of a faction. The cardinal's money transactions were objectionable. They used their power to squeeze profit from the wool trade, issue privateering licences to their friends, or pack local elections. Suffolk became a duke, Chamberlain, and Captain of Calais, with a mass of other grants and the guardianship of the Lady Margaret. Their monopoly goaded Gloucester to desperation, and drove into his camp the young York, who saw the Beauforts preferred in army commands and, he might well think, threatening his claim as heir to the throne, after Gloucester. It alienated men of moderation like Lord Cromwell, who was for ten years

Treasurer, and made an explosion certain unless they could make a success of their public policies.

Poverty was at the root of all evils. The debt in 1433 stood at £168,000, but at £372,000 by 1449. All revenues were loaded with pensions and annuities, and were dwindling through royal grants. The Household owed large sums, it was driven to use severe purveyance, and Parliament tried to earmark Duchy of Lancaster revenues to maintain it. The King drifted more and more into loans, especially from the unpopular Italians, whom he repaid by assignments on the customs or even a monopoly of trade to the Mediterranean. He was heavily in debt to the Staplers, who were in difficulties themselves, since wool exports had fallen since Henry IV's day by 30 per cent. The Calais garrison was mutinying for lack of pay, a cause which also led to soldiers at home robbing the countryside. Most of Henry V's ships were sold, pirates made the Channel unsafe and seized dwellers on the coast.

The opposition under Gloucester not only repelled any attempt at peace, but favoured a policy which would mean a larger war. For many years now mercantile opinion had tried to force government to drastic treatment of foreign merchants, and to put their transactions under English supervisors. They insisted that the Hanse must be treated as rigorously as it treated Englishmen; that Venetians and Genoese were capturing the Spanish and Breton carrying trade. The Staplers were indignant at infringement of their Calais monopoly and discontented by enforcement of the bullion laws, which crippled their bills of exchange; all the seafaring classes launched a campaign in Parliament, trading towns like Lynn contributing to the costs of this propaganda.

After long resistance the administration gave way. In 1435 Parliament suspended Henry V's statute against piracy, and during 1440–42 the mercantile school won a sweeping victory. When Gloucester issued manifestos against Beaufort and Kemp, accusing them of seeking peace at any price, estranging the King, and corruption, they silenced him by getting his unpopular wife Eleanor Cobham condemned for practising magical arts, but yielded to the business clamour which had given him popularity. Parliament laid a new poll-tax on aliens, repeated the most severe regulations on their trade, and committed the defence of the seas to a body of merchants, to be paid out of prize money.

This veiled war with all other commercial States made it the more urgent to close war with France, for neither York in the north nor Somerset in the south won any solid success, and hopes of help from French rebels faded away. Against Gloucester's protest the Council decided to seek peace, and in 1444 sent off Suffolk and Moleyns to make it; who, finding the French would not surrender Normandy or Maine, accepted a two years' truce, with the hand of Margaret of Anjou for the King.

After Margaret's arrival and under her influence Henry promised the surrender of Maine. But the French were still adamant against a permanent peace without Normandy, and the growls heard in London even before Suffolk's mission echoed over England. Long parliamentary sessions resulted in meagre supplies and angry protest. In 1447 the ministers determined to strike down Gloucester as the only way of carrying their policy, calling a Parliament to impeach him, perhaps on charges connected with his Regency, or even on an accusation that he was plotting for the throne, and summoning it to Bury St. Edmunds, in Suffolk's own country. There, under arrest, Humphrey of Gloucester died of a stroke, brought on with the shock to an enervated constitution; only the Yorkist popular legend of later days was to create the 'murder' of 'good Duke Humphrey'. Since Beaufort died the same year and York was honourably exiled to Ireland as Lord Deputy, the Suffolk circle stood supreme.

Within two years ruin fell on them all, weakness and violence encompassed them. The wild north and west were full of armed disturbance. Scottish bands attacked the Border castles; privateers in touch with members of Council seized the Hanse fleet and distributed the loot, in consequence of which our cloth exports fell to nothing. In Maine the government dared not face the outcry which performance of their promises would mean, and the captains on the spot surrendered the fortresses under protest. Somerset warned Parliament that the Norman cities, even if 'stuffed with men and ordnance', were too ruinous to defend, and the indiscipline of our mercenary leaders gave the French their pretext. In 1449 four French armies pierced Normandy; Rouen with many other towns rose against the English. In April 1450 a last expeditionary army was wiped out at Formigny near Bayeux; in the summer Somerset surrendered Caen and the last seaports fell. The ministry at home broke up in resignations; sailors at Portsmouth murdered Moleyns, Suffolk's nearest ally. Led by a Yorkist Speaker and organized by Lord Cromwell, the Commons fell on Suffolk himself and, breaking down the Lords' resistance, impeached him; bringing not only some false charges of conspiracy with the French or giving away Maine, but better-grounded accusations of rapacity and packing the Council.

The King, with a friendly party in the Lords, intervened and sentenced him to temporary exile. But an intense roar of popular hatred greeted his fall; ballads rejoiced

> *Now is the fox driven to hole,*
> *Ho to him, ho! ho!;*

down with 'Jackanapes', who had lost Maine and Normandy and brought over a penniless Queen to be his paramour, and by whose guilt the hero Talbot was a hostage in French hands. The Londoners tried to lynch him; in May, as he set sail for Calais, he was intercepted by a royal ship, murdered, and his body cast on Dover sands. And within a month, while ministers, from the safe distance of Leicester, redistributed offices among their own circle, news came that an insurgent army led by a man unknown, one Jack Cade, who said he was a Mortimer, had entrenched itself on Blackheath.

THE WARS OF THE ROSES

Placards and songs showed the people's despair, and the justice of their cause. Where, they asked, were the great houses and the war heroes? Good Duke Humphrey, and the Cardinal who 'covered us from many storms', both dead, Talbot a prisoner, and York sent to Ireland, while the King's ear was held by a ring of extortioners.

> *Many knights and little of might;*
> *Many laws and little right;*
> *Many Acts of Parliament,*
> *And few kept with true intent.*

How instinctively loyal the people were, was shown many times in the next twenty years. But Cade's rising revealed in a lightning flash that loyalty would fade if government were not reformed, and that opposition would take a dynastic shape. The King was childless, the Queen hated; failing their issue, Somerset was the male heir of Lancaster, and his niece Margaret the heiress if a woman could inherit. But the only other man of the blood royal was their rival York, whose Mortimer claim, if a woman could transmit it, was better than the Beauforts' and better than the King's; and whose York claim was also better than the Beauforts', if Henry IV's Act barring them from the throne were held valid.

Legally the position was altered in 1453 by the birth of Edward Prince of Wales, but at the same time the King fell into temporary insanity and had another seizure a few years later. Queen Margaret, passionately revengeful and without a spark of English feeling, became leader of her house and with the Beauforts would control a long minority. Their clear intention to crush York drove him first to take up arms, and then to claim the Crown.

Bloodshed, on a scale unknown since Stephen's reign, filled English politics for the next generation. If we take Speakers of the Commons as representative, the Yorkist Tresham was assassinated in his native Northamptonshire, the Lancastrian Thorpe killed by the London mob, a younger Tresham and Wenlock both killed in battle. Three Beaufort dukes of Somerset, two Stafford dukes of Buckingham, three Neville earls, a de Vere earl of Oxford, Owen Tudor, grandfather of Henry VII, the Lancastrian Prince of Wales, Richard of York and his son Clarence, King Edward V and his brother Richard, all these perished by battle, murder, or sudden death, with a mass of barons and knights, before the slaughter ceased. Fear, superstition, and old memories haunted men's minds. Once again Thomas of Lancaster's shrine was sweating blood. The chronicles speak of comets, ' woe-waters ' mysteriously up-springing, and headless figures crying ' bows '. Thames watermen hunted down accused politicians like rats, apprentices battered Flemings and Italians, Norwich mobs roared ' kill them, head them ' at the county officials. Under cover of the public quarrel every ruffian in distant provinces broadcast murder, blackmail, and piracy. Yet the Wars of the Roses were not just futile bloodshed, nor a continuous civil war, serious fighting was limited to two sharp outbursts, 1459–61 and 1470–71. A middle party did their best to avert it ; including, for a time, the Nevilles, and even more the Staffords who, with their half-brothers the Bourchiers (one of whom was archbishop throughout), were related both to Nevilles and Beauforts.

Lines of division were both old and new. The Crown in Lanca-shire, Percy in the north, or the Mortimer house on the Welsh frontier, could raise hereditary armies. Most of the north-country baronage like Cliffords or Dacres followed Lancaster ; the rich south country, on the other hand, had as great a horror of these plundering Borderers, with their ponies and lances, as the German plains had of the Cossacks. The south-west too, its knights and pirates, held many Lancastrian partisans, often because they preferred a weak government to a strong. Yorkist aristocratic power, on the contrary, was concentrated in a few kinsmen ; York's brother-in-law Richard Neville, earl of Salisbury, who had married the Montagu heiress, his son Warwick the King-maker who married the Beauchamps', and his nephew the Mowbray duke of Norfolk. What gave them more lasting strength was the support of London, the Channel ports, and most of East Anglia, where wealth was greatest, where industry had suffered most from government incompetence, and public opinion was most alive. Business England admired Warwick's activity as Captain of Calais against their enemies at sea, and favoured the Yorkist policy of alliance with Burgundy.

Yet it was not a civil war in either the worst or, if that can be said, the best sense. If there was little loyalty to a cause, it was because the cause was dead and, if much materialism, material wealth might at least engender peace. There was little harrying of the countryside, and the armies engaged were very small. Business did not suffer as a whole, and as years went on it revived. The law courts were open and busy.

Most county towns stood aloof, sending soldiers only when they were compelled, to each side in turn; in fact, the people for the most part were waiting in suspense for a decent government.

Thus Cade's rebellion of 1450 was not merely an outburst of anarchy. Kent and Sussex came out under their parish constables, abbots and squires gave their support, so did a party in London, an Essex contingent came to Mile End. Elsewhere there were violent riots, especially against the clergy, the mob in Wiltshire dragging the bishop of Salisbury out of his chapel at Edington and stoning him to death. Cade's manifestos made a fearful case against the government; packed elections, the exclusion of York from Council, ruin of the cloth trade, low wages under the Statute of Labourers. The King's false Council, they said, ' have lost his law, his merchandise is lost, his common people is destroyed, the sea is lost, France is lost ';

> *God send us a fair day,*
> *Away, traitors, away.*

One skirmish near Sevenoaks, where knights of the vanguard were dragged by pitchforks from their saddles and killed, was enough to demoralize the royal army, who themselves began to shout for justice on traitors. The King fled to the Midlands, and Cade, in the armour and gilt spurs of the slaughtered knights, cut the rope of the drawbridge and was admitted into London. The chief victim whom he executed, Saye the Treasurer, was hated for his extortion, and even royal soldiers defaced his tomb. But the discipline which Cade long kept broke down into plunder and ransom; solid citizens rose against him and, after an all-night battle when London Bridge was set on fire, the rebels left the city under promise of pardon. As Cade himself did not lay down his arms, the sheriff of Kent pursued and killed him in the Weald, and the Kent and Sussex rising expired at the new year 1451.

Except in exposing the weakness of government, it had settled nothing. The two rivals, York from Ireland and Somerset from Calais, hastened to the King's presence with armed followers. Each side in turn packed the House of Commons. What exasperated London, however, and most assisted York, was the ruin of trade. Friction with the Hanse over privateering, and with Denmark over Iceland, ended in the closing of the Sound. The Calais garrison seized the Staplers' wool in default of pay. In 1451 Gascony went the way of Normandy, and though old Talbot temporarily recaptured Bordeaux, in July 1453 he fell in the battle of Castillon, his army shattered in a frontal attack on the French artillery. With such a cause York had no scruple in filling London with armed men or issuing circulars to county towns against Somerset, as the man who had lost Rouen and ' the worship, honour, and manhood ' of England. But the Court held firm. The Bristol member Yonge, who proposed that York be declared heir to the throne, was sent to the Tower, nor did the nobility relish the use of York's name in the Cade rising. In 1454, after the Prince's birth, the Lords, though opposing the Queen's claim, would not make York Regent and only conceded limited powers as Protector, as they had to Duke Humphrey thirty years before.

The King's recovery in January 1455 and his restoration of Somerset to favour brought the first bloodshed. In May the Yorkist army, marching on London, in one hour broke the royal forces at St. Albans and killed Somerset, Northumberland, and Clifford. For a second cycle of years the same weary round was repeated; packed Parliaments, a second imbecility of the King and a second recovery, sincere efforts on his part to keep the peace, passionate action by the Queen to raise a royal party and to win a Scottish and French alliance. Parliament in 1455 declared the loyalty of the dead Duke Humphrey; rumour said the young prince was a bastard. But after the King's recovery in 1456 the Queen showed her purpose of revenge. The Bourchiers, representing the middle party, were dismissed; young courtiers tried to murder Warwick and drove him finally over to opposition, while his exploits as Captain of Calais won him golden opinions, in contrast to the King's support of aliens and the plundering of Sandwich and Fowey by the French. London rose in riot against the Italians and the royalist Inns of Court. The streets were chained, the river was full of barges carrying armed men. Warwick brought over his Calais troops in red uniforms with his badge of the ragged bear and staff.

The Queen's armed preparations in the Midlands, a pitched battle between Percies and Nevilles on the Border, and a scheme again to exile York to Ireland, brought the next collision. In September 1459 Salisbury, on his way from the north to join York in Wales, beat off a royal detachment at Blore Heath in Staffordshire; the next month, however, the King defeated the Earl outside Ludlow, Warwick's Calais men deserting to the Crown. York fled to Ireland, his son Edward of March, Salisbury, and Warwick fled to Calais, while a packed Parliament attainted them and their following. Raids from Calais were welcomed in Kent, there were Yorkists plots in London, Yorkists seized Welsh fortresses, and enlisted west-country seamen. In June 1460 the Earls from Calais landed at Sandwich and entered London, setting out thence to bring the Court to terms, either by mediation or force.

Five decisive battles within nine months concentrated the climax of the war. At Northampton (July) Warwick and March captured the King. But Margaret was still at large, raising the north, and most Lancastrian partisans were with her, while Yorkists were divided. For York came over from Ireland, only to find Nevilles and Bourchiers firmly

in power, and the body of the peers opposed to his claim on the throne :
ill-content, he accepted a compromise, whereby Henry kept the throne
and he himself was named heir. That done, he went off to meet his
death, in battle with Margaret's superior forces at Wakefield (December);
his son Rutland was stabbed in cold blood, old Salisbury taken and
beheaded, and their heads set on the gates of York. With Scots troopers
and forces raised, by promise of plunder, from tenants of the northern
baronage, Margaret swept down the great north road; her army sacked
Grantham, Stamford, and Hertfordshire villages, pillaging even the
parish churches; in February 1461, at the second battle of St. Albans,
she surprised Warwick's army and recaptured the King, while the
young Prince of Wales passed sentence of death on the prisoners.
London seemed doomed to fall to the dreaded northerners, but Margaret retreated, whether persuaded by the merciful King or anxious at
another danger. For Edward of March had beaten the Welsh Lancastrian, Owen Tudor, at Mortimer's Cross (February) and joined
hands with Warwick in Oxfordshire. And as they marched on London,
Warwick's hesitations must have vanished; the cruel end of his father,
his own recent defeat, York's death, left him no choice — he must
crown Edward and rule with him.

In the first week of March a small assembly of London citizens and
a few peers crowned Edward IV; within a week his energy reorganized
the southern forces and he began the pursuit. On the 29th he brought
the Lancastrians to battle at Towton, by the river Aire in Yorkshire;
all Palm Sunday they fought hand-to-hand until blood marked the
falling snow, and Norfolk with fresh troops turned the scales. ' Many
a lady ', wrote a London chronicler, ' lost her best beloved in that
battle '; where perished the flower of the Lancastrian nobility. Henry
and Margaret fled to Scotland, while an enormous list of attainders
crushed their friends.

Edward IV claimed the throne as true heir of Edward III, his first
Parliament treating the last sixty years as a usurpation, and even repealing the sentences against Richard II and his favourites. But in truth
he reigned through a national decision, to accept any *de facto* revolution if it provided a government. Margaret's alliances alienated the
English; she admitted the Scots into Berwick, sold the Channel
Islands to the French, was ready to mortgage Calais, and roused the
Celts against the Anglo-Irish of Dublin. After a few years of raids and
treacheries round the Border castles, resistance ended in the skirmishes
of Hedgeley Moor and Hexham (1464), and a new mass of refugees
were dragged out of woods and coal-mines to execution. The Scots
came to terms, Margaret with her son fled to France, while King Henry
wandered in the Lakes and Lancashire hills until in 1466 he was
betrayed, and lodged in the Tower.

Though Yorkist law condemned Lancastrian rule as usurpation, step by step Lancastrian England came to accept Edward IV. Parliament soothed property-owners by confirming the judicial acts of the Lancastrian reigns; many of Henry's officials continued; Lancastrian nobles, even some with bitter wrongs, as Rivers, Saye, or the young Northumberland, served the new King; young de la Pole of Suffolk married his sister. Edward, a boy of nineteen, had much wherewith to win the popular imagination; six-feet-three, the best-looking man of his age, generous in pardon to his enemies, a masterly soldier, genial with the London citizens, and with a magnificent taste in building, clothes, and fine books. The people pinned their hopes on ' the rose of Rouen ', and though he was to disappoint them, it was not all through his own fault. For he inherited three dangerous problems: a ruling class eaten up with lawless pride, a dilemma in foreign affairs, and a ruinous war of trade, which between them brought about another violent burst of civil war in 1469-71. He owed his crown to the Nevilles and lavishly he rewarded them. Warwick had the Marches, the Calais captaincy, and the Cinque Ports; his brother John was given the Percy earldom of Northumberland; his brother George, the archbishopric of York and the Chancellorship. The King-maker was not a fighting baron or a good soldier like the King, but a nervous restless man, ' crafty as Ulysses ' according to an Italian envoy, whose activity had done most to overthrow the Lancastrians, and whose standing with the people rested on more than a princely household or vast estates. Though a ruthless partisan, he had real executive ability and experience of Europe, and considered the best way to solve two questions was to marry the King to a French princess, so closing the war with honour.

Here he clashed with the hereditary policy of the house of York and with national feeling, and in 1461 the question became dangerous, with the accession of a French King who was to prove a statesman of extreme subtlety and cold-blooded craft. What Louis XI had most to fear was a coalition between Yorkist England, the restless French nobility, and Charles the Bold, heir and from 1467 Duke of Burgundy, whose territories suffocated France and reached to within fifty miles of Paris, and were at the same time both the market and the rival of English industry. The failure of Queen Margaret and the Scots in spite of French assistance, Warwick's policy of peace, and revolt in France, decided Louis against any strong action; he even declared himself ready to arbitrate on Gascony, and offered Edward the hand of his sister-in-law in return for neutrality.

But Edward's roving eye was caught by the beauty of an English-woman, Elizabeth Woodville, widow of a Lancastrian killed in battle, and daughter of another, Lord Rivers, and of Jacquetta of Luxemburg, kinswoman of the Burgundian house and widow of the great Bedford.

In 1464 he married her secretly, only announcing it to his Council when Warwick's diplomacy definitely confronted him with the French offer. This marriage was hard for Yorkist feeling to bear, while for the Nevilles it was worse, when the Woodvilles, upstart and incompetent but attractive, mastered the fountain of honour. Rivers became Treasurer, the Queen's brothers and sisters were promised marriages into the great inheritances of Norfolk, Buckingham, Bourchier, and Herbert, and her Grey son by her first marriage was given the heiress of Exeter.

It was not, however, only the beauty of a colourless woman, or her family's greed, which impelled Edward to the Burgundian alliance. For both money and political support he depended on London and south-east England, which was obsessed with hatred of alien merchants and the desire for an active policy; moreover, his loans from the Staple involved the defence of Calais, which would be difficult if Burgundy were hostile, and the cloth trade was deeply depressed. In 1464 statutes forbade export of wool and undressed cloths by aliens, prohibited import of foreign cloth, silks, and French wines, and gave priority to English shipping. Not unnaturally this brought Burgundian retaliation against English cloth, but since a fierce trade war was raging with the Hanse, the Burgundian alliance was almost indispensable commercially and must be won by a political understanding. Moved by this popular feeling, and not uninfluenced by reports that Warwick was too friendly with Louis XI, Edward accepted the flattering request of Charles the Bold for the hand of his sister Margaret, and in 1467–8 a series of connected events accompanied the marriage. The King made an alliance with Brittany, the last powerful feudal menace to French unity, repealed the statutes against Burgundian goods, dismissed George Neville the Chancellor, and appealed to the Commons for help against the ancient enemy.

Whether this decision in foreign affairs was right or wrong, Warwick was too proud to be an ordinary subject, and used his Captaincy of Calais as a power which no subject ought to hold. The least he would accept was the dismissal of the Woodvilles, and he began the dangerous game of influencing Edward's brother Clarence, whom he would marry to his own daughter Isabelle. Discontent against favourites was an invariable mediaeval feeling, and there were riots against the Woodvilles in Kent, where Warwick was a hero. Moreover, there were genuine Lancastrians in Wales and the north; plots even in London, from discontent at heavy loans, executions, and unrest. It was easy for Warwick to encourage this spontaneous feeling, but at midsummer 1469 he came out in the open. After publicly announcing the forthcoming marriage of his daughter with Clarence, he adopted a manifesto issued by rebels in the north under the signature of ' Robin of Redesdale ', which denounced the expulsion of noble blood from the Council by favourites and pointed to the fate of Richard II.

After a rebel victory at Edgecote near Banbury (July), the savage execution of Rivers and the King's nearest friend Herbert earl of Pembroke, and the betrothal of Warwick's nephew to Edward's daughter Elizabeth, showed the Earl's unscrupulous ambition. As yet, his intention was not to dethrone the King, but to master him. But he found himself unable to suppress the Lancastrian north, there were solid Yorkist families like the Stanleys who would stand by the King, and London was mainly loyal also. At the New Year 1470 he, therefore, plunged into a new plot with the apparent object of making Clarence King, a hopeless policy which was scattered by a skirmish at Losecoat Field (March) where Edward struck down the Lincolnshire rebels. Warwick fled with Clarence to France, so entering on a third scheme, the tempting revenge held out by Louis XI of a Lancastrian restoration.

Seven months from his return in September 1470 to his death in April 1471 were enough to end this wild dream. Surprised with the rebels landing in the south while he was far north, Edward IV was forced to flee for his life overseas to Holland, but the marriage of Warwick's second daughter to the young Lancastrian Prince of Wales robbed Clarence of his hope and decided him on a second betrayal, nor did it make for cordial relations between the Yorkists and pure Lancastrians like Oxford, Jasper Tudor, and Somerset. Londoners watched apathetically the huddled figure of Henry VI led forth from the Tower; perhaps the birth at this moment of Edward V in the Westminster sanctuary helped the Yorkist cause. It was impossible to win mercantile England to an anti-Burgundian policy, and when Louis began the war, Charles the Bold helped Edward to restoration: assisted by the Staple merchants, he landed in Yorkshire in March 1471. Purporting to claim only his hereditary lands, and leading cheers for King Henry, he was not at first resisted; the Percy earl of Northumberland, whose title he had restored, kept the north neutral, old Yorkists joined him, so did the perjured Clarence, and London opened its gates. In April, showing all his old military superiority, he defeated and killed Warwick, in a furious rambling battle in the fog, at Barnet.

The day that Warwick fell, Margaret and a Lancastrian detachment landed at Weymouth. Within three weeks Edward penned her between Cotswolds and Severn, and on the 4th May annihilated her army at Tewkesbury. Within, or without, that glorious abbey rest those killed in fair fight, or by summary execution after battle — Edward Prince of Wales, a third Somerset, Courtenay earl of Devon, and many more. A few days later London beat off an attack from the Kentish men. It was the end of the Lancastrians; on the 21st May Edward entered London in triumph, with Margaret of Anjou drawn behind him as a prisoner, and next day the body of Henry VI was exhibited in St. Paul's. How he had died no man can tell, though Edward's youngest brother Richard of Gloucester was supposed to know.

So the new monarchy triumphed, not only against the old, but against its own over-mighty subjects, triumphing both by what was evil and what was good. It was founded in crime, and continued in bloodshed. Nothing more bestial had been seen in England than the impalement of prisoners in 1470 by the Constable Tiptoft, the cultivated patron of Caxton. There was a savage judicial commission in Kent. The country continued so lawless that the King was always on progress, while detachments of Council were set up at Ludlow and York, which later developed into the Councils of Wales and the north. Judges were dismissed for refusing to give unrighteous sentence, Yorkist nobles were every bit as bad as Lancastrian in land-grabbing and intimidation. The King's yeomen of the guard, his new cannon, the use of torture, a curfew in London, and orders against carrying arms, all this pointed to a state of siege. And Lancastrianism, though not the root of disorder, was not all dead; the Earl of Oxford held out in St. Michael's Mount in Cornwall for a hectic six months, while until the end of the reign there were arrests of pilgrims to Henry's tomb at Chertsey.

Yet it would be unjust to deem Edward a systematic tyrant, and wrong to underestimate the degree of acceptance which he won. He conciliated many families by reversing attainders, pleased the parliamentary class by increasing magistrates' powers. Lancastrians of high character, chief Justice Fortescue and the future Cardinal Morton, served him faithfully, and sober London families like the Mores mourned his death. The last thing which mediaeval men wanted was frequent parliaments, yet it is important to be clear that, though the Yorkists evaded Parliament, they never suppressed it. Though he called only two after 1475, they gave him generous grants when he appealed to their patriotism; they would not, however, part with their money till he made war in earnest, and put his Household on a fixed revenue. Confiscations gave him some revenue, French pensions gave him more, and he squeezed his middle-class supporters for loans or the free gifts which were nicknamed ' benevolences ', taking them indiscriminately from monasteries, country towns, foreign importers, or Oxford colleges. He was a private trader also on his own account, as were the magnates Warwick and Howard; exporting cloth and tin, and importing Mediterranean luxury goods, through Florentine agents and in his own ships. He distributed many knighthoods, some to London merchant princes, with whom and with whose wives he never lost his easy popularity. It was indeed a new monarchy, for the force of events was manufacturing all the means of Tudor government. The King would make a pleasant English speech to his Commons, or issue a government statement against Warwick's faction. His Council was small and dependent on salaried officials. His servants patched up the gaps, or cut through the delays, of the common law by more drastic action — by the Council in Star Chamber, the Chancellor's remedies for trusts and contracts, or the summary procedure for poor suitors which made the germ of the Court of Requests. There were signs also of that anti-clerical policy which the sovereign State must involve, partly because the upper clergy and abbots were usually Lancastrian at heart. Though the King was loudly orthodox against the few Lollards who appeared above ground, he taxed his clergy to the hilt, attacking also the privilege of sanctuary and the Church courts.

A lull at the end of the reign was mainly due to some restored prosperity. Merchants, often indistinguishable from pirates, were breaking into larger markets. The Genoese forcibly crushed a Bristol enterprise to get access to Mediterranean wealth ; Portuguese and Spaniards heard with disquiet that English ships were fitting out for Guinea and Brazil. There was always collision in the Iceland fisheries between English and Germans, so that in 1468 the murder of the governor of Iceland by Norfolk seamen ended in a ruinous trade war. But though London supported it and Yorkist nobles hit hard at German shipping, solid business on both sides was pacific, and Hanse money assisted Edward's restoration in 1471. Their reward three years later was the peace of Utrecht, which reinstated them in the London Steelyard and their other factories, and their old immunities from taxation. If this was a setback for our Baltic trade, at least the peace allowed enrichment of our Merchant Adventurers in the Netherlands, and an upward curve in the trade figures. Cloth exports rose to the highest peak of the century, while miscellaneous trade doubled its volume in the fifty years ending with 1483.

Just, then, as Edward kept a hand-to-mouth order in the State without healing its financial weakness or constructing new organs of government, so he maintained a comparative prosperity which postponed decision. Part of this came from peace with France, at which he steadily aimed after one brief effort at a spirited policy. Whether or no his vicious life led to a growing lethargy, he seems to have decided like Charles II that he would not again go on his travels. Pride and the goadings of his Burgundian ally induced him to seek revenge on Louis XI, but he hesitated so long that, by the time he moved, Charles the Bold was fatally entangled in war with Germans and Swiss, and when Edward with a fine army reached Calais in 1475, he showed he was ready to be bought off. After a little skirmishing and a drunken orgy at Amiens, he signed a peace at Picquigny ; Louis promising the Dauphin's hand for the Princess Elizabeth, assistance against rebels, 75,000 crowns down, and 50,000 a year while both Kings lived. Annual donations from France to Hastings and other councillors gilded this peace, against the dishonour of which Richard of Gloucester protested, and, selling even their horses, the English ended their nine weeks' war.

The death in battle of Charles the Bold in 1477, an instant attack by Louis XI on his territories, the marriage of his daughter Mary to the Hapsburg Maximilian, who was also heir to the Empire, opened a new immense epoch in Europe, of the struggle which lasted till 1713 of France against the Hapsburgs. Its early stages did not disturb the inactivity of Edward IV. After hesitating whether it were better to go shares in the Netherlands with France, or to rebuild against France the English-Netherland-Breton alliance, he concluded that French cash was more safe than the promises of Maximilian, who was in difficulties with rebellious and democratic Flanders; rejecting warlike counsels, he merely used the emergency to screw more money out of the French. His decision was assisted by a Scottish war, which Louis partly instigated to keep England quiet; from which came in 1482 the one military achievement of the reign, the recovery of Berwick. But that very year Maximilian and Louis made an agreement over his head in the treaty of Arras, which not only extended French territory northwards but promised to Maximilian's daughter the hand of the Dauphin, who was pledged to marry Edward's. The breach of faith and the insult were glaring, and heavily Edward went to Parliament the month before he died, to get money with which he might stir up Scotland and Brittany against perjured France.

Charles the Bold's death contributed also to a last domestic tragedy, for Clarence, the favourite brother of Charles' widow Margaret and now himself widowed of his Neville wife, aspired to the hand of the young Duchess Mary. For one so suspect, who had once lost Edward his throne, it was a dangerous ambition. He was sulky because Gloucester had married Warwick's younger daughter and claimed half the inheritance; his followers were accused of conspiracy in calling the King a bastard. In 1478 Edward himself accused Clarence to Parliament as ' incorrigible ', and he died, no one knows how, in the Tower. The star of Gloucester rose higher. He took command in the Scottish war, and charge of the whole north; an extraordinary grant made him and his heirs wardens of the West March, with palatine rights over conquests in Scotland; one of his servants was Speaker in Edward's last Parliament. So that the reign of Richard III had in a sense already begun when Edward IV, exhausted at forty, died in April 1483.

Of Richard's short two years neither drama nor research have exhausted the possibilities. That he meant to be King from the first many men always feared, and in any case conflict between him and the Woodvilles was certain over the Protectorship, for Edward V was only a boy of twelve. They were hated in Yorkist circles, had risen on the fortunes of great families and on some of the Clarence forfeitures, while their effort to raise troops and hurry on the coronation gave Richard an opening, in which Hastings and Edward IV's friends were ready to join. The ease of this first victory decided Richard to seize the Crown; there were men ready to support him, his brother-in-law Suffolk, the young Buckingham, and Howard, tempted by a promise of the Norfolk inheritance. He executed not only the Queen's brother Rivers and one of her Grey sons, but Hastings too; appealed to London against Edward's children as illegitimate; sent the two little princes to the Tower, imprisoned Morton, ordered up northern and Welsh troops, and was crowned. Another month passed and he touched the lowest depth: his two nephews were murdered in the Tower.

' From the devil we came ', said Cœur de Lion of his Plantagenet house, and to the devil they returned in Richard III. Henry VI and his son, Clarence, many Lancastrians, and now the Woodvilles — it is not possible to clear Richard of the blood of them all; this businesslike ruler whom Yorkshire and the north followed to the end, who set to work vigorously in conciliating Scotland and the Kildares in Ireland, besides making commercial treaties and a survey of Crown lands. But men turned cold when they saw his nervous ringed hand for ever half-drawing his dagger from its sheath, and the teeth gnawing his lower lip. Like Louis XI he founded Masses and chapels to purge his sins away, and in all sincerity issued proclamations against the licentious life of Edward IV's friends.

It was no Lancastrian reaction that overthrew him. Vengeance began instantly in plots by surviving Woodvilles, former yeomen of Edward's Household, and friends of Clarence, at first to liberate the princes and then to avenge them. It was extended by the ability of the Lady Margaret, in blood half a Beaufort and half a Stafford, whose present, and third, husband was Lord Stanley, head of a house whose self-seeking had protected them through the civil wars, and who could sway the fighting area between Dee and Ribble. From Margaret it spread to the widowed Queen Elizabeth in the Westminster sanctuary, and through the prisoner bishop Morton to the Stafford duke of Buckingham; both sides agreeing on a standard of union in a marriage between the Yorkist princess Elizabeth and Margaret's son Henry of Richmond, who for twelve years had been an exile in Brittany. The rising of 1483, however, was badly timed. Buckingham's Welsh revolt was crushed and his head struck off, before Richmond's ships touched the Devon coast.

But the execution of the King's brother-in-law St. Leger and a long list of attainders in many shires proved Richard's danger, which in 1484 was redoubled by the death of his only son. For the moment he took his nephew John de la Pole as heir, but began to detach the weak and foolish ex-Queen Elizabeth; early in 1485 he had to repudiate rumours he had poisoned his wife Anne Neville, and that he meant to marry his own niece. Decision had passed from the vacillating Woodvilles. There was still a sense of shame in England, and resentment that Richard, like the wild boar on his coat of arms, ruled and dishonoured the realm with his murderous gang, Catesby, Ratcliff, and Lovel. Placards in St. Paul's voiced it:

> the Cat, the Rat, and Lovel our dog
> ruleth all England under a hog.

The Stanleys had now joined the conspiracy. Richmond, after taking oath to marry princess Elizabeth, escaped from Brittany, which was hard pressed by Richard to surrender him, and rode for France. There, after some hesitation, he was made welcome and there gathered round him not only Lancastrian veterans such as Oxford and his own uncle Jasper Tudor, but those who were to be his special councillors in Morton, Foxe, Bray, Poynings, along with several hundred English gentry and yeomen. He had promises of support from Wales, and of men and money from the French.

On 7th August he landed in Milford Haven, hoisting the banners of St. George and Caedwallader against the 'unnatural tyrant'; by the 22nd, when he had made his way by Shrewsbury to Market Bosworth, his 2000 men had risen to 5000, including Welshmen and Lancastrian Talbots, but Yorkist names too like Bourchier and Hungerford. The Stanleys, he knew, would abandon Richard; when the battle was joined they showed their hand, while the Earl of Northumberland's wing of the royal army also made no move. Thus betrayed, Richard fell fighting, and Norfolk with him; his crown, taken from a thorn bush, was set on Henry's head by Lord Stanley, and his naked body, thrown over a horse's back, was sent to Leicester for burial.

CONTEMPORARY DATES

1423	Council of Siena.
	Foscari becomes Doge at Venice.
1424	Death of the Hussite leader Ziska.
1426	Jan van Eyck painting for the Court of Burgundy.
	Foundation of University of Louvain.
1428	Philip the Good of Burgundy acquires Holland and Hainault.
1429	Joan of Arc raises the siege of Orleans.
	Capture of Salonica by the Turks.
c. 1430	Aztec supremacy dominates Mexico.
1431-49	The Council of Basel.
1431	Joan of Arc burned at Rouen.
1433	The Compacta signed at Prague.

1434–64	Cosimo de' Medici rules Florence.
1435	Peace of Arras between France and Burgundy.
1437	Death of Sigismund ; succeeded by Albert II, Hapsburg.
	Foundation of All Souls College, Oxford.
1438	The Council of Ferrara.
	The Pragmatic Sanction of Bourges.
1439	French Estates-General grant the taille to the Crown.
1440–93	Reign of the Emperor Frederick III.
1440	Gutenberg invents printing.
1441	Foundation of King's College, Cambridge.
1442	Foundation of Eton College.
1444	Ladislas of Poland and Hungary killed by the Turks at Varna.
1447	Election of the humanist Pope Nicholas V.
1448	By negotiation of Æneas Sylvius Piccolomini, a concordat signed between the Papacy and Germany.
1449	Alberti working for the Malatesta at Rimini.
1450	Formation of the Vatican library.
	Nicolas of Cues is Papal legate in the Netherlands.
1451	Beginning of the Lodi kings at Delhi.
1451–81	Mohammed II rules Turkey.
	Foundation of University of Glasgow.
1452	George Podiebrad becomes regent of Bohemia.
1453	Fall of Constantinople to the Turks.
1450–66	Francesco Sforza rules Milan.
1458–64	Pope Pius II.
1458–90	Matthias Corvinus rules Hungary.
1458	Foundation of Magdalen College, Oxford.
1459	Turkish conquest of Serbia.
1460	Death of Prince Henry the Navigator.
1461–83	Louis XI rules France.
1462–1505	Ivan III rules at Moscow.
1463	Death of Villon.
1466	The Pitti conspiracy at Florence.
	The Teutonic Knights surrender West Prussia to Poland.
1467–77	Charles the Bold rules Burgundy.
	Birth of Erasmus at Rotterdam.
1469–92	Lorenzo de' Medici rules at Florence.
	Marriage of Isabella of Castile to Ferdinand of Aragon.
1471	Ladislas of Poland rules Bohemia, and from 1490 Hungary, till 1516.
1474	Mantegna working at Mantua.
1476	Caxton's press at Westminster.
1477	Charles the Bold killed at Nancy. His daughter Mary married to the Archduke Maximilian.
1478	The Pazzi conspiracy at Florence.
	Union of Moscow and Novgorod.
1479–1516	Ferdinand I rules Aragon.
1480–99	Lodivico Sforza rules Milan.
1481–3	Botticelli, Ghirlandaio, and Perugino painting in the Sistine Chapel.
1482	Death of Mary of Burgundy ; second peace of Arras.
1483	Organization of the Spanish Inquisition.
	–1498. Charles VIII reigns in France.
1484	Estates-General meet at Tours.
1485	Printing of Malory's *Morte d'Arthur*

CHAPTER VII

HENRY VII: OLD THREADS AND NEW
˙1485–1509

So began the Tudor monarchy, in treason and a lucky skirmish. The King's title, as heir of the half-legitimated Beauforts, was very weak, but after surviving ten years of Yorkist conspiracy he was saved by events in Europe, which brought to England unexpected political and commercial profit. In 1494 Charles VIII of France, forsaking the shrewd tactics of his father, Louis XI, plunged into war to prosecute a claim on Naples, which brought him into collision with a newly-united Spain, armed with prestige by its capture of Moorish Granada, and ready to fight for the old stakes of Aragon in Italy. In 1496 the marriage of the Spanish Infanta Joanna to the Archduke Philip, Maximilian's heir, linked Spain with the Hapsburgs and menaced France with encirclement. Meantime internal convulsions rent the Germanic Empire, while Turkish pressure on the Greek islands and Egypt struck at the life of Venice.

Yet it was Henry's character and ability which turned this good fortune to account, and buried old discontents. His personal loyalties were constant; there are few more touching letters than those of his mother the Lady Margaret, when he had long been King, to ' my own sweet and most dear King, and all my worldly joy '. He kept the advisers of his exile in his service till their death, Morton now Cardinal and Chancellor, Bray, and Poynings, continuing the same unbroken trust to their successors, archbishop Warham and bishop Foxe. Delicate and reserved, he impressed individuals more than his people at large, but natives and foreigners alike came to believe in his wisdom and lucky star, and a blend of kindliness and contempt enabled him to conjure enmities away. A personal interview won over the Irish rebel Kildare, he completely enthralled Spanish ambassadors, and the only nobles to whom he entrusted large powers were both ex-Yorkists, Northumberland and the Howard earl of Surrey. In comparison with his predecessors he was both a civilized person and a man of business; incessantly in Council, smooth and firm in diplomacy, with French and Latin secretaries for foreign affairs, and his own pen ticking off his Chamber accounts. He was fond of hunting, though not less fond of music and card-playing, while his books and the careful education he gave his children showed his mother's son. If avarice grew on him as he got older, when he allowed his servants to find money by straining the law, a stately ceremonial and great buildings, like the Savoy and his gorgeous chapel at Westminster, proved a royal dignity. Careful memoranda reveal his interest in new endeavours, like Cabot's exploring of Newfoundland or the making of gunpowder, in dwarfs and fools and jewels, in the French tongue which he spoke well, and in the songs of the Welsh whose blood he shared, and whose loyalty he carefully nursed. When he died, unbeloved, at fifty-two, directing his burial to be ' without pomp and outrageous superfluities ', he had done more for Britain in his quiet way than any sovereign since the first Edward.

If his reign opened a new age, it was the fruit rather of character and efficiency than of new invention. Those evils which he combated had pressed on the Yorkists before him, and he used the same machinery against them. He, too, ruled through Council and developed further the branch Councils set up at York and Ludlow; his famous act of 1487 (only later called the ' Star Chamber Act '), which systematized the powers long used by Council against riot, maintenance, and corruption of juries, was not so important as the fact that its penalties were actually enforced. His Parliaments were few and far between. Despite Richard III's act against them, he continually used ' benevolences ' to tax the rich, and forced loans, which he repaid. In religious observance he was conservative, devoted to the Franciscans and stern in suppressing Lollards, took Churchmen as his leading advisers, and used Papal bulls to support his title or to punish Irish bishops. His economic legislation was more active, but unchanged in principle. His so-called Navigation Act, ordering that French wines be imported in English ships manned by English crews, looked back to measures of Richard II; laws against usury and export of bullion, or those which fixed maximum wages or forced the unemployed to accept work, carried on common ideas of the mediaeval State; his tariffs in defence of the cloth and silk trades merely extended those of Edward IV. Yet under his eye the State loomed larger, and worked with more intelligence. Various statutes, for instance, relaxing the severity of imprisonment, insisted on the return of the vagrant poor to their own neighbourhood; allowed a freer flow of apprentices into the Norfolk worsted trade; were the first to take action against the increasing abuse of enclosures and gave to the judges supervision of the gilds.

The King and his advisers had that ability to take first things first, without which the most high-minded government must fail. Not only the past but every present year showed that they would perish, if they could not restore internal order, external peace, and prosperity, and that these three were bound together. With the instinct of true statesmen they aimed, even in the first years, at those objectives which they finally secured ; peace with France, a new ally in Spain, settlement with Scotland, damping down the fires in Ireland, expansion of markets, and stern order at home.

Though his first Parliament entreated Henry to fulfil his pledge to marry Edward IV's daughter Elizabeth, the union of the two Roses was strewn with thorns. His marriage was indispensable but he postponed it until it was clear that he was King, not in virtue of it, but by hereditary right, by the judgment of God shown in battle, and (at some distance) by the consent of Parliament. New attainders and reversal of old ones, restoration of property and grants to those who had fought with him all the way from France to Bosworth, discontented the White Rose party. Though Clarence's son Warwick was instantly sent to the Tower, Edward IV had left other daughters than Elizabeth, besides a stepson in the Grey marquis of Dorset, and nephews in the de la Poles ; more than all, he left a sister, Margaret the dowager duchess of Burgundy, who was hatred incarnate. So the world might turn again, and the King's papers are filled with reports of Islington rioters waving ragged-staff banners, conspirators in Exeter churches who took each other by the thumb as a secret sign, white roses being stitched on jerkins in Bedfordshire, seditious speech in the Calais garrison and even in his own Household.

Yet the true danger, masked under Yorkist conspiracy, was that outer fringe of north and western Britain, whence most of the long anarchy had come, where something like feudalism was still part of men's lives, where the central government was distant and law distorted by the strong hand. Since the north knew no King but a Percy, Henry gave its government over to the Earl of Northumberland, who in 1489 was murdered when trying to collect a royal tax in Yorkshire. His successor Surrey had to rule for some years sword in hand, at the head of a Council founded upon Richard III's palatine powers and financed from his old estates. In 1497, rather than pay taxes towards a Scottish war, Cornwall rose in revolt, and under a blacksmith, a local lawyer, and a discontented peer, marched 15,000 strong the whole breadth of England to Blackheath, before they were dispersed by hasty levies of gentry and yeomen ; sending out again, before that year ended, 7000 or 8000 rebels to support the last effort of Perkin Warbeck.

Lambert Simnel's rising of 1487 first showed the wider contacts of this rebel fringe. The impostor, an Oxford boy schooled by the local clergy, was figured as the true Earl of Warwick, sent to Ireland where he was made welcome by Kildare and the Parliament, crowned in Dublin cathedral, and joined by the de la Pole earl of Lincoln, together with German mercenaries sent by Duchess Margaret. Crossing from Ireland to Lancashire, their force made its way as far as Stoke near Newark ; Lincoln and the Germans to meet their death in battle there, while

Simnel received a contemptuous pardon and employment in the royal kitchen.

In the long-drawn episode of Warbeck the threads ranged much further. The conspirators had made sure of sympathy from the young James IV of Scotland, who would use the impostor to recover Berwick, and of Charles VIII of France, with whom Henry was at war. So, coached in deportment by an English Jew, and accompanied by a Devon customs officer and by Henry's French secretary, whom they had bribed, this able and attractive Belgian, posing as ' Richard of York ', who had been murdered in the Tower, appeared at Cork in 1491.

Peace in Europe would remove half this danger; why then had Henry drifted into war with France? For the reason that politics, and especially foreign policy, are a choice of evils, and that Henry had objects worth many risks, if the risks could be limited. The formal cause of war was the Duchy of Brittany, the last fief unsubjected to the French Crown, with great seaports looking out towards England, and where the succession would soon be open, its last Duke having only young daughters. Through this Breton gap the enemies of France could recoup themselves for the provinces taken by Louis XI. The war already revived between Maximilian and France threatened another English interest, when French armies, joining with Flemish rebels, struck out towards Ostend, and might encircle Calais. English feeling being always against ' the French dogs ', even in 1488 volunteers crossed to help the Bretons and to share in their smashing defeat. And another vital reason influenced Henry, for when he proposed to get the hand of the Spanish princess Catherine for his heir Arthur, the Spaniards made alliance against France a condition. With such aims, then, he went to Parliament for large supplies, and shipped small expeditions to Brittany and Flanders during 1489–91. He was soon convinced, however, of Breton disunion, Maximilian's perfidy, and the egoism of the Spaniards, who only wanted England to occupy the French while they recovered their Pyrenean provinces. This sort of alliance could not resist the French artillery, and in December 1491 the marriage of the Duchess Anne of Brittany to Charles VIII took away the pretext of war. While Charles was only eager to buy freedom for his Italian plans by any concession, Henry, on his side, thought he had done enough for prestige and his allies, for his wars (as Bacon says) were always ' iron at the top, and gold and silver at the bottom '. His arrival in France in 1492 with a large army was only meant to clinch the negotiations. Within a month the French signed the peace of Étaples, promising not to support English rebels, and to pay by perpetual annual instalments Henry's expenses and the arrears of Edward's pension.

France was closed as a depot for conspiracy, but now the Spaniards, having got their provinces, were cool about the English marriage, so that the most dangerous years were still to come. The flighty Maximilian, arguing that Henry had abandoned him, welcomed Warbeck, and trade between England and the Netherlands was suspended. By the new year of 1495 the King's spies tracked down a long-simmering plot, which embraced peers and knights and finally Sir William Stanley who had largely won Bosworth, and whose head, with many others, now fell on the block. An attempted landing of Warbeck in Kent was beaten off by the country folk, and when he sailed on to Ireland he was stoutly resisted by the people of Waterford. But the Geraldines and O'Donnells smuggled him safely to Scotland, where in November he received a royal welcome with the hand of Lady Catherine Gordon. The Scots twice raided England in the next year, and in 1497, when the Cornish rising was hardly over, despatched Warbeck to join the rebels with any assistance he could get from Ireland. Hidden in a barrel on a Spanish ship, the Pretender reached Whitsand Bay, vainly attacked Exeter, fled to sanctuary at Beaulieu and was captured. The leniency of his treatment did not content this wandering spirit or the Yorkists who employed him. A second effort to escape in 1499 doomed to execution not himself only, but the innocent Warwick, last direct male stem of the Yorkist house.

Through these years of peril, when every European power was bidding high to get Warbeck into their hands, and English money was bribing Scottish nobles to betray their King, the rivalries of Europe and his own great skill took Henry safely. The League formed to resist and revenge the French invasion of Italy hoped that England would assist by prosecuting her old French claims, though they would be content with English neutrality. In 1496 Maximilian and his son Philip agreed in the *Intercursus Magnus* to reopen the Netherlands to English trade, while Spain, once so insolently cool, was now all complaisance. That year they pressed the marriage treaty for Catherine and Arthur to completion, and in 1497 through their mediation Scotland agreed to peace. It was Spain who insisted that the Hapsburgs must drop Warbeck, or hinted that only Warwick's death would make Catherine's throne secure. In 1499 the seizure of Milan by a new French King, Louis XII, further alarmed Spain and the Hapsburgs. Under such auspices Henry reached the two goals to which he had so cautiously advanced : the marriage of Arthur in November 1501, and in June 1502 that of his daughter Margaret to the Scottish King.

Royal deaths and mighty events in Europe were again to unsettle this edifice, but meantime the King, step by step, dealt with the dangers nearer home. To reduce Yorkist Ireland to better order was a matter of life and death. Ground between English neglect and Celtic revival, the Anglo-Irish governing class had become native princes, ruling through armed Irish clans ; since the warrior Talbot no English Lord Deputy had dared to offend this aristocracy, which had seized the opportunity of the Wars of the Roses to proclaim the independence of their parliament. Ireland was ' Yorkist ' in this sense only, that Richard of York and his sons had accepted this state of things, surrendering the reality of power to the Geraldine earls of Kildare. Against the eighth earl, the supporter of Simnel, and his Desmond kinsfolk, arch-supporters of Warbeck, Henry tried to employ the Lancastrian house of Ormonde and the Irish bishops, but with faint success. The evil lay, not in the holders of government but in its complete collapse outside a few walled towns, and in 1494, determining to try a drastic remedy, he sent a few hundred troops and some artillery under one of his oldest servants, Edward Poynings, with a staff of his ablest administrators.

It would take a generation, a large army, and heavy expense, to carry out the programme he planned ; that is, centralization under the Deputy and a single military command, a resumption of all lands granted since Edward II, and revival of a royal revenue. Without force, it was empty to decree that ' St. George ' or ' King Harry ' should replace the native war-cries of ' Cromabo ' or ' Butler Abu ', and Henry could not face the financial drain which his agent's measures involved. Yet in his one year Poynings achieved some substantial results. He sent Kildare as a prisoner to England ; he beat off Warbeck's attack. Acts of his Parliament declared great offices to be held at the King's pleasure, ordered annual accounts to be laid before the English Exchequer, imposed military service on the landowners, gave royal castles to English governors, and finally, by what is known as Poynings' Act, subjected Irish legislation to the veto of the English Council, and also applied the English judges' ruling that existing English law bound Ireland also. Once again there should be an Anglo-Irish garrison, but this time under a real control. If possible at all, however, it must be done by stages, and Kildare duly returned as Deputy. Yet he came back sworn to Poynings' laws, and if Henry did not make Ireland more Anglicized, at least he forced it to better outward obedience.

Poverty, the obstacle in Ireland, was also the grand weakness in England, which Henry set himself to overcome. That he was much the greatest surviving landowner took him a long way in overcoming the new feudalism ; for he inherited estates of Lancaster, York, Beaufort, and Mortimer, and increased this mass by the resumption of royal grants since 1455 and by attainders like that of the wealthy Stanley. These great lands he administered himself with the sharp eye of a bailiff. His agents drove hard all feudal dues and wardships, exploring every nook and cranny for arrears of taxes or exploitation of Crown estates. The west country alone paid £10,000 in fines for its share in the rising of 1497. He had the ancient customs, and tonnage and poundage, for life, besides benevolences and forced loans — taking, for example, £58,000 for one Scottish campaign. His credit was good, for he repaid his borrowings, and by the end of the reign his permanent income had increased threefold, to about £142,000. So he was able to heap up a great hoard of jewels, money, and bonds, to make loans to other Kings, and to avoid, as all the Tudors tried to avoid, frequent taxation, only calling on Parliament for assistance twice in his last seventeen years. To receive all these revenues he followed the Yorkists in reviving the power of the Chamber, which he reinforced with a Court of Surveyors, and by such means almost supplanted the Exchequer.

Peace abroad being the key alike to the defeat of pretenders and to trade and contentment, he manipulated foreign relations as an economic weapon. Their aim was to satisfy those desires, disappointment of which in the last century had antagonized the trading class; to win independence of foreign capitalists, to carry imports in our own ships, and secure more markets for our cloth. His success, however, was only partial. Antwerp was almost at the peak of its greatness as the financial capital of Europe; a temporary English triumph in 1506, which the Flemings called the *Intercursus Malus*, allowing for the retail sale of our cloth, was soon lost in political bargains. The Hanse was, indeed, suffering from the growing strength of Russia and Poland, and a cleavage between its Netherlands and its German branches, but Henry's treaties with Denmark and Riga to capture their outlying markets ultimately failed. He had to withdraw his contention that Hanse privileges in England did not cover the goods they carried from other countries, and English shipping made no recovery in the Baltic. In the Mediterranean he had more success. He appointed consuls to look after our interests, and when the Venetians retaliated against the monopoly he gave to English ships in the wine trade, he brought them to heel by heavy tariffs, or by stopping their supply of English wool.

While he thus sturdily protected commerce, using every negotiation to ask for better treatment, he encouraged the efforts of English trade to break out of the mediaeval routes, now fast being narrowed by Turkish aggression, into the outer Atlantic. In Edward IV's time Bristol ships had explored for Brazil; Columbus, who knew Bristol, asked Henry for assistance before he accepted it from Spain. And it was with the help of Bristol money that another Genoese, John Cabot, received letters patent in 1496, authorizing him to plant the English flag in new-discovered lands. He brought back from his voyages to Labrador and Newfoundland an assurance of magnificent fisheries, and the hope of a quick route to Asia. In spite of Spanish protests that these voyages encroached on the hemisphere assigned to them by the Pope, Henry continued to reward English sailors who struggled on to find a north-west passage to the East; Eskimos were exhibited at the Court where More and Erasmus were discussing Italian learning.

Whatever came, in the future, of the King's interest in these voyages, immediately his throne depended on the order he could keep at home. His very title lay in the fact that he represented a reconciliation of the two Roses. Whatever legal theory said, he fully accepted the legality of Edward IV's measures, and emphasized by his own laws that revolution was over. His statute of Fines, for example, forbade any questioning of title to landed property after a five years' tenure; his carefully guarded *De facto* Act of 1495 relieved from any charge of treason those who faithfully served the King for the time being. Yorkist sentiment, however, was not nearly so dangerous as the lawlessness revealed in his Star Chamber, the knives, bows, and bills brought out in scores of market towns over the election of a council or the fees at a fair, or brandished by many a landowner to terrify his rival's tenants; nor was the remedy to be found in new law so much as in Henry's determination to enforce the old. His major legislation carried three decisive marks. Law was to be open to all; private persons might accuse justices of the peace before the assize judges, the poor could get writs without payment, and special commissioners looked after their interests in the court held in the White Hall, which became the Court of Requests. Law, again, was to be uniform; Henry regulated town government by statute, cautiously extended the common law in Wales, co-operated with the Pope to close sanctuaries to fraudulent debtors, and deprived of their monstrous privileges those laymen who claimed benefit of clergy on the ground that they could read. Law, finally, was to be armed, and its execution committed more immediately to the central government. Several measures implied that corrupt juries were the root of the evil and in some cases, notably maintenance and livery, dispensed with them. A single justice was given powers of arrest; they could revise jury panels and fine them for false verdicts; appeals against perjury lay to judges of the High Court, who also controlled the magistrates by their writs; both giving and taking of liveries were made liable to crushing fines. In this developing detail, still more in its regular enforcement, consisted the growing peace of the country.

' Young for his years but old for the sorrowful life he has led ', so an ambassador described the King, for though Henry was still in the forties in 1500, the strain of conspiracy had aged him and his sorrows increased. Many nearest to his throne, if not to his heart, died between 1500 and 1503, the Queen, Prince Arthur the heir, the shrewd, humorous Morton, and his business adviser Bray, and no one replaced them. Henceforward the odium for harsh assessment and avaricious government fell on the King, and though his most hated agents, Empson and Dudley, had long been employed, now they had a freer hand; Empson, in particular, scandalously abusing power to feather his own nest and to intimidate juries. London suffered considerably, some of its leading aldermen being sent to the Tower, so that young men like Thomas More waited impatiently for a more liberal reign.

Two considerations mitigate any condemnation of the money-making tone in the last stage of his foreign policy. He kept the peace, obstinately resisting the pressure put on him by Spain and the Hapsburgs to make war against France, while the international revolutions of those years were enough to explain a good deal of his shiftiness. The unsettlement of Europe by Louis XI's ambition was deepened tenfold by the Italian wars, the fantastic falsehood of the Emperor Maximilian, and the cold perjury of Ferdinand of Spain. The marriage of Maximilian's son Philip to Ferdinand's daughter Joanna had brought an heir, now growing up to manhood, the later Emperor Charles V, who would inherit all the Hapsburg lands, the inheritance of Burgundy, and the Empire of Spain. On which pivot of that huge mass the policy of his parents turned must decide the peace of Europe. In 1504 Isabella of Castile died, her widower Ferdinand and her son-in-law Philip disputed Castile and the future of the young Charles, France and England would turn the balance of power. Amid these uncertainties Henry's policy was cautious, discreditable, but determined. Though Spain procured a Papal dispensation so that the young Henry could marry his widowed sister-in-law Catherine of Aragon, the King delayed the marriage on the ground that her dowry had never been paid, keeping the unhappy Catherine on such short-commons that she had to sell her jewels. Though he dallied with ideas of an alternative French marriage for his son, more and more a Netherlands alliance became the heart of his scheme, for the cloth trade was worth many marriages and much prestige. In 1506 a great storm, which blew down the weathercock on St. Paul's, threw on the English coast the Archduke Philip; the opportunity was taken to get out of him not only the *Intercursus Malus*, but a promise to hand over the Yorkist earl of Suffolk, on Henry guaranteeing his life, and a pledge of the hand of Philip's sister Margaret, regent of the Netherlands, for Henry himself.

Before the year ended Philip died; his widow Joanna was mad, and Henry considered the advantage of marrying her, again with an ample money equipment. But his essential scheme did not change. In 1507–8 he achieved the marriage by proxy of his daughter Mary with the Archduke Charles, ordering bonfires in London, for now he would have sons-in-law throned in the Netherlands, Scotland, and Castile, with a safe cloth trade. As to his own marriage, somehow he hoped to have the guiding hand, whether as stepfather or uncle by marriage, over the Archduke's wide and wealthy territories. Secure in such achievement or such dreams, his dying injunction was that young Henry should complete the Spanish match.

At the end of 1508, temporarily united by the masterful Pope Julius II, Maximilian and Ferdinand and France joined in the League of Cambrai, to bury their differences in a partition of the territory of Venice. Henry VII alone stood out, true to his policy of a waiting and gainful neutrality. In April 1509 he died, having restored order and prosperity to England, before she entered the storms blown up by the failures in mediaeval civilization and the raging ambition of modern States.

CONTEMPORARY DATES

1486	Breton resistance to the French Crown.
	–1525. Frederick the Wise, Elector of Saxony.
1488	Murder of James III of Scotland.
1489	Philippe de Commines begins his memoirs.
1491	Savonarola becomes prior of St. Marco, Florence.
1492	Death of Lorenzo de' Medici.
	Columbus lands in the Bahamas.
	The Spaniards capture Granada.
	–1503. Pope Alexander VI (Borgia).
1493–1519	Reign of the Emperor Maximilian I.
1494	Charles VIII of France invades Italy.
	Beginning of the Aldine press at Venice.
1495	The French, on retreat from Naples, win the battle of Fornovo.
	The Imperial Chamber founded in the Empire.
	Ximenes becomes primate of Spain.
1496	Marriage of the Archduke Philip to Joanna of Castile.
1497	Vasco da Gama passes the Cape.
1498	Savonarola burned.
	Erasmus at Oxford.
	–1515. Reign of Louis XII of France.
1499	The French and Venetians expel Lodovico Sforza.
	Amerigo Vespucci discovers South America.
1500	Portuguese settlement begins in Brazil.
1502	Foundation of Wittenberg University.
1503	Collapse of Borgia power; accession of Pope Julius II (–1513).
	Leonardo paints ' Mona Lisa '.
1504	Death of Isabella of Castile.
	Raphael painting at Florence.
1505	Portuguese settlement at Mozambique.
1506	Death of the Archduke Philip.
	Bramante rebuilding St. Peter's, Rome.
1507	Titian and Giorgione painting at Venice.
1508	Michelangelo begins work at the Sistine Chapel.
1509	Birth of Calvin.
	The League of Cambrai attack Venice.
	The Hindu kingdom of Vijananagar opens its great age.
1511	Foundation of St. John's College, Cambridge.

CHAPTER VIII

THE CONSTITUTION, 1400–1529

THE outstanding merit of the fifteenth-century Constitution was that it did not die. Good fortune and good rulers had already so far modified the weaknesses of all mediaeval government — a Church independent of the State, a loose society of franchises, boroughs, and Marches, a personal kingship without whose initiative not a wheel could turn, and fixed notions of custom — that it made a long stride towards the modern State without passing through the despotism which captured Burgundy, France, and Spain. These modifications, though often called ' Tudor ', originated in pre-Tudor days, so that the Tudor change was one not of principle but of efficiency and degree.

It would, then, be false to picture a constitutional Lancastrian rule degenerating into despotism. Ebbings and flowings there were, of course, for war exalted a warrior King, civil disturbance strained the law and Parliament, but the real process was continuous and less simple — the conversion of a loose bundle of rights and powers nearer to the modern shape of sovereignty and definition.

The English Middle Ages had established one great doctrine: that government was a rule of law. Common law, the rules of the Angevins' court, had become a law which bound even the King, at least in fundamentals like inheritance and capital punishment. And the King's highest court, it was now admitted, was Parliament; ' so high and mighty in its nature ', said the judges of 1453, ' that it may make law, and that that is law it may make no law '. This universal feeling, which was seen in the charges against Richard II and every utterance of Lancastrian ministers, received testimony even in the worst time of Yorkist England, whose special character was not the absence of law but its abuse. The Pastons and their rivals sometimes used guns and bows, but much more often a bribe, or the endless possibilities of the law's delay; even the Crown did its most lawless deeds through the law, as Henry VII's agent Empson took royal yeomen to overawe the Yorkshire county court: the very Henry VII who declared ' nothing more joyous than to know his subjects to live peaceably under his laws ', made ' by the authority of many and divers Parliaments ', one law for rich and poor, ' which be to him all one in due ministration of justice '.

Two things, however, stood in the way of an easy passage to the supremacy of the King in Parliament: the nature of mediaeval government, and the moral ideas amid which it had been formed. Mediaeval government was one, making no clear distinction between executive, legislature, and judicature. Law was there to do justice, but that could be done in many courts, which had come to the King at different times and from different sorts of rights — his Council and its provincial branches, judges on assize and magistrates holding his commission, his courts in Westminster Hall, but also his Duchy court of Lancaster or his jurisdiction of Admiralty. There were many rooms in or round the royal palace, besides the ' starred ' chamber for Council looking on the river and the Commons' room in the chapter-house, and government passed easily from one to another.

And since they all had sprung out of the Crown, the lines between them were blurred. ' Great Councils ' of peers often met to discuss matters in advance of Parliament, and raised money both for Yorkists and Tudors. Henry VII's judges drafted in Council the statutes which they afterwards construed freely in the courts, besides acting as ' auditors ' of petitions for the Commons or assisting the Lords in committee. The instructions they received in Star Chamber before going on assize covered matters of policy, like wage-rates, as well as justice. So long as right was done, the precise channel seemed to be indifferent, Henry VII telling those injured by livery and maintenance to complain either to Council, Star Chamber, or King's Bench. Proclamations in Council changed the law as well as applied it, as by altering the coinage or raising customs duties. Despite the conflicts between King and nation since Edward II, law had never attained a distinct frontier between the King's public and private capacities; rents from his manors were pooled with benevolences or customs, his chamberlain and secretary were part-public, but even more private, servants. The Crown itself was an office, but the succession to it was argued as if it were a private fief.

All this went back to the ideas of the Middle Ages, which made moral and not legal distinctions. Though they reckoned the difference between a King and a despot as profound, for the King's office was to do right and take counsel, such moral checks would only very slowly take outward shape. Henry IV's ' regality ' was not, in the eyes of Parliament, opposed to the good customs; the law, said his grandson's judges, was ' his highest inheritance '; his known prerogatives formed as much a part of the law as the right of the humblest copyholder. Law being thus seen as a fundamental and inherited thing, men still looked on Parliament as reasserting or amending rather than as making law, and had no notion of a sovereign legislator. Parliament was, in fact, much more than a legislature, while in ordinary men's view there were fields, above all the Church, outside its authority. If it were, then, the supreme court, it was not the only one; if common law was the highest, it was not the sole law.

A whole literature testified to this universal, tough sense of law. The four great Inns of Court made a legal university, where the best counsel of the day, like Thomas More, expounded the practice of the courts. The Year-books, which in manuscript had circulated since Edward I's time, had fifty printed editions before Wolsey died; Littleton's book on tenures, the first great law-book in English, was printed in 1482; soon there followed printed treatises on the justice of the peace or manorial stewards, and editions of the statutes. A fair sample of such constitutional teaching may be found in the work of John Fortescue, chief justice to Henry VI and councillor to Edward IV. Aristotle and the schoolmen were still the root of his thought, a scheme of natural law to which national law should bow, statute being simply a selection of good custom. The King had his rights, the people were bound to give him revenue, but this was precisely because he, every bit as much as the Pope, was 'servus servorum Dei', — a public servant set up for the good of his people. It was not, therefore, any limitation on his office that he could not change the law, or impose taxes, without Parliament; for this distinguished the 'rex politicus' of England from the despotism of France, whose wretchedness impressed Fortescue during a long exile. He gloried in a system which rested on trial by jury, which forbade torture and standing armies, and instead of the French peasantry, — ground down by taxation, living on rye bread, — whose wives and children ran barefoot, gave us a stout middle class, archers ready to defend their country.

Yet even Fortescue admitted there were cases where the King must have a discretionary power, and as the century went on we see signs of the new State, with more authority and continuous life. A Yorkist parliament declared valid all judicial acts done under the 'usurper' Henry VI; the *De facto* act of Henry VII put obedience to the existing State above the claim of a legitimist pretender. His Parliament fixed penalties on soldiers who deserted, and forced a uniform law on old 'liberties', as when, for instance, they brought wild Tynedale into the county of Northumberland. Lawyers were turning boroughs, churches, even the King himself, into legal corporations, and discussing their relation to the State. They were speaking of 'prerogative' in a new and more vague sense, as of a superiority to reinforce the law; Parliament might protest it only wished to uphold old custom, but its deeds and its prestige meant that its supremacy was getting near to a new sovereignty. Yet neither the full idea, nor the conflict it would mean between King and King in Parliament, had reached fifteenth-century England; a period of contradiction but of vital importance, for in it what was old was blended with what was new, in indestructible strength.

In spite of civil war and change of dynasty, the position of Parliament was without doubt higher in 1529 than in 1399. No King allowed that he had only a parliamentary title, but Henry IV, Richard III, and Henry VII all used Parliament to affirm it. Many times under the Lancastrians they named the Council or appointed a Regent. Though there were incessant forced loans, benevolences, and extortion by privy seal, no general tax was laid on the subject without their assent. They continued to earmark taxes, especially appropriating tonnage and poundage to defend the seas. They audited the royal accounts. It was through Parliament that Henry IV entailed the succession; it was to acts of Parliament that the Lords appealed in 1460 to refute York's claim. They limited the power of Council in raising loans, repeatedly warned it off encroachment on the common law, and tried to regulate the martial law of the Constable's court. Even the Yorkists evaded Parliament rather than defied it: Richard III thus making his sinister agent Catesby the Commons' Speaker, just as Henry VII made both Empson and Dudley, and all three dynasties took pains to bring their Household servants into the House.

The Commons' prestige and *esprit de corps* had risen correspondingly. They had recommended their procedure to the Parliament of Ireland. Twelve new boroughs were created in this century, and it was important now to define the rights of electors. Many Acts aimed at independent elections; to check the sheriffs varying the towns to which they sent writs; to insist that members must be resident and men of substance, and, by the Act of 1430, to clear elections of pressure by restricting the county vote to solid freeholders with property worth not less than 40s. a year. Even the effort of county families to pack elections was some tribute to parliamentary power.

'It is necessary', wrote the Duchess of Norfolk in 1455, ' that my lord have in the Parliament his menial servants ', but great though the power of such magnates was, it was now more indirect, being either filtered through the Commons or coming from their connection with the Crown as hereditary advisers. And though the number of lay peers quickly rose again from the handful of twenty-nine who first met Henry VII, the Wars of the Roses were a landmark in their decline, for they left the greater fiefs in the hands of the Crown. They continued, however, to amend the Commons' bills freely, to reduce (though not to increase) taxes the Commons had proposed, and to tax themselves at a different rate.

The Commons advanced more steadily, though not so clearly as they wished. Henry IV refused to admit that redress of grievance must always precede supply, and, though agreeing that grants must finally be presented by the Speaker, still left the Lords a right of initiating taxes. Henry V did not accept their claim that any legislation needed their assent. They got their way, up to a point, not so much by frontal attack as by ways round or accumulation of precedent. So they would postpone their supply till the end of a session, asked repeatedly for a conference with the Lords, and drafted their petitions in the form of a bill providing a specific remedy. Their 'privileges', which may always be taken as an index to their power, showed them in course of transition. Being by origin a part of the royal court, their Speaker and clerk were paid royal officials, their contested elections were settled in the royal Chancery, their freedom from disturbance was that claimed of old for any court of the King. Defence of such privileges as against the King was therefore not easy. The Lancastrians allowed freedom of debate in general terms, and they usually succeeded in getting members, or their servants, released from arrest during a session; the judges declared privilege too high a matter for them to decide. But when privilege touched high politics, as when Yonge, member for Bristol in 1451, asked that York be declared heir and was sent to the Tower, or when York in his turn had the Lancastrian Speaker Thorpe arrested, the Commons remained without a remedy.

They were, therefore, subject to power, yet it cannot be said that they were wholly subservient, either to the magnates in Lancastrian times, or the Crown later. Before 1450 the Commons always championed the common law, pressed for an increase of the powers of justices of the peace, and clamoured for free elections. Their House was used as a channel to push borough charters and trade laws, and to transmit a mass of miscellaneous requests, which were endorsed as 'Commons' petitions. If, with the Yorkist and Tudor Kings, government itself began to initiate most important public bills, it was because government had in a real sense become more parliamentary, with its confidential servants in the Commons. By 1500 they shared equally with the Lords the control of private bills; their procedure of three readings was nearly settled.

Though there were fewer Parliaments after 1450, only six short sessions under Edward IV, one only between 1497 and 1509, and none between 1515 and 1523, this was not entirely a bad sign, for it meant that the administration of King and Council was succeeding. It meant also that some of the work hitherto done in the mixed court of Parliament was being transferred, in the interest of efficiency, to other organs.

Government, then, at the end of the Middle Ages, though not in our sense constitutional, was severely limited by law. Though Parliament had devised means, by impeachment or attainder, to check ministers, it could not in ordinary times appoint them, and while there were ample powers in the law to curb the King, he kept the initiative. If Parliament and the old departments which it had mastered or protected, — common-law courts and Exchequer and Privy Seal, — held firmly the ground which they had won, what made this century a turning-point was that the State now had to break new ground. How this new business was distributed would be vital ; in England alone it was adjusted, inch by inch, to mediaeval liberties.

The Council, still the reservoir of all authority, was increasingly called upon to deal with matters for which Parliament and common law had neither capacity nor time. Some things demanded special training, like commercial or Admiralty business, Church questions in-volving Civil or Canon law, or intricacies of trusts and contracts. Common law and the jury proved incapable of stopping the worst evil of the day, livery and riot, and the Lords (the Council in Parliament) were too busy or self-occupied to be a good court. Lancastrian Parlia-ments, therefore, asked Council to take over the individual petitions not disposed of at the end of a session, recognizing also that there were cases in which there was ' too much might on one side and too much unmight on the other '. By an Act of 1453 it legalized for seven years the Council's writs *Sub poena*, through which rioters were summoned on unspecified charges and interrogated without a jury.

Yorkists and Tudors thus built upon tendencies already existing. Henry VII's ' Star-Chamber ' Act created no new court ; like the Act of 1453, it regularized Council's severe process, specified the offences (livery, corruption of juries, and riot) which the jury had failed to crush, and named a quorum of Council ; for Star Chamber was only the Council acting in a special capacity. And though from 1526 Henry VIII made a further distinction by assigning councillors who must be in attendance on himself, whence came ' the Privy Council ' later, Star Chamber continued to be Council till it was destroyed in 1641 ; a chair was set for the King, it heard cases far beyond those named in 1487, and other councillors attended than those named in the quorum by that Act.

Here then was the working heart of government, Council sitting day by day, whether in the King's presence or in Star Chamber ; putting every other court to work, speeding up or transferring cases, taking charge of anything which might endanger the State, — violence or libel, enclosure or printing, or the food supply. The great men who decided the government of Ireland, or munitions for Calais, would equally take steps to prevent the Harcourts breaking into their neighbour, Eynsham Abbey, or to reconcile some Cornish family feud.

In the late fifteenth century Council changed, not so much in legal power as in composition and strength. Political reasons had made it possible for Lancastrian Parliaments to name the Council and assign its functions, but political causes broke that sort of control down. Yorkists and Tudors composed it as they pleased, Henry VII hardly allowed any nobles on it, and its usual attendance was a small circle of about ten officials and lawyers, with an outer ring of ' ordinary Councillors ', whose work lay in the Star Chamber or on special commissions. Yet we have seen that the contact of Tudor councillors with Parliament was at least as close as that of the Lancastrian magnates.

Efficiency at the centre was the greatest need, and the greatest success, of this growing State. Richard II had appointed a clerk of Council; Henry VIII revived the keeping of its records. The speed and control required was found in the King's Secretary, an office developed from the secret seal or signet, which earlier Kings had employed to escape from control. Freed from the routine of Chancery or Privy Seal, and in direct relation with the King, the Secretary naturally became the mainspring of prerogative in dealing with new business.

From the Middle Ages, and from the civil wars of this age, the monarchy had acquired or built up many other jurisdictions. One branch of petitions, of old referred to Council, touching matters of equity or conscience, from Edward IV's reign went to the Chancellor, acting alone. An Admiralty court was emerging out of the tangle of the law merchant and the Cinque Ports' jurisdiction, to control piracy, wreck, or prize law. A committee under the Privy Seal, accustomed to take poor litigants' cases, developed by Wolsey's time into the Court of Requests. Special councils were framed for the wild frontiers. The Prince's Council for Wales was one nucleus, enormously increased by the fiefs which fell to the Crown by confiscation of Marcher lordships, and was commissioned by Edward IV as the Council of the Marches, which was continued for Henry VII's son Arthur. In the Lancastrian north Richard III set up a council to overrule the authority of the Wardens of the Marches, which was reorganized in 1525 under Henry VIII's natural son Richmond. And there were older courts of which the new State made use: the Constable's, the Chester palatinate court, or the Stannaries' court over the Cornish tin-miners.

Strains there would be, and collision, between such jurisdictions and the mediaeval frame, but in some vital respects the mediaeval frame already controlled them. Old statutes had forbidden Council to touch freehold, treason, or felony, and a convention grew up that, while it could torture, fine, or imprison, it could not take life. Moreover, Council's action was usually indirect, applied through the older machinery which was entirely controlled by the common law.

While dynasties rose and fell, the justices of the peace grew in strength. Edward III's statute created quarter-sessions, empowering them to determine felonies short of treason, and to arrest. They had to apply the Statute of Winchester for police and defence, and the Statute of Labourers for industry. The Lancastrians gave them control over gilds, Lollards, and livery, the Yorkists transferred to them all the sheriffs' powers. Parliament armed even a single justice with authority to arrest, or allow bail. Since Richard II's time they had a paid clerk of the peace ; as judge of a royal court, one of them, the *custos rotulorum*, was responsible for keeping the rolls. While ' stacks of statutes ' ordered them to look after everything in life, from vagabondage to roads and bridges, Henry VII used them to assess taxes, to revise jury lists, to certify maintenance to Council even if the jury failed to convict, and in one drastic Act, which his son repealed, to try felonies without a jury's indictment. Their numbers increased in proportion to their business, an average shire having now perhaps thirty, who had to possess land within it of substantial value, and members of the King's Council sat commonly on the local bench.

But these administrators, far from being bureaucrats or royal tools, were embedded in an old legal system. Their main powers were given by act of Parliament, they could be curbed by writs from the common-law courts, while for their chief functions they used the method of the old communal courts, of presentment and verdict by a jury. And the whole of local government showed the same mixture of royal super-vision with ancient liberty. The State had not extinguished the immemorial petty communities, but harnessed them to its service. Though common law had planed down mediaeval ' liberties ', from the great Durham palatinate to petty townships, and though the Crown remodelled boroughs by charter, local government was still self-government. Large boroughs had a commission of the peace of their own, almost indistinguishable from their old moot. Statute had given duties to the constables, who had originally been the servants of hundreds or feudal courts, but who were now really responsible to the justice of the peace. In countless manor-courts, in sworn bodies for the coroners' ' views ', or watch and ward, and in the ecclesiastical parish, communities of the Middle Ages still did their work of petty police, owned corporate property, farmed land and admitted tenants, ' presented ' to magistrates or judges of assize their crimes, poverty, or grievances — all buckled to every ascending tier of government by their rights and duties, ascertained and protected by custom and stated law. From the county juror had evolved the county voter, and the parish Dogberry, sworn with his community to keep the King's peace, set in action through magistrates and assizes the King's rule of law.

All these tiers led up to the King, from whom all courts had come, whose prerogatives were so large and becoming, through new needs of State, so undefined, and whose public and private rights were so con-fused. He was a servant of law, yet against him personally there lay no legal remedy ; he could make new courts and issue new commissions, as he had issued them to local magistrates or a Council in the north ; the discretion was his, which of his many courts he would employ.

Common law and Parliament tied him in many directions, but in many the field lay open, while in others he could strain his powers. As arm and conscience of the law, he had a dispensing power, to waive the penalties of a statute. Responsible for national defence, he could push far the common-law right of impressment, whether to get ships or men in time of war, or to conscript masons for the building of Eton.

Nor was it the wish of Parliament that a King in whom they trusted should be weak. That he should be able to ' live of his own ' was their aspiration. Over and over again they begged him to resume royal grants, and the Wars of the Roses acted so much like a great resumption act that Henry VII built up a landed revenue of £30,000 a year. Parliament gave Henry V, Edward IV, and the Tudors, tonnage and poundage and the wool-custom for life. And though Parliament was the King's highest court, he alone could call and dissolve it; in its long intervals King and Council supplemented statute by proclamations, and when it met they took the initiative in making law by public bills.

Yet our last word must be that neither in theory nor in fact was the New Monarchy a despotism. The Lancastrian king had no standing force except some Cheshire archers; the Tudors, none but a few hundred yeomen of the guard. Their most arbitrary actions were filtered through public opinion and self-governing agencies, whom statute and old law protected. Instead of dwindling, parliamentary action had increased. The Yorkists won the business class by initiating legislation; from Parliament Henry VII got power to reverse attainder, and Henry VIII authority for the Surveyors' Court. Fierce resistance to Wolsey's enormous taxes, mutters that ' England should be bond and not free ', came from the unpaid political class on whom this unarmed, restricted, and discretionary Kingship must depend. And it was not a despotism which insisted, as did Henry VIII in his early years, that the Commons must attend regularly, or forfeit their wages.

BOOK IV

MAKING OF MODERN ENGLAND
1509–1660

CHAPTER I

HENRY VIII: OLD PROJECTS IN A NEW AGE, 1509-1529

B Y the end of the reign of Henry VIII modern England was in sight. Printing and discovery, Renaissance and Reformation, revolutionized alike thought, the method of opinion, and the ruling class; a crisis of prices speeded up changes, long inevitable, in the economic structure. These processes, taken together, forced on a resettlement of England's relation to Scotland and Ireland; combined with others abroad, — religious war, Turkish advance, conquest of the Orient and the Americas, — they reconstructed the map and the meaning of Europe and diverted power from the Mediterranean to the Atlantic. By 1640 much of the fabric of nineteenth-century England was well above ground; of a seafaring, industrial, Protestant, middle-class State.

The first stage was conducted under Henry VIII, who, if greatness can be irrespective of virtue, must be held a great man. He outshone all his subjects, and for better reasons than because he was, as the Venetians reported, ' the best dressed sovereign in the world ' or, as he himself thought, the handsomest. He was a horseman and musician, spoke three foreign languages, was as skilled in theology as in ship-building, could make a pathetic speech, and put his finger on the weak spot in an act of Parliament or a despatch. His force as a politician was great, for he had ruthless craft to match ruthless foreign sovereigns, he bought base men and terrified the fearful, and yet could diagnose in his bluff way the motives moving the average English heart. He chose able servants and trusted them, though the only two men to whom he gave much power, Wolsey and Cromwell, were both men without soul, but from first to last the King was supreme when he took the trouble. Personal motives predominated in him always and his appetites grew with success, until in the end he became his own law, to whom all morals and counsels must bow down; ' if my head could win him a castle in France ', said More, ' it should not fail to go '. Yet high among his desires was one for popularity, and this masterful animal was not a despot. In the last resort he ruled without an army and through the House of Commons, keeping a great majority of his subjects loyal to himself and his policy through a bitter revolution.

The scholars who taught him, and the young men his contemporaries, cherished joyful hopes of a new age. That the reign of avarice was over seemed proved by his immediate execution of Empson and Dudley, and the cancelling of many bonds in the old King's coffers. A hunger for learning, an age of peace, they hoped, should launch reform in Church and State, for this was an age of unrest and men's minds were ready for new remedies. Until his death in 1491 Caxton went on printing the books that Englishmen demanded: chronicles, devotional literature, and older poets like Chaucer, far outnumbering a few translations from the Latin, and this went on another half-century, while European presses were producing the works of Rabelais, Ariosto, Vasari, or Ronsard. Yet Caxton and the early printers did two fundamental things: picking their way between classical borrowings and native dialects, they created a standard English speech, while simultaneously the volume of their work made public opinion. Printers like More's brother-in-law Rastell published editions of the statutes. Wynkin de Worde issued nearly seven hundred books in thirty years, while in the single year 1520 one Oxford bookseller sold over two thousand. From such figures we see that, for the full effects of Renaissance, England had long to wait; but the truer comparison is with Lancastrian days, when a few dozen manuscripts, painfully passed on and recopied, represented the annual intellectual harvest.

The turning-point was Henry VII's reign, and in the second half of it, for before 1500 organized Greek teaching was almost unknown. Among its pioneers, Grocyn returned from Italy to lecture at Oxford on Greek, and afterwards on the higher criticism as a London rector; Linacre acquired Greek at Florence and Venice, and the science which made him founder of the College of Physicians; from Oxford too went to Italy John Colet, dean of St. Paul's before Henry VII died and later founder of St. Paul's school, together with Lilly its first high master, whose Latin grammar disciplined generations of schoolboys for the next hundred years. Two greater men came round them at Oxford, and later in London; Erasmus of Rotterdam, the supreme scholar of Europe, and Thomas More the most original of his English contemporaries, who long hovered between the life of a monk or the application of Christianity to politics. The new learning was in high favour. Under the protection of the Lady Margaret and the direction of her confessor bishop Fisher, Cambridge University received it ardently. Erasmus became one of her professors, archbishop Warham was a loyal patron, and within a few years Cambridge was breeding a long line of Protestant leaders, Cranmer and Latimer, the Bible translators Tyndale and Coverdale, the earliest Protestant martyrs, and those, like William Cecil, whose old age was to make Protestantism victorious. At Oxford bishop Foxe founded Corpus Christi College, with Greek and Latin lecturers and a library of printed books, while Eton and Winchester were introducing Greek lessons. Immense new influences beat upon those pioneers; travels telling them how Amerigo Vespucci had discovered a new world, the study of Plato which cardinals and Florentine princes had revived, the text of Aristotle, and the Roman minds who taught moral conduct and the majesty of the State.

This first generation of English reformers, — for here Erasmus may be reckoned English from his repeated visits, — believed that Catholic reform was possible. Their method, whether in Colet's Oxford lectures or those sermons at St. Paul's which even Lollards gladly heard, or in Erasmus' great edition of the New Testament, was ever the same; to find the original books of their religion, to treat them as historical texts not less than as spiritual instruction, to throw overboard both the claim for verbal inspiration and the far-fetched allegorical meanings which mediaeval scholars had forced on the divine word; to allow also for development in religion, and not to anchor themselves to any one doctor of the Church; to reconcile God's purpose with human reason and, as Erasmus said, ' not to narrow what Christ meant to be broad '. Holding fast to the Bible and the creed of a historic Church and the person of Christ, they severely attacked the materialism which had overlaid Christianity, — the worship of relics and images like the milk of Our Lady at Walsingham, or the rich shrine of Becket at Canterbury, the sale of indulgences, ceremonial observance by ignorant monks, and the wire-drawn dogmas manufactured round the God Who was a spirit. Their work was instinct with freedom. More's early writings breathe a hatred of tyrants; Colet preached against war to the King's face. And it was their grief that the heads of the Church in their time were Popes like the warrior Julius II, and the Medici politician Leo X who acted, Erasmus said, ' as if Christ were dead '.

Nor was this generation deaf to the sorrows of English society. While Dudley lay in prison waiting death, he wrote in *The Tree of Commonwealth* of the decline of education, the laymen who appointed bad priests, and the oppression of the poor. Enclosures and discharged soldiers filled the roads with vagabonds who were being whipped back to their villages, or who flocked in thousands to a great man's funeral for the broken meats; every year capital punishment for violent robbery and horse-stealing sent hundreds to the gallows. How far was all this from the Platonic community of which the reformers dreamed! With such a contrast in his mind, in 1516 More published his *Utopia*. Every page flashed out a reproach against the reactionaries, whose refuge was the argument ' these things pleased our forefathers ', and whose practice resulted in a ' conspiracy of rich men procuring their own commodities under the name and title of a Commonwealth '; a State making a profit out of ' moth-eaten laws ', and covering iniquity over with the word ' prerogative '. *Utopia* aimed to show how different a society ruled by natural reason would be, and how more different still one which was really Christian. More warned men against hopes of sweeping reforms; ' if you cannot even as you would remedy vices which use and custom hath confirmed, yet for this cause you must not leave and forsake the Commonwealth ' but, rather, ' that which you cannot turn to good, so to order it that it be not very bad '. Essentially he preached reform within the Catholic framework; of a community which would insist on religion, without persecution of those who disagreed, though only if they disagreed in silence, and one leaving room for reformed monasteries; a community which aimed at felicity and leisure for all, and with so little regard for wealth that ' Utopia ' used gold only for prison fetters and chamber-pots; a land where men ' count nothing so much against glory as glory gotten in war '.

To either side of these reforming aspirations lay a mass of conservative interests and a small body of revolutionaries. In 1512 Colet's address to Convocation denounced the bishops as the root of all evil, together with the worldliness of clergy who haunted taverns and lived the life of farmers or office-hunters, and their grasping Church courts. Some bishops replied by attacking St. Paul's school, or by efforts to convict him of heresy; Cambridge colleges forbade the use of Erasmus' *Testament*, while at Oxford ' Greeks ' and ' Trojans ' fought in the streets. And at the other extreme stood Lollardy, which had burned under the surface continually since last we saw it in the Lancastrian age. Some of it was radical or visionary; some were pacifists; on the other hand, in Huntingdonshire an armed band were found, under oath to destroy antichrist; there were women preachers, and others who disbelieved in marriage or thought all good men were priests. In general their appeal was to Scripture, but when bishop Pecock of Chichester tried to refute this by appealing to reason, his fellow-bishops in 1457 took alarm and suspended him for heretical leanings. There were a few burnings under Edward IV, there were more, and even more recantations, under Henry VII, above all in Buckinghamshire. London women began to jeer at the famous shrines of Bermondsey or Willesden; there was repeated refusal to pay tithe; many clergy were involved in the agitation.

In 1515 two famous instances proved the common hatred of the Church. A London jury found that the bishop's officers had murdered in prison one Richard Hunne, a suspect heretic, and the bishop declared a London jury would condemn any clerk, ' though he were as innocent as Abel '. And the Commons, who showed their sympathy with the jury, had another opportunity of proving it, for they were about to renew a temporary Act of 1512, taking away benefit of clergy from criminals in minor orders. The King's confessor Standish defended this legislation, but Convocation argued no temporal court could try the Lord's Anointed. Lords, Commons, and judges, vowing that Church courts should protect no more murderers, declared Convocation had violated the Act of Praemunire, and when Wolsey advised referring the case to Rome, the King's reply was that ' kings of England have never had any superior but God alone '. To such lengths had the new age in England gone, two years before Luther roused Germany into a blaze.

For eighteen years, however, Henry VIII did nothing serious for religious or social reform, but rather cherished the ambitions of Henry V and ruled in the spirit of Henry VII. Fears for his dynasty were expressed in brutal action. He carried out his father's wish in marrying Catherine, though his sons were born dead or instantly died, and only one daughter, Mary, lived. In 1513 the prisoner Edmund de la Pole was executed, since his brother was in the French army, and in 1521 the Duke of Buckingham was brought to the block on a trumped-up case and Lady Salisbury was threatened, for the first was Edward IV's nephew and the second a daughter of Clarence. Government could still only survive by using the iron hand; Wales was full of disorder, and Northumberland a mass of gentry in league with brigands. In 1517 the anti-alien cry, roused by business rivals and popular preachers, was strong enough on ' evil May day ' to bring out several thousand apprentices with their clubs in the London streets, who broke open the prisons and sacked foreigners' houses, all of which had to be put down by the Howards' soldiers and many executions.

Though he sometimes intervened in his wrath, the King in these years was much given over to pleasure; given over, says one report, to ' girls and hunting '. Much of his father's economies poured away in gorgeous pageants, when in Moorish dress or decked out as Robin Hood he fascinated his Court; as time went on, his fidelity to Catherine broke down, one liaison giving him a natural son whom he made Duke of Richmond and loaded with honours, while soon after 1520 his ruling favourite was Mary Boleyn. Among the leading ministers two of his father's appointment, Foxe and Warham, soon retired, leaving two outstanding and opposed figures: Thomas Howard the Treasurer, earl of Surrey, made duke of Norfolk for his victory at Flodden, and Thomas Wolsey, the butcher's son whom Foxe had trained, and who by 1518 was archbishop of York, Chancellor, Cardinal, and Papal legate.

If the nobility and courtiers hated the Cardinal, who hauled even the greatest like Derby before the Star Chamber, common lawyers criticized the powers of his Chancery court, reformers lost faith in him, London and the parliamentary middle class hated him too. Yet he was realist enough to see the need of reform. He called on bishops and abbots to put their house in order, from the Pope he procured restrictions on the taking of minor orders, which would dry up the class of criminous clerks, and got a bull allowing him to visit the monasteries, some thirty of which he dissolved and tapped others for heavy subscriptions, wherewith to endow an Oxford college, Christ Church, now his chief extant memorial. Here a hundred canons, with a full equipment of professors, were to bring a reformed Church to the service of the State, and should be recruited from his other foundation at Ipswich, his native place. In Council and its branches his administration was strenuously directed to the keeping of order, and especially to the interests of the poor. By statute and commissions of enquiry, he tried to check enclosure. After other experiments he definitely organized the Court of Requests for poor men's cases, extended the commission of Council in Wales over the Marcher lordships, and raised the status of the Council in the north by bringing the Scottish March under its jurisdiction, and putting the King's son Richmond at its head. His energy stretched over all worlds ; whether to call the Spanish humanist Vives to teach at Oxford, or to urge City companies to finance exploration for the north-west passage to Asia.

But his soul, not without grandeur, had a gross and fleshly side, taking the form of vast pomp, banquets, and a huge household : while the palaces he rebuilt at Hampton Court and Whitehall became the dwelling-place of kings. He had natural children, upon one of whom he accumulated Church livings and archdeaconries ; he took large pensions from foreign sovereigns, while his ambition to be Pope influenced his policy. Yet all his centralization of power — the legateship which he used to crush the bishops, his threats of praemunire against Papal envoys, his menace of the new law of the Star Chamber — was infinitely precarious, since it existed only on the sufferance of the King. Moreover, the policy which he and the King together carried out in Europe brought about a breach with English feeling and constitutional tradition.

There was war without and within Europe. The iniquitous League of Cambrai, aimed at Venice, ended as might have been expected in the allies quarrelling between themselves, and in 1511 the Pope and Spain formed the Holy League, later joined by the Emperor Maximilian, against France. Mingled motives made Henry join it too. He was jealous of French military success, anxious to show off his navy, much influenced by his father-in-law, and a sincere son of the Church. There was opposition in Council, if only because a French war would certainly mean a Scottish war too, but the King was determined and now discovered his instrument in Wolsey. A first year of ill-success only made him set his teeth, and 1513 was full of triumph. The King in person defeated the French at the ' Battle of the Spurs ', at Guinegate in Artois. In September Surrey, now seventy years old, with great skill threw himself between the Scottish army, which had occupied Flodden ridge in Northumberland, and their line of retreat; tempted James IV on to the lower slopes, and the Highlanders into a precipitate charge, and in a hand-to-hand twilight battle, which artillery helped to decide, killed the King, the flower of his nobles, and 10,000 of his men. Having done enough for glory and forced France to terms with the Pope, Henry abandoned his selfish allies and in 1514 made a peace, whereby Louis XII married his sister Mary and left Tournai in English hands.

This rather thin triumph was shipwrecked the next year, when Louis XII died and his widow made a love match with Henry's friend Brandon, duke of Suffolk. The new King Francis I determined to recover supremacy in Italy, sent Albany the heir to the throne to stir up trouble in Scotland, which drove out Queen Margaret, crushed Milan and the Swiss at the battle of Marignano, and forced peace on Pope Leo X. In 1516 old Ferdinand of Aragon died, to be succeeded by his grandson Charles, who at once made terms with France until he was more sure of his new throne. To all this the first English reaction was bluster and defiance. Henry claimed to be ' protector of Scotland '; considerable sums were spent in subsidizing the Emperor Maximilian, who achieved nothing. In view of much opposition in Council to these wasteful adventures, at last King and Cardinal were persuaded to hold their hand, until France and the Hapsburgs inevitably quarrelled again. Their retreat was turned into a half-triumph in the so-called ' universal peace ' of 1518, whereby Francis paid an indemnity for our surrender of Tournai, promised his infant son's hand for Henry's daughter Mary, and withdrew protection from Albany, also greasing the wheels by pensions to Wolsey and other councillors. It was marked further by the grant of Wolsey's legateship: for through Rome he hoped to reach all his objectives.

So far all this costly unsuccessful policy had flowed from Henry's youthful jealousy of France, or his grievances against unfaithful allies, but in what followed the choice was more deliberate. Though Wolsey's ambition to be Pope was real, it would be inaccurate to explain all our moves by that; he himself always argued that neutrality was impossible, and that alliances were necessary to prevent bargains at our expense. Both he and the King were much influenced by a wish to work hand in hand with the Pope, while Henry often spoke of capturing the lost French provinces; though his real object seems rather to have been to pick up a few fortresses cheap, and sell them dear. Their actions were too impulsive to allow us to see any design of a balance of power; finding Europe at war, they meant to get prestige and profit, by siding with the stronger side or menacing him into giving England a share.

The fatal war which destroyed Wolsey was introduced by two

notable events. At the end of 1517 Luther began that resistance to the Papacy which within four years captured half Germany. In 1519 Maximilian died, German national feeling triumphed, and the Archduke Charles added the Empire and Hapsburg territories to what he already held in the Netherlands, Italy, and Spain.

Against this encirclement France would certainly strike, but the Pope would side with the Emperor, who could protect his hereditary state at Florence and crush the heretic Luther, and England soon reached the same decision. Henry had half-heartedly dabbled as a candidate in the Imperial election, mainly perhaps to stop a French success, but if we were to abandon neutrality at all, the Imperial alliance would be the popular choice. For all the fighting classes hated France, business men insisted on peace with the Netherlands, Catherine of Aragon's influence went in favour of her nephew, and Henry was ardently writing his famous book against Luther, which brought him the title he had long asked of ' Defender of the Faith '. So the ' field of the cloth of gold ', the negotiation with France held in 1520 with extraordinary pomp near Guisnes, was a mere deception, since interviews between Henry and the Emperor both preceded and followed it, and in 1521 a treaty was signed for the marriage of Charles and Mary, an invasion of France, and suppression of heresy.

War raged throughout 1522-5, with no satisfaction for Wolsey's ambition, as two Popes died and the Emperor's promised support for his election did not materialize, and far less with any military success to justify intervention. Our war was always feeble, our diplomacy insincere. Ravaging raids into France, like John of Gaunt's long ago, accomplished nothing, though the King hoped to conquer all north of the Somme. Even Margaret Tudor could not resist Scottish patriotism, while our devastation of the Border hardened the Scots' heart. In 1524 English diplomacy hesitated towards peace, and we let our ally the Emperor fight on alone. In February 1525 he took Francis I prisoner at the decisive battle of Pavia, and for a few months Henry and Wolsey hoped that here was the chance to partition France. But the Emperor had won all he wished from France and expected nothing from England, which he marked by throwing over the Princess Mary and marrying a Portuguese wife. The final act from 1525-9, ending in the crash of all Wolsey's policies, proceeded by two stages : a first, of making peace with France, and the second, of alliance with France against the too victorious Emperor. Of these results the two chief causes were a national resistance to war and Henry's determination to divorce his wife.

This war policy resulted in a most tyrannous financial government. The King's Chamber, which spent about £65,000 in an average peace year, in 1513 soared to nearly £700,000. To fill the gap Wolsey invented a new tax, the subsidy, on both land and goods, far more productive than the mediaeval tenth and fifteenth, but the grumbling of Parliament and its fierceness against the Church in 1515 did not encourage him to call others. Various unpopular economies helped him to dispense with taxation, though some were to cost England dear, like the reduction of expense in Ireland. When war broke out again in 1522, special commissioners took a new valuation, on the basis of which a forced loan was levied which brought in about £150,000. In 1523 Wolsey in person asked the Commons for £800,000, threatened individual members, and marshalled the votes of the King's servants against the unwilling town representatives. After four months of debate, much muttering in streets and ale-houses, he got about three-quarters of his demand, in a subsidy which touched even the wage-earning class; while as legate he compelled the clergy to promise the half-value of every benefice.

In 1525, before the subsidy was all collected or the loans repaid, news of Pavia spurred him to a last effort. Under the name of an ' amicable loan ' and on the plea that the King would himself lead the army to France, the Cardinal asked no less than one-sixth of lay, and one-third of clerical, wealth. Orders to prepare the way by bonfires for Pavia met with sullen looks. The clergy refused to pay except in Convocation. Royal commissioners were assaulted in Kent; the squires refused to use force against their neighbours; industrial England began to discharge labour; church bells were rung and markets closed, and only the good sense of the Dukes of Norfolk and Suffolk, and the big clothiers like Spring of Lavenham, warded off rebellion. Bills were posted up saying that nothing came of French wars, or that the Cardinal sent their money to Rome; while to Wolsey's face the London aldermen declared the loans were against act of Parliament. So government retreated and made peace with France, with ample pensions for the King and Cardinal.

For another year yet they were content to stir up Francis I to break the severe terms imposed on him after Pavia, and to incite Italian resistance to the Emperor. Early in 1527, however, Wolsey arranged a French marriage treaty; in May the fearful sack of Rome by the Spanish and German troops decided him to support the French and Italians further. For a time the balance in Italy wavered to and fro, but in 1529 his allies met with final disaster; the French and the Pope came to terms with Charles V, by the treaties of Cambrai and Barcelona, which saved Medici rule at Florence but left Italy and the Papacy under control of Spain. Such was the military end of these eighteen years of spirited diplomacy.

For years now there had been protests against it. What was the good, a new member of Parliament, Thomas Cromwell, asked of winning ' dog-holes ' in France which we could never hold, while an enemy Scotland lay at our door ? After all this expenditure, the tax-payer grumbled, Henry VIII had not a foot of French land more than Henry VII : why should they pay these forced taxes, which would make England ' bond and not free ' ?

When it came to open war against the Empire, which killed the City's best trade and shivered credit in Antwerp, the clamour rose higher. The French ambassador confessed that Wolsey was the only man who wished the alliance ; Protestants hated conflict with Germany ; Norfolk led opposition in Council ; unemployment and riots testified to the national fear and anger. Only military success could save the Cardinal, and perhaps not even that ; for he was in a trap. He was spurring on desperately to force the Pope, or to have the Papal powers trans-ferred to himself so long as the Pope was a Spanish prisoner, with one object ; to procure the divorce on which the King finally decided during 1526, and to recover the balance of power by French marriages for the King and his daughter. But it soon appeared that the King was bent on marrying Anne Boleyn.

Whenever war broke out, there was always talk of arresting the survivors of the Yorkist blood royal. Such fears for the succession, and doubts always held in some circles whether his marriage had been valid, marked as it was by the death of all his children except Mary, deter-mined Henry in his conscience that his marriage was null, and enquiries among the bishops showed that others besides Wolsey would support him. Surely, with his services to Rome, he could expect the Pope to sanction his divorce ? just as he had lately sanctioned the separation of Margaret Tudor from her second husband, Angus, or as he had allowed divorce for two recent kings of France.

There was, then, nothing whatever ' Protestant ' about Henry's enterprise in its first stage. Far from questioning the Pope's powers, he argued only that the dispensation for his particular marriage had been given on false grounds, and hoped to enlarge those powers for another dispensation, allowing him to marry Anne Boleyn, the sister of his former mistress Mary. On Wolsey's assurance of success, he acted not through any English court but at Rome, where his embassies and bribes vainly tried to extract a decretal commission, which would authorize Papal legates to declare the law without further appeal.

Though Pope Clement VII blanched under the violent language of the English envoys, often wiping his eyes and tying his handkerchief into knots, he refused to bind his hands. He would get rid of the responsibility if he could ; Henry might marry a second wife and con-front Europe with the fact, or pressure might be used to drive Catherine into a nunnery. Such advice broke down at once on her refusal, and her insistence that her marriage to Arthur had never been consummated. Moreover, behind her was ranged her nephew the Emperor, whose troops surrounded Rome, and to whom else could the Pope look for the destruction of Lutheranism, or protection of the Medici ? The commission which he granted to Cardinals Campeggio and Wolsey in 1528 was, therefore, carefully worded, the Pope's secret instructions being given to the first alone. When their court opened in May 1529 in the Dominicans' hall at Blackfriars, the Queen immediately appealed to Rome ; in July, without consulting England, the French made peace with the Emperor, Campeggio adjourned the hearing, and the Pope summoned the King to appear before him in person.

This, Wolsey had warned him, would not only destroy Wolsey himself but end for ever English devotion to the Holy See. The first came about in October, when the royal officials summoned the Cardinal in King's Bench for breaches of the Act of Praemunire as legate, for usurping the rights of bishops and patrons, and taking bribes from monasteries, and his palaces were taken from him. His innumerable enemies had captured the royal ear ; they were led by the ' night crow ', as he called Anne Boleyn, niece of his old enemy Norfolk, and included the King's favourite Suffolk, officials who hoped for his ruin, the high-minded Thomas More, who succeeded him as Chancellor, and most of the bishops.

Still worse might follow. For the King had taken to reading Lutheran books, was arguing that the Pope could not dispense against the laws of God and nature, and was hearing from the Boleyns' chaplain, Cranmer, that learned opinion was on his side. Protestant pamphleteers were goading him on to seize the clergy's wealth ; Tyndale, the translator of the New Testament, was urging the King's divine right to reform the Church ; a ' Christian brotherhood ' was hawking round English testaments. It was at least worth while trying the advice which the Pope himself had once given, to solve his ' great matter ' in his own realm. Within a fortnight of Campeggio's adjournment, he took into his own hands the control of writs for a new Parliament, to meet in October. Whose hopes would triumph was all uncertain ; whether a reaction of nobles, who hated the Cardinal's centralized power, and of bishops, who suspected his leaning to Lutheranism, or a revolution led by the reformers, carrying Parliament with them, to destroy not the Church riches only but the Catholic faith.

CONTEMPORARY DATES

1510   Albuquerque occupies Goa.
1511   Julius II forms the Holy League.
      Luther visits Rome.
      Albert of Hohenzollern elected grand master of the Teutonic
        Order.

1512	Battle of Ravenna.
	Medici restoration at Florence.
1513–21	Pope Leo X.
1513	Machiavelli writes *The Prince*.
	Balboa reaches the Pacific.
1515	Henry VII's chapel finished at Westminster.
	Accession of Francis I of France (–1547), who defeats the Swiss at Marignano.
	Raphael's Sistine Madonna.
1516	The Archduke Charles succeeds Ferdinand in Spain.
	His brother Ferdinand marries Mary, sister to Lewis King of Hungary and Bohemia.
1517	Turks conquer Egypt.
	Luther's 95 theses at Wittenberg.
1518	Linacre founds the College of Physicians.
1519	Charles V succeeds Maximilian in the Empire.
	Cortez reaches Mexico.
1520	Magellan circumnavigating the globe.
1520–66	Reign of Solyman the Magnificent in Turkey.
1521	Luther outlawed by the Diet of Worms.
	The Spanish communes defeated at Villalar.
1523–60	Gustavus Vasa, King of Sweden.
	–1534. Pope Clement VII.
1525	Battle of Pavia.
	Peasant rising in Germany.
1526	Battle of Mohacs.
	Baber begins the Mogul dynasty at Delhi.
	Holbein comes to England.

CHAPTER II

HENRY VIII: THE MODERNIZING OF ENGLAND, 1529–1547

BEFORE modern Britain — a united kingdom, Protestant, seafaring, and capitalist — could come into existence, a vast work of destruction had to be done. It is not given to the pure and lowly of heart to do such work, nor need we be surprised at the wickedness which accompanied Reformation. Henry's own moral decline was, indeed, unexpected. The young Christian sovereign, whose early letters had been headed ' In Jesus is my hope ', sank to a lustful animal, for whom a long succession of queens and mistresses were procured. His egoism and will degenerate into megalomania and ruthlessness, and as he tried to frighten Catherine with threats of poison and separated her from her daughter, so he executed Anne Boleyn and capered for joy at her death. He demanded of his servants not merely silent acceptance, but loud applause and unbroken success. Wolsey died in 1530, but he was on his way to the Tower, for he was growing faint in the divorce and trying to recover influence through foreign sovereigns. If he died lamenting he had not served God as he had served the King, More, whom the King had bidden ' first look unto God and after God unto me ', died for following this command too faithfully ; Cromwell, because his policy made Henry unpopular ; bishops, for trying to keep a Catholic predominance ; many humbler persons, for trying to speed on a Protestant reformation. But all alike were condemned, as ' faint to God, faint to the truth, faint to His Highness ' ; for even a passive deviation from the King's will.

His determination on his divorce was to involve the destruction of every link with Rome, the dissolution of the monasteries, and remaking of many old jurisdictions ; which, in turn, involved a great increase in the State's power, a revolution in the distribution of property, a closer union with Wales and Ireland, new claims of superiority over Scotland, a new threat from Catholic Powers, and consequently new needs of national defence ; all coincident with a revolution in money prices, which broke up society and brought a new problem of poverty. Only a government of remarkable force could have survived all this without much bloodshed, and Henry was a politician great enough to achieve it in the name of Parliament.

What previous governments had done, he did more thoroughly now.

By direct pressure, or indirectly through the local gentry, many royal servants were returned to the Parliament of 1529 and its successors; the King would harangue the Commons in Star Chamber, refuse writs to hostile peers, or threaten recalcitrant members. Yet he had to lead as well as to drive. Several times the Commons resisted statutes which touched property owners' interests; they guarded most carefully the common law, often amended government bills, and when they gave him power to change the succession by his will, they did it freely, for their genuine deference to his wisdom increased every year. This despot had no army, and it was with the unpaid militia of southern England that he put down rebellion in the Catholic north. He acted in Parliament on a scale never before known, keeping the Commons of 1529 in being for seven years, introducing more and more of his councillors into the House, while for every blow at the Church or in every matrimonial misfortune he boldly wielded the weapons of publicity and printed appeal.

What was the mind of England in regard to the Church, and what was the Church's true condition? These questions must be answered if we are to estimate the support which Henry found, the gradualness of his action, his justification or his iniquity, the loss and the gain.

Since Wyclif's onslaught the state of the Church, if changed at all, had changed for the better. Warham, Fisher, and Tunstall were better men than Arundel and his suffragans. Some evils like alien priories and benefit of clergy had been cut down, and the flow of money to Rome diminished. The printing press had poured out the religious books so long passed about in manuscript; 116 editions of the Sarum primer were now in print, some with English additions; Caxton and his successors produced volumes of the mystics like Rolle and Hilton; and on any broad test the religious feeling of the people cannot be doubted. All their corporate life, even their feasts and archery contests, centred round the village church. Hundreds of wills and testaments survive to show that Catholic piety was the binding force of society : wills that bequeath money for an altar, a vestment, or loans to the poor. A mass of benefactions in gilds and chantries, schools and alms-houses, all the mystery plays and innumerable religious songs and incessant building by parishes and monasteries, showed that all the people's hopes, amusements, and charities, flowed in the channel of the faith.

Against this must be set weaknesses which urgently demanded reformation, whether it came without revolution as in Spain, or with the violence of Luther in Germany. Worst of all was the condition of Rome itself. Englishmen were aware that money asked for jubilees or crusades was often used in raising armies, while ambassadors reported on the immorality of the Vatican and the all-powerfulness of money in its courts. Erasmus and the new scholars spread a scorn of these warrior or dilettante Popes, and criticized the historical origin of their claims. Within the last century English independence had shown itself in sharp refusals to admit Papal legates, and in growing pressure from the common law against Church courts.

Moreover, the English Church was the victim of those evils which since Avignon had marked the Church as a whole. The machine was costly, overloaded, and undisciplined. Though the laity did not suffer much directly, they resented the drain of money through annates (the whole first year's income taken from a bishop), fees from new abbots, the £1000 paid for his pall by a new archbishop, and costs of appeals to Rome, which were multiplied by Papal ' provisions ', litigation over livings, and sale of indulgences. The Church was also bitterly divided. Many bishops would favour the suppression of monasteries, and Lutheranism had touched a good many of the friars, who attacked the wealth of bishops and monks. Again, there were far too many un-beneficed clergy, while too many of the beneficed were miserably poor, which led to a hateful jostling after money, and to pluralism and absentees. For such evils the government and the laity were largely responsible. Most bishops were promoted for political service, which meant, for instance, that Fox never saw two of the cathedrals he successively ruled, or that the bishop of Bangor had not been seen there for fourteen years. Wolsey piled upon his natural son a deanery, two archdeaconries, five prebends, and two rectories. Landowners put priests into their livings on account of their merits as farm managers or boon companions ; as a Devonshire cleric sang :

> For if one can flatter and bear a hawk on his fist,
> He shall be made parson of Honiton or Clyst.

Monasteries also bore a heavy responsibility, since they held scores of livings where they appointed a curate on a starvation wage, and farmed the tithes through a layman.

The clergy lived too much like the world, and by the world. Long before Protestant pamphleteers showed up the evils, Cardinal Morton reproached their hunting and haunting of taverns, and Colet preached against their covetousness. Priests, especially those without tithes, demanded fees for every sacrament, the communion of the sick or the Easter communion of the poor ; most hated of all being the mortuary, whereby a priest would claim the garment of the dead, even the candles round the bier. But the clergy incurred equal hatred for privileges which sprang from their claim to be not of this world. Church courts took heavy fees on the probate of wills ; their officials entered private houses to make men attend church, or to spy out their vices ; in heresy trials their inquisitorial oath and process without a jury confounded every ordinary idea of justice, while heresy was stretched to cover anything which the clergy disliked. Benefit of clergy still meant that a villain in priestly orders might go scot-free, and sanctuaries like Westminster sheltered many murderous rogues. In London above all, and most of southern England, there was a violent anti-clerical feeling coupled with a great deal of cynicism. Jeers at unworthy priests or fat monks in mediaeval literature had not dissolved the faith, but the Renaissance was full of a deeper scepticism, and Erasmus taught many the dangerous habit of laughter.

Yet the Commons, who brought such charges, repudiated any suggestion that they were heretical, and those who in 1529 wished a change of faith were very few. Though Lollard practices and books now and then came to the surface, the numbers accused in the large London diocese seem to have been under fifty in the preceding twenty years; nor can any sentence of death be traced there after 1511. This humble evangelical movement, however, was followed by something more formidable, the rapid spread from about 1520 onwards of Lutheran teaching, which through the seaports first tinged East Anglia and the theology students of Cambridge. Some who were taken thence to fill Wolsey's new college infected Oxford; others, Latimer and Cranmer included, were rising to high positions; Tyndale fled to the Continent and by 1526 had finished his translation of the Testament, while scurrilous pamphlets attacked the clergy as robbers, ' idle lubber ', and the pest of the realm. Bonfires of such books were the official answer. Yet the King was arguing privately that, on their political side, there was much to be said for Luther and Wyclif.

For three more years, however, he did his utmost to get his way within the framework of the Church. And with good reason : France would not for his sake sever its alliance with the Papacy, voices even in the Commons asked him to take back his wife, and his new advisers, Norfolk, More, and Gardiner, were sturdy conservatives. So while embassies and a manifesto from the lords went to Rome, and opinions gathered from foreign universities were used to frighten the Pope, the King on one side allowed the burning of a few Protestants and on the other excited anti-clerical feeling in Parliament. Various small Acts reduced the fees for probate and mortuaries, and did something against pluralism and sanctuary. But the bishops' resistance led Henry to strike harder in 1531, when by a threat of praemunire he forced the Convocations to admit he was the Church's protector and ' as far as the law of Christ allows even Supreme Head ', and to buy their pardon by an immense fine. By 1532 it was certain that nothing could be hoped for at Rome, and opposition at home was stronger. Information from the north-country reported grumblings that the King was governed by a whore. The Commons were resisting taxation and asking a dissolution of this long Parliament. Against much opposition the King in person drove through a bill making the threat that annates would be stopped, and bishops consecrated without Papal bulls, unless Rome came to heel. His servants in the Commons, marshalled by Cromwell, inspired the ' supplication against the ordinaries ', which complained of Convocation's power of making canons, of the spiritual courts and oppressive heresy trials ; under which threat Convocation surrendered in the ' submission of the clergy ', whereby no new canon should be made except by royal consent. Even so, the opposition in the Lords refused to turn this into a statute ; More resigned the Chancellorship and took up his pen against the Protestants ; while just before his death Warham too was menaced with praemunire.

In January 1533 the long balancings were ended by a human fact : Anne Boleyn was with child and Henry married her secretly, for her child must be cleared of stain. His diplomacy and his pressure were severe and successful. The Papacy, bribed and threatened, issued the bulls to make Cranmer archbishop. Convocation affirmed that no Pope could grant dispensation for such a marriage as Henry's with Catherine, and Parliament passed an Act of Appeals declaring ' that this realm of England is an empire ', competent to settle all cases in its own courts. Cranmer then pronounced the marriage with Catherine void ; in June Anne was crowned, and in September gave birth to the Princess Elizabeth.

The gospel light that dawned in Anne Boleyn's eyes, or rather in those of her child, could not stop here. For a Papal sentence of excommunication was posted up in Flanders, the new marriage implied new succession laws, Latimer and other reformers were questioning Catholic doctrine, and the Boleyns patronizing Lutherans. Each side appealed to old principles, the clergy to Becket and the King's side to Henry II and John. Already Henry had envoys in Protestant Germany and appealed to a council against the Pope. Conservative circles were discussing prophecies of his death, coming from Elizabeth Barton, a nun of Canterbury, whose visions and moral influence had long made her famous. It was known that the Emperor would protect the interests of Mary, and his hand was traced in contacts with Yorkist families, the Scots, and the Irish.

In this emergency Henry relied much on his new secretary, Thomas Cromwell, a self-made business man who had done useful service for Wolsey in suppressing some monasteries. He had furthered his own fortunes by Wolsey's fall, while his carefully padlocked house in Austin Friars and his private note-books held many secrets. In travels abroad he had acquired a liking for Italian literature, with an admiration for Machiavelli's teaching of the sovereign State. Of any ideal except this, or any scruple, he seems to have been devoid, and he conceived a great contempt for the slowness of parliamentary government. He had some personal links with Protestants abroad and would use them for the profit of the commonwealth, coming to argue in later years that ' a Papist and a traitor were the same thing '. He told the King he would make him the richest in Christendom, and the most obvious source of these riches would be the Church.

Master and man made sure of success in 1534. Cromwell took pains over parliamentary candidates and elections; once at least members were summoned to the King's presence. A lucky run of empty bishoprics, and the forced resignation of some abbots, put safe men in important places, while inspired pamphlets tuned the press.

By such contrivance the government passed five important measures. The Annates Act executed the threat of two years back, that this payment should cease; no bishop should get bulls from Rome, and henceforward if a cathedral chapter did not elect the King's candidate, he would nominate by letters patent. The Dispensations Act forbade payment of Peter's pence, or the procuring of dispensations and licences, hitherto granted at Rome ' in great derogation of your imperial Crown '. A third made statutory the ' submission ' of 1532, and strengthened the Act of Appeals by making Chancery the final Church court. The Act of Succession declared Henry's first marriage void, settling the succession in his sons by Anne and thereafter in sons by any other marriage, and next in the Princess Elizabeth; offences against which should be treason, though Parliament secured that merely treasonable words should carry a less penalty. Finally a heresy law modified the Lancastrian Acts, by bringing in the State and making a royal writ obligatory.

Before this legislation passed, a Bill of Attainder sent the Nun of Kent and her sympathizers to the block, and though More's name was cut out of it at the last moment, both he and Catherine's special champion, bishop Fisher, were called on to swear to the succession. To the succession itself both were ready to swear, but not to the preamble of the Act, which denied the Pope's power and Henry's first marriage. They were, therefore, sent to the Tower, their promises of silence not being enough for the King.

Refusals to swear from the friars most respected for saintliness and many reports of seditious speech drove Henry to desperation. In the autumn Parliament tightened up the oaths, transferred first-fruits and tenth to the King, while an Act of Supremacy made statutory Convocation's surrender and gave the King power to correct heresies. A fierce treason Act condemned all who, even by words (though Parliament inserted the feeble safeguard ' malicious '), impugned the royal title or called the King heretic or tyrant. Armed with such powers and putting remorseless pressure on the juries, early in 1535 the government executed the friars of the Charterhouse and Sion. If any doubt existed about Fisher's fate, it was extinguished by the

Pope making him a cardinal; Henry swore he would send his head to Rome to fit the hat, and a jury sent him to execution, with more Carthusians, still more of the same order being starved to death in prison. In June a special commission, assisted by perjury from the law officers, condemned More for words against the supremacy; his defiant challenge, the last challenge of the mediaeval ideal, being that the Act violated the law of God and Magna Carta, and that the act of one realm could not prevail against all Christendom and the general Councils of a thousand years. What Henry's separation from the Church meant had now its evidence, in the heads of More and Fisher looking down from London Bridge.

Two pronouncements of this year defined its meaning further. In his *True Obedience* bishop Gardiner taught the divine right of Kings as the rule of Scripture, Roman law, and English history; that Church and State were one body, and that Christ Himself had disclaimed an earthly kingdom. On the other side Reginald Pole, whom his cousin the King had frequently tried to win over, issued from his refuge in Italy the manuscript of his ' Unity of the Church '. Henry, he argued, had destroyed the meaning of Christendom in usurping the office of the Vicar of Christ; broken his coronation oath, plundered his people, and sacrificed the flower of his subjects to his lusts. ' Is England Turkey ', he cried, ' that she is governed by the sword ? '

But the new State led by Cromwell, who vowed he would make Pole ' eat his own heart ', drove the revolution on. It enforced new oaths on the clergy, abjuring the Pope. Cromwell became the King's Vicar-General, in which capacity he began to take a strict valuation of Church property; ' first-fruits ', moreover, were now to be payable not only by bishops, but from every benefice. His friend Coverdale was working on an English version of the Bible. A visitation of the universities destroyed the study of the Fathers and the Canon Law. And, after considering the possibility of seizing all clerical wealth and putting the clergy on salaries, another visitation began the destruction of the monasteries.

After many partial suppressions of alien priories in time of war, or of small monasteries to endow colleges, there still remained over six hundred foundations, holding about seven thousand fully professed monks and friars, and some two thousand nuns. Their net income was in the neighbourhood of £135,000, or nearly £2,000,000 in modern values; their buildings, shrines, and moneyed wealth were of enormous value. Twenty-seven mitred abbots were peers of the realm; heads of famous houses like Fountains, Reading, or Bury, were figures to whom many dependants looked up. What Cromwell's visitors reported is beside the point, for they were men of low character sent to make a case and their information was a farce. But it is certain that the monks' influence for good had declined, many small houses were so empty that Wolsey took powers to suppress them just before his fall, while from the reports of bishops and visitors well before Cromwell's time three or four trustworthy impressions can be gathered.

The high purpose of monasticism had sunk into worldliness; sometimes into the pomp of rich parlours and abbots' outriders with gilded bridles, or nuns with silk waist-bands and pet dogs; sometimes into a more or less harmless domesticity, as at Eynsham where the abbot's sister kept house, or at Norwich Priory where barbers and tailors with their families lived in the cloister. The lay world all round them was much to blame. Kings, and descendants of their founders, insisted on board and lodging for themselves and their followers; neighbouring gentry and attorneys acted as stewards of their courts, or managers of their lands. So, losing the direct management of the soil, many houses made long leases of their demesnes; many made friends with the local Mammon, creating annuities and handing over their parish livings, thereby making a vested interest which would certainly demand satisfaction when dissolution came. Their finances were chaotic; partly because, like other corporate bodies, they were robbed by their servants, partly because of a vicious system of separate departments, and most of all from their dependence on the character of the reigning abbot, who might sink his abbey into debt for a generation. Westminster had been long bankrupt, while the Abbot of Bury lived in London for economy.

When, as was generally the case, they were conservative or lazy landlords, they did not prosper in the new world; while those who followed the enclosure policy incurred more hatred, like Peterborough, which had turned out a hundred tenants. They had many casual dependants in receipt of doles, but their regular payments to the poor were not large. Their rôle in education was not insignificant; the monks of Sion were producing books, many sent promising men to the universities, some kept schools for boys and choristers, while nunneries like Winchester boarded daughters of the gentry. But a lack of discipline weakened all their order. Visitations often show trivial punishments; an abbot deposed for grave immorality but comfortably pensioned, or recitation of the psalms as a penalty for haunting taverns, or vicars-choral of cathedral churches found absentee, or working as small farmers, with impunity. Finally, they were isolated; with bishops and friars, both old enemies, and the laity resentful of their wealth, they were standing or falling with Rome, to whose authority most of the greater houses claimed to be directly subject. Such seems the broad picture; to be seen neither as the vicious life discovered at Walsingham, nor the holiness proved at Glastonbury, nor the usefulness of Hexham in its lonely frontier. But on the whole, and on the scale in which it survived, as something relaxed from its dedicated life, something which had outlived its environment.

What should be done with them aroused disagreement in the King's circle. If Cromwell wanted their total destruction, Cranmer and Latimer would have continued some for clergy training or for charity, as local squires also sometimes asked. The compromise Act of 1536, which dissolved some three hundred and seventy houses with an income of £200 or less, met little objection in Parliament. But it was coupled with severe ' injunctions ', which were meant to make monastic life almost unendurable; younger monks were encouraged to denounce their seniors, and by 1540, under stress of terror, the connivance of individual abbots, or their share in Catholic resistance, the great majority surrendered, even before Parliament swept them away.

Here, anticipating the end and some of its effects, it would be false to describe the dissolution as a dead loss, or as inhumanity. For some years the Court of Augmentations, set up to handle their finances, controlled wealth which brought the Crown an income of £100,000, and six new bishoprics were raised on monastic churches. A great number of the monks were pensioned; many married, and a surprising number continued even to Elizabeth's time as parish priests. In the eight previously monastic cathedrals many monks continued as canons; the abbot of Westminster became its dean, and the abbot of Peterborough stayed on in his old home as its bishop. What was sheer loss was the result on education, and some aspects of charity. Not only were the monastic schools, the means of educating women, and many avenues to the university destroyed, but Henry seized most of the London hospitals, and on the ground of ' superstition ' Edward VI's government dissolved most of the schools attached to chantries or parish gilds. The figures of ordination for the clergy fell sharply, one aftermath being the scanty Elizabethan clergy which made room for Puritanism.

In the benefits of the dissolution all the ruling class shared, Catholics like Norfolk and Paget participating with the rising politicians of the new order, Cecil and Russell. So were laid the foundations of many political families; as at Hinchingbrooke by Cromwell's nephew, ancestor of the great Oliver. By his death Henry had disposed, more often by sale than by gift, of about two-thirds of the monastic lands, the rest remaining on Crown leases, and though his original grants were made to about one thousand persons or corporations, City speculators were soon busy and an immense amount of land passed by resale to the middle class. Here was the pledge for a vested interest in Reformation. A spirit of loot seized all ranks, from the highest officials down to the visitors' grooms who made saddle cloths out of church vestments, villagers who stripped an abbey roof of lead, or farmers who built up a cow-shed from its stones. Reformers under Edward VI united in denouncing the harshness of the new landlords, the decline of charity, and the disillusionment of seizing the abbey lands; ' it had been more profitable for the commonwealth ', wrote one, ' that they had remained still in their hands '.

Even before this dissolution the original cause of Reformation, Henry's marriage, was merged in greater consequences. In January 1536 Catherine of Aragon's death relieved Henry from fear of war; in May, Anne Boleyn was executed on charges of adultery, the evidence for which is non-existent but which we can only say was not impossible in her character. Henry was weary of her, her death would conciliate Imperialist and conservative circles, and within ten days he married Jane Seymour. A new Parliament, the elections for which were carefully nursed, echoed Cranmer's sentence that Princess Elizabeth was a bastard, and gave the King power to settle the succession by will.

Yet there was no reaction in the Reformation, which was too deep a thing to be changed by the ebb and flow of Henry's whim. Catholic faith could not survive an attack on Catholic institutions. For hundreds of years there had been an opposition to Roman supremacy, and always turning on the same points: an evangelical religion claiming the individual's right to live by the rule of Scripture ; or the claim of national societies to reduce clerical power ; or the superiority over the Pope of Christendom as a whole. The last might satisfy theorists, the second be enough for politicians, but the fire of the Reformation, as in earlier religious revivals, turned on the first alone. By a necessary sequence of ideas, what began as mere anti-clericalism, or a Puritan dislike of ceremony, always worked back to St. Augustine's thought : to the faith of those justified and a Church of the elect, saved not by sacraments or ' works ', but the merits of Christ alone, a salvation which those predestined would find by this all-saving faith.

The Supreme Head thus found himself obliged to define faith as well as jurisdiction. Though he burned Anabaptists alongside Catholics, it was in vain that he ordered silence, for the whole country was a din of religious quarrels. East Anglians were burning roods, Puritans attacking vestments and organs, all the German and Swiss disputes, which were tearing Europe to pieces over a married clergy or scripture-reading, now seized upon England. In 1536 government took two steps towards more control. The Ten Articles, forced by the King on the rival camps among his bishops, were a conservative document; though they set forth only three sacraments, they approved transubstantiation, allowed good works as well as faith, condemned purgatory but permitted the use of images. Cromwell underlined them with injunctions, which distinguished between articles of faith and ceremonial, urged that work and charity were truer religion than pilgrimages or relics, and ordered the teaching of the commandments in English and an English Bible in every church. He had hardly issued them, however, before Catholic England at last rebelled.

It was the crisis of the reign, for Catholicism might unite Henry's greatest dangers: the daughter Mary whom he had wronged, the Yorkist blood of the Poles, a coalition between Charles V and Francis I, a Papal excommunication, and old lawlessness in Scotland and Ireland. But his star shone out triumphant. The Empire and France continued at war till 1538, and in competition for English friendship ordered the Papal legate, Reginald Pole, out of their territories. Ireland was suppressed before the English north rose, the north had no centre and Yorkist nobles no head, and both were crushed before the Pope issued his excommunication.

The rebels who called themselves ' the Pilgrimage of Grace ' represented not only Catholic England, but all the older England which felt itself under sentence of death. Beginning in Lincolnshire in 1536 in protest against the suppression of the abbeys and new taxation, before long it spread over all Yorkshire, taking in peers like D'Arcy on whose influence local government depended, great abbeys like Fountains or Bolton, and the country gentry, Tempests, Constables, and Cliffords whose violence was always bringing them into Star Chamber. Their confused battle-cries showed the divided elements in their cause. Catholics who asked the refounding of monasteries, peasants who resisted enclosure, and yeomen of the Border who came out in defence of their tenant-right joined the squires, to whom those things meant profit but who in hatred of the new centralization called for the dismissal of Cromwell and Cranmer and a freely elected parliament to meet at York. This very year some new laws irritated many classes. The gentry had found in the legal devices of trusts, or ' uses ', an excellent way of bequeathing land and evading taxation; Cromwell had long tried to induce the Commons to stop it, but only this year succeeded in the Statute of Uses. Other sweeping Acts transferred the jurisdiction of the few surviving palatine courts, Durham and Hexham for instance, to the Crown, and made life uncomfortable for the criminals who filled the famous sanctuaries at Ripon or Beverley. New regulations against fraud in their industry brought out Bradford and Wakefield clothiers to join the peasants. A sharp rise of prices and rents unsettled every rank. There were wild cries of ' thousands for a Percy ', and threats they would bring back the loot of Cheapside. Religion, which was sometimes the mask, might be also the cement of these discontents, inflamed as it was by compulsory preaching of the royal supremacy, by evicted monks, and all that north-country political piety which still brought offerings to the shrines of Thomas of Lancaster and archbishop Scrope. Sometimes it was the pure motive, as in Lancashire, whence probably came the peasants' song :

> *Christ crucified,*
> *For Thy Wounds wide,*
> *Us commons guide ;*
> *Through Goddes grace*
> *For to purchase*
> *Old wealth and peace.*

But this conservative revolt never breathed disloyalty. Its hatred concentrated on Cromwell, whom the Yorkshiremen called Haman, and its typical leader was D'Arcy, veteran servant of the Crown, whose motto was, ' one God, one faith, one King '.

The Lincolnshire rising was all over in a fortnight, broken by the gentry's loyal hesitation, and by the King's blend of reproach and threats. How dare the commons of one shire, ' and that one of the most brute and beastly of the whole realm ', dictate the choice of his councillors ? Let them keep their allegiance, which God ordered, to a prince who had spent himself thirty years in their governance : ' Sirs, shame not your native country of England '.

But Yorkshire was of harder metal, and found a leader of men in Robert Aske, a lawyer of the East Riding, with the power both to inspire and to restrain masses of illiterate peasants. By the end of October his forces entered York, each wapentake marching under their church cross ; Hull and the royal castle of Pontefract surrendered ; the Kendal men entered Lancaster. He had now 40,000 under arms, not only from all Yorkshire, but the Bishopric men under St. Cuthbert's white and crimson flag and wearing badges of the Sacred Wounds, and with riders from the dales that lead to the Lakes. The archbishop was a more or less willing confederate ; Northumberland's brother Thomas Percy was out, with half the peers of the north and more than half the squires. Aske was strong enough to force a truce on Norfolk's army, to hold back the extremists who wanted civil war, and to brush aside Henry's evasive answers.

In December the Pilgrims drew up their full programme. It asked destruction of the books of Wyclif, Luther, and Tyndale ; with a part-restoration of the monks and of sanctuary, and of the Pope's purely spiritual supremacy. It asked the King to legitimize Princess Mary, to repeal the statutes of Uses and Treason, to dismiss Cromwell, to check the encroachment of Council on the common law, to stop enclosures, and to hold a Parliament in the north, with seats for new boroughs like Beverley or Kendal. Ordered to play for time, Norfolk promised a full pardon and a Parliament, and the Pilgrims melted away ; while Aske went to London to plead with the King, and to be persuaded by that master of deceit that he would keep his word.

But the wild north was too strong for the moderate idealism of Aske. The King's game was not difficult; to provoke resistance by his military preparation, and to drive a wedge between the rebels. He used the gentry against Aske, this ' pedlar in the law ', while the peasants had always feared betrayal; ' Commons, keep well your harness, trust no gentlemen ', ran a bill fixed on Leeds church. Encouraged by some of the clergy, a few squires and yeomen took up arms again in 1537 and, though Aske and D'Arcy did their best to stop them, the King had the opportunity to repudiate his promises. Martial law sent seventy-four persons to death at Carlisle; with those condemned by packed juries elsewhere, the total rose to nearly two hundred. Norfolk could not satisfy the King's call for blood, his demand that monks should be ' tied up ', or his anger even against women who, under cover of night, cut down their men's hanging bodies. The air of London, Lincoln, and York was poisoned by the heads and quarters of the leaders, Aske, D'Arcy, Constable, Percy, the abbot of Jervaulx and a former abbot of Fountains, together with the abbot of Barlings and another thirty of the Lincoln men. So fell the Catholic revolt; though not without D'Arcy's outburst to Cromwell, ' yet shall there one head remain that shall strike off thy head '.

There were two direct aftermaths. The first was the final constitution of the Council of the North, freed now from relics of a prince's household or the influence of local magnates, and administered by paid officials, with powers as executive and supreme court over five counties, overriding all franchises. A contributory step was that, under pressure, the Earl of Northumberland had made the Crown his heir, while the archbishop of York surrendered his liberties of Ripon, Beverley, and Hexhamshire. A second result was the taking of vengeance, long-threatened, on the Yorkists; who had for years dabbled with the Imperial ambassador, whose power might again be dangerous now that France and the Empire were at peace, but whose fate was sealed by Cardinal Pole's effort to combine Catholic Europe. Indiscreet words, their known Catholic sympathies, their power in the west country were enough to condemn them though no treason was proved. Montagu, eldest of the Poles and Clarence's grandson, the Courtenay marquis of Exeter, and Edward Neville of the Abergavenny line, were executed. The Poles' aged mother, Lady Salisbury, was attainted, and in 1541, when a new plot disturbed Yorkshire, was beheaded without trial, running round the scaffold to escape the axe.

And the Supreme Head continued to flourish. Though his illegitimate son Richmond died in 1537, Jane Seymour gave him a true heir in the future Edward VI, whose birth, however, killed his mother; now, Latimer exulted, God's Word was safe, ' verily, He hath shown Himself the God of England, or rather an English God '. Steadily master and man pressed on at their work of unifying the commonwealth, which the Reformation made terribly urgent. They must incorporate all Britain in the same law and the same Parliament. Not content with destruction of the old feudal franchises, Henry continually added members to Parliament; from the garrison towns Berwick and Calais, from his own Palatine of Cheshire, and eight more members from Lancashire. A great statute annexed Wales to England, merged the surviving Marcher lordships in old or new shires, made the common law, justices of the peace, and the English tongue supreme, and added twenty-four Welsh members to the Commons. The Council of the Marches, tested and made terrible by a hanging judge, bishop Rowland Lee, was now regularized by Act of Parliament.

A policy of union, easy in Wales, which Henry boldly claimed ' is and ever hath been ' part of his Imperial Crown, was more difficult in Ireland. But Reformation forced on a new handling of the problem so long neglected, and which Henry had postponed to European wars. In 1534 the FitzGeralds headed a rebellion inspired by Catholic faith and Spanish advice; overrunning the whole country except Dublin, whose archbishop, however, was murdered. Painfully and drastically the Lord-deputy Leonard Grey and the royal artillery restored a certain area to law and order, and the Earl of Kildare with five of his uncles died at Tyburn in the same year as Aske suffered at York. Henry took the title ' King of Ireland and Head of the Irish Church ' and suppressed the monasteries, meaning also to enforce English land tenure and the English language. But the Cromwellian policy of frightfulness, which was very costly, was modified on his fall: moreover, Grey was connected with the Kildares by marriage, became immersed in Irish faction, and, like Cromwell, perished for his failure on the scaffold. As the reign ended, Henry tried a measure of conciliation, encouraging the Irish chieftains to take peerages and bribing them with new title-deeds for their land. Whether such union could survive his war against Irish Catholicism was for the future to decide.

So far had widened the circles first set up by Henry's divorce, and it was impossible to stand still, when religious upheaval had brought out all sorts of discontents. Cromwell's ministry had become a sheer terror, the slightest word spoken in an ale-house or a shop at Calais reaching his ear. Merciless execution crushed the least movement; fourteen died at one blow in Somerset for a corn riot, another dozen in Norfolk for criticism of the King's tyranny. Reformers declaimed the Bible in their parish churches, there were incessant brawls over images or processions, and since religion had driven a sword through Christendom, England might have to adopt a Protestant foreign policy in self-defence. Whenever the Empire and France drew together, English envoys approached the Lutheran princes, and about 1540 Henry's isolation in Europe was at its worst. His nephew James V of Scotland defiantly married the French princess Mary of Guise, the Emperor passed through Paris on his way to attack rebels in Flanders, and the Catholic invasion seemed at hand. Cromwell strove to sharpen the issues to the King, pointing out the difference between ' Evangelics ' and ' Papists ', for in the faction fight of the Council everything was at stake, — his own life, the future of the Church, and foreign policy.

Henry was the balance on which all turned. Not for a moment did he cease to destroy everything which could bind England to Rome. He sent to the bonfire the most sacred relics, the figure of Our Lady of Walsingham, the Holy Blood of Hailes, and the jewelled shrine of St. Thomas à Becket. He executed four abbots within sight of their famous houses, Woburn, Colchester, Reading, and Glastonbury. On the spoils of the monks he raised up national defence, building Hurst Castle with the ruined stones of Beaulieu Abbey, while in every village a broken shrine, or lands high-rented by a new farmer, brought home the violence of Reformation. Yet nothing turned the King from his Catholic faith. The Germans found he would not yield on the Mass or clerical marriage, and while he executed abbots he argued in person with heretics who denied the real presence ; for in his self-chosen creed the fixed point was the sacrament, ' yonder is the Master of us all, author of truth '. He would keep the faith which might yet regain the Imperial alliance and which, as the northern rising had shown, was still the popular faith of England. And a supplement to the Ten Articles (the ' Bishops' Book ') indicated a certain Catholic reaction.

The memorable session of 1539 showed the two facets of his policy — his astonishing hold over Parliament and the struggle in his Council. Cromwell and Gardiner, the heads of the two factions, each influenced the elections, and at Cromwell's insistence Henry began negotiation for a marriage with Anne, sister of the Duke of Cleves, who was allied with Lutherans against the Empire. But he cut short the angry discussions proceeding among his bishops, and in person recommended to Parliament the severe Catholic scheme known as the Six Articles. This ' Act abolishing diversity of opinions ' affirmed transubstantiation, attacks on which were to be punished at the stake, denied the Protestant claim for communion in both kinds, reaffirmed celibacy and vows of chastity, private Masses, and confession. The Commons' agreement with the King in religion was as genuine as their hatred of Cromwell. They passed an Act of Proclamations giving to royal proclamations the force of statutes, and in particular full power to define heresy, but after long debate defied Cromwell by elaborately safeguarding the rights of property at common law. Though the Six Articles were unquestionably popular — London juries alone accusing some five hundred heretics — the dismay in Protestant Germany and among English reformers was intense. Yet, in the face of an apparent Imperial-French alliance, Henry unwillingly completed his marriage with Anne of Cleves.

That marriage took place in January 1540; in July he dissolved it, and executed Cromwell. For not only to his indignation did he find himself married ' to this Flanders mare ', a plain dull lady who knew nothing of languages, cards, or music, but her brother Duke William, far from being an asset, was threatened by the Emperor and called for help. And even more : the menacing cordiality between the Emperor and France was breaking down on their old feuds regarding Milan and the Netherlands. With Henry in this mood it was easy for Cromwell's enemies, the base Norfolk and the ambitious, high-minded Gardiner, to represent his policy as a national danger and his Lutheran sympathies as heresy, and to produce in Norfolk's beautiful niece Catherine Howard a young and attractive candidate for the King's consolation. All the old aristocracy, of whom Cromwell had killed so many were on their side. So Parliament and Convocation entreated the King to put away Anne and re-marry ; an Act of Attainder put an end to Cromwell, flanked on one side by the execution of six friars who had worked for his Lutheran alliance and, on the other, by Romanists who denied the royal supremacy ; gilded, too, by the Statute of Wills, which pleased the country gentlemen by restoring the freedom to bequeath their land, which his Statute of Uses had taken away.

Nothing ever made Henry more popular than Cromwell's fall, and for the rest of his life he stood by this Catholic-conservative policy and returned to an alliance with the Empire. Hooper, the future Protestant martyr, grieved that the King had ' destroyed the Pope but not Popery ' and, if there was little persecution, it was mainly because the mass of the people preferred Catholic observance. Another declaration of doctrine (the King's Book) in 1543 finally insisted on transubstantiation. True, his marriage with Catherine Howard swiftly collapsed in the ignominious discovery that she had been immoral before marriage, and probably unfaithful afterwards, but her instant execution did not seriously affect policy, nor did her replacement by the Protestant-inclined, shrewd, and gentle Catherine Parr.

Yet the reign ended in disunion and discontent. Despotism reached its climax, hardly any prominent politician was not at some moment in the Tower, and the more so because Henry's health was breaking and those near the throne were manœuvring against the accession of a King under age. The practice of privately questioning prisoners, often under torture, became almost invariable. London aldermen were imprisoned, or sent on war service, for opposing forced loans. An immense rise of prices afflicted all classes, partly due to some bad harvests, but much more to an evil financial policy. Armaments against invasion and the war of 1543-6 speeded up the sale of monastic lands, and brought about another dissolution of hospitals and chantries. The last seven years of Henry's reign raised half as much again in direct taxation as his first thirty, not to mention heavy loans which were often not repaid. Government borrowed Antwerp money at the ruinous rate of 12 per cent and entered on a vicious debasement of the currency, not only lowering the standard of gold coins, but making the silver two-parts alloy; so making half a million profit, but at the price of decreasing the real yield of taxation and leaving the Treasury empty.

The war which caused this ruin suggested not only that Henry's egoism was approaching madness, but that his idea of a royal Catholicism was a dream. He seized the opportunity of renewed war between France and the Empire to intervene in Scotland, since James V had thrown off the Anglophil Angus clan and his minister Cardinal Beaton was a fiery Papalist. The Scots sheltered English refugees, rejecting Henry's advice to seize the monasteries and his demand that they should dissolve their French alliance. Once he toyed with an idea of kidnapping his nephew, and in 1542 the English raids grew into a war. His envoy Wharton, the Warden of the Western March, routed a much larger Scottish army at Solway Moss; in December James V died broken-hearted, leaving a widow of great courage and firm Catholic views in Mary of Guise, and a daughter a week old, who was to be Mary Queen of Scots.

Henry's claims at once advanced from suzerainty to full sovereignty; his agents ordered the Regent Arran to allow the use of the Bible in the Scots tongue, and in May 1543 extracted a treaty which provided for a marriage between the infant Mary and his son Edward, and her residence in England after her tenth year. This violence drove Scottish national-ism into the arms of Beaton, whose party soon repudiated the treaty, and whose triumph, with its savage punishment of heretics, did still more — in linking Henry to a Scottish interest bound together by Protestantism, in whose ranks John Knox was already a recruit. What the sword could do to force on this alliance, Henry did. Hertford, his Seymour brother-in-law, and the rising hope of his Protestant coun-cillors, burned Edinburgh, and in 1545, after one English army had been ambushed, ravaged the Border shires, burning great abbeys like Kelso and Melrose. Lennox, Arran's chief rival for the Regency, was wedded to Henry's niece Margaret, the daughter of Angus, and in 1546, after long encouragement from England, Beaton's enemies murdered him in his own castle of St. Andrews. Yet Henry died still at war with Scotland, whose independence defied his policy of British union and moderate Catholicism. Ireland, too, was to illustrate that such a policy must fail, for the new Jesuit Order had already planned the missions which were to bind Irish nationality to Catholic Europe.

Even the alliance with the Empire, which Henry used to restrain France while he dealt with Scotland, demonstrated that if he lived he would be compelled to make a choice. Though his campaign of 1544 won him Boulogne, the Empire made a separate peace and, though he defeated a French attack on the Isle of Wight, imminent bankruptcy drove him to make terms, leaving Boulogne in his hands but to be redeemed by, the French within eight years. His ally's desertion and the meeting of the Council of Trent left him once more a religious outlaw, and again he opened contact with the Lutherans of Germany.

This whirl of faiths and policies made the religious history of his last years a turmoil. Though Cranmer's influence with Henry was not shaken, he had to put away his German Lutheran wife, and his mind quivered like a needle to every breeze of German and Swiss theology; privately he disbelieved in transubstantiation, and was composing drafts of what was to be the prayer-book of Edward VI. Meantime the Catholic group led by Gardiner ceaselessly tripped him up, his own chapter and the Kent gentry informed against him, and a storm over the use of the Bible showed that yet another of Henry's weapons against Rome was slipping out of his hands.

Cromwell's Injunctions had taken over control of the printing of the Bible, independently begun by Tyndale. Yet the version finally adopted in Matthew's Bible of 1538, and the Great Bible in the next year, was two-thirds based on Tyndale's text, and in a few years its teaching had seized the people, — it was found in the hands of shepherds and artisans and their wives, it began to replace *Guy of Warwick* and old romances as the popular reading, democratic reformers read it in loud tones to disturb church services. Inch by inch the law had cut away the old observances of images and pilgrimages, lights and beads, until a great outburst of irreverence, parodies of the Mass, and scurrilous ballads, infuriated Catholic feeling. Gardiner and his friends vainly endeavoured to get a more Catholic version of the Bible, and though an Act of 1543 forbade women, yeomen, and artisans to read it, it allowed all to read the primer and psalms in English. This Englishing of religion steadily increased, until in 1545 Cranmer's glorious litany was first sung in St. Paul's.

Though burning for heresy went on, Protestant feeling against the Six Articles was clear in the Parliament of that year, to whom Henry made his last and most magnificent speech. Charity, he said, had never been so cold; ' one calleth the other heretic and Anabaptist, and he calleth him again Papist, hypocrite, and Pharisee '. If the clergy were in part to blame, the laity were even more, who abused Scripture to make it ' a railing and a taunting-stock against priests ', so that ' that most precious jewel, the Word of God, is disputed, rhymed, sung, and jangled in every ale-house '.

Next year these hatreds reached their climax, and though the Protestant use of the press was more violent, the Catholics got in their blow first. They examined some of the best-known reformers, imprisoned Latimer, and set up a search for Protestant books; seven persons were burned, among them a Lincolnshire lady, Anne Askew, who, by her own account, was tortured on the rack by the Chancellor and Attorney-general in person. Heresy was found in the household and Chapel Royal, and it was hoped to find information even against the Queen.

So passed the summer of 1546, but when Hertford and Dudley, his two best men of action, came back from the wars, Henry swung heavily to the other camp. He would not abandon Cranmer, or Catherine Parr, or Hertford, who would stand by his son and heir; and the poet Earl of Surrey, violent in riotous action, foolish in talk of his royal blood and insolent to the upstart Seymours, gave ground for a Protestant cry that the Howards meant to seize the regency. John Dudley, hero of the naval war, was on the Protestant side, and there was a rush of councillors, even including Gardiner's client Paget, towards the rising sun. In December the Tower closed on both Surrey and his father Norfolk. On the 30th the King completed a redrafting of his will, leaving the succession after Edward to Mary and Elizabeth, making the marriage of each subject to the consent of the Council named in the will, and after them to the daughters of his younger sister Mary, so cutting out of the inheritance the Catholic Scottish line. He assigned leading Protestants as Edward's tutors, and the Council to execute his will had a clear Protestant majority, while Gardiner was excluded. On the 19th January 1547 Surrey was beheaded and on the 27th the royal commissioners attainted Norfolk, who was to die next day; while the King, decisive to the last, discussed the partition of their lands. But in the small hours of the 28th, holding Cranmer's hand, Henry VIII died.

So great is the turmoil of his reign that it is difficult calmly to review its achievement. What he left to be amended or undone will appear later: a debased coinage, a new poverty, religious faction, Scotland embittered, Ireland unsolved. The traditional freedom of England was so strong that it might survive the strength of Henry's new State, in which Councils and Chancery had encroached on the common law, and in which Cromwell had talked of *lèse-majesté*, and the Church of the divine right of Kings. At any rate Henry, who could never abide his councillors speaking in whispers, had shouted his achievement aloud. He had destroyed the mediaeval Church and reconstructed society through incessant use of Parliament, whose discussions he had encouraged, and which had trusted him to change the faith, to plan the succession, or repeal tariffs, as he pleased. Printed Acts of Parliament were now on sale even in village shops, and it was by statute that he regulated his instruments of government: the Augmentations Court, the Court of Wards to deal with his feudal dues, the Council of Wales, or the Admiralty.

He was, indeed, a real ruler, whose own pen redrafted despatches and remodelled religious creeds, and who continually increased the efficiency of government. His arrangements decided a separation between the political Privy Council and the judicial council in Star Chamber. His statute of precedence determined the high position of the King's secretary, to whom he gave a second colleague. His temporary commissions created the later office of Lord-lieutenant, his statutes provided for the *custos rotulorum* with his servant the clerk of the peace, the poor laws and the civil parish, and the first civil law of marriage and probate. Neither his early wars nor his revolutions, however, allowed of continuous social policy. Yet the perpetual watchfulness of his councillors and statutes continued to transfer powers to the State; by fixing prices and wages, by Acts against enclosure, and by a close eye on local elections. He chartered merchants to Spain and protected them against the Inquisition, he would encourage particular industries like hemp and flax, and consolidated his father's Navigation Act.

If he left the country torn in ideas, he left it armed with many elements of national strength. From the first he showed an ardent interest in the sea and in artillery, by combining which he created sea-power. For his *Great Harry* was the prototype of a new battleship : loaded with cannon, not now on ' castles ' at bow and stern, but frowning through port-holes in the hull, discharging the broadside which, from Drake to Nelson, made gunnery the secret of victory. At his death the Navy had fifty-three ships carrying over two thousand guns, while by constant experiment he and his experts like William Hawkins of Plymouth were making vessels of modern design : flushdecked, longer in proportion to beam, and so faster than the mediaeval ship, while the galley type that carried light guns was now used only as auxiliary. To his father's creation of Portsmouth he added two more royal dockyards, at Deptford and Woolwich. He founded the Trinity House for the organization of pilots, and the Navy Board, true origin of the modern Admiralty. Much money was spent on batteries at Portsmouth, block-houses and fortifications at Deal. His statutes protected every means of defence, forbidding the export of bow-staves or the monasteries' bells out of which cannon could be cast, or authorizing the use of hand-guns as well as bows at the village butts. When the test of French invasion came in 1545, Dudley faced them under the cover of heavy artillery, by land and sea, and 100,000 men were under arms.

So Henry VIII's body was buried in St. George's Chapel, where Gardiner preached on the text, ' Blessed are the dead who die in the Lord '.

CONTEMPORARY DATES

1527 The sack of Rome.
Castiglione's *Il Cortegiano*.

1528 Death of Albrecht Dürer.

1529 Treaties of Barcelona and Cambrai.

1530 The Confession of Augsburg.
Knights Hospitallers settled in Malta.

1531 Zwingli killed at Kappel.
Negroes imported from Guinea to America.

1532 Pizarro invades Peru.
Rabelais' *Pantagruel*, Bk. I.

1533-84 Ivan the Terrible rules Russia.
Death of Ariosto.
Catharine de Medici married to Francis I's son Henry.

1534 Foundation of the Jesuit Order.
Anabaptists in power at Munster.

1535-49 Pope Paul III (Farnese).
Death of the last Sforza duke of Milan.
Final overthrow of the Hanseatic League by the Danes.

1536 Death of Erasmus.
Calvin appears at Geneva.

1539 The Spaniards take Cuba and invade Florida.

1541 Cardinal Contarini's negotiations for religious compromise
fail.
The Turks take Buda-Pesth.

1542 Francis Xavier begins mission work in the Far East.
Papal Inquisition organized by Caraffa.

1543 Cartier's fourth voyage to Canada.
Death of Copernicus.

1544 Discovery of the mines of Potosi.
Foundation of University of Konigsberg.

1545 Humayun enters Kandahar.
Paré's writing on surgery.

1546 Death of Luther.
Council of Trent, first session.
Royal foundations of Trinity College, Cambridge, and
Christ Church, Oxford.

1547 Birth of Cervantes.
Charles V, allied with Maurice of Saxony, wins battle of
Muhlberg.
-1559. Reign of Henry II in France.

CHAPTER III

ANARCHY, 1547–1558

1. EDWARD VI

REFORMATION was rising to its climax. Charles V had taken prisoner the Lutheran leaders, but the Spanish troops who dragooned Germany were raising the Princes' War, which was to undo most of his life's work. His Inquisition in the Netherlands, Seville, and the Indies was planting a seed still more bloody and enduring. Francis I of France having followed Henry VIII to the grave within two months, Henry II succeeded, who had none of his licentious tolerance and drew the sword against the Huguenots. The Council of Trent in its first sessions of 1546–50, looking away from the ideas of compromise which had inspired many at Rome, began the redefinition of Catholic doctrine, in which it found its mightiest support in the Society of Jesus, lately founded by Ignatius Loyola, and now beginning to recapture the souls Rome had lost by winning the ear of rulers and the heart of the young. Luther was just dead, his successor Melanchthon had not his elemental force, and the Protestant fire burned more radiantly in the Swiss and the South Germans, who had taken from Zwingli their learning, their democratic basis, and insistence on the primitive Church. For those ends they had lately found a leader of genius in the Frenchman John Calvin—who since 1541 had made Geneva his headquarters—besides others of weight in Bucer of Strasbourg and Bullinger of Zürich. Blood had flowed for religion in Italy too, in Poland and all the Middle East, almost invariably over the same controversy of the body and blood of Christ.

This conflict struck England fully for the first time when Henry VIII left his throne to a child of nine. Within a few weeks Edward VI's Council repudiated the balance by which Henry had tried to govern even from his grave. They appointed Hertford (henceforth duke of Somerset) as Protector without restriction, turned out the leading Catholics, and in their first Parliament repealed the Act which allowed the King, on coming of age, to revoke statutes passed during his minority.

Somerset had served the dynasty well since his sister Jane Seymour had married the King. He was an extreme blend of high idealism and sharp practice. Though he had taken a full share of monastic spoil —even trying to destroy Westminster Abbey, and built his palace of Somerset House out of ruined churches—for all that he had genuine flashes of religion, with a pity for humanity which raised him above the vultures of Reformation. He believed that the Scottish strife might be turned into an union of hearts as well as of governments, ' having the sea for a wall, mutual love for garrison and God for defence ' under a British Emperor ; he believed also that a religious truce might bring tolerance, and championed the cause of the peasants desolated by enclosure. His chief agent in this last, John Hales, who had already once been a religious exile and was to be so again, was a democrat who assured him an age of gold had succeeded to an age of iron ; it says something, too, for the Protector's character that he first brought into politics William Cecil and Thomas Smith, Protestants of the Cambridge school, who were to be famous Elizabethan ministers. But Paget, ablest of his advisers, who put peace of the State above religion, very early warned him where his optimism and delight in popularity would lead : ' Liberty, liberty, your opinion to be good to the poor, the opinion of such as saith to your grace there was never man that had the heart of the poor as you have '.

From the non-execution of the law, and the preaching of Cranmer's following, it was clear that the government were on a new tack ; London congregations were taking down images, whitewashing walls, and selling vestments to City tailors, while at Portsmouth others were breaking down altars, which their diocesan Gardiner called the act of ' hogs and Lollards '. Homilies which were published simply by royal authority ignored the sacrament, and encouraged the destruction of paintings and painted windows.

Parliament met in the autumn with London in a frenzy, apprentices mobbing the clergy and jeering at the Host as ' Jack-in-the-box ', and when the Protector came home in triumph from victory over the Scots at Pinkie, the government moved a long step forward. The money for his campaign was found in a new Chantries Act, confiscating not only those foundations to the number of some two thousand, but the property of all gilds so far as they were dedicated to ' superstition ', — threatening a great loss to education and charity, and rousing a strong opposition in the Commons. For the rest of Somerset's measures, however, there was much support. One Act ordered the administration of the sacrament, to all who so desired, in both kinds. Another, sweeping away the shadow of election, arranged the appointment of bishops by letters patent. One vast statute repealed all Henry's additions to the treason law, except those guarding the succession and the supremacy, adding that two witnesses must support any charge ; swept away also the Six Articles, all existing heresy laws, and all restrictions on reading the Bible, together with the Act of Proclamations. But how long would the calm weather last which this statute said justified ' a lighter garment ' ?

Action outside Parliament during 1548 showed how the government meant this freedom to be used. The royal chaplains set an example in reading their services entirely in English. A proclamation set forth an order for the sacrament, which added to the Mass an English communion for the laity. Meantime royal visitors and commissioners ordered the destruction of images, and set out to value chantry property.. Norfolk was still in the Tower and was now joined by Gardiner, who resisted Cranmer's injunctions as unlawful without statute, and would not be silent on the real presence.

In one of his general pardons Henry VIII had excepted what seemed to him the unforgivable sins, — of heresy against the sacrament, Anabaptism, pacifism, and communism, — but now these and manifold others ruined what he had called his ' pacification '. These doctrines came mostly from abroad, for Europe was full of refugees in flight from the Emperor, and Cranmer hoped to assemble a rival council to that of Trent. Throughout 1548-9 reformers poured into England; the illustrious German Bucer, the Italians Ochino and Peter Martyr, the Pole Laski who set up his congregation in the Austin Friars, a French church at Canterbury, and Strasbourg weavers who were given what was left of Glastonbury. Bucer became professor of divinity at Cambridge, and Martyr at Oxford, while Englishmen who had fled from Henry VIII also returned, like Hooper from Zürich.

So opened a conflict which for a century was to convulse Church and State. It went deeper than a struggle between new and old property-owners, and deeper far than its superficial pretexts, vestments or images or bishops. Between mediaeval Catholicism and Puritanism there might be found half a dozen stopping-places, but the gulf between Catholic and Protestant was already fixed : already Somerset's laws spoke of salvation and God's elect, and already Brinklow, London mercer and pamphleteer, had left money for the godly who laboured ' in the vineyard of the Lord '. Justification by faith alone, which the new homilies taught, meant an individual religion, which must diminish the weight put by Catholics on sacraments and good works. It might end in Luther's teaching of the priesthood of every Christian man, which Gardiner warned Cranmer was the curse of Germany : it would certainly end, as Cranmer himself ended, in a Presbyterian scheme of discipline. As developed at Geneva by Calvin, it taught the predestined salvation of the elect, which would not be impaired even by a life of sin. Again, this ' justified ' Church found itself through the Word of God, with no intercepting tradition between man and his Creator. It laid stress, therefore, on the pulpit more than the altar, the congregation rather than the priest, making the ' common ' element essential to religion : ' what great holiness was this ? ' asked one who ended as an Elizabethan.

bishop, ' to have matins at midnight when folk were on sleep in their beds ? '

But to what lengths would this dependence on Scripture go, or who should interpret it ? It led Hooper to talk of vestments and ceremonies as ' Aaronic habits ' and ' altars of Baal '; Cranmer, on the contrary, declared that the argument ' whatsoever is not commended in the Scriptures is against the Scriptures ', would mean ' a subversion of order as well in religion as in common policy '.

And logically, as mediaeval religion had often proved, this conflict between Catholics and Bible Christians rose to a height over the sacrament. The mystery of transubstantiation, whereby the great sacrifice was repeated and the bread and wine became the very Body and Blood, was not the only point of controversy; for Ridley had converted Cranmer from his belief and it had few active supporters except Gardiner. Zwingli's teaching, which Bucer finally adopted, was clear enough; that the sacrament was not a sacrifice but commemoration, a sign whose worth depended on the communicant's worthiness, ' a testimony of grace ', as Hooper put it. Christ's presence was, therefore, not in the sacrament in any different sense, or to a greater extent, than in any other act of worship. Between this extreme and Catholicism there were ranged all the solutions of Luther, and the Swiss and German schools. Cranmer's language was so cloudy that he left many different impressions, but though he moved to the left, he and Ridley never repudiated the real presence in some spiritual sense; in his words, the sacrament was only a memory and a representation, yet ' Christ is eaten with the heart '. This strife embittered the country. Cheap tracts derided ' a vile cake to be made God and man '. Lutheran translations issued from presses in Billingsgate; when one of Somerset's favourite preachers attacked the real presence at Poole, a local merchant rose from his pew saying, ' come from him good people, he came from the devil and preacheth devilish doctrine '.

With such a gale blowing through his gentle receptive mind, and arguing that Henry VIII had been ' seduced ' to retain Popery, Cranmer and his circle early in 1549 produced the first prayer-book, compiled from many sources, Catholic and Protestant. Many of the Commons went to hear a great debate in the Lords, to hear the Catholics arguing that the bread was ' the same Body that was wounded with the spear ', while Ridley spoke merely of ' common bread before, it is made a divine influence '. Opposition in Parliament amended Cranmer's draft in a Catholic sense, eight bishops opposed the twelve who helped to carry the Act of Uniformity, and this first Edwardian settlement was only a truce. Though transubstantiation vanished, Catholics like Gardiner could find a real presence; the service, for ' holy communion commonly called the Mass ', still spoke of the altar, and ordered the use of alb and cope. If the service was more congregational, Cranmer's English retained some of the greatest beauty of Catholic devotion; and if it was compulsory on the clergy, as yet it included no Articles, nor did the Act compel laymen to attend service. Another statute allowed clerical marriage, and new injunctions finally suppressed all that Catholic England knew, the last light on the altar, the holy sepulchre, and the sacring bell. Royal commissioners visited the universities, gave them new statutes, encouraged the destruction of organs and windows, and left them in a turmoil; at Oxford scholars of Magdalen hacked the old service-books with axes, while the market-place smouldered with bonfires of Catholic theology. But simultaneously many causes were destroying Somerset's government.

His foreign policy was a failure. France, unwilling to pay his price of the Anglo-Scottish marriage in return for Boulogne, was determined to recapture it by her own effort, and in 1547 a French force took St. Andrews, where Beaton's murderers had taken refuge; carrying them off, John Knox included, to imprisonment or labour in the galleys. That autumn Somerset invaded Scotland and won an overwhelming victory at Pinkie on the Esk, a battle which the Scots threw away by abandoning a strong defensive position. Dumfries and the chief Border shires fell to the English, who attempted to win Scottish democracy with Bibles and the aristocracy with bribes. But in August 1548 the young Queen Mary was sent to France to be betrothed to the Dauphin, while French troops steadily set about recapturing all that the English held in Scotland.

Internal trouble in England encouraged the French in this cautious advance to open war. The first exposure of Somerset's weakness was the conspiracy of his brother, Thomas Seymour. His marriage to the widowed Catherine Parr made him the Protector's rival, and he allied himself with those next in the succession after Henry's children, hoping to consolidate power by marrying Jane Grey to the King. He collected arms, used his position as admiral to go half-shares with the pirates of the Bristol Channel, and finally, when his wife died, aspired to marry Princess Elizabeth. Whether his crimes constituted treason or not, his execution in March 1549 was a heavy blow which the Protector's enemies were glad to inflict.

Meanwhile there were signs of a Catholic reaction: even in the previous year there had been Cornish riots against the loss of their church ornaments, and some thirty executions. The rising of June 1549 was much more formidable; it began spontaneously in Devon and Cornish villages against the prayer-book, winning support from some men of old family and the local mayors, and 10,000 rebels laid siege to Exeter. They demanded restoration of the Mass, the Six Articles, and of two abbeys in each shire, the Cornishmen also asking for the Latin service as they knew not English. It was not till August that, with artillery and foreign mercenaries, Russell and Herbert and Grey de Wilton forced their way, after severe fighting, into Exeter. Another belt of Catholic country rose round Oxford, where priests' bodies hanging from their church steeples showed the fears of the government.

Yet the real significance of the year lay not so much in this effort of the old faith as in the violence of Protestant democracy, which had for twenty years terrified Luther and German princes. It was the worst time of suffering for over two hundred years, for the English, like the Germans, were caught up in an economic revolution : silver from America, international combines, speculation on the Antwerp bourse, were all making the final destruction of the mediaeval plan. Prices, having risen steadily since Henry VIII began to debase the coinage, were soaring still ; as compared with 1530, the price level of 1580 was to rise over 200 per cent, and in Edward's reign the process was not half complete. The money system showed every feature which mediaeval men had detested ; landlords were evicting leaseholders by rack rents and crippled copyholders by raising fines, or nibbling at their rights on the commons, while deer from their new-enclosed parks broke into the farmers' corn. London merchants were buying up alleys and driving a ribbon development into the suburbs ; clothiers were crushing out small weavers, paying wages in truck and ' rotten cloth and stinking fish ', discharging journeymen and taking cheap apprentice labour. Charity had fallen away with the gilds ; there had even been embezzlement of the tiny village endowments bequeathed for the poor. The Chantries Act had destroyed many schools ; the cost of living was emptying Oxford and Cambridge of poorer students.

Sermons and ballads and pamphlets poured out from the reformers, disillusioned with reformation. Covetousness, preached Lever before the Council, had brought ' a common wealth into a common misery ' ; ' your hands are full of blood '. Where now, wrote a bishop to the King, ' were the ancient and godly yeomanry of England ? ' ' Expelled ', said Latimer the yeoman's son in his famous sermons, ' for a shepherd and his dog ' ; ' to lie naked ', cried a third, ' in the miry streets ' of London.

The ' commonwealth men ', as conservatives called them, exclaimed against the new lords who had exchanged their wooden cups for silver-plate, against those who were monopolizing the land which Christ had meant for all, against the ' jolly crackers and braggers ' who were winning parliamentary seats. So the radical Protestants made a protest for the old Catholic order :

> *An Hell without order*
> *I may it well call,*
> *When every man is for himself*
> *And no man for all.*

With his own tincture of pride and religion, Somerset took the side of the ' commonwealth ' against those whom he called ' lords of the dung hill ', and strenuously reopened Wolsey's attack on enclosure. His proclamations denouncing the ' insatiable greediness ' which caused this misery, a new tax on sheep, a commission of enquiry, extreme leniency to the western rebels, and setting up a private court in his palace to hear poor men's causes, all these infuriated the covetous, the legal-minded, and the conservative. Parliament continuously resisted him. It rejected bills designed to educate the poor, to stop evictions, to put down parks, and to punish ' regrating ' of food. Country gentlemen obstructed the enclosure commissioners, making it impossible for juries to convict. And while they complained that they dare not touch a peasant, and while Paget upbraided Somerset's ' spiced conscience ' or bade him quarter German troops on the Devonshire towns to ' make them sweat ', radicals on the other side satirized the new ' thirteenth commandment ' of the infallibility of Parliament, while Latimer desperately cried he might ' preach till his tongue be worn to the stump ', for the good laws were not carried out.

Anti-enclosure riots, ascribed by conservatives to government's veiled encouragement, culminated in the Norfolk rising of June 1549. Its leader, Robert Kett, a rich tanner, at first kept in fair order the 20,000 peasants who collected at Mousehold Hill outside Norwich, but in time they broke into the open country burning and pillaging, and tried to seize Yarmouth. Their programme asked reduced rents, an end of bondage, since Christ had died to make men free, and of enclosure and game laws. They asked also a preaching resident clergy who could teach the catechism and, while they kept captured squires in chains, they held a daily service under their oak of reformation. They had their sympathizers even in the Norwich corporation, yet any mediation was difficult with Kett, who demanded powers to enforce the good laws ' hidden from your poor Commons '. So Church and State drew together against those who had denounced ' the gentlemen '. One body of Italians was routed, but in August Warwick arrived with German mercenaries and Welsh gunners, and in hand-to-hand fighting broke the rebels, some 3000 of whom fell in pitched battle, and another 300, including Kett, died on the gallows.

This victory for law and order was immediately followed by the fall of Somerset, all of whose policies had failed, and who in emergency had produced neither coherent command nor pay for the troops. Warwick, Russell, and other victors enlisted the support of Paget, the Protector's shrewdest adviser, of the Catholics whom he had ejected, and all those offended by his imperious temper. Nor did his printed appeals to the mob offset the solid citizens of London. The new men, satisfied with overthrowing his supremacy, soon got rid of their Catholic fellow-councillors, and as the Commons showed some sympathy for Somerset, early in 1550 they restored him to the Council.

Warwick was the son of that Dudley who had been executed for his financial services to Henry VII, and father of Robert Dudley earl of Leicester, Queen Elizabeth's favourite. Of this sinister family John Dudley was the worst and, though a man of action, ' the new Alcibiades ', as a reforming bishop called him, turned out the basest figure of a base age. Yet the Puritan Hooper saw in him a ' most faithful and intrepid soldier of Christ ', for he gave the decisive trend in which Somerset had failed.

Under his lead Council and Parliament set about repression. It was made treason to plot against a privy councillor, or plan any alteration in the law, or break down an enclosure, and a felony to agitate for lower rents. Somerset's law requiring two witnesses in a treason trial was repudiated, and a paid cavalry force was set up to police the shires. Sheer poverty decided the government to end the war by the ignominious peace of March 1550, which restored Boulogne and abandoned Scotland; only the renewal of war between France and the Empire saved even more humiliation.

Warwick had done with Somerset's religious moderation. The Church was to be made thoroughly Protestant and entirely servile, and when Gardiner, Bonner, and other Catholic bishops were deprived, their successors were brought to heel. A new bishop of Winchester exchanged its estates for a fixed stipend; when Hooper after much boggling at vestments accepted a bishopric, he parted with many lands; the see of Gloucester was suppressed and Durham ' refounded ', which meant substantial gifts to Warwick. In part compelled and in part willing, the new bishops proceeded with reformation. A new Ordinal polished off the minor orders, and barely distinguished bishops from the priesthood. In London, Ridley set up communion tables, an order which, in spite of riots in St. Paul's, was soon enforced throughout the country. In defiance of old promises, and to the detriment of good terms with the Emperor, the Council vainly tried to force Princess Mary to abandon her Mass.

Nothing could exceed the general misery and chaos. Cecil testifies that two-thirds of the magistrates and the squires were against the government. A gallows stood at the end of every vista; Norwich sullenly watched Kett's mouldering body swinging from the Castle, like a dead beast ' for winter's store '; there were still perpetual riots, a ' captain Redcap ' up in Middlesex, and enclosure troubles in Essex which deprived Londoners of their favourite cheese. Somerset had fixed the alloy in the silver coinage at one-half, Warwick raised it to two-thirds, and called the value of the shilling down to sixpence. Prices climbed upwards, poverty drove the peasants towards London, proclamations drove them back again to the unkindly land. And while angry disputations between deprived Catholics and embittered Protestants, with a literary war over the sacrament between Cranmer and Gardiner, unsettled belief, the condition of the Church beggared description. While a clothier had his looms in the ruins of Malmesbury Abbey and young London gentlemen held pigeon-shooting matches in St. Paul's churchyard, Bucer and Paget agreed that, while the old religion was nearly dead, no new faith had replaced it. While government allowed only its own licensed preachers and tried to silence stage plays, cheap Testaments poured out from the press, with anti-Catholic commentaries, and conventicles spread many acid heresies in the home counties. Radical divines deplored empty pulpits and jeering congregations, and the guilt of the laity who appointed bailiffs and grooms to their parish churches; robbers like Barabbas, cried the honest Puritan Gilpin, ' a gentleman thief such as rob nowadays in velvet coats '.

A fearful ignorance filled the void of religion. Children of sixteen did not know the Lord's Prayer, and when Hooper visited his diocese he found that half the priests could not repeat the Commandments. Though some of the royal preachers were saints, and later martyrs, neither principle nor character dignified the bishops. Hooper did not believe in episcopacy at all, some excited contempt by squalid marriages, and some by profiteering in leases. Nor would the government accept the reform of Church courts for which Cranmer asked.

It was for some feeble efforts to recapture moderate support and to make capital out of this discontent that Somerset was finally destroyed; he would have pardoned Gardiner and been lenient to Princess Mary, and meditated an appeal to the Londoners and a Parliament. New honours for the victors accompanied his arrest in October 1551, a dukedom of Northumberland for Warwick and of Suffolk for Dorset, an earldom of Pembroke for Herbert and a knighthood for Secretary Cecil. A packed commission sentenced him to death. But the new cavalry could not silence the London cries of ' God save him '; there were bonfires on the hope of his acquittal, and he was hurriedly executed on an early morning of January 1552.

Next day Parliament was allowed to meet after a two years' interval and promptly showed their sympathy for Somerset. Northumberland's circle was very narrow; of Henry VIII's statesmen, Rich's nerve had failed and Paget was now disgraced. Catholic and conservative noblemen of the north stood aloof; moderates like Cecil, though accepting Somerset's fall as inevitable, disliked violence. But Northumberland had one mighty asset in the young King who, though not yet fourteen, had all the Tudor intellect and more than their usual cold-bloodedness. Already he was beginning to draft bills for Parliament, and had ideas in his head of imposing a moral reformation on a country which he thought overrun by ' hell hounds '. Under whatever influence, he showed a rigid Puritanism, and his name was behind those who demanded a long move forward.

The main business of 1552 was this second religious settlement, whereby a second prayer-book eliminated all that Gardiner on one side, or Bucer on the other, had found Catholic in the first. It abolished prayers for the dead and reservation of the sacrament, and ordered a communion table to be set in the chancel or choir. A new Ordinal took away the vestments. Extremists inspired by Hooper, Laski, and Knox had taken to sitting at the sacrament; under whose pressure Council added the famous ' black rubric ', to emphasize that kneeling did not mean adoration of a sacrifice. The new book was annexed to a new Act of Uniformity, which for the first time punished laymen who attended any other service. Neither the book nor the forty-two Articles which followed were put before Convocation, and though the government would not publish Cranmer's revised Canon law, he was, in fact, now ready for a semi-Presbyterian church.

Meanwhile economic ruin stared the country in the face. The depreciated coinage drove the exchanges hard against us, the royal debt was a quarter of a million, soldiers were without wages. Northumberland was in earnest for economy, but dared not ask taxes, though the French were planning to take Calais, in effect ruled Scotland, and were intriguing in Ireland. So the government pulled down forts, sold ships, prospected for silver mines in Ireland, borrowed at Antwerp, and in a last rush swept away more chantry lands, together with church plate, bells, candlesticks, and even alms-boxes.

And political ruin threatened Northumberland. He had kept his group together and made his own fortune by lands, salaries, sale of livings and tithe, to the tune of half a million pounds; he himself held nearly all the Percy domains. But he had lost the Catholics, and there was a moral revolt among Protestants. Pressure from London citizens and especially from bishop Ridley, who told Cecil that Christ was lying in the streets of London ' hungry, naked, and cold ', induced the government to restore a morsel of their confiscations; to allow some re-endowment of St. Bartholomew's and St. Thomas' hospitals, to found Bridewell as a house of correction for the poor, and to charter some grammar schools on a diminished scale. Some kindlier amendments were made in the poor law, and taking of usury was prohibited. Early in 1553 bankruptcy compelled Northumberland to call another Parliament, which he tried, not very successfully, to pack. It gave him a subsidy, though accompanied with an audit aimed at corruption, and he broke out in a violent speech against the radical preachers.

It meant ruin, indeed, for Edward VI was too ill to ride from Whitehall to Westminster, and lay dying of consumption. Could Northumberland face Mary, the legal successor ? He dared not, and embarked, as rumour had long said he would, on a scheme to alter the succession. In defiance of Henry VIII's will and statutes defending that will, he persuaded the dying King in the name of religion to exclude his sister ; to settle the succession on the heirs-male of Lady Jane Grey, daughter of his tool Suffolk, whom he now married to his own son Guildford Dudley. Even that would not do, for Edward was dying too fast ; so the ' device ' was doctored to make Lady Jane herself the successor, then her male heir, and then her sister. In June the Council pledged themselves to stand by the ' device ', the judges were browbeaten by Edward and by Northumberland saying that he would ' fight any man in his shirt ', and a hundred and one peers, bishops including Cranmer, and officials including Cecil, signed the letters patent. Other marriages were made, to win over the Herberts, Cliffords, and Hastings. The Emperor was fighting the French for his life in Lorraine ; the French, who might fight for Mary Queen of Scots, would never do so for the Emperor's cousin Mary Tudor. The King died on the 6th of July ; Northumberland, concealing his death, ordered Mary to London, but she had been warned and fled to Norfolk.

In a fortnight all was over : in a roar of revolt from a people loyal to the blood royal, and miserable and oppressed. Even Protestants swore the good King had been poisoned, East Anglia came round Mary, Paget reappeared and, with Cecil, won over the moderate councillors. Midland risings cut off Northumberland on his way to East Anglia from his London base, and he was arrested at Cambridge. The prisons speedily received him and his sons, with Lady Jane Grey and Ridley, disgorging those held in duress so long—Norfolk, Gardiner, and Edward Courtenay. Bells and organs, set free again, and weeping crowds greeted the new Queen, and in August, after recanting his Protestant faith and admitting his false charges against Somerset, Northumberland ended his life under the axe. And his more cautious confederates, Russell, Pembroke, and the like, made their peace with the successor and were loaded with riches.

2. MARY

The pendulum in unhappy England swung hard over. Two personal decisions of the Catholic Queen finally confirmed English Protestantism : her Spanish marriage and her burning of heretics, which fused religion and nationality into one.

If her policy failed like Northumberland's, it was less from hatred of the cruelty, great though that hatred was, than from the temperament of the political majority. There were servile men like Rich, who had destroyed the Catholic Thomas More and who now was an active informer against Protestants in his county of Essex, but the general attitude was more creditable. Firm religious lines were not yet drawn in England, any more than in France or Germany, and obedience to the State was a stronger feeling than any dogma. The councillors of Henry VIII and Edward, — Russell, Pembroke, Arundel, and Shrewsbury, — served Mary loyally and went on to serve Elizabeth; Cecil, once Somerset's secretary and Elizabeth's in days to come, was employed occasionally, attended Mass, and quietly busied himself with his plantations and deer parks. Ten of Edward's bishops continued, so did some three-quarters of the parish clergy, of whom many more were ejected for being married than for religious scruple. In short, Mary's hope of a Catholic reaction was smothered in a politically minded society which was determined to keep all that Henry had won for the State and the Church's property for themselves.

Though nothing could be more fatal, nothing was more natural than Mary's leaning to Spain, the home both of her injured mother and of the Emperor, her only friend when Englishmen had forsaken her. But her marriage meant a split in her Council. That stout hot-tempered Englishman, Gardiner, wished her to marry Edward Courtenay and thought first of restoring Catholic order from the chaos he used to call ' Kett's government '; while his personal rival Paget agreed with the Emperor, and thought more of an English bulwark for the Netherlands against France than of Catholicism, advising Mary to be lenient and show herself ' bonne Anglaise '. And as Cardinal Pole sided with Gardiner, the Hapsburgs, therefore, did not let him reach England until the marriage was safely over. But the marriage also meant a defiance of Parliament's protest and paved the way for serious rebellion.

Though Londoners shouted ' liar ' and ' Papist ' at priests who revived the Mass, no one suffered during 1553 except Northumberland and his tools. Foreign congregations departed in peace, leading Protestants went abroad with connivance from the government, even Cranmer was not imprisoned until he wrote against the Mass. In October, Parliament annulled the divorce of the Queen's mother and the religious laws of Edward VI, thus bringing the country back to the state in which Henry had left it, and in which Gardiner's principles would have left it still. But then the unsuccessful pleadings of Parliament against the Queen's marriage and the open influence of the Imperial ambassador angered the country, and in January 1554 rebellion began. Breaking out precipitately because Courtenay betrayed it, it missed fire in the west, Suffolk vainly excited the Midlands with rumours of Spanish invasion, and only in Kent with the help of French money and arms did it come near success.

Sir Thomas Wyatt, the leader, was a ruffianly though valiant soldier; some of the London trained-bands deserted to him and, after

one failure from Southwark against London Bridge, he crossed the
river at Kingston; there was confused fighting round Charing Cross,
and the rebels' arrows rattled into the courtyards of Whitehall before
Wyatt was trapped at Temple Bar. The Queen was saved by her own
brave spirit and the loyalty of the Protestant nobles. Wyatt's defeat
brought death not on himself only, but on the innocent victim Lady
Jane Grey, her father Suffolk, and her husband Dudley. It brought
Princess Elizabeth to temporary imprisonment in the Tower; which
made her the hope of a party, for the Spaniards pressed for her execution,
while the rebels had hoped to marry her to Courtenay.

In the summer a good many Protestants' ears were nailed to the
pillory, while an Oxford assembly shouted down the prisoners Cranmer,
Latimer, and Ridley. Yet Catholicism struck on many rocks. The
Lords threw out bills to revive the heresy laws and the Six Articles,
mainly because they feared heresy charges against owners of church
property, while Paget and the Spaniards agreed that too much zeal
might endanger the marriage. The Commons proposed a bill to
safeguard those who held abbey lands, nor would anyone support
the scheme of the Queen and Gardiner to cut Elizabeth out of the
succession. Mary complained that days went in ' shouting at her
Council ', until the Spaniards advised her to dissolve a Parliament
which had jealously inspected every clause of the marriage terms.

On paper they were admirable. The child of Philip and Mary
would inherit Burgundy and the Netherlands as well as the English
realm, only Englishmen should hold office in England, while on Mary's
death Philip would lose all his rights. So with much jollity passed the
wedding at Winchester and the entry to London, and though Mary
had warned him to bring his own cook to guard against poison, Philip's
conscientious attempt to swallow English customs, even English beer,
and cartloads of Spanish gold for Mary's dower, spread a mantle over
the national displeasure.

A third Parliament was called for the winter of 1554–5 to complete
reconciliation with Rome. Mary's order to choose members of ' a
grave and Catholic sort ' was coupled with a pledge she meant no alteration of property, but the 40 per cent of old members returned, as indeed
all their proceedings, showed little submission. In November, equipped
with Papal leave to confirm the new landlords, Cardinal Pole returned
and absolved the realm from its schism. Parliament repealed Henry's
laws against Rome, but only under stringent safeguards to protect
holders of church land, and though they restored Papal jurisdiction
and church courts, they would not surrender impropriations or repeal
the laws against church fees. In other directions they were more
placable, passed a savage treason Act in part aimed at Protestant conventicles, and revived the mediaeval Acts against heresy.

Even so, Parliament turned a deaf ear to Philip's wishes for recognition as successor to the throne, and for co-operation in war against France. Englishmen were displeased to see a multitude of foreign guards and Spanish grandees who, they noted, even in their sport thought only of killing, and sneered at the Spanish galleys as ' mussel-shells '. They hated the stiff Spanish manners, and the translation of all business into Latin or Spanish for Philip's eye. Londoners read gladly ballads jeering at the King, and saw with fury Englishmen on the Fleet Street gallows, ' hanging all the day in the rain '. England, pamphlets repeated, would soon share the enslavement of Flanders or Naples.

It was not, however, by Spanish advice that the Queen embarked on persecution, within a month of reviving the heresy laws. Not on the Spaniards, for Philip left England in September 1555 and did not return except for a few months in 1557, and not on Gardiner, who burned no one in his diocese and died in November, but on Mary herself the responsibility must lie. Seventy were burned this year, and the rate was maintained until just on three hundred had died by the end of the reign; they were massed in the Protestant area, 238 suffering in the London diocese, East Anglia, Sussex, and Kent. They included women and boys, the aged and blind, many artisans, and the flower of the Protestant divines who had not fled abroad, but few, if any, of the political class. Hooper was burned in his old diocese at Gloucester; Ridley and Latimer in the town ditch at Oxford; and many more of the Edwardian preachers. Under cruel pressure Cranmer signed several recantations, which the government hoped would make other Protestants fall away, but when brought to the stake he repudiated them, putting first into the fire the hand which had signed. How English human nature would take these executions was the problem. Sometimes we read of crowds come to see a spectacle, with sellers of bags of cherries and drinks, and occasionally of brutality to the sufferers. Far more often there were infinite pity and anger, crowds echoing ' Amen ' to a dying prayer, bags of gunpowder brought in mercy to shorten their tribulation. These barbarities were a political blunder as well as a moral crime, and these weavers, apprentices, or widows, even more perhaps than the bishops, lighted a candle which, as old Latimer said to Ridley when they suffered, would never be put out.

Part of this persistent persecution was due to the violence of the Protestant exiles. Though not great in numbers, those who filled Strasbourg and Frankfurt, Zürich and Basel, were representative, active, and organized. Among them were five bishops, and an array of Elizabethan bishops-to-be in Jewel, Grindal, Horne, and Cox; Knox, who at Geneva in his *Blast of the Trumpet against the Monstrous Regiment of Women* denounced the Queen as Jezebel and predicted ' the day of vengeance is already appointed in the counsel of the eternal '; a few magnates like the Duchess of Suffolk; rich business men like Cecil's father-in-law, Cooke; and solid congregations of Essex weavers. There was Foxe, whose *Book of the Martyrs* was to blow the Protestant flame for a hundred years; and two future ministers of Elizabeth in Knollys and Walsingham. Their propaganda often preached armed resistance and a radical philosophy, while their fierce dissensions over the surplice or communion reached even the English prisons which held other fathers of Puritanism.

Mary, having to work through the parliamentary system of her father, continued his method by creating twenty-seven new seats, ten of them in conservative Yorkshire, but the session of 1555, after Gardiner's death, showed Parliament increasingly difficult. For Councillors, who had thought a severe lesson would restore Catholic faith, wearied of persecution when it was seen to harden Protestantism. The Commons rejected a bill confiscating the exiles' property, and discussed another for the exclusion of placemen from their House. The Queen, again, wished to restore to the Papacy the first-fruits and tenths which her father had seized, and to the English Church the tithe and livings in her possession. But the bill, as it emerged after narrow divisions, extinguished first-fruits entirely, and while allowing the Queen to surrender Crown livings, the laity kept a tight grasp of their own.

After this no Parliament was called for two years, and many members took a hand in the conspiracies detected in 1556–7. Elizabeth was suspected, some of her future servants were certainly involved. Protestant feeling showed increasing violence in mutilating images and assaults on priests; heretic congregations met stealthily in Essex woods and Islington inns; a Whitechapel bricklayer preached weekly to large numbers in his garden; there were secret Protestants in the Queen's guard. Excluded by Philip from trading in Spanish colonies, English adventurers sent ships at their own risk to Africa and Brazil, or swept the Channel as privateers, while heroic explorers reached Archangel and the court of Moscow. In short, a new England was growing up, in complete detachment from their blind and foreign government.

The unhappy Queen's hope of a child had faded, her waning health and Philip's unfaithfulness reminded her that she was eleven years older than he, while Spanish policy in 1557 broke her ideals and infuriated her people. A fiery new Pope, Paul IV, a Neapolitan patriot and hence anti-Spaniard, joined hands with the French. Philip returned to carry the Council for war with France, and though Pole opposed it, the Pope deprived him of his legateship. And while Philip won a great victory over the French at St.-Quentin in August, he took no steps to defend England against the Scots. Government could neither man nor finance the fleet, a forced loan was resisted, the French landed in the Channel

Isles and in January 1558 inflicted the blow which Mary, and England too, felt written on her heart. Long threatened, penetrated by French sympathizers, with crumbling defences which every public servant for years had reported as hopeless, Calais fell, the pride of the realm for two hundred years.

Parliament, in effect, washed their hands of Spain and Philip. The taxes they gave were miserly, though government were borrowing at Antwerp at 14 per cent. They would not even expel Frenchmen from England, and Council refused to send troops to the Netherlands. And Philip did not return to Mary, who ardently restored some endowments to the Church, a few nuns to Sion and a few monks to Westminster, and conscientiously burned over fifty heretics in this year. Everything alive seemed either to have gone into exile or to be menacing the Queen, and Protestant congregations met with more impunity. Both the Queen and Pole were said to be dying, so that all eyes turned towards Hatfield, where Elizabeth sat reading the classics under the English oaks. Early in the morning of the 17th November, Mary, this most upright of the Tudors, died and, as the Londoners lighted bonfires that evening, Cardinal Pole died also.

CONTEMPORARY DATES

1548	The Interim in Germany.
1549	Poets of the Pléiade writing in France.
1550	Vasari's *Lives of the Painters*.
1551	Palestrina in charge of Papal music.
	Second session opens of the Council of Trent.
1552	Maurice of Saxony and the French defeat the Emperor.
1553	Servetus burned at Geneva.
1555–59	Pope Paul IV (Caraffa).
1555	The religious peace of Augsburg.
1556–64	Reign of the Emperor Ferdinand I.
	–1605. Reign of Akbar at Delhi.
	Death of Loyola ; succeeded by Laynez.
1557	Battle of St.-Quentin.
	National bankruptcy in Spain.
1558	Marriage of Mary Queen of Scots to the Dauphin.
	Death of Charles V.

CHAPTER IV

THE REIGN OF ELIZABETH: I. 1558–1573

IN this age Europe passed through a fiery furnace, thereafter gradually cooling into what was to be its eighteenth-century shape, while England reached a destiny which three centuries had prepared. The wars of religion crystallized the division of mankind; counter-Reformation, organized by a Papacy reformed at the Council of Trent and politically directed by Spain, turned against Protestantism. But historical hatreds and commercial rivalries cut across religion; under great rulers, and finding allies in Protestant Holland, Germany, and Scandinavia, Catholic France set out to destroy the Catholic Hapsburgs. Eliminating her own religious feuds, France reached her great age, while the artificial Spanish Empire collapsed under the weight of its inheritance, its economic inability, and its crimes.

Sheltered from a joint Catholic attack by this Catholic rivalry, England made its own religious settlement, won a partnership with the Scottish Protestants which finally brought about a union of the Crowns, and crushed the Catholic outpost in Ireland. Her new wealth flowed out to every sea and made the foundations of an Empire, while at home she developed into a moderately capitalist society. The classes who had risen so steadily to supremacy, merchants and country gentlemen and lawyers, made Parliament the point of union and the decisive power. And, having at last absorbed the new learning of Europe and won for a brief space a spiritual equilibrium, English thought and letters rushed out in a harvest of perfection. Stresses of a new age of national sovereignties divided this small society of less than five million English folk, but neither these nor the folly of the Stuarts could arrest the tide which had set so long and risen so high. Reformation and Renaissance, continuous self-government and steadily evolved wealth, the Catholic Henry VIII and the Protestant House of Commons, had accumulated this great body of waters; upon which moved the vessels of Drake and Shakespeare, Hooker and Bacon, Jonson and Milton, the Cecils and Pym and Cromwell.

Revolution ended with a supreme gift of fortune, that Elizabeth reigned forty-five years, during forty of which she depended in the last resort on one minister, William Cecil. At first they could not dispense with those who had survived the anarchy, the Russells, Arundel, and Winchester, while the Queen from first to last made political favourites of men who made love to her. Robert Dudley, son of the evil North-umberland, was less forceful but as self-seeking as his father, and ' the gypsy ', as nobles of older blood called him, frightened the Queen's best servants by the fear that she might marry him for love. Though her reason asserted itself, he never entirely lost her confidence, but his nerve always failed at a pinch, while the mysterious death of his first wife, Amy Robsart, cast a shadow over his name, just as the crimes of his stepson Essex ruined him in his turn at the end of the reign. Neither these nor the arrogant charm of Raleigh seriously weakened the influ-ence on the Queen's better nature of the Cecils' tested services, or her leaning upon men connected with her own Boleyn family, like Knollys, Walsingham, the Careys, and Mildmay.

The Queen and her first minister made a formidable pair. She had her father's royal sweep and temper, which in small moments made her throw beer in a courtier's face or imprison maids-of-honour who preferred marriage to the torment of her service, but which also em-powered her to overawe remarkable men, to melt the House of Commons and inflame a nation. Skilled in using every advantage of her sex as a political asset, the Queen to whom Ascham had taught Greek, and who could address universities in Latin and foreign ambassadors in their own tongues, combined the brutal Italianate intellect of the Renaissance with a bluff pleasure in popularity, progresses among gaping crowds, jewels, and innumerable dresses. Her character kept her Court not moral, but guarded, lofty, and a thing of awe. Her conservative and catholic mind made extreme Protestantism suspect to her, separated her foreign policy from any enthusiasms, and fitted her to be the real maker of Anglicanism. An avarice deeper than that of Henry VII, the hesitations of a lonely woman, and a sceptical intellect saved her ministers from many mistakes, for when the storm rose she herself took the helm. Years of glory brought the people to agree with and admire her own confident self-portrait — ' if I were turned out of the realm in my petticoat, I were able to live in any place in Christendom ' — to love the Queen who proclaimed herself ' mere English ', and make true her boast, ' I have reigned with your loves '.

Cecil supplied a ballast of purpose, moderation, and enormous industry to the Queen's wayward greatness. Though, like all his class, he had obeyed the State religions of three reigns, he played a moderating part, and his family relationships were Protestant. As the age went, he was notably clean-handed, as careful a steward of national economy as of his own manors, and whatever shifts he used in his profession, at bottom he was a sober citizen, with a dislike of courtiers and garish clothing, and full of proverbial saws and instances. His mind was stolid, inclining to reach decision by cautious memoranda, but his positive qualities were admirable, and the Tudor and Stuart monarchy never had a more constitutionally minded minister, one more ready to consult the judges or to admit the legal powers of Parliament. He had two other attributes of his generation in a high degree, a dislike of clericalism and an ardour for economic prosperity, as his private investments showed. If his temper was conservative, and if he yielded, as busy ministers often do, to the pressure of business interests, he honestly applied his toil to rebuilding the national wealth, which made him a man of peace who realized the inferior, inconclusive character of war.

There was a third ruling figure, of Cecil's appointment. Matthew Parker, the new archbishop, was a product of Cambridge learning, a client of the Boleyns, a learned and conservative statesman. It was he who, with the Queen and Cecil, in the seventeen years of his tenure at Canterbury reconstructed an Anglican Church strong enough to hold a middle way between Rome and Geneva.

Though the problems of the reign were continuous, all that Elizabeth and Cecil laboured for was nearly shipwrecked in a crisis between 1569–72. Taking the years before that as a first stage, we find a tangle of urgent, inseparably connected questions. If she did not marry and have children, the succession must fall either to the Catholic, half-French Mary Queen of Scots, or to some Protestant claimant like Catherine, sister of Lady Jane Grey. Any such result must affect and be affected by the Church settlement, it must determine her choice of allies, and would divide the country. A few more candles in the royal chapel, a few moss-troopers loosed on the Scottish Border, or Devon corsairs on the sea; such were the various symptoms as policy changed in tune with votes in the Commons, or with far-off events of the balance between Catholics and Huguenots in France, between Mary and the Protestant lords in Scotland, with a Dutch rising or a Turkish war.

In this web of international complication there were some fixed points. A new epoch, which began with the religious peace of Augsburg in 1555, was clinched by the death of Charles V and by his will, which partitioned his great Empire, giving the Netherlands and Italy to his son Philip of Spain, Germany and the Austrian lands to his brother Ferdinand. Philip thus held the lands most devoted to Catholicism and those surrounding France, while the Austrian line ruled Germany, where Lutheranism was officially recognized, and where their own interests looked eastward to Poland and the Balkans. Defeated in a sixty years' struggle for Italy, France must necessarily try to break the strangling Hapsburg encirclement by thrusts towards Belgium and the Rhine, but the Italian wars and the Reformation had plunged her into turmoil, with which the last feeble Valois Kings could not cope. Henry II was killed in a tournament in 1559 and left a widow, Catharine de Medici, whose political ambition excelled Elizabeth's, and who would

exploit all religions and parties to save her children's Crown.   On which
French party was uppermost the English policy would largely depend,
so, too, would the Spanish attitude to England and the Scottish balance
of power.   But this decision in the French wars of religion would turn
on many other factors, the relations of the Huguenots to the Dutch
and to German Protestants, and the Huguenots' ability to win over a
Catholic people.   One other set of circumstances was rising in importance, an expansion overseas of the Great Powers, which was promptly
entangled in religious rivalry.   In the end, after many set-backs, a
diplomatic revolution came to pass between 1570 and 1580.   The
converging of all the causes mentioned broke down the old alliance
between Tudor England and Spain, substituting for it an understanding
between England and France, which lasted without essential disturbance for a century.

Such political enmity between Spain and France enabled Elizabeth
and Cecil to take some vital decisions during 1559-60.   The first
and indispensable gain was peace, and though the treaty of Câteau
Cambrésis (April) involved our surrender of Calais, the Hapsburgs
stood between Elizabeth and France, and intercepted an excommunication from Rome.   And though she refused Philip's offer of marriage,
acceptance of which would have imperilled her throne, and though his
envoys reported her a ' daughter of the Devil ' and Cecil an ' accursed
heretic ', all these things he was forced to overlook.   For, from July
1559, Mary Queen of Scots and her husband Francis II were sovereigns
of France, with her uncles, the Guises, in command ; better, Philip
argued, have England and Scotland heretic, than France, England, and
Scotland under one Crown.   So it was that Elizabeth was enabled to
settle the English Church and to make Protestant Scotland.

Many small signs — sharp words to bishops who would elevate the
Host in her chapel, and ' tuning ' of the pulpits — showed at once
that she would at least go back to the ways of her father.   But the
two intervening reigns had made his compromise solution impossible.
In the Parliament that met in January 1559 the Commons' majority
(though half of them had sat under Mary) insisted on the second prayer-
book of Edward VI, a committee of returned exiles urged Council to
go even further, while on the other side Convocation and the bishops
were unyieldingly Catholic.

It was only after three months' debate, and deadlock between Lords
and Commons, that a settlement was reached, bitterly disappointing
the extreme reformers, and representing the mind of the Queen more
than that of the Commons, and political necessity more than a religious
ideal.   It was a State settlement—for Convocation was ignored and every
bishop voted against it—yet a conservative one.   The Act of Supremacy,
reinstating Henry's legislation and repealing Mary's, avoided the

aggressive title ' Supreme Head ' and enforced on all clergy, officials, and university graduates an oath to the Queen as ' only supreme governor ' in spiritual and temporal causes ; while the commissioners whom the Act empowered her to appoint were limited in their definition of heresies to those determined by Scripture and the first four Church Councils,[1] or determined by Parliament with the assent of Convocation. The Act of Uniformity, passed in the Lords by only three votes, compelled the laity to attend their parish church, but though it took the prayer-book of 1552 as its basis, it made some important changes. It dropped the clause in the Litany against the ' detestable enormities ' of Rome, abandoned the rubric which explained away kneeling at communion, restored from the first book the sentence which made it possible to see the doctrine of a real presence, and ordered that clerical vestments should be those, including albs and copes, used in the second year of Edward VI. Injunctions issued before the end of 1559 ordered the holy table to be ' set in the place where the altar stood ' but to be moved into the chancel for the communion service, bade reverence at the name of Jesus, and forbade the clergy to marry, except with the consent of their bishop and a justice of the peace.

This compromise did not satisfy the Catholic clergy ; all but one of Mary's surviving bishops were deprived, together with some two hundred parish priests, rising to a total of perhaps a thousand over the next ten years. Nor did it satisfy the reformers ; it was with laments over vestments as ' relics of the Amorites ', with groans over a ' mingle-mangle ', and doubts whether primitive Christians had recognized the office of bishop, that the exiles, after consulting their foreign advisers, accepted bishoprics. But it kept the peace in England, and saved face in Europe, to whose diplomats Elizabeth would argue that her Church hardly differed from that recognized by the peace of Augsburg. Visitations struck at the Catholics, depriving, for example, sixteen heads of Oxford and Cambridge colleges, and forcing the clergy to sign a declaration that the prayer-book was according to the Word of God. In 1563 Convocation authorized the thirty-nine Articles, while the publication of Foxe's *Martyrs* reminded men out of what suffering their faith had come. But it was uphill work. Enforcement of the law rested with the magistrates, who, in the north, were half-Catholic ; Border families would not let their parishes attend the royal visitors ; at Hereford torch-light processions welcomed ejected priests. An Act of 1563 tightened the process, extending the supremacy oath to members of the Commons and teachers. Nor did the Queen make her bishops' path easier. The ceremonial in her chapel offended Protestant feeling ; she poured out her scorn on married clergy whom she would order out of cathedral

[1] *I.e.* the Councils of Nicaea, Constantinople, Ephesus, and Chalcedon, A.D. 325–451.

precincts, and showed her disgust at the Norfolk parsons who could hardly be got to wear a surplice. She plundered the Church by forcing bishops to exchange good estates for poor Crown livings, thereby adding to the fundamental problem of her Church; the poverty and lack of discipline, fruit of twenty years' plundering and revolution, which was shown by empty livings and an ignorant clergy, so few that they had to be eked out by still more ignorant lay-readers.

This struggling establishment, however, was one buttress against Catholicism, and in Scotland Elizabeth helped to make another. Writhing under French domination and the regency of Mary of Guise, a section of Scottish nobles turned to Protestantism, the lords of Congregation making a ' band ' in 1557 to defend their faith. Early in 1559 John Knox returned to Scotland; in May revolution broke out at Perth and the abbey churches went down in flames and hacking of axes; the Congregation appealed to Elizabeth. Dare she, then, break the peace she had just made, and risk war with all Catholic Europe? Yet, if she did not, the new Queen of Scotland, who this July became a Queen of France and boldly quartered the royal arms of England, would catholicize Scotland and northern England too. In the teeth of Arundel and conservative advisers who wanted a safe marriage for the Queen with the Austrian archduke Charles, Cecil ardently and Elizabeth with many hesitations decided to act. Beginning with underhand gifts of money, they then sent Admiral Winter to take the responsibility of stopping the French landing, and in the énd, finding the Scots too weak to act alone, in February 1560 they sent an army. They counted and weighed every step with admirable knowledge, being aware that Philip had rebels in the Netherlands and had suffered a defeat in Tripoli, while in France they had encouraged a Huguenot outbreak. In June the gallant Mary of Guise died, and in July the English army and Scots rebels achieved the treaty of Edinburgh, providing for the dismissal of French troops and that Mary should cease to use the English royal arms, while the Scottish parliament drew up a Protestant confession. Small wonder that Elizabeth now curtly refused the Pope's invitation to the Council of Trent, and sent some Marian bishops to the Tower.

It was the great quality of this administration that in war it never ignored the arts of peace, and made it their business to deal with fundamentals. And first with finance. One of her Secretaries of State described briefly the recipe for good government as ' peace, quietness, little taking of their money, few parliaments ', which justified Elizabeth's economic horror of war; taxation, men thought, should be kept for emergencies, while all Tudor experience proved how easily the political class evaded payment. When her reign began, the ordinary revenue was only some £200,000, rising at the close to about £300,000, and over the whole reign parliamentary grants did not average over £80,000 a year. Mary had left heavy debt, empty arsenals, commerce in decline, and now this Scottish campaign had swallowed a whole year's revenue. To reduce costs and break the vicious circle was Cecil's perpetual thought, as shown in his earliest notes of ' things to be performed ', which descend even to dinner allowances for the Queen's maids.

A first great work was completed in 1561, to call down the value of the base money minted since 1543, to call it in and issue a whole new silver coinage, which was achieved within a year and at a profit. With the assistance of the expert Thomas Gresham, and by punctual repayment of borrowings, the debt charges fell, and soon most of her loans were raised in London and not abroad.

Having reduced ordinary expenditure, Cecil began a second necessary task of rearmament, to make the country independent of foreign supply in gunpowder, metals, and naval stores. He embarked on a vigorous policy of mining for copper and tin, and raised the brass industry with zinc mines newly worked in the Mendips. Above all he thought of the Navy, and passed a statute to stop the destruction of timber, developed the growing of hemp, and paid bounties on shipbuilding. He conscripted labour to work on the repair of harbours; his additions to the law made the people eat fish not in Lent only but two days a week all the year round, for fisheries bred mariners.

It was his belief that trade did not flourish through forced channels, like navigation acts or bullion laws, or shipping by the ' detestable ' craft of piracy, but rather by freedom, new markets, and experiment. Hence his later insistence that Drake's piracy did not compensate for loss of the Spanish market; and hence, from the very beginning, his encouragement of immigrants, Saxon miners or Italian and Fleming textile workers, and the liberal grant of monopoly patents, as for saltmaking and glass. In the doubling of the Customs revenue in this reign may be seen the justification of his policy.

This enlightened conservative inherited and maintained a conservative society. Heavy tariffs, aiming at a balance of trade, prohibited absolutely many foreign goods, like cutlery or caps, and also the export of our wool, while an immense amount of regulation tried to keep a balance between town and country, consumer and producer, employer and employed. In 1563 the great Statute of Labourers, summing-up the changes of two centuries, fixed the frame of industry for two centuries more. By special advantages for skilled crafts it revived the boroughs from their long decline. The London practice of a seven years' apprenticeship was made generally compulsory. All persons not of independent means, and not in a craft, could be compelled to work on the land. No engagement was allowed for less than a year, and no person could leave his parish except under testimonials. Wages, the Act declared, were too low in regard to prices; abandoning uniformity, it ordered the J.P.'s to fix local rates yearly, subject to appeal to Council. Other statutes of this decade recognized the new conditions, with precautions against their abuse. Capitalism gained powers of taking large numbers of apprentices, the mediaeval usury law vanished, interest being allowed up to 10 per cent. But corn might not be exported if the home price rose to over 10s. a quarter, Council intervened to fix prices or increase supply, the law of forgery was modernized to meet a new world of trusts and insurance, and the Poor Law of 1563 for the first time authorized a compulsory rate.

Indeed, the eye and the arm of this government were everywhere, searching out all the nooks of a provincial country. A High Commission Court for religious offences, following precedents since the commission given to Thomas Cromwell, was set on a permanent footing; the Council in the North was reorganized with more summary powers; the rule over the Marches was taken away from the local magnates, Percies or Dacres. Once more the Church of Ireland was officially Anglicanized, and the Bible put into Welsh. And so, sitting in Council three days a week from 9 A.M., Cecil drove on towards unity and reform.

Yet all his hopes were precarious while the succession hung on the solitary life of Elizabeth, which gives the clue to the ten years of mortal danger on which is stamped the name of Mary Queen of Scots.

How sharp was the peril was already shown in August 1561. Mary, a widow at nineteen, returned to Scotland, and by refusing to ratify the Edinburgh treaty staked her claim, if not to the English throne, at least to the succession. The same month Elizabeth found that Catherine Grey, her legal successor by statute and her father's will, was secretly married to the son of Protector Somerset, for which offence she sent both to the Tower. Meantime, though smirched with ugly talk about the death of Amy Robsart and her flirtation with Leicester, she had dismissed several suitors, Arran whom the Scots Protestants wanted, the Archduke Charles the Catholic candidate, and the mad Eric of Sweden, with all his portraits.

There were men on the Scots' side, Mary's half-brother Moray and Maitland of Lethington, as well aware as Cecil that union of the two kingdoms was the true hope for both, and who were even hopeful of Mary's conversion to Protestantism. But Mary would not advance a step without an admission that she was next in the succession, which Elizabeth refused to give. Did they think, she asked, ' I could love my winding-sheet ? ' For that, she repeated to Parliament, it would be if she declared her heir, who would become, as her own experience in her sister's reign had proved, a centre of plots, even against her will. Moreover, to declare a Catholic the heir would split England in two.

Indeed, though both Queens probably wished an honourable settlement, events were too strong for them. In 1562 massacres by the Guises and new wars in France tempted Elizabeth to help the Huguenots, who surrendered Havre to her as a pledge for the restoration of Calais, and though the English army was decimated by plague and her policy was rejected by French patriotism, ardent Protestantism marked the Parliament of 1563. A strong section in Council supported the Grey claim, while Elizabeth's narrow escape from death by smallpox alarmed the country.

Mary, for her part, could not help becoming more Catholic, though hitherto she had cared more for her pleasures. The bigotry of Knox and his friends outraged her, she despaired of winning Protestant England, and a great marriage might intimidate Elizabeth. But the English Queen took her proposed marriage with Philip's son, Don Carlos, as a threat of war, and would do nothing for her unless she married an English subject; to which end she offered her own favourite Leicester. Even then she refused to make promises on the succession, until her own marriage was decided, one way or another.

In 1565, against Elizabeth's opposition, Mary married her cousin Darnley, a Catholic who would counterbalance the Protestant Arran and her brother Moray, and would win Catholic England, and who was himself a descendant of Henry VII. It was an act of defiance, but Elizabeth would not make the war which her Scottish experts advised, and once more considered marriage with the Archduke Charles as a reinsurance. Within a year, however, Mary's new Catholic zeal, her thirst for revenge on her Protestant nobles, and a bitter quarrel with the husband whom she found out to be a fool and a decadent, ended in March 1566 in Darnley conniving at the murder of her Italian secretary, Rizzio. But though English agents were aware of the plot and welcomed Moray's restoration to power, the birth of Prince James of Scotland (June) overshadowed the succession, which daily became deeper sunk in faction. Members of the Commons spoke of the ' villainy ' of the Scots' claim that their infant prince was Prince of England, and tried to make their money grants dependent on the Queen's marriage. Alva's barbarous persecution had driven 30,000 Flemish refugees to England; the moderate bishop Jewel preached against the Queen's proposed Austrian marriage as apostasy; the base Leicester, still not despairing of marrying her himself, defeated the scheme in Council and swords were drawn at court.

A second time Mary's passions threw away her advantage to Elizabeth, who could always postpone passion to policy. In February 1567 the house in which Darnley was lodged, at Kirk-o'-Field outside Edinburgh, was blown up, and he was found strangled outside it, a doom in which most of the Scots Council had a hand. But Mary's part in it was owing to her passion for Bothwell, the most violent desperado of his time, and when in May she married her husband's murderer, Scotland rose in revolt; Kirk, soldiers, and Edinburgh mobs called out ' burn the whore ', Bothwell fled to Denmark, the Estates forced her to abdicate and crowned James VI, with Moray as Regent. After nearly a year's imprisonment on Loch Leven she escaped in May 1568; her forces were routed at Langside and after a ninety-mile ride, sleeping on the ground and living on oatmeal, she crossed the English frontier, and appealed to Elizabeth to help a lawful sovereign against rebels. To the fury of Moray and the amazement of her nearest advisers, Elizabeth turned a favourable ear; she disliked the triumph of rebels, feared that an extreme policy would excite the French, wished to use her rôle as mediator, and dreaded the presence of this woman on English soil and to have her winding-sheet so attractively displayed. Even after the conferences of this winter, when Moray produced his charges against Mary, with black suggestion of murder and adultery, in the famous Casket letters, Elizabeth would make no clear pronouncement and clung to restoration on some terms or another.

Her instinct was right, for the prisoner was more dangerous than if at liberty, and her policies were desperate and depraved. For Bothwell her passion was entirely spent; ' revenge in hope of victory ' and a ' bloody passion ' were the comments of Knollys, her first English custodian, and while she professed a leaning to the English Church, she secretly appealed to the Spaniards, and of abdication would not hear. She was assured now of much sympathy within England; the project was launched of her marriage to the Duke of Norfolk. While the Cecil group convinced Elizabeth that restoration to Scotland or exile to France were equally suicidal, and that honourable imprisonment was the only possible policy, a triple movement of Mary, European hostility, and internal discontent rose to the desperate emergency of 1569-72.

The offensive-defence, which Cecil used as the means of safety, had nearly brought about war with Spain, England answering Spanish intrigues with English Catholics by propaganda among the Netherlands rebels. A tariff war ended in the Merchant Adventurers deserting Antwerp for Hamburg; pirates who benefited by English harbours cut the communications between Spain and Belgium. The Spanish Inquisition persecuted English traders, and late in 1568 word reached England that a Spanish fleet had treacherously attacked the squadron led by Hawkins and Drake on the Mexican coast. The English retaliation was to seize a large consignment of treasure, shipped by Italian bankers to pay the Spanish troops in Flanders; the Spanish embassy in London became the link between Mary and all Cecil's enemies. Meantime the third war of religion was raging in France, English volunteers and munitions being shipped to help the Huguenots.

Those who opposed Cecil ranged from personal dislikes, or sincere opposition to a policy which seemed to mean war with half Europe, down to feudal prejudice and downright treason. To combine peace abroad, settlement of the succession, and the fall of Cecil, brought together old conservative peers like Arundel, the opportunist Leicester, and the Catholics of the north, with the marriage of the Protestant Norfolk to Mary as their point of agreement. Though most of them designed neither a threat to the Queen nor to restore Catholicism, they went to extreme lengths; urged France and Spain to stop English trade, discussed the arrest of Cecil, and wrote to Mary their promises of support. Leicester, however, would not break with the Queen and Spain decided against open war, while Cecil disintegrated this faltering opposition. It broke finally on two fixed resolutions : Elizabeth's, against the Norfolk marriage, and Moray's, never to allow Mary's return to Scotland. In October 1569 Norfolk, originally a patriotic gentleman, but now brought by weakness and pride into conspiracy, was sent to the Tower ; the political plot had failed.

But those whom foreign Powers and English politicians exploited, the Catholic earls of Northumberland (whose father had been executed for the Pilgrimage of Grace) and Westmorland, and the gentlemen of Yorkshire and the Border, had gone too far to believe in pardon, and lost grip of their extremists. The north was poor, hard-hit by loss of the Netherlands trade, and exasperated by the new standards of government, which expected noblemen to attend the Court and summoned litigants to York. Their way of life, where young horsemen found a career in the Percy or Dacre households, was dying, but they would still follow their lords and cling to the old Church. Some of their sons were religious exiles, both religion and habits of life tied them to Scottish Catholics over the Border, and they feared that government would soon enforce the supremacy oath which hitherto their magistrates had evaded.

In November they rose, Percy and Neville, Tempest and Swinburne, and Norton, one of the Council of the North, while even the Yorkshire squires who stood neutral usually sent a son to fight under the banner of the Five Wounds; they heard the Mass in Durham cathedral, English service-books were burned on many village greens, and then they marched south as far as Selby in the hope of rescuing Mary. Caught between the southern armies and others at Berwick and York co-operating with Moray, they quickly retreated, but had hardly fled over the Border when in January 1570 Moray was murdered, and the Scottish Catholics tried to reopen contact with the English north. Elizabeth's cousin Hunsdon crushed Dacre in his own Naworth country before they could arrive, and after some eight hundred executions the rebellion was over.

In May Pius V's bull excommunicating Elizabeth was posted up in London, Scotland was torn by civil war, Spain and France pressed Mary's rights. Again Elizabeth hesitated, between the Cecil group who would have done with Mary and the Leicester-Arundel party, her own solution being to restore Mary under pledge of an alliance, and surrender of the little James to be brought up in England. But the Regency stoutly refused either, while Mary entered on another conspiracy. Its centre was Ridolfi, a Florentine banker in London; the programme which he took to Rome and Madrid included a Spanish army, the seizure or murder of Elizabeth, and Mary's marriage with Norfolk who, in spite of most lenient treatment, was captivated by Mary's sentimental letters. All was soon known to Cecil, and Norfolk was attainted, though for another six months the Queen postponed execution.

In this, as in other matters, religious divisions drove her forward. In the intensely Puritan House of Commons of this year she stopped with difficulty a bill to exclude Mary, and her heirs, from the succession; in 1572 they extorted the execution of Norfolk, and pressed for the attainder of Mary. 'The axe must give the next warning', said one member; 'a notorious whore', declared the Puritan Peter Wentworth. But even their milder proposal, to take away Mary's rights and hold her life liable for further conspiracy, was vetoed by the Queen.

None the less, two considerable things had come about, which were taking her on a new road. Though two Regents had died after Moray, by the end of 1572 Scotland was firmly Protestant under the grim rule of Morton, and Elizabeth for ever abandoned the restoration of Mary. Moreover, since France had in effect abandoned her also, a diplomatic revolution was forcing its way, in spite of reactions at the French Court, and even despite the massacre of St. Bartholomew this August. The French monarchy might kill the Huguenot leader Coligny, but they must follow his policy of alliance against Spain with the Protestants of the Netherlands and England. For England the Spanish alliance, having long lost its popularity, was now losing its usefulness since Alva had killed the commerce of Antwerp and, with the seizure of Flushing, the Dutch sea-beggars this year began the campaigns out of which William of Orange was to make a nation.

The axe, natural death, and official change in the next few years marked a divide. Northumberland, handed over by the Scots, followed Norfolk on the scaffold; Henry VIII's old councillors gradually died. Cecil's supremacy was underlined by his new title Burghley, and his new office of Lord Treasurer; his secretaryship fell to Protestant Sir Thomas Smith, while a second was made for the even firmer Protestant Walsingham, brother-in-law to Peter Wentworth. In 1573 Drake first gazed on the Pacific; two years later wise archbishop Parker died and made room for the Puritan Grindal, and the first Jesuit missions came to re-win heretic England. The prisoner Mary, no more put forward by any considerable English party, and less every year by the French, was drifting into the rôle of high priestess of the counter-Reformation, an instrument of Spain. She and the exiled English Catholics in Belgium waited for the day when Philip, slowly annotating the mass of documents that reached him from Mediterranean seamen, Irish chiefs, Mexican viceroys, and French Catholics, should decide that only open war could save the Faith and the Spanish Empire.

CONTEMPORARY DATES

1559	Peace of Câteau Cambrésis.
	Compilation at Rome of the Index.
1560	Foundation of Westminster School.
	Catharine de Medici becomes regent for Charles IX.
1561	L'Hôpital's efforts for toleration in France.
	Foundation of Merchant Taylors' School.
1562	John Hawkins voyages for slaves.
	Third session of Council of Trent.
1563	Murder of Francis, Duke of Guise.
	Foxe's *Book of Martyrs*.
1564	Death of Calvin.
	Birth of Galileo, Shakespeare, and Marlowe.
1565	William of Orange and Egmont lead resistance to Philip II.
1566–72	Pope Pius V.
	Gresham founds the Royal Exchange.
1567	Centralizing of government in Japan.
	Alva reaches the Netherlands.
	Foundation of Rugby School.
1568	The English Catholic college at Douai.
1569	Mercator's map of the world.
	Condé killed at Jarnac.
1570	Coligny's supremacy in France.
	Palladio writes on Architecture.
1571	Battle of Lepanto.
1572	End of the Jagellon dynasty in Poland.
	Massacre of St. Bartholomew.
	Revolt in Holland.
1573	Drake sees the Pacific.
	The Turks take Cyprus.

CHAPTER V

THE REIGN OF ELIZABETH: II. 1573–1603

THE last thirty years of Elizabeth, building within a scaffolding raised in dire emergency, decided the whole British future in policy, religion, government, and power. Much of this turned on events outside English control, on the growing strength of the Huguenots, the break between Holland and Spain, the Spanish conquest of Portugal, or activity of the Popes. And though for clearness' sake it is necessary to divide the strands, we must never forget how completely all were intertwined: the drift towards war with Spain, the rise of English sea-power, conspiracies of the Scottish Queen and English Catholics, the strength of Puritanism, opposition in Parliament, and Irish war.

In foreign affairs two stages can be distinguished: a period of armed friction and a period of war, separated about the year 1585 and marked by a division in the Council. In a sense the head of the peace-party was the Queen. Her economy hated war and the taxation it would mean; she complained bitterly of the expense of Walsingham's secret service and the gross corruption in her armed forces; and wrangled over every loan to foreign Protestants. If she thought also that a war postponed might be a war averted, it was partly because she had cooler nerves than most of her ministers, and a justified confidence in her own arts; she would order her band to play ' the Bells of Pavia ' to please a Spanish ambassador, while all the time she was taking her profit out of Drake's voyages and, though determined never to marry, discussed marriage with the French for ten useful years, finding also perhaps a certain pathetic pleasure in flirtation with ' her frog ', the Duke of Anjou, who professed to love her for her own sake. Near her stood Cecil, her ' spirit ' as she called him, more anxious than herself for her marriage but thinking first of peace and trade. The fire of the other side came from the impulsive, optimistic Walsingham, who saw Europe as a battlefield of ideologies : ' Christ and Belial can hardly agree ', let them unite Protestant Europe against ' the proud Spaniard, whom God hath long used for the rod of his wrath '. With him usually went Leicester, opposed (for auld lang syne) to marriage for the Queen, and finding Puritanism useful to the popularity which he loved still better.

St. Bartholomew's Day, the accession of the warlike Henry III in France, and pressure from business interests, brought about in 1574 a commercial treaty with Spain and English assistance to the Huguenots of La Rochelle. Then a lull in the French religious wars and, in 1576, a union of the Netherlands under William of Orange changed the tone, and the main theatre, of politics ; the Spanish plan, first attempted under Philip's brother the dashing Don John of Austria, and after his death achieved by the great soldier Alexander of Parma, was to break this union by winning back the Flemish Catholics. While Walsingham called for the full Protestant policy, the Queen's scheme was cautious and cold. Her favourite solution would probably be a weak Netherlands under Spanish sovereignty, with guarantees for the Protestants ; she long refused to admit Orange's belligerent rights which would impede English trade, and by her coolness drove him to fulfil his warning that, if England failed, he would turn to France. Here was a danger of the first order, for a French mastery of the Netherlands would be worse than a Spanish. Yet a restricted French assistance would have great merits. It would exalt Anjou, the heir to the throne on whom moderates and Huguenots counted, it might involve France in war with Spain, and save the Dutch without squandering English money. Events outside the Netherlands in 1578-9 also attracted Elizabeth to this veiled intervention — a Catholic revival in Scotland, a Spanish advance against Portugal, Philip's threats against the seamen who were attacking his American empire, and the arrival of Spanish troops in Ireland. The French marriage scheme was therefore revived ; twice ' her frog ' visited the Queen, and though she finally broke off on the ground of religion, and though the romance of her gifts of garters and rings dwindled down to a cash subsidy, she steadily encouraged France in the Netherlands. But under careful safeguards : if the French looked too successful, she then subsidized German Calvinist princes to intervene, nor did she ever entirely drop her mediation with Spain. To occupy Spain thus by Anjou's army and by sending Drake to sea with Don Antonio — the Portuguese claimant — was a cheap, though not a very lofty policy, nor was it a popular one, for Puritan members and writers exclaimed against the apostasy of a Catholic marriage. It was for this that John Stubbe, a substantial lawyer and brother-in-law of the Presbyterian leader Cartwright, lost his hand in the pillory.

For many years the Queen's ' prolonging and mincing ', as Burghley called it, succeeded because Philip was occupied elsewhere, and because the policies of Elizabeth and Catharine de Medici largely coincided, and it had the merit of postponing war until England was more at peace within itself. Yet indefinitely to sail so near the wind, to expect the best both of war and peace, was not possible ; Elizabeth's economies destroyed the Protestant leaders in Scotland, her anger at the Dutch not repaying her loans almost outweighed her service to them. In 1580

Spain acquired Portugal with its harbours, and its colonies in Africa, India, and Brazil. In June 1584 Anjou died, which made Henry of Navarre heir to the throne and a new civil war certain; the same month William the Silent was murdered, and though Elizabeth would not accept the Dutch sovereignty as the Walsingham party wished, Parma's taking of Antwerp in 1585 was a danger signal, magnified by the open league of Philip with the Guises. She, therefore, adopted a policy which for the next thirty years plunged England deep into the Low Countries, sending Leicester with an army of 6000 men, while some Dutch ports were surrendered as a guarantee for her expenses. Though Leicester was an unwise and unsuccessful commander, Philip Sidney's death in battle this year at Zutphen was one of many heroic exploits, which apprenticed some of the best English soldiers in the Dutch school of war. Simultaneously Drake sailed to sack Vigo, Cartagena, and Florida. These easy victories and his return with £60,000 in loot revealed the defencelessness of the Spanish Empire, and brought very near the great Armada. Behind the crisis, however, was a larger pattern of cause and effect.

The Catholic problem had changed since the Holy See had forbidden the faithful to attend Church of England services, and since the Papal bull of 1570 encouraged rebellion. It was still, however, a twofold problem. First, there were the lay recusants who would not attend church and generally moved house to avoid their Easter communion, and whose treatment varied in accord with the ups and downs of policy; in the north particularly magistrates and juries disliked troubling their neighbours or harrying the old priests sheltered in manor house and farm. But a different and much more dangerous side was raised by Catholic missions from the Continent. In 1568 William Allen founded a seminary at Douai, which later moved to Rheims, and another was afterwards set up at Rome: by 1580 over a hundred of these devoted priests had reached England, landing in disguise in all the rivers round the coast or from French ships that came for Newcastle coal, while the same year two remarkable men led a Jesuit mission, the saint Edmund Campion whose object was the winning of souls, and Robert Persons, political conspirator, whose contacts included a ring of exiles, in great part north-country rebels now assembled at Louvain, and Mary Queen of Scots who, Walsingham was convinced, was the key to it all. A terror began which was to infect England for the next century; in 1581 Campion was caught in Berkshire, racked, and executed, while Persons' printing press was tracked down in Essex and he fled to the Continent. Before the reign ended nearly two hundred Catholics had been executed, while many more lay in prison.

Yet there was solid substance in Burghley's defence that they perished not as Catholics, but as traitors. For the first twenty years of the reign the government had not taken half a dozen Catholic lives. The law of 1571 was severe, making it treason to deny the Queen's title, and a crime under praemunire to bring in beads, crucifixes, and other Catholic ornaments; that of 1581 was more drastic still, raising the fine for recusancy to £20 a month. Both, however, distinguished between those professing the Catholic faith and Catholic propaganda, and it was to this last that they assigned the death penalty. Her Council deplored the Queen's unwillingness to strike, and she vetoed a sacramental test; Catholics were rounded up, crushed by fines and often imprisoned, but government kept firmly to its difference of treatment for Catholics native-born and the missioners ordained abroad.

What made it almost impossible to distinguish between religion and treason was the action of Pope Gregory XIII, who set himself to execute literally his predecessor's bull. In 1579 Nicholas Sanders, a leader of English learning at Louvain, reached Ireland as a papal legate, together with Spanish soldiers. Rome sanctioned teaching that the murder of Elizabeth would not be a sin, and approved schemes devised by the Guises and Spain for invasion through Scotland and the release of Mary; Sixtus V made Allen a cardinal, and promised to contribute to the expense of invasion.

Philip's long delay and Scottish fluctuations frustrated these plots, and for the last time Elizabeth explored the chance of reconciliation with Mary, while Burghley stoutly opposed Walsingham's project for armed intervention in Scotland. The information reaching Walsingham was enormous and won at great hazard : one of his spies was killed in the streets of Paris ; he had another disguised as a Catholic at Bayonne ; and he was getting others out of the hatred between Welsh and English, and between seculars and Jesuits, among the exiles. Year by year he got nearer to the heart. In 1582 the seizure of a Spanish agent on the Scottish March, disguised as a dentist, revealed Mary's knowledge of the Spanish scheme. Next year a spy inside the French embassy led to the seizure of Francis Throgmorton who, under torture, gave up the detailed plans for a French landing at Arundel ; the Spanish ambassador was ordered out of the country. In 1584, just after the murder of Orange, the government got hold of the Scottish Jesuit Crichton, with full knowledge of the previous conspiracies. The Council circulated an ' association ' which thousands signed, pledging themselves to take revenge on any person whose steps to the throne were advanced by an attempt on the Queen's life. In 1585 Parliament legalized this association in a milder form, and forbade the mere presence of Jesuits and priests in England ; it was found that one member, Parry, had the approval of Mary's agent for murdering Elizabeth. This year Mary was moved to a safer prison at Chartley under a Puritan keeper, Paulet.

Here in 1586 the trap was baited with final success. All her accumulated correspondence was intercepted and at last, with the aid of a spy educated in the exiles' seminaries, and by using the prisoners' supply of beer as the channel for letters, Walsingham arrested two advocates of assassination, the priest Ballard, and Babington who had been Mary's page. Their trial revealed her approval of the plot, a special commission found her guilty, and both Houses petitioned for execution. The Queen procrastinated for months, testing Paulet whether he would not save her trouble by a private murder, which some foreigners thought would be a more decent way of killing a crowned head. But all Protestant England was in Paulet's answer, that he would not so shipwreck his conscience. At length Elizabeth signed the warrant, which the Council sent off without consulting her further, and on the 8th February 1587 Mary was beheaded in Fotheringay Castle, reading her prayers aloud to silence the Protestant ministers. For fifteen years only Elizabeth had stood between this and the English people, who felt the very life of England unsafe while Mary lived. Though Elizabeth imprisoned Secretary Davidson who had acted on the warrant, she could safely reckon that neither Scotland nor France would do more than protest, but the execution which set bells ringing in London confirmed the decision Philip had lately taken to invade England, for was not his claim on the throne as good as that of the heretic James VI? It came on top also of other dangers and provocations, the larger English armaments in Holland and the furious fighting in France, where the heretic Navarre was winning his first victories. And not in Holland and France only did he find the same force, carrying troops, running munitions, keeping all his rebels alive — the same English sea-power which had begun to cut the communications of Spain and the sinews of Spanish America.

Except in a few exceptional minds no vision of Empire inspired Elizabethan seamen. To find wealth or to invest capital was the aim of the London syndicates who financed them, as it had been the motive of the Bristol group who in Henry VIII's time sent agents to the Canaries and traded to the Levant. But since the age of Columbus and John Cabot the whole world had changed. Turkish conquest had blocked the overland trade; the Portuguese assisted by finding the Cape route to India and the East Indies. Meantime the Spaniards, ill-content with the discoveries of Columbus, extended the share allotted to them by Pope Alexander VI, until their Empire girdled the globe. Between 1519–22 Cortez conquered Mexico, Magellan found the south-west route into the Pacific and his ship circumnavigated the world; in 1532 Pizarro overran Peru. Eastern spices enriched Portugal, American gold and silver poured into Spain.

Before Elizabeth's accession various English books discussed these discoveries, and there were other signs — conflict with the Turks and the Spanish Inquisition, besides the decline of the Staple and Hansa — all

pointing towards new markets. Their enterprise looked in two directions. The first was put before Edward VI's government by the
veteran Sebastian Cabot, who had voyaged with his father long ago,
to find a northern route to the riches of Asia, shorter than Portugal's by
the south-east or the Spaniards' by the south-west. Hence the foundation in 1552 of the Muscovy Company, and the memorable voyage of
Chancellor of Bristol and Willoughby to find a north-east passage.
Willoughby was frozen to death with his crew on the Murman coast;
Chancellor reached Archangel and was received by the Czar at Moscow.
And though after twenty years the struggle for a sea passage to Asia
had to be dropped, his voyages and those of Anthony Jenkinson between
1557–64 opened up the Russian market, and for a time stretched to the
Caspian and Persia. The difficulties of this trade led to the devising of
another, a treaty with the Turks in 1580 and the origin of the Levant
Company, and so in 1583–91 to the journey of Ralph Fitch to Aleppo,
on to the Persian Gulf, India, and Malaya. Such enterprises had
reached ' Cathay ', though not by the north-east passage, and were
bringing in the East on the back of Spain.

In 1530 William Hawkins, later member of Parliament for his
native Plymouth, opened up a new and politically more dangerous
trade of breaking into the Portuguese monopoly, exchanging combs and
bracelets for ivory and negroes on the Guinea Coast, and trading with
them to Brazil. In 1553 a London syndicate launched the first of several
expeditions to Guinea and the Gold Coast, which clashed violently with
the Portuguese. In 1562 John Hawkins, William's son, began to turn
his experience of Spanish trade to a scheme which he argued need
not involve war; that is, to get negroes in Africa and sell them in the
market, only too anxious for them, in the Spanish Main and West
Indies. Strict orders from Spain, however, stiffened resistance, and
on the third of these voyages, in September 1568, Hawkins and Drake
were treacherously attacked at St. Juan de Ullua, where they lost their
flagship and 300 men.

The next fifteen years' exploits turned round three ideas : a north-
west passage to Asia, since the north-eastern had broken down, reprisals
or defence against Spain, and the foundation of colonies. In 1576–8,
inspired by the writings of Humphrey Gilbert and mainly financed by
a London merchant Michael Lok, the wild illiterate Yorkshireman,
Frobisher, sailed three times to the north-west, to Baffin's Land and
Hudson's Straits; though his discoveries were impeded by an impression that he had found ' gold ', lumps of which were soon being used as
road-metal in England. John Davis's three voyages, 1585–7, went still
further north and charted Greenland and Labrador, though ice blocked
the passage he claimed to have found. Simultaneously many motives
induced many minds, like Gilbert and the geographer Richard Hakluyt

(the first edition of whose *Voyages* appeared in 1582), to insist that trade was only safe under the flag, and to press for the foundation of a colony. In 1583, after several false starts, Gilbert sailed, claimed Newfoundland for English sovereignty, and after disastrous exploring further south had to turn home, to die in his ten-ton frigate the *Squirrel*, leaving the memory of his last heroic words, ' we are as near to Heaven by sea as by land '. In 1585 his half-brother, Walter Raleigh, planned at Roanoke the first of several unsuccessful attempts at what he called ' Virginia '.

Neither this exploration nor this struggling Empire decided Philip of Spain, but the activities of Drake. He embodied a doctrine which the English had steadily maintained against Portugal, and was enough in itself to destroy the Spanish Empire : that neither a Papal bull nor vague prescription could prohibit English traders, but nothing else than an effective occupation. To this Drake added a determination on reprisals, taking up the rôle which French seamen had long played, of attacking Spanish shipping wherever it was found. And though he was a bad colleague, without Hawkins' civic spirit or the scientific and loyal qualities of Davis, his was the most undoubted genius for war, ever insistent on unity of command ; a man of action of the class of Clive, and a very few more.

After two years of careful reconnoitring, in 1572 he struck at the strategic centre of the treasure-trade, where mule convoys carried the Peru silver across the Isthmus of Panama ; broke into Nombre de Dios, crossed the Isthmus, saw the Pacific, and returned with some £40,000. One of his shipmates, Oxenham, in 1576 repeated the game on his own account, launched his pinnaces on the Pacific, but was caught and hanged at Lima. Drake, meantime, during the years of better relations with Spain took service in the Irish war, and before he sailed west again in 1577 larger things were in the air. English geographers had decided that the Straits of Magellan were the best opening to Asia, they believed an unknown continent existed in the south Pacific, and some had hopes of a colony. Walsingham and perhaps the Queen were also ready to attack Spanish America, which Burghley would probably have opposed.

In December then, armed with such elastic instructions, Drake went off in his *Golden Hind*, on the voyage which was to last nearly three years and turned into a circumnavigation of the earth. After crushing a dangerous mutiny he passed the Straits of Magellan, heard of the hopelessness of attacking Panama, took what he wanted from Valparaiso and all Chile and Peru, ran up the Californian coast to look for the exit of the north-west passage, and at midsummer 1579 began to cross the Pacific. In the Moluccas he got spices and a treaty with a local Sultan, on which were founded many later claims, and so on by Java, the Indian Ocean, and the Cape, to reach home in September 1580. In 1586–8

Thomas Cavendish, a private Suffolk gentleman, circumnavigated the globe again by Drake's route, coming up the Thames, a month after the Armada had perished, with blue damask hoisted on his masts, while the Queen waved her hand from Greenwich Palace.

Four political points stand out in this enterprise. The sea-leaders were passionate Protestants; the Spaniards, Drake wrote, were 'enemies of the truth and upholders of Baal', while Oxenham's lawless crew had decked themselves in captured vestments and taught the Indians to call themselves Lutherans. If their triumphs continued, they would, moreover, make it impossible for Spain to finance her armies or to recover the Netherlands. Again, though Elizabeth might protest her innocence, she had taken shares even in Hawkins' early ventures, constantly lent a royal ship or two, and took a large share in the profits; while the syndicate which financed Drake's world voyage included Walsingham and Leicester, besides John Hawkins, now treasurer of the Navy. And most of all, the men who led and the ships engaged in these expeditions were the nucleus of a professional fleet. The fleet of Henry VIII dwindled in the next weak reigns and during the poverty of Elizabeth's early years, but though in 1587 there were only twenty-five royal ships of the line, as fighting units they were vastly superior. Under the lead of Hawkins they were built, or cut down, to different lines; longer in proportion to beam, lower than the 'tall' ships with their fore-and-aft castles that held soldiers for boarding; with crews better paid and less in number and therefore, being economical in victualling, capable of keeping the seas longer, and more heavily gunned. With Burghley's constant support Hawkins also reformed Henry VIII's Navy board, and checked some of the corruption which had rotted dockyards and contracts. The experienced seamen, who made up the Admiralty administration on Tower Hill, knew that they could outsail and outgun anything afloat, so that in comparison with this Navy the Armada was only a floating army.

Their confidence was justified in 1587, the year for which Philip had planned invasion, while Parma was deepening the Flemish canals to pass out his flat-bottomed boats. Drake's attack on Cadiz in April did much more than 'singe the King of Spain's beard'. His masterly strategy forced the Spaniards to postpone action for a year, his guns wiped out a whole division of the Armada, half convincing the Spanish captains they were beaten before they sailed. All our commanders were urgent to strike another blow while the demoralized enemy was strung out in half a dozen ports, and bitterly reproached Burghley, 'a long grey beard with a white head'. But the Queen insisted on continuing peace negotiations, the cost of mobilization alarmed her, she hoped Philip might drop the whole design. In the result, orders for an offensive in Spanish waters were released too late, and the Armada caught the English fleet in the very position that Drake dreaded, acting on a passive defensive and divided between a main force at Plymouth and a squadron in the Channel.

At last the day had come for which the Catholic world waited. Rome reissued its excommunication of Elizabeth; Cardinal Allen denounced her as an 'incestuous bastard'; his information assured him that all Catholic England would revolt; the Spanish flagship sailed under a banner of the Virgin and her crucified Son. Fortunately for England Philip drove his commanders on into the most improbable scheme of operations — an undisturbed passage of Medina Sidonia's fleet up the Channel to seize an English port near Margate, there to convoy Parma's troops from Flanders. For this reason the Armada carried 22,000 soldiers as against 8000 sailors and, hoping to avoid battle, advanced past Plymouth, sailing at only about two knots in stately procession.

The English commander, Howard of Effingham, had under him, to be conciliated and used together, Drake as vice-admiral, Hawkins, Frobisher, Fenner, besides great nobles and soldiers; ' a grand fleet ' it could not be, when half the ships were volunteer merchantmen, and when tactics were applied by squadron leaders at their own will. But eight days of continuous fighting proved the English mastery of their craft, from the 21st July 1588 when the fleet warped safely out of Plymouth to the all-day battle of the 29th off Gravelines.

This use of wind and weather-gage, the key to fighting action until Trafalgar, came from confidence in their experience and their ships; with guns that could outrange the Spaniards, they passed and re-passed in line ahead, using the broadside, so that the Spaniards wrote that their own fastest vessels ' looked as if at anchor '. And so, avoiding the only action which the Spaniards could understand, they drove them off their first intention of seizing the Isle of Wight and, almost intact in numbers but badly shaken, on to Calais; where the English could join hands with their squadron in the Downs and make good their shortage of gunpowder. At midnight on the 28th July Howard forced them from their anchorage with fire ships, sank four and damaged many more on the 29th, and drove them on again past their meeting-point with Parma, only a change of wind saving them from shipwreck on the Zealand shoals. With their objective lost, supply failing, without water and throwing their horses overboard, the Armada fled desperately north, under orders to pass round Scotland, refit in some Irish port, and make for home. It was beyond the power of ships manned for a military progress, battered by gunfire, and in wild gales, and though in battle they lost only nine or ten, fifty at least were wrecked in this fearful voyage, and the Irish shores were heaped with corpses and broken timber. Weeks elapsed in England before the fear of invasion passed away, but a great tide of patriotic feeling rose round the Queen. ' Let tyrants fear ', she said to the army at Tilbury ; she was come among them resolved ' to live and die amongst you all, to lay down for my God and my kingdom and my people my honour and my blood, even in the dust '.

The victory saved Protestantism for the time, but it only began a war which outlived Elizabeth. They were fifteen years of gloom and disappointment. By 1596 the Queen's old companions Leicester and Knollys and Hatton, with the war leaders, Drake and Hawkins, Frobisher and Walsingham (' good news ', noted King Philip), were all dead, and in 1598 Burghley also. There were severe attacks of plague, an Irish war opened, most dangerous and costly, while Henry of Navarre, abandoning our alliance, made a separate peace. And there was a change in the atmosphere of politics. Though the Queen's health was wonderful, the days of Gloriana were over, and a young generation were getting impatient. The Protestant feeling which had defeated Spain pressed the Queen on to a Puritan programme which she hated, while from the very success of her government the nation was outgrowing the rule of Council. So that her last years passed in resisting much opposition in the Commons, who were only reined in by respect for her age, her glory, and ancient charm. In Council there were sharp differences between the advocates of war to the knife by sea and those who would only subsidize allies in Europe and seize any chance of a moderate peace. Elizabeth, indeed, continued assistance to the Dutch and the Huguenots on a considerable scale, sending over £300,000, or more than a year's revenue to France in the five years after the Armada, and here were trained and tested, under excellent soldiers like the Norreys and the Veres, the troops who made the germ of the standing army. But to spend her treasure on armies was never Elizabeth's intention ; her allies were bad debtors, and the countless small expeditions to Normandy, Brittany, and Holland were just enough to hold some strategic point, or stop the Spaniards making a permanent base in France. Parma's death, and in 1593 Henry of Navarre's conversion to Catholicism, eased the pressure, since a united France and the ability of Maurice of Orange were capable now of resisting Spain.

Nothing was more disappointing than the naval war. In part this was due to rival policies, but even more to a great increase in Spanish efficiency. English deserters were teaching them to build better ships ; strong galleons of the ' Indian guard ' and swift treasure-carrying cruisers, excellent fortifications in the Islands, convoy from St. Helena for the carracks coming from India — against these Drake's method of surprise had lost its power. His expedition of 1589 against Lisbon and the Azores was a failure, Portugal showed no desire to rise in favour of Don Antonio, and he lost 10,000 men. This left him under a cloud, and for some years naval action dwindled to a search for treasure or destruction of commerce, financed by syndicates or rich individuals, like the adventurous Earl of Cumberland.   There were single exploits of great skill and gallantry, less famous but more success-ful than the Azores battle of 1591, when Richard Grenville in the *Revenge* refused to retreat before a whole enemy fleet.   It was mag-nificent but it was not war, and the Spaniards' taking of Calais and their burning of Penzance proved how little effect these raids had on the centre of strategy.   Drake was therefore called again into service, ' el Draque ', the dragon whose name in Spain, so an English spy reported, was ' more feared than ever Talbot's in France '.

Unhappily his last voyage was one long disaster; he failed in the Canaries, was beaten off at Puerto Rico, and found Panama a very different matter since his glorious days, and in 1596 the fleet returned, having buried at sea both the old heroes, Hawkins and Drake.   The same year the strongest expedition of the reign, under Howard, Essex, and Raleigh, seized Cadiz and its treasure, and forced the Spaniards to burn the Indian fleet.   But this was the last operation on a big scale. The island voyage of 1597 to the Azores missed the treasure ships, and broke on quarrels between Essex and Raleigh.   In 1598 Philip II died, and with him what remained of the Catholic crusade, while the with-drawal of France from the war made it imperative for England to con-centrate on helping the Dutch, and a great Irish war distracted every other effort.   Yet individual enterprise never ceased.   Raleigh sent ships to the Orinoco to explore the fabulous wealth of El Dorado, a kingdom of gold somewhere in the Guiana highlands, for which the Spaniards were also prospecting.   Most important of all, building on information from Cavendish's voyage and Hakluyt's garnered knowledge from foreign sources, and spurred on by Dutch rivalry, a body of London merchants equipped several ventures to India and the Spice Islands. James Lancaster, who reached them first in 1591, ten years later led the first fleet of the East India Company.

Besides Ireland, Elizabeth's government failed in another political problem of the first order; failed, that is, to maintain the unity of Church and State which Henry VIII had rebuilt.   Indeed, by the time of her accession it was probably too late; for if the Puritans did not, as they claimed, go back to Wyclif, they had absorbed, in their triumph under Edward and their exile under Mary, Calvin's views of Church government and a Bible doctrine which made compromise impossible. Elizabeth's first generation of bishops would not accept any idea of an apostolic succession, looking on their office as only a spiritual police, and warmly disliked the Queen's preference for candles, crucifixes, and ritual.   From the very first many ministers refused to wear the vest-ments ordered by the rubrics; in 1563 the Lower House of Convocation rejected by only one vote a petition against kneeling at communion, organs, and all outward signs of Catholic order. Under the deepening influence of Bible reading and hatred of Rome and Spain, Puritanism threatened to sweep the country away. Preachers attacked the stage, even the village gild plays; condemned the keeping of May Day, and would not baptize children except under Scripture names; while for the old English Sunday, which had allowed music and dancing and football out of church time and harvest work in summer, they substituted an austere Sabbath. For heresy and adultery they proposed the penalty of death. Not a session passed without a move in the Commons against the prayer-book, ceremonies, and church courts. Burghley himself would have compromised, and many of his family circle were more ardent. Walsingham, Knollys, Mildmay, were passionately Puritan; those who loved popularity, Leicester and Essex, hoped to rise on the Protestant wave; powerful noblemen like Huntingdon who made Leicestershire a Puritan stronghold, officials like Paulet who upheld it in his government of the Channel Isles, merchant colonies at Antwerp and Middelburg, Drake on his ships — half the vitality of Elizabethanism was Puritan at heart. Only the Queen's determination saved the Church; ' by the grace of God and His servant Elizabeth, we are ', was the verdict of Hooker, greatest of her divines.

Two facts in particular explain the difficulty of the problem, and of suppression. The great majority of men clung to unity and abhorred toleration as an offence against the truth, their claim being not a liberty to leave the Church, but that they were the Church. The heart of the matter, therefore, was not with the two extremes, Roman Catholics on the right and the little minority on the left who asked for no State Church at all, but with the centre. It included, no doubt, a small section who willingly accepted the Queen's settlement, but also two much larger bodies, the one shading into the other, who made up probably three-fifths of the laity. There were conforming churchmen who disliked bishops, preferred their minister to wear a Geneva gown instead of a surplice, and often received the communion sitting, who yet would not for such matters break up the Church; and there were, again, the Presbyterians proper, who followed the fixed model of Geneva or Scotland. The second governing fact was the patronage system. A landlord of Puritan sympathies, like the Rich family in Essex, would appoint parsons of their own colour, or like Peter Wentworth of Northamptonshire build up round them a formal conventicle scheme. The practice of London, the Court, and cathedral towns was thus very different from that in many country parishes, and, moreover, any effort to evict such parsons would at once collide with the common law. Sooner or later these religious disputes must touch the constitution, for the Queen held the view firmly, and not without historical

ground, that the supremacy was a royal supremacy. As Parliament was
her highest court for secular matters, so she ruled the spirituality through
the episcopate and Convocation, and systematically vetoed religious bills
introduced in Parliament.

A first stage, ' the Vestiarian controversy ', quickly passed into a
second, which was much more serious. Enquiry showed there was
utter chaos in observance. In some dioceses even the surplice was not
worn. Sometimes the service was said in the nave, sometimes in the
chancel ; some received communion sitting, others standing ; some
read the prayer-book, some sang Geneva psalms. And when Catholic
plots threatened the realm, common feeling was hot against harsh
dealing with patriotic men whose only offence was that of being too
anti-Catholic ; ' shall we be used so for a surplice ', asked one of their
best leaders, ' shall we fight for the Popish coat, his head and body being
banished ? ' Two future archbishops were among those who petitioned
that the surplice should be optional ; Grindal apologetically defended
kneeling ' until the Lord shall give us better times ' ; only Parker,
unsupported by the Council and most of his brethren, insisted that
discipline must come first — ' execution, execution, execution, of laws
and orders '. In 1566 he issued his *Advertisements*, insisting on a
kneeling communion and the surplice as a minimum, and compelled
the clergy to subscribe to the prayer-book and Thirty-nine Articles.

The Puritans retorted with a model of their own, their leaders,
Cartwright the Cambridge professor and Walter Travers, being earnest
scholars, who spent much of their lives in contact with Geneva and
Heidelberg, or in ministering to English churches in the Netherlands.
In 1572 their group issued an *Admonition to the Parliament*, taking as
their principle that the word of God embraced discipline as well as
faith. The lordship of bishops must go, elders in every parish must
assist a minister elected by the congregation, and the prayer-book,
' picked out of the Popish dunghill ', must give way to the Calvinist
model. In 1574 Travers published a *Book of Discipline*, which became
the basis of several parliamentary bills.

There were good reasons for the popularity of this Puritan movement, for revolution had left the Church in a scandalous state. Clergy
were so short that in 1561 nearly a hundred livings were vacant in the
London diocese. From the top downwards there was rank materialism,
the Queen herself being an arch-offender, since she kept the see of
Oxford empty twenty years on end, and Ely eighteen, meantime taking
the revenues. Politicians got hold of bishops' lands, lay impropriators
and patrons grew rich on tithe, and appointed underpaid parsons, ' boys
and senseless asses ', Cartwright complained, or illiterate servants ; several
bishops, like Cox of Ely, speculated in leases to enrich their families.
And while riches were thus spent, elsewhere a grinding poverty killed

spiritual life. Nearly a fifth of the parishes had no resident priest, and with underpayment went pluralism and absentees, all of which, in Wales for instance, meant an almost complete absence of any Church life at all. Church courts still went on unreformed, taking money payments for penance, while a greedy set of officials lived on licences and fees.

Finding that the Queen barred the way through Parliament, the reformers set to work from the inside. In their public measure, the so-called 'prophesyings', they won much sympathy from the Church leaders. Beginning with moral reform and Scripture reading, in East Anglia and the Midlands they developed it into an unofficial Presbytery. They insisted on the sermon as the core of religion and set up courses of lectures that centred round Calvin's catechism; in some cases municipal officers and gentry acting with the minister to discipline the morals of communicants. Parker's successor Grindal and other bishops wished to continue such prophesyings under regulation, but in 1576 the Queen angrily intervened. She was coming to her final position that Puritanism was ' unfit for a kingly rule ', and on his refusal suspended the arch-bishop and kept him in disgrace till he died.

Thus frustrated in open reform, the Puritans set up a secret machinery whereby they overlaid the legal structure with their own ' classis ' system. Their ministers submitted themselves to the con-gregation's choice, merely accepting a bishop's ordination as a form, pledged themselves to the *Book of Discipline*, and left out any parts of the service they disliked. They held local synods, even national coun-cils, and began to work in parliamentary elections; between 1585-7 a Presbyterian settlement was openly advocated in the Commons, and they submitted to their political friends their own reports on the con-dition of the clergy, — their Warwickshire list thus reporting 120 out of 186 as ' dumb ', and another 48 as ' offensive to the Gospel '.

Their comparative failure was not due only to the Queen but also to the violence of some Puritans and a change in Anglicanism. Earlier in the reign government had discovered various sects, Anabaptists or the ' Family of Love ', holding meetings in alleys off the Strand or on ships in the Thames, but the Puritanism which was finally to prevail began about 1580 with Robert Browne. Taking religion as an individual faith and the Church as a congregation of ' the worthiest were they never so few ', his manifesto, ' Reformation without tarrying for any ', preached a total denial of State supremacy, and separation as the only way to freedom. Browne himself returned to the Church, but his extreme followers set up their own congregations, and their denial of the royal supremacy, with some wild talk of rebellion, brought several (notably the Welshman Penry) to execution in 1593, an Act of the same year punishing attendance at conventicles with banishment. And to exile in Holland many of these early Congregationalists fled.

Moderate Puritanism was damaged further by a scurrilous propaganda, which reached a climax in pamphlets issued by a secret press in 1588–90. The unknown authors, who signed themselves ' Martin Marprelate ', defied the government censorship, raked in the personal failings of every dignitary — asking, for instance, did not the bishop of London play bowls on the Sabbath ? — and derided ' petty anti-Christs, wainscot-faced bishops, and unpreaching parsons '.

Meanwhile the Church which they abused had found a new leader, and some old principles. Whitgift, who replaced the unhappy Grindal in 1583, was a man after the Queen's heart, whom she called ' her little black husband '. Though firmly Calvinist in doctrine, he laid hold on two Puritan points as particularly intolerable, the equality of ministers and the claim that Scripture was the only warrant for worship. Against the opposition of half the Council and remonstrance from Burghley, he compelled the clergy to subscribe to the Supremacy, and to declare that neither prayer-book nor Articles contained anything contrary to the Word of God. His instrument was the High Commission, so much enlarged and centralized that it practically swallowed up other Church courts ; its procedure, which Burghley said savoured of the Inquisition, was that of the old Canon law, the administration of the *ex-officio* oath which would convict a man out of his own mouth. And the penalty was deprivation, or suspension from their livings, which he pressed on in the teeth of the Commons and magistrates. Yet he was a reformer as well as a martinet. He allowed modified ' prophesyings ' to be revived, and put some check on pluralism, non-residence, and abuse of excommunication.

At the turn of the century there came about a certain Catholic reaction in all Europe. It was a generation which respected learning, and the method of learned bishops like Parker and Jewel justified Englishmen in believing that the middle way of their Church was a good one. Alongside the Scriptures they put the authority of the first four centuries, before Rome had encroached on primitive order. Whitgift's right hand and successor, Bancroft, led a new school who argued that episcopacy was an essential mark of the Church, and an Anglo-Catholic piety was developing, represented by the saintly Lancelot Andrewes. Such men filled with a deeper meaning the idea stated in many Tudor Acts of Parliament, that the English Reformation had been not revolution but restoration, and in 1593 Richard Hooker, after many years' controversy with Travers, published the first books of his *Ecclesiastical Polity*. From this deep well of wisdom the Church, as years went on, drew its final justification : that law, the voice of God, was the scheme of creation ; that it must include reason, God's gift to man, which Scripture had not come to supersede but to re-enforce ; that, though Scripture contained all things necessary for salvation, it left to reason and civil wisdom a wide field of things ' indifferent ', whether a surplice or outward government; and that the Church was an organic society, with a capacity of development.

Such reasoning might, it was hoped, one day conciliate Puritanism, but meantime the feud of religion strained the Constitution. The Commons indeed felt sincerely, as they told the Queen, that ' Your Majesty and your faithful Commons are but one body politic ', and her wisdom in keeping some principal Councillors in their House was some guarantee against conflict. Yet the very benefits of her reign enhanced their self-conscious power. Years of peace, with Burghley's constitutional moderation, increased respect for law, while the mass of important business put before them spurred them to develop their own procedure. It was in this age that they worked out their committee system : the ' committee of the whole House ', when they put the Speaker, the royal agent, out of the Chair; and special committees for privilege and elections.

Religion more than any single thing hastened this constitutional conflict. Elizabeth's insistence that supremacy belonged to her alone came out clearly in the history of the Articles. To the thirty-nine drawn up by Convocation in 1563 she herself added a vital clause, ' the Church hath power to decree rites and ceremonies, and authority in controversies of faith '; and though the Statute of 1571 ordered the clergy to subscribe only to the Articles of 1563, and then only so far as they concerned doctrine, in practice the archbishops compelled subscription to them all, as amended by the Queen and themselves. What, again, was the legal validity of Canons, when duly sanctioned by Convocation and the Crown, and were they binding, especially on laymen, without parliamentary consent ?

What touched men's lives more nearly, their daily bread, and their legal sense, was the Court of High Commission. After many temporary commissions issued by her predecessors, Elizabeth's Act of Supremacy set up a permanent court. Were its powers then, as common lawyers argued, strictly limited to that statute and the scope of the mediaeval Church courts which it replaced ? Actually her letters-patent repeated those of Mary, giving the Commission power to fine and imprison, and its *ex officio* oath was borrowed from the Canon law. All such argument came to a head in 1591 in the case of Cawdrey, a parson holding one of Burghley's own livings, who had refused the surplice and called the prayer-book a vile book, and whom the Commission therefore deprived; their powers were legal, the judges of the Queen's Bench decided, even if in conflict with statute, in virtue of the Crown's supremacy.

So thirty years of struggle confronted an angry House of Commons with a doctrine and ceremonies which they disliked, maintained on legal grounds which they denied. The Queen's repeated suppression of Church bills and imprisonment of members enlarged the quarrel to the whole of parliamentary liberty. Their privilege, she told them, was freedom to say ' yea and no ' with their reasons, ' a liberal but not licentious speech ', but not to ' frame a form of religion or a state of government '; not under ' vizors of liberty ' to encroach on the royal province of Church, succession, and policy. Every kitchen-maid, she once scornfully said, took it on herself to condemn ministers of religion; and so the Commons, ' overbold with God Almighty ', presumed to criticize her government under the ' veil of God's word '. It was against this that Peter Wentworth led a loyal but bitter opposition. ' Sweet is the name of liberty ', began his famous speech against these royal messages; he would not refer doctrine to the bishops, for that were to make them ' popes '. Parliament, he declared, was a place of free speech for all the griefs of the commonwealth, no other Council could make or change law, and the Speaker was its servant. After several previous imprisonments, in 1593 he was sent to the Tower for propaganda in favour of a succession bill, where after nearly four years he died.

The Council's activity was, moreover, raising a general clamour against all the other courts — the Admiral's, Council of the North, Church courts, or Court of Requests — whose power rested on ancient prerogative or special commission; was, indeed, raising the largest of questions, to a claim that there was only one sovereign rule, that of Parliament and the common law. It was nourished on grievances other than religion. The war period was one of general strain. Taxation after 1589 raised three times the amount of the previous thirty years. There was constant conscription of county trained-bands or of Cornish miners for service abroad, a seizure of recruits even during their Easter communion, sometimes soldiers maimed in the wars dogged the entrance to Parliament. Government demanded ships from the coast towns, forcing those inland also to assist, as for instance York to assist Hull. Upheaval abroad and change of markets increased unemployment. Commerce and industry had begun to defy regulation; Yorkshire clothiers attacked the Council of the North; interlopers challenged the monopoly of the chartered companies. Voices in the Commons muttered that anti-enclosure laws were ' moth-eaten ', merchants objected to the Church's condemnation of usury, and the public service, now becoming a career, suffered the evils of crude youth. There was no notion of proper salaries; men sought office or military command to make their fortune; and even a high-minded man like Walsingham made large profits out of farming the customs.

Of one economic grievance the Commons complained over many sessions, the monopolies assigned by the Crown, either as a patent for a

new industry or as a controlling licence, to reward officials and favourites. It was a chief grievance in the angry session of 1597–8, during
which the Queen vetoed ten bills, and the next in 1601 was more angry
still, ' more fit for a grammar school ', said Robert Cecil, ' than a court
of Parliament ', while the Commons ' hawked, spat, and hemmed '.
The Queen, who had passed some patents against the Cecils' protest,
had not kept her promise to try them ' by the touchstone of the law ',
while some monopolies concerned necessities of life like salt, coal, or
leather. Raleigh alone held them for playing-cards, tin, and sweet wines.
' Is not bread there ? ' asked one member. ' What purpose is it ', said
another, ' to do anything by Act of Parliament, when the Queen will undo
the same by her prerogative ? ' So the Queen made the most glorious of
her retreats : speaking to the Commons for the last time, she said with
truth she had never been a ' grasper ' or a ' waster ', and withdrew the
monopolies she had allowed ' for lack of true information ', though
stoutly affirming her ' prerogative royal '. But the Parliament whom
she dismissed, weeping and fascinated, was not yet trained to defy
prerogative, and the opposition, as seen in 1601, was expressed in an
older and less constitutional form.

Essex concentrated the pride, the quarrels, and popularity of the age.
Grandson of Knollys, stepson of Leicester, husband of Philip Sidney's
widow and Walsingham's daughter, he was heir at once to the war-
party and to the magnates who had contested power with Burghley. He
had fought gallantly at Zutphen, Rouen, and Lisbon, and made himself
the nation's hero by the sack of Cadiz. Burghley was very old ; of his
rivals, Raleigh was put in the shade by an unlucky marriage, and the
younger Cecil was no courtier and a hunchback. Essex aimed at
political supremacy, spent money lavishly on an intelligence system in
Europe which would impress the Queen, and collected round him
soldiers and wits ; they would make the old fox Burghley ' crouch and
whine ', said Anthony Bacon. Steadily he amassed the offices which
immediately surrounded the Queen and controlled the army, those of
Master of the Horse, Earl-Marshall, and Master of the Ordnance. But
the Queen resented this pressure, and his monopoly of power ; she
twice passed over the younger Bacon, Francis, for legal office, and after
Burghley's death gave her chief confidence to his son Robert.

It was not a happy thing for England that this daring soldier could
come so near supremacy through popular arts and royal favour. But
his lack of character soon destroyed him. He was not one of those who
took calmly a box on the ears from the Queen ; he began to speak of her
lightly, and threatened to use force. In 1599, as head of the war-party
and to vindicate his criticism of others, he took command of the Irish
war. He asked enormous powers, appointed his own staff, yet accomplished nothing, except to create some sixty knights and to decimate his

army by mismanagement. He then opened treasonable negotiation with the rebels, and planned to march from a Welsh port to overthrow his enemies. He was recalled and condemned to the loss of his offices, though soon allowed to return to Court. But he could not stomach any place except the first; he tried to induce Mountjoy, lover of his sister Lady Rich and now commanding in Ireland, to send him troops, opened contact with James VI, drew round him Puritan preachers who offered public prayers for their ' noble Barak ', and some of the young Catholics who later took part in the Gunpowder plot. Young nobles of high names and talent joined him : Shakespeare's patron Southampton, Bedford, Rutland, and a ring of soldiers. Wild heads from the Mermaid tavern clamoured with rapiers in the streets at night, and staged at the Globe theatre Shakespeare's *Richard II*, the play that spoke of deposing a sovereign. Their scheme was to seize the Court and force the Queen to dismiss Cecil, and in February 1601 Essex rode in revolt through Cheapside with wild cries of Spanish plots. But the people would not rise against the Queen, and he was arrested ; Francis Bacon, who had warned him against men of war, led against him now as Crown prosecutor, and his peers condemned him to death.

Ballads and sightseers long showed the people's grief ; for, traitor though he was, he represented their growing discontents. Nothing, however, shook their loyalty to the Queen, or overturned the motto the dying Burghley left his son, ' serve God by serving of the Queen '. Her high spirit, her health preserved by spare living, lasted till she entered her seventieth year. And with it a confidence, which her subjects shared, that she was indeed an instrument of God ; for the Church, ' whose over-ruler God hath made me ', and for the soldiers and sailors to whom she promised victory, ' in His name that ever hath protected my righteous cause '. In this faith — that evil rewarded those who encroached on her sceptre — she struck down Essex whom she loved, and held power fast while her strength endured ; her last years being illumined by victory in Ireland and by triumph for the soldiers who helped the Dutch to win the battle at Nieuport that saved Ostend.

But all felt that a new age had begun, her courtiers were secretly agreed that the Scots king must be her successor, and post-horses for Edinburgh were ready saddled. She died on the 24th March 1603, keeping Whitgift, so long as she was conscious, praying by her side.

CONTEMPORARY DATES

1574-89	Henry III of France.
1575	Akbar conquers Bengal.
1576	Pacification of Ghent.
	Opening of first London theatre.
	-1612. The Emperor Rudolf II.
1578	Alexander Farnese succeeds Don Juan of Austria in the Low Countries.
	Lyly's *Euphues*.
1579	Duplessis Mornay's *Vindiciae contra Tyrannos*.
	Socinus in Poland.
1580	Russian venturers enter Siberia.
	Spanish conquest of Portugal.
1581	Anjou accepts sovereignty of the Netherlands.
1582	The Gregorian Calendar introduced.
	Hakluyt's *Voyages*.
1584	Murder of William the Silent.
1585	Spain and the Guises attack Henry of Navarre.
	Shakespeare settles in London.
1586	Sidney killed at Zutphen.
	Camden's *Britannia*.
1589	Accession of Henry IV in France.
	Arminius teaching at Amsterdam.
1590	Spenser's *Faerie Queene*.
1592	Death of Montaigne.
	The Japanese invade Korea.
1593	Henry of Navarre goes to Mass.
	Hooker's *Ecclesiastical Polity*.
1595	Death of Tasso.
	Dutch settlement in Java.
1596	Birth of Descartes.
1597	Maurice of Nassau resisting Spain.
	Bacon's first *Essays*.
1598	Edict of Nantes.
	Death of Philip II.
1599	Sully reforming finances of France.
1600	Founding of the East India Company.
	Gilbert's work on electricity.
	Shakespeare's *Midsummer Night's Dream*.
1602	Opening of Bodleian library.
1603	Champlain sails for Canada.
	Shakespeare's *Hamlet*.
	Althusius on political theory.

CHAPTER VI

SCOTLAND, 1370–1603

MEDIAEVAL England had failed to destroy the independence of Scotland, which won a new security by the Hundred Years' War. And for both peoples it was well that Union was postponed until they were nearer in character.

The country was poor, its population even in 1500 being under a million, covered with forests where the wolf could still be found, and divided by nature into its four original components — the mountainous Highlands where had ruled the Picts, Argyll and the Islands where had come the Scots of Dalriada, the hilly south-west which had been Strathclyde, and the south-eastern plain filled in turn by Angle settlers and Norman barons. There was a rude export trade in wool, hides, and fish, largely going to the Staple in the Isle of Flushing; and the Scots were good shipbuilders and fishermen. But trade and industry were at the mercy of a rude rural society, subsisting on the bread and ale made from their oats, on their fisheries and herds, and little organized except for war. To these causes of division must be added the inflammable English frontier. It ran for seventy miles aslant northeastward over moors and deep valleys, where armies were lost in fogs and where driven cattle and outlaws hid in safety. Here the Armstrongs, Elliotts, Fenwicks, and Graemes plied their wild life, taking a head for a head, defying the March Wardens of both governments. Houses fired, bloodhounds in chase, Coldstream nuns or Redesdale outlaws in English pay, women spies, — so the frontier smouldered from Solway and the Debatable Land to the upper Tyne, blazing up every few years into the bale-fire beacons, which flamed their warning from hill to hill until it reached Edinburgh.

Imported from England in the twelfth century, the feudal system of Lothian never succeeded in unifying Scotland, or expanded as in England into parliamentary government. Robert Bruce summoned burgesses to pay for his wars, and three Estates were accepted by the end of his son's reign : but to collect taxes was almost impossible, the Estates' attendance was irregular, and several efforts failed to secure representation of the lairds. Indeed, the Scottish Parliament had a history more like that of France or Spain. It remained mediaeval. It was a single chamber, the Commons having no Speaker or organized life ; a body, in fact, of feudal estates representing only tenants-in-chief, each estate voting taxes separately and distinguished by wearing different robes. Like its English sister it began as an expanded royal Council but, unlike her, never rid itself of that origin. The first general Councils, later called Conventions, were used to do all parliamentary business except justice, and it was easy to pack such bodies, while a full Parliament, which was comparatively rare, was always more like a court of registration, or a congress, than a legislature. For the royal burghs had a Convention of their own which prepared edicts touching their special interests, while from the first it was customary to delegate business to commissions, which developed by the fifteenth century into the Lords of the Articles, a small body usually composed of officials, who predigested legislation and acted in the intervals of Parliament. Meantime David and his successors developed out of another committee the law court which became the Court of Session, though Parliament itself continued as a court of high justice.

Robert Bruce impoverished the Crown by grants to his party, David by the strain of his ransom, and poverty continued with the granting away of royal lands and rights to the nobility. National weakness came in part, however, from sheer ill-fortune. When David died, he was succeeded, as long arranged, by his sister Marjorie's husband Robert the Steward, head of that branch of the Shropshire FitzAlans who had for a hundred years made their office hereditary in Scotland. But both Robert II and his son Robert III came to the throne when old and having little energy; then James I was a prisoner in England for eighteen years, as against thirteen of rule in Scotland; thereafter every reign, up to and including James VI's, began with a minority; an unhappy sequence which gave opportunity to two sorts of feudalism which in Scotland lived side by side. Real feudalism, the powers of the territorial chief and often the still older power of the clan, was the lesser evil, strong though it was proved times without number in the Isles and the north. The supreme danger was what the French called the ' appanaged ' feudalism, the power of members of the royal family married into old houses, and enriched by offices and lands. In this way rose the lordships of Douglas, Lennox, or Hamilton, a circle of royal kinsmen suffocating the King. Besides this, something of the politics of the harem corrupted the throne, the heirs of first marriages warring with sons of the second, and ambitious bastards fighting for a lordship or a rich abbey. Nor could any unwarlike King control this nobility who lived by war, and won themselves glory in French armies, or on Spanish and Prussian crusades.

While Robert III merely reigned and while James I was a captive, Robert's brother Albany as Regent shared power with the Earls of Douglas. Whether he was responsible either for the mysterious death of his elder nephew Rothesay or the long captivity of James, is unproven, but under him Scottish power did not deteriorate. Richard II's pacific policy, the Lancastrians' difficulties, and then the French war, allowed the Scots to hold their own; in 1411 a victory at Harlaw near Aberdeen broke the almost royal power of the Lord of the Isles. After the Regent's death two Kings of real force measured their power against the nobles. James I returned from England with his Beaufort wife, a high standard of government, and a wish for revenge. Within a year he executed his cousin the second Albany, got from Parliament a *quo warranto* inquiry into baronial titles, and suppressed the earldom of Lennox; March and Mar soon followed. He drove his people hard with legislation, showed his Parliament at Inverness, published his laws in the Scots tongue. A few nobles were made hereditary lords of Parliament, and the King tried to enforce attendance of the lairds. He was only forty-three when in 1437 he was murdered at Perth, by a conspiracy of his kinsman Athol with the nobles whom he had wronged.

James II succeeded as a boy of seven, and his ministers, fighting for power through his name, first attacked the mighty Douglas. The supremacy of the Black Douglas over all south-west Scotland, and along the Border to Jedburgh, went back to Robert Bruce's companion, the good Sir James. James the second earl was a hero of song and killed in the renowned night battle of Otterburn in 1388. The third, Archibald the Grim, had fought against Albany; Archibald the Tyneman, the fourth, lost an eye fighting against the Percies at Homildon, fought on their side against Henry IV at Shrewsbury, and received a duchy from the French Crown. In 1440 the Livingstones and Crichtons, who ruled for the young King, seized and executed the sixth earl and his brother, but soon a vigorous new Douglas had the ability to divide them and prepared revenge by political marriages and a Highland alliance. Then James II came of age, married a strong-minded Burgundian princess, and challenged this threat to government. Assisted by the admirable James Kennedy, bishop of St. Andrews and benefactor of its University, he attacked the Douglas castles; in 1452 he demanded the cancelling of their ' bands ' with the tigerish Earl of Crawford and the Lord of the Isles, and when Douglas refused, the King's dirk struck the first blow which, oft repeated by his attendants, tossed the Black Douglas's body into the courtyard of Stirling Castle. His brother, ninth and last earl, flung himself into alliance with England; the King drove him into exile there, bombarded his strongholds with artillery, and raised on the ruins of the Black Douglas the fortunes of the Red Douglas, Earls of Angus. Acts of resumption brought back many lands to the Crown, while alliance with Henry VI restored in 1460–61 the hundred-year-old losses of Roxburgh and Berwick.

It was while testing one of his cannon in these sieges that James II was blown to pieces, and the minority — and afterwards the character of James III — showed how weak a thing even now was Scottish government. When the Queen-Mother and bishop Kennedy died, a single knightly family, the Boyds, were able to dominate King and Parliament. The King grew up solitary, a lover of the arts, despised by his nobles, surrounded by companions of low birth, and in sharp contrast with his warlike brothers. For many years he had good fortune. Lancastrian plots and French wars kept Edward IV moderate, and allowed the Scots to hold off the exile Douglas, while by marriage with a Danish princess they were able to redeem the Orkneys and Shetlands. But from 1479 troubles ran together in a flood. The royal favourites incited James to attack his brothers, one of whom died in prison; Albany the survivor joined Edward IV, against whom Louis XI of France stirred up a Scottish war. So came about an English invasion, the violent execution of the King's friends, and in 1482 the loss of Berwick. Edward's death, a new exile of Albany, strife in England, for a time saved the King, yet his passion against the barons raised against him a new coalition. Though Douglas was now a prisoner and the Lord of the Isles reduced, the newer families raised up in their places — Angus, Argyll, and Hepburns — had the same ambition. In 1488, encouraged afar off by Henry Tudor, they stimulated the heir against his father and, after a skirmish near Stirling, James III was caught and murdered.

From the days of James IV we enter a new epoch, which ended in the Union. Hatred of England was never more bitter, yet strong reasons were raising a generation with a new outlook. Scottish civilization advanced very rapidly in the fifteenth century; three University foundations, St. Andrews (1414), Glasgow (1451), and Aberdeen (1495), reduced the migration of students to Paris; James IV ordered the sons of landowners to be taught Latin and chartered the first Scottish printing press. In his day flourished the poets Dunbar and Gavin Douglas, who did for Scots what Chaucer had done for English, and the national historians Boece, first principal of Aberdeen, and John Major. Another curious proof of prosperity lay in the pirate traders, Andrew Wood and the Bartons, who scourged the North Sea, took ships to help the King's Danish kinsmen against the Swedes, and threatened communication between England and Ireland. Fishery laws and some Flemish immigration increased national wealth, and a third fact indicated that mediaeval Scotland was passing away. The century was young when Lollards both from England and Bohemia reached Scotland and in a few cases testified their faith at the stake, and in 1494 a swarm of heretics was found in Ayrshire, where later Presbyterianism took on a fanatical form. Not unconnected with such things was the sentiment which opposed war with England, having more interest now in trade and low taxation than the old French alliance.

Though like Solomon in his love of women, and much his inferior in wisdom, James IV was an ardent, active man. An iron chain that wore his flesh, and journeys to many shrines, marked remorse for his father's murder, but when his soul was free he was a man of action. After many visits he crushed the wild men of the Islands, dividing authority over their vast spaces between the new houses of Huntly and Argyll. His passion for shipbuilding and diplomatic activity raised Scotland in Europe, while the general loyalty of the nobles showed that a King with spirit could hold the country together.

But there was one exception to this general obedience. Angus, inheriting the ambitions of Douglas, became a pensioner of Henry VII, who began the Tudor policy of penetration. Yet Henry would get his way by peace, if he could, and very early offered James his daughter Margaret, and when James at last abandoned Warbeck the marriage came about in 1503, so giving England a direct interest in the succession. Unhappily, Henry VIII's aggression against France, his high-handed treatment of Scottish shipping, the death of Andrew Barton at English hands, and perpetual frontier trouble, all confirmed James' chivalrous desire to cling to the French, of which Flodden was the result, and much more than a military defeat. With the King fell on the field twelve earls, fourteen lords, and ' the flower of the forest '; which for a generation extinguished the nobility. The overweening power of England strengthened those who would not fight England again, and the future of Scotland became, as never before, a part and parcel of international politics.

While James V grew up in infancy, power was bandied about between rival claims, the Frenchman Albany, son of James III's brother and rival, Arran head of the Hamiltons, and the wilful Margaret Tudor, the queen-mother, who within a year of Flodden married Angus. Fifteen years of chaos followed; of fleeting visits from Albany and his final retreat to France, Margaret's speedy quarrel with Angus, and street-fighting in Edinburgh between Douglases and Hamiltons. English money debauched half the lords of the south, Henry VIII hoped to get his nephew into his hands, and sent Surrey to make a desert on the Border.

His violence hardened the Scots, and the monopoly of Douglas power brought a great welcome for the young King when in 1528 he drove out Angus. But his attacks on the Armstrongs and other Border reivers, on the Isles and Argyll, his dependence on bishops and his two French marriages, challenged the nobility, while the Reformation created a decisive influence for Henry, whose nightmare was a Catholic coalition and who knew of the Scots' assistance to the Irish. In vain he tempted his nephew with the English succession, or incited him to break with Rome. James V, with his second wife Mary of Guise and his adviser

Cardinal Beaton, stood true to old causes, and against his barons' advice pressed on war, and hence the disaster of Solway Moss. It broke the King's heart and within a month he was dead, only thirty years old, grieving most at his favourite Oliver Sinclair's death : ' ever he harped ', says John Knox, ' on his old song, " is Oliver ta'en ? all is lost ".' He lived a week after the birth of his daughter Mary, later Queen of Scots, and since both his sons were dead, declared that the Crown, which had come to the Stuarts by a lass, would pass from them in another.

What seemed predestined and natural, a union of the two kingdoms by the marriage of Mary and the English heir Edward, was made impossible by Henry VIII's claim of sovereignty, and his army's burning of Edinburgh and Holyrood, which almost killed the English party ; he would not be false to the English alliance, said the Laird of Buccleuch, even ' if all Teviotdale were burned to the bottom of hell '. The assassination of Beaton, which Henry encouraged, brought in a French army and in 1548 Mary was sent to France. Somerset's Pinkie campaign and Northumberland's ignominious peace of 1550 strengthened French supremacy, which rose to its height with the appointment of Mary of Guise as Regent, and the accession of the younger Mary to the French throne in 1559, with a secret promise that, failing heirs of her body, Scotland should fall to France. How that combination was destroyed by Elizabeth, in alliance with Scottish Protestantism, has been seen.

The Scottish pre-Reformation Church was nearer to the German than the English type. Its bishops were great magnates, ministers like the Beatons, or sons of great houses like Douglas and Hamilton, and the nobles had large interests in Church land and patronage. Its extortions were cruel ; the peasantry suffered much from tithe, widows and orphans had their cow, or their last coverlet, taken for a mortuary. The churchmen's morals were infamous ; Hepburn, bishop of Moray, admitted to ten natural children. All through the 'twenties Lutheran books and Tyndale's Testament had come in, and in 1528 the Church burned Patrick Hamilton, despite his royal blood, who brought back heresy from Wittenburg. Several friars suffered in the 'thirties, while many reformers escaped abroad, including Buchanan the future tutor of James VI. David Lindsay's *Satires*, which made him almost a Scottish Erasmus, showed some of the universal irreverence. The English example and a Bible in the Scots tongue increased the excitement, which was carried high by the preacher George Wishart in the west and at Dundee ; higher still by his martyrdom in 1546, with the murder of Beaton that followed it. With Wishart had worked John Knox of Haddington, who joined Beaton's murderers in St. Andrews Castle, suffered for it by imprisonment in the French galleys, worked in northern England, and at Mary's accession fled to Geneva. If from this experience and Calvin's teaching he got his model of Church government, the force which made him the Scottish Luther was all his own; an absolute assurance that, while ' light and darkness strive ', light would defeat the dumb dogs of Romanism; an assurance, wrote Elizabeth's envoy, ' as though he were of God's Privy Council ', with a voice ' able to put more life into us in one hour than five hundred trumpets '.

Before his exile Protestant ballads were singing ' the night is near gone ', and before Queen Mary returned from France, Protestantism made itself invincible. During 1555–6 Knox won the sympathies of Lord James Stuart, Argyll, Lethington, and the lairds of Fife, being protected also by the plain fact that the Regent's French government, threatened by England and Spain, dared not persecute at home. In this alliance of the aristocracy with the reformers lay the Protestant victory ; the lairds coveted the Church's broad lands and, though it was an alliance not favourable to pure religion, it was the only one which could save reform. So rose the Lords of the Congregation, whose campaign was a triumph of skilful audacity. Entrenching themselves at first in a demand for mere liberty of worship, by 1558 they were strong enough to defy the Regent's effort to silence their preachers, and to enforce a religious truce. They could count on much pure zeal like that of the Ayrshire contingent, though they also attracted Catholics into the political side of their movement, which they based on resistance to a French servitude.

The revolution which began in May 1559, with the reappearance of Knox and the destruction of churches at Perth and St. Andrews, was accomplished in 1560 in the treaty of Edinburgh and the Parliament that followed. Meeting without the Queen's leave and swollen by an unusual attendance of lairds, the Estates adopted a Knoxian confession of faith, abolished Papal jurisdiction and all practices of ' that horrible harlot, the Kirk malignant ', and forbade the Mass under penalty of death. The first Book of Discipline accepted the liturgy that Knox had used at Geneva, setting up a fabric of church government that descended from a general assembly down to the Kirk session of minister and elders in every parish. But on the question of endowment the ministers had to give way to the aristocracy. The Council arranged to divide a third of church revenues between the Crown and Protestant ministers, leaving two-thirds nominally to maintain the old Catholic interests but, in fact, going to the laymen who had dipped their hands deep in church property.

Such on paper was the Protestant settlement which had to fight another twenty years for its life. It had three obvious weaknesses. English armed intervention might still have to protect it, — a protection odious to patriotic feeling. Outside Edinburgh and the southern towns it represented only a minority. And it contained the elements of a deadly struggle between Church and State.

In all countries the Reformation corrupted religion by the rivalries of politics, but never more than in Scotland during the years 1562-90 : through the character of Mary, a succession dependent on the life of one child, the policy of England, individual ambition and clan feuds. A Scottish patriot would wish to see peacefully accomplished the union of the Crowns and to avoid religious war. Such was the first thought of the Queen's early advisers : her bastard brother James Stuart (later the Regent Moray) who was a sincere Protestant, and Maitland of Lethington whom Elizabeth called the flower of the wits of Scotland. But Elizabeth and Mary between them doomed Scottish peace. If Elizabeth's refusal to name her successor was intelligible from an English point of view, it goaded Mary to desperation, and though Mary died a martyr of the counter-Reformation, the Papacy severely noted she was ' the slave of her passions '. Indeed she was first a woman, then a sovereign, and only last a Catholic. Her first instinct on arrival in England in 1568 was to send for her hairdresser, and new clothes occupied her imprisonment as much as the old faith. Her ready gift of tears and her exultant courage in galloping with men-at-arms, the power that won back the sulky Darnley to betray his fellow-plotters or could fascinate her jailors, were not incompatible with a hard heart and a lust for revenge. She lost her love for Darnley in six months, equally rapidly forgot Bothwell, and tried for a divorce to recover her throne. That she plotted Elizabeth's assassination is certain ; that she at least connived at Darnley's murder is certain also, rather from the general evidence of her actions than from the unproven testimony of her letters and poems which were captured in the casket taken from Bothwell. She was, in fact, a *politique*, like her mother-in-law and enemy, Catharine de Medici. In her first years, though insisting on her own Mass, she made no attempt to upset the revolution. Public causes, however, Catholic temptations from abroad, Catholic loyalty in the Highlands and the bigotry of the Kirk, drove her on to use the Darnley marriage in order to ruin the Protestant lords and re-establish Catholicism. Even so, she employed Protestants to slay Darnley and married Bothwell with a Protestant rite.

In the whirlpool set up by her passions all public decency perished, and the Scottish ruling class combined the murderousness of Afghans with the cynicism of renaissance Italy. The ' Catholic ' Huntly who had resisted Mary of Guise joined with the other master of the north, the ' Protestant ' Argyll, to restore Mary. The Protestant lords who combined with Darnley to kill Rizzio, and were betrayed by him, joined Mary to kill Darnley, and then dethroned her for the crime, moved not by the murder but by her marriage to Bothwell. Lennox, who had crowned his son Darnley on a Catholic platform, lived henceforth to revenge him by Protestant assistance. The Hamiltons, never dropping their ambitions on the throne, first proposed the execution of Mary; then, finding themselves in danger, rallied to her, murdered one Regent, Moray, and killed another, Lennox, in battle. In archbishop Hamilton, the brain of their house, who began his career as a boy abbot, who saw the Church's weakness and composed an admirable catechism, whose mistress when he was archbishop was ordered out of Edinburgh, and who was hung for his share in the murders of Darnley and Moray, — in this life appear the vices and contradictions of that Scotland. The struggle, therefore, which began with Mary's marriage to Bothwell and the Protestant victory, alike partook more of politics than religion.

Knox and the Kirk would have executed Mary, who was saved by English pressure and Scottish politicians; James VI was crowned in 1567 and Parliament confirmed the Acts of 1560. But the bare fact that Moray was made Regent was enough to make the Hamiltons plan Mary's escape from Loch Leven, and for five years plans for her restoration threw Scotland into civil war. Though most of the middle class stood by the King, a majority of nobles were on Mary's side, some through ties of blood, some for fear of disclosure if Darnley's murder were investigated, and even more from hatred of England, like Lethington who swore he would make Elizabeth ' sit on her tail and whine '. The decision came in the crisis of 1569 which convinced both Cecil and Moray that the restoration of Mary must be stopped. When Moray was murdered in 1570 by a Hamilton, the Border was still alight, and again it was an English army which installed Lennox as Regent and stopped a Catholic restoration. But it was not till the end of 1571 that, on discovery of the Ridolfi plot, Elizabeth dropped the idea of restoration by agreement, and by that time Lennox had fallen in battle.

Through the brief regency of Mar, 1571–2, the King's party slowly gained ground; when Knox died in October 1572 the Protestant political victory was assured. The next Regent was the sinister Morton who, in 1573, aided by English guns took Edinburgh Castle, with which, and with Lethington's death, the national cause of Mary expired. The diplomatic revolution of better relations between England and France, moreover, assisted the Scottish revolution, and Morton's regency, 1572–8, triumphed. This leader of the Douglas house had been the strong man behind Moray's suave pondering diplomacy, and he proceeded now to crush opposition by force, just as he had once agreed to the butchery of Darnley. By taking hostages and raising a standing army he stamped out anarchy on the Border and among the northern clans. But though he spoke the language of the Puritans, he stood for only a political Protestantism, simply using the Church's wealth to build up his own party. Against Knox's dying protest he made the Church retain the bishoprics, those ' tulchan ' bishops whose revenues flowed into the politicians' pockets.

In 1579, however, he was overthrown by a combination of God and Mammon, from the young King's circle, the Kirk leaders, and the surviving Marian nobles. ' All the devils in hell ', wrote the veteran English envoy, were loose again; so it was for the next ten years, while the young King was directed by dangerous adventurers — Esmé Stuart whom he summoned from France and made duke of Lennox, the soldier of fortune James Stuart, to whom he transferred the earldom of Arran and who betrayed Lennox, and the infamous Master of Gray who betrayed Arran. Under these men the counter-Reformation tried its last fall. A third of the nobles were Catholic, the north was almost solidly so under leaders like Huntly, and pockets on the Border under the Maxwells and Kers. To suppress them by force was not in James's power, nor his desire. While his mother lived, a Catholic scheme was possible in England, and from Elizabeth he could neither get recognition as her heir nor a fixed income. And since the Catholic danger drove the Kirk to make enormous claims, his loathing of the presbyters increased his wish to stand between the factions. He could not commit himself too deep but he dabbled in dangerous promises to Rome, and Scottish Protestantism was saved, not so much by its own strength as by English intervention and the quarrels between French and Spanish agents.

So came about an ugly pattern of crime and reaction; Morton's execution in 1581, the uncertain Raid of Ruthven in 1582 when the Protestant nobles took James prisoner and expelled Lennox, James' escape the next year and the ascendancy of Arran, and again the overturn of Arran in 1585 by Protestant exiles from England. These oscillations diminished as the King became his own master with Elizabeth's grant of an annual pension and the execution of his mother. He had never much heart, but none at all for her who had promised his throne to Spain, and so he offered no more than a mild protest. Not only did the defeat of the Armada anchor him, but he found a congenial subject in exchanging notes with Elizabeth on the menace of the Puritans, for while his Kirk publicly prayed against ' the tyranny of bishops in our neighbour land ', the English extremists took refuge in Edinburgh. By 1600 he had a full understanding with the younger Cecil. And yet, as an Englishman wrote of his weak legs and perpetual pacing round the room, ' his walk was ever circular '. In the early 1590's Protestant Scotland was in a frenzy of anti-Popery. Scottish Jesuits and a Papal nuncio came to incite the Catholics to avenge Mary, and there were plots for a Spanish invasion. But while the Kirk demanded fire and sword, James shielded and finally reconciled the Catholic peers; it was not only that he declined to reopen civil war and hated the Kirk more than the Catholics, but that against a Spanish candidate for the English Crown, or the rival claims of his cousin Arabella Stuart, he wished to have the Catholic voice.

So threatened by violence from his cradle, trampled on and reduced to tears by the factions — 'better bairns greet than bearded men', the Ruthven group told him, — James was falseness incarnate, vain beyond words, tyrannical to those at his mercy, but withal a man of real ability, who had thought out his plan for winning the English succession. It involved a settlement with the Kirk; the democracy, as he saw it, which had challenged his mother and his grandmother, which divided Scotland, and would divide it from Anglican England. Accordingly his attitude to Presbytery became the measure of his power.

To the Kirk Scotland owed the defeat of the Catholic schemers and, in the long run, of absolute monarchy also. This was the work especially of Knox's successor Andrew Melville, a man of learning and unbreakable courage. In a famous interview, telling James he was only 'God's silly vassal', he expounded the Kirk's teaching that there were 'two Kings and two kingdoms in Scotland', and how of the superior kingdom of Christ James himself was merely a subject. For though claiming only independence, the Kirk really asked supremacy. Its ministers must be free to speak of all things touching Christ's kingdom without interference from a lay court; in its ministers the King must 'reverence the majesty of God speaking by them'; the civil power must carry out its sentence of excommunication. In its general assembly the Kirk had an organ more representative of the middle class than Parliament, while its pulpits performed the work of the press, and it resolved to undo the imperfection of Morton's system and in 1580–81 staked its claims. By setting up presbyters it completed its structure and control of ordination; the second Book of Discipline condemned episcopacy and asserted the Kirk's independence. James took up the challenge, pursuing it for fifteen years. His first victories were the 'black acts' of 1584, which declared the King head of the Church and empowered him to appoint bishops, and though at the height of the anti-Popery excitement in 1592 he passed the 'golden' Acts accepting the presbyteries, they did not check his triumph.

In part it was due to the fact that the Kirk was a tyranny, unrepresentative either of all Scotland or of human nature. Its pulpit denunciation of the King's profanity or the Queen's neglect of the Word, the dragging of political enemies to do open penance, its growing sabbatarianism, incitement to witch hunting, savage Acts of Parliament against immorality and oaths, all these made for a reaction. In the north particularly there was much dislike of the 'Popes' of Edinburgh and St. Andrews, and not only did the King play on this division but, by an act taking all Church temporal property for the Crown, bribed the nobility with Church lands. His marriage to Anne of Denmark, the birth of Prince Henry, his escape in 1600 from the alleged Gowrie conspiracy against his life, these also strengthened him. In 1597–8 the Kirk's violence gave him his chance. Packed general assemblies, held far from the capital, set up a Church commission under royal control and allowed him the final choice of bishops, to whom he assigned seats in Parliament.

His English experience after 1603 confirmed his maxim of ' no bishop, no king '. Melville after three years in the Tower was exiled for life, while ministers who denied royal powers over the assembly were sent to the Hebrides. Inch by inch James inserted episcopacy into the Presbyterian system, merging the assembly's commissioners into bishops, until all illusions could be torn away. In 1606 he appointed ' constant moderators ' over every presbytery with salaries from the Crown, then extended this to the synods, restored the bishops' pre-Reformation courts, and consecrated Scottish bishops in England. In 1612 the Scottish Parliament cancelled the ' golden ' Acts of 1592, and the election of lay elders lapsed until the revolution of 1638. The King then proceeded to attack ceremonial; after a personal visit from himself, in 1618 the Articles of Perth ordered kneeling at communion, confirmation by bishops, and due keeping of festivals. On paper the uniformity and the royal Church were at last achieved, nor must this entirely be ascribed to the bribes, packing, and force which the King had used. To feudal Scotland episcopacy was not uncongenial, either in spirit or for their material interests and, more-over, there was as yet no absolute gulf between the two systems. The early Elizabethan Church had been full of Calvinists, Knox's younger son died an English parson, while most of James' bishops, who carried out his plans with reluctance, were not of the school of Laud. Thus, though the dangers were great, nothing had made revolution inevitable when he died.

And the less so because his long reign had left Scotland a much more settled country than he found her. True, there were still episodes of barbarism. Huntly murdered a younger Moray, the Macgregors in Lennox and the Border Graemes were so atrocious in butchery and forays that the King ordered their extirpation. Political robbery crippled the Church, so that four hundred parishes had no minister. But the King's efforts at remedy had some effect. He compelled the chieftains to give bonds for the good behaviour of their clansmen, encouraged the Western Isles to accept Protestant ministers and the English tongue, suppressed the earldom of the Orkneys, and set up magistrates on the English model. With the union of the Crowns the Border began to fade away and its private armies were disarmed.

Union also naturally assisted the economic development which James had begun; there was an active export both of cloth and coal; service in Swedish and German armies took off many wild spirits, and the plantation of Ulster attracted Scottish capital. Though the Kirk had not yet achieved its ideal of a school in every parish, Edinburgh University and High School, and Marischal College, Aberdeen, were founded in this reign, and there were Scots famous for their learning all over Europe, among them the King's tutor Buchanan, Napier of Merchiston the mathematician, and the poet Drummond of Hawthornden. The generation who fought and argued through the civil wars, Montrose and Lauderdale and the Presbyterian ministers, could hold their own in any company.

It was, therefore, unlikely that Scotland could last much longer with the loose despotism which James bequeathed. Its Parliament, vitiated by the system of Lords of the Articles, had become a farce, rarely meeting, irregular in membership, and powerless over the executive. As half the older nobles had been extinguished and the others bribed by the Church wealth, the feudal vitality had gone, yet no popular government had replaced it; for though James had given some representation to the lairds, he packed elections both in shire and borough. The removal to England made the Scottish Privy Council an absolute ruler; ' here I sit ', James boasted, ' and govern it with my pen '. His boasting was premature: for one thing, his government was still a system of balancing rival forces, and exercised in the Highlands, for instance, through the power of Argyll. In any case, it depended on what the pen ordered, whether there might not rise again a cry for the sword.

CHAPTER VII

IRELAND: THE PROBLEM SET, 1460–1633

' I F the Kings of England had any one thing heavier on their souls than another ', wrote one of Elizabeth's Irish governors, ' it is that they have not made a thorough conquest of this realm.' It was, indeed, the weak spot of English power, for centuries so mismanaged that it became the point of entrance for Spain or France, the area where English factions were transplanted and magnified, and by examples of cruelty and corruption demoralizing public character. So much so that the very names greatest in England for exalted virtue or courage, Humphrey Gilbert or Spenser or Cromwell, in Ireland only added to the total of infamy.

Before the Tudors at least one question had been settled — that the Anglo-Norman conquerors had definitely failed. Connaught and western Ulster and the Leinster hills had slipped back to the Irishry. There was still the garrison, especially in the eastern towns that lived by English trade, but on the whole, except for the Ormondes, Irish chieftains and Anglo-Normans had become one. FitzGeralds of Desmond and Kildare were bound by marriage and alliance to O'Neills and O'Donnells. They had blended together feudal power with Irish customs, such as coign and livery, which allowed them to maintain armies by quartering troops and taking food and payment. Even the English speech of Dublin had become half unintelligible to the English of England, while the Church was more purely native than ever, especially the friars. Since Richard II's time the utmost ambition of most English governors had been to keep intact the small area of the Pale, and even that they only saved by paying ' black rent ', which was indeed blackmail, to the Leinster clans, while treaties with those of the north and west only admitted a nominal paramountcy.

War and conspiracy forced Henry VII to intervene and assert royal rights by Poynings' laws, but the Crown grudged the money needed for a conquest and, in effect, the Earls of Kildare still ruled Ireland. Their power convinced Henry VIII's strongest governor, Norfolk, that only a large army and a planned colonization would succeed. Scots from the Isles had settled in Antrim, which they could reach in four hours' sailing and for whose beacon fires they watched, and for two hundred years they provided the ' gallow-glasses ', the stout soldiers with axes who made the flower of every Irish army, so that from Warbeck's time until Flodden Scotland and the Ulster Irish worked hand-in-hand. After Henry VIII's divorce, rebel Irish found a ready ear at Madrid and Rome, while on the other side the Boleyn family, having claims on the Ormonde earldom, were anxious for action. The arrest of Kildare, his death in the Tower, and the siege of Dublin by his son ' Silken Thomas ', brought about the ruin of that house in 1537, and Henry enacted for Ireland the anti-Papal measures he had carried at home. Yet all this was not a policy. Royal artillery and a few armed troops who could scatter Irish bowmen and the horsemen riding bareback never reached them in their pathless forests and bogs ; again, failing a well-paid army, English Deputies were forced to take sides with one faction against another, as the case of Leonard Grey proved, whose Yorkist blood and Kildare sympathies cost him his head.

At length economy and statesmanlike enquiry induced Henry to try a wiser scheme. Taking the title, King of Ireland, he swept aside the mediaeval policy of two nations, which had excluded the Irish from English law ; offering to chieftains a secure title as tenants-in-chief and a share of monastic land, in return for which he expected them to attend Parliament and army, to give up their black rents, keep open the passes, and let him educate their sons. For a few years the new plan showed fair promise. The O'Neills for the first time crossed the dark sea and received the earldom of Tyrone, MacWilliam Burke that of Clanrickarde, and O'Brien that of Thomond ; Irish kernes fought at the siege of Boulogne. St. Leger, the Deputy who most inspired it, wrote that if the policy could last ' but two descents ', it would succeed.

But it broke down, and not mainly through the Protestantizing of Edward VI's government, with its burning of St. Patrick's staff and other relics, hateful though that was. For power and the land came before religion, and it was the Catholic Mary who confiscated the land of the rebellious O'Mores and O'Connors, so beginning the plantation policy by carving out King's County and Queen's County for Crown tenants. The root of the trouble, however, was that, as in eighteenth-century India, the English tried to regulate a totally different society through one section of it, and that the one which was not the most important. An Irish chief was not a feudal lord, since the land belonged to the clan in gavelkind, which meant a periodical redistribution of the soil ; no primogeniture chose the chief, but the clan elected the strongest available man of the male line, as ' tanist ' or successor. Henry's system was therefore one which no Irish chief could enforce. On the other hand, when Elizabeth went direct to the sub-tenants, and spread an English local government through shires and assizes, it was to challenge all the chieftains' power.

On top of this, her Irish policy had every vice of an absentee government. It was arbitrary, for she called only three short Parliaments
over forty-three years and oppressed the Pale by the ' cess ', which was
a worse equivalent of purveyance. It was vacillating and hand-to-
mouth ; immoral, for her Deputies advocated assassination and used
kidnapping ; full of corruption, exploited by captains who took pay
for non-existent soldiers, land-grabbers, and family factions. A
deliberate debasement of the coinage led to a rise of prices and a
collapse of trade. The Irish wars were a scene of horror ; ' the Englishman's grave ', as a foreign ambassador wrote, and certainly so for the
wretches picked up from the gaols and streets and huddled over to
Ireland to fight without pay, to follow through burned crops and
poisonous bogs an enemy that melted away and whom, an Englishman
wrote, ' hounds can scarce follow and much less men ', to live on bad
beef and mouldy biscuit and the milk of the cows they could capture,
and to die by thousands of scurvy and dysentery. As for the Irish, the
poet Spenser, himself a Munster colonist, has written of their misery ;
how they died of famine, how they crept from the woods looking like
' anatomies of death ' ; credible eye-witnesses describe cases of cannibalism, bodies found with mouths green from eating nettles, a return of
the wolves, and miles of country where not even the lowing of cattle
was heard.

Elizabeth's first war was an inheritance — the struggle of Shane
O'Neill, the choice of his clan, against an English nominee. Murder
rid Shane of his rival, the English shelved an awkward question, and
though he lay howling at Elizabeth's feet on his visit to Court, he
intrigued with foreign powers and by 1565 was master of Ulster.
But his crimes united against him the O'Donnells with Henry
Sidney, most vigorous of Deputies, and with the Scots, who in 1567
assassinated Shane when he fled to them for refuge, and sent his head
in pickle to Sidney. If one chief could so tax English strength, far
more so the mixture of dangers in the second crisis, the Geraldine war
of 1569-83.

One root of it, no doubt, rose simply from their immemorial jealousy
of the Ormondes. A second was the new hostility between England
and Spain, the country from which Irish chiefs boasted their race had
come, and with which the west and south did most of their trade ; so
that one ominous sign was a falling away in the old loyalty of the
Munster towns. Worse still were the proofs of a new unity in Irish
feeling, for which two particular causes must account. Religion was
the first. The condition of the official Church was tragic ; Sidney
reported 105 out of 224 parishes in Meath, most Anglicized of all
bishoprics, as being without a parson, with wretched curates starving in
others and very few speaking English. Some bishops were disloyal and

others enormous pluralists, hundreds of churches were in ruins, not till the end of the reign were service-books printed in Irish, and a year after the Queen died the Irish attorney-general noted ' no more demonstration of religion than among Tartars or cannibals '. It was not a case of persecution, for the government did not force Catholics to take the oaths, but rather a religious desert. But from 1561 on this desert was filled by the Jesuit missioners, the zeal of the Franciscans, or priests trained in the Irish colleges, newly set up at Douai and Salamanca. The missionaries, prepared to face death and torture, preached revolt against the heretic Queen and obedience to the Pope, Ireland's true sovereign, held large field meetings in the glens and opened schools in the towns.

Their success was the more rapid because the Irish felt a new pressure on them under Henry Sidney. His arrest of Desmond, his pushing on of the shire system, and an organization of Connaught and Munster as Presidencies (1567-9), meant a real control, which would end the chiefs' game and take away the livelihood of their fighting men. The new Presidents forbade wearing of the national mantle, or their hair in long locks; fixed rents were to conciliate the peasants, who hitherto had paid in cows and would offer ten cows for an English musket. Devonshire gentry, Carews and Grenvilles, came to push their claims for Irish land. At every point English law clashed with the Irish Brehon system — a venerable tribal code administered by a hereditary caste, and which only punished murder and cattle-lifting by lenient fines — it set in the stocks the bards whom the Irish highly honoured, and forbade the fostering of children which bound the clan together by the dearest ties.

In Desmond's absence his ambitious cousin James FitzMaurice led the southern rising, and after one rambling and cruel war went off to appeal to Catholic Europe. In 1579 he returned with some foreign mercenaries, and with Nicholas Sanders as Papal legate; when he was killed, Desmond himself took the lead; in 1580 Catholic nobles rose in the Pale itself, and Spanish troops landed at Smerwick in Kerry. There they were encircled and massacred to a man, Desmond was caught and executed, and the way lay open for the plantation of Munster.

In principle it was to be an armed Protestant colony, the ' undertakers ' being pledged to take no Irish tenants, to build castles, and provide a garrison; and great tracts were awarded to famous men, from Raleigh's 4000 acres to Spenser's 3000. In actual fact some planters did nothing, many were of poor character, while the Irish had a hunger for the land and a keen scent for litigation. So that, in spite of much advertising, the colony was in bad odour, and there was a thin veneer of settlers over dangerous distances; without cheap Irish labour they could not live, and soon, with bagpipes triumphantly blowing, the

Irish returned as rack-rent tenants. In Connaught, however, a little
real progress was made in the milder policy of regranting land on a
fixed rental, which explained the comparative loyalty of its leaders in
the dark days coming.

Compelled by urgent danger to handle this older civilization, dealing
with infinite treachery, with peasants who tied their ploughs to their
horses' tails and who slept in the smoke of their huts with their
cattle, many English officials came to a sinister conclusion : that Irish
life was barbarian and must be blotted out. Almost any solution, however, would have been better than the choppings and changes that
actually occurred. The Deputies were always being undermined at
Court, yet government frowned on any drastic use of force, without
doing anything for their real difficulties. It grudged money and therefore encouraged the raising of Irish troops, who could never be depended
on. The old English interest in the Pale was narrowly selfish, bickered
with English officials, refused to loosen their hold on Church land,
profited by gun-running to the rebels, resisted the cess but offered
no alternative tax. And the divisions, physical and moral, between
the Pale and the Irishry were very thin. Racial feeling bound even the
Ormondes to their countrymen, rebels from Dublin crowded into the
neighbouring hills, whence the O'Connors would descend at night to
send the thatched roofs up in flame and cut out the cattle from the stone
courtyards. Catholic missions had a deep effect on the Pale also. Mass
was often heard in public, priests were sheltered in country houses, and
Dublin leaders ostentatiously absented themselves from the thanksgiving for the defeat of the Armada.

But the problem for government was seen in its darkest shade in
Ulster. ' Choke up the sink at once ' was the advice of the stout
Deputy Perrott, who advised a three years' campaign ; but a government
so distracted in Europe only tinkered at this seemingly minute Irish
question. While Shane's successor Turlough played with revolt,
government allowed adventurers to try a conquest at their own expense.
Most persistent and ruthless among them was Essex, father of the
favourite, whose doings in Antrim brought him into collision with the
Scots, and who after some cold-blooded massacres of his enemies failed
and was superseded. Yet Ulster was mainly quiet in the crisis of 1580
because O'Neills and O'Donnells were divided, and English policy
divided the O'Neills among themselves. To balance Turlough they
set up his cousin Hugh in Armagh, rewarding his loyalty with the earldom of Tyrone and liberty to arm his men. It was a dangerous game
and too transparent a one, for their intention to govern Ulster as they
had the south was clear, and Tyrone decided to resist. Marriage reconciled him to the O'Donnells, whose rising leader Hugh Roe, his
son-in-law, was kidnapped by the English ; his escape in 1591 and

Turlough's resignation of the chieftainship to Tyrone began the hardest testing time the English in Ireland had known.

O'Donnell was a single-hearted Catholic, Tyrone a diplomat of resource; they had the full support of the Papal bishops and promises from Spain. Their demands, on which Robert Cecil curtly noted ' Utopia ', did not openly ask for separation from England, but liberty of conscience, withdrawal of garrisons, and complete control over their vassals. A fiercer racial hatred was shown by the killing of all who could not speak Irish, or who wore English dress. While Spanish munitions came in and Spanish officers sounded Irish harbours, the Earls stirred up war in Connaught, harried Louth and Cavan, and for two years, waiting until Spain could send an army, Tyrone fended off the Dublin government in negotiation. In 1598 he wiped out the main English army at the battle of the Yellow Ford, near Armagh. All over Ireland new chieftains, a Desmond or O'Brien or McWilliam, sprang up in revolt, O'Mores and O'Connors broke into the Pale, and the Munster colonists, sometimes with tongues and noses cut off, straggled into Youghal and Cork, Spenser having his house burned and a child killed. Essex's feeble campaign of 1599 and a plea for a truce encouraged Tyrone to raise his terms, asking an uprooting of all the plantations, and the next year he appeared in Munster.

English dominion was saved by the Deputy Mountjoy, not only because the government had at last woken up and gave him a large army with decent financial backing, but because this indomitable man, with his thick waistcoats and endless tobacco, had both determination and a system. He would refuse all truce, keep the field in winter, which would deprive the Irish of cover and keep their cattle on the run, blockade them systematically by forts, and take Ulster in the rear from Lough Foyle. He had thus already worn Tyrone down before, in September 1601, a Spanish army reached Kinsale and drew the English away to Munster. Our sea-power bottled up the Spaniards there and cut their reinforcements, and after a long siege Mountjoy crushed Tyrone's relieving army and forced the Spaniards to capitulate. Munster was soon restored to order and O'Donnell fled to die in Spain. In 1603 Tyrone pleaded for pardon, and in 1607, involved in fresh disputes and conspiracies, together with the new O'Donnell left Ireland for ever. The conquest had taken five whole years of English revenue, but the flight of the Earls decided the fate of Ulster.

From the victory rose seventeenth-century Ireland. The chieftains' power was broken, and the wars which made their glory; ' no more ', their harpers sang, ' no more the shield is seen slung on the broad back, nor hilt girt to the side at the coming of the moon '. Even Ulster peasants made the judges welcome, and could now give over their habit of sleeping facing the door, which might open on an unknown foe. Assizes and shires covered the country, and with security came in English money. Rich houses, export of friezes and timber, enriched the eastern ports; Richard Boyle, first earl of Cork, spent a large fortune raised from plantations, ironworks, and fisheries in building harbours, colleges, and towns. Some real Anglican religion slowly spread outwards from Elizabeth's foundation of Trinity College, Dublin. Administration was more unified with an Irish Star Chamber, and more centralized law courts. Yet the fundamentals were still unresolved: the constitutional and economic relationship of Ireland to England, and the racial feud within Ireland itself. All three elements still existed in sharpened form, of an Irish aristocracy in the Pale, an Irish swarming nationality outside it, and the Castle or official interest; to which a fourth had now been added, in the solid and Presbyterian Scots of Ulster.

Mountjoy's successor Arthur Chichester had served in many wars without losing his lenity, and his remedy for the Ulster plantation went on the basis that the substantial Irish could be won over, and should be provided for as freeholders. The English government overruled him, ordered the removal of the swordsmen, several thousand of whom were shipped off to serve in foreign armies, and priority was given to English and Scots, whether the 'servitors' (that is, officials) or 'undertakers', who should take no Irish as their tenants. Eligible settlers hesitated, thinking they might get better value for their money than by having their throats cut in lonely plantations. But the City of London took up 400,000 acres, whence sprang Londonderry, the Irish were allowed some 50,000, and the rest of the six counties (Donegal, Tyrone, Armagh, Coleraine, Fermanagh, and Cavan) gradually fell to English and Scots planters. Yet Chichester's doubts were justified in the result. The undertakers found it impossible to do without the Irish, who would offer more for grazing-rents than others would for tillage, and the transplantation proposed never really took place. Thinking more of profit than defence, a few thousand British families were widely scattered, dependent on Irish labour and threatened by the kernes in the woods; evicted and legally inferior but far outnumbering the British, this cloud of Irishry hung over the new province, while the years brought another danger from the precisely opposite quarter. For the Scots, who prospered more than the English, took their civilization from Presbyterian ministers who had been driven by royal policy from Scotland, until the formidable shape appeared of a new Ulster, hateful to the Irish but alarming to the Crown.

Experts noted that the 'rivers of blood' which had flowed between the Irishry and the aristocracy of the Pale were forgotten now in the common bond of Catholicism. Mountjoy's warning not to press the religious question was realized in passive resistance and riot; priests taught the peasants to expect a return of the O'Neills; monks and friars

worked openly in Dublin. That Catholicism bound Ireland together
was made clear in the Parliament of 1613–15, the only one of James'
reign ; which, indeed, might claim to be the first true Irish Parliament,
since all Ireland was now shire land and the Commons had risen in
numbers from 98 to 232 since 1560. Though the government offset the
Catholic peers by its 19 bishops, and created 39 new boroughs, Lords
and Commons met in agitation against the Protestant laws they dreaded,
and by secession, deputations to England, and obstruction prevented
any such laws passing.

A great deal, however, was done against individual Catholics by
prerogative action, while the legal campaign against landowners never
ceased. There was a new regulation of land titles in Wexford and
Leitrim, with the effect of leaving some Irish clan landless or discontented, and only carried through by pressure on the juries. Each
such new settlement left a fringe of outlaws who, wrote an Irish
bishop, ' would rather starve on husks at home ' than take better
land elsewhere. In James' last year the titles given in Connaught
forty years earlier were declared invalid, and there was talk of a large
plantation. In 1627 Irish agents, however, made a direct settlement :
in return for a grant of £120,000, sorely needed for the wretched
Irish army, the King agreed that sixty years' possession should guarantee
owners against claims from the Crown, that the Connaught titles
should be recognized, and that the oath of supremacy should in certain
cases be waived. Had these ' graces ' been honoured, there was just
a chance of peace in Ireland, though its revenues were bankrupt,
its army unpaid, its ports ravaged by pirates, and its plantations unfinished. But in 1633 Wentworth came as Lord Deputy, intent on an
active policy of power, revenue, and reform.

CHAPTER VIII

THE ELEVENTH HOUR, 1603–1629

WHILE the sixteenth century had been an age of revolution, in the seventeenth the interaction of new forces thus released brought about those decisions which, taken together, made the structure of Europe till 1789.

In Great Britain the problems were those which Elizabethan government had evaded or postponed, of religion, economic life, foreign policy, and Ireland, the sum of which had already posed the even deeper question of sovereignty. Yet when James I died no one in England supposed that it could only be settled, as Germany was settling it, by civil war, and though he left an inheritance much deteriorated, it was not irreparable.

In several respects the year 1603 marks a real epoch. No King of full age had sat on the throne for sixty years, and James, as he never ceased to inform his new subjects, was ' an old and experienced king '. Again, his accession united two Crowns and eliminated the Border. And, thirdly, it exalted monarchy; not only because the King was the sole link between two kingdoms, whose jealousies, nobles, and Parliaments he played off against each other, but in that the parliamentary title of the Suffolk line was passed over and the Stuarts reigned in virtue of hereditary right.

If these conditions changed the nature of the problem, his character did so almost as much. The first British sovereign whose writings were printed in his lifetime, he had a sincere belief in the superiority of reason; *beati pacifici* was his genuine feeling in regard both to war and religion, while his championship of Union was a better thing than the English bias against ' beggarly Scots '. But if some of his ideas were larger, his practice was always meaner than Elizabeth's and his character an infinitely smaller one. ' Who seeketh two strings to one bow ', she had warned him, ' may shoot strong but never straight '; he had no principle, and after long blustering always yielded. Where she was careful, he was profuse; she ruled by the intellect but he by affection, which he gave not to public servants but to favourites, with little qualification save a shapely body or a glib tongue. Though timidity saved him from fatal resistance, he took opposition as an insult and tyrannized where he dared. Having read widely and reached in the unopposed arena of his mind some fixed views on every subject, from freewill down to that ' vile weed ' tobacco, he had an author's pride, telling the Commons he was ' the great schoolmaster of the whole land '.

As such he preached, alike in parliamentary speech and printed treatise, a theory of divine right, dangerous and exasperating however he guarded it, and defying the law if it were literally applied ; a theory evolved from wrestling with the Scots' Kirk, and followed up in later years against Cardinal Bellarmine and other champions of the Pope's deposing power. Elizabeth's Church homilies condemned resistance to the Lord's anointed, but James would forbid even discussion. The King was ' above the law ', though a good king would conform to it ; like God Himself, kings have ceded part of their original and parental power to human law, but as ' it is atheism and blasphemy to dispute what God can do '. so it was sedition in a subject ' to dispute what a king may do in the height of his power '. The Tudors had spoken forcibly of their prerogative, just as James forbade Parliament to ' meddle with the main parts of government ', but he went on to define it as ' absolute ' or ' a mystery ', ' no subject for the tongue of a lawyer '.

Though this querulous theorizing quickly damped the joy at his accession, it takes much to stir a comfortable aristocracy to resistance, and there were other strong factors to prevent it. The younger Cecil, who now became earl of Salisbury, was chief minister till he died in 1612 and, though a narrower man than his father, believed in parliamentary government and knew the native instincts. To him was due the negotiation of peace with Spain in 1604 ; which was not popular, for Spain still barred trade to the Indies and the Inquisition continued to persecute British seamen. Financially, however, it was a necessity, moreover it stipulated for English trade with the Dutch, who with the help of some English regiments remaining in their pay were now strong enough to stand alone.

Two of the royal family also diverted part of the growing distrust of the King. Prince Henry, the heir but curiously unlike other Stuarts, was manly, uncompromising, and full of warlike Protestant feeling ; when an early death from typhoid fever carried him off, national hopes were transferred to his sister Elizabeth, by her charm the darling of the nation, in whose praise Cavalier and Puritan united, and whose unhappy fortunes hurt the people's pride. Besides, the groupings of this reign, like men's minds and their manner of motive, were still Elizabethan. Older churchmen were in doctrine Calvinist, as was Abbott for instance, archbishop from 1611–33, so that the future lines between Church and Puritan were not yet defined. Diplomats like Henry Wotton had seen Spanish Catholicism at too close quarters to weaken in sympathy for Holland or the persecuted Vaudois. Bacon thought more, as his uncle Burghley had, of the State than the Church, and like him advised concession to the Puritans.

This sort of temper was prolonged by the conspiracies of James' early years. The disappointed and the adventurers of the dark ' bye ' and ' main ' plots of 1603 discussed getting Spanish troops to back the claim of Lady Arabella Stuart; though innocent of this, Raleigh was incriminated, sour at the loss of his rich places, and sent to the Tower. Far more serious was the Gunpowder plot. For many years government had distinguished between the extreme Jesuit group and the secular priests, whose feud divided the recusants even in their prisons, and in the counsels of the Vatican. In his anxiety for the succession James had given a half-pledge of toleration, and when he reached England, finding both Rome and Spain willing to keep the Catholics quiet, began suspending the fines for recusancy. Several causes, however, during 1604-5 drove him back on persecution, — a clamour in the Commons, an alarming increase of recusancy, Catholic influence on his queen who became a secret convert, and reluctance at Rome to admit his distinction between loyal and disloyal Catholics. His change of policy determined a section, who had long discussed Spanish invasion, to dally no more; their leaders, Catesby and Tresham and the Winters, had conspired with Essex and kept touch with English Catholics serving in the Spanish Flanders army; one of whom, a Yorkshireman, Guido Fawkes, had served with the traitor Stanley who had once betrayed a Dutch garrison. The details of this plot for killing King and Parliament together were worked out eighteen months before it took effect; the cellar was taken and the powder laid. Garnet, head of the English Jesuits, heard the whole in confession, and in outline by other ways, but kept silence. Betrayal by Tresham, who would not see his kinsmen among the Catholic peers destroyed, led to the discovery of Fawkes a few hours before Parliament was to meet on the 5th November 1605, and so to his execution, with Garnet too, while others were hunted down and shot by the sheriffs' forces in Warwickshire and Stafford. So the 5th November was ordained as a day of thanksgiving for ever, and new laws added new servitudes, providing that recusants could only escape fines by receiving the Anglican sacrament, forbidding them to move over five miles from their home, barring them from the public service and learned professions.

James' early relations with the Commons ended with the dissolution of the ' addled ' Parliament in 1614; a story of barren wrangling, with faults on both sides. Unlike Elizabeth, he had no principal minister in the Commons, who were thus left free to find leaders of their own, as in Edwin Sandys, for example, a leader of the City, and to work out their own procedure. His lecturing was very provocative, especially the claim that the Commons' privileges were derived from himself and that Chancery must settle a disputed election.[1] On the

---

[1] The case of Goodwin v. Fortescue.

other side, the Commons' ' Apology ' of 1604 showed the temper long
repressed by Elizabeth, with a determination to break down prerogatives and to teach a foreign king a lesson. ' In regard of her age and
sex ', they told him, they had not pressed the Queen for remedy of
' sore oppressions '; their privileges, which were their ' right and due
inheritance ', meant they could ' speak freely their consciences without
check '. As for religion, they went on, with reference to Convocation's
canons of this year against the Puritans, he would be ' misinformed '
if he was advised he could make laws ' otherwise than as in temporal
causes by consent of Parliament '. None but Peter Wentworth had
spoken thus to Elizabeth. They gave offence also by a cool reception of
his schemes for Union; reiterating that beggarly Scots would ruin
trade or that England was overpopulated already, they rejected freedom
of trade between the kingdoms, offering naturalization to the Scots only
on condition of their exclusion from many offices. Only a later judicial
decision [1] settled that the ' *post-nati* ' (Scots born after 1603) had *ipso
facto* the rights of English natives, and no more was heard of Union. But
the widening of the gulf went on through more immediate differences.

Religion was first and foremost. In the same spirit of hopefulness
as the Catholics, the Puritans promptly demanded much that Elizabeth
had refused. In the so-called Millenary petition of 1603 a number of
ministers merely asked what they had asked for thirty years, such as an
optional use of the surplice or restriction of the *ex-officio* oath. But they
circulated papers commending a discipline like that of ' other reformed
churches ', while in a conference at Hampton Court with King and
bishops their spokesmen mentioned prophesyings, and a bishop's synod
' with his presbyters '. At which the King flared up that ' presbytery
as well agreeth with a monarchy as God and the Devil ', the conference dissolving with no other positive result than the steps taken
towards the authorized version of the Bible. But though James rejoiced
that he ' peppered them soundly ', calling them a ' sect ' of ' persons who
never receive contentment ', the Commons took up their cause. Vowing they had ' no Puritan or Brownist spirit ', in the interest of peace
they asked for a yielding on ' some few ceremonies of no importance ',
and for no compulsion to subscribe the Thirty-nine Articles, except
those that touched on doctrine. Despite county petitions, the government ejected some, though no great number of, nonconforming clergy.
In each successive session the Commons challenged some bulwark
of Elizabeth's settlement, whether the powers of Church courts or
the right of King and Convocation to pass canons binding the laity;
they spoke much of the Sabbath, and for their own prayers went to
the Temple church or St. Margaret's, rather than stomach the Abbey's
vestments.

[1] Calvin's case, 1607.

Their distrust of royal control of religion was the source of that attack on other branches of royal supremacy, which their predecessors had begun. The law courts, led by Chief Justice Coke, who was obsessed with jealousy for the common law, launched a concerted campaign of ' prohibitions ' against High Commission, Chancery, Council of the North, and the Admiralty's commercial jurisdiction. Their detailed complaints, that High Commission had no right to imprison or deprive except for heresy and schism, or that a royal commission could not create a new court, sink into insignificance beside their guiding principle; namely, that only Parliament could alter the law, and only common-law judges could interpret Acts of Parliament. This new claim for one over-riding law was fought out in many disputes between King and judges. It defied the whole Tudor argument, which had made the Crown's discretion the arbiter of many co-operating jurisdictions ; it was for him alone, said James, ' to keep every court within his proper bounds ', and to decide which channel of the law he would employ.

In 1610 the judges reined him in tighter by ruling that his proclamations could not ' create any offence which was not an offence before ', adding ' the King hath no prerogative but that which the law of the land allows him '. All of which, contrasting sharply with Coke's own views under Elizabeth, was stoutly reaffirmed by the Commons, who declared the Act of Supremacy was ' of dangerous extent ' and that offences could not be determined by other courts ' than by those trusted by Parliament '.

Two parts of the government, though not yet consciously, thus each claimed a new power of sovereignty, and this was seen clearest in finance. James' inherited debt of £400,000 rose to £1,000,000 by 1608, mostly explained by bad administration. For though prices were rising against him and though Elizabeth had sold a mass of Crown land, his peace expenditure was as large as hers in a year of full war, much of it being dissipated in jewels and junketing at Court, or £200,000 in gifts to Scots courtiers. As the Commons stinted their grants till grievances were met, government developed to the utmost the customs revenue, whose steady rise proved the national wealth, and this expansion, already resisted in the late reign by enemies of the chartered companies, led to another conflict.

Bate's case concentrated it all. The Levant Company, paying a heavy sum in return for its monopoly under Elizabeth's charter, was allowed to levy a duty on non-members who imported currants, and when it surrendered this charter the Crown continued to take the duty, in consultation with the merchants. Bate's refusal to pay brought the Exchequer judges' decision of 1606 that the duty was legal, in which even Coke acquiesced. Foreign trade, they argued on Tudor precedents, was as much in the royal province as peace and war, and the seaports

were the ' King's gates ', to open or close. Going further, they declared
such a prerogative inseparable from the Crown ; whose powers were
double — ordinary powers exercisable through common law and
statute, and an absolute power of *salus populi*, guided by rules of
' policy '.

When two years later Salisbury added the Treasury to his secretaryship, armed with this decision he set about a new customs rate-book and
new impositions, again after meeting the merchants. But though by
such economies he halved the debt, a deficit continued, so that the
Commons of 1610 were asked for a permanent increase of revenue. By
the ' great contract ' he offered to abolish some ancient grievances,
especially the purveyors who, the Commons said, ' rummaged and
ransacked ' the realm, and the feudal dues and wardships, for which
he induced them to offer another £200,000 a year. But they took the
opportunity to insist on their right to discuss prerogative, and voted
that impositions were illegal without their consent. One decisive note
rang in the debates, that the essence of law was certainty. Proclamations
had submitted them to ' courts of arbitrary discretion ', ' policy ' could
not correct inconvenience by illegality. All taxation, said Whitelocke,
using the critical word, belonged to ' sovereign power ' ; and where lay
that ? — not in the King, but in the King in Parliament, whose office was
a public ' trust '.

To such fundamentals had religion and taxation driven things by
1610. The King, though offering to lay no more impositions by himself, would not restore deprived Puritan ministers or commit himself
against High Commission, asking also for more payment of his debts ;
of which the Commons would not hear, failing a remedy for their
complaints.

In 1614 a new House met, which the Crown had endeavoured to
pack ; Salisbury and Prince Henry were dead, the despicable Ker, earl
of Somerset, was the reigning favourite, and another motive, besides
repetition of old grievances, impelled James to dissolve this Parliament.
A struggle was dividing Council over a proposed Spanish marriage for
Prince Charles, and James acted after reassuring talks with the Spanish
ambassador Gondomar, to whom he confided his surprise that his
predecessors had allowed the Commons to come into existence. One
of the four members whom he now sent to the Tower had warned him
against imitating foreign tyrants.

While the next seven years passed without a Parliament, two
schemes of government and two policies swayed round the King.
Salisbury had kept on good terms with France and Holland, and James
married his daughter Elizabeth to a strongly Protestant choice, Frederick
Elector Palatine. But to preserve his own power Somerset allied himself to the Howards ; of whom Nottingham (the Howard of Effingham

of the Armada) was senile and had allowed the Navy to sink into corruption, Northampton was brother of the Norfolk whom Elizabeth had executed and himself a Catholic and Spanish pensioner, while Suffolk, who had fought with Grenville of the *Revenge*, was led by an ambitious wife in Spanish pay. Under such influence James reopened the question of a Spanish marriage, which from the first had entered into his self-portrait as the peacemaker. Though hitherto both Rome and Madrid had refused this heretic match except on impossible terms, such as the education of the royal children in the Roman faith, Gondomar believed that James could be induced to suspend the penal laws and supported a negotiation which would at least paralyse Protestant Europe. So the King entered on the steep slope down which many of his house were to follow, of an understanding with a foreign Power against his subjects; the Spanish faction — resisting those who, like Bacon, urged him to give Parliament another trial — pointed to prospects of a rich dowry. This meant a withdrawal from Elizabeth's alliances. Spain was on the aggressive against Venice and Savoy and aiming at the Alpine passes to make contact with her Austrian cousins, while religious re-action at Vienna and many collisions portended revival of war in Germany. In 1610, on the very eve of attacking the encircling Haps-burgs, Henry IV of France was assassinated, leaving a widow who began to plan Spanish marriages for her children. At any moment James might be forced to decide. He was bound by defensive treaties to the Dutch and the German Protestant Union, both of whom were nearly involved in war against the Empire in 1614 regarding the Duchy of Cleves, the key to the lower Rhine. English and French mediation for the time averted it, but meantime James was bitterly opposing Dutch efforts to bar our merchants from the East and accused them of poaching on English fisheries.

While thus severing himself from the allies who could keep him independent of Spain, his policy shifted with every change of wind. Somerset's enemies, Abbott and Bacon among them, had patriotic motives, but to evict this favourite they had to bring forward another, George Villiers; who within eight years rose from the penury of a too numerous Leicestershire family to be Duke of Buckingham and supreme minister. Somerset's ascent had been assisted by a scandalous marriage to Suffolk's daughter, who by the King's pressure was divorced from the young Essex, son of Elizabeth's favourite and himself later the parliamentary general; his fall in 1616 came from the discovery of a fearful crime committed by his countess, who instigated the poisoning of her husband's friend Thomas Overbury, courtier and man of letters.

But the collapse of the Howards and their hangers-on was due less to public causes than to Buckingham's greed for power, and Spanish influence remained almost unshaken. Raleigh was indeed released from the Tower, with wild ideas in his head of recovering favour by discovering treasure; to be harvested by involving James in war with Spain with the sympathy of part of the Council, and for himself, at worst, a refuge in France.   James approved an exploration for the mines which Raleigh had heard of in earlier voyages, on one clear condition, that this welcome money must be got without a clash with the Spaniards. Such a clash proved unavoidable, and when, in 1618, after a fatally tragic voyage, Raleigh came home with empty hands, he was executed on the old charges of 1603, on Gondomar's pressure.   So the last Elizabethan venturer went to his ' dark and silent grave ', not entirely undeservedly, but nevertheless as a sacrifice to a policy which the country loathed.

This was the date when the Thirty Years' War broke out in Germany, with the Bohemians' revolt against Austria and the acceptance of their Crown by James' son-in-law, Frederick of the Palatinate.   By what means now could the King reconcile the safety of his daughter and Protestant interests with a Spanish marriage ?   His protest against Frederick's aggression was justified, but he valued his own fame as a peacemaker more than peace, and while he mediated and sent forth many diplomats, weakened resistance by his friction with Holland. While he persisted in hope that Spain would put peaceful pressure on the Austrians, Spanish troops seized the Palatinate, the ' winter King ' was crushed at the battle of the White Mountain outside Prague in 1620, and his wife, the elder daughter of England, fled with him to begin a long life of exile.   And cartoons filled the shops of European capitals, depicting the English King with empty pockets, or brandishing an empty scabbard.

In this Court, sunk in gambling and intrigue, and in a Council manned with second-rate secretaries buying the good-will of Buckingham, the one man of shining ability was Francis Bacon.   He held a lofty conception of the Crown, unafraid of Parliament but ready to initiate reform, and giving a large place to the intelligence which could not be expected in country gentlemen, or common-lawyers rusted by precedent. Freed from his cousin Salisbury, the ' deformity ' he hated, he hoped for a rôle worthy of his talents, and achieved his ambition when he became Lord Keeper   But his old rival Coke, who had defeated him alike in love and official life, again stood in his way, and conflict raged till 1616 when Coke was dismissed from his chief-justiceship.   In one case [1] when an elderly clergyman was arrested for treason and tortured for a violent sermon against misgovernment, Coke objected to the Crown asking the judges for their individual opinions.   In others [2] Bacon argued that common-law judges should not proceed with a case touching the royal interest or prerogative until the King had been

---

[1] Peacham's case.
[2] The writ *de rege inconsulto* ; the case of commendams.

consulted, or his Chancellor, the 'principal counsellor and instrument of monarchy'. In his view, judges were prerogative's guardians; lions, as his essay said, 'yet lions under the throne'.

But Bacon, who loved to live softly in cloth of gold, and in whom intellect and a towering optimism dulled his moral sense, must look for support to Buckingham; as, indeed, Coke tried to recover favour by marrying his daughter to a Villiers. The favourite was not all bad. As Lord Admiral he did something to stop the canker of peculation, and to rebuild a fleet. Lionel Cranfield, the City apprentice who under his auspices rose to be Treasurer and earl of Middlesex, by his ability reformed the Household and balanced the accounts. But public life was poisoned by the King's surrender to his favourite, — 'Christ had His John', he said, 'and I have my George' — through whom and his greedy family all power and titles flowed. Before his time James had begun the prostitution of honours, which helped to range the older aristocracy against him. He created in all some 2300 knights, raised £90,000 to pay for an Irish army by selling the new order of baronetcies, increased the peerage from 59 to about 100, and after 1614 began selling peerages through his courtiers, Buckingham above all. So the Cornish tin-master Robartes, for instance, paid £10,000 for his.

Lack of parliamentary money and the favourite's rule alienated the business world as well as the aristocracy, especially when government in 1615 began to interfere with the chief national industry. The Merchant Adventurers' main export was 'undressed' cloth, since foreign countries, and in particular the Netherlands, kept the finishing process in their own hands. Our fullers and dyers always wished to recapture it, while Dutch competition spurred on the argument that here was a chance of increasing home employment. The King, therefore, forbade export of undressed cloth, transferring the Adventurers' monopoly to a London syndicate who promised him £300,000 a year and bribes to the courtiers. The result was a great disaster; a refusal by Europe to take the dyed cloth, prolonged unemployment, some permanent loss of markets, and finally a restoration of the Adventurers with more bribes.

While cloth exports sunk to half of what they had been in 1610, fury was rising against the monopoly patents, which Elizabeth had promised should be left to the common law. There was much to be said for corporations like the East India Company, developing in areas where trade went hand-in-hand with armed protection, and where no real native government existed. Nor was there serious objection to some government control by licence; as, for example, of the hundreds of ale-houses, which were the headquarters of criminals and footpads; nor, again, to genuine patents, such as those given to the glass industry for coal furnaces. The root of discontent lay, rather, in rises of price,

corruption, and intimidation. Thus import of foreign glass was prohibited; Mompesson, a Villiers kinsman, exploited wine and ale-house
licences to extort fees, and to jail those who refused to pay them;
Buckingham's brothers were promised an income from a monopoly in
gold and silver thread; another group, controlling the Irish fisheries,
set out to crush rivals in the Thames. Lawyers offended by commissioners who searched private houses, county magistrates, goldsmiths,
mercers, and consumers were all united. Moreover, the stiffening of
tariffs, warfare in the Indies, and unpaid debt ended in all the signs of
a crisis, — low prices for farmers, starving wages for weavers, a slump in
the foreign exchanges, a fall of 25 per cent in exports, and no credit for
the Crown.

Such was the atmosphere in 1621 when James was forced to summon
Parliament, if he would save the Palatinate; when he and Buckingham
had oscillated between two poles, from discussion with Spain for an
attack on Holland, or rejection of a French marriage for Charles, to
patriotic appeals for volunteers for Germany. And here may be said
to begin the reign of Charles and Buckingham, who dragged the old
King through their maze of folly.

Anxious to get the Commons' taxes and to save himself, the Duke
threw over the monopolists, the most hated patents were called in, and
Mompesson was impeached. This revival of impeachment, for the
first time since Henry VI's reign, was a deliberate step by the Opposition, which would link the two Houses together and assert the Lords'
superiority over any court outside the common law. Accidentally their
enquiry convicted Bacon of taking bribes, though money had not
affected his judgments; again Buckingham retreated, the Lord Keeper
was impeached, and stripped of his office.

Much else in the debates showed the Commons' grievances, their
remarks on the ' skip-jacks ' who bought baronetcies, their indignation
against informers, and a move led by the Virginia Company against
royal control of Colonial commerce. But religion was in the forefront.
' Never more Papists ', broke out the fervent Phelips of Dorset, ' never
more insolent; I beseech God, that chose this corner of the earth to
plant His truth in, to preserve it. ' Was not Protestantism, asked
another, ' martyred in Bohemia, wounded in France, scattered in
Germany ? ' Ignorant of the aggression of the Elector Palatine, of
his mercenary troops' barbarism, and the pacifism of Spain, Puritan
England could only see the unhappy facts. While apprentices hustled
Gondomar's staff and preachers poured out sermons, the Commons,
without a shadow of right against a man not one of their members,
pounced on an old Catholic barrister Floyd, who had spoken contemptu-
ously of ' that poor lad ' and ' good man Palsgrave ', howled for branding
and cutting out his tongue, but were forced to leave sentence to the

Lords, who were content with a whipping and life imprisonment.

When they reassembled in the autumn, they knew that the Protestant Union was dissolved and Spanish troops in the Palatinate. Asking the King to cut out ' the bitter roots ' in England, they begged him to attack Spain and marry Charles to a Protestant. If this went unpunished, said Gondomar, he was no king, and James denounced the ' fiery and popular spirits ' who meddled with ' deep matters of State '. When they claimed that by their privileges, ' our ancient and undoubted right and our inheritance ', they might freely discuss religion and the kingdom's safety, he declared their privilege derived only ' from the grace and permission of our ancestors and us '; when they repeated that free debate was their ' birthright ', he dissolved Parliament, tore the offending page from their journal, and in a proclamation upbraided their usurpation of the Crown's ' inseparable rights ' and their lack of respect in attacking ' any anointed king '. Sandys was already a prisoner for his lead regarding the Colonies; Coke, Phelips, Pym, were now added to those in custody, then the premier earl, Oxford, for words against royal policy, then Saye and Sele for instigating refusal of a benevolence.

This dissolution, Gondomar wrote, was the best thing done for Catholicism since Luther preached heresy. For two years yet James clung to his dream that for love of the English match Spain would compel the Austrians to restore the Palatinate, and for two years the Spaniards under Olivarez prolonged negotiation in their desire to avoid war, hoping against hope that objections either from Rome or London would break off this heretic marriage. But the higher they raised their terms, the wilder seemed James' ardour. In 1623, by an exploit which he described as ' worthy to be put in a new romanzo ', Charles and Buckingham forced his consent to their journeying incognito to Madrid, where the Prince's calf love for the Infanta, Spanish confidence in his conversion, and James' passion to get ' Steenie and Baby Charles ' safe back again, brought about a final danger. James took oaths to allow private Catholic worship in his kingdoms and to ask Parliament to repeal the penal laws, while at Madrid Charles was swearing he would get repeal within three years and would entrust his children's education to their mother.

Two rebuffs happily touched the Prince's pride and determined his return: wishing to test his promises, Spain would not part with the Infanta till the next year, and refused to put pressure on the Emperor to restore the Palatinate. Giving pledges to the last moment in Spain, which they were privately resolved to break, Prince and favourite reached home to find themselves the centre of rejoicing, and persuaded James to violate his word and make restoration of the Palatinate a condition of marriage. Their next step was to overcome objections in Council and to summon Parliament to make war on Spain. With their invariable short-sightedness they threw overboard the treasurer Middlesex, who opposed it, abandoning him, against James' warning, to impeachment on charges of corruption.

So the old King's life closed in 1625 in this new diplomacy, with all hope of compromise over the Palatinate gone and Europe in a religious war. Resisting the Commons' wish to make our main effort at sea, Buckingham was deep in alliances with Denmark and German mercenaries, while a treaty was signed for Charles' marriage with the French princess Henrietta Maria, the secret articles of which promised to the Catholics all that had once been pledged to Spain.

Within three years this feverish scheming collapsed. Every English expedition failed. Troops sent to serve under the wild Ernest of Mansfeldt died like flies of disease at Flushing; Edward Cecil led an army of undisciplined conscripts, in royal ships whose sails dated back to the Armada and in pressed merchantmen, to a disgraceful failure at Cadiz; and our Danish ally was crushed at Lutter. Huguenot rebellion forced Richelieu to peace with Spain, and no pressure could induce France to take part in a Protestant crusade. As usual, Buckingham swung violently from a French alliance to war against her; for which ample materials existed in a disappointed diplomacy, the impossibility of making Parliament carry out the Catholic articles of the marriage treaty, dictation to France about the Huguenots, and seizure of French ships. His last expedition, led by himself, to the Isle of Rhé, failed like others before it; ' since England was England ', wrote Holles to his brother-in-law Wentworth, ' it received not so dishonourable a blow '. In 1628 Buckingham was murdered at Portsmouth by John Felton, an officer disappointed of promotion and inspired, by the outcry against the favourite, to view it as a religious act.

Beyond £60,000 of private debt, Buckingham's legacy was a final break between King and Parliament. Having forced upon James a reversal of foreign policy and carried an Act against monopolies, the first two Parliaments of Charles doggedly refused to pay for war without enquiry, while their hatred of Catholicism appeared in hints against his marriage and anger against divines who criticized Calvinism. But in suspicion of Buckingham they were unanimous, Coke and Phelips and the usual Opposition now being joined by young Wentworth, passionate for a reforming Crown and for peace, and wishing for the day ' when the King will cause his chronicles to be read, and then let Haman look to himself '.

The Commons of 1625, having defied precedent by voting tonnage and poundage for one year only, were dissolved, and when a new House met next year, Cecil's men were dying or starving in western harbours, pirates made the sea unsafe, war threatened with France. Never was Buckingham's sway more insolently violent: he had got Charles to keep out some members like Wentworth by making them sheriffs, to forbid attendance of some Opposition peers, and to dismiss a moderate minister in Lord Keeper Williams. But Eliot, once his client, who had previously tried to mediate, now took the lead. ' Our honour is lost ', he cried, ' our ships are sunk, our men are perished '; ' not by the sword ' but ' by those we trust '. When Charles silenced complaints with ' I would not have the House to question my servants, much less one that is so near to me ', and accepted responsibility himself, the Commons impeached the Duke; Eliot accumulating far-fetched charges of treason with well-grounded accusation of corruption and incompetence, crowned in the parallel he drew with Sejanus. So came about another dissolution, to the Lords' plea for delay Charles answering ' not a minute '.

Rhé followed Cadiz, but through 1627 the King pressed on. Soldiers were subjected to martial law, a chief justice for advising against forced loans was dismissed, archbishop Abbott who would not license servile sermons was disgraced, the magistrates' bench was purged. On a test case, that of ' the five knights ' who refused to pay a forced loan, the courts refused bail on their request for habeas corpus, accepting (as by Elizabethan custom they might) ' by His Majesty's special command ' as sufficient cause for a temporary remand to prison.

Charles' third Parliament of 1628 was the last chance for a peaceful amendment of the Constitution, as Elizabeth had left it. Against the evils most complained of, — unparliamentary taxation, martial law, billeting of troops, and unregulated powers of imprisonment, — all were united, but how to achieve their end without infringing the power which in any State must be entrusted to some one in emergency, on this they fell apart. A middle section of the Lords, who would reserve the King's prerogative ' intrinsical to his sovereignty ', were strongly represented in the Commons, above all by Wentworth; hoping that the question ' whether the King be above the law or the law above the King ' might be laid aside, he proposed a bill reciting the law, safeguarding habeas corpus, yet not taking away the royal right to commit, since there must be ' a trust left in the Crown '. But messages from Charles, demanding confidence in his word to keep the law ' without additions, paraphrases, or explanations ', wrecked this effort, and on Coke's suggestion the Commons framed a Petition of Right, demanding an immediate answer and preceding its four major points by a vehement catalogue of grievances.

Again the Lords tried a reservation of ' sovereign power ', which the Commons again rejected, and though, as Wentworth said, the Petition if strictly kept would ' give a blow to government ', the Lords would not help Buckingham to resist further. The King then accepted the Petition, though only on receiving an assurance from the judges that it would not prejudice his ancient power, or their willingness to remand prisoners in special cases; only also after furious words against Buckingham in both Houses, ' the grievance of grievances ', as Coke called him.

Neither the Duke's murder nor the Petition decided the question of sovereignty. Under Pym and Eliot the Commons impeached the Arminian Mainwaring for defending unparliamentary taxation, boldly claiming also that tonnage and poundage and impositions without consent were forbidden by the Petition. As to the last, Charles declared he had ' granted no new but only confirmed the ancient liberties '; while in religion he would never depart from Elizabeth's prerogative. The fall of Protestant La Rochelle was the last drop of humiliation. In 1629, breaking away from the peers, Eliot swept the Commons into the aggressive. They dragged to their Bar custom-house officers who had connived at tonnage and poundage. They complained of Popery with the swarming of Catholics in the Queen's court and, branding ' the Arminian faction ', challenged as illegal the ceremonies retained in virtue of Elizabeth's addition to the Thirty-nine Articles; in which debate was first heard the voice of a new member, Oliver Cromwell. At last, on the 24th February, they refused the Speaker's move to adjourn, and held him down in his chair; with locked doors, while the royal guards were called for to break them open, they voted that whoever brought in innovations in religion, or sought to extend Popery and Arminianism, and whoever advised or paid tonnage and poundage without parliamentary consent, were enemies to the commonwealth. In March, Parliament was dissolved, not to meet for eleven years, while Eliot and eight other members were sent to the Tower.

So broke down the mediaeval Constitution. It was in vain, though most natural, that each side claimed they were seeking nothing new; that Pym denied the very existence of sovereignty, or that Wentworth only asked ' our ancient, sober, and vital liberties '. For he broke with Eliot because he felt that, in the last resort, there must be a trust in the executive; Pym's talk of ' Saxon ' liberty and the appeal to earlier precedents merely clouded the issue, when in fact the Commons were claiming to force the dismissal of ministers and to overrule judgments of the courts.

In the King's speeches and proclamations, as in the argument of his law officers, there was ample reply, strained higher but in essence the position of the Tudors. He owed account to none but God, in His ' high court of heaven '. He was the Church's supreme governor. Under him, interpretation of law belonged to his judges. There were mysteries, *arcana imperii*, of which they must take account. His prerogative embraced necessity, the preservation of the State; he had taken tonnage and poundage like his predecessors, ' *de bene esse* ', for the common good. And the Commons' encroachments and roving committees were ' incompatible with monarchy '.

CONTEMPORARY DATES

1605   Cervantes' *Don Quixote*.
        –1621. Pope Paul V.
1606   Peace of Zsitva Torok between Turkey and the Hapsburgs.
        Sikh revolt against the Moguls.
        First charter of Virginia.
1608   Rubens painting at Antwerp.
        St. François de Sales' *Introduction à la vie dévote*.
1609   Scientific discoveries of Galileo and Kepler.
        First reforms at Port Royal.
        Death of the last Duke of Cleves.
1610   Murder of Henry IV.
        Henry Hudson discovers Hudson's Bay.
1611–32   Reign of Gustavus Adolphus.
1612   Death of Bartholomew Legate, the last heretic burned at
            Smithfield.
1613–45   Reign of the Czar Michael, Romanov.
1614   Meeting of the French Estates-General.
        Dutch settlers sent to New Amsterdam (New York).
1615   Marriage of Louis XIII to Anne of Austria.
1616   The Manchus invade China.
1618   Opening of the Thirty Years' War.
        The Synod of Dort.
1619   Execution of Oldenbarneveldt.
1620   Battle of the White Mountain.
        War in the Valtelline.
1621–65   Reign of Philip IV of Spain.
1622   Beginning of Richelieu's permanent ministry.
1623   Death of Fra Paolo Sarpi.
1625   Tilly and Wallenstein invade Saxony.
        Renewed Huguenot revolt in France.
        Grotius' *De jure belli*.
1626   Battle of Lutter.
1627   Siege of La Rochelle.
        War of the Mantuan succession.
1628   Wallenstein on the Baltic.
        Building of the Taj Mahal.
        –1658. Reign of Shah Jehan at Delhi.
1629   Edict of Restitution.
        Peace of Alais.
        Bernini, architect at St. Peter's, Rome.

CHAPTER IX

THE DECISION, 1629–1642

NATURE had not fitted Charles I either to organize victory or to heal by concession. Rickety and immature as a boy, by resolution he made himself a man of courage and character, high-minded, artistic, and devout, but his principles, with the prejudices he erected into principles, made him a disastrous King. Reserved and by temperament remote, when he lost Buckingham he found, after many jars, a passionate love for his wife, subordinated only to his stronger devotion for the Church of England. Of public questions and political men he was a bad judge, viewing them through the lens of his affections ; so he juggled with European Powers just so far as they would assist his family in the Palatinate, deferred to the Queen in choice of ministers, and could only see rebellion in critics of the Church.

As no one quite replaced Buckingham, Charles himself presided over an undistinguished Council, some of them Catholic in sympathy or secret practice ; among whom Weston, earl of Portland, was a competent treasurer and urgent for peace, which was arranged during 1628–9 with both France and Spain. Though this stemmed the tide of debt, England's position in the next ten years was humiliating. Aware that without Parliament Charles was helpless, the French refused to hear of restoring the Elector Palatine. Trading interests and a common regard for the future of Belgium drew them towards Holland, which was enough, taken with rivalry in the Indies, to make Charles explore a Spanish alliance or an attack on the Dutch. But while he loftily expected all other navies to give England ' the honour of the flag ' in the narrow seas, he could not keep the Channel clear of privateers or stop Dutch and Spaniards fighting in our waters. Meantime Puritan England watched with joy and grief the Thirty Years' War, the conquests and then the death of Gustavus Adolphus, many volunteers, especially from Scotland, finding in Swedish service the chance to strike a blow for Protestantism which was denied at home.

Royal poverty led direct to measures which offended every class. Trade recovered with peace, nor was the country poor, for it found £200,000 in the next decade to send emigrants to America and half as much for draining the fens. Yet though the King's revenue, independent of Parliament, had been driven up to £600,000, there was a regular deficit, so that any emergency threw all out of gear. The

Treasury, casting about for new sources and furbishing up mediaeval rights, compelled all with lands worth £40 in income to ' compound for knighthood ', screwed up the dues of the feudal court of wards, and reopened forest claims which had lain dormant since the fourteenth century. Farmers and landlords were heavily fined in the forests of Rockingham, Waltham, and Dean ; Lord Salisbury, for instance, paid £20,000, and lesser men in proportion, for ' encroachment ' on land they had long thought their own. More far-reaching was the interference with trade by raising the customs and by new monopolies. For some of the last, those on gunpowder or tobacco, something could be said, but taking advantage of a loophole in the Act of 1624 which had only prohibited individuals' monopolies, the Crown formed corporations to control manufacture and sale of some necessary commodities such as coal, salt, and soap. While a host of royalty-holders and projectors intercepted royal profits, a steep rise of price angered the consumer. From every laundress who complained of bad soap, every Londoner taxed by the Newcastle coal-ring, a stream of grievance mounted ; up to the great commercial interests of Colonial companies contesting the tobacco monopoly, or the East India Company against a rival body headed by the Flemish merchant Courteen, to whom courtiers in search of quick profit persuaded Charles to give a charter. This warfare of capital blended with religious and constitutional opposition. Puritan merchants and squires headed the American emigrants, and the flower of the future parliamentary captains, Warwick and Saye and Sele, Hampden and Cromwell, took shares in New England settlements, where they were building up a freedom which some of the royal advisers meant to challenge.

All this time Council's intense activity, its spurring of gentry and magistrates over the poor law or wage-rates, meant conflict with important classes, while this unparliamentary finance outraged all legal sense. Clearly the Petition of Right had achieved nothing. Interpretation of ' the ancient law ' by the judges meant that the Crown could swell its customs revenue without limit, and keep Eliot in the Tower, where indeed he died. This was re-emphasized by the ship-money writs, issued every year from 1634 to 1639, the first of which asked in Elizabeth's way for ships from the port towns, but which soon became a heavy tax on the country at large. The need was real enough, when pirates were holding up the Channel packets and the Newcastle coal fleet. Growing resistance, however, showed a right instinct that this was not the point, and induced Charles to get his judges to rule that he could impose such a charge when the kingdom was in danger, ' of which His Majesty is the only judge '. From 1636, when John Hampden, rich and honoured in Buckinghamshire, tested this ruling, partial resistance became universal, when men heard the language of the judges who, by a narrow majority, condemned him. For to the plea of Hampden's counsel that the King's power must descend through known channels, and in taxation through Parliament as ' the ordinary means of supply upon extraordinary occasions ', they replied that ship-money was not properly a tax, that the King was *lex loquens*, the law's embodiment in case of necessity, and that his supreme rights and duties were not ' flowers of the Crown ' which Parliament might take away, but so inseparably connected with it that ' no acts of Parliament make any difference '. Here, as the royalist Clarendon wrote, was ' a logic that left no man anything he might call his own ', so that resistance spread even to those who were to be Cavalier commanders.

Those who held the highest ideal of monarchy had no illusion about Charles — ' a gracious prince ', as Laud noted later, ' who neither knew how to be nor to be made great '. Wentworth, his constant correspondent, became president of the Council of the North at the end of 1628, next year entered the Privy Council, and in 1633 proceeded to Ireland as Lord Deputy. He was never ' the grand apostate ' that enemies styled him; in all his indignation against Buckingham and in debates over the Petition, he had never ceased to argue for a strong sovereign. He asked only for ' beaten ways of happiness ', with government a symmetry as the Tudors had left it, in which King and people would not be opposed. Alongside a nation ruled by ancient law he raised, in many eloquent images, the ideal of a king as the State's motive power or keystone of the arch, *pater patriae*, the steersman in the night watch. He wished for peace, always advising Charles against petty intervention in Europe, and for a government devoted to protection of the people's ' modest liberties ' against social tyrants and poverty. But the wear and tear of politics severed Wentworth from Pym and his friends of 1628. He was never a Puritan, becoming on the contrary a more and more devoted churchman, while he had in him a defect of charity and a searing scornfulness, which made him unable to reach the better side of other men. Two stiff pieces of administration at York and Dublin, and bad health, darkened this outlook. He came to argue that government was going downhill, that there was ' a cancerous malignity ' in the Opposition which must be cut out. Puritans became to him only ' Pyms, Prynnes, and Bens ', ' odd names and odd natures '; Hampden ought to be ' whipped into his right senses '. And so, though he deplored the breach with Parliament, he was one of those who valued strength for its own sake. He poured scorn on lawyers who ' snuffled ' on the prerogatives, holding that ship-money, for example, if asked for a real necessity, was a necessary ' property of sovereignty '; *salus populi, suprema lex*.

In its good and evil alike his conception was proved in Ireland from 1633 to 1639, in government of a primitive society where law stood in contrast to chaos, and where rival religions meant a fight for the soil. In some ways his was the first, even the most benevolent autocracy which Ireland has known. Insisting on direct access to the sovereign in the hope of intercepting court jobbery, it was his policy to make Ireland a strong, contented, and self-contained dominion. He created an adequate army, cleared the coast of pirates, founded the linen industry, doubled the customs revenue. And if he built up his surplus on severe government monopolies, he at least protected Ireland against the selfish English interests which in the eighteenth century reduced her to servitude, insisting on a fair market for her cattle and keeping at arm's length the rapacious soap corporation. In the long run he believed that only a Protestant Ireland could be loyal, yet at present its Parliament was mostly Catholic and he did not approve the bad old method of swelling revenue with fines for recusancy.

More dangerous signs than his storms of temper or threats of court-martial against important councillors, showed how unfit he was to represent England. Perhaps his repudiation of the promised ' graces ' of Connaught was his least offence, for to grant unconditional recognition of land titles sixty years old would be to condone the grabbing, especially of Church land, by a most unmoral political clan. These ' black eagles ', as he called them, were headed by the veteran Earl of Cork, who had, for instance, gripped all the revenues of the diocese of Lismore, installed cousins in two more bishoprics, and farmed several dozen rectories. Against this aristocracy, and against middlemen acting for English peers, Wentworth waged unceasing war. But he repudiated also the royal promise to recognize land titles in Connaught, claiming all was the Crown's by conquest and descent, and proposed a plantation of new settlers who would ' line ' with Protestant Englishry this Catholic zone, linked as it was by trade and tradition to Spain, and where Clanrickarde ruled like a king. Pressure induced most juries to find the royal title ; fine and imprisonment punished the recalcitrant in Galway.

So he drove all the different levels of Ireland towards one iron-cast mould. A standing revenue he would have, he told Parliament, they could not expect the King to beg annually ' hat in hand '. ' A few petty clerks ', he menaced Convocation, should not stop his scheme for reception of the English Thirty-nine Articles, so much less Calvinist than their own. His search for money led to collision with London, whose charter at Derry was forfeited for non-fulfilment of their obligations. In Derry, too, he put an iron bishop Bramhall, for he was determined to bring to uniformity the Scot settlers, whose pastors taught them not to receive the communion kneeling. When in 1638 the Covenanters' rebellion in Scotland made Ulster a touchstone, he imposed the ' black oath ' against the Covenant, and moved troops to the north ; though troops which, as he himself saw with foreboding, could not be recruited further except from Catholics.

This system of ' thorough ', which Laud and Wentworth confided in their private letters, had meantime brought England to a dangerous temperature. There could be no compromise between the rival principles which had divided the Church for the past hundred years, yet many things had delayed a conflict ; a concentration of all Protestants against Spain, the political outlook of Elizabeth and the Cecils, a predominance of lay control in the parish system, whereby patrons could appoint Puritan clergy, and the strong hold of Calvinist doctrine. Even when the Stuarts drove Puritanism underground there was little agitation. Richard Baxter, most normal of Cromwellian Puritans, tells us that in his youth there was little talk of leaving the Church and little Bible reading ; it was a grief to the pious in Somerset that the peasants clung to their wakes on Sundays, nor would London playwrights, from Ben Jonson downwards, have put ' Zeal-of-the-land-busy ' on the stage or jeered at good Lord Saye's town of Banbury, unless their audience had enjoyed it. Much the greater proportion of High Commission cases came not from Crown pressure but from individuals seeking a remedy, usually in matters of marriage or divorce, and though many ministers objected to ceremonies, the number who were deprived was small.

Nevertheless, not only was there an irreconcilable section, but various reasons were convincing most laymen that their Church was in danger. Calvinist teaching of election and grace, and the open printed Bible, had deeply affected the country ; some independent conventicles, surviving Elizabethan persecution, were ready to suffer all rather than submit. Two such rivulets, later to make one great stream, flowed from a group which centred round William Brewster, manager of the royal postal service at Scrooby in Nottinghamshire. One was the band who in 1608 fled to Holland and who later, picking up others in England, as the Pilgrim Fathers sailed in 1620 to America ; another developed, before James died, into the Baptist churches. Still other sects, such as the Family of Love or the Seekers, branched off in revolt from the rigidity of Calvinism, to follow some new mysticism or doctrine of an inner light. Brownists and Baptists demanded toleration, the heart of Puritanism being indeed found in this challenge for the individual soul.

But this passion forced itself out through some bitter channels. Rapt in a literal devotion to the Bible and fortified by feeling themselves of the elect, the extremists warred against all delights of the eye and lusts of the flesh ; love locks, images, theatres, and maypoles. The Commons of 1621 expelled a member who reminded them how David danced before the ark ; another member, recorder of Salisbury, was punished for breaking a window that represented God the Father, and John Endicott, a founder of the Salem colony, cut the ' Popish ' cross out of the English flag. While the Commons discussed bills for keeping the Sabbath, both James and Charles affronted the Puritan conscience by their ' declarations of sports ', which the clergy read from the pulpit, encouraging archery, dancing, and village feasts on Sundays after service-time. But Puritanism covered much more.

In a real sense it meant the moralizing of England. The Civil War found Puritan Cavaliers in plenty, with a religion as deep, and a dislike of bishops as intense, as that of their enemies, while on the other side there were Puritan gentry, the regicide Colonel Hutchinson for instance, or Algernon Sidney, as well-read and cultivated, as devoted to hawking or music, as the gayest spark who followed Rupert. The best lives on each side show the same high ideal, the same personal faith, and a morality much changed since the Tudor Court. And the true Puritan was much more than the ' precisian ', which royal edicts styled him. Taught to find faith through mysteries of grace, assured that the humblest seeker should be a finder, and alone with God in an alien world, his sin and distraction, doubts, and too often his charities, vanished in one spiritual fire. He had lived, said Cromwell, in tents of Kedar and been ' the chief of sinners ', but on his death-bed, knowing he had once been in grace, knew all was well. So Bunyan's thoughts tortured him like ' masterless hell-hounds ', so the first Quaker leaders saw the light or heard the irresistible cry — George Fox listening to a voice over Lichfield crying ' woe to the bloody city ', or James Naylor at his plough to ' get thee out from thy father's house '. This minority were the men who edged the Puritan sword. ' Kings and armies and Parliaments ', said one of them in the debates of Cromwell's soldiers, ' might have been quiet at this day if they would have left Israel alone ', while the wisest of Puritan moderates, John Selden, found the root of the war in ' *scrutamini scripturas*, these two words have undone the world '.

While this dearly purchased individual faith won souls up and down England, the Arminian movement captured the Church organization ; a grave moment, since it represented a reaction from individual faith. Predestination, dooming so many, offended their moral sense ; they argued that religion was no ' jump into glorification ', but the continuous membership of a visible historic society, bound together and warmed by charities and sacraments. In doctrinal outlook they were more liberal than the Puritans, who would enforce a fixed Calvinist platform and in a double sense violated their feeling for law. To take Scripture as the sole ground narrowed, they thought, the scheme of creation ; the endowment of reason, the tradition of generations, the prerogative of learning, the development of a living society. And, in its over-bold scanning of mysteries, Puritanism as they saw it made mountains out of things that should be ' indifferent ', while throwing away the outward order in which erring men could find spiritual union.

Few bodies, in truth, have produced more holiness and intellect than the seventeenth-century English Church; which embraced not these high churchmen only, but the broad learning of Usher the Irish primate; the charitable and enquiring minds of Chillingworth and the scholar-soldier Falkland, who defended Anglicanism as the cause of reason against infallibility, whether coming from Rome or Geneva; Browne the author of *Religio Medici*, whose sceptical humanity yet hoped to ' bring up the rear in heaven '; or Donne the poet, hardly saved from joining Rome. Arminianism had also its saints; in the ' divine ' school of poets like George Herbert, who might have been Secretary of State but died in Wiltshire as a parish priest, or Nicholas Ferrar, who left the Virginia Company to found a community at Little Gidding, dedicated to worship and good works.

But since the broadest system narrows as it reaches the summit, it was a fatal misfortune that the Arminians' official leader was William Laud, Charles' confidant from the first, bishop of London and from 1633 Abbott's successor at Canterbury. His virtues were great, no man being bolder in bringing powerful sinners before High Commission, or defending the poor. But, always a disciplinarian since he had governed his Oxford college, he used his power to concentrate the Church in a faction, dividing lists of clergy for promotion as O. (Orthodox) or P. (Puritan), and filling the bench with Arminian bishops. He so far mistook his age that he gloried in making bishop Juxon Lord Treasurer or in appointing clerical magistrates, while his heresy-hunting reached out to American emigrants or English regiments stationed abroad. And in Star Chamber his voice was too often raised, against his lay colleagues, for severe punishment.

Three measures in particular made men indignant. The first were those to impose silence, a press-censorship by Council, the archbishop's power over licensing for publication, and a forcible reduction of London printing, all of which merely made scurrilous libels sell more widely and drove extremists to print in Holland. Religious men found unendurable a series of orders to forbid preaching on predestination and other ' deep points ', that made the very heart of Puritanism, and others ordering that catechizing should replace the afternoon sermon. This was connected with a second campaign, against the lecturers whom Puritan towns and gentry endowed, sometimes by trusts that bought up tithe. But it was by the outward signs, which convince the masses, that Laud created most hatred. Finding a mass of irreverence, churchyards where the militia exercised or communion tables whereon every passer-by laid his hat, St. Paul's a rendezvous for brokers or lovers, village churches where men behaved like ' a tinker and his bitch ' in an ale-house, he set out to compel discipline. He often ordered, and always encouraged, a move of the communion table to the east end, where it could be railed in as an altar; so offending the conservative ways of many parishes and straining Elizabeth's Injunctions. His vicar-general visited and reported on the dioceses, goading on some unwilling bishops. From every parish where a popular preacher had been silenced, a churchwarden imprisoned for resisting a move of the altar, a farmer fined for eating meat in Lent, or an order issued for bowing to the east, there rose a stream of anger and aversion.

A few notorious cases illustrate both Laud's zeal and his victims' courage. For opposing a change in cathedral ceremony, a Durham prebendary was deprived of his orders. For his violent *Zion's Plea against Prelacy*, the Scot Leighton was whipped, branded, and lay for years in prison. William Prynne, most learned, patriotic, and fanatic of lawyers, lost an ear and his livelihood for an attack on stage plays, reflecting on the Queen; lost his other ear, and endured branding, for criticizing Sabbath-breakers and bishops. At this same trial of 1637 two others suffered the same fate: Burton, a minister, for denouncing altars, and Bastwick, an Essex doctor, for labelling the bishops as anti-Christ. Pitying crowds round the pillory escorted the victims on their road to distant prisons, where they were cut off from wives and children in the cells of Scilly or the Channel Islands.

More than anger at this butchering inspired the laity. In the decency, colour, and music which decked George Herbert's church for the King of Kings, they saw only weak devices, intercepting the true light; 'capping, ducking, standing, and kneeling', flared out Bastwick —'poisonous Popish ceremonies', said Cromwell years after, which would 'eat out the core of religion'. Unlike the Commons of 1604 who disliked the name of Puritan, Laud's contemporaries began to take a bitter glory in it, as embracing all who kept the Sabbath holy, who avoided oaths and drink, or opposed the court; on all such, Mrs. Hutchinson wrote, the drunkards made their songs, the stage and ale-house 'belched forth profane scoffs'. How many souls, said Oliver, were not driven into the 'howling wilderness' of America!

But those not reckoned as 'saints', yet through whom alone the saints could triumph, were moved by one conviction above all: that 'an Arminian faction', as the Commons of 1629 put it, was wresting the law to bring back Popery. It was ill-founded, yet it had some plausible ground. For by affirming that Rome, though in error, was a true Church, by condemning European Protestants as schismatic, and justifying 'innovations' by going behind the Reformation — summed up in Laud's sentence 'we live in a Church reformed, not in one made new' — the Arminians challenged all their fathers had told of the old time before them. Had not the Gospel light broken on the midnight? Had not God, as Milton was to ask, revealed Himself, 'as His manner is, first to His Englishmen'? But now, distrusting half the bishops as Romanizers, they saw Catholics high in office; Portland as Treasurer,

Cottington at the Exchequer, Windebank Secretary of State. The Queen's chapel at Somerset House, and her Capuchin priests, were open to all. Papal legates appeared publicly at Court, where the Scotsman Con, whom the King called ' George ', was a special favourite, and there was an English resident at Rome. The Queen was trying to get an Englishman made cardinal, while the English Franciscan Sancta Clara (Catherine of Braganza's confessor later) worked for reunion. Many converts were in the inner circle, such as Buckingham's mother, Walter Montagu who for years acted as Henrietta's agent, some of the popular Lennox Stuarts, the mystic Kenelm Digby, and the great architect Inigo Jones. Recusancy laws were practically in abeyance, and it was now that the young Milton wrote in *Lycidas* of what ' the grim wolf ' daily devoured, ' and nothing said '. Our Protestant alliances were destroyed, the Palatine family were wandering refugees, and across the Irish Sea did not a Popish army stand prepared ?

At length Scotland gave to Englishmen an opportunity of resistance. Devoid of his father's knowledge of Scotland, its factions and leaders, Charles undermined that alliance with the nobility which had allowed James to humble the Kirk. He gave his confidence, and political predominance, to the bishops. His Act of Revocation of 1625 at one stroke reannexed all Church lands and tithe which had passed into laymen's hands since 1542. And though the compensation allowed was not unfair, and a reorganized tithe system for the first time gave the ministers a decent competence, he outraged the ruling class who were, moreover, alarmed for their feudal jurisdictions.

In 1633 he paid Scotland his first visit since infancy ; manipulating Parliament through the ' lords of the articles ', he confirmed James' Church legislation and put a mark on nobles who opposed him. Laud was with him, both were shocked at the disorder of worship, and they made a beginning by ordering the wearing of the surplice. In 1636 a new book of canons pronounced the King head of the Kirk, ordered the communion table to be placed at ' the upper end ', and desired obedience to a new prayer-book, which was still being prepared. When next year it appeared, superseding Knox's book, its sacramental teaching was rather more Catholic than that of the English prayer-book. Finally, neither canons nor prayer-book were submitted for approval either to the Parliament or the Church of Scotland.

From the first riots in St. Giles' Church at Edinburgh in July 1637, when women pelted the clergy and a mob tried to lynch the bishop, defiance on both sides led to revolution, to the setting up of commissioners or ' tables ' representing all estates, and in March 1638 to the signing of the Covenant. Reciting the doctrine of their Church and the laws passed to uphold it, this bound its signatories, ' by the great name of the Lord our God ', to resist unconstitutional innovation and,

' fearing no foul aspersions of rebellion ', to maintain royal authority and true religion. Beginning with those who signed in the Greyfriars' churchyard at Edinburgh, the mass of Scots of all ranks and opinions put their hand to it, and while Laud spoke foolishly of ' a few milkmaids ', the Scottish Council warned Charles that only 40,000 troops could restore the prayer-book. The people, wrote a Presbyterian minister, seemed ' possessed with a bloody devil '. Here was none of the solid prestige of government which it would take much to uproot in England, but a feudal nobility, a Church hardened by persecution and self-discipline into a granite mass, and a people hardy and poor, full of soldiers who had served in German and Swedish armies.

Wavering between war against concessions that would leave him only ' a Doge of Venice ', and concessions made necessary by lack of funds, in the autumn Charles revoked the prayer-book and allowed the meeting of a Church assembly. But the Scots, asserting its sole suprem-acy over the Church, determined its composition in accord with the Presbyterian system, the gentry electing lay elders and the mixed Kirk sessions electing ministers ; in November it defied a dissolution ordered by Hamilton, the royal commissioner, and declared episcopacy abol-ished. In February 1639 the Scots appealed to England to join them in fighting bishops and Papists, in March seized Edinburgh Castle and other strong points, and in May Charles with his army reached Berwick.

War meant the exposure of the ' thorough ' system. Personal government had reduced Council to faction. Wentworth had long com-plained of ' hungry courtiers ' and ' vermin ', who attacked his Irish government in hope of pickings for themselves ; Henrietta Maria expected her share : her influence promoted vicious courtiers like Lord Holland, and clinched the appointment of the self-seeking elder Vane as secretary of State. To pay his raw mutinous army the King could only look to a dribble of ship-money, or gifts from courtiers and clergy, London refusing any substantial loan. Wentworth's troops had to watch Scottish Ulster, and he advised that Scotland would be ' a work of two or three years '. All this contrasted ill with the Scottish levies, camped on Dunse Law under blue standards blazoned ' For Christ's crown and Covenant ', and marshalled cheerfully under the ' old little crooked soldier ' Alexander Leslie, veteran of Swedish war. Ex-officers drilled them, committees raised money, Edinburgh ladies worked to fortify Leith.

Yet the Scots, uncertain how invasion would react upon England, hoped to get what they wanted without fighting. So came about in June the pacification of Berwick, an insincere truce which each side used to consolidate its strength. Beyond vague phrases Charles would not decisively uproot episcopacy ; a fact enough in itself to prevent the formation of the royal party for which Hamilton had worked, and to keep on the side of the Covenant men like Montrose, who were offended by violence and suspected Argyll's ambition. But the Scots' action during the next year implied revolution. They enforced the Covenant on every subject, gave the election of lords of the articles to each estate, claimed for Parliament the command of royal castles, and passed laws in defiance of a royal veto.

While this armed quarrel went on, Charles sent for Wentworth from Ireland, created him earl of Strafford, and accepted his advice; which was to summon Parliament, abandon ship-money, and in Scotland wage a war to the knife. The 'Short parliament' lasted during three weeks of April and May, 1640. Strafford could report generous subsidies from Ireland and counted on English patriotism against invasion, the more so because there was evidence that the Scots were asking help from France. He was speedily undeceived. Pym at once took the lead, gravely rehearsing the grievances of the last eleven years; stressing the breach of privilege, ceremonies giving the Church ' a shape and face of Popery ', unparliamentary taxation, and the abeyance of Parliament. A tax given by Convocation and a royal majority in the Lords stiffened the Commons' resolve that before giving supply they must have redress over ship-money, tonnage and poundage, and the ' coat and conduct ' money now being raised to equip an army. Against Strafford's advice Charles asked no less than twelve 'subsidies' and, finding them preparing to discuss the Scots' grievances, dissolved this Parliament. His rejection of the last chance of agreed reform delighted Puritan extremists, among whom Cromwell's cousin St. John commented, ' it must be worse before it could be better '.

Worse it rapidly became. The government had argued that if Parliament failed to give supply, the people were ' without excuse ', and Strafford broke out in Cabinet with words that were to cost him his head. The King, he said, must take the offensive, and, as Parliament had brought him to ' extreme necessity ', could do all ' that power might admit ' and use the Irish army to reduce Scotland. Desperately the Council enforced ship-money, discussed debasing the coinage, asked help of Rome and Spain, but in spite of violent threats to the ' flat caps ' of London the citizens would give no loan. Against Laud's warning Charles insisted that Convocation should continue sitting after Parliament was dissolved, and the canons it proceeded blindly to pass provoked public opinion. They taught that subjects taking up arms against kingship received to themselves damnation, defended the railing-in of the altars, and framed a new oath, binding clergy and teachers, against any endeavour to change Church government of ' bishops, deans, archdeacons, etc.'.

Universal resistance checked these wild courses. Apprentices mobbed Lambeth, placards insulted the Queen. The conscript soldiers of southern counties mutinied, Devon men murdered a Catholic officer, those of Berkshire swore they would not fight against the Gospel, those from Essex tore down altar rails, unpaid militiamen took to loot; one commanding officer reporting he had to teach 'men that are fit for Bedlam and Bridewell to keep the ten commandments'. Yorkshire resisted billeting as illegal, judges hesitated to condemn those who refused coat and conduct money. Charles had hardly reached the north in August when, in a first skirmish at Newburn to hold the Tyne, the English levies fled, and Strafford could only groan over 'a lost business'. Without money he could not move his Irish army, but in his absence Irish taxes were not forthcoming.

So Leslie's force had triumphed, not only because it had mastered Scotland or because the English army was contemptible, but because England would not fight. The Scots' manifesto appealed to an English Parliament; twelve leading peers petitioned the King to summon the Houses and make peace, they were backed by another from 10,000 Londoners. When Charles summoned a council of peers at York in September, Buckingham's old enemy Bristol took the lead, telling the King he had lost his people's heart, and that nothing but Parliament could 'shoe the horses of the army'. Only Strafford was for no surrender, ardent to arouse the north against their hereditary enemy and to use Irish Catholics to expel the Scots of Ulster. The Scots' terms were therefore accepted, leaving them in occupation of Northumberland and Durham till peace were made, and allowing them meantime £850 a day for their troops, payment of which should be recommended to the parliament of England, which Charles agreed to call.

When the Long Parliament met on the 3rd November, this demoralized government met an opposition well organized and representative. It centred round Pym who, with Hampden, had seen to it that the electors returned their following, with a very high proportion of re-elections of members of the Short Parliament. Their programme was settled in concert with the Scots and Irish opposition, — punishment of 'incendiaries', and measures to make impossible a repetition of the last few years, — and they acted with the Scottish army as their shield, which they would not pay off till that programme was achieved. The leaders, who kept them together in Pym's lodging behind Westminster Hall, were fiery, embittered, and eminent; Hampden, devoted to the memory of Eliot, whose energetic sense could combine politicians and inspire Buckinghamshire yeomen; St. John, once his counsel over ship-money; Holles, who had suffered with Eliot; the younger Vane, fresh from a share in the democracy of New England; Fiennes, whose father Lord Saye held Puritan Northamptonshire in his hand; and Oliver Cromwell, a silent member since 1628, with more than twenty kinsmen in the House, and a great name with Puritan farmers of the Midlands, whom he had championed against enclosure and Laudian clergy.

While the work of destruction lasted, they could have no better leader than Pym, who had grown with the growing structure of the Commons ; a man of incisive eloquence, though apt to paint his radical designs as conservative, and to use any tactics as if they were principles. Believing it was a fight for life, his majority stuck at nothing. They turned out opposing members on the pretext they were monopolists, created new borough seats in areas favouring themselves like Devon and industrial Yorkshire, and locked away any Irish witnesses who would testify for Strafford. The Commons welcomed petitions from all and sundry, held solemn receptions for Laud's victims like Prynne, maintained a perpetual legend that the Papists were about to cut their throats, and accepted an armed guard from the City. With doubtful legality they summoned ' delinquents ' to appear before them, heckled high churchmen like Cosin who had introduced ' Popery ' at Durham, and dismissed magistrates. Inhabitants of Beckington in Puritan Somerset, for instance, made deposition how they had been imprisoned for resisting an altar, or how the bishop of Bath and Wells had jeered at their talk of Parliament, saying, ' when the sky falls, we shall catch larks ' ; but now ' the wicked parson ', says the Commons' diarist, was summoned as a ' delinquent '.

Not that the fears, thus skilfully exploited, were entirely groundless. A royal force was in the north, unpaid, hostile to the Scots, and with many Catholic officers ; the Irish army was not disbanded ; Charles had thoughts of hiring foreign mercenaries ; wild schemes were abroad in the Queen's circle. Moreover Pym had acquired through the younger Vane a copy of his father's notes of the Cabinet of May, when Strafford had told the King he was ' absolved from all rules of government ' and could use an Irish army to reduce ' this kingdom '. But though the first debates produced a flood of grievances and asseveration of a plot ' to alter law and religion ', Pym's decisive action turned on a chance betrayal of Strafford's purpose to accuse the Opposition of conspiracy with the Scots. There and then, on the 11th November, behind locked doors, the Commons framed an impeachment.

The Lords' angry calls to Strafford to withdraw, and their sending him to custody, gave the first expression of a vital fact — that on more than half of its programme this Parliament were unanimous. Leaders of the future Royalist armies did much to carry the measures of the next six months. Digby fastened on Strafford the name of ' the grand apostate ', Hopton and Falkland led in abolishing ship-money, and Hyde in the Acts that swept away Star Chamber, High Commission, and Council of the North. There was no opposition to the triennial Act, making automatic a reassembly of Parliament after three years' interval, whether the Crown agreed or not, or to those against tonnage and poundage. Moderate men saw with pleasure the impeachment of Laud and the flight overseas of Secretary Windebank, together with Lord Keeper Finch, who had given the ship-money judgment.

This body of legislation, however, was every bit as negative as the Petition of Right. It put a mark on abuse of prerogative, and when it declared that the reasons for an extended Star Chamber jurisdiction had ' now ceased ', corrected Tudor encroachment on the law. But, save that it subjected the Crown to a triennial Parliament, it did nothing to determine sovereignty, for it left the Crown with its veto and initiative, the choice of ministers, and command of the forces.

What it left unsolved was forced to the front by the trial of Strafford. Not till March 1641 did this drama open in Westminster Hall, where for three weeks, before tiers of crowded seats and in a clamour of conversation, food, and beer bottles, he struggled for life. Never was there a worse parody of justice. The Commons strove to intimidate witnesses, counsel, and the Lords. Their charges were a medley of inconsistencies, collected indiscriminately from gossip, whether from Irish Protestant vultures like Lord Cork — ' old Richard hath sworn against me gallantly ', said the accused — or Irish Catholics whom the Protestants would gladly extirpate. None of them amounted to treason ; as for the crowning clause, the design of bringing in an Irish army to suppress England, not merely was it refuted by every councillor except Vane, but the two witnesses required in a treason trial were really only one, — Vane's own halting recollection and a copy of his notes filched by his son. Failing at every point to prove legal treason which, under Edward III's law, must be against the King, Pym extended treason to any offence as interpreted by a parliamentary majority, argued that accumulated misdemeanours amounted to treason, and that ' ill intent ' could replace proof. In speeches of immense power Strafford riddled these tissues. Was not this ' arbitrary treason ' worse than his supposedly arbitrary law ? ' Be not you ambitious to be more skilful than your forefathers in the art of killing.' If opinions, given under a councillor's oath, could be so wrested, he warned the sympathetic Lords, ' you, your estates, your posterity, lie at stake '. He warned England not to lose Ireland by breaking down the Deputy's power, and once more reiterated his conception of a ' trust ' in the Crown, justified in ' extreme necessity ' in using exceptional means, though bound to employ Parliament in ordinary times to keep up ' the just poise of prerogative and liberty '.

Finding no legal remedy, the Commons fell back on force and in April brought in a bill of attainder. With evidence of plots among the Queen's friends in the army and a design to seize the Tower, the City was beside itself with panic ; thousands, many of them armed, surrounded Whitehall calling for ' justice and execution ', crying to their favourites, ' God bless your worship ', but posting up the names of the Commons' minority as ' Straffordians, betrayers of their country '. It was known that the Queen meditated flight to France, where troop movements were reported. Charles, though yielding unwillingly to every important bill, still would not disband the Irish army, and intervened in the Lords with an announcement that he could not accept the attainder. For some time there had been efforts to detach Opposition members, strivings for peace on the basis of condemning Strafford without taking his life, and talk of office for Pym.

He, indeed, was bent on having the life of Strafford, whose policy he conceived would have put on England a ' character of servitude '. Fear and indignation gave the Commons over to the extremists, to St. John's brutal argument that ' beasts of prey ' might be knocked on the head. With 200 members absent, they passed attainder by 204 to 59; coupling with it an appeal to the nation, in a ' protestation ' pledging them to maintain Protestantism, and a bill against dissolution of the present Parliament without its own consent. Charles' intervention and army plots wrecked the middle party in the Lords, Catholic peers were frightened away, the moderate Puritan Bedford died, and Essex held fast to his motto, ' stone dead hath no fellow '. While the Lords gave way from mingled patriotism and despair, the King yielded in fear for his wife and children, for the ports were stopped and armed mobs accompanied the presentation of the two bills. On the 10th May he assented to both, and on the 12th Strafford's head was smitten off. If human conflict had to fulfil the law that one man die for the people, the old regime could not offer a greater victim.

Attainder, with the implication that Parliament was the new sovereign, broke the previous unanimity. On religion, dearer by far to them than all, that agreement had so far covered two points, a fear of Popery and a hostility to the bishops. The Commons thus welcomed petitions flowing in against Laud, Wren of Norwich, or the clergy who had refused communion to those who would not come to the altar rails. No one opposed the destruction of High Commission; Falkland and many moderates argued for a ' primitive ' episcopacy, stripped of their courts and political influence.

But while before Christmas all had agreed to impeach Laud, now a huge London petition for abolishing bishops, violent preaching from laymen, like the leather merchant ' Praise God ' Barbon who held forth in Fleet Street, and wild sects alarmed the conservatives. The country was exasperated by heavy payments for the Scots, whose crusade to force Presbyterianism on England irritated most Englishmen. Parliamentary debate and county petitions showed their dislike of ministers and elders, together with the instinct expressed by one anti-Laudian royalist, that ' if we make a parity in the Church, we must come to a parity in the commonwealth '. Selden and the lawyers abominated clerical control, and tactics decided Pym and Hampden that, till

Strafford were dead, their majority must not be broken up by quarrels about episcopacy. All therefore that was done was to pass a bill to exclude bishops from the Lords, and the clergy in general from any lay office.

While the Lords' majority were ready for compromise, on lines worked out by Laud's bitter rival, the former Lord Keeper Williams, bishop of Lincoln, and Usher the Calvinist primate of Armagh, whereby ministers would assist bishops in their functions, in their indignation at the sects they threw out the bill excluding bishops from their house. This encouraged the ' root and branch ' party, led by Vane, Cromwell, and St. John, to produce an alternative bill, abolishing the whole episcopal system, while Pym was driven on by the knowledge that Charles meant to visit Scotland with the design of forming a royalist party, just as he had begun to win over Englishmen like Hyde and Digby, who were alienated by Strafford's attainder and attacks on the Church. So in both kingdoms religion was forming rival parties. While the Argyll section arrested Montrose and rumour of a new army plot reached Westminster, Pym pushed forward the ' root and branch ' bill ; though so far modified to suit English feeling that nine lay commissioners were to control jurisdiction in the Church. The Commons also demanded the dismissal of ' evil counsellours ' and proposed to make the whole nation sign the ' Protestation ' — a vote which, when rejected by the Lords, they circulated to the constituencies, defending it as ' a shibboleth to discover a true Israelite '. So much suspicion grew round the King's Scottish journey and the Queen's activity that both Houses discussed military precautions.

There is no reason to think that Charles meant to undo the important statutes to which he had assented. He disbanded both English and Irish armies, dismissed the Papal legate, and left Essex in military command of the south. Yet no doubt he would resist any more concessions, counting on winning over the Scottish nobles offended by Argyll's overweening power and, by acceptance of their religious settlement, the old loyalty of his Scottish people. His hopes were increased by a real reaction in England. His remaining prerogatives, clear of Tudor accretion, now stood impregnably on the law. The Lords' majority were not ready to expel bishops and Catholic peers. Sober Londoners intensely disliked the cobblers and women preachers, and the mobs which, on seeing a clergyman, tore off his surplice or howled ' Canterbury's whelp '. By September religion had made a deadlock ; for while the Lords issued orders against disturbance of the present service, the Commons commanded the removal of altars, and cessation of sports on the Sabbath day.

Two distant events drove on a new cycle of panic and aggression. Among the more primitive Scottish politicians there were disappointed men, soldiers, and Catholics, ready to use violence against Argyll and

Hamilton who, they argued, had imprisoned the King in a parliamentary-Presbyterian supremacy. Whatever the true facts of this plot, styled 'the incident', it confirmed the English Opposition's belief that violence threatened them also; when Parliament reassembled, once more they set on foot the bill to exclude bishops and, when the Lords procrastinated, began to draft a 'grand remonstrance'. On 1st November, the day fixed to discuss it, news reached London of an Irish rebellion.

It was caused by the past fifty years of policy, which left half the Irish dispossessed of their land, and immediately occasioned by those who had destroyed Strafford's cadre of government, dismissed his lieutenants, and part-disbanded a part-Catholic army, without adequate pay; it was inflamed by the rabid anti-Popery of the English Commons, which inspired Irish priests to preach a holy war. Its first leaders came from the ruined families, the fanatic Rory O'More, and Owen O'Neill, a good soldier trained in Spanish service. It began as an agrarian war in Ulster, and by murder, burnings, or suffering in flight to Dublin, not less than eight thousand English and Scots perished. But a plot to seize Dublin failed; neither Munster nor Connaught had moved; and not till the New Year did the savage bungling of the Dublin government drive the Catholic aristocracy over to the rebels.

No details, no wild rumour of 200,000 Englishry killed in cold blood, had yet reached England when Pym seized his opportunity: carried a resolution that, if Charles did not appoint ministers whom they approved, the Commons would find a way of defending Ireland, and introduced the Grand Remonstrance.

This was an appeal to the people, not only against the King but against the upper House, where 'bishops and recreant lords' impeded 'endeavours for reformation'. Once more rehearsing every grievance since the reign began, it sounded the motif of a prolonged Popish design; though baffled till Strafford's death, this 'malignant party' had taken heart again, its machinations culminating in this Irish massacre; and, as the army plots proved, but for God's providence 'we had been the prologue to this tragedy'. With a mass of bitter allusion, to Eliot's blood which 'still cries for vengeance' and the Queen's evil influence, it demanded a synod to include foreign (plainly Scottish) divines, and declared the Commons would give no supply if Charles did not choose ministers in whom they could confide.

After warm debate this Remonstrance was carried by eleven votes, Cromwell saying as they came out, when 'the chimes of Margarets were striking two in the morning' that, had it failed, he would have sold all he owned and gone to America. Swords were pulled out and the House was full of shouting, for panic was becoming a frenzy. Rumours of priests and Frenchmen, a false report that the Irish claimed to be acting under Charles' orders, drove the Commons to declare that, as ' the representative body ', they could act independently of the Lords, who were but ' particular persons '. They would not join them in reproving the mobs rioting round parliament; who roared out ' no bishops ', thrust their torches into suspect coaches, or passed their favourites with cries of ' a good man '; ' God forbid ', said Pym, ' the House of Commons should proceed in any way to dishearten people to obtain their just desires '. Face to face with the immediate problem of an army for Ireland, they put forward a militia bill, giving authority to a general of Parliament's choice. They called for the execution of Catholic priests, voted they would never tolerate Irish Catholics, and printed the Remonstrance.

As usual, Charles halted between two opinions. Though he was bent on defending the Church, the latest bishops whom he named were anti-Laudian, and he was conferring office on men who had been foremost in destroying ' thorough '. Let him, was the counsel of Hyde, Falkland, Culpepper, and Nicolas, stand on the defensive, ' the known law ' which asserted his right of naming ministers and generals, and the legal existence of bishops. But on the other side was the Queen, fired by indignation at the attack on Catholics and by fear of the rowdies crying round Whitehall against ' Papists ' and ' redcoats '. Many voices encouraged him to stand up to ' King Pym ' and his mob, from soldiers and the citizens' hereditary enemies at the Inns of Court.

Under such influence he tried to put the Tower in safe hands, then retreated, then made two irreparable mistakes. In alliance with Digby, now a wild champion of the Queen and aristocracy, the bishops protested that, by reason of the mob, Parliament was no longer free; for which they were promptly impeached and imprisoned. On the 3rd January 1642, acting on sudden impulse, though on a well-grounded fear also that Pym's party would impeach the Queen, the King through his attorney-general impeached for treason Pym, Hampden, Holles, Haselrige, and Strode, with one peer, Mandeville (the future parliamentary general, Manchester); on the 4th, with several hundred soldiers, he himself came to the Commons to demand the five members.

The City sheltered the accused and flew to arms, the moderating position of the Lords was destroyed, thousands of Hampden's Buckinghamshire yeomen, Thames seamen, and apprentices poured out, and Charles left London, purposing to send his wife abroad and himself to seek the loyal north. The only test now was the command of the sword. While the Commons sent agents to seize the Hull arsenal, the Lords (by this time very low in numbers) joined them in asking for parliamentary control of forts and militia. By the end of February the Queen was in Holland and the Prince of Wales safely with the King, who refused to give up command of the militia for more than a year. In April a parliamentary commander refused him entrance to Hull, the Commons imprisoned those who petitioned in favour of the prayer-book, and enforced their own militia ordinance. When Charles forbade militia musters without his assent, Parliament declared that sovereignty was exercised ' in this high court of law and counsel after a more eminent and obligatory manner than it can be by any personal act ', and in the Nineteen Propositions demanded parliamentary choice of ministers and judges, control of the royal children, fortresses, militia, and the Church settlement, with punishment of delinquents. Only then did the King issue orders for raising troops by commission of array.

Blood must flow when men tried to execute these rival claims, and in July was first shed in a collision between Manchester militia and the royalist Stanleys. Each appealing to the fundamental laws and vowing that the other aimed at arbitrary government, two bodies, each professing a conservative defence, took up arms to settle the question of sovereignty. On the 22nd August Charles set up his standard at Nottingham.

CONTEMPORARY DATES

1630	Gustavus Adolphus attacks Germany.
1631	Tilly attacks Magdeburg.
	Death of Donne ; birth of Dryden.
1632	Gustavus killed at Lutzen.
	Van Dyck comes to England.
	Birth of John Locke.
1633	The Inquisition force Galileo to recant.
	George Herbert, *The Temple*.
1634	Murder of Wallenstein.
	Milton's *Comus* acted at Ludlow.
1635	The Peace of Prague.
	Foundation of the Académie Française.
1636	Foundation of Harvard University.
	Dutch conquest of Ceylon.
1637	Descartes' *Discourse sur la méthode*.
	-1657. Reign of the Emperor Ferdinand III.
1639	Tromp defeats the Spanish fleet.
	English factory set up at Madras.
1640	Portugal revolts against Spain.
	Three dramas by Corneille.
	Dr. Busby becomes headmaster of Westminster.
	-1688. Reign of the Great Elector in Brandenburg.
1642	Tasman discovers New Zealand and Tasmania.
	Death of Richelieu.
	Birth of Isaac Newton.

CHAPTER X

THE CIVIL WAR, 1642–1646

I T was with loathing that Englishmen embarked on what the parliamentary general Waller, writing to the Royalist Hopton, called ' this war without an enemy '. Throughout, many stood aside; whole counties sometimes enforced a truce; peasant ' clubmen ' rioted impartially against both plundering armies; the flower of Puritan soldiers, the New Model army, was largely made up of conscripts. Not for such reasons only, in so far as it was fought between fellow-Englishmen and Protestants, it was waged with rare humanity, never becoming a war between geographical areas or rival classes. It is true that the cause of Parliament predominated south of Trent and east of Severn, as it did in clothing towns and the urban middle class outside those frontiers, as at Bradford or Manchester; true also, that nearly two-thirds of the peerage followed the Crown, and that democratic fervour inspired many Anglian yeomen and London apprentices. But nearly half the country gentlemen, the political leaders of that age, supported Parliament; so did many of the greatest and most ancient families of the peers, Percies, Russells, Sidneys, and half the Herberts. Essentially it was a contest of conflicting ideals, expressed by natural leaders through their normal following, which meant that it was a provincial, and in a sense a feudal war. Saye and Sele could mass Puritans of the Midlands, so could Robartes in the north of Royalist Cornwall, or the Fairfaxes in Royalist Yorkshire, and the ideals that cut across counties sheared also through families, Cromwells and Fleetwoods thus fighting on either side.

For men took up arms from all manner of motives, and sentiment weighed as heavily as logic or law. The royal army held many who detested the bishops, as did the royal standard-bearer Edmund Verney, killed at Edgehill, who yet would not abandon the King whose bread he had eaten so long. It included thousands like Hyde who stood on the law, Falkland who saw liberty of mind on that side, peers like Newcastle concerned for an old social order, and many who despised the violent sects. Against them were aristocrats like Manchester, who equally disliked ranters and democracy but distrusted courtiers and swordsmen; solid squires who swore by Elizabeth, and believed they were defending her system; fanatical preachers who looked for a new heaven and new earth. As time passed, the religious motive rose to the top, because it was the ruling passion of the age, and because on it the part

taken by Scot Presbyterians and Irish Catholics must turn, as well
as from that apparent law of revolutions which concentrates emotion
towards one fiery pyramid.

Unless the King could deal a knock-out blow, the military decision
was doubtful, though Parliament had some overwhelming advantages
which time would increase. London was the first, ' city of refuge ' as
Milton wrote, and ' mansion house of liberty '. Here were the moneyed
men who could equip armies, the centre of trade, and the customs house.
Here was the armoury of opinion, the printing presses which put out
nearly twenty weekly papers and poured forth 30,000 pamphlets in these
twenty years. Here Puritanism was solidly massed, bound with the
eastern counties from which the city drew its food. London trained-
bands were better disciplined than any others, the City had pride and a
passion for the good cause, shown, for example, even after Restoration
by survivors of those who had fought at Newbury holding a commemoration banquet. And possession of the London area meant two other
inestimable gains. Strategically, it gave to Parliament the inner lines,
from which they could strike at the Royalist circumference. And
morally it diffused an impression that Parliament was, as it were, in
legal possession — the spectacle of the legislature and law courts in
peaceful session, attacked by a King in alliance with rebels and aliens.

London also contributed to a third element in victory, that the fleet
went over to Parliament. Warwick, their admiral, had a hand in every
seafaring and colonial venture since Raleigh's last voyage, and took a
keen interest in privateering. And since the west-country ports were
Puritan too, Parliament held not the centre only but some keys on the
circumference, their command of the sea enabling them to intercept the
King's munitions from Europe and to hold the harbours from Hull to
Lyme Regis, by which they could take him in rear.

War was spun out because both sides at first were civilian, untrained,
and uncentralized. County associations thought only of self-defence ;
local forces would manœuvre to collect a large landowner's rents or to
revictual themselves on a local market-day. Outside London the first
forces were raised on almost a feudal principle, powerful individuals
recruiting the ranks and appointing officers, as Newcastle did with his
Yorkshire Whitecoats or Cromwell with his East Anglian horse. War
lingered on because local levies hated leaving their own county, the
famous Cornish Royalist army above all, though even the Londoners,
their first commander reported, were always crying ' home, home '.
This sort of warfare damaged the King most, recruiting as he did
especially from the north and Wales ; his striking force was reduced and
his tactics deranged by pressure to defend some great country house such
as Lathom, the Stanleys' castle, or frittered away in private garrisons,
most famous of which was the Catholic Lord Winchester's at Basing.

In the long run victory must go to professional soldiers and the longer purse, in both of which Parliament had a superiority. Having no settled funds, Charles scattered his garrisons as the means of raising supply, and while he depended on the private fortunes of great nobles, such as Newcastle or Worcester, with levies and plunder from agricultural England or Oxford college plate, or while the brave Cornish only lived by selling tin to France, Parliament controlled rich industrial areas and the customs revenue. Ultimately they raised also a special assessment on counties in their area, rising to £120,000 a month, and could pay their cavalry troopers 2s. a day. Regular pay and success won over several thousand professional soldiers who, like Monck, had first served the King, while Parliament always had more officers with experience of foreign service. In time, both armies, but Cromwell's in particular, found out better ways of a mobile war. The number of pikemen was reduced, the clumsy matchlock musket replaced by a flint-lock, cavalry dropped the heavy cuirass. Above all, just as Cromwell insisted they must get rid of 'tapsters and decayed serving men' and recruit men of spirit, so he followed Rupert in new cavalry tactics, making his men reserve their fire, trust to their swords, and concentrate on shock.

Till 1644 Charles pursued one strategy with considerable success, a triple advance on London from the north, Midlands, and west. The first serious fighting was with Essex at Edgehill (October 1642) where Rupert, the King's nephew, threw victory away by diverting his cavalry from the main battle to pursuit. Its effects were indecisive, for though Charles got nearer to penetrating London than he ever did again, the City foot held him at Brentford and Kingston, and he retreated to make Oxford his headquarters.

But 1643 was a year of Royalist triumph. The Cornish army, well led by Hopton and raised by men of eminent character and courage, Bevil Grenville, the Slannings, and Godolphins, beat two armies at Bradock Down (January) and Stratton (May); pushed on through Devon, and in July stormed Waller's position at Lansdown, above Bath; a week later, with Oxford reinforcements, routed Waller again at Roundaway Down near Devizes. Meantime the Queen, landing in Yorkshire under fire, brought in munitions from abroad. Hampden was mortally wounded in a skirmish at Chalgrove in June; in July Bristol surrendered to Rupert. By a forced march with London regiments Essex saved Gloucester, making good his retreat again in the first battle of Newbury in September, where Falkland was killed. But the Royalists captured Reading; Newcastle defeated the Fairfaxes at Adwalton Moor near Bradford; his detachments, with others from Midland garrisons, passed through Lincoln and reached King's Lynn.

Even so, the stars fighting against Charles shone already in the sky.

Newcastle dare not advance boldly while Hull was untaken, and Hull could be reinforced by sea ; Fairfax was able to ship his cavalry to join Cromwell, who won many local successes in East Anglia and in October a substantial victory at Winceby, on which Newcastle broke off the siege of Hull. The Cornish army insisted on returning home, for Parliament's hold of Plymouth was a perpetual threat, and by the beginning of 1644 Hopton's advance, the right horn of Charles' scheme, was definitely held up in Sussex and Hampshire.

While local armies fought, and small points like Reading or Lincoln changed hands without a real decision, each side took steps to acquire new strength. Pym decided to make a political sacrifice for military salvation and in August asked Scotland for an army, in return for a religious settlement in both countries, ' according to the Word of God and the example of the best reformed churches '. If Vane, the chief English commissioner, drafted these words to protect the sects, to the Scots they seemed a fair opening for Presbyterianism in England ; in September both countries accepted the Solemn League and Covenant, a last legacy from the supreme politician Pym, who died in November, and a Committee of Both Kingdoms was given direction of the war. Charles took two counter-measures : first, the ' Cessation ' (September), a truce for a year with the Irish Catholic Confederates, which would release some of his troops for England; and then an acceptance of the plan long urged by Montrose, to rouse Scotland from the north, in collaboration with an attack by Antrim through the Western Isles.

This scheme, news of which immediately determined the Scots, was finally to turn all England too against the King. His only present gain lay in a few undisciplined Protestant Irish regiments, the first of whom were beaten at once by Fairfax at Nantwich, and who constantly deserted to Parliament. But Antrim's levies would be Catholics, which was enough to import a new savagery into the war. Irish women following the troops were often butchered, while off the Welsh coast captured Irishmen were tied up and drowned.

Moreover, such tactics were a symptom of a deep division in the royal counsels. At Oxford there were some seventy peers and about one hundred and seventy of the Commons, all ardent for peace and detesting any truck with Popery. But against Hyde and soldiers like Hopton, representing this English conservatism, was cast the influence of the Queen and her group, who were ready for any political combination, intriguers led by Digby and Jermyn ; while the army's morale was weakened by commanders of the type of Goring, whose lives outraged decent men, who would take orders from no one but the King, and whose plundering troops converted many neutrals to Parliament.

1644 was the turning-point. Fears of being caught between Leven's advance and a sally of the Fairfaxes from Hull drove Newcastle to evacuate Durham, and soon he was beleaguered in York, outside which the Scots made contact with Manchester's eastern army. Rupert dashed to the rescue and forced battle at Marston Moor, early in July. But he chose his position rashly, his 17,000 men had 27,000 against them, and though on his left Goring broke Fairfax, the Scots in the centre were staunch, while Cromwell rolled up his right and then took his centre in rear. ' God made them ', he wrote, ' as stubble to our swords.' Newcastle's army had ceased to exist, he himself fled abroad, York fell, and outside Lancashire and a few garrisons Charles had lost all the north.

A month later Montrose, unaided except by McDonnells and Macdonalds from Ireland and the Isles, began his campaign ; broke one army at Tippermuir, sacked Aberdeen, and in February 1645 destroyed at Inverlochy the force of Argyll and the Campbells. But this came too late to melt the solid obstacle of Leven's army between himself and the King ; while he was perpetually menaced by the Scots' hatred of his Irish Catholic allies who, they said, ' killed men with no more feeling of compassion than they killed a hen ', and not less by the drift homewards of his Highlanders after each campaign. No unprofessional soldier ever showed more genius for war, no leader was ever greater in handling ill-equipped infantry, with a bare handful of horse, against much larger forces ; in exalting them to suffer incredible hardship in mountain warfare over roadless snow, in long marches barefoot or in raw-hide sandals ; and no one was a greater master of surprise. But he had for ever to be harking back north to raise new levies, while the Highlands were divided by sore feuds ; if he depended on Macdonalds, Mackenzies and Frasers would bar his path ; clan chieftains like Huntly would not join till assured they were on the winning side ; Macdonalds and Macleans cared more for harrying Campbells than for a Lowland war : though only the Lowlands, or a junction with the King, could make all this heroism serve the cause.

Yet the parliamentary victory of 1644 was part-destroyed by the incompetence of the parliamentary parties. Nothing had pulled together the local county associations, while quarrels among the generals threw away Marston Moor. Detaching Waller to follow the King, who was manœuvring between Oxford and the Severn and who soon dealt Waller a smart blow at Cropredy Bridge on the Cherwell, Essex obstinately insisted on marching to rescue Taunton and other outposts in the west. Charles pursued, blockaded him in the Fowey peninsula, and at Lostwithiel compelled the surrender of all his foot.

The victors of the north did nothing to retrieve this defeat. Leven, worried by Montrose's activity, had also much to clear up on the Trent and the Mersey. So the King was allowed to march, unattacked, from Cornwall till he came to Newbury ; even then, after infinite fumbling by Manchester, the battle was broken off, when if pushed home it might

have decided all, and Charles was able to mass in or round Oxford what
was left of Rupert's forces and his own. For all this the reasons were
more grave than a lack of military ability, for that autumn the supporters
of Parliament were within an ace of turning their swords on one another.

After three years' indecisive fighting, universal weariness of war
filled the country. London women had shouted in Palace Yard, ' give
us that dog Pym ', plots had been discovered among London business
men, and the Oxford ' parliament ' was eager for peace. True, in the
repeated negotiations no compromise seemed possible between demands
for a Puritan Church with punishment of the royal advisers and
Charles' vow that three things he would never surrender, ' the Church,
my crown, and my friends '. Yet a strong group of parliamentary peers
did not believe in victory by the sword, Essex and Manchester joining
Leven and the Scots in a move for Presbyterianism and peace. Against
both parts of this programme there was passionate feeling in- and outside the army. Vane, parliamentary head of the war-party after Pym,
already spoke of deposing the King. Since 1643 the Westminster
Assembly of divines had been in constant session, pursuing the task of
finding a religious settlement ; for though episcopacy was abolished and
altars and windows had been hacked to pieces, in doctrine and order
there was a void. While the Scots' commissioners and their ministers,
led by Alexander Henderson, pressed the full Kirk scheme and redoubled their pressure after each Scottish military success, Independents
headed by Vane and lawyers represented by Selden fought them at
every point ; contesting in particular a centralized Church, the institution of lay elders, and the use of excommunication to exclude from the
sacrament.

An air of democracy was blowing. Milton now published his
Areopagitica in protest against the Presbyterian press censorship, while
John Lilburne, type of the army democrats, began his long life of
championing the sovereign people against tyranny, whether by King,
Parliament, or Protector. All this, in the winter of 1644–5, coincided
with a crisis in the army.

At its centre stood Cromwell, ' Ironside ' as Rupert called him,
maker of the cavalry who were the flower of the forces, darling of men
in the ranks ; still the same as he had been when a Royalist member
noted his clothes made by a bad country tailor, with the ' rustic carriage '
and the touch of horseplay, the love of horseflesh, and the generosity to
an honourable foe which the private soldier loved. Enemies said
that his command was ' a mere Amsterdam ' ; at least he made the
core of his regiments out of ' the godly ', God-fearing men under
good discipline, who would follow, he said, any ' plain russet-coated
captain, who knows what he fights for and loves what he knows '. He
answered the clamour for peace and against the sects by angry words

against the Scots, and by purging his troops of those who would not fight for clear victory. Now they were full of officers and men who would preach in any orchard on the march, just as hundreds were seen later listening to a soldier-preacher on the steps of Christ Church Hall in conquered Oxford; Baptists and Anabaptists, Seekers and Fifth Monarchy men serving alongside sober Independents. There was free talk among them that the nobility only sprang from ' William the Conqueror's colonels ', that Charles was a tyrant, and that Providence destined them to resettle the State.

While the Scots spoke of impeaching him as ' an incendiary ', from his place in Parliament, Cromwell charged Manchester with incompetence at Newbury and an unwillingness to bring the King too low, and events played in his favour. Charles' refusal of terms at a conference at Uxbridge early in 1645 demolished the peace-party, who themselves contributed to its failure by executing Laud, and by setting up a new ' directory ' instead of the prayer-book. As regards army reform, Waller was as insistent as Cromwell, who wisely damped down personal feuds and concentrated on a policy to save a nation ' bleeding, almost dying '. Against the peers' obstruction, by April, his group achieved the passage of the ' self-denying ' ordinance and the formation of a ' New Model ' army. Members of both Houses were to resign their commands ; Fairfax became general, and Skippon major-general, of a new force 22,000 strong, with pay secured on the taxes. It was not as much an anti-Presbyterian as a professional army, for Fairfax commissioned its officers, mostly Independents and quite irrespective of social standing, and though an oath was taken to the Covenant it was not enforced on the ranks. This army was clothed in the red coats which the Eastern Association had been adopting, over a third of the men were ' pressed ', and many had fought for the King. Within a month a demand from the ranks brought about the choice of Cromwell as lieutenant-general, commanding the horse.

Hesitating between advice to join Montrose and an impulse to protect Oxford, Charles divided his army, struck north and stormed Leicester but then, alarmed at Goring's blunders in the west, turned south again, only to be caught near Market Harborough by Fairfax, with an army double his own in strength. Here on the 14th June was fought Naseby. Once more Rupert had let the enemy take a stronger position ; once more he swept away the wing opposite him and returned to find the battle lost, for once again Cromwell rolled up the other division of royal horse and took in flank the gallant, outnumbered, Welsh infantry. The victors captured 5000 prisoners, with all the King's munitions and his private papers which, soon printed for the world, revealed his schemes to repeal anti-Catholic laws, introduce an Irish army, and hire foreign mercenaries.

Before the year ended Fairfax disposed of Goring in a galloping fight at Langport and captured Bridgwater, Cromwell mastered the intervening Wiltshire garrisons and the famous ' Loyalty House ' at Basing. Rupert surrendered Bristol, declaring the cause lost, as Charles himself confessed, for the west was gone and Wales would recruit no more, but ' as a Christian ', the King wrote, ' I must tell you that God will not suffer rebels and traitors to prosper '. Though once and again he dashed at each face of the closing circle, to Doncaster north and to Huntingdon south, he could not break through to Montrose ; who in September was himself lost.

Since Inverlochy he had almost mastered the Highlands, twice crushed forces hurriedly detached from Leslie's army, and in August 1645 crossed the Forth, cut the Covenanters in two at Kilsyth near Stirling, and entered Glasgow. But Naseby had been fought, and his promised land faded. His Highlanders were jealous of the recruits from the Lowland gentry, resented the discipline necessary to humour the south, and drifted home, so that it was with a bare handful of his veterans that he now marched for Tweedside, to win the watchful waiting families on the Border. No signs of support came from the middle class of the towns and, having reached Kelso, he turned back in hope of better fortune in the west. On the 13th September he was surprised at Philiphaugh near Selkirk by Leven's brother David Leslie, his army was destroyed, and he fled to the Highlands. There he found the Gordons unwilling to move again, while a butcherly execution of his friends showed the Covenanters' decision. Vainly trying to raise new levies, he survived a life of wandering through a hard winter, only to hear, when spring came, that Charles had destroyed all he had fought for.

Ruin came from Ireland and the hopeless policy of reconciling the Catholics to the Crown. The rising of 1641, which began as an agrarian revolt and in less degree as religious reaction, turned in 1642 into a racial and political war. The English Parliament and their Dublin representatives disarmed the gentry of the Pale, silenced the Irish Parliament, declared for no tolerance to Catholics, and granted millions of Irish acres to those investing funds in the Irish war. While this war raged with massacre and harryings, — ' duck hunting was nothing to it ', wrote one English captain of this fighting in bogs — five elements of anarchy emerged : a Dublin government holding out for Parliament, a Scottish army defending Ulster, Ormonde fighting for Charles, and the Irish Confederates, organized in a supreme council, striking coins and levying taxes but subdivided between nationalists like Owen Roe O'Neill and nobles who, on terms, would stand by the King. Those terms were revised as the King's need became desperate, and the Cessation of 1643 settled nothing ; Ormonde, loyal to England and the plantation policy, would not admit a supreme Roman Church or help to destroy Ulster. In 1645 Charles' Catholic agent Glamorgan, assisted by parallel steps from the Queen, made a compact with the Papal legate Rinuccini, promising a Catholic lord-lieutenant, Parliament, Church, and university. In vain he tried to square the circle with Ormonde; he was disowned by the King, and early in 1646 the fall of Chester and Hopton's surrender in the west closed the ports of England to an Irish army. In September O'Neill heavily defeated the Scots at Benberb, the Legate arrested the more moderate confederates, and in 1647 Ormonde saved Protestant Ireland by handing over Dublin to the Puritans.

Before this climax, Charles had given up the English struggle. As the enemy closed in on Oxford he escaped, dressed as a servant, and in May 1646 reached Leven's camp in Nottinghamshire. In June Oxford capitulated; the Prince of Wales, leaving Scilly for Jersey, finally embarked for France; the Duke of York was a prisoner. Raglan, the last royal garrison, fell in August, and Montrose, who two years before had entered Scotland as a groom, now left it in a Norwegian ship, as a minister's servant. The King's flag was down, and the first civil war was over.

CONTEMPORARY DATES

1643	Sir Thomas Browne, *Religio Medici*.
	Battle of Rocroi.
	Beginning of the supremacy of Mazarin.
	–1715. Reign of Louis XIV.
1644	The Manchus depose the Ming dynasty in China and set up their own.
	Milton's *Areopagitica*.
1645–69	The War of Candia.
	In Brazil the Portuguese throw off Dutch rule.
1646	Turenne invades Bavaria.
	Henry Vaughan, *Poems*.

CHAPTER XI

THE FALL OF THE MONARCHY, 1646–1649

To all the meanderings of Charles' policy, between the downfall of his armies and his own execution, the key lay in his words before leaving Oxford, — ' not without hope that I shall be able to draw either the Presbyterians or the Independents to side with me for extirpating one another, that I shall really be a king again '. And as he rode from Newark to his new captivity at Holdenby, the bells ringing and sick men coming to be touched for the ' evil ' confirmed his fixed idea that England could not do without him. To that end he multiplied inconsistent promises and played desperately for time, yet without breaking his vow never to abandon the Church and never so far to yield his sovereignty and sword that, one day, though perhaps only under his son, they could not be fully restored.

A first stage ended when the Scots in January 1647 took £400,000 to liquidate their claims for pay, and handed the King over to Parliament. This was not the ' Judas ' act that gritted the teeth of Cavaliers. For the Scots were disappointed to find that Charles would not, as his assurance had led them to expect, see the Presbyterian light; they feared he would strike up alliance with the Independents; the politic Argyll worked for an understanding with the Cromwellians; nor was Scotland ready for civil war. Feeling between the two countries being so bitter, the two English parties deferred fighting out their own differences, and the terms sent to Charles in 1646 in the Propositions of Newcastle struck the old unyielding note: he must proscribe long lists of his friends, give up the militia for twenty years, and accept a Presbyterian Church.

While Cavalier churchmen like Hyde felt it would have been better to hold Oxford ' to the last biscuit ' than buy Puritan support by a surrender of principle, the Queen and the unscrupulous men who advised her in France put intense pressure on the King. When they begged him to throw the Church of England overboard, he replied he would not again violate his conscience, as he had in letting Strafford die, and that, as obedience rested on principle, ' religion would much sooner regain the militia than the militia will religion '. But, advised by the French, who linked up the Scots with some English Presbyterians, early in 1647 he offered a compromise: an establishment of Presbyterianism for three years and thereafter an agreed religious settlement, with surrender of the militia for ten years. Here was the germ both of the second civil war, and the Restoration of 1660.

English Presbyterianism was much wider than the Assembly of Divines and those directly influenced by the Scots. Negative rather than constructive, it embraced the thousands who detested sects, dreaded a levelling revolution, and hated army rule. Groaning under the heaviest taxation it had ever known, the country cried out for disbandment. Essex was dead but other commanders, Manchester, Waller, Skippon, and Massey, were on their side; their parliamentary leaders were tenacious men, representing the more political and conservative elements in Puritanism; men such as Holles, one of ' the five members ' who lived to be a Whig leader against Charles II; or Maynard the lawyer, who lived to give a Whig welcome to William III. Now war had ceased, they recovered their majority in the Commons. On paper their Church system was in working order, with elected elders and the ' Directory ' as the legal service-book; against Independent opposition they forbade lay preaching and ordained the death penalty for anti-Trinitarianism. Even Cromwell's old recruiting-ground of East Anglia petitioned against the sects, while London was ever more Presbyterian than the leaders; strong in its own militia, obedient to its preachers, and loyal to the memory of its favourite Essex.

But the Presbyterians threw their advantage away by their disbandment proposals, of which the political object was transparent. No general officer should be retained except Fairfax, no member of the Commons should serve in England, no infantry except local militia serve in English garrisons, while Skippon and Massey were to command a new army for Ireland, in which every officer must swear to the Covenant. By rank injustice Parliament killed any hope of volunteers for this new army, and united against themselves all the old. Though pay was badly in arrears, the cavalry's not less than forty-three weeks, Parliament offered a mere six weeks' instalment, ignored a request for indemnity for acts done in war, and voted such petitioners ' enemies of the State '.

The result in April 1647 was a mutiny, with the formation of what amounted to a rival army-parliament, composed of ' agitators ' or delegates from every regiment. Their motto was ' all or none '; suspecting a plan to break them piecemeal, they petitioned their general and persuaded volunteers to desert. Democratic pamphlets were circulating against Lords, tithe, and all established institutions, while it was openly mooted whether the army should not seize the King and settle with the ' tyrants ' in Parliament.

Meantime Parliament received Charles' offer of compromise, in which some of their politicians had taken a hand, and Lauderdale was coming to promise the Scots' help. In May it was decided to move

Charles from Holdenby either to London or Scotland, while the Prince
of Wales should come from France, and they began to build up trustworthy forces in case of resistance from the army, the disbandment of
which was ordered to begin on the 1st June.

If even the moderate Fairfax resisted disbandment without redress
of grievances, the rôle of the lieutenant-general was more decisive.
Hitherto Cromwell had stood by Parliament, warning his officers that,
' if that authority falls to nothing, nothing can follow but confusion ';
so much so that the democrat Lilburne concluded that Parliament had
bought him with riches and estates. But his letters show a weariness of
' a quarrelsome age ', and indignation at forgetfulness of the blood so
freely shed, and he warned Parliament of the ' deep sense ' of suffering
he found in the ranks. Voices were heard in the Commons crying for
his arrest, and he knew of the plan for a Scottish invasion, which the
agitators would resist by force. On the 31st May he ordered Cornet
Joyce to prevent the King being carried off from Holdenby and to seize
the artillery at Oxford, and in a few days was himself off to join the army
at Newmarket, whither Joyce, alarmed at rumours of a rescue, was
simultaneously bringing the King.

Another stage thus opened, lasting for the remainder of 1647, of
army efforts to compel a settlement by pressure on Parliament and
negotiation with the King. For a time Oliver succeeded in subduing
the agitators, disguising from himself the use of force by arguing that
they were acting not as soldiers but as citizens. But the ranks would
not trust the Commons further unless the Presbyterian leaders were
expelled and, much influenced by Cromwell's son-in-law Ireton, asked
for an early dissolution and shorter parliaments. As they moved in a
wide sweep from Newmarket to Reading and Bedford, carrying the
King with them, it became plain that the Presbyterians would not give
up their plan of war, nor would the eleven members whom the army
denounced withdraw, — Holles, Massey, Maynard, and Waller among
them. Once more we find Cromwell opposing the march on London
which extremists desired, arguing that ' that which you have by force,
I look upon it as nothing '.

If he proved right about Parliament, about London he was wrong.
The Common Council discharged soldiers of the old armies, apprentices
agitated for the Covenant and restoration of the City's own militia, and
the mob invaded the Commons, forcing them to invite Charles to
London. But while they set up a committee of safety and made Massey
their general, the army marched; bringing with them some sixty
members of both Houses who had taken refuge with them, they entered
the City on the 6th August and, while cavalry filled Hyde Park, the
Presbyterian leaders absconded or fled abroad.

All this was the more urgent because Scots agents were active round the King, who counted on playing off army against City. Through all the summer the army commanders had done their best to conciliate him, allowing him to see his children and his chaplains, entreating him to be frank, and to believe they asked nothing for themselves. Their scheme, the ' Heads of the Proposals ', in part amended to meet his own suggestions, was the most liberal settlement as yet proposed. The clauses for immediate security included parliamentary control of the militia for ten years and exclusion of Royalists from office and Parliament for five, though only five names were excepted from an act of oblivion. Coercive power in any ecclesiastics and the Covenant were both to vanish, and there should be tolerance for all Protestants. Ireton introduced some of the reformers' ideas, for better justice or reconsideration of tithe, but his chief basis was what he had mooted long before : a parliament, elected every two years, on a proper redistribution of seats, and having the nomination for ten years to great offices of state.

Charles would not look at it, confident that the Scots would give him better terms and that the army were at his mercy. And in one sense he was right, for a longing for peace was making Royalist feeling, nor could the army commanders safely depend on Parliament.

Of the private wish of Cromwell and Ireton to come to terms, there can be no doubt, but they were dealing with two fixed poles, the King and the narrow Presbyterians, and these long delays confronted them with a third. The Independent party in Parliament split, one section swinging over to the Levellers among the soldiers who declared for a republic, and inch by inch we see Cromwell driven back upon a second tactic of welding together Presbyterians and moderate Independents. But by October there were signs that he was moving towards a third. In long debates and searchings of heart in Putney church, the army Council explored their divisions. They had sinned in these ' fleshly ' negotiations, so reasoned the Levellers, and ' gone to Egypt ' for their help ; in their ' Case of the Army ' and ' Agreement of the People ', they put forth a vision of a democratic republic, built on universal suffrage and fundamental laws, which would make the people sovereign, and reserve religious toleration and other such indefeasible rights from meddling by Parliament.

Two rival political conceptions contested these debates. The Levellers spoke of revolutionary ideals. Property, said Wildman, depended on natural right, while Rainsborough championed the vote for all, saying ' the poorest he that is in England hath a right to live as well as the greatest he '. Ireton, the lawyer, answered with the sanctity of contracts, and the ' permanent fixed interest ' which alone deserved the vote. Between them, arbitrating with firm courtesy, stood Cromwell. He admitted his doubt of an appeal to faith, which might be self-deceiving and only a ' carnal reasoning ', nor did he like abstract logic, claiming to be

infallible, which might break England into Swiss cantons. He was not
' wedded or glued ' to forms of government, which were only ' dross and
dung in comparison with Christ ', yet ' the affections of the people '
inclined him to favour a monarchy.

Yet by November there was a change in his tone, and a move to the
left by the commanders ; ' extraordinary dispensations ', he had said,
would alone make him decide, and now we hear, ' I cannot but
think God is beginning of them '. Though the army Council clung to
the ' Proposals ', they were ready to radicalize them by adopting the
democrats' demands for a speedy dissolution, against a royal veto, or for
fundamental rights, and would give a vote to all who had fought against
the King. But they accompanied this advance by a severe restoration of
military discipline.

While the Levellers drove Cromwell on, their threats of violence
persuaded Charles on 11th November to escape from Hampton Court ;
a step to which many advisers had long urged him, as likely to bring
either the Scots or the army to better terms. He rode off to the Isle of
Wight, hoping to win over Hammond, governor of Carisbrooke. So
far as England went, no miscalculation could have been more deadly,
for fears for their existence pulled the army together and impelled it
towards agreement with Parliament, many of whom were equally
affronted by the menace of the Scots. Yet it needed a threat of military
force to drive through a thin House of Commons the ' four bills ',
which were sent to Charles to test his sincerity ; one of which took away
the militia from the Crown for good, while a second allowed Parliament
to adjourn to some place outside Presbyterian London. On 24th
December Charles rejected them, and on the 26th signed an ' Engagement ' with the Scots. Besides highly favourable terms for his ' ancient
and native kingdom ' in regard to share of office, war expenses, and
commerce, it established Presbyterianism in England for three years,
with a pledge to put down the sects, while the Scots promised to maintain his prerogatives over the militia and choice of counsellors, and the
royal veto. In January 1648 Parliament passed a vote against sending
more addresses to the King.

So it had come to the sword, against which Cromwell had struggled
for six months, for there was no unity of opinion to be found. Even
now the army leaders secretly gave Charles a chance to change his mind
and considered the alternative of crowning one of his sons ; which
vanished with the Duke of York's escape to Holland, disguised as a girl.
If England could have been polled, there would have been a large
majority for monarchy, as county petitions and bonfires on Charles'
birthday showed ; several thousand Essex petitioners marched to
London ; cavalry dispersed riots in the Strand.

But the army triumphed because its enemies were divided. They made it their business to humour London and the Presbyterians, Vane and many Independents agreeing in a vote not to alter ' the fundamental government ' by two Houses and a king. Again, though many Presbyterians wished agreement with the Scots, they dreaded the Cavaliers, and wished a royal restoration on conditions. In all directions there was the same hesitancy. Half the fleet mutinied, there were many local risings, but most countryfolk would not work with Cavaliers, and Scotland also was hopelessly divided. The Kirk's influence (and the Kirk, as Montrose wrote, was ' the gudewife that wears the breeches ') would not help to levy an army to be allied with ' malignants ' like Langdale and Musgrave, who had seized Berwick and Carlisle; Argyll would resist his rival Hamilton and those nobles who put the Crown above Church and people; David Leslie would not serve; and it was not till August that, having cleared the Border, the Scots reached Kendal and struck out for Lancashire.

By that time, though Fairfax was held to a long siege at Colchester, the home counties were brought to order, little came from the Prince of Wales' squadron blockading the Thames, Cromwell had disposed of south Wales after a troublesome siege at Pembroke and made forced marches to join Lambert in Yorkshire. Striking over the hills, on the 17th August he pounced at Preston on the ' Engagers ' army, miserably led by Hamilton and straggling from Kirkby Lonsdale to Wigan, forty-five miles away. In three days' fighting he crushed it with heavy casualties, forced surrender of the infantry at Warrington, then captured Hamilton and his broken detachments of horse. While he pursued the survivors northwards, the Covenanters of western Scotland marched on Edinburgh and, joined by Argyll and the Leslies, made terms with Cromwell. Early in October he entered Edinburgh, where he received pledges that Engagers should be excluded from power.

In Ireland two admirable soldiers, Michael Jones and George Monck, held Dublin and most of Ulster for Parliament, nor was it till October that Ormonde reappeared to endeavour reunion with the moderate Catholics whom the Legate had antagonized. He now accepted terms, sooner than accept which he had, the year before, handed over Dublin to Parliament; practically conceding an independent Irish parliament and a supreme Catholic Church. But though Rinuccini left Ireland in disgust, nothing could reconcile the factions; Ulster and Leinster Catholics were furiously jealous of each other, while both feared the Munster Protestants whom Inchiquin brought to help Ormonde.

While the army had dispersed to fight, the Presbyterian majority at Westminster passed a fierce ordinance against heresy, readmitted the members turned out in 1647, and repealed their vote of ' No Addresses '. Some political Independents, Vane and Saye included, joined them, and in September conferences were opened with Charles at Newport, in the Isle of Wight. Holles on his knees begged him to accept Presbytery and Vane pleaded for toleration, but Charles pursued his old path of piece-meal, but never honest, concession. He offered a Presbytery for three years, at the end of which a ' primitive episcopacy ' should be restored, the militia for twenty years, and control over offices for ten ; terms, he meantime wrote, which ' only an escape can justify '. At the end of October, unsatisfied without definite action, the Commons refused them, but already Ireton had suggested to the unwilling Fairfax a purge of Parliament.

Fanaticism was burning hotly in the army which, at their prayer-meeting at Windsor before departure to battle, had declared they would call to his account ' Charles Stuart, that man of blood '. Its heat, and dire emergency, infected the generals. Fairfax disgraced himself by executions after taking Colchester, while Cromwell sold his prisoners into West Indian slavery. They viewed this as a different war, not waged with men of honour, but one raised, Cromwell wrote, by those sinning against the light, to ' vassalize us to a foreign nation '. His letters, as he marched north, registered the rising fever in his mind. God, ' so terrible and so just ', had broken the oppressors ' as in the day of Midian ', to save the ' despised jeered Saints ' ; let Parliament, he adjured the Speaker after Preston, root out the ' implacable ', and not hate ' His people who are the apple of His eye, and for whom even Kings shall be reproved '. By November, when for a month he lingered round besieged Pontefract, this fever had cooled to decision. If neither legality nor worldly necessity was a just plea, there remained faith, the ' chain of providences ' which pointed all one way. He upbraided Vane who distrusted ' outward dispensations ' ; how could peace come about by the ' ruinous hypocritical agreement ' of Newport, or ' by this man against whom the Lord hath witnessed ? ' Any sort of Puritanism was better than ' meddling with the accursed thing ' ; Scotland encouraged him to think that Presbyterianism had learned its lesson ; he advised Ireton to make contact with the Levellers, and accepted their view that Charles must be brought to trial.

Charles' reply to the officers' ultimatum in November, showing his hopes for a return to London and playing off Parliament against army, gave more power to the fanatic wing, represented by men like Major-General Harrison, the visionary Fifth Monarchy man. Now Ireton and Cromwell's brother-in-law Desborough joined them, sweeping away Fairfax's hesitation. Under the shadow of his authority they arrested Charles' custodian Hammond as unreliable, transferred the King to lonely Hurst Castle, marched into London and seized money for the army's pay, while manifestoes demanded a dissolution and the King's trial.

Civilian England resisted, and not Presbyterians only ; Independents like Fiennes would accept Charles' terms, Vane and Algernon Sidney would not hear of taking his life. On 5th December a last free vote declared, by 129 to 83, that his reply was a ground for a settlement. Early next morning Colonel Pride arrested or turned back 143 members, and that night, the *coup d'état* over, Cromwell reached London.

Till the year ended, the victors hesitated ; Fairfax and Presbyterian clergy and lawyers were all against them, but a last approach to Charles, now at Windsor, showed he would never surrender the future by giving up his veto or allowing the sale of Church lands. In the first week of January 1649 the ' rump ' in the Commons, claiming that the Lords' assent was unnecessary, set up a high court of justice, of 135 persons ; of whom only 59 could be finally induced to sign the King's death warrant.

Under the presidency of Sergeant Bradshaw, for no judge would act, the charge was brought in Westminster Hall that the King, having been ' admitted ' to wield ' a limited power ', had attempted to erect a tyranny and ' traitorously ' made war on his people. In law the King's reply was unanswerable : that no court, least of all this court set up by one House acting under force, could try the King. He stood for ' the true liberty of all my subjects ', which must perish if ' power without law may make laws '.

What the country thought was shown by cries in the hall of ' God save the King ' and tears in the streets, or by Lady Fairfax's voice from her gallery crying that Cromwell was a traitor. But against protest from the Scots, the Assembly of divines, the Dutch Estates-General, in the face of faltering colleagues among the judges, and of a blank paper from the Prince of Wales offering any concession, the minority, of which Cromwell and Ireton made the centre, pressed on. On 30th January, accompanied only by bishop Juxon, Charles stepped from the banqueting-hall windows on to the scaffold in Whitehall ; his words could not reach the thousands there assembled across the soldiers massed round him, with their pikes and muskets pointing outwards. He said that ' God's judgements are just ', remembering still with grief how he had let Strafford die ; that the people's freedom was not a share in sovereignty but in ' laws by which their life and goods may be most their own ' ; that, as he stood there because he had resisted change by ' the power of the sword ', he too was ' the martyr of the people '. When his severed head was held up, says one onlooker, there came from the people ' such a groan as I never heard before and desire I may never hear again ', and cavalry troops rolled them back in two waves towards Charing Cross and Westminster. A week later he was buried at Windsor in the tomb of Henry VIII, without any religious service, as the words of the prayer-book were forbidden.

In this spirit of exaltation the masters of the army washed out the blood which they thought defiled the land, not in a corner, as one of them said in the Commons later, but ' in the face of God and of all men '. They did not repent, nor doubt of the need. ' Be not offended ', Cromwell wrote, ' at the manner of God's working, perhaps no other way was left.'

CONTEMPORARY DATES

1647   Massianello's rebellion at Naples.
        Accession of William II of Orange in Holland.
1648   The Peace of Westphalia.
        Outbreak of the Fronde.
        George Fox founds the Quaker organization.
        Gauden, *Eikon Basilike*.
        Herrick, *Hesperides*.
1649   Condemnation of Jansenism by the Sorbonne.
        Maryland ordains religious toleration.
    –1687.   Reign of Muhammed IV in Turkey.

CHAPTER XII

DESTRUCTION AND RESTORATION, 1649-1660

So began, in words engraved on a new great seal, the ' first year of freedom by God's blessing restored '.   Monarchy had gone, soon the Lords were abolished as ' useless and dangerous '.   This ' freedom ' was to rise to a climax of Puritan democracy, to decline by reaction into military dictatorship, and at last to expire through faction. But it left a legacy.   Puritanism released an energy which called for liberty in religion and every department of life, with an efficiency greater than anything England had seen.   It left behind a professional navy, a standing army, and British influence in both Atlantic and Mediterranean.   It took long strides towards union with Scotland and Ireland.   Its administrative machinery pointed towards the Cabinet. Its economic doctrine led to the capitalist Britain of the next two centuries.

Till 1653, however, the Commonwealth had to fight for life.   Despotic Russia severed relations with the regicides, at Madrid and the Hague Cavalier exiles assassinated its envoys with impunity and applause.   Scotland raised armies to serve Charles II, Ormonde was rewinning Ireland, Virginia and Barbados repudiated Parliament's authority.   At home the cause was split from top to bottom.   Fairfax would not take the ' engagement ' oath of loyalty, in and near London Levellers decked out in sea-green ribbons clamoured for a radical Parliament or a rule of the saints, stirring up army mutiny.   Only wholesale packing of the Common Council kept the City safe, while the sole legal authority was the ' rump ' of the Long Parliament, indissoluble save by its own consent, annually electing a Council of State as its executive, usurping the rôle of a supreme court, yet representing nothing but a fraction.   Lancashire had no members left, London only one, less than a hundred was the usual attendance.   But the Rump would not listen to demands for a dissolution, or reform of the suffrage and constituencies.

In March 1649 Cromwell was given the command in Ireland, where Ormonde's army and Rupert's ships might soon be joined by Charles II. But, in fact, Royalism was doomed by the direct effect of the Irish war, that nothing now could reconcile Protestant and Catholic.   Before Oliver landed with 12,000 fresh troops, Michael Jones crushed Ormonde at Rathmines, and Protestant royalists began to swing over to Parliament.

In September Cromwell stormed Drogheda, giving no quarter to the
garrison and killing the clergy; next month Wexford suffered the same
fate.   It was a judgment of God, he declared, on those ' who have
embrued their hands in so much innocent blood ', and ' He thus breaks
the enemies of His Church in pieces '.   By 1650 nearly all the coast was
won from Londonderry to Cork, though before Oliver could reduce the
inland places of Munster he was recalled for more urgent tasks.   Storm
and siege were continued by his best officers, Ireton who died in 1651
after taking Limerick, and then Ludlow and Fleetwood.   Regicide
colonels fought from point to point, burning crops, bridging rivers,
their horsemen penetrating bogs in single file.   When O'Neill, the
ablest Catholic soldier, died, his cause fell into the hands of a bitter
priesthood, who drove Ormonde from Ireland in despair.

After Galway, the last strong fort, had fallen, the Puritans wrote
an epitaph on a ruined country.   Their two Acts of Settlement and
Satisfaction of 1652–3 were the final words of the plantation policy.
They condemned to death and forfeiture all who had assisted rebellion ;
those who had resisted Parliament were to lose two-thirds of their land,
all who had not shown ' constant good affection ' should lose one-third,
and for the remaining proportion were to be transplanted to Connaught.
By infinite labour this transaction was pushed through ; though peasant
labourers were often kept to help the new owners, two-thirds of the soil
went either to Cromwellian soldiers or the ' adventurers ' who had
financed Parliament since 1642, and this mostly at the expense of the
Anglo-Irish of Leinster and Munster, who had been least guilty.

Ireland, in Vane's words, was to be ' a province ', and its new owners
a favoured garrison.   In 1653 by the Instrument of Government the
country received representation at Westminster, though her ' members '
were Puritan soldiers, since no Catholic could vote, and was given
equality of treatment under the English customs and navigation laws.
Puritan preachers were brought in, Trinity College, Dublin, was more
richly endowed, and the mild Henry Cromwell, Oliver's younger son,
relaxed some of the severity of the Baptist Fleetwood.

Yet some three thousand petty garrisons and never less than sixteen
thousand troops had to hold Ireland down, even though thirty thousand
of her fighting men were exiles in Europe and the remains of her
aristocracy clamped fast in Connaught.   Court-martials superseded the
law, English land surveyors were often murdered.   War and famine had
destroyed a third of its population, English officers wrote of riding
through desolate silences to which the wolves had returned, while
rewards were offered for catching a priest or killing a ' Tory ', the name
given to the bandits who kept up guerilla war.   Only the priest, moving
at his peril from one ruined cabin to another, was left to console the
peasants, while seeds of hatred for England blossomed in all countries

where Irishmen had taken service or in those transported to the Indies, even in the children whom Irish mothers, against the law, bore to Oliver's soldiers.

Among the causes which ruined Charles II's cause in Ireland was his alliance in 1650 with the Scots Covenanters, to which he only came after bitter heart-searching among his advisers ; humiliating to the Cavaliers, it would mean abandonment not only of Ormonde but of Montrose, who had just sailed from Sweden to the Orkneys. But Charles had no alternative. The winter of 1649–50 he spent in Jersey, only to hear of Cromwell's victories and that Blake had driven Rupert's little squadron to refuge in the Tagus, and when he returned to the Hague, Europe offered no hope. So he patched up terms with the Scots, getting from Argyll a promise of safety for Montrose, but the mere report of these terms destroyed such chance as Montrose ever had and, when he crossed to Caithness and made his way to Dornoch, the northern clans dare not move. In April Leslie's horse crushed him in Carbiesdale, on his flight he was betrayed, and on the 21st May was hanged as a felon at Edinburgh. It was too late, however, for Charles to draw back and, before he reached Scotland in June, he swore to impose the Covenant on his three kingdoms.

On the fate of Ireland nine out of ten Britons were agreed, but the Scottish problem divided the Puritan world and on it the British future turned. In England it brought about the supremacy of Cromwell, since Fairfax refused to invade the sister kingdom. In Scotland the ruling party, led by Argyll, had of late trampled on the Engagers who followed the Hamiltons and Lauderdale, and passed the ' Act of Classes ' to exclude them from office and Parliament, and though forced by national feeling after the King's execution to drop their understanding with Cromwell, they hoped to retain power by making Charles II a king of the Kirk. Such was the first phase of 1650. Cavaliers and ' Engagers ' were banished from Charles' counsels, while he was made publicly to admit his father's sin and his mother's idolatry.

Cromwell's manifestoes to the Scots received no response, and within a month of his invasion he was very near defeat. Leslie, checking the English plan to master Leith and cross the Forth, drove him back on his fleet, pinned him down with tired troops and short supplies at Dunbar, and with twice his numbers barred a retreat on Berwick. But on the 2nd September, spurred on by the clergy and confident that the English were embarking, Leslie came down from the Lammermuirs into the broken plain south of Dunbar ; here, at dawn on the 3rd, Oliver attacked him and, repeating his usual manœuvre, rolled up his right flank nearest to the sea, driving it back on the main body which was pushed against the hills. At the sun-rising an officer heard him say, ' let God arise and His enemies shall be scattered ', and in little over an hour the Scots lost 3000 killed and 10,000 prisoners.   Never had Cromwell's army snatched a greater victory, nor one deeper in political effect. ' The Kirk ', he wrote, ' has done their do ' ; victory was impressed on England by Scottish colours in Westminster hall and the issue of a Dunbar medal, the first in the army's long line.

While Leslie recruited another force, a long pause followed, for Cromwell fell ill and Scotland was torn by faction.   The western Covenanters, who refused to serve a ' malignant ' King, also rejected Cromwell's advances, but these ' remonstrants ', though defeated in the field, took all heart out of the Kirk.   To save himself Argyll was forced towards Charles and the Engagers, while ' resolutioners ' against the western bigots dominated the Estates, who repealed the Act of Classes and crowned the King.   Reinforced by the mass of the nobles and the Highlands, Charles had thus triumphed over the Kirk, yet by that very fact cemented Puritanism and entered England as a foreign king.

Having mastered Edinburgh and Glasgow, Cromwell decided to drive Leslie from Stirling, for a second winter campaign would exhaust both his army and parliamentary finance.   In July 1651 his sea-power enabled him to cross the Forth and move on Perth, so cutting Leslie from the Highlands but also, deliberately, leaving open the road to England.   Within a week Charles' army acted as expected and, as Hamilton wrote, ' with one stout argument, despair ', struck south by Carlisle, passed through Lancashire, and so south-west in hope of recruits from Wales.   But Lancashire Presbyterians would not fight for Cavaliers, a universal rally of county militias showed the English hatred of the invaders, Lambert and Harrison harried the King's march, and when he reached Worcester on the 22nd August Cromwell was hot in pursuit ; having left Perth on the 2nd, on the 27th he was ringing Worcester round, with 30,000 men to the King's 16,000.   Lambert and Fleetwood crossed the Severn to sever the Royalists from Wales, bridges of boats over Severn and Teme linked up the circle, and on 3rd September Cromwell stormed into Worcester.   After fierce fighting the Scots broke ; Derby, Massey, Hamilton were captured or killed in the pursuit ; almost all the leaders, indeed, except the King who, sheltered by Royalists and Catholics in an epic flight from Boscobel to Sussex, in October found a ship at Brighton which carried him to France.

In a military sense the Commonwealth was saved, and Worcester, as Cromwell called it, ' a crowning mercy ' ; for meantime Monck had done wonders in Scotland, capturing Stirling, storming Dundee, seizing the committee of Estates.   He completed his work finally in 1654 when, to break a Highland rising led by the Cavalier Middleton, he marched his troops in a great sweep to Lochaber and Inverness.   Garrison fortresses and heavy taxation bore down a passive, resisting country.   Though the Presbyterian system continued, the Kirk assembly was not allowed to meet, and some Independent congregations were set up. If material things could have satisfied Scotland, it now had free trade with England, the law courts were reformed and Highland jurisdictions abolished, and thirty ' Scottish ' members went to Westminster. But as Cavaliers and Engagers were disfranchised, the ' members ' were commonly English officers, nothing was left of native liberties, and the Scottish regalia were buried in a parish church. The Borders were restless, half the nobility were in exile, and Scotland waited for a Dutch war or any other opportunity to revolt.

All this time its sea-power, with the tireless and selfless Blake as its leader, was saving the Commonwealth. It mastered Royalist garrisons in the Scillies, the Isle of Man, and the Channel Islands, and brought to heel the colonists in America ; Blake forced Portugal to cease helping Rupert, while for the first time a fleet convoyed trade in the Mediterranean. Indeed the Navy, which essentially dates from the ship-money levies, was now enormously advanced. Instead of some noble lord-admiral eked out by a vague parliamentary control, the Council of State put an Admiralty committee under Henry Vane, and below them an expert board of Navy commissioners. The Commonwealth built 41 new warships before 1652, which by 1660 had risen to 207. Better pay and victualling, with some care for sick and wounded, was making a fleet with something of the spirit of the New Model.

Yet the government, whose servants did such great things, was dying at the top. The burden it laid on human weakness was heavy, theatres were closed, severe penalties struck at Sunday travelling or profanity, while for adultery the legal punishment — which juries refused to award — was death. Heavy too was the burden on the flesh, with an excise and a monthly assessment of £90,000, a frequent ' press ' for the Navy, 50,000 troops to be maintained, and sinking trade. Nothing was done to conciliate the Royalists, who were paying heavy fines to ' compound ' for delinquency and often thereby forced to sell their fathers' lands ; lands of the leaders, with those of the Crown and Church, were confiscated outright ; their clergy were silenced, and every ' delinquent ' was made incapable of holding office or giving a vote. Nor did the State even embrace all the Puritans. Many Presbyterians refused to take the ' engagement ', moderates like the Verneys joining Royalists in the exile of France or Holland, and nothing would make them swallow the sects. But the most bitter feeling against the Rump came from disillusioned democrats and the army who had set them up. What right, asked the tireless pamphleteer Lilburne, had this small minority, defended only by the sword, to supplant an elected Parliament, ' the very marrow and soul of all the native rights of the people ' ? And his enthusiastic acquittal by a London jury echoed over England. There

was a clamour to reform the law and to give it more speed, to heal
wrongs piled up by ten years of upheaval, vagabondage, poor debtors,
the many thousand cases waiting trial. But it all expired in verbose
committees. Some members had profited much by confiscations,
Londoners bought some 60 per cent of the Church lands, while speculators traded in the debentures, assigned to soldiers in lieu of their pay,
on Cavalier estates.

As for religion, it was in chaos. The Long Parliament's establishment of Presbyterianism never took root, there was general dislike of
the lay-elder system, justices of the peace obstructed its work. Parishes,
county committees, and patrons were competing in Church livings,
while Independents attacked the tithe system and yet offered no substitute. New sects multiplied, 'ranters' and Socinians and Anabaptists,
fanatics who claimed to incarnate the Lamb, Antinomians who said no
sin could damn the elect, visionaries and women preachers. John
Bunyan the tinker was working with a Baptist congregation at Bedford,
while among Baptists and Seekers George Fox found a welcome for
his doctrine of an inner light. His Quaker movement had spread far
from north and Midlands since the war ended, goading magistrates to
persecution by their interruption of preachers and their refusal to take
an oath, and by its pacifism disturbing the army. Nothing could so
much divide Puritanism as this problem of toleration. Though the
Rump abolished, except for Catholics, penalties for non-attendance at
church, it passed a blasphemy Act against extremists, and John Owen,
Cromwell's favourite divine, supported the ideal of an established
Church with punishment for those who attacked Christian fundamentals. To which the mass of the army would be intensely hostile.

From such various angles a call had long been swelling, redoubled
after Worcester, that the Rump should be dissolved, but the utmost to
which it would agree was to fix a date three years ahead. And in 1652
an army petition for dissolution and a purge brought the clash near, for
the Commonwealth plunged into the Dutch war, which Cromwell and
Vane and half England detested.

Though Cromwell and Blake had exalted this revolutionary State
in Europe, its international policies must be difficult and dangerous,
for the earlier lines between Catholic and Protestant were blurred
by political or economic rivalry. In 1648 the real Thirty Years' War
ended with the Peace of Westphalia, when the Austrians stepped aside
from the Catholic cause and the Dutch abandoned their Protestant
allies, and it was now nothing but a political conflict between France and
Spain. Once having broken the Hapsburg encirclement, Mazarin was
directing French policy to a greater motive, the succession to the
Spanish Empire, which the wretched debility of its royal house seemed
likely to open, and which involved the future of the Low Countries and

all the Indies. Northern Protestantism, meanwhile, was shivered by the hatred between Denmark and Sweden, and the far-sighted egoism of the Great Elector of Prussia.

To the bigoted Puritans and keen business men now ruling England it was tempting to fling their sword into the scale, especially when France in 1650 fell into the civil war of the Fronde and Spain leaped at its opportunity. On the whole, the prevalent mood was to attack France, which had encouraged the Scots throughout, sheltered Charles II at Paris, seized our shipping, and oppressed the Huguenots for whom every Puritan prayed. While rival agents approached England from all the combatants, Cromwell led a party who sought a French alliance, on the basis of favourable arrangements for the Huguenots and the cession of Dunkirk. Mazarin, however, would not yet pay this price and in 1652 the plan fell through when we attacked Holland, the client and trading partner of France.

For many years England had cried out upon the ingratitude of Holland, whose existence Elizabeth had saved, while many conflicts had obliterated the old religious sympathy. Dutch civilization was at its height. Without natural resources and wholly dependent on trade by sea, they had raised a wonderful fabric of economics and science, banking, shipbuilding, and colonial companies, far in advance of our own. But their spirit of monopoly was intense. In Europe they contended that the seas were free, for they could not live without the herring fisheries in British waters and, as the world's carriers, demanded that the neutral flag should cover even enemy goods; so challenging the essence of British sea-power which involved the sovereignty of the narrow seas, with a law of contraband which would stop food and munitions reaching our enemies, and a right of searching neutral ships. In Asia, on the other hand, the Dutch were jealous Imperialists. England had never ceased to demand compensation for the massacre of her seamen at Amboyna in 1623, and for our eviction from Pulo Run in the Banda Islands. Dutch factories far outnumbered ours in India, they were winning the relics of the Portuguese Empire, and had lately occupied the Cape of Good Hope; they held Portuguese Brazil, dominated the West Indies, and by their colony of New Amsterdam cut our American plantations in half.

Yet one bond might bring together the two republics, — the relationship of the royal houses of Orange and Stuart. In 1650 Charles II's warlike brother-in-law William II died, leaving only a posthumous son, the future William III, whereupon power fell to the republicans, who promptly abolished the Stadtholdership. Could not, the English Council asked, an alliance extinguish Orange and Stuart together, and perhaps even make a closer union? But negotiations revealed that Orange sympathy was still strong, and that Holland thought more of commerce than religion. Seizure of their goods on French ships annoyed them, a Dutch-Danish treaty threatened our trade in the Sound, and as 1651 ended, Parliament, urged on by the chartered companies, passed the first Navigation Act, confining our imports from the non-European world to British ships, and European imports to such ships or those of the producing country. Early in 1652 an English claim for the salute to our fleet brought about a chance collision.

In the long run England held decisive advantages, lying as she did athwart the Dutch trade routes, and being far less dependent on imports. Protection of convoys reduced the Dutch striking-power and, together with Orange-republican friction and jealous provincial admiralties, outweighed the magnificent skill of their seamen under Tromp and Ruyter, while if Dutch ships were more numerous, the English were larger and more heavily gunned. Our sea-power was greatly increased under the soldier-sailors, Blake and Dean and Monck. They made the navy a profession, instead of a nucleus of State ships among hastily commandeered merchantmen ; articles of war and fighting instructions restored discipline, while an organization by squadrons prepared the tactics of the future, the ' line ahead '.

But a first year of indecisive war, the cutting of the London coal supply, and heavy trade losses, doomed the Rump ; which only took on a greater complacency when in February 1653, in a three days' battle between Portland and Cap Gris-Nez, Blake and Monck re-won command of the Channel. For weeks Cromwell had discussed a way out, ' something of a monarchical power ' for choice, perhaps to crown the young Duke of Gloucester ; even desperately asking, ' what if a man should take upon him to be King ? ' All this winter he resisted soldiers and preachers who wished to use force, and at last persuaded the Rump leaders to a dissolution. In April, however, Vane led a movement whereby existing members should keep their seats, with a veto on the qualifications of those newly elected ; it was thought they would bring back Fairfax as general, and the Presbyterians to power. An unscrupulous effort to rush this scheme through decided Oliver to act and, with a file of musketeers, he held the House while he denounced their oppressions, private vices, and neglect of religion, turned both them and the Council of State out of doors, bidding his men take away ' that bauble ', the Commons' mace.

Except for his power as general, no legal authority was left. After many weeks he decided, as a temporary measure, on a more generous edition of what the army extremists had always urged, that is, a picked body of ' Saints '. He asked the Congregational churches in each county to submit suitable names, from whom he with the Army Council selected 129 for England, with a handful from the other kingdoms, who met in July as ' Barebones parliament ', so called from the enthusiastic

Barbon, leather-seller of Fleet Street. They were to sit for a year and then choose their successors, though some day, he told them, all the people would be the Lord's people and fit to choose a Parliament. Meantime, through ' strange windings and turnings ' God had called them, ' a people called and chosen and faithful '. Yet let them show the spirit of Paul, ' not a spirit for believers only, but for the whole people '.

From July till December this nominated assembly sat on, manifesting many high ideals but not a jot of constructive sense. They established civil marriage and parish registers, relieved the poor debtor, spoke of codifying the law into a small pocket-book. Their projects, however, alarmed the country. For they abolished the court of Chancery without finding a substitute, declared Church patronage at an end, proposed abolition of tithe, while in the face of war and conspiracy they questioned every tax and would not set up a high court of justice. Preachers at Blackfriars declaimed that the fourth Roman monarchy was passing, that the army must take the sword to set up Christ's and replace English law by that of Moses, and that Harrison must replace the sinful Cromwell; Lilburne's group asked universal suffrage. Disgusted by men who could only ' fly at liberty and property ', Oliver turned sharply to Lambert and the right wing, not the less because he was anxious for peace with Holland. In December Lambert's supporters engineered a carefully staged resignation by the majority of the assembly.

It was the end of Puritanism as a revolutionary movement; whether it could keep what it had won, remained to be seen. It was clear from many signs that the country's strongest interests desired stability, from London demonstrations against the preachers, or the intense wish for Colonial expansion, for in every department the Protectorate revealed an energetic efficiency unknown in Stuart government, before or after. It was seen in the Navy commissioners, in Monck's Scottish government, in the universities, or in the handling of intricate transactions like the disposal of Cavalier lands. A new ability got its opportunity; William Petty, economist and founder of the Lansdowne family, the poor clothier's son who carved out the Irish land settlement; Wren the young genius of a new scientific Oxford, Downing the scoutmaster from New England who became ambassador at the Hague, or Pepys the future navy secretary. If these men were unlike the Puritan sects, so, too, were Cromwell's nearest councillors; his Secretary of State Thurloe with his rare moderation and City connections, aristocrats like Ashley Cooper and Montagu who, as Shaftesbury and Sandwich, were to serve Charles II, realists like the ambitious Lambert, and sober, honest Skippon.

The ' Instrument of Government ', framed by Lambert's school, was itself a step backwards. Cromwell, indeed, declined the title of king, but his Protectorship became a limited monarchy. Throwing aside notions of democratic sovereignty, the Instrument narrowed the county franchise to holders of property worth £200, made no meeting of Parliament necessary except at three-year intervals, and forbade legislation in conflict with itself, especially with its guarantee of religious liberty to all except ' Popery and Prelacy '. Outside those limits Parliament could make laws without a veto, but most sovereign powers were shared between Protector and Council. The first councillors were nominated for life, while with them the Protector could issue ordinances, raise money, declare war and peace. In the intervals of Parliament they jointly controlled army and militia, with enough fixed revenue to provide for 30,000 soldiers, a navy, and civil administration. Finally, Council would name Oliver's successor.

Though superficially Cromwellianism was swept away in 1660, its work was permanent, and his own contribution of real importance. ' God and the people ', he always argued, had called him to his place, and certainly a great volume of opinion acquiesced in the circumstances which had brought it about. His strength lay, however, less in his political origins, for the country hated the army, than in himself, and much less in his ability than his character. His vision was limited, blind to the Catholic world like every Puritan's, and in foreign affairs short and sometimes reckless. But he was, in the first place, a very human being, with most human affections, and the normal tastes of his age and class. He loved his horses, hawking, and music. In battle and council he showed his touch of rough humour, his gift of inspiring men, conciliation, and courtesy. He continued still the civilian who had so long resisted military intervention in politics, believing that ' what you get by force is nothing '. ' Healing and settling ', he told his first Parliament, was their duty ; or, again, he was ' a constable in the parish ', ' the father in this family '. This disciplined tolerance, as great as Abraham Lincoln's, which tried to make the best of all men from Cavaliers to Quakers, had its boundaries. He was an Elizabethan squire, who found Levellers ' little better than beasts ', with their philosophy of nothing but ' overturn ' ; an aristocrat, unable to contemplate liberty apart from property and inequality. But he was also a fiery gospel Christian. The ' godly people ', it was for them he had fought and still would labour ; would win even ' the most mistaken Christian '. As he read English history and that of Protestantism, he would ask ' who is a God like ours ? ' and find ' Christ's cause ' in a piratic attack on the Spanish Indies.

Before meeting Parliament at the end of 1654, his policies and legislation settled the trend of the Protectorate. Do what he would, it meant a great narrowing of the cause. Lilburne the democrat was in a Jersey prison, Harrison was cashiered, Ludlow and Vane would not accept the new government, Leveller conspiracy sapped even Cromwell's own regiment. And though his repeal of the engagement oath was a gesture to the Royalists, among whom he employed as a judge the admirable Mathew Hale, the Instrument cut out of the franchise any who had acted against Parliament in the wars. Their plots became more formidable, directed by a secret committee styled 'the Sealed Knot', and it was possible they would win over the Presbyterians.

At any rate the Protector accomplished much in which Parliament and the Saints had failed. Long blockade had brought Dutch trade to ruin, Tromp was killed in action, and though Oliver still harked back to a closer union, hatred of this war and financial stress induced him to offer reasonable terms in 1654. The Dutch admitted our right to the salute in the narrow seas, pressed no longer for repeal of the Navigation Act, and accepted arbitration in the Indies; each State would exclude the other's enemies, the houses of Orange and Stuart respectively. Next, commercial treaties with Sweden and Denmark opened the Sound for Britain on equal terms with the Dutch; while another with Portugal gave English shipping priority and relieved our merchants from the Inquisition. It was, in part, this last question which by the end of 1654 tilted Oliver, after long hesitation, away from Spain, which was too bankrupt to finance him against France, and too Catholic to meet his zeal for the Huguenots or to give Englishmen rights of worship in their ports and free trade with the Indies.

Meantime his Council's ordinances developed Puritan reform and made some order out of chaos. He put down race-meetings because they collected Cavaliers, forbade cock-fights and duels, reformed Chancery, and pursued John Owen's plan for a religious system. Though Presbytery was the law, neglect of its discipline forbade its growth; sometimes rival sects shared churches in a friendly way, sometimes there were local squabbles over appointments. What Cromwell did was sincerely to follow the ideal of the Instrument; that is, an establishment comprising the chief religious groups, supported by tithe until a better way could be found, with a generous tolerance for those outside so long as they did not upset civil order. Private patronage often went on, but he appointed a body of 'triers', drawn from Presbyterians, Baptists, and Independents, to certify the fitness of ministers, with a body of 'ejectors' in each county to deal with the inefficient or scandalous. Backed by many voluntary associations, this organization built the strong character of Nonconformity. As for toleration, though the Mass and the prayer-book were both legally forbidden, several London churches and many private meetings kept Anglicanism alive, Catholics were at least freed from recusancy fines, while the Protector often intervened to prevent punishment of the extremer sects and stop the persecution of the Quakers. 'If thou and I were but an hour of a day together ', he said to Fox, ' we should be nearer one to the other.'

But when he met his first Parliament, the brittle basis of his power
was exposed. The Commons' majority instantly claimed every ancient
privilege of their House ; over a quarter were excluded for refusing a
pledge not to alter the government. The survivors attacked the notion
of unalterable ' fundamentals ' and asked the power of naming the
Council ; after months of debate they challenged the points he laid down
as vital, by asking control of the army after his death, by using their
financial power to reduce it immediately, and threatened the toleration
he most prized with a list of ' damnable heresies '. ' Circumstantials ',
he told them, he would surrender, but the mixed government by
Parliament and Protector, above all the guarantees for the army, were
the ' esse '; a barrier against a perpetual Parliament that would destroy
free religion and all they had fought for. Rather than consent to the
' wilful throwing away ' of this government, he would be rolled into
his grave. And so, when the bare legal minimum of five months had
gone, he dissolved them.

1655 was a year of imminent danger. The Royalist outbreak, which
he had warned Parliament would be the fruit of their obstruction,
showed itself in armed assemblies, though it only took serious effect
in Wiltshire where, under Penruddock, the conspirators seized on
the assize judges at Salisbury. Thurloe's espionage broke up every
Royalist move, corrupting even members of the ' Sealed Knot ' and
of Charles' court. Prisons were filled with Cavaliers and Levellers
alike, many of the humbler sort being transported to work on West
Indian plantations. Many legal-minded men doubted the very foundation of the Protectorate, five judges, for questioning the legality of
ordinances, were dismissed or resigned, merchants sometimes refused
to pay customs duties if unauthorized by statute, and their counsel
were sent to the Tower.

Indeed, every measure proved that Cromwell's power rested on an
armed minority and increased his isolation. A ruthless censorship cut
down the press to two government newspapers. Municipal councillors
were freely dismissed, some new charters being expressly devised to
build up a local majority. To all this despotism a climax came in the
appointment of the major-generals. England and Wales were divided
into eleven military districts, each under a picked soldier, assisted by
county commissioners and backed by a new mounted militia, the
expenses of which were met by a ' decimation ' or 10 per cent tax on
Royalists ; a proclamation, denouncing them as irreconcilable, forbade
them to bear arms or to keep Anglican clergy as chaplains and tutors.
The major-generals set out vigorously to put down ale-houses, arrest
suspects and round up vagrants, suppress race-meetings and bull-
baitings or observance of ' superstitions ' like Christmas day.

Moreover, though he reduced the army, Oliver launched into a costly foreign policy. Against Lambert's advice he convinced himself that the Protestant cause, and employment for his arms, called for a war in the Indies, where, in fact, the Spaniards had maltreated our seamen, and that this need not imply war in Europe. He lived again in the reign in which he was born, and which he commended to Parliament, of ' queen Elizabeth of famous memory '. No English government yet had accepted the Spanish claim to control the Indies in virtue of a Papal bull, or would prevent our settlers seizing territories not effectively occupied by other States. To Oliver, however, this motive was secondary to the other, that Spain was ' a natural enemy ', ' the underpropper of Babylon ' — ' the Lord Himself ', he urged on a sailor, ' hath a controversy with your enemies '. So came about the ill-fated expedition of 1655. The commanders, Admiral Penn and General Venables, quarrelled, while their force was made up of undisciplined drafts and wretched levies raised in the Indies. Their first attempt, against Hispaniola, was beaten off ignominiously, and though they took Jamaica, it was at first a ruinous possession, a graveyard of dysentery and yellow fever, without any prospects to attract New England settlers, as they had hoped. In October Spain declared war, but Oliver showed no intention of stopping until, as he said, he reached the gates of Rome.

In fact, he always hoped to realize that Protestant league which he urged on the Dutch, and for which a new chance seemed to open with the accession to the Swedish throne of Charles X, nephew of his boyhood hero Gustavus; the Protector applauded his plan of attacking Catholic Poland, and incited him to reopen the Thirty Years' War by marching on Vienna. His schemes and his prestige grew ever greater. Blake's fleet rescued captives from the galleys of Algiers, bombarded Tunis, and cut off treasure ships, while in his last and most glorious action, in April 1657, he destroyed the Spanish fleet at Santa Cruz in Teneriffe. Oliver spoke of seizing Gibraltar, and from the Swedes asked Bremen as a base.

By the same rough means he reached at last an alliance with France. Not hesitating to attack her traders, launching a New England expedition on her colony in Acadia, and still determined to be free to help the Huguenots, in 1655 he showed his teeth when the troops of Savoy, which was under the protection of France, massacred the evangelical people of the Vaudois villages. By this time, though still hoping for Spanish concession in the Low Countries, Mazarin was eager to neutralize English hostility; a treaty signed late in 1655 closed the commercial war, removed the English fear of a French-Dutch understanding which might partition Belgium and cripple our trade, and excluded the Stuarts from France. The consequent removal of Charles II to Brussels, his alliance with Spain, threats from Belgian privateers, all induced Oliver to pull tighter the French connection; which early in 1657 was converted into an offensive alliance, promising us the possession of Mardyke and Dunkirk.

Without a Parliament it was not possible to finance these operations, while English money had also to maintain government in Scotland and Ireland. Expenditure was much higher than under Charles I, rising to nearly two and a half millions a year, but the largest revenue Cromwell ever received was under two millions, the landed gentry resisted an increase of the monthly assessment, and the excise was detested as inquisitorial. When he therefore called in 1656 his second Parliament, the elections revealed, not least in shires once the most Puritan, a deep-seated opposition, in part republican but much more a reaction against rule by the sword. Though a hundred members were prevented from sitting by Council and about fifty more in consequence seceded, those who were left, whether veteran politicians like Lenthall, lawyers like Whitelocke, or solid squires like the Onslows, fought against the major-generals. To insolence like Major-General Desborough's that ' blows, not fair words ' must keep the peace, they replied by throwing out the militia bill. Another bitter debate turned on the punishment to be given to the unhinged Quaker James Naylor, whom his disciples hailed with hosannas as a new Messiah, for it was clear that Parliament meant to claim all the judicial powers of the Lords and cut down the licence of the sects. ' If this be liberty,' said the Presbyterian Skippon, ' God deliver me from such liberty.'

Far from criticizing the Protectorate, the moderates looked for a remedy in offering Oliver the Crown, — the office, as Thurloe wrote, ' known to the laws and to the people ', — as part of a new Constitution, ' the Humble Petition and Advice '. Oliver was much in sympathy with them, telling his officers he had been ' their drudge ' long enough, and it was time to ' lay aside arbitrary proceedings '. Left to himself he would probably have accepted, for he looked on the Petition as reconciling his special charge, ' the people of God ', with the nation at large, whom he never ceased to praise as ' the best people in the world '. But the soldiers nearest him, Lambert and Fleetwood, were against it, while many of the rank and file considered it an apostasy. He would not offend the simple, who in that faith, he told Parliament, had been ' never beaten '; Providence had testified against monarchy and in May 1657 he finally refused the Crown.

Even so the Petition was a long step back towards civilian government or, as Henry Cromwell wrote, ' towards the freedom of these nations ', and a stride also towards Restoration. The Protector received the right to name his successor. An Upper House was to curb the Commons. ' Fundamentals ' no longer bound Parliament; in right of its ' ancient and undoubted liberties ', without its assent no members might henceforth be excluded. The Commons were to have a voice in appointing the Council; Parliament, formally claiming control of taxation, gave the Protector a settled revenue of £1,300,000, and ratified his ordinances. Finally, the religious settlement was markedly conservative. It promised a national 'confession of faith' which ministers must accept if they were maintained from public funds, menaced the Quakers who disturbed public worship, and cut out of toleration not Papists and Anglicans only but those who held forth 'blasphemy' or 'profaneness'.

But neither parliamentary government nor monarchy were consistent with the Protectorate, as the session of 1658 proved. Royalist plots were now incessant, often aiming at Oliver's assassination, but they fumbled between Spanish dilatoriness and their own factions. Nor did government find it difficult to break up the dwindling body of extreme fanatics, whose preachers were telling them to 'stand or fall with the Lord Jesus upon His red horse against the Beast'. Its real danger came from the contacts steadily becoming closer between Royalism and the Presbyterian leaders, including Fairfax and Manchester. For aristocratic England was drifting towards the King; Puritan peers would not accept nomination to the new House, gentry like Ashley Cooper derided Colonel Pride and the Cromwellian 'lords'. Moreover, this promotion of his loyalest men ruined Oliver's majority in the Commons, which was further diminished by the return of formerly excluded republicans, who declared the Petition the work of a 'forced' Parliament, and refused to admit 'the other house' as a House of Lords. When they organized petitions to attract the sects and joined hands with discontented units in the army, Oliver decided to dissolve them. These 'tribunes of the people', he said, were 'playing the King of Scots' game', it must end in 'blood and confusion'. But as he ended with 'let God judge between you and me', there were some defiant 'amens'.

Many arrests, a purge in several regiments, an order that Cavaliers must stay within five miles of their homes, showed the emergency. Abroad, too, the Protector had his disappointments, for the Peace of Roskilde which he mediated between Denmark and Sweden broke down in the summer from Charles X's threatening ambition. Hopes of a Protestant anti-Hapsburg league faded away, while our relations with Holland were bad as ever, over her help to Denmark, her hostility to Portugal, and resistance to searching neutral ships.

Yet Cromwell's last months had their glories. In pursuance of the French treaty, 6000 red-coats went to Flanders, and took Mardyke while our fleet blockaded the Belgian coast. In June the English played a decisive part under Turenne's command in the victory of the Dunes, north of Dunkirk, which was duly handed over to England, while our men went on to storm Menin and Ypres. With 'the keys of the continent at his girdle', as his foreign secretary said, Oliver could bring the Dutch to reason. Nothing shook his hold on the army ; he dismissed the dangerous Lambert without ill effects. Civilian feeling would certainly bring about another offer of the Crown, which, it was believed, he would accept at an autumn Parliament.

But the summer was sickly, fever and overwork and the loss of a favourite daughter wore him down, and in August George Fox, meeting him riding round Hampton Court, felt ' a waft of death '. On the 3rd September, his day of victories, he died, after a prayer to God for His people, — ' give them consistency of judgement, one heart, and mutual love '. He named his elder surviving son, Richard, to succeed him, and England trembled, while the exiles rejoiced. For the testimony even of those who hated him, from Clarendon down to the man in the street, within a few years bore out what one of his household servants had written, ' a larger soul, I think, hath seldom dwelt in house of clay '. What his sword had wounded never rose to its full life again, neither monarchy nor Lords, Scottish Kirk nor Irish Catholics ; while upon United Kingdom and Empire, sea-power, toleration, and democracy the mark of the Protector is plain to see. In him were concentrated and concluded the full effects of the English Renaissance and Reformation.

CONTEMPORARY DATES

1650 Death of William II of Orange.
1651 Condé in revolt in France.
     Hobbes' *Leviathan*.
1652 The Dutch settle at the Cape of Good Hope.
1653 De Witt becomes Pensionary of Holland.
     Pascal enters Port-Royal.
     Madame de Scudéry, *Le Grand Cyrus*.
1654 Christina abdicates from the throne of Sweden.
     Petty's survey of Ireland.
1655 Massacre of the Vaudois.
     Charles X of Sweden attacks Poland.
1656 Coalition, including the Great Elector, against Sweden.
     The Kiuprili period opens in Turkey.
     Harrington's *Oceana*.
1657 Aurungzebe, Mogul Emperor till 1707, asserts his supremacy.
1658 Mazarin makes a League of the Rhine.
     –1705. Reign of the Emperor Leopold I.
1659 Peace of the Pyrenees.
     Molière, *Les Précieuses ridicules*.
     Pepys begins to keep a diary.
1660 Death of Charles X, and Peace of Oliva.
     Marriage of Louis XIV to Maria Theresa of Spain.

CHAPTER XIII

ENGLISH CIVILIZATION, 1540–1660

THE people which did such great things was a small one, not more than 4½ millions in England and Wales in 1640, with Scotland adding perhaps a million more, and another 200,000 overseas. If their strength was out of all proportion to these numbers, one good reason was their social unity. In Britain the antagonism of noble against bourgeois or rich against poor had, as the Civil War showed, almost disappeared in an equilibrium reached after two centuries of change, wherefore, having reached agreement on fundamentals, this society was able to lay down policies capable of meeting the requirements of the next two hundred years.

It was at once capitalist and planned. A ' mercantile ' theory had grown out of the more crude mediaeval ideas ; teaching that the State must be self-sufficient, that by tariffs and regulations it must maintain a population fit to carry arms and in full work, that it must grow its own food, do its own carrying-trade, and hold the balance between town and country, plenty and power. Its index of prosperity would be the balance of trade, measured not by prohibition on the export of precious metals but by the total superiority of exports over imports.

This theory had followed the facts. England was no longer a purely rural country, for probably not over 50 per cent of the people lived by agriculture, but it was decidedly a provincial and a balanced one. Its capitalism was on a small scale, in which the normal unit was the market-town, and the characteristic figures neither the large capitalist nor the wage-earner, but the country gentleman, the yeoman farmer, and the craftsman with his few apprentices. Yet a large industry and oceanic trade already existed, making the age one of many contradictions ; thus the West Riding weavers, who owned their own looms and raw material, sharply contrasted with Wiltshire clothiers who sometimes employed a thousand men, and against many hundred thousand yeomen and home workers must be set the large landlords and the East India Company.

At its best the practice of the State was not far removed from the mediaeval ideal : that a true Commonwealth was so far a religious body that it must take active steps towards social justice. So Council under Elizabeth and the early Stuarts regulated wages and prices with an eagle eye ; many times ordering employers not to throw men out of work, since (ran its order in 1622) ' whomsoever had a part of the gain in profitable times ' must in times of distress ' bear a part of the public losses '. It watched and allotted the balance of interests, thus, for instance, forbidding iron mills in Kent, where they would burn up the timber needed for shipbuilding. It refused patents to new machinery that would cause unemployment; it denounced corn dealers as ' wolves or cormorants '. Its inspectors searched out dishonest goods, and the chartered companies, like the gilds before them, were responsible for the quality of what they sold.

These being the ruling ideas, while they kept their power they resisted the free play of economic force; so that the changes of this period were changes of degree within an old framework, of which the two pillars were still the same, the land and the cloth trade.

Except in times of famine the country fed itself, corn prices fluctuating according to the home harvest; a bad one meant that the poor ate more barley or rye bread, and that government rationed imports of Baltic grain. The enclosure movement never ceased, whether for the pastures that supplied London with meat or for the clothiers' wool, and here and there for new crops of hops and turnips. It caused perpetual rioting, sometimes against the makers of private parks like the Cecils' at Hatfield, while in the midlands, where enclosure was most common, there was almost a social war of ' diggers ' and ' levellers ' who tore down the new fences. The Acts against enclosure which Elizabeth's advisers had to the last maintained were, however, repealed in 1624; a mass of property had come into the hands of business men who were determined to raise the customary and often uneconomic rents, and put pressure on the copyholders to accept leases. Many pamphlets showed that opinion had changed; they urged the disadvantages of the open fields, the slow pace set by the bad farmer, the exhaustion of the soil, the misery of the squatters on the waste and heaths, struggling along with a cow or two and living on oatmeal and goats' milk, or the impossibility of large flocks or improvements on these broken plots. Actually another reason had diminished earlier objections. From James I's time the export of wool was prohibited and profits in wool were checked, while there was a rise in the price of corn and a recovery of arable farming, enclosure for which did not cause so much eviction, and was often arranged by mutual agreement. Yet until the Civil War the Star Chamber acted severely against depopulation, particularly during Charles I's personal government from 1630; ordering the ploughing up of grasslands, protecting the tenant-right of the Cumberland ' statesmen ', and taking £50,000 of fines in a few years from offending landlords. On the whole, in spite of the new squirearchy, the yeomanry held their own. Free movement of money meant that the larger men among them bought out their weaker brethren. And since Elizabeth's Statute of Labourers had soon been repealed, so far as it tried to restrict industry to the gilds, weaving spread through all the villages of the kingdom, and spinning by women and children brought money into most peasant homes.

So far several factors thus kept up a well-poised Commonwealth, though movements were already at work which finally destroyed that happy balance.

The long Elizabethan peace and turmoil in Europe raised Britain above her rivals. Antwerp's supremacy was over; Turks, Spanish conquest, and the discovery of the Cape route, between them extinguished the Venetians and the Italian power at Southampton. As for the Hanse, in 1560 Burghley put them on the same level of tariffs as Englishmen and forbade them to carry our cloths to the Netherlands, in 1578 their privileges over other aliens were removed, while the Merchant Adventurers, when forced to leave Spanish Antwerp, achieved a large German trade through Stade and Hamburg.

Meantime European refugees contributed much to British wealth. Dutchmen and Flemings set up the new draperies, ' bays ' and ' says ' at Norwich and all over Essex, the Bedfordshire lace-making, and the cotton fustians which rapidly made a niche in Lancashire. Immigrants created the glass industry and paper-making, Germans taught us mining and metal-working, Frenchmen new arts in silk and steel, and Dutch engineers were draining the Fens.

Foreign competition and example, and the necessity of finding international markets, involved business with which only a considerable capital could cope. Each stage of the cloth industry, for instance, demanded advances on credit, so did movements in the corn trade, and in each the middleman and broker were found indispensable. In fact, money called the tune. The big clothiers fixed prices for spinners and weavers. Bristol was the exporting centre for Wales and financed the Mendip mines, just as London capital was found for the Cornish tin syndicates or for working Northumberland coal. Even the very size of new shipping meant the decline of many small harbours.

All this continued the changes begun long ago in the internal structure. Many local crafts decayed, others like the building trades amalgamated under the stress of competition. There were some efforts by local industry in active centres like Shrewsbury or Norwich to resist the big money of London, efforts which the Crown sometimes helped by a new charter : of craftsmen to keep a local market, or by journeymen to defend their gilds against the masters. But generally money overflowed the old lines of the crafts ; the glovers, for instance, who dealt in hides usually traded in wool too, and steadily a normal industrial type was being developed, of a ' livery ' or company that embraced all sections of the trade, usually ranked in two chief divisions, the rich merchants in control and the ' yeomanry ' of small masters.

For similar reasons, and also for purposes of defence, foreign trade came into the hands of chartered companies, whose monopoly usually included the right to levy customs and arm their ships. The greater companies [1] were mostly of the ' regulated ' type, already existing in the Merchant Adventurers; a body of merchants, that is, carrying on individual trade but obeying common rules as to prices, apprentices, and markets, and sailing in common fleets. The East India Company was the first permanent body to set up a joint-stock system, trading as a corporation and distributing profits to its shareholders, originally by ' divisions ' after every voyage but later by dividends on a permanent stock. These companies were the survivors of countless temporary syndicates, like the Cathay Company which backed Frobisher, or the politicians who shared with Drake, and the company scheme had tight hold also of many undertakings within England. So the Mineral and Battery Works had a joint-stock to exploit brass-making; market shares were quoted of the New River Company which James I chartered in 1609 to improve the London water supply; and Shakespeare held a large interest in the syndicate of the Globe Theatre.

London was the centre of this new power. Here were concentrated the directors of the cloth trade; the City paid perhaps four-fifths of the customs revenue, and its merchant princes took a hand in every great enterprise; so Sir Thomas Smyth was governor both of the East India and Russia Companies, treasurer of the Virginia, and a power in the Levant. From Gresham's time such men controlled the foreign exchanges, government depended on their loans, while bill-discounting houses and marine insurance were both advancing. The City's population grew so fast that proclamations vainly tried to stop suburban building; it was full of foreign craftsmen, Irish costermongers, and of rogues lurking in the Savoy or sleeping in Islington brick-kilns; on London converged all the carriers of the south country, bringing cloth and foodstuffs, and all the gentry's younger sons apprenticed to trade or the law.

How rich was the stream of this new wealth became clear after the Armada. An ordinary revenue of about £200,000 in 1560 was trebled by 1630, and the Customs alone were over £300,000. In its first twelve years the East India Company invested half a million of money; for many years the Russia Company's profits exceeded 40 per cent, and a great treasure was sent to America. Brokers and scriveners were practising an elementary and extortionate banking business. Coal was fast becoming a mainstay of our exports and a Newcastle fleet of 200 ships supplied London, though Elizabeth forbade the fumes near her palace.

---

[1] Guinea Company, 1553; Russia Company, 1553; Eastland Company, 1579; Levant Company, 1581; East India Company, 1600; Virginia Company, 1606.

Power was finding out many inventions, in blast furnaces for the Sussex iron, in water for paper-mills, pumping-engines for mines. What may be called a factory system was already present in the coal mines and parts of the cloth trade, large breweries, and the tapestry works of Mortlake.

This small island shared the shocks as well as the gains of world trade. Since 1540 the price level had risen by perhaps 250 per cent, and several black periods proved how dependent English employment had become on Dutch competition or peace in Germany. And control of these problems by a personal government had some evil consequences. Its grants of monopoly often turned into profiteering by courtiers, while its agencies often abused their power; the Newcastle ' hostmen ', for instance, kept a stranglehold on the sale of coal, and the Merchant Adventurers' quotas drove up the price of cloth.

None the less, this government held the balance even with fair success. The absolute prohibition it enforced on some foreign goods, such as leather or silks, had employment as its sole object; anxious ministers' notes and a great deal of administrative action showed their fear of disorder and their social sense, whether one looks at the Elizabethan Acts to pension soldiers, or the subscriptions in which both Houses of Parliament joined to help distress, the municipal distribution of cheap bread and coal, or the favour shown to the consumer in restricting export of corn.

Working hours were very long, always twelve and sometimes fourteen a day, and child labour universal, but little complaint was heard of either. Government did its best to keep the principle of a just wage as laid down in the Act of 1563 ; another of 1604 implied, indeed, not only a fixed but a minimum wage, and sharp reminders from Council to the magistrates and many wage-earners' petitions prove that till the Civil War the system was alive. Other statutes ordered employment to be for not less than a year, and for several generations the farm servants, the carter with his whip, dairymaids and shepherds, appeared at the annual hiring fairs.

Pre-Reformation Europe in its gilds and fraternities had not neglected its duty to the poor, but before it perished the new capitalism had impressed on all countries the need of larger measures. The early Tudor State, however, made little advance on the Acts of Richard II, which had provided for fixing wages, licensing the impotent to beg, and severe punishment for able-bodied vagrants. Swollen by high prices and enclosure troubles, this mass of sturdy ' masterless ' men became the special horror of the poor laws. Idleness, declared the Act of 1531, was the ' root of all vices ' ; the able-bodied should be whipped ' till his body be bloody ', and returned to his native place ' to labour like as a true man oweth to do ' ; a temporary Act of Edward VI even provided for branding and reduction to slavery.

Their poor-laws, however, soon transcended this barbarity. Carefully distinguishing between the able-bodied and the ' poor in very deed ', they forbade the giving of doles, held every parish responsible for relief, and developed a regular system of alms from the old customs of the churchwardens. Actually, as might have been expected, the self-governing towns and especially London took the lead during the years of suffering in the middle Tudor period. Nor was there any break between Catholic and Protestant charity ; funds for orphans, loans for the poor, cheap bread, were administered by both, and Catholic hospitals like St. Thomas's were refounded by the Protestants as public institutions. It was on these local experiments that Elizabethan statesmen built a national code.

Under Burghley's active lead, and with discussion in the Commons by men experienced in local government, their measures determined one vital point after another : compulsion to contribute (1563) ; levying of a rate by new parish officers, the overseers (1572) ; a ' house of correction ' in every shire, where able-bodied and true poor alike should be set on work (1576). Following again the practice of towns like Norwich and taught by several terrible trade depressions, in 1598, after weeks of debate, Parliament passed the Act which for two hundred years made the kernel of the poor-law, and the principles of which are fundamental for an understanding of old English life and character.

(1) Independence was upheld as better than relief ; parents and children, if able to do so, were legally bound to support each other, while refusal to work or to accept reasonable wages constituted vagabondage.

(2) Begging became illegal.

(3) The able-bodied vagabond should be set to work in the house of correction, or the gaol.

(4) Relief was to be found for the aged and impotent, whether by alms or by work on the provided stock of hemp, wool, and so forth ; poor children should be apprenticed ; any parish might build ' houses of dwelling ' for the impotent poor.

(5) Immediate responsibility lay on the parish overseers, though the magistrates were responsible for their appointment and activity. And the ancient principle of ' settlement ' was accepted, whereby the area for relief was the individual's native place, or usual place of work.

(6) But in aid of a poor parish the justices might order a rate on the whole neighbourhood.

Such, evolved upwards from the experience of self-governing bodies, was the greatest achievement of Elizabethan society. The next generation proved its worth, but also that only the activity of Council made it workable, an activity which was at its greatest during the administration of Strafford and Laud. A committee of Council, local commissioners, volumes of orders, and reports from magistrates, brought together information and reprimand in regard to wage-rates, food distribution, relief, and apprenticeship. All this action built up an administration, rising from the humblest overseer and constable through the J.P.'s, divided for this purpose into special districts, and so up to quarter-sessions and the assize judges, on whose information Council would act. In one generation vagrancy was almost stamped out; and into this web were woven all the alms-houses and endowed charities, which this age was freely adding to their predecessors', down to the smallest flock of sheep which some honest yeoman bequeathed as a ' stock ' for the poor. A great number of poor folk received relief in their own homes. There were plenty of spinning schools for poor children ; Christ's Hospital in London maintained over seven hundred, Elizabethan Beverley was educating eighty orphans, Jacobean Norfolk apprenticed some five hundred children a year. Not merely was relief made a public duty, but for the first time, and for the last for some centuries, government insisted that, however it were done, work must be found for the workless. So Council drove on against passive resistance and selfishness ; they were given ' little rest ', complained Nottinghamshire squires. A grain shortage would bring a drastic order to shut down 50 per cent of the ale-houses, which used up barley ; when the rich fled from the plague at Worcester, they were ordered to pay double rates ; and James I's Chancellor scathingly told the magistrates they were not appointed to ' stand there like an idol and do nothing '.

Yet since in the teeth of public opinion even the most high-minded government will not work, this detailed control of life collapsed, in part because it was in advance of its subjects, and even more because it was mixed up with illegality, unsuccessful policy, and religious discontent. All its motive power came from above, without which rate-payers would not contribute or constables convict. The moneyed class increasingly resisted this system of planning. Provincial firms challenged the monopoly of the London Adventurers, East Anglians broke into the Baltic area of the Eastland Company, and interlopers defied the East India Company. The maximum rate of interest, fixed by statute in 1571 at 10 per cent and reduced to 8 per cent in 1623, was freely evaded. The Commons began to attack monopolies as against ' natural right '. Honest doubts, as well as material selfishness, were seen in the magistrates' attitude to the whole policy ; in some counties they made no change in wages until they were compelled, while there were many complaints that fixing the price kept corn from the market. The Puritan ardour, which defied the State's right to compel their conscience, also challenged its right to dictate morality ; it was arriving at its argument that religion was not of this world but of a better one, and that here a man had a right ' to do what he liked with his own '.

These revolutions, which were making a new civilization, operated with varying speed on a country only lately united. What it had been since the decline of feudalism, such substantially it remained till the Civil War, a bundle of self-governing communities, directed by their own aristocracies. Nature was still enough man's master to keep mankind apart. In 700,000 acres of the Fens yeomen and squatters took boats to round up their cattle, living by the wild-fowl they could kill and the peat on which their villages were raised ; travellers could be lost on Newmarket Heath as easily as on Exmoor, where bandits like the Doones ignored the King's writ. In Cumberland fortified houses testified to the fear of the moss-troopers, while escorts with broadswords guarded Charles II's judges on assize. Though new industries in search of fuel, iron-founding and glass and salt works, and a short-sighted Crown revenue policy, were swiftly reducing the woodlands, there were still considerable forests in the Sussex Weald, Nottinghamshire, and the north ; while over heavy lowland soils the waters of neglected streams flooded the roads, except where benefactors or municipalities had carried them over bridges and causeways. Heavy traffic used the rivers for choice, the Cotswold stone descending the Thames to London and the eastern corn coming by the Lea ; sea-going craft went up Severn as far as Tewkesbury, and by the Ouse to York.

So life went on in its mediaeval compartments, though their inhabitants had changed. In the old order its last abbot had given Cirencester its fulling-mills ; in the new, the clothier Blundell endowed Tiverton with its school, and Francis Drake gave Plymouth a new water supply. Sons of good Lancashire families wore the Stanley livery till the days of Naseby, while the whole of local government preserved its mediaeval communal character. Parish and county had taken over from feudalism its unpaid obligatory services, whereby duty on juries, service as constables, or the upkeep of roads with their teams of horses, were laid by neighbours on each other. The parish church remained the heart of the village : the centre of bell-ringing contests, the Sunday sports abhorrent to the Puritan, and of countless charities, — suppers for the poor, collections for distressed Huguenots or for some timbered town burned down. And Jacobean England still observed the folk-festivals over which Catholicism had thrown its mantle : mummers and masques, May Day, beating of the bounds, and harvest home.

All men's dearest feelings were wrapped up in this ancient setting. The tie of blood was very strong, for it meant the perpetuity of the family estate, so that marriages were commonly arranged by the parents as Oliver Cromwell settled his son Richard's. Children uncovered to their parents to ask a blessing, as the chancellor Thomas More kneeled to ask his father's, the judge of a lower court. Reverence for ancient birth and a reverence for order marked the generations that heard Cranmer's Litany and Elizabeth's homilies, and this was shown as much by the Cromwellians as by Shakespeare, whose ideal republics were of the aristocratic type set forth by Plutarch, or practised on the serene lagoons of Venice. It was Cromwell who expounded to Parliament the ' good interest ' of ' a nobleman, a gentleman, a yeoman ', and a typical lawyer who uttered a famous lament for the great families perished, ending with ' most of all, where is now de Vere ? '

Their immediate loyalty went to their ' countrymen ', their fellow-Yorkshiremen or Cornishmen. To be a good ' housekeeper ', to keep up hospitality, were the virtues preached by good parents like Burghley or in the royal proclamations that ordered country gentlemen to leave London, while York or Exeter were real capitals with town houses of the county families, and their social magnets of races and assemblies. Local rivalries drove on the Saviles and Vanes to ask for Strafford's blood, the tie of kindred bound together Hampden, Cromwell, and St. John, while west-country members would vote as a solid body in the interests of their woollens, whatever their views on Church or King.

The countryman living in London had provisions sent up from his home, which was almost a self-subsisting unit ; where his own corn and beef, fish-ponds and game, malt and fat and wool furnished food and drink, russet coat and candles, while the wife made her medicines and preserves from herb garden and orchard. They hunted rather to kill than for the glory of the chase, used nets to trap deer, and treated the fox as vermin, for whose masks the churchwardens would pay a reward. Despite their pride of birth and a tincture of education at the university or Inns of Court, most of the squires were purely provincial, enjoying their petty power as justices, consuming the same beef-puddings and the same ale, speaking the same dialect as their farmers, and only marked out by their coat of arms or by the touch of leadership they got from marriage with greater men's daughters or the politics of the bowling-green and quarter-sessions. Their influence and Church patronage moulded many of the clergy in the same image ; Parson Welsh of Exeter, who was hanged in the rising of 1549, had been famous as a woodman and for skill with the bow, and many a later parson was a peasant farmer, working to glean his tithe sheaves, and brewing ale with the wife he had found in the waiting-woman at the squire's hall.

This rude but real society, the type of England outside the home counties, kept a high spirit and a vigorous standard. Foreigners noted the meat food of all classes, the beer which must be shipped with English soldiers abroad, the silver cup or dish in any good inn. Antiquaries and politicians boasted of the yeomen who, as the Elizabethan parson Harrison wrote, ' in time past made all France afraid ', while his contemporary Thomas Smith, secretary of State, declared the English would not endure servitude or torture, being ' free, stout, haultie, prodigal of life and blood '. From Angevin times they had been trusted with arms, and ordered of late to make themselves good archers, and though nothing could be less efficient than the militia musters held by the justice Shallows, or the constables marshalled by the Dogberries, they kept the elements of disciplined freedom among the whole people.   Hundreds of self-governing parishes and manors fixed their church rates and their routine of husbandry, electing constables, churchwardens, beadles, neat-herds, and surveyors to manage their daily life.   We read how in voyages on the Spanish Main or in the Arctic this people reproduced their home, how Hawkins read evening prayers in his slave-ship, Drake's men set up bowling-greens, and Davis' played football among the Eskimos.

Life, despite the poets, seems to be more ruthless when it is short, and Englishmen then were short-lived.   Rightly the Litany's heartfelt prayers asked for mercy on women labouring of child, young children, and prisoners, for all alike were mown down by death, and to be wounded in battle was not far from death by gangrene.   Though the College of Physicians was founded by Linacre in 1518, medicine was dominated till about 1600 by Galen and the ancient schools, easily degenerating into quackery of ' humours ' in the body, astrology, and noxious compounds like those stirred by the witches in *Macbeth* ; only under James I did better things begin, with the charter given to the Society of Apothecaries, borrowings from French surgery for wounds and amputation, and with William Harvey's discovery of the circulation of the blood.   Meantime men took one wife after another, and bred large short-lived families, like Dean Colet's twenty-one brothers and sisters ; and epidemics raged at will, however much in time of pestilence they fled to refuge, as the Westminster boys were sent to Chiswick, or however much the law courts were strewed with sweet herbs, or courtiers carried oranges and pomanders.   The sweating-sickness, which often drove Henry VIII to his forest lodges, was called ' stop-gallant ' in Edward VI's day, when ' there were some dancing in the court at nine o'clock that were dead at 11 ' ; at one Oxford assizes the gaol fever killed judges, jury, and nearly 300 in all, while in the year of Elizabeth's death the plague slew 38,000 Londoners.   Newgate and the jails were dens of horror, with earthen floors and straw to lie on ; whence issued lean arms and lamentable voices begging food.

Brought through many perils and ever menaced by sedition and sudden death, this society counted life too cheap to spare enemies and weaklings.   It held out the whip and the bloody back for the ' Egyptians ', highway robbers, masterless men and their doxies, whose confederacy with innkeepers made the roads unsafe.   It was used to see criminals hanged in dozens, and to hear the penitential psalm of those driven off to Tyburn.   Its moral code was low and yet severe ; the London theatres were next to a nest of brothels which the apprentices would often raid and pull down ; they kept a ducking-stool for light women, pillory and stocks for the pilferer or the baker of light bread. Corruption ran through all government service, military musters, university posts, and all places of emolument, for salaries were mean and perquisites many, and great men were all-powerful. When human beings tortured each other, they would not think of animals, and loved to watch a cock-fight or the Tower lions tear a mastiff to pieces or to bait a bull, while generations knew by name all the bears at Paris garden, until Colonel Pride killed them. Old superstition and streaks of new science delivered them over to alchemists, love-philtres, and the philosophers' stone, and the common folk to a frenzied fear of ' witches ', of whom some two hundred were executed during two years of the Civil War in East Anglia alone.

With riches and peace, however, there had come changes of life, sinking downwards some new shafts of thinking. Their habits were simple, the ways of country-bred folk, who held summer quarter-sessions at 7 A.M. and took their dinner before midday, who had no night raiment but their shifts, no habit of bathing, and even whose great houses had not a rudiment of sanitation. The most peaceful citizen wore dagger or sword, delicate scholars journeyed much on horseback, while poor university students rose at dawn, lived on a penny slice of beef and oatmeal, and never saw a fire except in the common hall. And long centuries had hardly changed the lives of the really poor. Though they were freemen now and not villeins, their bread was more often barley or rye than wheaten, their hovels still thatched, with wattle and daub walls, their fuel peat or furze, their furnishings wooden stools and trestles, wooden trenchers to eat from, with a few pewter pieces and, for chief treasure, a feather bed. Except that its materials were better and its cut changed, the peasant's dress had altered little since his Saxon forebear's. Though his leggings might, if he had prospered, be the worsted stockings worn by plain gentlemen like Cromwell, and a felt hat had replaced the hood, his shirt was coarse canvas like his smock, his coat was homespun in russet or grey, his working shoes often the wooden clog. But in the ranks above him the old compartments had given way.

For life and death were settled no more by the baron, and though in the fifteenth century a few strong keeps were raised as at Warkworth and Tattershall, they were survivals. Building like the Vernons' at Haddon Hall was rather for a great house than a castle, though for many years the hall remained the house centre, gate-houses and moats showing the need of security, so that dozens of country houses could stand a siege in the Civil War, as Lady Harley defended Brampton Bryan against the Royalists or Lady Derby held Lathom against the Puritans. But, all through the fifteenth and sixteenth centuries, at one end of the hall its single solar made way for parlours, withdrawing-rooms, and guest rooms, while at the other, beyond the screens, more rooms and a gallery would cover the kitchen and buttery. Fireplaces became common, with flues and clustered chimney stacks, while ample glass windows, heedless of arrows, replaced the slits closed of old by wooden shutters or horn. Gradually the wealth of the clothiers, of London, and new markets poured itself out into the manor and farm houses, churches, and borough buildings, of which England yet is full, into richness of panelling and timbered ceiling, plaster mouldings, bay and oriel windows, and on the clay soils in the new art of brickwork.

While Gothic forms exhausted their last vitality in prodigies of fan tracery and vaulting like Henry VII's chapel, a plain strength marked the new Perpendicular style, whether in the church towers of Suffolk, the Wiltshire Avon, and Somerset, or brick houses like Sutton Place and Layer Marney. Looking for line and light and utility more than to mass, religious meaning, or protection, it raised long church windows which dispensed with the triforium and flattened out the pointed arch, while straight broad staircases instead of the winding turret, and straight lines of transom and mullion, gave a symmetry reinforced by the horizontal battlement, and even the ornaments breaking this line, oriel or pinnacle or porch, themselves stressed the measured proportions. All that light and height and ornament could do may be seen in the Bell Harry tower at Canterbury, East Anglian churches like Lavenham, King's College, Cambridge, or halls at Eltham and Hatfield; an endless chain of new houses in stone, brick, and timber, show into what tranquil strength even local builders were bringing window and cornice, gable and chimney.

After many earlier borrowings of Italian and Flemish ornament, the servants of Elizabeth and James set the example of building to formal design, sometimes with architects who had studied Renaissance models abroad. Hatton built a palace at Holdenby, the Cecils built or renewed Theobalds and Hatfield and Cranborne, the Howards Audley End, the Sackvilles Knole, and were followed by a great number of squires and merchants, such as the Dorset Phelips who raised Montacute. A direct renaissance came from the influence of Vitruvius, as taught by learned Englishmen like Henry Wotton, until with the banqueting hall at Whitehall, the one fragment built of Inigo Jones' large scheme, the classic style achieved the dominance it held for a century and a half. Sashed windows, wide cornices, dormers, pillars, and proportioned wings revealed a new way of thinking.

With this new frame of civilian life there disappeared the weapons and distinctions of dress in mediaeval society. Changes in the art of war had displaced the various sorts of chain mail in which Vikings and

Normans had conquered. With each improvement in weapons of attack, armourers devised pieces of plate to cover vital places, until in the fourteenth century they reached the full suit of plate armour, artfully made to distribute its weight, and made flexible by separate pieces, rivets, and hinges. But there was a limit to thickening protection or piling up weight in the great helm and complete horse armour. Lighter and more airy pieces replaced the helm with a salade or bascinet or morion; archers, and the rank and file, were content with brigandine or ' jack ', the quilted coat sown over with small plates. Fire-arms, infinitely more penetrating than crossbow bolts, were the final blow, and though at Elizabeth's death the Tower stores held many bows, and yew-staves were still imported from Germany or Danzig, the archer's day was over; infantry depended now on bills, matchlock, and the sixteen-foot ash-shafted pike, on fire effect and mass tactics which did away with the armoured defensive. Breast- and back-plate, and the half-helmet, passed into the cuirass, buff coat, and big boots of the seventeenth century, while weapons of speed and lightness, pistol and flint-lock instead of the heavy musket with its prop and burning match, and Toledo rapier instead of the edged sword, testified that battles were won by mobility and mass.

All this involved a specialization which divided soldiers from civilians, most of whom melted into a fluid society unmarked except by gradations of wealth. No sixteenth-century sumptuary laws could enforce class barriers in dress, — the apprentices' flat cap and white cloth breeches, or the Puritans' linen bands, signifying rather a trade or a religious calling. Broadly speaking, the world of fashion had grown larger and more uniform, more practicable and cosmopolitan. Short cloaks and doublets, breeches and stockings, took the place of the Plantagenets' long gowns and tight hose, though fancy copied every extravagancy in sleeves and swellings from Europe; the Elizabethan fop had turned the collar into a giant ruff, he had a German cloak and a shirt of Holland, roses on his shoes, breeches bombasted out to great width, a jewel in his ear, and a mirror in his tobacco box. While women of the middle class wore gowns, aprons, wimple and coif, Elizabeth's Court ladies were as extravagant as those of Richard II, though horned head-dresses had given way to farthingales mounted on whalebone, jewelled stomachers, and wired ruffs, with fans and masks from France. A better and quieter taste came in with the restraint of Charles I's Court and Puritan influence, when Van Dyck's models succeeded the gorgeous figures painted for Elizabethan homes by Flemings and Spaniards.

At its summit it was a rich, sophisticated world, which spent enormously on food and servants, and washed out its ailments at the spas of Bath and Buxton, and for whom new luxuries had been brought, like tobacco and potatoes, from new seas. Many of its leaders, Dudleys or Howards, were corrupt in all ways. From their literature, Donne's satires for instance, there emerge the selfish ambitions, loss of faith, cynicism, and the scorn ' which patient merit of the unworthy takes ', while reaction from controversy and weariness unsettled in many their Protestant faith. Usurers and enclosers and greed broke up the ideal of an ordered State, new-bought peerages and ' dunghill knights ' debased it. So that Faustus and Iago, Hamlet and Brutus, darkened the stage between the ardours of Renaissance and the moderation of Restoration England, wandering between two worlds and, like Falkland in battle, vainly seeking peace.

Thomas More reckoned two-thirds of the population in his day as illiterate, and British civilization lagged behind France, Italy, and the Rhineland. Without foreign immigrants neither English trade, architecture, nor letters could have developed so swiftly, and though their rooms were hung with tapestries, or the humbler painted cloths that showed the worthies of Christendom or the story of Lazarus, Protestant zeal whitewashed over the church frescoes, and English painting hardly revived till the seventeenth century. Yet the native culture was full of strength.

Since Wyclif's age education had become a passion, all the Tudor reigns being marked by foundation or re-endowment of schools, and that much less from any government activity than from a general zeal ; foundation not only of schools for the fairly well-to-do, — Harrow, Uppingham, St. Paul's, Merchant Taylors', Repton, Christ's Hospital, Shrewsbury, and Westminster all being products of this age — but of countless others, even in small villages, well enough equipped to send boys to the universities. This renaissance could be illustrated further by new colleges at Oxford and Cambridge, the Gresham lectures in London, the foundation of new chairs and the Bodleian library. Certainly the century ending in the Civil War produced more learning and learned men than any equal period of British history, beginning with More and Tyndale, proceeding through the geographer John Dee, the antiquaries Stow and Camden, scholars in public life like Sidney, Hakluyt chronicler of the discoveries, the philosophers Bacon and Hobbes, the lawyers Coke and Selden and Prynne, a wonderful school of divines from Hooker to Ussher and Jeremy Taylor, the virtuosos Thomas Browne and Burton, down to the writers with whom the age closed, Milton, Cowley, and Dryden.

It was at the turn of Reformation, between 1551 and 1573, that Spenser, Raleigh, Sidney, Shakespeare, Marlowe, Bacon, Ben Jonson, and Donne, were all born ; before them the English renaissance showed solid performance rather than imaginative power. Some of its best prose turned on religion, from More to Latimer and Foxe's *Martyrs*, while Sternhold and Hopkins made those metrical versions of the Psalms which Puritan England sang for a hundred years. There was marked interest in history and antiquities, to which testified Berners' translation of Froissart, Leland's *Itinerary*, the chronicles of Hall and Holinshed, and *The Mirror for Magistrates*. Quite as remarkable was the flow of publication on every matter of public interest, such as Thomas Wilson's *Discourse on Usury*, the *Schoolmaster* by Jane Grey's teacher Ascham, Hawkins' account of his voyages, and important books on geography and mathematics. After 1580 there followed works on the same lines, of more enduring quality; of which it is enough to think of Hooker's *Ecclesiastical Polity*, Camden's *Britannia*, Stow's survey of London, and Bacon's essays.

The strength of Shakespeare's England came, in one sense, from the form taken in England by Renaissance and Reformation, which meant that no gulf divided our modern from our mediaeval letters. More stood in the direct tradition of Rolle and early devotional writing, and among the text-books most widely used into the seventeenth century were the works of the Catholic humanists Erasmus and Vives, the ' colloquies ' of the Norman Calvinist Corderius, and the Latin poems of Colet's acquaintance Mantuanus. The universities kept up the old oral disputations and the supremacy of Aristotle, many schools made their boys speak only Latin in working hours, while two great streams of influence united to make education not of the mind only but of morals. This ideal of active virtue was taught by the best Italians, Castiglione for instance, whose book was translated by Thomas Elyot in 1531; it was the doctrine of Roger Ascham, who was as ardent for archery as for Greek, and was verified by the sword and pen of Philip Sidney. Meanwhile, no less than the Catholics, the school of Geneva and Puritanism gave education a religious basis, so that public prayers, hearing and annotation of sermons, ceaseless moral responsibility, were the daily discipline of English youth.

Within this classical background and habit of religion worked three native literary products. The country was full of ballads, hawked by Autolycus and pedlars at market crosses, or hung on inn-walls; some the rude relics of *chansons de geste*, Anglicized to fit Robin Hood and Guy of Warwick; some a minstrel's theme like Chevy Chace, for ever being made anew in honour of Drake or Essex; others the songs that Shakespeare loved, ' King Cophetua ' or ' Greensleeves '. Nor had English lyric ever ceased to flow, in alliance with a passionate love of music.

Composers of Henry VI's time, of whom John Dunstable enjoyed a European fame, considerable Flemish influence, and a host of carols and airs, marked the fifteenth century. Henry VIII and his chapel-master Cornish carried on the tradition, and under Elizabeth and James

English church music, centring round the cathedrals, touched the heights in Tallis, Byrd, Bull, and Orlando Gibbons. The airs found in early Tudor song-books swelled after 1580 into a flood of madrigals and part-songs, noblemen and squires patronized the song-makers, one of James I's lutenists wrote the music for *The Tempest*. All England was singing, and every gentleman must play the lute or viol; the Queen played the virginals, all Shakespeare's characters ask for music, even if it is only a catch or a Lincolnshire bagpipe, Milton acquired Henry Lawes' music for *Comus*, and Cromwell's troops hummed their surly hymns.

The English companies of musicians and actors, who during Shakespeare's life toured northern Europe, bore witness to the mingled origins of the drama. It had come from morality and mystery plays which had begun in religious festivals and then become gild or village feasts, from interludes and masques of all sorts played by the Inns of Court or for the diversion of kings and nobles, from humble Christmas mummers who wandered to manor houses, or from Scripture scenes and classical plays acted at colleges and schools. These old diverse influences amalgamated together, no sharp change distinguishing the work of More's Catholic friend Heywood from that of Udall, headmaster in turn of Eton and Winchester, whose *Ralph Roister Doister* set English comedy on its course.

But before English literature rose to its climax, two other facts had to be absorbed, a conscious acceptance of the national language as equal to any other, and a borrowing from other tongues to make English and its message more flexible, formed, and profound. Every national speech in renaissance, from Dante's advocacy of Italian onwards, had shown the same pride as Caxton and Tyndale took in their English, or which Tottel displayed in publishing his miscellany, of Wyatt and the first modern poets, ' to the honour of the English tongue '. Meantime, before Elizabeth reigned, the great Italians' work was done, Rabelais was in print, and the new poetry of Ronsard and the Pléiade had appeared, from whom Wyatt and Surrey, Spenser, Shakespeare, and the unnumbered makers of the sonnet, drew theme and form. In their age translations were made of every major classic, Latin and Greek and modern European, sometimes in memorable versions such as North's *Plutarch*, Chapman's *Homer*, or Florio's *Montaigne*. Definite foreign influences are easy to trace, whether the Italianate which affected Marlowe and later made a pagan set among the Cavaliers, the Pléiade's vogue in Elizabeth's court, or the Spanish mysticism stamped on Laudian churchmen.

These forces, and the Latin borrowings especially, changed the national tongue, added to its vocabulary, deepened its structure, and created that range which might turn to pedantry but which, in the hands of the masters, became an instrument never surpassed in variety and power. The best English teachers, Ascham and Mulcaster, gloried that English had become all that Greek and Latin had been. Criticism explored all literary forms and the relation between art and morals, in the controversies marked by Lyly's publication of *Euphues* (1578), Sidney's *Defence of Poesy*, and angry pamphlets of the poets Nash and Greene against literary dictators and unlearned playwrights.

In this age so filled with riches and victory all the forms were achieved, the drama and the lyric by hands too many to number, the essay and the ' character ' by Bacon and Earle, satire and criticism, and the novel in Sidney's ornate *Arcadia*, or Greene's and Dekker's comedies of life. Literature became a national power, noblemen rivalled each other in patronage of men of letters, as Shakespeare worked for the dramatic company controlled by the Queen's cousin Hunsdon, or as the poets Lodge and Chapman followed the star of Essex. An actor like Alleyn, who ' created ' the parts of Tamburlaine and Faustus, died a public figure, leaving his wealth to found Dulwich College. How powerful was the stage may be measured by the Puritan attack upon it, and how mighty the pen by the deference paid to Jonson, or the public life of Milton.

The drama triumphed, even over Puritan resistance, because it contained and catered for all the facts of society; its very existence depending on the favour of the Court, which could not do without its festivals, of Leicester and the magnates, and the City audiences. Overlapping and assisting one another, local mystery and rough chronicle plays for the people and university drama for scholars went on side by side with the resplendent work being done in London. Shakespeare's predecessors, Greene and Kyd, wrote, as he did, for their living, and broke the conventions which Sidney and classical purists would have imposed. But though they wrote of real life, for a real audience who were munching apples and nuts, whose demand they supplied in murderous tragedy, low comedy, and topical allusion, they borrowed from the classical school their instrument of blank verse. They ranged all literature for their plots, created (Lyly in particular) a prose dialogue, and made an unrestrained analysis of character the key of their craft. When Marlowe, not yet thirty, was stabbed in a tavern in 1593, he left work which proved the energy of this renaissance. His Tamburlaine, who rides with captive kings drawing his chariot through conquered Persepolis, his Faustus who counts religion ' but a childish toy ', and will sell his soul for knowledge or a kiss from Helen of Troy, alike ask supreme power, without thought of God or pity of man; ' still climbing after knowledge infinite ', they have torn the stars from the ancient heavens, and destroyed all barriers to the might of man's mind and the glories of his flesh.

A multitude of more normal names measure the breadth and spiritual sources of this literature; an astonishing array of playwrights, Greene, Marston, Webster, Massinger, Ford, Beaumont, Fletcher, Middleton, Shirley, and in a class to himself Ben Jonson, severely classical, censorious, and analytic; several thousand songs and lyrics in every metre and on every theme, written not only by these great men, and by others of wonderful dexterity like Campion, public men like Wotton, bishops like Henry King, Puritan journalists like Wither, but often shown by lines of perfection, from men otherwise unknown, in the midst of long conventional stretches on the model of Petrarch or the French. There were all-round craftsmen, of whom Drayton, the Daniels, and the Fletchers were good types; a memorable school of divine poets in George Herbert and Crashaw and Vaughan; a Cavalier-classic group exemplified by Carew and Suckling, Lovelace and Herrick, all of whom adorned Charles I's court or suffered for him; and the schools who made poetry didactic, who tortured words and strained conceits, or clouded it with metaphysic. Where all cannot be comprehended, it may find its representatives in four names.

Those who ask genius will turn from Edmund Spenser, but no one more representative of Elizabethanism could be found. Here met the learning acquired at Cambridge, the literary cliques of London, the imitation of the French and Tasso, the thirst for fame, the conscious modelling upon Vergil, the deification of the Queen as Gloriana or Belphoebe. With a new mastery of liquid rhyming metre and sweeping all the forms of sonnet and satire, elegy and epic, his masterpiece *The Faerie Queene* faithfully reflected the Queen's England. The moral virtues which Plato drew must be typified by Arthur and British knights, the ' courteous love ' of mediaeval poets transferred to Elizabeth's court, Catholic Christianity fused with the Platonic vision and reconciled to Protestant faith, and all built up in a pageant of his own age; in the warfare of Britomart queen of chastity, type of Elizabeth, the sins of Duessa or Mary of Scots, and Archimago, by whom he meant the Pope. From this mirrored lake flowed the many streams that fertilized the next half-century, for if Spenser was unknown to the people, all the poets except Jonson agreed to idolize him, ending with Milton who, says Dryden, was his ' poetical son '.

We know that Shakespeare was born in 1564, that he left home for London before 1590, and that within some ten years he made a name enough to be abused as ' an upstart crow ' by Greene, though reckoned by others among the masters; and won fortune enough to become a leading property-owner in his native Stratford. That he had an interest in the Lord Chamberlain's company from 1594 and kept it to the end, that all who knew him liked him well, that he loved unhappily a woman other than Anne Hathaway his wife, that his plays filled the theatres, that Falstaff and Shallow and Caesar were proverbial and his plays acted on the Continent in his life-time, and that he died in 1616 at the age of fifty-two, — beyond these facts we know little of the man.

As to his fame and meaning, like that of all great things it is not less significant for what posterity read into him than for what he meant to say, but criticism has established an upward course of his genius. There is a first Shakespeare who wrote the affected beauty of *Venus and Adonis* and the bloodthirsty *Titus Andronicus*, who had some hand in the unequal *Henry VI*, and patched up other men's work in *The Taming of the Shrew*. There is a second who, to the best of our knowledge, between 1597 and 1606 made at least some of the sonnets, created Falstaff, Rosalind, and Malvolio, and within seven of those years staged *Julius Caesar*, *Hamlet*, *Measure for Measure*, *Othello*, *Lear*, and *Macbeth*. And there is a third Shakespeare of the end, of *Cymbeline*, *The Winter's Tale*, and *The Tempest*, who had left London for home and after storms found a haven. Yet the first Shakespeare produced Richard II, Juliet, and Holofernes.

Attested facts may help to explain his craftsmanship : that he acted himself, perhaps before he wrote ; that Stratford's ancient school could have given him a fair education ; that he freely adapted older men's work, as he found an earlier Lear, or borrowed from sources like North's *Plutarch* and Holinshed's *Chronicles*. He shared in his contemporaries' common atmosphere, the steady background of a rural society, in their knowledge of country sports or legal lore, which indeed in his prosperous days he often enforced to protect his rights. He was no better read than others in romances of Latin Europe, or more deeply versed in the Shallows and Dogberries, or had drunk deeper at the Mermaid. He held most of their deepest convictions, believing in the fixed order of society, the might of religion, the huge destiny but the petty scale of man.

But neither experience nor facts can explain why he alone became the mirror of the English temper and humour for all time. No other Englishman has added, to an immense volume of the highest poetry, supreme powers both of creating and analysing character, and of so welding romantic creation into reality that both artist and creations are merged in figures known to all men's consciences and hearts. Who, wrote his dramatic partners in publishing the first collected edition of his plays in 1623, ' as he was a happy imitator of Nature, was a most gentle expresser of it ' ; his nature, indeed, being so wide that he won the ardent worship of Milton and a perpetual reading, during his captivity, from Charles I.

John Donne, dean of St. Paul's and ' the first poet in the world in some things ' according to Jonson, was perhaps the greatest writer between Shakespeare and Milton. Some of that age's force might be found in Jonson's satiric drama, some of its grace in the verse of Herrick, the Devon country parson, but Donne covered more territory than either. For he had sunk low in sensuality like Carew, sought peace in the Roman Church like Crashaw, and explored as many philosophies as Bacon. No man has with equal power described the winding stairs of that ambitious, gross society, and also packed into intense poetic form so much of its intellectual wandering, its brutality and passion. All the new science, all its perpetual thinking on mortality, which sets a carved skull on its most lovely monuments and watches the flowers open only to fade, its astonishing and overwrought imagination, and the final offering of its treasures before God in humility or weariness, all are assembled in Donne's poetry and prose, making him more representative of what endures in Jacobean England than the masters of Puritanism.

Within seven years of Donne's death Milton issued *Comus* and *Lycidas*, but thirty years of war and revolution intervened before *Paradise Lost* and *Samson Agonistes*. How delicate and rare a spiritual force, how learned and disciplined Puritanism could be, his early poems show, nor could the claim for reason find more magnificent expression than in *Areopagitica*, the demand for liberty of printing issued against the Presbyterian Parliament. In his work before 1650 shine out the decencies and liberalism which this new England had achieved, the tranquillity of its homes, the pieties which are carved on brasses and monuments in its churches, its self-respect. Then came the Commonwealth in whose service, as secretary for the Latin tongues, Milton used up his eyesight and dipped his pen in venom to write against priests and kings. At the Restoration the blind poet turned to the great theme long pondered, publishing *Paradise Lost* in 1667 and in 1671 its sequel *Paradise Regained* together with *Samson Agonistes*; in this last commemorating ' the plain heroic magnitude of mind ' by which Cromwell and the soldier-saints had defeated the insolent sons of Belial, and how reviving it was to fight for liberty against an oppressor. But *Paradise Lost* has a wider significance than the Puritan scheme. For with it ended not only the peculiar character of this century, its mixture of ordered scholarship and Protestant faith, but also the last glint of the English mediaeval mind; which had sought to bring under one formula of salvation all experience and all learning, to rationalize revelation and confidently justify the ways of God to man.

Never, as Milton's example shows, has English prose more nearly partaken of the character of poetry than in English writing between 1580 and 1660. Their moral outlook, learning, and classical training, the cosmopolitan influences playing on them, their love of music and instinct for order, made their written and spoken word memorable; magnificent in Sidney and in Hooker, it was carried as high as harmony can go in Burton's *Anatomy of Melancholy*, Browne's *Religio Medici*, or Donne's *Sermons*. No one book so impressed the people at large, or so fully represented the standard of the language, as the Authorized version of the Bible, built essentially on the older version of Tyndale, and using a vocabulary simple and conservative, almost entirely free of Latinism. But this prose's strength, its spiritual imagination and its rolling waves, can be found also in parliamentary speeches, in men of all sides, in Strafford's letters as well as in Fuller's *Worthies of England*, its grandeur in Raleigh's *History of the World*, as in Clarendon's *History of the Rebellion*, its increasing precision and grace in Selden's *Table Talk*, or Izaak Walton's *Lives*, or in the books that all men read, Baxter's *Saints' Everlasting Rest*, or the unknown author of *The Whole Duty of Man*. When we pass from form to matter, the range of English learning, apart from Hooker or Milton or the Bible translators, was proved by the astonishing talent in the Church, whether in Jeremy Taylor or archbishop Ussher's chronology, in Henry Saville's edition of *Chrysostom*, in Walton's Polyglot Bible in nine languages, or again in the learning of parliamentary antiquaries like D'Ewes, Coke, and Prynne, or Urquhart's translation of Rabelais. But how men of that age, quite removed from being scholars, had learnt to think and write appears in all they wrote down for their families or posterity, in men of action like Montrose or Falkland, or the Puritans Whitelocke and Ludlow, in familiar letters, and the epitaphs on their tombs.

A century of science and philosophy had found out a new earth and unsettled the heavens. A great output of geographical and mathematical study in Elizabeth's reign came from men who accepted the discoveries of Copernicus and Galileo. William Gilbert confirmed it from another side by his work on magnetism and electricity; the Scottish laird Napier, the English parson Oughtred, the university teacher Wallis armed scientists with a new power of exact mathematics. In political thinking the notions of a fixed order and the law of God were first blended with, and then yielded to, ideas of a law of nature, into which men could read whatever they wished to take as fundamental. Francis Bacon gave the glamour of his name and his curiosity to the advancement of learning, claiming that knowledge was increased only by experiment, and rejecting the dogmas which, in the name of Aristotle or the Church, kept it enchained. One of those who did secretarial work for him was the young Thomas Hobbes, who in a very long life acclimatized in Britain the new philosophical teaching, which was coming from Spinoza and Descartes abroad. His mechanical philosophy, which derived conscience and morals from experience and outward sensation, could not be reconciled with the divine teaching held for many generations, and many signs showed that a new mentality had arrived, rational and exploratory and scientific. The first half of the seventeenth century built no more churches, its music became secular, its drama abandoned moral teaching.

A swarm of travel-books and travellers testified to the new curiosity, and to be a ' chymist ', an antiquary, or a collector seemed almost the mark of an intelligent man.   The Cavalier marquis of Worcester began his experiments in steam and, while the Puritans ruled at Oxford, the Protector's brother-in-law Wilkins with his young friends Robert Boyle and Christopher Wren laid the foundation of the Royal Society.

' The seat of the British Empire ', wrote Camden, was London, where were concentrated 600,000 of the country's five million souls, and a disproportionate part of its wealth ;   the centre and hive of these centuries of change.   It long kept its open spaces, Hatton's famous garden or Milton's garden house outside Aldersgate, while hostels and palaces along the Strand, taken over from abbots and bishops, descended to the Crown and its favourites.   Its pomps and powers kept their ancient place.   Pageants and arches still on great occasions decked St. Paul's and Temple Bar, the trained bands were exercised in the Finsbury Artillery garden, Lord Mayor and City companies processed the river in their barges.   Its traders were still massed in their mediaeval quarters, the goldsmiths in Cheapside or the booksellers in Paul's churchyard ; the Thames was its main thoroughfare, where Dekker heard the water-men cry :

> Oars, oars, oars, oars,
> To London hey, to London hey.

But time and transport had changed the City.   Its monasteries had gone ;   the Charter-house to make Sutton's new school, while the Black Friars' site now included a theatre.   The town had covered Holborn ; the green churchyard which Stow had known in Cornhill and hedgerows in Bishopsgate had disappeared ;   on the south side Southwark, where John Harvard was lately born, was teeming.   Royal palaces, ringing London round, took trade and fashion outwards, Greenwich and Oat-lands and Nonesuch, along with the houses of the new rich such as Gresham's at Osterley.   On the roads that bound all England to London came the carriers' waggons — rumbling over cobbles while Charles' Wain stood over the chimney — and dreading the footpads of Hounslow or Gad's Hill ;   but by the Civil War a post-horse system promised a weekly letter-post to all principal towns, a coach-rank stood in the Strand, and before the Restoration regular coach services ran to Southampton and Chester.   In vain royal proclamations tried to stop London growing, in vain the Puritan City fathers strove to banish the theatres, with their loose audiences and godless trumpets, to the suburbs or Bankside.   A new ' Globe ' replaced the one burned down during a performance of *Henry VIII*, when fire caught its thatched roof ;   its fellows on Bankside were the ' Rose ', the ' Swan ', and the ' Hope ' ;   there were soon to be the ' Red Bull ' in Clerkenwell and the ' Phoenix ' in Drury Lane.   A mass of rogues and paupers continued to flock towards the seat of wealth, to rendezvous in St. Paul's, and to prey on country gulls at Bartholomew's Fair.

In London and Westminster were accumulated all the layers of this civilization. Here was the loud criticism of government, from the theatre gibes at James I's Scottish accent to the Commons' attack on his Scottish policy, and here were the printers whose pamphlets called out the censorship of the High Commission. Before James died pamphlet and broadside were supplemented by the news-sheets of the Swedish and German wars, till the Civil War gave birth to a weekly press. Here worked and lived the capitalists whose support made or unmade successive ministers: Elizabeth's Thomas Gresham, or Edwin Sandys, leader of opposition in the Virginia Company; the East India Company was installed in Leadenhall Street. In the 'Devil Tavern' at Temple Bar, the 'Mermaid' in Bread Street, at the 'Sun' or 'Triple Tun', Shakespeare and Jonson, Beaumont and Herrick, spoke of life and letters, until under the Commonwealth taverns made room for the coffee-houses. The Inns of Court were at the height of their influence, full of the best character in England, disciplined by Coke and Calvinist preachers, producing gorgeous masques for the Court, flaring up in their ancient feud with the apprentices. Here, too, were the Londoners' great schools, Christ's Hospital and the Charterhouse, the Merchant Taylors' which had educated Marlowe, St. Paul's which educated Milton, and Westminster which under two great headmasters, Camden and Busby, had begun a magnificent life. In London were the heights and the depths. Here were the red-latticed haunts and stews of the suburbs, and all the common sights from the lions in the Tower to the lunatics at Bridewell, or Drake's *Golden Hind* now rotting at Deptford. Here also were Lord Arundel's collections of marbles, Charles I's pictures which the Commonwealth sold, and Robert Cotton's manuscripts whence came in a later time the British Museum. Here was the heart of the realm, though the blood coursed slowly to its extremities in the north and west, where dialect and custom and unchanging loyalties lingered for another century.

When Charles II, a man of this modern world, returned in 1660, men waited to receive him whose minds proved the end of the old order; Cowley and Dryden in whose hands English became the language of Addison and Swift, Muddiman the journalist in Monck's employment who was to found the *Gazette*, and Wren whose art was to stamp its character on a new capital. At last the Middle Ages were gone, with their binding cement of faith and order; in place of which had come London's sixty printing-houses, toleration in religion, and long strides towards *laisser-faire* in society. What would hold together this new scheme, and how would it answer Milton's prayer, 'let not England forget her precedence of teaching nations how to live'?

BOOK V

EQUILIBRIUM
1660–1760

CHAPTER I

THE REIGN OF CHARLES II: I. 1660–1667

I F Britain could settle down under Richard Cromwell, it meant a
constitutional monarchy, for the new Protector, though not without
a dignity of his own, had no powerful personality or weight with the
Army, having taken no active share in the wars. For that very reason he
was welcomed by the moderate Presbyterians and ' sober gentry ' whom
Monck recommended to him, and the Parliament he summoned, chosen
on the old electorate and franchise as before 1654, had a majority of
such men, many of whom would prefer the Stuarts to the soldiers.

Edward Hyde, already Charles II's chief minister, was clear that
restoration could not come about through Royalism unaided, nor
through foreign arms, which would be fatal, but only when the Puritan
factions became ' each other's executioners '. So it proved; Richard
fell a victim to the Army because the republicans would not stomach a
protectorate; the republic because it stood out in its dour way against
government by the sword; finally, the Army itself fell through a split
between its ' grandees ' and the rank and file, and because the forces in
Scotland and Ireland, together with the fleet, joined the civilians.

In this crumbling process a first stage ran from Oliver's death to
the dissolution of Richard's Parliament in April 1659. His own relations, Fleetwood and Desborough, began his destruction by surrendering to their officers' pressure that the Army should control its own
discipline and promotions; the republicans, Vane and Heselrige leading,
continued it, with attacks on Richard's veto and his ' lords ', and on the
Scottish and Irish members as government nominees. So, incited by
rejoicing Royalists, the factions turned on each other. If the Humble
Petition had been made by a ' forced ' Parliament, what then could be
said of ' Pride's purge ', and if, as some members continued, no Parliament had been free since war began, where could they stop short of the
monarchy? In any case a majority attacked the Army for illegalities,
paid no regard to their pay, and forbade officers to meet without leave
of Parliament. Both ' grandees ' and rank and file thereupon demanded
a dissolution from Richard, who gave way rather than renew civil war.

But the grandees, who hoped for a puppet Protectorate, were swept
away by a frenzy among the ranks and the preachers for the ' good old
cause ', with which Lambert adroitly associated himself, and in May
were compelled to recall the Rump, of whom never over seventy-six

were present, and to re-establish the Commonwealth. Now it was the army's turn to be disappointed. Vane, Heselrige, and Ludlow, high-minded and blind as ever, would not obey the swordsmen, packed the Council, and promoted or dismissed officers freely. Beyond agreeing on a dissolution for 1660, Parliament ignored the army's wish for new ' fundamentals ', held to the ideal of one Church as against sects, and flattered themselves they could restore the sovereign Commons of 1649.

Royalism proved incapable of seizing this golden chance. Neither France nor Spain, who were now making the Peace of the Pyrenees, would commit themselves to the exiles; there was still treachery, still disputes between a party for immediate action and ' the Knot ' who advised waiting until the army disintegrated. So that, when in August Sir George Booth rose in Cheshire, his fellow-Presbyterians hung back, doubting the sincerity of a Cavalier King's pledges, and Lambert swiftly overwhelmed this rebellion. This daring, attractive opportunist, and not the weeping, praying Fleetwood, was now the soldiers' favoured leader.

In short, not Royalism but the Army brought about the Restoration. Its petitions demanded military autonomy, a full measure of toleration, a purge of magistracies, and when Parliament, fired by messages from Monck in Scotland, in October cashiered Lambert, he marched on Westminster and expelled them, to set up a military Committee of Safety. This was the climax, and instantaneously the republic fell to pieces. While one section under Vane and Ludlow debated with the soldiers on new constitutions, another led by the resolute Heselrige persuaded the fleet and provincial garrisons to declare for Parliament, the City and the army in Ireland did the same. And all were cemented together by the commander in Scotland.

George Monck, a professional soldier who had in turn served the Dutch, the King, Protector, and Parliament, and of solid Devon stock, had all the English civilian's hatred of the ' slavery of a sword government '. As yet, though Charles had approached him, he simply stood for legal authority and, when he saw the Rump threatened by Lambert, wrote to Speaker Lenthall ' obedience is my great principle '. All November and December he kept his own course : lulled Lambert by negotiation, purged his officers, organized propaganda, arranged with the Scots gentry to keep the peace, and made contact with the commanders in Ireland, London clergy, and Fairfax, who could answer for Yorkshire.

In the last days of the year, hearing that the Army had collapsed and recalled the Rump, he left his camp at Coldstream and in February 1660 reached London. The King's agents had no notion which way ' this clouded soldier ' would jump. He found the Rump imprisoning or dismissing its enemies, but quite incorrigible, refusing to readmit

members ' secluded ' by Pride's purge or to allow the election even of
Royalists' sons, and expecting him to do their dirty work. On one side
lay the City, angered by trade depression and rioting against the
soldiery, backed by a flood of petitions for a free Parliament; on the
other, his own army, with its loathing of monarchy. To avoid civil war
he must throw the responsibility on a free Parliament, to get which he
must swamp the Rump by insisting on the admission of the ' secluded '
members. That done, on 16th March the Long Parliament at length
disappeared, and in the name of the keepers of the liberties of England
writs issued for another, for which Royalists were allowed to vote.

Only now did Monck agree to receive Charles' letters, and even so
the terms of restoration were uncertain. While the secluded members
tried to entrench their Presbyterian clergy, powerful Puritan politicians,
Holles and Ashley Cooper and Lady Carlisle included, were discussing
revival of the terms offered in 1648 to Charles I; even when the Convention met they attempted to unseat Royalists and to exclude all but
Puritan peers. But the incoming tide swept their resistance away.
Except in a few family seats the electors would not choose anti-
Royalist candidates, and when, during the elections, Lambert escaped
from the Tower, not a thousand men joined him; he was easily rounded
up; and it was clear that the military Commonwealth was dead. Yet
every day's delay was a danger, and that restoration came about
speedily, and without conditions, was due both to Monck and to the
policy directed by Hyde.

This policy had laid down that pledges must be avoided, and the
onus laid upon Parliament, though the ground was softened by bargaining with individuals. So, for example, one decisive influence had long
been secured, that of the Cromwellian admiral Montagu, later Lord
Sandwich, who brought over the fleet. Though Monck was in favour
of large concessions, he brushed aside the conditions the Presbyterian
magnates would have imposed, and, as he dared not wait for a public
treaty, accepted from Hyde's hands his own formula. The Declaration
of Breda, which Charles issued on the 4th April, held forth the extinction
of factions in ' a free parliament ', with whom he promised to legislate
for arrears of army pay and for tender consciences, for any exceptions
to a general pardon and the thorny question of Cavaliers' lands.

On these terms the Convention declared the ancient government
restored, and on the 29th May, his thirtieth birthday, Charles II passed
on Blackheath through the army which had taken his father's life, and
by streets tumultuous with bells and bonfires reached Whitehall.

The Restoration was thus a transaction between Royalists and
Puritans against revolution and the Army, and a restoration rather of
Parliament than the King. Charles inherited the foreign and colonial
policy of Oliver, his Council included not Hyde only (henceforth Lord

Clarendon), Ormonde, the Treasurer Southampton and Charles I's Secretary Nicolas, but Monck, Montagu, and Ashley Cooper. Thurloe drew up advices for Clarendon on foreign alliances; George Downing kept the Hague embassy which Cromwell had given him. For many such appointments, as in local government also, there was this compelling reason, that the exiles had nothing like the ability or experience of the men who had controlled and centralized government under the usurper. But even in the largest instance the moderates who controlled the settlement showed their power. Henry Cromwell lived untouched, popular as ever with many Royalists; and though Richard had to go abroad, he returned during Charles' reign, to live obscurely but peacefully till 1712.

What was restored was thus not the prerogative but the normal development of the monarchy. Nothing could bring Crown, Lords, and Church back to the position they had held before their ten years' abolition. New business interests were much more powerful, eager in colonial ventures, resentful of government restrictions in industry, giving to foreign policy a sharper edge with their markets and tariffs.

It was to Clarendon that the country chiefly owed this peaceful restoration, for he knew better what must and could be done than those who, calling themselves ' the loyal party ', asked an eye for an eye, and the turning out of every Puritan. His aim was to restore government to its situation in 1641, when he had been a progressive Royalist; in short, to Elizabeth's monarchy, though stripped of abuses like Star Chamber or ship-money. His mind, however, was a rigid one, his body worn out by strains of work and crippling gout, and he was incapable of understanding a new age. His conservatism saw the keystone of government in the Privy Council, though by this date it was an over-centralized dilatory machine, which in days of more business and specialized departments soon made chaos. For him the safeguards of common law and the rôle of the Commons, confined to the production of taxes and legislation, were enough; forgetting that the House was full of men who for a generation had been a sovereign body, appointing councillors and directing policy through their committees, and blind to the new channels of opinion in newspapers and coffee-houses. Even the ablest younger Royalists, George Savile later marquis of Halifax or Pepys' friend William Coventry, were to him suspect.

But this lonely, prematurely ageing, figure had high virtues. He hated violence, he reverenced the law and the pledged word; from the exile onwards he resisted the evil influence of Henrietta Maria's group, led by Jermyn, who would make her children Catholics and sell English liberty of action for French money; that, also, of the vile second Duke of Buckingham, whose amusing gifts, Yorkshire property, and marriage with Fairfax's daughter gave him a footing in several camps. True, Clarendon enjoyed wealth, his daughter Anne's marriage to the Duke of

York increased his arrogance, and he was too proud of his own righteousness. But if he dreamed, it was an honourable dream, of ' the good old
frame of government ' and a nation brought back to ' its old good
humour ', and when he fell, it was through his virtue as much as his
faults.

At the opposite pole stood the King, who in these early years left
the drudgery to his minister but kept the last word, and whose character
determined history long after Clarendon's fall. War and exile had
battered him. A roué even as a boy, he had been forced to sacrifice
loyalties like those of Montrose, he had often been penniless, he became
untrustworthy and ungrateful and irreligious, without belief in men's
honour or women's chastity. Yet the grandson of Henry of Navarre had
royal gifts, which sometimes made him, as he claimed, ' the man of his
people '.

For he was, as one of his later councillors wrote, ' both merry and
merciful ', inclined to let people alone just as he loved his own ease,
convinced that God would not damn a man for a little pleasure. His
repeated advances towards religious toleration, proved for instance in
regard to the Quakers, came rather from this temperament and his
political sense than from any Catholic zeal. Though happier with
Catholics or sceptics than with average Englishmen, there is no proof of
a conversion until his death-bed ; yet he openly thought it was the best
religion for a monarchy, and often hinted to Rome that in return for
money he would consider the question.

In spite of his vices, he could hold his own in most companies,
could work hard, especially in foreign affairs, and was the most accessible
of kings. For the Navy he had a passion, with some intimate
knowledge of shipbuilding, and made real sacrifices for it ; he was
interested in trade and colonization, dabbled in chemistry and was,
in short, a modern man. He prized his prerogatives but, having a more
elastic mind than Clarendon, would work for them through the Commons
and accepted the necessity of the press. One other motive could call out
his reserve of resolution, and that was his family affection, for he
honoured his father's memory, always supported his brother James,
whose stupidity he deplored, was led into his most fatal course by love
for his sister Henrietta, and much swayed in latter years by Monmouth,
his illegitimate son. On the whole, the danger he might bring on his
people came not so much from any dark design as from the fact that
he never appreciated and, off the sea, hardly ever met their average
opinion.

King and minister faithfully co-operated to carry through the urgent
tasks of the hour. The Convention, having declared itself a legal Parliament, dealt with the pledges given at Breda. Against the regicides,
Presbyterians and Cavaliers were equally bitter, and it required all the

King's effort to carry through a reasonable act of Oblivion. Ultimately ten regicides were executed in 1660, while three more were kidnapped in Holland and executed in 1662; in which year also suffered one who was not a regicide, but of whom Charles wrote that he was ' too danger-ous to let live ', Sir Henry Vane. These fourteen lives requited two civil wars; of other leaders, Lambert and Heselrige died as life prisoners, Ludlow and one regicide group lived as exiles in Switzerland, a few more clustered in New England.

Though the Commonwealth's laws were deemed null and void, Clarendon made no break in the legal order. Not only did he continue several Puritan judges in office, but an Act confirmed the Common-wealth's judicial proceedings, which in itself solved the burning question of landed property. Crown land, Church land, and estates outright confiscated were restored, but in the much more common case where a Royalist had been forced to sell, in order to ' compound ' for a crushing fine, he got no remedy. So, to the bitter indignation of his party, Clarendon allowed a vast mass of property to remain in Puritan hands.

Most urgent of all was it to disband the Army, which caused (a Secretary of State wrote) ' a perpetual trembling in the nation ', and ruined the finances. By 1661 nearly the whole, 35,000 men, had dis-appeared, paid in full, and without disorder, taking their discipline into civil life and making a strong element in the future Whig party. Charles merely kept up some of those raised in exile to form his guards, together with the Coldstream regiment taken from Monck's army, and the garrison of Dunkirk.

This paid for, the Convention arranged a revenue for Charles' life, estimated to bring in £1,200,000 a year. Since they confirmed a Long Parliament bill abolishing the Court of Wards and swept away the feudal dues, and since Crown lands never recovered their old level, this income mainly depended on the customs and excise. But for many years it never brought in over £800,000, Parliament did nothing for Charles I's debts or those of the exile, and the Crown's poverty, which in war would mean bankruptcy, coloured the entire reign.

There was another pledge of Breda which the Convention failed to honour: that for religious toleration. Though Restoration necessarily implied some sort of government by bishops, Charles would prefer tolerance, Presbyterians were strong in the Commons, and all that Clarendon dared to hope was that the Church might ' by degrees recover what could not be had at once '. As a temporary measure the King issued the Worcester House declaration in October, which associ-ated presbyters with bishops, waived the obligatory use of the surplice, and planned a synod to revise the prayer-book; Puritan leaders received offers of bishoprics and deaneries; Reynolds accepted the see of Norwich. But when an effort was made in the Convention to make this settlement permanent, it was defeated by jealousies between Presbyterians and Independents as much as by the King's disgust at their anti-Romanism, and to some extent by the feeling that this should be left to a regularly elected parliament.

With the new year of 1661, after the Convention was dissolved, the atmosphere changed; thousands watched the regicides die and Cromwell's bones cast out of the Abbey, saw all the royal family return, prepared for the coronation, and were terrified by armed Anabaptists (Venner's plot) attacking the guards and proclaiming the kingdom of Christ. In such an air of excited revenge the elections were held, resulting in the Cavalier Parliament whose life was to last till 1678.

Before its work seriously began, the Savoy conference met, between bishops and Puritans, and parted without effect. Sheldon, bishop of London, who soon followed the aged Juxon at Canterbury, had a will of iron and a rigid platform; the Church would stand on the law as it had been in 1641, secure in the support of Cavalier patrons and magistrates who had already begun to turn out ' intruders '. Not over fifty Puritans were returned to the new Parliament, which instantly plunged into reaction; goaded on by petitions from all who had lost relations, wealth, and limbs in the royal service, and kept at fever-heat over the next few years by rumours, true and false, of plots among Cromwellian soldiers, Quakers, and conventicles. During 1661–2 they passed a treason Act forbidding criticism of the King's estate, a militia Act giving sole control of the forces to the Crown, an Act against petitions when signed by more than twenty persons, Acts to restore bishops and Church courts (though not High Commission), together with a licensing Act, setting up a censorship of books and printing. Their Corporation Act confined municipal government to those who would take the Church sacrament and, like the militia Act, compelled an oath against any right of resistance to the established government.

Not Clarendon but the Commons and the bishops were authors of the so-called ' Clarendon code '. The Act of Uniformity of 1662 imposed a prayer-book revised, and made more anti-Calvinist, by Convocation; henceforth every minister must receive ordination from a bishop and, with schoolmasters too, take an oath of non-resistance. While King and Lords vainly suggested milder terms, with financial provision for those ejected, Clarendon, who feared rebellion, joined Monck in trying to suspend execution of the Act. But Sheldon's fierce temper carried the day. In August, on what they called ' black St. Bartholomew's day ', at least fifteen hundred ministers gave up their livings, and perhaps another four hundred had been squeezed out before.

This fanatical churchmanship became the binding cement of the Cavaliers, and was soon linked up with the feud between Clarendon and

his rivals. In the winter of 1662–3 the King, encouraged by the
Catholic Bristol, Arlington, and the former Puritan Ashley Cooper,
invited Parliament to approve his ' inherent ' power of dispensing with
penalties, for ' the peace of our dominions '. Though he undertook to
keep Catholics out of office, many Dissenters opposed this indulgence,
rather than take sides with what Sheldon called ' the whore of
Babylon ' ; the Commons told Charles he was trying to establish schism
and used their money-power to make him withdraw. Their bitterness continued in the Conventicle Act of 1664, forbidding religious
meetings where five persons outside the family were present, and in the
Five Mile Act of 1665, prohibiting the residence of Nonconformist
ministers and teachers within five miles of a corporate town, unless they
had taken oaths against any alteration of Church and State. So the
statute-book perpetuated the civil war, in the spirit in which new
churches were being dedicated to Charles the Martyr, which made one
of the kindliest of officials tell the Commons he would never receive
' the blood of my Saviour from the hand that stinks with the blood of
my master '.

Happily the letter of the law was worse than its practice. Persecution there was, of Quakers in particular, while Bunyan was twelve years
in jail, and a vile crop of fines and informers flourished. But it varied
from one diocese, even from one magistrate, to another, sprouting again
in times of excitement. Puritan peers and gentry insisted on keeping
their family chaplains or hearing their famous preachers, Manton or
Calamy or Howe, John Owen himself ministered to Fleetwood at Stoke
Newington, and bishops told Sheldon that justices and juries would not
convict. As the Cavalier heyday passed, many forces combined to
reduce persecution ; the notorious disinclination of the King and most
of his ministers, the increasing strength of the broad churchmen and
rationalists, a conviction that persecution damaged trade, and, finally, a
realization that all Protestants had a common enemy in Louis XIV.

Such feelings affected even the Cavalier Parliament, which, however
rancorous against the Puritan, had not the least intention of diminishing
its own power ; moreover, before its seventeen years ended, 300 seats
changed their members. Its constitutional outlook was as firm as that
of any of its predecessors. Three successive ministries fell before its
threat of impeachment ; it destroyed two prerogative declarations of
indulgence. The Commons refused to the King a right of creating
new seats, and their resolutions of 1670–71 permanently did away with
the Lords' right to amend a money bill. Though they repealed the
triennial Act of 1641 in so far as it set up automatic machinery, their
measure of 1664 left intact the triennial principle ; their distrust showed
itself in keeping Charles short of funds, in appropriating supply, and
examining the war departments' accounts.

While Clarendon would never accept such 'usurpations' and cut their sessions short, others realized that Parliament must be manipulated through a ministerial party. His isolation increased. Ormonde had gone back to govern Ireland, Southampton was ailing, Nicolas soon had to surrender his secretaryship to the King's friend Arlington. Lauderdale, representing the Presbyterian politicians whom Clarendon most detested, replaced his nominee Middleton in Scotland; Buckingham's group in the House included notable younger Cavaliers in Osborne and Seymour. Others like Arlington's client Clifford attacked him from the King's angle, some like Ashley from sympathy with Dissent, and some, notably the able William Coventry, because administration was breaking down. Disliked by both reactionaries and Puritans, his old-fashioned quality brought him into collision with the Commons, where a mercantile element insisted on excluding Scotland and Ireland from colonial trade, and where landlords ruthlessly kept Irish cattle out of the English market. Charles was weary of this strife and of the old man's lectures, angry because he ignored his mistress Lady Castlemaine, indignant at the failure of his own toleration schemes. All his ministers were to find out, as one of them wrote, that ' Charles Stuart would be bribed against the king ', but in this case the King was being told by serious politicians that he would never get a united people and a better revenue till Clarendon disappeared. And the end came from the quarter of his worst failure, in foreign affairs.

Peace for the sake of recovery was the first thought of his government, and it seemed assured, in the north by the peace of Oliva and the death of the warlike Charles X, and southward by the peace of the Pyrenees. Soon, however, it became clear that the marriage of Louis XIV to a Spanish Infanta was being used to stake his claim on the Spanish succession, and that the Polish succession would revive the feuds of the north. Nor could Charles stand apart from Europe; he must marry, restore commerce by treaties, and perhaps get a promise of help against Puritan rebellion. Such arguments brought him in 1661 back to the general policy bequeathed by Cromwell. Negotiation showed the difficulty of continuing friends with Holland; Spain stoutly refused to drop her claims on Jamaica and Dunkirk, or the war she had long been waging against Portugal. The Portuguese, on the other hand, offered a dazzling bargain, — the hand of Catherine of Braganza, which mattered little, but with a dowry of over £300,000, commercial advantages, Bombay and Tangier. If it involved sending our troops to defend Portugal and more tension with the Dutch, who had taken half the Portuguese Empire, it brought a blessing and subsidy from France, a new understanding strengthened by the marriage of Louis XIV's brother Orleans to Charles' sister Henrietta, and in 1662 by the sale to France of Dunkirk. Once again English poverty, and a price of

5 million livres, settled the issue, to the indignation of all Cromwellians and Protestant Europe. Though Monck and Sandwich approved of getting rid of a costly garrison and a bad harbour, the people never forgave Clarendon, and if their reasoning was false, as they pointed to his palace in St. James' as ' Dunkirk House ', their instinct was not unjust. Fears of Puritan conspiracy and for his own position induced him to stake everything on the French alliance, and a promise of French troops in case of need.

Many things were always drawing Charles II towards France, — admiration for a great monarchy, Catholic leanings, pressure from his mother and his beloved sister Henrietta; much, too, could be said for reasoning that the French army was less dangerous to us than the Dutch fleet, or that Britain's opportunity lay in taking a share of the dying Spanish Empire. Despite all this the French alliance made no progress. Inspired by the great Colbert, they were raising their tariffs and redoubling overseas activity; claimed restoration of Cromwell's conquest in Acadia, attacked our settlers in the West Indies, and made a treaty with Holland which threatened Charles' proud claim to be sovereign of the narrow seas. For twelve years from 1662 onwards the director of foreign policy under the King was Arlington, whose sympathies were Spanish, who knew Europe much better than his colleagues, and whose marriage to a lady of the house of Orange gave him another outlook. Under him and his under-secretary Williamson the secretary's office was overhauled, its archives put in order and the Gazette established; and he it was who first employed some men of mark, such as William Temple and Sidney Godolphin. In a negative way no influence was to be greater than his on the next decade. For though he loved power and wealth, and though he lived a sceptic and died a Catholic, the root of the matter was in this odd, timorous man. For knowledge and timidity combined to make him first resist the King's dangerous excursions in foreign affairs, and finally to bring them to an end.

To construct an anti-French entente was a work of enormous difficulty. The Hapsburgs were on ill terms with each other. Spain would not hear of surrendering Portugal, her finances were bankrupt, her Belgian province was defenceless. Germany was soaked with French money, while its wisest prince, the Elector of Brandenburg, loathed the Hapsburgs and dreaded the Swedes who disputed his influence in Poland. Sweden had long been a French client and nourished a blazing hatred of Denmark. Although, then, there were influences in Europe hostile to France, and among them the Emperor Leopold and his best diplomatist Lisola, and the great Elector, a dozen jealousies divided them, not to mention the tension between Protestant and Catholic. Finally, one necessary member of such an entente stood aloof, Holland, between whom and Great Britain there broke out in 1664 a long-expected and bitter war.

To this war, which was to destroy him, Clarendon was opposed, as originally was the King, but its causes were greater than any individual and not limited to one people. To the English the Orange matter was a detail; Charles' sister Mary died in 1660, leaving young William III to his guardianship, while the Dutch repealed their Act of Seclusion and the question of the prince's authority would not for some years arise. To Dutch republican feeling, however, it transcended every other, for an Orange restoration would destroy their power. Of this the incarnation was the great John de Witt, grand pensionary of the State of Holland, who was filled with suspicion and some contempt of everything proceeding from England, and who against the Orange cause would look towards France, in whom he recognized the best market for his country, and with whom the future of the Spanish Netherlands must be arranged.

But the root lay in the causes which had already caused war with Cromwell. The treaty of 1654 had settled nothing essential, the two East India Companies still collided, the Dutch had never surrendered Pulo Run, English settlers overflowed into the territory of New Amsterdam. War had nearly broken out again under Cromwell; the Convention defiantly repeated his Navigation Act; while to his Cavalier successor the ex-Secretary Thurloe handed on an overwhelming note, declaring that Dutch maxims of trade and Dutch monopoly threatened our very existence. A new treaty was painfully achieved in 1662, but again only by slurring over the burning questions. So the story went on, in clamours from the Council of Trade that only war could save our fisheries, from the East that Dutch contracts with native rajahs made trade impossible, in protests from the chartered companies and the Commons. There were rumours of Puritan exiles conspiring on Dutch soil, and complaints of unfair competition while the seeds of rival empires sprang to life. In western India the Dutch eliminated the Portuguese factories except Goa. New England called for a campaign against New Amsterdam, which separated her from the southern colonies and made the Navigation Act unworkable, and in August 1664 an expedition took possession, rechristening it New York. This armed violence was at its worst on the Gold Coast, where the title-deeds of every factory were in dispute, and where government was disputed between slave-selling tribes. After many armed reprisals, at the end of the same year the Dutch made war certain by sending out Admiral Ruyter, who recaptured almost the whole Gold Coast and then crossed the Atlantic to attempt New York. As in so many wars, each side believed that the other would yield, such always being the view of Downing, our ambassador at the Hague, who was confident that what had paid under Cromwell would pay again.

In England it began as a popular war amid great enthusiasm of the seafaring classes, and on the whole the English fleet showed itself superior. In 1665 Sandwich failed badly in an effort to seize a rich convoy in the neutral Norwegian harbour of Bergen, but the Duke of York defeated a Dutch fleet off Lowestoft with great loss. In 1666 an ill-judged division of the fleet left Monck much outnumbered, to fight alone a murderous four days' battle in the Downs in June; in July and August, however, he and Rupert drove the enemy to their harbours. Such fighting between well-matched navies was very severe, so that we lost thirty-nine flag officers in eighteen months; yet the leadership was good in the main, while the tactics, the close-hauled line ahead, gunnery, and initiative showed how much the Navy had advanced. But even success could not save a people unnerved and a discredited ministry.

Twice the hand of God visited England with enormous calamity. In May 1665 began the Great Plague, which that year killed 68,000 Londoners alone, spreading next year to the provinces. Colchester, for instance, lost nearly 5000 people, and at Portsmouth crows pecked at graves outside the dockyard. While Parliament moved to Oxford and the Court to Salisbury, Monck and archbishop Sheldon held on in London; a wilderness of closed houses, of doors marked with the red cross and inscribed, ' Lord have mercy on us ', bells ringing for carts to take away the dead, and torchlight burials. Trade, disorganized by plague and half-destroyed by war, had not recovered, when, in September 1666, the Great Fire destroyed old London. Breaking out in the small hours in Pudding Lane, east of London Bridge, after a long drought and fanned by an easterly gale it leapt across this city of lath and timber houses, with its lanes so narrow that a coach could hardly pass under the overhanging gables. For four days it burned, first the riverside and bridges, then northward to Cornhill and the Royal Exchange, and westward to Blackfriars; by the third day it had demolished Cheapside, St. Paul's, Fleet Street, up to the Inner Temple, and so to Newgate. Amid an endless roar of falling walls and churches, under a pall of smoking ashes that coloured the sunset even at Oxford, the people of London fled by boat, or camped out in Moorfields and the Highgate hills. Thirteen thousand houses were destroyed and eighty-four churches, together with the customs administration, the Post Office, and the reserves of the cloth trade; nothing but shipping was as yet covered by insurance, and £60,000 of rents vanished. From a ruined city, where you could stand in Cheapside and see the river, and which a man from the Borders compared to the heaped grey stones of his Westmorland fells, members of Parliament stumbled to Westminster over the hot ashes, with wild talk of a plot by Papists and Frenchmen.

Their hearts were hot within them also. They had begun war with a grant of £2½ millions, given for three years but which disappeared in one, and in granting £1¼ millions more they earmarked it for the war. After the fire they gave nearly £2 millions again, raising taxation to Cromwell's highest level, but demanded the production of all accounts. Sooner than give way, Charles prorogued Parliament; Buckingham's group led the opposition, and he was dismissed. Credit was unobtainable, seamen's pay was months overdue, lack of convoy cut off London's coal supply, though the Thames was full of ice. Only the pressgang kept up our crews, there was much desertion, and much sympathy for the Dutch among Puritans, most of all in Scotland, where this November a Covenanters' rebellion had to be crushed by force. Catholic Ireland was being fomented by the French, who had now joined Holland against us.

For our diplomacy had failed. We could make no progress in patching up peace between Spain and Portugal. The Danes were true to their Dutch alliance, neutrality was all we could obtain from Sweden. Our one ally, the Bishop of Munster, did nothing but swallow money and was driven to surrender, especially by the Great Elector, who believed in Holland as the bulwark of his own dearest interests, Protestantism and resistance to France. As for Louis XIV, he had tried to mediate, but when both combatants were obstinate he preferred to keep his treaty obligation to Holland; even if the Dutch turned cold, a prolonged war would weaken both the maritime powers. While, then, his squadron gave some slight assistance to Holland, his menaces kept off every ally from England. Arlington's endeavour to turn this into a war against France by exploiting the fear of France in every quarter: Protestant feeling, or Orange conspiracy, all alike broke down. De Witt would not be separated from France, and while the Dutch took our settlement in Guiana, the French seized St. Kitts, Antigua, and Montserrat.

Bankrupt, broken into factions, without allies, King and Cabinet determined on peace; peace on almost any terms, because men said Clarendon dared not come before a Parliament. The French faction, Clarendon among them, persuaded Charles to put himself in the hands of Louis, and in April 1667 a treaty was signed whereby France restored her West Indian conquests in return for our promise of neutrality for a year in her war with Spain. On the strength of assurances that the French would bring Holland to reason, and driven by financial ruin, our government took the fatal decision of laying up our fighting ships, and restricting the war to protection of commerce.

Terrible disaster followed. While the peace conference opened, in May the French armies invaded Belgium, but with iron nerve de Witt preferred to let that danger wait until he had forced England to peace. In June a Dutch squadron entered the Thames, bombarded Sheerness, and broke through to Chatham; their fire-ships destroyed half the fleet, the flag-ship *Royal Charles* was towed away as a prize. Once again Monck was called to the post of danger, but he could do nothing with unmanned guns, no ammunition, and dockyards rotten with corruption. And while men spoke of Oliver's days in sorrow, and the guns were heard at London Bridge, there was a run on the banks, placards were posted against Clarendon and ' Dunkirk, Tangier, and a barren Queen ', there were howls against Popery and meetings of the Puritan lords.

In July peace was signed at Breda. France restored her West Indies conquests in return for Acadia. England kept New York, New Jersey, and Delaware; the Dutch retained all West Africa except Cape Coast Castle, besides Pulo Run and Guiana. On the question of saluting the flag we reduced our claim to the Channel alone, while the Navigation Act was amended to allow Holland to re-export the products of Germany and Belgium.

This was an ignominious peace, and the country demanded a victim. Not entirely unjustly the lot fell upon Clarendon who, when the Dutch were in the Medway, had resisted the calling of Parliament. Spurred on by the leaders in the Commons, in August Charles dismissed him, telling Ormonde that otherwise he could not ' do those things with the parliament that must be done '. In the autumn he was impeached, on charges the details of which were absurdly untrue, but with the backing of an almost unanimous Parliament, and of the countries opposed to France; on the King's pressure he fled to Normandy, followed by a bill to banish him for life. He lived an exile till he died in 1674, revising and completing his great *History*, wherein he handed down to generations of conservative England his happier achievements, — the revival of Church and State on the basis of the law, in a lenient restoration.

CONTEMPORARY DATES

<table>
<tr><td>1661</td><td>Death of Mazarin; rise of Lionne, Louvois, and Colbert in Louis XIV's councils.</td></tr>
<tr><td>1662</td><td>Building begins at Versailles.</td></tr>
<tr><td>1664</td><td>Defeat of the Turks at St. Gotthard.</td></tr>
<tr><td>1665</td><td>Foundation of the London Gazette.</td></tr>
<tr><td></td><td>–1700. Reign of Charles II of Spain.</td></tr>
<tr><td>1666</td><td>Newton discovers law of gravitation.</td></tr>
<tr><td>1667</td><td>Milton's Paradise Lost, and first important works by Racine and Leibniz.</td></tr>
<tr><td>1668</td><td>Peace of Aix-la-Chapelle, and secret treaty between France and the Emperor Leopold.</td></tr>
<tr><td>1669</td><td>Fall of Crete to the Turks. Death of Rembrandt.</td></tr>
<tr><td>1670</td><td>Hungarian conspiracy against the Hapsburgs. Locke drafts a constitution for Carolina.</td></tr>
</table>

1672   Murder of John de Witt.

1673   The Hapsburgs join in the Dutch resistance to France.
      Frontenac becomes governor of Quebec.

1674   The Mahrattas under Sivaji declare themselves independent of
      the Moguls.
      Murillo painting at Seville.
      –1696. John Sobieski, King of Poland.

1675   Turenne killed on the Rhine.
      Prussian victory over the Swedes at Fehrbellin.

1676   Ruyter killed in battle with the French.

1677   Publication of Spinoza's *Ethics*, and his death.
      Racine, *Phèdre*.

1678   Peace of Nimwegen.
      Bunyan's *Pilgrim's Progress*.
      La Salle exploring the great Lakes.

1679–1726   Maximilian II, Elector of Bavaria.

1680   Kneller succeeds Lely as Court painter.

1681   French seizure of Strasbourg.
      Founding of Pennsylvania.
      Dryden, *Absalom and Achitophel*.

1682   Declaration of Gallican liberties against Rome.

1683   Sobieski relieves Vienna.
      Louis XIV marries Madame de Maintenon.
      Dampier begins his voyages.

1684   Locke expelled from Oxford.
      Truce of Ratisbon ; France retains Luxemburg.

1685   Revocation of the Edict of Nantes.

CHAPTER II

THE REIGN OF CHARLES II: II. 1667-1685

CLARENDON'S fall left the King face to face with the Commons, and the result was memorable. A period of six years in which personal government reached its height ended in 1673 with the triumph of Parliament, and the deepening of responsible government by the beginnings of organized party.

They were squalid and dangerous years. The King was in his lowest stage of vice, and York much the same, while before 1669 he became a Catholic. Of the Cabinet or ' Cabal ' (which the initial letters of the five leading ministers chanced to spell), no other King would have allowed such influence to a man so empty-headed as Buckingham. Two of the others were to show that power or revenge could make them criminal; Lauderdale, who would follow the King in any course demanded and trampled on everything that Scotsmen prized, and Ashley, now Lord Shaftesbury, a man of supreme ability, intellectually a convinced champion of toleration and with a real grasp of administration, especially of its economic aspect, but determined to be high on the winning side, and therefore equally ready to bring the King plans for his divorce, or to play on the passions of the mob. Clifford was only a fiery Cavalier, of upright character though no parliamentary gifts, interested in religion, and pining for another Dutch war. Only Arlington had in his luxurious soul the calibre of a statesman, with some realization of what England could do in Europe and what the King dare not do in politics. Most of the minor ministers were representative Englishmen and several were ex-Cromwellians, but the government rocked on its base, because the King was weak, on ill terms with his brother, and so gave full play to the mortal hatred between Arlington and Buckingham.

With, or soon after, Clarendon ended others of his régime. Monck's death removed a national figure, Ormonde was jockeyed out of his Irish lieutenancy, Sheldon and the bishops were out of favour, since the King pressed on his notion of toleration. Only the Commons showed themselves unchanged. They angrily refused a bill for ' comprehension ' in religion, passed another still more savage Conventicle Act, and were increasingly suspicious of Papists. But though these Cavaliers would persecute their Puritan rivals, there was a deeper line in politics, of the ' country ' against the Court. Session after session they enquired who

had divided the fleet or left Chatham defenceless, threw out officials, or
pressed investigation into the King's accounts. He was now £2 millions
in debt, they were jealous with supply, and stood much on their privileges. So that, although they were broken into factions and individuals
were bribed, ministers feared them and called them as little as they
dared; until in April 1671 they were prorogued for nearly two years.
This was because the King had now engaged his Cabinet in a secret
design.

Within a year of the peace at Breda Arlington's diplomacy achieved
several seeming triumphs; an important commercial agreement with
Spain, peace between Spain and Portugal, the famous Triple Alliance
between Britain, Holland, and Sweden, and the peace of Aix-la-
Chapelle which stopped Louis XIV's war against Spain. But this
triumph was very deceptive. The Cabinet did not instruct William
Temple to make the Triple Alliance in January 1668 out of love for
Holland but out of fear of a Franco-Dutch understanding, which might
ruin our trade and give our rivals power over the Spanish Low Countries
and colonies; moreover, they came to it only after ascertaining that
Spain could not finance a fight, and that the terms which Louis XIV
would offer for a joint war against Holland were lower than they could
accept. And though de Witt feared France, French help was invaluable
to him in the measures he was taking to keep the Prince of Orange out of
power. He distrusted England from the bottom of his heart, he thought
Spanish power in the north was doomed, and it seemed easier to let
Louis take the fraction of Belgian territory with which he announced he
would be content. When he made the Triple Alliance, he therefore
viewed it as only a corrective in the balance of power; its greatest
attraction for him perhaps consisting in an English concession on the
disputed point of contraband.

The first part of this treaty was a mere defensive alliance, but by the
second the allies agreed to force on both France and Spain the terms
which Louis had once offered. There was no more talk of enforcing
the renunciation he had once sworn to, of his wife's claim on the
Spanish succession, and de Witt made it clear that, so long as war did
not engulf Belgium, he did not care what happened to Spain elsewhere.
Having thus gained a strong line of Belgian fortresses, Louis made peace
in April, and had already signed a secret treaty with the Emperor
for a partition of the Spanish dominions if their infant King died.
In substance, then, the alliance was an empty framework, for the third
partner, Sweden, had to be won over by subsidies which were still to
be collected from a bankrupt Spain, yet the framework might be filled
if Arlington could keep both Charles II and the Dutch in the scheme
to which his own instincts drew him.

It was not to be so, and within two years plans were laid for the third

Dutch war. Material for it could never be lacking, for our East India Company protested against the commercial terms arranged by Temple, and the old discussions began again on blockade and the flag. Revenge for the humiliation of Chatham carried away many politicians, and tempted the King. The Dutch attitude was stiff, nor did they show any wish to bring the Hapsburgs into a wider league; which told against them when, as a pro-Dutch Cabinet minister in England wrote, England was undergoing ' the greatest temptations that ever were applied to princes '. For Louis XIV had decided that, for his future plans, he must break Holland who had betrayed his friendship, and sent his ablest envoy to win over Charles and convert Arlington.

Until his deathbed Charles II managed to live without the Catholic faith, yet Catholicism touched both his affection and political appetite. His sister Henrietta and his brother and heir, Lady Castlemaine and the Queen, all of them were Catholic. It was the faith of kings, and it seemed the winning faith, for the great Turenne had just abandoned the Huguenot religion to which he was born, and German Protestantism seemed to be collapsing. It was the faith of some of his most loyal subjects, and might it not be possible to frame a policy with all the maximum advantages; religious harmony in England, French money to save him from bankruptcy, punishment of Holland and yet protection of his nephew Orange, Colonial markets, and safety for Belgium? Spurred on by his sister, he began a secret correspondence in 1668; apart from mere agents, York was the only Catholic in whom he confided, neither Clifford nor Arlington having yet been converted.

To make Arlington a political convert was more difficult and months of negotiation followed, in which the English showed immense jealousy of French sea-power, actually asking that England might receive Ostend, Minorca, and Spanish America, if France acquired territories by the King of Spain's death. In May 1670, a month before her sudden death, Madame herself came to England to witness the signing of the memorable treaty of Dover; the terms of which showed Charles' hesitancy and limited objectives. They stipulated that, at a time named by himself, he would declare his conversion to the true Church, for which contingency France would provide 2 million livres within the next six months and, if required, 6000 troops. Only after this conversion took place would France fix the date for beginning war upon Holland, in which York should command the allied fleet and England receive a subsidy of £3 millions a year. From this conquest England should receive Walcheren and the ports commanding the Scheldt; Orange's interests should be safeguarded. Louis promised never to attack Spain, but if on the Spanish King's death he acquired ' fresh claims ', England would co-operate, which Charles intimated was to mean Ostend and the Indies.

But in June Madame died of consumption, and the full scheme, which contemporaries rightly associated with her, soon perished also. To carry his Council and to humour Parliament, Charles confided the secret, except its Catholic part, to his Protestant ministers, which of course involved giving a priority, as the French had always wished, to the war over ' Catholicity '. In a second treaty, of December, drawn up for the benefit of Buckingham and Ashley, the spring of 1672 was fixed for the outbreak, two more seaports being added to our proposed gains, while Charles masked the ' Catholic ' subsidy by adding it to the payment for the war. If he had ever seriously meant the Catholic design, certainly he dropped it now, putting off on various pretexts the proposals to the Papacy which the French urged, and which the ardent Clifford pressed. Any thought of making the country Catholic by force of arms had, indeed, never occurred to the wildest of his advisers, and the anti-Catholic frenzy of the Commons convinced him the whole was a folly.

Yet the secret treaty, charged with such black guilt in an English King, was to be the nemesis of his life; putting him at the mercy both of Louis XIV and the Whig Opposition. For by 1671 its secrecy had nearly gone, angry squires hearing from foreign ambassadors and Buckingham's loose tongue of a secret treaty, with rumours of French troops and Popery.

If Spain had been cordial or if Holland could be browbeaten into surrender, Charles and Arlington might even now have retreated, and anxiously they tried to make Spain believe they would protect her. But a war-party, York and Clifford and Ashley (now earl of Shaftesbury) included, predominated, while both French determination and fears of a French-Dutch settlement to the injury of his nephew pushed the King on. In March 1672 an attack without warning on a Dutch convoy began what Arlington, for one, hoped would be ' a short war '.

Short it was to be, though not in the sense he meant. After conversations with Dissenting ministers Charles combined his declaration of war with a Declaration of Indulgence, in virtue of his ' supreme power ' over the Church, suspending penalties against Protestant Dissenters and allowing Catholics to worship in their houses. Within a year he licensed some fifteen hundred Dissenting preachers and released many Quakers. Yet many Dissenters boggled at a liberty that extended to Papists, while the Indulgence threatened the Cavaliers and challenged many acts of Parliament, and meantime a ' stop ' at the Exchequer shook credit by suspending payment of interest to the bankers on their advances to government. In Scotland, Lauderdale had raised a new army, carried the King's supremacy over the Kirk, and issued another Indulgence; and since Ormonde's fall it was suspected that Popery was being officially favoured in Ireland. Though Parliament was not allowed to meet, everywhere men heard of French money being stored in the Tower; that the Triple Alliance was broken, that York had ceased to attend church, and that his wife, Anne Hyde, had died a Catholic.

Nothing could have saved government but success in war, and that failed them. Taking the initiative, Ruyter surprised York's fleet in Sole Bay, and after a desperate fight, in which Sandwich was killed, crippled the English design to land an army in Zeeland; which bad storms and his defensive strategy prevented for the rest of the year. Even more alarming was the success of France. With great forces Turenne and Condé swept over Meuse and Rhine, overran five provinces and reached Utrecht; the Hague was menaced, the States-General sued for peace, a revolution installed Orange as Stadtholder, and de Witt was assassinated.

To stop the French seizing all Holland and to end the war by agreement with his nephew, Charles sent his chief ministers to tempt Orange with an offer of sovereignty, on condition of yielding to England some seaports, — at least for a term of years, — a large indemnity, and satisfaction in India. But the young William III showed his greatness of character; rather than accept such terms, and far less the mere vassalship offered by the French, he would ' die in the last dyke '. As winter approached, the Cabal found themselves loaded with a barren hated war and an empty exchequer, and pleas to Louis for another million for ' Catholicity ' were rejected.

In February 1673 they faced the dreaded Parliament, which was bombarded by Orange's envoys and by pamphlets in his interest. Disdaining Arlington's caution, Charles declared he would stick to his Indulgence, and in Shaftesbury's phrase, ' delenda est Carthago ', appealed for supply in order to force an honourable peace. The loyal Commons offered large grants, but only at the price of withdrawing the Indulgence and its doctrine of a power to suspend the law. While Lauderdale and Buckingham spoke airily of using troops, Shaftesbury of a dissolution, York and Clifford of resistance, Charles at last accepted the view of Arlington and the French that money mattered more than religion, and cancelled the Indulgence. But the Commons pressed on. After proposing a bill to ' ease ' Protestant Dissenters, they drove through the Test Act, which imposed on all office-holders not the oath of supremacy only and an obligation to receive the Anglican sacrament, but a declaration against the dogma of transubstantiation. The summer proved they had begun a revolution. York left the Admiralty, Clifford resigned and within a few months died. In his place as Treasurer came Osborne, soon to become Lord Danby, a Protestant and anti-French Cavalier; with Edward Seymour, another of the same tough type, as Speaker; old Ormonde reappeared in Council. All was broken. Arlington was decided that the ' grand design ' must be dropped and peace be made; Shaftesbury spoke for the Test Act and already was pondering on a Protestant succession, to be secured by legitimizing the King's natural son, Monmouth.

The campaign of 1673 sealed their ruin. Both Hapsburg Powers joined the Dutch, who also retook New York, and Orange pushed the French back to the Rhine. After heavy fighting off Flushing, Rupert in August brought Ruyter to action off the Texel, but lost all hope of a decision when the French squadron failed to support him. Orange meant to drive us to a separate peace; Spain threatened war if we refused terms. It was not a wise moment for York to make another Catholic marriage, as he did with Mary of Modena, through the good offices of France.

In the winter session of 1673–4 Parliament finished off their work. Protests against the Duke's marriage and against standing armies, detailed allusion to the Dover treaty, and refusal of supply unless peace were made, were followed by a move to impeach the guilty ministers, and a first hint of excluding a Catholic heir. Shaftesbury, having re-modelled his rôle as a champion of Parliament and peace, was dismissed; Buckingham, after worthless attempts to trim his sails, was removed. Arlington successfully defended himself against impeachment, and after doing much to break the French alliance retired to the safer post of Lord Chamberlain; much though he hated Danby, on the necessity of peace they were agreed. So came about in February 1674 the peace of Westminster, by which the Dutch paid a small indemnity, restored New York, and conceded us the honour of ' the flag ' north of Cape Finisterre. This meant the real end, though unfortunately not the last word, of Charles' ' travels ' in foreign policy.

Danby's four years of power till 1678 were the most constructive of the reign, illustrating the forces which, below the surface of faction, were making a real advance. Though he and his nearest colleagues were narrow Cavaliers, he had high administrative ability. With the help of a good trade cycle he raised the King's standing revenue well above its nominal total of £1,200,000, tightened up the customs and all departments, and began to restore credit by part-payment to those damaged by the ' stop '. With no parliamentary grant till 1677, he still made possible the building of a powerful fleet. His own interest in stocks and shares was characteristic of a new age, which gives the reign its importance for the making of the solid Britain of the next century.

It was an age of experiment, venture, and reform, the mingled product of Puritanism, a larger capitalist system, and rational intelligence. Most striking of its material achievements, perhaps, was the administration of the Colonies, fully organized now under a Committee for Trade and Plantations. Now, too, were laid the foundations of a civil service, under clerks like William Blathwayt, who was to organize the campaigns of William III. The best talent of the country was harnessed to this service : Evelyn the diarist and Locke the philosopher in Colonial matters, Temple and Godolphin in diplomacy, and William Petty the economist, who was founding public statistics and advancing the Royal Society.

That the State required a permanent armed strength was recognized in the measures taken for army and navy. Directed by a great naval architect, Anthony Deane, and a masterful Admiralty secretary in Pepys, the fleet was rebuilt and reinforced, Charles himself contributing largely from his privy purse to the thirty-ship programme of 1677. Its lasting traditions were being made : in a cadet school at Christ's Hospital, examinations for officers on promotion, and a beginning of half-pay and pensions. Though the army was much more spasmodically recruited and disbanded, here also conditions of active service, as in the Tangier garrison, and constant alarms of war raised the whole question of its rôle in a civilian nation. Necessities of discipline produced a rudimentary military law, and the foundation of Chelsea Hospital for aged or sick soldiers was the first recognition of a standing army to whom the nation owed a debt.

To read the diaries and letters of Pepys and his generation is to feel oneself in a modern age, under a King whose most wholesome interests were his laboratory and his dockyards. Two Chancellors in succession, Finch and North, were consolidating the law of equity. Robert Boyle the chemist, Isaac Newton, and Halley the astronomer were changing the very basis of men's minds. Drastic regulation was rebuilding the City ruined by the fire; Christopher Wren was achieving his fifty London churches.

In short, with the Danby ministry we breathe the air of the revolution of 1688, and find present all the elements, though in different respective strength, of our government as it stood till the reign of George III. The stage was cleared for the duel between York and William of Orange, representing two rival systems of religion and policy, with Charles II in the ring between them, defending his prerogative but never to the point of explosion, determined that the deluge should come after his day. ' Men usually become more timid as they become older,' he said to Shaftesbury, ' it is the opposite with me.'

Parliament had nearly reached its transitional stage, of constitutional but not really representative government. Always now in a state of smouldering suspicion, during this ministry the Commons claimed the right to control expenditure in detail, challenged the King's control of foreign affairs or his nomination of the Speaker, and finally drove Danby from power as they had driven the Cabal; while their attacks on a standing army, and proposals to eject royal placemen from their House, raised problems only settled under William III. The King was in Parliament, in a sense deeper than of old. His influence must in part depend on getting members of his own, or ' King's friends ', elected in dockyard towns or the Cornish Duchy. Ministers were of his choosing, but they too must work through parliamentary groups, and it was to public opinion that final appeal must be made; as was shown by the censorship of the press, and the pamphlets of Shaftesbury, Marvell, and Halifax, which made the propaganda of that small world of squires, clubs, and coffee-houses.

Thus Danby stood, even as Walpole in a changed degree stood later, between two political worlds. The King might cross his policy; York, or Lauderdale, or the reigning mistress the Duchess of Portsmouth, might dispute his appointments, but fundamentally he rested upon Parliament and opinion. He made it his business to build up a majority by distribution of place and patronage, and by a party programme, even more than by developing the bribery which the Cabal and foreign ambassadors had used before him. Such a programme, for instance, in 1675 included many arrests of leading Dissenters, and a bill to impose an oath of passive obedience on members and office-holders. It was defeated by the machinations of Shaftesbury, who spent his fiery soul in organizing a rival party which would force a dissolution of this Cavalier Parliament. Thus came into existence the rudiments of our two-party system. By 1680 each had acquired its historic name, from terms of abuse; the ' Tory ', or Irish outlaw, because York and pre-rogative were supposed to depend on Irish Papists, and the ' Whig ', or Scottish Covenanter, because loyalists said that Shaftesbury's followers drew their politics from the Covenant and the doctrines of 1641. Printed manifestos, choice of candidates from headquarters, red rosettes for Tories and true blue for Whigs, Shaftesbury's ' Green Ribbon ' club in the City answered by ' loyal ' societies, rival news-papers, all the paraphernalia of party were in formation.

In this building of the Whig party there was something more than the defiance of an aristocracy proud of its governing tradition, or a merchant class that detested Frenchmen, both as Papists and commer-cial rivals. Protestant Dissent, in spite of bouts of persecution, never looked back from the Indulgence of 1672. It flourished in growing industrial centres like Birmingham which, not being boroughs in law, stood outside legal penalties and magistrates' control. Towns where Dissenters predominated, such as Yarmouth, simply defied the law. Though there was much ' occasional conformity ', — that is, Dissenters taking the sacrament in order to qualify for office, and others attend-ing their parish church, — the great mass had given up all thought of reunion. Rich London congregations maintained public lectures; regular general meetings were held by the Baptists, and even by the much-persecuted Quakers, whom Fox and Barclay and Penn were organizing. Dissenting schools and academies were many, and gave an excellent education from which, for instance, benefited both Robert Harley and Daniel Defoe. Altogether, then, a concerted defiance, a general feeling too that trade demanded tolerance, sometimes an interview of Penn with the King, or a Secretary of State's letter to stop local persecution, undermined Danby's official policy.

Politically he moved in a vicious circle; for he could not hold the King without getting parliamentary grants, while Parliament stinted its grants because it distrusted royal policy. In one memorandum after another he protested to Charles that prerogative could not finance him without Parliament, which could only be won by resisting France. He must raise his throne by saving Europe from ' thraldom ', and bitterly he deplored the bribes which his master accepted; ' if Cromwell were here ', he said to the French envoy, things would be different. He saw in Orange the hope of the future, trying to bring in Temple, the Prince's warmest admirer, as Secretary of State.

Though England had made its separate peace, the war raged on between France and Holland with her Hapsburg allies, always threatening, like all wars, to spread wider. Parliament called on the King to recall the few English troops, with whom young John Churchill was serving, still fighting alongside the French, and urged we should rejoin the Allies. So began a many-cornered struggle of infinite complication, with every State in Europe trying to influence the English Cabinet and Parliament. The King had valid reasons against joining the Allies. He feared the Commons would either not give him enough money, or else land him in a war and then attack his prerogative; whereas Louis would bid high even for a continuance of our neutrality, which was also most profitable to trade. He gravely suspected, too, the contacts of Orange with the Whigs; he realized the gaping cracks in the alliance, the poverty of Spain, the Hapsburgs' jealousy of Dutch encroachment on the Spanish Low Countries, and the peace-party of republican Amsterdam. Which policy would do most to help his brother's succession, his own finances, and British sea-power? Vacillating more every year, he went on balancing one against another.

He thus embarked on a new series of secret treaties, though now without mention of the Catholic faith. The first initiative from France marked the true adversaries, for they stipulated as a condition of payment that Parliament should be silenced, and brought about a prorogation for fifteen months. But Charles' private policies always included some element of a public object, and when Parliament met again in 1677 Danby nearly persuaded him to take up the national cause. As against the French, York, and the Shaftesbury Whigs, the minister was struggling to prevent a dissolution, and his tactics were unscrupulous but determined.

Finding the King decided that summer to accept another French subsidy for yet another prorogation, a business which he declared ' no money can recompense ', he would at least extort from France the largest possible amount. And as Charles was alarmed at Louis' threat to Flanders, and feared a separate understanding between France and the Dutch republicans, Danby converted him to a measure which, at the lowest, should enforce a reasonable peace. This was a marriage between Orange and James' daughter Mary, first attempted by Arlington some years before. In Charles' eyes it had a double merit, that it might humour Parliament to give him supply and also bring Louis nearer to reason. Simultaneously with the marriage in November, Charles and Orange presented joint terms of peace, and when Louis refused them Charles recalled Parliament and signed an offensive treaty with Holland. British troops were sent to Ostend ; the session of 1678 promised to decide all the future.

But Danby's endeavour failed ; Louis was determined to destroy this troublesome minister and this dangerous Prince of Orange, and he did so in their own countries. The Whigs, believing Charles was again deceiving them, pressed for disbandment of an army that they feared might be used at home. Shaftesbury and Russell made alliance with the French agents, whose money was used to win votes ; the Commons attacked the King's prerogatives of war and peace, and demanded removal of the ministers. Meanwhile the Dutch, to Orange's indignation, accepted Louis' terms ; the separate treaty which he signed with them at Nimwegen gave him Franche Comté but at least set up the barrier in Flanders on which Charles had insisted. Yet, for the time being, by his double game Charles had lost both parliamentary supply and French subsidy ; the league against France was divided, and Danby's majority in the Commons perished.

In September 1678 an extraordinary event came to complete the destruction which the Whigs and France had begun. This was the revelation of a ' Popish plot ' to kill the King and set York in his place, under cover of a French invasion. The arch-informer was one Titus Oates, an adventurer whose vices had already cost him expulsion both from an Anglican living and a Jesuit seminary. Though his main story was pure invention, as the King at once saw and always insisted, he had stumbled on some truths ; as, for example, the date on which the English Jesuits had held a meeting in London (though not the place, which had been St. James's Palace), and the fact that Coleman, the Duchess of York's secretary, had dabbled in treasonable letters to French Catholics. The seizure of Coleman and his correspondence confirmed the alarm, and then the murder, or suicide, of Godfrey, the magistrate who had taken Oates' statement, sent all England plot-mad.

When Parliament met in this frenzy, the Opposition leaders resolved to use the plot, in which some of them seriously believed, to work their own ends. While Oates became a national oracle on a lavish pension, and while Coleman and some Jesuits went to the scaffold, Parliament impeached the Catholic peers, passed an Act to exclude Catholics from both Houses, proposed to disband the army and call up the militia, and asked the dismissal of York from the royal counsels. In furtherance of Shaftesbury's old plan for a divorce, Oates charged the Queen with treason. At first Danby hoped to weather the storm, getting Charles to promise any guarantees that would not touch the line of succession, but Louis XIV came to the assistance of the Whigs. Instigated and financed by him, Montagu, lately our ambassador at Paris, betrayed the secret negotiations in which he had himself urged Danby on. The minister was immediately impeached, and on his advice the King dissolved Parliament.

Two years followed of anarchy, iniquity, and panic. Oates became a rival king, other informers arose to share his profits and his fame, producing the tittle-tattle of Catholic colleges at Lisbon or St. Omer, and concocting murderous charges in London taverns. To breathe a doubt of Oates' veracity, or to deny that the Papists had fired London, meant instant arrest, and terrified citizens carried an ugly weapon for their protection, called ' the Protestant flail '. The Commons from terror degenerated into tyranny, listened obsequiously to evidence from chimney-sweepers or rat-catchers, expelled doubting members, sent their sergeant, quite illegally, far and wide to seize ' delinquents ', impeached judges who tried to be fair, and sent Pepys and Deane, the makers of the Navy, to the Tower. The evil maxims reappeared of the Civil War, and Cromwellian names again in the Commons, another Hampden, the Leveller Wildman, and the proud aristocratic republican Algernon Sidney.

In the new Parliament of 1679 the Commons brushed aside Danby's hope that the tide could be stayed by sending York out of England. Infuriated at the King giving his minister a pardon, the Commons imprisoned him in the Tower, where for five years he remained. In vain the King formed a new Council that included Monmouth, Shaftesbury, and Opposition leaders; in vain produced a scheme of ' limitations ' whereby a Catholic King would lose many powers. The Commons responded with a bill to exclude James from the throne, spoke of an association, like that of 1585, to avenge themselves on Papists, and pressed for Danby's trial. In July, therefore, Charles dismissed them.

Alone and in deadly peril, he showed the brain and courage that he possessed. He gave the Opposition all the rope they needed, submitted to have Oates at dinner, consented to the execution of many innocent victims, including eight priests guilty of no other offence than the mere presence in England which an Elizabethan Act made illegal. But two facts encouraged him. There was a reaction against Oates' violence, and the Opposition had broken in two.

Shaftesbury had decided for exclusion, and thereafter a divorce for the King, with the recognition of Monmouth as the heir. This summer the Scottish Covenanters rose in rebellion, and Monmouth commanded the army to repress them; from his victory at Bothwell Brig, and by his mercifulness after it, he returned a stronger candidate than ever. On the same side was Lord Russell, lofty and fanatical, bent on bringing York to trial; the body of the Commons; and London. Not merely the City council who backed Shaftesbury's petitions, or manipulated the choice of sheriffs and jurors to cries of ' No Yorkist, No Papist ', but in the alleys of Wapping or Southwark thousands of ' brisk boys ', ready for rebellion.

Charles found support in others of his new Council; in the moderate but rather timid Temple, and Essex, a high type of the liberal Cavalier; above all, in George Savile, Lord Halifax. The ' Trimmer ', as he named his famous pamphlet afterwards, had the finest political head of the age. Nephew of the great Strafford, and taught by the greatest commoner of this reign, William Coventry, he was one of the many younger Royalists whom Clarendon had antagonized; of religion he had little, of ambition much, of intellect and eloquence abundance. Though he had been a steady member of the ' Country ' party against the Cabal and Danby, the sheer destructiveness of the present left wing alarmed him; the choice of the bastard and unintelligent Monmouth affronted one who was a pure patrician, while his instinct told him that the hope of the future lay in Orange. By blood he was related to half the political leaders, including Sidneys and Spencers. Of this last family the head was now his brother-in-law Sunderland, whom Charles had made Secretary of State.

How great was the national peril was proved in the autumn of 1679 when the King fell gravely ill. The moderates recalled York from exile at Brussels, and when, on Charles' recovery, they sent him abroad again, they exiled Monmouth also. But their policy of balance broke down when York persuaded his brother to let him change Brussels for Scotland; he was incessantly preaching that any more concessions, ' the same faults Lord Arlington committed ', would make the King ' less than a doge of Venice ', and his platform of firmness was winning many Cavaliers. At the new year of 1680 Charles dismissed Shaftesbury and prorogued the new just-elected Parliament, and when Monmouth came home without leave, deprived him of his commands. The Cabinet broke in pieces. Essex and Temple resigned, Halifax left London in despair. York had recaptured the King, and nothing could be weaker than the group of new ministers nicknamed ' the Chits ', — Clarendon's second son Laurence Hyde (later, Lord Rochester), a bigoted Tory Churchman; Sunderland who would swallow anything if he kept his place; and a shrewd young man from the Household, Sidney Godolphin.

All that year the two parties stood to arms. Monmouth went about on a royal progress, touching for the evil, running races with yokels, and winning many hearts, while rumours were set about that the King had really married Lucy Walters, his mother. Shaftesbury went from one outrage to another. His following ' presented ' York to a London jury as a recusant and the Duchess of Portsmouth as a ' nuisance '; he was ready to light civil war by extending the plot to Ireland, and his informers brought to the block the innocent Oliver Plunket, Catholic archbishop of Armagh. They were responsible too for the execution of Lord Stafford, an old and innocent Catholic peer. His ' Green Ribbon ' club in Fleet Street, besides exploiting a scurrilous press, organized petitions for the speedy meeting of Parliament; which were answered by Tory addresses of ' abhorrence '. Civil war, Halifax told his friends, was likely, and it was a common saying that ' 41 was come again '.

Though the young ministers made some play with an anti-French policy, Sunderland and Godolphin despaired and went over to exclusion. So had Essex, so had the Duchess of Portsmouth, so had Nelly Gwynne, who called herself ' the Protestant whore '. Their cause had become European. Immense pressure was put upon Orange to agree to it, and both the Dutch Estates and Austrian ministers begged Charles to meet the wish of his Parliament.

In November 1680 the Commons passed a second exclusion bill; it was beaten in the Lords after a seven-hour debate, during which hands were laid on hilts of swords, and mainly through the oratory of Halifax. Furiously the Commons demanded his removal from office, and tacked to their exclusion bill an association to reserve all places for Protestants of 'known affection', even suggesting that Parliament should hold certain towns as guarantees. Refusing to give way, Charles dissolved them, summoning another to meet in March 1681 in the more free and loyal city of Oxford.

Before it met he showed his decision by dismissing Sunderland and reinsured himself by opening a new treaty with Louis XIV, who after long hesitation had determined to back York as the champion of Catholic monarchy and the best instrument to perpetuate English divisions. Oxford looked like a camp, royal horse-guards lined the Windsor road, Whig nobles with armed escort were billeted in some colleges, the London members had hatbands with the legend ' No Popery, no slavery '. With the King's consent the moderates brought forward a sweeping solution, the banishment of York for life and during his reign a regency, under the Prince and Princess of Orange. It was rejected, Shaftesbury in person asking Charles to nominate Monmouth as successor and to abandon the cause of the Church. They had thrown away their last chance ; in a fortnight Charles completed his French treaty and dissolved this, his last, Parliament.

His instinct was right that the country dreaded the spectre of civil war, and agreed with him ' better one king than five hundred '. The reaction was so strong that he was able this summer to arrest Shaftesbury, though a London jury acquitted him, and to execute some of his underlings. Next year York came back from Scotland, henceforth to urge his yielding brother to stand firm, and it was decided to break opposition at its heart by the appointment of Tory sheriffs in London who could pack juries, and to challenge the City charter on a writ of *Quo warranto*. Following on this, charters were so remodelled in many boroughs as to put local government in the hands of loyalists. Dryden's *Absalom and Achitophel* led off a whole literature against the plot and all Whig principles, a base press called for punishment, sermons and fly-sheets denied any right of resistance, and again declared passive obedience the teaching of the Church.

With this sword over them many Whigs, and Cromwellian officers among them, took to conspiracy, extreme men like the mad Scot Ferguson plotting to murder the royal brothers, while Monmouth and Russell discussed the chances of a rising. Their exposure and their doom came in 1683. Shaftesbury fled abroad, soon to die at Amsterdam. The plot to kill King and Duke as they returned from Newmarket, at the Rye-house at Hoddesden, was betrayed, and led to the arrest of the nobles who had done no more than talk of resistance. Essex killed himself in the Tower; Russell was executed, Charles saying ' he would never have given quarter to me '; on even more flimsy evidence Algernon Sidney died, glorying that he fell for ' the good old cause '. And Monmouth, their wretched tool, took refuge in Holland.

Though in all this violence most of the councillors had a hand, several elements may be distinguished among them. There were base climbing men like Sunderland, who had soon made his Court again, or the furious drunken Chief Justice Jeffreys, ready to find their own fortune in reaction or to serve a Catholic king. There were also the dominant Cavalier group; Hyde the brother-in-law of York, Seymour the Tory leader of the west country, and the aged Ormonde, all ardent to stand by Church and King, but uneasy at the advance of Catholicism and the suspension of Parliament. Further to the left came Halifax, who had pleaded for Russell and dreaded the next reign.

Their contests were bound up with the politics of Europe. In 1681 Louis completed his ' reunions ' of supposedly French territories by swallowing Strasbourg, with most of Alsace ; in 1684 his military might, in a state of undeclared war, forced recognition of his right to Luxemburg; his hold on Italy was increasing; in 1685 his long persecution of the Huguenots ended in the revocation of the Edict of Nantes. Nothing could stop this mighty machine but a European league, but no remonstrances of Halifax and Seymour could make Charles face a Parliament which might begin a Protestant war and end in a Protestant succession. He would not reopen his years of humiliation. It was not for him, he implied, to defend the Empire; he married his niece Anne to George of Denmark, an ally of France, and ingloriously abandoned our Mediterranean outpost at Tangier, sending Pepys on the mission that blew up its fortifications. He had some excuse in the feuds dividing Protestant Europe within itself and from the Catholics, in the deadly hostility of Prussia against Sweden, or the bitterness between Austria and Holland.

High among the reasons for the danger of civil war during the Plot, and the reaction after it, were conditions in Scotland and Ireland, in each of which a terrible inheritance was accumulating. For the divisions, which in England fired debates of Whig and Tory, in more primitive societies would mean fire and sword.

In Scotland the Restoration had been popular, in that it swept away the Cromwellian union and garrisons, and brought back a Scottish Parliament. As head of the government Clarendon had chosen Middleton, who had led the risings against Cromwell; while Argyll, the brain of the Presbyterian politicians, who had finally submitted to the Protector, was sent to the scaffold. A ' rescissory ' Act declared void all legislation since 1633, others gave the King a revenue for life and proclaimed his supremacy over Church and State. Episcopacy was brought back, together with private patronage in Church livings, and the Presbyterian agent during Restoration, James Sharp, won undying hatred by accepting the archbishopric of St. Andrews.

In this reaction Middleton's group showed themselves meanly vindictive and incompetent; moreover, they clashed with Lauderdale, who had won Charles' friendship in the civil wars and never lost it. In youth the Kirk had looked to him as their rising hope, he was deeply read in theology, and the correspondent of Baxter. As years passed, however, he degenerated, allowing no opposition to his passions and having but one political rule, to keep his power by making the King absolute. His cynical temperament and brawny wit commended him much to Charles, while his high abilities kept in his following some of the best Scots of the day, Tweeddale and Kincardine and, above all, his agent in London, the accomplished Robert Moray. His policy coincided with the national pride, for he disliked Clarendon's settlement of Scottish problems at the English Council board, and had advised against restoration of bishops.

His supremacy dated from the year 1663, when he induced Parliament to raise a militia which the King might use even outside Scotland, and to revive the method of choosing the lords of the Articles, devised under Charles I, which gave the Crown the initiative in making laws. So he went on until he could tell his master ' never was King so absolute as you are in poor old Scotland '. But he spoke too soon.

For though the Kirk had not won most of the aristocracy, and by its fanaticism had lost influence on moderate men, its hold was still immense on the masses. To forswear the Covenant, to accept the silencing of its Assembly and the rule of the apostate Sharp, against this betrayal a remnant would fight to the death. A third of the ministers refused Middleton's settlement and threw up their manses. Fines and quartering of troops could not force the Covenanters to church ; in the south-west from Lanark to Ayr they gathered in conventicles in the glens, where masked or disguised preachers held forth, with sentries posted to watch for the dragoons.

This cruel repression brought about the rising of 1666, when the Dutch war cut off the Scots' best market; against all advice a few thousand fanatics made their way from Dumfries to the outskirts of Edinburgh, and were crushed in their retreat at Rullion Green in the Pentland Hills. Led by Rothes and Sharp, the panic-stricken Council tortured and executed their victims, giving the west over to the barbarism of soldiers like Thomas Dalyell, who had learned ways of terror in Russian service ; the fines that made husbands and wives mutually responsible, the carrying off of cattle from the byre, dragoons to eat the accused out of hearth and home, and a lighted match between the fingers to make them speak. Now was seen the exaltation of the martyrs, as in the boy preacher Hugh McKail who, after torture with the boot, died ' in a rapture of joy '.

Commissioned to end this chaos, Lauderdale began by an indemnity and a reduction of the army, and in 1669 issued an Indulgence. He could not entirely overturn the bishops, whom he took as a piece of political machinery and expected the Covenanters to do the same. No English liturgy was forced on the Kirk as in Laud's time, ministers could meet in their presbyteries, and those once ejected were allowed to occupy their old livings, if vacant, on a bare acceptance of episcopacy and royal supremacy. But since the true Covenanter would never be ' a King's curate ' or admit his supremacy over Christ, neither indulgence nor efforts at an agreed comprehension rewarded the high-minded men, the saintly bishop Leighton and the young Burnet included, who advised lenity, and Lauderdale accordingly began a new persecution.

The world, as personified in him, could not crush the Covenanting spirit, and another powerful reason condemned his policy : that England and Scotland could not be ruled in two compartments. With a population of less than a million, Scotland was poor and overtaxed, while English Acts had excluded her from the Navigation system and ended the free trade in corn and cattle, enjoyed under the Commonwealth. Many minds thought of returning to Union and, though the negotiation of 1670 broke down on objections from English traders and Scottish pride, inevitably the Scottish Opposition had English contacts and borrowed English principles. Lauderdale's tyranny in his own country was matched by his part in the violence of the Cabal, and, influenced by Shaftesbury, from 1673 a powerful Opposition, with great names among them like Hamilton and the young Argyll, attacked his corrupt hold over Parliament.

A minister who thus cut himself off from the feelings of the Lowlands was always tempted to look for support beyond the Highland line, where war was an honourable profession and Catholics and Episcopalians were in force. Inflamed by the brigandage of one such Highland army, in 1679 southern Scotland broke into revolt. One band of fanatics, meeting archbishop Sharp by chance on the moors west of St. Andrews, hacked him to death with their swords. Another in the west routed Claverhouse, the best soldier of the King in the north, at Drumclog. Charles wisely sent Monmouth to take command, strong in his royal presence and marriage to the Buccleuch heiress, and the rebels, torn by their feuds and almost without gun-powder, failed to hold the Clyde at Bothwell Brig, and were scattered like sheep.

All this, and the Popish plot, brought the downfall of Lauderdale, but soon Monmouth fell also, and York became from 1680 the effectual ruler. Resistance continued; the extremists, called from one of their preachers the Cameronians, declared Charles excommunicate and repudiated his government. A hideous war went on in the moors and moss-hags, columns of Claverhouse's horse dealing out martial law and no quarter, while the famous Sir George (or ' Bluidy ') Mackenzie led prosecutions for the Crown. Gradually the Opposition leaders made their way abroad, to join Shaftesbury and Monmouth. Argyll was joined in Holland by Monmouth's evil genius Ferguson, by the wise divine William Carstares, who after suffering torture in Edinburgh escaped to be Orange's Scottish adviser, by Burnet the historian, and Stair the head of the Bench.

So the reign ended with all the makings of civil war, a silenced Kirk, and a servile Parliament. Hitherto the connection had been a curse to both kingdoms, heightening the danger of absolutism in England and to Scotland bringing suppression of faith and liberty.

To Ireland also the English connection brought untold evil, but in this case far less through any doing of the Crown than through the English Parliament and British settlers. The King's Deputy for most of the reign was the admirable veteran Ormonde who, though an Irish

Protestant, put the interests of Ireland above persecution or English mercantile gain. But whatever the King, Ormonde, and Clarendon might wish, they could not uproot the Cromwellian settlement and its armed settlers. No amount of Irish land could satisfy all the claims, English and Irish, made upon it, and all they could do, after long enquiries, was to restore a small number of ' innocent Papists ' to their property, by the Act of 1665.

Since in Ireland too the Cromwellian union was undone, rule through an Irish Parliament meant, unless it was to be sheer force, a measure of tolerance for Catholics, who in this reign enjoyed more liberty than they had enjoyed, or were to have, for a century. No Test Act as yet barred them from office, and secular priests were generally left to work in peace. Yet Ormonde had to contend with the embers of several revolutions and the hatreds of two peoples. There was an extremist Catholic party, whose most reckless leader was ' mad Dick Talbot ', later Duke of Tyrconnel, whose aim it was to overturn the land settlement. At the opposite pole were the British settlers, not only the vested Tudor families like the Boyles, but the Scots of Ulster, and Cromwellian soldiers. Such men exclaimed against Ormonde's clemency, there were plots in Ulster, and no militia could safely be raised from such material. The Deputy's difficulties did not end here. From the King he had to endure attempts to raid the revenue for grants to favourites, like Lady Castlemaine, or use of the dispensing power to put Catholics into corporations. Worse still was the English Parliament, which cut Ireland out of any direct trade with the Colonies, and by a whole series of selfish laws closed the English market to Irish cattle and butter, and confined the whole export of Irish wool to England.

Then with appalling recklessness Shaftesbury plunged Ireland into the fever of the Plot; she was ' the snake we have harboured ', he said, and he would treat Ormonde as ' another Strafford '. His informers made their base fortunes by vamping up conspiracies, Jesuits and convents were suppressed, archbishop Plunket was executed on false charges. Yet Ormonde's steadfast equity brought the country through this storm. Trading channels were opened in other directions; the revenue nearly doubled during the reign; Dublin was a fair city of 50,000 people. Though the land upheavals had disturbed nearly every family, and though a good deal of ' Tory ' brigandage lingered on, another generation of even-handed government might have saved Ireland.

It was not to be, and between them Shaftesbury and York set the country alight at all its corners. No Parliament was held after 1666, nor would the real country have been represented if it had met. Active friars and Roman instructions kept government and people apart, while Catholic Ireland sought the aid of France. Before Charles died, Ormonde was recalled, and under York's influence the army command was separated from the lord-deputyship in order to introduce more Catholics; on the other side, Protestant Dissent, denied a voice in local government, was sending emigrants to New England. If York hoped that Catholic Ireland could be kept loyal to Protestant England, he was blind to the facts, nor was it certain that even Protestant Ireland could be kept in control.

In all three countries Charles' last year passed in this atmosphere of expectant waiting. Danby was at last released and tended to give his influence to Halifax, even in the royal circle some like Godolphin kept up good relations with Orange. There were signs that the King was again shifting to a change. His French treaty expired. The Treasury was taken away from Rochester, Monmouth secretly visited his father, and it was believed that York was again to be exiled.

But in February 1685 the King had a stroke of apoplexy and on the 6th he died, after receiving from Father Huddleston, who had helped him in his escape from Worcester, the last rites of the Roman Church. In London his people mourned him sincerely; not least, perhaps, because they felt, as Charles had often himself predicted, that his successor would bring with him stormy days.

CHAPTER III

JAMES II, 1685–1688

NEITHER the struggle in Europe nor the future of Britain could wait longer on the wearer of the British crown. Charles might have prolonged indecision in yielding by degrees, but James made decision take the form, within three years, of a revolution.

No two brothers could be a greater contrast. James had none of Charles' brain and still less of his charm, while conversion to Rome had not as yet improved his morale or mellowed his temperament. Both his father's fate and his brother's troubles he put down to making concessions and, as Burnet noted, was not born under a pardoning planet. He had pressed for no quarter to the plotters, ruled Scotland very severely, and began his reign by sending Oates to the pillory and imprisoning Richard Baxter. He was, however, a better man of business than Charles and had directed the Admiralty well, and however much his subjects deplored his religion, they believed him to be a man of his word.

This word he pledged to the new House of Commons summoned to settle his revenues, which from the new-modelled boroughs and by government influence on the elections had a large loyal majority; he would, he told them, protect the law and the Church. And this loyal temper was redoubled in the summer by a double invasion.

No more bungling and ill-starred rebellions were ever made. Without agreement either in object or timing, the Scots and English exiles set out from Holland. Argyll lost weeks in the Orkneys and found his own Inveraray country held down by Atholl, nor would the Cameronians rise for a Highland chief. And as disputes among his following gave government ample time to hunt them down, he was soon captured in a desperate dash over the Clyde and executed on his old sentence.

Before Argyll died Monmouth had landed at Lyme Regis on the 11th June; on the 15th July he, too, died on the scaffold. Not a sign appeared that England had forgotten 1649, or was ready for 1688. While Tory Oxford sent loyalist volunteers, Orange despatched his British auxiliary regiments to help his father-in-law; the Whig nobles made no move, and Monmouth's lieutenants were either Cromwellian captains or desperadoes of the Rye-house Plot, with here and there an angular idealist, such as the Scot republican Fletcher of Saltoun.

Even so, under other leaders, much might have been made of the 'old cause'. In this Puritan country stretching from Lyme to the Wiltshire border, full of textile workers and Mendip miners suffering a good deal of unemployment, evangelical Protestantism was a living faith, as the duke's humble followers proved to the bitter end. But their scythes and fowling-pieces could not face the fierce veterans just brought back from Tangier, styled 'Kirke's lambs', or Churchill's horse-guards, and when Monmouth in desperation took the title of King, he got no response from Bristol or the solid clothiers of Wiltshire. After stabling his horses in Wells cathedral, he retreated on Bridgwater; whence on the night of 5th July he sallied out to attack the royal army on Sedgemoor. There he was held up in the mists by its deep watercourses, his ammunition failed, and at dawn his men were cut to pieces. Riding for life, he was taken in Cranborne Chase and after a pitiable interview with the King he was executed.

Such were fortune's first gifts to James, who proceeded to throw them away and to alienate the Parliaments of two kingdoms, who had shown themselves passionately loyal and voted him large revenues for life. Moderate men were sickened by the shocking use made of victory. Chief Justice Jeffreys carried out his 'bloody assize', which made the west country a shambles; in which some three hundred prisoners were executed and hundreds more transported to the Indies. The crusade was pushed back to kill Whigs who had been under suspicion in the last reign, to arrest many more, to burn the aged Elizabeth Gaunt at Tyburn for sheltering fugitives, and to behead Alice Lisle, a regicide's widow, in Winchester market-place for the same offence.

Fresh from news of these atrocities or of the tarred bodies swinging in gibbets on the Somerset moors, the Commons assembled to hear James' demand for a larger standing army, his intention to keep the Catholic officers he had illegally commissioned, and to repeal the Test Act and habeas corpus. Popery seemed at their door. The King expected his ministers to attend him at Mass, a Papal nuncio was in London, Huguenot refugees were swarming to England. With the dismissal of Halifax, plain speaking in both Houses, and a sharp prorogation of Parliament — which was not to meet in this reign again — James cut the bridges behind him.

With the events of the next years before us it is impossible to argue that all he sought was toleration for Catholics. For that, in some measure, he could certainly have obtained, and a repeal of the penal laws was all that was asked by old Catholic families and the Papacy itself. What James demanded, however, was not liberty but power. The choice of Tyrconnel as commander-in-chief in Ireland was followed by the cashiering of Protestant soldiers and the selection of Catholic judges and councillors; in Scotland the Catholic duke of Gordon held

Edinburgh Castle, while two converts, the brothers Perth and Melfort, controlled the ministry. Not merely did an immediate purge begin in the Household and the army in England, but in 1686, in the collusive case of Godden *v.* Hales, a packed Bench upheld the legality of the King's power to dispense with acts of Parliament.

On the strength of that he brought four Catholic peers into Council, including one agent in the secret treaty of Dover, and appointed Catholic heads to two Oxford colleges. A new High Commission court was set up in defiance of several statutes, and its first measure was to suspend Compton bishop of London, who would not silence his clergy. A large army was quartered outside London on Hounslow Heath, new Catholic chapels and schools were opened in the City, and a mission to Rome asked a bishopric for the King's Jesuit confessor, Petre.

And that it was not liberty he sought was further proved by his transparent tactics. His Cabinet was composed at first of two elements, one led by his brothers-in-law Rochester and Clarendon, and another of the political servants, Sunderland and Godolphin. Sunderland's ability was great, and found indispensable by William III later. He was not prepared to lose office for a few scruples, for he lived in state and gambled high, and he would go very far, even to a nominal conversion to the Catholic faith, if he could outbid his rivals. Though there is no reason to think he would betray James, he would not risk his head. Much the same seems true of Godolphin, a public servant of much higher calibre, a Stuart servant since his boyhood as a royal page, devoted to Mary of Modena, but wise enough to see that the future lay with Orange. Others in the inner circle thought the same, and notably John Churchill, who some years back had written ' sooner or later we must be all undone '.

Now the King's first hope was to achieve his design through the Tory Churchmen, with a severe persecution of Dissenters as part of that policy. In 1687 he abandoned it, finding that neither through such ministers, nor with the existing electorate and Parliament, could he get the security he wanted for Catholicism in his own lifetime, and beyond. Rapidly there followed one stroke after another in a new plan. Rochester was dismissed, Clarendon replaced in Ireland by Tyrconnel, the Tory Parliament in England was dissolved, while a sweeping Indulgence in both England and Scotland suspended all tests and allowed public Catholic worship. He hoped to form a bloc of Dissenters, Catholics, and courtiers and to carry repeal of tests through a packed Parliament. From top to bottom he turned out the Tories who had restored the Crown and beaten exclusion, the families who had fought in debate and on battlefields, Finches and Berties and Bagots, loyal London aldermen, Herbert Vice-Admiral of England. The sheriffs set about remodelling Tory corporations, every justice of the peace in the country was canvassed to vote for repeal of tests and scores were dismissed, while the magnates of the kingdom, the last de Vere earl of Oxford, Derby, and Somerset, had to resign lord-lieutenancies and regiments. Tyrconnel was doing the same in Ireland, Protestants were in flight from Dublin. Catholics, including Father Petre, now made a majority of his Council, and a royal semi-Catholic nominee was forced as President on Magdalen College, Oxford, by a stormy visit from the King, breaking open of doors, and troops of horse. In December 1687 it was announced that the Queen was with child, and ardent Catholics predicted that a son would bless the Church's champion.

Sooner or later resistance was certain, but its form and season were determined by events in Europe. Louis XIV's reign of terror and undeclared war had overreached themselves, accomplishing what had not been seen since the Reformation in a coalition of Catholic and Protestant States against him. Pope Innocent XI was resisting his arbitrary rule of the French Church, his menaces to Rome itself, and threats to Catholic Germany; while after fifty years of bullying and bribes German national feeling had wakened, making a bridge between the Protestants of the north and the slow-moving Catholic Emperor Leopold. The time-honoured French scheme of raising up enemies in the German rear was breaking down. John Sobieski, King of Poland, who had won immortal glory in 1683 by saving Vienna from the Turks, had abandoned his French alliance ; the Hungarian rebels whom Louis had incited were being crushed; the Austrians had recovered Buda-Pesth from the Turks. It was clear that, once the East was safe, the Empire would turn west upon France; against whom in 1686 the League of Augsburg, for defence of the Rhine, combined the Hapsburgs, Bavaria, and the German lands held by Sweden and Spain. The Great Elector's self-seeking hesitation and anti-Catholic feeling were now swallowed up in his German patriotism, while in the governing motive of all this age, — the Spanish succession, — Leopold had won the last round. His daughter had lately married the Elector of Bavaria, one of the heroes of the Turkish war, and though father and son-in-law had yet to determine their respective claims in Spain, for the time being they were solid against France.

At the centre of this whirlpool was William of Orange, who had dedicated himself to this cause, and whose wife was heiress to the British throne. A double set of pressures drove him on. A civil war, to which England seemed to be drifting, might end in another Commonwealth, once again anti-royal and anti-Dutch, or again might not James induce Anne to turn Catholic and pass Mary over ? As for Europe, without English neutrality at least, he dared not move, while many Dutchmen feared a second 1672 in a sudden onslaught from England and France combined.

In actual fact such fears were groundless, for James was bent on avoiding a war which would necessitate a parliament, and destroy his Catholic scheme. And though at first he gladly took the small sums doled out to him by Louis, he did not like his quarrel with the Pope or his sabre-rattling to the Netherlands, being, moreover, too proud a man to be treated like a German princeling.

These incessant reactions between England and Europe came to a head in 1687, when William replied, to an enquiry from James, that he could not support a repeal of the Test Act, and sent over agents to sound the English leaders. Their answers were various. The Hydes were non-committal, Halifax was for giving James rope enough to hang himself, Churchill answered for the Protestantism of the Princess Anne, and his own. But Danby was for action; a strong party argued that the King might successfully pack the Commons, swamp the Lords with new creations, and stand on his Catholic-officered army. In April 1688 they sent Edward Russell to ask the Prince's intention.

For him it was, as he told the Dutch, 'now or never'. James had demanded the return of the Scots regiments in the Dutch service, and accepted French money to equip his fleet. A French candidate to the great archbishopric of Cologne, cruel oppression of the Huguenots, and a vindictive French tariff, were overcoming the ancient feud between Orange and the peace-and-trade party at Amsterdam. Advice for action reached him from the Great Elector, and from Schomberg, the Huguenot marshal in Prussian service; he had hopes also of peace in the East, and therefore of Austrian help. In May he told the Englishmen that, if formally invited by some of those ' most valued ' in the kingdom, he could come to their help in September.

That very month of May James turned this secret aristocratic conspiracy into a national cause by issuing a second Indulgence, coupled with the promise of a parliament, and by ordering it to be read in every parish church. The sure shield of Cavalier and Tory loyalty, the Anglican Church, would not cover this. Breaking with their teaching of a hundred years, archbishop Sancroft and six bishops [1] petitioned for withdrawal of the Indulgence as violation of the law; they were sent to the Tower and put on trial for seditious libel. Arguments from their counsel declared that the King could only legislate through Parliament and that illegal deeds of his ministers could be resisted, and they were acquitted amid amazing rejoicing, crowds on their knees as the bishops passed, cheers even in the Hounslow camp, bells and bonfires all over England.

Their trial was not over before, on the 10th of June, the son and heir expected was born to the Queen, and on the evening of their acquittal

[1] Turner of Ely, Ken of Bath and Wells, Lloyd of St. Asaph, Lake of Chichester, White of Peterborough, Trelawney of Bristol.

seven magnates signed the invitation for which Orange had asked : the Tories Danby, bishop Compton, and Lumley, and of the Whigs Devonshire the greatest noble of the Midlands, the young Shrewsbury a convert from Catholicism, of ancient race and great popularity, Henry Sidney brother of the dead Algernon, and the sailor Edward Russell, cousin of the martyred lord. For a month or two all that mattered of political England was at one. Except for a few individuals like the eccentric William Penn, the Dissenters had not been enticed by the Indulgence, conferences were exploring the possibility of prayer-book revision to conciliate them, and Halifax led the way in a swarm of pamphlets that called for unity among all Protestants. From Cornwall came the song ' And shall Trelawney die ? ', while all England was whistling ' Lillibulero ', for which the words, with their threat of ' a Protestant wind ', were composed by Thomas Wharton, wildest of Whig partisans, and for which an air of Purcell set the tune.

While James persisted in his insanity, punishing judges who had ruled for the bishops or filling up his army with Irish drafts, the con- spirators acted. They had promises of assistance from the soldiers Churchill and Kirke, from Tory pillars such as the young Ormonde or Lowther the stalwart of the Border, from Charles II's sailor son the Duke of Grafton, and from captains in the fleet. Orange had received an assurance that the troops of Prussia, Hesse, and Hanover would protect Holland in his absence, and pledged himself to the Emperor that he had no intention of deposing James or oppressing Catholics.

At last, moved by repeated warnings from France and the more moderate men in his Cabinet and Sunderland's terrified advice to retreat, James appealed again to Church of England loyalty. He did, indeed, cancel the Ecclesiastical Commission, restore some borough charters, and make amends to Magdalen College. But he was too late, too hesitant, too insincere. Tory nobles and magistrates would not come in again on the strength of partial concessions clearly extorted by fear; he would not summon Parliament till threats of invasion were over, and when a storm scattered Orange's first effort at sailing, the dismissal of Sunderland showed that the extremists were again in the ascendant. Finally, his petulant refusal of help from French ships doomed him. For Louis XIV England was secondary to the Rhine, while he thought he could continue the game he had played so long, and that civil war there would occupy both English and Dutch over the winter. When in September his armies turned east to the Palatinate, the Dutch felt they could safely accept Orange's plans. Preceded by a declaration for a free Parliament, to vindicate the law and to decide the disputed legitimacy of the Prince of Wales, on 5th November Orange landed in Torbay with a cosmopolitan army of 24,000 men.

His voyage was a gamble, and only on its course did the wind decide him to sail west and not north, as Danby had urged; his welcome was most uncertain, and the solution undecided, perhaps even in his own mind. Fortune saved him at once from what would probably have been ruin,—a clash with the English fleet,—for the gale that blew him west kept Dartmouth and his ships tethered to the Gunfleet in Essex, while no sooner had he landed than it changed and drove the pursuing Dartmouth back into Portsmouth.

Even so, perhaps nothing could have destroyed James if he had listened to the advice of his loyal Tories and bishops, and not abandoned his own cause. His refusal either to call a Parliament or to negotiate crippled his supporters; his irresolution whether to fight or flee dispirited his fine army. Before he went to Salisbury Plain to meet the invader, half the gentry of the west had joined William and signed an association for a free Parliament, and when he decided to retreat, Churchill and Grafton and George of Denmark went over to William. Slowly but instinctively the political sense of the country clarified itself, on the platform of 'a free parliament and the Protestant religion'. Under cover of this cry Danby and his friends seized York and Hull, and Devonshire raised the Midlands, whither Compton escorted the Princess Anne; it was assisted even by the King's loyal admiral Dartmouth, who stoutly disobeyed orders to carry the infant prince to France.

So things stood early in December, when James under pressure from the peers promised a Parliament and opened a negotiation, and so they might long have stood but for his own desperation. On the 9th he sent off his wife and son to France, and on the 11th himself took ship at Sheerness, after destroying the writs for Parliament, ordering disbandment of the army, and telling Dartmouth to take the fleet to Ireland. So he abandoned a people struggling to be loyal and did his best to ensure anarchy. The London mob began to loot the Catholics, disbanded soldiers plundered in the Midlands, only the peers' prompt action saved the country. On negotiation with Orange for a 'free parliament' all were united, though even now, when the Faversham fishermen intercepted James in flight and he was brought back to his palace, sentiment and legality might have brought about a sort of restoration. The first flight had probably decided Orange, his Whig followers were urging that it amounted to 'abdication', Halifax threw James over, and the Prince insisted he should leave London. But, in fact, the King's nerve had collapsed and, mindful of his father's fate, he was resolved to join his queen. On 23rd December he sailed from Rochester, and on Christmas day heard Mass in France. At the request of the Lords, and of a meeting of the members of Charles II's House of Commons with the City council, Orange took over the administration, pending the assembly of a Convention.

This meant revolution, for no one but a King could legally summon a parliament, and when a whole people has committed legal treason, it is unprofitable to bandy responsibilities. Resistance had run through all degrees : from high-church bishops like the saintly Ken, who had refused the Indulgence but would shudder at deposing the Lord's anointed, to Godolphin who had advised James against flight but equally advised against his return, to Tory squires who had signed the west-country association but had fought for the Crown against Monmouth, and so to the extreme Whigs, savagely thinking of 1680, who taught that the King had broken the contract with his subjects.

For months the electors had expected a parliament, and when in January 1689 the Convention met, a large majority in the Commons showed they had done with James. Outside a small clerical circle, talk of a restoration died away. But it was too much to expect that the Tories could shed all their beliefs overnight, or admit a theory that kings could be deposed ; led by the bishops and Church laymen like Nottingham, they put forward as their first solution the plan of 1681, a regency that would save the legal succession and their oaths. It was defeated in the Lords by two votes, being indeed open to one fatal objection, the impossible rôle of a regent acting for a King who, with his heir, was in the hands of a foreign Power. But defeat was in part due to a split in the Tory ranks. Assuming that the Prince of Wales was no prince, and agreeing that James' ' desertion ' relieved them from allegiance, a school headed by Danby and bishop Compton argued that Mary was already Queen by hereditary right.

Here they collided with the Commons' resolution, which laid down that James had ' abdicated ', and that ' the throne is thereby vacant '. By 5 votes the Lords disagreed, and by a majority of 131 the Commons adhered to their resolution ; a deadlock which was broken by the voice of the Prince and Princess, and by the country's instinct that an imperfect government was better than none. William let it be known that he would not serve as regent, nor as a mere prince consort ; indeed, to the fury of Englishmen, his intimate friend Bentinck was breathing, as was Halifax, that William should be sole sovereign. Mary sent word from Holland that she would not reign above a husband whom love and religion impelled her to obey, and the Churchills persuaded Anne to postpone her claim to William's for his lifetime. There were fears of the Commonwealth men rising, trade and markets were paralysed, while a strong wing of Churchmen under Nottingham, whose conscience would not allow them to assist revolution, would accept the powers that be as ordained by God's providence.

So the Lords, many of them abstaining in order to avoid bloodshed, gave way. Setting out from such different angles, Tories and Whigs combined to vote that William and Mary ' be and be declared ' joint sovereigns, with succession in turn to the survivor, then to Mary's issue, then to Anne and her heirs. They drew up a new oath of allegiance, making no mention of legal title, which the *de facto* school of Tory could accept. They accompanied their offer of the Crown by a declaration of rights, later elaborated into a bill, which not only made incapable of reigning any Catholic or one married to a Catholic, and imposed on the sovereign a drastic declaration against transubstantiation, but rehearsed — pell-mell and incompletely, since they were acting in a crisis — the main offences of James II ; declaring illegal henceforth the suspending power, the dispensing power ' as it hath been exercised of late ', courts like High Commission, and keeping a standing army in time of peace. This done, they passed an Act styling the Convention a legal Parliament. In April 1689 William and Mary were crowned ; by that time, France was at war with the Empire, Holland, and Spain, and Claverhouse was raising the Highlands for James, who was himself on his way to Ireland with French officers.

CONTEMPORARY DATES

1686	League of Augsburg against France.
	Buda-Pesth taken from the Turks.
	Bayle's work of rationalism begins.
1687	Venetians destroy the Parthenon.
	Newton's *Principia*.
1688	France declares war on Holland and the Empire.
	Death of the Great Elector.
	Halifax, *Character of a Trimmer*.

CHAPTER IV

WILLIAM III, 1689–1702

IN the oldest member of the Convention, Maynard, who had been one of the counsel against Strafford, we may see a symbol that 1688 sealed the meaning of events since 1641. Any sovereign henceforth must be what Charles II had once promised to be, ' the man of his people ', and no longer could pursue a policy or a religion which was abhorrent to them. Once for all, with profound consequences for posterity, Britain was declared a constitutional and Protestant State. In insisting on this fact the Revolution finally destroyed what new thought and new wealth had long been undermining; that is, the theory of passive obedience and of government as based on some divine order, together with all those ideas which since the time of Charlemagne had set kings apart as beings anointed, with sacred inherent prerogatives, and had made State and Church two facets of one unity. When William III ceased to touch for ' the evil ', when he was declared King by the voice of Parliament, when he made Presbyterianism the State religion of Scotland, and in England legalized toleration, the Plantagenet and Tudor conceptions of politics had plainly perished.

It was then a revolution, yet a conservative one, in so much that it reaffirmed the logic of the previous fifty years. Save for the Bill of Rights, which only clinched matters on which Charles II's Parliaments had insisted, not a change was made in the outward fabric. William used much the same methods as Charles, and George III much the same as William; who, in fact, employed all the principal Stuart ministers, Danby and Halifax, Sunderland and Godolphin. What this revolution did was not to innovate but to eliminate, not to destroy but to release the energies long-accumulating, which transformed the constitution from within.

This parliamentary order became the vehicle of a diplomatic revolution also. The broad scheme of policy formed by Elizabeth and inherited by Cromwell could not survive the ambitions of Louis XIV, and Britain embarked, hesitatingly in Arlington's day but under William with ardour, on a century of conflict with France. Even its early stages involved an increase and consolidation of Empire, with new measures to ensure sea-power and a standing army. It meant an enlargement of parliamentary sovereignty, for no doubts could be permitted as to where lay supreme power, and into that unity must be fitted Scotland, Ireland,

and the Colonies. The strain of William's wars, with budgets four times the average of Charles II's, decided the predominance of the Commons, creating, furthermore, a system of government credit, with more power for the moneyed class and a new industrial stimulus. In retrospect we see that all these things flowed in steady sequence from the fifteenth century, but now their triumph gave to the next stage of our history a continuous character.

In the shock of revolution it was Britain's good fortune to be ruled by so great a man as William III. True, he ruled unbeloved and died unlamented, and not unjustly. His heart was in the Hague, in the dykes he had defended, and to him England was never a fatherland, but a reservoir of men and money. Every year after 1690 he departed for six months to the theatre of war, even continuing to do so when war had ceased. He despised British faction, had bitter experience of British treachery, and trusted no Englishman as he did Bentinck, or his younger favourite Keppel. Nothing attached him to English feeling. He had no relaxation except furious hunting. His religion was undogmatic, contemptuous of men's intolerance. Arts and graces he had none, except some taste for formal gardens. His asthmatic cough drove him from Whitehall to Kensington or Hampton Court, and he was not seen, as the Stuarts had been seen, in the Park, the tennis court, or the theatre. Till her death in 1694 from smallpox, Mary counterbalanced her husband's unpopularity. Her devotion to the Church of England, her charity, some sense of remorse for the treatment of her father, and her gay courage, won some loyalty for the new régime, even from men who hated Dutchmen and Dutch policy.

But William's greatness outshone any shortcomings, or alien interests. He had a fiery heroism, patience that nothing could exhaust, a soul so generous that it was superhuman. In desperate fighting, in tempests on a lee shore, under threat of murder, he stood unmoved. He threw into the fire papers which would have convicted his counsellors of conspiracy, and chose false men if he judged them fittest to serve. Though happiest in the field, he was no great commander, except that he could inspire men to die, but of political preparation for war he was a master. To hold together two jealous States, to weld Catholic and Protestant Powers into alliance, to bring Louis XIV to a stop by an eight years' war and then to frame the lines and mass the weapons for a second mightier war, this was the achievement of William III.

Prior to, and continuing throughout, this struggle, were his tasks in Britain, where he must placate Whig and Tory, and settle three kingdoms; tasks which wholly occupied him till 1690. Revolution had relighted party passion. The Whigs counted on sole power, hoping for revenge not on James' circle only but on all who had opposed exclusion or persecuted Dissent, and once again the sinister face of Oates haunted

Westminster. Tories, on the other hand, were sore over their broken oaths, their Church threatened, the army demoralized and now broken into detachments, while London and its palaces were held by the blue-coated Dutch. The new sovereigns were hardly crowned when the Royal Scots mutinied, and had to be rounded up by Dutch dragoons.

But the last thing William designed was to be a king of the Whigs, and the one English faction he unnecessarily feared was the Common-wealth group. He would not yield an inch of the royal powers, and the type of minister that he liked best was a Godolphin, a civil servant above faction. In this uneasy stage of the constitution, when government was representative but not in our modern sense responsible, he used as his parliamentary manager the unscrupulous Sunderland. With such an outlook, and since Tories had shared in the Revolution, the ministry he chose first was shared between parties ; Danby offset Halifax, the amiable Whig Shrewsbury was one Secretary of State but the other was the high-Churchman Nottingham, — an appointment which the Whig Burnet asserts saved the Church, and thereby the State.

A Church settlement was vital, for from religious differences parties had sprung, and on them turned most bitter memories. True, the cause of toleration was already won, and on that understanding the bishops had received Dissenting support against the late King. The Toleration Act of 1689, however, was a limited solution, admitting no new principle but merely relieving Protestant Dissenters from most of the ancient penalties. It thus exempted their laymen, on taking the oaths of supremacy and allegiance, from the long series of Acts regarding church attendance and conventicles, while it relieved their ministers and teachers if they took the same oaths and subscribed the thirty-nine Articles, excluding those touching ceremonies and ordination. In the same way Baptists were freed from the article enforcing infant baptism, and Quakers on making an affirmation of Christian belief. But the Act expressly did not apply to Roman Catholics and anti-Trinitarians. While this met most practical grievances, a parallel bill failed for a ' comprehension ', on the lines attempted in 1641 and again at the Savoy conference of 1661. It was, indeed, out of date, for Church-men were more dogmatic now on episcopal ordination than before the Civil War, while Nonconformists, assured of reasonable liberty and financed by prosperous congregations, no longer wished to be included in the establishment.

Liberty of worship was less in the mind of either side than political power. The Test Act having become the bulwark of Anglicanism, even Whig politicians were averse from stirring up that hornets' nest ; on the other hand, they were determined so to apply the oath of allegiance as to clear the Church of Jacobites. The King's own proposal for a com-promise was therefore rejected. The Church kept the tests, which meant a legal monopoly of office for those who would take the sacrament, while those who could not bring themselves to break the oaths they had taken to James and his heirs were driven into the wilderness. Sancroft, Ken, 4 other bishops, and 400 of the clergy led the way, so beginning the sect of ' Non-jurors ', which survived as a separate Church well into the eighteenth century, a standing protest against what they deemed a national apostasy.

1689 was a year of disillusion, with Scotland at war, James seemingly triumphing in Ireland, ceaseless conspiracy, and suspension of habeas corpus. Most bitter was it to the advanced Whigs. Had they taken up arms to put in office the men who had executed Russell and Sidney ? They pressed on with blind fury, refused to give supply for more than one year, and drew up long lists of exceptions from the Act of Oblivion. As 1690 began, they introduced a bill to restore the borough corporations forfeited in the last two reigns, in which one of their number, William Sacheverell, proposed an additional clause to disfranchise for seven years all who had taken part in the surrender of the charters. In short, to give for that period a monopoly of voting-power to the Whig party.

Wearied of this vendetta and reassured by Danby and Nottingham, the King turned to the Tories; he dissolved Parliament, the elections resulted in a Church victory, Halifax and Shrewsbury resigned. For the next three years, at the head of a mainly Tory ministry, Danby testified that conservative England had swallowed the revolution.

In Scotland nothing had stirred till the English gave the signal, and till the departure of James' army made it safe to act, but when their revolution did come, it was more real and violent than in England. Here it was no case of a mere change of sovereign but the total reversal of a government, for if the majority of Scotsmen were to be satisfied, they would not stop short of destroying episcopacy, the despotism of the Council, and a packed Parliament. Scottish politics, moreover, were immersed in a primitive society, lacking the English discipline of compromise. Until the majority learned such moderation, — and it was the last thing they could have learned after twenty years of Lauderdale, — inevitably the defeated minorities would turn to conspiracy.

As in England, an assembly of nobles asked William to summon a Convention, but before it could meet the national temper was proved by riots against Catholics, barbarous treatment of episcopal ministers, and a swarming of armed Covenanters from the west into Edinburgh. This violence, their defeat in the elections, and James' arrival in Ireland, excited the Royalists, and Claverhouse (soon made Viscount Dundee by his master) rode off to raise the Highlands. Painfully pursued by General Mackay with the Scots troops so long in Dutch service, he reached Inverness, doubled south again to loot Perth, and in June 1689 rallied the clans at Lochaber.

Yet where Montrose had failed, Dundee was not likely to succeed, in the quest of winning the Lowlands from a Highland base. Nothing could have done that but substantial help from James in Ireland. If Catholics and episcopalians were more numerous in the north, the Highlands were moved much less by such principle than by feuds of the clans, for revolution had brought about a restoration of the house of Argyll. Those who mustered with Dundee were those who most hated and feared the Campbells — Cameron of Lochiel, many branches of Macdonald, Stewart of Appin, or Macleans from the Isles. Only action could hold those undisciplined forces together, and action was urgent to decide the mastery of Perthshire, the key to the Lowlands, whose natural leader Atholl was trimming between the two Kings. So came about on the 27th July, just north of the dark pass of Killiecrankie, a short and bloody sunset battle, in which the Highland claymores sheared their way through Mackay's infantry. But the victors, tarrying to plunder, made no pursuit, while Dundee had been shot dead in the first charge. Within a month a new-raised Covenanting regiment, ancestor to the ' Cameronians ', beat a much larger Highland force off from Dunkeld, and the clans melted away. A year later the government had firm hold of Inverness ; while Fort William was erected at Inverlochy to control the west.

Immediately Dundee had ridden north, the Convention resolved that James had ' forfeited ' the throne, and settled the royal succession as in England. They accompanied their offer by a ' claim of right ' to declare the law, in which they boldly inserted a clause that episcopacy was ' a great and insupportable grievance '.

Little was needed to convince William that only by acceptance of Presbyterianism could he keep the Crown, for Scottish politics went down to bedrock cleavages and a refusal of the oaths of allegiance by 200 ministers showed that episcopacy meant to survive by turning Jacobite. Yet Presbyterianism, all previous history demonstrated, could mean many different things ; the type William favoured would be both lenient and State-controlled, especially as only leniency for episcopalians in Scotland could maintain liberty for Dissenters in England. His advisers in this matter were the broad-Church Scot historian, Burnet, now bishop of Salisbury, the admirable William Carstares, the prudent Earl of Melville, and Sir John Dalrymple of Stair, whose high abilities, service to the Stuarts against the Covenanters, and cold temper, made him something more than the Danby of Scotland.

But the present session revealed a bitter Opposition ; of clergy who, not content with an Act abolishing episcopacy, demanded a sweeping purge ; and of dissatisfied Whigs, led by Sir James Montgomery and Fletcher of Saltoun, who called for an end to the ' lords of the articles ', and for parliamentary appointment of officials. These extremists of

' the Club ' did not stick at trying to carry their programme by offers to the Jacobites.

In 1690 William unwillingly gave way, hoping thereby to win over all Presbyterians, except the fanatics who would admit no King but Christ. Acts for the royal supremacy over the Kirk were repealed, presbytery was restored to the model of 1592, with the Westminster confession of 1646 as its formula of faith, and private patronage in livings was abolished. Though this was a partisan settlement, the restored Kirk differed fundamentally from the triumphant body of the Civil Wars, for the Covenant itself was not restored and laymen enjoyed complete tolerance. For the next few years the King tried to induce the Kirk to take in ejected episcopalian ministers on reasonable terms, ultimately contriving to set up a sort of indulgence, whereby a certain number kept their livings provided they recognized his *de facto* title.

Another concession of 1690 had dangerous results. The Lords of the Articles being swept away, henceforth a single-chamber parliament would appoint its own committees freely, in which royal ministers would have a voice but not necessarily a vote. No constitutional link would now connect the two Parliaments of Great Britain except the King, and if the Scottish Parliament chose to be neutral in an English war, or to name a different heir to the throne, there was nothing to stop them but the royal veto. If such dangers arose, they would find their best support in the unsubdued Highlands, where one fearful crime deeply marked this reign. While one school of administrators thought that bribes and lenity would keep the clans at peace, Stair and some soldiers believed that nothing could civilize them but the sword, reckoning that with the help of the Campbells they could scotch the wild Camerons, Macleans, and Macdonalds. Experimenting in both methods, government distributed considerable sums but also ordered that every chief swear the oaths by the new year of 1692. Stair had laid plans in advance for wholesale devastation in case of refusal, but when the day came all had sworn but one, Macdonald of Glencoe, who took the oaths six days too late. This accident was concealed from the King, who therefore signed the usual letters of ' fire and sword ', to which Stair added orders that action should be secret, and that the Macdonalds be rooted out. So came about the massacre in the early morning hours of the 13th February, by soldiers of Argyll's regiment, commanded by a Campbell. When, three years after, the facts came to light, Stair suffered no penalty but exclusion from office ; the soldiers engaged, no punishment at all.

If in Scotland the wheels of vengeance revolved slowly, in Ireland they whirled round in rebellion, war, and punishment. Unable for many months to spare a man from Europe, and tricked into negotiation with Tyrconnel, William did not seriously approach the problem till the middle of 1689. By that date James with French officers and money had reached Dublin; Protestants of Leinster and Munster fled to England or concealed themselves, those of Ulster took refuge behind the walls of Londonderry and Enniskillen. Tyrconnel raised an army of 50,000 men, lacking only arms and discipline to be formidable, and in April James formed the siege of Derry, which lasted 105 days, till the garrison were reduced to oatmeal and horse-flesh. There, by the energy of its citizens, a concentration of Scot and Cromwellian Ireland fighting with its back to the wall, was made and tested the personality of Ulster. Inspired by George Walker, an elderly Anglican priest, they resisted treachery, the barbarism of French generals, and hunger, till the spectacle roused the English Commons and in July the relieving ships broke the boom on the river Foyle. The same month the Enniskillen men routed the Catholics in the battle of Newtown Butler, and in August Schomberg, the old Huguenot who had led William's troops at Torbay, landed with his army in Antrim. But no decision came that year. His men were mostly raw recruits, thrown into the field without covering or pay, while commissariat and victualling were infamous, and the rains incessant. And though the best Irish soldier, Patrick Sarsfield, won successes in Connaught, James was in no better position to fight.

In most respects this expedition was the most ignoble part of his life. His courage seemed gone, Tyrconnel was dying, his Scottish adviser Melfort was universally hated. He moved also in a dire dilemma, in that the more he depended on the Irish Catholics, the worse his chance of retrieving Britain. All his counsels were divided. For if he thought of Ireland as a stepping-stone to England, the Irish were fixed to their national liberties, while his French advisers saw their best means of injuring William in a lingering Irish war.

Even before Londonderry was relieved, the Irish Parliament showed that James was their captive. Based on Tyrconnel's purge of the corporations, they represented only the Catholics, and their programme was a return to pre-Cromwellian, even to Elizabethan Ireland. They repudiated the supremacy of the English Parliament and, but for the King, would have abolished Poynings' Act. Their promise of toleration was belied when, repealing the entire land settlement, they declared that owners should be restored as in 1641, without compensation to the Protestants evicted. They attainted over 2000 landowners by name, under conditions that made it impossible to prove their innocence. If it was too much to ask them to forget the last hundred years, their bitter memory doomed their country for a hundred years to come.

In 1690 both sides massed for decision. Lauzun, who had escorted Mary of Modena on her flight, brought 7000 French troops; in June William landed in Ulster with 36,000 men, and his best Dutch generals. He had defied his Cabinet's protest, for the French fleet held the

Channel, but if victory was to come on the main front of Flanders, the French in Ireland must be beaten first. Within a fortnight of landing he reached the Boyne and on the 1st July forced battle, where the river twice loops between Drogheda and Slane; a crossing by his right wing opened up the Irish centre, and though the passage was desperate and Schomberg was killed, most of the Irish, unlike the French, gave way, and William at the head of many charges rolled up their left also.

Within the week Dublin fell and James fled to France, and excepting the south-west ports William mastered the coast, and advanced on Limerick. Here Sarsfield beat off his storming action and he could not be longer away from England, but with his unfailing skill Marlborough took Cork and Kinsale. The end came in 1691 when Ginkel turned the Shannon line by seizing Athlone, won control of Connaught after a fierce battle at Aghrim, and in August forced Sarsfield to surrender Limerick, under guarantees for religious freedom and property.

Neither English Parliament, however, nor Irish Protestants were in a mood for moderation. The first legislated to exclude Irish Catholics from office and parliament; then, over the years that followed, its twin at Dublin set in being the penal code which was faithfully enlarged by the Hanoverians. They banished bishops and monks, forbade Catholics to teach, to carry arms, or marry Protestants, and closed the law courts to actions against the land settlement. So the minority was set, sword in hand, over a conquered people, and 'Whig' and 'Tory' factions fought out in more primitive form the feuds of Westminster. Once again it had been proved that the Stuarts' effort to reconquer England from Ireland was as fatal for the Irish as for themselves.

It was not Ireland, so universally detested by the English, which shook William's throne. Early in the reign there were plots among some of James' old circle, including Dartmouth and Clarendon, Preston an ex-Secretary of State, Penn the Quaker, and the non-juror bishop Turner. Yet these fumbling conspiracies were dangerous only because they unsettled the Tories, whose sentiment drew them back to Church and King, and many of whom had kinsmen in exile. More disturbing, in fact, was the correspondence held with the Court of St. Germain by some of the most powerful men in the kingdom. Various motives drew Marlborough to intrigue in the army or to induce Anne to ask her father's forgiveness, Godolphin to hold out hopes, Shrewsbury to refuse office, or Russell to promise assistance in the fleet; sometimes disappointment at being passed over, sometimes old ties, sometimes reinsurance against a restoration. It is hard to think they meant much more, for these advances were reopened at every crisis till the death of George I, with little to show but fair words and a little money. In 1692 Marlborough was turned out of his commands; in 1694 he and Godolphin may have talked loosely to Jacobites of an attack coming on Brest, which, in fact, was an open secret, and which our commander Talmash foolishly attempted, with the loss of his own life and many others. But the Churchills' motive was mainly the interest of the Princess Anne, whom Mary treated rather shabbily, and when on the Queen's death William was reconciled to his successor, Marlborough was forgiven and again employed. There was, of course, another type of Jacobitism, inspired by the French, and manned by desperate or broken men. This came to a head in the plot of 1696, of which James' son (and Marlborough's nephew) Berwick was not ignorant, to murder William as he came back from hunting in Richmond Park.

Jacobitism hung over politics like a cloud. Tories thought with loathing of this apostate world, and of triumphant or tolerated sects, while Whigs seized every chance of branding Tories as Jacobites by efforts to force through new oaths ' abjuring ' James' title. Yet in action very few English Tories were Jacobite, though what would happen if James' son were declared a Protestant remained to be seen. For the present the plots confirmed the mass of the country in their hatred of France and ' Popery ', as was seen in 1696 in the association formed to avenge William's life. And the exiled cause was already disintegrating. St. Germain was split between Protestants like the Scot Middleton and Catholics like the Scot Melfort, or again between Irish extremists and those who argued that James must ' compound ' by guaranteeing religion and liberty.

It was not, therefore, dispute of his title which caused the angriest conflicts of this reign, but rather opposition to William's power and policy. Nor were they mainly conflicts of party. For, though by inherited feeling and the organization of Shaftesbury and Danby, Whigs and Tories were entrenched, they were not yet like modern parties, centralized and comprehensive. Party in that sense could not co-exist with a King who controlled the executive by ministers of his choice, and had supreme influence over the Church, armed forces, and bureaucracy; and though representative government had a firm hold, responsible government was still far away. The ideas of that day pictured the constitution as a division of powers, between a royal executive, a Parliament with guaranteed functions and duration, and a judicature applying the fundamental law. To such thinking the very essence of Cabinet government, an amalgamation of the executive in a sovereign legislature, would be alien; they knew the Council as a legal organ but detested Cabinets or ' Cabals ', as secret extra-legal bodies and as corrupting Parliament through placemen. A second reason obstructed any regimentation of parties, and that was the aristocratic and provincial nature of society. The families who sat, from father to son, for seats where they controlled all property and manned the local bench, would admit no responsibility to a wide electorate, or obedience to ministers. There was, therefore, little connection as yet between ministries and the Commons' majorities. An election did not make the ministry; on the contrary, ministers used royal influence at an election to create their majority. Thus in the House of Commons that sat from 1690 till 1695 the King began with Danby's ministry but by 1694 gradually turned it into the Whig 'Junto', while to the end of the reign fluctuating majorities proved the doubtful lines of party. Again, the Revolution had shattered both the original rivals. Whigs, who had spent their lives attacking standing armies or the royal veto, found that their liberator used them as forcibly as any Stuart, while Tories had driven their King to flight by their resistance and now had to put up with the prerogatives of a sovereign whom they judged an enemy to their Church.

In such a transition both ministry and Opposition came to be made up of coalitions and, if any line could be drawn across those politics, it must be the older line of 'Court' against 'Country'. The King controlled war and foreign policy absolutely, he rarely took abroad an English minister, the Commons contained at least a hundred placemen, and he had 100,000 men under arms for a policy of which Parliament knew little but the cost. A feeling grew that the Bill of Rights had large gaps in it, and had been signed too hurriedly.

From many motives, then, a majority could be found in the Commons to press for more liberties, and to use their power of the purse to obtain them. On their frequent meeting depended government credit, which made the sinews of war, while an annual Mutiny Act alone could legalize military discipline. Departing from precedent, they voted customs duties only for short periods at a time and assigned the King a limited civil list. They hedged in the Cabinet by roving enquiries into naval mishaps, or the alleged sacrifice of British troops by Dutch generals, and regularly set up a committee of accounts; another attempt compelled William in 1696 to establish the Board of Trade, to deal with commerce and the Colonies. They forced him to cancel a land grant he had made to his favourite Portland, carried their nominee as Speaker against his choice, and stretched their power to take in regions, such as the East India Company, hitherto reserved for the Crown.

Many times over, directly or by 'influence', William resisted. He twice vetoed a bill to exclude placemen from Parliament; once, a triennial bill to prevent Parliament sitting over three years, with another to make judges' salaries independent of the Crown. An important Act of 1696, requiring two witnesses in treason trials, was only forced through after three previous defeats caused by royal pressure.

The curve of his power rose to a height and then declined within the Whig Junto's time, 1694–8. Generally his choice of ministers coincided with the advice of the very able men whose ambition co-incided with national advantage. Godolphin was usually at the head of the finances, under whatever ministry; Sunderland advised a return to the Whigs; Marlborough would bridge a reconciliation with Anne. Tory administration, particularly Nottingham's at the Admiralty, was not successful, Danby (now duke of Leeds) was always unpopular; while the Whigs were more united as a party, had more contact with the City and foreign merchants, and were more ready to support his Continental war. So during 1693–4 he dropped Nottingham and Seymour, while Leeds was attacked for taking bribes and lost all influence.

So came into power the Junto. Somers was Lord Keeper, a man of luminous mind and great charm, though a political partisan. Charles Montagu at the Treasury was exceedingly able, ingenious, and conceited. Russell, now Lord Orford, at the Admiralty was imperious, selfish, and determined. Their party organizer was the violent irreligious 'Tom Wharton', who nursed his native Buckinghamshire as a Whig stronghold, and whose horses were the best, as his head at table was the strongest, of his time. For nearly twenty years these men led the party which was bequeathed to Walpole; with them, though not of them, was Shrewsbury, and in the background Sunderland. They induced William to allow the passage of the Triennial Act and the Treason Act, but pleased him by defeating another place bill. They exploited conspiracies so as to blend in one accusation Tories with Jacobites; in 1696 also passing an important Act that the Parliament in existence at a sovereign's death should continue sitting for six months thereafter.

They commended themselves most of all by their larger and more continuous war effort. From Montagu's receptive mind can be dated the real beginning of our public finance. From him came, as it lasted for another century, the staple of the revenue, — the land tax, — which he raised in these years to 4s. in the pound, together with the useful instrument of Exchequer bills. The question of public credit had faced every ministry since the Restoration, but the Stuarts had hardly changed the methods of Burghley and Gresham, borrowed from the goldsmiths at exorbitant interest, or squeezed loans from chartered companies. For thirty years reformers had recommended a bank, on the lines of those which had mobilized the wealth of Holland, Genoa, or Venice, and now, faced by the necessity of raising several millions every year, Montagu took the steps which in 1694 resulted in the Bank of England. Acting on the advice of the Scot financier William Paterson, he carried an Act incorporating as a joint-stock bank the subscribers to an 8 per cent loan of £1,200,000. From this limited and temporary origin it had far to go; it was given no monopoly till 1709, its notes were not legal tender, it had to combat rival syndicates and the prejudice of Tory squires, who thought City banks republican and tried to set up a Land bank instead. Its triumph tied finance to the Revolution, and the City to the Whig party.

One immediate crisis, however, all but extinguished it. Our silver coinage had become chaotic. The coins, crudely made by hand, were so reduced by clipping, and false coins so rife, that all values were uncertain, and though Charles II's government had made improved coins with milled edges, the bad coins had driven out the good, in part because silver was undervalued in relation to gold. Tests showed that, on the average, the coinage had lost nearly half its weight. Enlisting the help of John Locke and Isaac Newton, in 1696 Montagu carried through an immediate and total recoinage, the loss being borne by the Exchequer. But for another year there was such a currency shortage that local trade fell back on barter and it was difficult to finance our armies abroad, while the Bank, having over-issued its notes, only just survived.

Though the first triennial Parliament was elected in 1695 amid the enthusiasm for the taking of Namur, the Whig government began to disintegrate. Its abuse of power was violent. It refused to permit a meeting of Convocation, it tried to purge the magistrates' bench of Tories, and to make the East India Company surrender its charter in favour of a Whig syndicate. And there was always a cleavage in its ranks, between the pure Whigs and the great adventurers with a touch of Jacobite about them: Shrewsbury, Sunderland, and Godolphin. This came out strongly in the excitement over the arrest of a Jacobite conspirator, Sir John Fenwick, who revealed something of these contacts with the exiled Court. Shrewsbury was panic-stricken, the Whigs delighted in the resignation of Godolphin and, since ordinary means of proof failed, executed Fenwick by act of attainder. But what finally destroyed them was the strain of war, and its aftermath.

This war of 1689-97, which cost the country £40 millions and raised the army to 90,000 men, was inglorious and inconclusive, nor was there ever a chance of realizing its proclaimed object of restoring Europe as it had stood in 1660. A coalition, striking from a wide circumference against a centralized State, must always begin at a disadvantage, and the great French war machine was resisting a body broken by serious differences. Britain and Holland had guaranteed secretly the Austrian succession in Spain, a fact which must be concealed from the Spaniards and aggrieved Leopold's son-in-law, the Elector of Bavaria. Austria, distracted by the Turkish war, cared for little else but Italy; Spain was weak as ever, Catalonia rapidly fell to one French army, while a second occupied Savoy and pinned down its Duke in Piedmont. Prussia was already sparring with Austria over the fate of Silesia; Hanover was seeking an electoral title, separate interests took away all unity of command.

Decision therefore mainly turned upon what Britain and Holland could do, in Flanders and on the sea. The French fleet made possible the Irish ' side-show ', which for two years kept Britain away from the main front; in 1690 the Brest and Toulon squadrons combined to hold the Channel, forcing the Allies to a battle off Beachy Head, which the British commander Torrington fought against his own judgment, and for the loss of which he was unjustly dismissed. These fears of invasion were removed in 1692 by Russell's total victory at La Hogue, when he destroyed fifteen French ships in six days of fighting, and in 1694 the fleet was sent to the Mediterranean, with the effect of heartening Savoy and temporarily saving Barcelona. Though French privateering did much damage, we had driven their battle-fleet to take shelter. Yet this command of the sea was never complete, for efforts to blockade France broke down on neutral opposition, and even more on Dutch objections to severance of their French trade. The Navy was also torn by Whig and Tory faction, ill-found, and ill-financed.

On land the enemy set out with every advantage, in veteran troops, a great commander in Luxemburg, and their strategical position. This, the fruit of thirty years of victory, was based on a fortress line from Menin to Dinant, controlling the upper waters of the Scheldt, Sambre, and Meuse, and opening the Low Countries to easy invasion. In that classic arena of walled cities, streams, and woods, a skilled defensive could almost ensure victory, and in this Luxemburg was much superior to William and his Dutch generals; Marlborough never being employed after 1691. That year the French took Mons, and in 1692 Namur; William arrived too late to save it, was then diverted towards Brussels and beaten at Steenkirk, where the Dutchman Solms won lasting hatred by leaving the British infantry to suffer, almost unaided, some 7000 casualties. 1693 repeated much the same story. William was induced to detach parts of his force and then, outnumbered, was brought to battle in a badly chosen position at Landen, where he suffered another 12,000 casualties. Huy on the Meuse was lost, Charleroi, and the line of the Sambre.

In 1694 the tide turned as the Allied numbers rose, and more still in 1695, for Luxemburg was dead, and William won his solitary victory at Namur. By this time, however, the war as a whole was being lost. Louis made up his differences with the Pope, Catholic opinion was gathering on his side. He detached Savoy by generous terms, and both Hapsburg States accepted neutrality on the Italian front. Financial stress recalled the British fleet from the Mediterranean, while if their own security was achieved, the Dutch would fight no longer for Spain or Austria. With his eyes, as always, on the Spanish succession, Louis drove Spain towards peace by taking Barcelona, and in 1697 his diplomacy forced these divided Allies to terms.

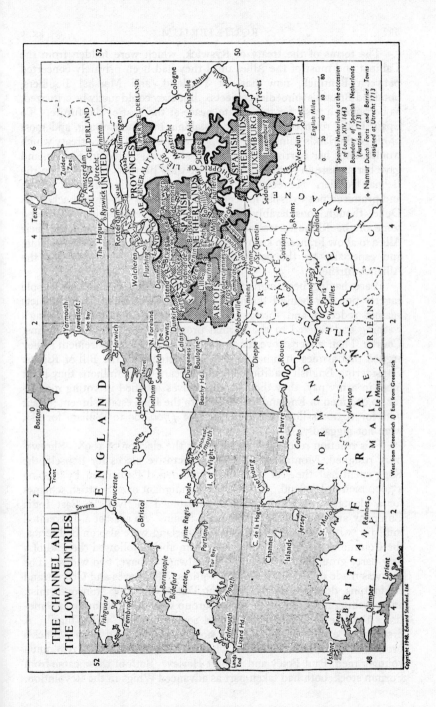

THE CHANNEL AND
THE LOW COUNTRIES

Copyright 1948. Edward Stanford. Ltd.

Spanish Netherlands at the accession
of Louis XIV, 1643

Boundary of Spanish Netherlands
(Austrian 1713)

Namur Dutch Forts and Barrier Towns
assigned at Utrecht 1713

English Miles
0   20   40   60   80

West from Greenwich 0 East from Greenwich

ENGLAND

Boston
Trent
Yarmouth
Lowestoft
Sole Bay
Harwich
London
Chatham
The Downs
N. Foreland
Sandwich
Nore
Calais
Dungeness
Beachy Hd.
Boulogne
Gloucester
Severn
Bristol
Thames
Portsmouth
Spithead
I. of Wight
Poole
Portland
Lyme Regis
Tor Bay
Exeter
Barnstaple
Bideford
Plymouth
Falmouth
Lizard Hd.
Lands End
Pembroke
Fishguard

C. de la Hogue
Cherbourg
Channel
Islands
Jersey
St. Malo
Le Havre
Caen
Dieppe
Rouen
Seine
Alençon
Le Mans
Rennes
Brest
Quimper
Lorient
Ushant

NORMANDY
MAINE
ORLÉANS
BRITTANY

FRANCE
DE FRANCE
ILE DE FRANCE
Paris
Versailles
Montmorency
Soissons
Reims
Marne
Châlons
Montreuil
Abbeville
Amiens
PICARDY
St. Quentin
Péronne
CHAMPAGNE
Sedan
Verdun
Meuse
Metz
Moselle

Texel
Zuider Zee
Amsterdam
Utrecht
The Hague
Ryswick
Rotterdam
Waal
Nimweggen
UNITED PROVINCES
HOLLAND
GELDERLAND
UPPER GELDERLAND
Arnhem
THE GENERALITY
Maas
Cologne
Rhine
Aix-la-Chapelle
Maestricht
Liège
BISHOPRIC OF LIÈGE
Walcheren
Flushing
Ostend
Bruges
Ghent
Antwerp
Brussels
FLANDERS
Dunkirk
Nieuport
Damme
Oudenarde
Audenarde
Lille
Tournai
Mons
Charleroi
Namur
Mouscron
Ath
BRABANT
HAINAULT
ARTOIS
SPANISH NETHERLANDS
Cambrai

SPANISH NETHERLANDS
LUXEMBURG
Luxemburg

The terms of the treaty of Ryswick, which were hidden from the Cabinet and most of the Allies until they had been privately concerted between Bentinck, now Earl of Portland, and Marshal Boufflers, obtained Britain's immediate objects. But they could justly be criticized, as betraying a wish for immediate peace at the cost of the future. To Spain Louis restored not merely Catalonia but Luxemburg, and most of his Netherlands gains since 1678. To Holland he gave a treaty which would admit her herrings and the salt she transported to France, and gave her a share in garrisoning some of the ' barrier ' fortresses on the Belgian frontier. He recognized William's title as King of Great Britain and promised not to assist his enemies. Lorraine was given back to its Duke, though considerably diminished, and the Austrians recovered some of the Rhine fortresses but, to their fury, were forced by their Allies to allow France to keep Strasbourg. So even in the peace-making, and especially by the generous terms to Spain, Louis divided the Alliance further.

Peace having been signed in September 1697, the British people eagerly put war behind them. In a bitter atmosphere of pamphlets against redcoats and foreigners, the Commons ignored the King's warning and reacted to the normal programme of ' Country ' against Court. Their anger drove the timid Sunderland into retirement; they argued that armies in time of peace conflicted with the Bill of Rights. Considering English tradition and the arrears of £2 millions they must meet in army pay, they thought themselves justified in voting moneys for 10,000 men in England, in addition to the Irish establishment; their vote for 10,000 sailors, and a civil list of £700,000 to William for life, were not niggardly.

This reaction reached its height after the election of 1698. Shrewsbury resigned, Montagu was devising lucrative places for himself, the King spent half the year in Holland and defied Parliament by keeping 15,000 men in England. The City was indignant over Scottish schemes for a plantation in Darien, which threatened to rival the East India Company and might involve war with Spain. As against a discredited ministry, with which the King and Sunderland were also on bad terms, the Commons, left without direction from above, followed the lead of a new party grouping. It had, and was always to have, two wings. The one was made up of old-style Tory squires, Musgraves and Gowers and Pakingtons, dead-set against anything Dutch, anything Nonconformist, and anything new; the other were a group who called themselves sometimes the ' new Country party', and sometimes the ' old Whigs '. A first leader of this second group, now just dead, had been Monck's brother-in-law Thomas Clarges, who had been succeeded by two much younger men, Paul Foley and Robert Harley. Both of these came from Puritan stock, both had taken part as advanced Whigs in the Revolution.

But they broke with the Junto on the old ' country ' principles, backed the triennial and place bills, resisted standing armies and the royal veto. So far they had fended off efforts to silence them by office; their letters spoke of ' a foreign interest ' pillaging the country, and criticized the King for violating the constitution.

In the session of 1698–9 Harley led his group to victory, carrying resolutions that the English forces should be reduced to 7000, all to be native-born (in addition to 12,000 for Ireland); they even rejected William's plea that he might keep his Dutch guards, which drove him to vow he would abdicate, and launched an enquiry into his grants of Irish land. Here he had a bad case, for contrary to an understanding that he would dispose of rebel forfeitures in concert with Parliament, he gave away large tracts to his foreign servants, Portland, Keppel, and Ruvigny, and his mistress Lady Orkney. After heated debate through 1699–1700, and tacking their votes to a money bill, the Commons forced the King to vest Crown property in Ireland in public trustees, and resolved to exclude aliens from the Privy Council. Meanwhile another revelation had shown that Somers and Orford had assisted to form a syndicate in favour of the notorious Captain Kidd, empowering him to put down pirates and reserving some of his booty to themselves. Unluckily Kidd turned pirate himself.

Step by step, but too slowly for parliamentary peace, the King yielded, until by 1700 all the Junto had fallen. Marlborough was brought into Cabinet and at the turn of the year 1700–1 Godolphin returned to the Treasury, Rochester took office, while after a dissolution Harley became Speaker. With this new system began, effectively, the age of Anne.

The new ministers inherited the greatest questions that could face a government, — the British succession and the peace of Europe, — and despite the previous angry years achieved on both a remarkable degree of national union. Anne's last surviving child, out of some eighteen born to her, the eleven-year-old Duke of Gloucester, died in July 1700, yet beyond her children the Parliament of 1689 had refused to look. At one time William had thought of the Duke of Savoy's children, descended from Charles II's sister Henrietta, but dropped the project when the Duke abandoned the Allies; and while James II lived no one pursued a scheme often mooted, to bring up his son as a Protestant heir. So all parties came back to another solution, mentioned ten years before, that after Anne's issue the succession should pass to the Electress Sophia of Hanover, daughter of Elizabeth of Bohemia and grand-daughter of James I. That security for a Protestant line made the first part of the Act of Settlement of 1701. But the new ministers also carried, without an opposing vote, clauses which summed up the ' Country ' party's criticism. They stipulated that any future sovereign must join in communion with the Church of England; no sovereign, not native-born, might engage England in wars to defend foreign territories, or leave the realm, without consent of Parliament. After the Hanoverian accession no alien, even though naturalized, could be a Privy Councillor or member of either House; no one holding office or pension from the Crown might sit in the Commons; all matters 'properly cognisable' there should be treated in the Privy Council, whose resolutions must be signed by the councillors consenting; judges should be irremovable except by a parliamentary address, and no royal pardon should bar an impeachment. Such, in Harley's words, was 'the ancient government of England', as the 'Country' party saw it; an executive rid of secret Cabinets, hedged in by a sovereign House of Commons freed from placemen, and subject to a law interpreted by judges, who had full security of tenure. Here, too, was a vote of censure on William's foreign interests and high-handed method, and full warning that no such foreign King would be stomached again.

For while this massive measure went calmly through, it was revealed that William had signed with the French two successive treaties, to partition the Spanish monarchy on its sovereign's death; the first had been negotiated by Portland and the Dutch minister Heinsius, Somers merely putting the great seal to a blank commission, and the second by Portland and Jersey, but neither treaty reached Parliament. On the top of a furious election the Tory majority, overruling their leaders, voted the impeachment of Somers, Portland, Orford, and Montagu. Yet while they wrestled with the Whigs entrenched in the Lords, and exploited this chance to destroy their enemies, the logic of facts drove them towards agreement with William on foreign policy under the united lead of Marlborough, Godolphin, and Harley.

France was exhausted, and Louis a man of sixty; the eyes of England were turned inward, and William was infinitely weary, feeling that his course was nearly run. Yet another war, in comparison with which that just closed would be child's play, was certain, unless the Spanish succession was peacefully adjusted before Charles II ended his living death of slow decay.

Every foreign office had been stuffed with documents on this matter since Louis and the Emperor Leopold had secretly agreed in 1668 on a partition, but the basic facts had remained the same. Charles II having no child, the succession would pass to his sisters' children. But the elder sister Maria Theresa, Louis' queen, had solemnly renounced her claim, though the French had very early invented pretexts to dispute this. The second sister Margaret, Leopold's first wife, having made no renunciation, her claim passed on her death to her daughter, married to the Elector of Bavaria, and so to the child Electoral prince. And though Leopold had extorted a private renunciation from his daughter, hoping to win the succession for the Archduke Charles, a son of his second marriage, neither Spain nor the Bavarians had agreed to it. So the broad rights of the question agreed with a broad political fact, that neither France nor Austria would, without fighting, surrender the whole inheritance to the other.

Thus came about the first Partition treaty of 1698, giving Spain, its colonies, and the Netherlands to the Bavarian; Naples, Sicily, some Tuscan ports, and the Biscayan province of Guipuscoa to France; and Milan to the Austrian archduke. It was followed by the Spanish adoption of the Bavarian prince as heir to the whole, though if Britain and France had held together, that crux might have been overcome, without any evil but a local war in Italy between France and Austria. But in February 1699 the boy Bavarian died.

Henceforth the chances of avoiding a major war were perilously lessened. Castilian pride, indignant at the pretension of others to divide its empire, stimulated the Emperor's hope that all might be reunited under a Hapsburg, the more so since with the peace of Carlowitz he had just triumphantly ended the long Turkish war. But since Austrian relations with the maritime States were embittered, and the British army seemingly dissolved, Louis' position was very strong and his attitude decisive, though moderate. He agreed that the Archduke should inherit Spain, Indies, and Netherlands; France should acquire, in addition to her assignment under the first treaty, Milan also, though this she was willing to exchange for Lorraine. This second treaty with William III was signed in February 1700.

Though the Austrians refused to abandon anything in Italy, the final cause of war came from Spain itself. Determined on no partition, swayed by the military preparedness of France and the influence of the Holy See, a party of his priests and councillors and a popular outcry induced Charles II to bequeath the whole, by his will, to Louis' grandson Philip; with a stipulation that, if declined by him, all should be offered to the Archduke. A month later, in November, Charles died and Louis XIV accepted the will. War with Austria was certain in any case, but if Louis had acted in the spirit of the will and left his grandson to rule as an independent sovereign, it is most doubtful whether either Britain or Holland would have struck a blow. It was not merely that his diplomatic position was so forceful, that Savoy was won over by a marriage for the new King of Spain, or that the Bavarian Elector, governor of the Spanish Netherlands and most hostile to his father-in-law Leopold, was now a French ally, together with his archbishop-brother, who held the strategical cities of Cologne and Liége. Some Dutch opinion and a majority of Britons held that the will was much to be preferred to partition; better, they argued, a French prince ruling in Spain, which would soon absorb him in its national pride, than to hand over all Italy to France itself, which would mean the Mediterranean closed by French fleets and tariffs.

Within three months Louis destroyed this dream. He did nothing to guarantee that France and Spain might not, some day, be united under one king. By agreement with the Bavarian Elector his forces occupied the barrier fortresses, garrisoned at present by the Dutch, between Ostend and Namur. He got the Assiento, or slave-trading monopoly for Spanish America, transferred to a French company, and almost closed the Spanish markets to English cloth. Refusing all notion of compensation for the Emperor, he sent an army to resist Eugène and the Austrians in Italy, where fighting broke out in May 1701.

Inch by inch the Tory majority came round to William's stand against this aggression; first, to promise support to Holland, if attacked; next, to authorize him to join with Holland and Austria for 'reducing the exorbitant power of France', Harley's speech putting their objective as 'a lasting peace' or 'a necessary war'. Even party interests pushed the Tories into a more warlike policy, for the Whigs, infuriated at the attack on their leaders, were denouncing them as tools of France and the Pretender, and organizing petitions for a new parliament. A spontaneous clamour arose for war, most of all in the City, and the Kentish grand jury petitioned the House to turn their resolutions into votes of supply 'before it is too late', for which the Commons, by a stretch of power, sent their representatives to prison.

Riding on this gale of popular feeling and cheered by Eugène's victories, in September William concluded at the Hague the Grand Alliance, Marlborough acting in the double rôle of plenipotentiary and commander of the British troops. Both Britain and Holland had recognized Philip V as King of Spain, and the terms of alliance in fact contemplated another partition, on a middle line steered by the British between Dutch reluctance and Austrian fury for war. As a 'satisfaction' for his claims, the Emperor should receive all the Italian provinces and Mediterranean islands that had belonged to Spain; the Spanish Netherlands should be organized to 'serve as a barrier for Holland', the awkward question being shelved whether Dutch or Austrians should rule them; Britain and Holland should enjoy commercial privileges in Spanish territories as in the late reign, and if war came might keep what they could take in the Indies; the terms of peace should provide against union of the French and Spanish Crowns.

They had not to wait for the two months during which Louis was given a chance of compromise. Not only did he prohibit British imports into France but, when James II died in September, violated the treaty of Ryswick by recognizing James Edward as James III. With English feeling roused to fury, William accepted the advice of Somers and his foreign counsellors to dissolve Parliament. It was against the instinct of Marlborough and Godolphin, and indeed a mistake for which, had he lived, he would have paid dear, for it clinched the Tory hatred of him and sent the country into a heated, scurrilous election. Nor did it succeed; the two parties returned equally balanced and Harley was re-elected as Speaker. The Tories being anxious to brush off the stain of Jacobitism, Parliament asked the insertion of a new clause in the alliance, that no peace be made until France made reparation for acknowledging James III. They passed another Act enforcing on members and office-holders an 'abjuration' of the Pretender and, as by Marlborough's wisdom full deference was paid to them in carrying out the treaty, voted supply for 80,000 soldiers and sailors. And though William dismissed his Tory ministers and Godolphin resigned, he did not recall the Junto but brought in some moderate Whig noblemen.

His work was done, and the British world would, in fact, be more united without him, to carry out what he had planned. In February 1702 his horse, stumbling on a mole-hill at Hampton Court, threw him heavily — 'the little gentleman in black velvet ' becoming the baser Jacobite toast. His weak consumptive frame had no resistance left and on the 8th March he died, leaving his throne and his task outwardly to Queen Anne but, in fact, to Marlborough, who was already called her 'grand vizier '.

CONTEMPORARY DATES

CHAPTER V

THE REIGN OF ANNE, 1702–1714

ENGLISH civilization, in its Renaissance phase, was now at its climax. Born of conflict between opposing principles and penetrated by native and foreign elements, it had achieved a poise which, in appearance rather than in fact, was prolonged for the first half of the eighteenth century. In Anne's reign the genius of Wren, Locke, and Newton won their calm satisfying victories, Dryden the master of the new letters had just died but Congreve and Farquhar carried on the drama, while Swift and Pope, Addison and Steele were writing, for a small individual society, prose and verse never surpassed in its clear horizon and ease of art. Here and there an older mentality contested the field, as in the non-juror literature which clashed with the pamphlets of the Dissenter Defoe, and it was now that his sons published Clarendon's *History of the Rebellion*. But the new lights steadily covered the firmament. Harley, by birth a Dissenting Whig, made himself leader of the Tories, Walpole was the rising hope of the Whig party, and in this reign John Wesley and Samuel Johnson, Benjamin Franklin, Fielding, Sterne, and Hume were born to fill gaps left by the death of Pepys and Evelyn, Locke, Danby, and Richard Cromwell. This age, which seemed to build for endurance, consolidated its heritage by victory; while the dome of St. Paul's rose, Louis XIV's monarchy was destroyed at Blenheim and buried at the peace of Utrecht, Gibraltar and Hudson's Bay were added to the Empire, and the Union at last created Great Britain.

Queen Anne, the first woman ruler since Elizabeth, was not of Elizabeth's calibre, so that the mere fact of this average, invalid, woman on the throne notably advanced our parliamentary system; though she sat often in the formal Cabinet, an inner ring of ministers supplied the lead which William III had given. Yet the Queen was no cipher. From her dislike both of William's memory and the prospect of the Hanoverians, from her first gift of £100,000 to the war funds down to her last effort for peace, from her devotion to the Church, her dependence on the Marlboroughs and subsequent quarrel with the Duchess, came the tone and the several crises of her reign. Many children she had borne, and buried them all, and the more ardently loved her husband George of Denmark of whom, however, Charles II had said, ' I have tried him drunk and tried him sober, and there is nothing in him '. She scandal-

ized her subjects by getting him £100,000 a year for life, and when she
lost him vowed undying unforgiveness to the Whigs, who had attacked
his Admiralty administration.   Though a Stuart princess, with some
uneasiness about the ' sin ' of the Revolution and some feeling for the
brother she called ' the young man in France ', and though a high-
Churchwoman who wished to bring back Ken as a bishop, none the less
she detested ' Popery ' and acted up to her lights as a constitutional
sovereign.   She would not be ' enslaved ', she protested, to ' the merciless men ' of either party, insisting on her free choice of ministers.   In
general she supported the proved sentiment of her people — the war,
the Union, and the peace — and leaned most upon those who, she
thought, would act as moderators.

Marlborough was fifty-two when he received supreme power, bred
from boyhood as a servant of the Stuarts and hence in what was in a
sense a Tory but, more truly, a pre-party outlook.   Though his steps
had passed through muddy places, for he had been one of Lady Castlemaine's lovers and his sister Arabella mistress to James II, he had lived
hard ; as a young guardsman he had fought in Tangier, in Flanders with
Monmouth, in Alsace under Turenne, finally holding high command
under William in Ireland and Flanders again.   Only one passion disturbed that collected mind, his love for his wife Sarah Jennings, and
here was the source of his relation to the Queen, for when William and
Mary had been harsh, Anne was propped by the affection of the invincible Sarah.   Sarah's husband had, indeed, some odd limitations.
With no money but of his own making, he died a millionaire, for as in
the parallel case of Warren Hastings his zeal for the State did not argue
any delicacy about riches.   So the enormous French bribes, which he
refused after Ramillies, he was ready to accept later when a good peace
was certain.   Nor, again, did he abandon almost to his last day correspondence with the exiled Stuarts, of late usually through his nephew
Berwick, in part perhaps from old sentiment but, one suspects, even
more as a political insurance.

Beyond the gifts which put him in the first half-dozen of soldiers,
Marlborough had many wonderful qualities.   With suspicious Dutchmen, grasping German princes, or the crude Charles XII of Sweden,
he wielded the charm of a genuinely conciliatory heart.   He won the
British rank and file by unshakable fortitude, and ceaseless care for their
food and welfare, and perhaps by the repeated spectacle of a commander-
in-chief, known to loathe useless bloodshed, heading a wild charge like
a cornet of horse.   He had a tenderness for Anne, ' the poor Queen ',
while England shone far more in his spirit than what he execrated as
' the detested names of Whig and Tory '.   Here, however, he clashed
with Sarah, so termagant, anti-clerical, and partisan, who hardened
and hastened what the war made inevitable, a break with his Tory

friends, and Sarah was reinforced by their ambitious son-in-law, the third Sunderland.

Another daughter's marriage, to Godolphin's son, bound them closer to their best political associate who, the Duke insisted in 1702, must be Treasurer at home, while he took the field. The Cornish Cavalier Godolphin had no more liking than Marlborough for the Whig Junto but, having to fight for Whig money through a Tory House of Commons, came earlier than Marlborough to see that, without alliance with the Whig party, the war could not be won.

Such was the inner group, already tested by years of suppression; of whom Anne wrote to Sarah, ' we four must never part, till death mows us down with his impartial hand '.

The reign was darkened by a revival of party, the product of reaction against the Dutch King, and the more unmanageable because of the Whig magnates and bishops in the Lords. With joy the Tories heard the Queen's first speech from the throne declare her heart was ' entirely English ', while the composition of her first Cabinet proved her sympathies. If its nucleus were moderates, in ' the triumvirate ' of Marlborough, Godolphin, and Harley, the majority, — the Queen's uncle Rochester, Nottingham, Seymour, and Jersey, — came from the right-wing of Tory Churchmen. Strengthened by the election of 1702, the Tories hastened to demolish all Dutch and Whig elements, reopened Montagu's accounts, questioned William's grants, and turned out Whig magistrates.

Party feeling still flowed most strongly through the churches, the universities which were largely clerical seminaries, the parish pulpit, or the Dissenting meeting-house. Embittered at the shipwreck of their old principles by revolution, and Toleration and Abjuration Acts, high-Churchmen were striving to recover a losing battle. They hoped the Queen, granddaughter of the royal martyr, was on their side; she revived the practice of ' touching for the evil ', while in 1704 her creation of ' Queen Anne's bounty ' restored to the Church, for the augmentation of poorer livings, the tithes and first-fruits taken away by Henry VIII. Tenison the archbishop, Burnet and other bishops of William's appointment, seemed to the lower clergy to be latitudinarians, whose undogmatic faith was hurrying England into infidelity. In their fear they raised once more the cries of the civil war, of Divine right and ' the church in danger ' from false brethren. In Francis Atterbury, later bishop of Rochester, they found an aggressive leader who fired Convocation to attack the bishops, and to claim that not Parliament, but their own body, was sovereign of the Church.

At the root of this passion was a fact, that the law was untrue to actual society. Formally cut off from all branches of government by the Test and Corporation Acts, the large body of prosperous Dissenters had found a way round, by taking the sacrament merely to qualify and ordinarily attending their own chapels; though Dissent was not yet altogether severed from marriage and burial in their parish church. This 'occasional conformity' gave grave offence. Religious minds felt it a blasphemy to misuse their holiest rite to qualify as a constable, while politicians saw they could wield this outcry to break the Whig machine. Led by men of either type, the religious member for Oxford University, William Bromley, and by young Henry St. John, a free thinker but a Tory partisan, in 1702–3 the Commons twice passed an Occasional Conformity bill to punish such offenders, and twice the Whig peers wrecked it. This controversy inflamed the country. Defoe was sent to prison for his pamphlet *The Shortest Way with the Dissenters*, in which he mockingly advised the use of fire and sword. Tory members voted against a resolution for the furtherance of Union with Scotland, which would seat Presbyterians in their own House.

To the leading ministers even more serious was the Tories' attitude to the war. Rochester maintained that Britain should fight not as a principal, but as an auxiliary; Nottingham, declaring a sea-war the only one suitable to British interests, would divert our effort to Spain and the Indies. This collision in Cabinet brought about deadlock between Lords and Commons. The peers hotly defended the policy of William, charged Nottingham with covering up Jacobite plots, and in the famous case of Ashby *v.* White took cognizance of the refusal of votes to some electors in Wharton's borough of Aylesbury, which the Commons resisted as a breach of privilege.

Seeing it was impossible to go on with violation of Cabinet secrecy and an annual threat to war supplies, Marlborough and Godolphin broke with the right wing. In 1703 Rochester was dismissed, Seymour and Jersey the next year, Nottingham discontentedly resigned, and the ministry was reconstructed. Harley became Secretary of State, while St. John, at twenty-five the best speaker in the House, was brought in as Secretary-at-war. But this coalition pleased neither extreme, while peril crowded in on the nation. In November 1703 'the great storm' wrecked fifteen warships, swept away the Eddystone lighthouse, killed the bishop of Bath and Wells in his palace, and did a million pounds worth of damage in London. Scotland was in almost revolution, Vienna was threatened by French armies, and nothing could have saved our government but a victory in the field.

The first two years of war had been disappointing, since Louis' measures of 1701 had given him every initial advantage. His forces held the keys to the Low Countries; by alliance with Cologne he controlled the lower Rhine. His Toulon fleet dominated the Mediterranean, he garrisoned Naples; Eugène was hard pressed in northern Italy. Savoy gave him one side of the Alps, the Bavarian alliance ensured the other.

All Spain was his, and Portugal was believed to be coming over.

Scattered round the circumference of this solid core was the Coalition. At the climax of the war the British troops in all theatres did not exceed 70,000, Marlborough had only 8000 at Blenheim, and though he technically commanded the Dutch as well, he had to convince not only their generals but the field-deputies detailed to watch their armies. The rest of his forces came from Denmark and German States, Prussia and Hanover in particular, unity of command thus resting on separate treaties and subsidies, and necessitating argument with jealous princes. Harder still was it to keep peace or patience with Austria, divided by such distances from the maritime Powers, and whose contingents were always in arrears, despite the Duke's loyal comradeship with Eugène. The Austrians looked first to their own objectives in Italy. Their misgovernment in Hungary kept rebellion alight there which tied their hand, they had one feud with Savoy about Milan, a second with Prussia, and a third, infinitely dangerous, with Holland as to the future of Belgium.

On good relations with Holland our success did, indeed, finally turn, and here Marlborough was indispensable through his staunch co-operation with the Pensionary Heinsius. Yet good relations were hard to maintain. The Dutch war effort was tremendous, since they undertook to provide a fleet and 100,000 soldiers, but to no country's economic structure could the war be more shattering. In fact, it proved impossible to prevent them trading with the enemy, so that no Allied blockade was entirely successful. Moreover, with war at their threshold and such bitter experience behind them, the Dutch took no interest in what happened to Spain, while to Austria their enmity was intense. They were determined to keep the Scheldt closed, which would submit Belgian commerce to their own, to enlarge their Barrier, and to resist handing over Belgian sovereignty to the Catholic Hapsburgs. Their trading rivalry with Britain was deep in their blood, and with some justice they complained of the economic concessions which Britain extorted from the Austrian claimant for Spain. Finally, once the Low Countries were cleared, a powerful peace-party raised its voice, representing the ties of Amsterdam with French markets, and led by Buys, a tireless politician.

On the rim of this jagged alliance loomed another danger, that more than once threatened to destroy it, the northern war proceeding all these years, of Charles XII of Sweden against Russians, Poles, Danes, and Saxons. To stop this storm engulfing the Danish contingents was one of Marlborough's first preoccupations; again, in 1707, when Charles threatened war on the Empire, he had to exert with that obstinate King his wonderful powers. So for ten years we find him ever travelling, to conciliate and inspire, from the Hague to Vienna and

Berlin, with all the gifts that made Bolingbroke write years after of ' the greatest general and the greatest minister that our country, or perhaps any other, has produced '.

Many reasons, too, in the military conditions of that age made vital the person of the commander. Never commanding more than the 90,000 men he led at Malplaquet, his forces could still be directed by one man — tactically moved by his telescope from a church tower, artillery placed under his own eye, a battle turned by his own gallop. Those small mercenary armies were carefully husbanded. Moving in precise deployment, his infantry taught to mass fire by platoons, and the cavalry to charge home with weight of steel, armed with new deadly weapons of grenade and bayonet, though with flintlocks and guns only effective at close quarters, with no margin of reinforcement and no communications more rapid than rivers or vile roads, Marlborough's army triumphed because he brought it intact to the decisive moment. But it could not be replaced, and the rate of casualty much exceeded that of modern war.

Through years of misfortune or distraction, his strategical thought remained constant. The French in the north must first be levered out of the Netherlands, and then brought to battle, so that he might open a way to Paris. But a back door must also be opened from the south, not only to cut off Spanish treasure fleets or to buttress our exports, but to force the Straits, master Toulon and, in touch with Austrians and Italians, roll up the enemy from the Riviera. This being the essential scheme, as time went on the objective of seating an Austrian prince in Spain had to be fitted into it, and hard it proved. As captain-general, master of the ordnance, and, through his naval brother George, with direct influence at the Admiralty, Marlborough alone could co-ordinate policy and war.

The sea-operations of 1702 were unfortunate, Spanish treasure fleets stole safely away, and though, in fighting on the Main, Benbow won the glory that made him a hero of inn-signs and ballads, two of his captains were shot for cowardice. A large expedition against Cadiz was a sorry failure, for Ormonde the general could not keep discipline, while Admiral Rooke made for home on the first pretext, only by luck destroying a Spanish fleet in Vigo Bay.

In the Netherlands that year Marlborough displayed in a few strokes both his own genius and the obstructions in his way. While his allies made a clearance on the Rhine by taking Kaiserswerth, he forced back the French between Rhine and Meuse by a threat to their communications and, having driven them into Brabant, manœuvred to fight them at advantage. But the chances were lost by Dutch deputies and Dutch generals. Even so, he cleared the Meuse and took Liége.

1703 told much the same story in both theatres. Rooke and the

Dutch accomplished nothing in the Channel; Shovell's squadron sealed up the French in Toulon but failed to make contact with the Huguenot rebels of the Cévennes. Marlborough meantime set forth what he called ' the great design ', a joint operation to win Antwerp and Ostend. But it demanded exact timing and good will, which he did not receive from the Dutch; the French retired into lines defended by water-ways and a trench system, and all the Allies won were Bonn and Lim-burg. Marlborough told Heinsius, ' I would rather die than put up with anything like it again '.

At the end of the year the Empire was at a standstill. In Italy the French drove the Austrians back on the Brenner, on the middle Rhine they recovered Landau, on the upper took Kehl and joined hands with the Bavarians; Augsburg, Ratisbon, and the upper Danube fell, and thence their armies could strike at Vienna, already menaced from the east by the rebel Hungarians. Prussia was shaky, the Imperial general Lewis of Baden in despair, all was at stake.

Here, in fact, the great war really began, for other events changed its whole character. Victor Amadeus duke of Savoy had spent a lifetime in balancing, a British envoy reporting he cared ' for nothing on God's earth but his own dear self '. But as he always reacted against a Power that might stop him acquiring ' leaves of the artichoke ' in the Milanese, he was infuriated by French patronage, and on a promise of British money and Imperial troops in October 1703 joined the Alliance.

King Pedro of Portugal also feared he might become a French vassal, realizing too that neutrality would not save his colonies from Allied sea-power. While our victory at Vigo pointed the arguments with which our envoy Methuen plied him, a greater influence came from Prince George of Hesse-Darmstadt, an excellent soldier who had governed Catalonia, and whose popularity would ensure support for an Austrian candidate in Spain. Portugal asked stiff terms in money and men, and made it a condition that the Archduke Charles should be declared King of Spain and show himself in person. After heavy grumbling the Emperor gave up his own claim, though he meant to keep hold of Milan, and early in 1704 allowed his favourite son to sail for Lisbon. A second Methuen treaty secured for British cloth a practical monopoly of the Portuguese market, providing in return that Portuguese wines should pay one-third less duty than the wines of France. So port and madeira became the taste of eighteenth-century English society.

Nothing could be more grave than the military effect of these treaties. Nottingham and the Tories worked for them, as conducive to the sea-war in which they believed, and indeed the great harbour of Lisbon was a necessary step, if the Mediterranean was to be held. Yet they made a vast departure from the original war-aim of a mere partition, and the programme of ' no peace without Spain ' was to become a grievous burden.

Our intervention accomplished nothing during 1704 in Portugal itself. After landing the Archduke, Rooke's fleet passed the Straits, found Savoy unable to co-operate, no sign of the promised rising at Barcelona, and failed to stop the Brest squadron entering Toulon. At last, though refusing to attempt Minorca or Cadiz, Rooke agreed to attack Gibraltar, upon which, since Cromwell's day, our seamen had kept an eye. With decayed fortifications and a minute garrison, it was an easy prey, and fell in one August day to our landing-parties, to be held in the name of the Austrian Charles. Ten days later the French, sallying out of Toulon to recover it, put themselves between the Rock and Rooke, off Malaga ; the British ships were foul with long cruising and short of ammunition, but the French broke off and retired. What the fleet had won, it saved. Twice in the next winter Admiral Leake brought reinforcements from Lisbon, that broke up the French and Spanish besiegers. But the full value of Gibraltar lay in the future ; within a fortnight of its capture, the present power of France was destroyed by Marlborough.

During 1703 he plotted the next year's campaign on his favoured plan, to strike towards Metz down the Moselle valley. By January 1704, however, he was speaking of the Rhine, by April under Austrian pressure he and Godolphin agreed with the Queen to take his army to the Danube. The risk and responsibility were enormous, the project was concealed from Parliament, he only extorted agreement from the Dutch by a threat to act without them. But his mind was made up, and for once his prosaic letters broke out that it was ' victory or death '. Of the Austrians he asked two things : a concentration to crush Bavaria, and the loan of Prince Eugène.

His march was a masterpiece of daring precision. Food and money, new shoes, and bridges of boats, all were ready at each stage, and in his eye the exact point where he would strike the Danube. From a point of departure east of Maestricht, he set out with 40,000 men on 19th May, reached the Rhine at Bonn, but on the 29th at Coblenz, instead of turning up the Moselle, turned left over the Rhine, on over the Main at Frankfurt, on 3rd June over the Neckar, on south-east through the Swabian hills, ten miles a day all these six weeks, with his men rested and confident, till on the 22nd he joined Baden and the Imperialists north of Ulm. By keeping the French guessing he had gained a start, but now Villeroy's army from the Netherlands was making for the middle Rhine, and Tallard on 1st July crossed it at Strasbourg.

He was too late. The Allied commanders agreed that, while Eugène held the Rhine, Marlborough and Baden should at once attack the Bavarians. The Duke persuaded Baden to attack the Schellenberg, the mountain fortress overhanging Donauworth, whence he would bestride the Danube, with good communications that, in case of need, would take him back on Nuremberg. At all costs he must strike before the French joined the Elector.

On the 2nd July the Allies stormed the Schellenberg in a bloody evening battle, then crossed the great river into Bavaria. Though they had slain 10,000 of the enemy, all Marlborough had come to do was in the air, for he had not the guns that could besiege Munich, and Tallard was coming through the Black Forest. Eugène, following him, boldly agreed with Marlborough they would sacrifice superiority of numbers to harmony by detaching Baden to besiege Ingolstadt. As they had expected, the French recrossed the river to attack Eugène, and on the 10th August the Duke moved to join him west of Donauworth.

Confident that the Allies were in retreat for Nuremberg, the Bavarian Elector over-persuaded Tallard to pursue them; on the 12th the French took up a strong position, having the Danube and the village of Blenheim on their right, the marshy rivulet of the Nebel across their front, and their left based on wooded hills. On the 13th, to their surprise, they were attacked at dawn, for fight the Allies must, before Villeroy and yet another army cut their line of retreat. And so, having taken the sacrament, Marlborough rode out on his white horse, in scarlet coat and the Garter.

In numbers the armies were almost equal, about 56,000 men in each, but the French artillery was superior and in that four-mile front Marlborough could not avoid fighting hand-to-hand. Though firing began just after eight, it was noon before Eugène had deployed the right wing up to the wooded slopes, and only then, after harassing French fire, could the British infantry under Cutts on the far left attack the fortified village of Blenheim. On either wing their attack was held and brought to a standstill till nearly three o'clock, and if Eugène fought a selfless containing action, it was the Duke's tactical genius which seized profit out of misfortune and the enemy's mistakes. For Tallard had overcrowded his infantry into Blenheim, and he waited too long to strike as the Allies passed, by pontoons and brushwood fascines, over the Nebel. Marlborough arrested the bloody assault on Blenheim, turning it into a passive defence which held the French foot in a vice; he himself took command of his left centre at the crisis of the day, when a wedge had been thrust between him and Eugène. That accomplished, and having brought his main body over the marshes, he launched a general advance, which out-numbered Tallard in all arms and broke his centre to fragments. While the Elector with his French colleague Marsin made for Ulm, and at last straggled through the forest to the Rhine, Tallard was taken with 10,000 prisoners; in battle and pursuit the enemy lost another 30,000 in killed and wounded. So, at a price of some 12,000 casualties, of whom about 2200 were British, Vienna was saved and France defeated as never since Agincourt.

Marlborough, recrossing the Rhine, prepared for the campaign of his dreams by passing through the Vosges and taking Treves. Prince of Mindelheim now in the Empire, he ended the year by visiting Berlin to prevent war between Prussians and Swedes, and came home to receive the royal manor of Woodstock, with the promise of a palace to commemorate Blenheim for ever.

In this way the coalition government was saved, in a rare moment of national feeling. London saw the French standards hung in Westminster Hall, while in the Lords the Duke gave the praise to the ' extraordinary courage ' of his men. But, soured by their enemies' triumph, the right-wing Tories came on again to criticize the ' betrayal ' of the Church, being insane enough to ' tack ' the Occasional Conformity bill to the land tax. The ' tackers ' were defeated, the Queen infuriated, and at the election of 1705 the weight of government was thrown against the Churchmen; the result being a Parliament in which the ' Queen's servants ', with independents and Whigs, outnumbered the Tories. Cabinet changes marked the swing-over, bringing in a rich Whig duke of Newcastle, a Whig chancellor in Cowper, and two rising Whigs in minor office, — the Norfolk squire Walpole and Joseph Addison, whose poem on Blenheim had been the success of the year.

Before that new Parliament ended in 1708, the reign and the war took decisive turnings. It was proved that, while Marlborough could defeat any army in sight, the Austrians were false allies and the Dutch longed for peace ; that the secondary war to install an Austrian in Spain was doomed ; that only union of Britain could save the Protestant succession ; and that no coalition could last between Whigs and Tories.

Marlborough's hopes of a Moselle advance faded in 1705, through Dutch and Imperial unreadiness, and he was recalled from the Saar to stop an attack on Liége. Patiently he obeyed, broke through the lines of Brabant south-east of Louvain, cut in between the French at Brussels and their own frontier, and near the later field of Waterloo faced them in superior numbers. But the Dutch vetoed an attack.

This year the Emperor Leopold died, but his successor Joseph continued the same selfish policy, massing all his force against Hungary, while his armies in Italy were beaten back to the Alps. The Dutch were turning one ear to peace proposals, for which the French offered Marlborough a bribe of two million livres. Courteously ignoring it, he went to Vienna and Berlin, for Prussia was wobbling and Austria bankrupt ; above all, he would lay foundations for a memorable scheme, to transfer his main army to Italy and invade France from the south.

The British government, having firmly told the Dutch we should never make peace without winning Spain, in the autumn gave some body to this dream by the capture of Barcelona. Hitherto the Portuguese front had failed ingloriously, — our commander Galway put no trust in his cosmopolitan forces, — but Hesse had hopes of Catalonia and in June a large expedition reached Lisbon, with elastic orders to explore the chance of helping Savoy or to attempt the eastern coast of Spain. For reasons still mysterious, except that his wit amused Duchess Sarah, the command was given to Peterborough, an active Whig venturer of 1688, factious, fanciful, and with no fighting experience. After innumerable changes of plan, it was decided to land near Barcelona.

After Shovell's fleet disembarked them north of the city, there was another long pause, passed in dispute whether it should be Italy or Spain, and in feuds between the Germans and Peterborough. At last they agreed to attack the citadel of Montjuich, south of the city; though Hesse was killed in the assault, Montjuich was taken, and in October Barcelona surrendered. Over the winter the Allies established themselves in Aragon and Valencia. Finding them so dispersed, in April 1706 a French force beleaguered Barcelona, but Leake saved it from the sea; Philip V retreated to the Pyrenees; Galway's Portuguese army, pressing Berwick back over the Peninsular fields where French and British were to fight again, in June set out eastward to march on Madrid.

Meantime Marlborough's Italian design had foundered, not because the Dutch would not send troops, or because the British Cabinet were nervous, but owing to an Austrian collapse both in Italy and Alsace. Gloomily the Duke set out for more fortress warfare. But Louis XIV, confident that one victory would bring the peace for which his exhausted country yearned, ordered Villeroy to seek a decision and in May the French took up position at Ramillies, midway between Louvain and Namur. Their right front rested on the Mehaigne river, the left was guarded by the marshy sources of the Geete, and in their centre was the cavalry's ideal open plain. In numbers about equal, but with superior artillery, after a night march the Duke attacked exultantly on 23rd May. Except that he was once unhorsed and nearly killed, nothing marred this, his happiest day, for never were seen better the simplicity of his design, his brilliance of decision, or the fighting power of British, Danes, and Dutch. The first cannonade fired at 2.30, and by 6 o'clock the final charge was ready. While the Dutch stubbornly attacked the enemy left, with such success that Danish horse broke through and outflanked the whole line, on the right Marlborough feinted with Orkney's British infantry and, while Villeroy was beguiled into taking it as the main assault, rapidly moved thirty-nine squadrons and some foot to the centre. The French broke; by midnight the Duke was himself twelve miles further on, sleeping in his cloak on the ground, with the summer before him. Villeroy lost 13,000 in casualties and several thousand more deserters, within a fortnight Brabant and Flanders as far as Ghent were in the Allied hands, and when the campaign ceased in October Marlborough held Menin and Ostend, with the Low Countries almost wholly freed. Even now this great year was not exhausted. Since Vendôme, the best French soldier, had been recalled from Italy to save Flanders, in September Eugène, by wonderful marching, came from Lake Garda to crush the enemy at Turin. In June Galway had entered Madrid. Outwardly, at least, the Dutch endorsed the British basis for peace, of conquering all Spain ; surely God had chosen him, the Queen wrote to the Duke, as ' the happy instrument of giving a lasting peace '. But here, save for a few more masterpieces of his sword, ended the years of glory, and from 1707 both the Alliance and the British Cabinet began to dissolve.

Reconquered Belgium at once divided the victors. Though professing to admit the claim of the Archduke, the Dutch proposed to carve out an enormous ' Barrier ', and treated the area as their conquest. Unable therefore to enforce their own sovereignty, the Austrians threw in an apple of discord by offering the governorship to Marlborough, and to this extent succeeded, that he was sore tempted, and that the Dutch never entirely trusted him again. Though in deference to their wish he refused it, they were not much more pleased by the joint control set up till the end of the war, nor could we accept the proposed extent of their Barrier.

If the Dutch were war-worn and exacting, the Austrians were incorrigibly selfish, having ' not one thought ', said the patient Godolphin, ' that is not directly opposite to the interest of the Allies '. Only an English loan had made possible the victory of Turin, but early in 1707 they signed a neutrality for Italy, which released 20,000 Frenchmen for other fronts. Next, they wrecked the Duke's design for the year : that is, a march on Toulon by Eugène and Savoy, assisted by the British fleet, which would draw French forces from Spain, where the Allies were threatened with ruin. But, jealous of Savoyard claims on Italy, the Austrians acted under protest and too late, and the siege was broken off.

Actually events in Spain had already destroyed most of the good designed at Toulon. Castile loathed the Austrians, with their Catalan friends and heretic allies, and heartily despised the Portuguese ; moreover, the Austrian cause deserved to fail. It was not until August 1706 that, after internecine bickering, Charles from Aragon and Peterborough from Valencia joined Galway east of Madrid ; by which time Berwick had reformed his army, retaken the capital, and cut the British off from Portugal. Wearily the Allies retreated on Valencia, their single good fortune being the dismissal of Peterborough who, Marlborough wrote,

had ' hazarded the loss of the whole country '. In 1707 they threw away
their last chance by dispersing their forces, Charles and Stanhope going
off to Catalonia, while Galway set out to retake Madrid. On the 24th
April he attacked Berwick's strong position at Almanza, and was
defeated with heavy loss. Though he beat a gallant retreat, outside
the walls of Valencia or such towns as the British fleet could reach,
Spain was lost, yet it was costing Britain a million a year.

This was only half the toll we had to pay to the Hapsburgs, who
continued to spend such energy as they spared from Italy on the
Hungarian rebellion. They were at feud with the Swedish King, whose
army was now near Leipzig; to conjure that cloud away required a
visit from Marlborough to Charles' camp, which he had hardly left,
when in May he heard that Villars had surprised the lines guarding
the Black Forest, broken into Germany, and raided to the Danube.

But nothing could induce the Dutch to let him offer battle. Having
got nearly all they wanted, they would not sacrifice more lives, either for
the hated Austrians or for the British who were mastering trade and
grudged them their Barrier. So all this late wet summer of 1707 he
guarded Brabant against Vendôme, patching up the rent on the Rhine
and with eyes strained on the Swedes, Vienna, and Toulon. But they
turned ever more anxiously to London, where party war threatened his
advice that, to get ' a good peace ', we must fight for one year more.

Those who had, so far, kept government together all in various ways
disliked party. The Queen burst out, ' why for God's sake must I, who
have no thought but for the good of my country, be made so miserable
as to be brought into the power of one set of men ? ' All parties are the
same, the Duke was always telling his Duchess, and his maxim was ' to
be governed by neither party but to do what I think is best for England ';
so spoke Godolphin also. In Harley, on whom they depended in the
Commons, this view was both a reasoned opinion and the working of a
nervous temperament. His whole life had been spent in making coalitions, in joining ' country ' Whigs with Tories to resist William III's
straining of the constitution, in carrying the Act of Settlement, or
breaking the violent Tories of 1703-4. Behind him was a brilliant
disciple, St. John, who signed himself ' your faithful Harry ' and who
also was preaching that party distinctions were removed.

When these men wrote of ' the party ', they meant the Whigs, who
were a much more defined body than their rivals. In part, this was
because they voiced the dissatisfied, such as the Dissenters excluded by
the tests, and, again, through the closer organization of their City supporters. But there were other reasons. Their leaders, — Somers,
Halifax, and Wharton, — were men of high ability, contributors to, and
profiting by, the fact that they stood for the forces of the future ; the
Protestant succession, toleration, the moneyed interest, and ascendancy

over France. They had the vigour and vices of a faction: some loved the spoils of office, and all loved power. And though we need not take literally their charge against the Tories of Jacobitism — with which Somers and Sunderland each flirted in their time — their grasp and determination shone out in contrast to the violence of Rochester or the crankiness of Nottingham.

Indeed, nothing so much assisted the Whigs as the folly of the Tories. Their press and their dull debaters went on hammering at Scots, Dissent, and Dutchmen; their cry of 'the Church in danger' antagonized the high-Church Queen; and their blind fury during 1706 entrapped them in an enormous blunder. Seeing the Queen hostile and her health failing, they proposed that the Electress Sophia of Hanover be invited to England; a prospect which Anne welcomed with the same resentment as that of Elizabeth at mention of her successor. In concert with Godolphin the Whigs outmanœuvred them; passing a Regency Act whereby holders of the principal offices would continue in power, while an extension of the Parliament existing at the sovereign's death would ensure a peaceful succession. They used this opportunity also to repeal those clauses of the Act of Settlement which had put the Privy Council above the Cabinet and would have excluded ministers from the Commons.

In return for their assistance in regard to the succession, Scotland, and the war, the Whigs asked, as a first instalment of their price, the admission of Sunderland to the Cabinet. His mother-in-law, Duchess Sarah, set out to convert her husband, who unwillingly agreed, and then the Queen, who only gave way under a threat of resignation from Godolphin, and Sunderland became Secretary of State, though not without Harley declaring that this would make independent members 'desperate'. But Godolphin must needs advance, driven forward by war in Europe and dread of civil war at home.

Nothing had reconciled Scotland to King William's settlement. The Kirk was not won by his State-controlled Presbyterianism; since Glencoe the Highlands were more than ever discontented; while the Darien affair inflamed the whole nation. This project, much assisted by William Paterson, who had done so much for the Bank of England, and designed as a Scottish Company for trade to the Indies, emerged in 1698 in a colony on the Darien Isthmus, south of Panama. The site was ill-chosen, English subscriptions were withdrawn under parliamentary disapproval, Spain would resist it as aggression, and William, then at the climax of his partition treaties, forbade Colonial governors to assist. After three expeditions had miserably failed in tragedy and farce, epidemics and discontents, periwigs and Bibles shipped for naked savages, and threats of war from Spain, the wretched survivors fled: after losing all the savings of hundreds of Scottish homes, the Company desisted. This coincided with some years of starving harvests, and henceforth, as William wrote, the Scots were ' raging madmen '. Union was therefore his dying recommendation.

Religion, race, and poverty were the three constituents of Scotland. Its population, even now a bare million, lived on the margin of subsistence; its land tenure was a mediaeval system of ' run-rig ' or short precarious leases, enclosure being almost unknown and improvement impossible. The landlord was a despotic patriarch, sustained in his grim fortified tower by feudal dues, the produce of his dovecot, salmon and game of his vassals' killing, eked out by rents in kind from the cottiers who scratched the hills with their teams of oxen. There was no money to drain the valleys, wheat was rarely grown, while for clothing they spun the wool of their sheep. Economic life, in short, resembled that of fourteenth-century England. Their busiest trading city, Glasgow, had just 12,000 people and less than twenty ships; their chief exports were rough cloth, fish, and the small black cattle sent over the Border; the revenue barely totalled £160,000. English mercantile jealousy excluded Scotsmen from the Colonies, while internal trade was blocked by mediaeval regulation and the privileges of royal burghs. Beyond the Highland line poverty was darker still, making part of a primitive political frame. Here the chief's order could bring out fighting-men who carried claymore and dagger, whose sentiment came from bards and pipers, and whom no roads could reach.

The Revolution of 1688 merely grazed this dangerous country. Though it formally established the Kirk and there was no Toleration Act, episcopalian ministers still held one-sixth of the parishes, mostly concentrated in Aberdeen and on the Highland line, and were the more bitter because, as they died out, they would be succeeded by Presbyterians. Men who in England would be Tories, in Scotland thus tended to be Jacobite, and this applied also to the aristocracy. Since Revolution restored Argyll to predominance, Atholl and rival clans of the north-west looked to a Stuart revival, and since William's agent, after Stair's fall over Glencoe, was the Douglas earl of Queensberry, his rival Hamilton, also half-Douglas but near the Stuart blood too, played with conspiracy. South-west, the Cameronians were still untamed, ever rioting against Erastians, English, and Catholics, and ever ready to march on Edinburgh.

Revolution made government more difficult when it abolished the easily manipulated ' lords of the articles ', leaving the Crown face to face with a single-chamber Parliament, suddenly aware of its power. A Court party was therefore maintained, based on the powers of councillors, hope of office, and corruption, and consequently liable to patriotic attack; yet strong in the ultimate fact that only the English connection could avert Stuart restoration and save Presbytery. Against it was ranged the ' Country ' party, in substance a national opposition but with a criss-cross division between Presbyterians and semi-Jacobites. It ranged from impracticable idealists like Fletcher of Saltoun, through disappointed officials and patriotic lairds to doubtful figures like Hamilton, beyond whom, again, were the Jacobites proper, both Protestant and Catholic.

At Anne's accession Scotsmen, still glowering over Darien, were further irritated by the Act of Settlement and the declaration of war. The Kirk was alarmed by the Tory hope of reviving episcopacy, while the ' Country ' party seceded from Parliament because the Convention of 1689 was kept in being, Scotland having no Triennial Act : and even that rump, though voting commissioners for Union, would not settle the succession. When the commissioners met at Westminster in 1702–3, a Tory majority controlled the English Commons ; there was bickering over Darien and rates of taxation, and the conference expired.

But the newly elected Scottish Parliament of 1703 altered the issue. While a change of ministers, — Atholl and some Cavaliers being added to the shrewd Queensberry and Seafield, — showed that government were angling for loyalist support, the election proved their miscalculation, for the ' Country ' party were in the ascendant and the session was disastrous. ' Country ' and Jacobite joined in an Act forbidding future sovereigns to declare war without assent of Parliament, and united to defeat government's demand that the Hanoverian succession be settled. After months of furious debate, sometimes with hands on their swords, they hammered out the Act of Security. By this, the successor should be a Protestant of the Stuart line, but not the same as the successor-designate for England, unless the Scottish Parliament had previously received such conditions ' as may secure the honour and sovereignty of this crown and kingdom ' ; which must include its religion, frequent parliaments, and free trade. The same Act provided for the arming of all able-bodied men. When it was vetoed, Parliament adjourned amid cries of ' liberty and no subsidy '.

In 1704 Scotland was plunged in rumoured or real Jacobite plots, which drove a wedge between Queensberry and his Cavalier allies ; Godolphin therefore dropped him and tried to work with moderates of the ' Country ' party, such as Tweeddale and Roxburgh, on the understanding they would support the succession, if coupled with some liberties. The majority, however, swollen now by Queensberry's discontented followers, again refused supply, if not given their Act of Security. Such was the situation on the eve of Blenheim. Except for an unpaid army — and to pay it from England would cause rebellion — Scotland was defenceless ; while if Marlborough failed, invasion was probable. As the lesser evil, Godolphin therefore advised Anne to pass the Act of Security, which, if unamended at her death, would divide the island into two kingdoms.

This hand-to-mouth policy was changed by his Whig alliance. Blenheim enabled him to defy the Tories, to settle Scotland was imperative, and for both purposes he reached an understanding with the Junto. Under Somers' inspiration the English Parliament passed an Alien Act in 1705, empowering the Queen to name Union commissioners, but also providing that at Christmas next, ' until a Union be had, or the succession settled as in England ', Scotsmen should be treated as aliens ; import of their cattle, coal, and linen would be stopped and the export to them of English wool.

How intense was the Scots' hatred was shown this spring by the judicial murder of an English mariner, Captain Green, and two of his sailors, charged with piracy against the Darien Company, who were sentenced to death under terror of the mob, in spite of the Queen's order for reprieve. This, and Whig insistence, confirmed Godolphin's purpose to remove the ' New party ' ministry and to act resolutely through the Presbyterian Whigs, led by the young Argyll, who had served bravely with Marlborough, and the experienced sense of Queensberry and Seafield. Their instructions were to attempt a settlement of the succession and, if that failed, to work for a ' treaty ' towards Union.

Scotsmen were shrewd enough to see that, without one or the other, their country would first be ruined and then reconquered. The ' New party ', however nationalist, were clear enough on this ; Stair reappeared, to throw his ability into the cause of peace ; Carstares, now principal of Edinburgh University, used his moderating wisdom with the Kirk. Even so, it was only by a process of exhaustion and intense management that it was decided to begin a treaty on the understanding that England would repeal the Alien Act.

Of the English commissioners who, in April 1706, began their sittings at the Cockpit, the most active were the Whigs and moderate Tories on whom the ministry relied ; Godolphin himself, Somers and Cowper, with Harley, who all this year kept at Edinburgh the cleverest of agents in Defoe ; the Scots, on the other hand, essentially represented one party only, the Whig Presbyterians. Here, after nine weeks of formal negotiation — for the two parties rarely met in person — the most successful of British organic unions was accomplished. The English, refusing to hear of any federal arrangement, from the first insisted on an ' incorporating union ' in a single Parliament, with one royal succession, one coinage, and St. Andrew's cross joined to that of St. George in one ' Union Jack ' ; admitting at the same time freedom of trade, as its logical complement. Discussion thus turned rather on the application of detail ; it being difficult to find an equal basis when Scotland, with a population one-sixth of England's, paid only one-fortieth of England's taxation. Unwillingly the Scots agreed that their members in the Commons should be forty-five only, and in the Lords sixteen elected peers; on the other hand, subject to an appeal to the Lords, Scotland kept her own courts and native law, while the Highlands retained their feudal jurisdictions. Tariffs and taxation were to be amalgamated, though Scotland was wisely given some temporary concessions. In recognition of her liability for the heavier English debt, she was to receive a cash sum of £398,000, known as the 'equivalent', part of which went to compensate those who had suffered through Darien.

The treaty was first put to the Scottish Parliament, in whose last session it was fought bitterly over the winter of 1706-7. For Union was not the work of democracy, most of the Scot middle and lower classes being hot against it. Petitions and pamphlets bombarded Parliament; Presbyterians feared the loss of the Kirk, Jacobites the last chance of recovering supremacy, Cameronians the downfall of religion undefiled. Defoe, posing as a merchant, heard growls of 'English dog' as he walked the High Street of Edinburgh, and dared not enter Glasgow at all, while Queensberry's coach was surrounded by soldiers on his daily progress from Holyrood to Parliament.

But his resolute circle had much in their favour. Their majority was greatest among the nobility, notably Argyll, Seafield, Stair, and Mar; moreover, discussion convinced the 'New party' or 'Squadron', whose help was invaluable, that there was no alternative. Their enemies, on the contrary, had no leadership and no union. It was a mockery to hear Jacobite professions of zeal for Presbytery, while a standing feud divided Atholl and the hesitating Hamilton, who had English estates to think of and shirked decision. A few more concessions on taxation won over enough of the burgesses and, most vital of all, under Carstares' influence the Kirk recognized that Jacobitism was their real enemy. Though unhappy at the English keeping their Test Acts, they were mollified by an Act of Security embodied in the treaty, that the Presbyterian establishment in Scotland should continue 'in all succeeding generations', and perhaps only their manifesto against violence made Union possible.

Passed in Scotland in January 1707, it became law in England in March without amendment, except a corresponding clause to safeguard the Church of England. Its testing time was still to come, whenever a Tory majority in England grated on sore feelings, or if Scotland were robbed of her promised prosperity. But Union had one immediate effect in the first British Parliament, that Scottish members reinforced the Whigs. The Junto thus entered on their dominance at the point of the succession, the motive alike of their Scottish policy and their wish to adhere to the Dutch alliance, while party strategy led them to press the Hanoverian succession home against the Tories.

Duchess Sarah's quarrel with the Queen had broken the inner circle, and she found favour transferred to a poor relation of her own, ' a woman I took out of a garret ', Abigail Hill, who this year became Mrs. Masham. Anne's failing health, shown by agonies of gout, may have contributed to a determination to assert herself, as she did, for example, in making high-Church bishops without consulting Godolphin. The Whigs were attacking George Churchill, the real power with George of Denmark at the Admiralty ; their leaders' ambitions were unsatisfied ; in short, as Godolphin put it, they would ' tear everything to pieces, if they cannot have their own terms '. Harley meantime, though urgent that touch be kept with moderate Whigs, dreaded the return of the Junto he had helped to impeach in the last reign. The two chief ministers long hesitated, for they too hated party and disliked the Junto, but when the session of 1707–8 opened a decision must be made. For both parties were attacking the Admiralty, each was intriguing at Hanover, and their united votes compelled the ministers to hold an enquiry into the defeat at Almanza. A Dutch peace movement was growing, there were signs the Tories might join it, some took up the cause of Peterborough as a stick to beat Marlborough, and to his fury asked a transfer of forces to Spain. In December a timely discovery, that a clerk in Harley's office had been selling secrets to the French, gave the last tilt. A rival scheme, that Godolphin should be dropped and Marlborough induced to coalesce with Harley, broke down in February 1708, when the two chief ministers resigned, and the Whig middle group, Newcastle and Somerset, refused to continue without them. Harley therefore retired, and with him St. John and Harcourt, their places being filled by the Whigs, Walpole and Henry Boyle.

Fortune continued to favour the Junto, when in March the French, too late to break the Union, despatched the expedition for which the Jacobites had asked. Their fleet, with the Pretender and 6000 troops aboard, broke out of Dunkirk when storms had driven off our blockading squadron, but Byng caught them up before they entered the Forth and drove them north ; whence, by way of Cape Wrath and Ireland, they crept back, much battered. This settled the election. Stirred by the Queen's proclamation against ' a Popish pretender ', the country sent up a good Whig majority, while yet another great victory came to bless the Whig-Godolphin coalition.

It was Marlborough's purpose to strike a decisive blow, for which end, leaving the Hanoverian Elector on the Rhine, he arranged that Eugène should bring his army of the Moselle to join him near Brussels. But the French, who also wished decision, planned a move which might destroy our alliance, — a conspiracy in Flanders against the hated Dutchmen. In July Vendôme dashed north to seize Ghent and Bruges, then south to threaten the Scheldt ; now they lay between Marlborough and his communications to the Channel, while eastward Berwick was following Eugène.   By extraordinary marching, on 11th July the Duke forced a battle, throwing his advance guard on to the Scheldt at Oudenarde to sever Vendôme from France ; Eugène had come, but as yet without his army, and it was a race for the bridgeheads.   Too improvised for fortification or artillery, this encounter battle was one of rank-and-file fighting, in which the future George II and the Pretender each had a hand.   Only darkness saved the French from destruction ; as it was, the Allies put 20,000 enemies out of action.

The Duke wished to mask Lille, bring reinforcements by sea to the Somme, and invade France, but since Eugène vetoed this as too risky they settled down to a laborious siege.   Lille citadel did not fall till December, having cost the Allies 15,000 casualties, and though Ghent and Bruges were recovered, France was still intact.

Elsewhere, the war had become a stalemate.   Conflict between Austria and Savoy doomed an invasion of France from the south ; on the Spanish coast one fortress after another fell to Philip V, until Charles held Barcelona alone.   But our sea-power achieved solid success. In August 1708 Leake took Sardinia, and in September convoyed Stanhope to take Minorca, which gave us the considerable harbour of Port Mahon.   The Mediterranean was under control ; far away in the Indies, Wager was destroying the Spanish treasure-ships.

Unhappily the British government was in confusion.   Before the election the Whigs called for admission of Somers to the Cabinet ; during it, the ungovernable Sunderland ran Scottish candidates against Godolphin, professing that he and Marlborough were secret Jacobites ; finally, the Junto turned their guns on to George of Denmark.   Once again Godolphin and Marlborough yielded, and threatened Anne with resignation ; once again she protested there was ' no washing a blackamoor white ' and that, her view of the Whigs being what Marlborough's once had been, she would not submit to these ' tyrannizing lords '.   But her husband's death prostrated her.   Somers came in as Lord President, Wharton as Lord-Lieutenant of Ireland, and a year later their triumph was completed when the Admiralty went to Orford.   They were blind enough to urge the Queen to a second marriage, and their politics were true to their old character.   A naturalization bill in favour of foreign Protestants flooded the country with refugees, raising the anger in different ways of wage-earners, clergy, and magistrates.   Their aims and their allies seemed to threaten the Church.   Wharton began a campaign in Ireland to repeal the tests ; the Scots were prosecuting episcopalians for using the prayer-book.   Somers was feathering his nest by extra salaries ; Halifax asked to be given charge of the peace treaties.   Most of all, while the country cried out for peace, their policy made peace impossible.

The strain of war was now telling, the costs for 1709–10 being

£13 millions. A long run of good harvests ended in 1709, when wheat rose to 72s. a quarter. Recruiting was drying up, despite a bounty to volunteers, and though the Commons rejected a scheme for conscription, parish constables put much pressure on the unemployed; yet while Godolphin was borrowing deeper in the City, the Allied contingents were in arrears. Shrewsbury, whose luxurious pessimism never blinded his political sense, had come back to England after long absence and was impressing the necessity of peace on Harley; to whom St. John's letters recommended ' for God's sake, let us once be out of Spain ' as the cry, and reunion with the Tories as their weapon.

Early in 1709, his armies shattered and his people starving in the cruellest winter within memory, Louis XIV seriously pressed the peace he had long dangled before the Dutch. But the Whigs' diplomacy combined the worst of all alternatives : the Austrian view of peace aims, which would give the whole Spanish inheritance to the Archduke, with an enormous bribe to Holland to win her support for those aims, which for her own part she detested. By the preliminaries submitted to the French in May, Charles was to receive the whole Spanish monarchy; Louis must acknowledge the British succession, cede Newfoundland, and dismantle Dunkirk; for their Barrier, he must surrender to the Dutch Lille, Tournai, Ypres, and other fortresses ; to the Empire, he would restore Strasbourg, Kehl, and many rights in Alsace. All this the French accepted, even promising to co-operate in forcing Philip out of Spain. But the Allies asked yet more ; Louis must make his surrenders at once, but if within two months all Spanish territories were not evacuated, the armistice would end and he would be called on to coerce his grandson.

This terrible decision was taken against the opinion of Marlborough ; but he was ageing fast, felt himself isolated at home, and made no serious resistance to terms in which he did not believe.

Determined on their policy of ' no peace without Spain ', nervous of the Dutch making separate terms, and bent on a Dutch guarantee for the Hanoverian succession, the Whigs proposed to buy their support by enlarging their Barrier. The Dutch held strong cards : not only the French offers, but their discovery that, in violation of the Grand Alliance, the British had made secret terms with the Archduke for possession of Minorca and trade privileges in the Indies. Hitherto Marlborough and Godolphin had kept one object in view, to bind up the Dutch Barrier with the general peace, making their reward thus depend on their loyalty. But the treaty of October made no mention of Spain — for which reason Marlborough refused to sign it — threw away our advantage, and dissolved the Alliance.

For the Barrier assigned included not merely fortresses on the French frontier, but cities making the heart of Belgium : Dendermonde, Bruges, and Ghent. It empowered the Dutch to garrison any other Belgian fortress in time of war and to raise revenues; to garrison the Imperial cities of Liége and Bonn; to take Upper Guelders, to which Prussia had a claim; to fix customs duties at the Flemish ports; Britain would see that the Dutch privileges in Spanish territories were equal to her own, and would not pursue her treaty for Minorca.

While the ministers and their agent Townshend were carrying through these transactions, Marlborough was seeking a military decision. But he took the field late owing to the negotiation; French national feeling had rallied, Villars put his rough energy into making a last army, and fortified lines of immense strength from La Bassée to Douai. Frontal attack being impossible, the Duke wished to strike towards the Channel ports but was overruled by his allies, and attempted the line's eastern end at Tournai. When this fell in September, he continued the outflanking movement by investing Mons, and it was Villars' effort to save it which brought about the bloody battle of Malplaquet. The French being given time to dig in deeply, it was only after fighting from dawn till the afternoon that their centre was pierced; the Allied casualties were 20,000 and nothing more could be done this year. Elsewhere, the Hanoverians were driven out of Alsace, Galway was beaten in Portugal, the Russians had crushed Charles XII of Sweden, and all German eyes were turned to this peril in their rear. All this winter British and Austrians were pushing the unwilling Dutch to exact the full terms; at the Gertruydenburg conference, broken off in April 1710, they would not hear of any scrap of Spanish territory going to Philip, still demanding that Louis should send French troops against him.

At home this deplorable ministry went on in its self-destruction. Somers hoped to replace Godolphin. Fearful and resentful, Marlborough made the mistake of asking for the captain-generalship for life, in which the Junto would not back him. From within the Cabinet Newcastle and Somerset reopened contact with Harley, at whose instigation the Queen began to promote officers without Marlborough's knowledge; Argyll and other generals were his bitter rivals. Protesting against ' the malice of a bedchamber woman ', the Duke put to Anne the alternatives of Mrs. Masham's dismissal or his own resignation, and once again the Junto failed him.

They united indeed in one action only, of extreme folly, when they turned the solemn weapon of impeachment against Dr. Sacheverell, a well-known Tory preacher against Dissent, who this winter vamped up an old sermon into a full-dress attack on the Revolution of 1688. It was to little purpose that the best Whig lawyers exposed the fallacies of passive obedience; what mattered was the Queen's presence in Westminster Hall, the cries of the mob for Sacheverell and peace, their riots against Dissenting chapels. The trial thus turned into an electoral demonstration; Shrewsbury, Somerset, Argyll, and a powerful ring of Whig peers joined the Tories in imposing on Sacheverell a merely nominal sentence.

This was the end. Confident now of national reaction and well aware of the feuds in Cabinet, Harley and Shrewsbury advised Anne to reconstruct her government by gradual steps — each artistic, measured, and more decisive than the last. In April Shrewsbury became Lord Chamberlain, in June Sunderland was dismissed, in August the Treasury was taken from Godolphin. The majority of the Junto did nothing except to seek terms for themselves in Harley's platform of ' moderation '. His earlier record, his request to Cowper and Walpole to stay in office, and assurances to the Dissenters, showed the policy he had in mind. But party passion swept him away. Wharton and Walpole were fierce against compromise; Marlborough got foreign Powers to protest against dissolving Parliament; the Bank threatened to withhold credits. On the other side, the Tories asked for changes in the bench of magistrates, guaranteed a victorious election, and grumbled against ' Robin the trickster ', who preferred a tepid Whig to good Churchmen. In September the decision was taken and Parliament dissolved. The furious Tory reaction was shown in wearing of the oak-leaf, testifying to the tree that had sheltered Charles II, and in flowers on his father's statue. Where elections were most free, the tide was overwhelming; the Tories captured all four City seats and eighty out of ninety-two county seats in England and Wales; altogether their majority was something over two to one.

If they needed confirmation for their peace policy, they received it in full this year and the next. Though still masterly in tactical skill, Marlborough had lost, he wrote, his ' sanguine prophetic spirit ', feeling himself ill-supported and that faction had tainted his own staff. With Eugène he broke the lines near La Bassée, but progress was slow in this fortified zone. Nothing of moment happened on the Rhine, where the Hanoverian Elector threw up his command in disgust at Austrian incompetence. In Spain all was lost, for the Allies were defeated by a patriotic revival against foreign invaders and rebels.

In July 1710 the Archduke's cosmopolitan army, goaded forward by Stanhope to invade Aragon, stormed their way into Saragossa. Unhappily Stanhope then induced him to invade Castile; they found Madrid deserted, Portuguese assistance did not arrive, guerillas cut their supplies. They determined to fall back on Catalonia, but in December Vendôme surprised Stanhope with the British rearguard at Brihuega and forced them to surrender; once more the Austrian King was reduced to his strip round Barcelona.

He was not to be there long, for in April 1711 his brother Joseph died, and he became the Emperor Charles VI; certainly Britain would not continue war to give the whole Spanish monarchy to a prince who already ruled Austria, Italy, and Belgium. Against that blank prospect, and aware that peace negotiations were engaged, Marlborough took the field for his last melancholy campaign. His army was much reduced, and facing him was the tough Villars, who had used rivers and earthworks to make lines from Montreuil right away to Namur. Having outmanœuvred the enemy and taken his army over the lines to seize Bouchain on the Scheldt, the Duke hoped to lay foundations for invading France in the next year, but found both his own government and the Dutch failing to maintain supplies. There was reason for it; peace was being made, and the Alliance was dissolved.

In the drama of the Harley ministry of 1710–14 there were three intermingled strands. There was the task of making peace, which involved abandonment of the declared aim of 'no peace without Spain', besides correction of the Barrier treaty. This task, again, must be performed by a government led by moderate Tories and moderate Whigs, dependent on a fiery Tory majority in the Commons. Each of these, thirdly, hung on the life of the Queen, whose health had broken, who detested the Hanoverian successor, and whose leanings to the highest Tories might so antagonize Hanover that the ministry might be driven towards the Jacobites. Even with the best of good will, good fortune, and good character, they incurred great dangers; with the worst, — the peace, the party, and the succession would all be engulfed.

To a great extent disaster came about through the nature of the leaders. The pace of each step would largely be determined by the Queen, who in her dislikes and hesitations showed herself a true Stuart. After enduring much insult she saw Duchess Sarah in a last hateful interview, but Lady Masham's favour was contested by the Whig Duchess of Somerset, and Anne's refusal to be hurried in ejecting Whigs from office and Household infuriated the Tories. On the other hand, at the end of the reign, Anne broke her government by siding with Lady Masham and St. John against Harley, and by offensive activities against Hanover.

Harley, who had twice broken the Whig Junto, and carried the Acts of Settlement and Union through the Commons, was not an insignificant minister. Succeeding to heavy debt and with the City against him, he restored public credit, and until his illness in 1711 conducted the peace negotiations; furthermore, in 1712 he destroyed the power of Marlborough. To defend his government in public opinion he employed all the talents in Swift, Arbuthnot, Prior, and Defoe. As an 'old Whig' he had begun life, and such in spirit he continued;

restraining his party from attacking Dissent, in close contact with Halifax for financial advice, ever seeking to put a moderate in office, disposed to mercy, and incorrupt. But there were in him, as Swift said, ' the greatest inequalities of any man alive '. He made private friends but no devoted public supporters, for he loved power, protested overmuch, and concealed secret tracks that all suspected but none could prove. He was not yet fifty when he came to supreme authority, but soon ruined his health by late hours and quiet drinking, and began to drift, clutching for protection at those who might ruin him, like the Jacobite vote.

The colleague whom he gave to Dartmouth, as the other Secretary of State, was his sworn disciple Henry St. John. Seventeen years Harley's junior, his eloquence and energy rested on a physique which defied his debauchery, and kindled the Tory commoners who, he knew, like hounds loved the man who gave them game. He had none of Harley's scruple, secretiveness, or moderation. Marlborough was his admiration, the throne his favoured theme and pathway to power, the country gentry the only class of whom he thought, and an insular triumphant Britain was his ideal. But just as the Secretary of State would fling himself into orgies, so to win power this politician, who disbelieved in Christianity and affected to despise party, would put himself at the head of the right wing of divine-right men and Jacobites, and assured the Whig victory by splitting the Tories.

A third great influence in their party was not a politician but a priest, and a genius. Jonathan Swift came of Whig stock, his upbringing had been in the service of Sir William Temple, and he had nothing in common with the divine-right school. But he was a devoted Churchman, whom the Whigs had alienated by refusing to restore the first-fruits in Ireland and by their attempt to repeal the Test Act; he thought, too, that Britain had been sacrificed to her Allies, and disliked government by soldiers. And though he was not all that a priest should be, so that the Queen refused a bishopric to the author of the *Tale of a Tub*, it would seem that the materialism of the Junto indeed offended his moral sense. At any rate, Harley and St. John had the sense to treat him as one of themselves, and in their ' brotherhood ' dinners, in which the Queen's wise doctor Arbuthnot, Peterborough, and Prior would join, much more was decided than the merits of Tokay or the deanery of St. Patrick's.

In 1710–11 the government was a coalition. Harley, St. John, and Lord Keeper Harcourt were survivors of Godolphin's coalition of 1705; Shrewsbury, Somerset, and Newcastle were Whigs; old Rochester and Ormonde were Tory high-Churchmen. The Queen and Harley, however, would not admit Nottingham, the high-Church leader, and when in 1711 Rochester and Newcastle died, the vacancies were filled up with

Harleyites, or officials such as Robinson bishop of Bristol, the last prelate to sit in a Cabinet.

But Speaker Bromley, an Oxford Churchman, was at the head of a rabid House of Commons, and while ' moderation ' was indispensable to smooth down the City and the Allies, the Commons showed they had learned — and forgotten — nothing. Their unwieldy majority broke into a centre and a right, Jacobites and extremists forming themselves into the ' October Club ' who, dining together over October ale, foamed against Harley and toleration. They clamoured for dismissals, produced a place bill, set up a committee of accounts which declared millions had been embezzled. While Harley openly or privily opposed them, they found more sympathy in St. John, who carried into law another of their old favourites — a property-qualification bill, by which a county member must own £600 a year in land, and a burgess £300; which, in theory, promised a permanent parliament of squires, but in fact was evaded by any solicitor.

In March 1711 Harley was stabbed by the émigré Guiscard, who thought himself ill-rewarded for secret service. During his long convalescence, St. John dominated the House and intrigued to make his own following; he forced on the Cabinet an expedition to attack French Canada, with troops commanded by Lady Masham's brother, and though it turned out a fiasco, it was believed that St. John had profited by army contracts. Harley's reappearance as earl of Oxford and Lord Treasurer deepened the feud, each party trying to claim him for their own. But Tory unity rallied to some extent over the making of peace, on which their very existence depended.

Since 1706 Harley had wished to get out of ' this ruinous war ', yet to set about it was immensely difficult. What prospect existed of the Hapsburgs giving up Spain, or agreeing with Savoy about Italy, or what of the Dutch surrendering their Barrier ? He and Shrewsbury decided to follow William III's example in the peace of Ryswick, to settle broad terms privately with the enemy and then bring their Allies to reason ; and the more so, since the French made the first approaches. By April 1711 these secret conversations resulted in agreement that Philip should keep Spain and the Indies, that Britain should have large commercial advantages, and that the Dutch should have a Barrier, though one ' agreeable to England ' : terms which were made to take the shape of an overture from France and, on Shrewsbury's insistence, were now revealed to the Cabinet and the Dutch. Harley's illness left St. John in charge, and all this summer, through his envoy Matthew Prior, he was pressing the French to complete the terms. The game was full of peril : to maintain a state of war, yet not to wreck the peace ; to have no break with Holland and yet to drive them to compromise ; to use Spain as a bargaining counter against France, and yet to make the Austrians drop their Spanish claim.

In October 1711 the preliminaries were signed. Those communicated to the Allies (and by them to the press) provided that France should acknowledge our Protestant succession; that the Crowns of France and Spain should never be united; that Holland should have a Barrier, and Austria also, and Savoy some unspecified advantages; that Dunkirk should remain unfortified. But other clauses privately secured for Britain enormous gains: Gibraltar and Minorca, St. Kitts, Acadia and Hudson's Bay, Newfoundland, though with certain rights for French fishermen, the Assiento or monopoly of supplying slaves to Spanish America, together with most-favoured-nation rights in Spain.

Though all was not known, the Allies were up in arms. But their disunity wrecked them; the Dutch agreed that Philip might keep Spain but disagreed with the Austrians over Belgium and, finding their own approaches to France rejected, dared not separate themselves from England.

These batteries of Europe and of party beat upon Parliament. While St. John called for a pure Tory Cabinet, the Whigs offered their alliance to Oxford if he would revise the peace terms, and on his refusal struck a bargain with the Tory Nottingham, who was indignant at his exclusion from office and the overthrow of war aims he had championed. In return for assistance over the peace, the Whigs helped him to pass a bill against Occasional Conformity. Meantime the Emperor sent Eugène to England to stand by Marlborough, while Buys came to fight for Dutch trade.

Many reasons had hitherto prevented an open breach between Marlborough and the Cabinet. The Allies begged him to keep his command; a wish to finish his task, knowledge that the building of Blenheim depended on Harley, a passion to shield his duchess — these motives perhaps contributed. Nor did ministers wish to bring about their ears the storm of his dismissal. But he had much to endure. Though he went on his knees to Anne, Sarah was turned out of her Court appointments, and embittered the quarrel by threats to print the Queen's letters. Some of his generals were cashiered for political demonstrations, while the *Examiner* and other Tory prints accused him of trying to prolong the war — 'stabs' which the veteran felt more than a hundred battles.

Three things probably decided him. Not so much the peace itself; as he had told Godolphin earlier it was necessary, so now he told Oxford ' our allies do by degrees so shift the burden of the war upon us that at the rate they go on the whole charge must at last fall on England '. But he would be revenged, especially for Sarah; would

' make some of their hearts ache ', he told her. He incessantly told Hanover that the Parliament was mainly Jacobite, and the Elector responded as he hoped. At the same time he heard that the Commons' committee of accounts reported that the army bread-contractor had paid him £63,000 ; nor even now had he given up hope of his Belgian governorship. So, part egoist and part great European, he took his stand.

Swift put the official case for peace in his ' Conduct of the Allies ', but in December by 12 votes the Lords resolved that no peace could be safe which left Spain and the Indies to a Bourbon. While Shrewsbury wobbled and St. John despaired, Oxford and the Queen took final action. Strong in the Commons' majority of 232 to 106 for the preliminaries, they produced the report against Marlborough, dismissed him from his appointments and dismissed Somerset too, created twelve new peers, and ejected Walpole from the Commons on a charge of corruption. The retirement of the Marlboroughs to the Low Countries in 1712 and Godolphin's death closed the Queen's earlier history. The high Tories, on whom Oxford had been forced back to make the peace, were in their glory, repealed the Whig Naturalization Act for foreign Protestants, and passed two acts most offensive to the Scots.

But the stress of the year lay in the congress at Utrecht, and there St. John was in his element. His problem was to work with France without suffering France to gain from a divided alliance, and here one danger suddenly became tremendous, when in 1712 both the Duke of Burgundy and his eldest son died, leaving only the infant life of the future Louis XV between the French throne and Philip of Spain. Oxford and St. John swiftly devised two alternatives : either Philip must keep Spain, renouncing all claim to France, or he must at once hand over Spain to the Duke of Savoy, taking the Savoyard territories and Sicily instead ; their hope was that he would resign Spain, which would please the Whigs and the Savoyard Eugène. When Philip decided to keep Spain, it brought the crisis. The embittered Austrians determined to fight, the Dutch proposed to join them in hopes of improving their Barrier. Without telling his colleagues St. John ordered Ormonde, our new commander, to avoid battle, and while our troops marched away in shame from the Allies with whom they had shared years of glory, the agreement was sealed by an armistice and the French surrendering Dunkirk. A total break with the Dutch was in part prevented by Oxford and Shrewsbury, though even more by events which compelled Holland to bow to the British lead, for in July Villars crushed Eugène at Denain and recovered some of Marlborough's conquests. In August St. John, now Viscount Bolingbroke, negotiated at Paris ; pressing the French finally by an ultimatum, till in February 1713 the terms were signed.

It was a good peace for Britain and a good peace also for Europe, which except for some redistribution in Italy kept the balance for half a century, and satisfied all essential points in the original alliance of 1701. While Philip V kept Spain and the Indies, Austria received the Spanish Netherlands, Milan, Naples, and Sardinia; Sicily and a better Alpine frontier being given to Savoy. The Dutch Barrier was, indeed, sharply reduced from that of 1709, though against France it was much stronger than in 1701; they could still garrison a line running through Furnes, Ypres, and Charleroi to Namur. It was not till 1714 that the Hapsburgs were induced to sign; when France gave up Kehl, but kept Landau and Strasbourg. Not till after Anne's death did the Catalans, whose liberties Britain had rashly sworn to defend but whom she now deserted, surrender to the hated Castilians.

So Britain was at last out of ' this ruinous war ', and if better ways were almost impossible, Bolingbroke's ways were morally ruinous and raised up powerful enemies, whom only united effort could defeat.

By this time, however, the Oxford-Bolingbroke feud was past remedy. Bolingbroke had asked an earldom and got a viscounty; Oxford had the Garter, he had not. Even in ordinary days it would have tested all their art to amalgamate Oxford's politics with those of the October Club, but now this clash was caught up in the personal feud and attached itself to other divisions. While Oxford negotiated with his Whig friend Halifax, Bolingbroke and Harcourt asked bishoprics for the bigoted Sacheverell and Atterbury, and differences over the peace further shattered the party. It was not merely that the manner of its making offended Shrewsbury and Argyll, the magnates who had helped Oxford to power; a definite group was formed, nicknamed the ' Whimsicals ', Tory but Hanoverian and anti-French, some being Nottingham's followers but also including powerful independents in Hanmer, a later Speaker, the Irish Protestant Anglesey, and an eloquent young Lord Carteret. This spring of 1713 they joined with Whigs and business men to throw out the commercial clauses of the French treaty, which it was alleged would destroy our Portugal trade and woollen exports. And the Bolingbroke group accused Oxford of inciting this revolt.

Oxford still held the upper hand. He sent Shrewsbury to Ireland to soothe the growing religious strife; by making Mar Scottish Secretary, he bought off one of his rival's circle; he promoted the Tory Bromley to be Secretary of State. His government carried the general election, even in the City, without serious loss, the Peace being still all-powerful. But the new Parliament did not meet till March 1714, for at Christmas the Queen fell desperately ill and it became clear how the succession had swallowed up all the politics of three kingdoms.

Scotland was a danger of the first magnitude. Though Glasgow and western ports were beginning to profit by Colonial trade, the immediate economic effects of Union were hatred of English customs officers, universal smuggling, and decline of domestic industries. Both English parties treated Scottish grievances with cynical violence, straining the spirit and sometimes the letter of Union. In 1711 the Lords upheld an episcopalian minister, whom the Kirk had imprisoned for using the prayer-book, and affirmed their right to hear Scottish appeals; next year, Parliament passed an Act of Toleration and restored private patronage. While the Kirk was thus offended, the nobility were outraged by the Lords' decision not to admit any Scottish peers, over and above the elective sixteen, even if they were granted a peerage of Great Britain. The Whigs were ready to exploit the outcry, and in 1713 a motion to repeal the Union was barely defeated. These measures of faction, carried against Oxford's will, inflamed Presbyterians like Argyll who were convinced the succession was in danger, while Scottish Jacobites believed that the Queen was on their side.

In Ireland, even more than in Scotland, faction struck down to fire beneath the surface. William III's conquest and the anti-Catholic code had, indeed, crushed the body of Ireland. One priest was allowed in each parish, but ordination was forbidden, while most professions and landownership were closed to Catholics by law. On Irish Protestants the effect of this suppressed majority was to sharpen their zeal, Irish Anglicans being much more Whig than their English brethren, while Ulster Presbyterianism was a standing challenge to the Tories.

There was, however, a double aspect in the Irish ruling caste. Economically they were oppressed by the English commercial code; Colonial trade and cattle trade had already been killed, and in 1699 the English Parliament forbade the export of Irish cloth to Europe. Constitutionally they were vassals, their legislation being filtered through the English Council under the operation of Poynings' Act, and the best places in Church and State were given to Englishmen. They resented this inferior condition. In 1703, the Irish Commons petitioned the Crown, either to restore their lost liberties or admit Ireland to a Union.

Worse still, English faction fomented Irish religious differences. In 1704 Nottingham got the Test Act extended to Ireland, a few years later the Whig Wharton set about to repeal it. Then a Tory administration under Ormonde brought faction to its height, so that in 1713-14 the country was torn between Tory, semi-Jacobite, officials patronized by Bolingbroke, and a Whig Protestant party and Whig Dublin, looking to Shrewsbury and Oxford for moderation.

So all roads came back to the succession. The house of Hanover were convinced that Anne had decided to restore her brother; their agents here, and Marlborough, reported that government had settled plans to bring it about with French aid. Neither of these propositions was true. The Pretender began to write to the Queen in 1712, but never received an answer; for three years, he complained, he had stopped his friends conspiring and only received fine words in exchange. There were pure Jacobites in the Highlands and among Irish Catholics, but in England a large majority of the people were merely Tory: in the sense that they liked the Church of England, rejoiced in the Peace, and hated foreign Kings, but were firmly Protestant and anti-French.

In London, and in the reading class of coffee-houses and clubs, public opinion was being organized, and often brilliantly expressed. Several newspapers, usually appearing twice or thrice weekly, had a wide circulation, and each group of partisans employed the best talent. Oxford used Swift to defend the peace and Defoe's *Review* to preach moderation; Addison had been an under-secretary with the Junto; Steele was a Whig member ardent for the Protestant cause; Duchess Sarah kept her tame journalists. How strong was the press is proved by the stamp tax passed by Bolingbroke, and the constant arrest of printers.

Yet though such opinion must win its way in the long run, in that age political initiative came from above: from the Queen, the Elector, and the Pretender. So long as their wishes were uncertain, ambitious politicians would insure or reinsure for safety; Marlborough, for instance, being active now at his old game of asking pardon at St. Germain but also investing money in Holland.

Hanover raised this temper to the point of fever. Unlike his old mother Sophia, who spoke English and hoped for burial in the Abbey as an English Queen (and would have been a great one), the Elector George Lewis did not care a rap for England. But he was a German prince, stoutly anti-French, who thought that the Peace meant a French and Catholic supremacy, marched his troops indignantly away from Ormonde, and never forgave the peacemakers. Not content with the succession clauses in the treaties, he requested more guarantees; when the Pretender was driven from France to Lorraine, wished him driven further still; asked a parliamentary grant for his mother, and in 1714 accepted the view, long urged by some Whigs, that his son should reside in England. Since the Queen would give no such guarantee, this matter was, Oxford truly said, ' driving him to the wall '. We find then this jealous, devious, and procrastinating man, though the maker of the Hanoverian succession and, as Hanoverians admitted, never a Jacobite, beginning secret conversations with French agents. And very odd they were. The Pretender, he said, should travel in Italy and, like Charles II, be patient till he was called home. Using Jacobite votes to carry the Peace, and French influence to keep Jacobites quiet, he would neutralize conspiracy. Having encouraged the Pretender to accept Marlborough's advances, he later betrayed them to Hanover, and having enquired whether he would turn Protestant, on his sharp refusal Oxford drew away. He was ' as great a villain ', said Marshal Berwick, as the Sunderland of 1688.

Bolingbroke, from whom he hid these conversations, was an egoist of a more desperate die. He stood high at Paris, and had been insolent to Hanover, while his scheme would range Britain with France, Spain, and Savoy against all Germans. He too believed that the Pretender stood no chance if he did not turn Protestant, but he cared neither for King nor Church, only for party and himself. ' To fill the employments of the kingdom down to the meanest with Tories ', to put those ' who may outlive the Queen beyond the reach of Whig resentment ', such was his programme; in virtue of which he inflamed the Commons against Scots and Dissenters and began, as Ormonde did in the army, to weed out moderates. Those on whom he counted had not been always Jacobite, — Mar and Atterbury, Ormonde and Wyndham, — but some were weak, others vindictive, and all resentful of Oxford's dallying and partiality for Whigs.

From the new year of 1713–14 the succession made part of his vendetta against Oxford, which perhaps helped the Hanoverians even more than the Pretender's loyalty to his faith. Bolingbroke won Lady Masham and through her the Queen, and Oxford no doubt was deteriorating fast, but his fall was probably hastened because he swung definitely towards Hanover. When Hanover asked that a writ of summons to the Lords be issued to their Electoral Prince, he got the Cabinet's assent, against the Queen and Bolingbroke. The parliamentary majority tilted the same way. Whimsicals, and even a majority of the bishops, joined hands with the Whigs; Shrewsbury returned from Ireland to work with Oxford, and to make contact with Somerset and Argyll. Oxford might have swept his rival away if he had resolved on clear terms, but he could not bring himself to share power and trimmed between the two Courts. In June the Electress Sophia died.

To divert discussion to safer ground, Bolingbroke against Oxford's opposition carried the Schism Act, an iniquitous measure which would kill Dissent by forbidding any but Anglican teaching; it was even to extend to Ireland, where enforcement in Ulster would have meant bloodshed. There was need for him to haste, for Oxford and the Whimsicals were brewing against him a charge of corruption.

The crisis developed in swift strides. Parliament was adjourned on the 9th July. On the 27th, Anne dismissed Oxford, who left her presence with accusations against Bolingbroke and warnings against a return of Marlborough. But Bolingbroke had no plan ready. That very night he sounded Stanhope and other Whigs for support; turned first to an arrangement with Marlborough, then thought of a semi-Jacobite ministry led by Ormonde and Atterbury, sometimes plied Hanover with soft words, sometimes breathed to the French ' if only the Pretender would find Protestantism '. Fate could not wait for his calculations. The Queen's gout flew to her head, on 30th July she was in danger.

There was no need for the Whigs to raise the troops they had organized ; the law and English political sense asserted their strength. The Whig dukes appeared at Kensington to reinforce Shrewsbury in Council, by whose advice the dying Queen named him Treasurer. On 1st August she died ; ' Sleep was never more welcome ', wrote Arbuthnot, ' to a weary traveller than death was to her '.

The box was opened that held the names of the regents, a great majority of them Whigs and not including the suspect Marlborough, nominated by the new King ; by whose order they dismissed Bolingbroke and sealed up his office. In September George I reached his kingdom, for which he appointed a purely Whig ministry, with Townshend at its head, and including Stanhope, Cowper, and Walpole. Their first step was to recall the envoys, Strafford and Prior, concerned in making the Peace, and their next, in January 1715, to dissolve Parliament, with a royal proclamation that asked the return of members who had stood by the succession ' when it was in danger '. Divided, discredited, and with all the armoury of government against them, the Tories were routed.

So ended a distinct epoch of our history, with loss as well as gain. The national will had declared against the Stuarts and their religion, and was evolving instruments of constitutional government to make that will prevail. It was not possible that an intolerant Church and an executive above parliamentary control should continue in the new age, and a broader life, with a greater respect for law, triumphed with the Hanoverian succession. But those who handle the instruments of power mould them in their own image. In the rise of the moneyed class and industrial interests to predominance, a decay of dogmatic religion, and an increase of materialism, in the association of Britain with a German princedom, in mishandling of Catholic Ireland and adolescent Colonies, there was peril for the Commonwealth and its spirit.

CONTEMPORARY DATES

1703   Foundation of St. Petersburg.
        Death of Pepys.
1704   Newcomen's steam engine.
        Beau Nash begins his sway at Bath.

1705   Vanbrugh building Blenheim.
      Death of the Emperor Leopold I.

1706   Execution of Patkul.

1707   Charles XII joins Mazeppa.
      Death of Aurangzeb.
      Isaac Watts' *Hymns*.

1709   Battle of Poltowa.
      Pope's *Pastorals*.

1710   Formation of South Sea Company.
      Swift begins his journal to Stella.
      Handel reaches London.

1711   Steele and Addison edit the *Spectator*.
      Swift, *Conduct of the Allies*.
      –1740.   Reign of the Emperor Charles VI.

1712   Death of the Duke of Burgundy.
      Birth of Rousseau.

1713   Peace of Utrecht.
      The bull ' Unigenitus '.
      Berkeley's *Dialogues*.

1714   Charles XII returns home from Turkey.
      Peace of Rastatt.
      Philip V of Spain marries Elizabeth Farnese.

CHAPTER VI

THE BRITISH EMPIRE, TO 1714

THE first British Empire, planted between 1600 and 1660 and organized between 1660 and 1714, rose from two interconnected causes, — an increase and redistribution of wealth, and war with Spain. These causes entered in varying proportions into Elizabethan ventures of every type, whether into Drake's strategy of a place of arms on the Main, Gilbert's more idealist voyages, Raleigh's search for wealth in Ireland and America, fishing fleets on the Newfoundland Banks, or capitalists who staked their savings in Eastern spices or search for El Dorado on the Orinoco. Their conviction that Spanish power must be cut at its root, which must involve English settlement overseas, was reinforced in the new century by economic discontents at home, breeding a generation who asked a better world and persuading serious thinkers that the mother-country was overpopulated. This surge outwards was doubled again by religious passion, anon in the form of zeal to carry the Gospel to the heathen or, more commonly, in the Puritan wish to find a land where undefiled religion might live in peace. These ardours were poured into the mould of the Elizabethan wars, embracing those vast areas of which Spain and her vassal Portugal claimed a monopoly.

Europe, based for so many ages on the inland seas, had found the oceans, and British expansion only followed a universal search for precious metals and raw materials. While our first colonists were struggling for bare existence, Champlain in 1608 took Quebec for France; in 1609 Henry Hudson in Dutch service discovered the Hudson river, and in 1611, this time serving his own country, met his death in Hudson's Bay. In 1621 the Dutch founded a West Indian company, to which they gave control of New Amsterdam on the Hudson; in 1642 Tasman circumnavigated Australia; Gustavus Adolphus sent Swedes to the Delaware; all nations competed furiously on the Gold Coast. Before 1714 a great part of the Spanish and Portuguese Empires had thus been conquered by Atlantic Powers. Within a hundred years of its first colony's foundation, the British Empire embraced thirteen of the future American States; Newfoundland, Novia Scotia, and Hudson's Bay; a chain of islands covering the southern ports of North America and the Main — Bermuda, the Bahamas, Barbados, Jamaica, some of the Leewards, Trinidad, and a half-settlement in Honduras;

West African harbours on the Gambia, at Cape Coast Castle, and Sierra Leone; St. Helena; Surat and Bombay, Madras and Calcutta; besides factories at Bandar Abbas, Ormuz, and elsewhere in the Persian Gulf.

Though the British view of colonies obeyed much the same mercantile theory as that of their rivals, which subjected them to the mother-country and preferred power to well-being, two facts from the first gave this Empire a different character. In contrast to the centralized government of New France or French India, not a single British colony was founded by the State; the Empire was a body of separate ventures financed by the savings of individuals and companies, and painfully made by their exertions. Nor again was it, as the Dutch possessions, merely a ring of trading-posts, but a number of self-governing communities. Not only did English law teach that Englishmen carried it with them wherever they went, but within a few years, in the most unlikely surroundings and often without sanction, elected assemblies sprang into being, among Virginian tobacco-planters and in tiny islands, or even among the broken men and Jews who attempted a colony in Guiana. A period of neglect, civil war, and then William III's pre-occupation in Europe left this self-government alone, too strong to be uprooted, so that, as it were, an older England defied the later English officials who tried to force a closer union or a neater shape.

In the phase before the Civil War, inspiration came from men full of Elizabethan experience: Sir Thomas Smyth, the London financier who was successively governor of the East Indian and Levant Companies; Southampton the fellow-conspirator with Essex; Hakluyt the geographer; and Rich earl of Warwick, the Puritan admiral. Taught by earlier voyages, and finding their original channel blocked by the peace with Spain, in 1606 this group set up the Virginia Company to do the work that Raleigh had relinquished, though still with the same objects of finding gold and a short route to ' Cathay '. Their settlement at Jamestown slowly took root after years of suffering, saved by the energy of John Smith and ruthless governors trained in the Dutch wars. Their first elected assembly met in 1619, with an ex-member of the English Parliament as Speaker, but in 1624, much reduced by Indian massacre and torn by faction, they surrendered their charter, to become a royal colony. Prosperity was soon assured, for they had found a mine of wealth in tobacco, which was first exploited by John Rolfe of Norfolk, who married the Indian princess Pocahontas. The same group of interests had also occupied Bermuda, which was held by its own chartered company till 1684.

These were years of many half-beginnings and experiments by seamen and soldiers, fishing firms, fur-traders, and Puritans, and much stirred by the new war with Spain. A Council set up under Buckingham, for the area christened by John Smith as ' New England ', in 1620 made its first land grant to the Pilgrim Fathers, who that year crossed to Cape Cod in the ship *Mayflower* of 180 tons. This little settlement at Plymouth, springing by origin from those Nottinghamshire Puritans who took refuge in Holland, was doubly important; in that it represented a new motive, of God-fearing men desirous of a new home under the English flag, and because the settlers drew up their own form of government. Further north, other grants before 1630 made the core of Maine and New Hampshire. North yet again, though ever since Gilbert's time settlement had been tried in Newfoundland, it had never succeeded, and clashed with the fishing fleets. But in 1621 James I handed over Nova Scotia to Sir William Alexander, expecting him to finance it by selling baronetcies, and by 1629 Alexander's agents had seized French Acadia and David Kirke occupied Quebec. When the French war ceased Charles I restored these conquests, but a few years later Kirke made a permanent settlement in Newfoundland; whose importance, however, lay rather in the fisheries, which annually employed some ten thousand men from western England, whose daring was a recruiting-ground of the Commonwealth navy, and whose catch made a vital trade to southern Europe.

Yet another of these ' proprietary ' colonies, set up between New England and Virginia, was christened Maryland in honour of the Queen by Sir George Calvert, later Lord Baltimore. The fact that the proprietor was a Catholic directing a province mostly Protestant led to more tolerance than elsewhere, and though their patent was modelled on the palatinate of Durham, the sheer facts of colonial life soon resulted in the rule of small landholders through an elected assembly. Another group, at the opposite pole of thought, established a company in 1630 to plant Providence Island, off the Mosquito shore, directly challenging the Spanish trade routes, with Warwick at their head and John Pym as their treasurer. Though the Spaniards soon overran it, here was the germ of Cromwell's ' western design '.

Amid all these efforts there was one of decisive importance, the foundation of the Massachusetts Bay Company in 1629. They developed an earlier settlement, inspired by a Puritan rector of Dorchester, John White, who had in mind a bulwark against the kingdom of antiChrist, while their first leader John Winthrop, Suffolk squire and magistrate, had reached clear conclusions with his friends, the chief of which was to transport the government of their colony bodily to America. They acted on a large scale; 1500 colonists crossed in 1630, and within ten years 10,000; for here, as one of them wrote, they were safe from ' wolfish prelates ; we have not known what an excise means, we have almost forgotten what tithes are '. Their leaders' ideal was no democracy, but a disciplined religious commonwealth. Basing their franchise on membership of approved Churches, their society swiftly suppressed the youthful enthusiasm of Sir Henry Vane, who was for a time their governor, and expelled the radical Roger Williams to make his own commonwealth for Christ, which developed into Rhode Island. Compact on the water-front and wrestling with a hard soil, they built their State on the self-governing township, while their swarming numbers hived off to find more space southwards in the future Connecticut, and thence spilled over the Dutch frontier. Godly and ungodly suffered alike. They began life in log huts, with locked palisades, oiled cloth for windows, and cotton yarn for lamps; they had to live on shell-fish and wildfowl; all the time watching for the Indians, creeping from the woods with bows in their mouths. They had to contend with adventurers who sold drink and arms to the Indians, and with transported felons and sweepings of the London streets. But as they moved backward to clear the wilderness, driving their cattle before them, they took with them an English frame of life, English Bible, common law and parish, jury and view of arms. The New Englanders quickly set up schools, many university men came to Massachusetts, and at a new Cambridge they founded in 1638 Harvard College, one of whose first graduates was Winthrop's nephew George Downing, who went home to found a fortune under the Commonwealth, and to buy house property that was to give his name to the seat of Empire.

Meanwhile other settlers roughly seized what they could of the West Indies. Disappointed after many endeavours in Guiana, one set of venturers occupied St. Kitts, Antigua, and others of the Leeward Islands. One syndicate in 1625 took Barbados where they began the planting of sugar, tobacco and cotton which raised their number to some 18,000 by 1640, and put government in the hands of an aristocratic assembly. Economically the basis of their wealth was the importation of slaves which, beginning in Virginia, led to capitalist management of large estates. In the first half-century of the trade, exports from Barbados grew until by 1700 they exceeded in value those of all British North America together, and West Indian riches turned an essential wheel of our Imperial system. Slave merchants of Bristol or Liverpool picked up on the Gold Coast, or the Gambia, the negroes brought by camel caravan from the interior, taking thence, when enough had been collected in the fort compounds, about 5000 slaves annually to the West Indies, on whom they might hope for a profit of £10 a head.

Charles I's weak government took alarm at the frontier disputes of America, the volume of emigration, and Puritan independence, but a colonial commission under Laud, with plans for a royal governor-general, lapsed with the Civil War, and for ten years the colonists went their own way. Massachusetts denied that English laws could bind them and, with Plymouth, Connecticut, and New Haven (a little Scripture commonwealth founded south of the last), set up a federation for defence. Barbados repudiated the Navigation Act on the ground that it was unrepresented in Parliament; Royalist parties in Virginia and Maryland declared for the King.

With their usual decisiveness the Puritans sent a fleet to stamp out this revolt, while from the Council of State of 1650–60 emerged an Imperial organization, in a permanent council for the plantations, and in committees which included the principal merchants dealing with the Colonies. After the Restoration this continued through divers experiments, taking final shape in a Privy Council committee as the ' lords of trade '. The officials concerned were the best men available, like Evelyn and Locke, or William Blathwayt who took the tradition on to William III, while all through that age the most powerful politicians of all parties, Vane and Downing equally with Danby and Shaftesbury, took a hand in Imperial development.

Beyond some short-lived settlements in Surinam (part of Guiana), and in Acadia, which were surrendered to Holland and France respectively at the peace of 1667, Cromwell's only addition to empire was Jamaica. Its first emigrants were inferior and unsuccessful, New Englanders declined to move there, and it was not till after Restoration that, by migration from Barbados and importation of slaves, it settled into its stride.

Here, as elsewhere, Restoration Colonial policy was liberal and enlightened. Jamaica was given an assembly, others had evolved in the Leewards, Connecticut and Rhode Island regularized their existence by royal charters on generous terms, even giving them the right of electing their governors. In 1663 a large grant of land south of Virginia was made to some proprietors, of whom Shaftesbury was most active, and here also, as in Rhode Island, religious toleration was guaranteed and an elected assembly assumed; gradually, two far-divided settlements of North and South Carolina arose, the one by migration from the north, and the other, round Charleston, peopled from Europe and the West Indies. In these years too a clean sweep was made of the proprietary interests which had restricted the West Indies, whereby Barbados and Bermuda and the rest became royal Colonies. In the far north, after much vacillation, protection was given to Newfoundland against the French, with whom a new dispute was launched by the chartering in 1670, at Prince Rupert's instance, of the Hudson's Bay Company. Their overland journeys to extend the fur trade led to the great lakes and direct contact with the Indians, so challenging French Canada, while another inlet was being driven from the south by conflict with the Dutch of New Amsterdam.

Cromwell had thought of it and it could hardly be postponed, for English settlers crossed the border in such numbers that the Dutch had an English secretary to deal with them, nor was it possible to enforce the Navigation Act while the Dutch, separating New England from Virginia, distributed their goods through the best harbour on the coast. So came about in 1664 the grant of this territory to the King's brother, an easy conquest of New Amsterdam, and its renaming as New York. After a brief Dutch reoccupation in the war of 1673, this cosmopolitan Colony was fitted into the English frame; strategically it was of vast importance since the Hudson river system took its rise in the Iroquois country and almost touched the Canadian lakes.

Out of the New York hinterland, or its borders, three later Colonies were carved. New Jersey, running south-west to the Delaware, was made over by York to courtiers, who resold it to a Quaker syndicate headed by Penn, who by yet another transaction got a tract on that river which in 1702 became the government of Delaware. But his largest acquisition was in 1681, of the great section west of Delaware and north of Maryland, which Charles II named Pennsylvania. Here, with his extraordinary gifts of propaganda, and after spending two years on the spot himself, he founded a mixed colony of Quakers, Swedes, Germans, and Swiss, who prospered in full religious liberty and soon asserted their self-government against his own fanciful loftiness.

So were sketched in outline, save for Georgia which was added under George II, the coastal Colonies of our old American dominion, whose population rose from some 63,000 in 1660 to 350,000 by 1713. Another 200,000 in the West Indies, of whom two-thirds were negroes, completed this Atlantic empire.

Yet ' Empire ' is hardly the word, for the system broke down whenever it was defined. Its ingredients, such as they were, were first pulled together by the legislation of 1650–73. These represented the current ideas that a favourable balance of trade was the index of national power; that trade rested on sea-power; that plantations should be so used as to increase shipping and a seafaring population, and so regulated as to supply what the mother-country lacked and swell the customs revenue. The Navigation Act of 1660, developing the Commonwealth's ordinance of 1651, provided (1) that no goods might be carried to, or from, the Colonies except in English or colonial ships, the crews of which must be three-quarters English; (2) that certain ' enumerated ' products of the Colonies — sugar, tobacco, indigo, cotton-wool, dye-woods — might only be exported direct to England or other English Colonies. A third principle was added by the ' staple ' Act of 1663, whereby products of Europe bound for the Colonies must first be landed in England and thence reshipped. Finally, in order to equalize rates in England and the Colonies, and to make unprofitable any illegal shipment, an Act of

1673 enforced a plantation duty on exports, and the taking of bonds that the law would be observed.

Later the ' enumerated ' list was much extended, as for instance to the rice of Carolina, yet it would be wrong to suppose that, as yet, the Colonies suffered unduly. Only tobacco much affected their producers; New England's fish and lumber could be exported freely. Again, these enumerated goods were given a monopoly of the home market, tobacco-growing in England, for example, being forcibly put down for their benefit, while our customs rates gave a large preference to Colonial products, notably on West Indian sugar, which paid only a third of the duty levied on the foreigner. It is, of course, true that the mother-country held the balance in her own interest; her favoured children were the tropical Colonies which did not drain away white labour, and whose products could not compete with English goods. But, in addition to our expenditure on their defence, there were many mitigations to this apparently rigid scheme — the salt needed for their fisheries, for example, being allowed to pass direct to America. It was recognized that the northern Colonies performed a vital function in feeding the West Indies, and when in face of short supply from the Baltic the all-important naval stores of masts, hemp, and tar were ' enumerated ' in 1705, they were subsidized by a bounty; many a New England tree was marked by His Majesty's broad arrow. From its primary point of view, the ' encouragement of the navigation of this nation ' which, said the Commonwealth Act, was ' under the good providence of God ' its principal safety, the system was justified. Under the two last Stuart kings our tonnage was doubled, by 1700 the American trade made one-seventh of all our commerce, about 80 per cent of it being with the sugar and tobacco Colonies.

In New England particularly, however, there was a wholesale breaking of the acts of trade, and at home there were signs of a desire to tighten up this ramshackle empire. The lords of trade multiplied their instructions to governors, aiming especially at fixed revenues, so that salaries and establishments might be independent of the assemblies' grants. In Virginia they enforced payment of quit-rents; they tried, and failed, to subject Jamaica to a sort of Poynings' Act; while customs officers appointed from England, and Admiralty cutters, fought the smuggling that flourished in the creeks of Chesapeake Bay and the Carolinas, or the running of negroes and sugar between the French islands and British Colonies. But the arch-offender was Massachusetts, where juries refused to convict offenders, and whose charter, after ample warning, was forfeited in 1684. And since there was other good reason for a stronger administration, to adjust frontiers and to resist the Indians, James II placed New England, New Jersey, and New York under a governor-general who, with red-coats and a surpliced clergy, set about him with a high hand.

But James fell and his projected ' Dominion of New England ' with him, there was clamour in America against Popish and French plots, and armed risings against royal officers. A period of national war followed in which British and American interests coincided. The French opened continuous attacks on New England, there was fierce fighting in Hudson's Bay, twice the Massachusetts militia captured Port Royal in Acadia, twice British expeditions unsuccessfully penetrated the St. Lawrence. Ultimately, Marlborough and British sea-power saved the Americans in Europe ; at the Utrecht peace of 1713 Britain received Nova Scotia, Newfoundland, and Hudson's Bay, while the Iroquois were recognized as British subjects. Yet France still held Canada, Cape Breton, and fishing rights in Newfoundland, and while that was so, the Americans must cling to the mother-country.

Our own revolution of 1688 implied a Colonial reaction against the Stuart system. Rhode Island and Connecticut recovered their original liberties, and though by a new charter of 1691 Massachusetts had to accept a royal governor and a wider franchise, it was allowed to absorb Plymouth and control Maine. Maryland and Pennsylvania continued under proprietary government, but these were the only exceptions to a new uniformity, by which New Hampshire, New York, and New Jersey all became Crown Colonies before 1702, as the Carolinas did under George I. But many fundamental reasons left British-American relations in a difficult stage.

A new epoch had opened in both countries. A sovereign Parliament might mean a harder master than a sovereign King, and already industrial interests at Westminster excluded New England woollens from the home market. Assembly government was well-grounded in America but the executive was of British appointment ; both William and Anne freely vetoed American bills, and Parliament's right to legislate for America, as it did, for example, by establishing an Imperial system of posts, was unquestioned. This dual government would feel any period of strain, more especially since America had grown very unlike the home they had left. Virginian revolt against their planter aristocracy, movement in Maryland against their absentee proprietor, a great increase of Germans and other non-British stocks, were all symptoms of a new society. It must change all the faster as pioneers worked further west into the Indian wilderness, where new soil and debts and murderous war made their background, and where memories vanished of the ' dear England ' of the Pilgrim Fathers.

At the same time mercantile interests at home were aggressive and alert. In 1696 a new salaried Board of Trade came into existence, which lasted as the advisory and initiating body to the end of the old-Empire ; the same year a new Navigation Act increased the power of the British customs service, and ordained British registry for American shipping. Within a few years twelve courts of Admiralty, from Massachusetts to Barbados, were condemning violations of the trade laws, often without a jury. Efforts to suppress the few remaining charter-Colonies, and a clash with the Colonial courts, were ominous evidence of an official view that the Colonies were not parliamentary governments but subordinate bodies, no freer than an English municipality, subject to the sovereignty both of the Imperial Parliament and the King in Council.

For the West Indies also the peace of Utrecht marked a stabilizing of the map, with a closing of some ancient history. The only addition of territory was the French share of St. Kitts, but the treaty transferred to Britain the 'Assiento', the coveted contract for supplying the Spanish colonies with negroes, which Portuguese syndicates and then the French Guinea Company had held before; with it went the right to send one ship annually to the Porto Bello fair. The age of anarchy was closing, which had made the Caribbean a sink of iniquity. The buccaneers' golden age was in its prime when Henry Morgan sacked Panama in 1671 and then rose to govern Jamaica, but many picturesque ruffians still sailed the seas during William III's wars, like 'Blackbeard' whose base was Carolina, or Captain Kidd who first made his name in New England.

West Indian prosperity was great, though changing in character, and linked to Britain in a different relation from that between Britain and America. Without British capital and sea-power they could not survive. They had struggled through early days, against misgovernment by proprietors' officials, French and Spanish hostility, and dangerous native Caribs; much was due to two successive gallant Lords Willoughby of Parham, and much to an admirable governor of the Leewards, Sir William Stapleton. But, as the war of 1666–7 showed, one hostile squadron in command of the sea could ruin them, and they could only be rich by living dangerously. Barbados' early prosperity was feverish and accidental, every inch of its black volcanic soil was cultivated, but the island was no larger than the Isle of Wight, and its surplus inhabitants must migrate when sugar prices fell. Planters, and the planter-governors whom they preferred, blamed the acts of Trade which confined them to the home market, though over-production, soil exhaustion, and competition from the rich French islands were equally responsible. By the early eighteenth century its white population was stationary, its original type of small planter squeezed out by large estates with many mills, and its labour supply was now less usually the white servants hired under indenture than masses of negro slaves.

Jamaica, half the size of Wales, had larger resources. It was not so dependent on the single crop of sugar, while it was also an ideal centre for privateering, for the log-wood trade with Honduras, or illegal shipping to the Spanish Main. The little Leewards (St. Kitts, Antigua, Nevis, and Montserrat) went their own way, with mixed crops and trade to the Americans; for a brief space Stapleton got them to elect a federal assembly, which did not survive their local jealousies. But their fate, like that of all the West Indies, lay in metropolitan and European events, in the London committee of planters, the power of their ' nabobs ' in the Commons, and British relations with France. It was, however, their market which kept alive the settlements on the Gambia and Gold Coast. Many ventures rose and fell; finally, the Royal African Company was chartered in 1672. But interlopers broke in on the slave trade from the first, in 1697 it was thrown open, and though the Company lasted till the trade was abolished, only parliamentary grants and the royal Navy maintained any hold on West Africa.

When Queen Anne died, the East India Company hardly ruled a foot of Indian soil, but its factories were already the germs of the future presidencies; Surat (1612) and Bombay (1668), Madras (1639), and Calcutta (1686). This development on the mainland, however, was pursued only when their first objective had failed, which had been a share in the spice trade of Java and the Moluccas; there the Dutch had a good start, their ships were better, their Company was almost a department of State, and their methods were brutal. In 1623 a massacre of our merchants at Amboyna marked the end of English fortunes in the islands, and as the Dutch also ousted all other Europeans from the Far East, the English Company turned to easier prey; to force a trade in India, where the Portuguese were breaking down. As part of this process Charles II negotiated for the inclusion of Bombay in his queen's dowry, which he could not afford to defend himself but transferred to the Company. Even here Dutch competition harried them, the rival factories fighting each other on both Indian coasts until their feud swelled into the wars of Cromwell and the Restoration.

Two facts long delayed the Company's growth as a territorial power. Though the Mogul Empire was decaying and the Bombay factory already had to defend its life against the rising Mahrattas, till the death of the last mighty Mogul Aurangzeb, in 1707, India did not fall into the chaos upon which Britain and France later raised their strength. Nor, again, could the Company prosper till its basis was secured at home.

Though the capital invested was great for that age — just on half a million being subscribed for the voyages from 1601 to 1612 — and though profits on pepper, indigo, and the rest might average 20 per cent, the Company had at first no assured continuity. Each voyage was a closed joint-stock venture, separately wound up; the Crown accepted money from ' interlopers ', or rival syndicates; there was an outcry against the

Company's export of bullion, or its calico imports which menaced the cloth trade. The Protector saved it from extinction in 1657 by enforcing its monopoly, broadening its shareholder basis, and making its joint-stock a permanent holding. A second crisis began late in the reign of Charles II when, under its masterful chairman Josiah Child, the Company went into politics on the side of the Court, and political clamour assisted the Whig merchants' anger at its monopoly. After a contest of bribes, parliamentary faction, and erection of a rival body, at last Godolphin brought about an amalgamation in 1708 in a United Company.

Its monopoly was now secured until 1733, and it exported annually over half a million in goods and specie, yet its Indian future was uncertain and nothing much yet distinguished it from many settlements which had perished. Indian warfare and the extortion of Indian officials forced it to use its legal power of raising troops and fortifying factories. But Fort William at Calcutta, Fort St. George at Madras, and Bombay were isolated from each other — each leading, within its locked gates, its separate small edition of English life, with its church, municipality, and magistrates. The profit-making motive ruled their lives, and the Company's greatest difficulty was to keep within bounds private trading by their servants.

Yet in several ways it was already more gravely involved than in the mere volume of its imports to England: of piece-goods, dyes, silks, indigoes, or saltpetre from Bengal. Sea-power alone had secured it; not only because it could cut the Mogul trade with the Persian Gulf, or its pilgrim traffic to Arabia, but because it found in the Indian coasting trade, and in shipments further afield, means of payment for its Indian purchases and of doubling its homeward cargoes. Mocha coffee and China tea were two large items in this roundabout trading. Its wealth had brought it into the arena of Parliament, which had remodelled its charter and borrowed its funds, and though, except in Ceylon, Dutch overseas possessions were declining, French factories at Pondicherry and Chandernagore warned Leadenhall Street that the sinews of war might be severed in the Orient.

CHAPTER VII

HANOVERIAN AND WHIG SUPREMACY
1714–1724

After nearly a century of fever the political temperature fell in the forty years after Anne's death to normal, or even below it; though not before the patient had lost some blood. Nothing perhaps could have avoided a rising of the Highlands, but for the rebellion of 1715 in general the rigour of the new government was largely responsible.

In British eyes the Hanoverians had little to recommend them, except that they embodied the Protestant succession. George I was now a man of fifty-four, hard-set in the mentality of a German soldier and the egoism of a German prince. Like all his line he had courage, proved in the Empire's wars since the great siege of Vienna but, except for a shrewd instinct against a knave, he had no qualification as a British king. He had not troubled to learn English, arguing with his ministers in French or dog-Latin, while a very casual weekly service showed his lack of interest in the Church. The centre of life and government had always been the Court, but now in effect Court there was none. George lived meanly in a few rooms at St. James'; his wife Sophia Dorothea had been held prisoner the past twenty years in Hanover on suspicion of adultery, and remained prisoner till death; and in her place the King brought to England two mistresses, one of whom played some part in politics as Duchess of Kendal. His political confidence went foremost to foreigners — his confidential secretary the Huguenot Robethon, Bernsdorff the sour veteran of his Electoral ministers, and Bothmar who had been his liaison officer with London before — and both ministers and mistresses were accused of selling their influence. This foreign dynasty made probable a new foreign policy. It seemed as if war between Sweden and Hanover would involve Britain, and the Tory cry that a new Junto would bring new wars was justified by Stanhope's effort to refurbish the alliance against France.

Though this was unpopular, what made rebellion inevitable was the clear intention to have no truck with half the nation. From top to bottom, from Ormonde the commander-in-chief or Mar the Scottish secretary, down to local excisemen, government applied the spoils system to turn out every Tory. The Commons set up a packed committee of secrecy, on whose report they impeached Oxford, Bolingbroke, Ormonde, and Strafford, for their share in making the peace; though they had not found out the full facts, and on those before them the charges were unprovable. One effect was that in March 1715 Bolingbroke escaped to France in disguise, afraid for his head, and frightened away by messages from Marlborough, but Oxford stood his ground and was sent to the Tower. Foreign ambassadors agreed that the country had become more Jacobite within six months than in all the last reign; there were incessant riots in London and along the Welsh Marches, demonstrations for Ormonde as against the unpopular Marlborough, mob attacks on Dissenting chapels. It was now that it was found necessary to pass the Riot Act, making assembly by over twelve persons punishable by death, on a refusal to disperse. How unsafe the throne was thought can best be measured by a single fact, that Marlborough and Shrewsbury once more transmitted their courtly messages to St. Germain.

Jacobite hopes must depend most upon France, which was stultifying its treaty obligations by work on a naval base at Mardyke and allowing Jacobites to raise arms. But when in September 1715 Louis XIV died, the regent Orleans would look to Britain to maintain his position against Philip of Spain and other princes of the blood. In any case the Jacobite cause was conducted badly. Hopes of an English rising disappeared when in July Ormonde fled to France; Bolingbroke, now the Pretender's Secretary of State, was convinced no Scottish movement could conquer England and would have put his master ' at the head of the Tories ', to win England over by pledges to respect the Church and constitutional liberties. But the Prince, he tells us, had ' the spirit of a Capuchin '; all secrets were betrayed, Ormonde reconnoitred Torbay and found no response, Wyndham and five other members of Parliament were arrested. Finally, without waiting to see what England would do and without Bolingbroke's knowledge, the Pretender allowed the Scottish rising to begin.

Mar, who raised the standard at Braemar in August, had been a chief agent of the Union but, rejected and despairing, reverted to conspiracy in the usual style of the Scottish nobility. ' Bobbing John ', as he came to be called, had no quality of decision, while against him was the jealousy of a greater Highland potentate, Atholl. His dilemma was the old one which had ruined both Montrose and Dundee : to raise a Highland army and yet defy the Campbell power in Argyll; to cross the Forth and master Edinburgh in the face of Lowland Presbyterian feeling and English sea-power; and to make speedy contact with the English plotters who, under the Northumberland squire Forster and Lord Derwentwater, were up on the Border. A large array of nobles joined him ; not Atholl and Gordon themselves but their elder sons, the Earl Marischal, Drummonds and Ogilvies, along with those from the north, Mackintosh, Invercauld, Grants, and Camerons. By October he held

Perth, entered Fife, seized the east-coast ports, and threw a vanguard forward to occupy Leith. There was a chance that Argyll, with the small royal army at Stirling, might be taken in a net.

But many things prevented even that problematic victory. The rebels had no artillery, and every town held out against them. Having failed to surprise Edinburgh Castle, they dared not assault the city from Leith, Dumfries defied the Lowland group, and Fort William resisted the Highlanders, whose rush on Argyll's Inveraray was also beaten off. For a whole month Mar hesitated, hoping for the Pretender's arrival, and not even assured that a hostile north would not rise behind him, for Sutherland was loyalist and Lovat took some of the Frasers into the government camp. So the rebellion broke into two distinct campaigns.

Three contingents met in October at Kelso; Highlanders from over the Forth, a Lowland force led by Kenmure, and that of the Northumberland gentry, in all only some two thousand men. Disregarding Mar's advice, the English decided to cross the Border and, though some Highlanders deserted, made by Penrith to Kendal, and so on to Lancashire by the old route of 1648. Except for a few local Catholics not a man joined them, and at Preston they were driven to surrender on the 13th November.

That same day Mar met his separate fate. After much waste of time he had marched to seize Dunblane, as a first move to the Forth, but Argyll outstripped him by taking the high ground at Sheriff Muir north of the town, and after a rambling fight Mar retreated. This check and news of Preston sent many Highlanders homewards, and all was already lost when James Edward in January 1716 landed and joined Mar at Perth, for Cadogan simultaneously reached Scotland with the Dutch troops, guaranteed by treaty for the Protestant succession. The Scots found their Prince ' heavy ', noting he was never seen to smile; nor had he much cause to, since his advisers insisted on retreat over the frozen Tay to Dundee, and Mar declared the game was up. Within a month he sailed for France and the Highland army scattered, pursued in a trail of destruction by the Dutch.

Such punishment as was inflicted could not be called excessive. Of the leaders impeached, only Kenmure and Derwentwater were executed, together with less than thirty of the rank and file, though several hundred more were transported to the Indies. In Scotland there was a bitterness left behind, in which Argyll himself shared; and since juries would not convict, or Scots profit by confiscation, many forfeited estates passed to English speculators. But, except that foreign powers occasionally encouraged the Pretender, politically Jacobitism was dead. And the more so since, under Catholic counsels, the Pretender dismissed Bolingbroke, who swore his arm should rot before he raised it for the cause again, and promptly approached the British government, urging his friends like Wyndham to drop a doomed dynasty. Torn between English and Irish, Catholic and Protestant advisers, Jacobitism degenerated into the squalid factions of exile, while under British pressure James Edward was driven out of France to Avignon, and then to Italy. Only the fierce Atterbury headed a knot of conspirators at home, though when Oxford was released from the Tower he began dabbling in his old, empty promises.

Rebellion had this other important effect that, rather than face an election within two years, in 1716 the government passed the Septennial Act, which by a great stretch of parliamentary sovereignty prolonged the life, not of future Parliaments only but of the existing one, from three to seven years. At the same time the dismissal of Nottingham, on account of his open sympathy with the prisoners, cleared the ministry of its solitary Tory. Yet, before this year ended, the Cabinet was broken up.

One reason for this was to colour, in various forms, the whole Hanoverian age, — the feud between the King and his eldest son. The Prince of Wales had fought bravely at Oudenarde, and had more human spirit than his father, while his witty clear-sighted wife, Caroline of Ansbach, was the one living figure in this drear Court. He had championed his mother, he was accessible to Englishmen, and the Tories had hopes of him. Again, the quarrel between Marlborough and the Junto Whigs had revived, though the great Duke was himself an aged invalid, and Halifax and Wharton just dead. But his Duchess lived on, venomous as ever, and together with his son-in-law Sunderland, his favourite general Cadogan, and his old agents the self-made Craggs, father and son, besides some Tory recruits like Carteret, made the nucleus of a party. The immediate reason for a break came, however, from a clash between British and Hanoverian interests.

Foreign affairs were in the hands, — under the King, — of Stanhope, whose long Spanish experience had made him ' Austrian ', so much so that in 1714 he advocated renewing war to revise the terms of Utrecht. Yet, though like all Whigs he dreamed of reviving the ' old system ', he soon discovered that Oxford and Bolingbroke had their justification : that the Dutch were opening their jaws for the whole Barrier of 1709 ; that to make a compromise between them and Austria would mean forceful mediation ; that Charles VI would not admit the title of Philip of Spain, and that British commerce depended, as of old, on peace within the wide Spanish area. Moreover, the Regent's need of support in France provided us with a balance, as Bolingbroke had designed, against Austrian pride and Spanish fury.

Stanhope's work in 1715–16, a good deal done by his personal missions abroad, steadied the peace, but not by any wholesale revival of the Junto system. Thus the third Barrier treaty took away from the Dutch some important fortresses, though they were left in control of the Scheldt, and in November 1716, after negotiation with the Abbé Dubois, Britain and France signed a treaty, which the Dutch joined the January after, so making a triple alliance. This confirmed the successions to the British and French thrones, as settled at Utrecht, providing also that the fortifications of Dunkirk and Mardyke should be really destroyed, and that the Pretender should be forced over the Alps. On this central balance peace was to poise for a whole generation.

But George I had hurried this treaty on for the sake of Hanover. When Sweden had collapsed in the northern war, he had taken his share of the spoils as Elector, in Bremen and Verden, while Russia, Prussia, Poland, and Denmark were scrambling for pickings from the Swedish Empire. In 1714 Charles XII returned from his Turkish exile to fight and, though Britain was at peace, each year a British squadron sailed to the Baltic to defend the interests of Hanover. Though Sweden responded by Jacobite intrigue, in fact Hanover's nominal ally Russia was much more formidable, and hence the urgency to get France on our side. The negotiation was put through in 1716 during a long stay of the King at Hanover — the clause of the Act of Settlement, forbidding the sovereign's absence abroad, being this year repealed — whither Stanhope accompanied him, and it represented a triumph for the Hanoverian councillor Bernsdorff.

The brothers-in-law Townshend and Walpole protested against this long absence and this use of British ships, mortally offending the King by asking that he should delegate larger powers to the Prince of Wales; Sunderland took the opportunity to join the circle at Hanover, and work against them. Early in 1717 Townshend was dismissed, Walpole resigned with other Whig ministers like Pulteney, leaving Stanhope, Sunderland, and Craggs to carry on a much weakened administration.

This was demonstrated when they attempted to pursue a Whig policy. As usual, the party feud was most fiercely expressed in the quarrel of the Churches, Oxford University was a nest of Jacobites, and nonjuror literature kept alive the principles of divine right. On the other side, a mass of secular writing, from Addison's kindly moralism in the *Spectator* to outright attacks on Christ's divinity, the doctrine of the Trinity, and miracles, announced the advent of an undogmatic age, of the Deists who made Christianity little more than a supplement to natural philosophy, and revelation an unimportant sequel to reason. Naturally the royal appointments went to liberal Churchmen; Wake, the new archbishop, had used his great learning to champion the State's authority against Atterbury and Convocation, and Gibson of London, later called ' Walpole's Pope ', was a determined Whig. But the angriest clamour was roused by Hoadley, once Sacheverell's opponent and now bishop of Bangor, who by a notorious sermon plunged the Church into the acid ' Bangorian ' controversy. The Church, he taught, was not of this world, not a visible society resting on the apostolic succession and authorized to maintain its authority by tests, but merely a collection of individual believers. When Convocation in 1717 censured him, the government stopped its sitting — not, as it proved, to allow it again for over a hundred years.

In this heated atmosphere government pressed on to redeem their pledges to the Dissenters. They got a Toleration Act passed in Ireland for Protestants and made perpetual another of William III, allowing Quakers to ' affirm ' in the law courts instead of taking an oath ; Stanhope was preparing to repeal the Test and Corporation Acts. But he found Parliament, with the Walpole group in opposition, determined to uphold the tests, so that all they could do, and that with difficulty, was to repeal in 1719 the Occasional Conformity and Schism Acts of the last reign.

Though weakened at home, Stanhope's ministry won some more solid success in Europe. Since the Triple Alliance could never be stable till the hatchet was buried between Austria and Spain, he planned a whole programme of treaty revision. Charles VI must renounce all title to Spain, but to round off his hold on Naples he should be given Sicily, Savoy being compensated by receiving Sardinia from him. Spain, in turn, would renounce all its lost territories but in lieu of them a son of the all-powerful Spanish Queen, Elizabeth Farnese, should be admitted as successor to her ancestral Duchy of Parma, and also to Tuscany, whenever those two small States fell vacant, as might soon be expected. All this with infinite patience he completed in the ' Quadruple ' alliance of 1718, though actually Holland never joined Britain, Austria, and France in full acceptance.

But his difficulties were enormous. The Dutch were anxious not to lose their Spanish trade. The Emperor hoped to evade giving up the Italian duchies to a Bourbon. Only British support upheld Dubois in the Regent's favour as against a strong pro-Spanish party, reinforced by the remarkable Scot John Law, who was reforming French finance, and who through his Mississippi Company was bent on challenging British expansion. In Spain itself an outstanding man, Cardinal Alberoni, a native of Parma like the Queen, had brought about a national revival, which he would use to recover the Italian provinces.

Sooner than he deemed wise, Philip and Elizabeth persuaded him to action. In 1717 the Spaniards seized Sardinia ; in July 1718 they attacked Sicily, and a visit of Stanhope to Madrid, even a promise to restore Gibraltar, could not stop war. In August our squadron under Byng destroyed the Spanish fleet off Cape Passaro, in south-east Sicily ; simultaneously our mediation brought about the peace of Passarowitz that closed a Turkish war in triumph for Austria, while through Stanhope's insistence a French army crossed the Pyrenees. Alberoni's

diplomatic web was broken.   A Spanish conspiracy to overthrow
the French Regent was foiled, Russia and Sweden could not work
in agreement, and Charles XII's death ended the project for a
Swedish-Jacobite invasion of England.   Though the Pretender
reached Madrid, a storm wrecked the fleet carrying Ormonde's army,
and only a few hundred Spaniards under the Earl Marischal reached
the Isle of Lewis and crossed to Kintail in August 1719.   Very few
Highlanders joined them, and they were soon rounded up in the
valley of Glenshiel.

    This universal failure, and a conviction that France would get them
honourable terms, induced the Spanish sovereigns to make Alberoni
their scapegoat.   In December he was dismissed, and in February 1720
Spain accepted the terms of the Quadruple Alliance.   Another stage in
pacification had been passed, mostly through Stanhope's resolution and
British sea-power, but the war was most unpopular, nor did the rifts in
the alliance heal.

    In the north, after Charles XII's death, it was Stanhope's object to
get agreed terms among the enemies of Sweden, which might safeguard
the Baltic against Russian supremacy.   Here he had to contend with
George I's jealous hatred of his son-in-law of Prussia, and to prevent
Bernsdorff's Hanoverian policy imperilling a peace that was vital to
British trade ; he must struggle also against the traditional French plan
of using Sweden as her lever within the German Empire.   Over the
Hanoverian councillors he prevailed.   A new treaty with Prussia, an
energetic mission of Carteret to Stockholm, and a British fleet settled
by 1720 the concessions that Sweden must make, giving Bremen and
Verden to Hanover, Stettin to Prussia, and something for Denmark.
But Russia still stood out, and neither Turkey nor any other would
listen to Stanhope's wild inducements to open a new war against her.
Hence our pledges to Sweden were dishonoured, and in 1721 the peace
of Nystad transferred Esthonia and other Swedish conquests in the
eastern Baltic to Russia, who henceforth held the dominance of that sea
through the ports of Riga, Reval, and Narva.

    Domestic politics in these years were vindictive and debased.   The
feud in the royal family was scandalous : the Prince and Princess were
driven from the palace to set up their own Court at Leicester House,
and separated from their children ; the King even thought of passing a
statute to separate Britain from Hanover, and left a will, which George II
later suppressed, to the same effect.   Party principle disappeared in
this faction.   Walpole joined forces with the Prince's friend Argyll,
even with Oxford and Tory Churchmen, while the Stanhope group
thought of enlisting Bolingbroke.   Stanhope and Sunderland schemed
unscrupulous measures to perpetuate their power.   They discussed a
visitation of the universities, vesting all appointments to fellowships in

the Crown, and only their colleagues' protest stopped an amazing proposal to prolong the life of this Parliament beyond seven years. But their Peerage bill was enough exposure. Plausibly dwelling on the objections taken in 1712 to the creation of the twelve ' Utrecht ' peers, their real motive was to deprive their enemy, the Prince, of this prerogative when he became King. The bill provided that the sovereign should not be able to add more than six to the existing number of English lords, while Scotland would exchange her elected sixteen for twenty-five hereditary peerages. Little was heard of the modern argument, that removing the safety - valve of new creations made certain, sooner or later, an explosion between Lords and Commons. But though the Lords, responding to an appeal to their caste, carried the bill, even there Oxford and Cowper criticized this limitation of the prerogative; outside, Steele led a press attack on a closed aristocracy, and Walpole brought out the vital change in the constitution and this insolent closing of the door. The Commons' rejection of the bill was chiefly due to his oratory.

A series of such defeats, threats to their foreign policy, and Bernsdorff's intrigues, at last convinced ministers that they could not survive without reconciliation with Walpole and the Prince. This was accomplished half-way through 1720, Walpole and Townshend re-entering the government. And only just in time, for the South Sea Bubble was about to break.

British public finance being still in its infancy, the method of paying for the wars since 1689 had been casual and extravagant. The ' tallies ' issued, an early equivalent of Treasury bills, were at a heavy discount; loans were devised on an annuity system and at a high rate of interest; much was borrowed from the Bank and other corporations. At the end of the war the public debt of £54 millions was thought alarming, especially as a good deal of it was irredeemable, held at varying rates up to 9 per cent. Walpole made a beginning by getting Parliament to accept a sinking fund and to fix 5 per cent as the rate for new loans, though Stanhope took additional borrowings from the Bank and the South Sea Company.

This last corporation had been founded by Harley in 1711 to clear a large unfunded debt, and was assigned a monopoly of our trade with Spanish America. This trade, however, never materialized, the Company was over-capitalized from the start, and in 1719, influenced by the apparently successful speculations of Law, it put forward a scheme to retrieve its fortunes. This was nothing less than to take over £31 millions of the national debt. Government were tempted by the interest offered and hopes of converting a mass of long-dated annuities, and tempted too by the company's bid of £7½ millions, cash down. But bribery also played a large part, in the allotment of fictitious stock to

Craggs the elder, his son the Secretary of State, the King's mistresses, and Aislabie, Chancellor of the Exchequer.

Rejecting, against Walpole's protest, a better assured scheme from the Bank, the Commons accepted that of the Company, the success of which would entirely depend on keeping the price of their stock high.   To achieve that, the directors used every fraudulent device. The stock rose from 130 in February 1720 to a maximum of 1050 in June, the nation went mad with gambling, in one week of August there were lodged 36,000 transfers.   A swarm of bubble companies buzzed into life, including one for ' importing jackasses from Spain ', in which millions were pledged.   But the directors overplayed their hand.   It was impossible for ever to ' peg ' the price of a stock not covered by assets, they overloaded the market, and struck the first blow at their own safety by getting government to proclaim as illegal some eighty rival companies.   A rush to realize those worthless shares spread the panic to South Sea stock also, which tumbled between July and September from 1000 to 400, and in November was back at 135.

The crash destroyed the ministry, but made Walpole.   Hounded on by a secret committee, the Commons sent Aislabie to the Tower and confiscated the directors' estates.   Only a party vote acquitted Sunderland, the elder Craggs killed himself, the younger was fortunate to die of smallpox ;   early in 1721 Stanhope died of apoplexy.   Townshend replaced him as Secretary of State, Carteret succeeded Craggs, and Walpole, now first Lord of the Treasury, began to salve the wreckage. Preserving the one solid thing done by the Company, the conversion of irredeemable stock, he induced the Bank to take part over, and enforced a settlement which, at a cost to the holders averaging about 30 per cent, at least saved the State from repudiation.

He had many rough passages before his power was put above question, but good fortune and unscrupulous resolution carried him through.   The death of Sunderland and Marlborough in 1722 relieved him on one flank.   Carteret, too, was one of Stanhope's dynasty, ready to work with Hanoverian mistresses and ministers, or to angle for Tory support, and his removal to govern Ireland in 1724 was perhaps Walpole's greatest single victory.   In his place came in the rich young Duke of Newcastle, together with his brother Henry Pelham, both loyal followers of the minister.   From the Tories he had little to fear.   In the election of 1722 Tories and Jacobites often fought each other ;   in that year too the arrest and exile of Atterbury for conspiracy enabled Walpole to brand all Tories as Jacobites, while a special new tax of 5s. in the pound crushed the Catholics and non-jurors.   Yielding to the King's pressure — for the Duchess of Kendal had been bribed — he took steps for the pardon of Bolingbroke and release of his estates, but refused restoration of his peerage, which would have freed that dangerous voice in the Lords.

His greatest moment of danger came in 1727 when the King died at Osnabrück, on his way to Hanover, for George II could not begin by liking his father's servants. But the new Queen had more sense, the transparent incompetence of the King's choice, Sir Spencer Compton, drove him back on Walpole, and a handsome increase in the royal civil list settled the question. After six years of struggle, Walpole was seated in power for fifteen years to come.

CONTEMPORARY DATES

1715 A third Barrier treaty signed.
      Pope's *Iliad*.
      -1774. Reign of Louis XV.
1716 The Turks finally expelled fom Hungary.
1717 John Law, Minister of Finance in France.
      The Bangorian controversy.
1718 Peace of Passarowitz.
      Battle of Cape Passaro.
      Death of Charles XII of Sweden.
1719 Dismissal of Alberoni in Spain.
      Defoe's *Robinson Crusoe*.
1721 Treaty of Nystad.
      The Czar appoints the Holy Synod.
1722 Formation of the Moravian brotherhood.
      Bach's Fugues.
1723 Fleury begins to dominate French politics.
      Voltaire's *Henriade*.
      Death of Christopher Wren.
1724 Birth of Kant.
      Burnet, *History of His Own Time*.

CHAPTER VIII

WALPOLE AND THE PELHAMS, 1724-1754

Thirty years passed of Whig rule, broken towards their close by rebellion and war, but outwardly years in the main of content and prosperity. In truth, however, matter was being heaped up for explosion. An industrial revolution was proceeding, the realm was weakened by social injustice. Methodism began to perturb the apathy of religion. Ireland and the American Colonies were both possessed by a passion for self-government, Scotland sorely needed reform, our foreign policy bought peace only by putting off the day of settlement. We may measure the scale of such dangers by considering the nature and working of this Whig government.

Its power must not be exaggerated, for it was an accident, which time would correct, that temporarily Jacobitism had put the Tories out of court and the Crown had no alternative. Nor was Walpole a Prime Minister in our modern sense. His predominance ebbed away after the death of the Queen, and with the entry of the Prince of Wales into opposition. Constitutional government had not yet arrived, some of George II's ministers were selected by his own choice, and twice, in 1744 and 1757, he endeavoured to form a whole Cabinet of his own. Royal influence was paramount in Church appointments, army commands, and Court patronage, and doubly so in foreign affairs, since the King was also a foreign sovereign. In forty-six years George I and George II paid eighteen visits to Hanover, most of which proved prejudicial to British interests.

Government was therefore a partnership, in the sense that royal influence and a mass of heterogeneous patronage were used to mould and hold together a government ' interest ' out of the country gentlemen in the Commons. It was this which kept a party in existence, much more than any independent life in either Whig or Tory which, as memories of the Revolution faded, steadily lost their original meaning. The so-called ' Tory ' opposition to Walpole and the Pelhams was much what opposition had been to William III, or even to Charles II, a struggle of the ' country ' against the ' court ', and its programme was much the same. In this age it turned on protests against standing armies and high taxes, executive action like the suspension of habeas corpus, pensioners and placemen and excisemen, against the ' Hanover rats ' who took good English money, Dissent, and the moneyed men of the City. It was this blend of conservative obstruction and constitutional notions that descended to the first Radicals. Such 'Toryism' flourished most in the seats that government could hardly hope to shake, in the large constituencies of the counties or the little boroughs that went on from father to son, sometimes unbroken for two hundred years. This was true especially of the broad belt stretching back from the Bristol Channel, through Staffordshire to the Scottish Border.

The new holders of the Crown were better people, or at least better for England, than the last. George II was vain, avaricious, a domestic tyrant, and fonder of Hanoverian guards and pleasures than things English. But he was brave as a lion, he could speak English, and knew the country before he was too old to learn, and though prejudice often directed his choice of men, when he gave his confidence he gave it honestly. The Queen's word was often decisive with him, and it was a misfortune for both the King and Walpole when she died.

Sir Robert had, however, come to the top before this reign began by eminent powers of his own which made him Prime Minister for twenty-one years, a longer span than any before or after. He was a cruder type than his Eton schoolfellow Bolingbroke, but a stronger man, even a more upright one. If that is a curious word for a minister who talked bawdy down to his audience and married his mistress, and lowered public life by cynical acceptance of corruption, it is true of a policy which was always loyal to a few principles: the Protestant succession, coupled with the Whigs, and British native interests in preference to Europe. There was, too, a finer side to his dexterity, in a hatred of bloodshed and a wholesome view that what is doubtfully wise is best left alone. 'Tranquilla non movere', that was his answer to Dissenters who begged him to repeal the Test Act, or to officials who advised laying taxes on America. He evaded these ugly questions. From 1727 onwards annual bills were passed to indemnify Dissenters who had 'forgotten' to take the Anglican sacrament before accepting office, while no serious attempt was made to check the Americans' defiance of the Navigation Act. But his positive qualities were very real. He was the best debater of his generation. His Cabinet supremacy was in its way unerring, and often ruthless. Personality and circumstance together made him the founder of our modern government, being the first minister who built power purely on party, and the first who treated the Commons as the dominant partner. With the tastes of a rich Norfolk squire of old family, for field sports, building, and the bottle, he combined an understanding of an increasingly business age.

On this, the source of his early reputation, his lasting fame must depend, yet even here he was eminently the politician. Though he maintained the principle of a sinking fund to reduce the debt, he regularly raided it when hard pressed for revenue. As a contented country gentry was politically desirable, he cut down the land tax from its war-time level of 4s. to 1s., preferring to retain a salt excise that burdened the poor, nor did he tackle any comprehensive scheme of debt reduction. For trade he did much more. Mercantilism was still the national policy, measuring prosperity by a favourable balance of exports, and the virtue of any particular trade by its effect on the volume of industry. Walpole at least applied these doctrines with some attempt at consistency. For the first time since the Restoration the customs rates were thoroughly revised. In 1721 alone he freed more than a hundred classes of goods from export duty, while he reduced import charges on raw materials, relaxing also the ' enumeration ' rules that confined Colonial exports to Britain. Looking for more revenue, he found his best instrument in developing the excise, borrowed by the Common-wealth from the Dutch and since then much extended ; by taking duty on exit, not from the port but the warehouse, he might hope to curb the smuggling which filled all the coasts with riot and corruption, help the carrying-trade, and adjust taxation to consumption. Measured by the figures available for this small population of six millions in Eng-land and Wales, trade moved sharply upwards, exports rising by about one-third between 1720-40.

But he did nothing to protect the wage-earner, shirked dealing with the grievances of the Colonies, and surrendered to any powerful interest, as he did in his Molasses Act of 1733 which, to please the West India planters, clamped high sugar prices on both Britain and America. Standing for vested, though solid, interests he would not probe into corruption, or consider minorities, so gradually accumulating an oppo-sition not to be despised, coming from many angles.

In Parliament the Tories were divided between a small Jacobite wing, led by an honest wooden man, William Shippen, and the larger body under Sir William Wyndham, whose stately presence and eloquent patriotism made him the type in which the Commons took delight. But unaided they could not hope for a majority, and it was Bolingbroke's aim to make a coalition with the opposition Whigs, in alliance with whose leader, the witty but inefficient Pulteney, he founded the ' Crafts-man ' as their organ in the press. Here first appeared his ' Dissertations on Party ' and the germs of his ' Patriot King ', in which he repolished for a younger age what he had learned from Harley. Totally repudiating divine right, he attempted to rebuild Toryism on acceptance of the Revolution ; Jacobitism being dead and the pretexts for Whig against Tory removed, all should unite under a King who would rule above party, in restoring the constitution to its first principles. They should recover liberty by putting down Walpole's corruption, septennial Parliaments, and standing armies, and make the Commons a mirror of the nation by a wider franchise and the suppression of rotten boroughs.

But few Tories would listen to one whom they regarded as a ' Judas ', nor was it easy to keep in one lobby Tory Churchmen and City Whigs. As for Pulteney, whose motive was disappointed ambition, he was really a Whig unsympathetic to the Tory programme, which tilted at the very essentials of eighteenth-century government, septennial Parliaments, and placemen. Opposition, therefore, could not profit by the chance with which Walpole presented them in 1733, in a bill to extend the Excise to wines and tobacco, uniting all who disliked inquisitorial methods with the City vested interests and the smugglers. After riotous demonstration, with cries of ' no wooden shoes ', fears of disaffection in the army, and a mob assault on the Prime Minister, the bill was withdrawn.

Though his majority held good in the election of 1734, he added some influential names to Opposition by the dismissal of mutineers against Excise. One was Chesterfield, an aristocrat of high ability and husband of a natural daughter of George I, whose fame as a letter-writer has obscured his power as a political journalist and his grasp of foreign affairs. Another was Cobham, one of Marlborough's generals, who led a group of young kinsmen christened the ' Patriots ' or the ' Boys ', including his nephews the Grenvilles, George Lyttelton, and William Pitt. Firmly Whig and Protestant, they were ambitious and high-minded, jealous for themselves and for British good fame, contemptuous of Hanover and foes to corruption. A third notable element was a group of Scots, headed by Argyll and Stair, partly antagonized by Walpole's packing the election of Scottish peers. And how hated English government was in Scotland was proved again in 1736, when an Edinburgh mob lynched Porteous, captain of the city guard, which had fired on and killed some would-be rescuers of a popular smuggler. Finally, and broadly speaking, not only was the City anti-Walpolean, led by its particularly able member Sir John Barnard, but the whole world of wit and fashion. There were survivors from the brilliant society of the Augustans, the Hyde Duchess of Queensberry or John Gay the poet, whose *Beggar's Opera* was filled with sarcasms against government, together with a younger generation in Henry Fielding and Samuel Johnson. The Prime Minister took steps, besides his own paid organs in the press, to put down this literary opposition, one result being the Act of 1737, from which dates the Lord Chamberlain's censorship over the stage.

But in the conditions of that day the most dangerous fact for Walpole was that Opposition found a figurehead in the Prince of Wales, for however weak and ridiculous in himself, the heir-apparent had a high political value and could at least acquit the Tories of Jacobitism. In fact, Frederick had some real grievances, for he had been isolated in Hanover, kept short of money, and disappointed in a marriage on which his heart was set. Having taken the wife his father chose for him, Augusta of Saxe-Gotha, he turned to Opposition to get more generous allowances; in 1737, rather than have his child born under his father's roof, he hurriedly removed his wife, to her great danger, and was forbidden the Court, and set up his own establishments at Kew and Leicester House. In November the Queen died, which removed Walpole's best shield, and the more so since his foreign policy had divided the Cabinet.

Ten years passed from Stanhope's death in 1721 without any real European settlement, years which the Whig Lord Hervey described as 'broken peace and undeclared war'. The death of the Regent Orleans and his adviser Dubois removed the personal motives keeping France loyal to Britain, shifting her back towards her natural affinity with Spain, so that she supported the Spanish charge that George I had promised to surrender Gibraltar, while a Spanish Infanta was sent to France as destined bride for Louis XV. His teacher Cardinal Fleury, now the leading minister, was a wise, determined statesman, who preferred peace to war, yet would never lose sight of French objectives and would strive to shake off British control. Meantime Elizabeth Farnese was bent, furiously as ever, on Italian lands for her sons, and the Emperor Charles as obstinately set against it. But he had a sore grudge against Britain and Holland for trying to suppress his Ostend Company, established to develop trade with the East, and another grudge against Hanover for interference in the Baltic, championship of Protestant causes, and approaches to Prussia. Peter the Great was dead, but Russia was an incalculable force; terrifying Prussia like a thunder-cloud on its flank, and nourishing schemes, not without attraction for Austria, of partitioning Poland.

Townshend, who directed foreign policy, had Stanhope's hot temper and Hanoverian leaning without his magnetism, besides some insular contempt for foreigners, especially Austrians. In 1725 Spain and Austria agreed to sink their feud in an amalgamation of their grievances, a decision clinched by the French insultingly discarding the Infanta and marrying Louis XV to a Polish princess. Austria promised to work for restoration of Gibraltar and Minorca to Spain, who, in turn, would give Austria commercial privileges; the arrangements were believed to contemplate a restoration of the Stuarts; while Ripperda, the Dutch adventurer now advising Elizabeth Farnese, schemed Hapsburg-Bourbon marriages to shape the future of Italy.

Against Walpole's instinct, Townshend set about constructing a rival system. By the treaty of Hanover of 1725 Britain, France, and Prussia made a defensive alliance; money was poured out to subsidize small States; Townshend spoke of partitioning Belgium. But though the Spaniards began a siege of Gibraltar, the great war was fended off again. A British squadron under Hosier blockaded Porto Bello on the Main, though he had orders to avoid battle and, with most of his crews, perished of disease; while the Emperor was powerless against our sea-power in the Mediterranean. While Walpole was anxious to avert war, the real maker of the peace was Fleury, who would have no war that could only serve British interests, and skilfully disjointed the temporary entente between Austria and Spain. By the treaty of Seville of 1729, France and Britain agreed that Spanish garrisons should occupy Parma and Tuscany, Spain silently waiving the matter of Gibraltar, and it was now a question of enforcing these terms on Austria, as Walpole insisted, without a war. In this he fought and defeated Townshend, who in 1730 resigned. In 1731, by the treaty of Vienna, the Emperor accepted them, giving up his Ostend Company in return for a British guarantee of the Pragmatic Sanction, which he designed to ensure the succession of his daughter, Maria Theresa, to the Empire.

Though on paper the Stanhope system seemed to be restored, it was not so in fact. None of the deeper questions, the future of Italy and the Empire, were settled; Holland, now on the downgrade and deeply pacifist, had really dropped out of the alliance; France had acted unwillingly at every stage, and a growing school at Paris looked on Britain as the enemy. Indeed, even putting aside Colonial rivalries, there was a fallacy in a British policy which expected France to sit still, while Austria and Russia were carving out spheres of influence in the Balkans and Mediterranean.

So the next years proved. While Walpole was immersed in domestic opposition, the French rebuilt their influence at Madrid, and in those other capitals — Stockholm, Warsaw, and Constantinople — which they had always employed to curb the Hapsburgs. In 1733 the war of the Polish succession tested this new position. While Austrians and Russians backed a Saxon vassal of their own, France championed their King's father-in-law Stanislaus; though for him or Poland they cared little, their aim being to thrust forward Spain and Sardinia against the Austrians. Having detached the timid Dutch by promising no attack on Belgium, and having in the first Family Compact undertaken to restore Gibraltar to Spain, they were rewarded by Walpole repudiating our guarantee to Austria. When this war closed in 1738, Spain had recovered Naples and Sicily, and France had won Lorraine, whose duke Francis, husband of Maria Theresa, was transferred to Tuscany. Against the wish of the King and some ministers like Newcastle, Walpole had insisted on non-intervention; war, he contended, must finally mean a French invasion and Jacobite revolt. It is true that a war postponed may be a war averted, — ' I never heard it was a crime ', he said, ' to hope for the best '. But a policy which abandoned diplomatic initiative to France, threw Austria over, and aggrandized both the Bourbons, was taking great risks, if and when real cause arose for war.

So far as Britain was concerned, such causes were sure to be economic and connected with markets overseas. In Walpole's last years our exports were depressed, not least by French competition, but the immediate difficulty was that one most vital market, Spanish America, was only kept open by force; by our monopoly of the Assiento for supplying slaves, and the South Sea Company's privilege of sending one ship each year. Older quarrels lingered on, too, in the West Indies. British contrabandists carried on a huge illegal trade; British settlers staked out a claim to Honduras by cutting log-wood on the coast; our colony of Georgia clashed with Spanish Florida. Both sides practised fraud or violence. The British abused the ' annual ' ship by refilling it from so-called supply vessels, while the Spanish *guarda-costas* arrested many traders, innocent or guilty. In 1738 Opposition swept Parliament into protest against this right of search, producing evidence which inflamed all England, especially one Captain Jenkins who showed the ear torn off by the Spaniards with words that became a battle-cry, that he committed ' his soul to God and his cause to his country '. Under fear of reprisals the Spaniards in 1739 agreed to the Convention of the Pardo which, balancing the respective claims for damage, assigned to Britain the minute sum of £27,000, leaving the right of search to future discussion.

In both countries public opinion had outrun their governments' endeavours for peace, and in the Cabinet a war-party was led by Newcastle, who reasoned that the showing of our fleet would bring Spain to heel. Since Spain would not negotiate under threats, war was declared in October 1739.

It was made against Walpole's will, and it was the end of him. He wished to resign but this the King would not allow, and he continued, only to obstruct a divided Cabinet. His fall did not come about from the Tories, for the Bolingbroke-Pulteney partnership became less and less cordial, their natural leader Wyndham died, nor did they wish to replace Sir Robert by another Whig. By the time the next election came in 1741, our policy had turned to disaster. There was a gleam of victory in 1739 when Vernon captured Porto Bello, but the admiral was a Tory, neither ships nor men to man them were ready after the rust of peace, and the expeditions sent out in 1741 failed ingloriously, both on the Main and against Cuba. More serious was the attitude of France, who warned us against aggression in the Indies and won a diplomatic triumph by negotiating an Eastern peace, that robbed Austria of her gains from the two last Turkish wars. At the end of 1740 the Emperor died, and his Pragmatic Sanction with him. Throwing pledges to the winds, the young king of Prussia, the great Frederick, invaded Silesia, a war-party bore away Fleury, and in 1741 France and Spain joined hands with Prussia to partition Hapsburg lands and to raise the Bavarian Elector to the Imperial throne. Before that year closed, Maria Theresa was driven into Hungary, one French army occupied Prague, a second on the Rhine frightened George II into declaring Hanover neutral, while an unresisting British fleet saw the Spanish invade northern Italy.

In such dark days took place the election in which, partly by the Prince's exertions, Walpole's majority was whittled away, so that when Parliament met it disappeared. Avowing that his resignation was necessary to save both the party and the throne, his colleagues the Pelhams and Hardwicke the Chancellor came to terms with the Opposition Whigs, on the understanding that they would check any persecution of Walpole. In February 1742 he resigned, becoming Earl of Orford. While his old rival Spencer Compton, now Lord Wilmington, was nominal First Lord of the Treasury, Pulteney came into Cabinet as Lord Bath, Carteret became a Secretary of State, while the Prince was bought by some money for himself and a few places for his friends.

Though driven out as the scapegoat, till his death three years later Walpole's advice to the King decided the balance among his successors. The ' deserters' Pulteney and Carteret threw overboard the deck furniture of their ' patriot ' days, — place and pension and triennial bills, — suppressed the secret committee that was searching for evidence against Walpole, and made no serious effort to get Tories or ' patriots ' into place. In short, the new government was split between irreconcilable temperaments and policies. Pulteney, indeed, soon effaced himself in his peerage, his nerves, and his wealth, leaving the future between Carteret and the Pelhams. The first was a man of great gifts, classical scholar, diplomatist, and boon-companion, whose knowledge of German commended him to the King, and who ' in the upper departments of government ', the great Pitt said later, ' had not his equal '. But he was a natural dictator, believing royal favour could defy party and Cabinet, while his liking to ' knock the heads of the Kings of Europe together ', and his bold schemings, meant risks and expense that terrified his colleagues. This was not the way to keep an eighteenth-century party together, and when in 1743 the dim Wilmington died, Walpole advised that the lead should go to Henry Pelham.

The new Prime Minister was a much reduced Walpole, composed of economy and pessimism and human kindness. He was a pacifist, a creditable financier and party manager, but without a spark of fire. Actually his power was less than that of his brother Newcastle, for whom the King had always supreme contempt, but who for all that held office almost on end for thirty years. Personally the Duke was a petty creature, as much afraid of a damp bed as of the barest demonstration by a mob, insanely jealous of power, ridiculous in his tearful embraces and gabbling ejaculations.   Yet, as 300 volumes of his correspondence testify, he lavished his wealth and industry on the patronage, rotten boroughs, and lobbying which kept his party in being, and, though nothing ever proved him a statesman, long experience had taught him something of Europe.

Thrusting themselves into this cleft, late in 1744 all wings of Opposition joined with the Pelhams to overthrow Carteret's power behind the throne.   Chesterfield took office ; so did the Duke of Bedford, who represented by connection and type the more martial and Marlborough school of Whigs, together with his follower Sandwich ; of the Tories, Gower, head of a famous once-Jacobite house ; of the ' Patriots ', Cobham with two of his ' boys ', George Grenville and Lyttelton, and with hopes for a third, the rising orator William Pitt. This ' broad-bottom ' ministry, which ended the party of the old Tories and prolonged the Whigs in a sort of evaporation for another decade, came about through the war, Carteret's policy, and the last Jacobite rebellion.

For what began as a Colonial war with Spain enlarged into a war in Europe, aimed at France.   To abandon Austria a second time was out of the question, though to help her was difficult, and not least through the King's Hanoverian selfishness.   His declared neutrality for his electorate made it impossible to press Maria Theresa to make concessions, while his hatred of Prussia encouraged Frederick to seek an ally in France. Nothing could galvanize the Dutch, who were bent on neutrality, while our obvious ally Sardinia could only find expansion in Austrian Lombardy.

For a year Carteret's energy overcame some of these enmities.   At least he persuaded George to let Hanover fight as an auxiliary to Austria — though Britain was to pay for Hanoverian troops —, while in the Netherlands he got on foot a cosmopolitan ' pragmatic ' army. Our Navy kept the Bourbons of Naples passive ; most of all, by the Breslau treaty of July 1742 he induced the Austrians to eliminate their worst enemy by yielding Silesia to the Prussians.   The tide of war turned.   Early in 1743 the last French troops straggled out of Bohemia ; by June the Austrians held Munich and the Bavarian Emperor was a fugitive.   The pragmatic army was at last got on the march to cut the French retreat from Bavaria, but George II halted on the Main and under harassing attack it retired northwards.   So came about on 16th June the collision at Dettingen, the last battle in which a King of England took the field in person.   And lucky indeed he was to win it, only just escaping encirclement through hard fighting of his English troops and bad mistakes by the French command.

Actually he fought as Elector, wearing the yellow Hanoverian scarf, since officially France and Britain were not at war, but now it was Carteret's purpose to turn the war into a great anti-French coalition. His plans included a reconciliation between the Emperor and Maria Theresa, who should find her compensation in Alsace and the spoils of France, while in Italy he negotiated the treaty of Worms, whereby Austria should grant some Milanese territory to Sardinia.

This spirited diplomacy, criticized in Britain as 'Hanoverian', was very expensive, involving subsidies in all directions, which the Cabinet refused. A first effect was to drive the Bourbons closer together in a second Family Compact, which included a project to restore the Pretender. And a second was to infuriate Frederick II, who feared that in a reconstruction controlled by Austria and Hanover he might be robbed of Silesia. In 1744 France declared war on us. Though a storm dispersed a convoy destined to carry an army into the Thames, their brilliant general Maurice of Saxe entered Flanders and took Ypres; Frederick once again invaded Bohemia; fumbling action under elderly admirals and insubordination discredited our Mediterranean fleet; in Italy there was a military stalemate.

So, to the King's indignation, Carteret was forced out of power, denounced by Pitt as the 'Hanoverian troop-minister', who had made England 'a province to a despicable electorate'. But his successors found that without Hanoverian troops and subsidies to Hanover they would be powerless, when in 1745, on the Emperor's death, the storm of war passed from Germany to Britain.

In the Netherlands the British commander was now the King's favourite son Cumberland, a dogged but inexperienced soldier of twenty-four, the Dutch were unwilling to fight, and in April Saxe laid siege to Tournai. On the 30th, at Fontenoy, five miles away, Cumberland dashed his force against entrenched positions, and though the British infantry did wonders, had to retreat with severe loss. Ghent, Oude-narde, and Ostend fell. Half Piedmont and the whole Milanese were overrun by Bourbon armies. In June Charles Edward sailed from Nantes, rounded the Lizard, and reached the Macdonald country at Moidart with seven companions.

There is no more severe condemnation of Whig Britain and George II's government than the '45, in which the Young Pretender was able to keep the field for a year, and with a few thousand Highlanders to reach the Midlands. In itself Jacobitism was nearly dead. 'James III' lived in Papal Rome, devout, dreary, and discredited by domestic bickering, only a trickle of English money occasionally reaching him from loyalists like the Duke of Beaufort, and now, but for a few Lanca-shire Catholics, not an Englishman moved. Only French arms could make invasion succeed, but France had made her effort the year before, and less than 1000 French troops came late in the day to help Charles

Edward. Yet in Britain there was almost universal incompetence and panic. The King behaved disgracefully, insisted on going to Hanover, and tried to revive a Carteret government. Early in 1746 the Pelhams resigned in a body and in forty-eight hours compelled him to surrender, one condition being a minor office for Pitt. On the ' black Friday ' that Charles Edward left Derby, there was a run on the London banks and, except in a few individuals like the archbishop of York, energy seemed dead.

A better government could have made the Lowlands impregnable, for Union had deepened the gulf between them and the Highlands. Covenanting feeling against England was much diminished, while government grants to the linen industry and a share in Colonial trade brought some new prosperity. Glasgow was solidly loyalist, no Lowland town willingly surrendered ; Edinburgh and Stirling castles defied the Pretender throughout ; nor could his pledges of tolerance do away with the Kirk's hatred of Rome. On the other hand, there was a good deal of cool indifference, for the Porteous affair and English taxation rankled with the burgesses, and government manipulation of elections with the political class, while its supporters were divided by jealousies between the Argyll interest and their rivals. Little, too, had been done since the '15 to change the Highlands. General Wade had constructed about 250 miles of military roads, a few clansmen like the nucleus of the Black Watch had been enrolled in the army, a few more Presbyterian ministers had found a foothold. But cattle-lifting and blackmail went on as of old, while a nominal disarmament only meant that the loyal gave up arms and the disloyal hid them. For some years a group of Highland gentlemen had been in close touch with Paris and Rome.

Yet even the 3000 recruits garrisoning Scotland could have held up rebellion, if General Cope had shown ordinary sense or the troops any spirit. As it was, instead of holding Stirling and the Forth, Cope dashed into the Highlands where, finding the Prince stronger than he liked, he took shelter in Inverness, and thence shipped his force to Dunbar ; only to find Charles in occupation of Edinburgh.

It was, in fact, Charles' personal triumph, and little more. He had sailed from France against his father's wish and the best advice, and only his own qualities bore down the objections of the Highland chiefs. In his youth he was the first Stuart since Charles II who bore himself like a king, always wearing the kilt and marching on foot with the ranks, winning all women's hearts, ever ready for a fight or a reel. He was already drinking too much brandy and, like all his house, listened to flatterers, his tutor Sheridan and other Irish whom the Highlanders despised. But when he came among them as their guest, their loyalty responded, his first success sweeping all doubts away. Young Lochiel and the Clanranald Macdonalds were first out when he raised his red standard at Glenfinnan, but when he reached Perth some of the clans, and some of the very men, who had been out in the '15, joined him; the Catholic duke of Perth, Stewart of Appin, Glengarry, and Macdonalds of Glencoe, with the Lowland peers Kilmarnock and Nithsdale. Unhappily his two ablest men hated each other; his secretary Murray of Broughton, who was to be the Judas, and the Atholl soldier Lord George Murray, to whom Charles owed his military success but to whom he never gave his trust.

Levying money on the towns as he passed, he crossed the Forth near Stirling unopposed, and so by Linlithgow to the outskirts of Edinburgh. A few shots routed the royal dragoons in the ' canter of Coltbridge ', after which he entered the city and slept in Holyrood. Then he issued out to meet Cope, advancing from Dunbar, which he did some nine miles east at Prestonpans, where on 21st September the clansmen broke through the morning mist on the stubble fields and cut the enemy infantry to pieces, Cope flying with the horse to Berwick-on-Tweed. Now the real decision must be made.

Charles himself urged immediate advance into England, for only an English rising would bring the French help on which he counted, but for a month the Highland chiefs resisted him, by which time the aged Wade with 18,000 men was at Newcastle and Cumberland brought home reinforcements from Flanders. Delay made desperate what was in any case a hard venture, and the odds had turned against him when in November he made for the western route, to reach the Jacobites reputed to swarm in Lancashire and Wales. Many Highlanders having now deserted, it was with less than 5000 men that he forced the surrender of Carlisle and so, through ill-omened Preston, moved to the bells and bonfires at Manchester. Derby was reached on 4th December, when his officers refused to go further. Not a man of weight had joined them; Cumberland's army from Lichfield and Wade's from the north were closing the jaws of the trap; they turned and, beating off Cumberland's advance guard, on Christmas day entered hostile Glasgow. Unless the French came in force, all was lost, for all the conditions were present which a century earlier had doomed Montrose. Being without money, Charles had to pay his men in meal; lack of artillery paralysed the assaults on Stirling and Fort William. Influenced by the wise loyalist Duncan Forbes, some important chiefs like Macleod wavered; in the north Seaforth and Sutherland, Mackays and Grants, held to the Crown, while the Navy cut off all but a few Frenchmen. Yet one more success kept the rebel army together a little longer. Joined by new levies of the Gordons, on the 17th January 1746, in twilight and rain, the Prince routed General Hawley at Falkirk.

Before the month ended, however, Cumberland reached Edinburgh, and once more his council forced Charles to retreat, through Perthshire to Inverness. With the fleet on his right Cumberland followed, passed Aberdeen in February, and in April prepared to cross the Spey. The Highland army was now so short of food that it scattered to get supply or sow for the harvest, but against George Murray's advice to seek the hills Charles determined to accept battle, north of Inverness, on the plain of Culloden. His night attack having failed, on 16th April his hungry army was attacked by Cumberland, shot through by immensely superior artillery, encircled by cavalry, and destroyed. Having lost 1000 killed, including the chiefs Maclachlan and Macdonald of Keppoch, they dispersed. For six months Charles disappeared in the Western Isles, guided by the loyal like Flora Macdonald and never betrayed, though £30,000 was on his head, until in September with Lochiel he escaped to France. Some eighty of the rank and file were executed, and of the peers Balmerino, Kilmarnock, and the treacherous Lovat, who was himself betrayed by Murray of Broughton. A host of Scottish leaders went into exile, while disgrace draggled the last romance of the white rose. Young Glengarry turned spy for the government; Charles Edward steadily drank away his character, though his strong body lasted out till 1788.

Rejecting the plea of Duncan Forbes for lenience, Cumberland earned his name of 'Butcher' by a savage suppression, harrying cottages, shooting suspects, burning crops. While a few large estates were confiscated, two statutes of 1747 cut at the root; one abolishing the chiefs' jurisdictions, and another substituting money rents for their vassals' military service. A stringent disarming Act forbade the wearing of the tartan and kilt, save by soldiers of the Crown.

In the chronicle of the Pelham ministry, however, the '45 made only one item in the mounting ruin of war. On the whole, the British effort assisted very selfish allies to victory, though totally unsuccessful in her own area. In December 1745 Frederick, by the treaty of Dresden, finally retired from the war, Maria Theresa sullenly accepting the loss of Silesia. This released Austrian forces for Italy, and with the Sardinians they cleared the north, when in 1746 Elizabeth Farnese lost power on her husband's death. But they hated each other too keenly to co-operate, as the British asked, in invading France; their failure against Genoa leaving the Bourbons an invaluable base. Nearer home our military objectives seemed unobtainable. Saxe swept on in 1746 to take Brussels, Antwerp, and Liége. In 1747 he invaded Holland and, at the other extreme, pressed up the Meuse to defeat Cumberland at Lauffeldt, in front of Maestricht. Holland was near collapse and ardent for peace; the Austrians were little interested.

Against this picture could be set other events which tokened the future and which, well-used, might have been turned to advantage. In 1745 Massachusetts despatched an army which, with a few British ships, took Louisburg on Cape Breton Island, the key of the St. Lawrence; but the vantage was not driven home. Anson, the hero of a voyage round the world, restored some vigour to the Admiralty, and both he and Hawke did great damage to French fleets and commerce. This sea-war reached the East. In 1746 La Bourdonnais captured Madras; in 1748 the great Dupleix beat off Boscawen from the French Indian capital, Pondicherry.

Though Maria Theresa would fight for ever at other people's expense, France was hard hit and weary of burning her fingers for Spain. Holland was entreating peace, pessimism dogged half the British Cabinet. ' Dear brother, we are conquered ' Newcastle heard in a letter from Pelham, whose economic soul shivered at a debt risen to £78 millions; Chesterfield had resigned in protest, Cumberland advised that the Netherlands could not be saved.

So came about in October 1748 the peace of Aix-la-Chapelle, arranged by Britain and Holland in concert with France, for whom it was a marked triumph, and then forced upon Austria and Sardinia. Frederick received international guarantees for Silesia, Sardinia won part of the Milanese as promised her at Worms, and Philip the young Spanish-Farnese prince obtained Parma. Elsewhere it was an ominous truce. Britain restored Louisburg as against Madras. Nothing was said about frontiers in America; war between rival East India companies still proceeded; the weak Dutch rule was restored in the Barrier. There was silence on the original pretext of war, — the right of search, — while the British Assiento privilege was given up within two years. We had lost the Austrian alliance. Burning to recover Silesia, Maria Theresa had already turned towards France, while eastward she looked for help to the new might of Russia. It was in vain that in the next few years Newcastle, following the King about Germany like a clucking hen, multiplied subsidies to German electors who were to buttress the ' old system '; for its mainstay, the Austrians, had secretly sold the pass.

Divided, weak, and well-intentioned, the Pelham government went on its twilight way. Patiently Pelham protested against his brother's costly policy, cut down the Navy to 8000 men, and halved the land tax. He did a good stroke in scaling down interest on the debt to 3 per cent, besides passing some useful legislation. Hardwicke's Marriage Act did away with the scandal of Fleet marriages and the abduction of heiresses, setting up our triple ' calling of the banns '. By reforming the calendar, British dating was brought into line with the Gregorian style long used abroad, eleven days of September 1752 being omitted, to the alarm and fury of ignorant voters. Money was found to establish the British Museum. On the suggestion of London magistrates, especially the novelist Fielding, the Bow Street runners became the germ of a much-needed metropolitan police. Another act at last checked what magistrates, doctors, and clergy agreed in calling the worst evil of the age, the drinking of gin, which alternate licence and severity had hitherto failed to reduce. London was said to have 17,000 gin shops, while 6 million people consumed 11 million gallons of spirits every year.

In matters of greater weight there was neither vision nor courage. Severe acts stopped working-men's combinations to improve their wages, and suppressed New England manufactures which competed with the home market. A conflict had begun over the right of the Irish Parliament to appropriate its taxes. In 1753 a bill passed to make easier naturalization for foreign Jews, but was repealed the same year under clamour from the mob. Principle in politics, or real party, was almost non-existent. Much damaged by the '45, the Tories lingered on as a collection of squires, proclaiming their independence against Hanover, placemen, and courtiers, championing the militia against the army, or the Church against Dissent. Bolingbroke died in 1751, all his influence gone, and half his followers like Gower had joined the Pelhams. What, in fact, divided politics now was not party, but personal jealousies and rival courts. Newcastle's thirst for monopolizing power drove out the Bedford group in 1751, and the same year died Frederick Prince of Wales; whose last acts had been, in jealousy of Cumberland, to attack the peace and Hanover and to collect round him a faction of office-seekers like the notorious Bubb Dodington, a few Tories, and some disgruntled Whigs.

The 'court' he had thus begun was continued by his widow, who wished to protect her son against the King and Cumberland. While Bedford and his ablest follower Henry Fox followed the Duke, the Pelhams tried to keep on terms with the Princess and Bute, her intimate adviser. For the King was old, and there might be a contest for the regency of a new reign. In the background the greatest man in England, William Pitt, now paymaster, was kept out of important office by the unrelenting malice of the King against the man who had helped to overthrow Walpole, had ejected Carteret, and held up Hanover to ridicule.

While Pitt, thus eating his heart out, watched Fox aspiring to the lead, in April 1754 Henry Pelham died. The Whig grandees, fearing Fox as Cumberland's man, and that the choice of Pitt would offend the King, put the lead of the Commons in the hands of a nonentity, the decent diplomat Sir Thomas Robinson, while recommending Newcastle to the King as chief minister. Such a system could not long live under the contempt of the King, Pitt, and Fox. Much less when news was coming in, that meant a new war; of rival sepoy armies in India under French and British officers, and of a reverse, at French hands, on the Ohio to the Virginian militia, under command of Colonel George Washington.

CONTEMPORARY DATES

1725　Death of Peter the Great.
　　　Vico's *Scienza Nuova*.
　　　Foundation of Guy's Hospital.
1726　Fall of Ripperda in Spain.
　　　Swift, *Gulliver's Travels*.
1727　Siege of Gibraltar.
　　　Gay's *Beggar's Opera*.
1729　Treaty of Seville.
　　　The Wesleys begin meetings at Oxford.
　　　Birth of Burke.
1732　Pope's *Essay on Man*.
1733　War of the Polish Succession.
1734　Don Carlos in Italy.
1736　Butler's *Analogy of Religion*.
1737　End of the house of Medici at Florence.
1739　Nadir Shah of Persia sacks Delhi.
　　　Hume's *Treatise of Human Nature*.
1740　Death of the Emperor Charles VI ; war of the
　　　　　Austrian Succession begins.
　　　Thomson's *Rule, Britannia*.
　　　–1786.　Frederick the Great rules Prussia.
1741　Dupleix begins his government of French India.
　　　Handel's *Messiah*.
　　　Russians under Behring open up Alaska.
1742　Pope completes the *Dunciad*.
1743　Voltaire visits Frederick the Great.
1745　American troops take Louisburg.
　　　Death of Swift.
1746　Diderot's *Pensées philosophiques*.
1747　Ahmed Shah Durani founds the Afghan throne.
1748　Montesquieu's *Esprit des lois*.
1749　Kaunitz becomes chief minister in Austria.
　　　Fielding's *Tom Jones*.
1750　Pombal in power in Portugal.
　　　Johnson edits the *Rambler*.
1751　Mason and Dixon drawing frontiers in America.
　　　The Encyclopaedia edited by Diderot and d'Alem-
　　　　　bert.
　　　Linnaeus, *Philosophia Botanica*.
1752　Great Britain adopts the Gregorian calendar.
1753　Duquesne on the Ohio and Mississippi.
　　　Horace Walpole building Strawberry Hill.
　　　Richardson's *Sir Charles Grandison*.
1754　Wall becomes principal minister in Spain.
　　　Rousseau's discourse on ' Inequality '.

CHAPTER IX

THE ELDER PITT AND THE SEVEN YEARS' WAR, 1754–1763

A NEW British Empire, revolution in Ireland, and new British parties were the fruits of the epoch from 1754 to 1783, of which the central figures were William Pitt, later Lord Chatham, and George III. And the minister was supreme before the accession of the King.

He was of that order of political genius which transcends all rules. There was a fluency in the Pitt blood, shown in his fierce grandfather Governor Pitt of Madras, who had used in pocket boroughs the money raised by selling the great diamond he brought back from India, and in some cases this temper turned to madness. His grandson, strained physically by gout and nervous lassitude, had a scornfulness and pride which made him almost impossible in Cabinet; Achilles must lead the host, or he would take to his tent. Seeing himself as actor on a tragic stage, he was theatrical even at his greatest, making ' properties ' out of his crutches and black velvet, and dramatized life even in his most private letters. Of money he had no sense at all, squandering it on building or estates. From vaulting ambition he was not free, as he showed during weary years when George II kept him down, in manœuvring with several party camps or the rival favourites, Lady Yarmouth and Lord Bute.

Bred a soldier, he was not a law-giver but a man of action, who by a rare combination was also the greatest British orator of perhaps any age. His eye was compared to a hawk's, he seems to have scorched up opponents in debate as if by fire, his speeches blazing up in sudden inspiration, as when he saw death riding on the white horse, the badge of Hanover, or pointed the Lords to the Armada tapestries. His sympathy went out to men of his own type, Frederick the Great or Clive, and young commanders of his choice, Wolfe, Murray, Keppel, Amherst, Howe, were the heroes of the war. In policy he united audacious strokes, being ready, for instance, to exchange Gibraltar against Minorca, with sweeping strategical conceptions, whether a threefold invasion of Canada, or an extended use of sea-power, and both of these again with painstaking mastery of detail in troop movements and supply.

Often impatient, prejudiced, even ignorant, within he was a man wishing for affection, high-minded, and religious; who, much unlike

Fox, refused to take the immense profits open to the paymaster. The ideas which inspired both England and America were few and simple; that the Whigs could only survive if they stood for the people, that France was the enemy, that the liberties of Magna Carta belonged to all Englishmen and all Americans, that Protestantism was the faith for men who loved liberty. Appealing to motives that are deepest in a people's heart, he raised magnificent fighting-men from the lately rebel Highlands, and behind the regular army built, in effect for the first time, a second line of defence by his Militia Act of 1757. Never afraid of publicity before Britons who forced George II to put him at the head of the State, or Americans who raised statues to him, he pronounced broad policies to which he penetrated rather by instinct than thought; contempt for placemen, dislike of Hanover, or the inseparateness of taxation and representation.

Spending his life in denouncing faction and calling for ' measures, not men ', he did at least as much as George III to disintegrate parties. His marriage to Hester Grenville cemented a strong clan who had attacked Walpole's corruption and the Hanoverianism of Carteret, and despised the feminine nerves of Newcastle. He was a Whig, in that he was a stout anti-Jacobite Protestant, a quality which he used to suppress one possible rival, the brilliant ' silver-tongued ' William Murray, of a Scottish Jacobite family, who as Lord Mansfield was a power later in George III's counsels. But he was poles apart from the place-hunting aristocracy; whose veteran enemies, Bolingbroke whom he knew well, and the old Duchess of Marlborough who left him a legacy, fixed on him as their hope. He had links with more radical persons, Beckford and other City merchants, and the adventurous John Wilkes, member for Aylesbury, and also found much to attract him in the Tory independents, not merely their ' independency ' or dislike of Hanover, but the belief he also shared in a strong Crown. This explains his temporary alliance with the young Prince George's court. Many patriotic men, indeed, found their best hope in this partnership between Pitt and Bute; especially when in 1755 Newcastle, in deference to the old King, took into his Cabinet Henry Fox, the special representative of the King's beloved Cumberland, whose joint influence hastened the outbreak of an inevitable war.

Strained financially by the war of the Austrian succession, dislocated by internal quarrels, and with a necessity of rebuilding her navy, France had little wish for a new struggle. But two sets of causes were making the origins of two wars, which turned into one. The first was the rancour of Austria against her late Allies and a resolve to recapture Silesia, in which she could count on help from Frederick's neighbours, Russia and Saxony. George II was ready to connive, if only Hanover were safe, but even Newcastle's wish to keep the old alliance could not persuade Parliament to support another war of Carteret's sort, which would involve expensive subsidies and, perhaps, a partition of Prussia. Late in 1755, protesting against an ' inundation of subsidies and German measures ', Pitt was dismissed, and George Grenville with him.   Before that, a second set of causes pointed to war with France ; yet Britain saw Austria unsympathetic and Holland decided on neutrality.   Casting about for allies, they found Frederick II in alarm at the threat from Russia.   Hence came in January 1756 the Convention of Westminster, providing mutual guarantees for Prussia and Hanover.   This, in turn, impelled France to the famous ' reversal of alliances ', long dangled before her by the Austrian minister Kaunitz ; the first treaty of Versailles in May arranging for Austrian neutrality in an English-French war, and mutual assistance against attack from Prussia.   So far already was English diplomacy driven, by need of security, towards a break with France.

That war rose, however, from causes long accumulating, beyond the desire of either government.   In India fighting had never ceased since 1748, little wars in which rival companies supported rival rajahs, in return for grant of a fortress or trade concession.   The scene was the east coast in the Carnatic and Hyderabad, and the chief actor the brilliant governor of Pondicherry, Dupleix, who thought expansion of territory indispensable for commerce and, assisted by Bussy, a soldier-diplomat of genius in dealing with Orientals, raised sepoy armies under French command.   Further south, however, two remarkable Britons, Stringer Lawrence and Robert Clive, stemmed the tide.   In 1751 Clive first made his name by seizing the Carnatic capital Arcot, and holding it triumphantly.   Dispersal of forces over this huge area and broken finances crippled the French ; Dupleix was recalled in 1754 and, though India was left an unsolved problem, it was not the occasion of war.

This came from America where, whatever their immediate acts of aggression, essentially the French were on the defensive, for their people in Canada numbered only some fifty-five thousand against nearly two million Americans.   Nothing could have kept the map as it stood.   The peace of Utrecht gave Britain the outer bastions of Canada, in Newfoundland, Nova Scotia, and Hudson's Bay, but with no clearcut frontiers.   To seaward of Nova Scotia the French held Cape Breton Island, on which they fortified a powerful base at Louisburg, and when it was restored to them in 1748, the British planted a military colony opposite it at Halifax.   Nothing reconciled to British rule the French Acadians, who were kept in turmoil by Catholic missions.

These losses in the north inclined the French to develop communications with an outlet, far south, which the great La Salle had found in the bay of Mexico.   There a new province arose, Louisiana, with New Orleans its capital at the Mississippi mouth, and to make contact between this and Canada, hitherto merely linked up by fur traders or missionaries, now became a fixed purpose. From their Canadian capital at Montreal their trading-posts radiated in three directions. Westwards a line by Detroit reached out to untraversed lakes and prairies. South and south-east they pushed down the Richelieu river to Lake Champlain, on whose shore they built forts at Crown Point and Ticonderoga, so reaching the territory of New York. Between these two prongs they passed round Lake Ontario to the Niagara peninsula, that links it with Erie, where they were within fifty miles of the Alleghany, and thence, all the way by water, made for the Ohio and so, by its junction with the Mississippi, to their distant goal. If their plan were completed, it would throttle American expansion westwards and pin our Colonies to the sea ; at each stage they clashed with pioneers from New York, Virginians who were pushing an Ohio land company, or Carolina traders. A clash was the more certain because this debatable land was the area of the ' six nations ', the Iroquois Indians, who at Utrecht were declared to be British subjects, but were indignant at American land-grabbing and skilfully excited by French agents. Under their inscrutable eyes rose rival French and British forts, while trappers and surveyors cut into the wilderness.

There was a third conflict, vital to America, over the West Indies, whose products made an essential exchange for American food-stuffs, and whose harbours could shelter rival navies. Here the French in Martinique and Guadeloupe were prospering more than the British, who had exhausted their best plantations and over-concentrated on sugar. Moreover, the possession of St. Lucia and three other islands was still in dispute.

The collision came in 1753–4, when the Virginians decided to make a fort where the Alleghany joins the Ohio, only to find the French already there building Fort Duquesne, and Colonel Washington was driven back on the mountains. In 1755 the British took two decisive steps, by deporting the French inhabitants of Nova Scotia into New England and sending royal troops under Braddock to help the Americans. In June Boscawen's fleet failed to intercept French reinforcements entering the St. Lawrence ; in July the gallant, old-fashioned Braddock was ambushed near Fort Duquesne and perished with half his army. War flared up all over America and in reprisals at sea, though Newcastle still hoped it might be kept out of Europe ; a hope that failed in 1756, when in April the French attacked Minorca, and in September Frederick the Great, anticipating his enemies, occupied Saxony and called on Britain for aid.

War broke up the government of Newcastle, whom Pitt compared to ' a child driving a go-cart on the edge of a precipice '. In that divided Cabinet Hardwicke headed a peace-party against Cumberland. The regular army was hardly 20,000 strong, yet government rejected a militia bill and brought in German mercenaries. Panic of invasion delayed the sending of assistance to Minorca, and its loss showed up our spineless command. The island had an insufficient garrison, the Gibraltar forces refused to help, a relieving squadron was weakened by dispersal in convoys, while Admiral Byng was inexperienced in war. After one indecisive action he abandoned efforts to harass the French or cut their communication with Toulon, though even so Minorca held out another month.   While politicians strove to lay all responsibility on the Admiral, national fury demanded a scapegoat; there was loathing of the foreign mercenaries, corn was rising to a starvation price, the French under Montcalm captured the forts of Ontario.   The Cabinet fell to pieces, Fox resigned, the timid Murray took refuge in the chief justiceship as Lord Mansfield. By refusing to serve with Newcastle on any terms Pitt drove him into retirement, and in November with his followers came into office, under the nominal lead of the Duke of Devonshire.

Another year went by, in chaos at home and disaster abroad. After trial by court-martial Byng was shot, King and people being equally decided, though Pitt attempted to save him. With difficulty a Militia bill was passed to raise a tiny force of 32,000 men, and much rioting was caused by the first levies. True, some assistance was voted to Frederick, foreign mercenaries were sent away, but the Cabinet could not survive the royal hostility. In April 1757, on the demand of Cumberland, the King dismissed them and, in the teeth of public opinion and the spirit of the constitution, spent eleven precious weeks in trying to instal Fox and Cumberland with a ministry of his own choice.

Fortunately national opinion and the calculations of the political groups coincided. While cities showered their freedom on Pitt, the Leicester House men dreaded the supremacy of Cumberland, and the Newcastle Whigs reckoned they had better close with a young prince than an old king. In part by Bute's agency a coalition was at last formed : Newcastle and Hardwicke representing the old Whig ' corps '; Pitt, Secretary of State and leader of the Commons, with his brothers-in-law Temple and Grenville ; Cumberland's followers like Bedford relapsed into minor places, while Fox ended his career by taking the paymastership in hope of riches.

Its first prospects in 1757 were black indeed. One effort to take Louisburg failed miserably, Montcalm came down beyond Lake Champlain. News reached England also that in the previous summer the new Nawab of Bengal had captured Calcutta, many of whose garrison had perished in ' the Black Hole '. After some first successes Frederick was defeated by the Austrians at Kolin, and evacuated Bohemia.

One French army invaded Saxony; in July, a second beat Cumberland at Hastenbeck and drove him out of Hanover, and in September he signed the convention of Klosterseven, interning or disbanding half his force. The same month our attack on Rochefort, near La Rochelle, collapsed; even Pitt declared ' the Mediterranean lost, and America itself precarious '. Neutrals grumbled at our rough use of sea-power and our extension of international law by two famous doctrines: the ' rule of 1756 ' which forbade, for example, Dutch ships to perform a carrying-service for France which would not normally be done in time of peace, and the doctrine of ' continuous voyage ', which would prevent neutrals carrying French colonial goods to France from a neutral port.

But in November the dauntless Prussian king turned the tide. Though compelled by the Russians to abandon East Prussia and threatened by the Swedes in Pomerania, and though an Austrian force temporarily held Berlin, he crushed the undisciplined French at Rossbach in Saxony and then, striking eastwards for Silesia, in December annihilated an Austrian army at Leuthen.

From 1758 onwards the war became a blaze of victory. This was made possible because, in effect, Pitt was sole war minister, often, for instance, issuing fleet orders without recourse to the Admiralty, and again because his system of war fully realized the meaning of sea-power. This it was which dried up French reinforcements for Canada and saved British India; drove first the French, and then the Spanish, navy from the seas; won an Empire and bargaining values which could be used in making peace; and so waged war that both exports and tonnage actually increased. Seen in this light, Germany became a secondary theatre; though the Klosterseven convention was repudiated, though money and men were sent to Frederick and diversion attacks made on the French coast, all were designed to contain the enemy while the mortal stroke was delivered overseas. Cumberland's successor in command, Ferdinand of Brunswick, was a good soldier but under this system Frederick bore the brunt; Swedes, Austrians, and hordes of Russians beat in on his State, he lost Saxony, Silesia, and Pomerania, more than once he thought of suicide. Only the death of his bitter enemy the Czarina Elizabeth in 1762 saved him, for it brought Russian neutrality.

Pitt lifted our war effort to a new scale. British troops alone rose to nearly 150,000, and the fleet to over 400 ships. Ten millions were voted in 1758, the budget of 1760 climbed to fifteen, while over a million was paid to the American Colonies. Even more, Pitt's breadth of vision, and power of raising men to united effort, made this the first Imperial war. His appeals wrung considerable taxes out of unwilling Colonies, his recognition of American commissioned officers and choice of some for high command called out a loyalty unknown before.

In Europe during 1759 our sea-power warded off serious dangers, for a great French minister had attained power in Choiseul and their ports were full of troops for invading England. But, reinforced through the port of Emden with superbly fighting British infantry, in August Ferdinand of Brunswick saved Germany by a great victory at Minden; marred only by the failure of the British cavalry under Lord George Sackville, a Leicester House favourite, who for this matter was dismissed the army. That same month the Toulon squadron, passing Gibraltar to join that at Brest, was destroyed by Boscawen off Lagos in Portugal; in November the Brest fleet broke out to convoy transports from the Loire, but Hawke pursued it in a storm into the shoals of Quiberon in Brittany, destroyed many ships, and left the rest crippled.

While the centre was thus firmly held, on all the circumference France was obliterated. Some British successes had, no doubt, little immediate bearing on the war. Among these was the seizure of French West Africa, and the same might even be said of India, weighted though that struggle was with future destiny. Having retaken Calcutta, in 1757 Clive and Admiral Watson seized the French settlements in Bengal and in June scattered Siraj-ud-Daulah's forces at Plassey. In 1758 the fiery Lally reached Pondicherry, took Fort St. David to the south, and then turned north to besiege Madras. Our sea-power forced him in 1759 to raise the siege, while one of Clive's best lieutenants, Forde, expelled the French from the northern Circars. In 1760 Eyre Coote beat Lally at Wandewash, between Madras and Arcot; pinning down the French squadron far off at Mauritius, by command of the sea we could bring the reinforcements which in 1761 forced Pondicherry to surrender.

By that date decision had been reached on the American scene. The campaign of 1758 did not achieve all that was hoped, for though the fleet helped Amherst to take Louisburg, it came late in the year to attempt Quebec. On the mainland two blows were struck at Canadian contacts with the Ohio, by the capture of Fort Duquesne and destruction of Fort Frontenac on the north shore of Ontario, but the main force was repulsed by Montcalm at Ticonderoga. Much had been learned, Pitt made drastic changes in the command, but even the glories of 1759 did not fulfil his objectives. To the west, indeed, one striking force reached Niagara and swept the French off the lakes, but Amherst's move on Montreal was delayed by resistance on Lake Champlain, and the army of the St. Lawrence had therefore to fight its campaign unaided.

This strong force of some 9000 regular troops and a powerful fleet was fortunate in its leaders. Saunders, one of Anson's best captains, by magnificent navigation brought ships of the line through the rocky narrows, and at every stage the fleet alone made victory possible. General James Wolfe, though he had fought at Dettingen, was still only thirty-three years old, but he had made a name at Louisburg, was renowned for training of troops, and though frail in body and temperament had an iron will for victory. The subordinates on whose appointment they insisted were a memorable team — the soldiers Murray, Monckton, Townshend, and Carleton, James Cook the navigator, and Jervis, the future St. Vincent. Their task was arduous, working as they must to a time-limit set by the date when the river would freeze, while they found the element of surprise was lost and Montcalm prepared.

Quebec stands where the St. Lawrence is hardly a thousand yards in breadth, at the strong angle where it is joined from the north by the St. Charles; a few miles further east the Montmorency made an outer defence. Montcalm turned this area into a fortified camp; though various in quality, his troops were numerically superior, and he hoped to wear the British down. Seizing the Isle of Orleans just below, and Point Levis opposite the city, Wolfe first pursued the idea of forcing the French left on the Montmorency, combined with a frontal landing near the St. Charles. But one attack was a dismal failure, Wolfe fell ill, and time was getting short.

The solution, which did not come till the end of August, was the product of several minds and new circumstance. With great daring Saunders passed some ships upstream under the batteries and his landing-parties threatened Montcalm's connection with Montreal, so that he began to string out his garrison; Wolfe's brigadiers, in agreement with the sailors, convinced him that somewhere above Quebec was the best hope. But he himself insisted on the exact spot — not, as they proposed, eight miles upstream but at a precipitous cove, the Anse du Foulon, leading direct to the heights of Abraham, only a mile north of the city.

Premonition that the path of glory leads to the grave held Wolfe as he drifted downstream on the night of 12th September, when he quoted to his officers from the Gray's *Elegy* which his betrothed had given him before he sailed. But whatever doubt haunted his mind, his inspiring ability carried through a great feat of arms. By dawn on the 13th he had placed 4500 men on the heights, mounting single file up the steep path. He had completely surprised Montcalm, yet if he was not to be caught between the Quebec garrison and troops upstream, he must win an instant action. Fortunately Montcalm gave it to him; at eight o'clock the battle began, by eleven all was over, a victory won by the discipline of the infantry and the tactical skill of his brigadiers. It ended in a hand-to-hand clash, Wolfe was twice hit, and then by a third in the lungs mortally wounded. But so was Montcalm, who lived till next day, long enough to agree that the city must surrender, and demoralized French soldiers fled towards Montreal. Winter was coming, the fleet had to go, and Murray was left to hold Quebec.

So the final fall of Canada was left over till 1760, although it was certain; for France could not reinforce Levis, commander at Montreal, and many Canadians were disloyal. Yet Quebec, with a garrison halved by winter and disease, was nearly lost again, and Levis was besieging Murray when in May our fleet returned. By August Murray had worked up the river to the outskirts of Montreal, where he was joined by a second force from Lake Champlain and then, from the west, by Amherst, who had sailed over Ontario and descended the St. Lawrence rapids. On the 8th September Montreal surrendered.

Sea-power was simultaneously expelling France from the West Indies, where Guadeloupe, Dominica, Martinique, and St. Lucia all fell by 1762; it even struck France herself, when the British occupied Belle Isle in the Bay of Biscay. For five years Pitt made Britain accustomed to victory, to see bells of Cherbourg or colours from Louisburg in Hyde Park, and to hear of continents won by generals in their thirties. But now a new scene dawned, which within ten years reduced this victorious kingdom to a second-class Power.

It opened with the death of the old king in October 1760. George III, as yet a boy of twenty-two, was during sixty years to show that he had private virtues which served the country well. Yet all were so twisted by his weak mind, and unhappy circumstance, that they became public disasters. Extremely immature for his years, in this first stage he simply echoed his mother and Bute, who had brought him up in a persecution-complex, taught him never to forgive the Whigs who had suppressed his father, to distrust his uncle Cumberland and his ' black-hearted ' followers like Fox; with a prejudice against ' German ' measures and wars, which they used to inflame the insular Tory squires. Proud of their own motives, the King's advisers encouraged him to push the Crown forward, as the barrier against a corrupt aristocracy who had kept the Crown in chains. Yet they had no deep design of remodelling the constitution, or refounding the Tories. All they claimed was what the first Georges had tried and William III had achieved — the King's unquestioned right to choose his ministers, to have the last word in policy, and to use those means by which government could influence Parliament, in the interest not of a faction but the whole realm.

It was a conception with much justification at the time, and a strength which was proved well into the nineteenth century, but the choice of Bute as its first instrument was enough to destroy it. Beginning with the unpopularity of a Scotsman, he was a courtier without political experience, full too of theatrical notions and self-righteousness which he imparted to the King. Pitt obstructed their first intention that Bute should become principal minister, but Pitt's predominance depended on war. They therefore decided to work for peace, the making of which could be used to drive a wedge between Pitt and Newcastle. Many signs showed the new tendency. With difficulty Pitt stopped a denunciation in the King's first speech in Council of a 'bloody and expensive war', though a declaration to Parliament that he 'gloried in the name of Britain' was enough to show he would abandon Hanoverianism. Encouraged by the old politicians long out of power, by Pulteney (Lord Bath), Dodington, and Egmont, a press campaign praised Bolingbroke's principle of a government above party, while Tories were made welcome at Court or placed in the household. Early in 1761 Bute became Pitt's colleague as Secretary of State.

Peace had now been under discussion for a year. The Newcastle group thought ruin stared us in the face, for war had doubled the debt, raising it to £150 millions. Even Pitt recognized the danger of prolonging it, especially from the attitude of Spain, where in 1759 Charles III came to the throne, formerly King of Naples and an old enemy, determined to resist our supremacy at sea. But Pitt was resolved that peace must be won sword in hand; Frederick must be supported to the end, not for loyalty's sake only, but because a ruined Prussia would have to be resurrected by bargaining away our conquests. There were innumerable arguments over what to keep and what to part with; measuring the wealth of Guadeloupe or Martinique against the fact that they competed with our own sugar islands or, again, reckoning the markets of America against the belief that only if Canada were French would America be loyal. Finally Pitt decided to keep all Canada, including the Newfoundland fisheries which, together with some of the West Indies, would permanently cripple France at sea.

Negotiations in 1761 showed a gulf it would be difficult to bridge. Choiseul would not give up the fisheries or the Mississippi line, nor commit Austria to restore her German conquests; most provocative of all, he dragged in the grievances of Spain. The Cabinet majority compelled Pitt to make concessions, but in September the break came, for Choiseul had signed a third Bourbon family compact. It was from his reading of intercepted despatches, giving the substance of this agreement, that Pitt proposed an instant attack on Spain. Except for his brother-in-law Temple, the whole Cabinet was against him — even Anson and the soldiers who argued we could not fight France and Spain combined. In October Pitt and Temple resigned.

If his popularity was momentarily dimmed by accepting a pension and peerage for his wife, his policy was instantly justified. Spain refused all approaches, Britain declared war, and Pitt's plans proved triumphant, not only in completing conquest of the West Indies but by the swift surprise of Cuba with its treasure at Havana, and the seizure of the Philippines. Moreover, freed now from the Russian menace,

Frederick made progress and British troops occupied Cassel. Bute, however, was not the man to make use of victory, and by this time the peace-making had become part and parcel of his supremacy. Of the older ministers Bedford, whose hot temper found Pitt intolerable, thought our ruin came only from ' the obstinacy and insolence of one man ', whose aim to drive France off the sea was ' fighting against nature '. But Newcastle and Hardwicke resigned when our subsidies to Prussia were cut off, and the two brothers-in-law with whom Bute patched up his Cabinet, George Grenville and Egremont, were trying to prevent his yielding even more to France.

To suspend the Prussian subsidy was abrupt, though perhaps defensible, but Bute also allowed Austria and Russia to see he meant to force peace on Frederick, who therefore became his mortal enemy. His secret negotiation through the Sardinian envoy and notorious weakness in Cabinet exposed him to pressure from Choiseul, who inch by inch extracted concessions. Revolt in the Cabinet, the City, and the streets threatened Bute with ruin ; since the Newcastle Whigs refused to come back in subordinate office, he persuaded the King to replace the more warlike Grenville in the Commons' leadership by Fox, who for a peerage undertook to carry the peace terms. Some secret-service money was employed, though the pacific feelings of most country gentlemen needed little persuasion, and drastic steps were taken to crush the old Whigs, who were now in the royal eyes ' an audacious faction '. Devonshire was struck off the Council, Newcastle and Rockingham dismissed from lord-lieutenancies, many lesser men from the customs-service and other departments. By these combined measures the peace of Paris went triumphantly through Parliament and was signed in February 1763.

Apart from its method of making, it was open to just criticism. Canada and Cape Breton became British, with the territory to the Mississippi line, though this was diverted to exclude New Orleans in Louisiana, which was now transferred to Spain. France kept her fishing-rights both in Newfoundland and the St. Lawrence, with the islands of St. Pierre and Miquelon. To Spain we surrendered Cuba in exchange for the inferior province of Florida, and the Philippines without compensation, though our rights of log-cutting in Honduras were recognized. In the West Indies Britain kept only St. Vincent, Tobago, Dominica, and Grenada, restoring to France the much richer Guadeloupe and Martinique together with the strategical base of St. Lucia. Minorca returned to Britain in exchange for Belle Isle. In India the French recovered their settlements, though without the right of fortification in Bengal ; in Africa Britain kept Senegal, but restored Goree. Except for some vague clauses, Frederick was left to make his own settlement.

This peace was no sooner made than the nerve of its authors gave way. Fox went off with his peerage, and the money of the paymastership. Bute was in ill-health and could not face a people's hatred; mobs were attacking his carriage or hanging him in effigy; the press poured out libels and ballads on the Scot favourite and the Princess-mother; he felt he was endangering his master. At Easter 1763 he retired; the new Prime Minister was Grenville, assisted by his brother-in-law Egremont, by the followers of Bedford, and a few of those who, like Halifax, had served under the Pelhams. For a few years more Bute lingered in the wings of the stage but, though he lived long, seems never to have seen the King alone after 1765. The episode of the favourite was over, though not its effects.

CONTEMPORARY DATES

1755	Paoli frees Corsica from the Genoese.
	Johnson's Dictionary.
1756	Opening of the Seven Years' War.
	Siraj-ud-Daulah takes Calcutta.
1757	The Reversal of Alliances.
	Battles of Kolin, Rossbach, and Leuthen.
	Thomas Gray's *Odes*.
1758	Choiseul becomes Foreign Minister in France.
	Quesnay leads the school of physiocrats.
1759	Battles of Minden, Lagos, Quiberon, and Quebec.
	Expulsion of the Jesuits from Portugal.
1760	Macpherson's poems of Ossian.
	First part of Sterne's *Tristram Shandy*.
1761	The third Family Compact.
	Defeat of Hindu India at Panipat.
	Gainsborough's first exhibition of paintings.
1762	Rousseau, *Contrat social* and *Émile*.
	Calas broken on the wheel.
	–1796. Reign of Catherine the Great of Russia.
1763	Peace of Paris.

BOOK VI

INDUSTRY AND EMPIRE
1760–1852

CHAPTER I

FRAMEWORK OF A NEW AGE

THE old mechanism faltered, sagging more heavily under each new overseas acquisition or economic crisis at home. Many had lost faith in the institutions which had carried the nation over the Reformation and two revolutions. There was a meaninglessness about party, a decline of religious ideal, a scepticism whether anything was worth while except peace and comfort. And overseas trade had brought an economic scale which was dissolving the old society of squire, village, and market-town. In short, if Britain was to become a great State, a revolution there would have to be : new government, new faith, and new social arrangements. Whether that came about by peaceful reform or in catastrophe, or in time to bequeath the inheritance without loss, lay in the hands of Providence, or at the hazard of events. If the long reign of George III accomplished a part of the changes required, the clues will be found before 1788 — after which date his personal government lost its grasp — in the conditions which surrounded that government and transformed it.

This parliamentary monarchy was destined to pass into the sovereignty of the middle class, who rose on the effects of industrial revolution. Judged by outward evidence, Georgian England was very rich. It was the age of Vanbrugh's palaces at Blenheim and Castle Howard, with innumerable other palatial houses ; of Chippendale and the Adams decoration ; of the Woods, father and son, who built Bath for the delight of the ruling class ; of 'Capability Brown' and a host of amateur landscape gardeners and planters of woodlands ; of an aristocracy who, like Henry Fox, ransacked Italy and France for marbles and pictures, or like his son Charles gambled away thousands at a sitting — an aristocracy whose interests were landowning, horse-flesh, and politics, whose painters were Reynolds and Gainsborough, whose God was reason, and whose spiritual homes were modern Paris or ancient Rome. It was an age also of new-rich men, Indian nabobs such as Clive, who bought up half the boroughs of Shropshire, or West Indian nabobs like Alderman Beckford, who built Fonthill and whose City influence assisted the elder Pitt to power.

Yet in the half-century before George III's accession the national advance was slow and uneven. The population of England and Wales, estimated at $5\frac{1}{4}$ millions in 1689, had risen only to about $6\frac{3}{4}$ millions in

1760, the 675,000 souls of London in 1700 barely increased in the next generation, while neither Glasgow nor Liverpool surpassed 30,000. Shipping cleared at the ports did not exceed 800,000 tons; exports roughly doubled in value between 1700 and 1770, but the latest total was only about £15 millions in value, while the Acts of trade had driven a third of our commerce into the single channel of the Colonies. Even in 1789, the last pre-revolutionary year, a minute revenue of some £15 millions showed the petty scale of the British State.

This limited progress was much due to the fact that the whole mechanism of life was antiquated. Internal trade was crippled by primitive communications. For though on main thoroughfares the turnpike roads were rapidly growing, taking tolls which trustees applied to their upkeep, others were left to the Tudor laws which bade parishes maintain highways by compulsory labour; with the result that scores of roads were simply mud tracks, in winter becoming torrents or bogs in which carts were stranded and coaches broke their axles. Many a time only the sound of church bells saved John Wesley from being lost on his journeys. A great mass of trade, even grain and coal, was therefore carried by pack-horse, while the fastest coach was three days travelling from Manchester to London.

As to government, it was not merely outmoded, but the central machine had almost ceased to function. Having revolted against the planning of the Tudor-Stuart monarchy, Parliament had done little or nothing to supply the void. Whig political thought from the time of Locke onwards, the best economists after the Restoration like Petty and Davenant, and the business men so strong in the Commons, all agreed in basing liberty on private property and sincerely objected to State interference. Not only did the State not contribute a penny to police, health, or education, but it let fall several functions it had once performed. The Elizabethan assessment of wages was dropped, save in a few special cases such as the silk industry; Acts of Walpole and the Pelhams forbade workmen to combine in unions to raise wages. Except in the case of parish pauper children, apprenticeship was now rarely enforced. Ancient machinery for fixing prices, such as the assize of bread, had lapsed, and though 5 per cent was the maximum legal rate of interest, it was freely evaded. Most serious of all, administration was left to the mercy of justices of the peace and municipalities.

This local government, devised by the Plantagenets and overloaded by the Tudors, collapsed when it was asked to meet modern problems. Manor courts were still managing husbandry for open-field villages, which themselves deserved to die. Outside London there was no paid police; no officials except the county clerk of the peace and overseers of the poor. Parish self-government, never broadly based, had usually sunk to some 'select vestry', of the squire with the parson and a few farmers; Tudor and Stuart charters had narrowed government in most boroughs, whose small corporations and hereditary freemen plundered them for private profit. There were some good magistrates, not least among the clergy, but in general they were harsh against poachers and Methodists, and quite unalive to economic change; at their worst they were infamous, as with the ' trading justices ' in the London suburbs, who set up a caucus of mercenary underlings in dealing with ale-houses, building, and the poor. The very instruments of law and order themselves corrupted the national character. Since barracks were thought ' Cromwellian ' or despotic, soldiers were freely billeted in ale-houses and, being scandalously underpaid and brutalized by flogging, demoralized every area where they were quartered. The most innocent passer-by might be forcibly pressed for the Navy; Charles II's Militia Act was a farce, an annual promenade for the squires and their tenants. Capital punishment for over 160 offences, many recently added, showed the panic of the ' haves ' or the deterioration of the ' have-nots ', while perpetual rioting, over Jews or turnpike tolls or shortage of bread, exposed an increasing lawlessness, a State that had no weapon but soldiers, and a people whose heroes were smugglers and highwaymen.

As yet, our ancient economic scheme stood almost unaltered. In 1700 cloth still made up half the exports, in the clothiers' interests the export of wool being totally prohibited. From the same motive import of Indian silks and calicoes was discouraged; not until 1736 was Man-chester allowed to manufacture printed linens and mixed cottons. In spite of economists and Walpole's relaxations, protection continued all-powerful, of which a strong instance was the virtual prohibition of trade with France. Bounties encouraged a few exports such as sail-cloth, and import of some colonial products, those for the Navy especially, like tar and masts. Agriculture was protected by law also, though hitherto there was no serious competition from abroad and Britain exported grain on a considerable scale. The law of 1689, which pro-vided a bounty of 5s. per quarter exported, long stabilized prices, wheat averaging only 34s. 11d. in the fifty years ending with 1764. But they had to feed a growing population, and in 1773 Lord North repealed the export bounty and allowed import on a nominal duty when the price touched 48s.

Agriculture perhaps best showed both the improvements and limitations of this age. Never had landownership been politically more powerful, or economically more rewarding. The enclosures made in the Stuart age by mutual agreement had continued, strengthened after 1700 by many private Acts of Parliament; how the process was hasten-ing was shown by the increase of those Acts, from some 280 between 1702 and 1760 to over 4000 in the next twenty years. Though it was estimated 2 million acres had been taken into cultivation, the effect hitherto was cumulative rather than revolutionary. In some areas, especially in the north, where it took the form of enclosure of commons or waste, small landowners actually increased. But on balance, above all in the heart of the open-field system, the midland and middle-east belt from Yorkshire to Dorset, there is little doubt that they diminished— some by reabsorption as tenants, some by departure into industry, some unable to face the cost of enclosure or to stand up to a capitalized agriculture. Fashion and profit both brought money to the soil, and it was the large owners who made possible the expansion of the food supply, which was to carry a much larger population through war and revolution. These improvers, indeed, created modern agriculture. Landlords like Townshend and the Bedfords advanced the use of turnips, clover, and sainfoin, which set up a new rotation and avoided the waste of mediaeval fallows, kept alive cattle which had previously been killed in winter, and enriched the soil by their manure. Robert Bakewell of Leicestershire began scientific breeding of cattle and sheep, for meat and not for wool or hides. The Berkshire man Jethro Tull was the pioneer of farm machinery, introducing the horse-hoe and the drill which made possible systematic sowing and cleaning of the soil. As in France, a philosophy sprang up in praise of the land as the mother of virtue and prosperity, and in 1768 Arthur Young, a reformer of extraordinary energy, published the first of a series of notes on tours through England, in which for thirty years he preached enclosure and big farming against the ' Goths and Vandals ' of open fields.

The ally of this new farming was the industrial revolution. In its largest sense no less time-limit can be given than the three centuries from about 1500, but in its concentration, the triumph of machinery, transport, and power, some such date as 1760 marks its birth. In a continuous process which took so long the speed was sometimes swift, but more often slow, and even to the middle of Victoria's reign we meet the co-existence of old and new. All we can say is that by a given date certain trends are becoming victorious ; we have already seen that by 1660 capitalists controlled many industries and most export trades, that gilds and small masters were being replaced by companies, domestic production, and wage-earners, and that new industries and invention were redistributing the population.

In the stage now before us these movements proceeded at a faster pace ; capable of endless expansion, but only if they broke through the old social frame. Unlike the Elizabethans, Englishmen now believed their country was under-populated, and a more generous immigration policy reaped a rich harvest ; much, for instance, was due to the 30,000 Huguenots who fled from Louis XIV. Facing the severe competition of France, one invention after another transformed the textile industries.

At Norwich in 1718 the Lombe brothers borrowed from Italy silk-making machinery, which was to make the future of Macclesfield and the Derwent valley. In the cotton trade the Lancashire man John Kay in 1733 invented the fly-shuttle, which doubled the speed of weaving; the Huguenot Louis Paul patented a carding machine, which the first Robert Peel took into Lancashire calicoes. But weaving could not expand far without improvements in spinning to provide it with yarn. Working on the inventions of Paul and others, Arkwright of Preston, a man of audacious ability, in 1769 patented his water-frame, a spinning machine driven by power; next year, Hargreaves of Blackburn patented the spinning-jenny, while by 1799 Samuel Crompton had combined Arkwright's and Hargreaves' principles to make his ' mule '.

The year 1785, when Arkwright's patent expired, so that his frame could be freely used, and when the first steam spinning-machine was erected, may be taken as our present limit in the history of cotton. Each invention had made a technical advance: Arkwright's for a stronger warp, so that pure cotton goods could be made successfully, as indeed by the Act of 1774 they were first allowed by law; Crompton's, for a finer thread, by which was created the muslin industry. Taken together, their social effects marked a transition; for while Arkwright's engines had to be concentrated in workshops, both the jenny and mule began as home industries, and since power was not successfully applied to weaving till after 1790, textiles had struck a balance as between men and machines. This pause before the power-looms conquered was the first cotton age of Lancashire, when there was a rush to install jennies in every cottage, when weavers walked on pay days with five-pound notes in their hat-bands and their wives drank tea out of Staffordshire china, and thousands of the best yeoman stock flocked into the towns to make a fortune.

Cotton, which called out most of this inventiveness, symbolized the first stage of our industrial revolution. Though the process was brought in by Dutch refugees before the Civil War, it long remained a struggling industry. Unlike cloth, its raw material of cotton-wool had to be imported from Levant and West Indies, while for the linen yarn mixed with many of its products it depended most on Hamburg or Ireland. Its first dangerous rival was the Indian industry; its best export market lay among the negroes of Africa and American plantations. Steadily it ousted cloth because it was cheaper, East India goods opened British eyes to these gayer cleaner materials, and the range of goods which Lancashire had invented or copied before Queen Anne died — fustians, calicoes, printed linens, checks, velveteens, muslins — covered every need and every class, from aprons and smock frocks to the luxury of the Bath Assembly Room. Its structure also made part of a new age, for from the first it demanded capitalist management, coming at a time when domestic producers had beaten the closed gilds, and growing up in an area exceptionally free from such restrictions. Once Manchester was made free by law and troubles in India damaged its old competitor, the progress was rapid. Imports of cotton-wool rose from £3 millions in 1750 to near £28 millions in 1791, while exports in the same period increased tenfold.

This inventive concentration affected other industries and areas. Birmingham, in law only an open village and therefore welcoming all comers, was never troubled by apprenticeship or the law of settlement, and all its region, close to coal and iron and with the Severn for its exit, was full of invention in metal industries which, like pin-making or buttons, carried division of labour to extremes. Since the sixteenth century the Midlands hosiery trades had also had their frames, now usually leased out by big employers. There, and even more in Lancashire, domestic industry had weakened; though cottage hand-looms and spinning, small forges, and nail shops abounded, this population was increasingly giving up their plots of land, and modern forces diminished Yorkshire weavers of the old school, who took the piece the family had made into Halifax, brewed their own ale, and farmed a hillside holding. Silk mills, jennies working a hundred spindles, and water-frames were concentrating more and more industry under supervision.

Even so, the real industrial age had not arrived. It was not merely that technical progress was only partial, that woollen textiles, for instance, lagged behind cotton. For though the structure was almost entirely capitalist, in that the big man owned the raw material and very often the tools as well, most of it had not yet attained a factory system, work being put out by middlemen to domestic workers and collected in comparatively small shops. It had not as yet created an urban civilization. If the population of Lancashire and the West Riding doubled between 1700 and 1770, at the last date Manchester had still under 30,000 people and Leeds under 20,000. Paul's first spinning-machine had two donkeys as its means of power, while the fly-shuttle was unknown in west-country industry till after 1790. Not only was movement thus provincial, but it had been dictated rather by commerce than industry. Liverpool and Glasgow reached their wealth before Manchester or Lanarkshire were industrialized; so far, both the capital that fed industry, and changes in the structure, came rather from merchants than industrialists, from investment which could be spared from the slave trade or the Indies, and from marketing for export. Industry pure and simple could not expand without larger means of transport and power.

Till the middle of the century, iron and coal were backward industries. In the south particularly, mining remained a country occupation, as in the Forest of Dean, where 90 small surface pits averaged 20 tons a week. Even on the Tyne and Wear, where shafts had been sunk 600 feet, there was no proper pumping machinery, no science against damp and gas, and everywhere the instruments were elementary — children watching ventilating doors, women carrying coal in baskets up long ladders, wooden rails on an inclined plane to run the loads away. Except by sea, transport was ruinously expensive, while in winter the state of the roads stopped internal movement. But if these were some reasons for the minute production, — $2\frac{1}{2}$ million tons in 1700 and not over 6 million in 1770, — a greater obstacle still lay in the iron trade.

As practised since Roman days in the Sussex Weald or Gloucestershire, iron-working depended on timber for its charcoal furnaces, to convert the ore into pig-iron and the pig into bars. But the timber supply was practically exhausted, by 1720 the country produced a bare 20,000 tons of pig a year, and forges depended for two-thirds of their bar-iron on foreign, mainly Swedish, imports.

Several generations failed to overcome the objection to coal for smelting, that its fumes made the metal brittle, but this was achieved after 1709 by the coke furnaces of Abraham Darby, at Coalbrookdale. Almost simultaneously Newcomen, a Devonshire blacksmith, perfected a fire-engine, which was at first used to pump mines, and then to turn water-wheels for a stronger blast; in 1740 a Yorkshire clockmaker, Huntsman, discovered the crucible method, to blend iron and carbon into the hardness of steel. From this time forward iron and coal, with their products steam and steel, helped each other in invention, supply, and demand. By 1788 production of pig-iron had risen to 68,000 tons, though full expansion waited on further inventions which allowed refining into wrought iron by a process cheap in fuel and large in volume. It was an Admiralty servant, Henry Cort, who in 1784 patented the process of puddling, using pit coal as his fuel, and a rolling-mill which multiplied many times the speed of hammering and variety of shape. The neighbourhood of coal and water transport made possible Josiah Wedgwood's extension of the Potteries from 1739 onwards into a great industry, while it was to be near iron and water-power that the Carron works in 1760 opened on the Forth.

A whole generation of ironmasters, by applying science to industry, revolutionized it : the third Darby, who made iron rails and threw an iron bridge over the Severn, Roebuck of the Carron works who quadrupled output by air blast, Bacon and Crawshay who founded Dowlais and Merthyr Tydvil, or Wilkinson of Broseley who controlled collieries and tin mines, launched iron barges, cast the water-pipes of Paris, and was buried in an iron coffin. It was he who made possible Watt's triumph by boring his cylinders and using steam for hammer and lathe.

For steam was the final achievement of this first industrial period. Fire-engines made by Newcomen and his successors were wasteful in fuel and heat, being little better than pumping-engines, and the true steam age began with the genius of the Greenock man James Watt, and the business ability of his partner Boulton, head of the Soho works at Birmingham. In 1769 Watt patented his invention, economizing heat by separating cylinder and condenser, and by making steam and not atmospheric pressure drive his piston, and for thirteen years with his assistants went on experimenting, till they perfected engines for every purpose. Collieries, Cornish tin mines, the New River Company, and rolling-mills, all used them; in 1782 the Wedgwoods, and three years later the first steam spinning-mill.

Steam began the end of the stage of water-power, which provided transport for the new industry. Though business men of the north had long been anxious to improve their rivers, the real step forward again came through the coal trade. In 1759 the Duke of Bridgewater engaged the engineer Brindley to make a canal to carry his Worsley coal to Manchester; the Liverpool-Manchester canal halved transport costs between those cities, by 1777 the Trent-Mersey canal made a through traffic from the north to the Irish Sea, a third creation of Brindley's linked the Black Country with the Severn. This network brought coal to new areas, halving its price at Birmingham, and enabled the Potteries to get china clay from Cornwall. It was in canal workings that a new race of engineers, disciples of Watt and Smeaton, tested their material and invention, which after 1790 Telford and Rennie poured forth on high-roads, aqueducts, and bridges. Even before this, 450 turn-pike Acts in George III's first ten years, with the labours of self-taught engineers, like blind John Metcalfe who transformed the West Riding, had doubled the speed of road traffic.

Such were some elements in this incomplete revolution; incomplete, because mills and machinery only covered part of the field, and steam was in its infancy. Nor was there any centralized economic plan. Though local merchant houses, like the Birmingham ironmasters the Lloyds, had begun banking business, so far the Bank of England had a legal monopoly of joint-stock operations, and though the Stock Exchange opened official headquarters in 1773, ever since the ' Bubble ' Act of 1720 the law had discouraged speculation. Even so, this revolution had already immense consequences, though hard to measure exactly before the first census of 1801. The population of England and Wales, which had been roughly 6 millions in 1700 and only 6½ millions in 1750, in 1801 nearly touched 9 millions. As compared with 1700, Middlesex kept its place in the five most populous counties, London having grown from about 675,000 to 900,000 people, but Somerset, Gloucester, Wilts, and Northampton had been replaced by Lancashire, Yorkshire, Stafford, and Warwick. This migration had not risen to its high tide, and was still an overflow of country people into neighbouring towns. Yet, accompanying it and the breakdown of old regulation, came evils which made the age of George III revolutionary, evils so great that it is the hardest thing in the world to remember one outstanding fact : that the century was one of social progress, not social decline. Of this there is weighty evidence, in the stability of prices, a slight increase of wage-rates, a larger consumption of wheaten bread and tea, and one even more decisive sign — that, if the birth-rate rose slightly up to 1790 and then began to pause, the death-rate declined much more, and more continuously. If one generation suffered more than another, it was probably those who were young between 1720 and 1750, but throughout this age sections of the people suffered cruelly from preventable causes.

In London, indeed, the existence of the poor could hardly be considered life. Until 1750, burials stood to baptisms as 3 to 2 ; the same year St. Margaret's, Westminster, found that 83 of 106 individuals in its workhouse had died ; from 1730 to 1749 London infantile mortality averaged 74 per cent. This was the age of cheap gin, to be bought from any grocer or off any fruiterer's barrow, and though great progress was made before 1790, typhus and gaol fever swept the City. Part of this mortality was due to antique regulations and short leases, which drove the population into cellars and single rooms ; much to lack of sanitation, old graveyards heaped-up and overflowing, night soil dumped on the streets, and contaminated cess-pits ; something, again, to the window tax, barbarous laws of imprisonment for debt, and immigrant Irish who lowered wage-rates.

It must also be said that the amount of sheer evil in eighteenth-century England was high. Its records are full of cruelty, of apprentices beaten and murdered, children taught to rob, or sold to the Indies, and of mobs whose favourite festival was a hanging-day at Tyburn. They are steeped in drink : parish officers celebrated when they fixed the poor rate ; wages were paid in public-houses ; trade unions had their houses of call. As in other classes, working men's amusements were brutal too, such as the three days' cock-fighting advertised between Oldham collieries and Manchester weavers. What a mob meant was evidenced by ' kicking ' matches in Lancashire, pitched battles between sailors and coal-heavers on the Thames, the stones which rained on Wesleyan preachers, repeated riots over food prices (as in 1740 when miners sacked Newcastle gild-hall), or attacks on machinery (which destroyed Arkwright's mills). Elementary education had not advanced since Stuart times, being almost restricted to charity schools inspired by religious societies, or to that provided in large parishes by the workhouse.

Yet the age was one of growing philanthropy. Private citizens of

London and Bristol inaugurated the workhouse. Thomas Coram set up the Foundling Hospital in 1745. General Oglethorpe led Parliament in exposing the iniquities of the prisons, and emigrated poor debtors to the colony he directed in Georgia. From 1773 onwards John Howard, a Dissenting Bedfordshire gentleman, carried this much further, persuaded Parliament to abolish gaolers' fees, and brought before the country a mass of information gleaned by visits to the prisons and many European journeys. Jonas Hanway saved thousands of lives by inspiring the Act of 1767, which insisted that London parish children be sent to the country with proper allowance for their board. Many new hospitals were added to the Catholic or Tudor survivals — the Westminster, Guy's, St. Thomas's, the Middlesex, the Lying-in hospital, and Queen Charlotte's, all between 1719 and 1752 — and after that a movement began to establish dispensaries. But this enlightened humanity needed time for its effects, which could never have materialized in an outworn frame.

For the century had inherited the Elizabethan scheme, built on paternal control, a country of small rural parishes and family industry, but the first of these conditions had lapsed, leaving the others ill-suited to an age of large-scale mobility. When assessments by the magistrates broke down, wages were left to the mercy of competitive markets. And though monopoly or special skill kept some, like the Northumberland hewers', at a decent level, wages in domestic industries would collapse when their by-occupations went with loss of their land, while urban domestic work, especially in London, became sweated labour. Agricultural wages varied immensely, being assisted by piece-work and many pickings, but the basic rate about 1770 was from 1s. 2d. to 10d. a day, which left little margin. A Leeds weaver, or a London labourer at 10s. a week, might manage if his family helped, but the Lancashire woman spinner at 5d. or 6d. a day pointed to the evil of this new capitalism, that its cheap labour meant labour by women and children; in which there was nothing new. In the north, children had long been made useful in woollens and cotton, as the infant Crompton was first set to tread out cotton-wool steeping in water, while women had always worked in the Scottish mines, though rarely in the south. The worst days came when water-power was set up in more distant valleys, and the children's homework changed to a ten- or fourteen-hour day in the mill. But life was brutal enough, in any event, for boys who began at the age of seven in Northumberland pits or at six as London chimney-sweeps, London tailors expected by Parliament to work from 6 A.M. till 8 at night, or families living in cellars at 1s. rent a week.

In addition, the state of the Poor Law was a monstrous evil. In a time of growing trade men watched with puzzled exasperation the rise of the poor rate from about £695,000 in 1695 to £1½ millions in 1756, and we see them in two minds, resulting in a conflict of systems. The doctrine which had triumphed in the Civil War and 1688 was individualist : that a man must save himself by his own exertions, and that unfettered trade would bring prosperity if the poor were virtuous and made to work. But the governing fact was this : that, having eliminated Tudor State control, they retained the Tudor parish unit. Uncontrolled from above, the magistrates practically let the parish overseers do as they pleased, and they, often unpaid, usually degenerated into corruption, sometimes into tyranny, and always into a parish-pump outlook. Their ruling passion was to economize on the rates, for which purpose they would often farm out their poor to a contractor, who could use them as he liked.

Their most abused power descended from the mediaeval principle of settlement, that relief must be given in the recipient's home ; which meant that, in a new age calling out for fluidity, the Act of Settlement of 1662 with its later amendments empowered the overseers to remove those who were not ' natives ', or had not acquired a ' settlement ' by a tenement worth £10 a year, apprenticeship, or employment for a year. Every parish desired to stop new-comers acquiring a claim to relief, proceeding to evade the law by short terms of employment, to pull down cottages, and turn out women with child as if they were cattle. Thousands of public money went in transporting paupers and litigation. Poor areas were kept poor, for it was safer to beg in your own parish than to risk a whipping or being turned back ; marriage was discouraged, so was housing, and bastardy flourished. The worst effect was to distort the purpose of the Elizabethan rule that poor children should be bound as apprentices ; designed to educate and make decent citizens, it became a weapon to lower the rates. To get responsibility off the parish, children were hired to any who would take them, any small weaver or chimney-sweep tempted by the £5 premium ; they were poured into the worst sweated industries (Spitalfields silks or Midlands hosiery), or carried off by the hundred to northern mills. An Act of 1778 divided premium payments into two periods, which might give a little protection, but the records abound with runaway, starved, and oppressed apprentices.

Relief of the aged and sick, apprenticeship for the young, work for the able-bodied, were the three parts of Elizabeth's code, and in country parishes the first two still sometimes operated with success. Small pensions, house rent, coal, or money allowances to make up wages could be watched and given without ill effect in the small units for which they had been meant. But in large towns and industrial areas opinion was swinging towards a greater discipline, and after many experiments the workhouse became the usual panacea to cure idleness and restore employment. Many were set up by private Acts, and others under the

Act of 1723, which provided that those who refused to enter the house should not be entitled to relief. In some cases rates were sharply brought down, but at its best the workhouse test demands detailed administration, in the absence of which the eighteenth-century workhouse became a byword. The Act was only permissive, and few parishes united with others, as it allowed, to build a union house for an economic area. In most of them old and young, gin-sodden and virtuous, vagrant and unemployed, were huddled into a promiscuity of long hours of spinning or oakum-picking, vice, dirt, and corruption. Pauper labour was never made self-supporting, outdoor relief necessarily continued wherever there was no workhouse or the house was too small, while decent feeling condemned the breaking up of families and the suffering of the sick and innocent.

Amid this changing atmosphere, an age of swelling industrialism and rising prices, in 1782 a reforming member, Thomas Gilbert, carried the Act called by his name, which restricted the workhouse to the aged, the sick, and orphan children, and required the parish to find work for its able-bodied outside the house, paying allowances if necessary to bring wages up to a decent level.

Those who grew up amid these changes describe the miners or mill hands as almost a savage race; indeed, English Christianity was almost at its lowest ebb between 1720 and 1750, and if the industrial poor did not turn revolutionary, it was not due to the Church. It had, indeed, lost both the ability or wish to persecute, and though Test and Corporation Acts nominally excluded Dissenters from office, annual indemnity bills in fact protected those elected, while excellent Dissenting academies largely made up for exclusion from the universities. But two principal causes made the Church weaker for good under the first two Georges than ever before. In an age of expanding demand it was encumbered with inherited evils, which the Reformation had, if anything, increased, and to the reproach of the laity, the great mass of clergy were miserably poor, some 6000 livings being valued at £50 a year or less. The result of such poverty was pluralism, and of pluralism, absenteeism, so that hundreds of livings had no resident priest, while the building of churches was neglected in the growing towns. Nothing had been done to increase the number of bishops or equalize their incomes, so that Lincoln still contained over 1300 parishes, and while Durham was paid £6000 a year, Oxford received £500.

The political element in Anglicanism was at its height. Whig governments counted on the twenty-six bishops' votes as they did on the Scottish peers, with the result that most bishops were out of their dioceses half the year, and some never there at all; so bishop Hoadley never saw Bangor and Hereford in eight years. The Duke of Newcastle carried this patronage to a feverish art, his correspondence being stacked with promotions to royal chaplaincies, translation of bishops and deans, the use of the clergy in elections. Since these were the qualifications wanted, Whig principles or a tutorship in a great family or a comely edition of some Greek classic dictated the choice; kinsmen of the great houses were planted in the best places, a North or a Keppel or a Cornwallis, and after Wake's death a line of respectable mediocrities ruled at Canterbury.

As the Catholic teaching of the Caroline divines was rejected, together with their political doctrine, the latitudinarianism taught by William III's bishops and the philosophy of Locke captured the mind of the Church. It ceased to think of itself as a divinely-founded society, set apart by an apostolic succession, built on revelation and unbroken tradition. The new generation stressed the ' reasonableness ' of Christianity, for they wished to conciliate it with modern thinking; it was, as Tindal's book said, ' as old as the creation ', simply the vessel of a ' natural ' religion. Pope's friend Warburton, the most powerful man on the bench when George III succeeded, taught that the Church was the moral police of the State, and though here and there a few highchurchmen or nonjuring clergy carried on an older ideal, generally speaking, sermons and lectures seem to have lost all notion of redemption and sacramental faith. Their denunciation was not of sin but of vice, their philosophy was common sense, and their theology almost limited to apologies for the miraculous, Butler's *Analogy of Religion* (1736), the outstanding Anglican book of the age, making a theory of probability and induction from nature the best evidence of Christian belief. This watering-down of faith and distrust of enthusiasm showed itself even in outward arrangement — in the whitewashed walls and unlighted altar, heavy private pews, neglect of daily services — and there was little difference between an average sermon and a charge to the grand jury at quarter-sessions.

At the same time, it seems, the older Dissenting sects had gone down in numbers. Calvinist faith, the original fire of Puritanism, had grown cold, while the effect of Deist teaching, with its emphasis on nature as God's only revelation, was to leave many of them Unitarians. Christian faith in political leaders was almost extinct. The materialist Walpole rebuffed the ideals of bishop Berkeley for a Christian college in Bermuda; his son Horace had no beliefs; Bolingbroke was a Deist. David Hume, the most acute British mind of the century, demolished the Supreme Being whom the graceful thought of Locke and Addison had left intact, and reduced philosophy to scepticism.

After 1730 an Evangelical movement began to sweep into these placid valleys and intellectual coteries. Since religious revival defies any order of time, earnest Christianity had, of course, never ceased and issued in many new activities. Societies for the ' reformation of manners' were set up in most big towns, to attack irreligion and drunkenness; while from the Society for the Preservation of Christian Knowledge (1696) rose both the charity school movement and the Society for Propagating the Gospel in foreign parts. This Christian life was not limited to any one school of thought. No religious book, perhaps, so influenced the age as the *Serious Call to a Devout and Holy Life* (1728) of the nonjuror William Law, whose hermitage in Northamptonshire recalled the example of the friars; no single life, perhaps, so strongly assisted the continuance of all that was best in the seventeenth-century as that of bishop Wilson of Sodor and Man (1698–1755), a leader of austere and sensible discipline, whose prayers were some of the most beautiful in the language. More immediately powerful effects came, perhaps, from the other side; in this age, for instance, the Dissenting minister Isaac Watts published some of the greatest of English hymns (including ' O God, our Help in Ages Past ', and ' When I Survey the Wondrous Cross '). Arising both in and beyond the establishment, this revival broke down the frontiers. Before the Wesleys began work, the parson Griffith Jones' preaching and founding of schools set Wales on a religious course that swept most of her people from the Church; the layman Howell Harris and the curate Daniel Rowlands, catching their motive from him, founded Welsh Calvinist Methodism.

The Wesleys also rose within the Church, of which indeed they professed themselves members to their death, and out of its right wing, their father Samuel, rector of Epworth in Lincolnshire, having come from a Nonconformist upbringing to be a high-churchman. Both famous brothers got their learning at Oxford where both were fellows of colleges, both were ordained priests, and owed much of their inspiration to Thomas à Kempis and William Law. The younger brother Charles collected round him the first ' Methodists ', a few young Oxford men determined to make a new method of what they thought the oldest Christian duties, to pray and read together, visit prisoners in gaol, fast, and make regular confession; his brother John (1702–91) came back from a curacy to lead the movement, which was soon joined by George Whitefield. There was a diversity of gifts among them. Charles, more conservative as regards the Church, was the greatest of English hymn-writers but, though heroic in action, no man of business. Whitefield, a more robust type, was the pioneer of field preaching and apparently the greatest orator of them all; always defying the division between Church and Dissent, his greatest triumphs perhaps were won in America, where the more fastidious Wesleys failed. But that Methodism became a strong permanent community was due to the sheer greatness and organizing power of John Wesley.

Like all his family he had a tumultuous temper and a strong colour

of superstition, while there were whole tracts of human nature —
women's nature especially — which he did not handle wisely. Curious
streaks crossed his soul — a belief in Mary Queen of Scots, a view that
only ' rigorous discipline ' could save Ireland, a conservatism which
made him the King's ally against American rebels or French radicals.
But he had the greatness of an invincible spirit, certainty of his calling,
and ruthless decision. Even to older and illustrious men he could be
rough and pugnacious ; his annihilating pen could tell the quietest of
his sisters that she ought to view herself, ' whores and murderers not
excepted, the very chief of sinners '. It was his unbending will which,
in a revival that brought out backsliders and false prophets, purged the
movement by drastic measures and built it on individual salvation. To
the left was Calvinism, which easily became antinomian, an over-
confidence in those who conceived themselves as the elect ; to the right
were mystic beliefs and quietism, which might end in spiritual indulgence
and a scorn for order. On this last ground he quarrelled with the
German Moravian brethren, with whose teachers he had first begun in
London. And over predestination of the elect he broke, though never
in affection, with Whitefield and the Welsh leaders, so that Methodism
split into Calvinist and non-Calvinist branches.

In 1739, following Whitefield's example, he began open-air preaching and the foundation of chapels, with Finsbury, Bristol, and Newcastle as his first centres, and rapidly developed his essential machinery :
edicts that implied discipline, division into bands which became the
class meeting, individual investigation, and visiting the sick. For his
followers he provided not only libraries of theology but medical care,
loans, and ministers' pensions. His first general conference of 1744
resolved against separation from the Church, whose sacraments he
urged his followers to attend. But as few clergy would let Methodists
use their pulpits and fewer still joined his ranks, practical reasons, as
well as his own resolution that, come what may, he would preach the
Gospel, drove him towards the schism he deplored. His lay preachers
began to celebrate the sacrament ; he was himself obliged to ordain
clergy, especially for America. The scorn and hostility of early days
were much diminished, but if the Church could not expand its organization, a struggle there must be, and the law could hardly recognize a
body which was neither Church nor Dissent.

That a break must come was proved by the evangelical movement,
which spread from Methodism into the Church established. Some of
his most famous followers held Church livings, such as Fletcher, vicar
of Madeley in Shropshire, whom a rich patroness, Lady Huntingdon,
made head of the training college she founded at Trevecca in Brecon.
But she divided herself from Wesley on the Calvinist quarrel ; the
chapels built for her connection collided with the law, so that most

evangelical clergy preferred to stay within the establishment. By 1770 their influence was very great, even on politics ; devoted ministers like the Venns, and business men like the Thorntons, led the group long called the Clapham sect, which was to cut deep into the history of religion and philanthropy.

When Wesley died in 1791 as a national figure, he left behind 75 circuits in England and Wales and over 70,000 followers, he had preached 40,000 sermons and ridden a quarter of a million miles. Wherever life was most squalid or resistance most dangerous, he and his preachers had done most — among miners of the Mendips and the Tyne, Plymouth dockyard-hands, or Cornish wreckers. To these ignorant, abandoned people he had preached in all seasons and places, whether from his father's tombstone at Epworth, in storms of lightning on the moors, or among crowds hurling stones. And always in substance from the same text, ' Why will ye die, O House of Israel ? ' ; always that the ' lover of God and man ' might count some day on ' assurance ' coming, perhaps in the ' twinkling of an eye ', a perfection of moral happiness which at any moment might make heaven in the soul. In its early days the movement was full of rhapsody and almost mania, of groaning men struck by ' the arrows of the Lord ', shouts and fainting and screams, and there was natural resentment when, without authority, lay preachers held demonstrations in churchyards or gathered love-feasts at night. Yet whatever the temporary extravagance of emotion, the work done was memorable and immense. For in what Wesley, preaching before his university for the last time, called ' a generation of triflers ', he half-recreated a sense of the burning need and majesty of righteousness, which he planted most deeply in those classes and areas oppressed by industrial revolution and present neglect.

Though his was not a democratic movement — indeed he made political arrangements a minor matter, and preached obedience as the Christian's duty — it did powerfully assist to make a new order, ardent for justice and filled with self-respect, in industrial and middle-class England. This brings us to a fact of the first importance : that Wesleyan-ism made one facet of a broad-based movement flowing towards re-form, which had existed a full generation before the French Revolution. In part it came down with the old ' Country party ' agitation against the Court, which Bolingbroke continued in his writings, a clamour against placemen and pensions, and a demand for parliamentary reform. It was assisted by philanthropy, or criticism of the poor law, and multi-plied by the press ; for daily papers existed now in most large towns, and were used, for instance, by Lancashire working men to state their grievances. Organization was growing fast in the working class, in their friendly societies and, among the aristocracy of labour, in trade unions. True political principle was reappearing in increasing conflict with the Irish Parliament and American assemblies. In short, from manifold causes, to the left of the Whig party there appeared the Radicals.

Into such an uneasy frame had now to be fitted the outward responsibilities of Britain, and the evolution of political groups.

THE GOVERNMENT OF GEORGE III
1763–1782

Georg III's personal government covered the years from 1763 to 1782, some of the most ignominious in our history. With his marriage, at first a happy one, to Charlotte of Mecklenburg he fast matured, both his virtues and shortcomings developed, his indolence was replaced by feverish exercise and tireless activity in politics. Watching votes like a party whip, he perfected the system begun under Charles II, and since much grown, of using the Crown's influence — patronage in the Church, the Colonies, and Ireland, military promotion, pensions and local jobs, or frowns at a levée — to induce country gentlemen to follow his ministers.

With all his sense of duty and morality, respect for learning, and interest in agriculture, George proved a disastrous king. He took personal vendettas into public life, which made him capable of protesting against a State funeral for Chatham as ' offensive to me personally ', and undermined Cabinets by encouraging disloyalty. If he had decision, he almost always decided wrong. His mind, which was weak, became excitable under stress, until at last it toppled over; his conservatism was blindly complacent, so that in Radicalism, industrial strife, or American rebellion he saw nothing but wanton attack on the most perfect of governments.

The Parliament elected in 1761 by the pains of Newcastle was directed, before it dissolved, by four different ministries: Bute's from 1761 to 1763, Grenville's 1763 to 1765, Rockingham's 1765 to 1766, and then Chatham's. These years of what North called ' choppings and changes ' were by no means only due to the King. Party in its old sense was stone dead. There were no Jacobites left, Church against Dissent was no longer a serious question, no social conflict divided this rich self-chosen aristocracy. Even if real controversies did arise, they must pierce through a layer of pocket boroughs, with a few dozen voters, till they arrived at a House of Commons which allowed no printing of debates.

In such conditions the genuine ' Tories ' now consisted of about a hundred members, holding half the most independent seats in counties and large towns. In fact, ' independence ' was their only surviving principle, a boasted independence of ministers and placemen. They differed, therefore, by a whole world from the followers of Bute and

Grenville, whom the Whigs abused as ' Tories ', for these ' sunshine gentlemen ', as Burke called them, were not Tories at all but the last logic of the Whigs.

In truth, the old Whig party had perished as a result of its triumph. Jacobitism having made the Tories impossible, the ' Revolution families ' monopolized power, so that till 1770 everyone in office was a ' Whig '; not merely Newcastle, or his rivals Pitt and Grenville, but Bute and his secretary Jenkinson, chief organizer of the ' King's friends ', and North who first took office under Newcastle. Whig principles having become universal, the party dissolved into groups which they called ' interests ' or ' connexions ', based on the rivalry of a few noblemen, and carefully cemented by government patronage. Nor could anything be more contemptible than the last years of the Newcastle group, or further removed from the future Whig party. After obstinately resisting Pitt's war policy, they could not stomach Bute throwing over the German alliances to which Hanover had accustomed them, and, when they connived at his elimination of Pitt, were caught in a trap set by themselves. When George III defeated them, they called his ministers ' Tory ', though his agents were old colleagues of their own like Fox, while his means were precisely those they had induced George II to use in their own interest. So the officials turned out after the Peace of 1763 were old clients of Walpole and the Pelhams, and George III spent no more in bribes, made no more use of placemen and Scottish members, than the Whigs before him.

Out of office, they had no notion of keeping a party together. Elder statesmen like Hardwicke could not approve ' a formed Opposition ', while to confront the King with a list of ministers or a fixed programme was called, in the jargon of the day, ' storming the Closet '. It was, therefore, not money or patronage only which accounted for the numbers supporting the King's government; in the absence of organized party, their constitutional ideals and their ' independence ' alike prompted this deference to the executive. But that outlook was prolonged by some temporary circumstance, and the influence of one great man.

Apart from the fact that, for the first time under this dynasty, there was no Prince of Wales of full age, and hence no rival Court, a genuine reaction had risen against the exclusive incompetence of Newcastle's system. Jacobite families and Tory independents cherished new hope, nor were those who followed Bute entirely servile courtiers. They included the remarkably able young Shelburne, high-minded Scots such as Gilbert Elliot founder of the Mintos, and some of the best brains of a civil-service sort in politics, notably Jenkinson and Dyson, clerk of the Commons. What direction such men would take depended on the answer to another question — was collaboration possible between the King and Pitt ?

No one was more the champion of monarchy than the great Commoner, who promised ' the breaking of parties ' as ardently as the King denounced ' banding together '. Some of his strongest support had always been among the old Tories and, though he attacked Bute in 1761–2, within a year or two he was ready to use Bute's influence to make a coalition. He would never serve again under Newcastle, indignation against the Peace divided him from Bedford as one of its principal makers, while he had no patience with the younger Whigs led by Rockingham — having scorn for their rigid view of party, a greater respect for the Crown, and an infinitely more democratic mind. Genius that he was, he was winning disciples on either side — Shelburne and young Grafton — but his inability to work with the Whig body was the fundamental reason for the chaos of these years. Yet out of them came a hardening and reshaping of both Whig and Tory.

Grenville soon disappointed the royal hope that he would be a figurehead for a concealed Bute, for with all his verbosity, woodenness, and family pride, he was not a mean figure. His passion for the House of Commons and his zeal for economy and peace commended him to conservatives; Treasury and Board of Trade admired his zest for organization ; he was the last man to bow to an irresponsible favourite. The King made a first effort to get rid of this mulish lecturing minister when Egremont died, late in 1763 ; but as Bute dared not bring back Pitt and the Whigs clung together, Grenville returned, strengthened by Bedford himself taking office, with Sandwich his follower. This last had good ability and long experience, but his bad private character damaged the government. Bedford linked Grenville closer with the right-wing Whigs, for as an old follower of Cumberland and head of the greatest ' Revolution family ' he detested Bute, and hoped for Whig reunion.

As soon as he could, the King would overthrow such ministers, though already two questions were raised which in the long run were to make Bedford and Grenville his allies. The first centred round John Wilkes, member for Aylesbury and a former associate of Pitt against Newcastle, who had also distinguished himself with Sandwich and others in some blasphemous orgies at Medenham Abbey ; for all this, an adventurer of wit, courage, and charm. Of late, with his friend the debauched but brilliant poet Churchill, he had shone as leader of a press campaign against Bute, the cider-tax which laid a heavy excise on the most Tory counties, and the abandonment of Prussia, and in 1763, in No. 45 of his *North Briton*, denounced the ' ministerial effrontery ' which put praise of the Peace in the mouth of the King. Instigated by their master, ministers arrested Wilkes with nearly fifty others on a ' general warrant ', an order, that is, issued by a Secretary of State and specifying no names, and lodged him in the Tower, charged with seditious libel. With Temple's assistance Wilkes demanded a *habeas corpus*, carefully selecting a sympathetic judge in Chief Justice Pratt, who declared the arrest illegal because privilege of Parliament covered all offences save treason, felony, and breach of the peace, and that general warrants were against law. Wilkes was freed amid riotous rejoicing, juries also awarding damages against the Secretary's office and the police to others of the accused.

In the winter of 1763-4 ministers tried to retrieve in Parliament this rebuff by the law courts. The Whigs were divided, for to Pitt's indignation Hardwicke and his son Charles Yorke, the Attorney-General, defended the arrest. Their privileges, the Commons voted, did not cover libel, while the Lords demanded the prosecution of Wilkes for blasphemy in *An Essay on Woman*, privately printed and seized among his papers. Dogged by spies and bullies, wounded in a duel by one of Bute's clients, Wilkes went to France; in his absence he was outlawed and expelled the House.

'Wilkes and liberty' was the first battle-cry of Radicalism. Though hatred of the royal system was most concentrated in London, from the Corporation down to the mobs who burned jack-boots and petticoats in ridicule of the favourite and the Princess, the popularity of Pratt testified to a more dangerous matter: a gulf between the nation and its representatives, who had taken on themselves to define libel and voted away their privilege to please the Crown. Only intense Court pressure, however, kept the Commons on their fatal course. A bare majority of fourteen rejected a resolution (February 1764) that general warrants were illegal, the mercenary members from Wales and Scotland outweighing the solid country gentlemen; by the King's order, those of the minority who held military appointments were dismissed, including Shelburne and the popular Whig Conway.

While the Whigs quarrelled among themselves, Grenville took up another question which permanent officials had long been pressing. Experience had proved the American Colonies incapable of uniting for mutual defence, an experience repeated in 1763 when the Indian rising of Pontiac threatened all the forts from Detroit to the Ohio. To meet this danger, and another from the Spaniards in Florida, it was agreed during Bute's ministry that America should be garrisoned by 10,000 royal troops, and pay part of the cost, seeing that the British national debt had been doubled by a war to save America, and that the land-tax still stood at 4s. in the pound. War had exposed another ancient weakness in systematic defiance of the Acts of trade: Massachusetts, in particular, lived by trading with the enemy, while an army of officials, often absentee, cost a good deal more than the revenue produced.

Grenville agreed with his colleague Halifax, who after long administration of the Colonies urged that all this must be stopped. The measures brought forward in 1764, on the ground that an increased revenue from America was ' just and necessary ', included a lowering of the sugar duties, a tightening-up of machinery for collection, an Act for quartering troops, and another taking power to levy stamp duties in America and the West Indies. He postponed action on this last bill while he consulted the Colonies on a possible alternative ; none being forthcoming, the Stamp Act passed in 1765, with no protest except from a few merchants. In America there were fierce resolutions in the assemblies, boycott of British goods, burning of the stamps, but before details could reach England the Cabinet fell in August, on a different question.

Furious at Grenville's economies on the new Buckingham Palace, Bedford's blunt charges of bad faith, and their joint campaign against Bute, the King asked help of his once-hated uncle Cumberland. He was ill this year and his ministers' handling of a Regency bill finally decided him, for they deliberately attempted to exclude his mother from the list of possible regents. A first effort to restore Bute broke down on Pitt's firmness, but the ministers' insistence against the favourite drove the King on ; moreover there was an industrial crisis in London, and as Bedford was attacked by the mob for opposing a bill to protect the Spitalfields weavers, the King saw a prospect of popular support. In a second negotiation he made some concessions over Wilkes and America, but Temple, on whom Pitt counted to lead the Lords, had reconciled himself with his brother George Grenville, and without him Pitt would not proceed. Only then, as a last desperate expedient, did the King turn to the Whigs.

So came in the first Rockingham government, built on the Whig aristocracy, not so much old Newcastle as the rising men in Grafton, Portland, John Cavendish, and Conway. It was doubly weak, because it represented not the King's choice but his necessity, and because Pitt repeatedly refused to join. While this kept away his followers like Shelburne, ambitious politicians such as Charles Townshend would not anchor themselves to a doomed system, so that Rockingham could not dispense with the King's friends, the Chancellor Northington and the able, bitter, Egmont.

Yet though Rockingham was dumb in debate and inexperienced, and though his ministry lasted less than a year, with this decent plain man began the Whig party of Fox and Grey. If it had the defects of a narrow aristocracy, only aristocracy could in those days resist the Crown and, spurred on by the pen and power of Rockingham's secretary Edmund Burke, the Whigs gave a new meaning to party. Loyal to each other, they declared for measures on which they would stand or fall, looking for support rather to the people than the Crown.

Their actions satisfied many popular desires. Pratt became a peer as Lord Camden, one Act made general warrants illegal, another protected the Spitalfields weavers, the cider-tax was repealed. On the other hand, Cumberland's death removed their friend at Court, the King's men obstructed them in Cabinet, Grafton threatened resignation unless Pitt came in — which he would not do, except in supreme command ; particularly since, over America, the Rockinghams rejected his advice.

Early in 1766 they framed a compromise, to end American defiance without destroying legal authority. The King and several ministers wished to amend the Stamp Act but, carried away by Pitt's eloquent speeches and pressure from the merchants, the majority agreed on total repeal; they coupled it, however, with a declaratory Act, safeguarding in rather vague terms Parliament's right to tax America. A strong right wing had resisted repeal, recruited from the followers of Grenville, Temple, Bedford, Bute, and the King's friends.

Sniped at from right and left, the Cabinet lost heart, and Grafton resigned. Pitt now declaring himself ready to act independently of Temple and any party, in July the Rockinghams were dismissed, and he took office, with Grafton as titular head of a ministry which Burke compared to a mosaic pavement. For now it was seen how Pitt and the King between them had splintered the political groups.

He dealt his own influence a deadly blow by going to the Lords as Earl of Chatham ; a second, and mortal one, was delivered by destiny. In December 1766 he buried himself from the world, not to reappear until July 1769 ; gout, Bright's disease, and bad medical advice had for the time unhinged him. He dreaded the human voice, sat in darkness, lavished thousands in rebuilding one house at Hampstead, and thousands more in rebuying the house he had sold at Hayes. In his absence the Cabinet dissolved into the chaos which was always possible from its composition.

Indeed, his attitude to party was obsolete. Northington was the only King's friend in the Cabinet, but Chatham and his group, Grafton, Camden, and Shelburne, were flanked by the Whigs Conway, Granby, and Townshend, while each section he excluded put pressure on their friends inside. Irritated by his ban on Rockingham and Burke, Portland and the Cavendish group threw up their places ; Chatham vetoed the Bedfords as a body, and when he tried to detach some individually, their loyalty resisted, which drove him to fill up the lower rungs with courtiers. So matters stood at the time of his illness, though his name was so indispensable that the King humoured his moods, for Grafton, his deputy, made a deplorable leader, often abandoning his duties to race at Newmarket, or to love in a cottage.

Before 1767 was out, the large policies in which Chatham had his heart were ruined. Led by Grenville, the Opposition cut the budget to ribbons. Choiseul was rebuilding French armaments, but Frederick the Great had not forgotten Bute's desertion and, like Russia, was more concerned with destroying Poland than with building an anti-Bourbon league. To deal with the scandals and conquests in India, Chatham wished a rigid enquiry and perhaps a transfer of the Company's powers to the Crown, but one section in the Cabinet cut down reform to a restriction of dividends. It was led by Charles Townshend, whose fame is inexplicable to posterity, and whose ambitions lay in bringing together the Whig houses. The last serious act of this light man, in defiance of the Cabinet, was to persuade the Commons to lay more taxes on America. Chatham had always distinguished between direct taxation like the Stamp Act and tariffs to unify Imperial trade, and so far the Americans had accepted the distinction; Townshend took them at their word. His Act of 1767 set up a new customs-board and levied new duties, in particular one on tea, which were to pay for the civil list and garrison; in September, leaving this legacy, he died.

To end this futility one of two things was required, either a reunion of the Opposition groups to force a change of government, or the junction of some one group with Grafton. Though there was much common ground between the Bedfords and the conservative Rockinghams as to the East India Company or sovereignty in America, the hardening of party divided them. If the Bedfords no longer stood by the unpopular Grenville, they would not accept Rockingham's demand for a totally reconstructed ministry, and turned to Grafton. They found him accommodating, for he was not ready to surrender Chatham's position, and the reconstruction kept a fair balance of the groups. To Townshend at the Exchequer succeeded Lord North, who came of a Tory courtier family but had been offered a place by Rockingham; a Shelburne man in the lawyer Dunning, and a Rockingham Whig in 'Tommy' Townshend, were matched with four 'Bedfords'—Gower and Weymouth in the Cabinet, Sandwich and Rigby outside it.

In 1768 came the general election, in preparation for which the Cabinet delivered a blow at Portland, one of the Whig leaders. As a borough-owner on the Border he was the chief rival of Bute's son-in-law Lowther, for which reason the law-officers now discovered a convenient flaw in the title to his estates. This stroke was answered by the Opposition's 'Nullum Tempus' bill, giving protection after sixty years' possession against Crown claims—which was only just defeated now, and carried the next year. Like most eighteenth-century elections, this, though involving huge expense, hardly altered the strength of factions. Yet the choice of 164 new members, the death of Newcastle, and the fact that only half of the House had sat before 1761, testified to the beginning of a new stage. One old member, however, John Wilkes, returned from exile and was elected for Middlesex, and he it was who put the match to the fire which consumed the government.

There was universal discontent. Chatham, the national hero, had vanished. His successors, men said, were truckling to France, which was scheming to conquer Corsica, then in revolt against their masters of Genoa. American disorder was producing unemployment, trade had never recovered from the last war, bad harvests and high prices were stimulating a series of strikes. Lancashire was bad but London much worse—full of disbanded soldiers, Irish immigrants, discharged apprentices and weavers. These made the lower strata of those who elected Wilkes, forced every house to illuminate, and chalked ' Wilkes and liberty ' on every door.

If the demagogue was insolent, the conduct of government was imbecile and illegal. Wilkes was vindictively sentenced for his old offences, and in a clash outside his prison in St. George's Fields the hated Scots Guards fired, killing or wounding some twenty persons; soon all London was rioting — sailors and Irish coal-heavers, tailors on strike, weavers breaking looms. Coroners brought in verdicts of murder; mutiny was feared in the army; at a bye-election the second Middlesex seat went to Wilkes' lawyer. The King demanded his expulsion from the House as a step ' whereon almost my crown depends ', and after months of hesitation the Cabinet agreed. Early in 1769 the Commons expelled Wilkes by a majority (half composed of Scot and Welsh members) of 219 to 137. Two of the charges were old, ' No. 45 ' and the *Essay on Woman*, while the third turned on his attack on Weymouth, Secretary of State, who had told magistrates not to hesitate to ask for troops. Though none were offences against themselves, the Commons thus punished what had been punished before, and took on themselves to define libel. To expel was their legal right; but not so their resolution, when Wilkes was re-elected, that expulsion created an incapacity to serve. In April, after a third re-election, they vitiated the very essence of Parliament by declaring the Court candidate Luttrell, though in an enormous minority, duly elected.

While the people's favourite, loaded with gifts, lay in prison, law and order disappeared, the Whigs renewed contact with the nation, and Radicalism was born. Rioters fought with the Guards outside St. James' Palace; Bedford was savagely assaulted in Devon. The City made the King listen to petitions against a ' secret and malign influence ', chose Chatham's friend Beckford as mayor and Wilkes himself as sheriff. In their slower stately way the Whigs, energized by Burke and Sir George Savile, a pattern Yorkshire member, organized county meetings for reform. In this revival of party the Dissenting leaders were prominent, while the best head among the Radicals was Horne Tooke, the Brentford parson who inflamed Middlesex. A new society of ' Supporters of the Bill of Rights ' directed a campaign for a broader franchise and shorter parliaments, and a scurrilous cheap press dragged every grievance to light. For three years from November 1768 the dreaded pen of ' Junius ' held up the King, Grafton, and the Bedfords to popular hatred; though his anonymity was half his power, it may be taken for granted the author was Philip Francis, at this time a War Office clerk. He wrote without any democratic feeling, rather in an icy contempt for inefficiency and disregard of law and, most of all, with a malign pleasure in hurting his victims.

While Parliament was dumb, seven daily London papers — by 1777 they were seventeen — rose to defend free opinion, which yet had no security if government could define libel as it pleased. Not only was it the law officers' custom to lay ' informations ' against the press, which would dispense with a grand jury; following his predecessors, Chief Justice Mansfield declared it no part of a petty jury's duty to determine libel, but simply the facts as to publication. In consequence, the hatred of government was extended to the judges, and no London jury would convict for libel.

In 1771 the Commons collided with the press and thereby, again, with the City and the common law. They sent their own messengers to arrest printers of debates — those messengers were themselves arrested for violating the City privileges; fearing to touch Wilkes, they then sent to the Tower other City members, and arbitrarily quashed the ruling of the City court. Ungovernable mobs swarmed round the palace of Westminster, once nearly lynching North, and nothing could stop the printing of debates.

Troops sailing for America and more troops lining London streets, to this had come the King's system; ' a pretty system ', as Chatham said, ' — jurors who may not judge, electors who may not elect, and suffering subjects who ought not to petition '.

Meantime Grafton's Cabinet had fallen. The Bedfords' entry and differences about America quickly brought the dismissal of Shelburne (October 1768), ' the Jesuit of Berkeley Square ' as they called him, with whom no one ever wished to work twice, in spite of his shining ability. His master Chatham resigned at the same time, but late in 1769 reappeared in public, frail in body but with nerves restored. That winter his speeches demolished the government. This ' novice ' Grafton had betrayed him, the Middlesex election was ' laying the axe to the root of the tree of liberty ', the Lords must stop ' the arbitrary power of a House of Commons '. Influence, ' something behind the throne ', had made the King ' a stranger in England ', but some portent would yet tear back his curtains like old Priam's and tell him   half his Troy was burned '.

Under these reproaches the timid Camden resigned, followed by the brave soldier Granby. Through the King's merciless pressure the Whig Charles Yorke accepted the Chancellorship, the dream of his life, but within a week took his own life, unable to bear his friends' indignation. George Grenville and Chatham made their peace after a ten years' quarrel, and joined all those, from the Rockinghams to Junius, who were attacking government; in January 1770 Grafton resigned. Yet when this storm had passed, it left North in power for twelve years and the King's system seemingly strong as ever.

One reason for this was the choice of North, a shrewd, lovable, humorous man, and a capital debater. In sheer conservatism and love of economy he stood near to Grenville but disapproved of party, taking the view that ministers were individually responsible to the Crown. Yielding more and more to the royal firmness — and it was a bad transaction that the King paid some £20,000 of his private debts — under stress he bent like a reed in the wind and let each department go its own way. He was much directed by the Treasury secretary, John Robinson, who worked closely with the King's agent Jenkinson.

As Radicalism and the American question grew pressing, the Cabinet moved towards the right. On Grenville's death in November 1770 his mediocre follower Suffolk joined it, then Grafton (though he resigned again over America later), but the Bedfords were the strongest group, though the old Duke himself had died. Among them Gower was sensible and popular, Weymouth an able rake, Sandwich an experienced head of the Admiralty but a partisan who split the Navy into factions. The worst appointment was George Germaine (formerly Sackville), already damaged by his record at Minden and in Ireland, who as a supposed man of action replaced North's religious step-brother Dartmouth as American secretary. The ablest men, and the most self-seeking, were holding office outside the Cabinet, the ' Bedfords ' Thurlow and Henry Dundas, the ' Grenville ' Wedderburn, and the King's man Eden.

These ministers profited by a genuine reaction, sickened of mobs and a base press. None were more bitter against the Radicals than the Rockingham Whigs, both from their cast of mind and their borough interest; they viewed Wilkes as a firebrand, and stoutly resisted shorter parliaments or a wider suffrage. Taking party as the weapon of an aristocracy, who alone could successfully defy the Crown, their aim was to crush the King's resources by what they styled ' economical reform '. His civil list revenue was £800,000 and, as his family were large and costly, Parliament twice paid off his debts. Then there was the parliamentary influence of government contractors, and that wielded in the constituencies by excisemen and revenue officials. Placemen, pensions, and government money at elections were much the same as under the Pelhams, though boroughs cost more now in competition with ' Nabobs ' and new money. To root out this influence would make possible a real party government, but at any more fundamental change the Rockinghams would stop, stiffly rejecting the alliance of the Radicals. On the other flank, their co-operation with Chatham ended after Grafton's fall. He would have outweighed ' the rotten part of the constitution ' by adding county seats and was a convert to triennial Parliaments ; he wished also a declaratory Act to repudiate Mansfield's rulings on libel. In India the Whigs defended the Company, while he desired control by the Crown. In Ireland many of them were rich absentee landlords ; he championed the rights of the Irish Parliament. They were aristocrats, using party as their weapon ; he a nationalist, believing in a strong Crown. While he derided the moderation of these ' warblers of the grove ', their prophet Burke attacked the ' cant ' of ' measures, not men ', calling Chatham an ' artificer of fraud ', a stalking-horse for the King's designs.

North was therefore resisting a divided Opposition, and a Radical movement which easily turned to mob rule. Besides, neither he nor the two Parliaments between 1770 and 1780 were mere reactionaries. Their conservatism was more liberal in religious questions than the old Tories, for ' church and king ' had lost its power until the French Revolution revived it. A broad-church group petitioned in 1772 for relieving the clergy from subscribing the thirty-nine Articles and, though this was defeated, in 1779 North carried an Act allowing the same relief to Dissenters. His Cabinet were equally liberal to the Catholics. Overcoming Chatham's unworthy cry of ' no Popery ', they established the Catholic Church in Quebec, and in 1778 assisted to pass Savile's• Act which repealed some of the persecuting code in Britain, allowing Catholics, for instance, to own land or keep a school.

Nor were these Parliaments entirely blind to the ills of society, as the Spitalfields Act, a statutory wage for weavers, a more liberal corn law in 1773, and the poor law of 1782 all testified. Both the Regulating Act for India of 1773 and the Quebec Act of 1774, each carried against Whig opposition, were constructive measures. And the storm ridden by Wilkes and Junius had changed the relation of Parliament to the public. Grenville's last deed was to carry in 1770 an Act to reform the trial of election petitions, transferring decision to a committee chosen by ballot instead of a partisan majority ; other measures reduced the much-abused immunity of members from judicial actions, and the freedom of their servants from arrest. The press won its triumph in reporting debates, and in 1774 Wilkes took his seat without challenge.

Nor again could the royal influence, of which Opposition made so much, drive Parliament against its will. How many independent members existed was seen in the measures described above, or again in the passing of the Royal Marriage Act of 1772, which was brought forward on the King's command in consequence of secret marriages between his brothers, Cumberland and Gloucester, and commoners. The veto it gave the King in such cases, and the German notion of a royal caste, were most offensive to English feeling, and it was carried after angry debate and narrow divisions. In short, the position of the King succeeded only so long as it did not antagonize the majority, of which an outstanding proof was the American war.

From the beginning there had been a dilemma in American government, the same as in England before and in Canada after, between representative assemblies and the central executive. Though forms varied greatly, from Pennsylvania's proprietary government to the almost republican charter of Rhode Island, in general a royal governor with a Council assisting him as executive, second chamber, and sometimes as supreme court, confronted an elected assembly. In this struggle the assembly held the winning hand, the power of the purse, on which depended the public revenue and official salaries. Charters, custom, and the governor's instructions did, indeed, check the assemblies' progress. The Imperial Parliament also freely legislated for America, to decide terms of naturalization, deport convicts, or commandeer timber for the Navy and, outside the trade laws, asserted its right to tax ; setting up, for instance, an Imperial post-office system and a tax in aid of Greenwich Hospital. Colonial laws had to pass the governor's veto and, if they survived that, could be ' disallowed ' by the Crown, or checked if, on appeal to an Imperial court, they were found repugnant to statute or common law. By many evasions, however, the assemblies had usually got their way, and this strained relationship had lately reached breaking-point.

For one thing, America was now much less British, its population having risen to over two millions, many of whom were of foreign stock. French Huguenots were strong, especially in the south, Germans were dominant in Pennsylvania : while of those coming from Britain many had endured great suffering, whether Welsh Quakers, or Highlanders after the rebellions, or Irishmen ruined by British law. This rapid migration created a revolution within a revolution. Though the older coast Colonies, and the aristocracies ruling them, had many increasing quarrels with Britain, and above all New England which held one-third of the whole population, a high proportion of them were to be Loyalist in the coming war. Very different was the pioneer fringe to the West, hostile to both the old world and older Americans, asking for rapid land settlement, radical laws, and paper money to scale down their debts, and always encroaching upon the Indians whom Imperial agents protected.

This frontier problem took on a new urgency after 1763, a year marked by an Imperial proclamation drawing a line at the Appalachian mountains, beyond which it forbade private acquisition of Indian land. This conflicted with several colonial charters and barred off some land-speculation companies. But 'inland' Colonies offended against the ideal of the trade laws; while champions of the Indians were joined by the fur interests of Montreal, as well as by Carleton and other soldiers who would extend Canada southwards for reasons of defence. This policy was realized in the Quebec Act, which brought Canadian boundaries to the Mississippi and Ohio.

This restriction on American expansion was the more galling, because any favour to Canadian Catholics roused the old fervour of New England. Their ministers, more fanatical than any branch of Dissent, were irritated also by discussions proceeding for appointment of bishops over the many episcopalians in the middle and southern States. But it was not religion which caused rebellion, the root of which was a growing incompatibility between two societies.

Granted two assumptions, that the Acts of trade kept the Empire together and that America should contribute to its own defence, there were four possible alternatives. One was to continue the old appeals to thirteen separate assemblies, which produced neither enough money nor enough men. At the opposite pole was an ideal put forward by some governors and approved by a few British thinkers, including Adam Smith, for American representation at Westminster. But this no American desired and, as Burke declared, nature herself was against it. A third scheme, often suggested in earlier days, was repeated in 1754 at the Albany Congress by the ablest living American, the Pennsylvanian scientist Benjamin Franklin, for an inter-colonial union for defence : but not a Colony would have it. So there remained only the fourth expedient, of taxation through the Imperial Parliament.

Broadly speaking, despite sharp differences of tone, the basis of British action remained the same under all governments, for repeal of the Stamp Act left the fundamentals unchanged. That basis was to conciliate by lowering duties but to demand a revenue through the Acts of trade, to insist that those Acts be really enforced, to apply the resulting revenue to purely American objects, and to maintain an army by Acts for billeting. In 1770 the North Cabinet made a further gesture; they silently dropped the quartering Acts, repealed the Townshend duties except one on tea, which was maintained to assert the legal principle, and informed the Colonies that no more taxes for revenue would be imposed. But the question had passed from grievances to principle.

Economic grievances were real enough. Though the trade laws had been lightened by more bounties and a freer permission to export direct to southern Europe, they plainly checked American manufactures; as by the Act of 1750, which encouraged export of raw iron but forbade the Colonies to keep rolling-mills. Restricted to Britain as their chief market, they found it hard to pay for their imports, being indebted often on long credits and hit by an unfavourable exchange. On the top of a depression following the war came Grenville's Acts, threatening the triangular commerce with the West Indies, by which New England got specie to pay for their British imports and to finance the African slave trade. Another irritant was an Act of 1765, forbidding them to issue paper money.

Yet the material burden was light, tea, for example, being half the price it was in England, and America revolted not so much against the revenue Acts as against accumulating signs of what they considered a ' new sovereignty '. Their leaders protested they would gladly obey laws passed in the interest of Imperial trade, but now the admitted object was revenue, and a revenue which was actually collected. A central board of British customs officials, the use of naval officers for revenue purposes, trial of such cases without a jury, a standing army, an establishment making judges and officials financially independent of the assemblies, ' writs of assistance ' to search private houses — these they denounced as inconsistent with their ancient liberties.

Their notions of liberty came down from their seventeenth-century fathers, and in particular from John Locke. They appealed first to their charters but, increasingly, to broader ideas which, like the Puritans, they read into the constitution : that the common law summed up ' fundamentals ' and the ' law of nature '. They had inherited, said Pennsylvania, a ' free ' government ; Virginia declared the Stamp Act ' destructive of the constitution ' ; James Otis of Massachusetts, leading the case against writs of assistance, said ' an act against the constitution is void '. Standing on these principles, they could not agree that their legislatures were subordinate corporations. Step by step they began to deny the supremacy of the British Parliament or any idea of ' empire ', until they finally pictured a loose federal bond in which American and Irish legislatures, though obeying a common king, in their own territory would be supreme. Their origins made them unable to accept the view that British subjects, whether directly represented or not, must obey Parliament. For by ' representation ' they envisaged what by painful effort their townships and counties had achieved in a wilderness, a democratic system whereby every landholder had a vote and a true local representative. Even the Englishmen warmest for conciliation, Chatham and Burke, would never surrender parliamentary sovereignty, or take ' representation ' in this sense.

Though from 1765 there was a small group, at least in New England, working for independence, the general symptom was rather a growing disorder, a strain which any emergency would snap. ' Sons of liberty ' hanging officials in effigy or tarring and feathering tax-collectors, a boycott of British goods, Boston ladies refusing to drink tea — such signs degenerated into mob rule. Massachusetts would not pay compensation for the Stamp Act riots, New York refused to quarter troops, crowds at

Boston goaded the soldiers to fire. Committees of correspondence testified to a new unity between the Colonies, while in 1768–9 many assemblies were dissolved for joining the Massachusetts protest against the trade laws.

Except for some attacks on revenue cutters there was a lull between 1770–72, for non-importation broke down after the part-repeal of Townshend's Act, and sober merchants, heavy losers already, feared disorder. But, badly advised as ever, in 1773 North tried to rescue the East India Company from bankruptcy by a temporary monopoly of selling tea in America, which offended the usual dealers and undersold the smugglers. Universal resistance turned back the tea ships, Boston citizens disguised as Indians tilted the cargo into the sea — a small act of violence which proved the occasion of a great war. Weary of lawlessness and informed that the mob was in command, the government decided to punish Massachusetts. Acts of 1774 not only closed Boston harbour till compensation was paid but remodelled the charter, to make both the governor's council and juries mere official nominees, and to take away the right of public meetings. By a coincidence the Quebec Act passed at the same time, which in American eyes encircled them with a ' Popish ' military government.

British policy was based on the belief that Massachusetts could be isolated; the reply was the Continental Congress at Philadelphia in September. In the name of ' the immutable laws of nature and the principles of the English constitution ', it demanded repeal of the Boston Acts, the Quebec Act, and all revenue measures of this reign, asking too the control of the judges and disposal of the army in time of peace by the assemblies. On each side of the ocean the extremer feelings gained ground, anti-Americanism was loud in the British general election, while New England terrorists expelled the loyal and brought the law courts to a stop. On each side men believed that pressure would make the other give way, America counting on trade stoppage or Chatham's influence, Englishmen on American disunity, or arguing that an American army would be contemptible. As to conciliation, Burke's famous speech would have repealed all revenue Acts and appealed, as of old, to the separate assemblies; Chatham, going more to the root, wished to recognize Congress as the taxing authority. North's majority, decisively rejecting both, in 1775 unwillingly accepted his offer to relieve from taxation any Colony that provided for defence and the civil list. This came too late, for in April General Gage, blockaded in Boston, sent out a force to seize munitions, and first blood was shed at Lexington. The Americans seized the Canadian frontier posts; in June the British at Boston occupied the dominating height of Bunker's Hill, but at the cost of a thousand casualties. So broke out the war which destroyed North's ministry, the King's full influence, and the old Empire.

For another year the moderates held to avoidance of a final break, but their desperate need of foreign help reinforced the arguments expressed by the English Radical Thomas Paine in his *Common Sense*, and on the 4th July 1776 Congress passed the Declaration of Independence.

In its first stages this was a civil war. A majority of upper-class Americans, especially in the middle States, were Loyalist, fourteen regiments of them fought for the Crown, many thousands preferred exile to surrender. On the other side, some British officers would not fight against America, Radicals were loud in American sympathies, and such a war of principle instantly revived British party. While North's men attacked ' the American faction ', Chatham praised ' this glorious spirit of Whiggism ', and the Whigs, now led by Charles James Fox, borrowed from the American buff and blue uniform their party colours.

For two years, or more, most opinion supported the King, not only churchmen and squires but many Dissenters under the lead of Wesley, and many merchants, since the industrial revolution was opening other markets than America. Military success prolonged this attitude. Though Montreal was temporarily lost, Carleton recovered it and held Canada secure, both French-Canadians and Indians leaning mostly to the British side; Boston was wisely evacuated, and in 1776 our new commander, Howe, occupied New York. But then a year of disaster forcibly converted British feeling.

No war was ever worse handled in British military history. In men and munitions there was an absolute unpreparedness. In a civil war, moreover, it was a base thing to employ German mercenaries; much worse, whatever the provocation from the American side, to use the scalping redskins, or to raise negroes in the south. As to our commanders, Burgoyne was able but factious, Howe missed many chances by his dilatoriness, North's weakness dissolved the Cabinet to atoms. The service chiefs argued that our true policy was a naval blockade, yet we scattered armies from Montreal to Florida and the Indies. Germaine attempted to dictate strategy from Whitehall, while one admiral after another refused to serve under Sandwich.

The military problem was, of course, most difficult, for nothing final was gained by occupying large cities, or by extended lines in a country of vast spaces, where self-supporting settlements could take to the forests and renew resistance immediately a British column had passed. Meantime, all along an immense deeply indented coast, one of the hardiest of seafaring races poured forth as privateers. On the other hand, local liberties and jealousy made Washington's one of the most undependable of armies, ill-paid and short of arms, raised on short enlistment and riddled by desertion. So that Britain might hope to achieve decisive success on two conditions : that New England could be isolated, and that we kept command of the sea.

Howe's sloth allowed Washington to escape from New York, and though he followed him south to the Delaware, 1776 ended with a smart British reverse at Trenton. The scheme for 1777 was for a move from Canada by Burgoyne, down the Lake Champlain route to Albany, there to join hands with a striking-force from New York. But Germaine approved an eleventh-hour change of plan, whereby Howe, leaving Clinton in New York, went off in July with his main army to Pennsylvania. That month Burgoyne took Ticonderoga and got within forty miles of Albany, but his supply broke down, New England raised large forces, and Clinton failed to break the circle.

In October Burgoyne surrendered at Saratoga, and this was final ; even though Howe had gone into Chesapeake Bay, beaten Washington at Brandywine, and retaken Philadelphia. For it decided the French to intervene, which meant that ships and reinforcements were diverted from America to other theatres. Howe having resigned, Clinton evacuated Philadelphia in July 1778 and retreated overland on New York, another army still held Rhode Island, a third began a promising campaign in Georgia. More than one leading American soldier, above all Benedict Arnold, a hero of Canada and Saratoga, lost hope, and plotted with the British. But from the next new year a factor began to operate, fatal whenever it has appeared in British history — the loss of command of the sea.

Chatham's old rival Choiseul had re-established French sea-power to wage a war of revenge, his successor Vergennes saw that America had brought the opportunity, with hopes of recovering the St. Lawrence fisheries and the West Indies, and he found an ardent ally in Charles III of Spain. In 1778 the two Powers menaced the Channel, and Keppel could only fight an indecisive action off Ushant ; in 1779 the Spanish fleet reinforced the French, threatened invasion, and blockaded Gibraltar.

Swiftly the effects passed across the Atlantic. While troops were retained in England, French fleets convoyed armies to help Washington and locked up our West Indian garrisons ; Dominica, St. Vincent, and Grenada fell, and then the harbourage of Rhode Island. Fears of French superiority in 1780 broke off Clinton's southern offensive, and he left Cornwallis to master the Carolinas. New enemies assaulted our sinking cause. War was declared against Holland who, as of old in Stuart days, refused to admit our practice of searching neutral ships, while the same causes brought together Russia and the Scandinavian States in an ' armed neutrality '.

In 1781, while Rodney watched over his last conquest, the rich Dutch island of St. Eustatius, a French fleet under de Grasse eluded him, and in August landed troops in the Chesapeake. This decided Washington to strike, not at New York but at Cornwallis's force, which, leaving dispersed garrisons and struggling north into Virginia, was entrenched at Yorktown on Chesapeake Bay. There, after six weeks of inaction and ill-supported from the sea, he was surrounded by double his numbers, and in October capitulated.

Yet Clinton had 30,000 men in New York, while when de Grasse sailed away the Americans were weak as ever, and it was not at Yorktown, but on the high seas, that America was lost. The French retook St. Eustatius, adding also Tobago and St. Kitts; one Spanish force mastered West Florida, another in 1782 compelled Minorca to surrender. Gibraltar, held with glorious courage by General Elliott, was enduring a third year of siege. French squadrons covered assistance to Hyder Ali and the huge coalition threatening to uproot Britain from India. Always outnumbered and short of stores, our fleets could not prevent loss of convoys, and hardly averted invasion; rotten timber sent to the bottom Kempenfeldt and his flagship the *Royal George*. The enemy had taken 3000 British merchantmen; £100 millions had been added to the national debt; the industrial north and Liverpool with its slave trade were ruined; Wesley described the people as ' exasperated to madness '. Stripped of British troops, Ireland was boycotting our trade and, under cover of a volunteer movement, claimed self-government; ' a voice from America ', said one of her orators, ' had shouted to liberty '.

To such peril had obstinacy and soft weakness reduced an empire lately so mighty. In 1778 North offered terms, a repeal of all laws passed since 1763, but infinitely too late, as the American-French alliance was in being. But the prolongation of war was mainly the doing of the King. When the whole nation cried out for Chatham, he refused to make ' that perfidious man ' his minister, and in 1778 Chatham fell in a seizure as he spoke to the Lords against ' the dismemberment of this ancient and most noble monarchy ', to die that May. When North spoke of resignation, the King reproached him with desertion, would not drop Germaine and Sandwich, would abdicate rather than give up ' my person, my principles, and my dominions '.

In 1779 Gower, by resigning together with Weymouth, really destroyed the Cabinet, declaring there was ' no discipline in the State, the army, or the navy ', and that he saw ' impending ruin '. Telling the King he agreed with Gower, the wretched North patched up with a few placemen, and reeled on. His majority was crumbling, clamour for reform became a torrent. County meetings and bills in the Commons asked action to root out placemen and contractors. Wyvill, a Yorkshire squire, organized mass petitions, the reformers founded county associations, Radicals got up societies for universal suffrage, and a new line began of leaders of public opinion; men like the Unitarian philosopher Priestley of Birmingham, or the ex-naval officer John Cartwright, who was to live for a long age as father of reform. A majority of independent members helped Shelburne's follower Dunning to carry his resolution in 1780, that the Crown's influence ' has increased, is increasing, and ought to be diminished '.

Three reasons, however, enabled North to survive the election of that year. A patriotic people, fired against the old enemy of France, would not willingly endure the loss of empire. Opposition was divided as ever, Rockinghams against both the Radicals and the Chatham Whigs led by Shelburne. But what helped him most was the disorder of the Gordon riots.

Anti-Popery, a national instinct and always an easy pretext for trouble, had burst out again at the recent concessions to the Catholics and, after much violence in Scotland, in 1780 reached London, which was infected by hatred of government and economic misery. The demand was for repeal of the Act of 1778; the leader, Lord George Gordon, was beneath contempt. In June thousands of the mob, decked in blue cockades, besieged Parliament and attacked obnoxious members, pillaged Catholic chapels, burned private houses, demolished Newgate and freed the prisoners, tried also to storm the Bank. Allowed to go their way by timid City magistrates, they were easily suppressed when ministers, acting on the courageous initiative of the King, nerved themselves to use the soldiers. But when the cavalry had charged up Downing Street and London looked like a city put to fire and sword, the government profited by a natural reaction.

Neither this, however, nor election expenditure could keep their majority when the seas were lost and Yorktown fell. Fox was now member for Westminster, Chatham's son William Pitt was in Parliament too and denouncing the ' diabolical ' American war, while new men like Sheridan and Wilberforce reinforced those on the fringe of the Cabinet, in particular Dundas, who were determined that war must end and North must go. Rockingham declined to take office without guarantees for American independence and economic reform, Shelburne refused to be separated from him, and in March 1782 a revolt of independent members drove North to resign. After much stiff resistance the King had to face ' the fatal day '. Thurlow the cynical Chancellor, who had ever despised North, was the one minister whom he was able to retain and, using Shelburne as his intermediary, he accepted the second Rockingham administration.

CONTEMPORARY DATES

1764 America rises against the projected Stamp Act.
Death of Madame de Pompadour.
Wincklemann's history of Ancient Art.

1765 Clive's second administration in India.
Blackstone's *Commentaries on the Laws of England.*
–1790. Reign of the Emperor Joseph II.

1766 France acquires Lorraine.
Goldsmith's *Vicar of Wakefield.*
Lessing's *Laocoon.*

1768 France acquires Corsica.
Captain Cook visits Botany Bay.
Foundation of the Royal Academy.

1769 Birth of Napoleon Bonaparte.
Letters of Junius.

1770 Marriage of the Dauphin to Marie Antoinette.
Birth of Wordsworth.

1772 First Partition of Poland.
Warren Hastings made governor of Bengal.

1774 Turgot becomes controller-general.
Peace of Kutchuk-Kainardji.
Goethe, *Sorrows of Werther.*

1775 Battle of Bunker's Hill.
Sheridan, *The Rivals.*

1776 Turgot replaced by Necker.
Adam Smith, *The Wealth of Nations.*
Gibbon, first volumes of *The Decline and Fall.*

1778 Death of Chatham, Rousseau, and Voltaire.

1779 The peace of Teschen.
Johnson, *Lives of the Poets.*

1780 Galvani's discoveries in electricity.
Hyder Ali overruns the Carnatic.
Bentham, *Principles of Morals.*

1781 Dismissal of Necker.
Kant, *Critique of Pure Reason.*

1782 Treaty of Salbai, and death of Hyder Ali.
Mrs. Siddons appears in London.

CHAPTER III

RECONSTRUCTION, 1782–1792

G EORGE III's reign was not half over but his power was much diminished after the fall of North. At last a beginning was made in disposing of the problems so long neglected — peace with America, a settlement with Ireland, economic reform to meet the ruin of the Navigation system, reconstruction in India, and at home measures to check the Court and satisfy a new industrial community.

There were not yet two clear parties, which would emerge only in the solving of these problems, and what confronted the King in 1782 was a loose coalition. Rockingham and Fox controlled half the Cabinet, Shelburne and Camden the other half; Thurlow and Dundas, originally Bedford Whigs, continued respectively as Chancellor and Lord Advocate, while the leader of that group, Gower, gave his benevolent support. The younger Pitt, who called himself ' an independent Whig ', refused anything below Cabinet rank, to which the Rockinghams would not admit him.

Two considerable steps were speedily taken. England accepted *en bloc* the Irish demands, as put forward by Grattan. That part of Poynings' Act which subjected Ireland to the British Privy Council was repealed, together with the Act of 1719 maintaining the British Parliament's sovereignty and the appellate jurisdiction of the Lords; other measures gave Ireland a mutiny Act and repealed more of the anti-Catholic code. Furthermore, a great part of the economic reforms for which Fox and Burke had moved became law, in statutes which forbade government contractors to sit in Parliament, disfranchised thousands of excise men and revenue officers, abolished forty places in the King's gift, and cut down the pension list and secret-service money.

In July, however, Rockingham's death opened the long-threatened rift. His followers always viewed Shelburne as the King's minister, while Fox continued a special hereditary feud. Their wish was to have a party man in every important place, — to replace Hastings in India, for example, by the malignant Philip Francis, — Burke, in particular, being a pure partisan, jobbing his Irish kinsmen into office. Claiming that not the King but the Cabinet majority should appoint the Prime Minister, Fox's group refused to serve under anyone but the insignificant Portland, which would mean a Fox supremacy. This the King would resist to the end, not least because Fox was as thick as gambling and debauchery could make him with the Prince of Wales, who was just now embarking on the familiar Opposition rôle of an heir-apparent. Shelburne therefore received the office of Prime Minister, which he had waived in Rockingham's favour four months earlier; Pitt became Chancellor of the Exchequer, his cousins Temple and William Gren-ville had office also, while the Whig leaders Fox, Burke, Portland, Cavendish, and Sheridan resigned.

Shelburne was that rare type in politics, the intellectual aristocrat. The founder of his family fortunes, William Petty, economic adviser both of the Commonwealth and Restoration governments and one of the clearest minds of his age, married his heiress into the Irish Fitz-Maurices, and if Shelburne was perhaps the most distinguished, he was also the least English mind among Hanoverian ministers. In administrative discernment he was above all his rivals; experience of the Board of Trade, discipleship under Chatham, friendship with Priestley, Bentham the founder of the Utilitarians, Franklin, and the best brains in Europe had given him knowledge, principle, and liberalism. Unlike the Fox Whigs he despised party and distrusted aristocracy, believing in the Crown, if purged of corruption, as the necessary executive. He proposed to reform not the Crown's influence only but every government department, which would be much less congenial to the Whig aristocracy. Already Pitt had brought in one bill for parliamentary reform, only to be beaten by a coalition of the Burke Whigs with North's following, and Shelburne was ready to give this move another chance. In statesmanship he outshone, wherever he differed from, the Fox group. On Ireland, he was urgent that some bond of union must follow on destruction of the old system. He would grant America independence if he must, but keep it in hand to bargain for what he hoped was still possible, a federal link or at least a close commercial treaty. Unlike the curiously conservative Fox, he hoped for good relations with France, having no confidence in Prussia, Russia, and the other possible members of an anti-French alliance.

In the peace, which was made the pretext for his fall but on which his rivals could not improve, he achieved much more than could have been expected. He was much assisted by Rodney's victory off the Saintes islands near Dominica (April 1782), when he destroyed De Grasse's fleet, and in September again by a brilliant success at Gibraltar, where Eliott beat off a last attack and Howe brought in a relieving convoy. For our sea-power was now restored, and the national fighting spirit. But Shelburne's best good fortune was to discover and exploit the divisions among the enemy. The Americans justly distrusted their allies. France meant to exclude them from the fisheries, and, with Spain, to keep a hold on the Mississippi; while French finances and diplomatic sense both forbade a prolongation of war simply to win Gibraltar for Spain. Shelburne would have accepted some large compensation for the Rock but sharply resisted the enemy's larger demands—the Americans' for the whole of Canada or the French for a complete restoration in India—and in November won a diplomatic triumph in a separate signature of terms with America. So the truce of January 1783 was to become in September the final peace of Versailles.

The Americans won thereby their independence and the country assigned to Canada in 1774 that lay between Ohio and Mississippi. They received liberty to fish in the St. Lawrence Gulf and on the Newfoundland Banks, while a compromise was hammered out for their northern boundary, from the Bay of Fundy and by the high lands north of the St. Lawrence, westward through the great Lakes. On the bitter controversy over the Loyalists, Britain could get nothing but an empty promise of an endeavour for fair treatment by the several States.

The French received nothing additional in the West Indies except Tobago; slightly enlarged their fishing rights in Newfoundland, keeping also the isles of Miquelon and St. Pierre; in Africa they recovered Senegal which they had lost in 1763; and in India their forts and factories, as they had stood in that same year. Spain recovered Minorca, she also won all Florida, but British rights were at last recognized in Honduras. The terms with the Dutch showed their isolation and our revival of strength; they were forced to surrender Negapatam, the best harbour on the south-east coast of India, and to admit, what for two centuries they had disputed, our right to trade in the East Indies.

But the makers of peace were thrown out of office in February 1783, when the Commons by sixteen votes condemned these preliminaries. Shelburne's masterfulness and secrecy offended his Cabinet, his reforming programme alarmed conservatives, his favour with the King affronted the Whigs, while the concessions to France, and, above all, the hardships of the American Loyalists made the terms most unpopular. With no clear majority of his own, only some sort of coalition could save him; but on this point his colleagues were divided, for while Dundas and the King's friend Jenkinson advised alliance with North, Pitt and Grafton tried to regain Fox. Fox, however, would not serve with Shelburne again and was ready for that combination with North to which he had leaned some years before; North for his part was alarmed at the threat of a dissolution, or of a Pitt-Fox coalition demanding reform and punishment of the man who had lost America.

In this manner Fox made the coalition with North, whom he had threatened to impeach, pushed on from both sides, both by Burke and by North's underlings, Eden and Wedderburn—an alliance of King's friends and King's enemies, of those for conciliation with America and those who would have fought America to the end. It came about because Pitt resisted the King's pressure to take office, being determined to have no truck with North, and its chance of survival was never great. The terms of their union, for Cabinet government instead of royal control and for dropping both economic and parliamentary reform, alienated alike the King and the reformers, while public opinion was severe against them. The new Prime Minister, Portland, was a worthy nonentity; Burke turned out a hysterical and partisan minister. The new majority threw out bills moved by Pitt for parliamentary reform and against administrative abuses, and only the King defeated their monstrous proposal to give the Prince of Wales a parliamentary income of £100,000.

His chance came in the autumn when ministers took up the problem of India, which they could not escape. For British India had been engaged in a fight for life against Mysore and the Mahrattas, the feud between Hastings and his councillors had crippled government, and the ill-gotten wealth of the ' nabobs ' infuriated Englishmen at home. Unhappily, Indian patronage and control of the East India House had become bound up with party. A clear assertion of parliamentary supremacy was necessary, but Fox's India bill was drawn up by Burke in concert with Francis, the defeated rival of Hastings, and would have replaced the Company's control by a party machine, naming seven commissioners, who could be members of Parliament and to whom both government and patronage were given for four years, all seven being followers of Fox or North. Though the Commons carried the bill by 102, Company and City roused a campaign in defence of chartered rights; the King's advisers Thurlow and Temple told him that the Lords could be won over to reject it; Pitt and Dundas were ready to make a Cabinet. In December the King authorized Temple to tell the peers that he would not view as a friend anyone who voted for this ' unparliamentary and subversive ' bill, the India House and Gower used their influence, many North peers deserted Fox, and the Lords rejected it by 19 votes.

The weapons used were those of the day, or of Walpole's time; for if Pitt's cousin Temple spurred on the King, Fox brought the Prince of Wales to vote. But the crisis decided the future of politics for half a century. Pitt's first step, an offer of collaboration with Fox if he would drop North and modify the bill, was instantly refused. His second was equally unsuccessful, since his father's followers Grafton and Camden declined to serve. Temple lost his nerve and resigned. In this desperate pass Pitt therefore formed an emergency Cabinet, consisting of two Bedford Whigs, Thurlow and Gower, who had abandoned North, the sailor Howe, the radical Duke of Richmond, and a few young friends of his own. Dundas and himself were the only commoners of ability, and with this weak team he defied a hostile majority through the winter of 1783–4.

Though this crisis made a long stride forward, constitutional conditions were far removed from democracy. The Commons' majority, Fox claimed, were sovereign and could name ministers, but few agreed with him, and Fox himself rejected the logical conclusion of an appeal to the electors. A dissolution in this sense was unprecedented since the exceptional year 1715; Fox's object, rather, was to deny the King's right to dissolve and to force Pitt to resign. He thus played into the enemy's hands, for what had happened between 1761 and 1763 or 1768 and 1770 now happened again, as the Commons' majority steadily shifted towards the ministers in power. North's old election expert, John Robinson, advised Pitt that, given some time and a good deal of money, eighty seats could be won.

Many addresses of thanks showed the swing - over of opinion. Independent members were angry at the Whig refusal to consider coalition between Fox and Pitt, and their constitutional ideals argued that the King's ministers should be given a chance. When, therefore, in March 1784 Pitt at last dissolved Parliament, popular favour certainly accounted for his victory more than royal money; seventy of Fox's group lost their seats, including many leaders such as Eden and Coke of Norfolk. By universal admission there was a dead-set against Fox and the ' seven kings ' of India and a delirium for the name of Pitt, two elements being especially marked — the business world and the reformers of Yorkshire and Middlesex. But if royal influence and public opinion had coincided, how long could they march together ?

The first Pitt government lasted seventeen years, his contest with Fox until they both died in 1806, and it was Britain's felicity to find two such men to found the modern parties. Their rivalry has coloured history to our own day. Reason might argue that their destiny was to work together, for each execrated the American war, each believed in parliamentary reform and in conciliating the Irish Catholics, each abominated the slave trade. But apart from the fact that a reformer in opposition is not the same as a reformer in power, — a distinction which divided them throughout the strains of French Revolution, — temperamentally and by their gifts they were entirely opposed. Their fathers, also rivals both in politics and character, had brought up their best-loved sons on different models: Fox, to have all he wanted so long as he loved, to run through his own fortune and others', to drink and to gamble ; Pitt, to have a lofty and self-conscious sentiment of virtue, to be proud of his character and ' independence ', to scorn delights and live laborious days. The soul of gaiety with the few he loved, Pitt unbent only to a few idealists like Wilberforce, to close colleagues such as Dundas or his kinsmen the Grenvilles, or to young disciples like

Canning; Fox, with the Prince of Wales and Sheridan, innumerable women, and hosts of friends. While Pitt laboured and hoped and trusted, Fox loved and hated and despaired in turn, and if humour, vitality, and lovableness were enough to make a leader, he had infinitely more winning power. The one was always ' Charles ' but the other ' Mr. Pitt ', and what Grattan called Fox's ' negligent grandeur ' won more hearts than Pitt's frozen Grenville air.

The eloquence of each was extraordinary, Pitt never failing in the art and sometimes inspired to marvellous heights, but more often, as years passed, over-exhausted into a monotonous, mechanical, competence; Fox, supreme and sinewy in debate, often unwise but always fertile. More than accident decided his long exclusion from office. His mistakes, as in the coalition with North or his zeal to make the Prince unfettered Regent in 1788, were on the same large scale as his virtues. He could be monstrously partisan; his power was to see clearly and stoutly defend a scheme of dear British liberties, but sometimes he seemed to see nothing else, and the patriotic feeling, which he once offended by joy at American victories, he wounded again by sorrowing over French defeats. Of the economic talent, in which Pitt abounded, he was entirely devoid; indeed, in some important ways he was the reactionary and Pitt the progressive.

In judging these men it must not be forgotten that they did not possess the organized mandatory power of a modern minister. Burke's reforms and the competition of new wealth had much reduced royal influence, so that placemen in the Commons in 1800 did not number half those of 1760, but the King was not a figurehead and far less the aristocracy. Of this truth one instance is enough: in 1788, when Pitt's secretary analysed the Commons' majority into 52 Pittites, 15 East Indians, 10 Scots, 9 following Shelburne and 9 Lonsdale, 108 independents, and 185 as ' the party of the Crown '. It was these last who in 1801 followed the King against Pitt in refusing to emancipate the Catholics.

Thus, although the Revolution made Pitt the founder of a second Tory party, he was not a party man and never a Tory. He soon brought old Camden into his government, tried to bring back Grafton and to find office for Cornwallis, the honest Whig administrator in turn of India and Ireland; and twice in his last years strove to induce the King to allow a coalition with Fox. So that the party he founded was never a unit, being always divided between Liberals of his own sort, like Canning, and Conservatives like the King's friends or the right-wing Whigs, and finally broke in two in 1827.

With all its limitations, however, Pitt's was the first modern ministry. It was not merely that with him ended the worst corruption; that, for instance, he refused the £3000 a year clerkship of the Pells, which his successor Addington took for his own son, or that he put government loans out to tender instead of placing them with political friends. If any one man did so, he created the rôle of Prime Minister. The King's activity declined after his first serious attack of insanity; moreover, Pitt was his only bulwark against Fox and the Prince, and the Cabinet, therefore, steadily concentrated round its leader, though not on party lines. His loyal brother Chatham took over the Admiralty. Dundas was his right hand in the Commons, being manager for Scotland, treasurer of the Navy, effectual ruler of India, and finally Home Secretary when Pitt's cousin Grenville received the Foreign Office in succession to Leeds and became leader in the Lords in 1792. This last step was associated with the ejection of the Chancellor Thurlow, Pitt terminating his long disloyalty by an ultimatum to the King. His other appointments seemed to turn not on party, but on personal or practical considerations. His friend Wellesley went, viâ the Treasury, as governor-general to India. At the head of a reconstructed Board of Trade Pitt put the King's friend Jenkinson, later first Lord Liverpool, whose economic gifts were considerable, and employed Eden, later Lord Auckland, originally a follower of North and a self-seeking talented man, in negotiating commercial treaties.

He centred his power in the Commons, for to the indignation of the aristocracy he made 95 new British peers during his first ministry in addition to 77 peers of Ireland; some of whom, like the banker Robert Smith, came from the business circles where he found his best support. Till the outbreak of war this newer England of reform, business, and philanthropy voted Pittite, including the ' Saints ' led by his friends Wilberforce and Bankes, and the evangelicals represented by the Thorntons of Clapham.

From Pitt, again, may be said to proceed modern administration which, through the young men he promoted, Canning and Huskisson and the second Jenkinson, passed on to Peel and to Peel's disciple Gladstone. Following Shelburne's example, he set up commissions of enquiry into every department of State, substituting salaries for fees and reducing the endless sinecure jobs which had made life pleasant for Whig politicians. To him and his officials, Jenkinson or George Rose, are due much of the modern State's activity, whether the London magistrates, the friendly societies, or the Board of Agriculture. Most of all, he introduced eighteen successive budgets which revolutionized public finance.

What he inherited was a funded debt of £238 millions, nearly all in 3 per cent Consols, the price of which had sunk to 54, and the interest on which swallowed three-quarters of the revenue; trade ruined by loss of America; an antiquated tariff, so complex that one class of goods might pay on ten different scales, and so choked by high duties (that on tea averaging 119 per cent) that smuggling was a powerful, armed, profession; an administrative chaos of ear-marked taxes, and a separate treasury for each main service. Before revolution and war interrupted his work he had restored Consols to 90, raised the revenue by one-third, paid off £11 millions of debt although he had rebuilt the fleet, and laid the foundation of all future reform.

He admitted his debt to Adam Smith, the wise Glasgow professor, whose *Wealth of Nations* found in freedom the way to prosperity. He made smuggling unprofitable by reductions of duty and by extending the excise, as Walpole had intended, to wines, tobacco, and many other articles. What this modernizing the tariff involved may be judged from one fact, that in the single year of 1789 he moved on this question over 2500 resolutions. Since no government yet contemplated anything so inquisitorial as an income tax, for direct taxation he depended on the land-tax and certain taxes on spending, — servants, carriages, horses, and so forth, — which he brought under one control as ' assessed taxes '; many a blocked-up window still testifies to efforts to bring them down to less than seven, at which a house escaped window-tax. He devised the scheme of a modern budget by creating the Consolidated Fund, into which all permanent taxes were paid, and from which issued payment for all permanent charges, such as the debt interest or civil list. A beginning also was made in the full audit of accounts, which later was put under the comptroller-and-auditor-general, a high independent official.

For the restoration of confidence public opinion demanded a reduction of debt, and in 1786 Pitt established a sinking fund, with ample safeguards against the raids which Walpole had practised. An independent body of commissioners were each year to apply £1 million, voted by Parliament, to the purchase of government stock, and hold it till the reinvested interest brought their income up to £4 millions; after which date all debt purchased would be cancelled. Though this optimism as to the results of compound interest was undermined by the heavy borrowing necessitated by war, it would be wrong to write off Pitt's sinking fund as a mere delusion. The principle itself was a contribution to credit, and £238 millions of debt were cancelled in 1813.

First of a new school of finance ministers, he aimed to restore prosperity by freer markets. As Shelburne's Chancellor of the Exchequer he had brought in a bill giving the Americans almost all the privileges they had held while British Colonies; but shipping interests protested, the Portland government excluded American ships from Canada and the Indies, and British-American relations were long poisoned by other disputes, American obstruction in regard to the Loyalists or British debts being answered by a British refusal to evacuate the forts south of the Lakes, and by Canadian incitement of the Indians. It was only under pressure of the French war that the British decided to make a settlement with America, which after all was one of our best customers, taking 90 per cent of their imports from Britain. So came about the treaty of 1794, negotiated with Grenville by Chief Justice Jay, by whose name it is usually called. In America it was highly unpopular; though the British at last gave up Detroit and other disputed forts, and frontiers were more clearly demarcated by joint commissions, the treaty still excluded American shipping from the Indies and Canada. A still larger question, of neutral rights at sea, was left over to the politics of war.

Strong vested interests, goaded on by the Fox party, broke several of Pitt's fiscal measures. His Corn law of 1791, which in effect prohibited import when the price fell below 50s. a quarter, was criticized by the Whigs as not giving enough protection. Again, he imposed a legacy duty, but the country gentry would not allow it to be applied to land; big business leaders, Wedgwood for the Black Country, Boulton the iron-master, and the cotton firms, combined to defeat his proposed low-tariff treaty between Britain and Ireland. His one great success in international trade was the treaty of 1786 with France, negotiated by Eden. Business men were confident they could beat the French on the equal terms of much-reduced duties of 10 per cent or 12 per cent, which woollens and cottons, cutlery, and pottery would henceforth pay on either side. And if French wines were now to pay duties no greater than those imposed on Portugal, French silks were still prohibited. Such solid advantages, and this large market to compensate for the loss of America, drowned Fox's beating of the drum against France as an ancient enemy. But French industrialists rebelled, and in 1793 the revolutionary government denounced the treaty.

In yet another immense problem Pitt devised a long-term settlement: by his India Act of 1784, which survived as the basis till the Mutiny. But here it is necessary to recall how India entered British politics.

Nothing could be more false than to suppose that Britain or its East India Company set out to conquer territory; ' the perilous and wonderful paths ', as Warren Hastings called them, were not of our making. From 1707, on the death of the last great Mogul, India became a land without a master. Hindu reaction against Moslem cruelty had, long before Aurungzebe died, begun with Sivaji, founder of the Mahratta power. His dynasty continued as rajahs of Satara in the Deccan, though lately overshadowed by mayors of the palace styled Peishwahs, whose influence centred at Poona; other chieftains of this warrior people, the Gaekwar, Scindia in Gwalior, and Holkar in Indore, spread out fanwise until Mahratta States ranged from the west coast across central

India.   From the Punjab a more austere Hindu revival, of the Sikhs, threatened Delhi on another side.   Meanwhile Moslem lieutenants of the empire turned their official position into hereditary thrones— the Nizam of Hyderabad, the Nawab of Oudh, and the Nabob of Bengal—and Moslem soldiers forced their rule on Hindu populations, notably in Mysore, where from the Seven Years' War onwards Hyder Ali, a master of amoral ability, raised a power which threatened Bombay and overhung Madras like a cloud.   Lastly, as always happens in a weakened India, the gates of the north-west passes opened before new conquerors.   Rohilla Afghans settled down north of the Ganges, Nadir Shah the Persian looted and massacred in 1739, the Afghan Ahmad Shah annexed the Punjab and in 1761, in his fourth invasion, obliterated the Mahratta armies in battle at Panipat, outside Delhi.

It was in this scene of force and iniquity that European traders were compelled to arm in self-defence, that ambitious governors intervened in Indian war to bargain for fortresses or markets, and that clerks and merchants found unlimited opportunities of wealth. French possessions were scattered from Mauritius in the Indian Ocean to Chandernagore above Calcutta, but their headquarters was Pondi- cherry, south of Madras, from which during the Austrian Succession war Dupleix set out to make French influence all-powerful.   Peace came in Europe but in India war continued, with native thrones being put up and down, until it passed again into the Seven Years' War.   The English triumphed through the incompetence of the French company and its friction with its great servants, Dupleix, Bussy who long held Hyderabad, and Lally, defender of Pondicherry ; even more, however, through their superior sea-power and the fact that they controlled the Ganges, main artery of India, so that Bombay and Madras could be saved by armies sailing from Bengal.   Lastly, they found a genius for action in Robert Clive, a writer in the Company's service at Madras, who was under thirty when he first won fame by the defence of Arcot in 1751.

A transformation of the Company to a political State was thus almost inevitable, and the hour struck when in 1756 a young Nabob succeeded to Bengal, Siraj-ud-Daulah.   A slave to passions and fear, he quarrelled both with Hindu financiers and Mohammedan soldiers and, suspicious of European aggression, in June attacked Calcutta.   Its defences were worthless, most of the English councillors were chicken- hearted, and in four days they surrendered.   Nearly 150 prisoners were shut up for the night in the ' black hole ', a prison room in the Fort, less than twenty feet square, and only 23 survived.

Though faced by the certainty of a French threat to themselves, the Madras Council despatched Clive and Admiral Watson to the rescue.

In January 1757 they recovered Calcutta, then seized Chandernagore, and in June, convinced of the Nabob's intrigues with the French and aware of his subjects' hatred of him, set out to depose him in favour of his kinsman Mir Jaffar. On the 23rd, with 800 Europeans and only 3000 men in all, Clive routed the Nabob's 50,000 at Plassey; Siraj-ud-Daulah was betrayed and murdered. This revolution carried with it recognition of British sovereignty in Calcutta, and of their ' zemindari ', or land revenue rights, in a large tract outside ; before Clive left India he also suppressed Dutch power in Bengal and sent an expedition to seize the Northern Circars, the coastal area which linked land communication between Bengal and Madras. Few Englishmen as yet had so trained Indian sepoys to fight, and his courage and decision never failed. But he did not shrink from any weapons, even forgery of treaties, while his greed set off the new Bengal on a torrent of corruption.

The conquest was carried further by Coote's victory over Lally at Wandewash in 1760, the fall of Pondicherry, and the peace of 1763. Revolution, massacre, and corruption in Bengal brought about war with the Mogul emperor and Oudh, and in 1764 Hector Munro won another decisive victory at Buxar. Once again Clive was sent out to restore order, and though his success was limited his measures were vital. Ceding some more territories in full sovereignty, the Mogul emperor also granted to the Company the ' Diwanni ' of all Bengal, that is, the right to collect and administer the revenue ; henceforth, under a puppet Nabob and through the agency of Indian officials, the British were in fact sovereign.

From Clive's final departure in 1767 the problem took on dimensions which no British government could ignore : his enormous wealth, struggles by political groups to win control at the India House, great wars won by a merchant company, and the fortunes displayed by returning ' nabobs ' — all this aroused public indignation and private enmity. English servants of the Madras presidency, lending money at an enormous interest to the Nabob of the Carnatic, became involved in his feuds with Hyderabad, the Mahrattas, and Mysore. Mahrattas, making the Moguls at Delhi their tool, pressed upon the Rohillas and then on Oudh, the outer bulwark of Bengal ; dynastic strife of the Peishwah's family encouraged the Bombay government to intervene in hopes of winning more trading-posts. Parliament shirked the larger issue in 1767, merely taking a tribute from the Company. But in 1770 a ghastly famine slew a third of the people of Bengal, India stock fell like a stone, all three presidencies were on the verge of war, and the Company begged Parliament for a loan.

One result was the Regulating Act of 1773, the first large vindication of parliamentary sovereignty. It compelled the Company to lay its accounts and correspondence before parliamentary ministers, named a governor-general with a council of four in Bengal who were in ordinary cases to control the foreign relations of Madras and Bombay, and set up a supreme court in Bengal over ' His Majesty's subjects '. The governor-general appointed was Warren Hastings, the Company's governor in Bengal since the previous year.

British India was, indeed, created between that date and his final home-coming in 1785. What he inherited was simply an anarchy of force, no system, and universal corruption. He it was who by experience arrived at the fundamentals : that India could not exist without a paramount power, and that, in the absence of another, Great Britain must take that place ; that British India must be an Oriental Power, ruling through Indian means and Indian law, and doing justice to the tillers of the soil ; that this government in India must be one, and saved from fluctuating faction at home. Measures innumerable besides his chief governmental acts — codification of Indian law, famine relief, encouragement of map-makers, exploration of Tibet, foundation of the Asiatic Society and of a Mohammedan college at Calcutta — show his extraordinary range and the nature of his ideals. He almost alone saved the British Empire and character during the ignominy of Lord North ; his achievements were so great, and so bitter his sufferings, that he may be forgiven his own conclusion, ' I gave you all, and you have rewarded me with confiscation, disgrace, and a life of impeachment '.

Sent to India as a boy, Hastings went through the worst days with clean hands but not without effects which later exposed him to attack. Like all his contemporaries he speculated, spent money recklessly, and acquired the Oriental view of what in England would be called a bribe. Bitter opposition, and ingratitude in his employers, made him inflexible and ruthless, with the autocrat's leaning to take short cuts towards great ends.

In the two years before the Regulating Act reached India, he did much of lasting importance. On the directors' orders he swept away Clive's double government ; the Nabob became a pensioned figurehead, Calcutta became the capital, English collectors controlled local revenue and justice under a revenue board and courts of appeal. Pending enquiry into the tangle of old systems, the land revenue, which was the mainstay of Mogul power, was fixed for five years, though unhappily at too high a level, and functions of government were separated from management of trade. Finding the Emperor was simply the tool of the Mahrattas, he repudiated Clive's treaty, refused further tribute, and made Oudh the buttress of Bengal by increasing its territory and putting a British force in its pay. These arrangements led directly to the war of 1774 when Oudh asked for help to suppress the Rohillas, who would neither keep the Mahrattas off his frontier nor act effectively against them, and Rohilkhand was annexed to Oudh by British aid. But while

Hastings was experimenting in every branch of government, at the end of this year his work was cut short, by the Regulating Act, the futility of the home government, blunders in Bombay and Madras, and, finally, an enormous war. The Act itself made openings for great mischief, if the ill-will were there. It gave the governor-general no overriding power but only a casting vote. It gave Bengal no initiative but only a vague veto over Bombay and Madras, which they could overrule on a claim of emergency. It left obscure the relation of the supreme court to the council, the law it would apply, and who were subject to its jurisdiction.

Spurred on by various influences, North's hope to win votes, Clive's bias against Company rule, many directors' dislike of wars of conquest, and some honest zeal, three new councillors from England arrived with minds fixed against Hastings and all his work, outvoted him, and paralysed government. Two were mediocre self-seeking soldiers, the third was self-seeking on a giant scale but a man of ideas —Philip Francis. The rancour and arrogance he had shown in the *Letters of Junius* he now applied to India, of which he was bent on being governor-general, and which he deemed he had been sent to save. This evil man stuck at nothing to destroy Hastings and to achieve his own ambition, encouraged natives to libel the governor-general, worked on a party at the India House, and convinced Burke, hitherto a Company champion, that its corruption was infinite and that Hastings was the oppressor of innocent millions. His own ideas were in part derived from Clive, and partly from his own ignorance. He would establish direct English sovereignty in Bengal, but merely as a tribute-receiving power. Our contacts should be limited to the zemindars, the revenue-collectors of the Mogul system, whom Francis would recognize as an hereditary aristocracy, fixing their revenue liability on a permanent settlement; we should divest ourselves of responsibility for justice or protecting the peasants, while the Company should fall back to the rôle of merchants. Sovereign in this sense of Bengal, we should not interfere in the rest of India, leaving friend and foe to fight it out. Such was the ignominious part which Francis thought possible and impressed on British politicians by years of industry and hatred.

Hastings was not the man to abdicate, and war to the knife disgraced Calcutta. Among the charges encouraged by the majority against him were some of bribery, brought forward by a Brahmin official Nuncumar, who had been for twenty years a byword; the resuscitation of a charge of forgery against Nuncumar, the verdict of the supreme court against him and his execution, though all in themselves defensible, came so opportunely to save Hastings that they roused a dark suspicion. The majority removed his officials, and undid his settlement with Oudh; once they claimed he had resigned and seized the Calcutta fort. Death swept away Francis' associates but not death could take away his revenge, and in 1780, at the height of the great war, the governor-general engaged in a duel with his senior councillor. Scandalous contentions broke out between council and supreme court, terminated by an arrangement which had some sense in it but could be represented as more scandalous still, whereby the court's chief justice, Elijah Impey, was to be head of the Company's ordinary courts also. Here, murmured Hasting's enemies, was Impey's reward for hanging Nuncumar and saving Hastings from ruin.

Never was British control more weak and squalid. While North and his secretaries encouraged the Francis group and the Company proprietors refused to recall Hastings, envoys from home thrust their oar into Mahratta politics; creditors of the Carnatic Nabob had representatives in Parliament and were strong enough to arrest a governor of Madras. Exploiting this weakness and contradictory orders from home, the two smaller presidencies plunged into war. In 1778 the Bombay government sent an army to put up its candidate at Poona, which was ignominiously defeated. By temporizing with the Mahrattas Madras offended Hyder, while by its favouritism to the Carnatic Nabob and encroachment on the Circars it affronted both him and Hyderabad. Even before war broke out with France in 1778, both the Nizam and Mahrattas had French officers drilling their troops, a great confederacy threatened Madras, and in 1780 Hyder drove back our armies.

In these years Hastings saved India. He sent one force under Goddard across India from Bengal to the west coast, another under Popham stormed Scindia's fortress at Gwalior; Pondicherry was taken. He stopped the Company's home investment and suspended the government of Madras, sending Eyre Coote to save that presidency. His diplomacy gradually detached the Mahrattas, who in 1782 signed the treaty of Salbai, and recovered the friendship of Hyderabad; Mysore was isolated, Hyder died the same year, the peace of Versailles rescued us in the nick of time from the French admiral Suffrein, and in 1784 Hyder's son Tippu was brought to terms.

While Hastings laboured and while forgotten regimental officers fought heroically, the presidencies bickered, the aged Coote and most commanding officers proved their incompetence, and even after Francis left India the inner councils were full of faction. Amid these storms Hastings took steps which were to bring on his head some grave charges. Desperate for funds and suspicious of treachery, he demanded large sums from Chait Sing, Rajah of Benares, whom he regarded as a vassal, and on his recalcitrance arrested him in person, at the cost of a rebellion in which he nearly lost his own life. A new arrangement for subsidy from Oudh led to harsh demands on the Nabob's relations, the Begums, suspected of intrigue with Chait Sing and owners of much treasure, and the peace settlements of 1783-4 involved Hastings in a fierce quarrel with Macartney, governor of Madras.

Such were the facts, great and small, good and bad, which were before parliamentary committees from 1782. The Commons called for the recall of Hastings; the Company proprietors defied them. Opinion was fairly general that there must be drastic reform and a new council, but what the Dundas school would have made a compromise and peace with honour was turned by Francis' influence on Burke into a party fight, and a campaign against Hastings as a ' cruel and desperate man '.

Pitt's India bill of 1784 differed from Fox's in two essentials ; that it was composed in agreement with the Company, and that it left to the Company their patronage and appointments. It made the State predominant, however, by setting up the Board of Control, two of whom must be Cabinet ministers ; they would approve all political despatches, and could issue orders through a secret committee of the directors. Government in India was relieved from the weakness under which Hastings had suffered, for Bengal was made supreme over the other presidencies, and a subsequent Act of 1786 empowered the governor-general to override his council and to be commander-in-chief. So the State and the Company entered into partnership, to work together with fair harmony for the next seventy years.

But the Act declared conquest and extension of dominion ' repugnant to the wish, the honour, and policy of this nation ', it forbade intervention between native States until a war threatening British rights had actually begun, and expressly declared for the zemindars and the revenue policy which Francis had championed. Seeing in this his own condemnation, Hastings resigned, came home in 1785, and challenged the impeachment for which Francis and Burke were working, and which hostile votes from Pitt and Dundas on the Benares and Oudh charges made certain. From 1788 to 1795 his trial intermittently dragged on, becoming at every stage more of a party vendetta, until the Lords finally acquitted him on every point—broken in fortune by costs of £70,000, but justified in his major policy by all intervening Indian history, and vindicated before his death in 1818 by a later House of Commons. Yet all was not the malice of Francis ; what Burke had honestly felt, though monstrously exaggerated, and what Pitt found himself unable to clear, were acts which might be pardoned in one great man in imminent peril but not made the standard of British rule.

Canada also owed to Pitt's government the first stride in its modern history. The peace of 1783 transformed the problem by the migration of the American Loyalists, for some 35,000 crossed the line into Nova Scotia, whose demands brought about the creation of another Colony in New Brunswick, while 20,000 more entered Canada itself. These New Yorkers, western pioneers, and Highlanders, reinforcing the

British traders at Montreal, insisted on a larger self-government than the French of Quebec had received, or desired. After long consultations with the veteran governor Carleton, now Lord Dorchester, Pitt and Grenville decided to divide Canada into an Upper or British, and a Lower or French province, each with an elected assembly. As a transition measure and to avoid racial dispute, this scheme had advantages, but it left in Quebec a discontented British minority and awkward economic rivalry between the provinces. Yet the logic of self-government would work itself out, proceeding from Pitt's express wish to bring Canadian government ' as near as the nature and situation of it would admit to the British constitution '.

Several failures to keep his parliamentary majority, as over the Irish Commercial Treaty or a scheme to fortify some big ports, and strong resistance about India, warn us that Pitt was by no means omnipotent, and on two great questions he had to retreat. Disappointed reformers called him an apostate but the true explanation seems clear : this lack of power, coupled with that mercurial side of his character, and due perhaps to his weak health, which made Dundas grumble he was always ' in a garret or a cellar '. In 1785 he redeemed his pledge on parliamentary reform in a bill for which he canvassed widely and got the King's promise of neutrality. Disclaiming ' unlimited notions ', he merely proposed to enfranchise the small class of copyholders, to buy out thirty-six rotten boroughs and allot their members to London and some counties, and to form a fund for the future compensation of boroughs, whose representation should be extinguished with their own consent. Half his Cabinet voted against him and more than half his party, besides North's following and Burke and conservative Whigs, so that he was defeated by a majority of seventy-four . In fact there was no popular demand, and till that was changed he would not again court the charge of ' innovation '.

Abolition of the slave trade was likewise caught up in considerations of party and fear of revolution. Since the Asiento treaty of 1713 British ships had transported several million Africans, even after the loss of America carrying nearly 40,000 slaves in an average year, and the trade was a powerful interest — a mainspring of the wealth of Liverpool and Bristol. Until the age of Chatham hardly a protesting voice was raised save that of the Quakers, but condemnation from John Wesley, a new spirit of philanthropy, and the Evangelical movement brought about a change. In 1772 Mansfield's judgment in Somerset's case laid down that a slave became free on British soil, while in the 1780's Thomas Clarkson and Granville Sharp began their propaganda, founding the Abolitionist Society with mainly Quaker support. Wilberforce, who joined them after his own independent enquiries, was one of Pitt's nearest friends, and in concert with

him Pitt in 1788 brought the question before Parliament. Opposition
was obstinate, from the King, many of the Cabinet, West India and
shipping interests, anti-reformers, and from those who pointed to
refusal from France and Spain to take simultaneous action. Only Pitt's
threat of resignation carried through a small bill to improve the foul
conditions of the slave ships, while before the main enquiry was completed the Revolution spread ideas of equality to the Indies, which
brought about slave insurrection. In 1792, resisting both Pitt and Fox,
Parliament accepted a resolution of Dundas for gradual abolition, and
when in 1794 the Whigs of the right wing made their coalition with
Pitt, he deferred to their wish for no immediate move. Opposition
from colonial legislatures and the conquest of slave colonies during the
war swelled the party for postponement, and abolition was set down as
' Jacobinical '.

One episode above all showed how uncertain was the power
of this powerful minister. The Prince of Wales' feud with his
father had deepened ; his character seemed incorrigible, and he owed
half a million pounds. Rumours were current, of what was indeed
a fact, that in 1785 he had married Mrs. Fitzherbert, a widow of high
character, in defiance both of the Royal Marriage Act and the Act of
Settlement, which forbade the succession of a prince married to a
Roman Catholic. Fox in all innocence denied the rumour, but when
later, knowing the truth, Grey and Sheridan denied it once more, it had
become part of a larger crisis.

From November 1788 to February 1789 George III was out of his
mind, a violent maniac. Yet the doctors agreed that his recovery was
probable, on which view Pitt's Cabinet framed their bill : a Regency
regulated by Parliament, limited in powers of making peers or creating
offices and in its control of the Household, so that if the King recovered he would be restored to all his means of influencing government.
If in logic and law their steps were curious, — that is, the passage of a
bill under the great seal by a commission which itself was created by the
two Houses, — they seemed to the mass of the people nearer to the spirit
of the constitution than the extraordinary attitude of Opposition, whose
whole behaviour was a series of error. For they declared that the King
was legally dead, that the Prince had of right stepped into the full power
of sovereignty, and that Parliament had nothing to say but to fix the
date of the transfer. Armed with many proofs of popular favour, Pitt
swore he would ' un-Whig them for ever ' and carried his scheme of
limitations for three years. But many deserted him. Thurlow intrigued with the Prince, lists of new ministers and new peers were
bandied about, and the Irish Parliament adopted Fox's view. Burke's
language was so violent that he seemed out of his mind, the Prince's
callousness outraged decent feeling, all seemed to be over, and Pitt was

preparing to return to the Bar. Then the King recovered, and the election of 1790 showed the ministry more powerfully entrenched than ever.

Its work of reconstruction demanded peace, but Europe was full of rumours of war. Two pillars of experienced wisdom, Frederick the Great and the French minister Vergennes had died in 1786–7, leaving most inadequate successors. Of the other Continental powers, Russia was ruled by the calculating Catherine the Great, and the Empire by the rash doctrinaire Joseph II, who had lately reached agreement on a programme to give Russia Constantinople and push deeper the partition of Poland begun in 1772. Joseph had been defeated by German resistance in his project of getting Bavaria in exchange for Belgium, but his schemes of centralization unsettled the proud Hungarians and threatened the old liberty of Flanders, while on the ground of ' natural rights ' he swept away the Barrier treaties and challenged Dutch control of the Scheldt.

When Pitt first attained power, Great Britain was isolated. France, with Spain in tow, had new colonial and economic objectives, and through her other ally, Austria, made contact with St. Petersburg. During the American war Russia was offended by the claims of our sea-power, while her Oriental ambitions threatened our Mediterranean trade and might reach to India. The old Whig scheme against France seemed irrevocably gone, with Austria in the enemy camp, while in Holland, torn as ever between an Orange and an Amsterdam party, the predominant group leaned to France, looking for protection against Joseph.

Though peace was Pitt's primary object, all the more while he restored the finances and rebuilt the fleet, and though the Middle East was not a direct British interest, his government felt bound to oppose any change in the Low Countries; with the further possibilities of joint French-Dutch action against India or of France bargaining with the Eastern despots to attack Turkey with Egypt as her reward. A first chance of resistance came when Frederick William II succeeded to the Prussian throne, for he resented French supremacy in Holland and the insults inflicted on his sister, the Princess of Orange; and in 1787 Turkey's declaration of war upon Russia meant that France would have to fight her Netherlands battle alone. Prussian troops entered Holland, and in 1788 Prussia, Great Britain, and Holland signed a defensive triple alliance. This diplomatic defeat for France, which was greatly owing to her crumbling finances, was followed the next year by the Revolution, which seemed to destroy her for the time being as a great Power.

But this combination drew Pitt into deep waters. Gustavus III of Sweden, despotic and mercenary and capricious, flung into the strife to recapture the lands long lost to Russia, so that Britain had to damp down a Baltic war. It was more serious that Prussia tried to convert a defensive alliance into a scheme for changes of territory, which in effect meant that, at Turkey's ultimate expense, Poland would give Danzig and some more to Prussia. But, security being Pitt's sole object, he had no wish to make an enemy of Russia, nor to profit by the Belgian revolution which Joseph's reforms caused in 1789; for a triumphant Belgian democracy might join Paris, and if defeated might cause a general war.

Early in 1790 he secured an ally for his aim of restoring the *status quo* when Joseph was succeeded by his more sensible brother, Leopold II. Their joint pressure was strong enough to make the Prussians hesitate, while a firm British stand induced Leopold to give the Belgian rebels decent terms. One other event of this year raised British prestige. True to their old maxims of monopoly, the Spaniards had arrested British ships harbouring in Nootka Sound, Vancouver Island; both sides armed, and Spain appealed to the French National Assembly. The vigour of our armaments, and perhaps bribes in Paris, carried the day, Spain for the first time admitting our right of navigating the Pacific.

In 1791, however, British policy was seriously rebuffed. Suvoroff, Russia's general of genius, won decisive victories over the Turk. Prussia had backed us loyally over Nootka Sound, so that Pitt now supported their claim to Danzig, but the Poles would not hear of any concession; Prussia was therefore ready to sell Turkey, if Russia would support her Polish scheme. Moreover, Revolution was affecting all Europe. Gustavus III made peace with Russia, preparatory to a crusade for monarchy; revolutionary decrees touching Imperial rights in Alsace, an army of French *émigrés* on the German frontier, appeals from his sister Marie Antoinette, all stimulated the Emperor to intervene; he could bury his ill-relations with Prussia and rid himself of Russian pressure by a pact for another partition of Poland.

When, therefore, advised by our over-sanguine ambassadors abroad, Pitt demanded that Russia should restore all conquests except the Crimea, and notably the fortress of Oczakoff between the Dniester and Bug, he found allies who protested, his Cabinet divided, and Parliament alarmed. Opposition were particularly virulent, a visit from Fox's friend Adair convincing Catherine that England could not move, and Pitt had to retreat, losing Leeds his Foreign Minister in the process, whose successor Grenville was firm for neutrality. This retreat meant the doom of Poland, and perhaps a despotic alliance against France.

CONTEMPORARY DATES

1783   Peace of Versailles.
       Russia seizes the Crimea.
1784   Joseph II demands the opening of the Scheldt.
1785   Mozart, *Marriage of Figaro*.
       Paley, *Moral Philosophy*.
1786   Death of Frederick the Great.
       Burns' *Poems*.
1787   Meeting of the Notables in France.
       Impeachment of Hastings begins.
1788   Triple alliance between Britain, Prussia, and Holland.
       Godoy's supremacy in Spain.
       Russo-Austrian invasion of Turkey.
       John Walter founds *The Times*.
1789   Meeting of the Estates-General.
       Rebellion in the Austrian Netherlands.
       Washington President of the United States.
       Blake, *Songs of Innocence*.
1790   Joseph II succeeded by Leopold II.
       Burke, *Reflections on the Revolution in France*.
       Goethe, *Faust*.
1791   Death of Mirabeau, meeting of Legislative Assembly.
       Declaration of Pillnitz.
       Paine, *Rights of Man*.
1792   France repulses the Allies; meeting of the Convention.
       Birth of Shelley.

CHAPTER IV

REVOLUTION AND WAR, 1792–1801

ARLY in 1792 Pitt reduced taxes and cut down armaments, saying
that Europe never had more reason to expect fifteen years of
peace. He protested against the threat to Poland but, having
burned his fingers once, felt no call to intervene, while for France he
wished nothing better than liberal reform on the English model. So
wrong was the judgment of Europe, and its ablest statesmen.

For the French revolutionary fires inflamed every neighbouring
country, embroiled Britain in a twenty years' war, cut short Pitt's
peaceful liberalism, and divided the country into two camps. By the
time that war ended, Britain had scarcely avoided internal revolution,
civil war in Ireland had compelled a Union at the expense of the
Catholics, the speed of industrial revolution was redoubled, sufferings
and passion raised a new democracy and made every institution tremble.

When the Bastille fell in July 1789, most Englishmen felt something
of Fox's enthusiasm for this ' greatest and best event that has happened
in the world ', and when the National Assembly went on to sweep away
feudal rights, disestablish the Church, and put democracy in power, and
made these changes in the name of the rights of man, all that was young
and progressive rejoiced in this appeal to principles. Here seemed to
be coming to life everything that reformers had dreamed of; these were
' golden hours ' in which the young poets, Wordsworth and Coleridge
and Southey, found it ' bliss to be alive ', seeing rainbow visions of a
new age which would restore righteousness to the earth. Older political
societies, fresh from the centenary of 1688, blossomed again, while in
every seat of liberal opinion and industry, London and Sheffield and
Manchester, new clubs sprang up to demand reform and to acclaim
France. But the bloody-minded Paris mobs, the looting of the châteaux,
persecution of the Church, and arrival of penniless refugees alarmed
conservative and religious England, causing in 1790 a decisive rejection
of bills for parliamentary reform and repeal of Tests. This division in
the nation involved the breaking of the Whig party, driven on by the
very man who had remade it, Edmund Burke.

His life (1729–97) covered the changes which marked the difference
between the eighteenth century and modern times and, having the
largest mind ever given to politics in these islands, more than any other
single man he produced and expounded them. His character was so

far below his genius that many thought him an adventurer, or a madman. It was lamentable that he depended on borrowing to buy estates that he could not afford; or that, when he was legislating for India, he would be surrounded by kinsmen deep in Indian speculation; while it would have been better for the champion of America not to have been a paid agent of New York State. He swallowed whole Francis' malignant version of Warren Hastings, and both on that impeachment and in the Regency crisis his speeches were insanely violent. Towards the end, when his face, it is said, ' wore the look of one pursued by murderers ', he became unable to escape from the image of his fears. Yet speeches, acts, and correspondence proclaim him the most informed monument of wisdom, the most benevolent of men. Coming from Ireland to seek his fortune, he went on from journalism to be Rockingham's secretary and the brain of the revived Whig party; he died the high priest of resistance to revolution, the inspiration of a second party of Tories.

Despite that contrast, however, he held a continuously consistent faith, that of the conservative moralist. His first discourse defended civil society against those who rhapsodized about a state of nature. His *Present Discontents* (1770) attacked the Bute system and glorified 1688 and British liberties, for the first time justifying party as an agency of freedom. His economic reforms of 1778–82 would amend the old fabric without touching its essence, for he steadfastly refused to hear of parliamentary reform, equal suffrage, or the right of electors to impose a mandate. Just as his solution for America was local self-government, a return to the liberties which Englishmen had won for themselves, so he saw in Catholic emancipation the best hope of raising an Irish conservative aristocracy. In the first half of his career he defended the vested interest of the East India Company against what he viewed as State confiscation; in the second, against a corrupted Company, he conceived he was defending native rights and venerable religions, and if he was often feverish or misled, the needle of his mind pointed always to the same truths.

He found divine right in something larger than had the seventeenth century : in the whole order of nature, as disposed by God. The State was not a material partnership of existing individuals, but ' a partnership in all perfection ' between the living and the dead. Men had their liberties, but all liberties were inherited; politics were a moral art, not dealing with abstract rights on formulas deduced from experience or reason; not deriving right from mere human will but from more venerable, consecrated forces. The ' little platoons ' in which men really live, their village or church or shire; the affections of the hearth, the physical bonds of parent and child, husband and wife, which turn into spiritual ties; the prejudices which clothe the bare bones of reason, — property and aristocracy and all the organization in which men prove their unequal diversity; all that time had sanctioned, everything that made for enjoyment, ' a liberty connected with order ', — here was the God-sent scheme of things, a mysterious incorporation of the race, to be amended only with prudential care. ' Never did nature say one thing and wisdom say another '; no man, no revolution, had the right wantonly to tear to pieces this long-tested texture of society.

In this spirit Burke instantly denounced in his famous *Reflections* (1790) all the work of the Revolution, and in his *Appeal from the New to the Old Whigs* (1791) broke with its English defenders. ' Fly from the French constitution ', he cried to the Commons; yes, ' there is loss of friends ', was his reply to Fox's tears. With much exaggerated praise of the old régime, much inaccuracy in detail, he nevertheless taught a doctrine with prophetic fire. It was ' a civil war ' of principles; there could be no compromise with ' this strange nameless wild enthusiastic thing ' at Paris; the Catholic peasants resisting in La Vendée were ' the Christian army '. So till his death he preached a new crusade, spending his dying strength for the *émigrés*.

Radical England replied to his attack on ' the swinish multitude ' in scores of pamphlets, but soon adopted as its text-book Thomas Paine's *Rights of Man*, which sold in a cheap form by tens of thousands. As his American career had shown and his later life was to show again, Paine had not a rudiment of English feeling, nor was he a thinker. But he dealt in good plain English some hard blows at Burke who, he said, had praised the French Court, ignored the people, pitied the plumage but forgot the dying bird; government was for the living and not the dead, and each generation had a right to alter it. In a second part of his book he declared for a republic, alliance with the democracies of France and America, and penal taxation of the rich.

In 1791 this controversy passed into riots; at Birmingham the mob attacked a reform banquet, wrecked Dissenting chapels, and hunted the Radical philosopher Priestley out of the city. The Society for Constitutional Information, a survivor of the radicalism of 1780, was revived and, with the London Revolution Society, began to correspond with clubs in every part of France; early in 1792 the shoemaker Thomas Hardy founded the London Corresponding Society, on a subscription of a penny a week, embracing several thousand members in provincial branches, with a programme of universal suffrage. Through these and through working-men's clubs, as at Sheffield, Norwich, and Dundee, Paine's writings and French propaganda descended to cottagers, weavers, and miners.

This passion was brought to a height by the approach of war. When Louis XVI in July 1791 fled from Paris to Varennes and was brought back a prisoner, the Girondins determined on war to save themselves, and to end a monarchy accused of intrigue with foreign states. After long hesitation the Emperor Leopold, just before he died in March 1792, took up their challenge; Prussia was ardent, and Russia anxious to divert her rivals from Poland. In April France declared war on the Empire.

Invasion doomed the French King, volunteers flocked to save democracy, the mob was inflamed by Danton, and in September the Terror began with a massacre in the Paris prisons. A Convention was summoned to make the republic; the French held the invader at Valmy (20th September) in the Argonne, and were welcomed by German revolutionaries into Mainz. The Belgian revolution, suppressed by Leopold, flared up again and in November French troops, breaking the Austrians at Jemappes, entered Brussels. Savoy and Nice were declared annexed, together with the Papal fief of Avignon.

This triumphant revolution and British radicalism joined hands. Bonfires and tricolours in Britain greeted French victories, British addresses and deputies assured the French that Britain would never allow her armies to be used against them, Paine and Priestley were elected members of the Convention. Some reformers were prepared to follow the French model, and a Scottish Convention, after hearing an address from the newly founded society of ' United Irishmen ', took an oath to ' live free or die '.

Until November nothing budged Pitt, Grenville, and Dundas from their resolve to be neutral, which made them decline approaches from both France and her enemies. Declaring that England would remain the same ' till the day of judgement ', this very year Pitt helped Fox in the passage of his Libel Act, which would empower a jury to judge on the limits of political discussion. But increasing excitement, riots by both parties, especially in Scotland, and French armies in Belgium, compelled them to take precautions; a proclamation against seditious writings, some prosecutions, especially of Paine (though he had fled to France), an Aliens Act to control the thousands of exiles now in Britain, and a part-embodiment of the militia. All these, which were supported by the mass of the Whigs although opposed by Fox, did not involve war, nor was it occasioned by the execution (21st January 1793) of Louis XVI. It was decided by the actions of the French government.

Their decrees of November and December 1792 offered assistance to all peoples wishing to recover their liberties, announced they would sweep away anti-revolutionary institutions wherever their armies went, and in virtue of the ' laws of nature ' declared open the navigation of the Scheldt and Meuse. Such decrees, tearing up half a dozen treaties, would equally justify a seizure of Belgium and Savoy; the French plainly hoped their propaganda would crumple up our ally

Holland and counted on British democrats preventing intervention. Our ministers' warnings were plain; they encouraged no plan of meddling with the form of French government but insisted that France must withdraw her invading troops, ' without insulting other governments, without disturbing their tranquillity, without violating their rights '. France decided otherwise. On the 31st January, flinging down to the kings, in Danton's words, the head of a king as gage of battle, the Convention decreed Belgium united to France, and next day declared war on Britain and Holland.

This war, so unlike older wars, a war as Pitt said against ' armed opinions ', had annihilating effects on British politics. Fox detested European kings only less than he did George III; he distrusted Pitt, loved the independence of the Whig party, and believed that France stood for liberty. But as most Whigs loathed French principles and felt with Pitt on the war, negotiations began for a coalition; first Wedderburn (now Lord Loughborough) joined Pitt as Chancellor, and in 1794 Portland, Windham, and Spencer entered the Cabinet, while Fitzwilliam became Lord-Lieutenant of Ireland. All the eloquence of Burke was behind them, most of them were more panic-stricken of revolution, and more anti-French, than the Tories. The lines of party hardened; while one side spoke of the ' rabble ', the other denounced ' tyrants ' and ' pensioners ', and for the first time a class war poisoned politics. In this atmosphere reform became tainted with revolution, and Windham's argument was accepted that we could not mend our house in the hurricane season. So Grey's motion on parliamentary reform was rejected in 1793 by an enormous majority, and despite Wilberforce, Fox, and Pitt, Parliament would not hear of abolishing the slave trade.

This panic was unreasonable, for the great mass of the people were anti-French, testifying to their loyalty in clubs and addresses ·and volunteer services. Yet the reformers must bear part of the responsibility; some continued to correspond with France after war broke out. If men feared civil war, it was most likely in Scotland, where parliamentary unrepresentation and economic suffering were at their worst. The Scottish judges passed harsh sentences of transportation; and yet Muir, one of the victims, had stayed in the enemy capital of Paris and linked the Scottish movement to Irishmen who were planning a republic; his fellow-victim Palmer circulated a pamphlet condemning this war, as waged against the French ' merely because they would be free '. A second Edinburgh Convention was broken up after resolving it would reassemble secretly if Parliament forbade its meeting or suspended habeas corpus; London mass meetings pledged themselves to stop the landing of Hanoverian troops, and declared it right to resist oppressive laws by force. A few wild heads urged the use of arms, and in Sheffield they were making pikes. Such were the grounds which determined government in 1794 to suspend habeas corpus, and to prosecute Hardy, Horne Tooke, and others for treason; of which the London juries decisively, and rightly, acquitted them. Bad harvests, high prices, conscription under the militia ballot, brought more strain, and in 1795 mobs crying ' bread and no war ', ' no royalty, no Pitt ', stoned the King. Huge majorities therefore passed the two ' gagging ' bills, one against treasonable practices and the other a seditious meetings Act, by which meetings of over fifty persons could not assemble without the leave and presence of a magistrate. This severe repression, and the social machinery of magistrates, property-owners, and innkeepers, drove the societies underground; though two other factors much assisted their decline. The first was the resistance of the Churches to atheism and the ' reign of reason '; the second was the transformation of the Revolution itself, first into the Terror and, after 1797, into a military despotism over other nations. This it was which sickened idealists of the crimes done in the name of liberty.

All these years it was a grim disastrous struggle in which, organized by the great Carnot and led by soldiers of genius, the French out-matched the Allies. The Prussians speedily withdrew most of their forces to Poland, and in April 1795 (treaty of Basel) made peace, abandoning everything west of the Rhine. Before that date the Austrians were thrust out of Alsace and Belgium; the Duke of York's army was first ejected from Dunkirk (1793), then out of Flanders, and finally driven back to the border of Hanover (1794), while the French occupied Holland. British efforts to help the French royalists fared no better. Toulon welcomed Hood and a British fleet, but our Bourbon allies Spain and Naples were inefficient, Austrian reinforcements did not materialize, and before 1793 ended the French recaptured the port. Another chance of driving a wedge into France was afforded by the anti-revolutionary movement in Brittany and La Vendée, just south of the Loire, which Burke and Windham urged with all their might. But the *émigrés*, princes, and local leaders were bitterly divided, La Vendée was beaten in 1793 before British troops could be collected, and an expedition to Quiberon in 1795 was a fiasco.

Grave faults marked the British conduct of war. As usual, the army had been rashly cut down and was short of equipment; raw recruits were hastily raised, on no adequate system, in a mass of new units, and the liberty to pay for a substitute ruined the militia ballot. York was a hard-working courageous prince, but inexperienced and unintelligent, while Pitt's brother Chatham at the Admiralty had no enterprise. A better control began in 1794 with the Coalition. Relieved of Home Office work by Portland, Dundas became Secretary for War and the Colonies, while two good administrators, Spencer and Cornwallis, respectively took over Admiralty and Ordnance, and on

Pitt's insistence York was brought home to be commander-in-chief, where his zeal for the soldiers' welfare made him a useful public servant. But changes of personnel could not compensate for mistakes of policy.

There were four fields of war open, — Flanders, western France, the Mediterranean, and a war by sea, — with something to be said for each, but nothing for scattering our forces among them all. The strongest men in the Cabinet disagreed, for while Grenville thought most of the balance of power, Dundas cared passionately about India and colonial power, Pitt also leaning to that side through his interest in trade. To fight in Europe by subsidizing our allies had been his father's policy; moreover all of them, convinced that France could not endure a long war, thought much of winning bargaining counters towards making the peace. There were other inducements to concentrate on the sea and colonial side. When Holland fell to France the Prince of Orange took refuge in England, and action must be taken if the Dutch Empire was not to assist the enemy and their intrigues with Tippu in Mysore. Hence came about in 1795 the successful expeditions to seize the Cape and Ceylon.

But the chief strain came from the West Indies, where revolutionary propaganda had excited the negroes, especially in Haiti, the French half of San Domingo, whose trade exceeded that of all the British islands rolled together; the West Indies, too, would deprive France of much raw material and were the strategic key to the Atlantic. In answer to appeals from the French planters British forces in 1794 occupied the ports of Haiti and soon held all the French islands, except Guadeloupe; on the ' glorious first of June ' Howe intercepted a convoy 300 miles west of Brest and destroyed a quarter of its fighting strength.

Yet these ventures drained away the forces which might have brought decision in Europe, a deadly climate and disease costing 40,000 British lives within three years, while refusal to settle the question of slavery spread negro revolt. In 1798 Haiti was evacuated, though not before it had contributed to a break with Spain.

This was a serious disaster; when Flanders was abandoned, it was all the more vital to curb France from the Mediterranean with the aid of Spain, Naples, and Sardinia. But the Spaniards were irritated by our seizure of Haiti, and of Corsica in 1794, while the favourite Godoy, who ruled its wretched sovereigns, was tempted by French offers of spoils in Portugal. Spanish peace with France in 1795 exposed Sardinia to the hammer-blow with which Bonaparte knocked her out of the war in 1796; his Italian victories brought Spain right over to the French side, together with the British evacuation of the Mediterranean. Except for Austria, who was fighting a losing battle in Italy, Britain stood alone. On the ocean circumference, it is true, our power was supreme. Pondicherry and French India had fallen, during 1796–7 General Abercromby captured St. Lucia and practically all the remaining West Indies, Spanish Trinidad, and Dutch Demerara. But France held all Europe from Holland to Rome.

The years 1797–8, the crisis of the first half of the war, make a point of departure for a change in its character. Invasion threatened us from all the harbours of the Low Countries, France, and Spain. Advised by Irish refugees, in December 1796 the French sent off Hoche with 16,000 men, who eluded our fleet, but mercifully a month of storms broke the expedition to fragments, so that the ships which reached Bantry Bay could not land their troops. In February 1797 Jervis and Nelson off Cape St. Vincent, near Cadiz, crushed the Spanish fleet, which was to make the second horn of invasion.

War subjected the country to terrible strains. Bad harvests and the loss of the Baltic market raised wheat to famine rates, 108s. a quarter in 1795 and a few years later sometimes 120s., while prices in general had risen by about 100 per cent. Rapid enclosure of land, large migrations into the cotton and iron areas, were dislocating the old small-scale England. Besides minor remedies, such as bounties on imported grain or encouraging the people to eat non-wheaten bread, Parliament passed an important Act, nicknamed from the ' Speenhamland ' magistrates in Berkshire who, like others, extended what had long been an occasional practice, of raising wages by payments from the rates. If this measure perhaps averted revolution, it was at the price of doubling the poor rate and debasing the people's morale.

By this time Pitt had raised £100 millions in war loans, but invasion scares caused panic, much gold had gone abroad, country banks were breaking, and Bank of England reserves were dangerously low. In 1797 the Bank was consequently authorized to refuse cash payments for sums over £1, and a period of paper money began which was to last till 1819. Various patriotic loans showed there was money to spare, but there was not yet any proper machinery for direct taxes, and a great deal of evasion. The reforms of 1797–8, however, firmly redistributed the burden. Pitt trebled the assessed taxes, made permanent (with an option of redemption) the land-tax at 4s. in the £1, and introduced an income-tax, beginning on incomes from £60 upwards and rising to 2s. on those of £200 or more.

Poverty also partly caused the most deadly danger of 1797, the naval mutinies which brought Consols down with a run to 48 and exposed us to the enemy ; yet not poverty only, for the treatment of the Navy was a national disgrace. Regularly reducing the crews in peace-time, Parliament recruited them in war by the press-gang, or by emptying the gaols. Able seamen's pay of 22s. 6d. a month had not been increased since Charles II's reign, while even this pittance was withheld until a ship was paid off, leaving wives and children to starve meantime ; rations

were bad and fraudulently administered, every ordinary liberty like
shore-leave was almost non-existent. As private petitions were ignored,
in April the squadron at Spithead put into action a deliberate plan,
refused to put to sea, made many officers prisoner, and appointed
delegates to negotiate. When their chief demands were met through
the agency of their favourite admiral ' black Dick ' Howe, this
squadron, which behaved with steady moderation, returned to duty.

But the excitement, influenced by some London supporters, carried
away the squadron at the Nore, led by an ex-officer and natural rebel
in Richard Parker ; their manifestos spoke much of the age of reason
and notions of fraternity, to which a large Irish element in their ranks
probably contributed. This was a fearful danger, for they were joined
by nearly the whole North Sea fleet based upon Yarmouth, so that
Duncan was left off the Texel with only two ships to resist invasion ;
it was not improved by Fox and Grey choosing this moment to move for
household suffrage and, when heavily beaten, to announce their secession
from Parliament. But the redress of grievances, stern measures, the swing
of public opinion against them, rallied nine-tenths of the sailors, and in
October Duncan led them to crush the Dutch at Camperdown. Only a
small remnant, after sinking to pillage and terrorization, fled to France,
while Parker and a score of others paid the penalty with their lives.

This almost coincided with the final breakdown of Pitt's efforts for
peace, which he had pursued since 1795. After the Thermidorian
reaction and the failure of the *émigrés*, there seemed more hope of
making terms with a stable French government, which the collapse of
Prussia, the enmity of Spain, the defeat of Austria, and the strain on our
finances made doubly urgent. The Directory curtly rejected our first
proposals, but by 1797 we were prepared to yield more. For Catherine
of Russia died and was succeeded by the madman Paul, on whom no
dependence could be put, and all our efforts failed to patch up the feud
between Prussia and Austria, the last of whom surrendered to Bonaparte
in the peace of Campo Formio, sacrificing everything west of the Rhine
in return for a share in the spoils of Venice.

This compact, made in defiance of our protest, drove Pitt to open a
separate treaty, offering to surrender all conquests except the Cape
and Trinidad, and to leave the French in possession of Belgium,
Luxembourg, and Savoy. But the ambitions of Bonaparte and the
Jacobin lust for power swept away the peace-party in the *coup d'état*
of Fructidor (September 1797) ; our ambassador Malmesbury being
ordered out of Lille if we would not yield every single conquest. This
was the turning-point, signifying that the Directory meant to despoil
Italy and surrender to Bonaparte. In 1798 the French invaded Rome,
imprisoned the Pope, and killed a last democratic illusion by extinguishing the freedom of Switzerland ; postponing the invasion of England as

impossible without naval supremacy, at midsummer Bonaparte seized Malta and proceeded to Egypt. This brought about a vital English decision, to re-enter the Mediterranean. After twice missing Bonaparte, on 1st August Nelson blockaded him in Egypt, annihilating his fleet amid the sandbanks at the Battle of the Nile. Under cover of our victory the over-confident King of Naples marched on Rome, while one of our best soldiers, Sir Charles Stuart, skilfully occupied Minorca.

So began the war of the second Coalition. Austria, repentant and disillusioned, raised new armies with English money, and pushed the French back to the Rhine. The Czar Paul, who looked on the Middle East as his own preserve, did the same and his great soldier Suvoroff swept the enemy out of Italy. Driven back once upon Sicily, the Bourbon government soon returned to Naples, Nelson's great name helping to cover its barbarity to rebels. But these hopes swiftly faded. Russia, like others, found out the pure selfishness of the Austrians, who let Suvoroff exhaust himself in hard Alpine fighting, while they schemed to outweigh Prussia and seize Piedmont for themselves. All pretence of co-operation broke down; an Anglo-Russian expedition to Holland hopelessly failed, for a supposed Orange revival never arrived, the Duke of York was once more an unhappy commander, and by the Convention of Alkmaar agreed to evacuate our army.

This year of ups and downs of 1799 ended in October with Bonaparte's return from Egypt, in December with the revolution of Brumaire which made him Consul, and with his approach to Britain with an offer of peace. Disbelieving in the duration of his power, seeing one French army locked up in Genoa and another in Egypt, and building on unity with Austria, our Cabinet rejected it; not without reason, but not also without making the mistake of replying that the best guarantee of peace would be a Bourbon restoration. To the intrinsic power of Bonaparte and the recovery of French morale our Foreign Office were blind, depending too much on dreams of Royalist risings or on Austria, which cared nothing for our two main points of a strong Belgium and a French restoration. Our miscalculations were exposed in the great French victories of 1800; Marengo, where Bonaparte crushed the Italian group of Austrian armies, and Hohenlinden, which opened the road to Vienna. By the treaty of Lunéville (February 1801) Austria fell out of the war, leaving Germany to be rearranged by the conqueror, who was further fortified by vassals in the Cisalpine, Ligurian, Helvetian, and Batavian republics. Meanwhile the Czar Paul was equally infuriated by Austrian claims in Italy, the fiasco in Holland, and our hesitation on the future of Malta. Drawing nearer to Prussia he prepared to play a waiting game, to explore the possibility of partitioning the East with France, and set up a new League of the North to resist the British blockade of Europe.

Through these darkest years Pitt kept the vessel of State head on to the storm. In spite of misfortune and misjudgment his position at home was never greater, reinforced by the election of 1796 and the following of young men, Canning, Castlereagh, Perceval, and Huskisson, who were to succeed him. The monstrous oppression of the Swiss and Italians had converted most British democrats, but a dangerous sediment remained; 'United Englishmen', relics of the Corresponding society, were found in contact with those in France and Ireland who planned an invasion. New measures of 1799 therefore suppressed certain societies by name, and habeas corpus was again suspended, under cover of which democrats were arrested and imprisoned without trial. Political fears as well as economic doctrine brought about the same year an Act against 'combinations' or trade unions. Party took on almost the fierceness of civil war. Pitt accused the Whig Tierney of obstructing the public service and fought him with pistols in a duel near Putney Common; while, for toasting the 'sovereignty of the people' at a public banquet, Fox was struck off the Privy Council.

Now that the Revolution was revealed as merciless to other nations' liberties, anti-revolutionary feeling brushed aside those who, like Wilberforce, aspired to peace. There was a warlike cheap press led by a great journalist in William Cobbett, and in 1798 Canning and his friends began to issue the *Anti-Jacobin*, full of wit and fire and fury against cosmopolitan philanthropists or a defeatist peace, and passionate in defence of Britain, 'this little body with a mighty heart'. Year in, year out Pitt's speeches rang the changes on the peril of reform which might endanger all, on the 'union of liberty and law' in happy Britain 'the temperate zone' of political States, the destructiveness of abstract formulas, or 'the virtues of adversity endured and adversity resisted'.

Of their fortitude they had sore need, for Europe had collapsed. Our military effort during 1800 evaporated in unsuccessful expeditions on the whole sea-front from Brittany to the Riviera, and the Austrians had reason for their complaint that we did nothing from Minorca or Sicily to cut the French communications. The Cabinet was tired and torn, Dundas and Grenville leading rival camps, and its members differed as to the terms of peace, the King and Grenville, Windham and Portland, heading a group for no compromise. Yet extraordinary triumphs showed that in her proper element Britain was invincible. Wellesley broke the power of Mysore, Tippu himself falling in the storm of Seringapatam, and carried British territory from sea to sea; Malta fell to us in August 1800; early in 1801 Ralph Abercromby lost his life but gained the day at Aboukir, which forced a French surrender of Egypt. Exhausted by his frenzies, his own courtiers murdered the Czar Paul, whose son Alexander I leaned to neutrality, and in April the Northern league, which was becoming a French instrument to destroy the Baltic supplies on which our Navy's very life depended, was wiped out by Nelson's triumph at Copenhagen. Threading his way through narrow fortified waters and putting the telescope to his blind eye when his commander-in-chief signalled retreat, he placed the Danish fleet between his own and the shore batteries, and part-forced, part-persuaded, the Danes to capitulate.

Before these successes were complete the Pitt ministry had fallen, mortally wounded in the Achilles heel of British government since the Tudors — Ireland.

The Irish Problem, 1782-1801

Nothing fundamental was changed by the storm of 1778-82, either by the reforms extracted from the North and Rockingham governments, or by Grattan's Parliament which followed. True, some of the penal code both in religion and commerce disappeared, the Test Act of 1704 was withdrawn so far as Protestant Dissenters were concerned, while the repeal of Poynings' law, with the acknowledgment that Irish Parliament and courts had a final authority, left Ireland in name a free dominion under the Crown. These changes, however, which left a void in the Anglo-Irish connection, healed neither the recent fever nor the old-standing disease.

English rule since 1650 had cruelly restricted Irish prosperity and deprived two-thirds of Irishmen of all reasonable life. The country was forbidden to export her natural products of live cattle, butter, and woollens, and cut off from direct trade with the Colonies. And what economic jealousy began, was fulfilled by religious hatred. Such Catholics as had not been evicted, by conquest or plantations, were prevented by law from buying land, holding long leases, or making a will, from becoming freemen of a corporation, owning a horse worth over £5, and bearing arms ; they were excluded from the vote, the Bar, the magistracy, the university, and not allowed to keep a school. English law poisoned life at its very source ; by providing, for instance, that an eldest son who turned Protestant should inherit the whole estate, by making mixed marriages illegal, and setting up the Charter schools, which would indeed educate children and save them from famine but only on condition they became Protestant and never saw their parents.

From this evil proceeded the demoralization of a whole people. With no legal or free outlet in either industry or commerce, Irishmen could not save capital. Catholic landlords let their estates down to pasture as the cheapest way out, lived by exporting meat or a little wool, and cleared off all the inhabitants they could ; large absentee

English owners took the better part of a million in rents farmed through middlemen. Driven back upon small plots in the mountains and without any security of tenure, the small farmers and peasants drove up rack-rents by their competition. But they had no motive to make improvements, and no money to grow much except potatoes; when that crop failed, famine caused hundreds of deaths from starvation. Yet since their standard of living was abject, and their religion very real, they multiplied exceedingly, a population of some two million in 1700 having more than doubled a hundred years later.

This community of beggars were crushed by rents, tithe to Anglican parsons and dues to Catholic priests, and every affection inspired them against the law. Their heroes were the minstrels, often blinded by the smoke which never escaped from their hovels, highwaymen and smugglers, the ' wild geese ' or fighting-men in exile who served in the armies of France and Spain, or the masked secret bands of ' White Boys ' and others, who houghed cattle and burned houses in protest against rent, tithe, and enclosure.

Ulster was better off, if only because it was Protestant, and because their coarse linens were encouraged by English law, and their tenant-right permitted improvement of the soil. But they too had bitter grievances, being excluded from all offices and Parliament till 1780 and downtrodden in their civic life, so that evictions, subletting, and trade laws set up a tide of emigration to America.

Though the ' ascendancy ' was, as it had been in the middle ages, a foreign garrison, it was itself subordinate to the supreme command. Not only was the Irish Parliament tied hand and foot, but Ireland had none of the standard British liberties; no habeas corpus and no mutiny Act, judges only held at pleasure and, till the Octennial Act of 1768, Parliament sat for a whole reign. Some two-thirds of the Commons represented small boroughs, absolutely controlled by about a hundred landowners, while a third were placemen or government pensioners. The pension list rose to over £80,000 a year and most of the revenue was fixed in perpetuity, independent of a parliamentary vote; in Britain's interest Ireland paid for an army of 12,000 men. Twenty-two bishops, almost invariably Englishmen, took a great income, though some 800 Anglican clergy, usually very badly paid, ministered in churches, often in ruinous condition, to a mere fraction of the population.

As of old, this alien rule had raised an ' Irish interest ' among both races and all creeds. In 1698 a famous book by Molyneux, member for Dublin University, claimed that Ireland should either be given her old liberties or equal rights in a Union. This agitation of Irish Whigs was brought to a head in 1722 by the greatest of Irish Tories, when Swift in his *Drapier's Letters* pronounced that this ' government without the consent of the governed is the very definition of slavery '. The scandal which he attacked was the flagrant case of ' Wood's halfpence ', a job perpetrated for the royal mistress the Duchess of Kendal, foisting a superfluous copper coinage on Ireland at an extortionate rate. The great dean compelled its withdrawal and from this time on constitutional opposition grew continuously, while the Protestant bias of 1688 had much declined. The aristocracy and ' undertakers ' who controlled so many seats, Boyles, Ponsonbys, or Beresfords, were self-seeking enough, but not ready to follow blindly the English archbishops who usually directed the Castle interest. Between 1750–70 it became impossible to stop the Commons agitation for more power over money bills, shorter Parliaments, and more appointments for Irishmen, an agitation in which the later leaders Grattan and Flood served their apprenticeship. A greater prosperity, seen in an increase of tillage, fanned this spirit of liberty. Magnificent building in Dublin and country houses, an active press, a powerful Irish bar, the many Irishmen of genius like Burke and Goldsmith shining in British life, all testified to a new national spirit.

Nothing, however, so swiftly advanced Irish feeling as the American war; a strain, because loss of markets meant economic distress, — an opportunity, since England had to withdraw her garrison, — and a battle-cry, when Ireland saw America winning only what she asked for herself. Ulster was specially determined, from parliamentary families like that of the young Castlereagh down to Presbyterian yeomen, and as government had no funds to pay a militia, it was impossible to refuse the service of those ready to defend Ireland against French armies and American privateers. Under Protestant leaders like Charlemont all Ireland drew together in the volunteer movement, nearly 80,000 in number, who demanded a freer government and freer trade, while the Protestant Grattan called for emancipation of the Catholics. This irresistible force and a boycott of British goods drove government, despite angry mercantile opposition, from the petty concessions of 1778 to the great ones of 1780–83 ; by the end of which time Britain had renounced its legislative supremacy, flung open the colonial trade, and admitted many Irish goods to her market. That this change was brought about so rapidly and in peace was greatly owing to the broad loyalties of Grattan and Shelburne's liberal wisdom.

But the problem of six hundred years and the crimes of the last two centuries could not be so lightly liquidated, and great questions remained. The American example and the volunteers roused a clamour for parliamentary reform. Again, though Catholics had lately been allowed to buy land and to keep schools, and their priests were freed from many restrictions, a cry had risen for full emancipation. Both of these were conditioned by a third problem, the ownership of the land.

Finally, whatever shape Ireland itself might take, no English statesman believed that its legal relation to Britain could be left as it was; some treaty or union must end this dangerous uncertainty, whereby two independent parliaments might take contradictory decisions.

The next stage from 1783–9 was disastrous. We have seen that Pitt, postponing the large questions of union, emancipation, and reform, which must rekindle every passion, tried to unite the two peoples in trade and defence; his commercial propositions of 1785 thus planning a scheme of low tariffs in return for a permanent Irish contribution to the Navy. They were defeated by British industrial interests and Irish indignation against a money tribute, on each of which motives in turn the Whig Opposition played. The same jealousy, and the same evil effect of party, was seen in the Regency crisis of 1788, when the Irish Parliament followed Fox and the Prince of Wales. Indeed, as all history before and after proved, Ireland could not continue half slave and half free, or a sovereign Parliament co-exist with an irresponsible foreign executive. The Castle could only get its way by corruption, and successive Lords-Lieutenant taught rival Irish groups to look to rival British parties. Meantime the internal situation went backwards. While agrarian war and riot continued, secret societies began to form on religious lines, Protestant ' Peep-of-day ' boys against Catholic ' Defenders '.

Then the French revolution blew every spark into flame; a republican movement swept the north, and, since the rights of property reopened the whole ownership of the soil, the Catholics demanded emancipation. A young Protestant lawyer, Wolfe Tone, sympathizing with their claim and disappointed in his hopes of a career under government, in 1791 founded the Society of United Irishmen; nominally to force through reform of Parliament, but in fact to work for independence. By 1792 it had made contact with British democratic societies and the French Convention; simultaneously an aristocratic Catholic committee, much inspired by Burke, petitioned the Crown.

Both Pitt and Dundas were convinced that emancipation could not indefinitely be refused, though they would prefer to postpone it till war was over; and, again, it bore directly on the question of union which they had now decided was essential, if only for security against France. Their Irish officials told them that emancipation could not safely be given in an Irish Parliament, where it would unite the democrats of both religions in favour of reforms which would destroy Castle influence and obstruct union. They therefore played for time, and compromised. They gave Ireland some real benefits, a share in the East India trade and a libel Act on the English model. But the concessions which they forced on the unwilling Irish government in 1793 did not touch the rotten boroughs, though they reduced the civil list and excluded place-men, and though seats in Parliament and offices were denied, the Catholic forty-shilling freeholders received the vote. In the same way, while they did not proceed with a scheme of State payment to the Catholic priests, they subsidized the foundation of a seminary at Maynooth.

In the throes of a desperate war their burdens were enormous, but the Cabinet procrastinated because it was divided, and such half-measures only increased their difficulties. Westmorland, their Lord-Lieutenant, assured them that without Protestant supremacy Ireland would be lost; Irish Protestant officials, led by the most resolute of men, the Chancellor Fitzgibbon, later Lord Clare, resisted a reform which would destroy their supremacy. On the other hand, no Catholic would be content with the vote if unaccompanied by seats and office, while the half measure simply made a more corrupt electorate without admitting the conservative Catholic aristocracy to power.

Revolution and war, thus mingling together elements of quite separate origin, wholly demolished the position of loyal Whigs like Grattan. The United Irishmen, founded by Protestants, made their first converts almost entirely among the middle class and Dissenters of Dublin and Ulster, who were angered by denial of reform and fervent for the Revolution. Ulster was hot against the war and deeply infected by Paine's teaching; Belfast commemorated the fall of the Bastille, parading portraits of Lafayette and Franklin. But this political movement co-existed with something more native and more dangerous. Perennial agrarian war, of a peasantry on the margin of starvation, flared up again from the late 'eighties; Catholic 'Defenders' began to drill by night and seize arms, Protestants armed against them, and from Armagh lawlessness spread southwards. High prices and a driving-up of rents turned these troubles to extremes, and the United Irishmen's principles overspread every local feud of land and religion.

Till 1795 there was a bare chance that England might keep the sympathies of the Catholic Church and aristocracy; the United Irishmen of Dublin were broken up, and Tone, morally weakened by a confession, joined others in exile in America. But this chance was destroyed by party politics. The Whigs who joined Pitt in 1794 being bent on alliance with Grattan, their representative the new Lord-Lieutenant Fitzwilliam plunged into a reversal of policy, for within a month of his landing he dismissed the leading Protestant officials and encouraged the introduction of a Catholic emancipation bill. This breach of a Cabinet understanding led to his recall which, for the peace of Ireland, proved a major disaster. Fitzgibbon and his friends in England convinced the King that emancipation would violate his coronation oath, and Pitt's circle decided it would be unsafe apart from a union. While disappointed Catholics threw themselves into conspiracy, Protestants drew together in a solid block, survivors of the volunteer movement and farmers of Armagh founding in 1795 the Orange Order. Faced with Irish racialism and a new Catholic electorate, the northern Whigs reverted to their origins, of Protestantism as the bond of union with Britain and the badge of their own supremacy; Ulstermen poured into the newly raised yeomanry, turning it into an instrument of terror, and under their threats several thousand Catholics took flight to the west.

If this Protestant crusade swelled the United Irishmen's ranks, it was a still graver matter that government in self-defence felt bound to endorse what the Orangemen had been doing. An indemnity bill covered their stretches of the law, while the insurrection Act of 1796 empowered government to ' proclaim ' certain districts, apply a curfew, search houses by night, and ship the accused, without trial, to serve in the navy. In 1797 martial law and disarming, boycott and house-burning, crowds assembling on the pretext of funerals or potato-planting, orange cockades against green ribbons, marked an anarchy which spread south into civil war. Tone had returned from America to France, to inspire Hoche's unsuccessful expedition, while Lord Edward Fitzgerald and Arthur O'Connor negotiated at Hamburg with French agents.

Early in 1798 the Rebellion at last broke out, forced into the open by the severity of disarming and demoralized by the arrest of its leaders. O'Connor was caught on his way to France, the Leinster committee were taken in one swoop, Fitzgerald was given away by an informer, to die of wounds received in a desperate resistance. In May the rank and file rose, without hope or concert. No French assistance as yet reached them, the scheme to seize Dublin was betrayed, Ulster and Connaught hardly moved, so that rebellion was, in fact, almost limited to Leinster and Wexford. Though the fiercest leaders were often priests, the leading Catholic prelates and gentry were against it, and it was not so much a war of religion as an outburst of fanaticism and despair. Many enlisted believing that the Orangemen meant to wipe out all Catholics ; many more were goaded on by martial law, burning of their homes, or floggings to force a surrender of arms ; and many by hope of loot. It soon degenerated into mob-law and massacre by half-armed peasants, whom any good troops could destroy, and in June the centre of resistance in the south was broken at Vinegar Hill. It was only in August that a thousand French troops under Humbert reached Killala Bay in Mayo and, though their bayonet charges routed the militia at Castlebar, within a month they were forced to surrender. A larger French force which sailed into Lough Swilly in October was dispersed, among those captured being Wolfe Tone, who was sentenced to death by court-martial but died of self-inflicted wounds.

At the height of rebellion Cornwallis arrived as Lord-Lieutenant and commander-in-chief, a man proved by his Indian record as one of lenient and judicial mind ; his chief secretary was Castlereagh, by origin an Irish reformer of Grattan's school.   They found a country black with burned houses and ruined towns, and loaded with debt.   At least 12,000 rebels had been killed in action, and many executed or exiled. Army discipline was almost destroyed, the militia perpetuated hatred, and the ruling class cried out against mercy.

Already the Cabinet had decided that only Union could offer a remedy, or save Ireland from invasion.   Like Shelburne before him, Pitt had always realized that the settlement of 1782 could not be final, the Regency crisis had driven this lesson home, the war clinched it, and he believed that only English wealth could heal the ills of Ireland. British politicians were emphatic that it was impossible to go on if their policy, even their military arrangements, were subject to Irish Protestant officials, who were not responsible in any real sense to either Parliament.   Such considerations carried the Union proposals at Westminster with ease, but at Dublin the case was badly prepared, and on a first attempt in 1799 the measure was defeated.

The great bulk of Protestant Ireland were now hot against it, for political consciousness had found itself since the American war ; Dublin was a capital with a brilliant society ; Ulster, fresh from victory in battle, wished to keep its supremacy.   But if Protestant Ireland proved unwilling, Union could only be carried by conciliating the Catholics ; Pitt and Dundas, as well as Cornwallis and Castlereagh, were convinced that emancipation must make part of the settlement, for the bulk of the Catholic upper class would support Union as the best means to win their own objects.   Yet against emancipation the Irish Parliament, and even officials like Clare who, on other grounds, would support Union, would fight to the last ; the King's scruples were notorious, and Protestant panic was already heard in Pitt's party.   It was therefore determined to work at present for Union alone, at the same time assuring the Catholics of government's good intentions ; emancipation, Pitt and his advisers were agreed, could only safely be attempted in a united Parliament.

Stunned by suppression and in dire poverty, the masses showed little passion either way, but 45,000 troops were none too many to keep order and at the least rumour of a French fleet the old disorders revived.   Among the political classes Union slowly made some ground. The Catholic prelates were particularly solid, agreeing with Castlereagh that, if the State paid the priesthood, it might have a veto on the appointment of bishops.   Most of Catholic Munster, especially Cork with its hopes for an enlarged trade, was with them ; even many United Irishmen preferred Union to their old Parliament.   Among the Protestants the Orange order was divided, but the Ulster linen merchants were generally favourable. Dublin, however, was irreconcilable, whether the Protestant stronghold of Trinity College or the Catholics in business and the professions, among whom a young Daniel O'Connell now first raised an eloquent voice. The immediate task was to retrieve the first defeat in Parliament, and to this the whole weight of government was turned. There were enemies who argued that Union would mean higher taxation, an increase of absenteeism, a deeper gulf between owners and tenants, and borough - owners who would not part with their power. But in this narrow self-elected body a majority could probably be won, by the corruption the Castle had always used.

When Union again came before the Dublin Parliament in February 1800, it was found that government had secured a majority of nearly fifty in the Commons. A new article that the Irish Anglican Church should be established ' for ever ' conciliated one vested interest. Two notable concessions won over many politicians; the number of county seats was not to be reduced, and owners of a two-member borough, if totally disfranchised, would receive a compensation of £15,000. But the majority was made safe by coarser means. A good deal was spent on bribing the press, while in its struggle against the Opposition campaign fund the government triumphed because it was the fountain of honour. Nearly forty creations or promotions being promised in the peerage, many patrons willingly replaced opponents of Union by Union supporters.

In August the Act received the royal assent. Making the two kingdoms one in regard to the royal standard, the great seal, and succession to the throne, it provided that Ireland should be represented in the Imperial Parliament by 4 lords spiritual, 28 lords temporal elected for life by their peers, and 100 commoners, of whom two-thirds would sit for counties. The royal prerogative would be restricted, so that the Irish peerage would gradually be reduced to a maximum of 100, though Irish peers could sit in the Commons. The Act also safe-guarded Ireland against economic shock during the transition. For twenty years the two systems of debt and taxation would be kept separate, Ireland meanwhile contributing to Imperial expenses in the proportion of 2 to 15; free trade was established as the principle, but for a term of years some important Irish industries, woollens and cottons in particular, were to be protected against English competition.

Within a month of the Union the Cabinet were discussing a measure to complete it and to fulfil their moral obligations. Catholics and other Dissenters should be admitted both to Parliament and office on taking an amended oath of allegiance, their priests and ministers should receive some State aid, and the tithe system should be revised. Loughborough the Chancellor betrayed this to the King, who fell into his old frenzy about his coronation oath ; intriguers for office like Auckland exploited it, the archbishops were busy too, Protestant agitation and the royal wishes swept away Portland, the Jenkinsons, and the weaker men in Cabinet. Pitt was ready to give the King time for reflection, though only if he preserved neutrality in public, and on that condition to stay in office till the question of peace or war were settled ; but he demanded ' a full latitude on the principle ', and no reduction of his power as ' the minister '. Two criticisms of his action were made at the time, and have often been repeated. Why, it was asked, had he not done more to overcome the King's scruples, of which all were aware ? In part, it must be answered, because he was himself on the verge of a breakdown ; and again, that till the new year he hoped to carry with him a substantially united Cabinet. But why, Cornwallis then and posterity since have asked, did he offer resignation instead of persisting ? For he had with him the strongest men, both Whigs and Tories — Grenville and Dundas, Spencer and Windham, Canning and Castlereagh. Against this must be set the principle, on which all his life he stood firm, that ministers were the King's choice ; a growing certainty of opposition and probable defeat in the Lords ; his Cabinet divided, and his party too ; lastly, at the crisis of the war, the possibility of the King being driven back on the Whigs, and so to an unsatisfactory surrender to France. Whatever the value of this reasoning, its effect made it easy for George III to accept Pitt's resignation and appoint Speaker Addington as Prime Minister.

So ended Pitt's government, and so ended also the last hope of a just settlement in Ireland which was left, as Castlereagh said, to a continuance on the garrison principle. For even now George III had not filled the cup. In February 1801, immediately on the change of government, he again became mad ; his death was feared, and rather than cause this or a regency, Pitt impulsively promised not to revive emancipation during the King's lifetime. That being so, many of his followers, Dundas and Canning particularly, urged that he should return to office. But the King had found in Addington a man after his own heart, and a man who enjoyed power, while Pitt would not put pressure on them nor court an accusation that he had betrayed the Catholics.

Addington's Cabinet consisted of the ' Protestants ' in the old government, led by Portland, reinforced by a few able men on their promotion, the Chancellor Eldon and Perceval, and some mediocre friends of Addington such as Vansittart. This most weak government had now to decide whether to continue war or make an inconclusive peace ; in the face, Grenville wrote, of ' that despicable weakness which drives the powers of the Continent, from motives of fear alone, into the arms of France '.

CONTEMPORARY DATES

1793   Beginning of the great war.
       Second partition of Poland.
       Invention of Whitney's cotton-gin.

1794   Execution of Danton, and then of Robespierre.
       Toussaint l'Ouverture rouses Haiti.

1795   Peace of Basel.
       Third partition of Poland.
       The Speemhamland Act of Parliament.
       Birth of Keats and Thomas Carlyle.

1796   Bonaparte in Italy.
       Goya painting in Spain.
       Jenner introduces vaccination.

1797   Peace of Campo Formio.
       Death of Burke.

1798   Bonaparte in Egypt.
       Malthus, *Essay on Population.*
       Wordsworth and Coleridge, *Lyrical Ballads.*

1799   Suvoroff and Nelson in Italy.
       Tippu killed at Mysore.
       Brumaire.
       Banks and Davy at the Royal Institution.

1800   Battles of Marengo and Hohenlinden.
       Jefferson President of the United States.
       Beethoven, First Symphony.

1801   Peace of Lunéville.
       Concordat between France and the Papacy.
       The first census in Britain.
       –1825.   Reign of the Czar Alexander I.

CHAPTER V

THE STRUGGLE FOR NATIONAL EXISTENCE
1801–1815

WHEN Addington finally settled in office in March 1801, the war had become a deadlock, leaving France mistress of the land and Britain of the sea. Yet though Austria seemed annihilated and Prussia was merely bargaining for compensations, the revolution which swept away the Czar Paul demolished Napoleon's hope of an accomplice in Russia; with which, and with Nelson's victory at Copenhagen, vanished his chance of closing the north to our shipping. At the same time the French surrender hourly expected in Egypt and the loss of Malta shut the avenues that led eastwards. Other objectives, moreover — to establish his position against royalists and republicans, revive French industry, win French conservatism by a concordat with Rome, make solid the striking points he had won from Holland to Italy, and build a fleet capable of fighting Britain — all disposed him to seek an interval of peace.

Britain, on her side, was without an ally. War had added £290 millions to the debt, we had lost hard on 3500 merchant ships, bread was again at famine prices, and Ireland dangerously discontented. On the top of war-weariness and business pressure for peace came one of those gusts of isolationism which have so often turned our policy — Britain would take care of herself and spend no more blood and treasure in saving Europe.

Yet if, as Pitt argued, a breathing-space was necessary, and if it was right to test whether Bonaparte would co-operate in the work of peace, nothing could be weaker than the making of the peace of Amiens by Addington, his Foreign Secretary Hawkesbury,[1] and his plenipotentiary Cornwallis. Their first proposal spoke of keeping Malta and all the Dutch colonies, with a complete restoration in Italy, but by the time the treaty was finally signed, in March 1802, nearly all such safeguards had disappeared. Great Britain's gains were limited to Ceylon and Trinidad, the Cape went back to Holland, West Indian islands to France and Minorca to Spain, and, though Turkey recovered Egypt, Bonaparte would not include her in the treaty. Portugal was nominally restored to freedom, though, in fact, she was forced to close her ports to British ships. Malta was given back to the weak rule of the Knights of St. John.

---

[1] Later, the second Lord Liverpool.

Though the French evacuated southern Italy, there was silence on Sardinia and the north, a vague flourish of indemnity to the Prince of Orange, but silence on the future of Holland and Germany, and silence on what British opinion would value most — a commercial treaty with France.

Indeed, over this ill-omened peace lay the shadow of party faction. As in Bute's time, only a peace could save a weak Cabinet of the King's making, but now the case was even worse, for all through 1801 the King's sanity was trembling in the balance, so that Pitt refused to endanger it by overthrowing Addington, or by risking a regency which would give power to Fox, who was rejoicing that the terms were 'glorious for the French'. To the indignation of his nearest followers, he therefore ranged himself in defence of the peace, which was endorsed by great majorities in Parliament.

Fourteen short months were given us before war broke out again, months of threats abroad and faction at home. By his own deeds Pitt had destroyed the party he had made, Catholic emancipation separated him from the King and Protestant feeling, and the election of 1802 showed that Addington was solidly established. Grenville might gravely denounce the 'degradation' of the peace terms, Canning might pour out sarcasm against the Prime Minister as 'happy Britain's guardian gander'; actually, demobilization of troops and repeal of the income-tax enhanced the popularity of Addington, with whom the country gentlemen felt more at ease than with the imperious Pitt. For the present, Fox supported Addington to prevent a return of Pitt and a renewal of war, his follower Tierney even taking office with 'the Doctor'.

Soon, however, it became evident that Bonaparte's design was to complete by an armed peace what had been left unfinished by war, so fulfilling Grey's prediction that he would 'make us drink the cup of our disgrace to the very dregs'. The sending of a force to reconquer St. Domingo and acquisition of Louisiana from Spain threatened our Atlantic colonies. Again, though his treaty with the Emperor promised independence to the small republics, every one of them was violated; French troops garrisoned Holland; to the indignation of British liberals a French army selected a new government for Switzerland; Bonaparte made himself president of the Cisalpine State, and annexed Piedmont and Elba outright. Meantime a 'scientific' expedition was exploring Australia, a military mission set out to inflame the Indian princes, French agents traversed Greece, while Bonaparte's official newspaper published a report from his Levant commissioner that Egypt was ready to fall into the arms of France. To Prussia he was holding out the bribe of Hanover, to Russia a partition of Turkey; to Britain, he alternated between blustering manifestos that we dare not fight, or hints that France and Britain might together rule the world.

While Addington declared he must wait till Bonaparte so ' heaped wrong on wrong ' that even the greatest peace-lover would be convinced, and Fox protested we had nothing to do with Switzerland or Egypt, Grenville, Dundas, and Canning argued that this weak government must be extinguished and that Pitt must return. But the King and party faction between them destroyed any such hope of a national government. A personal feud separated Dundas (now Lord Melville) and Grenville, besides a fundamental political difference, that Melville would resist what Grenville was coming to accept, a coalition with Fox. After long negotiations, early in 1803 Addington ungraciously offered to serve under Pitt, but he and his colleagues vetoed the Grenvilles and Windham. Pitt himself, in failing health and torn between the groups, did not share in their vendettas, but the path he staked out was almost as disastrous. As against Addington's weak policy and incompetent finance, he steadily hardened, nor would he accept any post but the highest. Yet he would not ' force ' the King, for that might imperil his reason and bring in a Fox government, while it would make him more obstinate in refusing a comprehensive Cabinet ; again, he would not be bound to exclude Grenville, but neither would he proscribe men like Hawkesbury and Castlereagh, or brand all those who had made the peace. With Grenville, then, he demanded a total new government and was ready to make the Catholic question an open one. But he demanded a free hand to form the best Cabinet he could, and both from principle and tactics would pay his old deference to the King, true to the ideas of his father and Shelburne.

By this time national feeling had driven the Cabinet to stand against Napoleon's veiled conquests. Though even now they evacuated Egypt and the Cape, they repudiated his ruling that Britain had no right to a voice on the Continent and, to balance his aggressions since the peace, insisted that we should occupy Malta for ten years, while the French should evacuate Holland and compensate Sardinia. But Napoleon, who had seen his West Indian army die of fever, and marked the surrender of his western plans by selling Louisiana to the United States, would not further cheapen his prestige by leaving Malta in our hands, or drop his eastern ambitions. Denouncing Britain as a violator of treaties, he would enforce a blockade to bring her to her knees.

From the renewal of war in May 1803 Addington's government struggled on another year, while Napoleon seized Hanover, invaded Naples, and prepared to invade Britain. The Grenville group, refusing to wait longer for Pitt, agreed with Fox that Addington must be overturned and a wide government installed, with no ban on Emancipation. In April 1804 Addington resigned ; the King, assured by Pitt that Emancipation should not be forced upon him, refused to admit Fox, though he was induced to accept the Grenvilles. But as, without Fox,

neither the Whigs nor Grenvilles would co-operate, Pitt was compelled
to take the course he had hoped to avoid, of making a narrow government; including Melville, Harrowby, Canning, of his own followers,
with Hawkesbury, Eldon, Portland, and Castlereagh from those who had
served with Addington. This was a weak team, throwing too great a
burden on himself in the Commons; half of his old party still looked
to Addington, while Fox's tactical sense kept emancipation to the forefront as the means of cementing a party against Pitt and the King. At
the new year of 1804-5 Pitt had to humiliate himself by restoring
Addington, now raised to be Lord Sidmouth, to the Cabinet, with some
places for his friends; this reconstruction, however, collapsed a few
months later, for feelings were too sore, and sharp tongues like Canning's
were always reopening the wound. Moreover Sidmouth knew his own
price, and when a commission on the Navy brought home to Melville a
grave laxity in administering public money, the Addingtonians declared
against him. He resigned and was impeached, but when Sidmouth
asked more promotion for his followers, Pitt declined and they left the
Ministry. Tarnished by these scandals, Pitt once more tried to make
the King take in Grenville and Fox, but again he failed; ground
between royal power and party feeling, he had to fight on alone in this
year of peril.

In May 1804, when Pitt took office, Napoleon became Emperor of
the French, and by kidnapping the Bourbon Duc d'Enghien from
Baden, and shooting him, defied Royalist conspiracy and the crowned
heads of Europe; next year he annexed Genoa and declared himself
King of Italy. Against Britain he would use three weapons, separately
or in combination — direct invasion, diversion by sea, and closing of
the Continental ports. Spain was forced to give him her alliance;
he closed the ports of Italy and Portugal, with the whole coast-line from
Hamburg to the Scheldt. He began to turn Antwerp into a vast
naval base, massed light craft and flat-bottomed boats between Ostend
and Étaples, while 160,000 men under Soult and Ney rehearsed em-
barkation and landing.

For over a year, fighting alone, the British set themselves grimly to
defence. Though economies had left only some eighty ships of the line
and though the eyes of the fleet, the frigates, were short in number,
squadrons were found to sweep in St. Lucia, Demerara, and all enemy
colonies, as well as to blockade enemy ports; for two years on end
Admiral Cornwallis lay before Brest, for twenty-two months Nelson
watched Toulon without a night ashore. The country was made ready
to receive invasion — in which most of our best sailors and soldiers did
not believe. Plans were laid to move the Bank and Woolwich Arsenal
to the Midlands, Martello towers and military canals and beacons
covered the coasts, Pitt himself as Warden of the Cinque Ports was one

of 350,000 volunteers.   The Duke of York had done much to improve army discipline and was organizing the foundations of the Staff College. But the recruiting system was still radically wrong, as volunteers were exempt from the militia ballot, and a regular army, enlisted for life, had to compete against militiamen who were paid higher bounties for a term of years.

This petty force of 175,000 soldiers and militia could not restore the balance in Europe, which nothing could do but another Coalition.   But very slowly did this come to pass, for Prussia held timorously back, Austria dared take no risks, the Czar Alexander hankered after Malta, not to speak of Poland and Constantinople.   Yet in that curious nature, destined so deeply to mark the next age, part made up of Slav racial passion and in part of liberal ideals, there were elements that bitterly resented Napoleon : a sense of mission to arbitrate a new order, a pride of royalty, the great ruler of his country.   In discussions with Russia in 1804–5 Pitt laid down the principles, taught by his experience, by following which his disciples were to overthrow the tyrant.   Revolution, he argued, had made it unwise to re-establish those petty states whose inability to save themselves had been painfully proved.   Holland must be restored but enlarged to include part of Belgium, Prussia expanded westwards to include Luxembourg at least, and Sardinia brought to the forefront in northern Italy, where Austria also must acquire more room.   This system of barriers would restrain France more or less within her pre-revolutionary limits, though he would leave France the free choice of her government.   The Allies should make no peace except by common consent, and protect peace by their joint guarantee.

On such a basis and sustained by British subsidies, came into being at midsummer 1805 a Coalition between Britain, Russia, and Austria, with Sweden on the flank.   But by mid-winter it had perished in fearful disaster.   To move the slow Russian machine over marsh and river would take time, nor could it safely advance to help Austria leaving Prussia in its rear, so jealous of Austria, so greedy for spoil, and undecided whether Hanover could be extorted more easily from the Allies or the French.   While one British force was wasted in southern Italy, another after dangerous delays was launched in Pomerania to co-operate with Sweden and a supposedly friendly Prussia ; to whom Pitt offered large bribes, even Belgium, or anything but Hanover.   Meanwhile the Austrians, rashly counting on Bavarian help, struck out for the Danube before Russian reinforcements could reach them ; Napoleon, they reckoned, was far off at Boulogne and could not march to the Danube under eighty days.   But within sixty days the 'army of England', now turned into the grand army, fell on Mack's forces, and on the 20th October compelled them to surrender at Ulm.   The next day Nelson won Trafalgar, which completed the process that saved Britain from invasion for the duration of the war.

Napoleon had long given up the notion that one dark night would be enough, and now asked of his sailors a larger gift — ' make us masters of the Channel for three days and we are masters of the world '. His orders now were that the Toulon, Brest, and Rochefort squadrons should simultaneously break the blockade, rendezvous at Martinique, ravage the West Indies, and on their return, picking up the Spaniards from Ferrol and Cadiz, clear the Channel with their joint force. But he could not collect sailing ships from scattered ports, or move them to a time-table through unmeasured waters, as he moved his army corps on land — least of all in the face of the British Navy as it then stood, inspired by its greatest fighting leader, Horatio Nelson.

From a Norfolk rectory Nelson had gone to sea as a boy of twelve and fought through the American war, by the end of which a school of great sailors, Keppel and Jervis, Hood and Howe, had reformed the Navy, improved its gunnery, perfected its signals, and re-created its spirit. As a boy in the Arctic, and as a boy-captain of twenty-one in the West Indies, fortune and his ceaseless courting of responsibility had given him experience in every type of command, boat-training and convoy, expeditions of all arms and blockade. His fame was assured during the Mediterranean command of Hood, the leader of his special admiration, his tactical intuition was proved at St. Vincent in 1797, and the next year, aged thirty-nine, he hoisted his admiral's flag to win the Nile. His right eye was blind since Corsica in 1794, in 1797 he lost his right arm in a night attack on Tenerife, his physical system threatened to collapse, his unhappy home and liaison with Lady Hamilton robbed him of peace and tarnished his name. Yet Nelson was much more than a master of his craft, for by love of his country and his countrymen, by patience and confidence and courage never dimmed, he was a spiritual force; what every man in arms would wish to be, happiest at the cannon's mouth, but a leader whose captains from Collingwood down-wards were a band of brothers — the darling of the nation as Marl-borough never was, and Wellington was never to be. Raised now to his full strategic insight, he encouraged the initiative which varied with all the conditions of sailing-ship warfare, and had long instilled the action by groups or columns, by which Trafalgar was won. ' Numbers alone can annihilate '; to bring the enemy to battle, to crush them by concentration of his whole on their part if that were possible, but in any case never to lose a chance of decisive action, even at the cost of crippling his own fleet.

While Napoleon's army lay round Boulogne, the time-table of what he called his ' immense design ' went awry. The Rochefort squadron broke out in January 1805 and reached the rendezvous, but, as no others joined it, returned to France; thus missing the Toulon fleet under Villeneuve, which got away in the last days of March and in May arrived at Martinique. And the Brest fleet was bottled up, till after Trafalgar was lost.

First making sure that Villeneuve had not sailed east towards Egypt, and that Ireland was safe, Nelson gave chase, knowing with the divination of long thought that he would find his quarry in the West Indies. In June he reached Barbados; on hearing which Villeneuve made for home, following Napoleon's latest order to join hands with the Brest fleet, falling back on Cadiz in case of difficulty. Fast on his track, and only missing him through false intelligence, sending his fastest frigate ahead to warn the Admiralty, came Nelson, who in late July touched Gibraltar and drew Cadiz blank, unaware that Villeneuve, brushing off Calder's effort to intercept him, had entered Vigo. The first half of August was decisive. For while Nelson's squadron joined Cornwallis off Ushant and he himself went on leave, and while Cornwallis rashly divided his fleet, Villeneuve threw away his superior numbers and chance of victory; after one vain endeavour to link up with the Rochefort ships, he abandoned the design of reaching Brest and made himself safe in Cadiz. It was on receiving this news, together with that of Russian mobilization, that Napoleon in the last week of August turned his back on the sea, and prepared to break Austria and win the Middle East.

In Cadiz lay the French and Spanish fleets with Collingwood observing them, from whom in September Nelson came to take over command; for, while the enemy in Brest and Cadiz were intact, Britain could not breathe, nor himself be satisfied. ' May the great God whom I adore ', he wrote in his diary on his last night at home, ' enable me to fulfil the expectations of my country.' Villeneuve, anxious to justify himself in Napoleon's new design, broke out to pass eastwards through the Straits, and so, on the 21st October, came about the battle of Trafalgar, fought from noon till five o'clock on an almost windless sea. Nelson's aim was annihilation; in two columns, himself in *Victory* leading one, and Collingwood in *Royal Sovereign* the other, his twenty-seven ships cut the middle of the allied line, so that their van never effectually came into action. Desperately Villeneuve tried to re-enter Cadiz, but his dispositions were confused, the Spanish contingent very passive, the English gunnery accurate and severe, while the resolute decision of individual officers justified all Nelson's trust. Out of thirty-three ships Villeneuve lost eighteen that day, captured or sunk, and four more were taken in the next fortnight. That made an end of the striking-force of Napoleon's navy, whatever it did later in raiding commerce, but to Britons the price paid, for a gain the fruits of which they could not yet see, seemed terrible; the log of the *Victory* summing

it up, ' partial firing continued until 4.30, when a victory having been
reported to the Right Honourable Lord Viscount Nelson K.B. he died
of his wounds '. Few places are better known in England than the
cockpit of the *Victory*, and few words than his signal before action of
what England expects, in the spirit of the last clear word he was heard
to say, ' Thank God, I have done my duty '.

On the 2nd December Napoleon forced decision and defeat on the
Austro-Russian armies at Austerlitz. The Czar retreated from Germany, Austria was driven to make peace, giving up the Tyrol, Dalmatia,
and Venice. The base Prussians made ready to accept Hanover at
French hands, vetoed any attack on Holland, and caused the withdrawal
of our Baltic forces. Under pressure of these calamities Pitt died in
January 1806, as much a victim of war from exhaustion at the age of
forty-six, as Nelson at forty-seven. His immense achievement in constructing the modern British State, obscured by the dark reactions of
war, was to be made good by his followers, and he too left behind in his
last speech a maxim of salvation : ' England has saved herself by her
own exertions, and will, as I trust, save Europe by her example '.

The Ministry of ' all the talents ', which replaced him, condemned
his Coalitions and made an effort to bring about peace. But Fox now
discovered that, however just his earlier defence of the Revolution, it
could not apply to Napoleonic despotism ; though the French dangled
before us a restoration of Hanover, he deemed no peace honourable
or safe which divided us from Russia, or allowed our Bourbon
allies to be robbed of Sicily. Napoleon's mild words were betrayed by
his deeds, the proclamation of one brother, Joseph, as King of Naples,
of another, Louis, as King of Holland, of a third, Jerome, as King of
Westphalia, by the confederation of the Rhine to suffocate Germany,
by plain intentions to form a Latin *bloc* which, by mastering the
Mediterranean, would ' avenge centuries of English insults '. Fox
had hardly died in September when Napoleon marched to punish the
treacherous Prussians, whom he scattered at Jena in October, issued
from Berlin the decrees which declared a blockade of Britain, in
February 1807 gripped the Russians in the murderous battle of Eylau,
and in June crushed them at Friedland. In July the Czar, obedient
to long-cherished dreams and sore at the lack of British assistance,
signed at Tilsit memorable treaties, public and secret. Prussia was to
become a petty State, losing her Polish lands to make a Grand Duchy
of Warsaw, which Napoleon would thrust between the eastern monarchies, and much in the west to make a Westphalian kingdom for
Jerome. Secretly it was provided that Joseph should receive Sicily, and
France the Ionian Islands ; the two emperors should then summon
Britain to restore her conquests and amend her maritime law, and if she
refused would compel all neutrals to close their ports against her. The

tempter pointed the Czar on to other gains, a share in the Turkish Empire, Finland, and a joint rule of the world. From this date till the end of 1810 the Napoleonic Empire was at its height, and though Britain fought on, it was with grievous incompetence, political and military.

Pitt's death having completed the demoralization of his party, his colleagues advised the King to call on Grenville. The nickname of the new government, ' all the talents ', was hardly justified by the admission of Sidmouth, or the Prince of Wales' favourite Moira, and, excepting Grenville, all its principal members were Fox Whigs. Fox himself, Grey, Erskine the Chancellor, Henry Petty (Shelburne's son, later third Lord Lansdowne), and Holland, were reinforced by those Whigs — Spencer, Windham, and Fitzwilliam — who had served with Pitt in the first war, but had left him when he capitulated over Emancipation.

Here then was something like a party, but the loss of Fox took away their one great man, and both parties were full of long-persisting division. The Crown was still powerful enough to make the King's prejudices, or his sanity, very formidable; the Prince did infinite harm to the Whigs by the scandal of his life and by giving confidence to the feckless Sheridan rather than the recognized leaders. Radicalism was rising, the advanced Whigs called ' the Mountain ' detested Grenville. On the other side, there was a solid block of Tories — Liverpool, Eldon the lawyer, Perceval — who had acted with Addington; some in the centre, Castlereagh for instance, who hoped to reunite the party; over against them were some pure Pittites — Canning above all, his friend Huskisson, and Wellesley now back from his government of India — whose views on the Catholic and economic questions were more advanced, and who believed they could reunite with Grenville and rebuild Pitt's party of progress. This confusion would endure until both parties closed their ranks, till Whig and Radical either agreed or separated, or till reabsorption of the Sidmouth, Canning, and Grenville groups of Tories broke their accidental relation with the Whigs.

The ' Talents ' had little success either in diplomacy or war. Just before Pitt's death General Baird had recaptured the Cape from the Dutch, but Windham at the War Office was as bad as Dundas in allowing dispersal of our effort. One foolish expedition captured Buenos Ayres and Montevideo, but only to lose them again, merely antagonizing Spain without helping Spanish colonies to rebel. With the dual object of relieving Russia from her Turkish war and Austria from fears of Russian expansion, in February 1807 Admiral Duckworth passed the Dardanelles. But he failed through general mismanagement on the spot, leaving France supreme at Constantinople, while yet another expedition to seize Alexandria was unsuccessful. In July 1806 the British victory at Maida, the first on land over the French since Minden, saved Sicily, yet Naples was lost. While the Russians fought from Eylau to Friedland, the Grenville government refused loans, did nothing in the Adriatic, and sent no timely assistance to the Baltic.

At home it was weakened by faction, and the washing of much dirty linen. The squalid quarrel between the Prince and Princess of Wales induced it to appoint the ' delicate investigation ', which convicted the Princess of nothing more than vulgar indiscretion, but alienated the Prince and offended the people. Meantime the Lords dismissed the impeachment against Melville. Fox's death broke Grenville's best link with Canning, whom he was trying to win, and the election of 1806 made no change except in reducing the Addington members.

This government was formed on the understanding that Catholic emancipation in its full sense should not be pressed on the King, and Sidmouth for one could not have joined it otherwise. But the younger Whigs were restive, the Lord-Lieutenant warned them that, if nothing were done, he might have to use martial law, and a Catholic petition would split the Cabinet. Early in 1807, therefore, Grey proposed to allow Catholics to hold commissioned rank anywhere in the Empire, to the extent already legalized in Ireland. To this modest reform the King agreed, though stipulating ' not one step further '. When Grey, under Irish pressure, moved on, with a bill opening the highest commands in both army and navy, the King had a right to protest; Grenville withdrew the bill, but reserved their freedom of future action. At this, conceiving that the bargain was broken, and aware that Sidmouth would be on his side, in March the King asked a positive assurance of no further demands, whereupon the government resigned.

Before doing so they had carried one important measure, Windham's Act to abolish enlistment for life, a first necessary step to army reform, and all but the last formalities of another infinitely greater, the abolition of the slave trade. In 1792, against all the oratory of Pitt, Wilberforce, and Fox, Dundas had persuaded the Commons to a gradual abolition, 1796 being fixed as the destined year. Since that time, however, opposition in the Lords, mingling of the problem with revolutionary dangers, apathy in the country, had set the clock back; the Portland Whigs would not hear of its being made a Cabinet measure, Addington was hostile, and though Pitt continuously backed up Wilberforce's almost annual effort, when he came back to power he was weary, and harried by enormous dangers. He therefore put this question aside and the Abolition committee suspended its meetings.

But from 1800 onwards the ruling conditions changed for the good. That very year the government gave a charter to the company which had been struggling at Sierra Leone, with a settlement for freed slaves, its brave local agent, Zachary Macaulay, being one of the Clapham sect, whose influence over the churches and politics was yearly increasing. Perceval, a rising Tory hope, was a deeply sincere Christian; Canning also was an abolitionist, as Grenville always had been, and the trade itself was much divided; some business men were genuinely converted, while others with West Indian interests would stop the trade before it could restock their rivals, the conquered French and Dutch colonies. Irish members after the Union also generally voted with the cause. And so at the end of 1805 a first step was taken, in an Order in Council to prohibit the trade to the former Dutch colonies, and the ministry of the Talents took the great decision, having what Pitt's ministry never had, nine out of twelve in the Cabinet for abolition. Fox threw his last ounce of strength into the balance and in March 1807, the new Cabinet co-operating with the old, this great and righteous measure became law.

Portland, old, ill, and passive, was the figurehead Prime Minister from 1807 till the end of 1809, but, in fact, power was shared between those who had served with Sidmouth and those who had opposed him, this latter section, led by Canning, refusing to admit Sidmouth himself. Sooner or later this balance must be determined. It would tilt either to Perceval, now leader of the Commons, a fighting debater, a high-principled man, but a bigoted ' Protestant '; or to Canning with his insatiable ambition, his devotion to Pitt's memory, his rich eloquence, and his leaning to coalesce with Grenville and Wellesley; or, perhaps, to Liverpool, who might bridge the gulf — as the son of a ' King's friend ' but also an old friend of Canning, who had done most to reconcile Pitt and Sidmouth and was a shrewd conciliatory politician.

Their first step was the bold one of another dissolution, within a year of the last, which swept the country to the cry of Church and King and ' No Popery '. Canning was at the Foreign Office, Castlereagh minister for war, and their resistance to Napoleon during 1807 was determined and in many respects successful. Piecing together information and intuition in regard to what had happened at Tilsit, in August they anticipated the enemy by demanding from Denmark either alliance or neutrality; on refusal, British ships bombarded Copenhagen, and seized the Danish fleet. Danish Heligoland and the Dutch West Indies were occupied, and a British squadron, outpacing a French army, escorted the regent of Portugal to Brazil.

Napoleon's Continental system, inherited from the Directory, was taking final shape, now that he controlled every port in Europe outside the Spanish peninsula. Believing that the bubble of British credit could be burst, his decrees would have made her a commercial leper, destroying the exports by which she lived, and draining away her gold. Grenville's government began reprisals, the long series of Orders in Council, which Portland much expanded. Their effect, taken with our interpretation of prize law, largely at the hands of Eldon's brother Lord Stowell, was to declare France and her allies in a state of blockade, to prevent neutrals taking over the carrying-trade between France and the outside world, and to ' ration ' neutral trade in accord with our war-needs. Though something was done by licence to attract cargoes to our ports, all neutrals were indignant, and the United States in particular, at loss of markets, submission to our prize courts, and the ' right of search ' to discover concealed goods, or take off British deserters. This strangulation of trade became a race against time. Which would snap first ? The will to war of an island state, to whom neutral trading with France meant destruction ? The patience of British exporters, deprived of livelihood by American reprisals and restricted to trade in scanty convoys ? Or the patience of the neutrals, at the mercy of two belligerents ? The patience of French allies ? Of Russia, for instance, robbed of American goods and with her Baltic exports blocked ; or the endurance of France herself, deprived of every colonial product from tobacco to cotton, starved by a prohibitive tariff, driven to use beet for sugar and chicory for coffee, painfully smuggling British goods through creeks and crevices, by way of the Channel Islands, Heligoland, or Salonica ?

It was the weakness of Napoleon's system that it could only survive if it were made total, which led to his annexation of Tuscany, Corfu, Holland, and the Hanse towns ; even in 1808 there were signs that the Czar was discontented, Austria rearming, and Germany catching fire. British effort that year began with another unhappy expedition to buttress Sweden against a Russian invasion of Finland, but in May it was presented with a new opportunity in the national rising of Spain. Exploiting the scandals in the Spanish royal house, Napoleon transferred his brother Joseph from Naples to this greater crown ; spontaneous risings flamed out over the whole country, one French army was defeated at Baylen, and the patriots appealed to Britain.

In August Arthur Wellesley with a small force landed near Lisbon and beat Junot at Vimiera, but the senile generals who took over command stopped the pursuit, signing the wretched convention of Cintra which allowed the French to evacuate their army. In return for the gift of Finland and the principalities that later made Roumania, the Czar acknowledged Joseph's title and with Napoleon summoned Britain to make peace. Our reply was to send a new force under Sir John Moore, the best trainer of troops in the army, which from Lisbon would act on the left of what was hoped might be a vigorous Spanish front. But the Emperor himself with 200,000 veterans broke through like a thunderbolt and in December entered Madrid ; disappointed but misinformed, Moore still pressed on, in hope of drawing off the French from southern Spain. Forced to retreat at last, he marched 250 miles in nineteen days to the ships at

Corunna; there on the 16th January 1809 he made his stand, at the cost of his own life, while his shattered army was embarked.

While the French overran the Peninsula, a weak British force held on to Lisbon, whither in April Wellesley returned; having convinced the government that it could be held, and that there, and not from Cadiz, our effort should be made. Having driven Soult out of Oporto north-wards, he struck out for Madrid and, though outnumbered, beat Victor at Talavera. But a new advance of Soult again forced him south of the Tagus, while the demoralized Spaniards fell back on Andalusia. Fortunately for us, Napoleon ordered Soult to follow them, postponing his main attack on Portugal.

Sea-power, which enabled us to cut this gash in the enemy's side, in 1809 ranged in its captures from Martinique and St. Domingo to Senegal. But the hardest stress, and our greatest missed opportunity, came on land, for Austria had rebelled against France and the first German revolts broke out in Westphalia. After two months of discussion the Cabinet decided to strike at the Scheldt with an army of 40,000 men. Lack of transport, however, prevented it sailing till July, secrecy was lost and the French fleet escaped above Antwerp, our commander Chatham was unenterprising, and co-operation with the navy very bad. A prolonged siege of Flushing, on the island of Walcheren, destroyed any hope of surprising Antwerp, the dykes were cut, the troops knee-deep in water, and in September, when a quarter of our strength were sick, the survivors were brought home.

Long before that, after desperate fighting, Napoleon crushed the Austrians at Wagram; the peace of Vienna in October assigned her Polish lands to the puppet duchy of Warsaw, and her southern Slav lands, with Trieste, to France. The compact was sealed by Napoleon's divorce from Josephine and his marriage to the Archduchess Marie-Louise; at the same time he declared Rome the second city of his Empire, annexed the Papal States, and held the Pope prisoner. Only Wellington's small and so far inferior army, with a Portuguese force being hammered into shape by British officers, and the Spaniards hold-ing out in Cadiz, defied this universal monarchy.

Walcheren destroyed the Portland government, already disintegrat-ing for other reasons. Canning despised his colleagues, his nervous tension could not stand failure and unpopularity, he had objected both to Wellington's appointment and Moore's expedition. He believed the conduct of war could be improved by bringing in Marquis Wellesley, and early in 1809 threatened resignation unless Castlereagh were removed. The King and Portland agreed in principle but asked some delay, other ministers insisted that Castlereagh must at least be allowed to carry out the expedition he had planned; to Castlereagh himself not a word was said. And if the convention of Cintra and Moore's defeat dispirited the country, it was driven to fury by the exposure of the commander-in-chief, the Duke of York, whose cast-off mistress, encouraged by Radical politicians, testified to the sale of commissions through her influence.

Like the breaking of a sluice-gate this scandal released all the waters of reform. Two Radicals, Sir Francis Burdett and the bold sailor Lord Cochrane, held the great Westminster constituency, Grey's brother-in-law Whitbread was advancing bills for a new poor law and popular education, and the York enquiry, coming on top of Melville's impeachment, caused a distrust of public men, revealed the hatred of the royal house, and spread into charges of universal corruption. The Radicals carried a bill to prevent the sale of parliamentary seats ; another forbade the grant of offices for life, or in reversion. From Scotland, so long held firmly by the Dundas influence, new forces were emerging ; Brougham was leading against the Orders in Council and turning the *Edinburgh Review* into a liberal organ, Horner was working for currency reform. William Cobbett, whose *Political Register* reached classes not touched by Perry's Whig *Morning Chronicle*, had begun as a war Tory, but his Toryism looked back to an older England of yeomen and allowed him to act and write as a Radical.

Amid such discontents fell the fiasco of Walcheren, a final breakdown in Portland's health, Canning's insistence that Castlereagh should go instantly, and his own ambition to be supreme. The Prime Minister, he declared, must be in the Commons, nor would he serve under Perceval. The Cabinet, however, agreed with the King that Perceval, already leader of the House, should have the succession, and as Canning's resignation was followed by that of Castlereagh, now at last aware of the decision against him, and by a duel between them, they looked round for means of recruiting more strength. But Grey and Grenville declined to serve with a no-Popery government, Sidmouth was too unpopular with the Pittites and his followers refused to come in without him, so that the only important change was the substitution of Wellesley for Canning.

With only three commoners in it, the Cabinet was miserably weak — except for Perceval himself and Liverpool at the War Office — living also under sentence of death, for in 1810 the King's madness became permanent and a regency would presumably doom them. Repeated efforts were made to bring back Sidmouth, Castlereagh, or Canning, separately or together, but all collapsed on calculation, pride, or ambition ; throughout they had to contend with the sulky pomp of Wellesley, who looked to the Prince, intrigued with Canning, and wished more done for the Catholics. At home an angrier agitation faced them than any since Wilkes' day ; press attacks, bills against sinecures, trade-union lawlessness, and breaking of machines. From the cross-benches they were

fired at by Canning and the ' Saints '; Horner and Huskisson inspired
the bullion committee's report of 1810, which demanded a return to
cash payments. Ireland was almost under arms. Orders in Council
and American embargoes on trade to Britain, together with over-
speculation, produced unemployment and high prices; poor rates had
doubled since the outbreak of war, within the year 1810–11 our exports
fell by a third.

Of large or constructive design this Cabinet showed not a glimmer.
True, in ' no-Popery ' they had a really popular cause, some grounds
also for refusing to consider returning to cash payments till the war
ended, and agitation for parliamentary reform was confined to the
Radicals. But discontent they merely answered with repression. A
solid majority in the Lords, led by Eldon, turned down Romilly's
proposals to reduce the monstrous amount of capital punishment.
When Burdett raised the question of freedom of printing and publicity
of debate, the Commons sent him to the Tower; this straining of their
privilege was dragged to light by the lawsuit he brought against the
Speaker; the brigade of Guards and artillery had to hold down London.
Prosecutions silenced the violent Cobbett and even moderate criticism.

Yet, despite such shortcomings, the Perceval Cabinet founded the
Tory dominance that lasted till 1827; by no means, however, merely on
their own merits, for Opposition were in evil case. Whigs and Radicals
hated each other. Grey was out of sorts and out of humour, Lansdowne
was too young, Holland too ailing, and as all these were peers, the Whig
lead in the Commons went to George Ponsonby, a stopgap imported
from Ireland by Grey. For Whitbread was passionate and unpopular,
Brougham young and patently insincere, Tierney shifty, Sheridan had
lost all character. It was perhaps more important that the Prince had
turned Tory since Fox's death; he hated Grey, had weakened on the
Catholic question, and would not be accused of making impossible his
father's recovery. When therefore in 1811 he became Regent, in the
first instance for one year only, he made no change in his ministers.

Most of this was the doing of Perceval, who proved a debater of the
first order and a leader of boundless courage. Almost single-handed he
fought through a long tussle to carry the Regency Act, on the same lines
as that of 1788, and Tories felt an enthusiasm they had not known since
the youth of Pitt. Round him assembled the young future leaders in
Palmerston and Peel, while the Regency, violence in Ireland, and
Canning's eclipse drew the Addingtonians back towards the government
fold. Above all, while Grenville, Grey, the *Edinburgh Review*, and most
leading Whigs except Holland, despaired of the war, jeering at Wellington as a mere ' sepoy general ' and demanding withdrawal from Spain,
Perceval and Liverpool reaped the harvest of cleaving to a cause which
roused fervour in the young and raised the national character.

Meanwhile the Navy stopped up every exit, seizing every source of raw material and every strategical place of arms. Guadeloupe and Mauritius were won in 1810, Java in 1811; occupation of Sicily and blockade of Corfu kept open our contact with Italy and Austria; Cadiz was made impregnable, and the army in Portugal supplied. If the Peninsular war restored morale to the Army and hope to the country, the prime credit must go to the Cabinet. Economically the cost dismayed them; to get specie to Wellington at times seemed impossible, but they stuck to Liverpool's ideal of ' a steady and continued exertion on a moderate scale '. Avoiding the old fatal dispersion of effort, they were decided that this should be the single military front, never faltering in their principle that while Spain fought for liberty, they would never abandon her.

As Napoleon never returned to Spain, Joseph's flabby civilian nature had to cope with the jealousies of the marshals, Soult, Ney, Marmont, and Masséna. Their superiority in numbers of seasoned troops could neither close a long coast-line against our sea-power nor ensure their communications against Spanish guerrillas. Wellington had rehearsed in India his power of discipline, his incessant capacity for trying, and attention to the transport and supply by which armies live. Given time, he would make his own army superlative and the Portuguese reasonably efficient, and time he first secured by making, north of Lisbon, the fortified zone of Torres Vedras.

This saved him in the campaign of 1810, when Masséna uncovered the entry to Portugal by taking Ciudad Rodrigo and Almeida and, though sharply checked at Busaco, pressed on west to Coimbra, and beyond. In October the British fell back within their triple lines while Masséna, through a countryside made a desert, prowled round all the winter, until in March 1811 with his starving army he beat a retreat. Soult, delayed in taking Badajoz, came north too late to prevent this, and then Graham's sally out of Cadiz and victory at Barossa recalled him to the south. Again Masséna invaded Portugal, only to be beaten at Fuentes de Onoro while, in the bloody fight at Albuera, Beresford or rather the British infantry again stopped Soult's effort to break to the north. Neither of these victories owed much to our high command, almost everything to regimental officers and magnificent courage in the ranks; ' our dead ', said Beresford's despatch after Albuera, ' particularly of the fifty-seventh regiment, were lying as they had fought, in ranks, and every wound was in the front '. From midsummer Marmont, superseding Masséna, made his way to the upper Tagus, and the year closed with Wellington in eastern Portugal, Soult still pinned down by Cadiz, but the French hold tolerably intact on north-eastern Spain.

The memorable year 1812 opened at home with the fact that the

Regency became permanent and unrestricted, in anticipation of which, to force on his own schemes, Wellesley resigned. The Regent's invitation to Grenville and Grey, which they declined, broke down like others this year on a plain truth, that party feeling had now so hardened that compromise was impossible, either on the Catholic question or the war. Perceval decided a first step by putting Castlereagh at the Foreign Office and bringing back Sidmouth, but in May, Bellingham, a half-insane and bankrupt merchant, shot him dead in the lobby of the House of Commons.

The survivors resolved to go on under Liverpool as Prime Minister, with Castlereagh leading the Commons but, their invitations to Wellesley and Canning being refused, a Whig and Canningite vote for a stronger and more ' Catholic ' government forced them to resign. Once more the Regent tried his own solutions. Neither Whigs nor Tories, however, would serve under Wellesley or Canning, or the Whigs under Moira, the Prince's personal representative, without the reality of power. Hence he fell back again on Liverpool and the Tories. Strengthened by victory abroad, agreeing to make the Catholic question an ' open ' one in Cabinet, and to repeal the Orders in Council the new government made one last endeavour to conciliate Canning, who most foolishly declined the offer of the Foreign Office unless Castlereagh also surrendered the lead of the Commons. The general election this year was a government triumph, in which several Whig leaders lost their seats, and in 1813 some of Canning's followers took minor office, while he buried his pride in a mission to Lisbon.

During those months of British faction, Napoleon fought his fatal campaign to compel Russia to become a French helot. He battled through to Moscow, to find it a desert ; in November he was in retreat, having lost half a million men ; Prussia took fire and in February 1813 reached agreement with Russia for resolute war.

The British contribution to this mighty turn of the wheel was at first indirect, though persistent. Lord William Bentinck was sent to end the intolerable Bourbon misgovernment of Sicily, which by strong measures was made something nearer the bulwark of our Mediterranean effort that it should long have been. At the other extremity of our military circumference, by accepting his wish to acquire the crown of Norway we pushed Bernadotte, the French marshal who had become Crown Prince of Sweden, towards a break with his master. Pressure was brought to bear on the Adriatic and Balkans by occupying the Ionian Islands and making contact with the stalwart Ali Pasha of Janina, and early in 1812, as the first exploit in a long illustrious life, our envoy Stratford Canning negotiated peace between Russia and Turkey. These done, we rejected a hint from Napoleon that we might make peace by deserting Russia and Spain.

In the spring of 1812 Wellington, having perfected his transport, stormed the fortress keys of Ciudad Rodrigo and Badajoz, though the last was taken at a bloody cost, and in July proved his tactical precision when he pounced on Marmont's careless manœuvring at Salamanca. But, though he entered Madrid, he was soon forced back on Portugal, his advance having drawn Soult to the north. This at least meant the permanent loss of southern Spain to the French, whose young conscripts were being engulfed in the morasses of Russia and Germany.

In that year, and all through 1813, an unreasonable war with the United States threatened to cripple our effort to liberate Europe. Canning had missed one chance of a settlement; the confusion after Perceval's death delayed another. Our public opinion was now set against the Orders in Council, Brougham leading a popular campaign, while our new allies Sweden and Russia would demand relaxation of our blockade. But our suspension of the Orders in 1812 crossed an American declaration of war. This, in fact, mostly turned on their domestic politics, in which the presidencies of Jefferson (1801-9) and then of Madison, with Monroe as Secretary of State, installed a southern dynasty, generally hostile to Britain. Though New England and seafaring States were for peace, the south was for war, so too was the west, which was ardent for expansion and in conflict with Indians and frontiersmen who, they claimed, were incited from Canada. Meeting with British stubbornness in the matter of impressment of sailors, and deceived by illusory concessions from Napoleon, in 1811 Madison prohibited trade with Britain, and in 1812 declared war.

The Americans' power at sea and their excellent gunnery came as a shock to Britain, bringing the loss of over 1600 merchant ships and also of the great lakes. But though they spent much energy in pressing to Detroit and the north-west, they failed in more vital moves on the St. Lawrence and Montreal; if Toronto was burned, Canadians of both races for the first time realized themselves as a nation, and did wonders with their small numbers. Fired by a born leader of men, General Isaac Brock, they firmly held the Niagara peninsula. In 1814 veterans from Spain came to their aid, our Navy blockaded the coast and carried a force up the Chesapeake to sack Washington, though at the end of that year Andrew Jackson crushed our assault on the Mississippi at New Orleans.

By that time a peace conference had assembled, for American seaborne trade was almost annihilated and the British government, much influenced by Wellington's common sense, decided to end this distraction and withdrew their previous stiff demands. With peace in Europe some nominal causes for war, such as impressment, automatically ceased, so that both countries determined to ignore them. The treaty of Ghent (December 1814) stated therefore little more than a mutual restoration of territories, with a reference to joint commissions of other controversies, such as armaments on the lakes, fisheries, and frontiers.

All this had been a petty episode, if measured by the peril in Europe. We welcomed the Russo-Prussian agreement of 1813, and assisted them with subsidies, but for months the probabilities seemed either another jealous coalition or a European settlement without Britain — even against her. Hanover still divided us from Prussia, there was much resentment of our belligerent rights at sea, and most dangerous of all was the attitude of Austria. Metternich dreaded the spread of Russia over Poland, and feared German pretensions; was it not better to preserve a counterbalance in France, from whom Austria might acquire a larger share in Italy and a partition of Turkey? Though Austria offered an armed mediation, the Eastern Powers ignored Britain's special objects, such as the independence of Spain, while expecting us to throw all our colonial conquests into the bargaining scales. Even in October, after the allied victory at Leipzig, they offered France her natural frontiers of the Alps and the Rhine.

This serious drift was arrested, and reversed, by Napoleon's juggling and blindness, Wellington's victories, and the resolution of a great minister of foreign affairs in Castlereagh. He adhered to the spirit of the State-paper on which Pitt had consulted him in 1805, which in turn ran back to Grenville's proposals of 1798. Only ' large masses ', its argument ran, could restrain France; Prussia therefore must be brought west of the Rhine; Austria must be built up in Italy; Holland must make another strong barrier, and Sardinia also. This point of view made the ' natural frontiers ' too wide; moreover, we must fulfil our pledges to Spain and Portugal, Sicily and Sweden, nor should we surrender conquered colonies until satisfied as to the shape of Europe. Finally, he reverted to the conclusion of all Pitt's experience, of no negotiation except in common, and after the peace a defensive guarantee.

Suspicious of Austrian sincerity, alarmed by the Allies' quarrels and our ambassadors' feebleness, in January 1814 the Cabinet sent Castlereagh himself to the scene of action. To reduce France to safer limits, to save Antwerp, to redeem our pledges, he had strong weapons in his hand : £5 millions to offer in subsidies, 200 ships of the line and 300 frigates, and Wellington's army.

In Spain the French held the north-east in force, in part because Bentinck had subordinated his duty of attacking from Sicily to his own notions of ' liberalizing ' Italy. But their supply difficulties were immense and, while they painfully chased the guerrillas, Wellington shifted his sea-base north to Santander and in May 1813 moved into Spain with astonishing speed. Pushing over the Douro, for ever turning the French right, in June he broke Joseph's army at Vittoria, and was soon investing Saint Sebastian and Pampeluna in the Pyrenees. Despite

Soult's skill in defence, through wild country the British had by November made their way over the Bidassoa and to St. Jean-de-Luz, in March 1814 entering Toulouse.

While these victories buttressed him on the south, and while an Orange revolt gave point to our insistence on freeing Holland, Castlereagh at the congress of Châtillon struggled through the decisive months that ended in Napoleon's abdication. He had to combat Metternich's wish for an armistice, and the Czar's dangerous alternatives of making Bernadotte King of France or summoning a French constituent assembly. To him was due, after Napoleon's last victories on the Seine, the treaty of Chaumont (1st March), by which each of the four Allies would keep 150,000 men in the field, Britain in addition paying £5 millions a year in subsidies, and bound themselves in a defensive alliance for twenty years. At this moment only the fortunes of war could decide the two fundamentals : what should be the frontiers of France, and with whom in France terms should be made. As to the first, the impetus of military advance and Castlereagh's pressure swept away the Austrian suspicion of their allies, and it was agreed to offer nothing more than the frontiers of 1792. If Napoleon had closed promptly with this offer, Austria certainly and perhaps Britain would have left him on the throne, but he refused to hear of giving up Belgium or the Rhine, and made himself impossible by insincerity. Once decided on this, Castlereagh was clear there was no mean between Napoleon and a restoration of the Bourbons, in whose favour British opinion was well in advance of the Cabinet, and some of whose princes had appeared at Bordeaux to raise the white banner of their house. All this, with Talleyrand's stage management in Paris, crumbling in the army, and desertion by some of the marshals, made it possible to say that the Allies were accepting the will of the French people. In April Napoleon abdicated and departed to the gilded cage assigned him in Elba, in May the Allies signed the treaty of Paris with Louis XVIII.

British and Russian policy combined to give Bourbon France a generous restoration. The peace asked no indemnities and, though the war had cost Britain £600 millions, her gains were limited to those vital for her life-line east and west, Malta and Mauritius, St. Lucia and Tobago, the Dutch colonies at the Cape and Demerara; for which Holland was to receive £2 millions in compensation. As to the ' just equilibrium ' so often declared, Holland was to be extended southward at least to the Scheldt, Sardinia would receive Genoa, Austria would get Venetia and part of Lombardy. But some most arduous questions, such as the future of Poland and Germany and Murat's kingdom in Naples, were left over to a future congress.

At last the horrors of war seemed gone, Napoleon was planting mulberries at Elba, the House of Commons rose to cheer Castlereagh, the allied sovereigns were richly feasted in London. Yet when the congress opened at Vienna in September, it was seen that peace was still unborn. It would be made and kept, Castlereagh wrote, not by insurrections but only by ' disciplined force under sovereigns that we can trust ', when a million Bonapartist soldiers resented the spectacle of a Bourbon throne, propped on foreign bayonets, and the Allies' concert was endangered by the ambition of the Czar, who claimed all Poland for his own. Against this double threat of France and Russia it was Castlereagh's object to construct a central barrier in Austria and Prussia. If Prussia, however, was to lose her share of Poland, she insisted on receiving the whole of Saxony, which would bring her to the edge of Austrian Bohemia. To this, under heavy British pressure, Metternich agreed, on the understanding that Prussia would help her to keep her old Polish frontier, and meet her wishes in the rest of Germany. But the King of Prussia went over to the Czar, and at the new year of 1814–15 the Allies were on the verge of war between themselves. Here was the golden chance for Talleyrand to divide his enemies, for the small States of Germany to rally round Metternich, and for the Whig Opposition in Britain to clamour for Polish nationality.

When the Prussian military party threatened war and the Cabinet sent instructions he must at all costs avoid it, Castlereagh boldly accepted the greatest responsibility ever taken by a British minister. In January he signed a secret treaty with Austria and France, which Bavaria and Holland should be invited to subscribe, for joint action against a Prussian attack. This was his clearest triumph. Prussia gave way, receiving only about two-thirds of Saxony but acquiring Thorn from Russia and the left bank of the Rhine ; Cracow became a free city, though the bulk of Poland was to be Russian under a pledge of separate institutions. Talleyrand also received his price, for it was agreed that Murat should be evicted from Naples.

But Murat had taken precautions to avoid this ; on the 1st March 1815, as Castlereagh was travelling back to England, Napoleon landed in the south of France. Within a week most of his marshals and the bulk of the army had come over, while Louis XVIII fled to Ghent. This counter-revolution, as Napoleon divined, could only succeed if it rested on the people. He took up again his rôle of 1799, dabbled in constitution-making, and protested his wish to keep the peace, as most Frenchmen certainly desired. Was Britain then, false to her own tradition, to force on France the reactionary Bourbons ?

In such a spirit Grey and Grenville, Wellesley and Whitbread, opposed renewal of war, but though the Allies hesitated to pronounce for the Bourbons, on Napoleon they spoke with unanimity. Declaring that he must be given over to public justice, they renewed the treaty of Chaumont and prepared a great converging invasion ; Britain, said

Liverpool, could not stand apart, ' without giving up all hopes of ever rallying Europe again '.

Powerful reasons, then, decided Napoleon to strike when and where he did. Action would anticipate the Allies' cumbrous mobilization, reward the enthusiasm of his soldiers, and silence doubters at Paris ; successful action in Belgium would crush the two best-prepared of his enemies, win the sympathy of his old Belgian subjects, and perhaps bring down the Liverpool government.

Disarmament and the American war had weakened the British forces, so that only some 21,000 British were in the 67,000 men under Wellington at Waterloo, and Napoleon found them and the Prussians strung out over 150 miles from Ostend to Liége. His masterly move caught them unready and uncertain of his direction when, on the 14th June, he struck at the hinge between their armies at Charleroi, whence ran the road to Brussels. Though neither his own energy nor the grasp of his commanders reached their old level, two fierce encounters of the 16th gave him a half success, and at Ligny he badly mauled Blücher's army, driving it north-eastwards. He was robbed, however, of the co-operation he counted on from his left wing under Ney at Quatre Bras, who dallied so long that he became engaged in a full-dress battle. For Wellington, fearful of a move to outflank his right and cut him from the Channel ports, began that day with a bare 7000 men in position, and though by nightfall reinforcements raised that figure to some 30,000, it was a chaotic battle, fought until both sides were exhausted. Retreat Wellington must, to keep touch with the Prussians, but the retreat on the 17th had some bad moments and was only made possible by Ney's incompetence.

The Duke now gave Blücher his word he would fight, if he got the help of even one Prussian corps, and had marked down the spot where to make his stand. Before the Charleroi highroad to Brussels passes through the forest of Soignies, in which the village of Waterloo lies, it rises very gently to cross the plateau of Mont-St.-Jean. From this ridge northwards the ground fell away, affording fair cover ; southwards a country road, protected variously by hedges and embankment, crossed the whole front from east to west ; forward of that again the stone farm-house of La Haye-Sainte in the centre of the slope and the château and wood of Hougoumont, some thousand yards forward from the British right, made outposts to a strong position. Behind in Soignies and away to the east were woods, but the valleys and the slope were full of corn, though now beaten down by pitiless rain. About 1300 yards south of Mont-St.-Jean was another ridge, and on it an inn called La Belle Alliance ; this was the destined centre of the French line, behind which they bivouacked this night.

When Sunday the 18th June broke, dull and showery, neither side had mustered all their strength. Still nervous of a turning movement round his right, Wellington had 17,000 men in reserve ten miles north-west at Hal. But Napoleon made two, much more false, assumptions. He believed that the Prussians were too demoralized to fight again at once and, misled by bad staff work, also believed they had retreated towards Liége and the Meuse; whereas they had rallied at Wavre on the Dyle, only ten miles or so east of the British. Meantime he had detached Grouchy with 30,000 men to follow them north-eastwards, as he did with dilatory literalness for twenty-four fatal hours. On the ground, then, Wellington had some 67,000 men against 74,000, with 184 guns against 246.

It was a desperate battle, — ' the nearest run thing you ever saw in your life ', said Wellington next day, — since both armies were fighting against time. The opening artillery began at 11.35, but it was not till 4.30 that Blücher struck on the French right and rear, and not till about 7 that another Prussian corps formed up on the British left. Twice the British seemed to be overwhelmed; once just after noon when the French reached the cross-road, only to be swept off it by a massed cavalry charge, and again about 7, when La Haye-Sainte fell, leaving a gap in our centre. But that success came too late.

Never did the French show themselves braver, but neither their high command nor their tactics were worthy of that courage. Instead of masking Hougoumont, or shattering it by artillery, they turned what Napoleon had intended as a diversion into a continuous battle, which used up thousands of their infantry. Again, their infantry attacks proved once more the mistake of pitting dense columns against the British deployed firing-line. Finally, Ney prematurely committed nearly all the cavalry, leading four charges packed in the narrow front between La Haye and Hougoumont, against unbroken infantry squares, enfilading fire, and the bayonet. Not till these were beaten back, exhausted, did he press forward his infantry again.

When he made the attack that took La Haye at last, the Prussians' arrival made it doubly too late. For Napoleon could not reinforce him, having to use some of the guard in repelling Blücher on his right, while other Prussian columns, reaching the English left, allowed Wellington to move troops to his breaking centre. It was against this reinforced front that Ney led the last crowded mass of the guards' infantry. The sun had just set when, at 8.15, the Duke ordered a general advance; by nine the French flight had become a rout. The British losses were nearly 15,000 in killed and wounded, the Prussians' about 6000, the French 25,000 and more thousands taken prisoner.

Napoleon having abdicated in favour of his son, the Allies' rapid advance, despair at Paris, and the management of Talleyrand and

Fouché, made a second Bourbon restoration easy; in July Napoleon surrendered to the British ships at Rochefort, and duly departed as a captive to the distant island of St. Helena. There still remained the settlement with France in which Britain, with assistance from the Czar, played the great part; though not Britain, indeed, so much as Castlereagh and Wellington. While the Allied troops pillaged, and while the Germans demanded Alsace-Lorraine, the Saar, and every powerful fortress, Wellington pointed to our pledges to the French people and argued that France, if stripped and held under, would turn revolutionary. Castlereagh criticized the folly of ' scratching ' a great Power, contending that our first object must be to ' bring back the world to peaceful habits ', while France could also be made a counterweight to the might of Russia.

Resisting British and Allied sentiment, these two men convinced the Cabinet, and carried through the second peace of Paris. By this France received, roughly, the frontiers of 1790, losing Landau, Saarlouis, and small strips in Belgium and Savoy; she paid an indemnity of 700 million francs and restored the artistic treasures looted in the long war. An army of occupation, under Wellington's command, was to hold certain northern fortresses for five years.

One other concession Castlereagh could now wring from Louis XVIII, which meant more to British feeling and the world's future than changes of territory. The national sentiment for universal abolition of the slave trade was ardent and organized, but in 1814 all that he had been able to achieve was an offer from France and all other States, except Spain and Portugal, of abolition within five years. Since then, however, Napoleon had ordered instant abolition and this the restored Bourbons accepted, together with our proposal for an international commission to give it effect. One or two other matters left over at Vienna had now solved themselves, or were quickly disposed of. Murat condemned himself by taking up arms against Austria and perished at the hands of the Neapolitans. For lack of a better custodian, and from disagreement between Russia and Austria, Great Britain became protector of the Ionian Islands. All the Powers guaranteed the neutrality of Switzerland.

It remained to clinch the peace by that wider guarantee which our ministers had long sought. To them the ' Holy Alliance ' put forward by the Czar, whereby all the Continental sovereigns pledged themselves to observe Christian principles, seemed meaningless, while they saw danger in Alexander's notion of guaranteeing the form of French government. The quadruple alliance drafted by Castlereagh, and signed in November, was more limited and rational; binding the Allies to maintain the treaty of Paris, to joint measures against a Bonapartist restoration, and to hold conferences at regular intervals to consider whatever seemed required for ' maintenance of the peace of Europe '.

This was the climax of the settlement of 1815. There were flaws in it, as liberal opinion thought at the time, and as later events were to prove; pledges given during the war which, when translated into fact, proved unpopular or unfitting, like the annexation of Norway to Bernadotte's Sweden, or subjection of Belgium to a Dutch dynasty; while Italy must, one day, so mature in strength and feeling as to throw off the dominance given to Austria. As a whole, it represented too narrowly the fears of a generation to whom popular institutions had come to mean anarchy, nor did the concert of Europe of Castlereagh's making contain the machinery for necessary change. But a great evil and a great despotism had been overthrown, and Europe had substantial peace for thirty years. During which Great Britain achieved, without bloodshed but amid turmoil and strain, her own long-postponed revolution.

CONTEMPORARY DATES

1802 The peace of Amiens.
      Marquis Wellesley makes treaty of Bassein.
      Foundation of *Edinburgh Review*.
1803 Reopening of war.
1804 Napoleon, Emperor of the French.
      Schiller, *William Tell*.
1805 Ulm ; Austerlitz ; Trafalgar.
      Walter Scott, *Lay of the Last Minstrel*.
1806 End of the Holy Roman Empire.
      The Sikh Ranjit Singh makes terms with the British.
1807 Death of Henry, Cardinal of York.
      Stein and Scharnhorst at work in Prussia
      Fulton's steamboat in the Hudson.
1808 Joseph Bonaparte, King of Spain.
      Beethoven, Fifth Symphony.
1809 Aspern and Wagram ; Corunna and Talavera.
      Metternich becomes Austrian Chancellor.
      Birth of Gladstone, Abraham Lincoln, and Charles
          Darwin.
1810 Republican governments set up in South America.
      Madame de Staël, *L'Allemagne*.
1811 Battle of Albuera.
      Jane Austen, *Sense and Sensibility*.
1812 Napoleon at Moscow.
      Badajoz and Salamanca.
      War with the United States.
      Hegel's *Logic*.
      Byron, *Childe Harold*.
1813 Rising of Germany ; battle of Leipzig.
      Elizabeth Fry visits the prisons.

1814   Napoleon in Elba.
　　　　Ferdinand of Spain overthrows constitution of 1812.
　　　　Treaty of Ghent.
　　　　Scott, *Waverley.*
　　　　Wordsworth, *Excursion.*
1815   Waterloo ; Congress of Vienna, and second peace of
　　　　　　Paris.
　　　　Macadam, surveyor-general of the roads.

CHAPTER VI

THE CONSTITUTION IN 1815

THE stages in the evolution of our government, last sketched in detail before the revolution wrought by Henry VIII, have appeared broadly in the unrolling of the two succeeding centuries. We survey it once more as it stood about 1815, before it passed through changes more radical than any since the Angevins.

What had been begun by the Tudors was completed as against the Stuarts, and never challenged again. Generation by generation, government was transformed from one of a mediaeval to one of modern type, in the sense that moral notions of custom or fundamental law made way for the legal concept of sovereign power; and this a power not resting in the Crown, but shared between King in Parliament and the common law. This particular solution of sovereignty, so unlike that reached in other countries, was due to the continuous strength in a small, undisturbed, and therefore conservative country of its mediaeval rule, that law and the consent of his people bind the King.

We have seen the last decisive clash in the Civil War — or, rather, on its eve in 1641. By the consent of both parties in that year the Star Chamber, High Commission, and Council of the North were swept away; so too were the arbitrary powers and the original jurisdiction (though not its powers on appeal) of the Council itself. Nor after the universal revolt against impositions and ship-money would it be possible to use unparliamentary taxation on a large scale. These protests of Parliament and the law triumphed even over the Protectorate and its military necessities. In 1660 we therefore enter a new constitutional epoch, which endured until 1760 at least, and in which the controversy was not whether King in Parliament and common law were supreme but rather the respective shares within that sphere as between the partners.

This supremacy carried within it some vital consequences.

(1) The life of Parliament became continuous. Between 1603 and 1640, for instance, its total sessions added up to only four years and a half; between 1681 and 1685 it did not meet at all. All this was changed at the Revolution of 1688 and driven home by the creation of credit as the means of financing government, which made regular meetings of the Commons imperative.

(2) Local government was brought within the same arena. The

judges' decision of 1610 that royal proclamations could not make new law; the downfall in 1641 of the Council's means of enforcing obedience; the end of forfeiting borough charters by *Quo Warranto*; by such steps local government was left to the administration of ministers, the rules of common law, and for larger matters to private bills in Parliament.

(3) Within the ambit of Parliament were incorporated, one after another, every new extension of sovereignty. This could be illustrated by Henry VIII's Church legislation or his statute of Wales, the Union Act of 1707 with Scotland, the Acts regarding Ireland of 1719 and the Union of 1801, the new charters issued to the Colonies after 1689 by Parliament, no longer by the Crown, or the revised charters given to the East India Company and the Bank of England.

(4) It was now in Parliament, rather than in the Crown, that the State was envisaged as an undying corporation. That was implicit in the Act of 1696, whereby an existing Parliament was to continue six months after the sovereign's death, as well as in the many Regency Acts, such as those of 1706 and 1788.

(5) A very large increase in the Commons' numbers testified much less to royal wish for influence than to a growing demand to be represented. There were only 298 members in 1509, but 467 by 1603, and 558 after 1707. From Charles II's time onwards any additions were made by statute, and no longer by prerogative.

(6) Time out of mind, the method of advance had been one of taking over royal prerogatives and absorbing them in the ordinary law. Sometimes this had come about by royal cession, as the Tudors brought the Welsh lords' marcherships under statute; sometimes by resistance from the common-law courts, as with their writs of prohibition against High Commission; sometimes, and more commonly in later days, by direct attack through statute. Such, for example, were the Bill of Rights' restriction on the royal dispensing power, the triennial and septennial Acts, or the clause in the Act of Settlement which forbade a royal pardon to bar an impeachment. One late instance arose over the Army, originally controlled by the royal constable and marshal. The Petition of Right had merely laid down that martial law could not be used in time of peace, but in fact military discipline was necessary, whether in peace or war. Since the Bill of Rights, consequently, Parliament has annually renewed its consent to the legal existence of an army and by many Mutiny Acts ratified a code of military law, at the same time providing by other statutes for the government of the militia.

(7) Not the powers only, but the structure of government went through the same process. Many times over, one part of government after another had gone ' out of court ' — Exchequer, Chancery, and Privy Seal; even the Star Chamber in its later days became a public

court, in which common lawyers acted as counsel. After 1689 any serious change or expansion was made by ministers after parliamentary debate; so in 1710 statute established the Postmaster-General, while in 1794 a third secretaryship of State appeared, for War, which in 1801 was given charge of the Colonies also. The Rockingham Whigs and Pitt, again, brought under Parliament the old prerogative organs of the Secretary-at-War and the Board of Trade.

(8) All this meant that the distinction which fourteenth-century reformers aspired to draw between the private and public capacities of the King had at last been determined. Of this a manifest proof lay in the royal civil list : the assignment by Parliament of revenues to the Crown for personal and ceremonial purposes, all other charges being borne by the Exchequer. It was fixed at £700,000 for William III, and at rather more for the Hanoverians, but it was not till William IV's day that it was finally relieved of all public payments, such as the salaries of judges and ambassadors.

So prerogative had gone, or been absorbed into parliamentary usage. No sovereign after William III vetoed a major bill, none after Anne any bill (except a bill of a Colonial legislature) at all. The prerogative of dissolving Parliament was used in 1784 at the discretion of the younger Pitt, in 1806 on the request of Grenville, and in 1807, within a year, in order to establish Portland. What remained to the King was the ' influence ' we have seen wielded by the Georges, a mixed mass of legal powers, patronage, and conventions, subtle and sometimes dangerous, but in the last resort defenceless against a resolute Cabinet or Parliament. All the King's influence could not have waged the American War or resisted Catholic claims without large support in Cabinet and people, while alike in 1757, 1806, and 1812 the Crown failed to form a government to its own liking.

Of this absorption of prerogative the supreme case was Cabinet government, a growth brought about by usage and in terms unknown to the law. Like all else in our central institutions it had come out of the Council, having descended from the ' foreign committee ' to which the old-fashioned privy council of Charles II left its vital or secret business. How unpopular this development was the Act of Settlement of 1701 had proved, by its attempt to restore the Privy Council as the working executive, but that clause was repealed in 1705 since experience showed that, whatever it was called, some such small body, amenable to Parliament, was indispensable.

Yet Cabinet government in our sense was unknown in the days of Walpole, and here, as in so many other ways, the decisive period came after 1782 ; in part from accident like the weakening mentality of the King or the general contempt for the Regent, but still more from the new stirring of party and positive action. Restriction of ' influence ' by the Burke reforms, and the fall of the King's friends, much enhanced the office of Prime Minister; the Cabinet became more coherent, without the old distinction between an inner and an outer group; the ejection of Thurlow in 1792 or of Sidmouth in 1805 illustrated the tighter bonds of discipline. Even so, it was very far to go to the modern system. Organized party being yet in its infancy, a high proportion of members were independents, totally uncontrolled by ministers or any machine; besides which the old view of the Constitution still prevailed, which made it one of separated powers, each with a proper legal rôle. How powerful was the Crown was yet to be seen in 1820–22, and in Lord Grey's struggle to carry the Reform Bill.

In this supremacy of the King in Parliament the share of the Lords had much dwindled since Tudor days, however great the local influence of individual peers. By a rule the reverse of that applying to the Commons, it had diminished in ratio with an increase of their numbers. There were 60 temporal peers when Elizabeth died, 176 just before the Scottish Union, and in 1806 just on 330. They had thereby come down from their lofty patrician estate to become part of a Prime Minister's patronage, or his route to power. With every wider diffusion of wealth the proportionate weight of the Commons must gain, and their power of the purse grow more decisive. By resolutions of 1670–71 they had refuted the Lords' claim to amend money bills, and though the number of peers in most Cabinets was much greater than it is now, the driving-wheel of every ministry after Walpole's was its majority in the Commons.

Such power was easily abused, for they were becoming increasingly unrepresentative, their debates were not printed until after 1770, and their own privileges were stretched out to tyranny. Freedom from arrest was extended to cover their debts, or offences of their game-keepers; freedom of election, to claim that their resolution could determine the validity of an individual's vote or, as in Wilkes' case, to declare a minority candidate legally elected; their power to commit for contempt was scandalously used against alleged ' Papists ' during the Plot, and against printers in the eighteenth century. But this danger from a tyrannous House of Commons was arrested by the same force which had curbed a tyrannous King — the common law.

Indeed everything, good and bad, most characteristic of the Constitution in the three hundred years from Henry VIII to George IV must be attributed to a historic fact — that it had grown like a coral reef round this venerable common law. Long before new Councils were devised to give remedies for new problems, its tough strength had decided that law in England is the law applied by a court, and had built up a frame-work of specific writs and indictment and punishment, within which justices of the peace or any other new legal engine must be fitted. From the fourteenth century onwards, until their triumph in the seventeenth, the courts insisted that there were some things which no royal council or new-fangled tribunal could do, as, for instance, to take away a man's life or freehold; except in the partial instance of Chancery, they defeated every attempt to apply any law but the single common law, added to by statute but interpreting each statutory addition as part of something larger and more venerable.

So in many memorable cases, and in ages when everywhere in Europe public liberties were being quenched, English law defended freedom. The Habeas Corpus Act of 1678 cleared of doubt, once for all, the principle of Magna Carta, that a prisoner is entitled to a speedy and public trial by his peers; henceforward to deny that right necessitated a suspension of the Act by Parliament, as happened in days of stress such as 1715 or 1817. Juries might, indeed, be stampeded by sentiment, but the mere existence of trial by jury was enough in 1794 to prevent Pitt's government proceeding to extremes against reformers, and often made the law officers hesitate to prosecute. Many an English family held slaves in Virginia or Jamaica, but if the nabob or planter brought a black boy on to British soil, to stand behind his chair in a silver collar or wave his mistress' fan, the slave became free; as Mansfield majestically laid down in Somerset's case in 1772.

This vindication of liberty was pursued against political majorities in Parliament itself, and that perhaps was the best legal achievement of the eighteenth century. Acting not in the name of high-sounding rights of man but by prosaic deduction from habeas corpus or the law of nuisance, the judges consistently protected the subject against ministers and Parliament. Thus Holt in the case of Ashby v. White of 1704 ruled that the Commons' resolution alone could not make law, or deprive a citizen of his franchise. So, in the controversies circling round Wilkes, Camden demolished the Secretary of State's supposed power to arrest on a general warrant — declaring, as Coke would surely have declared too, ' with respect to the argument of State necessity or a distinction which has been aimed at between State offences and others, the common law does not understand that kind of reasoning '. And so in 1798, even on behalf of the rebel Wolfe Tone, the Irish judges insisted that no such thing as martial law existed in the British realms.

As a defensive system, no stronger vehicle for the common good has been known than British law, but it suffered from the very virtue of its origins, that it had grown upward from the soil of vested right and was administered by immemorial self-governing bodies. These rights and bodies, having prevailed in the seventeenth century, had ever since gone their own way, till by 1815 we see plainly that they were wholly unfit to deal with a new age. Such modernization as had been achieved had been done piecemeal, as by Pitt's reforms of some central depart-

ments, by setting up ' improvement commissioners ' in large towns to
control water or drainage, by some statutory local bodies to deal with
the poor, or by giving London a few paid magistrates. But such steps
merely added new tiers or wings to an old fabric, antiquated beyond
repair. For the county franchise had not changed since 1430, distribution of seats had hardly altered since Elizabeth, the commission of the
peace kept the powers given in 1590 down to 1875, Stuart charters and
Laudian statutes governed Victorian boroughs and universities. Every
public office was full of mediaeval relics, as the Exchequer preserved the
clerk of the pells or the surveyor-general of green wax ; every ancient
endowment for charity or education was administered, sometimes
decently but more often ill, in accord with conditions long passed away.

It was certain that one thing only could close this gulf, or become the
pre-condition of all that must be done to harmonize government with
the new society ; that is, a reform of Parliament itself. As it stood
in 1815, the representative body was wholly unrepresentative. The
distribution of seats had been notoriously so, even under the Commonwealth. A quarter of the Commons were returned by the five south-
western shires, Cornwall alone accounting for 44 ; whereas the area we
now call Greater London returned only 10, and many large towns —
Birmingham, Leeds, and Manchester among them — were not represented at all. Of 558 members, 405 sat for English boroughs, but of
those 203 boroughs the 23 northern counties held only 74 ; some three-
quarters of the boroughs had electorates of less than 500, and a high
proportion of very much less. As for the franchise, for the 80 county
members in England the voting qualification of a 40s. freehold had not
budged since 1434 ; during which time an extension of leaseholds made
a freeholders' monopoly ridiculous. However, by dint of manufacturing
freeholds for each occasion and by growth of population, an average
county electorate was rather over 4000— reaching 20,000 in Yorkshire
— and the boroughs caused the real scandal. Except for a dozen or so
with a wide residential vote — Westminster being much the greatest —
they were divided into four classes of qualification, each of them
mediaeval or out of date ; those where freemen of the borough had
the vote, those where it went to citizens who paid ' scot and lot ' (the
equivalent of rates), those where it was restricted to members of the
corporation, and those where it was attached to the sites of mediaeval
tenements, called ' burgages '. Each type contained its own absurdities.
The burgage voters of Old Sarum were only 7, and the wide household
voters of Gatton numbered only 6 ; a pocket borough could be made
almost equally safe by multiplying freemen as by bribing a corporation.
On the whole, it seems that nearly half the English seats were in the
hands of patrons, the Crown included, though such government influence
had much diminished since 1782.

Scotland was in much worse case. Its total electorate was barely over 4000; the royal burghs were ruled by small, self-chosen councils; Walpole's and the Pelhams' administrations, and the long career of Henry Dundas, proved that, given time and money, a government could make of Scotland almost one large pocket borough.

If all this were not changed, the monarchy could still obstruct ministers who had no mandate behind them; provincial aristocracies, or effete corrupt corporations, would still go their own way; the law would still be exploited to block any change. Much good, no doubt, could be accomplished by a strong minister, even under the old system, as Pitt and Canning had shown, but not the essentials of popular government: of a real Cabinet, organized parties, and the dominance of public opinion.

CHAPTER VII

CONDITION OF THE PEOPLE IN 1815

As with their government, so both the outer life and inner thinking of the people continued little changed, to a surprisingly late date. Their real revolution, if dates can be applied to ceaseless growth, had not occurred in 1688 but about a century after. In early Georgian England we find still existing the fabric of the Cecils and the Protectorate, in masses of open fields, domestic workers and peasant farmers, tiny cottages of wattle and daub, universities more than half given to training a priesthood, and life set within the frame made by Renaissance and Reformation.

How economic pressures broke down that ancient scheme, we have seen in part, and are to see again, but there were other changes proceeding, equally important. For though history knows no rigid compartments, and though such terms as ' classical ' or ' romantic ' mask a hundred degrees and shades, it is possible to give a character of its own to the century following 1660 or 1688. More, indeed, by way of negatives than by positive quality; for it had lost much as well as gained.

Religion in its former sense, as the cement of society and justification of man, had disappeared, and must somehow be reconciled with the triumphant forces of natural philosophy, tolerance, and opinion. And we cannot measure their state of mind, as in older days, by illustration from a few great writers, since opinion had descended from the closet of Bacon or Donne to the street, even Grub Street, to the coffee-house, and public debate. Individuals may, indeed, outlive their age, and even after Restoration we meet with those — Sir Thomas Browne of the *Religio Medici*, Otway the dramatist, L'Estrange the Tory press censor, a few clerics of Anne's reign — who link us to what has gone before. But we have only to read the main body of Dryden, to open the Augustans in Swift, Addison, and Pope, or men whose fame was made under George II like Johnson and Chesterfield, to realize we are breathing a new air.

Its inhabitants over two generations included very great figures: Locke, Newton, Wren, Swift, and Pope; Johnson, Hume, Fielding, Burke, Reynolds, Blackstone, Warren Hastings, Gibbon, and Adam Smith. Men use such terms as ' Augustan ' of their literature, ' Palladian ' of their building, ' classical ' of their view of government; their achievements embrace St. Paul's, the building of Bath and many hundred superb houses, the school of portraiture which went on from Reynolds to Gainsborough, Raeburn, Romney, and Lawrence, the human arts of Hogarth, Fielding, and Goldsmith, the philosophy which assisted America and France into revolution, as well as the energy of inventors and men of commerce. Varying infinitely from man to man, these powerful individuals, unregulated by any uniform education, standardized press, or all-absorbing civil service, did nevertheless all partake of a certain fixed outlook. Their philosophy, and often their religion, was one of common sense; the Deist school, and for that matter many divines, had argued away the miraculous or transcendental, they shunned and disliked enthusiasm, and one feels that their heavenly citizens would be clad in broadcloth. Their classical training, the teaching they took freely from France, and their new science, all alike induced them to search for system; their instinct was to take the broad sweep, to plan thought as they planned landscape gardening, to generalize from their reading of experience to the rights and properties of man, his reasonableness, and his benevolence. They were, again, a generation of aristocrats, not by noble blood, much as they admired it, but in spirit; and that was inevitable, considering the dearth of elementary education and the barbarity of an eighteenth-century mob. They had, finally, a sense of satisfaction, of complacency, in the civilization of their age and country, as we may judge from the serene portraits of their leaders and the undoubting prejudices of their thought.

They were therefore apt to write off the Middle Ages and paint earlier history as ' Gothic ', and to dismiss what was obscure or embittered, as Johnson dismissed the seventeenth-century poets; what was original could not make appeal to those who admired the sweet platitudes of Addison, or pruned Shakespeare to fit their rules. The vehicle of their thought was an admirable prose, that of Dryden, Tillotson, Swift, and Hume, plain and sinewy and persuasive. They had rationalized everything, Christianity included, even the strongest Christian treatise of the age, Butler's *Analogy of Religion*, defending dogma on the ground that it conformed to the teaching of Nature; from and by Nature's gift to man, of Reason, they deduced the laws of conduct and civic rights. In all this they were much swayed by the liberal thought of France, of Voltaire, Condorcet, and the economists, who were sweeping their country clean of all but a few strong dominant ideas.

Nowhere was the change since the passionate seventeenth century better seen than in Scotland, whose intellectual golden age covered the reigns of the second and third Georges. Scotsmen, in particular Hartley and Reid and Hutcheson, polished this philosophy of the senses and common sense; a moderate school, under men like Robertson the historian, captured the high places in the Kirk; Adam Smith founded modern economic thinking. Most dynamic of all was David Hume, who pricked all the bubbles in the once venerated abstract rights and original contract, and by pushing the rule of reason into scepticism put an end to the classic system. For this ' eighteenth century ', whose real dates ran from about 1670 to 1760, ignored or minimized two things which cannot be ignored for long : past history, and the full content of human nature.

From about 1760, but in some earlier symptoms too, we light on those spiritual forces which had by 1815 broken asunder the genial half-truths of the eighteenth century. ' Nature ' is not a creature which submits to be docketed by man, and there are plentiful signs in the early poetry of the century, in Collins for instance, of what was later called the ' romantic ' spirit. In Cowper and in Richardson's long novels we have the sensibility of which the age was full, besides the philanthropy which they were extending to animals ; a new quality which we might measure if we compare Gilbert White's *Natural History of Selborne* with the spirituality of a seventeenth-century nature poet like Henry Vaughan. There were marked expressions of a new interest in the Middle Ages, much deeper than the amateur patronizing of Horace Walpole ; bishop Percy's *Reliques* of old ballad poetry, the cult of James Macpherson's spurious *Ossian*, or Gray's borrowings from the Welsh bards, indicate a public that would welcome ' romance '. Well before the French Revolution, old springs which had long seemed dry had flowed again. Methodist and Evangelical revival prepared a religious renewal, which would strain the decent political machine of the establishment. From the Dissenting academies leaders like Priestley delivered a teaching which would insist on reform. The long public life of Jeremy Bentham had begun, for his *Fragment on Government* appeared in 1779, already inspired by his rule of ' utility '.

Such influences, first reaching the upper air of public life in the circle which Shelburne assembled round him, were visible in Pitt's measures, and about 1809–12 we become conscious that no government can stand which resists reform. Forty years of passion had bequeathed three powerful schools of thought. There were the utilitarian and philosophic Radicals, led behind the scenes by Bentham and James Mill, and most volubly represented in politics by the Edinburgh advocate, Henry Brougham. There were the ' revolutionary ' group — though violence was rarely their object ; these would include the survivors of the societies which Pitt had repressed, like Major Cartwright, intellectuals of the Left like Godwin and his son-in-law Shelley, or Hazlitt, William Cobbett the Hampshire yeoman — who had begun as a war Tory and looked back to an older England which had not known enclosure, war debts, and poor-law doles — and a little minority in Parliament such as Whitbread, Romilly, and Francis Burdett. Finally, the revolution had produced by way of reaction those whom religion, or natural conservatism, would incline to detest it; led by the great names of converted revolutionaries in the Lake poets, the long-lived legacy of Burke, and the new fame of Walter Scott. Such men would perhaps only agree with their formal political leaders, Canning and Peel, in one point : in their repudiation of reason, the revolutionary formula, and dependence on quite another set of motives, sentiment and the affections, custom and conscience.

Even during the necessities of war, reform sprayed over the survivals which had become abuses; there was, for example, new legislation against the sale of seats and sinecures, while in 1812 the East India Company's monopoly was removed. There had been reform too at the universities, Oxford and Cambridge both organizing their examination systems soon after 1800. Fundamentally, however, the old educational regime, and its gaps, stood almost unchanged. Except in Scotland, no public money was spent on elementary teaching, most of which was done by charity schools or village dames, or by the Sunday-school movement lately begun by Robert Raikes of Gloucester, or private effort, as by the Tory high-churchwoman Hannah More's village classes in the Mendips. Since 1811 it had been taken up by rival Churches, the National Society for Anglicans and the British and Foreign School Society in the interest of Nonconformists.

As for higher education, it would be absurd to dismiss lightly all that was taught at the public schools to boys like Canning and Peel, but their teaching was almost restricted to the classics and their life often brutal and undisciplined. Though there were some good grammar schools, a mass of them suffered, as scores of endowed charities and corporations suffered too, from the absence of any central body to see they were honestly administered.

In truth, almost every institution had been made for a smaller and different England. The poor law was made for Elizabethan parishes. The Anglican Church in Ireland represented a Tudor monopoly. In England and Wales it had lost much ground to the Wesleyans and neglected newer, populous areas; its structure had not been overhauled since the Reformation; its revenues were unjustly distributed, hundreds of parishes giving their priest a starvation wage. It monopolized the universities, where none but an Anglican could take a degree, while Test and Corporation Acts still legally, though not in fact, excluded Dissenters from office.

We have, then, a people fundamentally changed in spirit but enclosed in an ancient governmental frame. Drastic reform there was bound to be; and how much more certain if we consider the effect of the twenty-three years of the great war, and of the industrial revolution which had now entered on a larger stage.

By the first census of 1801 the population of Great Britain was found to be just below 11 millions, but had risen to 16½ by 1831. Its distribution was in course of a vital change, for in those years Lancashire grew by 98 per cent, the West Riding by 74 per cent, and Lanark even more than these. Manchester's 40,000 people of 1770 were 187,000 by 1821; Leeds, Sheffield, and Birmingham all doubled in thirty years. Outside these great concentrations the whole face of the country altered. In the century ending in 1821, for all practical purposes, all that had been left of its mediaeval common-fields and commons was enclosed, or some 6 million acres. While our exports before the war ranged in value between £25 and £20 millions, the figure of 1830 was round about £70 millions; iron production and cotton imports had both risen several hundredfold per cent. The national debt, which before the war had been under £250 millions, in 1815 stood at £861 millions.

Though each item in this process of revolution and suffering has been controverted, and is still subject to intense examination, in some directions we can limit the controversy. In the first place, this revolution was nothing like complete, and for years to come the scale of industry was petty, if compared with late Victorian days. Robert Owen's New Lanark mills, the most famous landmark of George IV's reign, employed only 1600 persons, and both in London and the Birmingham region the common unit was the small workshop. Mechanism grew very gradually; even in cotton, which was far ahead of other textiles, as late as 1830 hand-looms were reckoned to outnumber power-looms by four to one. Revolution had also been a lengthy process, though so much was concentrated in the Napoleonic period that contemporaries could hardly see beyond their own agony. Investigation seems to show that four-fifths of the smaller landowners had disappeared before 1780, while the clothing trades of the eastern and middle-western shires had long ago lost ground to the north.

Nor again is it possible to describe the period from 1780 to 1830 as one of sheer social evil. It is now established that the British birth-rate reached its peak about 1780-90, thereafter slightly falling; in other words, that the increase of population was principally due, not to the birth-rate, but to an astonishing fall in the death-rate, of something like a third between 1780 and 1820. This too had begun earlier, for the middle-eighteenth century saw the first great extension of hospitals and dispensaries; we have also to take into account a greater variety of food, better meat, and drainage, that accompanied agricultural improvement. Moreover, any vision of a population pressed down into deepening poverty is beside the mark. Over the whole period of upheaval from 1790 to 1850, industrial wages as a whole rose by about 40 per cent, which was well above the corresponding rate in the cost of living.

It was a matter, rather, of conflict and confusion. As the new system rose, grievous suffering fell on the weakest survivors of the old, notably on the hand-loom weavers of the north and the southern agricultural labourers, and it was a suffering with which the existing machine proved unable to cope. At the same time, most men were ruled by an economic teaching that State interference would do more harm than good.

Let us first look at the land. Whereas the enclosure movement under the Tudors had been carried out in the teeth of government and against many of the best minds of the age, the exact reverse obtained in the eighteenth century. It was part of that spirit of improvement which had begun to revolutionize farming, spurred on by Parliament and applauded by experts, and in particular by the active Arthur Young and the Board of Agriculture founded by Pitt. Without it, certainly no improvement would have been possible, and much less the feeding of a greater population. For open fields kept farming at the pace of the slowest, made good drainage impossible, and forbade crop experiments, while no good stock could be raised on the commons, where every commoner turned out his wretched beasts without stint or selection. So far, the reformers' case was impregnable. But this phase of enclosing, as carried out, destroyed any chance of preserving a peasantry at all. Unlike the Tudor stage, this was concentrated on the wastes and commons, the loss of which to a poor man meant loss of all that made his holding profitable — of cheap fuel, of keeping a cow or two, or turning out his geese. Enclosing expenses, the fencing involved for instance, were beyond his means, so that even if it were carried out fairly, which it very often was not, his small share became an uneconomic unit. And as simultaneously new industries were swamping the village craftsmen — smiths, saddlers, glove-makers, and weavers — a peasant family was left with a hard battle for existence.

Another considerable item in its downfall was the poor law, which had become the worst abuse of society. Import of grain being impossible during the war and no large supply being yet available from America, with any inferior harvest the country was immediately confronted by starvation prices. North's government had legislated for wheat prices of less than 50s. a quarter, but for the ten years ending with 1814 they averaged 75s., and for the next ten, 93s. If the labouring poor were not to starve, there were only two possible remedies. The one, to raise their wage to a legal minimum, ran counter to the reigning economic theory; the other was adopted, at first by local magistrates like the Berkshire J.P.'s at Speenhamland, and then by Parliament, to assist wages by cash payments, or some other method, from the rates.

In its full evil this system never prevailed in the north, but in the east and south the damage was growing every day. Before the war the total of poor rates had been rather under two million pounds, at the peace it was near seven, and this increase was hideously concentrated, the county of Sussex thus spending more than all Wales. A minimum subsistence according to a bread scale being fixed and pauper wages brought up to that point, normal agricultural wages naturally sank to that level. Farmers were thus guaranteed getting their work part-done from parish labour; that being so, the only way by which an independent labourer could be sure of keeping employment was by going on the parish. This burden of rate-aid broke down many a small employer. By many devices this pauperized labour-supply was partitioned out; sometimes as ' roundsmen ' billeted on each ratepayer in turn, and sometimes auctioned out like animals.

While the south sank in this deadly penalty for a legislation lacking administrative safeguards, the new industrial order was also full of evil. Experience seems to show that the mass of humanity must be protected either by the State or their own organized effort. But in this era both methods were ruled out. The paternal system, developed by Tudors and Stuarts from mediaeval precedent, had included fixed wage-scales and defence of labour standards by regulating apprenticeship; but many appeals to fix minimum wages were now rejected, and in 1813–14 the last relics of wage assessment and apprenticeship were swept away. Meantime, the coincidence of the new industrialism with war and revolution doomed the alternative method of defence. Trades unionism, already heavily attacked in the Pelham period, was put outside the law by the Combination Act of 1799; it is true that many unions secretly continued, masked as benefit clubs or friendly societies, but open strike action was illegal and defence could be wrested into conspiracy. Left without any weapon except violence, the poor passed through a phase of sharp suffering. Wage-rates were driven down, in Lancashire in particular, by hordes of Irish immigrants; in fact, the increase of machinery was delayed for the very reason that employers had a cheaper alternative, in the hand-loom weavers who would accept 9s., or less, a week. Hours were monstrously long, the factory bell would clang at dawn, and its doors would not shut for fourteen or sixteen hours. Mills, mines, and factories employed women and children, and parish apprentices from the south ; children of seven years old and upwards were bound to the first textile mills until they were twenty-one. Barbarities inflicted on chimney-sweeping boys were at least limited by their scanty numbers, but in the new towns many thousands lived in cellars or over cess-pits, to die miserably of ague and fever. Their children ran wild; even in the 1830's over half the Lancashire mill-hands could not write. Into this morass individual charity seemed to be draining, without serious effect.

In this first quarter of the new century the social thinking of the ruling class was perhaps made up of three dominant strands. There was the anti-revolutionary teaching of Burke, prolonged in the hands of Canning, Liverpool, and other ministers, who had to resist open violence. Second, came the very great power of Evangelical religion, within and without the established Church. Reaching politics largely through the long devoted life of Wilberforce, it had done and was still doing much good, so that religion and private life were far better things than in the age of Walpole, Wilkes, and Wesley. But not only had this Evangelical-ism an other-worldly ideal, a certain passivity about the evils of this life on earth, but it made its chief objective the individual's worthiness and salvation. It had absorbed a good deal of that Puritan theology which insisted that the ' elect ' must be left free, to prove their justification, even by their material success. Yet probably neither of these forces was so strong as that of the economists.

It must be remembered that the generation for whom Adam Smith wrote, and Bentham soon after, was violently critical and coming out of a tangle of ancient regulation and local ignorance. All their in-fluence, therefore, was directed to making economic life free; or ' natural ', as they put it. If things were left alone, they argued — rents, interest, profits, and wages — they would find their true level. Smith's disciples, notably the Jewish banker David Ricardo, worked out the laws of the distribution of wealth ; the doctrine of a wage-fund, found in the ratio between the capital available and the number of labourers competing, which could not be increased by ' interference ', and whose distribution could not permanently be altered by combina-tions of wage-earners.

These men lived through the pressures and half-starvation of the great war. In 1798 Malthus, a Hertfordshire parson, published the first edition of an *Essay on Population*, perhaps the most influential English book of the next half-century. Human numbers, he reasoned, were for ever pressing on the food supply, and unless positive checks of war and famine arrested this pressure, nothing could do so but moral restraint. Wages must therefore always tend to hover round about the cost of the wage-earner's subsistence, and could not for long be kept above that rate by any ill-judged, benevolent ' interference '. This bogy of a swarming, improvident, and unprovided population, driving down all wage-standards by competition, coloured the thought of England till half-way through Victoria's reign, affecting alike its currency policy, its zeal for emigration, and its harsh poor law.

Against this fatalistic philosophy many voices had already been raised. Some were those of idealists such as the Lake poets ; Words-worth with his conception of Nature's purer plan, Southey in fierce attacks in the *Quarterly* on mills and factories, Coleridge with his defence of Christianity as the truer political wisdom. There were voices from the new democracy also, seizing on some half-truth, and often doing as much harm as good. Owen had shown by example in his Lanark mills that a humane environment was compatible with business profit, though now he was wandering off into utopias of small self-sufficing Socialist units. To Thomas Spence, and his followers the Spenceans, nationalization of the soil was the panacea; others imagined that labour was the sole source of wealth. Most popular of all was William Cobbett, whose remedies ranged from repudiation of the national debt to abolition of the poor law or juggling with a paper currency, whose notions of history were fantastic and his ignorance profound, while he antagonized the Whigs and Radicals by his inconsistent violence. Yet his vitality and popularity were immense, he was a born pamphleteer and publicist, and in 1815 reduced his *Political Register* in price to twopence, which brought its sale to 50,000 copies a week. He put his strong finger on one essential, that the way to improvement was not revolution, but parliamentary reform.

Taken all in all, the effect of this momentous age had been to cleave the nation in two. Under the surface of the classic Constitution, with its fixed liberties like trial by jury, its monarchy, established Church, chartered boroughs and privileged universities, was a new, unorganized, part-disinherited, part-conservative, swaying mass; of new craftsmen and dying small industries, landless peasants, followers of 'Captain Lud' breaking machines, and an unrepresented middle class. This struggle was at its height when a war of twenty-three years had left government exhausted, reforms long deferred, a vast debt, and prices driven high by a depreciated currency. It was too much to hope that men would rein in their aspirations and hungers until, as the economists argued, these jostling forces found their level.

CHAPTER VIII

THE LIVERPOOL GOVERNMENT, 1815–1825

FROM the turning-point of the war in 1812 Britain was conducted to victory, peace, and massive reform by one and the same government until 1827; not without reproach, but at least with a moderation which no other country could match.

In experience and ability it was one of the strongest of Cabinets. Its original core was the proved partnership of Liverpool, Castlereagh, and Bathurst, respectively at Treasury, Foreign Office, and War Office; Canning was brought back in 1816, Wellington joined in 1818; in its lower ranks were Peel, Huskisson, Palmerston, and Aberdeen. Its weak spots were the iron conservatism of Eldon the Chancellor, the depressed rigid ideas of Sidmouth (Addington) who as Home Secretary would have to deal with internal disturbance, and the incompetent Vansittart at the Exchequer. Sometimes it has been argued — Disraeli made it a popular view in his novels — that this government took on a new and liberal life from 1822, when Canning succeeded to Castlereagh, and Peel to Sidmouth. Closer investigation suggests that this contrast is strained, and that the real difference lay between the bitter aftermath of war and the slow dawning of peace and prosperity.

They could congratulate themselves on one piece of good fortune, that the Whig opposition was so ineffectual. Its allies, the Grenvilles, by 1818 returned to the Tory camp. Grey's leadership was idle, and ultimately he retired in favour of Lansdowne, who stood much closer to the right; their leader in the Commons till 1818, Ponsonby, was insignificant; few trusted Tierney, no one trusted Brougham; two of their best men, Whitbread and Romilly, committed suicide, Horner their economist died young. Personal questions apart, there was no hope for them until they had cleared up relations with the Radicals. Riot and violence repelled Whig peers like Fox's nephew Holland and Fitzwilliam, and so long as the Radical leaders, Burdett and Cartwright, 'Orator' Hunt or Cobbett, spoke of manhood suffrage, Grey could not take up parliamentary reform again without breaking his party.

On the whole, the ministry's greatest embarrassment was the evil condition of the monarchy, which more than any other single cause, perhaps, brought the country near revolution. The Regent's private life was notorious, his wife had gone abroad and he already meditated divorce; his demands for money for his comforts were incessant. The

Duke of York was childless and tarnished by old scandals; the other brothers were making haste to marry, but Cumberland's character was fearful, Kent and Clarence were weak and absurd. And when the Regent's only child, Princess Charlotte, died in childbirth in 1817, the nation looked with disgust at a prospect of this battered series of roués succeeding to the throne.

Government's first duty was to keep the peace of Europe, which was indeed maintained, in so far that major wars were avoided, until 1848. But the prevailing mark of this period was that it formed a truce between two eras of revolution; if nationality had finally triumphed over Napoleon, the French conquests bequeathed ideas which were to divide Europe as with a sword, the revolutionary ideas of the rights of man, anti-clericalism, and self-government. As so often before and since, before Britain lay a choice between isolation and alliances; the first so dangerous and, as Castlereagh rightly argued, so impossible when Europe was still trembling, yet the second involving such hateful possibilities. When, therefore, the restored Bourbons and Hapsburgs, the military Prussians and the Czar Alexander, now fast turning a religious mystic, tried to force the clock back and stamp out all liberal movements, an inevitable clash came about between Britain and her Allies of the war.

In all this, it is now clear, the supposed contrast — taken too often from a few bitter lines of Byron and Shelley — between Canning and Castlereagh lacks substantial foundation. Their methods were different enough, but not their ruling idea. We find Castlereagh advancing from point to point in resistance to Metternich and Russia, and the Congress system, on which he had depended, swiftly wilting away. Like all British ministers after such wars, he had two necessary pre-occupations : the enemy must not be allowed to revive in strength, yet their overweening power must not merely pass to one of our Allies. In other words, at that time, a British minister must guard both against revival of French imperialism and against a European despotism of Russia, and we deduce from many words of both ministers that Britain was taking up her usual rôle of mediator, refusing to be imprisoned within any ideology. ' We shall be found in our place ', said a famous paper of Castlereagh in 1820, ' when actual danger menaces the system of Europe ; but this country cannot, and will not, act upon abstract and speculative principles of precaution.'

We find him, then, at Aix-la-Chapelle in 1818, the first meeting of the Congress arranged by treaty, concerned to decide the evacuation of France by Allied garrisons, but also to prevent the Alliance becoming an international police, pledged to uphold all existing governments and territories. By the date of the conference of Troppau in 1820, liberal revolt in Spain and Metternich's repression of liberalism in Germany forced the breach wider; at Laibach a year later, though admitting Austria's special rights in Italy, Castlereagh refused point-blank to allow a general right of intervention. But the division of Europe between liberal and despotic States was that year cut across by new events: in the Greek rising which put Russia and Austria in rival camps, and French intervention in Spain.

He did not live to attend the Congress of Verona in 1822, at which our cleavage from the Holy Alliance was made final, but his papers prove that, at his own pace and in his own way, he had reached the conclusion followed by Canning. For he left behind instructions which meant recognition of the South American republics now rebelling against Spain, and an admission that, though our interest was to preserve the Turkish Empire, some scheme must be found for Greek self-government. Carrying these burdens, besides the lead of the Commons and a feud between King and Cabinet on his shoulders, he broke down and killed himself.

Until nearly that date the internal condition of Britain was a much more grievous strain than conflict in Europe. They had to meet the ruin left by war, and the sudden depression brought by peace. War had raised the debt from £240 millions to £861 millions, the interest on which absorbed over half the budget expenditure. Both corn prices and rents had doubled, the paper currency had depreciated, and peace knocked the bottom out of this flimsy structure. Gold prices fell by 50 per cent between 1813 and 1816, Continental demand ceased, iron dropped from £20 to £8 a ton. All the new cornlands, often enclosed on borrowed money, threatened to be dead loss: the Navy was cut in one year from 100,000 to 33,000 men; demobilized soldiers flocked home, to swell an army of starving weavers.

The Commons' measures show what clashing influences were beating on them, and shed a sad light on the fabric of government. Their first instinct being to save the landed interest, the Corn Law of 1815 prohibited entry of foreign corn till the price reached 80s. the quarter, with 67s. as the corresponding figure for Colonial wheat. Their second, wherein members of both parties joined, was to reduce taxation, clamour rising loudest from the Radicals Brougham and Hume. So, against the will of the Cabinet, the income-tax was repealed, which directly led to higher duties on necessaries of life.

Indeed, *laisser-faire* economics had captured the mass of all parties. Liverpool himself, and the ministers who under him dealt with finance and commerce, Huskisson and Wallace and Robinson, believed in levelling all barriers, and this many years before the supposed change of 1822. So the East India Company was deprived of its Indian trading monopoly, the bounty on corn export and the apprenticeship laws were removed, and after long Cabinet conflict it was agreed in 1819 to accept the recommendation of a committee, under Peel as chairman, that the Bank should resume cash payments. In time, when world trade revived, such remedies might assist prosperity, but at the moment they meant a grim deflation, a tussle for employment, and distress.

1816–17 and again 1819 were miserable years of bad harvests and high food prices and violent strikes ; there was machine-breaking among the peasants of the east Midlands and the hosiery frame-workers of Nottingham and Leicester. This strife was conducted, in the main, between two equally hopeless extremes, of a panic in the possessing class, in ministers like Eldon and Sidmouth or even in Canning, and on the other side a leadership ruined by some irresponsible demagogues. Hence the violent meetings held by Orator Hunt, folly like the Lancashire ' blanketeers ' marching on London, seizure of arms, a few mob murders, a great deal of cheap sedition and blasphemy in a very base press, red flags and all the insignia of 1789. Secret committees of the Commons, of both parties, reported that schemes existed to overturn the Constitution, habeas corpus was suspended in 1817–18, informers were used to detect points of danger, and yeomanry called out to reinforce the army.

An exposure of the part played by one such informer, Oliver, brought against this alarmed government a charge that *agents provocateurs* were fomenting disturbance with their approval. This was untrue, and even in this period government did not watch distress with entirely folded hands. They found money for public works, as for the Caledonian Canal ; paid a million, in this Evangelical age, for building new churches ; supported the elder Peel's Factory Act of 1819, which at least stopped employment of children under nine in factories and mills and the sending of pauper apprentices far from home. It is true also that the darkest spot of all, among the hand-loom weavers, was hardly curable by any government.

But though they were bound to keep order, the older men among them seemed to think repression was a cure, nor had they the vision or vitality to see that parliamentary reform had captured the artisan class. The Combinations Act had broken down, trade-union action was incessant, but government did not discern that the sting could be taken out of industrial action by meeting democracy on its political side. That was illustrated by the events of 1819, when the unrepresented city of Birmingham elected an unofficial ' representative ', and when political unions spread over Lancashire. It came to a head in August at ' Peterloo ', the famous meeting in St. Peter's Fields, Manchester, when something like 80,000 persons marched in to hear Orator Hunt, where the magistrates most culpably used the local yeomanry to arrest him after the crowd had assembled, and, when the yeomanry were resisted and surrounded, employed the regular cavalry. Government then stood on the worst possible ground; eleven persons had been killed and many score injured, but the magistrates pleaded self-defence; that the crowd had been drilled and bore threatening banners, and that the yeomanry were first attacked. The Cabinet, Canning included, felt their action had been wrong, but that, if they condemned them, no stand for law and order would be possible again; publicly, therefore, they commended them, and introduced the Six Acts.

Of these the aim was conservative, not reactionary, and in part they still stand on the statute-book. One forbade unauthorized drilling of private armies, a second empowered magistrates to search for arms. As regards meetings, they left the familiar county and borough meetings untouched and, accepting a Whig amendment, left indoor meetings free also. What they were concerned to prevent were mass meetings in the open, embracing persons from wide areas, and these they made subject to the magistrates' licence. Their other bugbear was the violence of the cheap press, which they struck at by a stiffer stamp duty and by allowing a court to confiscate the whole issue, if seditious or blasphemous.

Such revolutionary violence as existed came to its climax in the Cato Street conspiracy of February 1820, when Thistlewood, leader of the London extremists, organized a gang to murder the Cabinet, and was caught red-handed. After that the worst days were over, and though there were fluctuations in the cost of living, it never rose to the terrible peak of 1816-19. The poor-rate sank, exports rose, and trade revival carried off the people's discontents; which were also distracted in other directions.

When the old King died at length in 1820, it at once brought to the forefront George IV's determination to get a divorce from his hated Queen, Caroline, and this set up a furore which shook the throne and resulted in a remodelling of the Cabinet. To them the divorce scheme was abhorrent; though they believed the Queen guilty, they warned George that this public exposure, resting on the evidence of Italians, would endanger national peace. It was their hope that Caroline might be bribed by a large income into a continuance of her life abroad; it was only when she returned, defied all compromise and abandoned Brougham, her previous adviser, for Cobbett and the enthusiasm of the mob that, much against their will, the Cabinet introduced a bill of pains and penalties.

After this scandal had dragged on through 1820, they dropped the bill, for their majority in the Lords fell to nine and they could certainly never pass it through the Commons. While the Church resented the view that Parliament could declare the marriage annulled, mob demonstrations and deputations to the Queen and threats of mutiny in the army expressed what Liverpool himself and half the Cabinet felt as well, — that it was unendurable that the monarchy and all government should be strained to please a King who had treated his wife as had George IV. How little the people cared for the Queen personally was soon seen when she accepted a parliamentary income, again when she was kept out of the coronation, and finally in August 1821 when she died.

Canning had resigned rather than endorse the penal proceedings, the King was furious with his ministers, Peel was out of office and very ambitious, and Castlereagh's death in 1822, leaving open both the Foreign Office and the lead of the Commons, crowned this mounting crisis. Its solution was as important, alike constitutionally and in immediate effect, as any event between the appointment of Pitt in 1783 and Gladstone's return in 1880. Against a persistent campaign by the King, supported by some ministers like Eldon, Liverpool laid down that this ' principle of exclusion ' must stop once for all, and with a threat of his own resignation carried the appointment of Canning.

This, together with the elimination of some older men, brought about in 1822–3 a recasting of the Cabinet; Canning replaced Castlereagh, Peel replaced Sidmouth, Robinson succeeded Vansittart at the Exchequer, Canning's follower Huskisson took the Board of Trade; some of Grenville's supporters were brought in also. All of which, with the choice of Marquis Wellesley as Lord-Lieutenant, much strengthened the ' Catholic ' element in Cabinet.

Now Liverpool had formed his government on one principle, taught by all experience since Pitt's sad failure, that the Catholic question must be left ' open ', ministers being free to vote as they pleased; moreover, it was a government held together for national purposes, to end the war and ensure the peace. Gradually, however, great questions arose in addition to the Catholic matter, which could not indefinitely be held in suspense; questions of the currency, corn, and parliamentary reform, indeed, all the principles of foreign and social policy. Between 1820 and Liverpool's resignation in 1827 we become conscious of one paramount fact, that these new issues were transforming the old parties; that the Tory inheritors of Pitt were irretrievably divided, and that this cleavage was destroying the Cabinet, within which one section was willing to coalesce with moderate Whigs. Liverpool was thus poised between two hostile bodies; the one including Canning, Robinson, and Huskisson, and the other led by Wellington, Eldon, and Peel.

In two particular directions these were years of fundamental reform. The first was especially the work of Liverpool and his subordinates Huskisson, Robinson, and Wallace; to carry further the task which Pitt had begun but which had been interrupted by war, and which Peel and Gladstone were destined to complete, a gigantic task, of remodelling the whole economics of the State. Encouraged by Ricardo and other economists, they took action in advance of business opinion, and in defiance of sullen opposition from their own back-benches. The old system of high protection, high prices, and monopoly for British shipping had become out of date when America was independent, when the Spanish colonies became free nations and new States like Prussia competed with British industry, and when we our-selves were part-dependent on imported food.

In principle our ministers were converts to *laisser-faire*, free ex-changes, and cheapened costs. Having restored cash payments in 1821 they stood staunchly by it, despite clamours both from agricultural and democratic quarters for a return to inflation, and were rewarded by the cheapness of money which allowed them to convert part of the war debt. Each year Robinson's budgets remitted taxation, yet revenue increased.

One part of their campaign being against internal barriers, they swept away the tariffs separating Britain from Ireland, freed the coal trade from several ancient duties, abolished excise on salt, and repealed the last relic of fixed wages and prices in the Spitalfields silk industry. A second achievement was an immense revision of the tariff. Duties on raw materials were cut low, bounties were cancelled, while on manu-factured goods a level of 20 per cent duties was their aim. If Britain continued a protectionist State, it was moderate protection, and imposed on some principle, while in structure the consolidating Act of 1825, repealing over a thousand statutes, made the first modern tariff for the United Kingdom.

Huskisson's own feeling was more deeply engaged in a third task, the revision of the commercial system of Empire. Plainly the Navigation Acts were obsolete. By the end of 1825 both Americas were allowed to send their products direct to Britain, in their own ships; goods from Europe might henceforth come, not merely in British ships or those of the country of production, but in ships of the exporting country; our Colonies were allowed to trade direct with foreign States. Government were empowered to make, and freely did make, reciprocity treaties with foreign countries which gave the equality of treatment, as regards port dues and charges, which we offered to them. As Huskisson left it, however, it remained an Imperial system. Not only our own coastal trade, but all inter-Imperial commerce, was reserved for Imperial ships, non-European goods might not be imported from Europe in foreign vessels, large preferences were given to colonial exports and imports. Many substantial privileges thus protected West Indian sugar, Canadian timber, and the new-found wealth of Australian wool.

A commercial crisis in 1825–6 threw light on all this activity, for it was mainly caused by over-speculation in South America and led towards another reform on which Liverpool was decided. This was in the banking system, or rather the lack of one, wherein England lagged much behind the Scots. The Bank of England's privileges were great but its obligations were few, it held a monopoly of English joint-stock banking, its note-issues and reserves of gold were laxly controlled. Beneath it were some sixty private banks in London and some eight hundred in the provinces, going their own way, on whose notes most business outside London turned. Every crisis exposed their weakness, nearly two hundred failed between Waterloo and 1830. On Liverpool's insistence government rejected the panic measures, such as a new suspension of cash payments, for which many called; his Acts of 1826 instead forbade issue of English notes under the value of £5, and authorized the establishment of joint-stock banks in the provinces.

One other economic measure, though not inspired by the Cabinet, was of great future import. This was the repeal, by Acts of 1824–5, of the Combination Act of 1799, so far at least as to make it legal for trade unions, by strike action or otherwise, to combine for improvement of working conditions. This move was, in fact, directed by Francis Place, the remarkable Radical tailor, who had for years been the master behind the scene in the great Westminster constituency. Even so, trade unionists had still to walk delicately along the vague edge of the law of conspiracy.

Meantime, at the Home Office, Peel was conducting a parallel series of reforms, of equal value to national welfare; for, though not himself a man of originating insight, his mind was just and open to reasoned conviction. Of all the heterogeneous subjects under his department, public feeling was offended most by the criminal law. As it stood, there were over two hundred offences for which death could be imposed, including shop-lifting or cutting down a tree; a code so ridiculously barbaric that, for many years, no jury had brought a conviction under two-thirds of its clauses. The Whigs Romilly and Mackintosh had first taken this in hand, but had been able to accomplish little against the bigotry of the Lords, led by Eldon. No one but Peel, at this time the rising hope of the right-wing Tories, could have overcome that opposition, and his Acts of 1823 abolished the capital sentence for a hundred offences.

He proceeded to reform the prison system, though imprisonment for debt lingered on, and hence, among others, the trials of Mr. Pickwick; to modify the severe Aliens law which had come down from the war years; to overhaul the much-criticized, dilatory court of Chancery; to give the judges proper salaries instead of ancient perquisites and fees; to examine the evil of transporting convicts; to consolidate the whole criminal law. In his earlier office of Irish Secretary he had set on foot the Royal Irish constabulary, and was already busied with enquiry as to organizing a new London police, which came into being in 1829. This was almost his greatest service; for hitherto there had been no medium between decrepit parish watchmen and using the military.

So the government was borne along on a tide of change. But change was detestable to a large part of its following and the Cabinet itself broken by divisions which sooner or later must destroy it.

CONTEMPORARY DATES

1816   Chief Justice Marshall interpreting the Constitution of
          the United States.

1817   Bolivar defeats Spanish troops in Venezuela.
          Third Mahratta war.
          Ricardo's *Political Economy*.
          Coleridge, *Biographia Literaria*.

1818   List plans the German Zollverein.
          The first steamer crosses the Atlantic.
          Keats, *Endymion*.

1819   The Carlsbad decrees.
          Shelley, *Prometheus Unbound*.
          Byron, *Don Juan*.

1820   Revolution in Italy and Spain ; Congress of Troppau.
          Slavery in America ; the Missouri compromise.
          Lamb, *Essays of Elia*.

1821   Revolution in Piedmont, Greece, and South America.
          Death of Napoleon.
          Hegel, *Philosophy of Right*.

1822   Turkish invasion of Greece.
          Heine, *Poems*.

1823   A French army in Spain.
          The Monroe Doctrine.

1824   Mehemet Ali intervenes in Greece.
          Death of Byron at Missolonghi.
          –1830. Reign of Charles X in France.

1825   First railway runs between Stockton and Darlington.
          Foundation of University of London.
          –1855. Reign of Nicolas I in Russia.

CHAPTER IX

CANNING, EMANCIPATION, AND REFORM
1825–1832

SEVEN years, ending with the great Reform bill, determined the character of nineteenth-century Britain and its rôle in the world. They were years full of paradox, total uncertainty as to the future of parties, and unpredictable parts played by human beings.

They were years of incessant movement, spiritual and mechanical, and of striving for reform, in which all the products of the revolutionary age, long distorted or pent-up, overflowed in a sudden release. During the 'twenties death took away three young men of genius, Byron, Shelley, and Keats, but the first writings of Carlyle, Tennyson, and Macaulay appeared in those years also, the *Christian Year* of John Keble, and the Whig classic of Hallam's *Constitutional History*. Physical movement was being revolutionized by Telford and Macadam on new trunk roads, great works like the Menai Bridge or Caledonian Canal, and George Stephenson's locomotives on the first passenger railways, between Stockton and Darlington, and from Manchester to Liverpool.

It was a serious-minded society, whose three most typical forces — evangelical Christians, skilled artisans, and Utilitarian thinkers — clamoured for wider education and a broader highway for the talents. That the State should control a compulsory system would have seemed wholly wrong to an age which believed with all its heart in parental responsibility and the individual's duty to find his own salvation, while in any case such a proposal would have clashed on the friction between Church and Dissent. Much, however, was done for higher education, to which was given the most disinterested energy of the ferocious egoist Brougham. He it was who brought to London the work which the Glasgow professor Birkbeck had begun in the north, of mechanics' institutes and working-men's colleges ; he founded a society for ' diffusion of useful knowledge ', which set about the publication of text-books ; and inspired enquiry into the scandalous waste of old endowments, which later led to the Charity Commission. Under his influence and that of the Radical thinkers, University College, London, was founded in 1827, free from religious tests and with the special purpose of teaching science, economics, and modern subjects ; the same year Dr. Arnold was appointed headmaster of Rugby, whose example made a new usefulness for the public schools. Bentham was now a very old man, but his fame had reached its height and was being extended by his disciples, James Mill at the India House and John Mill, his son; their group had just founded their own organ in the *Westminster Review*.

Closely connected with them were the philosophic Radicals : Ricardo the economist, Grote the historian of liberal Greece, John Austin the teacher of modern law, and the school — Durham, Charles Buller, and Gibbon Wakefield — who would apply Radicalism to home and colonial politics alike.   Wilberforce was still alive and, with Fowell Buxton, his successor as leader of ' the Saints ', was meditating a last crusade to abolish slavery as they had abolished the slave trade.   In the swarming industrial areas of Lancashire and the Midlands an intense energy of mind, as in the young Richard Cobden, demanded manifold changes.   And though a heavy tax on newspapers, raised to fourpence in 1815, and extended to periodicals like Cobbett's *Register* by the Six Acts, made knowledge dear, the press was more powerful and much more independent of government than before the war.   *The Times* in particular, under an editor of high aggressive quality in Thomas Barnes, worked strenuously for reform.

Yet while such elements gathered force there was a curious halt in politics, and that was associated with the condition of parties, which in its turn depended, first and foremost, on the personality of Canning.

He was one of those few remarkable men, dominant in the British party system, who have strained that system beyond endurance, and it is not surprising that the majority of his own party distrusted him deeply.   Launched first by the Whigs, in whose brilliant society he was happiest, he had been the favourite disciple of Pitt, but had sorely troubled his master's last days by inflaming the quarrel with Addington and the orthodox Tories.   He had tried to be Premier in lieu of Perceval, wrecked the Portland government by his feud with Castlereagh, and in 1812 destroyed his apparent future by refusing the Foreign Office unless it were coupled with the lead of the Commons.   Subsequently Liverpool, always loyal to their old Oxford friendship, had brought him back, and in 1822 risked all to give him the second place in his government.   All this reads like the record of an ambitious self-seeker, and there were leading men on either side, as Wellington and Grey, whose dislike of him was incurable.   In fact, however, he was pre-eminently an orator and an intellectual, hypersensitive, contemptuous of second-class brains, and not disposed to sacrifice to party his own future and ideals.

What is it that makes this short space the age of Canning, the idol of earnest families like the Gladstones and of Liberal Europe? He was no Radical and disbelieved in parliamentary reform, adhering always to Burke's teaching that democracy was one form of tyranny and that liberty implies variety, an inherited society, and private property as the instrument of talent. He had no informed interest in the economic schemes of Huskisson and Peel. He was, rather, an opportunist, intensely insular in the higher sense that he felt the England of his master, Pitt, had saved Europe, and was worthy to be preserved in her historic character. His abilities were especially those of a parliamentary statesman. His eloquence was magnificently elastic, and he was the first of responsible ministers to use modern publicity, laying before his constituents, or exposing by publication in ringing defiant tone, his quarrel with the despots of the Continent.

He was fortunate in that his epoch of power began when trade revival and reform had removed the heaviest social misery, and when the policy inherited from Castlereagh had come to an open breach with the Holy Alliance. But he it was who opened that breach wider, by his immense skill exploited it to divide the despotic Powers, and by his speech so expressed it as to elevate Britain in the eyes of her own people and all the world. He was hardly one of the rare foreign ministers who harmonize the long-range interests of their own country with others. He disclaimed notions of regenerating the world as romantic, dealt with the United States as a counter in his game rather than as a natural partner, and reduced his objective to the interest of England. Yet his nationalism had a high and intelligent content, of a Britain neutral between what he called ' the two conflicting bigotries ' of despotism and democracy, not interfering in other peoples' brand of government, and only intervening, but then ' with commanding force ', when British interests were in peril.

Two particular questions tested this flexible ability during his five years at the Foreign Office : revolution in Spain and Portugal, with the connected effects in their overseas Empires, and the rising of Greece. In themselves the wretched politics of the Peninsula and the infamies of the Spanish Bourbons could not concern us, but the Czar Alexander spoke of an army to crush revolution, while the French were resolved to save another Bourbon monarchy and to assert their own restored status. The French invasion in 1823 did, indeed, destroy the Spanish constitutionalists but there it stopped ; for in a published despatch Canning threatened war if they menaced Portugal, or took any Spanish colonies, and poured scorn on the whole gospel of legitimism. To go further was not possible in the condition of the Cabinet, and of our defences, while such separate French action was a different thing from action by the Holy Alliance. But their invasion led direct to Canning's pressure for recognizing South American independence ; to which referred the most famous words in his own justification later, ' I resolved that if France had Spain, it should not be Spain with the Indies ; I called the New World into existence to redress the balance of the Old '.

This claim is more accurate if applied to his struggle within the Cabinet, rather than to his diplomatic activity. For inside the government the disagreement was furious. Wellington felt himself the representative of the order settled in 1815, and that democracy might upset everything for which he had fought. He and those who naturally sided with him, Eldon and Bathurst included, asked what could underpin peace if the Alliance were removed. The King, obsessed with the threat to all monarchies, took counsel with Metternich, foreign ambassadors like the Russian Lieven and his intriguing wife, and Hanoverian ministers, to whom he and Wellington maligned the baleful advice of Canning. It was, in fact, only the decision of Liverpool and Canning to resign if their policy was beaten which impelled the Cabinet in 1825 to recognize the Argentine, Mexico, and Colombia as independent States.

It was, indeed, inevitable. Those rich countries could not be left in chaos, and British sentiment was as deeply engaged as British wealth. Bolivar, the Colombian liberator, had British officers on his staff; Cochrane, our best leader of light craft and Radical member for Westminster, organized the navy of Chile; thousands of British and Irish adventurers fought over those jungles and mountains. That the Spanish monarchy could ever recover the great spaces between Cape Horn and San Francisco was most unlikely, but whether European Powers would seize parts of them, quite another question. Russia was proclaiming that her Alaska stretched down to Oregon, and Canning feared, rather unduly, that France meant to plant out Bourbon princes. Such causes had contributed to the United States giving recognition to the rebels, more widely than and in advance of Britain, and contributed also to their enunciation, in December 1823, of the Monroe doctrine. While disclaiming all intention of interference with existing Colonies, the President's message declared the American continents ' are henceforth not to be considered as subjects for colonization by any European powers '.

This message was, in fact, the work of a more formidable man, Monroe's Secretary of State, John Quincy Adams, and though the immediate interests of Great Britain and the United States coincided, and in Liberal eyes Canning's fair words about the mother and the daughter seemed to offer a vista of Anglo-Saxondom, actually the objectives of Canning and Adams were far apart. Adams wished to seal off America, to make universal a chain of free republics, of which some day his country must be the presiding force ; Canning had no passion for democracy, dreaded a world in which Europe would be lined up against America, and hoped to bring about independence by peaceful arrangement with Spain and Portugal. He was zealous also to get trading advantages, and suspected an American design against Cuba.

Yet if all this comes out in his private utterances, what mattered outwardly was that he forced recognition on King and Cabinet, compelled France to repudiate any purpose of interfering, and made it plain that what protected South America was not the Monroe doctrine, but the British fleet.

Much the same story was repeated in the parallel case of Portugal and her dependency, Brazil. Here he stood on stronger ground, for we were pledged to Portugal by ancient treaties, and British ships had brought their government to Brazil out of the French clutches during the war. This virtual independence of Brazil while the seat of government, revolution in Lisbon in 1820, French invasion of Spain in 1823, and dynastic ties between Portugal and Spain, all made it a test case between despotism and liberty. Never was better seen Canning's power of conciliation, with force in reserve, than when he showed the sails of our fleet in the Tagus, to reinforce our ambassador against the French. Our mediation secured in 1825 both a peaceful acceptance of Brazil's freedom, and its preservation as a monarchy. A year after, Pedro the Emperor became by his father's death king of Portugal also, but made over that kingdom to his young daughter Maria, at the same time granting a more liberal constitution. Canning had not inspired this move, but when Pedro's brother Miguel took up arms against his niece and Portuguese deserters were organizing forays from absolutist Spain, he sent off troops and a fleet in December 1826; not, ran his speech in the House, ' to prescribe constitutions, but to defend and preserve the independence of an ally. We go to plant the standard of England on the well-known heights of Lisbon.' While Wellington threatened resignation and Metternich explored the chances of resisting Canning, Liverpool stood staunchly at his side, promising that if Spain declared war, we should not hesitate to ' play the whole game of liberal institutions '. But indeed Canning had made sure of Portugal by dividing the despotic Powers over Greece.

As in the West, so in the Middle East the French revolution had revived nationality, and showed up the weakness of cosmopolitan empires. Serbia had half broken away from the Turk, Albania was in arms under Ali of Janina, the principalities which now make up Roumania claimed self-government, and from 1820 it was the turn of Greece. This long Eastern question was to trouble Great Britain for a century, stirring many conflicting chords in her policy. Pitt and his successors had committed her to the defence of Turkey, guardian of the Straits and barrier against the Russian strides towards Persia and India, but all the sentiment of liberty, all the devotion of English minds to the glory that was ancient Greece, and the zeal of Christian against Moslem, deflected our course to the other side. Here too our commercial interests were engaged, since they must suffer from anarchy, and here again

Castlereagh had held that the Greeks must have some sort of self-government.   Meantime ships and money and volunteers were raised for the rebels, Byron threw himself into the cause, and died in 1824 at Missolonghi.

Nothing could so instantly divide what was left of the Holy Alliance. The Czar Alexander's horror of revolution was counterbalanced by Russian ardour to save members of the Orthodox Church, and by their aim of controlling the Straits, but when he died in 1825 his brother, Nicholas I, made an end of such balancings.   Austria must view a Russian advance on the Danube, and far more one to Constantinople, as a mortal danger, while France had vested interests in the Levant which the decay of Turkey might assist.   Once again Canning was not determined by sentiment, and not going to fight, he said, for either ' Aristides or St. Paul '.   His first step was to recognize the Greeks as belligerents, his first hope was to mediate and prevent any great Power using force. That hope vanished in the atrocity of this war, which redoubled when the Turks called to their help the armies of their rebel and ally Mehemet Ali, Pasha of Syria and Egypt; for this made it certain that the Czar would strike, even if alone.

Early in 1826 Canning, then, decided to limit such a war by agreement with Russia; by the protocol of April, Greece was to become self-governing but remain a Turkish dependency, neither Russia nor Britain would seek anything from Turkey, and other Powers should be asked to join in their mediation.   At midsummer 1827, with the adhesion of France, it was converted into a triple alliance to enforce an armistice.

At each stage of this policy Canning had to fight the right wing of his party, and other causes were bringing politics to a crisis.   Parliamentary reform, indeed, seemed to be shelved.   If Liverpool agreed to disfranchise one particularly corrupt borough, Grampound in Cornwall, and add its members to Yorkshire, he would not face the general principle, and Canning agreed with him.   As for the Whigs, young John Russell made several attempts, but though Grey privately believed some drastic measure was necessary, involving a hundred seats, he had thrown off his extreme proposals of earlier days and feared reform would break his party; moreover, he was getting old and liked his country happiness, and in 1826 gave up the lead to the more conservative Lansdowne.

The root of division lay rather within the Tory party than between Tories and Whigs, and less in parliamentary reform than other matters. One was corn, in which Liverpool and Huskisson defied the pig-headed squires, telling them that the reason of their trouble was over-production on inferior land, and that they must accommodate themselves to lower prices.   In 1822 they insisted that prohibition must be replaced by a sliding-scale; in 1825 they admitted Canadian corn at a 5s. duty, and in the hard year of 1826 took power to import corn by order in Council. The Cabinet agreed to legislate in the next session for a sliding-scale, pivoting round a normal price of 60s. a quarter.

Furthermore, the Catholic question, on which they had agreed to differ in 1812, was with them still, and demanding solution. From a party point of view this was more serious. For on it the Whigs were united, and so were the survivors of Pitt's intimates, in Huskisson, Grenville, and Canning. Many narrow divisions, on motions sometimes brought forward by Radicals and sometimes by leading Irishmen, like Plunket and Grattan, had proved that an increasing number, especially of younger members, favoured emancipation, and though Liverpool hesitated and older men in the Cabinet, together with the leading young man in Peel, were against, it became certain that no purely ' Protestant ' Cabinet could be formed again.

Yet the intricacies of the question were much greater than in Pitt's day. In part this was due to a hardening religious bitterness. Evangelical England was rigidly anti-Roman, and so at present were the high-church school rising at Oxford, where the University had just elected Peel for their member as against the older claim of the ' Catholic ' Canning. But in Ireland a more democratic, ultramontane, element was now dominant, which rejected the guarantees, such as State control over the choice of bishops, which were acceptable to older Irish moderates and English politicians. The Catholic aristocracy, on whom both Pitt and Peel depended, had seen influence over their tenantry captured by the eloquent Daniel O'Connell, who was preaching not emancipation only but a repeal of the Union. It was in vain that Liverpool had sent over, as Lord-Lieutenant, Wellington's brother, Marquis Wellesley of India, who himself favoured emancipation; religious differences were hopelessly bound up with racial hatred and a land war. The population, now growing at the rate of a million each decade, were struggling for existence, paying tithe to the hated Anglican besides dues to their own priest; they were riddled by secret societies, while almost every year the same weary round revolved of eviction, boycott, cattle-maiming, murder, and then coercion Acts, which imposed a curfew, a search for arms, and suspension of trial by jury. A large British garrison could not enforce order, and the Protestant north was organized in Orange Order lodges. In short, the uncrowned King of Ireland was O'Connell, who in 1823 founded the Catholic Association, which in effect became a quasi-legislature, levying a ' rent ' in every parish.

In 1825, when Cabinet friction was at its height over foreign affairs, the Radical Burdett carried another emancipation bill, in which Canning, the Whig leaders, and O'Connell all had a hand; to disarm opposition it proposed to make some State payment to the Irish priest-

hood and raise the county franchise qualification to £10. The Crown's
influence was cast against it, York the heir to the throne fulminating
in the Lords, who threw it out. A clamour for a prompt anti-Popery
election rose from the Tories, led by Wellington, while Canning broke
up the ' open question ' basis by declaring that he held himself free to
initiate the question whenever he pleased.

Several years had thus passed in a tacit coalition between the
Cabinet's liberal wing and the Whig opposition, to forward liberal
notions in corn and currency, the Catholic matter, and foreign affairs.
It was then natural that the election of 1826 showed in a flash the
division of the Tories and the strength of ' No Popery ', nor surprising
that hard-bitten Tories were convinced of Canning's purpose to make
his alliance with the Whigs open and definite. In February 1827 the
decision arrived when, after years too much forgotten of invaluable
service to the State, Liverpool was struck down by paralysis and, after
a month's hesitation, George IV invited Canning to form a government.

The long-delayed break in Pitt's party came about when seven
ministers refused to continue under Canning, Eldon naturally among
them but also Wellington and Peel. Their mixed motives embraced
the Duke's hatred of Canning's foreign policy, a belief in aristocracy,
Peel's pride in his own consistency and his link with the churchmen of
Oxford. Yet the Cabinet was to continue on Liverpool's lines, with
emancipation ' open ', nor was there any good ground for the view that
Canning had intrigued with the Whigs. It was only now, after this
rebuff from the right wing, that he definitely worked for coalition.
Grey stood aloof; he despised Canning as a *parvenu*, disliked his
record, held that his policy had sacrificed liberal Spain, and refused
support unless binding pledges were given on emancipation. But very
few Whigs followed him. Brougham insisted that here was a golden
chance to break the Eldon school for ever; Lansdowne, Tierney,
William Lamb (later Melbourne), Stanley, all accepted office, while
John Russell was willing to support; of the Tories, Canning still had
with him Huskisson, Robinson, and Palmerston, brought in the unscrupulous, brilliant Lyndhurst as Chancellor, pleased the throne by
giving the Admiralty to the Duke of Clarence, and left the Irish government in ' Catholic ' hands. So both the old parties seemed to be
dissolved.

The omens were not propitious, and when, at Wellington's bidding,
the Lords mutilated a corn bill, Canning broke out that they were
inviting a mortal struggle between ' property and population '. But
whether he would have moved farther leftwards or induced the King
to swallow emancipation, or prevailed over the fury of the Tory peers,
all such questionings were silenced in August by his death. The King
endeavoured to carry on his system by making Robinson, now Lord

Goderich, Prime Minister, who lingered on till January 1828. How confused party had become may be judged from the fact that Goderich served later both under the Whig Grey and the Conservative Peel, but that very confusion allowed the King to interfere in Cabinet construction in the style of his father. This and party rancour together proved much too hard for this tearful, amiable Goderich, who resigned without ever meeting Parliament, to be succeeded by Wellington, with Peel leading the Commons, at the head of the last Tory government.

Yet, though their master was dead, the scales over the next few years were tilted by the Canningites — Huskisson, Melbourne, and Palmerston — or, rather, by the middle body of opinion on which Canning had played, and which would assuredly demand a forward move. Peel was clear that what he called ' the mere Tory party ' had had its day, and Eldon and other veterans were dropped, while to the indignation of Canning's close friends the Duke got Huskisson, Dudley, Palmerston, and Melbourne to enter his government. But this apparent reunion of Liverpool's party did not last long.

Wellington's ministry of 1828–30 was, indeed, a great failure, but then so was nearly all his career in domestic politics. He performed, of course, some services which no other man could have done, standing on such an eminence that he could reduce George IV's folly to order, or curb the influence of Cumberland, most hated of the royal brothers. But he was lonely, easily flattered by second-rate people, and as deaf to public opinion as to party feeling. Moreover he could not help identifying himself, or being identified, with the settlement of 1815. The battle of Navarino in November 1827, when the British, French, and Russian squadrons under Codrington destroyed the Turkish fleet, had horrified him ; he was not ready to use force further, and wished to reduce this rebel Greece to the smallest possible frontiers. He also withdrew from Portugal the troops Canning had sent, declining to intervene while Don Miguel worked a merciless reaction. Abroad and at home, he thought first in terms of administration and defending established order, so gradually alienating every ingredient of parliamentary support.

His partnership with the Canningites only continued from January to May 1828, the actual occasion for a break being a confused wrangle over the transfer of the franchise from two rotten boroughs, Penrhyn and East Retford, to large cities. The Canningites felt bitterly the overthrow of Canning's foreign policy, Huskisson spoke openly of freer trade, the Duke replied their attitude was ' mutiny ', and seized on the first chance to force their resignation. His new appointments were very weak, including that of Aberdeen to take Dudley's place at the Foreign Office, while one consequence was a bye-election in County Clare, where Vesey Fitzgerald, though an Irishman who approved emancipation, was beaten by O'Connell himself.

Before that happened, skilful Whig manœuvre had forced the question forward, for on Russell's motion the Commons passed, and government were compelled to accept, the repeal of the Test and Corporation Acts, so far as they excluded Protestant Dissenters from office. And if this outflanked the Tory logic — for if religion was not to bar Protestants, why should it bar Catholics ? — Wellington himself, caring little for religious differences, was persuaded by the hard facts in Ireland, where the Lord-Lieutenant doubted whether he could safely depend on a partly Catholic army and police. But he could not have faced the storm without Peel, so long the ' Protestant ' leader. By mid-summer 1828 Peel had convinced himself that an ' open question ' Cabinet was the worst of all things, and that the concession he had condemned in Canning ought to be made ; by the new year of 1829, — that it was his duty to help the Duke, on the grounds that nothing else could withstand the opposition of King and bishops, and that Grey could not form an alternative government. In April the bill passed, admitting Catholics to Parliament, and to all offices except those of Lord-Lieutenant and of Chancellor in either country ; it was accompanied by another to raise the Irish freehold qualification for a vote from 40s. to £10.

This made an end of the old Tory party, of whom 173 voted against emancipation, and their undying anger was natural against leaders who for months elaborately tricked them. Wellington fought a duel with Lord Winchelsea who charged him with deceit, Oxford University turned Peel out of their seat, while to avenge themselves some ' Ultra ' Tories were ready to combine with the Whigs, even if it resulted in parliamentary reform. For the next year party confusion was worse than ever. As the Duke had carried out the first plank in the Whig platform, some Whigs joined him in minor office, while Grey himself, in personal relationship and some questions like the Corn laws, stood much nearer to the Duke than the Canningites. Peel's police and law reforms, reduction of taxation, and peace abroad, pleased many Whig critics. Blind to the future, Wellington seems to have thought he could ignore party, and continue his course of enlisting individuals. And, indeed, no one in the first months of 1830 could have predicted how that year would end.

It began with many partial strikes, and some revival of cries for parliamentary reform ; in Birmingham, for instance, the Tory economist Attwood founded a political union for that purpose, while Cobbett was championing universal suffrage. There was no united Opposition but ceaseless criticism, though one not very well-founded when it demanded economies in the services, coupled with a strong rôle in foreign affairs. But the first stage only amounted to this, that unless the Duke reconstructed his Cabinet, they would oppose him openly.

George IV's death in June advanced the crisis, not merely because it was hailed with relief, or because William IV had some inkling of national feeling, but in that it eliminated the hated Cumberland and removed the late King's veto on the employment of Grey. Moreover, it legally involved a general election. Hardly had this dissolution taken effect when the French rose in arms against Charles X, and in the first week of August drove him into exile; in the last week of that month the Belgians began a revolt against their Dutch rulers, which turned into a demand for separation from Holland. At the same time, through the combined effects of corn laws, poor laws, over-capitalization, and market depression, all agricultural England was troubled, and a labour revolt rose in Kent, which spread north and west as autumn came on. Gangs of labourers moved about, sometimes a thousand strong, calling for no reduction of poor-law doles, or for higher wages and abolition of tithe, breaking up threshing-machines and firing ricks.

In the middle of this excitement and embittered feeling the election took place, with damaging results for the government. Reformers swept the county seats, at that date the only constituencies which could truly represent opinion; Brougham came in for Yorkshire on a platform of reform, cheap bread, and abolition of slavery, while the Tories were angrily divided between Peelites and ' Ultras '. Though parties were unorganized and many members would reckon themselves independents, the moral on which all observers agreed was that without drastic changes Wellington was doomed.

In September Huskisson was accidentally killed at the opening of the Liverpool and Manchester railway, and this — for he had not been trusted — made easier a coalition between Whigs, Canningites, and independents like Stanley and James Graham. Though some of them, notably Palmerston, had not the least enthusiasm for reform, they were not blind to the national danger and national desire. Their remaining doubts vanished with the crass folly of the royal speech opening the new Parliament, its praise of the unpopular Dutch government, and the Duke's vow that he would resist any change in our perfect constitution. Amid many revolutionary threats, plans to refuse payment of taxes, and violence against the police, the end came on 15th November, when the various sections in Opposition, Tory ' Ultras ' included, defeated Wellington over a vote on the civil list; rather than face a direct debate on reform he resigned, and the King sent for Grey.

The new government of 1830, destined through its Whig-Liberal offspring to direct the country for most of the next fifty years, was formed as a coalition. Grey and his near allies, Holland and Lansdowne, were the political children of Fox; John Russell and Althorp belonged to the historical Whig stock. Grey's son-in-law Durham was

Radical, so too was reckoned Brougham, who fought his way in as Chancellor. But Goderich, Melbourne, Palmerston, and Grant were Canningites, Stanley and Graham were very conservative Whigs, and many of these, besides those ruling Ireland, had served under Liverpool ; Richmond represented the temporary alliance with the extreme Tories. Its character, and its fate in the present unreformed House, were undecided until it produced the Reform bill, the one purpose for which they had universal support, and to which Grey wisely bent all his powers.

He was now a man of seventy, on whom the gods had showered gifts of fortune, beauty, and charm, but hitherto his career had been uneven and disappointing. Perhaps even now he could hardly have succeeded without Althorp, the leader in the Commons, a wretched financier and a wooden speaker but a character infinitely sincere and lovable, best type of the country gentleman. Yet Grey's achievement entitles him to perpetual fame. His was the choice of men, on his conciliation and high-mindedness fell the strain of managing the ferocious temper of Durham and the unscrupulous intrigues of Brougham, while only his instinctive wisdom could manage an eccentric and easily frightened King.

It was not any vision of democracy which moved him, as indeed the composition of his Cabinet suggests, and as their extreme severity against popular violence bears out. Melbourne at the Home Office set up a special commission which dealt out heavy sentences of death and transportation against the agricultural rioters ; Cobbett and other extreme journalists were prosecuted. Grey held, rather, to the teaching of the earlier Burke and the later Fox ; that peoples do not rise without good cause, that arms and force are no remedy, and that liberalism means the timing of just concession. Having decided long before coming to power that any reform must be thorough, he instructed those drafting the bill that he wished for ' an arrangement on which we can stand ', a reform, that is, to last a generation, based not on abstract rights of universal suffrage but on property, and the historic divisions of counties and boroughs. For this committee he chose men whom he could trust not to be too moderate, Durham, Russell, Graham, and the party organizer Duncannon.

The first bill, brought forward in March 1831, had been hammered into a compromise in Cabinet, vote by ballot and the shortening of Parliament's life from seven to five years thus being dropped in return for a sharp reduction of the borough franchise. It would make an end of the anomalies and varieties of seat and vote, which had grown up haphazard over four centuries. At one blow it extinguished rotten and nomination boroughs ; 60 of which, with less than 2000 population, would by schedule A lose both their members, while another 46, with a population between 2000 and 4000, would lose one member by schedule B. If this was the most popular side of the bill, the franchise changes were quite as revolutionary. For all the varieties of voting in boroughs — some widely democratic, some restricted to the corporation, some to owners of a few tenements — the bill substituted one uniform test, of a vote for every occupant of a house with a rental value not under £10. In the counties the 40s. freeholders would keep their vote, but the franchise would also be given to leaseholders with property worth £50 and to £10 copyholders.

In the largest recorded division of the old Parliament the second reading of this bill was carried by one vote, but it was too strong meat for a House elected under Wellington, and the Tories carried Gascoyne's amendment not to reduce the number of members for England and Wales. Whereupon Grey, in April 1831, induced the King to grant a dissolution; which was decisive. The electors angrily threw out the leading ' Ultras ', and Grey came back with an ample majority, which in July carried the second reading of a second bill, by 136. After weeks of debate, with no substantial change except the Tory Chandos' clause to give the county vote to £50 tenants-at-will, in addition to long leaseholders, it went up to the Lords; who in October rejected it by a majority of 41.

This winter was the crisis, not for the government only but the whole future. The deadlock between Lords and Commons was complete. The King's good will had given way to alarm. Though the two most powerful Radicals in the country, Francis Place with the Londoners and Cobbett for the provinces, stood by the bill, they took it as a minimum; more extreme men, like Doherty the Lancashire trade-union leader, despised it as a mean bourgeois thing, to be repudiated. At Birmingham the political union declared against paying taxes if the bill did not pass, some unions were preparing to use force. The wild men who orated at the Blackfriars Rotunda were out of control, there were threats against the monarchy and the supposed influence of poor Queen Adelaide, ' the German frow ', and several acts of violence against the bishops, of whom twenty-one had voted against the bill. Mobs broke out at Nottingham, where they fired the reactionary Duke of Newcastle's house, and at Bristol, where the weakness of mayor and military allowed them to sack the centre of the city; Radicals were drilling, nervous landowners like Peel were laying in arms.

There were only three possibilities — mob rule, a compromise, or surrender by the Lords, and the last was unlikely unless Grey received from the King a promise to create new peers. But to create the numbers needed, fifty at the lowest, was a revolution which William IV would not yet contemplate, nor as yet would Grey himself, being convinced that it would make as many enemies as it won friends. With immense patience he pushed along several paths. A new bill, it was announced, would be introduced, ' not less efficient ' than the old. That formula allowed him to meet the wishes of the moderates in his Cabinet, Palmerston and Melbourne and Lansdowne, and to explore whatever reality there might be in offers held out by the Tory group styled ' the Waverers ', led by the Canningite Wharncliffe and by Pitt's last surviv-ing friend, Harrowby. And while a sharp proclamation denounced political unions which set up quasi-military organization, private contacts assured London and Birmingham reformers that, given the keeping of order, ministers would persist with full reform. Much, too, was due to the loyal and constitutional rôle of the King's secretary, Sir Herbert Taylor.

Though the ' Waverers'' negotiation resulted in no formal agree-ment, it assisted to obtain some important concessions in the third version of the bill. The number of English members was not to be reduced ; not population only, but the amount of taxes and houses were to be reckoned in drawing the line between boroughs keeping and losing members ; though fifty-six were still doomed under Schedule A, the number in Schedule B was cut down to thirty ; if resident, freemen were to retain their borough vote. Negotiation had the further vital effect of making Grey confident he could manage the Lords. In January 1832 the King gave a rather vaguely worded promise to make what peers might be required, though only when the need was ' certain ', and on that point Grey had to resist a demand from half his Cabinet, Althorp, Brougham, and Durham included, for an immediate creation. How right his judgment was appeared when the Lords passed the second reading in April by a majority of nine, and it was proved right again by the last clash.

All through this story the Tories had been out-debated and out-fought, and in this May crisis their position was chaotic. Peel was well aware that reform was needed and that the Lords' resistance might shake the country, but he would not risk his own fame by a second charge of ' apostasy ', and fatalistically gave way to the Duke's blind resistance. But, now that the ' Waverers ' had so far triumphed that the Lords had accepted the principle of reform, too-clever men like Lyndhurst believed they could wrest reform out of Whig hands, remodel it in committee, and by this manœuvre reunite their party ; the Lords therefore carried an amendment to postpone the disfranchising clauses. At once Grey asked the King for power to make not less than fifty peers and, when this was refused, resigned office.

He was only out for five days, and Wellington's abandonment of an attempt to make a Tory government was not so much due to threats of civil war as to the passion of party, the English political sense, and Peel's refusal to join a Tory government committed to ' an extensive reform '. His own mistake had been grave enough for years past, in declining any reform at all; at least he would not commit another which would destroy all character in politics. And since in this the Whig majority in the Commons and the Tory rank-and-file agreed, the Duke's military notion of saving the King from any creation of peers rapidly expired. Radical posters in London — ' to stop the Duke, go for gold ' — wilder schemes of barricades and refusal of taxes, tricolours and pikes, were not needed to bring about his retreat.

Not to their own pleasure, for Grey and Althorp were ready to support a Tory government which would carry the bill, but on the clear demand of the Commons of both parties, the Cabinet returned to office; receiving from the King the full pledge he had evaded before. But making of peers was not required. William IV put pressure on Wellington, bishops, and moderates to abstain, and on the 4th June, to almost empty Tory benches, the Lords passed the bill.

It was the triumph, not of democracy, but of the Commons and the middle class. Not the King and Lords but the Cabinet, representing the undoubted will of the Commons, had carried it. To an existing electorate of about 435,000 in England and Wales it added less than 250,000 new voters, and those for the most part on a comparatively high £10 franchise, which actually cut out many who had voted before. It was the plain determination of the middle class which, more than mob violence, impressed Parliament; their huge but orderly meetings, the warnings received through Radical leaders like Place and Attwood, the refusal to act as special constables, resignations from the yeomanry, the overwhelming voice of the press and a firm lead given by *The Times* — these carried more weight than the whirling words of Orator Hunt.

Some of the Tory warnings, indeed, were just, and justified by later events. There could be no finality made in the franchise by drawing a £10 line, and if numbers were to be the test for distribution of seats, this principle must in time swallow up all others. Such were some of the penalties incurred by the Tory refusal, from Pitt's time onwards, to face up to this question. But, things having come to this pass, we must think the measure of 1832 both just and inevitable; in any case, it was a first condition for all that was done in Victorian Britain.

CONTEMPORARY DATES

1826 War in Portugal between Maria and Miguel.
1827 Battle of Navarino.
      Death of Blake and Beethoven.
      Dr. Arnold becomes headmaster of Rugby School.
1828 Russo-Turkish war.
      Andrew Jackson elected President of the United States.

1829   Treaty of Adrianople.
1830   Revolution in France ; Louis-Philippe elected King.
        Separation of Belgium and Holland.
        The French take Algiers.
        Lyell, *Principles of Geology*.
        Comte, *Philosophie positive*.
1831   Russian suppression of Polish rebellion.
        Charles Albert becomes King of Savoy.
        Victor Hugo, *Notre-Dame*.
        Stendhal, *Rouge et noir*.
        Founding of the British Association for Science.
1832   Otto of Bavaria, King of Greece.
        Mazzini founds ' Young Italy '.
        Death of Bentham, Goethe, and Walter Scott.

CHAPTER X

WHIGS AND CHARTISTS, 1832–1841

THE landowning caste had thus taken into partnership the middle-class manufacturers, tenant farmers, and skilled artisans; the industrial north at last found itself in power, representatives of Birmingham, Manchester, and Leeds balancing uneasily the highly protected landed shires. This new Britain had to adjust itself to its full inheritance in Europe and Empire, Ireland and India, yet its first essential work must be done at home — to complete those changes which Pitt had begun but the war had delayed, which Canning and Huskisson had advanced, but the fulfilment of which could only come through a reformed Parliament. And this epoch was a continuous one, for much the same work was done, first by the Whigs, then by the Tories.

With one six-month interval in 1834–5 the Whigs held office till 1841, under Grey till his retirement in 1834 and thereafter under Melbourne. In one sense their best days seemed to end with the passage of 'the Bill'. They fell into factions; with Irish and Radicals to either side, their central mass were ill at ease, while in years of deepening depression they never found a minister who gave a lead in finance. Economically this was a period of upward progress. Exports had stood at £47 millions in 1827, but were £102 millions in 1840; wheat, which in the decade ending with 1819 sold at an average of 88s. or more, averaged just under 56s. a quarter over the 'forties; the cost of living by 1849 was lower than since 1780, and industrial wages in the same span rose as a whole by some 40 per cent. But this progress was interrupted by fluctuations — 1838–41 and 1847 for instance being years of great suffering — and was subject to some terrible exceptions. There were flaws in our economic structure, besides political causes, not all of British making, which held the country in a sort of arrested march.

Intimate papers of Grey, Russell, and Peel inform us how statesmen's minds were still darkened by fear of a 'convulsion', of which the Chartist movement was to give some proof. The throne was most unpopular, certainly till after Queen Victoria's marriage, the Church often positively hated, while revolutionary notions of the French pattern had not yet died. Looked at on a large scale, the central problem was what would be the national future, whether it could be held by conservative influences to some kind of planned protected society, or whether it would turn, as all that was liberal in France was turning, to some Socialist scheme. The solution was found elsewhere; in the acceptance, even by the Tories, of *laisser-faire* and the remedies of Liberals and Utilitarians, and the slow absorption of the quasi-revolutionary working-men of the 'thirties into the Radical wing of a Liberal party.

A large majority was given to Grey in the election of December 1832, necessitated by the Reform bill. So far as the loose parties of the time allow us to calculate, only about 150 Tories were returned, but the 320 Whigs had to bargain with their allies, some 70 Radicals and the same number of Irish. Not that this left-wing thrust was yet immediate. By no means all Irish members followed O'Connell over Repeal, nor was Radicalism adequately represented in Parliament, though Cobbett had been elected together with leaders of the ' philosophic ' school, in Grote, Molesworth, and Charles Buller. In fact, of the first ' reformed ' House of Commons, one-third were the sons of peers or baronets.

It remained, then, till the Reform bill of 1867 an age of aristocracy, though Liberals and Utilitarians desired to make it an aristocracy of talent rather than of property. Yet the change of atmosphere since the 'twenties was decisive. Parties were so much altered as to be almost new; that which Peel was careful to call ' Conservative ', instead of ' Tory ', being changed out of all recognition.

After as before the Bill, Grey was beset by heavy problems in foreign affairs, his conduct of which, in junction with Palmerston, was strong and successful, as the Belgian settlement showed. He had to deal, too, with an ageing, soft-witted King, and a hostile majority in the Lords. His Cabinet was disunited. The fiery Durham, struck down by private griefs and impatient at any compromise, resigned in 1833, while Brougham was ever a brand of discord, but the mortal wound to his government, and again to Peel's in 1835, came from Ireland. O'Connell had given valuable aid in carrying reform, though his claims to office were neglected, but Ireland's essential evils went much deeper than mere law and order, being massed in a poverty-stricken population which swelled from $6\frac{3}{4}$ millions in 1821 to 8 millions in 1840, and in alien institutions, represented first and foremost by the Church of the Anglican minority. If Stanley, the Irish secretary, concentrated less on causes than on symptoms, such as the repeal campaign or the 242 murders of a single year, his transfer to the Colonial Office did not change the fundamentals. In May 1834, rather than allow that Irish Church revenues could be transferred to secular purposes, he resigned with Graham, Goderich, and Richmond — in July, finding that some of his colleagues, including Althorp, were in league with Wellesley the Lord-Lieutenant and O'Connell to obtain a milder coercion Act, Grey himself threw up office. Melbourne, sensibly rejecting the King's wish for a coalition with Peel, came in with a much weakened Cabinet, which collapsed on the first difficulty when Althorp, on his father's death, was removed to the Lords. Unwilling to see the Commons' lead go to Russell, which would mean an advance of Radicalism, in a weak letter Melbourne gave the King the chance he longed for, of dismissing his ministers, as Radicals put it or, more accurately perhaps, of leaping at their half-proffered resignation.

So came about in November the six months' ministry of Sir Robert Peel. It involved an election, preceded by a manifesto issued to his Tamworth constituents : declaring the Reform Act was irrevocable, and that the ' Conservative ' party was ready to reform Church and local government also. The Whig majority was much reduced, though they lost more ground to Radicals than Tories, but not enough to enable Peel to stand, and in April 1835, beaten on that very principle of ' appropriation ' of Irish Church endowments which had split Grey's government, he resigned. Melbourne returned to office, though now without Althorp, Brougham, Durham, Graham, or Stanley, and dependent on the so-called ' Lichfield House compact ' with the Irish vote.

One parliamentary epoch had ended, for the old Houses of Parliament, which had cradled the constitution and heard each great voice from the Cecils to the Pitts, were burned down on the 16th October 1834; the cause lay in another relic, the fire beginning in a careless burning of the wooden ' tallies ' used by mediaeval kings to count their revenue.

These events, when the acid of the Irish question played on British party, did not interrupt the great achievement of this decade, the passing of more vital statutory reforms than any since the Long Parliament. By no means all were due to the initiative of Whig ministers, for sometimes they were inspired by the Radicals, nor could most of them have passed without the support of Peel.

In this atmosphere of reform and a dead-set against privilege or monopoly, the steps were taken which Eldonian Toryism had refused, and which the split in the Tory ranks had further delayed. The campaign to amend the criminal law, begun by Romilly and Peel, was pushed deeper, and thus capital punishment was abolished in 1832 for horse-stealing and house-breaking. Brougham carried part of a great legal programme through a hostile House of Lords ; sweeping away sinecures, cutting at the jungle of common-law procedure, and erecting the Judicial Committee of the Privy Council as a court of appeal in ecclesiastical and Admiralty cases. In 1833, when the East India Company's charter was due for revision, its last monopoly of the China trade was thrown open and its famous fleet of East-Indiamen disposed of ; the India government now being empowered to legislate for all India, a legal member was added to the governor-general's council, with Macaulay as the first appointment. In 1834 it was the turn of the Bank of England, and henceforward joint-stock banks were to be allowed within the London region, as well as the provinces; on the other hand, the Bank was set free in determining its rate of interest, and its notes for sums. over £5 were made legal tender. In 1836 the newspaper stamp duty was reduced from fourpence to a penny, not only through a democratic agitation organized by the tireless Place, but as part of a Whig campaign to crush the predominance of the Peelite *Times*.

In one special case, fundamental for the transmission of knowledge and the assimilation of a varied society, the government could claim no credit. Our postal system dated from the Commonwealth, the post-master-general's monopoly being worked in practice through contractors, and though Pitt had insisted on fast mail-coaches to hasten delivery and give protection against highwaymen, the service did little to help either the public or the revenue. Its charges were enormous, a London to Edinburgh letter costing 1s. 4d., and the brunt fell on the poor, for through members of either House or officials most of the upper and middle class could get their letters 'franked' free. The result was wholesale evasion, in a smuggling of letters by every coach or travelling bagman. Moreover, postage was painfully calculated, and painfully collected, on delivery of each individual letter.

Government's slow enquiries and their officials' obstruction were stormed by the energy and vision of one man, Rowland Hill. He came from one of many remarkable families of the Birmingham region, trained in the tradition of Priestley and acquainted with the Utilitarian leaders, whose minds turned easily from mechanical invention to edu-cational and social reform. His ruling idea was simple, that postage should be prepaid, at a uniform rate irrespective of distance, and having failed with the government he appealed to the people. After three years' resistance Melbourne bowed to public opinion, and penny postage became law in 1840.

Of all ancient establishments the most unpopular with Radicals was the Church, and Peel was aware that only strenuous reform could save it. Already Grey, after abolishing ten out of twenty-two Irish bishoprics, had warned the English bishops that they too should 'set their house in order', while two Whig measures of 1836 executed the changes which Peel's government had explored. One Act commuted the much-disliked payment of tithe in kind into a fixed charge, calculated on the corn prices of the preceding seven years. A second set up the Ecclesiastical Commission, to redraw the boundaries and redistribute the endowments of dioceses. So the income of Canterbury, for example, was reduced from £30,000 to £15,000; it was made illegal to hold two benefices, if over two miles apart; cathedral chapters and their finances were brought under a central control. Thus surplus funds were found to amend the stark poverty of many livings, over two thousand of which still had an income of less than £100.

If strong enough to hold out on many points, the Church had to yield some of its ancient ground. London University was incorporated in 1837, to give degrees without those Anglican tests which Oxford and Cambridge retained. After several refusals by the Lords, the Marriage Act of 1836 allowed Dissenters to be married in their own chapels, also legalizing civil marriage before the registrars for births, marriages, and deaths.

Meanwhile the Whigs carried out the reform of local government, without which parliamentary reform would remain unreal. Ever since the Union Scotland had politically been in the pocket of every government of the day, the root of the evil lying in the corrupt burghs and their self-chosen councils. That was all ended by an Act of 1833, creating councils to be elected by citizens who had a parliamentary vote. For England and Wales the Municipal Corporations Act of 1835 was a much more sweeping measure, largely inspired by the Utilitarians; the secretary of the enquiry being an extreme Radical, Joseph Parkes, formerly a driving-force in the Birmingham political union. Its chief provisions were very drastic. By a revolutionary invasion of old charters the Act dissolved over 200 corporations, setting up instead 178 municipal boroughs to be governed by elected councils, and this municipal franchise was given to all ratepayers. Though the principle was approved by Peel, the Tory Lords added sundry checks and balances, such as the creation of aldermen, designed to curb what they feared would be local democracies. The Act had this great importance, that it restored for the first time, broadly speaking, since the fourteenth century a real urban self-government; ending the abuses which had grown up in the intervening ages, whereby petty self-chosen bodies had exploited the money and rights of thousands, or some local peer had flooded a corporation with his tenants. But it was by no means complete, for in many cases the improvement commissioners of the previous century lingered on, together with other special bodies set up to deal with paving, drainage, or light.

Most memorable by far of the Whig reforms, in the breadth of its effect, was the Act of 1833 to abolish slavery. Wilberforce and his friends had never rested content with the abolition of the trade in 1807. For, in the first place, this ‘ abolition ’ was not a fact; though this was no fault of Great Britain, whose taxpayers advanced £700,000 to Spain and Portugal to induce them to do the same, and whose foreign ministers from Castlereagh to Palmerston were urgent in the cause. It became clear that, so long as slavery existed, large profits could be made in an illegal trade, nor would the United States collaborate by allowing British

warships to search suspect traders. In the 'twenties, therefore, Wilberforce and Fowell Buxton raised the issue of abolishing slavery itself.

The Liverpool Cabinet did their best. In the new Crown Colonies,
such as Trinidad, regulations prepared the way for freedom ; abolishing
use of the whip in the fields or the flogging of women, and preventing
the break-up of slave families. But the mass of slaves were held in
ancient self-governing colonies like Jamaica, whose legislatures evaded
such regulation, and whose planters, feeling themselves outnumbered by
ten to one, ruthlessly put down the rebellions which rumours of freedom
excited, and persecuted missionaries who championed the negro. By
1830 it was clear that these legislatures would do nothing unless they
were forced, and other facts brought that compulsion nearer. For the
West Indian interest had lost much of its power in the Commons,
reforming Britain was on fire for abolition, and James Stephen, son of
one of Wilberforce's original helpers and a remarkable character himself, was high in authority at the Colonial Office.

The Act of 1833 arose, however, not merely out of this abolitionist
pressure but from a Cabinet crisis, Stanley being anxious to make a
success at the Colonial Office after his failure in Ireland, and its clauses
reflect a good deal of compromise. The West Indians were strong
enough to procure compensation for their slaves in a free gift of £20
millions ; on the other hand, the slaves' apprenticeship, which was to
precede full freedom, was to last for only seven years. As the Act
passed, Wilberforce lay dying ; a year later, in August 1834, all slaves
in the British Empire became free. This was an act of enormous faith.
The young member for Newark, W. E. Gladstone, whose father was a
leader of the Liverpool slave interest, was not alone in predicting evil
effects, both for the slaves themselves and the very existence of the West
Indies.

At the height of the Reform bill crisis, cholera reached England from
eastern Europe, and 50,000 deaths exposed the squalid lives being
dragged out by many thousands, and the limited extent of anything like
a social policy. As every Budget proved, this was the heyday of orthodox
political economy. The one overpowering clamour from all parties was
for retrenchment ; the house-tax was repealed under pressure from the
new urban vote ; the national expenditure of 1839-40, just under £49
millions, was well below that of ten years before, nor would Althorp
and his Whig successors at the Exchequer ever reimpose the income-
tax, repealed in 1815. One example of their economy was the nothing-
done for national education. Despite some Radical motions — Roebuck
bringing forward a scheme, as Whitbread had done twenty years earlier
— the State contributed nothing, except to grant £20,000 in 1833 to the
various Church societies. In 1839, however, a small wedge of State
direction was driven in, when a committee of Privy Council was given

control of educational grants and authorized to appoint inspectors. Much the same sort of tentative compromise held good as regards the police; a prisons commission, with government inspectors, was organized in 1835, but outside London the creation of an adequate police force was left to the whim of local authorities.

These ruling dogmas extended much beyond taxation. If private savings were thought all-important, if there was a wage-fund dependent on a ratio between the capital available and the number of wage-earners, and if, as Malthus taught, population threatened to outrun the means of subsistence, the approved social policy logically followed. State interference must do more harm than good, while efforts to subsidize wages or reduce working-hours would only diminish the wage-fund or swell the competing population. All this was reinforced by the powerful Evangelicals, who believed in the saving of men by their own exertions, and pronounced the Christian duty of charity a higher thing than State compulsion. By the same reasoning, a great majority of Dissenting Radicals vehemently objected to State-controlled education.

There was, indeed, a rival influence, that of the Benthamites, counteracting this policy of *laisser-faire*. Their power in the press and in organizing opinion was at its height, and how great was the energy of Bentham's disciples we could illustrate from the rugged figure of Edwin Chadwick, secretary to the poor-law enquiry and then to the poor-law commissioners till 1847, and later a leader in promoting national health. The Utilitarian method was to insist on science and statistics, to lay down principles for administration and enforce them by centralizing power. This authoritarian democracy, however, collided not only with individualism and many democratic sentimental forces, but with the ancient aristocracy of justices of the peace. So that the central and local structure of nineteenth-century Britain was the child of compromise.

Well before the Reform bill the humanitarian feeling, which was working for slaves and introducing the first laws against cruelty to animals, inspired another agitation, which brought about the factory Acts. Of those sponsored by Peel's father, the Lancashire cotton magnate, that of 1802 applied to the pauper apprentices sent up from London and southern workhouses; a process which ceased soon after Waterloo, for steam-power brought the factories from country valleys into the towns, where local child labour was plentiful. His second Act, of 1819, touched cotton mills only and, though forbidding night-work and setting up for these children a twelve-hour day, provided no real system of inspectors and was evaded wholesale. When the Whigs took office, adult labourers' hours were still entirely unrestricted, nor was anything serious done for children outside the cotton mills. In 1830 Richard Oastler, a devout Tory churchman, began a crusade in Yorkshire against ' child slavery ' in the woollen and worsted trades, finding allies in the strong Lancashire spinners' union who were pressing for shorter hours. Their first spokesman in Parliament was Michael Sadler, a Tory and a critic of the fashionable economists, and when he lost his seat the Tory Evangelical Ashley, later Lord Shaftesbury, took up his work.

Two separate questions were involved; the one, a movement to protect child labour, but the other, the real aim of most northern trade unionists, to get shorter hours for adults. They concentrated, therefore, on asking a ten-hour day for young persons and women, without whom the mills could not be kept running by the men operatives alone. But that the State should fix hours for grown men went against the teaching of Benthamites and economists, it was opposed by manu-facturers who feared foreign competition, and the Act of 1833 bitterly disappointed reformers. Yet it registered a great advance. It covered all textiles except lace, forbade employment of children under nine absolutely and night-work for all under eighteen, enforced a nine-hour day for those below thirteen, a twelve-hour day for those between fourteen and eighteen, and, what mattered most, appointed salaried government inspectors.

While factory reform slowly proceeded, a royal commission of 1832 attacked the worst of all evils, the poor law. An earlier enquiry of 1817 had shown how deep set was the disease; how indiscriminate subsidizing of wages from the rates, by several thousand timid parish authorities, had broken the spirit of independence, driven down wages, loaded agriculture with crushing rates, and put a premium on idleness and bastardy. Poor rates, which in 1803 cost England and Wales little over £4 millions, rose to over £7 millions by 1832.

The Act of 1834 was the greatest of Benthamite triumphs, carefully prepared by Place and Chadwick and the Mills, and marshalled with skilful publicity. Its principle, the commissioners claimed, was a return to the true purpose of Elizabeth's law, the relief of the impotent and the temporary relief of distress. Its professed aim was a total abolition of outdoor relief to the able-bodied, who could henceforth only expect to receive relief in a workhouse, and that under 'deterrent' conditions, since the pauper's lot ought to be worse than that of an independent labourer. But this Act, too, was a compromise. It did not, as some reformers wished, entirely prohibit outdoor relief, nor did it make the poor law a nationalized service; one objection to this, its authors argued, would be the cost, and another, that 'candidates for political power would bid for popularity by promising to be good to the poor'. Over and above its social objective, the Act was an administrative revolution, sweeping away the venerable powers of magistrates, parishes, and over-seers, to replace them by elected guardians for wide areas, working under orders of central commissioners. Such centralization was to that age most distasteful, being judged un-English or Prussian, and the commissioners were appointed, in the first instance, for only five years.

Ardently they and their pugnacious secretary Chadwick rearranged 15,000 parishes into some 600 unions, while in enforcing the ' work-house test ' they were assisted by some prosperous years and the great rush of railway-making. But in 1836 this prosperity ended, just as they were approaching the stiff problem of the industrial north. No law since the Six Acts had roused such bitter feeling, it was resisted by Tory idealists like the poet Southey, by Disraeli and Walter, chief proprietor of *The Times*, as inhuman and unchristian, and equally denounced by the dying breath of the Radical Cobbett. The commissioners' purpose being to make workhouse life disagreeable, their regulations separated husband and wife, cut off comforts like tobacco, and made their workhouses hateful as ' new Bastilles '; ' the house ' which, till a much later date, every decent working family abhorred. In the north their problem was quite different; that of an area where the Speenhamland dole system had usually been un-known, but which was now smitten by dire poverty. Was there to be no remedy for the artisan, unemployed by no fault of his own, except this semi-imprisonment in a Bastille ? Many thousands swore they would resist the setting up of Union houses by force, and their resistance became part of the Chartist revolution.

Chartism, which rose to its peak in 1839 and flared up again in 1848, had in itself a disappointing history, but possesses this double import-ance : that it linked the reforming movements of Paine and Cartwright with the later Radicalism of Bright and Chamberlain, and that it held up, as it were, a social mirror in which men of good will could see the shortcomings of their country. In its political platform there was nothing original, for the six points of the Charter drawn up in 1838 — annual Parliaments, universal male suffrage, equal electoral districts, the ballot, payment of members and no property qualification for them — had been ventilated in the time of North and were revived by the survivor of that early Radicalism, old Major Cartwright; who lived on till 1824 holding, his contemporary Place tells us, over his weak gin-and-water ' a vague and absurd notion of the political arrangements of the Anglo-Saxons '.

The fact that all these six points, except annual Parliaments, have since become law, does not mean they could have been carried then, or involve condemnation of the Whig government. Much in their social policy did them credit. Not the Factory Acts only, but others ; one for instance, not very effectual, to stop the oppression of chimney sweepers' boys ; another, to check the very old evil of paying wages in ' truck ', usually taking the form of inferior goods at dear prices from an employer. Althorp, that mighty and happy sportsman, carried an Act to reform the monstrous game laws, which had covered the country with armed gangs of poachers, and from 1831 the killing, sale, and purchase of game were opened to all who could obtain a licence. Unlike their predecessors, the Whigs also respected freedom of opinion. Meetings were rarely interfered with until they became torchlight meetings, calling to arms, while no Chartist paper, however violent, was suppressed. But they inherited the horror from French revolutionary days of a ' convulsion ', as was shown by Melbourne's administration at the Home Office and, best known of all, by the case of the ' Tolpuddle martyrs ', — the sentence of transportation passed in 1834 on the Dorset labourers, who were found practising secret oaths and ritual, as many early Labour bodies did, to uphold their union. Their fear was not surprising, for violence and some murderous crime dogged the early history of trades unionism, and Chartism covered several possibilities.

Its leaders included men of every type. Oastler was a Tory democrat, whose theme was ' the altar, the throne, and the cottage '; Stephens, who did in the Lancashire Factory Act agitation what Oastler did for Yorkshire, began as a Methodist minister. Some, like William Lovett of the London group, were primarily moral reformers; others were idealists with a streak of the crank, like Thomas Cooper of Leicester. Some were revolutionaries of a traditional sort: as Julius Harney, an intellectual, who thought of a *sans-culotte* night march on London; or Bronterre O'Brien, their best writer, a Jacobin who came to see that violence was useless. Their most powerful leader was also their worst. Feargus O'Connor began with the inherited notions of an Irish rebel family, found in the industrial north an avenue for his eloquence and an opening for his ambition, and from Leeds conducted the *Northern Star*, for which he enlisted the democratic writers. But no one could work long with this vain and unscrupulous man who, after leading thousands to the verge of revolution, perpetually backed down. Having no understanding of economics or industry, in his latter days he reverted to a typically Irish crusade, for an agrarian community of peasant co-operators.

Three other influences had blazed the trail. One was that of Robert Owen, an idealist believer in man's perfectibility, if his environment were improved; who, however, increasingly disliked political action, and disapproved the class war. For him the community life was to be found in a voluntary association of co-operative groups, and by men willing to be educated. Again, there was the economic theory, in part taken from Locke and Ricardo, by the first school of doctrinaire Socialists, such as Hodgskin, the ex-naval lieutenant who held forth at the London mechanics' institution, or the surviving disciples of the Newcastle schoolmaster, Thomas Spence, who preached land nationalization. Their teaching included the notions that Labour, as the sole maker of values, created the ' surplus ' seized by others in rent, interest, or profit, and that, under a capitalist system and Malthus' doctrine, wage-rates were driven down as by an iron law. Lastly, there were political democrats, particularly strong in Birmingham, represented by men like Attwood and the Quaker Joseph Sturge, who would welcome the alliance of moderate Chartists.

Chartist strength and its claim upon history, did not, in fact, consist in its leaders, but rather because it assembled all the protests against monstrous hardships. Against wretched wage-rates and long hours; worst in the case of the hand-loom weavers of Lancashire and the Border, who might earn a penny an hour for a seventy-hour week, or the knitters and stockingers of the Midlands. Against the injustice of an undis-criminating poor law; against cellar-dwellings and child labour; and how miserable was that life we can read not only in Disraeli's *Sybil* or Dickens or Charles Kingsley, but in the toneless figures of official reports. But though the Chartists forced these grievances on the mind of the nation, they did it in some wrong-headed ways, and themselves deservedly failed.

They were ruined by faction among their leaders, and by contra-dictions which they never solved. Was action to be political or in-dustrial ? Was it to be the class war, or a union of middle and lower classes ? There could be no solid truce between their extremists and men like Place, who believed in the workhouse test and thought that trade unions would disappear, while the Birmingham Radicals soon fell away, disapproving of physical force. Cheaper food was the remedy of the Anti-Corn Law League, but to most Chartists that was suspect as a body of middle-class manufacturers who wished cheaper food, only in order to lower wages. Violent signs of earlier days were present, secret collections of arms, wearing of the tricolour, with plans for a run on the banks and for a Convention to rival Parliament.

Chartism was preceded not merely by the Factory Acts and poor-law agitation, but by furious trade-union activity, seen in many strikes against wage-cutting and piece rates, or for all-union shops. From Lancashire James Doherty organized a national union of textile workers, there was a parallel movement in the building trades, and in 1834 Owen founded a ' Grand National Consolidated ' union of all trades, com-mitted to a general strike ; not for ' some paltry advance ' of wages, but to ensure to all ' the most advantageous exercise of all their powers '. This was said to have enrolled half a million members, but its huge vagueness was wasted in sectional strikes, and broke on the determina-tion of the masters.

Thus reinforced by a backwash of defeated resentful workmen, during 1838 the London moderate group under Lovett prepared the Charter, while schemes matured for a Convention and a national petition. But meantime O'Connor got to work on the *Northern Star*, violent men overcame the moderates, and early in 1839 the Convention, declaring a right to arm, moved to Birmingham as an easier contact with the north. In July there were heavy riots there, and the Commons refused to hear the petition; there were many arrests of leaders, and the armed rising, from which O'Connor now shrank back, petered out in a hopeless affray between the troops at Newport and the revolutionary miners of the Welsh valleys.

The early 'forties were hard years of depression and savage strikes, but the foreign revolutionaries then studying England, Engels and Karl Marx, found the country much too pacific for a proletarian rising. Trade unions in general had veered away from the general strike, the middle class were almost solid against universal suffrage. How indeed could true democracy come from a working-class of whom one-third, as statistics show, could not write their names? Self-improvement, both Owen and Lovett argued, must be the first step.

Yet, though democracy was not yet fitted to rule, we become conscious that the Whig contribution is nearing exhaustion; of which Melbourne, with his weary, tolerant cynicism, may be taken as symbol. Great forces, expressed in organized bodies, Chartists and Anti-Corn Law League and Irish Repeal association, were outrunning the government. They were plagued also by Canadian rebellion, Afghan and China wars, and threats of war with France, in all of which they made mistakes. They were tending to make large matters, like corn laws and vote by ballot, ' open questions ' in Cabinet; they carried their Irish Tithe Act, but only by dropping their principle of ' appropriation '. They could neither absorb nor come to terms with the Radicals, on whom their future majority must depend, while for fear of losing bye-elections they dared not reconstruct the Cabinet.

Dependent on the neutrality of O'Connell, the wish of Wellington to assist government against disorder, and on Peel's unwillingness to take power till assured his forces were disciplined, they went on without vitality till 1841. The accession of a new sovereign had helped them, giving Melbourne a rôle in which he shone, as the disinterested worldly mentor of a young woman, but their weaknesses were cumulative and their sap had ceased to flow.

CONTEMPORARY DATES

1833   Carlist wars open in Spain.
       Treaty of Unkiar Skelessi.
       Beginning of the Oxford Movement.
       The British abolish slavery.

CHAPTER XI

THE QUEEN AND SIR ROBERT PEEL
1837–1850

WHILE the weak Melbourne government laboured with rebellion in Canada and Jamaica, and disgusted their Radical
wing by concessions over Ireland to the Lords, their life was
prolonged by the death in June 1837 of William IV and the accession,
at the age of eighteen, of his niece Victoria. Many years were needed
to bring out the Queen's qualities, and nothing but the length of her
reign could have made it so vital. Even so, the immediate effects were
momentous. Her youth and innocence set up the monarchy again
in the eyes of the people, against the tarnished background of George
III's sons. Her dignity, with her decision to stand forth as Queen and
relegate her mother and her mother's advisers to obscurity, equally
impressed the political class.

On the other hand, until her marriage and sometimes after it, her
temper and excitement reminded close observers that she was granddaughter to George III. Lonely and inexperienced, her gratitude
for Melbourne's devotion made her see politics through Whig
spectacles, while nothing but her sex could have caused the crisis of
1839, and no male sovereign could have escaped from it so lightly.
Melbourne's weakness was so great that his resignation might have
come on any pretext, and he found one in a combined Tory and Radical
resistance to suspending the constitution of Jamaica. When Peel was
sent for to form a Cabinet, his reception was frigid, the Queen insisting
she could not agree to a dissolution, and when, as a mark of confidence,
he asked some change in the phalanx of Whig ladies in her Household,
it was refused. The ex-ministers' view of their constitutional duty was
curious, for when the Queen appealed to their chivalry, they advised
her to stand fast, and Melbourne returned to power.

Hitherto, the chief rival influence to Melbourne's with the Queen
had been that of her Hanoverian governess Baroness Lehzen, but with
the Queen's marriage this stage closed. Her mother had been a princess
of Saxe-Coburg-Gotha, sister to that Leopold who had married George
IV's daughter Charlotte and since had become King of the Belgians,
and all her early life was coloured by the advice of this wise uncle
and his confidant, Baron von Stockmar. This circle put forward as her
husband one of themselves, the Queen's first cousin Albert, son of yet

another brother of the Duchess of Kent. They married in February 1840 and, with the birth of the Princess Royal that year and the Prince of Wales the next, began the sequence of a large family.

This new monarchy was very German, and by no means popular. Parliament cut down the financial allowance which the Cabinet proposed for the Prince Consort who, moreover, was not as yet admitted to royal interviews with ministers. His laborious intellectuality did not appeal to Englishmen who felt, with some justice, the same dislike of alien influence as they had under William III. The Prince, declaring he was the Queen's permanent minister, applied to this country Stockmar's ideas of monarchical government, so that on occasions innumerable — above all over foreign affairs, — the Court's policy clashed with their ministers'. And numerous marriages in the Coburg family, with the royal houses of France, Belgium, and Portugal, built up a powerful diplomatic clan.

On the other hand, the slow recovery of respect for the Crown and the Queen's massive strength in after years both dated from her marriage. The Prince's political instinct was shrewd, his moral standard was austere, both Court and Cabinet changed greatly as compared with the last few reigns. The Queen's courage in facing two attempts made on her life, her progresses in Scotland and the disturbed Chartist regions, a decent and economic Court, and small children, began a domestication of monarchy unseen since the few happy years of Charles I. Ministers found a royal pair with firm well-documented views on Europe, an eye and ear for religion, art, and learning, and a punctilious ideal of their duty. Soon this Court found its perfect servant in Sir Robert Peel.

Two disastrous years for the Whig Cabinet followed on the ' Bedchamber ' crisis of 1839. Except that they made vote by ballot an open Cabinet question, they did little for their Radicals. Chartist discontent smouldered on, so did the ten-hour-day agitation, and from 1838 a severe depression darkened the country. Wheat stood round about 70s. all the next year; exports, cotton in particular, were stagnant; the Bank's reserve was dangerously low; wage rates were miserably forced down. To two unfortunate wars in China and Afghanistan were added, in 1840–41, a European crisis and fear of war with France, while nothing except a poor law on English lines touched Irish grievances over Church and soil. When four successive budgets had shown a deficit, in 1841 Russell, perturbed at the progress of the Anti-Corn-Law League, tried to capture the flagging gale with suggestions for a reduced colonial preference on timber and sugar, and a low fixed duty on imported wheat. This late-found liberalism did not impress Parliament or people. In June Peel carried by one vote a resolution of lack of confidence, Parliament was dissolved, he was returned with (for those days) the ample majority of 90, and at last the Whigs resigned.

His government of 1841–6 was one of the strongest of the century. It included five other past or future Prime Ministers, — Wellington, Stanley, Aberdeen, Gladstone, and poor Goderich; the administrative talent of Sir James Graham; four future Viceroys in Hardinge, Ellenborough, Dalhousie, and Canning. This powerful body was emphatically the instrument of Peel himself, who in the capacity of Prime Minister has never been excelled. As the business of State, much increased though it was, was still within the grasp of a man of high ability, his incessant preparation and continuous hold covered all departments, to control foreign affairs through Aberdeen, India through Hardinge, or tariff revision through Gladstone. His nearest counsellor perhaps was Graham, whom in temper he most resembled, in the same fear of revolution or what Graham called ' the grand blow-up ', watchfulness for economic symptoms, and comparative disdain for party. Yet however supreme as an administrator, it is arguable whether Peel reached the first rank of statesmen. His powerful mind was rather apprehensive than of ranging imagination, moving also more to the bidding of realized facts than of ideals. If high-mindedness in using patronage in Church and State, and a zeal to discover and reward merit, mark the great public servant, and if sagacity and moderation won homage from the Prince Consort, Leopold of Belgium, and Guizot, yet neither in social policy nor in problems of Empire did he seem to look far beyond the compromises which must tide over the next few years.

More than any other man he was the creator of the Conservative party. To him was due their reorganization, the new weapon of registration, and the Carlton Club, while for ten years he had kept them on his own restrained course, fending off both Wellington's pessimism and the folly of Tory peers. He was masterful as leader, as many cracks of the party whip showed, and in tactic and debate unrivalled. But he had two serious shortcomings. He did not win the heart of his following, and that not just because he ignored some human expectancies, — making, for instance, only six peers in these five years, — but because he was cold or deaf to some high sentiments in Tory tradition, whether religious passion or the vision of paternal government. And being both sensitive and secretive, anxious and proud, he would form ideas of educating his party into his own way of thinking, and try to force decision on men from whom his process of thought was concealed.

This very great politician registered like a weather-glass the change of atmosphere since Eldon, and in himself summed up what early Victorians held in highest regard. The ' spinning jenny ', as George IV called him, represented the new wealth of Lancashire and, when one of the richest men in England, still himself kept his household accounts. That origin he had ornamented by the highest academic

honours of Oxford, coming thence religious but anti-Puseyite, an
economist in mind but with the social notions of a moderate Tory, a
believer in progress yet with a rooted fear of revolution. Now he
had reached the full power, sought with such reserved ambition, to
make real what he desired, which was to modernize, conciliate, and
appease. Other chapters will illustrate parts of his task, — to renew a
pacific air in Europe, to dispose of unhappy Whig legacies in Canada
and Jamaica, and wars with China, Afghans, and Sikhs, or to fulfil the
logic of his own Emancipation Act in Ireland by alliance with moderate
Catholicism. His immediate duty at home was to dispel discontent by
eliminating the causes of depression, and to set in circulation the capital
and energy of the new industries. What was achieved of this by 1850,
though not all by Peel, sealed the political effect of the industrial
revolution.

Deficits totalling £10 millions for the five years ending in 1842, and
this on a budget averaging a mere £50 millions, dear bread, riotous
strikes, banks breaking, one person in every eleven a pauper, and
stationary exports, all testified to the need of what he described as
' permanent and comprehensive action '. The budget of 1842 showed
his resolution. In the teeth of Whig and Cobdenite criticism he revived
the income-tax at 7d. in the £, exempting incomes below £150, so as to
win a financial margin while he carried out a long overdue tariff revision.
Reducing duties on some 750 items, he produced a moderate gradation ;
cutting duties on raw materials to an average of 5 per cent, protecting
wholly manufactured goods by an average of 20 per cent, and increasing
the preferences which Huskisson had given the Colonies. He thus, for
example, reduced the duty on foreign timber to 25s., but that on
Canadian from 9s. to 1s. Meat and live animals were to come in at low
rates.

His prestige with his party was still great enough to make them
swallow much the same principles in regard to corn. The working of
the sliding-scale of 1828 was spasmodic, inducing speculators to hold
up supply for higher prices ; he contended that to continue the prices
of the last few years would mean social upheaval, and that what agriculture had most to fear was a lack of consuming power in the people.
The fixed duty which the Whigs favoured he would not have, since in
any scarcity it could not be enforced, preferring to reform the sliding-
scale downwards, to a pivotal price of about 56s. the quarter of wheat ;
Canada's would pay only a 1s. duty.

Good fortune rewarded his courage, the depression lifted, and credit
so much improved that in 1844 he was able to convert £250 millions of
debt from 3½ to 3 per cent. The budget of that year tackled sugar, a
thorny question with his party because West Indian interests were
strong, besides a persistent feeling that they had a right to protection

against slave-grown sugar from foreign colonies. In 1845, renewing income-tax for another three years, Peel repealed all duties on another 450 imports, including cotton-wool, dyes, and oils, and all duties whatever on exports, while the tariff on manufactured goods would henceforth range about 10 per cent.

Other economic measures showed his cautious experimental advance. Commissions of enquiry ordered by his predecessors resulted in the Coal Mines Act of 1842, forbidding employment of women underground, and of boys under ten, and providing inspectors to enforce it ; other reports on labour conditions revealed in Sheffield, Nottinghamshire, and the Potteries a mass of demoralized children, illiteracy, and immorality. If the Factory Act of 1844 did not meet those who wanted a general ten-hours day, for here Peel was of the same mind as Cobden, at least it fixed a 6½-hour maximum for children under thirteen and a maximum of 12 hours for women, besides the provision for fencing machinery. In social policy Peel stood broadly on the Benthamite maxims. He was firm in extending the poor law for another five years, and then, pushed on by the poor-law administrators, turned to public health. Chadwick had used an Act of 1837, setting up registrars of births and deaths, to investigate the causes of mortality ; his inspectors, Kay and Southwood Smith, with Farr in the registrar-general's office, were issuing one report after another on the pestilential condition of burial, water supply, and sanitation ; on the cesspools underlying most of London, the monthly cleaning of Manchester's mean streets, the four out of five Birmingham houses without water, corpses heaped in crowded churchyards, or the one-brick-thick, jerry-built houses set down on clay. Peel therefore appointed the commission on the state of towns, on whose reports of 1845 all sanitary legislation was to be based.

The 'forties were not altogether ' hungry ', as the saying has it ; on the contrary, though 1847 was a dire year, with that exception progress was decidedly towards that greater cheapness of living at which Peel aimed. Exports were valued at £47 millions in 1842, but at £60 millions in 1845 ; 5000 live animals were imported in 1842, but 216,000 in 1847 ; the growth in cotton and iron was portentous, and of coal great, though not so fast. The harvest of 1844 was the best for ten years, over the whole 'forties wheat averaged just under 56s. a quarter, and fell to 45s. in part of 1845 ; with the familiar exception of dying trades like hand-loom weavers and hosiery knitters, real wages in industry as a whole had risen perhaps by something between 20 and 30 per cent. When Peel left office, in fact, after two fluctuating and hard-tried generations, the cost of living had been restored to much the same level as before the great war.

If Nature, and Nature's recovery when man allows her, had assisted in this, man's invention and Peel's faculty for the minimum of sensible reform had contributed too. Cheapness, for one thing, was a child of cheaper transportation. After Stephenson's first triumphs at Darlington and Liverpool, ten years passed before railways much advanced : through doubts whether the locomotive had come to stay, or whether horses must not do the haulage on steep gradients ; through obstructive landowners, competition and wild speculation and battles over rival gauges. At the end of 1838 there were only 500 miles operating, of which the London and Birmingham line accounted for a fifth, and though Bradshaw's ' guide ' first appeared the next year, even in 1843 less than 2000 miles were working. Large development came only with Peel, and the cheapness and cheap money for which he worked. When 1848 ended, 5000 miles were working in the United Kingdom, while by amalgamation 200 scattered companies, some serving only a few miles, had sunk to 20 or 30 large units, such as the London and North-Western. This was the age of railway mania, the boom which broke in 1847 and ruined thousands ; the age of the railway-king, George Hudson, who began life as a York draper, rose to wealth and Parliament, and died a bankrupt. Stephenson himself lived till 1848 ; his son Robert, engineer to the North-Western, built the great bridges at Newcastle and the Menai Straits ; contractors like Peto had 10,000 men employed at a time in excavating and tunnelling, Thomas Brassey was launching out in the career which was to found the railways of Canada, India, and France. This enormous sprawling of competition brought in the State ; for though that age admired competition, practical dangers showed that railways could not be safely used like turnpike roads by private carriers, while only Parliament could adjudicate on the extent of a monopoly, or on rates, fares, and accidents. As President of the Board of Trade, Gladstone carried the Act of 1844, which created the ' parliamentary ' passenger train, bound to run at a third-class fare of 1d. a mile, with seats duly protected from the weather, and at a speed of not less than 12 miles an hour. But his wider proposals for State control were stoutly resisted, among others by Bright and Cobden, and though the State was empowered to buy up a railway when twenty-one years had elapsed since its charter, and a commission was set up to frame regulations, within a very few years such notions disappeared. By 1846 the electric telegraph, beginning as an accompaniment to the railways, was also being developed by private enterprise.

Though Peel's own instinct leaned to vested interests, he was no doctrinaire, and in one direction firmly exerted economic control. In every severe depression, not least in 1839–41, the banking system was found precarious, and quite incapable of guiding our much-expanded resources. The Bank of England's gold reserve fluctuated wildly, and was several times at danger-point ; uneven harvests and the tariff structure meant sudden drains, expecially from America. Some of the joint-stock banks, permissible in England since 1826, were mis-managed; private banks had fallen in number, but there were still nearly 300 which issued notes. Since his conversion to bullionist views in 1819, Peel had believed that the essential evil lay in this un-regulated issue, and his Bank Charter Act of 1844 enforced this definite, though narrow, point of view; to dangers of government monopoly and political money he was keenly alive, conceiving he could get the requisite safeguards without uprooting an existing system. The Act forced on the Bank a greater publicity of accounts, rigidly separated its banking and issue departments, allowed it to issue £14 millions in notes against securities but forbade issue above that figure, except on the basis of £1 in its vaults, in gold or silver, for each £1 note. No bank henceforth founded might issue at all, while those already existing were restricted to the total they issued in 1844 and encouraged to leave issue to the Bank of England. Against this Act much could be said, and was said by bankers at the time; as that its concentration on bank-notes ignored the greater, increasing share of cheques and mercantile bills in affecting credit, or that its effect must be to destroy any chance of expand-ing credit at the very moment when it was most needed. Indeed, at the first emergency in 1847, as twice in after years, it had to be suspended. But though warned of these possibilities, Peel feared inflation much more, and wrote that men must be trusted to act with sense at a crisis.

His pillars in Cabinet, now that the Duke was ageing so fast, were the pacific Aberdeen, the nervous Graham, and the restless Stanley. He had to contend with many severe ordeals; Ellenborough's unwise viceroyalty in India, aftermath of Afghan war, and preparation for Sikh war; tiresome pin-pricks with France; the Scottish Church disruption, which his political view of religion could ill judge; O'Connell's repeal campaign and his arrest in 1843; rumours of armed revolt from the Young Ireland party; bitterness of Orangemen; obstruction by the Lords to his schemes for Irish land, and by the Irish priesthood to those for education. Not being a man who could throw off his burdens, when attacked he grew autocratic; yet such attack needs must come, since his moderation isolated him between two extremes. Except for the ambition of Russell for power, he had little to fear from the official Whigs, who were discredited by manœuvring, divided by jealousies, and disunited on the corn laws. But to one side lay the Radicals of the Anti-Corn-Law League, and on the other the country gentlemen of the Tories.

Since its foundation in 1839, the League had grown to a giant. Money it was never likely to lack, having behind it the whole cotton interest of Lancashire, eager for cheaper raw material and enlarged markets for their finished goods. Its operations were on a great scale, £90,000 were spent in 1844, £¼ million asked for in 1845; tracts were distributed by the million; meetings were organized by the hundred in cities, farmers' markets, and villages, and often held in the face of riots, with speeches sometimes from a waggon, sometimes in a church. Though they found their orators in the Radical fervour of the north, and notably in the Quaker John Bright, the soul of the League was Richard Cobden, transplanted from agricultural Sussex to be a calico-printer in Manchester. In him were blended an extraordinary per-suasiveness of appeal, fiery energy, ardour for the tactics of battle, a passion of sincerity. But his limitations were as marked as his virtues. To the indignation of Gladstone his speeches, and the League press, held up all who defended protection for agriculture as monopolists, intent merely on upholding high rents or their class interest. He spoke of the navy as ' idlers ', believed that aristocracy encouraged war, and wished to loosen the tie with the Colonies by abolishing preference. Most of the Chartists opposed him fiercely, and not without reason, for his social policy held out little for democracy. He disliked trade unionism and State regulation of adult labour, and though in his own trade there were children of nine work-ing sixteen hours a day, he resisted Ashley's effort to legislate. Finally, within forty years every major point in his predictions was refuted. In short, the League triumphed because it had the art, and the single-minded passion, to exploit sentiments with which tariffs had little to do ; a feeling of middle-class manufacturers against the landed aristo-cracy, indignation at the hard lot of agricultural labourers and the lowest scales in industry, the moral feeling of that age against restriction, and a vague half-religious philanthropy, which believed cheapness was the Gospel teaching and a condition of international peace. Its campaign did not shrink from strong deeds any more than wild words, for in quite an eighteenth-century way it set about manufacturing freehold voters on a considerable scale.

Peel, who had begun public life as the hope of the highest Tories, ended it in unofficial alliance with Cobden and the progressive Whigs. He was not made to be a man of the past, as two Cabinet resig-nations of high Tories made clear. As early as 1843 he admitted to Gladstone he could no longer stand on agricultural protection as a principle ; defending it now on grounds which time might soon wash away, as that it was unjust suddenly to uproot a large investment, or undesirable to become dependent on the foreigner. Graham was an even more convinced convert, and if events had proceeded normally, it seems that Peel would in 1848 have proposed a final settlement, perhaps a low fixed duty. And just as every item of his tariffs made the landed interest feel itself abandoned, so his Irish policy, especially his increased subsidy in 1844 to the priests' seminary at Maynooth, alienated the bigoted Tories who had not forgiven the ' apostasy ' of 1829.

But neither was he a man of the future, and there was a rising Tory school who detested his brand of Conservatism as having no principle except that of making terms with Mammon. Part of that opposition came from sentimentalists of the ' Young England ' group who looked to a revived aristocracy, leading a people made happier by social justice. Some opposition centred round Ashley and champions of the Factory Acts, many others disagreed with Peel's union with Whigs and Bentham-ites over the poor law. All alike resented the concealment of his changing views and the strict discipline he enforced, in votes over Maynooth, sugar, or the ten-hour day. Such types of rebel found not a leader — for he was too much the adventurer as yet for that — but a voice of genius in the Jew Benjamin Disraeli, who, after shedding some Radical sym-pathies, entered the House in 1837 as a Tory, though standing nearer to the Bohemian Lyndhurst than to Peel. In 1841 he asked Peel for office and was refused, but nothing could have kept them long together. Though he sat for an agricultural constituency and believed in the land as the base of society, his speeches on Chartism, Factory Acts, and Ireland preached the same doctrine as his pamphlets and novels, — of which *Coningsby* appeared in 1844, and *Sybil* the year after : that a real Conservatism would conserve permanent principles, that these could be found by welding together Throne, Church, aristocracy, and people ; that, for the masses, social arrangements far transcended any mere mechanism like the franchise ; that first the Whig oligarchy, and now the capitalists of whom Peel was a type, had overthrown the national policy of Elizabeth and the first Stuarts, which Shelburne and Pitt and Canning had striven to revive.

Peel had overcome such discontents before in the 'thirties, and in 1845 his prestige might have driven the party forward, but he was worn down by labours, and in the autumn a crisis broke which tested his pride, his tactical sense, and high-strung nerves. Reports reached him, and scientists whom he despatched confirmed them, that the Irish potato crop might be a total failure, while in England a fair wheat crop had been thinned by ceaseless rain. Nothing seems more certain than Peel's agonized conviction that this meant famine, that nothing would meet the case except suspension of the corn laws, and that, once sus-pended, they could never be reimposed without fear of ' convulsion '. Almost equally clear, however, was his wish to carry these measures himself. In November, Russell, who since Melbourne's failure of health led the Whigs and had hitherto stood for a fixed duty, came out in his Edinburgh letter for total repeal, which spurred on Peel the faster. But he found many in his Cabinet, even of those agreeing, most reluctant, Stanley strong against, and in early December he resigned. Within a fortnight he was back in office ; Russell discovered a reason for inability to make a government in the refusal of Lord Grey (the third Lord) to see Palmerston return to the Foreign Office, though, in fact, the Whigs were beyond measure relieved to leave this ugly problem to the Tories. Peel came back without Stanley but having regained Gladstone, who had lately resigned from scruples over Maynooth; assured of Whig support and of enthusiastic approval at Court, in January 1846 he produced his repeal bill. It provided for a three-year interim, during which foreign wheat would pay a 10s. duty when wheat was under 48s., and thereafter a mere registration 1s. duty. It was not carried through the Lords until the 25th June, and the same night a combined vote of Whigs and Protectionists in the Commons against an Irish Coercion Act drove Peel from office. Nothing could have saved him long, for 231 Tories had opposed his corn bill.

In the capacity of a party leader his action had been hardly pardonable. The arguments by which he defended his change, the effects of his budgets or evidence that wages had not fallen in accord with prices, could have been put to his party before, and it is not surprising that the agriculturalists felt themselves betrayed. Nor can his famous eulogy of Cobden in June easily be reconciled with earlier declarations to the Court that he was striving to avert a Cobden government, or overrule the impression left by Graham's letters that one of their prime motives was to end the agitation of the League. That certainly directed the mind of Wellington, who disapproved repeal, convincing him that as 'the Queen's retained servant' it was his duty to keep out extremists. Apart from this, Stanley had some reason for asking why the corn laws should not be suspended, as they had often been in emergency before, and some ground for doubting whether it was indeed an emergency, of a sort to be mended by repeal. All through the next few years Ireland went on exporting grain and butter, the real stress of famine only arrived in 1847, while if her potato crop failed, how could it help her to expose her grain to foreign competition? On a longer view also Peel's justification is not to be found in his change of the tariff. For all through the 'forties corn averaged just on 56s.; years after repeal it sank only to 53s. 5d. for 1856–61, and it was only after 1878, under totally new circumstances, that immensely lower prices at once scaled down the cost of living and ruined British arable farming.

As it was, Peel parted in bitterness from the Tories; 'thank God', he wrote, 'I am relieved for ever from the trammels of such a party'. Lord George Bentinck and Disraeli organized the Protectionists against him, and Russell took office, politics thus returning to something of the aspect of the late 'thirties, of a Whig government ruling with the assistance of Peel.

He lived till 1850, while the Russell government continued Peelite measures, for the crisis had shattered parties, and even after the 1847 election the Whigs were dependent on Sir Robert's votes. Since

Graham and other Peelite leaders would not join him (and refused Disraeli's approaches also), Russell made a weak government, predominantly of peers, from old Whig material, — like Lansdowne who had served in the ' Talents ' of 1806, and a knot of the Grey clan ; its best vitality consisting in Palmerston at the Foreign Office and Grey's administration of the Colonies. Most of its energies were necessarily given to Ireland and the acute state of Europe after the revolutions of 1848, but it was burdened with a commercial crisis in 1847 and the year after by the last effort of the Chartists : their vast assembly on Kennington Common, the fiasco of their march on Parliament, and the stand of the middle class, who enlisted in thousands as special constables.

In domestic legislation they pursued what the parliamentary situation dictated, or completed what administrative experiment and public opinion asked. Bentinck, who lived only till 1848, was not a good leader of Opposition, for his mind was ill-trained and his giant industry unselective, yet he was strong enough to force government to a compromise on sugar, giving the half-ruined Colonies a small preference, to expire in 1854. In 1849, however, government demolished another Imperial interest by a total repeal of the Navigation Acts, with Peel's strong approval ; to which pressure from America and Prussia and Colonial resentment at loss of preference both contributed. In 1847 both parties, though Peel and Cobden were still averse, carried the ten hours Factory Act for which Ashley had worked so long, yet it was not till 1850 that the device of work by relay was fully scotched, and a compromise passed which, in fact, assured a day of $10\frac{1}{2}$ hours for factory workers of all sorts, with $7\frac{1}{2}$ on Saturdays. In 1847 too the poor-law commissioners' powers were transferred to a Board under charge of a minister, while in 1848 the strenuous crusade of Chadwick and his school achieved the Public Health Act, establishing a central directory, empowered to create local boards of health on petition.

Peel's death was a heavy blow to the government, removing their shelter from the Tory blast, while Palmerston strained their good relations with the Court, but in any case Russell was not a Prime Minister who could interpret opinion, and was always raising great friction over small issues. His own prejudices were fixed. His Church appointments, especially that of Hampden to the see of Hereford, showed how he minimized the Oxford Movement and the change in Anglican temper. In 1850 the Vatican set up a territorial episcopate in England, Cardinal Wiseman thus being styled archbishop of Westminster, to which Russell's reply was a quite useless Ecclesiastical Titles Act (duly repealed twenty years after), giving offence both to the Peelites and to Ireland. There were other signs that Whiggism had lost the elasticity needed for a liberal age. In deference to his Cabinet, though much against his will, Russell resisted a bill to extend the county franchise, was defeated, and in February 1851 resigned, but since the Peelites would neither join hands with Derby (the former Stanley) owing to protection, nor with the Whigs owing to the religious issue, he returned for another year of crumbling power. In December, under intense royal pressure, he dismissed Palmerston for his open approval of Louis Napoleon's *coup d'état* at Paris, and in February 1852 Palmerston took his ' tit for tat ', opposing a militia scheme which government wished to raise on a local basis, but which he rightly would bring under a central authority. Thereupon Russell made way for a weak and minority Tory government, led by Derby.

At that point, with Free Trade in being, the middle class in power, and the clamour for a second Reform Bill rising, with the Crystal Palace just opened to enshrine Cobden's vision of perpetual peace, the Queen on a firm constitutional throne, and Europe working through the effects of a second Revolution, we may leave domestic politics, and their adjustment to the new age since 1815. In Europe, Empire, and Ireland the new Britain had moved, not always happily, on parallel lines.

CONTEMPORARY DATES

1842	Treaty of Nanking.
	Disaster in Afghanistan.
	A Karageorgevitch wins the Serbian throne.
	Browning, *Dramatic Lyrics*.
1843	Disruption of the Scottish Church.
	The Sonderbund formed in Switzerland.
	Macaulay, *Essays*.
	Ruskin, *Modern Painters*.
1844	Maori war.
	Co-operative store at Rochdale.
1845	United States and Mexico at war.
	Newman joins the Roman Church.
	Wagner, *Tannhäuser*.
1846	Pius IX becomes Pope.
	The Spanish Marriages.
	Austria annexes Cracow.
1847	Gold found in California.
	Hampden made bishop of Hereford.
	Marx and Engels, *Communist Manifesto*.
	Emily Brontë, *Wuthering Heights*.
	Thackeray, *Vanity Fair*.
1848	The Second Revolution.
	Fall of Metternich and Guizot.
	J. S. Mill, *Political Economy*.
	Formation of Pre-Raphaelite movement.
1849	Mazzini and the Roman Republic.
	Kossuth a refugee in Turkey.

1849   Macaulay, *History of England.*
       Gibbon Wakefield, *Art of Colonization.*
       Death of Chopin.
1850   Cardinal Antonelli, Papal Secretary of State.
       Convention of Olmütz.
       Cavour becomes minister in Piedmont.
       Tennyson, *In Memoriam.*
       Death of Wordsworth and Balzac.

CHAPTER XII

BRITAIN AND EUROPE, 1827–1852

'WE have no eternal allies, and we have no perpetual enemies; our interests are eternal.' So said Palmerston, the Canningite, who more than any other dictated foreign policy for the forty years after Canning's death, during which the old order of 1815 and Metternich passed out of sight. Yet even eternal interests change character with changing mankind.

To preserve the sea-power which had been our salvation was made easier by our acquisition, at the peace, of Malta, Mauritius, Heligoland, and the Cape; yet the object of sea-power is commerce and safety of communication, which may be threatened by changes on land. So our Mediterranean communications involved us in the Near Eastern question, as did our Indian connection in finding secure routes farther east, as well as in commercial competition in the far Orient. New bases, Singapore (1819), Malacca (1824), Aden (1838), and Hong Kong (1841), mark steps in this extension. As for our second eternal interest, as men of the time would have deemed it, — that is, a balance of power to curb any over-mighty State or armed alliance, — that must always imply the opportunism which moved Palmerston. Even so, on the whole, Britain adjusted itself to change with much regard for principle and fixed objects.

That new age of liberalism and nationality, which Canning had championed in America, Spain, or Greece, strode fast forward in the movements of 1830. If the Italian risings were too weak to uproot Austrian and Neapolitan power, at least the accession of Louis Philippe severed France from the circle of legitimist despots, making another middle-class constitutional State with which reformed England might hope to work. An immediate secondary effect was the Belgian rising against their Dutch king, which at first strained Anglo-French relations, but this was surmounted by the patience of Grey and Palmerston, the insight of the aged Talleyrand, now ambassador in London, and Louis Philippe's understanding that his throne could not stand with Britain against him. By the end of 1832 this difficult creation of modern Belgium and Holland was made. At times the French put forward their King's son Nemours for the new throne, breathed ideas of partitioning Belgium, or claimed frontier fortresses: all these Palmerston judged were inadmissible; France should not get so much as ' a cabbage garden '.

But to achieve this, to wield the French army as a lever against the Dutch and the Eastern despots without increasing the French hold on Belgium, required rare and determined skill. In the end the partition was made along the Scheldt and Meuse, the Belgian Crown was given to Leopold of Coburg, once husband of our Princess Charlotte, and Belgian neutrality guaranteed by the Powers. It was not till 1839 that the Dutch swallowed these terms and were allowed to reoccupy Luxemburg, which, though remaining a member of the German federation, was to be ruled by the Orange House.

British interests in the Low Countries had been held vital ever since Edward I, but our efforts for settlement were explained also by the fear of revived war between revolutionary and anti-revolutionary States. This motive, real enough in days of military monarchies and Jacobin memories, in part justified our interference in the dreary vendettas of Portugal and Spain, where triumphant Bonapartism had been followed by the restoration of a repressive Bourbon monarchy. Palmerston was a man of an older age, inclined to think that France burned to avenge Waterloo, or might even seek to overturn the Utrecht treaties, which had separated the two Bourbon lines, and by some marriage make Spain her satellite. The quadruple alliance he brought about in 1834 with Britain, France, Spain, and Portugal, was devised both as a counterblast to the eastern despots and to harness France to Peninsular independence, one part of that object being immediately fulfilled by the pretender Dom Miguel leaving Portugal. Spain was another story. As against the young Queen Isabella, Don Carlos could build on Catholic fanaticism, provincial hatreds, and the wretched character of the queen-mother Christina, so that the Carlist war dragged on till 1839. Our government interpreted its doctrine of 'non-interference' in a strangely strenuous way, allowing Admiral Napier to enrol Portuguese sailors and De Lacy Evans to head a British legion; the Foreign Enlistment Act was suspended, so that many British volunteers found death amid the Spanish mountains, defending what Palmerston proclaimed as the constitutional cause.

While Louis Philippe swung between his need of peace and dynastic ambition or the restlessness of a country brought up in the glories of Bonaparte, a more massive rival overshadowed our Foreign Office. The prestige won by the Czar Alexander I in the peace settlement was fixed on a more solid base by his successor, the towering, rigid Nicholas I. Russia had done most to give life to Greece, her agents encouraged Slav racialism and religion in Serbia and Bulgaria; since the century opened she had advanced by way of Georgia and Armenia beyond the Caspian, outmatched British influence in Persia, flung a screen over Khiva and other khanates on the Oxus, and in the early 'thirties was inciting Persia to attack Afghanistan. Nearer still than this threat to

India, since Canning's death Russia had become supreme at Constantinople. By intervening between the Turks and their dangerous vassal, Mehemet Ali of Egypt, Russian arms saved the Sultan and in 1833 extorted the treaty of Unkiar Skelessi, a secret clause of which arranged that on a Russian request the Dardanelles should be closed to foreign warships.

Though Palmerston exaggerated both the Russians' immediate intentions and Mehemet Ali's scheme to extend Arab dominion from his acquisition of Mecca northward to Iraq, the realities were serious enough, and his achievement very considerable. For in 1839 the Turks and Mehemet Ali went to war again, the rebels advanced from Syria and routed the Turkish Army. Was the future to be settled by Russia, by the old French ambitions for Syria and Egypt, or a combination of the two? His resolution secured a settlement on the lines of his own choice, a conservation of Turkey by a concert of the Powers. He had discerned French encroachment spilling over from their new conquest of Algiers into Morocco and Tunis, and was determined to undo the Russian menace to the Straits.

Diplomacy must deal with the perils of its own day, which in this case were large enough to discount much later criticism; which suggests that, in proposing to save Turkey rather than win the sympathy of Egypt, Palmerston was blind to the future. His first aim, after all, was simply to prevent a general war. So came about the four-Power treaty of July 1840 between Britain and the three Eastern monarchies, — Austria being unwilling to see Turkey disintegrated in Russian interests and Russia being glad to see the Liberal Powers divided. For, though terms for compromise were put before her, French pride was committed to alliance with Mehemet Ali and a sphere of influence in the Levant and, led by Thiers, spoke violently for war.

If Palmerston's diagnosis of motive often erred, his gifts shone out this year as a judge of material forces. Convinced that Mehemet was a man of straw, whose communications could be cut by our sea-power, and that Louis Philippe would plump for peace, he drove forward. Though part of the Cabinet were hostile and Russell vacillating, and though intrigues in the civil service worked hand-in-glove with the press and the oldest of intriguers at Paris, Princess Lieven, he was proved right. In October British and Turkish forces mastered Beyrout and Acre, and Thiers made way for the more placable Guizot. In July 1841 the peace left Egypt, but not Syria, as a hereditary possession to Mehemet Ali, at the same time obliterating the ill effects of Unkiar Skelessi by reaffirming the 'ancient rule of the Ottoman empire' which closed the Straits to warships in time of peace.

That year, in which the Whig government fell, sealed Palmerston's European fame and his enduring popularity with the British masses.

Some of his shortcomings were peculiar to himself, including a habit of insolent language and a coarse-grained lack of sympathy with other nations. Others, on the contrary, were shared by many British public men. There was little to choose between his use of the *Morning Chronicle* to push his views and the godly Aberdeen's manipulation of *The Times*, while in sheer insularity or lack of scruple several ambassadors outdid their chief. To accuse him of lacking humanity is the reverse of truth, for no minister worked harder against the slave trade, while some of his unpopularity with foreign Courts, and with his own, sprang from humane sentiment; as when he publicly applauded the London dray-men who rolled the brutal Austrian general, Haynau, in the mud. Nor is it just to depict him as a lover of war. That may be disproved by his record in regard to Belgium, Italy, and the second French republic.

Personal defects apart, what may prevent us from thinking him a great statesman comes, perhaps, from his very length of days and the pre-judices that made one side of his virtues. The France he had known when an apprentice, as the source of revolution, was followed by the restored Bourbons, whose ambitions Marlborough and Chatham had fought to curb, while like all his generation he idolized constitutional government, thought little of kings, and despised priests. An immense national pride made the counterpart to his force and unwisdom. ' Our duty,' he told the Commons, ' our vocation, is not to enslave but to set free '; ' I may say, without any vainglorious boast, — that we stand at the head of moral, social, and political civilization '.

If there was something magnificent in this, driven home as it always was by homilies to small States and large, bidding them follow the British way of free government, in practice it comprehended strong measures which left a harsh legacy : one early example of which was the first China war of 1840–41. Once again his mistakes allowed enemies to build up a legend that this was just ' an opium war ', forced on a benevolent and self-improving Oriental people. The profits from opium did, indeed, enter into it, though only as a detail; really, the crux lay in the change of 1833 when the East India Company lost its China trade monopoly, whereby a merchant body, accustomed to the connivance and corruption of eastern trading, was replaced by the British Crown. Even more, in a European sense, China was not a State at all. For to restrict foreign traders to dealing through one gild at Canton, to refuse diplomatic contact, to make life impossible ashore for British agents, were devices which China could not enforce in the nineteenth century, while the clamour against Indian opium was a pretext, seeing that Chinese officials profited by the domestic crop, and that we offered to stop import as part of a settlement. Taking the war as one of reparation for injury, Palmerston asked guarantees for the future, which were secured by the next Cabinet in the Nanking treaty of 1842; which included the cession of Hong Kong to Britain and the opening of five treaty ports, Shanghai among them, to foreign trade.

His Tory successor at the Foreign Office between 1841–6 was Aberdeen, a disciple of Castlereagh, who had held this post before in 1828–30, and whose original sympathies had been with Metternich and the party of ' order '. His high-mindedness was transparent, his love of peace was passionate, but he lacked decision and exposed his hand to busybodies, like Princess Lieven who, in the last phase of a mischievous life, was living with Guizot. All the Cabinet desired to restore the good relations with France which the eastern crisis had jarred, but Peel and Wellington increasingly doubted Aberdeen's judgment in trusting the French, and demanded an active programme of national defence.

So the *entente cordiale*, in spite of some ecstatic royal visits and Coburg-Bourbon marriages, and despite Aberdeen's ingenuous admiration for Guizot, wore away. It was strained by evidence of French ambition in the Mediterranean and their contact with Metternich, their resentment over our occupation of New Zealand, their tariffs and their armaments. There was a sharp curve in 1843-4 when they annexed Tahiti and arrested Pritchard, an aggressive Congregational missionary, who had long encouraged the native rulers to take cover under a British Protestant flag. This was duly settled by an indemnity, though the French kept the island. But what finally destroyed the *entente* was the matter of the Spanish marriages ; the question, that is, of finding suitable husbands for the very youthful Queen Isabella and her sister, the next heir. Much harm, no doubt, was done by rival desires in the royal houses of Coburg and Bourbon, vicious Spanish factions, and active intrigue with those factions by foreign envoys, the British not least.

Aberdeen conducted policy with his usual good faith but, as Palmerston bitterly said, on ' a sliding scale ' ; retreating from the principle that Spain should be left with a free choice and always leaving to France the initiative, he first promised not to support a Coburg and finally in 1845 agreed the Queen should wed a Spanish or Neapolitan Bourbon and that, when she had children, a second marriage should follow between her sister and the French King's son, Montpensier. If danger really existed of a French prince staking out a claim to the Spanish throne, Aberdeen had clearly not conjured it away and, even before he left office, Guizot was decided to hurry on both marriages. This decision was accelerated by Palmerston's return, his hectoring despatches, and Bulwer's active assistance to one Spanish faction, all of which in 1846 led the French, in violation of pledges, to push on both marriages, of the Queen to her cousin Don Francis and of the Infanta to Montpensier, simultaneously.

Fierce and scornful was the wrath of Palmerston and Queen Victoria. Profiting by this disintegration of the *entente*, the Eastern monarchies arranged that Austria should absorb the republic of Cracow, last relic of free Poland, while only Palmerston's obstruction prevented their destroying the Swiss federation in the Sonderbund war of 1847 between Catholic and Protestant cantons. In this also France took the reactionary side. But the unctuous, ungrateful Guizot had dug his own grave, and when in 1848 internal revolt shook down the Orleanist throne, both King and minister took refuge in Britain, whose friendship they had cast away.

Severed in sympathy from the despotisms and alienated from France, Britain had to adjust her isolation to the second revolutionary epoch which now convulsed the Continent, leaving behind it, among other things, a second French Empire and a new kingdom of Italy. Those results were only reached after two years of chaos in 1848-9, during which civil war devastated Paris, risings in Vienna and Hungary brought the Metternich system to the ground, the Weimar parliament threatened the Prussian monarchy, Savoy headed Italian revolt against the Austrians, and only the Czardom survived from the Europe set up by the victors of Waterloo. Famous exiles, Mazzini and Louis Napoleon, left their refuge in London to tear up the settlement of 1815, while for a short space it was believed that a Liberal Pope, Pius IX, might reconcile religion and nationality.

Fortunately the conduct of foreign affairs during this upheaval was in the hands of the Whigs. For the sympathies of the Queen and Prince Consort leaned to Austria and established systems, so did those of Malmesbury, Derby's Foreign Secretary in 1852, though not Disraeli's ; Radical and middle-class opinion being overwhelmingly on the other side. Palmerston and Russell at least shared one sincere belief which, — in these conditions, though not in all conditions, — made a positive contribution to peace ; that liberties of the British sort would restore stability, and that it was our proper rôle to mediate. The despatch of Minto's mission in 1847 was thus meant to encourage a reforming Pope, our prompt recognition of the French republic and warnings to Austria were given to protect Liberalism in France and Italy. Palmerston, indeed, believed that Austria would do well to evacuate northern Italy and find compensation in the Balkans. On the other hand, as against an all-powerful Russia, he deemed a substantial Austro-Hungary to be indispensable, and consequently, much to democratic indignation, refused to support the Hungarian rising led by the orator Kossuth which, under a popular veneer, in fact aspired to Magyar predominance over oppressed Slav subjects.

He held office just long enough to see this storm of revolutionary violence subside. His autocracy in his department, strong gestures and forceful method, had raised a swarm of enemies at home and abroad.

He had allowed munitions from Woolwich to be diverted to help Sicilian rebels. He infuriated foreign ministers and our own ambassadors by provocative despatches. In 1850 he sent a blockading squadron to enforce payment of debts due from the Greek government to a British subject, Don Pacifico, a Gibraltar Jew, vindicating himself in the famous speech that swung over a hostile House by its keynote of ' Civis Romanus ', — of an Imperial flag protecting even its meanest subject. His horn was exalted over his old enemies, Louis Philippe and Guizot, Princess Lieven and Metternich, all now exiles in London suburbs. He won the plaudits of the masses by stout support of Turkey's refusal to surrender Hungarian refugees, and by showing that he approved the popular welcome to Kossuth. In December 1851, in advance of Cabinet decision, he let the French ambassador know his approbation of Louis Napoleon's *coup d'état* ; at last the fears and enmities he had aroused saw their opening, and he was dismissed.

Innumerable though his mistakes had been, he would not have fallen except for the hostility of the Court, which had worked for this result over three years. He had given just ground for complaint, sometimes taking important decisions of which he left them in ignorance, or sometimes altering despatches from the drafts submitted to the Queen. But there was a deeper difference — of policy and power. Taught by Leopold of Belgium and Stockmar his own tutor, Prince Albert was teaching the Queen that he himself was her ' permanent minister ' ; ' they labour ', said Lord Clarendon, ' under the curious mistake that the Foreign Office is their peculiar department ' ; indeed, when Palmerston fell, the Queen insisted she could veto any nomination of a successor and, against the wish of most of the Cabinet, selected the bland and courtly Granville. As for policy, the Court was distressed by the fall of Leopold's kindred, the house of Orleans. Victoria could see nothing but brigandage in the Italian war against Austria and secretly worked against her ministers. The Prince Consort was set on German unity under the presidency of Prussia, bitterly opposing Palmerston's successful effort to stop a German conquest of Schleswig-Holstein. Yet the minister had triumphed in essence, having done more than any man in Europe to prevent a general war, and to associate Britain with national democracy.

Time was to show on what a fragile base our diplomatic structure rested. While immense conscript armies paced the Continent, Palmerston's bold words were backed by an ill-organized regular force of some 130,000 men, of whom less than half were in Europe, and a small fleet slowly changing over from sail to steam. Whig financiers argued that Parliament would never stand an increased income-tax, recommendations from the Duke and Palmerston for a strong militia were evaded, while Cobden and the Radicals preached that increased defence was needless panic, and that disarmament was the road to peace.

CHAPTER XIII

THE NEW EMPIRE, 1815–1852

THE first Empire, with which Walpole would not meddle and out of which Chatham had wrought such marvels, was passed away. America was gone, most early Victorians believed Canada would follow, the West Indies were on the down grade. Yet within forty years of Waterloo the foundations of a second Empire were laid.

It must develop in a new body of ruling conditions. One lesson at least had been taken to heart, that government and taxation directly through the Imperial Parliament were out of the question ; on the other hand, modern transportation had brought means of contact, the lack of which Burke had declared fatal to any closer unity, and thus in 1839 the Nova Scotian Samuel Cunard launched a first British trans-Atlantic steam service. So that, though in the old Empire too there had been an exchange of men and ideas from the days of George Downing onwards, it was now much multiplied. But since such exchanges took place in a new Britain, fast becoming industrialized and evangelical and democratic, the Empire was subjected to new influences which might conceivably be fatal. After 1815, save for Hong Kong and some other bases in the Orient, this was not a period of extending territory, but rather one of consolidating principles ; and that not only in our way of ruling communities overseas, but in regard to commerce and Imperial relations with other States.

No vision of Empire had yet stirred the mother country. From 1801–54 one Secretary of State combined ' War and the Colonies ', for the department ranked low in the Cabinet and, except for one year of Huskisson, no man of the first order, primarily interested in the Colonies, held it before the third Lord Grey between 1846–54. Only too long these swarmings overseas were treated in an eighteenth-century style — ' the scum of England is poured into the Colonies ', wrote one of the ablest Victorian observers. Powerful Benthamite influence was cast against keeping any Colonies at all, while to Cobden and his Manchester school they were offensive as ' Imperialism ', or provocation to war ; even in conservative and moderate minds the prevailing mood sounded the line of *Marmion*, — ' erring sister, go in peace '. Economists grudged the cost of defence, and the price of colonial preference to the home consumer. Many times new annexations, as in Tahiti, were rejected, or frontiers, as in Natal, revoked and drawn back. Indeed, what the last Hanoverians inherited was still what Adam Smith had styled only ' a project of empire ', of scattered petty communities, ill-related to Britain and unrelated to one another ; not 500,000 in Canada, a bare 20,000 in Australia, not 50,000 in Cape Colony, while in each West Indian island a few hundred white men were engulfed among thousands of negroes and half-castes.

Three potent legacies, however, had come down from the old Empire. The first was the venerable binding force of English law which, legal maxims taught, Englishmen carried with them as a garment, and in virtue of which elected assemblies, magistrates, and trial by jury had flourished since the first germs of Bermuda or Virginia. A second was the system of the laws of trade, embedded in which was the principle of preference. And a third was the trusteeship of British administrators for native races, seen long ago in the protection of Red Indians against American pioneers, and rewarded, for example, by the Mohawks taking refuge in British Canada. But all three, shaken by violent change, had now to be readjusted ; to American independence, Radical politics, new economic units and methods, and humanitarian feeling.

In the sixty years following Waterloo some $7\frac{1}{2}$ million emigrants left the United Kingdom, about half of whom went to the United States, $1\frac{1}{2}$ millions to Canada, and 1 million to Australasia. As of old, in contrast to other empires, self-help was the general British rule. With the exception of a considerable migration to Australia, the mass of those seeking new homes owed little to government assistance, moving fastest in obedience to causes which governments did not control, such as famine in Ireland or gold discoveries in California and Australia ; the State doing little else for them except to pass some tardy legislation, to stop overcrowding or lack of doctors in emigrant ships, which had suffered almost as much as the slave ships before them. Thus the life blood of these settlements came from individual or community action, from below and not from above. From the Highland Society, or individual Scots like Lord Selkirk, concerned to remedy hardships due to land eviction ; from soldiers, such as Colonel Talbot in Ontario ; John Galt's land company in the Huron country ; or Scottish churches and English episcopalians, who respectively set up Dunedin and Christ Church in New Zealand. Indeed, not the Imperial government, but only Gibbon Wakefield and the company of his creation made New Zealand possible at all.

This Empire owed everything to families who staked their all for freedom and kept the faith ; to the Maryland loyalists, for instance, who migrated to Nova Scotia, or the children of soldiers and government servants, like the Australian statesman William Wentworth, born in Norfolk Island when his father was surgeon to the convict settlement, or to Caroline Chisholm and her husband, formerly of the Madras army, who worked at Sydney to give new life and citizenship to convicts. Our Dominions were made, as Anglo-Saxon England had been made, by blood and sweat of forgotten human beings. Wooden sailing ships, — forty days to Canada in 1840 and ninety in the clippers to Australia — timber-framed houses, blackened tree stumps round the new clearing; long journeys by horse or canoe to fetch stores, doctor, or priest; Maoris, Indians, Kaffirs, drought and ice and murrain; from such beginnings and in such trials they raised their small States above ground.

Yet, though this seems the main truth, it would be unjust to see Britain as wholly uninterested, or without any Colonial ideal. On the contrary, at least three strong schools of thought may be distinguished, to each of which this Empire owed much : administrators, radical reformers, and humanitarian and evangelical Christians who, sometimes blended but more often in conflict, together made a new Imperialism.

Like most other things in modern Britain, the new tone of administration was set by colleagues and disciples of the younger Pitt, and especially by Grenville, Dundas, Bathurst, and Huskisson, men who seem to belong to another planet than their immediate predecessors, whose rigidity had lost America. Never doctrinaire but in fundamentals liberal, they were concerned first to reconstruct a ruined Empire, and then to absorb the gains of war. As the Canada Act of 1791 shows, they meant to give to the Colonies the British constitution as then it stood, which left room for a strong executive. They aimed too, and this the great war forced on more urgently, at readjustment of the laws of trade to the loss of America. Results of victory added a third problem, how to absorb bodies coming from foreign systems; whether Trinidad and its Spanish law, the Dutch of Guiana, or the Maltese. In those cases, as well as in Ceylon, they added a new category to Empire, found out by experience and careful enquiry, of a Crown Colony type, the core of which was not in an elected assembly, but rather in the governor in council.

Perhaps their most continuous achievement was the working out of a new commercial system. They faced new powerful groups, in the United States, South American republics, and the German Zollverein, with whom bargains must be struck. New conquests, whether Trinidad or Mauritius, clashed with the old monopoly of West Indian sugar. A new supremacy in Britain of cotton and iron demanded cheap material, and was satisfied it could triumph through competition. We find therefore a long series of measures, particularly in the day of Huskisson, to relax the prohibitions of the Navigation Act. Thus all the Americas were allowed henceforth to send produce in their own ships to Britain; or again, since without North American commerce the West Indies could not live, here too after long struggles full freedom was given by 1830. Acts of 1822–5 repealed the rule that goods in foreign ships could come only from the country of origin, allowed the Colonies to export direct to Europe and to import direct also, and provided for reciprocity treaties. Trade with India had been opened to other nations for some time past. On the other hand, British and Colonial shipping retained a monopoly of all other inter-Imperial trade, while the whole system turned on the principle of preference; Britain, which gave a large priority to West Indian sugar or Canadian timber and corn, requiring in return a preferential duty for British imports.

Conditions after the peace, trade depression, and the overcrowding of Britain by demobilized unemployed soldiers, revived a zeal for emigration, which since the Restoration had always been discouraged. Five thousand ' 1820 settlers ', to hold the east of Cape Colony, were launched with a parliamentary grant, much the same was done in Upper Canada, and much land granted to companies who undertook to settle Ontario and Western Australia. Reports and enquiries in this period of experiment show a greatly increased competence at the Colonial Office; within whose ranks, and at its head from 1836–47, was one of the strongest men of the day, James Stephen, nephew of Wilberforce, who brought to Colonial administration all the ' Saints' ' dedication to the public good. The decisions taken, and the guidance given, were of lasting importance. It was the Colonial Office which, for example, laid down at the Cape the rule of racial equality, irrespective of colour, and by vetoing proposals for Oriental labour ordained the future of a ' White Australia '.

As with the mother country, the year 1830 began a new stage in the Empire, indirectly through the pervading effects of Reform but immediately as being the foundation date of the Colonization Society inspired by Gibbon Wakefield. This remarkable man, belonging to one of the families thrown up by revolutionary England who satisfied their enormous vitality in philanthropy and economics, had some defects of the pure adventurer; yet combined with an understanding and power of decision which went to the root. The title of his book, *The Art of Colonization*, gives a clue to his doctrine. Colonization must be systematized; new Britains could be made by conscious effort. No longer the haphazard product of the workhouse or misfortune, emigrants must be selected as a true cross-section of British society, and financed by an emigration fund formed from the sale of the vast empty lands, which were the inheritance of all the people. Hitherto those lands had been given away without thought, and could be bought for a song, so that no wage-earning class existed in the Colonies which could make possible large capital development. That process he declared could be arrested by selling lands at a ' sufficient ' price, which would compel labour to work for wages until it had some capital saved, and check the dispersal of emigrants in scattered lots.

But Wakefield's theory, often found over-rigid in practice, was less important than his inspiration. His power of persuasiveness and publicity converted Durham and Grey among ministers, and raised up many disciples, notably Charles Buller ; whose criticism described the famous, though too dark, picture of ' Mr. Mother Country ' and the ' sighing rooms ' at the Colonial Office, where aspirations died. From the energies of this group issued the colonization of South Australia and the New Zealand Company, parliamentary committees on lands and transportation, and the Land and Emigration commissioners created in 1840. But their greatest gift by far was something that contemporary statesmen, with hardly an exception, lacked : a faith that an Empire of free communities could survive.

Their crusade often collided with the then mighty force of evangelical religion. From the same body of ' Saints ' who had overthrown slavery came the London Missionary Society, the Church Missionary Society, the British and Foreign Bible Society. Stephen at the Colonial Office belonged to their inner circle, so did Glenelg, the Secretary of State at a crucial time, and individual missionaries, Marsden and Williams in the Pacific, or Philip the Congregationalist in South Africa, wielded as much power as any governor. Wilberforce's successor Fowell Buxton turned from his victory over slavery in 1833 to form the Aborigines Protection Society, with far-reaching effect. Missionary influence, it was even hoped, might evangelize Hindu and Mohammedan civilization, and the government of India was urged to abandon its wisely guarded religious neutrality.

Here, then, was an inherited frame of empire, admitting local liberties, yet defending executive authority and established Churches ; ready to relax restrictions but still attempting to direct Imperial trade as a whole ; rarely but firmly using old rights of veto, or disallowing Colonial law ; striving to protect native races, even against self-governing Britons ; pessimistic of final continuance, though not without new rays of hope. Its task embraced four elements of the first importance ; self-government, emigration and settlement, native races, and economic relations. Each in some degree entered into the history of each principal Colony, though each may here be tested by looking to each principal group in turn.

Canada came out of the American and French revolutions and the war of 1812 as a people neither American nor British, but of a character all its own. Since Newfoundland still ran its own course, and the great West lay in the hands of Indians or of the Hudson's Bay Company and its rivals, the core of the country consisted of three divisions between sea and lakes, — the Maritime provinces, Lower Canada or Quebec, Upper Canada or Ontario. As to the first, the original Nova Scotia was divided after the coming of the American Loyalists, in order to set up three additional governments in New Brunswick, Prince Edward Island, and Cape Breton. If the life of the two last was too minute to affect large issues, Prince Edward Island furthermore being almost given over to absentee proprietors, Nova Scotia and New Brunswick together made a stalwart society. Here was the sea-link with Britain, Halifax was a vital naval base, from the St. John river the royal Navy got its masts, in Halifax were settled privateersmen and ex-naval officers of the wars. Their chief ingredients came of vigorous stock, — soldier colonists, Highlanders of the Isles, and American Loyalists (had not its first bishop been a rector in New York?). Their civic standard was high; Dalhousie University and many grammar schools began life before 1820, and its teeming press produced in Joseph Howe a politician of a high order. Economically the Maritimes lived in the orbit of New England, being cut off from Canada proper by almost insuperable barriers of mountain, river, and forest, but their political temper was British and Imperial.

It was far otherwise with the two Canadas, whose differences had brought about their division under Pitt's Act of 1791. That severance had not healed their unkind relations, if only because, in commanding the St. Lawrence, Quebec's hold on the customs revenue galled Ontario. But behind this was a question immeasurably greater : whether political predominance was to be British or French. Every decade after the Loyalists' arrival tilted the scale; Ontario grew from 80,000 people in 1815 to 455,000 in 1841, while British immigrants overflowed into the eastern townships of Quebec. This racial conflict, inflamed by a British minority at Montreal, was reinforced by the French-Canadian passion to uphold a Catholic supremacy. And meanwhile each province was wrestling with a third internal strain, as indeed were the Maritimes too, the oldest and most inevitable strain of all : a conflict of elected assemblies with a half-alien, irresponsible executive. As with the lost American Colonies, so now the controversies turned on the powers of governors and their councils, provision of a civil list, control of patronage, the independence of judges, and distribution of the soil. There were glaring abuses. Sometimes the governor's council was simultaneously an executive and a legislative upper chamber; office-holders sat for life; Crown dues and quit rents took much revenue out of parliamentary control. Sometimes lands were rigidly tied up or, again, profusely alienated to speculators. Broadly speaking, in each province a party of reformers and recent immigrants was up in arms against an oligarchy, part-official and in part of vested interests, which monopolized power. Whether that local and social

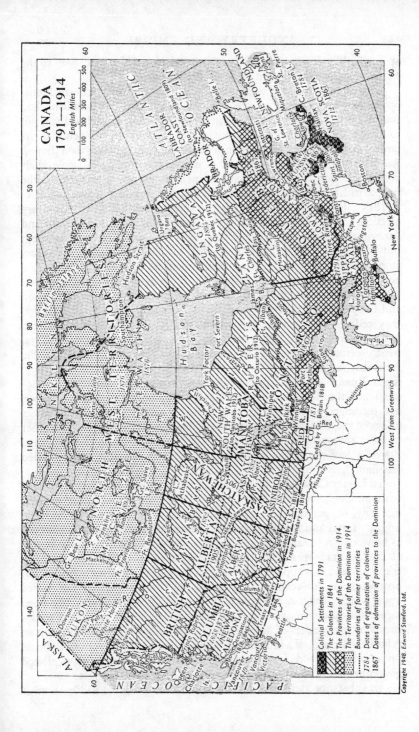

CANADA
1791—1914

English Miles

0 100 200 300 400 500

Copyright 1948 Edward Stanford. Ltd.

Colonial Settlements in 1791
The Colonies in 1841
The Provinces of the Dominion in 1914
The Territories of the Dominion in 1914
Boundaries of former territories
1784   Dates of organization of colonies
1867   Dates of admission of provinces to the Dominion

strife would coincide with resistance to British government, even to the British race, would depend on local circumstance.

The darkest outlook was naturally in Quebec, where constitutional opposition melted into a race war. Though French-Canadians had fought bravely in 1812 and the general loyalty of the priesthood was not in doubt, Quebec had passed out of the moderating influence of its landed seigneurs, on whom early governors had pinned their hopes. An illiterate peasantry, granted a democratic franchise, gave their confidence now to lawyers and journalists, finding a tribune of the people in Louis Joseph Papineau, who became Speaker of the Assembly in 1815. From that time till 1837 the party of his making carried every election. His contacts were flung wide with British Radicals and Americans, his models were the new republics, and his case was strong, but he had no constructive mind, while his abuse of impeachment and stoppage of supply must bring government to a standstill. Once the home government thought desperately of reuniting the provinces and suppressing political use of the French language, but under Huskisson and Grey their attitude was more liberal. Asking only a small civil list, they ceded all permanent revenues to the Assembly and excluded the judges from Council. Papineau's reply was the 92 resolutions of 1834, which demanded an elective Council, sole financial power for the Assembly, and a special court to deal with impeachments, and in 1837, when Russell declared responsible government tantamount to independence, the Assembly refused supply. Papineau's violence, however, had estranged English-speaking reformers, his anti-clericalism equally offended the Church, and only a few villages took up arms in November to resist the warrant for his arrest. After he had escaped to the United States, a few companies of infantry sufficed to suppress this so-called rebellion.

In Upper Canada we follow the normal sequence of Colonial history, without Quebec's racial hatreds, and in a province of more assured maturity, 80 per cent of whose inhabitants in 1815 were of American origin. Land and religion furnished some real grievances, though only as between Protestant sects of the same major nationality. Nine-tenths of the soil had been alienated, but only a fraction had been actually taken up, and this applied especially to the Clergy reserves ; that is, the proportion of one-seventh assigned to the Churches under the Act of 1791, which Strachan, the militant bishop of Toronto, claimed had been meant for Anglicans alone. This great abuse, which separated settlements by many miles of uncleared holdings, was one instance only, or so reformers argued, of a universal monopoly ; of a ' family compact ' made up of officials, old Loyalist families, and rich men, who exploited government and the British connection in their own interest.

In substance and spirit, however, Ontario's progress had been swift and solid. For strategic and economic reasons much had been spent on roads and waterways, as on the Welland, Rideau, and Lachine canals, which together made connection from Lake Erie all the way to Montreal. Rival religious bodies had organized their schools, Upper Canada College was on foot at Toronto, Strachan was pushing on towards a university. In him, and in Beverley Robinson of Virginian origin, the ' Compact ' group had leaders of distinction, whatever their prejudices, while another Loyalist, Egerton Ryerson, made the Methodists a nucleus of patriotism and educational zeal. Nor could the province justly complain of lack of response from Britain. Crown revenues were handed over, a fairer share allotted of the customs levied at Quebec, and restrictions on American immigrants removed. If some of the soldier-governors were wooden, Colborne (Lord Seaton) was admirably fair-minded, and on the whole the crux lay not so much in the British connection as in the blending with it of a social feud, within provincial society itself.

Opposition to the ruling caste found a voluble leader in the journalist William Lyon MacKenzie, in whose expulsion from the Assembly by a Tory majority they received the gift of a crowning grievance, and the antics of a foolish governor, Sir Francis Head, touched off the spark. In 1837 MacKenzie plunged into treason and after a mere fiasco of rebellion fled to the United States. Sensible men, notably Robert Baldwin, had already told the Colonial Office what they judged the only lasting remedy : that the governor's council should become a true Cabinet, selected from the majority in the Assembly and held responsible to it. In struggles over revenue the Nova Scotians had put this point to Downing Street as far back as 1830, while in this very year of rebellion New Brunswick acquired what was in fact, though not by admission, responsible government. Lord Durham's principal recommendation arose, therefore, on a ground well prepared.

His mission, first offered before the rebellion, was pressed on him anew in January 1838 ; he reached Canada in May, stayed there less than six months, and presented his report in February 1839. Whatever the share of his assistants, Buller and Wakefield, its thrust and final shape were his own, comprehending not merely a new government for the Canadas but schemes for land settlement, municipal planning, parliamentary procedure, and emigration. Its effect, perhaps, would not have been so immediate but for the circumstances of his resignation. For, armed with all-embracing powers, he used them to the full, so that enemies at home — Brougham in particular — and honest constitutional scruple seized on the ordinances whereby he banished Papineau and his fellows under pain of death and deported others without trial. When this was cancelled and his powers questioned, he resigned, appealing to Canada in a fiery proclamation over the head of the Imperial government.

There were shortcomings in this classic report. It exaggerated the
French disloyalty, it was based on a thin knowledge of Upper Canada,
its detail did not maintain its ground. But its logic was resolute and
decisive. If Canada was not to be swallowed up in America, she
must become a nation, and Quebec must become part of an Anglo-
Saxon State by merger in a larger unit. Federation he declared
against, for it would leave a French majority in Quebec intact, and
the larger Union he would have preferred was unwelcome to the
Maritimes and would take too long to achieve. He therefore pronounced for uniting Quebec and Ontario, which would involve a
British majority. But this new unit must be rid of the root cause
of friction. The governor must administer this united Canada through
men who commanded a majority in its Assembly; under instructions
that he could count on no aid from home in any dispute that did not
directly involve relations with the mother country. Those Imperial
relations should include amendment of the constitution, foreign affairs,
commerce, and public lands, in all of which the home government
should have the last word.

While this lofty recommendation exhilarated Canada and was
carefully studied by Australians, it took the better part of ten years for
its theory to become fact. The British Act of 1841 united the two
provinces, ordained a fixed civil list, gave Canada control of its own
lands, and made English the official language, but Russell, now Colonial
Secretary, flatly refused to accept ' what is absurdly called responsible
government '; a governor, so ran his rigid dilemma, who implicitly
followed the advice of his Cabinet, would be ' an independent sovereign '.
Stanley, his Tory successor, and Peel both shared this fear of an Empire
dismembered. Yet, as by Russell's own instructions officials were in
future to hold their places at pleasure, pressure on the spot soon forced
an admission that such changes in heads of departments must accord
with the majority opinion of the Assembly.

At first the problem was masked by the strenuous governor-generalship from 1839 to 1841 of Poulett Thompson, Lord Sydenham, during
which great public works, education, municipalities, and county courts
were all driven forward. In fact, however, he acted as his own Prime
Minister, selecting colleagues from any branch of moderate thinking,
and riding off the principle of a party Cabinet. The charm and diplomatic skill of his successor, Canning's friend Charles Bagot, sweetened
the atmosphere, and he took reformers of each race, Baldwin and
Lafontaine, into his government, but he was followed by Sir Charles
Metcalfe (1843–6), an Anglo-Indian administrator of heroic type, yet
inelastic and totally inexperienced in parliamentary arts. Conceiving
his mission as a last crusade to save ' the connexion ' from French, Irish,
and Republicans, he insisted that his final responsibility must be

exerted through heads of departments answerable to himself, and won a last election on this confusion of the real issue. His attitude brought admiring adhesion from Peel, Russell, and Gladstone, while James Stephen gloomily declared Canada was ' in everything but name a distinct State '.

Self-government was, indeed, finally achieved by Canadians them-selves ; by the steady stand of Baldwin and Lafontaine, and the staunch-ness of Howe in Nova Scotia, whose *Letters to Lord John Russell* laid down a clear strategy : ' we seek for nothing more than British subjects are entitled to, but we will be content with nothing less '. Year in, year out, this battery from the Maritimes broke on the Colonial Office, and was supported by Buller at home. At last the third Lord Grey, Russell's Colonial Secretary, lifted the ban which Russell had imposed, instructing the governor, ' it is neither possible nor desirable to carry on the govern-ment of any of the British provinces in North America in opposition to the opinion of the inhabitants '. The first true party government took office in Nova Scotia in February 1848, followed in March by a Baldwin-Lafontaine ministry in Canada.

Elgin, the governor-general who thus promptly applied Durham's principle, was Durham's son-in-law, and in his long term, from 1847 to 1854, Canada was made. He it was who put life into Durham's ideal, faithfully following out obedience to majority rule, at whatever risk or cost to himself. Pursuing what the kindly Bagot had begun, he set out to win the French, repealing the existing veto on their language for official use, and against British opposition at Montreal carried the Rebellion Losses Act of 1849, to compensate those who had suffered unjustly twelve years before. He discerned the depth of the conservative nationalism of Quebec, asking, ' who will venture to say that the last hand which waves the British flag on American ground may not be that of a French Canadian ? ' This faith in permanence induced by freedom he tried to instil in the doubting Whigs at home, whom he bade ' renounce the habit of telling the Colonies that the colonial is a provisional exist-ence '. Besides this grasp of fundamentals, his government pushed on with public works, chartered the Grand Trunk railway, created an un-sectarian university at Toronto, secularized the clergy reserves of land, and abolished seigneurial tenures in Quebec.

His most delicate task was one implicit in the triangle that history has made between Britain, Canada, and the United States. Intermixture of blood — even the same families — on either side of a long border, a vast immigration of Irish to America which rose to flood-height after the famine of 1847, economic dependence of the Maritimes on New England, the trend of Canadian waterways from the Great Lakes, all such factors offered a rival alternative to the British connection. American notions of government affected Papineau, American raiders in Ontario

demonstrated sympathy with the rebels of 1837, and a stiff knot of
diplomatic disputes had descended from the past. One, born with
the peace of 1783, concerned American fishing rights in Newfoundland and the St. Lawrence. A second of the same date, over the Maine-
New Brunswick frontier, was only compromised by the treaty which
Lord Ashburton negotiated in 1841. A third opened up the much
greater future of the West.

By the settlement of 1818 the frontier ran from the Lake of the
Woods along the 49th parallel to the Rockies; beyond, as the parties
could not agree on the tangle of Spanish inheritances, fur-trading posts,
and sea-captains' discoveries, they had agreed for the time to occupy
in common the great space known as ' Oregon ', that stretched to
the Pacific. To push along that parallel to the sea would deprive the
British of the Columbia river and their Vancouver settlement, but the
thinly stretched-out arm of the Hudson's Bay Company could not
resist a tide of American pioneers. The Presidential election of 1844
was won by the Democrat Polk on the cry of ' 54·40 or fight ', — claiming a parallel, that is, reaching to Russian Alaska; heavy negotiation
was necessary to bring about the adjustment of 1846, which left
Vancouver Island to Britain and made possible British Columbia.

For Elgin's immediate purpose, however, the crux was the commercial system. British preferences had determined the course of Canadian
trade, making, for example, the strong lumber interest of New
Brunswick, while Huskisson had allowed Canadian wheat to come in at
5s. a quarter, which in 1843 was reduced to 1s. In virtue of this policy
Canada developed her waterways, Britain treating American grain
ground in Canada as if it were Colonial; powerful American interests,
however, worked to draw Canadian exports through New York, by a
rival canal system and bonded warehouses. At the same time the
United States were taking something like a sixth of all British exports,
and a vehement agitation marshalled the British objection to buying
Canadian timber dear instead of Baltic timber cheap. Then Peel's
repeal of the corn laws jeopardized at a stroke the painfully built fabric
of Canadian transportation. Inflamed also by the racial issue, Canadian
merchants asked repeal of the Navigation Acts which increased their
freight charges, and argued that Canada's future would best be served
by annexation to the States. For this economic grievance Elgin sought
an economic remedy by the reciprocity treaty of 1854. To open
the American market to Canada's fish, lumber, and grain would
disperse many discontents, while the Americans, at some cost to Nova
Scotia, received free access to the shore fisheries and the St. Lawrence
waterways.

Thus principles and changes within reformed Britain assisted to
make a self-governing, self-conscious, Canadian State.

Far otherwise was their effect on the other survivor of our Atlantic Empire, the West Indies. Artificially prolonged in their old prosperity by the wars, the sugar islands even in 1830 counted for much more in our trade than British North America, but they suffered from many grievances and their life was precarious. They had, indeed, an almost monopoly of the home market, yet Navigation Acts and British duties kept prices so high as to keep consumption stationary. They were much afflicted by absentee owners, who left plantations to the mercies of attorneys and overseers. Suppression of the slave trade in 1807 imperilled their labour supply, exposing them too to competition from the slave-grown sugar of Cuba and Brazil, and a little later Britain made such competition even more severe by scaling down the duties on sugar from Mauritius and the East.

No part of Empire suffered more directly from the changing impulses, even from the highest motives, of the mother country. Slave emancipation in 1833 was a hard blow. The money compensation given was much less than the value removed, while the intermediate stage of apprenticeship till 1838 was a sorry failure. As wage-labourers the negroes proved — in general — hopeless, unwilling or incompetent to give the continuous labour on which crops must depend. Production fell away sharply, even before the equalization of duties with those on foreign sugar, slave-grown included, by the Whig government of 1846–52.

True, their local conditions varied much ; in some small islands like Antigua the relations of masters and negroes were different from the mutual hatreds in Jamaica, while some lately conquered colonies like Trinidad had both a better government and a less exhausted soil. Planters had often themselves to thank for their calamities, owing to generations of absentee or oppressive rule, and they often defied alike the Imperial government, the missionary interest, and humanity itself. Recovery was to come in due course, but only when conditions had changed, by an immigration of Indian labour, alternative crops, and mechanization. For the ensuing twenty years, however, while the white folk fell away steeply in proportion to negroes and coloured people, depression and demoralization descended on the once wealthy, proudly self-governing, West Indian interest.

On a smaller scale, and at a later date, than in Canada, the same problems of emigration, land, native races, and self-government were forced forward in Australasia. Here, however, it was no matter of diplomatic inheritance or rival European systems, but an imposition of British communities on what had, politically, been a void. The origin of Australasia was simply the need, when America was lost, to find some alternative area to receive British convicts, on which advice was sought from the scientist Joseph Banks and those who had sailed with Captain

Cook twenty years before. In 1788 Captain Phillip with 700 convicts reached Botany Bay and chose the site of Sydney, being under further orders to anticipate the French by annexing the eastern half of the continent. There for some twenty years this petty settlement went on, hemmed in on the west by what was reckoned an impassable range of mountains, with Van Diemen's Land, or Tasmania, as an outlier for the more desperate prisoners. To a late date the convict population predominated, for of 30,000 adults in New South Wales in 1828 some 23,000 were or had been prisoners, and while this endured, representative government could hardly arise. Yet never did the political instinct of the race triumph more signally over a hostile environment.

'Convicts' in those harsh days included men transported for snaring game, or some first slip for which now they would be merely bound over to keep the peace, and covered also many political offenders. Much good was done by the governor from 1809 to 1821, the Highland soldier Macquarie who, with all his pugnacity and limitations, seized on one great truth, that the settlement was meant not to punish but to redeem. Against ugly opposition and prejudice he consistently brought 'emancipists', prisoners who had proved their worth, out of the shadow, giving them land grants and making some of them magistrates. As such men rose, often to considerable wealth, their first wish was that their status as citizens should be recognized by allowing them to serve on juries.

Still earlier another Highlander, John Macarthur, had founded Australia's first prosperity, when he brought out merino sheep from the royal flock at Kew. By the early 'thirties Australian wool had driven the Spanish off the market and was overhauling the wool of Saxony, and here too Macquarie builded better than he knew. For he set on foot the first determined explorations which passed the Blue Mountains on the west and in time reached, west and south and north, unlimited grazing for flocks and herds. For two decades small bands of pioneers with boundless daring discovered passes, forded great rivers, or traversed deserts, — warned by smoke signals or spear-armed natives that man had been there, though never a white man; reckoning their next find of water by the flight of cockatoos or pelicans; sometimes with tall grass to their saddle girths, sometimes bound fast in sand drifts or wilderness of rock and iron-stone, with kites and eagles overhead; experiencing, in dried-up torrents and dead animals, natives with swollen tongues and their own suffering, what drought was to mean in the heart of this Continent. So Hume and Hovell discovered Victoria from the north, Allan Cunningham found the rich Darling Downs, Sturt tracked the Darling and its junction with the Murray, and the southward drainage of these rivers to the sea.

From this daring of botanists and geologists, sailors, sheep farmers, and Peninsula soldiers, came the break-out from New South Wales'

narrow confines, and a flood of free emigrants.   Defying all regulations
the squatters moved ever outwards, taking what land they could; on
the back of their sheep was the wealth of their country, once a year to
roll in bullock waggons to the seaports.   Meantime, the need to disperse
convict concentrations, fears of the French, and philanthropy at home,
assisted to make new Colonies northwards at Brisbane and in what, after
1826, was to be Queensland; from 1834 the genesis of Victoria round
Port Phillip, in 1829 the Swan river settlement out of which came
Western Australia, while in 1836, from another of Wakefield's enterprises, rose Adelaide and South Australia.   Progress in these last cases
was to be painful; in the west a small isolated body were wrestling with
hardwood forests and a forbidding hinterland, in the south the rigidities
of Wakefield's system and bungling government induced many settlers to
try elsewhere.

But the original colony of New South Wales was reaching maturity
in great strides.   Assisted immigration on a large scale, 48 per cent of
it being Irish between 1840 and 50, introduced a different society.   Old
social barriers passed into new economic division between the acquired
interests of settlers and squatters, whether springing from ' emancipists '
or not, as against the new arrivals, mechanics and shopkeepers, peasants
and wage-earners.   Every sentiment of this new class must rise against
transportation, and so did all the Wakefield school, and save in Tasmania
it came to an end in 1840.   Once in after years it was reintroduced to
save a desperate situation in Western Australia, where it lingered on till
1868, even longer than in Tasmania, but all proposals to bring it back
in the east were angrily resisted.   From the 'twenties onwards self-
government came to New South Wales in the usual gradual steps, the
first decided advance being the Act of 1842, which set up a legislative council, two-thirds elected on a property-owning franchise,
and made ex-convicts eligible both to vote and to be elected.   But
with all his liberalism the third Lord Grey was a man of rigidity.
His measure retained for the Crown the control of a civil list, while a
simultaneous Act enforced on all Australia the Wakefield programme
for land sales, and kept all that burning question under Imperial
direction.

All through the late 'forties Gipps, a very strong governor, was
combating a mixed Opposition, of squatter interests fighting against
fixed prices and demanding long leases, confused with the wholly
separate matter of Australian control of local affairs.   Wentworth, the
squatters' political leader, was out of touch with the new demands for a
broader electorate and an opening of the land to smaller men, and an
Imperial Act of 1846 gave the squatters a long respite by assuring them,
outside settled areas, long leases and prior rights of purchase.   Much
the same gradualness or compromise was impressed on the form of

government. The Australian Government Act of 1850 enlarged the franchise, created a new State in Victoria, and both there and in Tasmania and South Australia made legislatives mainly elective; on the other hand, lands and land revenue were kept under the Secretary of State. But Grey's most fundamental proposal, of a federal council for all Australia, was abandoned under opposition both in the British and Australian Parliaments.

While old Australia and young, the conservative Wentworth and the radical Robert Lowe, were equally asking clearer definition and more responsible government, in 1851 the finding of gold turned this stream into a torrent. The finds were of immense richness, both at Bathurst in New South Wales and at Bendigo and Ballarat in Victoria, and native-born and new immigrants swarmed to the diggings. 94,000 people entered Victoria alone in 1852, and in the first ten years after discovery Australia's population of 400,000 was trebled. In 1852-3 the Imperial government gave to this changing society all that it asked for; responsible government, control of their lands, and constitutions of their own devising.

While Australia had sprung from a government settlement, New Zealand was a pure product of individual enterprise, almost more so than any other Imperial community since the seventeenth century. Captain Cook had recommended the islands as suitable for colonization after circumnavigating them in 1769-70, but seventy years passed without effect. In that interval traders and escaped convicts and whaling seamen broke in, some to live among the Maoris, others just to debauch them with vice, drink, and muskets; French adventurers too, and French warships in the offing. Many missionaries of admirable devotion, Samuel Marsden among them, one of Simeon's Cambridge Evangelicals, and Henry Williams, crossed from Australia to save the Maoris from the white men, while vague land claims among primitive tribes, selling of arms, and violence were laying up a future collision. For the Maoris, immigrants long ago from Malaya, were cannibal, warlike, and intelligent. In the 1830's colonization was opposed by the missionary interest at home, and Glenelg and Stephen.

Wakefield's New Zealand Company was therefore at first refused a charter, but early in 1839 took the law into its own hands by sending out a shipload of settlers; a few months later, ' with extreme reluctance ', as the Colonial Office put it, government despatched a warship to deal with the Maoris, barely in time to anticipate the French. So came about in February 1840 the treaty of Waitangi, declaring the Queen sovereign, leaving the Maoris in ' full exclusive and undisturbed ' possession of their land, but giving the British government a right of pre-emption, if and when the Maoris wished to sell. Here was a first and long-remaining dilemma; between the word of the British government and the claims, part-recognized by that government, of Wakefield's Company, which suggested that terms signed with ' naked savages ' need not be honoured.

Before the Company was bought out in 1850, infinite harm had been done. The political influence of Wakefield's circle was strong enough to extort government recognition and land grants. But weak governors on the spot could not resist pressure for claims amounting to many million acres, while the great length of the two main islands, and the choice of Auckland as capital in the far north, set up rivalry with the Company's choice of Wellington. Land speculation defeated a fair trial of Wakefield's principles, and the Maoris, after many attacks on white surveyors and justly alarmed that Parliament wished to break the treaty, in 1845 began war.

This was confined to the North Island where the mass of the Maoris were concentrated, and perhaps it was the least of the troubles which confronted the new governor that year, the memorable George Grey. Son of a soldier who fell at Badajoz, he first made a name by exploration in Western Australia, and enhanced it by a resolute governorship of South Australia, where mismanagement had left a chaos. In some forms and circumstances of government this high-minded autocrat, as after-life showed, could not succeed, but in the New Zealand of 1845–53 he was worth much gold. By decision and justice he ended the Maori war. He far advanced the land problem in the South Island by large purchases and, — whether wisely or not, — speeded the growth of pastoral farming by reducing the price of Crown land. The Company's disappearance was for the best, but it had done essential work. It had killed notions of transporting convicts, chosen a good stock of settlers, and by its high-price policy secured in the South Island several prosperous settlements of middle-sized farmers ; especially the Otago group coming from the Free Church of Scotland, and the Church of England colony in the Canterbury plains.

Not the least of Grey's services was his refusal to put into operation the elaborate top-heavy constitution issued in 1847, his chief objection being the exclusion of natives from the franchise. His own scheme of beginning with small local councils was continued in the Act of 1852, which created elected bodies for six provinces ; above them, with exclusive powers over customs revenue, land, and native races, and with an overriding power over all, was to be a general assembly, the lower house of which would be elected on a low franchise. At its first meeting this assembly asked for responsible government, and this was granted in 1854. So a community of less than 60,000 Europeans, within fifteen years of their migration, were granted the utmost liberty that Victorian Britain had to give.

This growth outwards of self-governing areas had been complicated in Canada and New Zealand by pre-existing conditions; the fragment of another European race and a native population. In South Africa these conditions meant a more formidable danger.

By our second conquest of the Cape in 1807 we had taken over what we, like the Dutch before us, viewed as a half-way house to India and a military base, any idea of colonization only arising later in conditions unforeseen. For, having conquered a struggling settlement of some 15,000 Dutchmen and Huguenots, we found ourselves face to face with rival invaders from the north in the Bantu peoples — Kaffirs, Zulus, Bechuanas, and Basutos — who by the late eighteenth century had either exterminated the Berbers and Hottentots, or driven them toward the sea. Hence came our threefold interconnected problem; government of a British Colony, relations of British and Dutch, and a European contest with the natives. A fourth, or at least a ruling condition, must be added, the influence of the missionary.

Even before the Dutch downfall the tide of Christian effort began to flow, with the Moravian brethren and the Independents of the London Missionary Society, to be followed after 1815 by Wesleyans and Presbyterians, the Church Missionary Society, German Lutherans, and French Evangelicals. Their radius was immense, far beyond the Colony up to the Vaal, into Basutoland, and among the Kaffirs eastward to Natal, and their power, which matched their devotion, had in some ways a deplorable effect. If their standard of justice for men of all colours was admirable, it was upheld with an optimistic dogmatism and an ignoring of some essential facts, while their geese always seemed to be swans, and rival missions championed rival chieftains. With the Evangelicals so strong in colonial questions at home their advice was paramount, and in particular that forthcoming from a man of burning feeling and political ability, John Philip of the London Missionary Society.

Assisted by the ' 1820 settlers ' in the eastern districts of Albany and Grahamstown, the white population struggled upwards to about 54,000 by 1830, but there was neither scope, nor any united demand, for representative government. Though Roman-Dutch law continued for civil cases, the British set up new courts and magistrates, made English the sole official language, and brought land sales under the reformers' price regulations. But the native question was at the root, wherever one looked. Were they to be Europeanized, amalgamated, enslaved, or segregated ? An ordinance of 1828 gave to Hottentots and all free coloured folk rights of owning land, the colonists' wish for a severe vagrancy law being resisted by the Colonial Office under missionary influence.

This native question, in a land of no frontiers and an age of conquest, was controlled by forces far beyond the Colony. The last century's upheavals had left behind five centres of violence. Along and inwards from the coast, running north-eastward, were the Kaffirs, and beyond them again a half-empty four hundred miles, before reaching the handful of English traders and ivory hunters who were exploiting Natal. West and north of Natal the Zulu despot Chaka, by building up a military machine of disciplined ' impis ', had lately made a desolation, which drove the wreckage of other peoples far and wide. Circling west once more, over the Drakensberg mountains, was the well-covered and fertile Basuto-land, disputed by many chieftains, but with predominance going to the watchful, tolerant, and able Moshesh. West of Basutoland and north of the Orange river were several communities of Griquas, a congerie of half-breeds, Bushmen, and broken tribes, which politically were created by the London missionaries. North-east of these stretched unlimited grass lands, of the future Orange and Transvaal States, until at the Limpopo they touched the Matabele power, a Zulu offshoot who had fled from Chaka, lying in rear of the unused waste of Portuguese East Africa.

In 1834 it was first exemplified on a serious scale how the British people's high intentions jarred and twisted these new-spun skeins. When slave emancipation passed, the new governor D'Urban was sent out to enforce it, with instructions to avoid aggression and to make treaties with those whom the home government were pleased to call native ' States '. One such treaty he did make with Waterboer, the Griqua who under missionary guidance ruled the western districts round the Orange river, but on the east a Kaffir war changed his outlook. Kaffir society, he discovered, was not a ' State ' at all, but a disintegrating mass of tribal units, huddled together in panic of the Zulus, and in need of more living room. In short, his problem was not political but economic, of settlers and Kaffirs alike hungry for land with space for an economy that depended on cattle ; a matter of cattle-lifting, reprisals, and counter-raids, much like the Scottish Border centuries ago. After the experiment of a neutral belt had failed, he annexed the territory up to the river Kei. In 1836, however, the home government disavowed him and the frontier was drawn back ; the Commons' committee on aborigines, after hearing Dr. Philip, threw the blame for aggression on the colonists. With that, and in part from that, came the most decisive event in modern South African history, the Great Trek.

In one sense the Boers had long been on trek, for they were pastoral farmers and frontiersmen, whose pioneers pushed out to take land wherever they could find water springs, in all the wide areas not held by natives in force or armed bodies like the Griquas. These Boers of the frontiers had sat very loose even to their own Dutch government, and much more so to the British, whose measures they detested. Some of them owned slaves, and found the compensation paid most inadequate, or tied up in baffling red tape. All demanded a supply of native labour, nor were they ready to accept orders which would treat Hottentots as equals; they were affronted by the inferiority stamped on their language, the high government price for land, and new demands for taxes or commando service. They wanted large farms, 6000 acres or more, on which a patriarchal family could live, sufficient to itself, but found themselves forbidden to use force against the natives by a government that was incapable of protecting them. Their contempt was deep for an Empire which, as Glenelg's last exploit showed, shilly shallied with men's lives on dangerous frontiers. So in 1836 the trickle of migration broadened to a stream; many hundred waggons crossing the Orange, with wives and children and church ministers and household goods, to seek a promised land where they might live free. Among the fighting-men, the Retiefs and Maritz and Potgieters, was a boy of ten, Paul Kruger, with whom this vision was to end. Slowly, perhaps five miles a day, for their sheep and cattle could not be over-driven, the main bodies moved on; to divide in 1837 between some who drove north over the high veldt toward and over the Vaal, and others who descended the steep Drakensberg into Natal.

No more intractable problem was ever set a British government, and few movements have so swiftly deflected history. The map shows how the trekkers sheared right through, or cut behind, the divided Bantu peoples, forcibly collided with the fiercest of them, Zulus and Matabele, spread one tentacle over the missionary road to the Lakes, and another eastward to the Indian Ocean. Chaka's successor Dingaan massacred one section of them, for which they took a bloody revenge and overthrew him; passing through months of extreme strain and horror, — when their waggons were chained together to hold the laager, Zulu assegais wrapped in burning hay lighted the night, and shapes in ambush, looking like cattle, turned out to be the warriors' shields. One division thus overran Natal, others menaced the Basutos. In the heart of Africa they rooted this aggressive force, hostile to British dealings and stirring all native races into commotion. Yet in the eye of the law they were British subjects, whose doings threatened British security; though themselves broken into factions, and incompetent to make a stable government.

For fifteen years our policy veered between economy, humanitarianism, and Imperial feeling. Troops were sent to Natal in 1838, withdrawn again, reoccupied it again in 1842 when Boer violence threatened to convulse the Kaffirs, and in 1845 finally annexed it. The bulk of the Natal trekkers having consequently rejoined those on the Orange and the Vaal, much the same story was repeated here. As the home government forbade annexation, the Colony attempted new treaty arrangements to protect Griquas and Basutos, but the root question of the land was left unsolved, a chaos of titles bought from rival chiefs and with all boundaries vague, and certainly insoluble by a few British agents, who had no military force behind them. Another Kaffir war in 1846 and the arrival of a new governor, the dynamic Harry Smith, hastened the speed of events. Once more he annexed Kaffraria up to the Kei, and in 1848 declared royal sovereignty over all between Orange and Vaal, beating off an attack at Boomplaats from the Transvaal Boers under Pretorius. At that date the British might fancy they had overtaken the trekkers, and found a policy on which they could stand.

It was not to be. The line was too thinly held by Europeans, over great distances from the Vaal round to Durban, and a crack in one place would bring all the centre caving in. Moshesh the Basuto was antagonized, commandos of the Orange river sovereignty would not back up the British resident, extremists were pulled by sentiment toward their brethren across the Vaal. In 1850 yet another Kaffir war tied down our strength in the east, at a moment when we had intervened, most ingloriously, between Moshesh and his rivals. And the mood of Great Britain had changed. Ardour for native interests had dwindled. Self-government for the Cape was under close discussion, but on the assumption that a self-governing Colony would look after its own affairs, and that Great Britain could not bear the brunt of native wars, stretched ever farther from our base. Colonial reformers and Cobdenites brought pressure to bear on Russell and Grey. In 1852, by the Sand River convention, we admitted the independence of the Transvaal Boers; in 1854 the Bloemfontein convention did the same for the Orange Free State. Some 25,000 Boers in the first, and 15,000 in the second, were thus cut adrift, in the second case assuredly by no very solid wish of their people.

As for Cape Colony, it had over 200,000 European people in the 1850's and economically, largely by the wool trade, had lately prospered; it had organized municipalities, churches, and schools. By the constitution of 1853 it received an elected Council and Assembly, though not responsible government, the Colonial Office also insisting on a franchise low enough to admit men of colour. By 1856 Natal was a Crown Colony, with a part-elected Council.

Here, at least, was nothing more than a project of Empire; a sub-continent ruled on rival principles, divided between half a dozen petty European settlements, many solutions essayed but all cut short, and in the greatest matter of all an abdication. Questions prior to, and more vital than, self-government must be resolved, before South Africa could partake of the life achieved by Canada and Australasia.

CONTEMPORARY DATES

CHAPTER XIV

IRELAND, 1815-1848

NEARER home another subdivision of Empire was gripped in these same fundamentals of race and soil, which outstrip the formula of self-government or ask of it a fuller meaning. It has been seen from what causes the emancipation planned by Pitt had been delayed till 1829, how over those thirty years the Irish Catholic upper class had given ground to O'Connell, with the alliance of Church and peasant democracy that he created, and how the final concession was made in face of civil war. Yet it was found that, though emancipation increased Irish power in the British Parliament, it was irrelevant to the real ills of Ireland. After, as before it, the country was riddled with agrarian crime, riot, and murder, so that Castlereagh's coercion, suspension of habeas corpus, curfew and military courts, had often to be repeated by the Grey and Melbourne ministries.

Statistics give only the bare bones of the problem. In round figures a population of 5 millions at the Union grew to more than 8 by 1841, with perhaps the heaviest density in Europe, of some 365 to the square mile. Of these nearly 70 per cent depended on the soil for a livelihood, for the temporary protection given by the Union to Irish industries against British competition was withdrawn in 1823, since which date, save for Ulster linen, they had seriously declined. Though by British standards Ireland was lightly taxed, paying per head not a quarter of the British figure, there was little or no capital to spare, a high proportion of the soil was owned by absentees and notably by the Whig aristocracy, the squires had usually overspent and mortgaged, and even in 1846 there were hardly 100 miles of railway working. Some 50 per cent of the people could neither read nor write, and of the 8 millions about $6\frac{1}{2}$ were Catholics; the Anglican Church income was about £600,000, though a third of Irish parishes each contained less than fifty Anglicans.

Ireland was, in fact, a standing reproach and an ever-present danger. Every traveller testified how, despite large emigration to America and Australia, it swarmed with beggars; running barefoot, sleeping on straw in mud cabins, living on potatoes and water, still using the wooden plough. Dozens of reports and commissions proved that British institutions had provided no remedy. Crime, murder, and cattle-maiming fill the annals; gangs with darkened faces terrorized witnesses or tenants who replaced those evicted, no dependence could be put on a jury, the country was garrisoned as if it was an Indian frontier, guns and pikes were found under the wet thatch, and almost annual coercion Acts struggled through Parliament.

Pitt had justified Union not as a war measure only, but as a step towards making British wealth available for Irish poverty, and to meet Irish Catholic grievances in a wider and more tolerant arena. Human nature and political events had ruled otherwise. Emancipation, delayed so long, even in its concession seemed to have made little difference, for the magistrates' bench, constabulary, and corporations continued overwhelmingly in Protestant hands. If Union was to go on, O'Connell said, it must be made something more than this ' parchment union ', but to give it such reality would now be harder. He had himself made the Catholic priesthood politically minded, while from their Ulster fortress the Orange order, originally so passionate against Union, clung to it now as the sole means of Protestant ascendancy.

Anglo-Irish relations in the 'thirties and early 'forties make disheartening reading, for which some responsibility attaches to each of three forces, — Tory obstruction, British economic thinking, and O'Connell. The ' liberator ' had been educated in the seminaries of Flanders, he was to die on his road to Rome, but he was no political bigot and no revolutionary. Himself one of the feckless ' squireen ' class, he had taken no part in the '98 rebellion, disliked agrarian crime, and distrusted trade unions; while the inferiority of some who surrounded him, his tactics, and his compromises, pained the younger idealists. His oratorical triumphs, his hatred of bloodshed, and the sentiment that made him hail the accession of the young Queen, all combined to persuade him that he could restrain the mass emotion which he had set glowing, and repeat his success over emancipation anew over Repeal, by demonstration without using force. Though the coarse violence of his tongue made enemies of Peel and Grey, he was tactician enough to put aside any storming of Repeal and for many years to work by degrees.

Much to the disgust of the Whigs in general, he struck up an alliance with British Dissent and Radicalism, over repeal of tests, emancipation, and reform, continuing it in his unofficial understanding with Russell in 1835 which enabled the Whigs to overturn Peel. Russell's school, who were agreed that the Anglican Church in Ireland could not be defended, in 1832 suppressed 10 out of 22 bishoprics and abolished the Church ' cess ', or rate. Their next attempt, the tithe question, cost them five years of humiliation but could not be evaded, for tithe set up a war in every parish; even the peasant's potato plot, already obliged to help his own priest, being tithable for the Anglican parson. Furthermore, it reduced government to absurdity, hardly a month passing without the march of British soldiers to seize some wretched tithable cow from a mob armed with scythes and stones. The Act finally passed in 1838 meant in one sense a defeat for Russell and the Radical wing, for the Lords' long obstruction forced them to drop an ' appropriation ' clause, which would have transferred some of the Church's wealth to purposes of the State. Tithe, however, became a fixed charge on the land-owner, not the peasant, and that alone was a step towards local peace ; whether the landlord would not recoup himself by way of an increased rent, depended on other circumstances.

On the whole, once they were rid of the irascible Stanley as Irish Secretary, the Whig government of the 'thirties pushed on with some success towards a more liberal administration. In an engineer officer, Thomas Drummond, they found for under-secretary a masterful person-ality, bent on reconciling Ireland by making British institutions work equitably. Catholics were recruited in large numbers for the constabu-lary, paid magistrates were appointed to balance the biased local bench. Orangemen were held on the curb, and soldiers and police withdrawn from protecting any scandalous case of eviction. But Drummond's laborious life was cut short, while as regards legislation the Whigs could do little against the Lords, nor had they the insight to look deep. Schemes for State aid to railway development were laid aside, and so were the projects of a strong poor-law commission for housing and emigration. Firmly set in the prevalent economic notions, the Whigs were convinced that ' surplus ' population must be cleared off, holdings enlarged, and the peasant become a day labourer. They were content to pass a poor law in 1838 on the English model, in part, no doubt, to relieve England from supporting the impoverished Irish who came to England for work, but chiefly as the means of getting through a time of transition, during which estates should be cleared and relief applied strictly through the workhouse. Their other principal measure was the Municipal Act of 1840, which they passed only with help from Peel, and a grudging Act it was. True, the scandalous co-opted Protestant corporations were ended, yet the Act only established elected councils, on a high franchise, in ten large towns, keeping control of police and magistracy in the hands of government.

British policy thus ignored the crucial evil of the land, which previous history made it almost impossible for British experience to understand. Our legislation before 1782 had destroyed any other opening for Irishmen, while against open British competition very few Irish industries could stand. So in southern Ireland at least the soil was the one way of livelihood, and high corn prices in the war years increased that teeming rural peasantry, an increase all to the advantage of the political landowners after 1793, when the 40s. freeholders received the vote. Whatever their social charm or mental talent, and those were often great, economically this landowning caste was

one of the most disastrous in history. Inheriting large grants in a
poverty-stricken country but dependent on Britain for power, and often
absentees, many did not differ from the rent-receivers of West Indian
plantations. What they leased out was not, as in England, buildings
and land improved but the bare soil, and except in Ulster, where a
tenant-right custom protected the farmer, at the lease's end all improvements became the landlords', without compensation. Since the
peasantry furiously competed for the means to live, rents were forced
up to a figure that stripped the tenant of the whole surplus beyond the
sum indispensable to existence, and as the landlords commonly acted
through middlemen, such rents were loaded with intermediate profits.
But the peasant clung to his soil, content if on a minute conacre plot he
could get enough potatoes, and eager to subdivide that plot as his family
increased, ready to make his rent by walking to Dublin and taking
cheap passage to harvest work in England. More often than not,
perhaps, he received no money-wage but worked out his rent by field
labour, gambling his family's life on a crop often smitten with disease.
An added precariousness hit him when Emancipation swept away the
40s. freeholder vote, in consequence of which landlords reduced what
tenants they could to annual leases or tenancy at will, or cleared them
out to wastes and bog-land. The legal right of eviction was used often
without mercy, sometimes merely because the tenant voted for a
Catholic. Robbed of any motive to improve, the peasants hugged their
sense of ownership with the passion of a dispossessed people, thinking
any weapon lawful against the injustice of eviction on terms like these.
So we get boycott against new tenants, maiming of cattle, and murder,
and a hideous severance between Irish morality and the British legal
code.

As compared with this black background, most of the political
detail of the 'forties was of minor importance. The King's ' Protestant
minister ', as George IV liked to call Peel, had come to see that Ireland
could not be held longer on a garrison basis, and that force mended
nothing. Determined to wean moderate Catholics from Repeal, he
much increased the grant Pitt had begun for the priests' seminary at
Maynooth, and set on foot the Queen's Colleges at Cork, Dublin, and
Belfast. Catholics, however, would not make terms with these ' godless ' colleges, in which all religions were to be on equal terms, the
bishops mostly backed O'Connell, and though Russell would have given
some State payment to the priesthood, he found British Protestant
feeling invincibly opposed. On Peel's return to power O'Connell
resurrected the banner of Repeal, raised large sums, and organized a
national demonstration. But after his meeting at Clontarf was ' proclaimed ' in 1843, he drew back, was arrested and then released on a
technicality, and before he died, in 1847, his course was run.

Much the most hopeful step was Peel's appointment, in 1845, of the Devon Commission on land tenures. Its leading recommendations cut at the root; that the powers of eviction, or rent-raising without compensation for improvements, extinguished all hope and all justice. But they were themselves extinguished without further ado by the House of Lords, and in the famine of 1846–7 came the downfall, not only of the old land system but of any tolerable chance of bettering Anglo-Irish relations. After many previous warnings, the potato crop of 1845 partly failed, and that of 1846 almost as a whole, and, even when good crops returned, the weakened people were carried off by dysentery and fever. A population of over 8 millions in 1841 fell in the next ten years to $6\frac{1}{2}$, not less than 700,000 died of starvation or after-effects of half-starvation, while the survivors, crowding emigrant ships with their disease, fled their country at the rate of 200,000 a year. The famine thus increased a political fact of great future importance, — the Irish-Americans; at the same time, it seemed to have done the work of 'clearance' which British economists had called for. In the decade ending in 1851, three-quarters of the holdings of an acre or less disappeared, those of under 15 acres were halved in number, and 35,000 orders for eviction were issued in the three years of 1847–9.

British private charity did not fail, nor an advance of British public funds, for 700,000 men were employed on public works in 1847. But the major British remedies hardly touched the man on the soil. The repeal of the corn laws went through against many Irish protests, and it seemed a cruel paradox that Irish corn was exported throughout the famine. All the letters between ministers show that their chief concern was to cut down the numbers receiving relief; George Bentinck's scheme for railway development was rejected; and an amended poor law, though allowing outdoor relief, refused it to any one holding over a quarter of an acre. Russell himself would have wished legislation to control rents, but Cabinet and Parliament were against him, and the Encumbered Estates Act of 1848, though valuable in breaking up bankrupt properties, had the very opposite effect. Within ten years about a third of the soil went to new owners, 80 per cent of whom were Irish, but of a new and harsher class, not prepared to keep poor tenants or swell their own poor-rate, when by eviction they might get rid of them wholesale.

The famine years also deepened the inner rifts of politics. The organization of 'Young Ireland' was in a very different category from O'Connell; of its leaders, the fierce, tragic John Mitchel was an Ulsterman, the high-minded Thomas Davis and Smith O'Brien were Protestants. Their spirit and method were much nearer akin to the French or Italian movements of their day than to '98, or to O'Connell's Papal tradition, for they wished to make a united nation of all creeds, even including landlords, and were ardent for Irish history, arts, and language, of which they made much in their paper, the *Nation*. Much resenting the old Liberator's autocracy and even more the ensuing dictatorship of his son John, they equally disliked his clinging to some British connection and the clerical control which would estrange Protestants. Since they concluded that nothing could be got through Parliament, and believing the European revolutions of 1848 were their opportunity, they took to organizing armed resistance; Lalor and Mitchel perceived what could be made of the land by rent strikes and tenants' leagues. Their resources were small, their feuds were bitter, their aims openly declared, and their conspiracy was broken up; Mitchel, Meagher, and O'Brien were transported, all to end in America; McGee in the long run became a Canadian minister, and Gavan Duffy Prime Minister of Victoria. And Ireland, for whose self-government they had been ready to make war, continued for another half-century in the Union, receiving ideas, money, and arms from those whom the land system had driven overseas.

CHAPTER XV

THOUGHT AND RELIGION, 1830–1860

Not the Whig reformers only, but Peel and his successors too, worked in an arena changed, spiritually, out of all recognition since the reign of George III. Without some suggestion of these new forces, doubly powerful since the advent of a cheaper, more free press and a wider education, the Victorian golden age, or the duel of Gladstone and Disraeli, cannot be understood.

The British were still a religious-minded people, indeed more so, perhaps, in this age than at any date since the Commonwealth, the fate of many governments and composition of many Cabinets being determined by religious causes. Older divisions of Whig and Tory had always largely corresponded with the line between Church and Dissent, but now those divisions took on a sectional character, confusing each party within itself. This process could, of course, be traced in part to much wider causes, affecting all Europe, especially the rise of secularism and a new passion for nationality.

Even within Britain, however, the tone and framework of religion had changed fast. Wesleyanism, French revolution, Evangelical revival, and industrialism had shaken an old fixed order, forced men to search out their fundamental beliefs, driven some to the left or nearer to Dissent, others to the right or back on Catholic principle. In 1828–9, by the repeal of the Test and Corporation Acts, the Church's political monopoly was broken. They had to meet Radical threats of disestablishment; or again, while a few years back one quarter of the J.P.'s (and many of the best) had been clergy, that social rule could not be maintained. There had been variations of equal importance in the Dissenting bodies. English Presbyterianism had largely turned Unitarian, making centres of great intellectual and economic distinction, as at Birmingham and Norwich. Independency, abandoning one of its first positions, had set up a central authority over its congregations. Wesleyanism had dropped Wesley's hope of reunion with the Church he had come from, and itself became an organized body, rather than a spiritual protest.

Another general mark of the age was the decline of Erastianism, the unified structure of Church and State, originally characteristic of England and refortified by the Tudors. To defend that system on principle became very difficult after the events of 1828–9, for when religious uniformity had gone, it was hard in a reformed Parliament to insist on a monopoly which compelled every Dissenter to pay church rates, and to be married in an Anglican church. Though there were men of weight like Keble who would continue fighting for the old ideal, and though as late as 1839 Gladstone's book on *Church and State* tried to defend it, they were rowing against the tide, and had to reckon with Peel, political leader of the churchmen's party, who realized what concessions must be made.

If the Church were driven back for weapons on its own armoury, it would not find a sword of cutting edge among the Evangelicals. Before 1840 their major figures had died, such as Wilberforce, or Charles Simeon, whose net had been cast so wide from Cambridge, while their present representatives in politics were not of the calibre of Liverpool and Perceval. Besides, great though their holiness was and deep their influence, not least in founding the bodies which evangelized both industrial England and the Empire, — the Religious Tract, Church Missionary, and British and Foreign Bible Societies — their intellectual base was narrow; their essential doctrine of justification by faith and perseverance of the elect leaving little room for the never-extinguished Catholic element in Anglicanism. Religious revival, in response to the infidelity of the past century and the Revolution, had inevitably taken on a conservative and Catholic colouring, making part of the ramifying ' Romantic' movement of the human mind. It was a mental habit to which Walter Scott had given humanity, Wordsworth a sense of identity of man's working with nature, and Coleridge a search for ruling principle. But religion, though finding new channels, derives from the original stream; Newman himself imbibed the Evangelical thirst after individual righteousness, while two of Wilberforce's sons became Catholics, and a third a high-church bishop.

The Oxford Movement came out of the University's revived life in the first years of the century, which included the making a reality of its examinations, and award of fellowships on intellectual grounds alone. In that reform Oriel College was the pioneer, its members in the 'twenties including the future leaders of all schools — Keble the pure Anglican, Arnold of Rugby and Whateley the broad-churchmen, Newman and Hurrell Froude. A first open cleavage came in 1833, when Arnold put forth proposals for a liberal State Church, in which all Protestants could blend, but Keble, fired by the Whig attack on the Church in Ireland and threats of disestablishment in England, preached that sermon on ' national apostasy ', from which history dates the coming of the movement. That autumn Newman issued the first in a long series of *Tracts for the Times*.

Though the move began in this small arena, and its early landmarks were small matters of academic appointments, its principles cut to the heart of society. Its leaders proclaimed war against Liberalism as infidelity; war against notions that heresy was but mistaken thinking, or tolerance a virtue, or that the majority-will could decide what was right, or that the secular State could govern religion. Looking for a rock on which to stand, they could not find it either in human intellect or in the individual's sense of salvation, and groped their way back to firmer ground of the seventeenth century. Then the Caroline divines had taught an apostolic succession of bishops as the unbroken chain of the Church; a vision of a divine society, historically extending over all generations since the Apostles, and witnessed to by the discipline of its believers, whether wise or unlearned, in the sacraments. If this was conservatism, it was at least built on principles which were independent of living men, whether Peel or the administrator Blomfield, bishop of London, who had to resist the pressure of numbers and accept compromise.

While the learning of the *Tracts*, the challenge of such principle, and the outstanding quality of Newman and Keble and Pusey the Hebraist, filled the Church with new courage, this movement's course was diverted by external events and individual character. Clamour over the subscription to the thirty-nine Articles, which was enforced on all undergraduates, over Whig appointment of ' unorthodox ' liberals, such as Hampden, to chair or office, commemoration of Cranmer and the Protestant martyrs, a curious scheme for a Jerusalem bishopric under joint Anglican and Lutheran auspices, all these before 1839 broke the Church into factions. In front of the leaders skirmished the lighter troops, who asked instant action. Hurrell Froude, the historian's brother, died young, but the publication of his *Remains* revealed his equal scorn for compromise and Protestantism, and his place was taken by a Balliol philosopher, W. G. Ward, whose keener edge sharpened every controversy.

Five years longer Newman lingered in the Anglican communion. He was shaken within; St. Augustine's sentence, ' securus judicat orbis terrarum ', seemed to condemn the *via media* to which he had given his life, while a phrase from one of his early teachers, ' growth is the only evidence of life ', made the germ of a doctrine of development, by which he reconciled modern Rome with Christian antiquity. The extreme sensitiveness, pathos, and love for perfection, which made his writing unsurpassed and his preaching memorable, did not equip him to wait, as Pusey's greater learning and selflessness could wait in confidence, or Keble's more normal English temper, while a series of blows struck by the rulers of Oxford, some the natural reaction of timid men but some the fruit of a vendetta, drove in his sense of frustration. In 1841 he was condemned on account of No. 90 of the *Tracts*, in which he argued that the thirty-nine Articles did not conflict with the beliefs of early Catholicism. Pusey was suspended from preaching for his sacramental views, Ward condemned for a provocative challenge. The method whereby the Tractarians clung to their teaching that the English Church was Catholic, qualifications they inserted into plain statements, their defence of ' reserve ' in expounding religion, or of ' economy ' in using its terms, exposed them to a common charge that they were not to be trusted. At the end of 1845 Newman was received into the Catholic Church, where many of his disciples followed him, and in 1851 Manning, hitherto an archdeacon most combatant against Rome, went over too. This was directly due to the Privy Council's action in upholding a clergyman, Gorham, against his bishop's ruling on a point of doctrine — meaning that a lay tribunal could determine belief.

Church reform began long before the Tractarians and millions of money were found to build new churches, but when the storm over Romanism and ' Puseyism ' had blown over, it was seen how deep a mark the movement had made. Not, indeed, so much by its immediate acts as by its battle-cry and its example, for no movement so clerical and intellectual could be popular in England. But its learning, sanctity, and insistence on all that was Catholic in our heritage, altered the whole religious outlook, raised the standard of worship in every parish church, and undoubtedly assisted both the intensity and extension of religious life. In 1852 Convocation was revived, after being kept in silence since 1717; an incessant growth of Colonial bishoprics fortified Anglicanism in the Empire; by asserting its own principles in independence of the State, the Church became more fitted to cope with democracy.

But, whatever the distant value of this revival, in the early Victorian age Liberalism was all-triumphant. Macaulay's *History*, beginning to appear in 1849, marked its type, and proudly counted the blessings of Britain in that year of revolution. The historian had little to say in praise of democracy, while his speeches denounced the Chartist claim for universal suffrage as a delusion. What made him a representative mind was the glorification of the Whig platform, a robust Protestantism, an insular pride, and belief in progress through an expanding liberty. Steadily the legislature continued to strike off whatever they judged a fetter to ordered liberty; everywhere we find the creed that conscience must be free. In Scotland a revival of zeal after the Revolution had naturally revived the basic Presbyterian principle of the congregation's freedom and right to approve its ministers. Fired by Andrew Thomson and then by Thomas Chalmers, the reformers challenged the power of private patrons, and when the Church Assembly's act, giving the congregation such a veto, was found illegal by the law courts and the Lords, ministers obeying the State were deposed by the Kirk. After ten years of agitation, in 1843 Chalmers led over 400 ministers out in the ' disruption ', to found the Free Church of Scotland.

So one by one the prerogatives of establishments were broken down.

In 1844 Peel much enlarged the subsidy to Maynooth, the Irish seminary for Catholic clergy. In 1847 the election of Baron de Rothschild as member for the City challenged the barrier against the Jews, in the oath which every member must take on ' the true faith of a Christian '. But though the Commons wished concession, Disraeli and Gladstone joining hands, the Lords resisted, and it was not till 1858 that a compromise was hammered out, that each House should determine its own qualifications. In 1852, to the indignation of those who stood on chartered rights, the first royal commission on the universities began enquiries. By a long process of legislation their governing bodies were made electoral, fellowships released from many an antique restriction, the professoriate strengthened, and religious tests abolished for degrees. In 1856 the tide engulfed an innermost religious citadel ; a new lay court of Probate and Divorce replaced the Church's jurisdiction over marriage and last testaments, divorce was made accessible to men of small means — for hitherto it had required the expense of a private Act of Parliament — and the remarriage of divorced persons was legalized.

Thus Liberalism, in which the Tractarians saw their enemy, overcame them, yet it was not in England a teaching of revolutionary ideas. For a long generation, which we may take as ending with the death of their greatest leader John Stuart Mill in 1873, the most powerful political school of thought were the Utilitarians. ' They aimed low ', said Newman, ' but they achieved their aim ', and to pick holes in their philosophy is easy. Brushing aside all natural rights, and rejecting conscience or intuition, they looked only to outward experience, from which they deduced the sway of two sovereign masters, pleasure and pain. Making the criterion of action not its moral motive but its external effect, in the world's tangled skein they pursued one guiding thread, ' the greatest happiness of the greatest number '. Their bias was in favour of individual liberty, holding that for each to calculate and follow his own good was the safest way to the happiness of all. Like the French liberal thinkers on whom they had drawn, they suspected the State and were opposed to restraints on the individual, whether imposed by a caste or by Socialism, a vested interest or a trade union.

It was this common-sense utilitarianism which more than any other force inspired, yet limited, the principal legal changes from the Reform bill to 1870 ; abolition of usury laws, but a law of limited liability ; laws against truck and long hours, but no law to fix wages ; reform of legal procedure, and the many steps we have noticed to release energy and opinion.

John Mill's most popular works [1] revealed the Malthusian ideas in which he had been bred. Himself the most spiritual of men, he dreaded the debasement of a people by animalism or a multiplication of the

[1] *Political Economy*, 1848 ; *Liberty*, 1859 ; *Representative Government*, 1860.

unfit, his chief concern being to champion minorities and personality against convention and the tyranny of majorities. Hence his insistence that each man should be free in his ' self-regarding ' acts, his earnestness for second chambers, a plural vote based on education, proportional representation, and votes for women. On these foundations he did not change, though as time passed he widened the first crude ideas of his school as to what constituted happiness, and grew to allow more good in Socialism than had his father or Ricardo.

There was another body of opinion in existence, by no means yet grown to its full strength, but already a dangerous foe to dogmatic religion. The British Association for the advancement of science was founded in 1831; Lyell's studies in geology raised questions as to the antiquity of man, which the book of Genesis did not answer; all the great Faraday's personal piety could not conceal the truth that the theme he was exploring, of physical forces, magnetism, and matter, involved a world of progressive change. Even before 1840 Charles Darwin's voyage in the *Beagle* assembled data for those conclusions on evolution, to which he and others were converging.

In the 'fifties this wrestling between dogma and science came into the open, with the interpenetration of British Christianity by liberal influence. A Christian Socialist school, headed by F. D. Maurice and Charles Kingsley the novelist, coloured their Anglicanism with the emotion of democracy. Maurice was expelled from his teaching at King's College, London, for unorthodoxy; Oxford was rent by the warfare between Pusey and Liddon for the high-churchmen, Stanley and Jowett for the broad. In 1860 Jowett, Temple, Mark Pattison and others published their doubts in *Essays and Reviews*, and a plea for a less literal interpretation of Scripture, but their work was condemned by Convocation. The year before, Darwin's *Origin of Species*, reinforced by the independent enquiries of A. R. Wallace, had brought the Christian doctrine of creation into the region of doubt.

At that date, though the lives of Mill, Cobden, and Gladstone had still to reach their full effect, this liberal rationalistic scheme of things held the stricken field. Its momentum could be tested in all branches of intellectual activity; in the violent recoil from the Oxford Movement which made Froude's historical writing a glorification of political power; in Tennyson's *In Memoriam*, or in the grave un-Christian philosophy of George Eliot's novels. Only from a few elevated corners came protests of rebellion against the new order. In innumerable essays, and in his *Cromwell*, Thomas Carlyle questioned the individualist way of life, or the shallowness of political franchises as a remedy for deeper discontents; while, echoing his condemnation of material pleasure, Ruskin was searching for the spirit which had of old, in Gothic art or mediaeval gilds, made for human fraternity and a common ideal.

BOOK VII

A GREAT POWER
1852–1918

CHAPTER I

CLIMAX OF THE VICTORIAN AGE, 1848–1880

EW civilizations have left such enduring spiritual monuments, wielded such political power, or expanded in such rapid material progress, as that of Great Britain in the mid-Victorian age.

Between 1871 and 1875 our birth-rate reached its highest point, round about 35 per thousand, and the United Kingdom population, which had been 27 millions in 1851, rose in the next thirty years to nearly 35 millions. In much the same period they invested over £1000 million overseas, while 2½ million British subjects migrated to British Colonies and the United States. The tonnage cleared in our ports grew from less than 15 millions to nearly 60, almost one-third of the world's sea-going ships were British. In 1850 exports were valued at £197 millions but at £297 millions in 1874, imports rising even more, from £100 millions to £370 millions, while at the last date the total foreign trade of Britain and her Colonies equalled that of France, Germany, Italy, and the United States all rolled together. Except for the Crimea, the country was engaged in no major war. Much that had been tentative in the Empire of 1850 was made solid; Canada was confederated, Australian self-government determined, in India the Mutiny was suppressed and government transferred to the Crown. Memorable things were done for the life of the mother State. Universities were opened and reformed, the modern civil service created, education made universal, the parliamentary electorate doubled, the courts of law modernized, trade unions given their full status, and the position of women revolutionized. As for the achievements of the spirit, in the years between Wordsworth's death in 1850 and Carlyle's in 1881, a great body of immortal British literature and thought was made: by Tennyson, Browning, and Ruskin; Dickens, Thackeray, and George Eliot; Newman and Matthew Arnold; Macaulay, Mill, and T. H. Green; Darwin, Huxley, and Tyndall; Bagehot, Henry Maine, and Herbert Spencer; J. R. Green, Acton and Froude; Meredith, Thomas Hardy, and William Morris; Westcott, Lightfoot, and Martineau; Clerk Maxwell and F. H. Bradley.

Though no era is self-contained, since perils passed or decline in prospect leave uncertain its fringes, a certain stability defined these thirty years. Spaced out by some dates of decision, the Prince Consort's death in 1861 or Palmerston's in 1865, this age appeared to have left revolution behind. The Crown, which in 1830 had been discredited and which Peel had thought menaced even in the late 'forties, secured an essential rôle in a new Constitution, and a new rôle as well as a new style when in 1879 Disraeli made the Queen Empress of India. Threats against lords and bishops died away to mere party mutterings. Chartism as a militant force vanished. The Utopian or all-embracing Labour movement of Robert Owen's day changed into a regulated moderate trade unionism, recognized by law and employers, accepting the economic teaching of *laisser-faire*, and bent on improvement of practical conditions. Out of the storm of the Oxford Movement the Church passed into a comparative peace.

This was the last pure age of aristocracy, but also the one and only age of an ascendant upper-middle class. The electorate of 500,000, as increased in 1832, hardly exceeded 900,000 when the second Reform Bill passed in 1867, which raised it to nearly 2 millions. Pocket boroughs had not altogether died, for between these two Reform Bills no Tory was ever elected for the Duke of Bedford's close preserve at Tavistock, or the Lansdowne citadel at Calne; indeed, well after this there were many petty townships left with members, as at Woodstock, where a majority of its 873 voters in 1874 duly returned the Blenheim nominee, Randolph Churchill. Both ministry and Parliament accurately reflected this society. The small Gladstone and Disraeli Cabinets of the 'seventies were made up of peers and commoners in pretty equal proportions, and even in 1880 there were 160 members of the Commons who were related to peers. Till the agricultural depression beginning with the cruel harvests of the late 'seventies, the landed interest had rarely been so prosperous, for wars in Europe and America distracted rival grain-growers, and gold discoveries raised prices. Landed rents increased by about 28 per cent between 1851 and 1878, while the so-called ' New Domesday ' of 1874 showed that half the soil was owned by less than 8000 persons. On the influence of great landowners, and round their London houses, — Londonderry, Spencer, Devonshire, or Derby — many political manœuvres turned.

This aristocracy, notwithstanding, was much changed from that of the eighteenth century. Of its chosen political leaders not the Radicals only, Bright or Chamberlain, but Peel, Gladstone, and Disraeli were all the sons of new industry or raised simply by their own talent, political power now being equally shared between the land and business. Industrial revolution, evangelical faith, the Oxford Movement, and Utilitarianism had imported an earnestness into public life unknown in Horace Walpole's letters, or the circle of Fox and Devonshire House, even if all ministers did not move on the moral elevation of Aberdeen or Gladstone. Such a quality of public opinion pointed the power of the *Edinburgh* and *Quarterly Reviews*, when Jeffrey edited the first and

Southey was chief writer for the second, and later the proud independence of *The Times*, remade by two great editors, Barnes and Delane. If a majority of public men were still brought up on the classics and in the confines of Anglicanism, Bright in 1868 being the first Nonconformist in a Cabinet, their horizon had been much enlarged by science, economics, and history. Religion and science and reformed examinations had given new purpose to the universities; while in the twenty years after Dr. Arnold's death many new public schools, Marlborough and Cheltenham, Wellington, Radley, Haileybury and Lancing among them, followed the discipline and broader range of study which Arnold had given to Rugby. From the sons of the upper-middle and professional class trained in them came the human material which, by the opening of the civil service to competitive entry, first in India and then at home, could be turned to the benefit of the State.

Though that generation had a zest for improvement, this new mixed aristocracy was well satisfied with the progress made since their fathers' day, and on fundamentals were much agreed. The age was liberal, or liberal-conservative, not so much because Conservative governments filled only ten of these thirty years, as from the prevailing beliefs to which a great majority would subscribe. Liberalism, in the sense of breaking down privilege and equalizing opportunity, never ceased its steady advance. One result of the commission of 1851 on the universities was to open Oxford and Cambridge and their degrees to Dissenters, while the tests Act of 1871 opened their fellowships also. Admission of Jews to Parliament was settled at length in 1858; Gladstone abolished church rates in 1868. In 1871 vote by ballot, so long resisted by Whigs of Palmerston's type as un-English and 'unmanly', gave real freedom to electors; simultaneously the abolition of purchase of commissions in the Army widened the ladder for merit.

The minds most representative of the age, or those to whom it most deferred, show the blended influences contributing to its poise. Though the static religion of Church and State had broken down, Christian faith was all-powerful, or at least Christian ideals of conduct never so strong. Sabbatarianism was dominant enough to stop bands playing in the London parks, church-going and family prayers were habitual; the young Unitarian Joseph Chamberlain taught in Sunday school, as many Tory politicians did in theirs. Liberalism was led by Gladstone, a mind soaked in Latin Christian teaching and persuaded that politics were a religious vocation, and the Radical and Labour world owed most of its leadership to Dissent and chapel preaching. If discoveries like Lyell's in geology, and in biology those of Darwin, Wallace, and Huxley, shook parts of the faith severely, the age hugged a belief that science and religion could be reconciled, in an optimism that human progress made part of a divine plan. In his cloudy way this was the teaching of

Charles Kingsley, and of this Victorian faith no mind was more typical than Tennyson, Wordsworth's successor as poet laureate; awed by Nature's new revelations, yet refusing to discard the older gospel, creating in this world of doubts the figures of a spiritual aristocracy whose Victorian virtues he transferred to King Arthur's Court. The minds of artists more powerful and sceptical than his were charged with the same seriousness, as the novels of George Eliot and George Meredith, or the poetry of Matthew Arnold may show, this reasoned agnosticism of the 'seventies being very far removed from the jeers and juvenility of Shelley or Richard Carlile.

Liberal philosophy of that time had its high priests, of admirably pure and persuasive character. In the hands of John Stuart Mill utilitarian teaching had been enlarged and refined; if the note of his *Liberty* and *Representative Government* was increasingly one of democracy, it was democracy guarded against the tyrannies of ignorance and mobs. Before his death in 1873 his school's supremacy was passing to another, the idealists of whom T. H. Green of Oxford was a memorable leader; expounding from the metaphysics of Plato, Rousseau, and Kant the doctrine of a general will and the rule of reason, yet tinctured with an emotionalism which, in other hands, might unstring the fibre of the Utilitarians.

For the greater part of this age, however, individualism was still supreme, and more marked individuals this country has never known than Livingstone and the Lawrences, Richard Burton the explorer, Gordon, Herbert Spencer, the Mutiny soldiers, or the business leaders of Lancashire and Birmingham. Believing in liberty, not equality, and competition, not regulation, that generation, and no one more than Gladstone and Bright, looked on taxation as an evil and disliked State interference; strong in the core of their religion, that God most helps those who help themselves. This blend of religious purpose with the paternal tradition inherited from aristocracy resulted in a high ideal of public service, as might be illustrated from the founders of the Charity Organization Society in the 'seventies and of women's colleges at the universities.

Though their humanity was very real, as increasing legislation showed on behalf of women and children and merchant seamen, the province which they left to the State was minute, if compared with our day. Only £54 millions were raised by taxation in 1852, and in 1881 revenue was still below £70 millions. Any enlargement of public control proceeded slowly, by extension or from commonsense experience; the powers given to the Home Office, for example, in 1856 to inspect county police forces, or the creation in 1871 of the Local Government Board to combine powers over health and poor law. Substantially, health and housing, education and insurance, were all left to self-help, and rigorous administration ensured that, outside the workhouse, less than 80,000 able-bodied poor should be relieved in 1877. In consequence an immense structure of self-help had arisen in Friendly Societies, savings banks, and co-operators ; savings-banks deposits were doubled in these thirty years, societies like the Oddfellows and Foresters had a membership of half a million.

If there were still the ' two nations ' of which Disraeli's *Sybil* spoke in 1845, the gulf of sheer poverty he had painted was filling up, the deeper cleavages now lying rather between country and town, or between an aristocracy of labour and those below it.   Agriculture was the greatest single industry, employing a quarter of the working male population in 1850, though that proportion was falling with the growth of cotton, iron, and steel.   Far ahead of other industries in mechanism, the textiles then employed 1 in every 19 persons and made 60 per cent of our exports, cotton alone accounting for nearly 40 per cent even till 1880.   Mechanism and engineering made possible too a great growth of coal from deeper workings, its output rising threefold in this period, and the output per miner a year from 264 to 403 tons.   Based on cheap coal, the furnaces trebled iron production, turning out more than all the world together.   That golden age of the Black Country ended in the heavy slump of the middle 'seventies ; by 1880 steel had superseded iron on the railways, and increased fivefold with the inventions of Bessemer and Siemens.   If iron and steel exports that year are taken together, they make four times the figure of 1850.

Many different tests would show that those who worked with their hands took an increasing share of this new wealth.   Somehow between them the people of 1880 posted over ten times the number of letters of forty years earlier.   Railway mileage meant much for the poor in cheapening living and ease of employment, and the 5000 mileage of 1850 had come to 18,000 in 1880.   Money wages as a whole rose by nearly 50 per cent, and real wages not less, for prices fell fast in the 'seventies ; even the agricultural labourer's in the most depressed years was 20 per cent more than the rate of 1850 and the best agricultural wage in Europe.   In those industries covered by the Factory Acts, which were extended to cover many more than the textiles and mines originally protected, the law had almost established a working week of $56\frac{1}{2}$ hours, with a Saturday half-holiday ; trade-union action won a 54-hour week for most engineers and metal workers.   Trade unionism, indeed, had become a recognized part of the State.   Led by men of high ability, Allan of the Amalgamated Engineers, Odgers of the London Compositors, and Applegarth of the Carpenters, they revived their strength by avoiding strikes, and by regulating from the centre their branches' conduct of benefits and contributions.   Miners and cotton operatives were first solidly organized late in the 'sixties, the Trades Union

Congress began in 1868, while in 1874 the miners Burt and Macdonald became the first Labour representatives in Parliament.

All this came about by degrees, for many commissions proved the miseries endured by a people of countrymen who were becoming a people of townsmen. Between 1851 and 1881 London's population rose from 2,360,000 to 3,800,000, and some great towns elsewhere by 80 per cent; in rural England and Wales, on the contrary, population positively declined. At the last date 68 per cent of the people lived in areas defined as urban, nearly 100,000 agricultural labourers having left the soil in the last ten years.

With that process a new Radicalism came into our history, yet even so it was moderated by the prevailing temper, resolutions for manhood suffrage being often rejected at the Trades Union Congress. Some personal reasons help to explain, no doubt, this stability, as the prolonged lives of Wellington and Palmerston, while party lines had been blurred by the achievement of parliamentary reform and free trade. Since Peel's 'apostasy' had rent Conservatism in two, and religious differences sundered Whigs from Peelites, an era followed of party confusion, weak governments, and a House of Commons disposed to follow not measures but men. Eight different ministries filled sixteen years ending in 1868. Two governments fell in 1852, one defeated by nine votes and the other by nineteen; and the Commons elected that year sat successively under Derby, Aberdeen, and Palmerston. The first essential, a fusion of the able Peelite group with one party or the other, was only part-done by Aberdeen's unhappy coalition, and until the death in 1865 of Palmerston, a Conservative Canningite, Liberalism found no exponent in a Whig government. On the whole such impetus, or obstacles, as existed to party division, came rather from without than from within, — from the reactions of British opinion to Napoleon III or the colossus of Russia, Italian nationality, and American democracy.

Though the age ended with a new Conservative and a new Liberal party, the earlier careers of their leaders illustrate these transitions and possibilities. Disraeli began public life as a Radical, Gladstone as a high Tory; once the question of Protection was decided, as Disraeli did decide it in 1852, what was there to prevent a Conservative reunion? We find that Derby, under his inspiration, offered places both to Gladstone and Palmerston in 1852, and again in 1855; that Gladstone, who condemned Palmerston as ' by far the worst minister the country has had during our time ', was vehemently pressed to join Derby in 1858 and was voting for him a week before entering the Palmerston government of 1859; that Palmerston was prepared to invite Derby's son Stanley in 1855, and Derby ready to ask the Whig Clarendon in 1866.

When politics are so nicely balanced, decision turns on the personal

factor, or men's native bias. Gladstone long hesitated in which camp he
could best serve the causes which he had learned from Peel, but in the
last resort was less moved by historical than by moral ideas. Free trade
and economy with him partook of an almost religious character; his
published letter in 1851 on the persecuting government of Naples, ' the
negation of God erected into a system ', showed that he stood with
Liberalism in Europe; his personal reprobation of Disraeli as an
adventurer forbade him to sink the Peelites in Disraeli's party. Death
in that small Peelite body, of Aberdeen and Herbert and Graham, and
the national acceptance of Palmerston, left him no alternative except
the Whigs, yet it was not till the old man died and Gladstone lost his
Oxford seat that the Whigs passed into Liberalism.

Transition was also prolonged by the Crown, whose strength was
very different from what it later became, and exerted in ways often
reminding men that Victoria was granddaughter to George III. Her
reign, not in her heart only but for history, divided at 1861, when the
Prince Consort died at the age of forty-two. Since the days of their
engagement, when at the Queen's bidding he had worked through
Blackstone's *Commentaries*, he had strenuously set himself to elevate the
Crown, and morally had done so without doubt, yet under his guidance
the royal position was not without danger. Together they attempted to
keep the prerogative of dissolving Parliament in their own hand; the
Army was taken as a specially royal province and, after Wellington and
Hardinge had gone, the Queen in 1856 made commander-in-chief her
youthful cousin George, duke of Cambridge, in whose irascible, kindly
hands the office remained till 1895. The Prince Consort was a Liberal
of a Continental type, though profoundly a German, as his passion for
the cause of Holstein against Denmark showed; but he had also a
doctrinaire fear of democracy, spoke of Mazzini as ' insane ', and
always defended the Austrian cause in Italy. Drawn by dynastic ties
to the Orleanists, the Court at first frowned on Louis Napoleon, and
resented the genial British welcome given to Kossuth and Garibaldi.
These matters brought about a long vendetta against Palmerston, whom
they succeeded in ejecting from the Foreign Office in 1851, and kept
him out of it during Aberdeen's government. The royal prejudices
likewise vetoed a privy councillorship for Bright, just as for years they
excluded any one deemed a ' Puseyite ' from the Household.

When her ' dear angel ' was taken away and Windsor became ' a
living tomb ', the Queen's nervous system collapsed, and for some years
she became the petulant, exacting recluse of Osborne or Balmoral, who
could not be induced to open Parliament or appear in London, and
whose ministers had to seek her out by weary journeys. What had
been her husband's purpose was now a sacred legacy. Germany,
she was convinced in 1864, was ' our natural ally ' and, even in 1867, ' a

Power from whom no aggression need be feared '. Personal or feminine considerations moved her deeply, as when Disraeli's extravagant courtliness in caring for her comfort contrasted with Gladstone's lengthy memoranda and serious zeal; and she was quite without scruple in using a congenial minister like Granville against her Prime Minister. She continued to claim a chief share in church patronage, of which Tait's appointment as archbishop in 1868 was a strong case, while she incurred a heavy responsibility by excluding the Prince of Wales from important business. On the other hand, her husband had made her a dutiful and laborious public servant; indeed, her developed virtues and limitations were those of the industrious middle class that made the backbone of her people. As the Prince's lead in the arts and the great exhibition at the Crystal Palace represented their culture, so her pride of country, or her thought for the Crimean soldiers and her feeling for the afflicted, were worthy of the great Queens, her predecessors, and her own fervently patriotic generation. Her military pride during the 'seventies even made her miss the once detested Palmerston; several times her straightforward sense impelled Parliament or ministers towards a necessary solution, as in her instinct of 1867 that some speedy settlement of parliamentary reform was vital, or her recognition that disestablishment of the Irish Church was the national will.

In each recorded detail, whether her objection to ' women's rights ' or to vivisection, or in defending flogging in the Army, the Queen was intensely conservative. Her sentimentality, undogmatic religion, and fixed moral code, like her simpler preferences in the arts, were all characteristic of this virile, satisfied, and sententious age.

CHAPTER II

COALITION, CRIMEA, AND THE TRIUMPH OF PALMERSTON, 1852–1859

ERBY'S first government, of February to December 1852, was a mere interlude, weaker in personnel than any since Goderich's in 1827, and dependent even after the election on the Peelite vote. Doubts whether the minister and his party were sincere converts from protection made Palmerston decline to join, nor would any whole-hearted Peelite serve with Disraeli. Its fall was therefore pre-destined whenever Whigs and Peelites combined, and an opportunity was promptly taken on Disraeli's budget. True, he ostentatiously dropped tariffs as ' obsolete opinions ', but some concessions to the landed interest and an extension downward of income-tax allowed Gladstone, in a fiercely conservative speech, to overwhelm him.

Russell having become impossible to his own party and Palmerston being vetoed by the Court, the Queen sent for the venerable Whig Lansdowne and the no less venerable Peelite Aberdeen, appointed the second as her minister, and exerted herself to make a coalition government. On paper it was very strong, but never did the vices of coalition appear more clearly than in these thirteen talented men. Though the Commons contained only 30 Peelites as against 120 Whigs and about 150 Radicals, the Peelites managed to annex six Cabinet places; Russell conceived he had received a promise that in a short time he should become Prime Minister, a notion stimulated by his ambition and wounded party feeling; Palmerston, who would have preferred a more conservative Lansdowne ministry, was soon brought to the front by the stress of foreign affairs, out of the gilded cage designed for him at the Home Office. This high-mettled team was much too spirited for Aberdeen, who showed no capacity for keeping his Cabinet together on vital questions. Two years brought the Coalition down, and one of the two was passed in the shadow of war.

Whatever memorable they accomplished in the time of peace was done, pre-eminently, by Gladstone. His energy and knowledge, with his blend of Liberal and Churchman, pushed through the Universities Act of 1854, meeting half-way the aspirations of those who, like Stanley and Jowett at Oxford, or Henry Sidgwick at Cambridge, had worked for reform from within. For the future of higher education the pro-visions of this Act were revolutionary : that close fellowships and close scholarships were abolished; that the universities would henceforth be governed by the resident teachers; that powers were given to open halls for men of poorer means; that the obligation to take Holy Orders was much diminished. Gladstone again was in the forefront of a battle, fought against Russell's obstruction, which led from 1855 to an opening of the home civil service to competitive examination, and its recruit-ment by an independent commission, instead of by government patronage. But it was his first budget, of 1853, which set him in the first rank of ministers.

It was stamped with the hallmark of Peelite finance and the ideals of his age. Restriction must end, the necessaries of life be freed, and revenue be grouped in mass. One hundred and forty duties were abolished and another 150 lowered, the excise on soap and paper, for example, among the first, and in the second the duties on tea and life insurance. He had never held Peel's high view of the income-tax, thinking it easily evaded, and that by its ease of collection it encour-aged extravagant government. Taking it as a tax to be reserved for emergency, he now put it at 7d., which would gradually taper to extinction within seven years, but for the first time extended it to Ireland. But though for another twenty years he clung to his principles, income-tax was promptly doubled on the outbreak of the Crimean war.

Though this war has often been called unnecessary or fruitless, to his death Gladstone viewed it as one fought to vindicate the public law of Europe, while no modern British war was more strongly desired by the people at large. It is, indeed, probable that if Aberdeen had had his way, Britain would have stood aside, and equally possible that, if Palmerston had had his, Russia would have drawn back. But to declare that, because Turkey in the next twenty years failed to amend the griev-ances of her Slav and Greek subjects, we had ' backed the wrong horse ', is to beg a hundred questions, — whether, for example, some war would not have been fought even had Britain been neutral, and what in that case would have happened to Constantinople, — while it assumes that the Balkan States who achieved their independence in 1913 were capable of winning and maintaining it sixty years earlier.

The revolutionary age of 1848–51 had ended in a considerable reaction. Italian movements had collapsed; German Liberalism had broken down; Prussia had thrown away a chance of leading a united nation, the German case in Schleswig-Holstein had failed. The second French Republic was destroyed by its own factions, Louis Napoleon made himself President in 1851 and Emperor in 1852. High above this weakness stood the Czar Nicholas I, who had helped Austria to survive by beating the Hungarians, crushed Polish insurrection, and warned Germany off from attacking his Danish kinsfolk. He was all-powerful with the Prussian King, had brought pressure to bear both on Persia and Afghanistan, and never lost a chance of patronizing the Christian subjects of the Turk. But Palmerston's triumph of 1841 had arrested his influence there, while in Napoleon he found not only an offence against the sacred order of monarchy but a ruler who would revive French prestige in the Levant.

While at Jerusalem, Bethany, and the holy places, angry claims and outrages surged between Catholic priests and Greek monks, in 1853 Nicholas again stirred the view he had put forward in 1844 when Aberdeen was Peel's foreign minister, and with which, the Russians thought, Aberdeen had much agreed. The Turkish bear, he now said, was dying, and they must arrange division of the skin; how would it be if Roumanians, Serbs, and Bulgars became 'independent' under his protection, and Great Britain annexed Crete and Egypt? Like all British governments, Aberdeen's refused to make hypothetical commitments and, like other autocrats, Nicholas made the mistake of deciding that a particular Prime Minister, in this instance a weak and pacific one, could bind Cabinet and people. The Czar's responsibility went far beyond this; though not desiring war, he hoped by a forceful bluff to win the advantages that war would give, and took the first steps, from which retreat is so hard.

In February 1853 his envoy Prince Mensikov entered Constantinople with much show of armed might, and charged with severe demands; dismissal of the foreign minister, a new guarantee of the Orthodox Christians' privileges in the Holy Places, and recognition of Russia's right to protect the twelve million Greek Christians within the Turkish State, — all this coupled with an offer of a secret treaty, aimed against France. When these terms were rejected in May, Nicholas ordered his troops to enter the principalities that now make up Roumania. But not till October did Turkey declare war, and not till March 1854 did Britain and France follow suit.

During that long interval one influence, often in the past made the scapegoat, may be acquitted of inflaming the causes of war; that of Lord Stratford de Redcliffe, our ambassador, who returned in 1853 to Constantinople, where he had served as a junior as far back as 1808 and as chief between 1841–52. His life had been given to the cause of a Turkey saved by internal reform from external attack, believing that the penalty of failure would be a Russian aggression; he now threw his weight into saving peace by insisting on delay, and twice at least put aside the power given him of calling the British fleet into the Straits. Such responsibility as lies on Britain at all must fall, rather, on Cabinet, press, and people. Some falls upon France, whose ministers, more than the Emperor, often asked action outdistancing the British Cabinet; some, again, on the shifty court of Austria which, though directly concerned to prevent a Russian command of the Danube, would leave the effort to the western Powers. But most by far on Russia and Turkey, in both of which raged a fever for war.

When Russian armies neared the principalities in June 1853, a British fleet was sent to Besika Bay, lying well outside the Straits, though Palmerston and Russell thought it should have gone direct to Constantinople. By September not only had Turkey rejected the Powers' Vienna note, but it had become clear she was justified in doing so, since Russia had not given up schemes for a protectorate; and this swung our foreign minister Clarendon away from the pacific Aberdeen, nearer to those who wished for decided action. In October, refusing an Austrian effort of mediation, the Cabinet sent the fleet through the Narrows, but still refused Palmerston's view that it should forthwith enter the Black Sea. On 22nd October the Turks took the offensive on the Danube; on 30th November the Russians annihilated a light Turkish flotilla at Sinope, upon which British public opinion, calling this a wanton massacre, clamoured for war. We were now committed, six months after Palmerston's original advice, to defend Turkey against aggression, and in December he resigned, nominally because the jealous Russell chose this curious moment to push for a new Reform Bill. He was brought back to office in triumph on a wave of anger in the press; under which pressure, and more from France, late in December the Cabinet moved the fleet into the Black Sea, with instructions to stop Russian ships leaving Sebastopol, pending another endeavour for peace. Since Nicholas would not evacuate the principalities under this threat, war began in March 1854.

Whatever our apportionment of responsibility for the war, except for individual heroism it makes an inglorious page of history. Now was fully exposed, since for the first time press correspondents followed the Army, the unpreparedness of our military machine. Army administration was distributed between the Secretary of State for War and the Colonies, the Secretary-at-War who directed finance, the commander-in-chief, the Home Office which controlled militia and yeomanry, the Master-General of the Ordnance who managed artillery and engineers, the Treasury, and several other authorities. Parliament and its economists had scandalously neglected the Army. The private soldier's pay of 1s. a day left, after deductions, less than 3d. for himself; while how bad were barracks, sanitation, food, and disease may be judged from a single fact, that the rate of mortality in infantry regiments at home was twice that of civilians'. Troops were enlisted either for life or for a term of years, most taking their discharge after fifteen years; their present distribution in round figures being 65,000 at home, 40,000 in the Colonies, and 30,000 in India. Shortage of establishment, moreover, meant cruelly long spells of foreign service, so that a few years earlier fourteen battalions had been in India continuously for fifteen years. Some small steps had of late been taken to better conditions, at least flogging was restricted now to fifty lashes, but the private soldier was still probably the worst treated of all Her Majesty's subjects.

Though the Militia Act of 1852 set up a small reserve, with a mere three weeks' training in the year, and though a new Minie rifle was replacing the old Brown Bess musket, both armament and training were terribly deficient. Guns were short in number, musketry neglected, and though the Aldershot area was just being developed, large field exercises were almost unknown. There had been no experience in the field in Europe since Waterloo, while seniority clogged the higher command, Raglan the commander chosen for the Crimea being sixty-six years of age and not having seen active service for forty years. Purchase of officers' commissions chilled professional ambition in cavalry and infantry units; supply — which was largely in the hands of contractors — and army clothing were most disorganized.

Some of these evils had damaged the Navy too, but then the Navy was always on part-active service, and Graham had lately overhauled its administration. Parliamentary economy kept too many officers on half-pay without chance of promotion; Charles Napier, who was designated for the Baltic command, was as old as Raglan; and the fleet was in transition from sail to steam. As things turned out, though invaluable in the Crimea, the naval contribution in this war was small, for as it had not enough light craft to go inshore, it could do little in the Baltic against heavily gunned fortifications.

Even before the Russians evacuated the principalities, both the French and British governments pressed their unwilling commanders to attack the Crimea, and were warmly supported by the press. It was a risky decision, for from the sea Sebastopol was impregnable, and the armies, thrown ashore against an enemy of unknown strength, would have to race against the Russian winter. Moreover, Raglan's request for a transport corps was refused by the War Office, and his troops during their halt in Bulgaria were weakened by sickness. However, having landed in mid-September in the bay of Eupatoria, north of Sebastopol, they struck southwards and on the 20th stormed the heights south of the river Alma. The next week was fatal. Raglan's instinct to press the attack home at once was resisted by the French, and the Allies marched on to occupy the plateau south of the city. As their base the British were assigned a small inferior harbour, southeast at Balaklava, which threw on them not only the eastern part of the siege operations but the protection of those operations from the Russian field army.

Two immediate efforts were made by the Russians to save Sebastopol from investment. On 25th October they surprised the British holding

Balaklava, an onset which had to be held by our cavalry till infantry reinforcements could be sent from the plateau above. So came about the famous charges of Scarlett's Heavy and Cardigan's Light Brigade ; the first a brilliant success, though left incomplete for lack of support, but the second a consequence of bad temper and misinterpreted orders and in every sense a disaster, except the all-saving sense of immortal courage. This battle left the Russians threatening our communications to the sea, and on 5th November they attacked these lines in great force at their north-east angle near Inkermann. In this murderous, straggling fight in a morning fog the British regimental officers and ranks made up for loose contact between British and French and some tactical mistakes, and beat off the Russian sortie with immense loss. But winter was at hand.

The eight short miles from Balaklava to the front line were soon deeply engraved on British hearts. Transport and forage were almost non-existent, metalled roads there were none, fuel ran short, while with no change of clothing, freezing in trench and redoubt, no shelter in the rear but canvas, fed mostly on salt pork and biscuit, the Army was ravaged by dysentery, cholera, and pneumonia. So great was the wastage that casualties were filled by boys of sixteen, sometimes men were in the trenches six days in seven, and government were driven back, as George III's had been, on recruiting German mercenaries. Early in 1855 numbers on the sick list exceeded numbers in the line, and how many sick would not die ?—without ambulances, drugs, sanitation, or trained orderlies. This price we paid for neglect by Parliament, wooden routine in the high command, and the British conviction that war can be improvised.

However, long before Sebastopol was taken in September 1855, the worst had been overcome. Though much inferior in strength to the French, our combatant numbers were raised to 60,000, and given more hope and opportunity by new roads and a railway, a transport corps, the new Enfield rifle, and commissariat reform. Too late to assist this particular campaign, the Secretary for War was relieved from the Colonies and given the powers hitherto so disastrously divided over finance, militia, and ordnance. Florence Nightingale's masterful hand took over the iniquities of the hospitals at Scutari and, in the face of intense obstruction, revealed to the public its responsibility and the nursing profession as a public service.

That winter of failure and horror destroyed the Aberdeen government, eaten into as it already was by Russell's jealousy and the frustration of Palmerston. The choice of this hour to give Aberdeen the Garter showed the Queen's Peelite sympathies, doubly unwise when the Court was under heavy fire from the Radical press, which enlarged on the Prince's Austrian views and even avowed he had been sent to the Tower.

Declaring himself unable to defend their record and Newcastle's administration of the War Office, Russell resigned rather than face the Radical Roebuck's resolution for enquiry, which in January 1855 was duly carried by a majority of 305 to 148. The Queen's first explorations, with Derby and then with Russell, proved that no Cabinet could survive if Palmerston did not lead it; of the Peelites, Gladstone and Herbert and Graham joined him but promptly resigned when he accepted the Roebuck resolution, and he went on, therefore, with a ministry of Whigs, — Clarendon, Granville, and Cornewall Lewis included, — only later diluted by adding the Radical Molesworth.

Palmerston was now the man of the country, which demanded a tougher prosecution of the war. With his easy magnanimity he gave Russell office, but Russell destroyed himself anew at midsummer. Britain and France, declaring they sought nothing for themselves, had in concert with Austria drawn up what were called the four Vienna points; which would substitute a European guarantee of Roumania for a Russian protectorate, make international control of Danube navigation, reject Russia's claim to protect Turkish Christians, and restrict her naval power in the Black Sea. The last was the crux, and till his death in March the Czar had refused to hear of it. In May, however, Russell as our envoy accepted an Austrian plan for compromise, and it was when this was rejected by France and Britain, and his share was made public, that he was compelled to resign.

An Italian contingent sent by Cavour, alliance with Sweden, the fall of Sebastopol, and our reformed Army offset the Russian capture of Kars and inflamed warlike feeling in England; there was also the displeasing knowledge that the French storming of the Malakoff fort had done most to win Sebastopol, more than our own assault on the Redan. To retrieve that failure and to win lasting terms by more conquests being the prevailing mood, the war was ended against our will by Austrian mediation and war weariness in France. The new Czar Alexander II accepted the four points in January 1856, the crucial clause being enlarged to exclude all ships of war from the Black Sea, and peace was signed at Paris in March. Roumania received from Russia enough of Bessarabia to cover the mouths of the Danube, navigation of which would come under a permanent international commission; the two principalities of which it was composed, Moldavia and Wallachia, were to have self-government, like Serbia, under Turkish suzerainty. Both Dardanelles and Bosphorus were closed to warships; neither Russia nor Turkey might maintain fleets, or fortresses, in or on the Black Sea. Receiving a promise of reforms to benefit its Christian subjects, the Powers guaranteed the integrity of Turkey, and in accord with Palmerston's wish to draw ' lines of circumvallation ' round the enemy, Russia undertook not to fortify the Aaland Islands off Sweden and restored Kars to Turkey. The peace conference also made a notable advance in defining the rules of war. Privateering was forbidden, blockades were to be invalid if not effective, except for contraband of war a neutral flag would cover enemy goods, nor would sailing under an enemy flag expose neutral goods to capture.

At the cost to Great Britain of 25,000 lives and £50 millions, peace was thus won, on the basis that the future of the Turkish Empire was for Europe, not Russia alone, to decide. As often happens, we ended war on the worst of terms with our greatest ally. France, having borne the brunt of a war fought more in British interests than her own, was militarily predominant and, having designs against Austrian Italy and also having fears of Prussia, was concerned to make Russia a friend. We, on the contrary, were more anxious than ever to maintain a firm anti-Russian front, for the peace was barely signed when we declared war on Persia, and it was only a year old when the Indian Mutiny began, which was unextinguished when Palmerston lost power.

Both his strength and his weakness came from the fact that he led the country and not a party. Radicals must always oppose him whenever the time came for more parliamentary reform ; Cobden — whose letters accused ' the military party ' — and Bright had throughout resisted the war ; Russell and Graham, out of office, were always undermining him ; Gladstone, isolated from all parties alike, detested the war's prolongation and the slur cast on the Peelites, and criticized Whig finance. The minister's power really rested, within the present Parliament, on the help or neutrality of the Tories, but Disraeli was confident that Derby had missed a chance in 1855 and the time had come for his party's return to office. But in 1857 it was proved again that the people were solid behind Palmerston.

Late in 1856 a second China war began, in fundamentals much like the first ; as opium had been the pretext for the first, so the question of the lorcha *Arrow* was the pretext now, — whether this sailing ship was covering piracy under the shadow of the British flag, or whether its Chinese owner at Hong Kong had duly taken out a British registration. But once more the realities lay deeper. Plunged in civil war, the Chinese government could not control its agents ; anti-foreign agitation resulted in pinpricks and boycott, and if there was no doubt that European consuls connived at many abuses there was also no doubt that the Chinese steadily evaded the foreigners' treaty rights, while our wish for normal diplomatic access to Pekin was repelled. Weeks before the home government could be informed, Bowring the Hong Kong governor took the law into his own hands, with sympathetic support from the representatives of France and the United States. On this score, though against Disraeli's advice, a coalition of all parties in the Commons defeated Palmerston by sixteen votes. He dissolved

Parliament and came back triumphant, Cobden and Bright, besides some Peelite and Radical leaders, losing their seats. Indeed, Bright's pacificism and Cobden's doubts whether India were worth holding, or rightfully held, were hateful to the generation of Crimea and Mutiny.

Palmerston's downfall within a year, in February 1858, in itself proved the strength of Palmerstonianism. For the occasion was made by the bomb hurled at Napoleon III by the Italian Orsini, whose plot and its weapons had both been made in England; thence came furious demands by the French military for measures against this ' nest of assassins ', and Palmerston's consequent bill to tighten up the conspiracy law. The Commons' majority, who by nineteen votes drove him to resign, were led by personal opponents in Russell, Graham and Gladstone, and by Kinglake, the historian of the Crimea, who had a personal quarrel with Napoleon; their language accused him, of all men, of ' truckling ' to France, and appealed to the national pride he, of all men, had evoked. Disraeli pushing forward the reluctant Derby, the Tories took their opening, and were called on to make a government.

To the rule of a man without a party now succeeded something equally unstable, the rule of a party without a majority. Though stronger than in 1852, Derby's second government was a very weak one, no one but Disraeli and the two Stanleys being of the first rank, while it included too many cleverish, fanciful men like the foreign minister Malmesbury, or the novelist Bulwer Lytton. Ellenborough, another of the same type, whose querulous arrogance had led to his recall when Viceroy, had soon to resign the India Office now, for an equally arrogant attack on the present viceroy, Canning. Three times Gladstone was invited to join but always refused, so did Palmerston and Graham, and if other groups could make up their differences, the government's life would plainly be short. Though Disraeli's grasp on the party had increased, he was unable to convince them of some things he had at heart, such as ministries for education and defence; on the other hand, aided by the Liberal Stanley, he pursued objectives to which a majority of this factious house were committed in principle, a Government of India Act and a new Reform bill. On each of them his curious flights of fancy exposed a flank to attack, but by skilfully exposing the differences among Opposition he prolonged this dangerous life for a year.

The Reform bill he brought forward in 1859 was meant to satisfy the middle class and superior artisans. Leaving the borough franchise at £10, it would lower that in the counties to the same figure, and would have given votes too, by what Bright baptized as ' fancy franchises ', to graduates and teachers, solid savings-banks depositors, and others who on similar tests stood out above the general level. Its weak spots were plain. It was liberal enough to displease many Tories, for two ministers resigned, but too conservative to win over the Radicals. Though

Disraeli had wished to go further, all it did for redistribution was to take away 15 members from some small boroughs, while plainly an additional 400,000 voters, chosen on selective principles, did not meet the Radical claim for equal representation. An amendment of Russell, implying a lower borough franchise, being carried against them, government dissolved; their small gains did not give them a majority, and being defeated in June on a vote of no confidence, they resigned.

Four ministries had now fallen since 1852. Everything went to show that the electorate liked a sort of conservative Liberalism, that no vital matter divided Palmerston from Derby, and that parliamentary reform was rather a pretext than a passion. Conservatives were still rancorous against Peelites, the Manchester school equally bitter against Whigs, but the political class at large were thinking of other things. This spring Cavour, in concert with Napoleon III, launched the war of Italian liberation which would certainly win more sympathy from Palmerston, Russell, and Gladstone than from Derby and Malmesbury. Perhaps this, together with the conviction that in isolation the Peelites could do nothing of service, was the turning-point in the life of Gladstone, though to the end he had voted with Derby. That his morbid, self-examining conscience finally overcame his aversion to Palmerston, is good proof that Palmerston's personality was the representative or stabilizing point for this generation.

This, indeed, demolished the Queen's effort to escape taking either of the two, pro-Italian, ' terrible old men ', by asking the courtly Granville to make a government; her final choice of Palmerston being ruled by public opinion, Russell's proud claim that he must be either first or second, and perhaps the realization that Palmerston would better conciliate Conservatism. Each having agreed to serve under the other, he gave Russell the post he asked for at the Foreign Office, which the Queen had designed for Clarendon; and gave great place to the Peelites by putting Gladstone at the Exchequer, Herbert at the War Office, with other posts for Newcastle and Cardwell. The Radicals were given a pledge of a lower borough franchise, and though Cobden declined office, Milner Gibson went to the Board of Trade.

So at last was made the Liberal Party, compounded out of the Canningites from whom Palmerston long ago had come, the Whig patricians, Peel's followers, and the Radicals. At its head was a man of seventy-five who had lately hunted in his red coat with the Emperor of the French, who still walked miles after partridges, and rode regularly to the House of Commons, who wrote cheerfully of vote by ballot as ' sneaking to the poll ', and whose Tiverton speeches conjured up the vision of a manly aristocratic country of free men, ready to teach foreigners their duty about misgovernment or the slave trade. Had they not under his auspices already demolished Metternich and Mehemet

Ali, Louis Philippe and the Czar, Indian rebels and Chinese barbarians ? Stronger and larger than Russell in moral physique and worldly sense, conservative and middle-class England would follow him while his vital star lasted. The man of destiny in his government was Gladstone, just turned fifty, who had in youth imbibed the Canningite outlook in foreign affairs, and added to it what came from his own intense thought on Christian principle, a persuasion of the moralizing power of liberty. Profoundly he distrusted what he called the ' malignant ' genius of Disraeli and the policy of Malmesbury, while since the dissolution he could hope no more for alliance with Derby. Maintaining what the Peelites had long styled ' liberalism ' at home and abroad, he believed he could count on Palmerston and Russell, nor would he any longer live the life of a political Ishmael. To this partnership had the industry and liberalizing of Britain brought the Prime Minister, who had first held office under Perceval, and the Chancellor of the Exchequer, whose first speeches had defended the unreformed Parliament.

CONTEMPORARY DATES

1851 *Coup d'état* in Paris.
      Bismarck at the Frankfurt Diet.
      The Crystal Palace in Hyde Park.
      Charles Kingsley, *Yeast.*

1852 Napoleon III, Emperor of the French.
      Treaty of London, regarding Schleswig-Holstein.
      Thackeray, *Esmond.*
      Matthew Arnold, *Poems.*

1853 Commodore Perry opens Japan to American trade.
      Stratford Canning returns to Constantinople.

1854 Alma, Balaklava, Inkermann.
      Civil war in Kansas.
      F. D. Maurice and others found a Working Men's
          college.

1855 Italian troops in the Crimea.
      Tennyson, *Maud.*
      Death of Charlotte Brontë.

1856 Peace of Paris.
      British fleet bombards Canton.
      Pasteur teaching at Paris.
      Bessemer's steel process.
      Livingstone, Burton, and Speke in Africa.

1857 Indian Mutiny.
      The Dred Scott decision in the United States.
      Flaubert, *Madame Bovary.*

1858 Napoleon meets Cavour at Plombières.
      Creation of the Roumanian State.
      The Czar Alexander II frees the serfs.

1859 Battles of Magenta and Solferino.
John Brown executed after Harper's Ferry.
De Lesseps begins the Suez Canal.
Darwin, *Origin of Species*.
Mill, *Liberty*.
Meredith, *Ordeal of Richard Feverel*.
George Eliot, *Adam Bede*.
Death of Hallam, Macaulay, Tocqueville, and Metternich.

CHAPTER III

INDIA: FROM WELLESLEY TO THE MUTINY

PALMERSTON's life almost exactly coincided with the completion and the extinction of British India as the Company and Warren Hastings had made it. He was born in the year of Pitt's India Act; he lived to deal with the Mutiny, the fulfilment of Indian prophecy that in the centenary year of Plassey the British Raj would be shaken down, and to transfer India to the Crown. How the British attained their greatest achievement, their policy, prowess, and mistakes, must be traced from 1785 when Hastings came home to face impeachment.

For another generation after that event, and in a sense to the end of its rule, the Company strove to implement Pitt's declaration that schemes of conquest were repugnant to the nation, and to pursue that doctrine of non-interference which Philip Francis had preached against Hastings. It was in vain. Hastings' successor Cornwallis had to meet forces which made such an abdication impossible; a nominal Mogul power, so weak that a Rohilla adventurer could seize Delhi and blind the Emperor; a shadow Peishwah at Poona, dragged hither and thither by rival Mahratta chiefs, of whom Scindia almost controlled central India; at Mysore was Tippu Sahib, inflamed by ambition and Moslem fanaticism, and convinced that the British could be ignored. The second Mysore war of 1790–92 proved him mistaken; Cornwallis took up arms to protect the Company's allies and dependants, and the peace terms divided nearly half of Tippu's territories between Hyderabad, Mahrattas, and the Company. But resistance in his uplands had been desperate, the Madras government's inefficiency was again exposed, and in 1795 he joined the Mahrattas in attacking Hyderabad, our oldest ally. Now the fruits of ' non-interference ' were reaped. Cornwallis' successor, Sir John Shore, a Company servant of eminent merit in revenue policy, rigid, evangelical, and self-distrustful, stood aside. The defeated and resentful Nizam tried therefore to rebuild his strength with French soldiers of fortune. Tippu made contact with the French Republic, the Mahrattas threw central India into turmoil by aggression and civil war, our protected allies in Oudh and the Carnatic sank ever deeper in their weak corruption.

A turning-point came when Shore was replaced in 1798 by Pitt's friend Mornington, later Marquess Wellesley, an aristocrat of tireless ambition and outstanding ability, who saw India as one aspect of the war with France. Despising the cautious economy of the India House, he stamped his own notion of Imperialism on India, built a princely new government house at Calcutta, and set up a college to train young civilians on his own model; entrusted armies and diplomacy to his brothers Henry and Arthur, and formed in Malcolm, Munro, Elphinstone, Ochterlony, and Metcalfe, a magnificent dynasty of administrators. His first measures were to make safe the bastions of Bengal in Hyderabad and Oudh, by suppressing French influence and putting their foreign relations in our discretion; that done, in 1799 he turned to punish the proved intrigues of Tippu with France. A campaign from east and west, of two months, prepared with all the Wellesley laborious detail, ended the danger; Seringapatam was stormed, Tippu killed in its ruins, and his State swept away. Leaving a fragment of Mysore to the Hindu dynasty which Hyder Ali had ejected, Wellesley made over some territory to Hyderabad and annexed for the Company the mountain passes and coastal districts, both east and west. Annexation of Tanjore the same year, and in 1801 both of the huge misgoverned Carnatic and parts of Oudh, completed the British hold alike on the sea and the Ganges valley.

These victories brought us face to face with the Mahratta confederacy, whose wandering armies were incompatible with peaceful frontiers. Their factions gave Wellesley his opportunity in 1802 when the Peishwah appealed for help, and the governor-general concluded with him the treaty of Bassein, which obliged the Poona government to maintain a British subsidiary army and to give Britain control of his relations with other States. The inevitable result was the desperate war from 1803 to 1805, waged for their independence by the great Mahratta chiefs, Scindia, Holkar, and Berar. Though Arthur Wellesley defeated Scindia in the hard-won battle of Assaye and overwhelmed Berar, and though Lake entered Delhi and crushed Scindia's northern contingent at Laswari, Holkar continued resistance through 1804-5, and that resistance enlarged the war. For Wellesley meant to assert supremacy over all Bundelkund and Rajputana, and by alliance with their numerous petty States to wall off the Mahrattas from Delhi and Oudh.

This extension into the heart of India, some sharp reverses like Lake's failure to storm the Jat stronghold of Bharatpur, and the expenses of war, induced the directors to recall Wellesley in 1805 — with whose costly buildings and designs they had another quarrel — and for a last time to essay ' non-interference '. The aged Cornwallis, a dying man, was sent back to make the surrender; under his successor, Barlow, our southern boundary in Hindustan was declared to be the

Jumna, thus abandoning our Rajput allies and the fortresses of central India to Mahratta oppression. Only a few years, however, were required to convince the most unwilling that the facts could not be fitted into our formula.

For our Indian power, in the first place, must reach defensible frontiers, and our effort to find them involved collision with primitive and warlike peoples. Minto, the governor-general from 1807 to 1813, and of old one of Warren Hastings' arch-accusers in Parliament, found that the north-west barrier could not be drawn short of the Himalayas; the settlement which Metcalfe made for him in 1809 with Ranjit Singh, the Sikh conqueror of the Punjab, extended the British sphere of authority to the Sutlej. His successor, Marquis Hastings (1813–23), found that Bengal's northern border lay open to the inroads of the Gurkhas, and two years' hard fighting passed before, in 1816, Ochterlony made up for the incompetence of other commanders and carried that frontier firmly to the foothills. Hastings was responsible also for the decision to protect the Company's China trade by occupying Singapore in 1819, though the initiative had come wholly from their agent in Malaya, Stamford Raffles. Amherst, who followed him, had to make the north-east safe against the Burmese, who had seized Manipur and Assam. In that war neither British administrators nor the sepoy army showed to advantage, but our command of the sea brought in due course the capture of Rangoon and advance up the Irrawaddy, and the treaty of 1826 won for us Assam, Arakan, and the Tenasserim coast.

But the most urgent problem for ' non-interference ' lay in the very heart of India. It was not merely that conditions all over Rajputana and Bundelkund were a reproach; that Mahratta armies, supplemented by Pathan adventurers and gangs of Pindaris, broken men of all castes and origins, ravaged and ravished and tortured, or that the political officers of Wellesley's training reported appeals which they dared not answer, and the ruin of royal families we had sworn to defend. Since prestige in the East runs across frontiers, outside this area of anarchy currents of conspiracy rose in every neighbouring State. Hastings' successful campaigns of 1817–18 against the Pindari freebooters thus led directly to risings of the Mahratta chiefs, and to a permanent settlement. Baji Rao the Peishwah, a monster of iniquity, who had always intrigued against the Bassein treaty, attacked our resident Elphinstone, but was hunted down after stiff fighting; Mahratta sentiment was conciliated by preserving the small State of Satara, whose powers the Peishwahs had filched, but the Peishwahship was abolished and Baji Rao himself relegated, on a vast pension, to a long life outside Cawnpore; the name with which his adopted son, Nana Sahib, stands coupled in history. The Bhonsla rajah of Nagpur, having taken the same course, was deprived of his northern Saugor territories, Scindia had to surrender the strong point of Ajmer in Rajputana, Holkar's territories were cut down. A series of treaties, worked out by Malcolm and others, covered with our protection the Rajput States such as Bundi and Jaipur, and new-modelled others like Bhopal out of areas where the Mahrattas had tyrannized. Not only was the British paramount power thus asserted in all India, south of the Himalayas and east of the Sutlej and lower Indus, but the old entangling veils were torn away; from 1835 the Company's coinage, which for half a century had purported to show our vassal relation to the Mogul Empire, was stamped with the head of the British sovereign.

Indeed, though the Company went on, all was changed in its character since Warren Hastings' day. Parliament's hold, though indirect, had been made final by the Acts of 1784–6; the Board of Control's orders were issued through, but could not be altered by, the secret committee of the directors. And though the Company kept a nominal veto on the appointment of a governor-general, and in 1844 used its legal power to recall Ellenborough, in practice Pitt's compromise worked for the supremacy of the Cabinet, exerted through the President of the Board, who was almost always one of their own members : often, as in the case of Dundas, Castlereagh, Canning, or Sir Charles Wood, a minister in the first rank. At each renewal of the Company's charter something decisive was done to impose on India the will of the British people, and to make its service royal, not mercantile. In 1793 all appointments, except that of members of Council and governors, were restricted to the Company's covenanted servants, so sweeping away the patronage from home which had crippled Warren Hastings. The charter of 1813 took away their monopoly of the India trade, organized an Anglican Church establishment, and explicitly declared the Crown's sovereignty. That of 1833 deprived them of all commercial privileges, including the China trade, and laid down that no native of British India should be debarred from any office, ' by reason of his religion, place of birth, descent, or colour '.

From Cornwallis' day onwards, save for the exceptional case of Shore, the unhappy instance of Barlow, and the unique appointment of John Lawrence after the Mutiny, no Company servant was ever appointed to the governor-generalship, which was given either to men of high distinction or on the other grounds that govern Cabinet appointments; generally speaking, though Elphinstone and Munro were glorious exceptions, the same practice was applied to the Presidency governors of Bombay and Madras. The political prestige of this new type of governor-general, and their enhanced powers, allowed them to carry large legislation and reform. Rightly or wrongly, Cornwallis' ' perpetual settlement ' of Bengal land revenue was achieved, through the express will of the Cabinet and the advice of the expert Shore, taking the zemindars, the revenue-collectors of Mogul days, as being for revenue purposes the owners of the soil. More undoubted good was done by Cornwallis' measures to lay the basis for a civil service: by payment of proper salaries and stopping that private trade which had enriched two generations of ' nabobs '. A long series of experiments up to 1830 created the Bengal district system, each under a British collector with powers both executive and judicial. District judges, regular circuits, enlarged courts of appeal, spread a higher standard of justice, though not without many lapses owing to the Indian zest for litigation, an ill-paid police, and the crudity of Moslem law.

In a sense our administration was balanced, or hovered, between two traditions and schools of statesmanship. There were the great ' politicals ', of the type of Metcalfe, Munro, and the Lawrences, whose experience and sympathies lay with native India ; who came out as boys and took their first leave after twenty or thirty years, and some of whom had Indian wives and children. Their axioms were Wellesley's, of a British supremacy approved by victory, but their spirit was that of Warren Hastings. To these men were due the delicate net-work of alliance with innumerable States, at every level of power, which filled up the huge interstices between Delhi and the Presidency capitals ; they too were concerned in working out, in the Presidencies outside Bengal and in new-annexed territories, systems of revenue and justice more akin to Indian tradition and better suited to reach the root — the peasant on the soil. On the other side was the swelling tide of Anglicization, of European reforming ideals, which rose rapidly under the Whig governor-general of 1828–35, Lord William Bentinck. His first measure was boldly to abolish the burning of Hindu widows, known as *suttee* ; he supported William Sleeman in the extinction of the murderous secret society of Thugs. In part for reasons of economy, he much increased employment of Indians in office ; with Macaulay, the legal member added to his Council by the 1833 charter, and Metcalfe he took the decision to make the English tongue the vehicle, and education in English thought the basis, of progress. There were other instruments of Anglicization. Steam navigation between India and Suez became regular from 1843, cut short the length of exile, and brought more Englishwomen to India. Again, though missionary influence had been strong even under Warren Hastings with Swartz and the Baptist Carey, Christian influence now developed immensely ; evangelical faith was powerful with the Scot and northern Irish Lawrences and Nicholson, and among the greatest of our Indian soldiers, nor was it unknown for colonels of Indian regiments to hold Christian meetings for their men.

While the flower of the British race, still sword in hand and far enough from London to depend on their own initiative, slowly cut the shape of a British dominion, another twist was given to it by the necessities or fears of the Imperial government. Wellesley and Minto had been driven by the Napoleonic war to annex the dependencies and satellites of France in Ceylon, Mauritius, and Java, and when that danger disappeared with peace, we were faced by the greatest of our allies, Russia. This was to be the point, throughout the nineteenth century, at which the Foreign Office and the government of India met or conflicted, and both our Indian government and our policy of upholding Turkey enmeshed us in all Moslem politics and the swaying mass of petty States between the Himalayas and the Caspian. In increased Russian weight with the court of Persia Palmerston saw a potential threat, a fear which he impressed upon Auckland, the agreeable weak man whom the Whig Cabinet chose out of their own ranks as governor-general in 1836. At that date three States controlled most of the warlike peoples which lay between British India and Persia. The pivot of our north-western policy was alliance with the great Sikh Ranjit Singh, ruler of the Punjab and Kashmir. We had another with his southern neighbour, the Amirs of Sind, who controlled the lower Indus and the approach from Bombay to the mountains. Lastly, there was Afghanistan, fallen far from the power which fifty years before had shaken India, having lost Peshawar to the Sikhs and Herat to one of its own princes; for some ten years past its Amir had been Dost Mahommed, with a rule almost confined to northern regions round Kabul and Ghazni. At the end of 1837 the Persians, stimulated by a Russian agent, laid siege to Herat, whence sprang the first disastrous Afghan war.

For this the prime responsibility lay on Auckland and his advisers in India. Against Dost Mohammed personally we had no serious grievance; our agent in the north, Alexander Burnes, believed he could be made a friend, nor did the home government exclude that idea. But Auckland, inspired perhaps mostly by William Macnaughten, precipitately decided on a forward policy to win ' a permanent barrier '; this involved entering the Punjab and using the agency of the Sikhs, which must antagonize the Afghans. In this he persisted even after the Persians retired from Herat and, worst of all, chose as his instrument Shah Shuja, who had been dispossessed as Amir as early as 1809, had neither strength nor popularity, and had lately been defeated by Dost Mahommed. What might have been predicted came to pass. The Sikhs, suspicious for their own future, induced us to make our main effort across Sind, which meant violation of treaty with its Amirs, while after Ranjit Singh's death in 1839 their obstruction became open hostility. That year our main army struggled to Kandahar and thence to Kabul: Shah Shuja was propped up on our bayonets and the advice of Macnaughten but, though Dost Mahommed surrendered, our puppet's power only reached as far as the British arms. By 1841 it was sustained simply at four points, — Kandahar, Ghazni, Kabul, and Jalalabad which led back to the Khyber, — all alike imperilled in communication with India by perpetual rebellion.

Within Kabul itself every conceivable mistake was made in the tragic winter of 1841–2. The beginning of the end came in November when Burnes was murdered, and the next month Macnaughten also, when negotiating for evacuation. Though commanding 5000 combatants and 12,000 followers the British generals would not strike a blow, retreated in January under Afghan pledges towards Jalalabad, and in the snow-bound passes, save for a few taken as hostages and one military doctor who reached safety, were wiped out to a man. Not since the darkest Madras disgraces of the 1770's had there been such demoralization, and the first proposals of Ellenborough, the newly arrived governor-general, were for total withdrawal without an effort to recover the prisoners. The wretched Shah Shuja had been murdered. In the end honour and sanity were retrieved by the insistence of the generals — Nott who had held on to Kandahar, and Pollock with the northern relief force from Peshawar — together with Henry Lawrence's influence over the Sikhs. Kabul was entered, our prisoners saved, and Dost Mahommed restored.

During this war we had occupied the port of Karachi and decided that, to make the Indus secure, the Amirs of Sind must submit to our suizerainty. Ellenborough found them irritated by our encroachment and exalted by our defeat; he chose in Charles Napier a soldier who was convinced that, though Auckland had acted unjustly, the Amirs' rule, which was only seventy years old, was a vicious tyranny, and that annexation was the best rough justice. Fighting against great odds, in February 1843 he routed the Baluchi swordsmen at Miani, near Hyderabad in Sind. There were many in India, not least Napier's predecessor in that province, the heroic Outram, who thought our action unjustifiable, and it was formally condemned by the Directors. But to undo it was a responsibility that Peel's Cabinet would not face, and reluctantly they sanctioned it.

In this triangle the third factor, the Sikhs, drew their fate upon themselves. Ranjit Singh left a succession disputed between many incapable heirs and ambitious nobles, but he also bequeathed the pride of his life, an army 80,000 strong, armed with modern weapons and highly trained by European officers. After civil war and murders innumerable the army council of the Khalsa, ' the chosen ', accepted as ruler the child Dhuleep Singh, whose vicious mother with her lover attempted to control the State. Afghanistan and Sind perturbed the Sikh soldiers, who had seen our failure but feared our designs; moreover, many chiefs would not be sorry to see the Sikh army defeated. In December 1845 they crossed the Sutlej, with Delhi as their object.

Ellenborough having been recalled by the Company, he was replaced by the Peninsular veteran Hardinge, sane, unprovocative, and assured of Peel's affectionate confidence. He took wise defensive precautions, and victory was rarely better deserved than in this first Sikh war. By mid-February 1846 we had fought four battles against superior numbers, Sobraon being the last and gravest, and occupied Lahore; serving as a volunteer, Hardinge was able to counterbalance the recklessness of Hugh Gough, his commander-in-chief, whose impatient courage was apt to hurl troops against entrenched lines without artillery preparation. By treaties of this year the Sikhs surrendered all east of the Sutlej and the Jullundur district also, made over the Hazara frontier to us and Kashmir to the Hindu rajah of Jammu, ceding also their forts and final authority to a British agent and army, until their youthful Maharajah came of age.

Whether annexation could have been avoided in the long run must remain in doubt. In a bare two years our agent Henry Lawrence did wonders through the men of his choice, — his brother John, Lumsden who raised the Guides, Nicholson and Hodson, Herbert Edwardes who ruled one fierce frontier from Bannu, and James Abbott who ruled another in Hazara. That achievement was cut short when in 1848, during his absence on leave, the murder of some British officers grew into a second Sikh war. Whether this could not have been prevented by resolute action, as the Lawrences argued, or whether an opportunity was not seized to press on total annexation, are two of the many questions encircling the name of Hardinge's successor, Dalhousie. Since the Sikhs were given ample time to make ready, our losses at Chilianwala (January 1849) were so heavy that the Cabinet determined to supersede Gough by Napier. In February, however, Gough retrieved himself in the victory of Gujrat; the Sikh armies were broken, their Maharajah was deposed, and Dalhousie, declaring ' an act of necessity ', on his own responsibility annexed the Punjab. He committed administration of this great area, which included also what is now the Frontier Province, to a Board of three, of whom Henry and John Lawrence made two.

In Dalhousie and his memorable term of office from 1848–56 were gathered up the faults, dangers, and virtues of British India. The young governor-general was a Peelite, marked with all the caste signs of that school, their industry and ideal, their touches of autocracy and self-righteousness. With none of the imaginative sympathy of Elphinstone or Henry Lawrence, and seeing good and bad sharply defined, and good government as better than self-government, he thought the best British standard was one to which India must be compelled, and brought about an immense, efficient increase in railways and telegraphs, irrigation, public works, and schools. But the machine did not fulfil some of the best purposes of the government of men. Illustrious names among the Company's older servants had long predicted danger. ' Our administration ', Malcolm wrote in the 'twenties, ' though just, is cold and rigid '; ' all India ', the more pessimistic Metcalfe declared in the 'thirties, ' is at all times looking out for our downfall '. One reason, no question, came from the very speed of our growth, and the apparent boundlessness of our ambition.

After Wellesley's and Hastings' annexations there had been some reaction, yet even Bentinck, for all his *laisser-faire* principles, had annexed Coorg and taken over administration of Mysore. The higher the standard of government, the more unendurable seemed the effects of our subsidiary treaties, whereby British-controlled contingents garrisoned and upheld native States whose internal rule might be an orgy of incompetence or crime. By the 'forties the Company was ready to accept any ' just and honourable accession of territory ', and on that basis Dalhousie, though distinguishing between independent and tributary States, would act to the full. His chief device was the doctrine of ' lapse '; the rule in Hindu States that, if no proper heir existed, — and in Hindu faith adoption of an heir meant discharge of ceremonial, all-important to the dead — none could be adopted without leave of the suzerain. So, sometimes in accord with his Council and sometimes against their advice, he applied ' lapse ' to the Mahratta States of Satara, Nagpur, and Jhansi. Over and above that, when the old Peishwah died, he cut off payment of pension to Nana Sahib, his heir; abolished the royal title of Nawab of the Carnatic; took from Hyderabad the administration of Berar to ensure proper maintenance of the Hyderabad contingent; annexed from the truculent Burmese the province of Pegu; and, left to himself, would have suppressed the Imperial style of the Moguls at Delhi. Finally, on the eve of his departure, he took the decisive step of annexing Oudh. After two generations of warning, scandalous misgovernment and misery prevailed in that kingdom. But the Company's order for total annexation was a drastic measure against the Company's oldest ally, taken against the advice of Henry Lawrence and Sleeman, and pushed beyond what Dalhousie himself desired.

All this increased some inevitable enmities; of *talukdars* or landowners forced to drop their oppression, vested interests in palaces, and warlike classes left without occupation. Our revenue settlements from the 'thirties onward involved many resumptions of property and forced sales, Dalhousie's government confiscated many thousand estates wrongfully held, and other Indian interests than the landowners, whom Lawrence thought ill used, were perturbed by what we deemed was progress. Obliteration of caste distinction through railways, prison rules, and schools, and laws to permit the remarriage of Hindu widows, to stop infanticide, or protect Christian converts, alarmed the priestly order. An opium-tax irritated humbler folk. Afghan and Sikh wars, even if they divided our enemies, showed the British soldier not invincible, and roused Moslem passion. For in the historic divisions of Islam the Afghans were Sunnis, but Persia was Shiah, as was Oudh.

All these strains affected the very base of our power, the native army, or more accurately the Bengal army, that made up 60 per cent of the whole. With those of Madras and Bombay there was little trouble, as they were recruited irrespective of caste and part-composed of more placid peoples; the army of Bengal, however, was built on men of high caste, distinguished by legal privilege and good pensions. Since their heroic fighting under the Wellesleys, and in Mahratta wars, they had much degenerated. Mutinies had been frequent; on distant service in Afghanistan they grumbled for extra allowances; while to cross the dark sea to Burma would, they said, violate their caste. Rules of seniority brought to the top many too elderly officers, both British and Indian, and centralization had destroyed much of commanding officers' almost paternal prestige.

And now a high proportion came from Oudh, which they saw annexed, though not disarmed; while new levies from the north, Punjabis and Sikhs and Gurkhas, threatened to usurp their place of favour. They were, further, persuaded that government cared nothing for, and was even bent on undermining, their religion; a suspicion doubled when in 1856 Dalhousie's successor Canning ordered general enlistment for all recruits for service in India and overseas. It was roused to fury when they discovered that cartridges for the new Enfield rifle, the end of which must be bitten before loading, had been greased in England with beef fat. All the first months of 1857 were marked by refusal to use cartridges, mutiny, and burning of barrack huts; on 10th May three regiments in the Meerut garrison murdered every European they could seize, and marched for Delhi.

So began the Mutiny, in form but not in substance a military rebellion; marking, rather, as it was terribly to deepen, the gulf between Britain and India. It had, indeed, no unity whatever. In Oudh and the north it centred in Moslem fanaticism, bent on Delhi and exploiting the relics of Mogul Empire, the rebels coming to the assault led by priests and under the green flag. Nana Sahib, on the other hand, and the Rani of Jhansi would revive the Hindu Mahratta confederacy, and Brahmans were active on the Ganges from holy Benares to Bengal. One centre and one leader they never found, and its suppression became therefore a series of little campaigns. But countless cases showed the length of Indian memories, and how a shake to British power roused the instinct to desert a losing cause. A Rohilla, of those dispossessed in the eighteenth century, made himself master of Bareilly in Oudh; though Scindia stood loyal himself, his Gwalior troops fought fiercely against us; so too did the Jats of Bharatpur, and the Hyderabad contingent. There were murmurings even in the Bombay presidency, and only rapid, resolute disarming of native regiments saved Lahore and Peshawar in the north.

In the last resort the British people had themselves to thank for the duration of the Mutiny, which was directly due to the small ratio of European troops. Dalhousie's repeated urgency that this must be corrected had been ignored, in part because the Company would have to bear the Europeans' higher pay; and when the outbreak came, as against 230,000 Indian soldiers, there were a bare 40,000 European. Of these some were fighting in Persia, others quartered in Burma, and some 13,000 in the Punjab or the Sutlej area. Thus along the thousand miles between the Punjab and Bengal only weak European detachments were strung out, with none at vital points like Allahabad, and none guarding the Delhi arsenal. As the railway only ran a hundred miles up from Calcutta, to send reinforcements meant a slow process of marching, river steamer, or bullock train, and for many months there were none to send, a delay which, John Lawrence wrote, was ' very nigh fatal '.

Many times over it was proved that leadership would conquer any odds. The Punjab had not been subdued ten years, but John Lawrence, Edwardes, and their school could move it almost as a solid unit against Delhi; held it, indeed, so strongly that law courts and schools proceeded as in peace. Frontier valleys stood staunch which had heard the legend of Nicholson and his white mare; Bartle Frere's benevolent rule in Sind was so absolute that he could strip the province of European troops; none were more firm than the Sikh States like Patiala. George Lawrence held most of Rajputana safe; the courage of a few soldiers and a few civil servants stamped out what might have destroyed Bengal and Bihar; Henry Lawrence's time in Nepal had not been wasted, and invaluable help came from the Gurkhas. Colin Campbell with 4500 men broke into Lucknow, a fortified rambling city held by 60,000 desperate rebels. On the other side, when decision failed, the evil was instant, sometimes as at Meerut through old men in command, or sometimes through a clinging belief that Indians were loyal. Canning the viceroy was courageous and confident, yet made some mistakes, — dallying, for instance, in accepting Gurkha help, — which slowed decision down.

In the autumn of 1857 the extremest urgency was removed by the capture of Delhi and the relief of Lucknow. The first was the work of

British forces and civilians from the Punjab. A first advance in June had captured the Ridge, west of and commanding the city, but the assault had to wait long for reinforcements and heavy guns. There in September Nicholson was killed, the Mogul King taken and his sons shot by Hodson, and the backbone broken of Moslem resistance in the north. The suffering of the innocent and the fascination of great characters have made famous some places of less military importance. Mistakes of judgment at Cawnpore are obliterated in the memory of the 400 European combatants who, in the heat of June, endured three weeks' bombardment without cover from an overwhelming enemy force; when they surrendered, Nana Sahib gave them a safe-conduct to go downstream to Allahabad, but massacred them as they reached the boats. In July, hearing that Havelock's relieving army drew near, he had 200 women and children cut to pieces and hurled, live or dead, into a well.

It was only early in 1857 that Henry Lawrence had reached Lucknow as chief commissioner of Oudh, much too late for his prestige to prevent an outbreak, or to undo the hopeless distribution of our garrison. He was soon isolated, an effort at a sortie defeated, and his small force, with not above 1000 Europeans, driven back into the Residency, where in July he was killed. His successors held out until Havelock and Outram forced their way in, in September, and in November the new commander-in-chief, Colin Campbell, evacuated the garrison. But Lucknow itself he could not take until the spring of 1858; so small were his forces, and so serious the threat to his communications from the Cawnpore rebels, and from those in Central India under Nana's general, Tanti Topi, and the Amazon Rani of Jhansi.

In 1858 more troops had come, some diverted from the China war, with Peel's famous naval brigade, and at that year's end we had sixty-eight battalions of British infantry. The war turned to a piecemeal reduction of garrisons, or hunting down those who had put themselves beyond the pale; for the British it was as much a war against great spaces, sunstroke, jungles, and mountains. In this phase the best leader was Sir Hugh Rose, whose small Central India force took the strong keys of Jhansi, Kalpi, and Gwalior, and in sixteen battles within six months beat down resistance.

It had been, too often, a war of atrocity, provoked by murder of British women, prisoners, and children, to which the response was sometimes stark execution and lynch law. The choice between conciliation and punishment divided the Company's best servants, and Canning, nicknamed ' Clemency ' in the early stages, later issued a proclamation to Oudh which shocked Outram and much opinion at home. Yet there were many signs that what in British minds was conjured up by ' the Mutiny ' was not true of Indians as a whole. Many villagers, and a few landowners, sheltered our unhappy refugees; several hundred sepoys served faithfully through the siege of Lucknow; it was noted that mutineers often wore their British medals; while Nana could only get his worst work done by butchers and palace servants.

But, whatever its legacy, it was not to be managed by the Company, whose powers had long since been purely formal, and Great Britain, which had borne the shock and caused the emergency, must take up the full burden. The Act of 1858 transferred government to the Crown, replacing the Board of Control by a Secretary of State, to be assisted by a Council a majority of whom must have Indian experience. The Queen's proclamation, drafted by Derby, promised to respect the territories of Indian princes, — the doctrine of lapse being repudiated, — disclaimed any interference with religious convictions, and promised openings in her service to men of ' whatever race or creed '. Since the Punjab had saved India, John Lawrence was the man of the hour, in 1864 succeeding Elgin as viceroy, and the rising's chief lessons were taken to heart. European troops were increased and Indian diminished, till the ratios stood at about two to five; Sikhs and Gurkhas were enlisted freely, and men also of lower castes. Centralized administration, a better police system, penal and commercial codes, and the new public works department all deepened the uniform weight of government. The Act of 1861, by which some nominated Indian Members joined the Legislative Council, and much educational expenditure, represented another side of British policy.

Yet personal qualities had saved, or in some instances contributed to undo, British India, and for another generation the personal element in the Crown service was to be all in all. It had inherited, as the Company boasted with substantial justice, ' such a body of civil and military officers as the world has never seen before '.

CHAPTER IV

LIBERALISM, AT HOME AND ABROAD
1859–1874

THE first Liberal government, led by Palmerston till 1865 and then by Russell, was rich in many talents, — Whig notables like Argyll and Cornewall Lewis, Gladstone and the flower of the Peelites, with Goschen and Hartington to represent a younger school, both bourgeois and aristocratic. But its unity rested on the genial, flexible Palmerston who enjoyed, beyond his popularity with the middle class, three great advantages. National prosperity was increasing by leaps and bounds; Derby, having no wish for office, was ever ready to help the Prime Minister against the economics or pacificism of Gladstone; and public interest was concentrated on Palmerston's best field, foreign affairs. Though his differences with the Court were sharp as ever, they so far agreed with him that they too believed national defence was the most urgent matter before government.

It was then, so far as domestic reform went, an age almost blank; 'we cannot go on legislating for ever' was Palmerston's opinion, and a modest reform bill produced by Russell expired in 1860 in total apathy. Cabinet time was taken up by foreign policy, defence, and the finance that these involved.

One British war was proceeding when this government took over, the China war originating with the lorcha *Arrow*, from which the Mutiny had diverted troops. Elgin's first mission, by a blockade of Canton and bombardment of forts, had extorted a treaty in 1858, giving us on paper all we asked. But when the next year we sent an envoy to ratify, he was fired on, so in 1860 Elgin reappeared, with a mixed British-French army to enforce the treaty and additional compensation. This time the Chinese evasions, their treacherous seizure and torture of an allied mission, led to the forcing of the Peiho as far as Tientsin, entry into Pekin, and burning of the Imperial palace, the final terms ensuring diplomatic access and increased commercial advantages, including a regulated migration of coolie labour to British Colonies. Between his two missions Elgin had visited Japan, with whom a treaty was signed allowing British consuls and traders a few openings.

It was not, however, by this remote scene that British sentiment was gripped but by the outbreak in 1859 of war in Europe, when

Napoleon III fulfilled his pledge to Cavour and invaded Italy to expel the Austrians; a war that well might grow, if Prussia came in to assist the other German Power. It was in part this consideration which in July drove Napoleon, after two costly victories, to make the convention of Villafranca, giving Lombardy to the Sardinians but leaving Venice in Austrian hands. Though the Queen and Prince were aggressively 'Austrian', British sympathies in general were wholehearted for Italy, the strongest 'Italians' within the Cabinet being its strongest members, Palmerston, Russell, and Gladstone. Over the next two years, when Tuscany and central Italy rose to join Sardinia, when Garibaldi and his thousand sailed to make rebellion in Sicily and crossed to the Neapolitan mainland, and when the Sardinian army marched south to make contact with him but also to head him off from an attack on Papal Rome, the British actions were decisive. Russell's despatches preached the doctrine of 1688, that a people had a right to depose a bad ruler, and that, if Garibaldi were a 'filibuster', William of Orange had been another, while our minister at Turin, James Hudson, immensely assisted Cavour. Our influence was thus used to keep the ring, to let the central Italian duchies vote themselves into the new kingdom, to cover Garibaldi's crossing to Naples by our fleet, to deprive the Pope of temporal power except for Rome itself, and to prevent a general war by warning the Italians off Venetia.

Our diplomacy had the additional object of obstructing the ambitions of Napoleon. Against him were ranged British forces of most diverse character; the Liberal minds of Macaulay and Mill, and the young Radicals who had never forgiven the *coup d'état*; the Germanism of the Court; and Palmerston's conviction that, when the Emperor denounced the treaties of 1815, he meant to revive his great uncle's France. His scheme for a federated Italy was thought to mean an Italy under French control, and our suspicion was deepened when, as part of his bargain with Cavour, he annexed Savoy and Nice to France. Herbert at the War Office believed the French planned invasion; their rapid building of armoured ships harassed the Admiralty; while in the beginning of the Suez Canal by the French engineer, de Lesseps, Palmerston saw Egypt and India threatened.

From such reasoning came what Cobden called the 'panic' of 1859–60, in which, however, there was this justification, that steam had altered all the conditions of sea-warfare, and that our shortage of trained men in the Crimea had been terrifying. Napier, our naval commander in that war, pointed to the great base building at Cherbourg; a royal commission declared Portsmouth was defenceless and called for large expenditure on fortifications. Out of this controversy rose, spontaneously, the origin of the volunteers, who numbered 150,000 by 1861, and the collision of a war and a peace party in the Cabinet.

It was the hope of Cobden and Bright, and by them communicated to Gladstone, that a commercial treaty would contribute alike to free trade and peace, and Cobden volunteered unofficial negotiations. In France he found valuable support from the economist Chevalier; and the Emperor, when once converted, bore the brunt against protectionist interests, but in this country no one but Gladstone could have carried it in Cabinet. Convinced that the alternatives were this treaty or a ' high probability ' of war, he conceived his budget of 1860 as ' a European operation ', and displayed to their utmost his tenacity, ingenuity in finance, social ideal, and that mastery in debate which soothes an unwilling audience into a conclusion that sensible men can do nothing else. The treaty terms provided that France would lower duties on iron and all principal British goods to 30 per cent or less; Britain, on the other hand, would reduce hers on wines and brandy, and abolish duty entirely on French manufactured goods. This meant a sacrifice of £1 million of revenue, besides which Gladstone must face, mainly from war costs, a deficit of nearly £10 millions in all. Demonstrating that our taxable income had increased by over 16 per cent in the past seven years, he returned boldly to the method of Peel, as he had himself used it in 1853, to raise new revenue by reducing taxes, and made the French treaty his lever for the final advance to free trade. Such duties as he abolished on French goods he abolished for all nations alike; lowered duty on timber and currants, swept those away on butter, eggs, and various fruits, together with the excise on paper. His changes reduced the number of articles chargeable under our tariff from 419 to 48; for the time being he paid his way by keeping stiff duties on tea and sugar, and income-tax at 10d.

This parliamentary triumph, and his doctrine of a permanent addition to productive power by freeing production, made him the real head of the Liberal party, in part because it brought him into conflict both with Palmerston and the Lords. The national expenditure of £70 millions, small though it was, had grown by 20 per cent since 1853, and that mainly through the army and naval estimates, a process doubly horrible to a man who believed that money ' fructified ' best when left in the taxpayer's pocket, and to a Christian who execrated war. Though he fought Palmerston's plans for fortifications, several times threatening resignation, the old leader carried his Cabinet most of the way; if Palmerston wrote jauntily to the Queen that it was better to lose Mr. Gladstone than to lose Portsmouth, Gladstone denounced him in private, and in public drew nearer to Cobden and Bright. One bond between them was the fight over the repeal of the paper excise, which the Lords rejected, to Palmerston's pleasure. In 1861 Gladstone extended his revenge far beyond repassing that item, for by combining all the money bills of the year in a single measure he made it henceforth impossible for the Lords to do anything but accept, or reject, the Budget as a whole.

His policy of retrenchment prevailed in the succeeding years. Income-tax fell from 9d. in 1863 to 4d. in 1865, when the tea duty was halved also; total expenditure, which was £72 millions in 1860, was back at £66 millions in 1865. Creation of post-office savings-banks, the Exchequer and Audit Act of 1866, the Commons' committee of public accounts, part-exemption of incomes below £200, — by such performance and doctrine Gladstone impressed on the country his own high standard of public finance.

The impetus towards a broader democracy, which this prosperity and his stewardship encouraged, was hastened by the event in which he made his greatest mistake, the American civil war. In this our declared and right policy was to be strictly neutral; recognizing the rights of the South as belligerents but not their independence, claiming for ourselves the rights of a neutral trader but no right to break an actual blockade, forbidding British subjects to help either side. Had slavery been the only matter in dispute, practically all Britain would have sympathized with the North, but that was not so until, late in 1862, Lincoln declared for emancipation; as it was, Russell and Gladstone saw in the South a people asking the liberty of self-government, Palmerston rejoiced at the weakening of a Power he disliked, and upperclass sentiment felt at one with Lee and the gentry of the South. To Bright, on the other hand, and the Radicalism he represented, the North meant democracy, where all had a vote and where thousands of their own folk had found a home, while the religious mind of Liberal England cut through any constitutional dispute to the one question, slave or free? That faith was upheld all through 1862, by which time the cutting off of cotton from the South had thrown Lancashire out of employment and half a million people were living on the rates, or private charity.

Diplomacy was finely served by the ambassadors, Charles Francis Adams for America and for Britain the wise Lord Lyons, but some American statesmen, Seward the Secretary of State included, were at times ready for war. That possibility came nearest, perhaps, late in 1861 when two Southern agents, Mason and Slidell, were forcibly removed by a Northern warship from the British mail steamer *Trent*; one of the Prince Consort's last acts being an advice to send a milder protest, which allowed Lincoln to lead an honourable retreat. War was possible again because, intent on stopping the carnage, the British Cabinet often considered offering mediation, on which Napoleon III was even more intent for reasons of his own. For in 1862 he was involved in a military adventure in Mexico, which began in concert with Britain merely to enforce payment of debts but which, after Britain withdrew, developed into a scheme for a Mexican monarchy under a

Habsburg archduke. That year Gladstone went so far as to declare in public that the South had ' made a nation '; but the Southern victories were too costly for their people to endure, Palmerston wisely held his hand, both the Queen and the Opposition were against intervening. Yet another danger was narrowly avoided, arising from the commerce-destroyers, equipped and sometimes built in our ports, which the South used to break the blockade. Of these the most famous was the *Alabama*, which only escaped detention in the Mersey by hours and an unhappy combination of chances; some were stopped or bought by our government, but others got away, — one of them to sail 60,000 miles, untaken. In 1864, however, the victory of the North was assured, Lincoln's great stature was plainly seen, slavery had gone, and this dark possibility disappeared.

If Bright and public opinion saved the government from dire mistakes, in other directions our policy showed some of its frequent shortcomings, in lack of insight into other countries, moral indignation unsupported by moral force, and rank ignorance. What had lately begun was the age of Bismarck, who became chief minister in Prussia in 1862, yet no one in England, unless it were young Robert Morier, weighed the new forces aright. Faithful to her ' dear angel's ' vision, the Queen saw in Germany only a peaceful people resisting Napoleon's thirst for territory, Palmerston was much the same and built on our military men's view that the French could ' walk over ' the Prussian army. And though the very opposite of being isolationist in the sense of Bright, Palmerston and Russell helped to isolate their country. Their Italian policy antagonized Austria, Russia was still the arch-enemy, and when the Poles revolted in 1861 the Prime Minister told St. Petersburg that it was ' a just punishment of heaven '. Again, if Britain meant to make a stand against the Eastern despots, the one indispensable alliance would be that of France, and that would mean going half-way to help the French objective of a stronger frontier in Luxembourg and on the Rhine. But when Napoleon mooted a congress to eliminate these and other pretexts for war, like Venetia, Russell snubbed him in his loftiest style. To abstain in Europe might be wise; not so, to threaten and lecture and then to abstain.

This was seen at its worst in the weary tangled matter of Schleswig-Holstein, the two duchies part-Dane and part-German, bound to Denmark by the same royal dynasty, to each other by ancient history and, in the case of Holstein, to the German federation by law. After one outbreak in the age of revolution, the Powers had all recognized by the London treaty of 1852 that the succession both to Denmark and the duchies lay in Christian of Glucksburg, who in due course, a few months after his daughter Alexandra married the Prince of Wales, succeeded in 1863. But the Danes had broken their pledge of giving separate institutions to the duchies, Christian incorporated Schleswig in the Danish monarchy, and early in 1864, dragging a deceived, unwilling Austria with him, Bismarck declared war. Warlike language from Palmerston and the British press encouraged the Danes, but the Queen, Cabinet, and Opposition stoutly resisted the Prime Minister and Foreign Secretary, Derby denounced their ' meddle and muddle ', and we drew back in a cloud of high-sounding words, which did not affect the fact that Prussian troops occupied Schleswig and Kiel.

Though Opposition made capital out of this sorry business and the Queen found Palmerston ' extremely impertinent ', when in 1865 Parliament was dissolved in its usual course, the people again returned the old man to power with a comfortable majority. He was now over eighty years of age ; Gladstone, he said, would ' soon have it all his own way ', and that way had lately been shown not only by an almost open alliance with Bright but by a famous speech, the more impressive because half-musing and unrehearsed, in which he declared that every man was ' morally entitled ' to a vote who was not positively incapacitated by unfitness. His constituency of Oxford University, which had cast out his leader Peel, cast him out also in this election, and he found another in industrial Lancashire, to whom he announced that at last he came to them ' unmuzzled '. On 18th October Palmerston died ; this, Gladstone wrote to Russell, must be a ' new commencement '.

Immediately that could not be, for Russell, veteran and indispensable leader, was seventy-four and now in the Lords, nor could he conciliate diverse men as had Palmerston. The Cabinet was weaker through other deaths, of Cornewall Lewis and Herbert, nor did Russell's few changes bridge the gulf between Radicals and Whigs. Yet he stood nearer than his predecessor to Gladstone and Bright, and his personal ambition to pass a second Reform bill released part of the long-arrested Liberal flow ; on public grounds the case for it was very strong, for leaders in both parties were committed, and since 1851 one attempt after another had broken down. Changes in industry had made the existing distribution of seats ridiculous, Glamorgan returned only one more member than Radnor, and Cornwall as many as London and Middlesex north of Thames, while five out of six grown men had no vote. The bill produced in 1866 was modest enough, but badly handled and with the vices of a compromise ; to lower the borough franchise to £7 could never satisfy the Radicals, whereas many Whigs cordially disliked a proposed lodger vote. Some forty Liberals, led with outstanding eloquence by Robert Lowe, formed themselves into what Bright christened ' the cave of Adullam ' and worked with Opposition, between them they drove Gladstone's feverish leadership from point to point, and in June, on an amendment being carried to make rating and not rental value the basis for a vote, government resigned. Dissolution was avoided, not only on the public ground that the Austro-Prussian war had just begun, but because to dissolve on Reform would split the Liberal party.

Derby therefore formed his third ministry which, on his resignation in February 1868, became the first of Disraeli, and may historically be treated throughout as such. This was the first Conservative cabinet of any strength since the fall of Peel; having discovered considerable force in Cranborne (soon to be Salisbury), Gathorne Hardy who had beaten Gladstone at Oxford, Carnarvon, and Stafford Northcote. But since once again they were in a numerical minority if all the oppositions could agree, their business was to settle questions which both sides could accept; as they did, for instance, in the Act for the confederation of Canada, in extinguishing compulsory Church rates, and in transferring trials of election petitions to the judges from the heat of party committees.

To settle parliamentary reform, on which they had ejected Russell, was indispensable and not only for their party interest. Crowds crying for ' Gladstone and liberty ', an angry meeting which demolished the railings of Hyde Park, clamour in the trade-union world against prosecutions, the American example, and the influence of Bright and Mill, such symptoms and the long dallying with the question convinced the Queen and politicians that delay would be dangerous. But how the bill of this Conservative government grew into a measure of advanced Radicalism and split the Cabinet, revolved round the rivalry of Disraeli and Gladstone.

Disraeli quite plainly had framed no plot for an advanced bill, and even wished to stave the question off till it could be made a favourable ground for dissolution. But when convinced that it must be taken speedily, he wished it settled by the government, seizing with great skill the openings given him by Gladstone's difficulties between Whigs and Radicals, and his mistakes both of tactics and temper. As constructed after severe struggles in Cabinet, the bill of 1867 made its principal point the borough vote for every householder who paid rates in person; as a basis more solidly lasting than any attempt to rest on some middle figure between £10 and household suffrage. It would avoid the last extreme, for personal payment of rates would cut out the ' compound householders ', whose rates were paid by their landlord, and who in some cities, as in Birmingham, were numbered by thousands. There were to be other checks against democracy: additional votes for large taxpayers, holders in savings-banks or university graduates, besides a qualification of two years' residence.

Its final shape was changed because, in a House of many ' caves ' and a minority government, the House itself took charge, and especially the Conservative members who represented large towns. Faced with

their view that a large simple solution was the safest, and forced by
Gladstone's attack to grasp the knot of the ' compound householder ',
Disraeli persuaded Derby to stand on a household rating vote without
financial limit. On this matter Cranborne, Carnarvon, and General
Peel resigned, a shock which the Cabinet could sustain since the party
majority were for a decided measure. So the proposed safeguards of
the ' fancy franchises ' and plural voting were dropped, and the two
years' residence was reduced to one ; most of all, by an amendment
making compounding for rates no bar to the franchise, the working-
class vote was greatly increased.

The second Reform Act thus gave the borough vote to all rate-
paying occupiers and to those occupying lodgings of £10 value, and in
the counties to those occupying houses rated at £12. Its net effect was
to add some 938,000 new voters, in fact almost to double the electorate,
while 45 seats were redistributed by taking one member from each
borough with a population below 10,000. Such was ' the leap in
the dark ' of which Derby spoke, or ' shooting Niagara ', of which
Carlyle and Bagehot wrote with resignation and doubt.

A Reform bill involved a dissolution, but before it came both
Derby and Russell had given up the lead of their parties. Gladstone's
tactical sense, watching the sky for what he called a ' first streak of
dawn ', pitched on the Irish Church as a rallying-point, and perhaps the
way to a majority, even in this Palmerstonian Parliament, and early in
1868 he carried resolutions which would end the union of the Irish State
and Church. The ground was well taken, for it divided Conservative
feeling, Disraeli himself inclining to the old Pitt scheme of ' levelling
up ', or endowing the Catholics instead of disendowing the Anglicans,
but most Protestant feeling opposed him. In any case the Conservative
election cry of ' no Popery ', and ' Church and State ', failed to prevent
the return of Gladstone with a strong majority of 112.

This, the first of his governments, lasting till 1874, must be reckoned
his greatest. At fifty-nine his own powers were at their zenith ; by
including Bright, Hartington, and Lowe he united all sections of
Liberalism ; in Cardwell, Childers, and Goschen he had administrators
of a very high order, with a legal statesman of the first rank in the first
Lord Selborne, who became Chancellor in 1872. In the new Parliament, one-third of whom were elected for the first time, there were also
Liberal recruits who later won fame, including Harcourt, Dilke, and
Campbell-Bannerman.

Borne forward on his own portentous energy, their programme was
massive and connected. It had, indeed, some sharp limitations, for its
foreign policy was vague and its social outlook too set to impress democracy, but its spirit and performance were nineteenth-century Liberalism
at its best, and worthy of a country which had high hopes and un-

challenged power.   Much can fairly be said in criticism of Gladstone.
The future was to show how blind he could be to some deep British
sentiments, and how sometimes so obsessed with an immediate objective
that he ignored justice.   His way of thought was theological, of the old
Oxford sort, clouding every conclusion with a qualification or nicety,
and sometimes he took short-cuts that were indefensible.   For, like other
moralists, he was capable of confusing his own mighty voice with the
still small voice of Divine command.   When all, however, is said, his
gifts of mind and character combined were perhaps the greatest in the
annals of Parliament, uniting to magnificent oratory and financial genius
the best qualities of a ruling class and the devoted sense of a fervent
Christian.   ' The Almighty seems to sustain and spare me ', ran his
diary on taking office, ' for some purpose of His own, deeply unworthy
as I know myself to be '.

Within a year he passed two vital measures for Ireland, which all
parties were agreed could not wait.   Revived in America and assisted by
experience in the American civil war, Irish racial feeling had shown its
renewal in the revolutionary Fenian brotherhood ;   Fenians had raided
Canada, in 1867 an effort to rescue Fenian prisoners at Manchester led
to three executions, there were explosions in London, and in Australia
an attempt to kill the Queen's second son.   Gladstone had little difficulty in carrying his Irish Church Act, for many Conservatives thought
that Church was impossible to defend ;   working closely with the Queen,
archbishop Tait recognized that disestablishment was inevitable, and
wisely concentrated on saving as much Church property as possible
from disendowment.   The final compromise in the Lords, against
Derby's expiring effort in politics, — he died late in 1869 — was achieved
by the resolution of Cairns, Disraeli's favourite lawyer.   The Act of that
year, repealing what the Act of Union had declared should be perpetual,
disestablished the Anglican Church in Ireland, separated it from its
English sister, and made it a voluntary society ;   yet one well endowed,
even though it lost about half its revenues, some millions of which over
the next decade went to assist education, poverty, and arrears of rent.
Yet Disraeli's prediction is worth recording as to the distant result, —
' its tendency is to civil war '.

No Church question, however, could raise in Ireland the same
passion as possession of the soil, and after intense study Gladstone came
to much the same remedy as the Devon commission had recommended
in 1845, which Disraeli's colleagues had prevented him adopting in
1852.   This was to extend universally the customs which held good in
Ulster, and occasionally elsewhere, that the tenant must be compensated both for his improvements and for disturbance of his tenure.
That was the utmost he felt was attainable.   We find him wrestling with
his Irish secretary Fortescue, who would have gone further ;   with

Bright, who believed in buying out the landlords and making peasant proprietors; most of all, with Argyll, Lowe, and the typical British group, who would not strain the British notion of property. His Land Act of 1870 took therefore a great stride, but did not go to fundamentals. All tenants must be paid for their improvements; they would also receive compensation, if evicted for other reasons than non-payment of rent. As regards that vital matter, they would only be compensated — and the landlord restrained — if an increase of rent were proved to be ' exorbitant '. Neither fair rent nor fixed tenure, therefore, were guaranteed.

Two other measures which Gladstone designed for Ireland broke down, one on the Queen's resistance, for a royal residence in Ireland where the Prince of Wales might live, and another, for a mixed university, on objection from the Catholic bishops. Neither could have touched the root of discontent, which was shown by a vicious circle of land riots and coercion acts; in 1870 a Home Rule association began operations, and the question was already searching Gladstone's conscience whether Ireland could ever be reconciled within the ambit of the Imperial Parliament.

Meanwhile he had passed for Britain one most fundamental law, which bitterly divided his majority, the Education Act of 1870; not that in any sense it was principally his work, for he was absorbed in Ireland, and indeed not ardent on this matter except as it affected religion. Since a State education service would have offended every ideal of the previous generation, the system had been one of grants, administered by a Privy Council committee, whose secretary, Kay Shuttleworth, had pushed strenuously along those lines, sending out inspectors, organizing pupil teachers, and dovetailing public grants with local contributions. By 1860 the grant had risen from the £20,000 of 1833 to nearly £1 million, the committee was represented by a vice-president in Parliament, while the Newcastle commission of 1858 had recommended for large areas an elected board with power to levy rates. But they had not recommended compulsion, most children left school at eleven, and some two million did not attend school at all. The need then was sore, and it was Robert Lowe, bitter opponent of Disraeli's Reform bill but once vice-president of the Education committee, who cried ' educate your masters '; so echoed all those who were impressed by the northern victory in America, and those who, like Matthew Arnold, one of the committee's inspectors, realized what education had done for Bismarck's Prussia. Elementary education, universal and compulsory, non-sectarian and free, was the demand of Radical England, taking shape in 1869 in the National Education league organized by a young Birmingham manufacturer, Joseph Chamberlain.

Gladstone's education minister, William Forster, an admirably courageous man of Quaker stock, produced an Act radical in its long-range effect, but in Radical eyes intensely conservative. It was not national, because it aimed first at merely supplementing an existing system; Church schools would continue, if they had the financial resources to keep up the standard; the gaps would be filled by new schools, maintained by elected boards with power to levy a rate. It was not compulsory, except in so far as a board ' might ' compel attendance. It was not free, for parents who could afford it would pay fees. It was not secular, for religion was to be taught in all schools, subject to a conscience clause. In short, its policy was to get schools built, maintained, and filled by the easiest means, and the easiest parliamentary avenue.

This roused a storm, so that the Act was only carried by Conservative votes saving Gladstone from his Radical Nonconformists, who felt that, in single-school areas especially, they would be taxed for religious instruction of which they disapproved. In the end an amendment moved by Cowper-Temple forbade teaching of the catechism, or any denominational dogma, in a rate-aided school; on the other hand, the State grants to Church schools were doubled. Radical anger was long-lived and unforgiving, their candidates attacked government at bye-elections, and in the end helped to bring it down. Yet, after all, rate aid and local control, with the possibilities of compulsion and of remitting school fees, contained in themselves the future, while in time other ways could be found of harmonizing the Church and Dissent.

This ministry did a good deal more of value for an educated people. Their endowed schools Act of 1869 made a beginning, though not much more, in making good one of the worst shortcomings in secondary education, by creating commissioners to overhaul the grammar schools and endowments lavished by benefactors of old. In 1871 religious tests were swept away at the universities, except for degrees in theology and a few professorships, and a commission appointed to examine their finances. In 1870 steps were taken to complete the reform which, since 1855, the civil service commission had partially applied, and which Russell and the Queen much disliked; subject to approval by heads of departments, which in fact left the Foreign Office the solitary exception, all posts were thrown open to competitive examination.

Two other administrative measures cut deep into history. Our courts of law were in the dead hand of the past. Their jurisdictions clashed, they used different procedures, they terminated in different courts of appeal, equity and common law were rival systems. Since Benthamite influence had become supreme, one commission after another had nibbled at reform, but only the Judicature Act of 1873, mainly Selborne's work and coincident with the building of the new Law Courts, revolutionized the whole. By this, and as amended in 1876, the venerable courts of Chancery, King's Bench, Common Pleas, Exchequer, and

Admiralty, and the court of probate and divorce, were united to form one Supreme Court, divided into a high court and a court of appeal; distinctions between rules of common law and rules of equity, and of procedure, disappeared, and the age of Bardell *v.* Pickwick, or Jarndyce *v.* Jarndyce thus ended. Contrary to Selborne's intention, the House of Lords was retained as the final appeal court for Great Britain.

With that exception this had been an agreed settlement, but not so the forceful measures touching the army, in charge of Cardwell, one of Peel's most capable disciples. Until his day nothing systematic had been done, despite the Crimea, but Sadowa and the Franco-Prussian war roused Parliament to act. Political excitement was concentrated on what was only an important detail, the abolition in 1871 of purchase by officers of commissions and steps in rank; an abuse which Wellington had always championed, and was still defended by the Whig lords Russell and Grey as meaning a non-professional officer class, in whose hands liberty would be safe. Yet plainly it stopped promotion by merit and must strangle any reorganization; had not Lord Cardigan, of the Light Brigade, bought the successive command of two regiments of hussars? Against determined resistance from senior officers, and only supported by a few younger soldiers like the future Wolseley and Cromer, Cardwell drove abolition of purchase through the Commons; when it was obstructed in the Lords, Gladstone forced them to agree by persuading the Queen to cancel the royal warrant of George III that legalized purchase, and to declare it abolished.

Much more fundamental was the programme which Cardwell doggedly carried all through the years 1868–73. The prime lesson both of the Crimea and of Prussia's triumph was the necessity for a trained reserve, which must depend upon a short-service Army. He therefore introduced enlistment for six years with the colours, followed by six in the reserve; further improving the reservoir of man-power by bringing home 20,000 men from the Colonies, he assisted recruiting by stopping flogging in time of peace. His second vital measure was to develop recruiting-grounds, and to connect the regular Army with the Militia, by making it territorial; assigning to each historic, numbered, infantry regiment a local depot and a county name. Each regiment would have two linked battalions, one of which would be on foreign service, and would be associated with its county militia and volunteers. His third endeavour touched the higher command. An Order in Council at last definitely subordinated the commander-in-chief to the Secretary of State and brought him under the roof of the War Office; beyond this, reorganization of the staff could hardly go, for the Duke of Cambridge, commander-in-chief down to 1895, was a royal and obstinate prince. Over and above these came the rearming of the infantry with the Martini-Henry breach-loading rifle, an increased artillery, and twenty-five more battalions on the home strength, — all without increasing the estimates.

If this brought some strains with the Court and the upper class, the Licensing Act of 1872 made the government highly unpopular with some sections of democracy, as well as with the brewing and drink interests; some severe clauses as to closing hours and a police right of entry being attacked as un-English restrictions on liberty. But by that time its general unpopularity was obvious. Having offended the Churches by its Irish legislation, it had roused an angry Radical temper over education. Its Act of 1871 failed to satisfy the trade-unions' grievance against the uncertainties in which they were left by the law of 1825 and judges' interpretation, which taken together left their strike action and picketing open to the older view of conspiracy. Indeed, in many ways their social policy proved the near horizon of Gladstonian liberalism. Though the Local Government Board was created in 1871, it was dominated by the poor-law department with its austere tradition against extravagance. Nothing was done for housing or health; Goschen's plan to replace the magistrates by elected county authorities was dropped. While Chamberlain, as mayor of Birmingham, was pushing on a series of municipal controls over water, light, and open spaces, and while Joseph Arch of Warwickshire was helping to advance the agricultural labourers' wretched wage by union action, Gladstone's letters refer to such Radicalism with distaste; Bright's health had broken, and with it the Cabinet's strongest bond with its Left wing. Social advance meant expenditure, which all Gladstone's standards resisted; the last budget of his government, at £77 millions, was not higher than that of 1868, while income-tax had been reduced to 3d. For the first Liberal principle, as Gladstone saw it, was to enfranchise individual energy, as politically he did, for instance, by the Act of 1872 which at last conceded vote by ballot.

Beyond these various interests, thus disturbed or affronted, national sentiment was jarred by the government's record in foreign affairs. To offer armed mediation, even if other Powers had co-operated, in the Franco-Prussian war must have been doubtfully wise, for we had no adequate army to send abroad, and British action was confined to persuading both rivals to recognize the neutrality of Belgium. Yet the man in the street felt that a violent change had been made in the balance of power at our expense, and perhaps by our inaction, an impression which was deepened when Russia repudiated that clause of the 1856 treaty barring her naval forces from the Black Sea. Then came the long-pressed American claims over reparation for harm done by the *Alabama*, an extension of such claims to cover the whole prolongation of their civil war, and the international arbitration of 1872 which condemned Britain to pay £5 millions in damages.

Before that date we find Gladstone dispirited by failure and faction, as well as by the increasing coolness of the Queen; he tried vainly to break down her objection to bringing the Prince of Wales forward in business, and to overcome the shrinking which made her demand more time at Balmoral or Osborne; which in turn contributed to some academic advocacy of a republic by Radicals, like Chamberlain and Dilke. In 1873, making an effort to escape, he offered his resignation, but since Disraeli would neither take office in the present Parliament nor rule with a minority until a dissolution, he returned again. Bitter dissension between Radicalism and individualist Whigs of Harcourt's type, his party's lack of agreement over Ireland and local government, the land and education, departmental scandals, and continuous loss of bye-elections, led him to think that he could only reunite Liberalism in his own field of finance. Taking over the Exchequer himself, he proposed to abolish income-tax entirely and lower the sugar duties, but he could not get his Service ministers, Goschen and Cardwell, to accept the economies that this scheme would require, and early in 1874 dissolved Parliament.

Disraeli meanwhile, having defeated some cabals against his leadership, had reorganized his party machine by setting up a central office and democratic local associations. His speeches show his belief that democracy could be rallied to Conservative causes; to the throne as 'the security for every man's rights'; to a national profession of religion, since 'the traditions of a nation are part of its existence'; social reform, he had always taught, was the purpose of all political mechanics, 'the first consideration of a minister should be the health of the people'. He looked, in an age of international revolution, to the strength of 'an Imperial country'; arguing that we should have accompanied our grant of colonial self-government by measures for an Imperial tariff, defence, and councils.

From whatever causes, the electors of 1874 returned 350 Conservatives against 245 Liberals; though in Ireland the 46 Conservatives and Liberals combined were outnumbered by 57 Home Rulers. Within a few months Gladstone resigned to Hartington the Liberal leadership, declaring that he could not unite its different sections, and that he craved some interval 'between parliament and the grave'.

CONTEMPORARY DATES

1860   Cavour in Central Italy; Garibaldi in Sicily and Naples.
      Lincoln elected President of the United States.
      Burning of the Summer Palace, Pekin.
      Tolstoi, *War and Peace*.

Ruskin, *Unto this Last.*

1861　Outbreak of American Civil War.
　　　　Death of Cavour.
　　　　–1888.　Reign of William I in Prussia.

1862　Battle of Aspromonte.
　　　　Lincoln declares the slaves free.
　　　　Bismarck premier in Prussia.

1863　Battles of Vicksburg and Gettysburg.
　　　　General Gordon in China.
　　　　Lassalle makes workers' associations in Germany.

1864　War over Schleswig-Holstein.
　　　　Sherman marches through Georgia.
　　　　The Geneva Convention for the wounded.
　　　　Newman's *Apologia.*

1865　Lincoln murdered : surrender of General Lee.
　　　　Clerk Maxwell, *Treatise on Electricity.*
　　　　Manning becomes archbishop of Westminster.
　　　　Booth creates the Salvation Army.

1866　Prussian victory over Austria at Sadowa.
　　　　Venetia incorporated in Italy.
　　　　Dostoievsky, *Crime and Punishment.*
　　　　Swinburne, *Poems and Ballads,* I.

1867　Dual constitution arranged for Austria-Hungary.
　　　　Execution of the Emperor Maximilian in Mexico.
　　　　Siemens' process for steel.
　　　　Karl Marx, *Capital.*
　　　　Bagehot, *The English Constitution.*

1868　Grant elected President of the United States.
　　　　The Shogunate abolished in Japan.
　　　　Wagner, *Meistersinger.*
　　　　Browning, *The Ring and the Book.*

1869　Opening of the Suez Canal.
　　　　Foundation of Girton College, Cambridge.

1870　Franco-Prussian war.
　　　　The Vatican Council defines infallibility.
　　　　Death of Dickens and Dumas.

1871　The Commune at Paris.
　　　　Kulturkamf in Germany.
　　　　George Eliot, *Middlemarch.*
　　　　Manet and other Impressionists exhibit at Paris.

1872　Herbert Spencer, *Sociology.*
　　　　Death of Gautier and Mazzini.

1873　Macmahon President in France.
　　　　Republican rising under Castelar in Spain.
　　　　Brahms, *Requiem.*
　　　　Death of Mill, Livingstone, and Napoleon III.

1874　Russia enforces conscription.
　　　　Green, *Short History of England.*

CHAPTER V

DISRAELI, 1874–1880

Two facts beyond his control from the first weakened the Disraelian ministry. He achieved power too late, for this year he reached the age of seventy, while his health so rapidly gave way that in 1876 he was forced to retire to the Lords as Earl of Beaconsfield. Again, his taking of office coincided with the beginning of a great economic depression. First it was the turn of commerce with heavy price-falls and deepening unemployment; then followed, after four wet summers, what was more ruinous and permanent, a slump in British agriculture with farmers going bankrupt and wages tumbling, so that the 1881 census showed how in ten years 100,000 labourers had left the soil. Against these strains must be set one great advantage that, much unlike Gladstone, he could count on the fervent support of the Queen. Left most lonely by his wife's death he found in serving a woman sovereign, who was as lonely as himself, scope for all he declared that he lived for, — power and affections. On the great themes with which he had to deal of war and empire, they thought alike; he lavishly flattered her royal dignity, humoured or wore down her tantrums, and showed himself genuinely sympathetic to the woman's pain. And he used her influence without scruple to direct his Cabinet in the way that he intended them to go.

His quarter of a century in drilling his party in the wilderness, his courage, diplomatic craft, and magnanimity had their reward in the formation of a Cabinet very strong in statesmen and administrators; in the Commons, Northcote, Gathorne Hardy, Cross, W. H. Smith, and Hicks Beach; in the Lords, Cairns and Derby, and two of those who had left him in 1867, Salisbury and Carnarvon. He was large and wise enough to see in Salisbury, originally so hostile to him, the man of the future, and to make of him his central column. His skill in handling this team was immediately shown over what was in itself comparatively unimportant, the Public Worship Act of 1874, for which the bishops asked, to curb ritualism; which was disliked by Salisbury and all high churchmen, fiercely resisted by Gladstone but pressed on by the Queen, whose Protestant prejudice was so strong that she preferred preachers in her chapels to wear a black gown.

In domestic history the government's most decisive work was that social legislation on which from his first days Disraeli had insisted as a

Conservative party's function, and the condition of its survival; here the direct agent was the Home Secretary, the Lancashire banker Richard Cross. Disraeli told the Queen that the most important social laws of her reign were the two Labour Acts of 1875, which only his support enabled Cross to carry in Cabinet; one putting master and man on an equal level as regards breaches of contract, the other sweeping away the older view of conspiracy, allowing peaceful picketing, and permitting trade unions to do whatever would not be criminal if done by an individual. The 56-hour week was fixed in a consolidating Factory Act; much the same was done for health by the Public Health Act of 1875, the basis of all our modern legislation, which created a sanitary authority in every area. Housing was first seriously tackled by the State in the artisan's dwellings Acts, which gave local authorities power to pull down slums and which, for instance, enabled Chamberlain to do his work at Birmingham. Stirred up in the first instance by the angry humanity of the Radical Samuel Plimsoll, the merchant shipping Act of 1876 attempted regulation of the overloaded, over-insured, ' coffin ships ' which endangered seamen's lives. An agricultural holdings Act to give tenants compensation for their improvements, a friendly societies Act, a food and drugs Act to stop adulteration, these also were useful first steps. If we add Northcote's new Sinking Fund, by means of which £150 millions of debt were discharged before the century ended; the education Act of 1876, which much advanced compulsory and free education, or the gradual creation of six new bishoprics (St. Albans, Truro, Liverpool, Newcastle, Wakefield, and Southwell), it will be seen that this was an active, reforming ministry.

In Disraeli's vision the Crown was to be the warming fire round which would unite the peoples for whose happiness government must toil. For India above all he had, as far back as the Mutiny, thought this all-important, and in India he, first perhaps of British ministers, discerned a mighty lever to raise our position among the nations. Hence, after a visit of the Prince of Wales, came the royal titles bill of 1876, styling the Queen ' Empress of India ', which was much opposed as flummery by Gladstone and the Radicals. But then Gladstone also resisted Disraeli's purchase of the Khedive of Egypt's shares in the Suez Canal in 1875. They had been offered to Gladstone's government and rejected, and would have been turned down now but for Disraeli's insistence; who for £4 millions acquired rights which would allow us to lower the Canal tolls on our shipping and assure us a stronghold on another route to the East. The purchase money was advanced by the Rothschilds in advance of parliamentary sanction.

Part of his success here had come through being on good terms with France, and this because his government had made a stand against Bismarck. The calculation, the enormous diplomatic skill of the iron

Chancellor, dominated Europe in this generation as in the next. Always dreading a French revenge, he had brought about an understanding between the three military empires of Germany, Austria, and Russia and in 1875, it seems, contemplated another war rather than see France rise again. Unwillingness in Russia and protests from Great Britain assisted to check this continuing rule of the sword. But it was the Eastern question which enabled Disraeli, as it had Canning, to divide the three Emperors' league.

If the Crimean war had arrested Russian supremacy in the Balkans, in another objective the treaty of Paris had altogether failed; for Turkey never reformed, as she had pledged, her way of ruling her Christian subjects. In 1875 the chronic rebelliousness of Bosnia and Herzegovina boiled over; in April 1876 the Bulgars revolted and there followed the atrocities, in which some 12,000 were massacred by Turkish irregulars. This was not yet known in England when the British government declined to accept the Eastern powers' scheme, known as the Berlin memorandum; when fully divulged in July, at which time Serbia and Montenegro also rose in arms, Gladstone came out of retirement with a pamphlet which called for expulsion of the Turks, ' bag and baggage ', from the provinces they had desolated. Two years followed which divided British parties, shook the Cabinet, and brought Europe to the edge of a great war.

Foreign affairs were nominally in the hands of Derby. Always a more democratic Tory than his father, the former Prime Minister, he had been asked before this to enter a Whig government and was destined to join Gladstone's after 1880. In feeling he was strongly pacifist, and as his stepson Salisbury wrote of him as ' irresolute ' and ' dawdling ', control of policy passed to others. Disraeli brought the Cabinet to reject the Berlin memorandum, mainly because it asked us to accept point-blank a scheme arranged by other Powers, and was so far justified that Russia and Austria were found to be discussing a partition of Turkish provinces; he cared for the integrity of Turkey because its disintegration might mean Russia at Constantinople. He argued throughout that a firm tone would have prevented the Crimean war, and that the doctrine of peace at any price had ' occasioned more wars than the most ruthless conquerors '. There was a wide gap, surely, between this belief and the Queen's hysterical claim that war should be declared against the ' barbarians ' of Russia, or her orders for a letter to be read in Cabinet protesting we were becoming a third-rate power and even breathing her abdication.

In fact, however, the British attitude was fortunately determined by neither of these, but rather by the middle section of the Cabinet, notably Salisbury and the Opposition leaders Hartington and Granville, who did not care about Gladstone's crusade. Salisbury was as ardent as

Gladstone to protect the Turkish Christians, but without Gladstone's ardour to join hands with Russia against the Turk, and this moderation prevailed in the Constantinople conference of January 1877, to which he went as our representative. This meant that we had brought the question on to a European plane, and asked of Turkey concessions of self-government and territorial gain for her Christian provinces. When the Turks unwisely evaded these terms and Russia declared war in April, we kept our neutrality, but with a warning that we should not stand aside if Constantinople and the Straits, or Egypt and the Canal, were put in danger.

The British feeling of Christian humanity, which brought the Nonconformist north, churchmen, and the greatest men of letters round Gladstone, was counterbalanced, as 1877 wore away, by the gallant Turkish stand at Plevna and the sweeping Russian advance over the Balkans after Plevna fell, until in January 1878 their armies stood at the gates of Constantinople. A British fleet moved up to the Bosphorus; in March Russia imposed on Turkey the peace of San Stefano, which would not only demand a huge indemnity, with the concession to Russia of the keys of Armenia and Bessarabia, but would create a large Bulgaria stretching from the Black Sea almost to Salonica, to be garrisoned for some years by Russian troops, which would command Constantinople and strangle Greece. To stop this lop-sided tyranny and to convince Austria that we meant business, the Cabinet called up army reserves, summoned Indian troops to Malta, and decided to occupy Cyprus to offset the new Russian vantage-points in Asia. These steps brought about the resignation of Derby and Carnarvon.

Salisbury, taking over the Foreign Office, issued a masterful note which, while admitting the necessity of change, appealed to the principle that treaty changes must be made by European concert, and demanded that the San Stefano scheme should be recast. He spoke to the converted. Not merely was Russia exhausted by war; Austria, assured that we should not object to her control of Bosnia, was alarmed at the Russian triumph; Bismarck's preoccupation was to prevent a war between his two allies and he had always been ready to save the peace by partitioning Turkey, encouraging us moreover to occupy Egypt. Fortified by a secret agreement with Turkey over our acquisition of Cyprus and by Russia's secret acceptance of our broad principles, in June 1878 Beaconsfield and Salisbury went to complete their work at the Congress of Berlin.

The treaty signed there was a heavy diplomatic set-back for Russia. Serbia and Montenegro became independent but were reduced in extent from the San Stefano terms, and were both threatened by the right given to Austria to hold Bosnia and Herzegovina and

to garrison the Sanjak of Novibazar. Bulgaria had to restore Macedonia to the Turk, while the part of it south of the Balkans, to be
styled Eastern Rumelia, was to be self-governing but under Turkish
sovereignty. If Russia obtained Bessarabia from the Roumanians and
Kars in Asia, she promised not to fortify the port of Batum. Great
Britain received the right to occupy Cyprus, promising furthermore to
guarantee the Turks' Asiatic territories, the Turks in return pledging
themselves to reforms.

This was the settlement for which Beaconsfield claimed ' peace with
honour ', and peace between the great Powers did, indeed, endure for
thirty-six years to come. Nor was the cause of reform in Turkey fairly
tested, since the next Gladstone government withdrew the British
military officers on whom Salisbury relied. Against the harsh subjection
of the Serbs to Austria, racial conflict in Macedonia, and the disappointment of the Greeks, must be set the fact that Constantinople and the
Straits were preserved in freedom and a chance of development given
to several peoples. As to Gladstone's passionate criticism that Beaconsfield had looked solely to British interests, not the moral law, it was
inspired by a belief that Christian civilization would benefit by giving
full liberty to all the Balkan States. Whether he was justified in that,
future history was to judge.

While its whole attention was being given to the Eastern question,
agricultural depression clouded the country, and two other questions
embarrassed it of which the full development was yet to come. After
ruining his country by maladministration, the Khedive Ismail of Egypt
was deposed in 1878 under pressure from France and Britain, who
jointly took over control of the finances ; the same year Parnell succeeded to the lead of the Irish Parliamentary party and a revolutionary
movement of the Land League opened a new chapter of civil war.
Meantime, many thousand miles away, in another old volume of empire
a new page was turned. Since Dost Mahommed's return after our
disasters of 1839-40, and through his shrewd balancings during the
Mutiny, our relations with Afghanistan had remained peaceful ; in the
anarchy which came of the twelve sons left at his death, we recognized
Shere Ali, the one amongst them who finally in 1869 made himself
Amir. But the question of the Indian frontier had reached a determining phase. To expect stability from Afghanistan was out of the
question : ruled only by the sword, dogged on its frontiers by exiled
princes of its royal house, defied by wild tribesmen and half-independent
nobles like the Khan of Khelat. There was, again, its old feud with
Persia, and for us to pronounce between them, as for example in regard
to the fortress of Herat, must antagonize one or the other. But what
had done most to transform this central Asiatic problem was the
advance of Russia's armies over the thousand miles separating the

Caspian from the Indian frontier. One after another between 1868 and 1875 the keys of Turkestan fell into their hands, — Samarkand, Bokhara, Khiva and Khokand — and though Russia admitted Afghanistan lay outside her sphere, the effect on Afghan-Indian relations was immediate. It brought to a head an old controversy between two schools of Indian administrators, the one represented by John Lawrence who would leave things alone, and a ' forward ' school who thought that the frontier and Afghanistan must somehow be brought under more control.

Shere Ali's repeated request for a binding agreement to protect him was, against the advice of the Indian government, rejected by the Gladstone Cabinet, and British policy throughout seems open to this criticism, that it expected the Amir to maintain a friendly neutrality without offering him any adequate compensation. When Lytton was sent by Disraeli as Viceroy in 1876, the Turkish dispute with Russia being in full swing, he was instructed to make the frontier more secure, and to pierce the curtain concealing what was going on in Asia by insisting that a British agent should be resident in Afghanistan. But though there was a military school in India who believed that war must come, and had better come soon, this was not the attitude of the Cabinet. Nothing could be more damaging either before or after the Congress of Berlin than a war in Asia ; Salisbury, first as Secretary for India and then for Foreign Affairs, was sceptical of the Russian danger and begged the country to use ' large maps '. One part of Lytton's task was speedily accomplished : by a treaty with Khelat, Baluchistan was brought under our protection, and British troops occupied the invaluable post of Quetta, commanding the roads to Kandahar. But, in negotiating for a British resident, Lytton's threatening tone created the very atmosphere which Salisbury had hoped to avoid. In 1878 a Russian mission was received at Kabul, which inevitably decided the Cabinet that a British mission must be admitted too. Even so, with the exception of Gathorne Hardy, now Lord Cranbrook and Indian Secretary, they thought Lytton precipitate and were only forced into war by a point of prestige, when the mission he insisted on sending through the Khyber Pass was refused entry.

The first campaign of 1879 was a brilliant success ; three columns, operating by the Khyber, the Kurram, and Quetta, pierced Afghanistan, Shere Ali fled to Turkestan and died, vainly asking Russian aid. A treaty with his successor made over to Britain the control of Afghan foreign affairs and supremacy in the Khyber, and by ceding Kurram, Sibi, and Pishin, gave us two alternative frontier bastions. In September, however, the massacre of Cavagnari, our resident at Kabul, and his following threw all again into confusion. General Roberts advanced to Kabul and Donald Stewart to Kandahar ; but Afghanistan was without an Amir and Lytton had a wild idea of breaking it up into petty

States. In 1880 a British force was wiped out at Maiwand, and only a wonderful march by Roberts' army saved Kandahar. Two simultaneous events restored the situation; the advent of the Gladstone government, and the emergence from exile of an Afghan prince of ruthless ability, Abdur Rahman. The agreement between them of 1880 to this extent vindicated the forward policy, which Gladstonians had so furiously attacked : that it pledged the Amir to follow British advice in his foreign relations, promising him in return our protection and a larger subsidy.

Unhappily for the Beaconsfield government the costly campaigns and reverses in Afghanistan overlapped disastrous years in South Africa. Though the full story must wait for a more decisive stage, enough to say that the two continual factors remained what they had been since the '30's, — Great Britain's refusal to take the position of a paramount Power and the disintegration of native society. Here also we meet, as over Afghanistan, two damaging elements in our conduct of Imperial affairs: a dangerous departmentalism in the Cabinet, and action by men on the spot committing the Imperial government.

Since the conventions of the 1850's, by which Britain abdicated control in the Boer republics, it had become clear that Cape Colony and Natal, as they stood, could never feel secure. It was not merely that they were separated by immense territories, part-annexed to the Crown after Kaffir wars and part-held by swarming tribes; and not only that our native administration veered between segregating natives in reserves, or downright amalgamation, or making a chequer-board of black and white. The Boers' trek had not made a clear break, but had left a wound or contagion. Boer families both in the Cape and Natal, religious bonds of the Dutch reformed Church, the dependence of the interior on the commerce of the coast Colonies, all these ran across frontiers; above all, there was the universal colonial view as to white men's relations with the natives. There was, indeed, a great difference between the policy of the Natal administrator Shepstone, with ambitious schemes for control by an enlarged Natal, and the crude view of the average backveldt Boer, who would simply make the natives hewers of wood and forcibly apprentice their children. But both were united by a common fear.

Already one governor of the Cape, the stalwart George Grey who had federated New Zealand, had insisted on attempting union with the Orange Free State, and was recalled in 1859 for doing so. Since then every year made it more certain that closer union of some sort would come, the one doubt being whether it would be British- or Boer-inspired. One school in the Transvaal planned union with the other Boer State, with an exit eastwards at Delagoa Bay. Transvaal society was anarchic, lawless, and oppressive to the natives; it was made worse in the '60's by the discovery of gold and diamonds, Boer pressure turned westwards on to the Griquas, with whom we had old treaties, and threatened to close the road to the far north. Missionary influence, and Livingstone's, thereupon asked for Imperial action to safeguard the natives. Meanwhile, Boer relations with Basutoland, which touched every South African State, brought about repeated wars, and in 1869 the Cape governor Woodhouse fixed the frontiers and took Basutoland for the Crown. Despite its protestations of standing aside, the Imperial government also intervened to stop chaos in the diamond-fields, overruled the Boer claims, and in 1871 annexed Griqualand West. In fact, like many leading men of Afrikans race at the Cape, such as De Villiers or Hofmeyr, the Colonial Office had come round to accept some form of union. But the home government chiefly desired it in order to lighten their own burden, as they showed by cutting down Imperial garrisons and by forcing representative government on a much-divided Cape Parliament.

There was another swelling danger, the Zulu power, which threatened eastern Natal on the Tugela river and northwards constantly clashed with the Transvaal. Succeeding to the milder Panda, Cetewayo ' washed the spears ' of his fighting-men in the blood of weaker tribes, but with each British annexation he felt himself more hemmed in, and resented our frontier awards between him and the Boers.

This was the African background when Disraeli gave the Colonial Office to Carnarvon, who in the last Conservative government had completed the federation of Canada. It was Carnarvon's misfortune always to be skirmishing ahead of opinion, and to precipitate a crisis by putting himself in the hands of men on the spot. For federation there was, indeed, much to be said, — to solve the native question, control of railways, and the whole economic life of South Africa, — but nothing for Carnarvon's way of bringing it about. The speeches of his agent the historian Froude, the adjournment of the conference at Capetown, and its reopening in London, showed that he meant to drive on the question from outside, and the measures he finally took in 1877 were hasty and ill-connected. For while he sent out an eminent Indian administrator, Bartle Frere, as High Commissioner for the express purpose of bringing about a ' South African dominion ', unknown to Frere he also despatched Shepstone with orders to discuss federation with the Transvaal and, if he judged fit, to annex it.

Boer opinion was much divided, but prompt guarantees for their self-government were needed to overcome the sturdy opposition led by Paul Kruger, which appealed to the Imperial government against this blow to their independence. Such guarantees were not forthcoming, and annexation helped to destroy any chance Frere ever had of achieving an agreed federation. He turned therefore to his other immediate purpose, of averting the danger of a native war. All through 1877 and 1878 he was busied suppressing risings on many frontiers, in the course of which he acquired a conviction that the root of disturbance was the Zulu Cetewayo. Beaconsfield, and Carnarvon's successor at the Colonial Office, Hicks Beach, distrusted his policy and, in unwillingly sending him reinforcements of British troops, instructed him they must be used only for defensive purposes. He disregarded them and, on his own responsibility, in December 1878 issued an ultimation which must almost certainly mean war; demanding the disarmament of the Zulu army and the admission of a British resident. On 22nd January 1879, the incompetence of our commander, Chelmsford, led to the annihilation of a British force at Isandhlwana; only the defence of Rorke's Drift by a bare company of the South Wales Borderers redeemed that dreadful day. In due course Chelmsford's victory at Ulundi in July, Wolseley's arrival, and the capture of Cetewayo ended the Zulu problem, but too late for the Beaconsfield government. For the year which began with one massacre at Isandhlwana ended with another at Kabul, and we entered upon 1880 beset by these two inglorious wars.

These, coming on the top of Bulgarian atrocities and Cyprus, made the theme of Gladstone's campaign of speeches in Midlothian that winter, binding together Bulgars and Afghans and Boers and Zulus as the victims of Tory reaction, and by the spell of his oratory convincing millions that in this contest was concerned the whole welfare of mankind. With this moral weight the pendulum swung hard over; its speed was assisted by economic depression, crime in Ireland, and obstruction by Parnell's group in the Commons; it was carefully watched and accelerated by the much superior organization of the National Liberal Federation, which Chamberlain inspired from Birmingham. When in March 1880 Beaconsfield took the dissolution, making his appeal especially on the danger from the ' destructive doctrine ' of Home Rule, the electors returned the Liberal party with a clear majority of 100 over the Conservatives, though 60 Home Rulers were returned from Ireland. Hoping against hope that this ' shamefully heterogeneous union ' of Whigs, Radicals, and Irish would collapse, the Queen in vain asked both Hartington and Granville to form a government. On their advice she was compelled to summon Gladstone, the clear choice of the electorate.

Disraeli, to give him his lasting name, lived only until April 1881. His last government had come too late for his physical powers, and what he had done, or rather what he had foreseen, was to be better justified in the quarter-century that followed his death. ' Above all things ', Salisbury said, ' he wished to see England united and powerful and great '; to that end, his insight had lighted on the deep feelings and real forces which could prolong Conservatism in a democratic State.

CONTEMPORARY DATES

1875	Constitutional revision in France.
	Tisza becomes premier in Hungary.
	Revolt in Bosnia.
1876	Abdul Hamid II reigns in Turkey, till 1908.
	Graham Bell invents a telephone.
1877	The Russians take Plevna and Kars.
	Diaz becomes President in Mexico.
1878	Congress of Berlin.
	Leo XIII becomes Pope (–1903).
	Ellen Terry acts with Irving.
1879	Death of the Prince Imperial.
	Austro-German alliance.
	Henry George, *Progress and Poverty*.
	Treitschke, *History of Germany*.
	Ibsen, *A Doll's House*.
1880	Abdur Rahman becomes Amir of Afghanistan.
	Death of Flaubert and George Eliot.

CHAPTER VI

THE EMPIRE, 1850–1880

ONE of those forces had been the conception of Empire, which so much changed its form and character that, well before Bright and Gladstone disappeared, it was certain that the British world would develop on lines very different from those they approved. Indeed, here in a sense began a dilemma within which the British peoples still move, how far Liberalism and democracy could cope with the necessities of Empire.

As yet, the ruling class were dead-set against Imperial expansion. How unwillingly they allowed annexation in South Africa, or how they frowned upon ventures beyond the Indian frontier, has been seen; in the same spirit they made over the Ionian Islands to Greece in 1864, resisted Australian pressure for the annexation of New Guinea, and rejected a golden chance of taking Zanzibar. Nevertheless, these thirty years saw and clinched some notable additions to British territory.

Of these the most important result was a deepening of the Oriental character of Empire, shifting its strategic centre to Egypt, Capetown, and Colombo. The matter of Egypt, and with it went the annexation of Cyprus, did not rise to its height till later, but long frictions and the opening of the Suez Canal had wide effects before Egypt itself was contested, as for instance in the occupation of Perim in 1857, in order to offset France and control the waters this side of Aden. The full development of British India, completed by the wars of the '40's with the Sikhs and Sind, fear of Russia, and the end of the Company's monopoly, all conduced to further extension, for the nature of Oriental States made security for trade and defence impossible without annexation. Of this one instance was the war into which Dalhousie was forced in 1852 by the barbarian arrogance of Burma, bringing about the capture of the Pegu province which covered the eastern bay of Bengal. On the other side of India, Outram's expedition of 1856 to the Gulf, provoked by a Persian threat to Afghanistan, illustrated the fact that the ruler of Bombay and the Punjab was necessarily concerned with the whole Moslem world; thus the family ruling at Muscat in the Gulf ruled also at Zanzibar, and the commerce of Persia and Arabia flowed to and from the Arabs settled in East Africa.

Furthermore, long before we colonized Australasia, the East India Company had made us a Pacific Power, for its China trade and the wild piracy in Chinese waters made urgent a safe route and good harbourage, while its ancient rivalry with the Dutch was redoubled when, in the revolutionary days, Holland became a French satellite. Out of that rivalry came our acquisition of Penang (1786) and Malacca (1824) in the Malay peninsula, and the astonishing career of Stamford Raffles who, after ruling Java till it was handed back to Holland at the peace, induced the Company in 1819 to occupy the empty island of Singapore. He had died in his forties, but his prediction that here was the Malta of the East was fulfilled; assuring us of free trade in the Eastern archipelago and free passage through the straits of Malacca, Singapore grew from a squalid fishing-port to a city of a hundred thousand people before Company rule ended. In 1867 it made the nucleus of a new Crown Colony, the Straits Settlements, and from the '70's the independent Malay States sought British protection.

Another footing deeper in the Pacific had been planted by another individual Englishman, James Brooke, once an officer of the Company's army. Sailing for Borneo in a 140-ton schooner, between 1839–42, with no arms but his character, he established himself with the local Sultan's good will as ruler of Sarawak, at the island's north-western corner. And there, after long struggles against head-hunters and pirates, he founded an independent hereditary State. But further into the seas separating Singapore from Australia the British government would not go, leaving the French to annex Tahiti and New Caledonia, and it was not till 1874 that, to stop exploitation of native labour for Queensland's tropical plantations, they finally agreed to take over Fiji.

While trade to India and China thus drew us into the Pacific, occupation of the Cape as a stopping-place for India first made us a Power in Africa, though a set of causes unconnected originally with the Cape were laying wider foundations. For there, as once before in India, our traders found themselves plunged in a debris of dying empires, shadowy States, and barbaric warfare; an ancient, demoralized Portuguese dominion on both coasts, fractions of every European race, sheer savagery in native States like Ashanti, Arab and negroid tyrannies scattered by history from the Sahara to Somaliland, and a vast interior of which Europe knew little save that it was given over to man-hunting, disease, and war.

In this anarchy the earliest British point lay in the chain of factories on the west in the Gambia river and the Gold Coast, which had come down from the Stuarts and their African companies, but the day of those monopolies was done, the last inefficient company being dissolved by Parliament in 1821. Many times over there was talk of evacuation, but Britain was kept on that coast through two principal causes : the obstinate resolution of British traders, and a settled national purpose to break slavery. To that end the ' Saints ' had set up the company which in 1787 colonized Sierra Leone, and was in 1808 transferred to the Crown. For yet another generation government was pulled in opposite directions, by the dislike of expenditure or new responsibilities and, on the other side, the evangelical passion against slavery ; for in Africa abolition of the trade had turned out an empty gesture, the few ships we could spare could not cover those thousands of miles of coast and inlets, and Wilberforce's successor Fowell Buxton showed that the numbers shipped over the Atlantic in 1837 was actually thrice the figure of thirty years before. Harsh experience proved that our cruisers must be supported by measures ashore, treaties with native kings and powers to pursue offenders beyond our own settlements, while the missionary world was learning that the best antidote to the trade was legitimate trading. Prestige added its weight ; one Gold Coast governor was killed by the Ashantis, who kept his skull as a royal goblet ; there were missions to defend, a growing commerce in palm oils and cotton, French activity to be feared. So, with many set-backs and protests, and in most damaging ignorance of local facts, our rule slowly extended. In 1850 the Danish settlements were bought out and in 1872 the Dutch ; in 1861 we annexed Lagos so as better to check the slave-trading of Dahomey and Nigeria. Finally, after ten years of humiliation, the Imperial government in 1874 despatched an expedition under Garnet Wolseley, to drive the murderous Ashantis back on Kumasi.

These were small things as yet, barely known to the mid-Victorian public, whose enthusiasm about Africa was concentrated on the dark centre and the shining figure of David Livingstone. Our exploration had, indeed, begun much earlier, and from many motives ; some who had served with Captain Cook supported the voyages of Mungo Park of Selkirk, whose last letter of 1805 declared ' the fixed resolution to discover the termination of the Niger, or perish in the attempt '. He perished in the rapids, as others were to perish in the desert, in efforts to solve the Niger's course ; simultaneously explorers of every nation had started from the north, to do the same for the Nile. The British achievement was to attack this Nile problem from the other end. In 1857–8 Richard Burton and the heroic Speke of the Indian army discovered Lake Tanganyika, and Speke reached Victoria Nyanza ; in 1862–3 he and Grant entered Uganda, and traced the Nile from its exit out of Victoria Nyanza at the Ripon falls to its passage into Albert Nyanza, where he joined hands with Samuel Baker, coming from the Sudan. But Livingstone, who preceded Speke, also outlived him, and though politics were not his motive, from him derived the first inspiration for one of the major British political triumphs.

In character this poor Lanarkshire cotton-spinner was as sheerly

heroic as any Drake or Nicholson, while in his life was signally represented the most continuous purpose of a moral age. Having won a
medical degree by study outside his factory hours, he took service with
the London Missionary Society in Bechuanaland under one of its
greatest leaders, Robert Moffat. There he was astride the road to the
north, and from that base moved among the natives, for ever acquiring
languages and geology carpentering or astronomy, every craft and
science, armed with which he might work in unknown country, alone.
On his first major expedition of 1852-6 he ascended the Zambesi,
struck the Congo tributaries, reached the west sea in Portuguese Angola
and passed down the Zambesi again, discovering the Victoria Falls on
his way. In the year of the Mutiny he was given every honour by the
nation and in 1858, now supported by government, set out on a five
years' journey. From that came the discovery of the Shire highlands,
the Murchison Falls, and Lake Nyasa. On his last, that of 1866-73,
wherein he died of his toils, he was seeking to determine the mystery of
the streams which flowed towards Nile and Congo.

Always a solitary and sometimes unaccompanied by any other
European, unknowing of fear, invincible through perpetual suffering,
Livingstone's first purpose was not so much that of the dogmatic
Christian but rather, in its purest essence, that passion for raising
humanity which was the highest Victorian attribute. On every page
of his books and journals, in speeches to every sort of audience, comes
the black portraiture of the slave trade ; the Arab and Portuguese half-
castes who had made central Africa a hell, their path marked by skeletons,
the interminable procession of slaves chained or clenched in wooden
yokes, everywhere ruin and death and lust, the tsetse-fly, fever, and
leprosy. To prove that white men could purify this abomination by
ways of peace was his task, yet thus to open the road was to open what
could not be closed. From the movements he inspired, such as the
foundation of the Universities' Mission, and the men he trained like
John Kirk, who as consul-general became all-powerful at Zanzibar, and
the increase of British trade which his trail made possible, proceeded
influences which the least expansionist government could not ignore,
and which in due course resulted in an empire.

While, haphazard or under protest, such vast unpremeditated beginnings were made, the logic of reformed Britain worked itself out in the
chief Colonies of British emigrants. They had become substantial
communities. By 1880 between $3\frac{1}{2}$ and 4 million Canadians exported
goods to the annual value of £30 millions. Australasia cleared 8
million tons of shipping and was swallowing millions of British capital.
To large and small alike responsible government was granted with lavish
hand ; to South Australia and New Zealand in the '50's, to Tasmania
and Newfoundland. They were given powers to amend their own

constitutions, Canada was allowed to make its legislative council elective, one Australian colony after another introduced manhood suffrage and triennial elections. In 1859 a decisive lead by Canada settled that self-government must include tariff-making, even against the mother country, while in the Australian Customs Act of 1873 Gladstone was unwillingly obliged to permit discrimination in favour of Australian products. This completeness of freedom extended to religion, the privileged position of Anglicanism thus disappearing in Canada with a settlement over the clergy reserves, and in the West Indies with disestablishment. Most of the bonds which Pitt's generation would have judged necessary, and nearly all the restrictions which the Durham school of the '30's had in mind, were thus removed.

There remained therefore only the powers of the Crown and its representatives the governors, restraints of English law, and the practical problem of Imperial defence. That the governor must be as impartial between parties as the Queen was at home, followed from the new doctrine; that he must check abuses of the constitution by party, equally held good, though this often exposed him to Colonial criticism. Local feeling, indeed, inevitably whittled away the governor's 'sovereign' rôle, Canada thus in 1876 obtaining changes in his instructions, so as to reduce his prerogative of pardon and the right to reserve bills for Her Majesty's pleasure. In 1865 the Colonial Laws Validity Act broadly defined the stage reached by the larger communities; those with representative legislatures had henceforth complete powers over their constitutions and courts of law, provided that their laws were not 'repugnant' to Imperial statutes which expressly affected that particular colony. Formally the governor might veto legislation or 'reserve' it, but this was ever more rarely used. But miscarriage of justice might still be corrected by appeal to the Crown, — that is, since 1833, to the judicial committee of the Privy Council.

As finally responsible for war and peace, the Imperial government retained control of the treaty-making power which, for example, touched the Colonies' tariffs or the Australian objection to Chinese immigration, but how in practice this prerogative would be employed was shown in 1871, when the Canadian Prime Minister was included in the British delegation that signed the commercial treaty of Washington. Missionary activity meantime kept well to the forefront the notion of trusteeship for native races, which officials of the best type had never lost, and this ideal successively protected Maoris, Basutos, and Bechuanas.

Many of these interconnected matters came together in Imperial defence. Until the '70's at least any such conception seems to have been unknown, for the good reason that common British opinion hardly thought the Empire could endure. We should do our duty in a passive sense; and so strong reinforcements were sent to Canada during the American Civil War. But not merely Radical politicians like Bright, or intellectuals like Goldwin Smith the historian, declared that separation was certain to come, and was in itself desirable; senior officials responsible for policy at the Colonial Office were equally convinced, at least of the first conclusion. In any event economy, strategical thinking, and constitutional outlook would all induce the British government to cut down their commitments. Why, Parliament murmured, should 40,000 Imperial troops be scattered in small detachments, at an annual cost of some £3 millions, largely to deal with native wars over the causes of which Parliament had no control? In the last resort Colonial defence must depend on the Imperial fleet and a concentrated striking-force, while Colonies which demanded responsible government must bear responsibility's burden, and do more to defend themselves. By 1871 all Imperial forces were withdrawn from Canada, except for small garrisons at the naval bases, Halifax and Esquimault, and from Australasia also, while only a few remained in the West Indies. This matter, in fact, delayed a grant of responsible government in Cape Colony, which could hardly contemplate a withdrawal of Imperial troops in the face of Boers and Zulus, Kaffirs and Griquas.

Thanks to good fortune, and the preoccupations of Europe and America till the later '70's, these communities were given time to mature their strength. One section of Empire, however, and one of the oldest, was stationary, if not in decline; the case of the sugar islands was almost desperate. Not so much by loss of their privileged tariffs in Britain, though it was severe and must take time to recoup; the more fundamental cause of collapse seems to have been the sudden emancipation of the slaves, who were not spurred by freedom to work for a good livelihood, but subsided into laziness on their own patches. Broadly speaking, prosperity returned fastest to sugar colonies most distant from the old West Indies and best able to use immigrant Indian labour, as in Trinidad, Mauritius, and British Guiana. But government was affected in these hardly tried islands as much as well-being. Emancipation, poverty, the slow replacement of absentee owners by a more business-like class, and the dwindling proportion of white to coloured population, showed up much incapacity and faction in their assemblies. After years of conflict with their governors, special committees, and clamour, the negro riots of 1865 in Jamaica and their severe repression by Governor Eyre, — nearly six hundred persons being executed by court-martial — led to the Assembly surrendering its powers; within a few years councils with nominated majorities were introduced in many other islands, and only Barbados and Bermuda retained the self-government which had come down from the seventeenth century.

Even in Australia self-government had not, within this period, produced results promising a future of power and progress. Till the early '70's exploration continued of the unknown interior, sometimes with tragedy like the death of Burke and Wills in 1861 in the salt-lake country far north of Adelaide, though more often with profit, as in John Forrest's expedition to link Adelaide with Perth. By such endeavour and painful degrees the true limitations of the country appeared — that roughly 40 per cent was tropical, that the rainfall over half of its area was less than fifteen inches, that white men could hardly work with profit in the northern territories, and that, though flocks and herds could be cropped on salt-bush and desert-feeding with comparative success, drought was a deadly enemy. Absolutely, population increased fast, yet a continent of three million square miles, or forty times the area of Great Britain, carried in 1871 little over a million and a half people, preponderantly massed in the south-east angle, New South Wales and Victoria.

Unmenaced as yet by foreign Powers, this handful of people — in blood the purest British community in the Empire — were economically doing considerable things and striking out many experiments. Their sheep increased sixfold between 1861 and 1881, gold and coal and copper had been found in abundance, South Australia was rich in wheat, tropical Queensland had a substantial sugar trade. The telegraph linked Adelaide with the British cable at Port Darwin in the far north; native mechanical invention showed that within reasonable limits arable farming could be made to pay. But politically Australia had not got over its growing pains. Separate in origin and even more in environment, and kept asunder by huge distances, these small States kept themselves still further apart by rival tariffs and different railway gauges. A British suggestion of 1849 for federation had been put aside, and though the strongest leaders both of New South Wales and Victoria, Henry Parkes and Gavan Duffy, favoured it, intense State jealousy stood in the way. Nor did responsible government bring about governments that could speak with authority. In the twenty years ending with 1876 Victoria had eighteen ministries, New South Wales seventeen, and South Australia twenty-nine; in the two first a squatter aristocracy, even in the face of hostile laws, had fought successfully to hold their power, and incessant conflicts between upper and lower chambers coincided with opposing notions of society.

Without doubt the outstanding achievement of Empire in this period was the making of Canada, by its confederation and its absorption of the West, into a great State running from sea to sea. The responsible government framed by Durham and put into practice by Elgin could not, it was found, in itself heal Canada's fundamental division, the united province set up by the Act of 1840 showing the same fissures as the former Upper and Lower Canada. While that union rested on equal numerical representation of the two provinces, that is, in effect, of British and French, immigration rapidly changed the proportions, so that British Ontario would soon far outnumber French Quebec, and from the Ontario Radicals, or ' grits ', led by George Brown, a demand grew loud for representation in accord with population. Moreover, the settlement had in other ways the character of a treaty between two races, for it was argued that a ministry ought to have a double majority, that is, a majority within each province. From Elgin's departure in 1854 responsible government did not result in party ministries of the British type. A great mass of all parties having come to agree in most great policies, such as reciprocity or the clergy reserves, there was little ground left for political principle in a society without class distinctions, and parties were in fact disintegrated into faction by distance, religion, and race. No continuous alliance could exist between Ontario Radicals, deeply coloured by Scot and Ulster feeling, and the so-called Liberals of Quebec, who were either influenced by American republicanism or swayed in the last resort by the Catholic Church. Yet without the good will of the French no government could be successful.

Such conditions gave his opening to a supple, genial, and wary opportunist, John A. Macdonald, who founded a ' Liberal-Conservative ' predominance in an understanding with the French moderates ; up to Confederation, and beyond it, government was thus normally held by a coalition — between Macdonald and a series of Quebec leaders, Morin, Taché, and Cartier. Out of this balance and inability to agree came about in 1857 the choice of Ottawa as capital, half-way between French Montreal and the rival British claimants at Toronto or Kingston, while perpetual controversy, as over the Catholic demand for separate schools, testified that Durham's hope of racial amalgamation had been a dream.

Since his day the values at stake had risen high. Population had doubled since the rebellions, and at Confederation stood round about $3\frac{1}{2}$ millions, of whom the $1\frac{1}{2}$ millions in Ontario much outstripped the French. Exports and imports together totalled some £24 millions in value, the country had over 2000 miles of railway working, the Canadian Allan line of steamships directly connected Montreal with Liverpool, while the greatest inland waterways of the world led from the St. Lawrence to the Lakes. Powerful banks and new protectionist tariffs revealed that factories and mechanism had replaced the little shops and looms and saw-mills of the pioneers. Yet by the '60's every principal politician, Macdonald and Brown, Cartier and the financier A. T. Galt, and the Irish ex-rebel Darcy McGee, were agreed that the present regime could not last, however much they differed on the means of

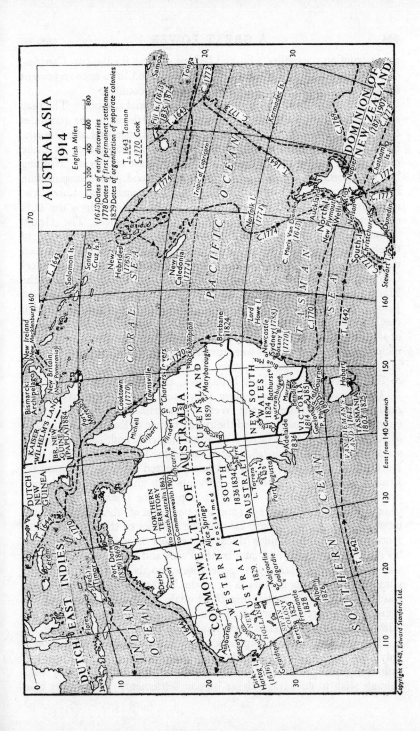

AUSTRALASIA
1914

English Miles

0 100 200 400 600 800

(1613) Dates of early discoveries
1778 Dates of first permanent settlement
1829 Dates of organization of separate colonies

T. 1643 Tasman
C. 1770 Cook

DUTCH EAST INDIES

INDIAN OCEAN

DUTCH NEW GUINEA

KAISER WILHELM'S LAND
Bismarck Archipelago
New Ireland (New Mecklenburg)
New Britain (New Pomerania)
BR. NEW GUINEA (PAPUA) 1884

New Holland

Port Darwin (N.S.W.) 1869

Derby
Fitzroy

Ashburton

NEW COLONY HOLLAND
Geraldton
SWAN COLONY 1829
Perth Fremantle 1828
Albany 1826

Dirk's I. Hort Hortog's I. (1610)

WESTERN AUSTRALIA
1829
Kalgoorlie
Coolgardie

COMMONWEALTH OF AUSTRALIA

NORTHERN TERRITORY
1863 to South Australia
1907 to Commonwealth

Alice Springs

SOUTH AUSTRALIA
1836 1834 Settle.
Proclaimed 1901

L. Torrens
L. Eyre
Port Augusta
Adelaide 1836

QUEENSLAND 1859 R.V Maryborough

Cooktown (1770)
Townsville
Michell
Gilbert
Flinders
Gt. Div. Range
Charters Towers
Curry Dividing
Rockhampton
Brisbane 1824

Murrumbidgee
Murray
Geelong
Melbourne 1851
P. Phillip
VICTORIA 1814 1851

VAN DIEMEN'S LAND
TASMANIA 1803 1825
Hobart T. 1642

NEW SOUTH WALES
1824 Bathurst
Blue Mts
Newcastle (1770)
Sydney 1788
Botany (1770)

SOUTHERN OCEAN

CORAL SEA

Solomon Is.
Santa Cruz Is.
New Hebrides (1768)
New Caledonia (1774)

PACIFIC OCEAN

Tropic of Capricorn

Fiji Is. (1613) 1835, 1874
Tonga
Samoa

Kermadec Is.

Lord Howe I.
Norfolk I. (1774)

C. Maria Van Diemen (1643)

TASMAN SEA

DOMINION OF NEW ZEALAND

Auckland
North I.
Napier
New Plymouth
Wellington
Nelson
South I.
Christchurch
Dunedin
Stewart I.
Chatham Is. 1787 1907

East from 140 Greenwich

Copyright 1948, Edward Stanford, Ltd.

reconstruction ; whether a limited federal scheme for the two Canadas, or something greater. Hitherto they had received little encouragement in this, financial or otherwise, from the mother country.

Three other problems urgently asked some final solution. The map shows not merely the distances between their settlements, the 400 miles of the St. Lawrence up to Quebec or the 500 thence to Lake Ontario, but also how both nature and man seemed in conspiracy to make connections run north and south, rather than east and west. Nothing but transportation could reverse this natural trend, but transportation had not as yet succeeded. American canal systems from Lake Erie, lower costs, and bonding arrangements via New York, drew the bulk of western production away from the St. Lawrence. The Grand Trunk railway, begun in 1852, ran from Lake Huron to east of Quebec, but then a gap of many hundred miles intervened between that terminus and Nova Scotia, and that crying need for an inter-Colonial railway raised another question — the whole future of the Maritime Provinces. The Imperial government had disappointed Joseph Howe's hope of a financial guarantee for such a line, and though the Maritimes felt that their fisheries had been sacrificed in the treaty of 1854 to please the Americans, their American trade had doubled under reciprocity. Their thoughts were turning, not to closer links with Canada, but to closer union with each other, the principle of which was accepted in 1864 by Nova Scotia, New Brunswick, and Prince Edward Island.

Graver yet, for it might have prevented Canada from ever being made, was the future of the West. The Hudson's Bay Company, chartered in 1670, had stamped the ruling names of Restoration England in Rupert's Land, York factory, or Fort Churchill and, surviving many wars with the French, in 1821 after some bloodshed absorbed the rival North-West Company, which had been erected after our conquest by British fur-traders of Montreal. Servants of both companies had done prodigies of exploration. David Thompson, for instance, over many years before 1812 had surveyed and mapped most of what became Manitoba and Saskatchewan, and crossed the Rockies to the Columbia and Kootenay rivers ; Alexander Mackenzie tracked the great stream bearing his name to the Arctic, and later by the Peace and Fraser rivers made his way to the Pacific. Many hardy generations, mostly of Scots, lived in the wilderness, searching for furs as far as the Yukon, among Indians whose chief glory was still in hunting the buffalo, and little settlements of *métis*, the half-breeds more often half-French than British, fringed the now well-used canoe routes from Hudson's Bay or Lake Winnipeg.

The bounds of the Company's grant were undefined, their monopoly was repellent to the leaders of Ontario who saw in westward extension their best hope, nor did those trading in the furs of wild animals wish to encourage closer human settlement. But in any case the Company could not cope with the scale of events. Though the Oregon treaty of 1846 saved its footing on Vancouver Island, discovery of gold and coal on the mainland brought in new numbers who asked representative government. In 1858 a new Crown Colony was set up of British Columbia, which in 1866 was linked with Vancouver Island. If here was the terminus of Canadian visions, much more urgently immediate must be the intervening space east of the Rockies, for Minnesota and other American States just south of the border were flooding with settlers, and by Lake Superior and the Red river American enterprise might capture the trade of the West. Some London financiers who wished to develop the Grand Trunk had a strong representative in Edward Watkin, who believed in extension to the Pacific also, while late in the '50's the government of Canada, claiming to have inherited the old French rights, challenged the Hudson Bay Company's title.

These different strands were pulled taut by the American Civil War. The Northern States' dislike of Britain was at its height, their Secretary of State Seward was ready for war, Irish Fenians threatened to invade Canada. When the reciprocity treaty ran out in 1864 the Americans let it expire, it was believed, as a lever to compel Canada to join the Republic; there was a resolution in Congress for peaceful annexation, a group on the frontier positively working for it, and in 1867 the Americans' purchase of Russian rights in Alaska closed another Canadian window on to the Pacific. But though needs of defence, and the economy of dealing with larger units, at last moved the British Cabinet from their lofty detachment, Canadian Confederation was mostly due to Canadian effort. In 1864 the fundamentals were accomplished, when George Brown and the Ontario Liberals volunteered to serve with Macdonald for this single purpose and when, by the initiative of McGee and the railway engineer Sandford Fleming, Canada was invited to confer with delegates of the Maritime provinces. At the Quebec conference that October agreement was reached on all essentials, Tilley and Charles Tupper from New Brunswick and Nova Scotia negotiating with Macdonald, Brown, Galt, Taché, and Cartier. But another two years passed before Canadian delegates assembled in London, for neither Newfoundland nor Prince Edward Island would come in, while it took all the influence of the Imperial government and Tupper's adroitness to overcome unwillingness in New Brunswick, and fiery obstruction by Joseph Howe. Certainly the last stage could hardly have been achieved except through the assistance of British ministers, and of the Church in Quebec. Its two natural sequels were the transfer of the Hudson Bay Company's rights to Canada in 1869, and in 1871 the admission of British Columbia as a province. In 1873 Prince Edward Island relented also, leaving Newfoundland the only British community outside the Dominion.

By the British North America Act of 1867 a new type of government was added to the Empire, in the federal Dominion of Canada. Though Macdonald had wished for closer union, nothing but a federal bond leaving self-government in local affairs could have reconciled either Quebec or the Maritimes, but warning was taken from the troubles of America to make the Dominion stronger than the Union, and the provinces much weaker than the American States. Certain specific powers were assigned to the provinces, direct taxation for example and public works, but the whole residue of powers went to the Dominion which would, further, appoint the provincial lieutenant-governors and judges and, subject to appeal to the Imperial Privy Council, could disallow provincial laws. If the Senate was organized to protect the provinces by giving equal representation to the three chief groupings, — Ontario, Quebec, and the combined Maritimes — representation in the Commons by population asserted a British racial supremacy. Yet, except for a supreme court of appeal created in 1875, the Dominion was given no federal courts.

In short, its constitution received no strictly federal character but bore rather that of a treaty, and its development has depended less on the letter of the law than on convention and interpretation. The distribution of members, for instance, is fixed by awarding to Quebec a perpetual basic figure of 65; without reference to the Imperial Parliament the Dominion cannot amend the Act of 1867; overlapping powers of Dominion and provinces, each of them sovereign bodies, have only been adjusted through the medium of the Privy Council.

In a country wrestling with sheer emergencies, of bridging rivers, growing food, satisfying settlers, and blasting mountains, politics must often be a rough and ready business, since government has in its hands the making of individual wealth. So that the early records of the Dominion have their darker side, nor was Macdonald the man to make them white. The true measure of his stature is that, with one five years' break from 1873, he remained Prime Minister from Confederation until 1891, which must be explained by much more than political arts. He had the statesman's first gift of managing other human beings; Howe himself in the end entered a Macdonald Cabinet. And he had a largeness, both of nature and vision, which his Liberal opponents had not; neither the upright wooden Alexander Mackenzie, the Prime Minister of 1873-8, nor the eloquent, fastidious, but factious Edward Blake. An electorate recognizes this scale and this staunchness, which enabled Macdonald to survive the scandal of 1873, of acceptance of party funds from contractors for the Pacific railway.

One moment of danger revealed how delicate a plant was the young Dominion, the Red river rebellion of 1869-70 led by Louis Riel. Round Winnipeg the French and half-French *métis* not only resented the transfer of their home to the Dominion, but feared for their land titles and their Catholic faith, and detested the new democratic type of settler. This discontent, being badly handled on the spot, might bring about either an Indian rising or some annexationist move from American pioneers. That it was settled speedily was much due to a few individuals, not least the Hudson's Bay representative Donald Smith, the future Lord Strathcona, but also to Macdonald's resolution in sending a military force under Wolseley, and his conciliatoriness in forming during 1870 a new province of Manitoba, with a due regard for separate Catholic schools. For another generation the rest of the prairies up to the Rockies continued as the North-West Territories, to whom in those early days government's best gift was the establishment of the North-West Mounted Police.

By the letter of the Act, Confederation was coupled with promises of improved transportation, both east and west. Helped by an Imperial guarantee, the inter-Colonial railway at length completed connection in 1876 between Halifax and the St. Lawrence. A railroad to the Pacific was a much greater proposition, but the commitment of 1867 was renewed as a definite pledge when British Columbia came into the Confederation. Its early years were obstructed by contention and scandal, the engineering difficulties were portentous, and costs gigantic, involving the thorny question of land grants and subsidies to the contracting companies. When Macdonald went down in 1873, the Mackenzie government continued the work but with a doubting spirit and ill-success, and it was not till 1880 that Macdonald came to terms with a new company, of which the ruling spirits were Donald Smith, J. J. Hill, and George Stephen, and the engineering minds were Van Horne and Sandford Fleming. In 1885 the first trains reached the Pacific, on all-Canadian soil.

By that time Canada's destiny was decided, though not perhaps by any great margin, or very long ago. Neither in East nor West was the annexationist temper extinct; many times over Canadian governments suggested a renewal of reciprocity to Washington, only to be rebuffed. The treaty of 1871, signed under severe pressure from the Gladstone government, convinced Canadians that the mother country would sacrifice their interests to get American good will, ceding, for example a perpetual right of navigation in the St. Lawrence as against a settlement of the *Alabama* claims. Bad harvests and deep depression in the '70's also drove Canada to seek a remedy in herself. Hence came about the ' Canada First ' national movement, and a demand for protection to safeguard Canadian industry, the banner under which Macdonald swept the elections of 1878.

Rising out of such accomplished fact and half-realized ideal, a new spirit about Empire was manifest by 1880. Disraeli, laying weight so often on ' an Imperial people ', had foreseen it and done something to foster it; not least by instilling this vision in the tenacious mind of the Queen. But it hardly had come about through the action of individual statesmen; much more by the amalgam of plain material interest and unconscious affections which made up Colonial sentiment. Self-government had removed any popular wish for separation in the Colonies; at home, a wish to let other Britons have what they desired, a growing cohesion in the face of rival Powers, and the unwavering claim of the middle class that British trade should be protected, combined to build up a defensive Imperialism, simply to hold in peace what they had won. It was not a system, had no high theory, and had grown in a score of different ways. It was seen in the poets and prose-poets of the age, Tennyson and Froude. It was seen in Dilke's Radical welcome for new communities; accepted in the fame of John Lawrence and great Indian administrators, now at the height of their autocracy; and exposed, under another form, in the national enthusiasm for Livingstone and the explorers. It had at least become so strong a thing that any British government which seemed to imperil or repudiate it would have to reckon with a new indignation.

CONTEMPORARY DATES

1850	Australian Governments Act.
1853	France takes New Caledonia.
1854	Burton and Speke in Somaliland.
1856	Speke on Victoria Nyanza.
	Livingstone on the Zambesi.
1857	The Mutiny.
	French conquest of Algeria.
1858	End of the East India Company.
1860	War in the Lebanon.
	British and French enter Pekin.
1861	Outbreak of American Civil War.
1863	General Gordon in China.
1865	Revolution in Jamaica.
1867	Federation of Canada.
	The United States buy Alaska.
1868	British army in Abyssinia.
1869	Opening of Suez Canal.
1871	Livingstone on the Congo.
1873	The slave market closed at Zanzibar.
	Russia conquers Khiva.
1874	Britain acquires Fiji.
1875	De Brazza extends the French Congo.
1877	The Queen proclaimed Empress of India.
1879	Formation of the Congo Free State.
1880	Roberts at Kandahar.
	The Transvaal Boers declare their independence.

CHAPTER VII

PERIL AND DECLINE, 1881–1914

I N this short quarter of a century fundamental changes, long prepared
and in 1914 not fully matured, affected the British State more gravely
than in any comparable period of time since the Reformation, leaving
on the mind, stamped with the assuredness and stability which had gone
before, a foreboding interrogative as to what the future might hold.
Forms and powers were all changed, spirit and outlook even more.
That Christian and classical culture, in which the English had been
nurtured, lost its pride of place. The town at last finally triumphed
over the countryside. Democracy, which every generation from Shakespeare to Wordsworth had rejected, made its victory sure. An Empire
of which Elizabethans had not dreamed and greater than that which
Rome had ruled, and the extension of Europe in overseas Imperialism,
challenged our political ideas, tested our institutions, and remoulded
our policy.

These influences, the velocity of which much increased with the
century's ending, were masked by the prestige of those who had
attained eminence earlier, and their long survival: of Tennyson till
1892, Huxley till 1895, Gladstone till 1898, the Queen till 1901, and
Salisbury till 1902. Not economically only, the race seemed to be living
on its capital, for equal successors did not replace the giants whose work
was done. Asquith and Lloyd George instead of Bright and Gladstone,
Balfour in lieu of Disraeli and Salisbury, Stevenson for George Eliot,
the Fabian Socialists in the room of Mill, — some elevated quality of
spirit seemed to have departed.

Those economic tendencies which had been gathering momentum
for a hundred years now rapidly advanced. The United Kingdom's
population, 31 million strong in 1871, passed 45 millions in 1911, of
whom nearly 80 per cent were concentrated in England and Wales, with
a density of 600 people to the square mile. In those two countries
roughly 80 per cent of the total lived in urban districts, often massed
in aggregates like the 4½ million of London, or the million apiece of
Glasgow and Birmingham. Indeed, in this generation one of the
greatest of all revolutions transformed Britain : that rural setting, within
which its arts and letters and political spirit had grown up, was broken
to pieces, and with it the beauty of country building and country crafts,
iron-work and lace-making, weaving and leather. The miracle, so long

deferred, of swift transportation came to pass, by sea and land from American prairies, and in import of refrigerated meat from the Argentine and Australia. Four million arable acres, £17 millions of landed rents, 150,000 agricultural labourers, disappeared; wheat, which so late as 1878 sold for 45s. the quarter, fell till it reached its lowest figure of under 23s. in 1894, and four-fifths of our wheat supply were now imported, together with 60 per cent of the butter consumed and 80 per cent of the cheese. If country wages were better than those of the '70's, they were at a wretched level in the southern counties, whose population was in some cases positively lower than fifty years before.

Though its internal balance had thus collapsed, economic revolution had given great power and riches to the nation. Our foreign trade amounted to £698 millions in 1880 but, allowing for a changed price level, about £1100 millions in 1913, while in the last year coal production, which in Gladstone's youth had ranged about 60 million tons, reached a peak of 287 millions. By 1880 steam had at length overtaken sailing craft, and in 1914 we still possessed 47 per cent of the world's iron and steel tonnage; 60 per cent of all Suez Canal traffic was British, and 65 per cent of India's imports. Our overseas investments were reckoned at over £1300 millions in 1885, indeed £226 millions were so spent in the single year 1912.

This great wealth, which increased the average individual income by about a third in this quarter-century, was better distributed, and the general lot had without doubt improved since mid-Victorian days. One proof of that may be found in the falling death-rate, and in particular the decline in infantile mortality. Such bettered health and homes must be connected with some plain economic facts; that working-class taxation had been halved between 1840–80, that real wages were better by 30 per cent at least in 1914 than in 1880, and that the Post Office and savings-banks deposits rose from the £30 millions of 1850 to more than £200 millions. Throughout the quarter of a century under discussion the pauperism officially relieved (which is not the same thing as poverty) very rarely reached 3 per cent of the population.

Outwardly society bore much the same aristocratic countenance as of old, to a degree barely credible to those who have witnessed a later change. Great Whig salons, Devonshire or Lansdowne House, still dominated society and politics, as they had under Fox and the Regent; the Church and the cadres of military officers were manned by much the same stocks as those who had won Waterloo or figured in Jane Austen's novels; formality of dress and regularity of church-going, the patriarchal village and a life of domestic service for its women, the graduates of the older universities and recruitment for the civil service at home and in India, all these changed little, to outward seeming, in the later Victorian age. Those were days when a Prime Minister's prestige was assisted by his horses winning the Derby, the golden age too of W. G. Grace and intense native patriotism in county cricket. Yet in so far as aristocracy rested on the land, it never in fact recovered from agricultural depression, while many tendencies were breaking the unity and dissolving the character of the propertied class.

Though till 1896 the period as a whole was one of falling prices, there were ever-increasing signs that the Free Trade era had evolved into a system which was both top-heavy and precarious. Foreign competition had obliterated our first easy supremacy. In 1880 the populations of the great industrial Powers, Britain, Germany, and the United States, were respectively in round figures, 35, 45, and 50 millions; but by 1911 they stood at 45, 64, and 91 millions. German steel output passed ours in the '90's, and ended twice as great; the growth in American exports was ours multiplied fivefold; the individual British miner produced 100 tons less a year, while the American hewer's product rose. Nor was agriculture the only shaky pillar in the British economy. Textiles had been nearly 60 per cent of our export values in 1860; by 1914 that was almost halved. The palmy days of Black Country iron were over, but the new districts nearer to the sea had not, by 1914, developed their full opportunities in basic steel. Moreover, one of Cobden's assumptions had been falsified, when first France, then Germany, and lastly America — especially by the McKinley tariff of 1890 — laid heavy duties on our goods. Excluded thus from their old primary markets, British manufacturers exploited Asia and Africa, but there too, as the period closed, appeared the beginnings of Japanese competition and the desire of India to protect her own textiles. British wealth, based in the first instance on a mass export of manufactured goods, tended henceforth to concentrate on those of higher finish and better quality, or to find its chief reward in investment and shipping services; to depend, that is, more and more on world conditions that were not within its own control. That instability, putting the fortunes of the urban millions in these islands at the mercy of gold production in South Africa, a slump in America, or an Indian famine, was certainly not lessened in a community which was allowing its own agriculture to sink or swim, as best it could.

Great, then, though our progress remained, its pace slackened. Whether considered as cause or as effect, the decline in the birth rate was important; from its highest recorded point of 36 per thousand in 1876, it fell smoothly but without faltering to 23 by 1913. What mattered more, the practice of birth-control that brought it about was most common among the upper and upper-middle classes; and the emigration of those vigorous stocks, and of artisans, reached a high level, rising from the annual average of some 50,000 in the '90's to 235,000 in 1907, — and higher still between 1911–13. There was a lag, almost a halt, in the growth of the national income after 1900, and a very distinct arrest of real wages, which in 1912 were not above the 1900 level, and in the miners' case probably below it. Housing development was checked too, and there were some dark social patches; nearly half the people of Scotland, for instance, lived in one- or two-room dwellings, and though the artisan had won a working week of 52 or sometimes 48 hours, the law permitted one of 70 and more for shop assistants. Public health could not be approved when a third of Army recruits were medically rejected, and when social investigators after 1900 declared that a third of the nation lived on, or below, a bare level of subsistence.

There were thus dangers of a slowing production, and some evils of a bad distribution, to which several causes were thought to be contributing; among them the conservatism of old-fashioned business, restrictions on work by trade unions, political threats to capital, and hostile tariffs. There was certainly a widening gap between the fabric of the State and the facts and ideals of society.

For though the third Reform Act of 1884 and the County Councils Act of 1888 extended the vote, and replaced the squires' local government by elected bodies, they did not accurately measure the change of social balance. Compulsory elementary education since 1870 — which in 1891 was also completely freed from school fees —was accompanied by the making of many modern universities, Manchester leading the way in the '80's, followed before 1909 by Wales, Birmingham, Liverpool, Leeds, Sheffield, and Bristol. The space between elementary and university, of technical and secondary education, had been too long neglected, but public money was found in several devious ways, and after the Act of 1902 rapid progress was made. By such avenues, opened up in a new urban life and reinforced by a cheap press, there grew up a new social democracy, which had never warmly accepted the Utilitarian and economists' notions of *laisser faire*. Gladstone once lamented that modern Liberalism favoured ' what they call construction ', ' taking into the hands of the State the business of the individual ', and the decline that this meant in ' public economy '. Our democracy had taken its views not so much from the German exile Karl Marx, who died in England in 1883, but in part from what Chamberlain had done at Birmingham and in his Radical crusade, in part from the Nonconformist chapels, and in part from Ruskin and William Morris, who taught that the good life, like good art, could not be measured by the volume of wealth, or achieved by a jostling competition.

Though Disraeli's social policies and public education meant higher expenditure, the average Budget of the early '70's of £65 millions hardly rose over £87 millions in the ten years after, and the real momentum came much later, between the £132 millions of 1901 and the £209 millions of 1914. In that increase the costs of defence had

risen by some £20 millions, but the civil estimates still more in proportion, and the State's enhanced power, both in central and local
government, was the outstanding fact as the new century began.
The Board of Agriculture was created in 1889, the Board of Education
in 1899, while the 1911 census showed how the number of public
servants had doubled within twenty years. Means were found to pay
for this new machinery through the rise of the income-tax from 6d. in
1888 to 1s. 2d. in 1909, and the creation of death-duties and surtax;
that is, in a transference of the burden from indirect to direct taxation,
and in taxing the richer minority for the majority's needs.

    While Conservative and Liberal governments slowly extended the
State's functions by working piecemeal at each urgent problem, a
doctrine of Socialism welled up from below; through Hyndman's
Social Democratic Federation, Morris' Socialist League, and the Fabian
Society led by Sidney and Beatrice Webb and Bernard Shaw. The
book of the American Henry George on *Progress and Poverty* inspired a
school who would tax the ' unearned increment ' of property values, and
assert national control of the land. Out of the miseries of the East End
of London and the dock strike of 1889 came the Salvation Army,
Toynbee Hall, and a swarm of philanthropic enterprises, and a passion
in many outside the working class to bring about a greater equality.
Two instruments of working-class effort combined to carry that doctrine
into political effect; the trade unions, whose membership rose from 1½
millions in 1892 to some 4 millions in 1914, and the Labour party which,
after much earlier striving led by the Scotsman Keir Hardie, came into
formal existence in 1900. The election of 53 Labour members to
Parliament in 1906 was the first decisive proof of this new power.

    Another force was running its course, parallel with democracy, and
this was Imperialism; indeed, in the hands of Dilke and Chamberlain
they were allies. Each took a lofty view of the State, each was bound
to clash with *laisser-faire* economics. Imperialism owed something to
the perception of Disraeli, the writings of historians like Seeley and
Froude, and the passionate convictions of Kipling, the Anglo-Indian
man of letters, and Cecil Rhodes, the South African adventurer and
idealist. But it was also bound up with sentiment fired by the Queen's
two Jubilees, and bonds between many hundred thousand emigrants
and their folk at home, while it was riveted by many clashes in Africa
and the threat of German militarism. Self-preservation and obvious
interest thus built reinforcing walls round what had been, of old, rather
a matter of honour or prestige. For over a third of British exports, and
over 70 per cent of British emigrants, went in 1913 to the Empire and
Colonies.

    If much had changed materially or in outward aspect since Peel
administered and Cobden resisted, the mental change had been greater

still since Newman and Mill had led rival schools of thinking. This quarter-century was full of life but of a life that had lost unity, and perhaps lost some sense of direction. It was a more impersonal life; in which inherited family firms were steadily turning into public companies, administered by experts and financed by a distant anonymous horde of shareholders. Amalgamations and trusts concentrated masses of capital as against large trade unions, each embracing the country as a whole; swift transportation, by steam and electricity and at last the motor-car, dissolved local units, and shuttled millions of human atoms in to work and out to sleep. This teeming loose-seated population was fast outgrowing the spiritual fixities which had persisted since the Reformation. Darwinism and natural science had destroyed the foundations of faith, criticism denied the inspiration of Scripture, and the public teachers of educated Britons, — Matthew Arnold, Huxley, John Morley the editor of the *Fortnightly Review*, Froude, Leslie Stephen, or the Oxford philosopher T. H. Green — taught a faith in which Christian dogma made no part. The Christian standard of conduct was strong — strong enough to drive both Dilke and Parnell from power — but church going and Sunday observance no longer ruled the mass of the people. Within the national Church the principles of the Oxford Movement may have won a majority of believers, but their effort to harmonize reason and revelation, as for instance in the *Lux Mundi* essays composed by Gore and the ablest High-church minds, recovered little of the ground lost with the laity.

In literature no single mind held the sovereign position of Scott, or even of Macaulay. That historian's assumption of the triumph of Liberalism was no more unquestioned, for his generation's belief in progress and tolerance was shaken in their successors. By the end of the age even the generalizing principles of Darwin's school and the idealist philosophers were both yielding to revolutionary questionings, to discoveries in forces of matter, radioactivity, physics and psychology, which made the destiny of the individual and the nature of his being, even the time and space within which human history was transacted, emerge as more mysterious, puny, and unprotected. One effect of the new conditions was that learning became more specialized and less catholic, and that the arts and letters once unified by national figures, the portrait-painters, Scott and Dickens, Tennyson and Macaulay, were divided into groups and categories.

Between some date like 1890 and Edward VII's death in 1911, we seem to find a culture in doubt, even in decline. The moral purpose on which Ruskin had insisted was denied. There was an amorality in some brilliant contributions, a disillusionment about Morley and Thomas Hardy and Samuel Butler; something most unconstructive in the would-be realists Wells and Shaw, and a new cynical and accomplished drama. The atmosphere of the Edwardian court, some motives in the Imperialism of Rhodes' school, and new wealth easily won in speculation, lowered the code of the mid-Victorians, while there was something sterile in the intellectual circles of the ruling class in the heyday of Balfour and Asquith. There was a deeper and more incalculable shifting of values in the changed relation of the sexes. Women's emancipation included their competition with men in the professions, relief from the severities of the old law for married women and their property, a rapid growth of divorce, a fierce demand for political equality, all of which must overturn the Victorian family ideal.

More damaging at the moment, more potent in the long run, was the mentality of a democracy, armed with new powers civic and scientific, but only lately given opportunities of full education. Human pity touched them nearly, they were played upon by gusts of emotion, and sensationalism was given them by those who wished to capture their minds. Under the special influence of Alfred Harmsworth, a vast cheap press aimed at circulation before accuracy, and popularity before a standard; a power capable of making a public opinion, but a power for evil if irresponsibly used.

By 1914 the paradox of democracy was not yet declared in Britain, whose political forms were not yet totally democratic; the paradox that equality is apt to destroy liberty, and that democratic power tends to coincide with the physical force of numbers and to find expression in dictatorship. It might be that the past history of the nation, something in its inherited character, the balance of its social forces, or the needs of its Empire, might hold this paradox at bay. All that could be said in 1914 was that a moral and material revolution had demolished nearly all the ideals and arts of life of our earlier history.

CHAPTER VIII

GLADSTONE AND THE IRISH QUESTION
1880–1886

AFTER many protestations that he must find a quiet space before death to shake off the world's trammels, at the age of seventy-one Gladstone was recalled to power by what he regarded as a divine call. He obeyed this call, indeed, for thirteen years to come.

His second ministry, though powerful in individual names, proved highly divided and unconstructive. Six of its original fourteen members came from his usual nearest counsellors, the Whig peers, who were also perfectly represented in the Commons by Hartington, while the new Radicalism only forced itself in at the bayonet's point, and even so Chamberlain was not reinforced by Dilke till the end of 1882. Bright, a Radical of an older school but now enfeebled, resigned when force was used in Egypt; within two years the Irish crisis drove out Argyll, Forster, and (outside the Cabinet) Lansdowne. Harcourt was a vital politician, a masterful debater, but insular and turbulent. In short, Gladstone alone held the Cabinet together.

Two facts from the first strained and exhausted him. The Queen's hostility was unceasing and indecent. She had done her best to keep him out of power, asking her secretaries if this ' half-mad firebrand ', who had encouraged Russia to imperil our place in Europe, was fit to lead her Empire ? Again, Disraeli had made her his confidant in the interior relations of Cabinet; Gladstone, who felt his very real loyalty ill used, brought her long arguments or Cabinet decisions, but concealed from her all knowledge of the process. But old age was confirming the Queen in her every aspect. Jealously she excluded her heir from the inner citadel of politics, fought for her influence over the disposal of the armed forces, and harassed the Prime Minister by letters innumerable, denouncing Chamberlain as ' a most dangerous man ' or defending the Lords. On the other hand, she several times displayed her insight as to the needs of Empire with a passion for the national prestige which reproached her Cabinet's indecision.

And, secondly, Gladstone had outlived his generation. Granville at the Foreign Office, courteous and dilatory, was terribly outmatched by Bismarck. Harcourt, a typical mid-Victorian, detested all notions of Empire. Finally Gladstonian Liberalism resisted, or was blind to, the social armies behind Radicalism who held up Harcourt and the Whigs as representatives of the propertied wealth that impeded progress. This conflict of two societies cut across the Opposition also, for Randolph Churchill and his small following, christened ' the Fourth Party ', defied the lead in the Commons of the excellent uninspired Stafford Northcote, and would answer Chamberlain with a new conception of Tory democracy.

Upon the government, thus set between two generations, fell a sequence of harsh ordeals; liquidation of Disraeli's foreign policy, a necessity for decision in South Africa, new burdens in Egypt, contemptuous hostility from Bismarck, Russian aggression, and in Ireland a disorder amounting to civil war. These tested their unity and capacity for action, with dire effect, and it is not surprising that their domestic legislation was so meagre. Urgent schemes for reordering the government of London, counties, and boroughs were crowded out, so too was most of Chamberlain's desired programme at the Board of Trade. Months of time went in disputation whether the atheist Charles Bradlaugh should be allowed to take the oath, which the House decided against him; many hours passed in organized obstruction from the Irish, to curb which the government in 1881 upset the Commons' old procedure by creating the closure. So that their sole legislation of substance was a third reform of the franchise and redistribution of seats in 1884, to which all Liberals were pledged, and which no Conservative of Churchill's type would resist. One controversy turned on the point whether the bill should apply to Ireland where, Hartington predicted, it would enthrone a Nationalist party; another, and larger, was bound up with the personality of Chamberlain, who made persistence with the bill the condition of his remaining in the government, attacked owners of inherited wealth as those ' who toil not, neither do they spin ', and cried out for popular control of the land. When the Whig section gave way, there still was the landed interest in the Lords, obstinately led by Salisbury against this ' Jack Cade ', and that, in turn, roused a Radical clamour to ' mend or end ' the peers' veto. In the long run, thanks both to the Queen and Gladstone, the bill reached an agreed settlement. It would extend to Ireland, but on the other hand the Conservatives had their way in establishing single-member constituencies. By extending the householder vote of 1867 from the towns to the counties, the electorate was raised by about two millions; seventy-nine small towns lost their members, thirty-six others lost one member out of two. This advance towards democracy was moderate, by no means satisfying to Radicalism, but it was not on such domestic issues that this government was to be judged and fall.

Forty years had passed since Gladstone had written of ' Ireland, that cloud in the west, that coming storm ', and nothing had conjured the storm away. No utterance of his in the '70's committed him, though some phrases about local government alarmed the Whigs; his intensity was always apt to fix wholly on one matter at a time and, being wrapped up successively in Papal infallibility, finance, and foreign affairs, led him to neglect what might have been for Ireland some useful reforms. But to ignore Ireland became out of the question with the agricultural depression beginning in 1877, for low prices and bad seasons, failure of the potato crop, and a calling-in of debts brought about a renewal of eviction — of 10,000 persons in 1880 alone — and, with eviction, soaring figures of crime. It was an old circle, but now revolving in a changed Ireland.

'Home Rule', as interpreted earlier under the genial lead of the conservative Isaac Butt, amounted to little more than an endeavour to induce the Commons to give Ireland more liberal treatment, with perhaps some federal basis for the conduct of purely Irish affairs. It came into very different hands in 1879 on Butt's death, those of Charles Stewart Parnell, descended from English Protestant landowners in Wicklow with a long anti-Unionist record, son of an American mother, and inspired by a cold hatred of English ascendancy. This singular man, intellectually so uninterested and humanly so remote, judged politics purely in terms of force. If the British had enough resolution, he believed they could coerce Ireland; as it was, he meant to coerce them. He set to work on two fronts; at Westminster, to make Parliament unbearable by obstruction until Ireland's claims were heard, and to bid one British party up against the other; at Dublin, to sap government by breaking the landlords. Hence his alliance with the Land League, founded in 1879 by a lately released Fenian prisoner, Michael Davitt. Eviction and unjust rents were to be stopped by force; the guilty party, whether landlord or new tenant, must be cut off from all human touch, Parnell taught, 'as if he were a leper of old'; which was the device christened from one particular victim, Captain 'Boycott'. And beyond the Land League, contact was made with a third circle of conspiracy, inspired and financed in large part by Irish-Americans, and terminating in the secret brotherhoods of Clan-na-Gael and 'Invincibles', whose means were dynamite and assassination. This was the situation inherited by the Gladstone Cabinet; war on the soil, and a breakdown of the jury system and civil government. Parnell had become something like the ruler of a foreign State, who in America was escorted by Irish regiments and invited to address Congress.

They were thus involved in a hard dilemma, simultaneously to pass remedial reform and to vindicate law and order. Inevitably it divided the Cabinet, between the Whig elements such as Spencer, Hartington, and Harcourt, and the Radical wing led by Chamberlain and Dilke, who argued that coercion must be abandoned if Ireland was to be conciliated. All Gladstone's own instincts must lean to this second course, yet all his mental training and his dominance in Cabinet inclined him against the Radicals. From this interior struggle, and from absorption in Egypt and the franchise bill, proceeded the delays, vacillation, and compromises which heaped up fuel for revolution.

The Lords having destroyed a first attempt to compensate victims of eviction, slowly Gladstone during 1881 arrived at the Land Act, built upon the ' three F's ' of fair rents, free sale, and fixity of tenure. His masterly parliamentary powers were, for the last time, triumphant. To fix rents for fifteen years by public tribunals, and to protect such tenants from eviction, was to revolutionize the British conception of property. But the Act had large omissions, — as of the 130,000 tenants whose rents were in arrears — and was coupled with a stiff coercion Act, giving to the Lord-Lieutenant most arbitrary powers. Parnell's reply was to use the Land League against the Land Act in order to force better terms, and in October he was arrested and put in Kilmainham jail.

1882 began with strenuous efforts for a settlement; by the ' Kilmainham treaty ', inspired notably by Chamberlain, Parnell was set free on an understanding that he would co-operate in checking crime, in return for a wiping out of rent arrears and an end of coercion. Rather than accept this, both Cowper the Lord-Lieutenant and Forster, Irish Secretary, resigned; Spencer replacing the first and Hartington's brother, Frederick Cavendish, the second. But within a week of Parnell's release Cavendish, together with Burke the Under-Secretary, was murdered by the ' Invincibles' ' knives in Phoenix Park. Whence came yet another coercion Act, a ghastly series of murders, cattle-maiming, killing of informers, and on the English side a refusal to hear of more concession. Yet under Spencer's firm government the Land Act bore some fruit. Parnell himself, distracted by his love for Mrs. O'Shea, was not prepared to allow the extremists to wreck his purpose of extorting an Irish Parliament from the rivalry of British parties. Vote by ballot, as he had long ago perceived, gave him his weapon, while the franchise Act of 1884 made his hold on Irish seats secure. Having defied the Catholic bishops by exploiting crime to manipulate British legislation, he would now defy the criminals by exploiting British party.

It would be shallow to understate the sincerity of the party leaders. Long before the crisis there were Conservatives of high standing, like W. H. Smith, who advocated State-aided land purchase to stabilize the peasantry, or who with Hicks-Beach attacked unceasing coercion. Subject to the supremacy of the Imperial Parliament, Churchill in one camp would go as far as Chamberlain in the other to meet the wish for local self-goverment, though both men were ardent tacticians who discerned one instrument of party victory in the Irish vote. But with the existing government no progress could be made ; the Whig element defeated one such effort in 1880, and early in 1885, against Gladstone and all the commoners in the Cabinet except Hartington, resisted the scheme Chamberlain had negotiated with Parnell for an Irish National Council, to be elected by representative boards and controlling land, education, and public works. The Chamberlain wing were on the eve of resignation when in June, nominally on their Budget but in fact by the Irish vote, government were defeated and resigned, on a division in which seventy-six Liberals abstained.

For the next half-year the situation was even more demoralizing, for Salisbury, the new Prime Minister, could not dissolve till the new register was completed and, pending the election, must manœuvre with his minority. In that memorable phase the decisive actors were Salisbury, Gladstone, and Parnell. Salisbury, like his rival, directed a party deeply divided, but as yet with less than Gladstone's authority, for he had only lately won recognition as leader, his own interests lay in foreign affairs, and with Tory democracy he was always out of tune. Yet his Cabinet's composition represented a considerable triumph for that wing and for Churchill, whose ally Hicks-Beach had the lead of the Commons, Northcote being ' kicked upstairs ' to the Lords. On Ireland Churchill's policy was to offer educational and financial reform, ministers began to criticize Spencer's coercion, and their first measure was the Ashbourne Act, advancing the whole price to peasants who wished to purchase their land.

All the evidence goes to suggest that Salisbury would never have agreed to Home Rule ; he was not prepared, he insisted, to repeat the rôle of Peel in 1846, or of Disraeli in 1867. Yet his personal responsibility was great, for the Lord-Lieutenant he appointed was Carnarvon, who had legislated on Canadian federation and attempted it for South Africa, and whom he now permitted not only to speak publicly of reconciliation but, unknown to the Cabinet, to hold a secret meeting with Parnell. On the Irishman the effect was natural, that he now hoped to get much more than Chamberlain's central board, and henceforth his speeches declared for an independent Parliament.

By August 1885 Gladstone had convinced himself that such a demand could not be resisted, above all if, as he expected, the new elections gave Parnell a great majority. He was aware of the Carnarvon interview, indignant at the Conservative attacks on Spencer, and his Whig colleagues saw with consternation how his mind was veering ; through Mrs. O'Shea he invited Parnell to say what he wanted. Another paramount motive governed his action this year, the future of his party, which open differences between Whigs and Radicals threatened to destroy. To keep it at one through the election, and to deal with the Irish question, which that election might make of ' commanding Imperial necessity ', he would keep a fast hold on the lead.

These two questions were bound together in the personality of Chamberlain, now undisputed leader of the Left wing, for Dilke was this summer caught up in the adultery charge which killed his political future. Gladstone was now seventy-six, but Chamberlain only forty-nine years old, and his election programme was that of a younger Liberalism; the ' unauthorized programme ', which held forth taxation for social purposes, manhood suffrage, compulsory acquisition of land for small-holdings, reformed local government, disestablishment, and free education. If some such essentials were not accepted, he would not take office. As for Ireland, he had broken off negotiation with Parnell and repudiated his claim for a separate legislature; the maximum he could contemplate being ' Home Rule all round ', by some federal arrangement of subordinate councils under the Imperial Parliament. The youth of Liberalism, a youthful Lloyd George included, were flocking to his banner, which might well destroy Gladstone's leadership.

By mid-December the election results were declared. The agricultural labourer had rallied to Radicalism, the Liberals had a majority of 86 over the Conservatives, but it was not the independent majority for which Gladstone had appealed. For Parnell had given the Tories many boroughs through the Irish vote, and had himself won 86 Home Rule seats in Ireland. At that very moment Gladstone's son Herbert, alarmed lest Chamberlain should dominate the party, allowed the press to publish the so-called ' Hawarden kite ', declaring that both his father and Spencer were ready for Home Rule. This was true enough, as Chamberlain had long suspected, but the revelation embarrassed the strategy which Gladstone had adopted, which was to induce Salisbury to legislate on Home Rule, with his support. In actual fact, the Cabinet had already decided to drop contact with Parnell, and to accept Carnarvon's resignation. Gladstone had kept Chamberlain at arm's length, concealing the degree of his own conversion; moreover, when he let it be known that he was pressing Salisbury to act, he strengthened Parnell's power to bargain. He was, in short, uninterested in — even hostile to — Chamberlain's social policy, and wholly possessed by Ireland, while Chamberlain privately denounced his scheme as ' death and damnation '.

If Gladstone's secretiveness demoralized his party, in January 1886 he was forced to show his hand, when Carnarvon's resignation and announcement of a coercion bill showed that Salisbury and his party meant to stand by the Union. On the 26th, selecting a small amendment by Chamberlain's follower Jesse Collings on the need for small-holdings — nicknamed ' three acres and a cow ' — Opposition ejected the government by a majority of 79. But 18 Liberals voted with Salisbury, and another 76 abstained.

So Gladstone, forming his third government, had the chance of producing the policy on which, privately, he had been bent almost since he left office seven months before. His reversal of view had destroyed his previous Cabinet; neither Hartington nor Goschen, Bright nor Henry James would serve — Chamberlain and Trevelyan consented only to wait and see what shape his bill would take, and that shape might already be guessed from his choice of a Home Ruler, John Morley, as Irish Secretary. Nothing could conceal the truth that he lay at the mercy of Parnell, with whom and Morley he prepared the bill; refusing Chamberlain the place he wished at the Colonial Office, he treated him as politically suspect. Abandoning any federal basis, the bill proposed to withdraw Irish members from Westminster, and to set up a single-chamber Irish Parliament with full control over all subjects, except those expressly reserved to the Imperial Parliament — foreign affairs and defence, trade and customs; thus leaving to the Irish government powers over the police and appointment of judges and magistrates. In March Chamberlain with Trevelyan resigned, taking as his tactical demand the retention of Irish members at Westminster. But his objections went much further, to the control of law and police, and the forcible subordination of Ulster to a Dublin parliament. He objected, furthermore, to Gladstone's second measure, a bill to buy out the Irish landlords by advancing British credits to a Home Rule government.

Not very justly Gladstone vowed he was appealing from ' the spirit and power of class ' to ' the upright sense of the nation ', but whatever the nobility or even the necessity of his objective, his method is hard to defend, while some grounds against his bill were very real. Forsaking equality of treatment between different sections of the kingdom, he had hidden his opinion from colleagues and electorate over many months, and now asked his party to swallow the policy of Parnell, who had spattered them with abuse and lost them many seats. The particular solutions he put forward could hardly have lasted long; Parnell was in active protest against the proportion of Imperial expenditure, of $\frac{1}{15}$, to be met by Ireland; how long, again, would an Irish tenants' Parliament have paid the 4 per cent interest on the credits for land purchase, or accepted taxation from an Imperial Parliament in which they would be unrepresented ? and would not Ulster agree with Churchill's slogan, that ' Ulster would fight and Ulster would be right ' ? In any event, Gladstone's conversion asked a political impossibility of his party and the British peoples; to forget in a trice the Land League and murder and boycott, to obliterate their Protestant bias and his own declaration for a settlement in independence of the

Parnellite vote, and to entrust their Imperial security to forces long hostile and still untried.

That this fateful question was bandied between British parties was deplorable, and that neither party shines in the annals of 1885-6 is clear enough, but his method destroyed his own party; not only the Whigs left him, but Bright's immense influence reinforced Chamberlain's. When in June the bill was beaten by 30 votes in the Commons, 93 Liberals voted against it; when in July Gladstone went to the country, 316 Conservatives and 78 Liberals Unionist were returned, as against 191 Liberals and 85 Irish Nationalists. At the end of a year's convulsion the old grouping of parties was thus shattered, and Salisbury was installed, for six years, at the head of an incipient coalition, whose character only events would determine. If the Whig element was destroyed, so too for the present the Radical social programme was paralysed. Rather than accept Gladstonian Home Rule, Chamberlain had sacrificed an almost certainty of becoming the next Liberal Prime Minister, and now, wresting his faithful Birmingham area from the Liberal machine, moved into a desert between the parties.

Simultaneously other causes besides Ireland had wounded Gladstone's fortune and fame.

CONTEMPORARY DATES

1881	Murder of the Czar Alexander II.
	Gambetta forms a ministry in France.
	France takes over Tunis.
	Death of Beaconsfield and Carlyle.
1882	Italy enters the Triple Alliance.
	Death of Gambetta, Garibaldi, and T. H. Green.
1883	French expansion in Madagascar and Tonkin.
	Maxim invents his gun.
	Death of Marx, Turgenev, and Wagner.
1884	Congo Conference in Berlin.
	Russia takes Merv.
	Founding of the Fabian Society.
1885	Russia at Penjdeh.
	Death of Gordon.
	Gold found in the Transvaal.
	Cleveland becomes President of the United States.

CHAPTER IX

SOUTH AFRICA, EGYPT, AND THE SUDAN

HAVING divided British democracy by his obsession with Ireland, Gladstone's course also ran counter to the second growing force of the age, British Imperialism. Taken together, his policies excluded his party from power for all but three of the twenty years ending in 1905.

The outstanding international event of the late nineteenth century was the partition of Africa between the Powers, a process which, though not fully launched by 1880, was already in use by the diplomatic master at Berlin as one means of dividing his enemies. Though Bismarck was uninterested in colonies as such, to embarrass Britain and to stimulate German trade and prestige he took advantage of our weak Foreign and Colonial Ministers, Granville and Derby; whence resulted in 1884–5 the German protectorate of south-west Africa, the seizure of Togoland and the Cameroons higher up the west coast, and on the east a German company mastering the hinterland of Zanzibar. Within this frame must be painted the chronicle of this government, on which are inscribed two words most injurious to its fame — Majuba and Khartoum.

Carnarvon had set forth his African policies at a bad moment for the Imperial government, which in 1877–8 was entangled in agricultural depression, danger of war with Russia, and a certainty of war in Afghanistan. And no man was more averse than Hicks-Beach, his successor at the Colonial Office, to extension of territory or war expenditure. Though our objects were morally excellent, and proved in the long run indispensable, to bring South Africa under one government and this not least in order to enforce one native policy, our measures were premature, our means ill-chosen, and our resolution faltering. All of which ended in a bad example of a bad thing, a retreat from incurred obligations under the stigma of defeat.

Federation had been damaged already by Carnarvon's attempt, via Natal and the Transvaal, to sidetrack the plain unwillingness of the Cape and the Orange Republic, and was killed outright by Shepstone's forcible annexation of the Transvaal in 1877, antagonizing leading Afrikanders at the Cape such as Hofmeyr and de Villiers, President Brand at Bloemfontein, and all the moderate element who hitherto had favoured union. Yet strong reasons for annexation could be found in

984

the hopeless Transvaal finances and native wars threatening its life; and yet stronger reasons against reversing it, once done. Gladstone's government therefore in 1880 declared it would be maintained. Many Boers were not unwilling, even Kruger himself hesitated longer than others like Joubert, but annexation had been coupled with promises that they should be governed in their own way, and through their own tongue. Nothing of this was done. Shepstone proved a stiffly incompetent ruler of white men, while the military governors who followed him advised against self-government. But practical reasons counted as much in this story as racial sentiment. Generous financial help and a railway policy, which might have accomplished much, were not forthcoming; British troops, a bare 4000 in Africa, were first engaged in Kaffir war and then covered with failure in Zululand.

This Zulu war of 1879 was the doing of the High Commissioner Bartle Frere, who put to a most unwilling Cabinet the propositions that annexations up to the Portuguese frontier were inevitable on both coasts, and that the Zulus must be dealt with once for all. Assisted by the absence of any direct cable between London and Capetown, he despatched that ultimatum which led to the murderous defeat at Isandlwana, and only the Queen and the Prime Minister stopped his recall there and then. As it was, a censure of his measures by Disraeli and his part-supersession by Wolseley were signs of retreat, which outweighed our victory (July 1879) over Cetewayo at Ulundi and, taken with Gladstone's Midlothian speeches, encouraged Kruger's group to hope that the annexation of their country might also be reversed.

Another year passed, the reforms promised did not materialize, our military governors so far disbelieved in resistance that they reduced garrisons, and then, late in 1880, taking advantage of the Cape being entangled in a Basuto war, the Boers rose. Defeating General Colley once at Laing's Nek, in February 1881 Joubert's marksmen annihilated him and his force at Majuba, and in July the Pretoria Convention handed back their country to the victors. The battle had been fought in the middle of armistice negotiations, and the Cabinet were probably right not to withdraw concessions previously decided. But though the root of evil lay in our inaction during 1879–80, the effect of surrendering, after defeat, what had been denied before it, was deadly. Surrender was indeed wrapped up in the formula of 'suzerainty', with a British claim to rule Boer relations with foreign States, while other clauses purported to satisfy our ideal of protecting the natives; these safeguards, however, and the word 'suzerainty' were dropped in the amending London Convention of 1884. True, in the same year hard facts vindicated some of Frere's maxims, proving that to abdicate intervention in native Africa was impossible, for the Crown took over

Basutoland and South Bechuanaland as protectorates, at the same time checking both Boer and German ambitions by annexing St. Lucia Bay. But South African unity, and hence unity in handling the native question, had disappeared; Kruger's republic was entrenched, while the Afrikander Bond party at the Cape set out to get rid of British paramountcy.

While this ancient, perpetually evaded, problem was so left incomplete and inglorious, the Cabinet took responsibility for a portentous addition to the burden of Empire by the occupation of Egypt. Our direct interests there, as the key of our route to India, were multiplied tenfold since Disraeli's acquisition of major control in the Suez Canal, and were forced into the open by the atrocious misgovernment of the Khedive Ismail, bankruptcy, and his deposition in 1878. With that began a period of ' condominium ' with France, whose historic stake in the Levant was great, and whose zeal for the bondholders of the Egyptian debt much exceeded our own; yet the only alternatives to this uneasy partnership were, as Salisbury pointed out, either to stand aside, or to take sole control. This foreign sway, insisting on reform before satisfying vested interests but also inclined to think of the European bondholder before the Egyptian taxpayer, necessarily swelled Moslem and Nationalist feeling, which was directed not only against the Europeans, but the Turks and Armenians surrounding the young Khedive, Abbas. Steady, agreed policy, which was indispensable, broke down on the faction of French politics, Gambetta, its initiator, falling from power in 1882 and his successor Freycinet drawing back in fear of Germany. An Egyptian colonel, Arabi Pasha, led the Nationalist movement and demanded a constitution, whose wilder followers murdered many Europeans and trained their guns on the allied fleets. The French declining to intervene, in July the British bombarded Alexandria; from which first step, taken to protect life and property, flowed the long British occupation.

This was a sore matter for a Liberal ministry, since Arabi's crusade could be represented, with part truth, as a basis for self-government. On the other hand, Egypt was vital to the security of the Canal; it was full not only of international wealth but of Christian communities of Greeks, Copts, and Syrians; and in all sincerity our government wished to restore the Khedive's authority and ' Egypt for the Egyptians '. That done, as this and many later Cabinets protested, we should withdraw. A first stage was taken successfully in Wolseley's easy victory in September over Arabi at Tel-el-Kebir, and a second late in 1883 when Sir Evelyn Baring was appointed as British agent. France and Italy both refusing to co-operate, we acted alone, but still admitted Turkish suzerainty and would not declare a protectorate.

To restore a government quite devoid of law, honesty, revenue, or a disciplined army, must anyhow take much time, but we were also at the mercy of a geographical fact, that Egypt depended for bare life on the Nile, and security in the Nile on peace in the Sudan. That vast area, spreading east to the Red Sea and south to the great Lakes, and only nominally conquered by Egypt in 1819, had under her misgovernment become a model of misery, a market for slave caravans, a hive of Arab fighting-men and petty tyrants. Out of its fanaticism rose in 1881 the Mahdi, ' the expected one ' or Messiah, in one Mohamed Ahmed, who from an island in the White Nile above Khartoum declared that the Prophet himself had bidden him lead a *jehad* against unbelievers; a war in which Egyptians and Turks also should be overthrown, and Mecca return to its old glory. In 1882 his forces overran the province west of the river, Kordofan, and in November 1883 an Egyptian army, under a British commander Hicks, was ambushed and exterminated.

So began an ever-extending responsibility of the British government, which could have stopped this rash expedition by a word. They stood aside and now found themselves forced by clamour at home to save the Egyptian garrisons in the Sudan, and indeed forced to employ a particular instrument, Charles Gordon. Never more than in this episode were the demerits of parliamentary government so cruelly exposed.

This colonel of engineers had first made his name in leading an ' ever-victorious ' army in Chinese service against rebels; since then he had served Egypt in the Sudan between 1874–80, far to the south of Khartoum; suppressing slavery, building the first elements of a government, never out of danger. His fearlessness, his charmed life, and contempt for the world's honours had made him a man of legend; the more wondered at because, in an age of dwindling faith, he acted and spoke openly as a man moved by one motive, that he was but the tool of a divine worker, ' the dust under His feet ', with something of Cromwell's feeling that he had been accepted into grace. This mystical hero, guided by impulse and contradictory moods, stood at a far distant pole from Baring, our watchful methodical servant at Cairo, who had demurred to his appointment, accepting it only under the pressure of government and public opinion.

Government policy, and one inevitable in view of British feeling and Egyptian weakness, was the evacuation of the Sudan. But having instructed Gordon to concert with Baring, and allowed him to be named governor-general of the Sudan with orders to bring out the garrisons and refugees, when they found that their own vague handling might involve military action, they accused him of departing from instructions. His request, backed by Baring, for the employment of Zebehr Pasha was refused, in deference to the House of Commons, for Zebehr had been a great slave-trader — though to abandon the Sudan was plainly to abandon it to slavery. Having sent Gordon by the Nile to Khartoum, where in March 1884 he was shut in by the Mahdi's overwhelming numbers, they refused his proposal that the forces at Suakin should be used to force open the eastern route to the Nile at Berber. His arguments that evacuation would mean fighting, and therefore reinforcements, were backed in March by Baring's warning that it was time to prepare a relieving force; Gladstone and Harcourt led a Cabinet section against it, and it was not till August that an ultimatum from Hartington compelled them to decide. They found reasons for their dilatoriness by fastening on Gordon's phrases, such as ' smashing up the Mahdi ', or by taking offence at his cry that to abandon the garrisons would be ' indelible disgrace '.

So, disagreeing with Gordon but not recalling him, nothing could be more purblind than Gladstone's bland insistence that Gordon was in no danger, or that war in the Sudan meant war on a people ' rightly struggling to be free '; this, of a fearful whirlwind of torture, death, disease, and lust, which in the next two decades was to obliterate three-quarters of the population; at a moment when Baring had reproached government as ' deaf to humanity and honour ', and when Gordon with only two other Englishmen held out in a siege of 317 days. But many eyes at home were fixed rather on the franchise bill than the Nile.

At length in October Wolseley's force set out from Wady Halfa, and on 17th January 1885 won a desperate victory at Abu Klea. On the 26th, storming in at an angle which the ebbing Nile waters had made it impossible to refortify, the dervishes entered Khartoum, killed Gordon and massacred all whom they could find. The first British steam-boats arrived two days later.

National indignation was burning, the government's majority falling to fourteen on a vote of censure, and even more lasting the anger of the Queen, who in open telegrams criticized the ' frightful ' delay and wrote of ' the stain left upon England '. For a month the Cabinet, returning to Gordon's view, declared for destroying the Mahdi and setting up an orderly government, but then reversed their decision; moved not merely by Baring's preference for a defensive and by Radical discontent, but by a sudden alarm of war. For some years Russia had pushed her advance over Turcoman territory, in 1884 occupied Merv, and in March 1885, moving in force towards a frontier at that moment under discussion, attacked the Afghans at Penjdeh, north of Herat. Gladstone asked large military credits, the Czar finally accepted arbitration, but this crisis enabled Gladstone to get rid of the Sudan. Though we retained a garrison at Suakin, the Egyptian frontier was drawn back to Wady Halfa. And though the Mahdi died this year, the Khalifa Abdullah and his slave-drivers ruled the central Sudan — the rest falling in time to other claimants: the fierce Senussi of the western desert, Menelik the aggressive conqueror of Abyssinia, one strip to the King of the Belgians' evil dominion in the Congo, and the port of Massowah to Italy. It was not till 1891, after several petty campaigns, that the Egyptian frontiers could be considered safe.

Meantime Baring wrestled with two sets of problems: corruption and forced service, the lash and the slave trade, irrigation and finance, all of which must be reformed if the people of Egypt were to be given life and hope, but also with the debt-holders and foreign colonies, and the capitulations and mixed courts that protected them. Every year he worked, the reasoning against speedy evacuation was strengthened. Gladstone sent out Northbrook to investigate in 1884 but rejected his advice when it tended to give Great Britain the last word; Salisbury's envoy Drummond Wolff in 1887 signed a convention with Turkey, which spoke of evacuation within three years. But as this was guarded by a clause giving us a right of re-entry in emergency, under the influence of France and Russia the Sultan eventually refused to agree.

Continuance in Egypt had, in fact, become intermixed with our position in Europe and Asia, and a touchstone of our security.

CHAPTER X

THE SALISBURY GOVERNMENT, AND FOREIGN AFFAIRS, 1886–1892

So long as Gladstone adhered to his Irish policy, the new Cabinet could count on the Liberal Unionists, whether Whigs or Radicals. Indeed, since their vote could turn the scale, Salisbury offered to take office under Hartington who, however, declined either to lead or to serve. And as any offer to Chamberlain would have been too sharp a curve, he made a purely party government.

Still keeping some of Disraeli's veteran administrators like Gathorne Hardy and Cross, it gathered strength as it proceeded, and not least, paradoxically, through what might have seemed a mortal blow — the resignation of Randolph Churchill in December. At the age of thirty-seven he was Chancellor of the Exchequer and leader of the House; his wise ally Hicks-Beach had the key position of Irish Secretary, while his aversion Stafford Northcote (now Lord Iddesleigh) held the Foreign Office under Salisbury's supervising eye. But whether his undisciplined egoism could ever have long led, or worked with, the party is questionable, even if he had not blundered, or if his health had not broken down. For his remonstrances to Salisbury and his speeches announced a programme nearer to Chamberlain than to his own party, Salisbury in vain warning him that it depended less on the masses than the classes, who asked 'a lower temperature', or that time would bring what his furious driving would imperil. His Budget proposed to get funds by increasing death- and house-duties, and by economy in armaments; whereby he would be enabled to lower income-tax, tobacco- and tea-duties, and to provide larger grants for a democratic local government. Both service ministers, W. H. Smith and George Hamilton, resisted his economies and, since the European situation was black, Salisbury supported them. Repeating his earlier tactics over the fight to capture the party machine, Churchill offered his resignation which, to his surprise, was accepted with relief.

Once more, in deference to his friends, Hartington declined the opportunity of leading a Coalition, though the gap at the Exchequer was filled by another Liberal Unionist, and a first-rate financier, in Goschen. At his instance Iddesleigh was removed from the Foreign Office, which was taken by Salisbury himself, and the shrewd business man W. H. Smith took the lead of the Commons. Hicks-Beach's health temporarily failing, Salisbury's nephew A. J. Balfour became Irish Secretary, in that post revealing the courage and power of debate which, on Smith's death in 1891, gave him the lead of the House. Another first effect of Churchill's fall was a loosening of the government link with Chamberlain and a move, soon proved vain, for Liberal reunion. Yet the Tory democracy which Churchill stood for, and which he declared ended by Balfour's elevation, did not in fact stand still, though he himself fell into a sad isolation and died, still under fifty, in 1893.

Ireland apart, there was much common ground between the parties, and if this government was not inclined to sweeping legislation, some of its measures had a large importance. Its method of enquiry by royal commission was to bear fruit later in many directions. The Hartington commission of 1890 recommended some vital Army reforms, in particular for an Army council and a general staff; though these were delayed for another generation. Naval reconstruction, urgently called for by new inventions in guns, armour plate, and design, took shape in the Naval Defence Act of 1889, which envisaged a building programme of ten battleships and sixty cruisers within five years. Goschen's finance essentially followed on Churchill's lines, in reducing sinking-fund charges, income-tax and tea-duty; in 1888 he was able to convert £500 millions of 3 per cent Consols to a 2½ per cent basis. Moreover, this Conservative Parliament achieved a good part of Chamberlain's Radical programme. Tithe became an obligation on the landowner, and no longer on the tenant A housing Act of 1890 widened the possibility of demolishing or buying-out slum areas. A technical instruction Act gave to local authorities some valuable powers, which Goschen furthered by increased Exchequer grants. The Local Government Act of 1888 ended the historic predominance of the country gentlemen by transferring all administration — though not judicial powers — from the J.P.'s to elected councils for counties and county boroughs. A parallel Act created the London County Council, and though its area was constricted and its power curbed by the City corporation and certain boards and vestries, in this arena its progressive majority fought the first battle for a practical Socialism.

In general the financial doctrine of Peel and Gladstone still held the field, that money did more good in the taxpayer's pocket than in the Exchequer; Churchill had only budgeted for £94 millions, and Goschen's never rose to £100 millions. But this government's life began in a heavy trade depression, unemployment produced several riots, and though trade then improved until 1891, there seemed less resilience in our recovery, and social discontent had much to feed on. The great strike of the dockers in 1889 for 6d. an hour, the publication of Charles Booth's statistics of London poverty, a Shop Act allowing a maximum of 74 hours a week, such illustrations expose it. A new and more democratic trade unionism, reinforcing the Socialist thinkers, found its opening in the new democratic local government.

As for the Union with Ireland, the cause on which this government was returned to power, the Cabinet went its way with some grave mistakes, yet with resolution and, from a party angle, some unexpected good fortune. The ' plan of campaign ' of 1887, to answer evictions by systematic refusal of rent, divided the extremer men like John Dillon from Parnell; the publication by *The Times* of letters accusing Parnell, and others, of contact with murder made the background for a permanent crimes Act, allowing the chief secretary to ' proclaim ' areas and suspend trial by jury. When Parnell took legal action against *The Times*, government offended constitutional tradition and justice by using a special commission of judges to supersede the ordinary courts, and to launch a political investigation. Damaged by that, they were injured further by Parnell's acquittal and proof that the letters were forgeries, but in 1890 were rescued by Parnell being found guilty in the O'Shea divorce proceedings, a revolt of the British Nonconformist conscience, Gladstone's announcement that Liberals must choose between Parnell and himself, and a resounding split in the Irish party, which was prolonged even after Parnell's death in 1891. Meanwhile Balfour accompanied coercion in Ireland by reform, a scaling-down of judicial rents, extension of land purchase, and the creation of a Congested Districts Board, with subsidies for the fishing, crofters, and village industries of the poverty-stricken west coast. It is not in domestic politics, however, that Salisbury's prime interest, and his historic fame, are to be found.

Destined to be the last peer at the head of a Cabinet but to hold that place for thirteen of the last sixteen years of the reign, this remarkable character was far removed from that of an average party leader. Not in the least ardent either for democracy or Imperialism, he deplored the damage done by the first to consistency in public life and steadiness of policy, while he resented the money-making and land-grabbing that accompanied the second. As devoted as his ancestor Burghley to the interest of England, he too was a man of European feeling, insistent that Great Britain must follow a neighbourly policy of understanding for others. The inner spring of his conduct was the Christian life, yet he saw Christianity as at incessant war with the heathendom of man, which must be met with human weapons. Though he despised the cries of party and was a radical in his acceptance of new invention and his scientific interests and contempt for muddled compromise, his fixed hostilities sometimes made him act like a partisan. Essentially, perhaps, he approached public life from the angle of loyalty, to the Queen especially, the nation and its institutions, colleagues, family, and Europe. His wisdom, admired by the public from whom he carefully hid himself, was a compound of several balancing forces; a realist disbelief in man's altruism, a view that evils usually cancel each other out if left alone, and a strategic preference for an uncompromising course. If he never despaired of the State, it was perhaps because it was not in him to hope overmuch.

In its ruling conditions foreign policy had been revolutionized since the death of Palmerston. Bismarck's Germany had replaced a supreme France, behind Germany was a more coherent Austria-Hungary, a kingdom of Italy had come into being, and Russia's ambitions had achieved much success. What mattered more was that every major Power was seeking markets and raw material in Africa and Asia. These factors resulted in an uneasy equilibrium, from the Berlin treaty of 1878 until Salisbury's return to power in 1886.

Towards the end of his life he described our diplomatic isolation as ' a danger in whose existence we have no historical reason for believing ', but though he struggled against commitments to which, he argued, a parliamentary government could not be held, ' magnificent isolation ', which was one of his casual explosive phrases, misrepresents his real attitude. The Gladstone-Granville regime, he thought, had left us without a friend, and with two dangerous enemies. The one was France, whose hatred he called ' incurable ', and who nursed or was manufacturing grievances all over the globe — whether Newfoundland fisheries, Indo-China, or the Congo; who had lately occupied Tunis and Madagascar, schemed annexation in Morocco, and was set on obstructing us in Egypt. Again, her internal instability always encouraged the rise of a war-party. Lord Lyons, whom Salisbury once invited to become Foreign Secretary, during a twenty years' tenure of the Paris embassy dealt with twenty-two foreign ministers; and in 1886–7 a melodramatic war minister, General Boulanger, seemed to be working up his country to take her revenge. Our second potential enemy was Russia, who had not forgiven her humiliation in 1878, had shown her teeth at Pendjeh, and whose tyrannous exploitation of Bulgaria suggested that she had not abandoned hope of Constantinople. In such a world isolation was unsafe, for in certain circumstances, Salisbury wrote, a European coalition might treat our Empire as ' divisible booty '.

Since every addition to Empire exposed a larger surface, our position in Egypt was full of danger. It antagonized Turkey, estranged us from France, and provided Bismarck with a weapon of precision. Till 1890 the German chancellor remained the mightiest figure in Europe, and though he declared Germany a sated Power and his sincere aim was to keep the peace, his manner of doing so was to dominate by the fear, language, and preparations of war. His trampling triumphs had left him with but one horror, of a war on two fronts : from France in revenge for 1870, and from Russia, sore at the defeat of her pan-Slav objectives.

To isolate France and keep Russia content he therefore constructed a close network : a secret treaty in 1879 with Austria, for in the last resort Austria must be preserved; the three Emperors' league, to keep touch with Russia; and the Triple Alliance of 1881, to harmonize the jealousies between Austria and Italy. With Great Britain he had no direct quarrel, yet everywhere he crossed our path. Indifferent to the future of the Balkans, he was ready to partition those small States into an Austrian and a Russian zone. Italian indignation at the French seizure of Tunis suited his book well, and so even more did the British occupation of Egypt, for with it he could foment French feeling to fever, or blackmail Britain in the Pacific and Africa.

Always distrusting Gladstone's ideals and his sympathy for the Slavs, Bismarck secretly arranged with the other Eastern Empires that the Straits should be closed to our warships, while in the dilatoriness of Gladstone's colleagues he found another opening. While Granville and Derby circulated his demands between the Foreign and the Colonial Offices, he protested against 'a Monroe doctrine for Africa', and in 1884 made South-West Africa a German protectorate, annexed Togoland and the Cameroons, and with French support challenged Anglo-Portuguese claims on the Congo. Karl Peters and a German company were probing in the interior behind Zanzibar; simultaneously, to the indignation of Australia, German stakes were being planted in New Guinea and Samoa.

To arrest this disintegration, to meet just grievances, and settle the immense question of Africa in peace, were the tasks which Salisbury undertook, and substantially performed. All through 1886–8 the atmosphere was highly charged: with the Czar's soreness over a free but ungratefully anti-Russian Bulgaria, Turkish intrigue, and the flamboyance of Boulanger. While Churchill gyrated between advocating the abandonment of Constantinople or a German alliance, Salisbury slowly made sure of what he judged were the minimum requirements. Of Turkey he had never taken the same view as Palmerston or Disraeli, finding in Balkan liberties a better buckler against Russia; but, he told Churchill, ' I draw the line at Constantinople'. He was equally ready to evacuate Egypt, if and when stabilization there was reached, realizing that without this any amity with France was unprocurable. But French colonial ambitions and feverishness provoked him. Two pacts of 1887 register his conviction that for the time being our interests lay with the Central Powers, above all with Austria, who might do our Middle Eastern work for us; though he signed them ' with regret ', for to some extent they committed us. In effect we undertook, in collaboration with Austria and Italy and with German good will, to maintain the *status quo* in the Mediterranean and Black Sea, the Straits and the Balkans.

Yet he would not listen either to Italy's request for an outright alliance against France, or to Bismarck's in 1889 for a public treaty. The German game, of making others pull their chestnuts out of the fire, was very visible, nor did he find in them any assured support against Russia. British constitutional tradition in any case forbade such a step, while at the moment British feeling was angry over Bismarck's feud with the dying Emperor Frederick and his English wife and offended by the first gestures of their son, the young Kaiser William II. With Bismarck's dismissal in March 1890, however, a new era began, destined to see swiftly realized what he had most striven to prevent, the dual alliance of France and Russia. But some last threads of the earlier age were tied in the Anglo-German treaty of June.

A great age of African exploration had just ended, in which Britons had done mighty deeds from Mungo Park down to Livingstone, our last important exploit being Joseph Thomson's march in 1883 from Mombasa over the Kenya highlands. Five forces, or magnetic points, had drawn Britain into the heart of the continent. These were our West Coast settlements; our base at the Cape, with its northern projections; the posts set up by Livingstone round the great Lakes; the Sultanate of Zanzibar, connecting with our interests in India and the Persian Gulf; and, finally, the claim of Egypt, lately strengthened by Samuel Baker and Gordon, to control the Nile from end to end. Hitherto our economic ventures had been left to fend much for themselves, our outstanding motive having been the suppression of the slave trade; to which end we had annexed Lagos, tightened relations with rulers in the Persian Gulf, and forced abolition of slave-trading on Zanzibar. To maintain this object, and to protect Christian missions, without increasing our territory, had been the Foreign Office doctrine.

But the new conditions made it obsolete. Explorer and missionary had been followed by trade, a traffic in fire-arms, gold, and diamond-diggings, and wars had transformed native Africa. Stanley's ruthless expeditions from coast to coast cut swathes through its tribal communities, a large Indian settlement at Zanzibar claimed our protection, and the Powers of Europe were using commerce as their spear-head; Leopold II of Belgium founded a Congo Association in 1878, while the French were reaching out arms, both from the west and Algeria, to embrace all north-west Africa in one empire. Germany had taken action, as we have seen; Italy was stretching southward from the Red Sea; even Portuguese Africa had stirred from centuries of sleep, putting forward what Salisbury called ' archaeological claims ' to an area reaching from Mozambique on the eastern sea to Angola on the west. How jealous were these rivalries we discovered in 1885 in the resentment against a separate Anglo-Portuguese agreement, and in the summons of the Berlin conference, which delimited the Congo State and arranged for navigation and trade in the million square miles of its river system.

With that partial exception, these claims and encroachments pierced a continent still almost unmapped and frontierless, in which a ' treaty ' with some savage chief or the hoisting of a flag represented the vanguard of some great Power, and in which some Belgian or French officer from the west might march without resistance to the Nile.

Salisbury inherited this explosive substance when it had been added to the fires of Europe, when Bismarck was pushing on colonies to rivet France against us, and when Gladstone had publicly wished ' Godspeed ' to Germany as a colonizing Power. What happened on the west in 1884 was the next year repeated in the east, when the German government took under its wing the annexations made by Peters in the hinterland of Zanzibar. Now that they held the capital port of Dar-es-Salaam, a naval squadron and a treaty demolished the ideals of our agent John Kirk for an independent Zanzibar under British guardianship. So far afield had ranged the effects of Majuba and Khartoum, Pendjeh and Ireland.

With events moving at this speed, Salisbury's method was to accept the inevitable, to choose his priorities, and to strengthen where we were strong. If France was to be warned off the Nile, she must be allowed to vent her ambition elsewhere : what could not be saved from Germany, might at least be shared. British enterprise, he believed, could regain ground if it were encouraged, and this conviction was marked by charters to the Niger Company in 1886, the East African in 1888, and Rhodes' Chartered Company in 1889. Territorial agreements with France and Portugal were followed by two much more considerable events, in a settlement with Germany and the beginnings of Rhodesia.

By 1890 our bargaining value was much raised. Egypt might, in a military sense, now be considered safe, Russia was getting loans and rifles in Paris, Italy desired our approval for her designs on Tripoli. In Africa itself there was urgent need for settlement, the whole east coast being in an uproar from Mozambique to Somaliland, with Germans and Italians staking claims by force of arms, and Peters invading Uganda to take us in the rear. Hence came about the treaty of July 1890. Heligoland was the price, which we had held since 1807 but which the Admiralty said would be indefensible in modern war, and for it the Kaiser's naval enthusiasm would bid high, since the Kiel Canal was under construction and the island would be its shield. Germany in return admitted our protectorate over Zanzibar, ceded her claims on the coast approaching Somaliland, and all east of a line drawn roughly from Mombasa to Victoria Nyanza, recognizing too the upper Nile basin as a British sphere. So was constituted British East Africa, out of which came Kenya and the Uganda Protectorate. On its west, German East Africa was barred from our missionary road connecting Lakes Nyasa and Tanganyika, though northwards its frontier was to meet the Congo State, which would intercept a Cape to Cairo through-line. German South-west was also extended, by the narrow ' Caprivi strip ', to reach the Zambesi.

These arrangements directly affected the territory which was to become Rhodesia, that immense area which, running north-eastwards, would restrict the Transvaal on both west and north, embraced the Zambesi's main course and the Congo tributaries, and met Germany and Portugal on both sides of the Continent. Its origins began when our Bechuanaland protectorate, declared in 1884, made contact with Lobengula, the Matabele king; they went much further in 1888, when he agreed not to cede territory without our leave and granted to a Rhodes syndicate a monopoly of minerals. This last passed to the Chartered Company, whose pioneers in 1890 entered Mashonaland, the northern Matabele territory. That in turn brought them into armed collision with the Portuguese, who in Delagoa Bay and Beira held the natural ports both for the Transvaal and Rhodesia, and whom Rhodes would have wished to expel entirely. Disclaiming this violence, Salisbury enforced in 1890-91 conventions on both parties, compromising the conflict on the lower Zambesi but admitting our protectorate over Nyasaland and Mashonaland. As he had also recognized French claims in Madagascar and in the Sahara between Algiers and Lake Chad, in return for our new position in Zanzibar and admission of our Company's advance inland in Nigeria, for a time at least the partition of Africa might cease to inflame Europe.

There our fundamental rôle did not change before his fall from power in 1892, or indeed during Rosebery's tenure of the Foreign Office until 1895. Austria and Italy being considered as valuable friends, the Triple Alliance was renewed with our good will; we continued to bicker with France, alike over Egypt, Newfoundland fisheries, and her expansion of Indo-China so as to menace Siam. Almost annual visits from the Kaiser, though exasperating his grandmother and her Prime Minister, and even more his unfriendly uncle the Prince of Wales, seemed to proclaim our adhesion to the old system; and events in Africa might be thought to clinch it. For Salisbury left to his successors the project of a Uganda railway, as part of his determination not only to maintain our hold on the Nile but to reconquer the Sudan.

Though the crash of Parnell halted the Liberal swing in bye-elections and though, save for Gladstone and Morley, ardour for Home Rule was now very tepid in the Liberal ranks, the government had lost much ground. Trade was slipping down again into depression, labour discontents were loud, and the Liberals' Newcastle programme of 1891 made large bids for the Radical vote; holding out prospects of Church disestablishment in Wales, triennial parliaments, abolition of plural voting, local option over licences to sell drink, allotments for labourers, district and parish councils. Salisbury was not the man to outbid such offers, and though his Liberal Unionist alliance remained staunch, Conservatives were slow in welcoming any of Chamberlain's Radical items.

The election results of 1892 promised neither strength nor stability. As against 315 Conservatives and Liberal Unionists, making a majority in Great Britain, Gladstone's 273 Liberals drew their strength from Scotland and Wales, but depended for their very existence on 81 Irish Home Rulers.

CONTEMPORARY DATES

1886   Boulanger, Minister of War in France.
        Under Russian pressure, Alexander of Bulgaria
            abdicates.
1887   The Grévy scandals in France.
        Beginning of the Kiel Canal.
        Crispi, Prime Minister in Italy.
1888   Accession of Kaiser Wilhelm II.
        Kipling, *Plain Tales from the Hills*.
1889   Menelek makes himself ruler of Ethiopia.
        British South Africa Company chartered.
        London dock strike.
        Bernard Shaw, *Fabian Essays*.
        Death of Browning and John Bright.
1890   Fall of Bismarck.
        McKinley tariff in the United States.
        French troops occupy Timbuctoo.
        Ibsen, *Hedda Gabler*.
1891   Suicide of Boulanger.
        Franco-Russian alliance.
        Hardy, *Tess of the d'Urbervilles*.
        Death of Parnell.
1892   Witte, financial minister in Russia.
        Zola, *La Débâcle*.
        Death of Renan and Tennyson.

CHAPTER XI

HOME POLITICS AND PARTIES, 1892–1905

THESE thirteen years, the last of the Victorian era, divide into a short Liberal and a long Conservative phase, though formally into four different Cabinets — of Gladstone succeeded by Rosebery, and of Salisbury continued under Balfour. Domestic politics were diverted and their solutions delayed by external events, war in South Africa and a series of international dangers which threw us, substantially for the first time since the seventeenth century, against the German Powers and on the side of France. In the permanent scales these were the decisive weights, yet there were other measures and changes, personal or social or administrative, of lasting importance.

Much more than superficially the scene was transformed at the death, in January 1901, of the Queen. A sixty-four years' reign had brought her from Wellington and Melbourne to Asquith and Balfour, during which the place of the Crown in the State had been elevated, in part by her sense and virtues, in part by the sheer majesty of time. With much acceptance to herself, she had become the symbol and connecting link of a diversified Empire; much against the grain, she lived also into the epoch of democracy. Her sex, her solitude, and the reign's triumphs encircled her with almost legendary reverence, taking final expression in the Diamond Jubilee of 1897, when the greatest sovereigns of Europe, Dominion Prime Ministers, Colonial and Indian soldiers, did homage to the granddaughter of George III. Her political qualities were ever the same. Strenuously hostile to Gladstone to the bitter end, she raised up Rosebery and vetoed employment of the malignant Radical Labouchere; declaring that the constitution had been ' delivered into her keeping ', she protested against any move to reform the Lords, and in 1895 seriously explored her right to order a dissolution of Parliament. She exerted herself to raise her youngest son Arthur, Duke of Connaught, to high Army command; wisely advised by Randall Davidson, dean of Windsor, she argued every episcopal appointment, even against Salisbury. Her sense of duty and fortitude lasted in extreme old age through the darkest days of South Africa and were displayed, too late, in a visit of 1900 to Ireland, for the first time since 1861.

Gladstone's long life and his large blind spots, the Irish matter, and swelling democracy, all cemented Unionism, in the junction not only of

Chamberlain's Radical Imperialist following, but of a majority of the Whig and propertied class, with the Conservatives. The results, both near and far distant, would be grave : that the Lords became a Conservative party body, whose resistance to Liberal bills must invite attack ; that parties were massed, as never before, largely on lines of class, and that a class party would arise, prepared to outbid, and in due course to extinguish, Gladstonian Liberalism. Imperialism, the other growing force, had comparable effects, dividing the Liberal party into two bitterly opposed sections and thus giving a decisive weight to Chamberlain, in whose hands Empire took on a new reality.

Gladstone's last government, of 1892–4, was a sad and sorry business. He was now eighty-three, handicapped by deafness and cataract in one eye, raised far aloft by age and fame, indisposed and too infirm to tolerate Cabinet dissension. Though he brought in two excellent administrators in Asquith at the Home Office and Acland for Education, the Liberal Unionist split had diminished the available talent, while the prospect of his retirement brought out every conceivable division. There was one long-continuing difference of principle ; between Rosebery, with others like Kimberley, who had imbibed Imperialism, wished to hold Uganda, and refused to pronounce for an early evacuation of Egypt, as against Gladstone, Harcourt, and Morley, with all those holding the view of mid-Victorian Radicalism, that such things meant waste, tyranny, and war. But the personal factor was too much involved. Harcourt, the commoner next in the succession, was irritable and intolerant ; Rosebery, a courtier peer who had never sat in the Commons, was moody and hypersensitive ; Morley was jealous and thin skinned.

There were two other points of danger. With a fatalism almost magnificent, Gladstone thought of nothing but Ireland, yet Home Rule was unpopular with half his colleagues ; Harcourt, for one, would have gladly seen it buried. Again, not a word of Gladstone in the election, except one of opposition to an eight-hour day, betrayed a gleam of interest in the social discontents which were fast rising. All through 1893–4 trade sagged, and wages with it ; in 1893 thirty million working days were lost by strikes, a six months' stoppage in the cotton trade being only ended by the Brooklands agreement, which was long to keep textile wages steady. That year also a fierce coal strike brought about the Featherstone riots in Yorkshire, when the troops fired and killed two of those wrecking the collieries, — an important incident for the career of Asquith, and important too for the British doctrine of martial law, which treats soldiers as citizens merely concerned, like other citizens, to preserve the King's peace. It brought about also the first important government intervention in a wage dispute for many generations. In this year moreover, under the inspiration especially of the

Scottish miner member, Keir Hardie, the Independent Labour Party came into existence, pledged to create a working-class Socialist party. The trade-union movement, once the nursery of Radical skilled crafts-men, was beginning, again with the miners in the lead, to organize *en masse* all those employed in each industry. But little of this could have been guessed from the Cabinet programme, or the Liberals' relations with Labour.

With no party enthusiasm behind him, though with unexhausted resource, Gladstone fought for his second Home Rule bill through 1893. Though this time it proposed two Irish chambers instead of one, once again it ignored the objection of Ulster, and once again illustrated the crux in finding any half-way house between Union and separation. For, to meet the point raised above all others in 1886, it was now proposed to keep Irish members at Westminster, though they would vote on Imperial questions only ; when that was judged impossible in practice, the government decided to keep them at Westminster for all purposes,—able, that is, to vote in English and Scottish business, whereas in Irish affairs neither England nor Scotland would have a say. This bill passed the Commons by a majority of 34 only, or, in other words, would have been beaten save for the Irish vote, and was rejected in the Lords by 419 to 41.

Here ended the political life of Gladstone, by no means as this great warrior would have wished. His government were carrying a local government Act, setting up district and parish councils, the finance of which was restricted by the Lords, who had already mutilated some smaller measures. Was this to be borne, and all hope to die of his re-introducing Home Rule ? He proposed a dissolution but his Cabinet would not hear of it, and at the turn of the year 1893-4 he was fighting an almost solitary battle, — as he had long ago against Palmerston — against an increase of naval estimates which Spencer and the Admiralty considered vital. In March he resigned ; his last speech to the Commons proclaiming that between them and the Lords there were ' differ-ences of fundamental tendency ', — a controversy ' which, once raised, must go forward to an issue '. So the member of 1832 for a Duke of Newcastle's pocket borough ended his sixty years with the battle-cry of the People against the Lords.

His advice on the choice of a successor was not asked by the sovereign ; whose own selection was a peer, yet not Spencer whom he would have named, but Rosebery. The Queen, indeed, acted as the Cabinet majority wanted, for the sufficient reason that they found un-endurable the prospect of Harcourt. But the choice was fatal. Rose-bery's great accomplishments of speech and writing, his wealth and social outlook, did not commend him to the bulk of his party ; a courtier in the sense of Disraeli or Granville, the friend of Randolph Churchill and

Cecil Rhodes, the husband of a Rothschild, on the side of his deeper affections and beliefs he had little in common with Radicalism, and less with Nonconformity. Some felt displeased that he twice won the Derby while Prime Minister, others because he admitted that Home Rule must wait till England, ' the predominant partner ', was converted, or because he proclaimed a protectorate in East Africa. And, though allowing the need of Lords' reform, he held a high view of a second chamber.

His government lasted only fifteen months. A Prime Minister in the Lords must depend on close understanding with the leaders in the Commons, but some never gave him the barest loyalty; Harcourt never forgave his own supersession, Morley was indignant at not getting the Foreign Office, Labouchere had desired the Washington embassy. The one solid performance of 1894 was Harcourt's Budget, framed to meet a demand of £3 millions extra for the Navy, and introducing the powerful weapon of a remodelled death-duty, while in another sense it was his triumph against Rosebery, who disliked this onslaught on landowners and the taxation of capital to acquire revenue. For the rest, government pursued Harcourt's plan of ' filling up the cup ', by bringing forward one item after another of the Newcastle programme of 1891 — Welsh disestablishment, a bill giving power to extinguish liquor licences without compensation, and another to abolish plural voting. That the Lords would reject all alike was tolerably certain, and perhaps the intention; not a process inspiring to the electorate, who would have respected a dissolution challenging the peers, and especially when for such bills there was little demand.

In this state of dispute they could not have lasted long; actually they fell in June 1895 on a chance vote, and on a false ground, that one of their best administrators, Campbell-Bannerman, had failed to equip the Army with cordite, or smokeless powder. Without unity or a programme they resigned, Salisbury immediately dissolved, and the electorate returned 340 Conservatives and 71 Liberal Unionists as against 177 Liberals and 82 Irish Nationalists. Both Harcourt and Morley lost their seats, while Rosebery let it be known that he would not serve with Harcourt again.

The Unionist party, installed in such strength, embodied a good deal more than antagonism to Home Rule. Though separate Liberal Unionist organization continued, in the Birmingham area indeed until 1919, outwardly the temporary alliance of 1886 had been consolidated. The leaders on either side, Salisbury and Balfour, Devonshire (as Hartington had now become) and Chamberlain, were loyal and conciliatory to each other, Chamberlain's followers thus giving up their crusade against Church schools, while Salisbury recognized that part of

Chamberlain's social pledges must be honoured. The high ability of the Liberal Unionist chiefs gave them Cabinet places, six out of nineteen, much exceeding their numerical ratio and, subject to Salisbury and Balfour leading the two Houses, they took office on their own terms, Chamberlain choosing the Colonial Office and Devonshire refusing the Foreign Office, which Salisbury again combined with the burden of the Premiership. Unchanged for the next five years, this Cabinet, though somewhat elderly, assembled many gifts, including besides those mentioned Goschen, James of Hereford, Hicks Beach, Cross, and Lansdowne.

If they came in on a boom which carried our figures of trade to a new record until 1900 and kept unemployment down to minute proportions, their administration was distracted by international crises, and dogged by the origins and process of the South African war. Though these did not strain their unity, for both Imperial sentiment and financial venture overseas were at their height, this Imperialism underlined the fact that Chamberlain shared power on equal terms. But it had also the reverse effect, of delaying Chamberlain's social reform. The only measures on a large scale were an important workmen's compensation Act of 1897 which put squarely on the employer the liability for accident to life and limb, and a large factory Act of 1901, rounding off the work lately done by Asquith for health and safety. Chamberlain had long wished to follow the German example in social insurance, and in particular to do something for old-age pensions, in which the social reformer Charles Booth had given a lead, but the modest proposals of 1899, for 5s. a week to the poor over the age of sixty-five, were extinguished by the war. A London government Act of 1899, though leaving the City corporation intact, replaced old boards and vestries by twenty-eight elected borough councils, and an agricultural rating Act of 1896 proposed to remedy depression by relieving farmers of half their rates.

In legislation, as in much else, a new activity came in with the new century : that was inaugurated by the so-called ' Khaki ' election of 1900, which used war sentiment to confirm the party majority ; by the Queen's death in January 1901 ; peace in South Africa in May 1902 ; and Salisbury's resignation in July. The old minister had aged much, having already made over the Foreign Office to Lansdowne, nor had he ever sympathized, except in housing questions, with domestic reform ; some older men had gone already in Cross, Goschen, and Chaplin, and now Hicks Beach, a Victorian who detested several aspects of Imperialism, went with his leader. Chamberlain's position had risen to new heights. He had made the Colonial Office almost the mightiest engine of State, created the Imperial Conference as a permanent institution, and laid before ministers from every Colony far-reaching schemes for unity, trade, and defence. Imperial soldiers gathering for the Diamond Jubilee and then serving in Africa, the atmosphere of war, and Australian federation, all swelled the tide. From the angle of Empire he struck into the web of foreign affairs and, outstripping Salisbury, forced an African settlement with France and a prolonged exploration of a possible German alliance.

As no Liberal Unionist could yet hope to lead a Conservative majority, Balfour's succession was undisputed, and government continued to rest on the relation between himself and Chamberlain; which, though loyal and co-operative, never had the strength coming from similarity of mind. Nor did Balfour's appointments much reinforce the Cabinet : George Wyndham, his own brother Gerald and his kinsman Selborne, Austen Chamberlain, Ritchie at the Exchequer, and Brodrick at the War Office. In some essentials he was deficient as a democratic leader, seeming to many solid members to lack conviction and having none of that capacity to fire the masses which had elevated Gladstone, Churchill, and Chamberlain. In legislation and administration, however, he achieved things with much more than a party value. Bridging the gulf by his intimacy with the best brains of the younger Liberals, Asquith and Haldane, he had a disinterestedness, a grasp of principle, an intellectual eminence, which in dark days and in the highest issues of government made him a counsellor of stout quality and fibre.

One lasting monument to this high character was the Education Act of 1902. Gladstone's measure of 1870, though providing the bare frame of universal elementary education, left its content disputed between elected school boards, financed from the rates and imparting an undenominational teaching, and the older voluntary schools, which were maintained by Anglican and Catholic churches and governed by their own managers. Secondary education it had left alone, though here, as German trade rivalry or Swiss and French models showed, was an urgent need. As time passed, while the self-governed public schools and endowed grammar schools catered for the wealthier classes, some uncoordinated steps were taken to provide secondary teaching for the less prosperous; sometimes by active school boards stretching their powers, sometimes by State grants through local authorities, or direct to schools.

Following on Acland's preparation during Gladstone's government, in 1899 the Salisbury Cabinet created the Board of Education, which at least united the means of direction under one minister. But not only was secondary education incoherent and fed by piecemeal finance; financial stress was driving the Church schools down to a lower level of efficiency. Yet any remedy would trespass on an awkward ground as between Church and Dissent, and raise indignation in Liberal Unionists.

It was then an act of parliamentary courage in Balfour to push forward a measure of drastic reform, inspired in particular by a civil servant of rare originality, Robert Morant.

In local government alone this was a landmark, in that it reversed the tendencies of the past century and replaced special *ad hoc* bodies by a single authority. Abolishing the school boards, the Act set up one organ for education, both elementary and secondary, in every area, that is, a committee of the county, county borough, or urban district council. These would finance both ' provided ' and Church schools from the rates, and manage all secular education ; on the other hand, Church schools would control their own religious teaching and appoint their own teachers. Educationally this advance was all-important, in making one channel for secondary education and raising all elementary schools to a uniform level, but politically the Act excited furious anger and a passive disobedience to the law. For Nonconformity saw the Church schools not only armed with Church endowments but also financed by the ratepayers, while in country areas, as in Wales, where no alternative school existed, Nonconformists would be paying for religious teaching to which they objected, and over which they had no control. Whether churchmen had an equal right to resent paying for the undenominational teaching in ' provided ' schools, whether the cost of maintenance would not finally crush the Church schools, or whether the interests of parents and children were not more important than these theological disputes ; on such questions controversy continued for ten years to come. On Haldane's initiative Balfour also moved in a direction which resulted in making a teaching university in London, and later on in Manchester, Liverpool, and elsewhere.

Since ' beer and the Bible ' were said by Radicals to be the props of Conservatism, the Licensing Act of 1904 was another measure that invited attack. Drunkenness in those days was a proved evil. By what means should it be checked ? If licences were extinguished, was it to be without compensation, or were they a legitimate form of property ? And should licences continue to be given by the venerable licensing sessions of the J.P.'s ? Legal opinion was divided ; the brewing and the temperance interests were both politically powerful. On the whole, Balfour's Act may be reckoned a fair compromise ; accepting compensation, save in cases of misconduct, but assessing the compensation fund on the trade itself, and transferring licensing authority to the stronger power of quarter-sessions.

Balfour's quality is best illustrated by his action to improve national security. Deep searchings of heart over our military failure in Africa, — absence of planning, starving of military intelligence, incompetence in the high command, and breakdown both in transportation and supply — led to the appointment in 1903 of a powerful committee headed by Esher. The Liberal Secretary for War, Campbell-Bannerman, had indeed at length ejected the old Duke of Cambridge, who was succeeded as commander-in-chief by the autocratic and difficult Wolseley. Once again the Esher committee, repeating the advice of the Hartington commission of 1890, recommended that this extreme centralization in one man be brought to an end, and this time with success ; the office of commander-in-chief was abolished, and an Army Council set up, much like the Board of Admiralty. Nothing, however, was done to create a general staff, and few things damaged this government so much as the successive contradictory paper reorganizations of Brodrick and Arnold-Forster at the War Office, and their almost total absence of result.

Much more positive construction was done for the Navy — and naturally, for the two German Navy Laws of 1898 and 1900 threatened the only power on which under Providence the safety of the realm depended ; Gladstone had resigned in 1894 in protest against naval estimates of barely £10 millions, but £31 millions was the figure of 1901. The vital changes were due primarily to a sailor of ruthless genius, Sir John Fisher, backed by two strong First Lords of Balfour's appointment, Selborne and Cawdor. One step which gradually matured was a redistribution, diverting our main force from the Mediterranean to the Atlantic and Channel fleets, and accompanied by the making of a northern battle-base at Rosyth. A second was the building of a new fleet of battleships and battle-cruisers, with *Dreadnought* and *Invincible* as prototypes, armed with big guns that could outrange torpedo attack ; with a permanent programme in each class which, if faithfully pursued, would give an ample margin of safety. A third was the creation of Dartmouth College and an overhauling of officers' training.

Towards all this enhancement of national preparedness Balfour's most personal contribution was the Committee of Imperial Defence, an organization carried much beyond the earlier defence committee of Cabinet. Henceforward its chairman would be the Prime Minister, while its permanent nucleus of service ministers and experts was given flexibility by calling in other advisers at will ; finally, unlike the Cabinet at that date, it had both written records and a permanent secretariat.

Such work as this, making the best justification of these ten years of Conservative government, was done under stress of one crisis after another ; in 1895 the Jameson Raid, a clash with the United States over Venezuela, and Turkish massacre in Armenia ; in 1896, German intervention in the Transvaal ; in 1897, Greek-Turkish war ; in 1898, German and Russian aggression in China, our reconquest of the Sudan, and the collision with France at Fashoda ; then three years of war in South Africa, Russian menaces in Persia, Tibet, and China, and behind it all the incessant blackmailing diplomacy of Germany. All of which involved, as we are to see, a revolution in our foreign policy.

Domestically, however, a deep and by no means wholesome mark was set on politics by the South African war. All the doings of Rhodes and his followers, the Matabele war and the Raid, a parliamentary enquiry with little fruit, war against two small republics, a suspected smear of diamonds and gold and big money over Imperialism, concentration camps for Boer civilians, — all this enlisted against government many honourable, scrupulous minds and fiery democratic feeling. The war had of course one opposite, though temporary, effect; that, coming on top of their own vendettas, it hopelessly divided the Liberal party. By 1898 Rosebery, Harcourt, and Morley had abdicated, and the leader chosen for the Commons, Campbell-Bannerman, divided this division further. For though he held that the war ought to end in annexation of the republics, he denounced Kitchener's burnings and camps as ' methods of barbarism ', worked for a peace by way of self-government, and leaned to the section of his party then called ' pro-Boer ', of which a young Welsh member, David Lloyd George, was the eloquent voice. That meant a break, not with Rosebery only, but with the ablest rising leaders, Asquith, Haldane, and Edward Grey who, if all had not approved the outbreak of war, admired Milner's work, and were decided that the war had become a national cause; in 1902 they joined Rosebery in founding a Liberal League, with a platform of its own. From this state of weakness Liberals were slowly rescued, in part by Campbell-Bannerman himself — who, though not comparable in intellectual distinction to the leaguers, had twice Rosebery's character and would never haul down his flag — but even more by the mistakes of the government. Liberals who were divided over Africa found grounds of reunion in the Education and Licensing Acts, and in others to come.

Though Ireland hardly made one of these, for few Liberal leaders retained Gladstone's fervour, none the less Ireland much injured the Unionists. Since the days when the chief secretary of the '80's, rarely parted from his loaded revolver, had won the name in Ireland of ' bloody Balfour ', it might be thought that what Salisbury had advocated, and what Parnell thought possible, had succeeded: twenty years of ' resolute government ', and of ' killing Home Rule by kindness '. From 1887 to 1905 three able chief secretaries, Balfour, his brother Gerald, and George Wyndham, pursued this path of order and reform, with at least this outward effect, that at the end of it Ireland was more at peace than for a hundred years past. Their work through the Congested Districts Board was extended by the Agricultural Organization Society, founded by Horace Plunkett, which through co-operation would make of this dairy-farming land another Denmark. An Act of 1898 at last gave to Ireland elected county and district councils, while from the Ashbourne Act of 1885 onwards the plan of buying out the landlords was pursued down to Wyndham's land purchase Act of 1903. By this last transaction £100 millions of British credit were advanced as a beginning, to make possible the sale of whole estates and the creation of universal peasant ownership, the price to be repaid by annuities spread over sixty-eight years. Before 1909 a quarter of a million such agreements were completed, and in these last years of the Union Ireland was a country materially almost remade, with exports risen from insignificance to over £150 millions a year, nearly all of which went to Britain.

Yet many symptoms suggested a doubt whether this prosperity was exorcising the Irish question, and Wyndham failed, as Gladstone and Parnell had failed, to settle its religious faction over education. His fall embittered and deepened that doubt. His heated, exuberant vitality made him an imprudent administrator; against Balfour's advice he took as his second-in-command Sir Anthony Macdonell, an Irish Catholic and Home Ruler. When Macdonell became involved with a reform association, promoted by Dunraven and other moderates, Ulster and Unionist suspicion fell heavily on his chief; the immediate objective, to combine the numerous government boards under some part-elective Irish control, might in itself be blameless, but the word 'devolution' and the man in charge raised the bogy of Home Rule. In March 1905 Wyndham was forced to resign. This deprived Balfour of a loyal friend, injured his position as leader, and excited the Irish parliamentary party, whose two wings, Parnellite and anti-Parnellite, had lately been reunited by John Redmond. Furthermore, it exposed that party to its enemies in Ireland. Part-product itself of the order made by Unionism and the self-respect instilled by Plunkett, an Irish national renaissance was in train, and was exalted by centenary celebrations of ''ninety-eight', so that the Gaelic League, the brilliant Irish theatre, and the organization of Sinn Fein ('ourselves alone'), had all come to pass by 1905. But Wyndham's fall followed on another split in the Unionist party, which proved its death blow.

Chamberlain, like his first ally Dilke, had never in his most Radical days shared the pacifism of Bright or the Gladstonian dislike of Imperialism, and since then, with perfect consistency, had taken his political life in his hand rather than accept Home Rule. Business experience, a self-made career, and temperament all separated him from the outlook of Salisbury and Balfour; his mind was always set on the future, inclined to see politics as a chequer-board of black and white, and coloured by the immediate task. Given at last the keys of power, he was led by international danger and Colonial Office pressures to conclude that our continued isolation meant deadly peril, but that in our Empire we possessed an undeveloped, potential, compensating strength. Imperial sentiment proved itself at the Diamond Jubilee and in

Colonial contingents for the South African war, but the two Colonial conferences of 1897 and 1902 set some limitations within which he must act. Nothing resembling Imperial parliaments or councils could be hurried on; Colonial contributions to Imperial defence were small, and plainly they meant to keep control in their own hand. It also became clear that his first vision of Imperial free trade was a dream, for Colonial tariffs had come to stay. On the other hand, Canada initiated the device of giving tariff preference to British goods, to facilitate which the mother country denounced her commercial treaties with Germany and Belgium; and the 1902 Conference invited Britain to give such preferential duties in return.

Inevitably this problem worked within the atmosphere of party politics. Chamberlain took a gloomy view, thinking that votes innumerable had been lost over the education Act, but while he openly spoke of free trade ' shibboleths ', at the Exchequer Hicks Beach, grim and formidable, brushed aside the Colonial suggestion. Before he retired, however, ' Black Michael ' had revived for revenue purposes a small corn-registration duty (only dropped in 1869), thereby reviving talk of protection, and in a casual, vague Cabinet of November 1902, just before Chamberlain departed for South Africa, they agreed, or such was Balfour's version, to consider favourably a grant of Colonial preference by this means. When Chamberlain returned in March 1903, however, it was to find that Beach's successor Ritchie had repealed the corn-duty. In May he took the field at Birmingham, declaring for Imperial preference and for retaliatory duties against foreign tariffs; by October the Cabinet was, in effect, destroyed.

If Chamberlain had been brusquely treated in his absence, his manner of retaliation is hard to defend; that is, to hold a pistol to the head of his colleagues by a direct appeal to the masses. Balfour's chief concern was to preserve the party; had they not often agreed to differ before, he asked, as over Catholic emancipation or the Corn Laws? Yet by conviction he was nearer to Chamberlain's way of thinking than to Cobdenism, nor did this split coincide with the division between Conservatives and Liberal Unionists, for the free-trade ranks included the elder statesmen of both camps, like Devonshire, Hicks Beach, and Goschen. In September he dismissed two free-trade ministers, Ritchie and Balfour of Burleigh, but also accepted Chamberlain's resignation; which was followed by that of two more free traders in George Hamilton and Devonshire. His policy was to repudiate a general protection and food duties, but to ask for a free hand to bargain against foreign tariffs, and he reconstructed his Cabinet accordingly; the choice of Austen Chamberlain for the Exchequer giving a guarantee that his father's views would not be neglected.

For two more years the party balances protracted this delaying game, and if public opinion was being ' educated ', it was also being annoyed. Balfour wished delay in the hope of party unity, though even more perhaps in the public interest, for he dreaded the coincidence of a Liberal victory with a European war. Chamberlain, with the aid of a tariff-reform league, was fast building an organization, hoping to spread the gospel outwards from faithful Birmingham. He pointed, prophetically, to one dark spot after another; silk gone, iron and wool threatened, ' the turn of cotton will come ', and bad employment during 1903–4 supported him. But in 1905 the trade figures turned unmistakably upwards, it was plain that his original cause of Imperial preference would be impeded both by Colonial tariffs and by the British refusal to hear of taxing food; more and more, consequently, his campaign was reduced to protection for home industry. Unionist free traders were a minority, though including some old pillars of the party and some, like Hugh Cecil and Winston Churchill, of its rising hopes, and they too were divided on tactics. For if some like Churchill predicted ' a gigantic landslide ', others who thought a Liberal victory certain were all the more anxious to delay a moment which would involve much more than free trade, in Radicalism and Home Rule. Nor, for that matter, was Campbell-Bannerman ready to bargain away his weapons by alliance with Unionist free traders.

Such motives paralysed the Unionists in their twilight, while Balfour wrestled with a fierce Curzon-Kitchener controversy in India over military reform and the Viceroy's powers, and while he and Lansdowne gradually constructed the Japanese alliance, broke with Germany, and made the Anglo-French *entente*. In January 1905 his formula seemed to be accepted : for a retaliatory tariff, measures to stop dumping, and a Colonial conference after the election to discuss means for ' closer commercial union '. But Chamberlain's impatience could not be restrained, especially when Balfour made the conference's proposals dependent on a second British election, and in November, with his programme of a general tariff, he captured the party machine. It was too late.

Cabinet breaks and a bitter feud within the party, education and licensing, the fear of ' dear food ' — to those some more injuries were added. One commission's report after another darkened the impression of ministers' incompetent handling of the late war, while one aftermath of that war gave the Liberals a new arm, of which they availed themselves to the full, the cry of ' Chinese slavery '. The grounds put forward by Milner for importing Chinese coolies to the Rand mines were a desperate economic situation and dire shortage of native labour, and though Chamberlain had opposed this step, his successor Alfred Lyttleton was convinced, and the ordinance of 1904 was duly passed by the Transvaal legislature. But the Rand mine-owners were figures highly distasteful to British feeling, and though the spectacle of 50,000 coolies, bound by indenture for three years to work at one task and to live in compounds, had earlier parallels in our Colonies, it smelled of slavery; some vice and outrage was inevitable and, when it occurred, was as easily exaggerated. And it affronted the deepest instincts of the British working class, which had grievances of its own.

For if trade was rising on the new price boom, industrial wages were almost stationary, and agricultural wages much too low; housing progress was slowing down, and overcrowding not being overtaken. Only two members of the Independent Labour party were returned in the election of 1900, but in 1901 two legal decisions seemed to undo the whole position won by trades unionism under Disraeli: by declaring that union funds were liable for damages where wrongs were done by their agencies, that unions could be sued, and that picketing could be ruled to be intimidation. A great increase in the numbers of the Labour party founded in 1900, and some Labour victories at bye-elections, showed that, against supposedly political judgments by the House of Lords acting in its judicial capacity, working men were furbishing their own weapons.

In December 1905, forced to act by Chamberlain's open offensive and hopeful of a Liberal split over Home Rule, Balfour at last resigned. And great was the fall thereof. At the election of January 1906 only 157 Unionists were returned, Balfour himself and several other ministers losing their seats, as against 377 Liberals, 83 Irish Nationalists, and 53 Labour members. It was now to be tested whether Gladstonian Liberalism could come to terms either with Imperialism or democracy.

CONTEMPORARY DATES

1893	French attack on Siam.
	End of Matabele power and death of Lobengula.
	Tschaikovsky, *Pathetic Symphony*.
1894	First arrest of Dreyfus.
	Hohenlohe, Chancellor of German Empire.
	Japan attacks China over Korea.
	Death of Froude, Pater, and R. L. Stevenson.
	–1917. Reign of Czar Nicholas II.
1895	Treaty of Shimonoseki in Far East.
	Armenian massacres.
	Siege of Chitral.
	Marconi invents wireless telegraphy.
	Death of Huxley and Pasteur.

1896 Revolution in Crete.
Italian defeat at Adowa.
Beginning of the *Daily Mail*.

1897 War between Turkey and Greece.
Russia occupies Port Arthur.
United States annex Hawaii.

1898 American-Spanish war.
Delcassé, Foreign Minister in France.
First German Navy bill.
The Curies discover radium.
Zeppelin invents an airship.

1899 Second trial of Dreyfus.
Peace Conference at the Hague.

1900 Bülow, Chancellor in Germany.
The Boxer rising in China.

1901 Death of Queen Victoria.
On murder of McKinley, Theodore Roosevelt
    becomes President.
Yeats, *Poems*.

1902 Peace of Vereeniging.
Anglo-Japanese treaty.
Death of Acton and Rhodes.

1903 Murder of King Alexander of Serbia.
Settlement of Alaska frontier.
The Wright brothers fly in the air.

1904 French-British *entente*.
Russo-Japanese war.
Hardy, *The Dynasts*.

1905 Resignation of Delcassé.
Norway and Sweden separate.
Treaty of Portsmouth.
Church and State separate in France.
Formation of Sinn Fein.
H. G. Wells, *Kipps*.

CHAPTER XII

SOUTH AFRICA, 1884-1914

COSTS' of war may be measured by many standards; materially, the war in South Africa lasted for the three years of 1899–1902, at a price to Britain of £200 millions and 20,000 lives. In both origin and result, however, it cut much deeper, for by it British Imperialism was judged, in some respects found wanting, and transformed; while it made part also both of an alteration of balances within Britain and of the causes of the world war.

It has been shown earlier how South Africa called out for unification, not merely as regards dealings with the natives but in adjusting the interests of two European races, which were broken into half a dozen petty communities, separated by great distances, and, in some instances, cut off from the sea. The sting of the first problem had now been drawn. Proclamation of Imperial protectorates over Bechuanaland and Basutoland (1884–5), annexation to Natal of what was left of the Zulu kingdom (1887), and to the Cape of the native fragments between Natal and the Kei river, had eliminated the chief danger of one Colony entangling the rest in a native war. But with each decade the second question grew more calamitous.

Politically it evolved within the Gladstone government's settlement with the Transvaal, by the two Conventions of 1881 and 1884, by the last of which the Boers' wish was gratified in the style of a ' South African Republic ', our claim to control their native policy was cancelled, and all mention of ' suzerainty ' vanished. On the other hand, the Transvaal was tied down to fixed frontiers, and without British consent could make no treaty with any but the Orange Free State, nor with native tribes to east and west; it was pledged also not to lay hostile tariffs on British goods. Furthermore, though the British had not pressed home the matter of the franchise, both Conventions guaranteed civil rights and equal taxation to all Europeans. But even if they had been unambiguous, — which they were not — they operated in an atmosphere wholly changed by Majuba.

Dutch racialism, never absent since the great Trek, rose high during the period of annexation, finding expression in the foundation in 1879 of the Afrikander Bond. The germs of this association were part cultural, an endeavour to save their tongue and literature, and part economic, but after Majuba its political possibilities became pre-eminent. Pride in their victory over the red-coats, indignation at their past treatment and, not least, at the British filching of the diamond fields, moved the Afrikander people which, it is vital to remember, was as strong in Cape Colony as in the Boer republics. Now the Cape leaders were as convinced as any Briton that South Africa must be made one and, whatever their far ideals, that at present the British connection was indispensable, and that somehow the two races must rub along together. De Villiers, the admirable chief justice, was ardent for one supreme court and one law; Jan Hofmeyr, distrusting the narrow Transvaal racialism, set out to make the Bond a force which, beginning with the Cape, would create a South Africa for South Africans, bound by federal relations with the British but freed from Imperial interference.

It thus became, as it were, a race between rival forces to head off racialism, and here much would depend on the Orange Free State. Its President from 1864–88, Brand, was a Cape Afrikander and a man of moderation, while its economic life turned on the Cape ports. Might not a customs union and a common railway policy extinguish these sterile feuds and integrate the whole country? But great obstacles existed in the Cape's jealous hold over the customs, and the parochialism of Natal; others, still greater, were becoming incarnate in two personalities, Kruger and Cecil Rhodes, and the future turned on which of the two captured the middle mass of opinion, British and Dutch alike.

Past history, frontier conditions, and Calvinist religion made the Transvaal a racial spearhead, and Kruger, its President continuously from 1883 to 1902, the point of the spear. Of his people he was a strong representative, of their invincible courage, their Old Testament conception of themselves as a people set apart, their ardour for freedom, and tough craft. His policy throughout was to whittle away the Conventions and reassert their country as a free State, above all by winning a port, whether Delagoa Bay or some other on the east coast, which would leave them independent of the British and make contact with other Powers. He wanted more soil, too, for his farmers and, most of all, to keep intact their character, which he would do by reserving all power to a rural oligarchy, and this made him look on liberal men like Hofmeyr as weaker vessels.

In every direction he found the British in his way. Bechuanaland and Basutoland barred extension west and south-east, their Matabele concessions barred the north, their acquisition of St. Lucia Bay took away another good harbour. In 1886, moreover, his whole outlook, and African history, was changed at a stroke when gold was found on the Rand in vast quantities, proving at deep levels in effect inexhaustible, so that the poorest State in South Africa suddenly became the richest, and the most individual the most cosmopolitan. Kruger's bargaining strength, his dangers, and manner of rule, all were changed. Refusing now to hear of a customs union or Hofmeyr's project of an understanding with the Cape, the President pushed on with his railway schemes for Delagoa Bay and in 1889 made, with Brand's successor Reitz, a close alliance with the Orange Free State, economic and military. But if the probabilities of collision with the British were thus redoubled, its timing came to depend on another individual, a Hertfordshire clergyman's son, Cecil Rhodes.

He had come to Natal as a delicate boy in 1870, and soon moved from cotton-growing to try his fortune in the Kimberley diamond fields, though periodically retiring to Oxford to work for a degree till 1881, when he entered Cape politics. From whatever source he derived them, whether his reading of Gibbon and Darwin, Oxford, or the open veldt, his ideas were spacious, and he set down, even in the '70's, that ' we are the first race in the world '; that he would work for a British settlement of all Africa and reunion with the United States, in the hope of an Anglo-Saxon federal Empire which would mean ' the end of all wars '. By 1890 his achievement and position were immense. With the help of Alfred Beit he had won for the De Beers company the chief diamond supply of the world; he also controlled the goldfields on the Rand. He took a leading hand in securing Bechuanaland, which he hoped might come to the Cape. He had founded the British South Africa Company, whose charter set no northward limit to its increase; his pioneers stirred up the diplomacy of 1890–91, through which Salisbury declared Nyasaland and Mashonaland under British protection; by influence with Rosebery he assisted in keeping our hold on Uganda. He was bent on driving the Cape railway system far to the north, on the route to Cairo, through the Transvaal if it agreed but, if not, then round its borders; whereby Britain should constrain the Boer republics to enter a united British South Africa.

Hitherto the outstanding merit of his triumphs had been to win them with the alliance of the Cape Dutch, with whose leaders he, as Prime Minister, formed a Cabinet in 1890. Like his friend Hofmeyr, though from another angle, he disliked the Imperial factor. For his hopes to secure northern Bechuanaland and all north of the Zambesi for his company brought him into conflict both with British statesmen who, like Chamberlain, suspected his finance and the Company's high-handed way with the natives, and with the school of officials who held that all extension should be ruled by the Imperial government. He subscribed to Parnell's campaign fund, on condition that Irish members were kept at Westminster, and to those of the Liberal party. Sympathizing with Hofmeyr's notion of economic union, both in South Africa and for the Empire, and the vision of two races uniting to rule, he made advances to the Boers both for agricultural protection and a firmly paternal native policy.

During his premiership of 1890–95, his duel with Kruger came nearer an open clash. In 1893 Kruger was re-elected President by a narrow margin over Joubert, candidate of the more liberal elements, and the same year Jameson and Rhodes' pioneers forced war on the Matabeles, so giving the Company a solid control of the Transvaal's northern frontier. In part because of this, and through Rhodes' growing Napoleonism, his links with the Dutch moderates were weakening. The railway war still raged, for while the Cape system reached Pretoria, Kruger's subsidized line was pointing towards Delagoa Bay, the owner of which, Portugal, was hard driven between Rhodes and a German warning against parting with it to Britain; on the west a Company line, approaching Mafeking, would soon envelop the Transvaal. One thrust countermatched another. Kruger's last hope of an eastern port vanished when the Rosebery government annexed Tongaland; on the other hand, German diplomacy in the Congo and with Portugal barred Rhodes off from north and east. Yet it seemed possible that a Transvaal civil war might make the Union, in a different way.

In the last resort the President's power rested on the unchanging Boer farmer, but as his diplomacy and industrialism both developed, he used Hollanders, notably one Dr. Leyds, and Germans to direct his railway, bank, and government monopolies; the hardest knot, however, was the problem of the Uitlanders, ' the aliens ' brought to the Rand by the mines, by no means all British but coming besides from other South African States and Europe. His attitude had already produced a remonstrance from the Gladstone ministry, and the facts were plain; that the gold industry paid some five-sixths of the revenue, but were totally unrepresented in Transvaal institutions. Immensely rich mine-owners might be little affected, though taxes and dynamite monopoly and corruption bled their profits. Their employees, on the contrary, had substantial grievances. They now outnumbered the Boers by more than two to one, yet Dutch was the sole official language in the law courts and education, and though they had a voice and fair regulation in the mining industry, laws of 1890–94 confined the vote in elections for the Presidency and legislature to those with fourteen years' residence, under a severe oath of allegiance. They had no confidence in judges dependent on the President, or in juries made up of Boer burghers. In 1892 they formed a national union, but their petitions were rejected; our High Commissioner at the Cape, Loch, in 1894 thought revolution certain, and asked for more troops, which the Liberal government refused. In 1895 a defiant pro-German utterance by Kruger, his increasing armaments, and laying of prohibitive railway rates on Cape goods, brought war nearer still but, taking his stand on the Conventions, Chamberlain sent an ultimatum before which Kruger gave way. The Colonial Office being well aware of what might happen on the Rand, it was arranged that in the event of revolution the High Commissioner should intervene, and summon a freely elected convention.

Unhappily the decision was distorted by Rhodes, who turned what might have been a reforming agreement into the scandal of the Raid. He had not got his way with Chamberlain, who refused to make over to the Company the Bechuanaland protectorate, granting it only a strip to carry its railway from Mafeking on towards Rhodesia. But in that strip Jameson assembled a small force who were to move on a signal from Johannesburg, while Rhodes' funds bought arms for the revolutionaries. It was, in fact, their aim so far to compromise the Colonial Office as to compel Imperial intervention.

Nothing could have been more dangerous in 1895 than a war in Africa, for the British government were locked in an angry dispute with the United States, and on the worst of terms with Russia and France, while Germany in warlike tones threatened to resist any change in the African *status quo*. If an Uitlander rising must come, Chamberlain indirectly advised Rhodes, let it either be at once or be indefinitely postponed, and to this extent his responsibility cannot be denied. What he did not foresee, and immediately repudiated, even while its result was in doubt, was Jameson's raid to force the issue. For though the ill-organized Johannesburg reformers, being divided on the point whether they would put their State under the British flag, asked for delay, on the 29th December Jameson took action, defying both their last advice and a direct order from the High Commissioner. On 2nd January 1896 he and his 500 were captured by Boer forces.

This unscrupulous bungled plot had fearful effects. The delicately wrought co-operation between British and Afrikander was killed at a blow. Steyn, an extremist, became President of the Orange State. Hofmeyr and the Bond broke with Rhodes, who resigned the Cape premiership ; his name was indelibly smirched, even his Company's charter put in danger, and the Matabele took their chance to rebel. Chamberlain's denunciation of this ' filibustering ' was immediate, but his degree of foreknowledge tied his hand, while his hopes to extort reform in the Transvaal and to induce Kruger to visit England vanished in the Boers' jubilation, and the weakness of the British case. Then the Kaiser's telegram of congratulation to Kruger and British indignation turned the sentence of our courts on the raiders, and Rhodes' appearance before the Commons' committee, almost into demonstrations of triumph, leaving racial relations worse than ever. That enquiry, in which Campbell-Bannerman and Harcourt took part, was itself unfortunate, for though its report acquitted Chamberlain, the committee did not force Rhodes to produce all the documents, — fearing, it seems, the effect on foreign opinion, — which left the British government under dark suspicion.

Thus delivered from Rhodes and strengthened against domestic rivals, Kruger was re-elected President and hardened his heart. He hastened on armaments, challenged the Conventions, and made a closer alliance with the Free State. Cape politics were poised between a Bond party, in alliance with those who had rejected Rhodes as a lost soul, like Schreiner and Hofmeyr, and Progressives who were still loyal to him and heated by sore British feeling. Rhodes, having lost his Cape basis, was working furiously to develop the north, for Chamberlain had safe-guarded the Company charter and publicly vindicated his services; through Rhodesia, Natal, and the Uitlanders, he hoped yet to force the Transvaal into Union.

Three questions filled the years, 1896–9, between the Raid and the war. There was the undoubted fact of Kruger's armament. There were his efforts to get an understanding with foreign Powers. Most of all, there was the internal condition of the Transvaal. Severe alien laws, suspension of the press, dismissal of judges, extortion, and conflict with a high-handed police, were raising a genuine democratic movement among the Uitlanders, whose petitions were now addressed to the Crown. 'To go to war with President Kruger in order to force upon him reforms in the internal affairs of his State', — that, Chamberlain told the Commons, would be immoral and unwise. Yet to that he came. For if, as he contended, under the Convention Britain was the paramount Power, it must be able to protect its subjects; moreover, what peaceful way existed of overturning Krugerism except by constitutional reform within the Transvaal? And if Kruger's demands for repeal of the Conventions and for foreign arbitration must be resisted, was there not a hope of assisting moderate Afrikander feeling and the British element?

There were, indeed, some signs of improvement, foreshadowed by Kruger's acceptance of some moderate ministers with a Cape training, such as Reitz and Smuts, and Steyn in the Free State saw the necessity for it; while Leyds himself realized they could not count on help from Europe. On the other side, Chamberlain, and even more Salisbury, Balfour, and Hicks-Beach, were determined to avoid war if they could, for none of them wished to be ruled by Rhodes, and the international scene was dark; until the end of 1898 our garrisons in South Africa were diminishing. Chamberlain was rejecting advice from our High Commissioner that war was inevitable and perhaps best brought to a head; replying that such 'a civil war' would throw back Union for a generation.

Milner was sent out in 1897 with the good-will of all parties, having made a great name in Egypt and at the Treasury, and being, like

Asquith, a high example of the public men who issued from the teaching of Jowett's Balliol. Pure, selfless, and arduous, he had some of the defects of his virtue and his German education ; laboured in speech, in his mind and his state papers he would set things in logical antithesis or anticipate a decision as predestinate, which made him apt to divide sharply the sheep from the goats, and refuse to go half-way with men whose final goal he distrusted. Finding himself in an atmosphere of racial strife, and soon with a Schreiner government at the Cape, he established no real relationship with moderates like De Villiers, and challenged the Cape Dutch to prove their loyalty. As for the Transvaal, he wrote, ' their hearts are black ', and by 1898 convinced himself that at least a show of force was required, and that inaction would merely lose our friends.

For over a year Chamberlain resisted him, deprecating a policy of challenge and urging the necessity of not alienating the Cape Dutch. A decided advance came, of course, when in April 1899 the Cabinet took up the Uitlanders' petition, but even so, in the tangled negotiations till September, their line was moderate. They welcomed the Bloem-fontein interview of June between Milner and the two Boer Presidents, nor did they boggle at details of the franchise offered to the Uitlanders, accepting, too, the principle of arbitration if it were operated through some Imperial tribunal. There was a moment when Smuts' offer of a five-year residence qualification seemed to remove what Chamberlain thought the root of the evil, the Transvaal's deliberate policy of keeping their British subjects as ' helots ' ; even so, and even if Kruger had not proceeded to water this offer down, it was accompanied by an impossible demand, that the British government should bind itself never to inter-vene again. At any price, even by refusing concessions which the moderates begged him to accept, Kruger would keep his people free, if he could not make them a sovereign State. He still reckoned on foreign assistance and believed the Liberal party in Britain would help him. Possibly, if what Milner had asked for, that is, large and early military reinforcements, had been realized, war might have been averted, or possibly a more conciliatory man than Milner might have avoided war entirely. But neither is probable. For the substance in dispute, far exceeding any detail of a franchise, touched, as Chamberlain said, ' our supremacy in South Africa and our existence as a great Power '.

Late in September the British Cabinet was preparing its ultimatum, demanding an assured franchise, a real independence for the law courts, and a negotiation for reduction of armaments. But on 9th October Kruger requested the removal of all troops landed since June, and the stoppage of all reinforcements *en route*. Confident in their superior numbers and the assistance pledged by their brethren in the Free State and the Cape, determined also to anticipate attack and seize the moment when the rains brought new grass for their horses, the Boers invaded Natal and Cape Colony; Kruger reminding his council of the Psalmist's promise, ' I will divide Shechem and mete out the valley of Succoth '. If in Britain at large there was some vainglorious over-confidence, it was absent in those holding power; it would, Chamberlain told Milner, be the greatest war since the Crimea, ' with no honour to be gained if we are successful '.

That in a military sense it would be a difficult war could be foretold from the map, the large distances badly served by rail, abrupt hills and defensible rivers, and extremes of heat and cold. Initially the Boers' advantage was great in the inner lines of their mountain-fringed republics, while their commando system was suited for a war of movement, and they were well armed and first-rate marksmen; their Krupp and Creusot artillery excelled anything which the British could produce. One such advantage, that they could live on the land as they moved, also embraced a political fact, that in northern Natal and northern Cape Colony they would be among fellow-Afrikanders, who might be neutral but would never resist them. As Schreiner's ministry hoped to keep out of the war, such conditions were a grave military obstacle to the British.

Reluctance to take the aggressive had made the Cabinet reject Wolseley's advice to speed reinforcements, and when the Boer ultimatum issued we had a bare 14,000 men in the country; a shortage all the harder to fill owing to the right decision not to employ Indian troops. The next few months exposed alarming failings. Lack of a general staff meant lack of any plan of campaign; there was a dire shortcoming in military intelligence; and an inability, from generals down to rank and file, to adapt themselves to strange conditions. Fortunately, under the old and cautious Joubert, the Boers threw away their best strategic chance, which was to ignore isolated garrisons and to sweep Cape Colony before British strength matured.

Four months of British failure, at its peak in the ' black week ' of late December, formed the first stage of the war. Outlying forces in Natal were driven into Ladysmith, to be locked up in a long siege. Our commander-in-chief, the gallant and incompetent Buller, aban-doned the scheme of a massed advance into the Free State, instead of which he sent Methuen westward to storm his way in by the Modder river, leaving Gatacre to defend the Colony and himself moving by sea to Natal. In one week, between 10th and 15th December, Gatacre at Stormberg, Methuen at Magersfontein, and Buller on the Tugela, were all heavily defeated. Buller advised the surrender of Ladysmith, and in January 1900, when again seeking to relieve it, was beaten in the scandalously mismanaged action of Spion Kop.

A second stage opened at the new year with the appointment of

Roberts as commander-in-chief and Kitchener as his chief of staff; the discovery of a cavalry leader in French, who saved the broken flanks between Methuen and Gatacre; a sober realization in Britain that a serious war had to be seen through; a mass of volunteers, and large contingents from Canada and Australasia. Returning to strategical values, Roberts struck out for the Free State; in February his cavalry under French raised the siege of Kimberley, Cronje's force was driven off and after severe fighting brought to surrender at Paardeberg, and White's Ladysmith garrison was relieved. In March Roberts captured Bloemfontein; after a halt to reorganize, to check ravages of disease, and to seek terms of peace, in May he advanced again; in the far north-west Baden-Powell was relieved after a long siege at Mafeking, Johannesburg was taken, Buller penetrated the Transvaal at its Natal angle, and in June our forces reached Pretoria; Kruger entered Portuguese Africa and sailed for Europe. From the first Salisbury had declared for annexation; this done, Roberts made over the command to Kitchener, to stamp out what seemed the dying embers.

But the Queen and Rhodes died, and Salisbury retired, before war ended, and Kitchener's 200,000 men had almost two more years of action against these 60,000 farmers. One overriding difficulty was that the Boers were a plain-clothes army; fading into space or reappearing as peaceful agriculturalists, yet only needing a horse and ammunition to re-emerge as soldiers. Forced to use up whole brigades in securing railways and fixed posts, Kitchener had to evolve a new arm of mounted infantry, together with new devices to concentrate the enemy between block-houses and barbed-wire lines. It is, moreover, vital to remember that this was a civil war, — the hardest of all, as history shows, to end. By information and food, running of ammunition and passive obstruction, any Afrikander might help the enemy; while over the raising of volunteers, disfranchisement of rebels, and courts-martial, Schreiner's government contested obstinately with Milner. If 'Krugerism' had been an original cause of war, a passion for liberty prolonged it; the Free Stater Steyn was even more bitter than the Transvaal leaders, and it was De Wet, a Free State commander, who was foremost in this guerrilla stage. Finally, on Joubert's death the supreme command fell to a steadfast hero, Louis Botha.

Yet the end, though slow, was certain. Kitchener was not only a great organizing soldier but a diplomat more conciliatory than Milner, whose stiffness for the punishment of rebels broke off one negotiation, and who wished to make victory and reconstruction easier by suspending the Cape constitution. In this he was resisted by Chamberlain and by protests from Canada and Australia, nor was there ever any intention in the Cabinet, however slow their pace, of refusing the Boers self-government. But necessities of war and party cleavages embittered the last phase. Burning farm-houses as he advanced, Kitchener massed civilians, women, and children, in concentration camps, in which a heavy death roll shocked British feeling. On the other hand Schreiner, who endeavoured to keep a middle path, was turned out of office by the Bond, and the Cape Parliament was prorogued for nearly two years.

At length peace came about in May 1902, in part by the influence of Liberal Imperialists against pressing for unconditional surrender, in part by the sheer necessity of retrieving the country from ruin, and directly rather through discussions between Kitchener and Botha than through Milner. Britain annexed the two republics, but with a promise of self-government by stages and a gift of £3 millions for reconstruction; Dutch should be taught in their schools, while until responsible government was reached there would be no decision as to the native vote. Rather than accept, the Free Staters Steyn and Reitz went into exile, but before the year ended Chamberlain was in South Africa, Botha and De Wet in London, all from their own angles striving to build a future of peace.

Seven years passed before what Rhodes and Afrikanders alike had wished, a Union of South Africa, was miraculously achieved out of bitterness and distress. Much was due to Milner's decision to work for Union, as he rebuilt agriculture and industry. His administrative mastery till his departure in 1905, and the high quality of the men he chose to implement it, were his most enduring service, while a scaffolding for union was set up in a customs system, a central railway control, and consultative machinery for education and native problems; united policy was implied also in an Imperial guaranteed loan of £35 millions. Something, too, was due to Jameson, Prime Minister at the Cape from 1905-8, who knew that racial groupings were fatal and who, both in the Cape and Rhodesia, was beset by economic depression. Much was unquestionably due to Campbell-Bannerman personally, who promptly suspended the Crown Colony governments which the Unionists had sanctioned, converted his Cabinet, and in 1907 gave fully responsible government.

But the chief impetus came from the hard facts, and the leadership, of Afrikander Africa. Milner had used Chinese labour to get the Rand working again, as the most vital necessity, and though the Liberals cancelled Chinese recruitment, the coolies had done the task. As the richest Colony, soon producing one-third of the world's gold output, the present seat of government, and the testing ground of Milner's administrators, the Transvaal took the lead and produced the leaders. By 1905 Botha had united his people in the Het Volk party, in 1907 he and Smuts took office as British ministers. Fischer and Hertzog did the same in the Orange Colony; Hofmeyr broadened the Bond into the South African party, and in 1908 Merriman succeeded Jameson, so that all three powerful communities had Afrikander ministries. War had hardened their sense of nationality, while the British were divided on other lines : between capital and labour on the Rand, or Company and settlers in Rhodesia; while Natal, oppressed by overwhelming native numbers, asked for more soil and a larger trade.

It was thus in concert with the Transvaal leaders that in 1907 Milner's successor Selborne, and Milner's ' young men ', took the first step towards Union; the causes driving them forward being many and urgent, — drought and depression, a Zulu war, Chinese labour, Indian immigration, disputes over railways and customs. All the leaders of both races welcomed it; in October 1908 the Convention opened, its proceedings lasted well into 1909, and from this body, presided over by De Villiers with Steyn next him, emerged what so many Britons had sought in vain. Instructed by their proved needs and admirable preparation, under the Transvaal lead the new constitution was made far less federal than Australia's, and even more unitary than that of Canada, despite Hofmeyr's opposition. Natal's desire for federalism was offset by a guaranteed share in railway revenues ; neither the equal representation given to each Colony in the Senate nor the establishment of each old Colony as a province with a local council prevented the overruling power of the Union lower House or Assembly. To the central government were given all powers over taxation, police, and civil service; provincial courts became subordinate divisions of the supreme court of South Africa. Equality between English and Dutch was maintained by providing that both should be official languages. As between the Colonies, it was determined that the executive should be seated at Pretoria, the supreme court at Bloemfontein, and Parliament at Capetown; one clause, specially protected against arbitrary amendment, preserved the Cape's non-European vote ; others ensured that, if and when the protectorates were made over to the Union, their identity should continue and native lands receive due safeguards. Substantially, however, it may be said that Afrikander notions prevailed. No native might sit in the Union legislature; in the distribution of seats the basis was that of white voters ; and the electoral machinery favoured the agricultural constituencies.

In 1910 Botha took office as the first Union Prime Minister, with a Cabinet drawn from his National party, though devised to represent every province and principal group, and including Smuts, Hertzog, Sauer, and Fischer. Racialism found plenty to feed on, not least in controversy over language and education, and within two years Hertzog went into opposition. But Botha's large nature and Smut's high ability, with the very universality of difficulties to be solved, kept the body of the ministry and the Union together ; struggling with the needs of defence, a violent conflict against Gandhi and the Indian immigrants whose political consciousness he had roused, the burning question of the land as between European and native, and angry strikes on the Rand.

Out of such matters, transcending race, and out of their new relation to Empire, new political divisions were forming, not coincident with the old cleavage of Briton and Boer. But in 1914 that ancient feud received another lease of life, when the Union was entangled in an Imperial war.

CHAPTER XIII

THE LAST OF LIBERALISM, 1905–1914

CONTINUITY of politics and party was broken after 1914 by war and upheaval, which telescoped into five years great changes which in ordinary times might have taken many decades. Cabinet government, Ireland, India, Egypt, and the standard of democratic life were transformed, old lines of division melted away, all making a process in which the party of Russell and Gladstone disappeared. Yet not without leaving many legacies to those who took its inheritance.

The general election of 1906 put the party in a very strong position, with a majority of eighty-four over Unionists, Labour, and Irish combined, while Campbell-Bannerman had formed one of the most powerful of modern Cabinets. It was not made without a struggle. For though his own claim was not disputed, being welcomed by the mass of the party whose unity he had preserved, and appreciated also by King Edward VII, his health was not good and his ability moderate, and the Liberal Imperialists wished him to take a peerage and leave the real lead to Asquith in the Commons. In this move Grey, Rosebery's heir in foreign affairs, and Haldane were the chief actors, but were overcome by Campbell-Bannerman's resistance, Asquith's influence, and their own sense of public duty. Yet, however distributed, statesmanship and administrative talent abounded in a Cabinet which, besides those names, included Lloyd George, Morley, Crewe, and Lewis Harcourt, and had among its junior ministers McKenna, Winston Churchill, Samuel, and Runciman.

They had the profit of an angry reaction against the faction and omissions of Balfour's government, and were carried in on a tide, long held back, of reforming zeal. What use they made of their great majority must determine the Liberal future; whether, as Asquith's outlook inclined, it remained content with the Gladstonian doctrine of peace, retrenchment and reform, or pursued policies more popular with democracy, more Socialistic, and more expensive. This cleavage underlies the two stages in their pre-war history, marked not so much by the resignation and death of Campbell-Bannerman in April 1908 as by Lloyd George's budget of 1909, and its after-effects. In Asquith and Lloyd George two types of Liberalism, two possibilities, were strongly expressed, complementary and as yet not rival. Asquith, by eleven years the older man and high in office when Lloyd George was a back bencher, represented a more traditional type: of Yorkshire professional and Nonconformist stock, polished and indoctrinated in a triumphant career at Jowett's Balliol, and matured by success at the Bar. His intellect was masterful, his lucidity of speech unmatched, he had loyalty and disinterestedness in a rare degree. Yet his performance, especially after becoming Prime Minister, was uneven, and his hold on the country not in proportion to his gifts. Moreover, he seemed to age quickly and stumble in delays.

David Lloyd George, the product of a Welsh elementary school, and a local solicitor, was much the reverse of all this. He had in abundance the endowments of his Celtic people, a voice of music and a delightful oratory, humour and ridicule, besides a passion for causes which he felt as a crusade, — the undeserved hardships of the poor, horror of war, and distrust of empire; together with inherited prejudices against Church, capitalism, and landlords. In mind, and even more in character, he was to Asquith as quicksilver to a plainer metal; immeasurably more flexible, both for good and ill, more egoist and less moralized, but also less fixed in party entrenchments. His speed of work, fertility in expedient, persuasiveness in negotiation, not these qualities only but a deeper impulse made him, much more than the professedly Labour man John Burns, the representative in Cabinet of the new democracy.

Much, however, was due in the first stage to Campbell-Bannerman himself, who at the age of seventy seemed to expand in sympathy with the youth of his party, and showed a leadership not previously suspected. From him personally came the decision to give immediate responsible government in South Africa, the challenge to the Lords, and the form taken by the trades disputes Act of 1906. This last, though hastened no doubt by the election of over fifty Labour members, proceeded from a general agreement, that the status of trade unions could not be left as it had been by recent legal decisions. Their position had always been anomalous; as corporate bodies and yet not corporations at law, composed of individuals whose actions their executives could not entirely control, having functions mainly economic but also partly political, with funds for distinct purposes and derived from different sources. It was not disputed that the Acts of 1871 and 1875-6 had been designed to save their funds from liability for damages, to permit a reasonable use of picketing, and to mould the law of conspiracy and agency in their favour. But, as it was, not only had legal interpretation prejudiced the minor points, but in the dispute arising from a strike on the Taff Vale railway in South Wales, the House of Lords had on appeal cast the railway servants' union in heavy damages, for a strike which it had not authorized and deeds of violence which it had not approved. The Labour world's passionate demand for a remedy, to restore the immunity which in practice they had long enjoyed, was adopted by candidates of all parties and partly endorsed by a royal commission; though what form the remedy should take turned on highly technical legal argument.   In the result Campbell-Bannerman intervened in debate, threw over the safeguards advised by his law-officers and approved by Asquith, and incorporated in the government bill a Labour amendment.   The Act of 1906 thus not only lifted from trade unions all liability to action for conspiracy, if done in furtherance of a trade dispute, and authorized peaceful picketing, but forbade any court to entertain any civil action whatever against a trade union.

In 1909 another event carried further these relations between the State and the unions.   This was the Osborne case, in which one branch of the railwaymen's union challenged its legal right to take a compulsory political levy for the Labour party, and was upheld by the Lords on appeal.   The government's first step was to make good the consequent gap in Labour members' livelihood, by carrying in 1911 the old Radical proposal for payment of members, in this case one of £400 a year; their second was an Act of 1913 permitting a political levy, if approved by a ballot and if individual members were at liberty to ' contract out '.

This legislation was some index of a greater question, which pursued the whole course of this government.   As a third party, Labour had not won seats in proportion to its voting strength; indeed, their representation was reduced in the elections of 1910, and their Left wing inclined to turn from political action to industrial strikes, or to revolutionary theories of foreign inspiration; whether of the German Karl Marx or American extremists or the French syndicalists, but all agreeing on a class war, direct action by economic groups which would somehow build up a Socialist State, and methods of violence.   The background of their action was an economic fact, that till the end of 1912 this was a period of rising cost of living and a lag in wages, and punctuated by trade disputes.   The scale of these became increasingly greater with the increasing centralization in powerful unions, reaching a climax in the national stoppages of 1911–12 by seamen, dockers, railwaymen, and miners.   In returning to the earlier part of this administration, this perpetual strain must not be forgotten.

Made independent of the Irish vote by the elections and not agreed among themselves on any larger solution, they did nothing for Ireland except to propose in 1907 a representative Council to administer the small matters of local government, education, and agriculture, which was disdainfully rejected by an Irish Convention.   Their other early measures naturally dealt with the contested questions of the past, — South Africa and Chinese labour, education and free trade.   Their persistence over education represented, almost for the last time, the historic rivalry of Church and Dissent. Birrell's bill of 1906, more drastic than many of the Cabinet liked, voiced the intolerance of their majority; the local authority alone was to provide elementary schools, might transfer church schools to its own direction, and would appoint all teachers; whether it gave religious instruction of any sort was left to its pleasure, and if denominational teaching was given in ' transferred schools ', it must not be by the teaching staff. This bill was rejected by the Lords. McKenna's of 1908 introduced a new principle of ' contracting out ' for church schools, but the most serious effort was made late that year in a scheme agreed on, in substance, by his successor Runciman and Davidson archbishop of Canterbury. This would have allowed church schools, if not in single-school areas, to ' contract out ', required local authorities to allow denominational teaching in all schools in all areas, and allowed assistant teachers to give it. But this effort broke down on the resistance of the church laity.

By that date education made only one part of a total deadlock. In 1906 the Lords threw out Birrell's education bill, a bill to abolish plural voting, and mauled several others; in 1907 rejected two Scottish land bills, and in 1908, against the advice of the King, turned down a licensing bill, Asquith's principal measure of the year. So moved towards a decision the cause on which Gladstone had wished to fight in 1893; plainly, Liberals could never accept as a reasonable second chamber a body which, under Conservative governments, registered an automatic approval but obstructed the most important bills of a decisive Liberal majority. That a purely hereditary chamber was hard to reconcile with a democratic age had long been recognized by men of all sides, and by Rosebery in particular, but proposals for change in its composition always ended in the same dilemma, that an introduction of elected or life-peers might make the Lords too strong. Campbell-Bannerman insisted that the essential was to reduce their powers, carrying in 1907 a resolution for the suspensory veto, which Bright had advocated years before, to ensure that ' within the limits of a single parliament ' the Commons' will must prevail.

Changes in holders of office, stress in international affairs, and reluctance to embark on a course in which they themselves might disagree, postponed a further advance, and Conservatives believed that they could wear down the government, as they had in 1895. Unemployment was growing, and many discontents; bye-elections showed a turning tide. But in 1909, by a fatal blunder, the Lords played into their enemies' hand.

Asquith's course at the Exchequer had been on the classic Gladstonian lines. He reduced taxation on tea and sugar, cut down expenditure on armaments, and kept his budget below £150 millions; free trade was jealously safeguarded in refusing to hear the Colonies' suggestion for

Imperial preference. His chief innovations were to draw a distinction between ' earned ' and ' unearned ' incomes, and in 1908 to fulfil what Chamberlain had desired by instituting a non-contributory old age pension of 5s. for those persons over seventy without other income of more than 10s. a week. When he became Prime Minister and made over the Exchequer to Lloyd George, not only was the man very different but the circumstances, for besides falling trade and the new pensions there was also an immediate demand for eight new battleships, the country having decided that the German Navy law was a serious threat. Lloyd George therefore introduced a budget, which was a social and political challenge. A Road Board and a Development fund would cover the new problems of motor transport and do something for natural resources ; more revenue from liquor licences and spirits would avenge the Lords' extinction of the licensing bill. Higher death-duties on estates over £5000, an increase of income-tax to 1s. 2d., and a new super-tax on incomes of £5000 and over, would all raise immediate revenue. But what excited most opposition was the expansion held out for the future, which embraced taxes on site-values and leaseholds, undeveloped land and mineral rights, and would involve a valuation of the whole country. This was proclaimed as ' a war budget ', a war against poverty, framed on the principle that values due to the community should be returned to the community ; it was also accompanied by much oratory about hen-roosts, dukes, and rich men who grew richer while they slept. Holders of property saw confiscation in this doctrine of the ' unearned ' increment, while tariff reformers feared the budget would kill their alternative plan for raising revenue. But the temper of Opposition was edged most against the personality of Lloyd George, as it had not been against any individual since Chamberlain, twenty years before.

Once more acting against the earnest advice of the King and their own veterans, St. Aldwyn and Cromer included, the Opposition leaders Balfour and Lansdowne allowed themselves to approve the Lords' rejection of the budget as a whole ; which was voted in November by 350 to 75. The Commons' immediate reply was to declare this ' a breach of the Constitution and a usurpation of the rights of the Commons ', which was an accurate statement of the facts over the last two centuries. So opened a serious conflict, involving the future of government, the rôle of the Crown, and the balance of society ; not to be settled without two elections, and a great shifting of political weights.

Looking back, it would seem that both successive holders of the Crown and Asquith as Prime Minister steered their course with wise moderation, in the spirit of the Constitution. The government were manœuvring on an impregnable ground, that the Lords' claim meant in effect the power to dissolve Parliament and overthrow a ministry, and that remedies must be found to make this impossible. If the Lords resisted and Liberals would not surrender, there was no way out except through the ancient safety valve, which Lord Grey had painfully induced William IV to threaten in 1832, a creation of peers in numbers sufficient (and in this case it would mean perhaps 500) to swamp resistance. Edward VII hoped that delay might avert what he viewed as a mortal blow to the Constitution, and perhaps to hereditary monarchy; turning a deaf ear to unwise voices which suggested that he might refuse to create peers, he stipulated that two elections must intervene before he was asked to do so.

The election of January 1910 sharpened the crisis, since the Unionists won back about 100 seats, leaving them at 273 against 274 Liberals, while Labour fell to 41. So the balance turned again on the 82 Irish, who proceeded to bargain, that they would only support the budget, in which they disliked the liquor duties, if assured of a bill to break the Lords' veto, which they would then employ to extort Home Rule. They got their way. In April 1910 Asquith introduced the Parliament Act: whereby (1) bills certified by the Speaker as money bills could not be touched by the Lords; (2) other bills passed by the Commons in three successive sessions, but rejected by the Lords, should, notwithstanding, become law two years after their first introduction; and (3) the duration of a Parliament should be reduced from seven to five years. The preamble of this Act contained a vague formula to satisfy those, like Grey, who wished Lords' reform coupled with restriction of their veto, and declared an intention of remodelling the second chamber on a popular basis. But on 6th May Edward VII died.

A general opinion that the new King, George V, should not be unduly pressed led to a conference between the party leaders which met periodically until November and was accompanied by unofficial negotiations of even greater importance. These were initiated by Lloyd George, who wrote in after years' 'we were beset by an accumulation of grave issues, — rapidly becoming graver'; unemployment, loss of markets, German armament, and Ireland. He therefore declared for a coalition to face these questions, including exploration of a tariff and the possibility of national military service. But this was too abrupt a curve for either party, and on Ireland, in particular, the Unionists stood firm. The formal conference broke off on their demand that Home Rule should be reckoned in the class of ' constitutional ' measures which, whenever the two Houses disagreed, should go to a referendum.

Indeed, apart from the merits or the proper rôle of a second chamber, nothing in the story is so clear as the political inferiority of the Unionists. Some were tariff reformers, some free traders; some would accept Ireland as one unit in a federal kingdom, but still more would yield Ireland nothing at all. Jealousies between Conservative and

Liberal Unionist divided the constituencies.   Joseph Chamberlain had been stricken down in 1906 by paralysis, but his name was still more dynamic than Balfour's; his son and representative Austen was a high-minded but unsafe counsellor. Unable to agree, they were dabbling in this weak notion of a referendum, which to Chamberlain's horror Balfour proposed to apply to food taxes.   Lansdowne was the soul of honour and patriotism but an indecisive leader, and an Irish landlord of a rigid pattern.   On the platform they had no speaker comparable to Lloyd George, while they allowed the issue to be diverted from the Lords as a revising chamber to a caricature, of the Lords as defenders of unearned riches.   Worst of all, their counsels were heated by those who, after advising rejection of the budget, declared that Asquith was abusing the Crown and urged the Lords to throw out the Parliament Act also.

Unless history yields further revelations, this reproach to Asquith seems groundless.   The conference having collapsed, in November 1910, when George V had reigned for six — and the controversy had been before the country for eighteen — months, he asked the King for an understanding that, if another dissolution returned the Liberals, he would allow the creation of peers.   To this the King agreed, subject to the condition that, before the dissolution, the Act should be discussed in the Lords.   It was not till July 1911 that this commitment was made public, — a secrecy indispensable, indeed, if the sovereign was to be kept out of discussion.   But it left the Unionists in the dark, apt to be captured by their extremists' argument that this talk of creating peers was a bluff.

This second election of November 1910 left party numbers almost exactly as they had been in January, for the Lords' alternative of a referendum and reform in their membership seemed little more than a death-bed repentance.   In May 1911 the Commons passed the Act by a majority of 121; a group of Conservative peers, christened ' Die-hards ', were still bent on rejecting it, led by Halsbury, Milner, and Salisbury, and supported from without by the Chamberlains, Cecils, F. E. Smith, and the Ulster leader Carson.   Revelation of the King's pledge, however, decided Balfour and Lansdowne that this would be suicide and in August, with the aid of 29 Unionist and 13 spiritual peers, the Act was carried by a majority of 17.

This two years' debate, a landmark in the evolution of the constitution, may too easily distract us from much else of note in this powerful government.   Two sides in a sense it always had : the one, Asquith and his intimate friends Grey and Haldane, with Crewe and McKenna usually in the same camp ; the other, with Lloyd George and Churchill leading, representing a younger age and less certain ambitions.   Lloyd George in particular sharply departed from Victorian Liberalism.   He was a son of the cottage, a Celt whose Nonconformity aggravated every nerve in English conservatism, and a political genius with great gaps of ignorance, who used every expedient of the platform and cheap press. Unionist detestation rejoiced when in 1912 it was revealed that he had done something which a minister of more delicate feeling would have avoided : that, at a time when the British Marconi Company, whose secretary was a brother of Rufus Isaacs the Attorney-general, was given the tender for an Imperial wireless service, Lloyd George and Isaacs acquired shares in the sister company in the United States. Not accused of corruption but saved by a party vote on a charge of what Unionists termed ' grave impropriety ', the ministry survived this storm ; though the departure of Bryce to be ambassador at Washington, of Morley and Haldane to the Lords, and other changes weakened the front bench in the Commons.

Apart from the Parliament Act and foreign policy, their outstanding work was a series of social reforms, which transformed and perhaps destroyed their party. In wages, hours, and health the condition of the working class had improved by great strides in the past half-century, yet the age of *laisser-faire* was closing in some disillusionment and decline. In 1909 the report of a poor-law commission reinforced the conclusions of private investigators and government departments. There was an increased, though still manageable, degree of unemployment ; under-employment and much casual labour ; a mass of lower labourers, both industrial and agricultural, badly paid and worse housed ; greater national wealth, yet an increase in pauperism and an increase in its cost ; finally, despite much effort, there were areas where one in every six children born died in infancy.

Not only economic but political facts called out for a new treatment of this poverty. Universal education had laid a foundation which ought not to terminate in a hopeless slum, democratically elected bodies now controlled local government, the Education Act of 1902 pointed the way to dealing with other social questions through specialist organs of that self-government, while a whole army of social workers (of whom the Chamberlain family might be taken as one type) were experimenting in wider reform.

It was the function of Asquith's government to put these ideals into action. Its pace was uneven, for Burns at the Local Government Board was not constructive, and since a Conservative majority and a Socialist minority of the commission had disagreed, nothing comprehensive was done for the poor law. But from Lloyd George and Churchill especially proceeded an impetus, which translated into law many projects for cutting at the roots of poverty. So came about old-age pensions, and an eight hours' day for miners, in 1908 ; in 1909, labour exchanges, and trade-boards to fix wages in sweated industries; other Acts providing meals for school children, school care committees, and medical inspection; the growth of the Borstal reformatory system for young criminals, and the Children Act of 1908, which made wide provision for their good treatment and prohibited imprisonment below the age of fourteen. In housing they made but small progress, for both Lloyd George's land-value duties and high-interest rates restricted building, and the town-planning Act of 1909, though giving more power of destroying unhealthy dwellings, shirked the question of built-up areas, and answered only vaguely to its name. But fertile law-making marked this government in almost every other branch. A small-holders' Act and a Scottish Board of Agriculture; a shops Act of 1911, reducing hours and enforcing a half-holiday; or the Act of 1912 to give the miners a minimum wage. This last was one instance only of what was incessantly increasing, a new intervention in industrial disputes by the State, usually represented by the stormy petrel Lloyd George.

Greatest of all, no question, was the National Insurance Act of 1911, borrowed from a German example but adapted to our conditions by civil servants and implemented by Churchill and Lloyd George. Like so much British governance before and since, its method was to harness together State machinery and voluntary action. Under Part I, dealing with health, all manual workers between the ages of sixteen and seventy, and earning less than £160 a year, were to be insured in a compulsory and contributory scheme, by contributions coming from the State, employers, and workers; controlled from above by a National Insurance commission, organized (as education had been) by Robert Morant; its benefits administered either by approved societies, that is, the friendly and assurance societies and trade unions, or by the Post-office, and supervised by local committees. So came into being the framework of a national health service: of doctors enlisted in panel work; guaranteed benefits in sickness, disability, and child birth; drugs and sanatoria.

Part II dealing with unemployment was more selective and experimental. On the same compulsory, shared, and contributory basis, it provided insurance against unemployment, though for certain trades only in which employment most fluctuated, as in building, engineering and shipbuilding; framed on genuine principles of insurance, not on any doctrine of 'work or maintenance'; with benefits much lower than wage-rates, and restricted to a maximum of fifteen weeks in any one year.

While all this was being done to humanize society and extend political equality into economic life, work at least as indispensable was helping to preserve the State's very existence. Here the dominating mind was that of Haldane, trained by Scottish civilization, a German education, and a philosophic grasp of law to look for quality and principle. In a fortunate hour for the country Campbell-Bannerman refused him the Lord Chancellorship and put him in that grave of political reputations, the War Office. He had to work through a party which distrusted militarism and only asked for an army on the cheap, and to work too with an army in fearful need of reform ; though he benefited from two of Balfour's measures, the Committee of Imperial Defence and the suggestions for reorganization by Esher's committee. The Army had no central brain. Its organization in peace bore no relation to its needs for war. Its brigades were not formed into divisions. It lacked transport, medical units, and guns. It had a second line, the militia, which could not be used abroad, and a third line of yeomanry and volunteers, formed in many local units, unorganized and half equipped. It was Haldane's work to connect defence with the political facts, which clearly meant a striking force, ready to the last button on mobilization, to take its place alongside the French army in resisting Germany and holding the Channel ports. Having formed a general staff by army order, he created an expeditionary army, with six infantry and one cavalry divisions. For the infantry he preserved Cardwell's creation of two linked battalions, but converted the militia into a third battalion or special reserve, to make good the wastage of war ; he got his second line by amalgamating yeomen and volunteers into a Territorial Force, of fourteen divisions and fourteen cavalry brigades : he established officers' training corps at the universities and schools. He collected round him on the Army Council, and in high command, men whose ability could make his schemes succeed, — Haig, Nicholson, French, Ewart, and Grierson. The Committee of Imperial Defence was systematized into sub-committees to consider every possible phase of emergency ; one of which, guided by its secretary Hankey, compiled the War Book for detailed action. By 1914, and at a cost less than in 1906, the country was able to mobilize within a few days a force of twenty divisions regular and territorial, ready for despatch abroad.

In view of German aggression there was a strong movement, much inspired by Roberts and backed by the Chamberlain influence, and one to which Lloyd George himself was not averse, for some form of compulsory service. But whether the Liberal party could have been won over to the principle, and its cost, remains doubtful ; in any case Haldane was convinced that sea-power was our proper rôle and a professional striking force our real military need.

Till 1910 the Navy was directed by the masterful Sir John Fisher, whose measures of concentration and creation of the Dreadnought fleet we have seen. But his acid ruthlessness divided the Navy into factions and it was only after this time that, in part through Haldane's pressure, something was done to make a naval staff, while the costs of shipbuilding disturbed ministers like Lloyd George who were ardent for social reform. Twice over, First Lords of the Admiralty had to fight hard for the margin of safety which they thought necessary; McKenna over the eight battleships voted in 1907, and Churchill in 1914. But the German threat was too grim to ignore. Our first gestures of reducing or delaying warship construction turned into the policy of ' two keels to one '; the naval estimates for 1913–14 thus reaching £51 millions, or an increase of £18 millions on those of 1905. Late in 1911, to restore unity of strategy between Army and Navy, Asquith made McKenna at the Admiralty and Churchill at the Home Office exchange their places; under the new First Lord the Navy continued reorganization in every direction, in improvement of sailors' pay, expanding the supply of officers, acceleration of building and the decision to equip new bases at Scapa Flow and Cromarty, and ensuring through the Anglo-Persian Oil Company a safe supply of the new fuel.

Never free from this dark shadow and strenuous in their social legislation, the government proceeded within the political frame as it was left by the elections of 1910, and the Parliament Act. One result of that controversy was Balfour's resignation in 1911 from the lead of his party, whose factions and the nakedness of the land were proved anew in the choice of his successor. Between Austen Chamberlain, nominee of the Liberal Unionists, ' die-hards ', and tariff reformers, and Walter Long, an honourable type of Conservative country gentleman, there was a deadlock, which was only resolved by both withdrawing in favour of Bonar Law. The new leader was Canadian by birth, a Scot by later domicile, and an iron merchant by profession; he had made his name in the fiscal controversy but had never held Cabinet office, having only entered Parliament in middle life. Time was to prove his sterling worth as a minister and his lovable character, but though a master of his own subjects and a strong debater, he had not the distinction or popular gifts to which the party of Disraeli and Salisbury were accustomed. In most respects a cautious and pessimistic nature, on the Irish question he was a fanatic, being descended from Ulster Presbyterians, and this, coupled with Lansdowne's rigidity and Chamberlain's loyalties, and a reckless element in the ablest rising leader, F. E. Smith, inflamed further an angry atmosphere.

For looking retrospectively over the years 1910–14, when Europe was descending into a universal war, we find that faction injured this country with a violence unknown since the 1830's. Each limb of it caught contagion from another. Conservatives incited first the Lords and then the Crown to stretch their powers, spoke openly of the King dismissing Asquith or of holding up supply, implied that Ulster would do well to fight, and army officers to refuse obedience rather than coerce Ulster. Syndicalists, among the miners particularly, were teaching that violence was justified against the slow-moving bourgeois, and that by perpetual strike action and sabotage profits could be drained away ; might not a triple alliance between miners, railwaymen, and transport force their will on the community ? Trade-union membership had increased vastly since 1905, assisted hardly more by its own campaign than by the Liberal government. Their Insurance Act swelled the movement by using the unions as approved societies ; their intervention, in railway and mining strikes, compelled the employers to give recognition and negotiate on equal terms with labour executives. Official trades unionism, however, was wrestling with a wave of lawlessness, unauthorized strikes often declared on small grounds, and rebel leadership by shop stewards ; in short, with all the growing pains of a new democracy, in many cases inadequately paid, and bent on using its power to change the economic facts.

Violent, impatient discontents were found in other areas of society. If the high-church clergy had ceased to resist the State's law, it was largely because they had triumphed by doing much as they pleased in ritual observance. But the greatest visible change, no doubt, was in the attitude of women, whose emancipation had begun in the reign of Victoria, who thought they should take no part in public life. John Stuart Mill had taken up their cause as a crusade, women's suffrage societies began in the '60's, and amendments to give them a vote were put before parliament in 1884. The married women's property Act of 1887 first gave them a legal independence. Colleges for women went back as far as the Christian Socialist movement of the '40's, and before 1880 were opened at Oxford and Cambridge, while London and several provincial universities gave them the degrees which the two ancient foundations refused. From 1894 they could sit on parish and district councils, and an Act of 1907 applied this to county and borough councils also. Many hundreds served on education committees, or as guardians of the poor ; government employed them as factory inspectors, they did invaluable work in setting up trade-boards. And now they pressed for the parliamentary vote, already familiar in Australia and New Zealand, which they argued, as men had argued before, was the necessary lever for improving their conditions and the just symbol of civic equality.

The violence of the new campaign came from the Women's Social and Political Union, founded in 1903, and now dominated by Mrs. Pankhurst and her daughter Christabel. This section believed that violence would pay them and compel government to produce a bill, and

they increased their violence every year till the eve of war, by interruption of meetings, attacks on public buildings, assault, bombs, and
wholesale arson. Its effect was to antagonize a Parliament which would
otherwise have been convinced; for though the question cut across
party and in the Cabinet Asquith led a strong opposing section, on the
other side were Grey, Haldane, Lloyd George, a solid Labour party,
and the fact that a principle already rooted in local government could
not be restricted.

Thus emancipation, which Gladstone's life had come to mean, was
faithfully pursued by his political dynasty in all directions, carrying
them to the verge which brings Liberalism to the danger zone of an
enforced equality. In 1912 they produced, but were forced by the
entanglement of women's suffrage to drop, a new reform bill, adding $2\frac{1}{2}$
million new voters. Lloyd George was preparing a land campaign,
applying to Britain the public control, fixed leases, and rent courts
which had changed Ireland. Morley had carried reforms in India, to
extend election to all councils and introduce Indians into the executive.
Cromer's successors were applying the same doctrine to another
Oriental people in Egypt. But their heaviest burden of inherited pledges
lay in Ireland, which during 1912-14 engulfed and embittered all the
feuds of Britain. Here, the Conservatives thought, they might take
their revenge for the budget and the Parliament Act; faced with
the doubts of northern England, Bonar Law abandoned food taxes as
immediate politics and bound his party to the cause of Ulster.

The Irish problem had changed greatly since Gladstone's second
defeat. Land purchase had been largely accomplished, peasants had
become prosperous farmers. Local government was largely in Irish
hands. Redmond, leader of the parliamentary party, had been a
Parnellite but was a man of parliamentary traditions, hopeful of winning
Liberal opinion and ready to see Ireland take her place in the Empire.
With the election of 1910 his chance seemed to have come and his
support of the Parliament Act must bring its reward; he could count
on open sympathy in the Dominions, besides the old pressure from the
United States and its massive Irish vote. There were, on the other
hand, new elements in Ireland, or old elements given a new life, which
menaced this parliamentary school. A continuous tradition of no
compromise ran through Irish history, from Wolfe Tone through
Young Ireland of the '40's, the Fenians, and Parnell, which would
reproach Redmond for any transaction with the ancient enemy. An
Irish republican brotherhood called for violence and the seizing on
any moment of danger to Britain. The Gaelic League was one
of many bodies, preaching a national revival. Arthur Griffith, of
a Dublin working-family, tenacious and selfless and dedicated, had
made his paper, *The United Irishman*, a vehicle of revolt, and

thence came the organization of Sinn Fein, which planned universal passive resistance as the first step to self-government. There was, furthermore, a growing industrial population in Dublin, poorly paid and badly housed, who were listening to syndicalist teaching of violence.

Augustine Birrell, the Irish Secretary from 1907 onwards, was ill fitted for resolute administration; it was also a misfortune that land-purchase finance had broken down, bringing sales almost to a stop. In 1907 they made the grave mistake of permitting the Act to lapse which forbade importation and carrying of arms. Their meagre Irish Councils bill of that year, and long delay before they produced a Home Rule bill in 1912, assisted Redmond's enemies. Moreover, their bill evaded the greatest issue, the matter of Ulster; a community of a million Protestants, rich in the rapid prosperity of Belfast, whom it was certain the British people would never compel by force of arms to be ruled from Catholic Dublin. Though Asquith was aware he would have to make concessions, for tactical reasons he held them back and introduced his bill as for all Ireland, underlining the importance of relieving the Imperial Parliament, and of Ireland as one unit in a federal Kingdom; as was implied by keeping a number of Irish members at Westminster. This bill was thrown out by the Lords in January 1913, repassed over their heads under the Parliament Act, and became law in September 1914 under very changed conditions.

Unionist resistance was always hovering between two schools; an opposition to Home Rule in any shape on the ground that, even if Ulster were satisfied, it was a crime to throw over the Unionists of southern Ireland, and an acceptance of Home Rule provided Ulster was excluded. Ulster's own policy, however, was declared before the bill was produced at all; that is, to prepare a provisional government, ready to defy Home Rule if it became law. Early in 1912 the Ulster Volunteers were organized, and in the autumn the Ulster Covenant was signed.

Their political leader was Edward Carson, who had been a law officer in the Balfour government, and now Bonar Law pledged his party to support Ulster to the end. Government would not take legal proceedings against Carson, if only for the good reason that no Ulster jury would convict, and after much negotiation, in which the Crown played a valuable part, early in 1914 they produced a compromise which Redmond accepted, that certain Ulster counties should be able to ' contract out ' for a term of years. This time-saving device did not satisfy Ulster, which put forward an alternative for the permanent exclusion of a fixed area, with the option of rejoining United Ireland later, if it so voted. In July an all-party conference called by the King failed to agree, and a week later war buried the question.

But it buried it as an explosive mass, for Ireland was repeating its earlier history. Under Birrell's weak governance boycotting, shootings, and cattle-driving revived, and the jury system could not be used. With Home Rule revived, too, the stark division on religious lines. In 1913 James Larkin led a transport strike in Dublin, assisted by a Socialist republican James Connolly, whence sprang up a citizen army. The Ulster Volunteers, now 100,000 strong, in April 1914 ran the blockade, landing masses of arms at Larne. Their example inevitably inflamed the South where a body of National Volunteers was launched by Sinn Fein and extremist organizations, which Redmond took under his own wing in order to bring them under control.

Not only were there these illegal armies, but the Irish question had demoralized the British Army too. Ominous naval and military movements gave an impression that Ulster was to be coerced, a strain not easy to put on an army in which men of Irish Protestant birth like Roberts held more than a proportionate power; one of whom, Henry Wilson at the War Office, was in close touch with Ulster resistance. In March, through a combination of his intrigues and some blundering by Seely, Haldane's successor at the War Office, and by the general commanding at Dublin, the Curragh incident forced this matter to a head; for, when unwisely confronted with a hypothetical choice between obeying orders to fight Ulster or dismissal, a majority of officers in the garrison preferred to be dismissed. By Asquith's taking over the War Office himself, order was outwardly restored, but infinite harm had been done, alike in British politics, class relations, Ireland, and the watchful mind of the German government.

On 24th July the King's summons to the conference declared ' civil war is on the lips of the most responsible and sober-minded of my people ', and two days later the Dublin Volunteers imitated Ulster by disembarking rifles at Howth. But on the 28th Austria declared war on Serbia, and the lamps began to go out in Europe. Neither for British Liberalism nor for British government in Ireland were they, in fact, to be lighted again.

CONTEMPORARY DATES

1906   Algeciras Conference.
        First meeting of the Duma.
1907   Edward VII in Paris and Rome.
        William James, *Pragmatism*.
        Synge, *Playboy of the Western World*.
1908   Opening of the Hedjaz railway.
        President Fallières in London.
        H. G. Wells, *The War in the Air*.

1909 Deposition of Sultan Abdul Hamid.
Bethmann-Hollweg, Chancellor in Germany.
Blériot flies over the Channel.
Death of Meredith and Swinburne.

1910 Accession of King George V.
Japan seizes Korea.
Arnold Bennett, *Clayhanger*.
Death of Tolstoy.

1911 Italy seizes Tripoli.
The *Panther* at Agadir.
Death of Charles Dilke.

1912 Poincaré, Prime Minister in France.
China becomes a republic.
Woodrow Wilson, President of the United States.

1913 Balkan wars.
Einstein's theory of relativity.

1914 The first World War.
Opening of Panama Canal.

CHAPTER XIV

FOREIGN AFFAIRS AND THE STEPS
TOWARDS WAR, 1895–1914

BEFORE Queen Victoria died, her people, all unwitting, entered on what was to prove one of history's most destructive epochs. After many earlier warnings the map of world politics, as Britain had fought to make it in the twenty years before 1815, was torn to shreds. The long security then won having proved illusory, once more we emerged from isolation and formed a new alliance system, contradicting all our maxims for the previous two hundred years. It was based on an understanding with our old enemies France and Russia, and aimed against Germany, so long our friend.

Mighty forces, transcending the will of any one people or the acts of individual statesmen, directed this change in the international order. The revolutionary principles of 1789 had worked out their logic in spreading the notion of liberty to one people after another, and binding this freedom to the ideal of racial nationality. This national passion, denouncing minorities and all else that stood in its way, was spread by the instruments of democracy, the press, and organized opinion, even in the most undemocratic States; massing the pan-Slavism of Holy Russia or the feuds of every Balkan people until it entered Africa through Egypt, and Asia through India and Japan. Simultaneously the free-trading epoch ended in the spilling of European capital over every undeveloped continent, in a scramble for colonies, raw material, and markets. The very progress of humanity redoubled its danger. For the concentrated power of each State had multiplied many times since the wars of the past, being now built on principles which called forth national unanimity and universal military service; years of peace, in Asia particularly, had accelerated the growth of huge populations which must expand or die; scientific invention, by steam and turbine, submarine and airship and explosive, enhanced the weapons of power. And all this in an age when the restraints of religion were disappearing from the human soul.

As the balance now stood, the weights had changed profoundly. The decadence of the Turkish Empire, so long predicted, seemed really to be nearing the hour of death, for which were watching the Roumanians, Greeks, Bulgars, and Serbs, and which might well give the signal for the break-up of Austria-Hungary also. That loose dynastic

Empire, shaken in 1848, mutilated in 1859, and humiliated in 1866, must dread any change, for a majority of its subjects were Slavs looking, like the Czechs, northward toward Russia or, like the Croats and southern Slavs, fomented from outside by Serbia. Bismarck's Germany was still master of the land mass of Europe but his successors failed to keep his golden rules; the French-Russian alliance of 1893 meant that his dreaded dilemma of two hostile fronts had not been solved, while the Triple Alliance was weakened by Italy's open resolve not to be involved in war against Britain. For the time being, however, the French Republic, which was never more corrupt and factious than in the '90's, hovered between two trends, the one of revenge against Germany and the other of an Imperial policy overseas, which must mean collision with Britain; while Russia, beaten off from the Balkans between 1878 and 1890 and held up in her penetration towards India, had turned her eyes to the Far East. This world of the '90's was infected, too, by empires in decline, the Turks' misgovernment of the outlying territories of Tripoli and Syria, or Portugal's huge spaces in Africa. But it was also shocked by new energies. Borrowing models and weapons from western Imperialism, Japan manifested the efficiency of a modern State; between 1890 and 1900 also, the United States so far dropped its old isolation that in Southern America and the Pacific it turned Imperialist.

If here were many possibilities of conflict, yet another clash of principle, well known to Castlereagh and Canning, disturbed the balance; a clash between democracy and personal government. The despots who ruled the eastern empires were more dangerous to peace through their weakness than their strength; through the vain incalculability of the Kaiser William II, the decrepitude of Franz Joseph, and the blind spots in the well-intentioned Czar Nicholas II. Such weakness, of listening to Byzantine flattery or dependence on soldiers and secret counsellors, killed many chances of reconciliation.

British policy during Salisbury's last ministry adhered to that non-commitment to alliances which we had followed so long, though still putting first on its list of possible enemies the same two Powers as it had since Waterloo. Russia's ambition to pass through the Bosphorus, though dormant, was undisguised, and her intervention in the war between China and Japan threatened our rich Far Eastern trade. As for France, we collided with her all over the world. Rosebery had hardly avoided a war over the boundaries of Indo-China and Burma; we disliked their fortification of Bizerta, the naval base of Tunis; boundary disputes over Niger and Congo were spreading towards the Nile valley, which a notable declaration of 1895 from Rosebery's under-secretary, Edward Grey, announced was a British sphere.

Non-commitment, however, though Salisbury preferred it to the end, was a much more uneasy business since the hardening of the two camps. The Concert of Europe was dead. This Salisbury first discovered during the Armenian massacres of 1895–6, for Germany stood out as the champion of Turkey, any disturbance of whose territories would set Austria by the ears both with Italy and Russia. He experienced it again during the Cretan rising, and the Greeks' unsuccessful war of 1897 against the Turk. But the peril of our isolation was shown most clearly in the Far East. In 1895 Russia, France, and Germany combined to force on Japan the surrender of what she had just extracted from China by the peace of Shimonoseki. China gave Russia a line across Manchuria, which would link the Siberian railway with Vladivostok; in 1898 Russia took the great harbour of Port Arthur, and Germany the port of Kiao-chau. To keep some balance in Far Eastern waters, Britain replied by acquiring a lease of Wei-hai-wei.

In addition, our differences with France all but ended in war. In 1896 the Abyssinians annihilated the Italian army at Adowa, the Dervish power we had left intact since Gordon's death was aggressive, and we determined to make a beginning of reconquering the Sudan. That year an Anglo-Egyptian force under Kitchener occupied Dongola, in 1897 Berber, and in September 1898 crushed the Khalifa's army at Omdurman and took Khartoum. All this time, under a determined foreign minister Hanotaux, the great French African Empire had been penetrating the hinterland of our West African settlements; it held the Niger at Timbuctoo, reached Lake Chad, touched the Congo watershed, and an expedition under Colonel Marchand was sent out to reach the Nile. He emerged on the White Nile and hoisted the tricolour at Fashoda, just before Kitchener reached Khartoum. This challenge to the policy we had laid down was deliberate, but it was not till March 1899 that Hanotaux's successor, Delcassé, gave way before our threat of war, and that a dividing line was drawn between British and French spheres of influence.

From yet another quarter, Salisbury's government received a warning of the change in the scales. Our relations with the United States had never been cordial, either before or after the American Civil War. Canada had been made a pawn in Irish Fenian conspiracy, while her tariff arrangements hesitated between reciprocity with America and preferential duties for the mother country. There were old disputes over Newfoundland fisheries, and a new American claim that the Behring Sea and its seal fisheries were a closed American zone. Finally in December 1895, on the eve of the Jameson Raid, President Cleveland, perhaps with one eye on the Democratic party's propects, claimed by virtue of the Monroe Doctrine to impose a settlement in an ancient dispute between British Guiana and Venezuela. His message was

violently worded, but British horror of what Chamberlain called a
' fratricidal war ' was deep, and this particular danger was conjured
away by agreement to arbitrate. Yet the Senate's rejection of a general
arbitration treaty left the Anglo-American future uncertain.

Throughout these years our greatest embarrassment by far was
the attitude of Germany. The Kaiser's personal influence was at its
height and was dangerous. His mind was restless and ill-balanced, as
his correspondence with the Czar may show, dwelling on fantastic
visions, sometimes of war between Britain and America as inevitable,
or very often an obsession that some day Britain meant to ' Copenhagen '
the infant German fleet. Foolish language about ' our old Prussian
god ', the God-bestowed right of kings, or the sharp gleaming sword,
irritated and alarmed other peoples. He declared that Russia and
Germany must stand together against the yellow peril, and from his
own angle shared in the scheme of Holstein, the most dangerous man
in his Foreign Office, that the Triple Alliance should be expanded
into a European confederacy, which could squeeze better terms out of
the complacent and declining British. In detail he was perfectly untrustworthy ; while negotiating with Britain, he would privately deplore
that France did not fight at Fashoda, and though he was decided to ' nail
Russia down in Asia ', he would reveal to the Czar what Britain offered.
That his personality offended his uncle Edward VII, was embarrassing ;
that it filled Salisbury with indignation, was more important.

Taking for granted that Germany pursued Bismarck's method, of
using Egypt as a nuisance value in order to dispute every frontier in
Africa, we come to three matters of first-rate importance. The first
was German policy in Turkey, a determined campaign to capture the
Turkish railways for a German syndicate, and the Kaiser's loud visit to
Palestine in 1898, with its utterance that in him all Moslems would find
a friend. The second was the appointment of Von Tirpitz as head of
the Admiralty and the passing in 1898 of a first Navy law, to produce
twelve battleships and thirty-three cruisers within six years. The third
was the scene in South Africa ; the German decision that Britain should
not control Delagoa Bay, and that the Transvaal should be supported.
This came to a crisis during the Jameson Raid round the New Year of
1895–6. Threats to withdraw the German ambassador, and the Kaiser's
congratulatory telegram to Kruger, made part of a scheme to land
German troops and declare a protectorate, together with enquiries
whether Russia and France would not assist to lower British pride.

Henceforth the atmosphere became much worse, for the flames were
fed by the press of both countries, while Tirpitz and the Kaiser had
reached a fixed view, that Germany's place in the world would never be
secure until her Navy was so strong that not even the greatest naval
power could defy it without serious risk. Our isolation reached a pitch

of extreme danger by the outbreak of the South African War, together
with discussions, initiated from Russia but pursued in Paris and Berlin,
whether or not to form a coalition to mediate. That this danger passed
away peacefully was due not only to the rooted anti-German feeling of
France, Russia's weakness, and Italy's uneasiness in the Triple Alliance,
but to British measures, — which would later have been called ' appeasement ', — to keep Germany quiet. These included a treaty, staking
out claims for Germany and Britain in the event of the bankrupt Portuguese Empire coming on the market, and a settlement in 1899 whereby
Britain, much against her Australasian Colonies' desire, evacuated
Samoa, leaving those islands divided between Germany and the United
States.

This long sequence of dangers brought some British ministers to
the conclusion that it was time to end isolation and to explore a settlement with Germany. Chamberlain was the leader but Devonshire and
Lansdowne supported him, and three times between 1898 and 1901
this negotiation was seriously pressed. By this date the chief German
minister was the bland amoral Bülow, who agreed in conclusion with
the Kaiser, Holstein, and Tirpitz. Time, they thought, was all that
was wanted to get Germany through a danger period, while her Navy
was being created, and time, they argued, was telling against Britain.
The fear underlying their thought was the immemorial German fear of
a giant Russia, and they asked what a British alliance could do except
to entangle them in a defence of the Bosphorus or the Indian frontier, or
what could the British fleet do to keep the Cossacks out of Prussia ?
Besides, what alternative remained to the British ? Holstein was sure
that a British alliance with Russia and France was an impossibility.
It would seem unjust to believe that any of them at this stage desired
war ; they wished to have their hands free, and to mould both groups
of Powers in the direction they pleased ; above all, to keep a close
link with Russia, who in time might bring France into a Continental
scheme, which would keep Britain, America, and Japan in order. They
therefore received coolly Chamberlain's notions of an opening for
Germany in Morocco, or a free hand on a Baghdad railway, or his public
appeal for a triple entente between Germany, Britain, and America.

As the discussions proceeded, the German methods left relations
still worse. Bülow played up to his press, and publicly turned down
Chamberlain's offer by carrying in 1900 the second Navy law, which
would result in a fleet of thirty-four battleships and fifty-two cruisers
within sixteen years. In 1899 the first Hague Conference was called
by the Czar to consider a limitation of armaments, but the German
attitude was purely obstructive. In China the Powers' combination to
put down the Boxer rebellion in 1900 added more dissension, while
it was soon clear that Germany would do nothing to resist Russian

encroachment in Manchuria. When, therefore, the last negotiation took place in 1901, the two nations were found very far apart. The utmost that the British would consider was a defensive treaty, with Germany alone; but the Germans asked all or nothing, — that is, a British adhesion to the Triple Alliance, with a commitment not only to keep Alsace-Lorraine German but to underwrite the position of Austria in the Balkans.

Chamberlain had warned the Germans that, if rejected by them, we should turn elsewhere but, if the years 1901–5 were indeed a turning-point, it was not because Great Britain deliberately made a diplomatic revolution. The Anglo-Japanese treaty of 1902, the Anglo-French entente of 1904, and the Anglo-Russian convention of 1907, did not follow logically in one harmonious scheme. They were, rather, separate parts of a defensive diplomacy which, even when completed, did not create one alliance, while in operation they were controlled by an unforeseen event, the crushing defeat of Russia by Japan in 1904–5. Yet, taken together, they meant a trend which every year it would be harder to reverse.

Our great trade in China would disappear if that country disintegrated and if Russian aggression closed the open door, nor could we keep in those waters a fleet strong enough, unaided, to protect our interests; to Japan it was life and death, if not to recover control of Manchuria, at least to keep Russia out of Korea. The treaty of 1902, however, was defensive and carefully guarded, binding each Power to benevolent neutrality if the other were attacked by one enemy, and only to active assistance if attacked by two other Powers. It was only in 1905 that a revised treaty provided for assistance in case of attack by any one enemy, and was extended to cover all eastern Asia and India.

In English eyes the original purpose of a settlement with France was similarly limited. For twenty years now British and French Imperialism had collided, sometimes over venerable matters like the French fishery claims under the treaty of 1783 and sometimes over new French penetrations, as in Siam, West Africa, and the New Hebrides. At the turn of the century French feeling was savage, humiliated by Fashoda, and distracted by the Dreyfus scandal, which threatened to array conservative and democratic France in rival camps, no less in foreign than in internal affairs. There were two more urgent controversies. Egypt divided us, being to the French an unhealed wound, and Cromer was insistent that French obstruction confounded the reforms which were indispensable. The second area was Morocco, a tangle of Arabs, Berbers, Jews, and foreigners, misgoverned by a spendthrift Sultan, an uneasy neighbour to the French in Algiers, separating French northern from French west Africa, and by its lawlessness a temptation to any rival Power.

If reconciliation was first discussed in 1902 between Chamberlain and Paul Cambon, who as ambassador in London played a great part for twenty years to come, its achievement owed most on the French side to Delcassé, minister of foreign affairs from 1898. In his hands it made a part of several moves to recompense France for the insincerities of Russia and her absorption in the East, which included a skilful wooing of Italy by matching her ambitions in Tripoli against French hopes in Morocco. Lansdowne found him a hard bargainer, but an agreement was signed at last in April 1904. French concessions over Newfoundland and Siam balanced some French frontier gains in Africa, but the core of it lay in the clauses referring to Morocco and Egypt. Subject to a mutual pledge for freedom of commerce, what Britain promised to France in Morocco, the same France conceded to us in Egypt, — a promise of diplomatic support. Secret articles insured a free hand in reforming the foreign colonies' privileges in Egypt; if Morocco disintegrated, the French would be at liberty to act, though Spain should be given a zone of influence and the coast opposite Gibraltar should not be fortified.

Germany could make a grievance of thus being ignored, and the crisis of the next two years came from an effort to reassert herself. It was true that Russia went staggering to defeat at the hands of Japan, which must weaken France in Europe; on the other hand, when the Russian fleet in October 1904 nearly caused war by firing on British fishermen, France mediated between her new friend and her old. The Germans therefore pursued a double policy. While they denounced French aggression and sent the Kaiser to visit Tangier, they also stimulated the Czar with hopes of assistance, drafted a treaty whereby Russia should compel France to join their Continental scheme, and by getting President Roosevelt to mediate obtained for Russia better terms than could have been expected from Japan. In short, France was to be intimidated and the Anglo-French *entente* broken.

They were so far successful that in June 1905 they forced the resignation of Delcassé, but in all else they failed. Britain had given France no pledge of armed support, but was ready to fight if France were attacked; Lansdowne authorized conversations between British and French military and naval officers, — an authorization continued by Campbell-Bannerman and Grey in 1906. In all essentials the conference of Algeciras that year was a German defeat, for Austria was tepid, the Italians' understanding with France was plain, and Russia failed them; the mandate of France and Spain in Morocco received international recognition. It was clear enough that the Franco-Russian alliance stood intact and that the Anglo-French *entente* was near to becoming an alliance also, and if the two were interconnected the encirclement of Germany would be complete.

Three processes of the first magnitude filled the years 1907–8. These were Anglo-German naval rivalry, the Anglo-Russian *entente*, and a re-emergence of Russia in the Balkans. In the British mind the first was always pre-eminent, so that for us it became the prime cause of war, for the national instinct asked, without ever getting a satisfactory answer, for what purpose the strongest military Power was also building a mighty fleet ? And that a fleet not preponderantly of vessels for commerce-protection or defence, but of battleships and battle-cruisers, massed in home waters. It was in vain that this pacific Liberal government reduced Cawdor's programme of 1905, or offered any device which would cut down armaments. A new German Navy law of 1906 answered with a larger programme and provided for widening the Kiel Canal; they rejected our proposals at the second Hague conference as a Machiavellian move, while another law of 1908 laid down construction of four dreadnoughts a year. All our remonstrances were waved aside by the Kaiser as an insult to himself and German self-respect.

Our adoption of the Dreadnought type temporarily reduced our superiority, which consisted in a great number of older ships ; we also believed that, by expansion of dockyards and rapid assemblage of guns and armour, the Germans were accelerating building in advance of the official dates. Hence came about the ' scare ' of 1908–9 when McKenna, backed by a Board of Admiralty threatening to resign, stood firm on six battleships as a minimum, and the Cabinet were finally compelled by national pressure to lay down eight. This was the intermediate answer to the Germans' two fallacies : their belief that the best means to win our respect was to out-build us, and a conviction that we were ready to make war in jealousy of their trade. Yet our exports to Germany were greater than to the United States, nor was any element in Britain so pacific as the City of London.

German fears were much aggravated by Anglo-Russian conversations in 1907. It had been Salisbury's conviction that a strong Russia was needed for the balance of power, though for a generation Russian hostility had everywhere embarrassed us. Reconciliation would not be easy, least of all for a Liberal government, many of whose supporters hailed with pleasure the Russian revolution of 1905 and resented the Czar's dismissal of the first Duma in 1906 ; it would also have to safeguard interests vital to India, for which Curzon as Viceroy had been fighting fiercely.

It was then a limited agreement, in making which Grey, and Morley as Secretary of State for India, played the chief part. Keeping benevolent silence as to the future of the Straits and the Persian Gulf, it made a compromise settlement in three dangerous areas. In Tibet the predominance we had won by Younghusband's expedition to Lhasa was, to Curzon's indignation, put aside and we contented ourselves with mutual pledges against interference. The same pledge was exchanged about Afghanistan, though Russia recognized it as outside her sphere. The crux was Persia, already deeply penetrated by Russian agents and money, where Grey had to leave the north as a Russian sphere, separated by a neutral belt from the British sphere which was designed to guard India and the Gulf. But Russia's perpetual encroachment here up to 1914 was enough to prevent this understanding becoming cordial.

We were, indeed, very far from a close alliance with Russia, where powerful ministers and courtiers inclined the weak Czar towards Germany, and that was proved by the gyrations of Isvolsky, Foreign Minister from 1906 to 1910, between those influences on the right and the pan-Slav pressures which drove him on in the Balkans. Meanwhile the year of 1908-9 marked an increasing danger, that each group of Powers moved at the pace of its least civilized portion. Some murderous band in Macedonia, or some frontier village on the Adriatic, was enough to perturb great capitals, and in this case a general war nearly followed, of which Britain and Germany and France all alike disapproved.

Once more the crisis broke in one of Europe's worse areas, where the Sultan Abdul Hamid still reigned. Macedonia was disputed between war-bands of Bulgars, Turks, Serbs, and Greeks, while an uneasy truce had reigned for ten years between Russia and Austria. The first impetus to war came from Aerenthal, the Austro-Hungarian minister, and that group in his country who saw their greatest danger in the southern Slavs; in particular since the new dynasty, which set itself up in Serbia in 1903, were conspiring with five million Serbs and Croats under Austrian rule. It was accelerated by the Anglo-Russian *entente*, which might agree to enforce reforms in Turkey and by a meeting of the Czar and King Edward in June 1908; it was touched off by the rising of the Young Turk party against the Sultan, a month later. Behind the back of his allies Isvolsky made a bargain with Aehrenthal; that Austria might annex Bosnia and Herzegovina, the two Serbian provinces she had garrisoned since 1878, if Austria in return supported the opening of the Straits to Russian warships.

But the Austrian betrayed his confederate and seized his own part of the spoil; in October Austria annexed the two provinces, at the same time arranging that Ferdinand of Bulgaria should declare his sovereign independence of Turkey.

These transactions would not stop short in this crumbling soil, and Grey's contention was that such breaches of treaty must be dealt with by European conference, — not that we were prepared to fight after Isvolsky's craftiness, or make a one-sided arrangement about the Straits. Germany, too, was outraged by the Austrians' treatment of her Turkish friends, but for them it became a trial of strength; for they could not abandon Austria, their one firm ally, in face of a warlike Serbia and the indignation of Russia. In the end the crisis passed off in 1909, in part by some financial compensation for Turkey, but even more through a German ultimatum to Russia. Not that Germany desired war at this moment, or on this matter ; but Conrad, the Austrian chief of staff, pleaded for it, and had war broken out Germany was pledged to stand, as the Kaiser later boasted, behind her ally ' in shining armour '.

What the fall of Delcassé had been to France, this Bosnian humiliation was to Russia, a defeat inflicted by a threat of war. It was the fatality of German policy not only to injure but to insult, and to make it impossible for other States to retreat again.

To what extent, while the Liberal government won the two elections of 1910, was Great Britain committed, as Europe moved towards the abyss ? Her destiny, to a degree perhaps unparalleled in the case of any Foreign Secretary since Canning, was directed for ten years by Edward Grey. This rare character had the entire trust of his countrymen, though no one did less to court popular favour. Wholly devoid of personal ambition, borne up in popular life by a sense of duty amid innumerable private sorrows, more radically minded than his nearest friends, he came from the Whig dynasties which had so often controlled our policy, and shared their attitude. Building on what Lansdowne had begun, his aim was peace and his method was to keep in being a Concert of Europe. It may be that his insularity, his almost total non-acquaintance with the countries of Europe and their rulers, blinded him in a measure to the effect of his policy, or exposed him to pressure from less disinterested men. On the other hand, this very detachment allowed him to speak with a voice which imparted a moral nobility to what his country was trying to do.

His rôle in an age of imminent danger was thus to steer a middle course, and to keep the body of British and, as he would have wished, of world opinion, united. On one side he was pushed at by colleagues who detested expenditure on armaments, Liberals and Labour men who hated contact with Czarist Russia, and a large mass of all parties who would resist commitments and distrusted French militarism. On the other, he was girded at by those who were convinced that Germany meant war, and exhorted to turn these *ententes* into clear-cut alliances. This second opinion was strong not only in the services but in the Foreign Office itself, where the powerful figure of Eyre Crowe, Nicolson's devoted purpose, and Hardinge's experience all converged in that direction.

It was, however, Grey's argument, as it had been Salisbury's, that the hands of Britain were and must remain free ; the military conversations which he and Campbell-Bannerman authorized with the French were to be non-committal, and when in 1912 they were revealed to the Cabinet, this point was emphasized in an exchange of letters. But it is possible to trace in Grey's papers a settled mournful conviction that Germany meant war, or at the least that their war party was too strong for the Kaiser and his civilian ministers. Always ready to look for ways of giving Germany her place in the sun and well aware of aggressive elements in Russia and France, in the last resort he could not antagonize allies on whom we might have to depend for our very life. He must turn a blind eye to Russian intrigues in Persia, stand behind France in Morocco, and connive at Italian encroachment in Tripoli. To a man of this type there was also another motive, more moral though perhaps more insidious, the motive of honour; that our name would stink in Europe if, having encouraged expectations in our allies, we let them down.

What sacrifices our Liberal policy would make for peace was shown in much besides our repeated efforts to reduce or stabilize naval armaments. It was shown by the discouragement poured on the campaign for conscription, and again by the Naval Prize bill which, following on the Hague Conference, our government put forward in 1911 and which was thrown out by the Lords. For this bill, much against the Admiralty's protest, would have crippled the right of search at sea we had always claimed in war, by exempting neutral ships if under convoy, and by making non-contraband some raw materials, such as cotton and rubber, which were vital for a modern war-machine.

In this, just as in a stand against the atrocious Belgian oppression in the Congo, Grey looked to moral ends, and a reconciliation of British interests with the world's sense of justice. This it was which guided perhaps his greatest achievement, the amendment of our relations with the United States. It had begun earlier in the hands of Lansdowne and Chamberlain, for we had shown our sympathy during the Spanish-American war of 1898, withdrew our previous objection to American control of the Panama Canal, and accepted their contention regarding the frontiers of Alaska. But though much was due to American statesmen, their Secretary of State, John Hay and the two Presidents Theodore Roosevelt and Woodrow Wilson, there were awkward corners during Grey's term of office, which he and Bryce, our ambassador at Washington, did most to turn. One was the naval doctrine of this greatest of neutral Powers, 'the freedom of the seas', which the Declaration of London was designed to meet. A second was our Japanese alliance, which was not agreeable to a Pacific Power with a strong sense of 'colour' and a zeal for the integrity of China. This determined the revision of that alliance in 1911, whereby we rid ourselves of any obligation to make war on a third Power with whom we had signed an arbitration treaty. For though the Senate in 1912 rejected Grey's first effort, he persisted until he brought about a general arbitration treaty in 1914. For this understanding that America and Britain stood essentially for the same things, he reaped a first reward in Woodrow Wilson's courageous deed in 1914 when he repealed the Panama Act, which had given preferential terms to American shipping.

After the Bosnian crisis a certain lull followed, and some important personal changes. Isvolsky left the scene of his humiliation in Russia, to be succeeded by Sazonov; Bülow at Berlin was followed in the Chancellorship by a more upright man in Bethmann-Hollweg; in 1912 Poincaré formed a strong French government, next year becoming President; in 1912 also Aehrenthal died and was replaced by the weaker Berchtold. But the essential forces did not change and the hardening of the lines proceeded. Russia still pressed her historic object, the opening of the Straits for her warships, and prepared for a Balkan revenge by nursing the ambitions of Bulgars, Serbs, and Greeks. Italy reinsured herself all round Europe. France steadily used the Act of Algeciras as a means of making a Morocco protectorate.

For Britain the barometer of all these moves was the German Navy, and nothing but the removal of that challenge could reassure us. From Bethmann-Hollweg's appointment in 1909 two years of negotiation passed, during which German ministers occasionally breathed the possibility of slowing up their shipbuilding. But the more these conversations were pursued, the clearer it became that the Tirpitz school were in the ascendant, and that as the price of naval concession even moderate Germans would demand a political agreement, which would mean the breaking of the Russian and French *ententes*. They came to an end in Haldane's mission to Berlin of January 1912; though he found the elements of fair bargaining over the Baghdad railway or Africa, even to the extent of our ceding Zanzibar, on the naval question there was a dead stop. When we offered a pledge of non-aggression, the Germans would only accept a binding formula of absolute neutrality if war were ' forced upon ' Germany. And not only so; it was found that the new German Navy law now passing would mean more capital ships, and a third squadron in home waters.

Since our offer of a ' naval holiday ' had no effect, the reply was inevitable. We should keep a 60 per cent superiority in Dreadnought strength and build two keels to one, while there were other momentous political results. The first was an ever-closer association with the Dominions in defence; the second, a far-reaching agreement with France. The reorganization on which our Admiralty insisted, basing the first fleet in home ports and concentrating our Mediterranean force upon Gibraltar, meant that for some years our security there must depend on the French, who transferred their fighting strength to those waters. In such a military decision there was involved a political effect. Such were the barren fruits of Tirpitz's triumph; of an expenditure of £200 millions on their fleet between 1900 and 1914, and a programme for thirty-five ships of Dreadnought type by 1920.

Half-way through this conflict came the next crisis of 1911, pivoting on Agadir. Once again, as Grey saw, Germany had a real grievance in which Spain also shared, that French intervention between rival Sultans in Morocco and their expedition to Fez destroyed the settlement of 1906. But once more the German method of negotiation imperilled what might be a proper claim, and set Europe on fire. Their despatch of a gunboat to Agadir, a closed port on the Atlantic, — the precise move already discussed at Berlin some years before; demands on France for great cessions in her Congo colony; a blank silence after our declaration that we must take part in any new settlement; all these brought the British Cabinet into the open with Lloyd George, the supposed leader of the peace party, as their spokesman. If, his Mansion House speech said, Britain was to be treated ' as if she were of no account in the Cabinet of nations . . . peace at that price would be a humiliation intolerable for a great country like ours to endure '. Since neither Germany nor the pacific Caillaux government wished a general war, a settlement was reached but only after dangerous recriminations, and the German recognition of a French protectorate in Morocco in return for a rich slice of the Congo plastered but did not heal the wound.

This crisis led direct to those which followed. For Italy, ever jealous of France, concluded the hour had struck for what all the Powers had unwillingly agreed must come, and in September 1911 made war on Turkey to seize Tripoli. Long before that war was done, the Balkan races decided to take advantage of Turkey's plight, and overturned the Young Turks who had lately deposed Abdul Hamid. The ambitious Ferdinand of Bulgaria, the new Greek minister Venizelos, and Russian agents, brought about early in 1912 a league of Bulgars, Serbs, and Greeks. Too late, under French criticism, Russia tried to avert the storm she had helped to raise, and in October the league, with Montenegro also, attacked Turkey.

The Balkan wars passed through two phases; a first from their outbreak until May 1913, during which the allies captured every strong point, from Albania to Salonica and Adrianople; and a second, from June to August 1913, in which they fell out among themselves, the Serbs and Greeks, aided by Roumanians and Turks, turning on the Bulgars. The map was thus revolutionized by force, and a peace made which left Bulgaria embittered, and every Balkan State discontented. What mattered much more was how a general war was again barely avoided.

Indirectly, the Slav states' triumph was a triumph for Russia and, therefore, an Austrian defeat; Conrad, their chief of staff, who a year before had wished to attack Italy, was now arming against the Serbs. But Russia's military preparations were in arrears, France wished for peace, Germany was not ready to be dragged into war at Austria's heels, and a London conference under Grey's presidency in the winter of 1912–13 damped down the flames. Its chief contribution was to create an independent Albania, which would meet the Austrians' wish to prevent Serbia reaching the Adriatic and there joining hands with Montenegro.

Yet the archives now make clear that henceforward the drift was out of control. Dread of it enhanced armaments, which in turn increased its speed; France raised her term of military service from two years to three, there was a capital levy in Germany, and larger armies in Russia. Each group was haunted by a fear that the loosing of one stone would bring its whole system toppling, and each prepared to fight, however rotten the individual stone might be.

Taken in themselves, Anglo-German relations were no worse in 1913–14 than in the last ten years. Lichnowsky the German ambassador found, as his predecessor had, no taste for aggression in Britain, the Germans were helpful during the Balkan conference, and Grey persisted in his patient patching up of weak places. The German scheme for a Baghdad railway involved numerous objections as regards Russia, Turkish finance, and the Persian Gulf, but all these interests were safeguarded, after arduous negotiation, by an agreement completed in June 1914. In principle, too, agreement was reached on the thorny question of the Portuguese colonies, dividing them into British and German spheres of influence for economic and, if Portugal parted with them, political privileges.

But the root of all evil lay elsewhere. Twenty years of blundering aggression had stripped Germany of every firm ally except Austria, while a waft of death had gone up against the Austro-Hungarian Empire. Its Slav subjects were deep in conspiracy; Italy was a jealous rival; the Roumanian alliance was lost, thanks to Hungarian oppression of its Roumanian areas. The Balkan War had meant a diplomatic defeat, with the magnifying of Serbia and Greece, and all who counted on Russian support. Gradually the influence of Conrad and the soldiers wore down the hesitations of the heir-apparent Franz Ferdinand, Berchtold the Chancellor, and Tisza the Hungarian minister, with a conviction that the Empire would perish unless Serbia were crushed, either by a diplomatic offensive or by war. All through 1913–14 we find Russia and the German Powers manœuvring for position, to win Bulgaria or Turkey, Greece or Roumania, and in the background the Kaiser's fatal decision, supported by his soldiers, that in the last resort, right or wrong, Austria must be upheld. If a great war of Teuton against Slav must come, and of that they were convinced, then better sooner than later; before Russian armaments and railways were complete, and before her campaign to reach the Straits matured. On the Russian side, if the army and the pan-Slav press and Isvolsky, now at Paris, worked for war, on the other hand the Czar, Sazonov, and the strongest voices were anxious to postpone it. Yet the dynasty could not safely suffer, nor national pride endure, another such ultimatum as in 1909.

Amid these primeval hatreds and in the throes of the Irish question the British Cabinet moved, its hands still free, on paper, from entangling alliances and giving warning to its partners against aggression. Though not sharing the belief, powerful in some of their official advisers, that Germany unquestionably intended war, we may take it that Asquith and Grey had minimum points on which they would stand to the last; not to suffer an attack on France, the Channel ports, or Belgium. Whether they kept their eyes too intently on Berlin and did not make close enough contact with Vienna and the Balkans, or whether they considered Berlin too much in terms of civilian ministers without taking due account of the soldiers, these are questions less easily disposed of.

The most brutal murder by two Bosnians with Serb connivance on 28th June of Franz Ferdinand and his wife at Sarajevo in Bosnia, the Austrian decision to seize their chance, the Kaiser's promise to support them on 5th July and on 28th July an Austrian ultimatum, so framed that no independent State could have accepted it, — such was the train of events which brought us to the issue of peace and war. The timetable of that fateful week is in itself enough to lay the immediate responsibility elsewhere, while the documents reveal both the double-headed government of Germany and its doubly mistaken diagnosis : to wit, that an Austro-Serbian war could be localized, if only it were quickly disposed of. As against Britain, it may be a real criticism that, as in the Crimea, Cabinet and party divisions let slip a chance of peace. For, it has been argued, if we had promptly declared our intention of fighting alongside France and Russia or, again, declared some days earlier our decision to fight if Belgium were invaded, the Germans would have drawn back.

Once a certain speed was reached in their military machinery's revolution, we may say that the second view became untenable, since the German effort was geared to carry out the Schlieffen plan for a vast envelopment of France through Belgium. And the first criticism, even if more just, is academic, seeing that our ministers' papers make it certain that an earlier declaration would have wrecked the Cabinet and divided the country. If Asquith, Grey, Haldane, and Churchill would think it disaster and dishonour to abandon France, some other ministers (as Morley and Burns proved by resignation) were against intervention at all. The majority, like the majority probably of the people, would decline to fight in a Balkan quarrel. Asquith and Grey then must move by gradual stages, if the government was to survive and the country to be kept at one.

Though on 29th July a German bid for our neutrality was rejected, in return for their promise not to annex French and Belgian territory in Europe, the Austrian and Russian mobilization and then a German ultimatum to Russia passed before our Cabinet could reach decision. It was not till 2nd August that, fortified by promises of Unionist support, they agreed that the German fleet should not be allowed to enter the Channel; though the Germans had already refused to pledge themselves to respect Belgian neutrality, even so it was not till that evening, when they had invaded Luxemburg and demanded a passage through Belgium, that Lloyd George and the Cabinet majority came round to resistance.

Though Grey, and Asquith with him, would have resigned if we had abandoned France, it was the Belgian issue which united Cabinet and country. Never was a national outlook better expressed than by Grey's speech on the 3rd August, backed not only by Bonar Law for the Unionists but by Redmond for Ireland. On the 4th, aware now that German troops were in Belgium, our ultimatum demanding assurances for Belgium's neutrality was sent off, and expired without a reply that night; and the Europe which our statesmen had known since the Tudors expired with it.

It would be easy to spread the responsibilities for this calamity to all mankind; to show that by offensive means Austro-Hungary was fighting a defensive war, or that the Slavs were defending a racial offensive, or to admit that British and French Imperialism often provoked a natural indignation. The chain of crime might be traced much further back in Turkish persecution, the partitions of Poland, or the aggression of Louis XIV. But for Great Britain in 1914 all doubts and questionings were swallowed in a plain instinct, which had driven them to fight Philip of Spain, Louis XIV, and Napoleon; that an overweening military strength threatened the balance of power, the open sea, and the liberty of nations, on which depended alike our safety, livelihood, and ideals.

TIME TABLE, 1914

28 June　The murder at Sarajevo.
5 July　Germany promises Austria her full support.
23　,,　Austrian ultimatum delivered at Belgrade.
25　,,　Serbia accepts the bulk of it, offering to refer two crucial points to the Powers or to the Hague Tribunal.

26 July   British fleet on trial mobilization is kept from dispersal. Grey suggests a Four-Power conference (Britain, Germany, France, and Italy).

27   „   Germany rejects the conference.

28   „   Austria declares war on Serbia. The Kaiser and Bethmann-Hollweg urge moderation on Vienna.

29   „   Partial Russian mobilization against Austria. Germany bids for British neutrality. Austria begins bombardment of Belgrade.

30   „   Russia accepts a conference, but orders general mobilization. On hearing this, Moltke urges the same on Austria.

31   „   General Austrian mobilization ; they refuse to stop operations in Serbia. German ultimatum to Russia, demanding demobilization within twelve hours, and another to France demanding a pledge of neutrality.

1 Aug.   Germany declares war on Russia. General mobilization in France. Germany declines to give Britain a guarantee for Belgian neutrality.

2   „   The Conservative Opposition urge the Cabinet to support France and Russia. Grey gives France a pledge not to allow the German fleet to operate in the Channel or North Sea. German ultimatum to Belgium.

3   „   Mobilization of British Expeditionary Force. Belgium asks for our diplomatic support. Germany declares war on France.

4   „   German forces cross the Belgian frontier. Issue of British ultimatum.

CHAPTER XV

THE FIRST WORLD WAR, 1914–1918

BY the end of 1914 the Germans had failed in their master plan, which was to break the life of France within six weeks and then, gripping the Channel ports to fend off Britain, turn their strength on Russia and wound that unwieldy bulk in so many vital places that it must collapse. On the contrary, the war was to last for fifty-two months. Its prolongation, sufferings, and universality brought about effects unpredictable when it began; the destruction not only of three empires, German and Austro-Hungarian and Turkish, but a total revolution in Russia and violent change within the British Empire itself.

In its first pattern the war, from our point of view, took the same form as those waged against Louis XIV or Napoleon; that is, a struggle against the strongest military Power, holding the interior lines and the land mass of Europe. To win victory we counted first, and as it proved justly, on the means which Marlborough and the Pitts had employed before; to use sea-power as our weapon for a relentless siege and hold the enemy armies through the force of our Allies, reinforcing them with whatever military effort we could afford on land, though even more by money and munitions. This British method of war, waged from the circumference against the centre, followed much the same sequence as in 1704, or 1805–15. While by blockade and commerce destruction we constricted the central mass from the sea, we sought to win additional allies, or to enforce neutrality, all round the circumference; with the result that, for every alliance gained, we also incurred some new and often conflicting political obligation. So the circle widened until a war, begun by a squalid murder in Bosnia, ended with British soldiers fighting in Syria, on the Caspian, at Archangel, in East Africa, the Alps, and the Caucasus.

Beginning, therefore, with an original understanding with France and Russia, which in September we converted into an agreement to make peace only in common, our alliance system extended outwards. Belgium was brought in at once by the German onslaught; Japan, by her wish to avenge and be rid of the obstacles Germany had put in her path. Serbia and her partner Montenegro being necessarily engaged, it was certain that the whole Balkans must sooner or later be engulfed. Nothing could have restrained those defeated in 1912–13, Bulgaria and Turkey, from taking an opportunity of revenge, except a decisive victory for the Russians or a swift agreement by the victors of 1913 on compromise. But not all the efforts of British diplomacy could induce Serbs and Greeks to loosen their hold on Macedonia. Roumania, it is true, passionately wished to seize Hungarian Transylvania, but they too had taken Bulgarian lands, and until 1916 kept their watchful neutrality. A war with Turkey was the last thing desired either by Russia, already in mortal danger, or by Britain, with her millions of Moslem subjects and her dependence on peace in Egypt, and Grey was therefore firm that Venizelos' offer of alliance must be declined, and the Allies promised to guarantee the integrity of Turkey. But the young Turks had long ago decided their course and in August signed a secret treaty with Germany; entering the war in October after the fast German cruisers, *Goeben* and *Breslau*, had escaped from Malta to Constantinople. Out of this Turkish war and its ups and downs came the long hesitation of Bulgaria, terminated by their joining the Germans in September 1915, together with a duel for power in Greece between the Kaiser's brother-in-law, King Constantine, and Venizelos.

Parallel with this haggling in the Balkans there proceeded a long bargaining with Italy. Her refusal to fight on the side of the Triple Alliance had been foreseen, and the question was whether she would fight against them. Her finances were weak, her German connections were very intimate, and a strong party led by Giolitti held out for neutrality; Salandra and Sonnino, however, and the young patriotic zealots voiced by the poet D'Annunzio, saw the chance of realizing every Italian's desire. Her price was enormous, much beyond what the Austrians would pay, and much resented by the Slavs, but at the date of the secret treaty of London in April 1915 the Allies' position was so desperate, that the risk was taken. Italy was promised the Trentino and the southern Tyrol, Trieste, Istria, northern Dalmatia, a practical protectorate over Albania, the twelve Aegean islands she had filched from Turkey in 1912, and full possession of Libya, together with a promise of expansion in Asia Minor and Africa if the Allies partitioned Turkey or took the German colonies.

Once again, therefore, as of old, this was a war of a scattered coalition against one central power; for the German staff soon took control of the inefficient Austrians. Between Russia and her western allies there was no direct physical contact, but every chance of misunderstanding; while, as between France and Britain, there was until 1917 no continuous unity of command but, on the contrary, a grievous degree of military jealousy. Many times over, the mutual hatreds or special objectives of our allies prohibited some operation of war, or impeded some step to peace.

If these were familiar difficulties in British history, this war was also changed and prolonged by new weapons and inventions. No Power had foreseen the hurricane development of artillery; in one battle the British used more shells than in the whole South African War. The power of the defensive, as the Germans proved, was multiplied by entrenchment, machine-guns, barbed wire, and grenades. Their use of poison gas, first employed near Ypres in 1915, and of Zeppelin airships to strike at industrial populations, imparted a new scientific savagery. Aircraft above the battle-fields eliminated tactical surprise. Possession of a single overwhelming weapon outweighed numbers. Warships firing at 20,000 yards obliterated their enemy without contact. Wireless from the Admiralty issued command, or transmitted intercepted messages, to battle-cruisers off Heligoland or the Dogger Bank. The laying of great mine-fields, and the use of submarines to sink passenger or merchant shipping without warning or rescue, confounded the laws of neutrality and pushed the war zone back to the outer oceans.

Subject to these new perils, British sea-power faithfully fulfilled its old mission. By the end of 1914 every German colony, with some notable exceptions in Africa, was in Allied hands. The expeditionary force was taken to France without loss of man or ship, a Canadian corps was brought to England, and Australian and New Zealand troops to Egypt, while regular troops in India and Territorials from Britain were interchanged. Except for a raid to bombard the Yorkshire coast the German High Sea Fleet kept in its protected harbours, only to emerge, indeed, five times in the first two years of war. The Channel and North Sea were firmly blockaded, by the Grand Fleet based on the Orkneys, the light craft on Harwich, and the Second Fleet on Sheerness. Strength was found to hunt down every German cruiser in distant waters. The *Emden*, after audacious ventures in the Indian Ocean, was destroyed near Java; in November, von Spee's cruisers overwhelmed Cradock at Coronel off the Chilean coast, but were themselves destroyed at the Falkland Islands in December by Sturdee's much more powerful squadron.

Most vital of all duties was to keep the sea-lanes open for food and munitions, on which our bare life must depend. This involved the handling of neutral States and the search of their ships for contraband, which would keep Germany alive, a task made infinitely more hazardous by submarine war. It soon became apparent that the proposals of the Declaration of London were incompatible with a successful blockade, which in these days of torpedoes and mines must be exercised from a distance; we must bring in suspect ships for examination, nor could we afford to let pass some war essentials like rubber and oil. It was Grey's achievement to reconcile what was necessary for our existence with the good will of the United States, whose munitions were indispensable, and whose good offices as mediator or, later perhaps, their assistance as ally, might turn the scale. To drive even a minor State like Sweden over to the German side might be dangerous for Russia, but to antagonize the United States might lose the war. The strains were innumerable and highly dangerous, for at one time, for instance, over a thousand American firms were on our ' black list ', as suspect of trading with the enemy. Much, then, was due to the close understanding between Grey and Walter Page, the American ambassador in Britain.

This tightening blockade, pushed outwards until it reached customs-houses in America or the West Indies, implied the keeping of watch and ward in all weathers and all waters, by a multitude of cruisers, mine-sweepers, and trawlers. Under Fisher, whom Churchill brought back as First Sea Lord when war began, a great building programme was launched of vessels large and small, which redoubled our Dreadnought superiority and immensely added to our destroyer and submarine strength.

One other general condition, for good and ill, overruled this new sort of total war. In the democratic States nothing could mass the people's purpose, or fire them to bear years of sacrifice, except public opinion, and the power which formerly descended from the speeches of Pitt and Canning, or Napoleon's bulletins, was now exercised through the press and government propaganda. The influence of the popular press, and its proprietors, rose to a degree before unknown, and not invariably for good, to which was due the ungrateful clamour which drove Haldane from office as supposedly pro-German, and the First Sea Lord, Louis of Battenberg, as a man of German blood. It was used also by politicians, rival generals, and even rival government departments. It was responsible later for much which was bad in the terms of peace.

Nothing, on the contrary, was more genuine, or in the long run more decisive, than the feeling we were fighting for causes much larger than our own; the cause of all small nations and all liberties. This flooded the recruiting-stations in 1914, and produced from this unmilitarized nation over three million volunteers. That voluntary sacrifice excited an idealism which helped to bring America to war, set up a contagion in the East, and bequeathed to the world of 1919 a short vision of a better world.

Historically the four years fall into two clear stages, dividing round the months between December 1916 when Lloyd George supplanted Asquith, and the spring of 1917, when revolution wiped out Russia and the United States declared war. But each large stage was subdivided into periods of deadlocks and periods of desperate action.

Of these, the first expired with the year 1914. All that Haldane had inspired was now justified in the immediate despatch to France of four infantry divisions and one of cavalry; in their highly trained quality and unsurpassed rifle fire; and in the administration which, by the next May, had expanded this vanguard of 90,000 to 600,000 men. But this army was immediately caught up in military disaster.

Hopelessly miscalculating the German plan, the French hurled themselves north-eastwards in a costly offensive; by the time, 22nd August,
that the British took up their place near Mons, seven German armies of
1½ million men were advancing, swinging west in a huge enveloping
movement, to drive the Allies back on either side of Paris and roll them
up against other German armies in the east. Day by day the British
were forced back, barely saved from the closing trap by Smith-Dorrien's
2nd Army standing at Le Cateau, until by 5th September they had
retreated over the Marne. French, our commander, was in fact hardly
prevented by Kitchener from crossing the Seine and moving his base
right back to the Loire.

A final defeat of the French, the loss of Paris and perhaps of the war,
were averted through the weak grip of Moltke, the German chief, and
the mistakes of his army commanders, which gave Joffre his chance.
The battle of the Marne, 6th–13th September, though not a triumph for
British generalship, was a decisive battle for the world, for the Germans
were driven back to the Aisne and the whole Allied front reformed.
They had not, either, been able to seize the Channel ports. Assisted by
a last stand at Antwerp, where Churchill rightly directed a minute
British force, what was left of the Belgian army was brought safely to
the Yser, while the British seized the Ypres salient. Here, in October
and November, pressed the brunt of overwhelming German numbers;
in this first battle of Ypres the British regular Army was half-destroyed,
but the Channel ports were saved and the flank could not be turned, for
it had reached the sea.

Open warfare raged in the east, for the Russians, in answering the
French appeal, were driven out of East Prussia with bloody loss, but
swept the Austrians back to the Carpathians. In the west a long line
of trenches and fortifications ran from the flooded coast of Belgium,
through Flanders mud, over the chalk downs of central France, away
through the wooded Argonne, through Lorraine and the Alsace hills,
until it reached Switzerland; and here, for more than three years, the
mass of British strength was held and suffered.

Dour indecisive fighting never ceased on this front through 1915.
At Neuve Chapelle in March, the second battle of Ypres in April,
Festubert in May, and Loos in September, the British Army in Artois
moved in accord with French attacks farther south, and never with
success. It suffered some 300,000 casualties this year; losing 60,000
at Loos alone, the most unhappy of our battles in its wastage of
inexperienced battalions. Soon after, French was superseded, and the
command given to Sir Douglas Haig.

French, no doubt, lacked the balance required in a commander-in-
chief, especially in one commanding what was a small section of an
Allied army. But the causes of failure went far beyond individuals.

To loosen the German hold on the richest industrial regions of France, to wear them down by attrition, was the strategy of the French soldiers, and often enough we fought against our better judgment, as we did at Loos against Haig's protest. Some responsibility also attached to Kitchener. His appointment as Secretary of State was brought about by popular clamour, his hold on the national imagination was unique, and the service he rendered was immense in impressing the scale of the war. But his eastern training and lonely self-dependence led him to over-centralize, with the result that, in effect, he duplicated the two rôles of Cabinet minister and chief-of-staff; nor was he equipped to understand Cabinet government, nor swift to grasp that only civilian assistance can make possible a total war.

The major cause was a simple one : that we were far behind the enemy in armaments. Our infantry began with only two machine-guns to a battalion; our artillery were armed almost wholly with shrapnel, not with the high explosive shells which could obliterate trenches and wire, and in that policy French too long agreed; our deficiency in heavy guns was disastrous ; in mortars, howitzers, and trench weapons, almost as bad. Our ordnance department and arsenals were slow to accept new ways. Production was obstructed by trade-union rules and fell behind contract, and though our munitions output had expanded twentyfold by the early summer, it was plain enough, and brought home by Northcliffe in the press with support from French, that our guns were not receiving one-fifth of the ammunition necessary. The Ministry of Munitions, inspired by Lloyd George and put in his charge in June, came too late to affect the campaign of 1915.

This deadlock in the west and this failure of armaments, which was handicapping Russia even more tragically, brought about conflict in the Allied councils. To France, with the enemy within sixty miles of Paris and holding her iron and coal areas, the west must be all in all, while to concentrate on the main front was the orthodox doctrine of our own soldiers ; above all, when that front might be reinforced by a flood of Germans, returning from a defeated Russia, or might even become a springboard for invading Britain. Yet to get round what could not be frontally taken, to use the amphibian power of our island in diversion ; to fall, not on strong Germany but on her weaker allies ; here were rival arguments of great weight. Fisher's notion of seizing German islands, or attacking in the Baltic, was deemed too risky ; but even in January 1915 Lloyd George pointed to the Balkans, as a back-door into Austria, and Churchill already advocated the Dardanelles. So developed the contest between ' easterners ' and ' westerners ', which was sometimes equivalent to a contest between civilians and soldiers, and sometimes between Britain and France.

When Turkey came into the war and hopes grew of enlisting Italy,

Greece, and Roumania and of preventing Bulgaria going over to the other side, this Dardanelles project came to new life, stimulated by Russia's appeal to her allies to take off Turkish pressure. Its history was unhappy, for it began as a diversion and ended in a large-scale expedition, entangled in the rival ambitions of the Balkans. Greek assistance might have been invaluable but our government, after consulting the Opposition leaders, in March promised Russia possession of Constantinople when peace was won, and the Russians vetoed the employment of a Greek army Again, our expedition, being opposed by Kitchener from one angle and by Fisher from another, opened as a military compromise, being originally viewed as a naval operation in which ships should silence the forts and force their way through the Narrows to Constantinople ; and since both the French and Kitchener were firm that troops could not be spared, it was looked on as a venture which could, if a failure, be broken off and, if successful, would only require a small landing-force. But by the end of March the sailors reported they could not get through alone, prestige was involved, troops from the East were now available, and in April Ian Hamilton with a considerable army was given the task of capturing the Gallipoli peninsula.

Our first advantage of surprise having vanished, our forces found garrisons massed under German command, beaches wired, and guns sited. The British at Cape Helles and other beaches round the peninsula's southern corner, the Australian-New Zealand Army Corps (Anzac) half-way up its western side, could make no progress, squeezed between open beaches and heavily defended hills, perpetually under fire even when in reserve, always short of water, and with serious wastage from disease. In May Hamilton called for large reinforcements, which he did not receive until August, in part owing to a change in the government at home.

Between 6th and 9th August he made his last effort, in a dual attack from Anzac and a more northerly landing at Suvla Bay. It failed by a narrow margin, and largely through the incompetence of his subordinate generals, after heavy losses in which the English yeomanry were half destroyed. By this time the Russians had met disaster in Poland, Bulgaria was ready to strike, a heavy battle impended in France, and the French decided to make their eastern effort at Salonica. Storms and frost-bite had now succeeded to the summer heats ; gun ammunition was as deficient here as in France, and German submarines were reaching the Mediterranean. After a visit from Kitchener, it was decided to evacuate, and this, by a miracle of skill and good fortune, was carried out in December without loss. Kitchener's preferred alternative, of landing in the neighbourhood of Alexandretta, was vetoed by the French and, against the advice of the general staff, our government sent forces to Salonica.

War with Turkey had results more wide-stretching than Gallipoli. It involved defending the Suez Canal, the artery through which the blood of Empire flowed ; it brought about our declaration of a protectorate over Egypt, and advice from Kitchener to rouse the Arabs against the Turks. It involved also a penetration by German agents of all the routes into Asia and efforts to engineer a rising in India. Most of all, it added to the other strains of 1915 the ill-starred campaign in Mesopotamia.

To hold the Persian Gulf, to secure the exit of the pipe-line which gave our oil fuel, was the proper duty of the Government of India, whose prompt occupation of Basra in 1914 was well warranted. The first forward moves up the Tigris and Euphrates in 1915 easily succeeded, and our officers on the spot were fired by optimism. By September General Townshend had reached Kut el Amara, 300 miles inland ; in October the Cabinet, against Kitchener's advice, approved an advance on Baghdad. As a political offset to the Dardanelles it was tempting, but as a military operation a bad risk. India had sent its best troops, British and Indian, to France and Egypt, its naval resources were meagre, and the date of reinforcements from Europe uncertain. After an immense loss in a headlong attack at Ctesiphon, Townshend retreated, to be besieged in Kut until it surrendered in April 1916. Every attempt at relief was beaten off, our casualties were portentous, our disorganization damaging, the break-down of medical services was complete, and the sufferings of the wounded a horror never seen in the West.

And the Salonica expedition did nothing as yet of what it was meant to do, for Serbia was destroyed by the new year of 1916, and Montenegro overrun.

This sequence of failure overturned Asquith's government, complicating every old problem and creating others altogether new. A party government could not expect a truce between parties when things went wrong ; shortage of shells, heavy losses in the West, criticism of Kitchener, and Lloyd George's restless conviction that the war was being lost, all these fires exploded in May 1915 when Fisher resigned, refusing to engage more ships in the Dardanelles. The new coalition government, which lasted till December 1916, kept Asquith, Grey, and Kitchener where they were, though Haldane's exclusion and the sinking of Churchill to minor office reflected the passions of the hour. Bonar Law's Unionist following included strong ability in Balfour, Curzon, and Carson, while Arthur Henderson represented the general steadfast support given by Labour to the war, which only a small minority, led by Ramsay MacDonald and Snowden, had repudiated. Nevertheless, this ministry showed coalition government at its worst.

A Cabinet of twenty-five was hopelessly unwieldy in any case, but the Unionists also felt that every key position was in Liberal hands, and that the Liberal outlook on some vital matters impeded the conduct of war. Asquith's caution seemed to have degenerated into dilatoriness. His contempt for publicity and his very virtues, his loyalty to friends and generals in the field, made him unfit to deal with a desperate crisis or a public opinion manipulated by newspaper proprietors. Carson resigned when Serbia fell unaided; Churchill, excluded from the War Council, left to command a battalion abroad; steadily an alliance gathered between Bonar Law, with Unionists asking more decision, and Lloyd George.

His own field of munitions was proving itself; 70,000 shells a week were forthcoming in May 1915, but 238,000 by the following January, 287 machine-guns in 1914 and in 1916 over 33,000. Yet round the Ministry of Munitions swayed the fiercest controversies; quick building and high wages, relaxation of trade-union rules, dilution of skilled labour by unskilled, employment of women, legislation against strikes, Labour's demand that private profits should be limited, production held up by drink, and looming through them all — compulsory service.

For, while some Liberal ministers protested that neither Kitchener's aim of seventy divisions nor our current expenditure could be maintained without ruin to industry, wastage in the armies proved that voluntary effort was not giving the necessary recruits. Munitions were held up by the flood of skilled men into the forces; a hundred anomalies, — of young men in well-paid munition work while fathers of families were in the trenches, or the return of the twice-wounded to face the holocaust, — offended the public sense of what was just.

Labour and average Liberal opinion were both opposed to conscription, and even more to industrial compulsion, but step by step sheer necessity broke down these doubts. Amid severe Cabinet disagreement a last effort to save the voluntary principle was made late in 1915, Lord Derby being appointed to canvass all men between eighteen and forty-one. It failed, with the refusal of nearly one million unmarried men to volunteer. After several false starts, and the resignation of Simon from the Cabinet, a Military Service Act was passed in May 1916, making all men up to forty-one liable to serve. Even so, its working was full of shortcomings; government departments, munitions in particular, would not give up their young men, and a mass of exemptions given by them and local tribunals kept alive a feeling of injustice and intercepted the needed recruits.

On this government also fell the strain of the Irish Rebellion. At the outbreak of war Home Rule was passed under the Parliament Act, but its operation was suspended until the war ceased, with a pledge that Parliament should be consulted on the treatment of Ulster. Though Redmond rallied loyally to the war, as Irish Catholics did in general for the cause of Belgium, the war destroyed his middle position; for his acceptance of even a temporary partition offended the Nationalists, while clumsy handling of Irish recruiting cooled their zeal. To the Sinn Fein party the war was an opportunity to revolt and, supported by German and Irish-American money, they enlarged their rebel army. In April 1916 a German attempt to run arms to Ireland, the arrest and execution of Roger Casement their envoy, the rising of the Sinn Feiners in Dublin, their suppression and the execution of fifteen leaders, forced a settlement of the question on this coalition government, made up of two parties whose most bitter difference had been over Ireland. Under this test their unity broke down. Carson and Redmond combined to accept the compromise which Asquith and Lloyd George proposed, that is, Home Rule to come into force but with the exclusion of six Ulster counties during the war; Balfour and Bonar Law agreed. But Selborne resigned, Lansdowne revolted, and the Conservative ministers bowed to this veto from their rank and file.

These strains and divisions bore hard on a government labouring under military calamity, for the triple offensive agreed on, from the West, Russia, and Italy, marched to disaster in 1916. The Central Powers believed that an energetic offensive might end the war before the British blockade became unendurable, and that Russia, now slipping into chaos, could be ignored; the German commander Falkenhayn therefore concentrated his strength against Verdun where, even if a break-through was not achieved, France might be bled to death, and was so far justified that the whole French force was pinned down from February till July, suffering 350,000 casualties. Meantime Conrad, the audacious Austrian, hoped to break the despised Italians, but in so doing exposed himself to a last hammer-blow from the Russians. Brussilov's offensive of June to August permanently damaged the Austrian fighting-power, though it also exhausted the armies of Russia, which were crippled by corruption and dearth of munitions.

Verdun bleeding, Kut falling, Salonica motionless, the Italians threatened from the high Alps or vainly beating towards Trieste over the desolate lime-stone of the Carso, the great Russian wave tiredly breaking, against that background must be set the British campaign on the Somme. To fight now was against the wish of Lloyd George and Kitchener, who would rather wait until our armies and armaments were trained and developed. Yet not to fight was politically impossible. The French effort being reduced after the horror of Verdun, the brunt fell on the British, especially on Rawlinson's 4th Army and the Kitchener divisions, and against long-prepared German defences, holding the high ground, Haig's optimistic calculations collapsed. Our casualties on the first day, 1st July, were 60,000, and 410,000 before the fighting died away in October; measured against a small advance along a thirty-mile front to a depth of six or seven. Yet from the Somme, and their appalling losses there and at Verdun, the Germans afterwards dated the beginning of the end; under the suffocating feeling of an unbroken enemy ring.

For the time being, however, darkness encompassed the Allies. Haggling to the last moment for more territories, deciding too late and making every military mistake, in August the Roumanians made their choice; by December Mackensen and Falkenhayn had cut them to ribbons, and opened to Germany rich areas of grain and oil.

The bitterness of failure was not assuaged by the clash of the British and German fleets in the Battle of Jutland, on 31st May. That it should be a decisive victory was improbable; for to Jellicoe, our commander, to expose the Fleet to destruction in mine- and submarine-infested waters meant a risk of losing the war in a day, while to Scheer a pitched battle must be a death-trap. On the day of this chance collision our superiority in gun-power and tonnage was great, but our losses were three battle-cruisers, three cruisers, and eight destroyers,— the Germans', considerably less in ships and lives. To measure Jellicoe's caution as against Beatty's bold handling of the battle-cruisers, to question an over-centralization of command, inferior disposal of our destroyer flotillas, or failure in our armour-piercing shells, any such controversy leaves unchanged the substantial result. Which was: that the Germans fought equally, ship for ship, and perhaps with better gunnery; that the British hold on the narrow seas, with all that meant, was left intact; that all notion, however, of grasping hands with the Russians through the Baltic was henceforth abandoned, and that blockade was accepted as the principal rôle of the fleet; and that the Germans, accepting the same moral, turned to the submarine as their saving arm. By the end of 1916 they were sinking 300,000 tons of merchant shipping a month.

One week after Jutland, on 5th June, another blow was struck at collaboration with Russia when Kitchener, on his way there, perished in the cruiser *Hampshire*, mined off the Orkneys. His death impinged directly both on the conduct of war and power in politics, for his place at the War Office was given to Lloyd George who now had to impress, if he could, his demand for a new strategy on Haig and on the rugged chief of staff, William Robertson. That struggle between the minister and the two soldiers, both of whom were convinced ' westerners ', was to rage long and with unhappy effects; a struggle no less of policies than of temperaments and codes, between this mercurial Celtic political genius and Haig, a soldier always growing in the scale, with a Calvinist confidence in victory and his own way of winning it.

This departmental struggle made one small part of a universal crisis, which was to decide whether the war could be continued at all.

Amid the slaughter, voices were heard breathing peace. Franz Joseph having died in November 1916, the new Emperor Karl wished to save Austria, if need be apart from her allies. Bethmann-Hollweg was fighting against the new war lords who had succeeded Falkenhayn, — Hindenburg and Ludendorff. President Wilson's private envoy, Colonel House, had already laid before us an offer of mediation with a hint that, if Germany refused moderate terms, America would join the Allies; and though our government believed no peace was possible without victory, and would not press the Allies who were bearing a much crueller burden, Grey's anxiety to conciliate America made him indecisive, while Lansdowne asked the Cabinet to consider whether a dictated peace was not impossible. In France a pacifist group was led by the able and cold-blooded Caillaux.

Through such hesitations Lloyd George drove his road to power. Many converging forces were brought to bear in his favour; the influence of the press magnates, Northcliffe and Beaverbrook, the conviction of Carson and the Conservative leader, Bonar Law; together with a general feeling that the essential matters of food, man-power, aircraft production, and anti-aircraft defence called for fiercer energy and unified control. His advocacy of the ' knock-out blow ' was the reply to vague German offers of a compromise peace, while his championship of a small war council was supported by those concerned in the conduct of war. In the end Asquith refused the pistol put to his head, that he should be excluded from presiding over this committee, and early in December resigned, refusing to serve under Balfour or Bonar Law, let alone Lloyd George; largely owing to a lead from Balfour the Conservatives agreed to join, in what most of them had not originally desired, a Lloyd George government. With this small War Cabinet, — Lloyd George, Bonar Law, Milner, Curzon, and Henderson — and parallel steps in France under Briand including the supersession of Joffre, the Allies brushed aside President Wilson's suggested conference and declared for continued war : to enforce reparation for wrong, and the freedom of all races from foreign domination.

Immense and tragic events filled the year 1917. In March revolution began to annihilate the force of Russia. In April the French offensive under their new leader Nivelle was beaten back with fearful loss. That month the loss of shipping by submarines rose to 900,000 tons and a bare six weeks' food supply was assured ; a rate of destruction which, unless remedied, would by the autumn either starve us out or paralyse our armies. True, Germany's declaration for unrestricted submarine war brought the United States in against her in April. Yet American troops could not reach us for a year, and would a year be given ? For France was crippled by bloodshed and now by military mutinies, Russia was perishing, in October the northern Italian armies were overwhelmed at

Caporetto, and their line of resistance pushed back to Venice. On Haig and the British Army all the present strain must fall.

Lloyd George's unquenchable spirit and endless power of expedient did, to an extent hitherto unknown, dedicate the country to total war. In his hands the office of Prime Minister became almost Presidential, since he dealt direct with departments, industry, the services, and the press. His small War Cabinet, on occasion expanded to a Cabinet of Empire by the addition of Dominion ministers, superseded our familiar system, Bonar Law being ordinarily left to manage Parliament while the Prime Minister gave himself wholly to the war. Here he did immense service. Through his insistence the greatest overriding danger of all, the submarine, was defeated and by August our monthly loss reduced below 200,000 tons; Beatty replaced Jellicoe, and the Admiralty accepted a system of convoy for merchantmen, which they had long resisted. Dictatorial powers were given to new ministries of food and shipping, home production was multiplied by financial guarantees, and food was rationed.

In this dark year a light dawned and slowly broadened in the East. In March under General Maude, a master of preparation and tactics, our forces entered Baghdad, while meantime our defence of Egypt had necessarily grown into an offensive-defensive, over the Sinai peninsula and the Red Sea. In the spring our coastal advance was severely checked at Gaza, but in June Allenby was sent from France to take command and, organized by a man of genius, T. E. Lawrence, King Hussein's Arabs were besieging Mecca and creeping up the Hedjaz railway. In October Allenby's victory at Beersheba outflanked the Turks' hold on the coast, and in December he entered Jerusalem. In June also the Allies had at last compelled the deposition of King Constantine, installed Venizelos in power, and from this much-divided Greece hoped to strike the Turks nearer home.

Lloyd George's belief never wavered that the war could be ended in the East. Twice in the winter of 1916–17 he worked for an offensive through the Italian front and so on to Vienna; which collapsed on French objections, Italian unpreparedness, and resistance from our own soldiers. But in truth the last chance of a decisive ' eastern ' solution had been lost at the Dardanelles two years before. Whatever the strength of his case then, it hardly corresponded to the present dangers, when Russia was in confusion and France crippled, and in any case he was himself temporarily converted by the over-confidence of the Frenchman Nivelle.

That offensive, of one overwhelming attack north of Rheims, and its dreadful collapse in April 1917, destroyed the coherence of all Haig had planned for an offensive on the Somme; which was disintegrated further by the German's skilful retreat to their shorter, immensely fortified, Hindenburg line. Haig's campaign of 1917 was therefore largely governed by political considerations, the demoralized state of the French armies, and a conviction that if Russia were knocked out of the war German reinforcements would be coming from the east. He was much influenced, too, by the Admiralty's despair at the submarine campaign which, launched from their nests at Ostend and Zeebrugge, might soon make the Channel impassable.

Taken as isolated operations, three strokes of this year were successful and significant for the future. These were the Canadians' capture of the Vimy heights in April; Plumer's long-prepared seizure of the Messines-Wytschaete ridge, south of the Ypres salient; and in November the first triumph of the tanks in Byng's advance towards Cambrai. On the other hand, Haig's main conception of a drive northwards to save the Channel ports vanished in the morass, from July to October, called Passchendaele or the third battle of Ypres, which was delayed too long, bogged in pitiless rain, and broken in bloody frontal attacks on Ludendorff's concrete gun-posts and elastic defence.

Lloyd George's distrust of the 'westerners'' strategy was henceforward confirmed. Unable in the face of public opinion to remove Haig, he changed his staff, vainly attempted to subordinate him to Nivelle, and reduced his fighting strength. Some 760,000 men were kept in theatres of war outside France, while another 300,000 front-line troops were held in hand at home. Robertson was removed from the post of chief of staff, which was given to Henry Wilson, whose doctrine was a holding war until 1919 or 1920, and concentration on eastern lines of victory through Syria and the Carpathians. An inter-Allied council was established at Versailles, with claims to control an army in reserve, but this clashed on the mutual suspicions of British and French, and equal refusal from Pétain and Haig.

Vitiated by this internal conflict, the Allies in 1918 faced the great German attack which Haig had predicted for months past. A truce in January was followed in March by the peace of Brest-Litovsk, which the Germans imposed on a crushed and Bolshevik Russia. By this date they had massed 192 divisions in the West, as against 173 Allied, and on the 21st March Ludendorff began the offensive which he hoped would split the Allied armies at their point of junction. When it opened, Haig had about 180,000 men fewer than a year before to defend a front now extended to 125 miles, a shield which in its southern rim, held by Gough's 5th Army, was perilously thin. Nearly half a million men would be needed to make up establishment and fill wastage, but it was not until the blow had fallen that government took the step, for which the soldiers had long pleaded, of calling up recruits by age-groups, cancelling exemptions, and ' combing out ' the munition workers.

Ludendorff's first blow shattered the 5th Army, which was taken

back behind the Somme ; by the 5th April the enemy had pushed a
great western bulge within ten miles of Amiens and weakened the hinge
between our 4th and 5th Armies.   The pessimistic Pétain actually
proposed to break contact with the British and fall back towards Paris,
and it was this emergency which drove Haig to take the initiative in
getting Foch made generalissimo, being ready to yield to a man what he
had refused to a half-political committee.   The second German stroke
was delivered in mid-April in the Ypres area, with such weight that
southwards the Messines ridge and Mount Kemmel were lost, and
northwards the vital junction of Hazebrouck threatened : it was now
that Haig told his armies that their backs were to the wall, and preparations were made to evacuate Calais.   In these two great battles
120 German divisions had fallen on 58 British, who suffered 300,000
casualties.   In May the third stroke fell, this time on the French along
the Aisne, and here by 1st June the Germans once more stood on the
Marne.   Yet by mid-August they were convinced that to fight on was
impossible, and in October were treating for peace terms.   If the gods
of history grind slow, the speed of their grinding is multiplied many
times in the last few hours.

Weighing in the scales the material and moral factors in this victory,
so far as they touch British history, we are right, perhaps, to eliminate
some particular achievements, brilliant and heroic in themselves.   The
naval attack of April on Zeebrugge, inspired by Roger Keyes, could not
in itself shake the German hold of Belgium ; indeed, it did not entirely
seal up their bases at Zeebrugge and Ostend.   Allenby's strategical
triumph in the battle of Megiddo, his advance with horse, foot, and
Arabs east and west of Jordan and his entry into Damascus and then
Aleppo in October, drove Turkey out of the war, as Bulgaria had been
driven out in September by an advance from Salonica.   But these
victories on the outer circumference came when Germany was already
toppling at the centre.

The ' westerners ', it seems, were right in their fundamentals, that
only defeat of the German mass in France could be decisive, and that
the morale of that mass was on the down-grade.   In many points, and
very seriously in obstructing the development of tank warfare, Haig's
fixed mind takes him out of the class of inspired commanders.   But
when, in June 1918, all statesmen and most soldiers would have postponed victory for another year, or even two, he (even perhaps before
Foch) declared it could be done here and now, and in the teeth of
an official warning that the country would not stand more casualties,
took on himself the responsibility.   To him was due the choice of
area on the Somme front ; the decision to turn the converging French-
American attack north-westwards towards the Argonne, rather than to
Lorraine ; and the never-relaxed offensive at one point after another.

He was assisted by the now developed arm of the Air Force, by abundant munitions, tanks in large numbers and, late in the day, large reinforcements : assured also of a stream of fresh American troops, who had risen to two million by the autumn. But in the final moral fact in all victories, the destruction of the enemy's will to resist, Haig's Somme victory of August was the beginning of the end and justified his permanent argument.

On the other side, while Ludendorff's mistakes were serious, in the last resort this moral factor came back to British sea-power. This it was which by blockade deprived Germany of war material, filled her home front with conviction of defeat, convoyed the food and coal which alone could keep France and Italy in the war, carried millions of American troops safely, took the means of victory to Palestine and the Balkans, and finally set up that desperation which appeared in the Germans' shattered discipline, even during their tactical victories at Amiens and the Marne.

While, then, from July to September parts of their armies disengaged themselves skilfully, so that by purely military standards they might well have stood another winter on their own frontier, first the German command and then the German people gave way. On 29th September our 4th Army broke through the Hindenburg Line, and the same day Hindenburg and Ludendorff were insisting on peace. On 5th October the German government asked President Wilson to arrange an armistice, accepting as the basis of negotiations the ' 14 points ' he had laid down in the previous January. While the President demanded guarantees against the continued power of soldiers and autocrats, revolution broke out in the German fleet and spread from the northern ports to Berlin and Munich ; on 4th November the British pierced the front near Valenciennes and pushed on to the Sambre ; on 9th November the Kaiser abdicated and a German Republic prepared to receive the armistice terms. These were more severe than Haig thought possible, though less severe than the American commander Pershing desired ; the British emphasis being on surrender of all submarines and the pick of their powerful ships, and on a refusal to accept Wilson's formula, fatal to our weapon of blockade, of the ' freedom of the seas '.

On 11th November the Armistice was signed ; on the 22nd, Lloyd George took the election for which he had long prepared. After a month, in which the electorate clamoured for extracting from Germany the whole cost of war and punishment of all war criminals up to the Kaiser, he returned to power with a vast, mainly Unionist, majority over Labour and Asquith's Liberals, and in January 1919 proceeded to Paris to make the peace.

When war ceased the British had 8 million men and nearly 1 million women serving in the Army, Navy, Air Force, and munitions ; they had spent £6000 millions, sold all their overseas securities, lent £1500 millions to our Allies, and lost over six million tons of shipping. They had saved themselves by increasing the pre-war harvests by one-third, and adding 3 million acres to arable cultivation. Our income-tax had risen from 1s. 2d. to 6s., sur-tax from 6d. to 6s., and an excess profits tax of 80 per cent governed industry; wholesale prices were 125 per cent higher than in 1914. Except in Ireland all men up to 50 had been made liable to military service, and at least 1½ million women had replaced men in vital employments.

The dearest cost to the British Empire was the death of almost 1 million of its best sons and leaders-designate: on the Western front alone, from February 1915 onwards, there were 115,000 officer casualties, or five for every two German officer casualties over the same period.

AFTERMATH
1919–1938

CHAPTER I

FRUITS OF WAR AND PEACE, 1919–1929

THE world's peace, extinguished in 1914 through the guilt of eastern Europe, was never in fact wholly restored. Ten million young men had been killed, many more human beings than that perished from disease, more millions innumerable had for four years thrown aside, or been forced to see abandoned, all the securities and codes which a thousand years of civilization and Christian order had toiled to build up. This world, thus spiritually enfeebled, was at the same time impoverished by the destruction of several generations' capitalized wealth, instruments of production, and means of transportation and, though charged with new greeds, depended for existence on a credit structure which was very near collapse. Meantime, the crash of Russia, destruction of Austro-Hungary, and mutilation of Germany and Turkey, left gaping voids in the frame within which Europe and nearer Asia had lived, to be contested now by every suppressed race, and alight at each corner with the glow of nationality.

We confront also once again, as in the age of Pitt, the peril of urgent matters laid aside under stress of war, and made more angry by the passions war had lighted. This set up turmoil in Ireland, India, and Egypt and strained the new fabric of South African union. For if it was a war for vital interests, it was also one for democratic ideals. The working-class demand for a new order, already clamorous in the strikes of 1911–12, advanced with every sacrifice demanded of them, and with the relinquishment of hard-won trade-union safeguards in the interest of war production; ceaseless strikes of munition workers, a challenge by shop stewards to union executives, were symptoms of this movement from below. In the Russian revolution many saw an example of the common people's might, a model for control even of the armed forces by the ranks, or a condemnation of the ' Imperialism ' which had arrayed workers of different races against each other.

History, perhaps, will record nothing more surprising in such an age than the fact that, except for three years, Great Britain was directed from 1919–39 by predominantly Conservative governments. For which it may find one overriding cause, that this restored peace was really a prolonged state of siege, in which Great Britain, as never before, was pressed in and blockaded by forces beyond her own control.

One great internal change was made instantly clear, that the democracy implicit in British self-government, and proclaimed by many theorists for a century past, had at length arrived. Since equal and universal sacrifice called for universal rights, our venerable equality before the law was transmuted into a claim for equality in social fact, and what might have been a long-term process was crowded into a single generation. Lloyd George, the first Prime Minister to rise direct from the ranks, never lost some of Cromwell's ardour for the common man, while it had always been his method to make direct contact with democracy's representatives. Having brought Labour leaders into his Coalition government, before the election he passed two vital measures for the democratic future. The Representation of the People Act of 1918 trebled the electorate, increasing its numbers to over 20 millions, setting up adult suffrage for all men of twenty-one, and giving the vote to women of thirty who were, themselves or their husbands, electors in local government. Property, therefore, hitherto viewed as a reward of skill or intelligence, and the basis of political power since Parliament began, made way for human equality; with it, of course, disappeared plural voting. So, too, did many ancient parliamentary seats, from boroughs with a population of less than 50,000. At the same time Fisher, minister of Education, brought forward an ambitious Act which, when brought into full operation, would raise the school age to fourteen, prohibit child labour, and continue part-time education to the age of eighteen.

War had hastened what this advent of economic democracy must soon otherwise have brought, an immense growth in the sphere of the State, a new centralization, and diminution of some old liberties. From it also dates an enhancement of the office of Prime Minister, which Gladstone would have rejected as weakening the Cabinet, yet the powers both of Cabinet and individual ministers had grown also, in relation alike to the Commons, the citizen, and the courts of law. Linked now by its secretariat with the Committee of Imperial Defence and with its decisions for the first time formally recorded, its corporate supremacy, so long as it acted in unison, was complete; while, to enforce the detail of a planned State, ministers were given by statute wide powers of regulation, which allowed them to make and interpret law. New permanent ministries were created for Health, Labour, Transport, and Pensions. Treasury control of banking and currency, innumerable controls over production, prices, and wages, a State subsidy to keep down bread prices, a war-time nationalization of mines, railways, shipping, and imports in bulk — all these had banished our individualist, Cobdenite, Liberal world.

This powerful machine had now to be adjusted to our historic government by party which turns, as the defiant Chatham had said, on an interplay of measures and men. An epoch had come again, as in 1794, when Coalition born of war-emergency superseded party, whose lines were transcended, as they had been by the two Pitts, by three men of rare political talent in Lloyd George, Churchill, and Birkenhead. Yet once again, as after 1815, the cardinal fact of post-war politics was the downfall of Coalition, a renewed struggle of party, and a redistribution of power between the two main bodies of Conservative and Labour. All of which, again, contributed to the fall of Liberalism.

Within four years of its triumphant election in 1918, the Lloyd George government was overthrown. Its basis was always shaky, for only 136 Coalition Liberals sat beside nearly 400 Conservatives, and by breaking the Liberal party Lloyd George had sapped his own independence. There were, indeed, Conservative leaders like Austen Chamberlain and Birkenhead who, with Churchill from the Liberal camp, hoped that Coalition might be permanent, welding Conservatives and Liberals into union against Socialism. That plan made too little allowance for the continuous causes and loyalties which, despite union in war, divided parties, and too little allowance also for a drift within Liberalism towards Labour. But since parties are moved by, or against, persons as well as by principle, Lloyd George's method and nearest associates offended the Conservatives quite as much as public causes.

Those causes were so tremendous that it is arguable no other government could have succeeded better. The peace treaties of Versailles, signed after bitter dissension in June 1919, registered the aspirations upon which the three principal Allies, Britain, France, and the United States, had found it possible to agree ; what was to come out of their shortcomings, had yet to be seen. Their terms, as directly affecting the British Empire, included the surrender of the German fleet and the destruction of German armaments ; a share of 22 per cent in the financial reparations demanded of Germany which were fixed, after many conferences, in 1921 at over £6000 millions ; and a lion's share of the Colonial territories to be held by ' mandate ' under the League of Nations, — Iraq, Palestine, Tanganyika, German South-West Africa, part of the Cameroons and Togoland, Samoa, New Guinea and other Pacific islands.

Several critical decisions, though not always decisions of our own, rapidly shook the peace, isolated Britain, and damaged the government. Our democracy's loathing of war and its burdens, rejection of conscription and a rush to disarm, meant our withdrawal from many areas and sensibly weakened our world influence. Repudiation by the United States of President Wilson and all his works left a deep void in the League, compelling us also to back out of the frontier guarantee which we jointly with America had given to France. Indeed, before Lloyd George left office, Anglo-French relations were cold, if not hostile.

For the map of Europe, as redrawn at Versailles, was a French map, designed to constrict Germany by a number of small States who should be French clients and, against Lloyd George's warning, gave several large German minorities over to alien government. British insistence alone prevented Poland taking all Silesia, but the boundaries of Poland, against our advice, were so extended as to make collision with Russia inevitable. In the eyes of British Labour the treatment of Bolshevik Russia was the darkest part of post-war policy : the assistance we sent through Archangel, Murmansk, the Crimea, or Siberia to anti-Bolshevik Russians, though originating in 1917 as the only means of preventing Germany acquiring Russian resources, was prolonged through 1919 at great cost, and with a total failure. By what right, our democracy asked, were we obstructing another people rightly struggling to be free ?

There were other burning questions springing out of the necessities of war, or the fever of peace, which rent the Coalition. Self-determination was a formula which leaped across continents and frontiers. India asked for it now in virtue of her war service, but the strains of army recruiting caused in 1919 riotous disorders in the Punjab, which were followed by severe repression, above all, by the firing on the mob at Amritsar, ordered by General Dyer ; uneasily, the Conservative majority swallowed that year the Montagu-Chelmsford scheme, for granting to India more responsible government. We had also given many pledges to the Arabs, but had simultaneously issued the Balfour Declaration, promising the Jews a national home ; each of which must somehow and some time be adjusted to the French mandate for Syria. Self-determination again and war strain roused Egypt to revolt in 1919, and in 1922 we declared our protectorate at an end and Egypt independent.

If these were unavoidable difficulties, in one instance Lloyd George's foreign policy was indefensible and largely personal to himself, being pursued in flat defiance of his foreign minister, Curzon. The treaty of Sèvres of 1920 not only deprived Turkey of Syria, Mesopotamia, and Palestine but neutralized the Straits, left Constantinople a small oasis surrounded by Greek territory, and handed over part of Asia Minor itself to Greek occupation. A new Turkish government, set up at Angora by Mustapha Kemal, the hero of Gallipoli, resisted this aggression, and in 1922 broke to pieces the Greek armies. When Turkish troops advanced on the British garrison which at Chanak defended the passage to Europe, it was revealed that our Allies, France and Italy, had made their own understandings with Turkey ; neither British nor Dominion opinion would tolerate this prospect of fighting alone in a dubious cause.

Meantime, the post-war boom had broken, unemployment on a scale hitherto unknown hit our basic industries, and a series of strikes pointed the contrast between Labour ideals and post-war facts. Staving off trouble by subsidies and wage concessions, the government put the helm hard over towards the economy which its supporters demanded; 'rationing' departmental expenditure, abolishing some war-time ministries, and repealing the Corn Production Act, which involved abolishing the guaranteed price for grain and the agricultural minimum wage. If all these tested the government's cohesion, for a Conservative-Liberal alliance no test could be so grim as the settlement of Ireland.

The convention of Irish parties summoned in 1917–18 failed to persuade Ulster, while a threat to impose conscription strengthened the hand of Sinn Fein; which, though proclaimed as illegal and its leaders arrested, was armed and defiant. In the general election of 1918 they won seventy-three seats, but refused to sit at Westminster and proclaimed a republic; the country declined into what amounted to civil war, a garrison of 60,000 British troops not availing to stop murder and pillage. A fourth Home Rule Bill was passed in 1920, offering two Parliaments in Belfast and Dublin, but Sinn Fein refused any such partition. Concession having failed, Lloyd George then attempted repression, and a wave of reprisals began, sometimes unauthorized and carried out by an auxiliary police, often called the 'black and tans', and sometimes on a system by the regular Army.

Though Bonar Law emerged from retirement to fight again for Ulster, public opinion would not stomach the continuance of these atrocities or the prospect of a pitched war demanding 100,000 men. So began the negotiations of 1921, ending in December in the Irish Treaty. By this, Southern Ireland obtained the status of a Dominion, British troops and police being withdrawn; the leading Irish signatories were Arthur Griffiths, chief founder of Sinn Fein, and Michael Collins, a leader of their guerrilla armies. Their work was done at the cost of their lives, through exhaustion in Griffiths' case, and in Collins' by political murder, but after savage warfare between supporters of the treaty and De Valera's republican army an Irish election in 1922 endorsed the settlement, which Cosgrave and O'Higgins proceeded loyally to carry out. In all this, though the Coalition Conservatives, Birkenhead and Austen Chamberlain especially, stood by Lloyd George, the mass of the party was sore at a spectacle of making 'truce with murder', abandonment of the southern Unionists, and the triumph of Home Rule outside Ulster.

Such causes meant that coalition under Lloyd George could not endure, and his effort to perpetuate it by a new election was angrily rejected. In the autumn of 1922 a revolt of subordinate Conservative ministers, led by Baldwin, defeated their party leaders, forced Lloyd George's resignation, and led to Bonar Law making a Conservative government; the dissolution emphasized the collapse of Liberalism, Lloyd George's section winning only 57 seats as against Asquith's 60, while Unionists returned 344 and Labour rose to 159. But two more years of confusion followed before politics attained stability.

When Bonar Law died in May 1923, the party passed over the proud and experienced Curzon in favour of Baldwin, a business man as yet almost unknown to the public. Deriving from experience of industry and his liberal nature a Disraelian view of Conservatism as a safe channel for democracy, his aims were to mellow and educate Labour as the alternative government, and to mend the rift in his party made by coalition. But he was a protectionist who, confronted at every turn by appalling unemployment, decided to press on with an extension of tariffs. Against the instinct of most leading ministers, and before party reconciliation had come about, in December he decided on an instant election. This precipitancy failed; the Unionists fell to 259, Labour rose to 191, and the combined Liberals to 158. Any party taking office must, therefore, govern on sufferance, and there were those who urged a Conservative-Liberal coalition. But the country had clearly pronounced against the Conservatives' principal policy, while Asquith and Baldwin were both decided that the proper course was to allow Labour, the strongest opposition party, to take office.

So came about the first Labour government, under Ramsay MacDonald. Its life was a bare year and was extinguished by the unwisdom of its Left wing, for since the war Labour had been divided between a main body, Radical or Fabian but constitutionalist, and an extremer section, touched by revolutionary ideas and moved by sentimentalists like Lansbury who, from his stronghold in Poplar, preached work or full maintenance for the unemployed, and pacifism among nations. Subjected to such pressure, yet dependent for its existence on Liberal votes, the government was driven into making a treaty with the Soviet, involving a loan to Russia, and was entangled also in damaging controversy with their Communist rivals. In October 1924 MacDonald appealed to the country; nothing probably could have saved him, but the exposure of some Russian propaganda, the so-called Zinoviev letter, was decisive. Labour's numbers fell to 151, the Conservatives rose to 413, Asquith was once more defeated, and Liberalism sank to a mere fragment of 40 members.

Baldwin's second administration from November 1924 to May 1929 makes a clear stage in our post-war world, a breathing-space during which some of its drifts and decisions can be judged. The party stream was returning to its old bed. Rid of the Irish members, British party divided once more substantially into two; most survivors of the Liberalism of 1906 going their several ways, some with Haldane over to Labour, but a greater part with Churchill, and later Simon, towards Conservatism. Thanks to the reconciling part of Baldwin's rising lieutenant, Neville Chamberlain, the Conservative coalitionists, —

Austen Chamberlain, Balfour, and Birkenhead — now rejoined the main body.

That the country should be restored to its old good humour, and the world to ways of peace, was Baldwin's aspiration, and a rôle for which he was in many ways perfectly equipped. Such hopes, however, were overruled by the aftermath of war, complicating and intermingling the threefold task of peace in Europe, readjustment in Empire, and recovery at home.

How hope of abiding peace was lost must be seen later, but already we observe how the peace treaties divided the victorious Allies. Reparations from Germany and war debts to each other poisoned their relations. Over six thousand million pounds were fixed as the debt due from Germany, but Great Britain had lent over £2000 millions to her Allies and owed £920 millions to America, and although by the Balfour Note of 1922 we proposed entire cancellation of this tangle, that was not agreeable to America and far less to France which in 1923, against our protest, occupied the Ruhr to extract reparations. Her complete failure to dig out German payments at the bayonet's point only extended the crash of the mark to the franc; with American help the Dawes plan of 1924 reduced the German liability to annuities of about £120 millions, while Britain gradually remitted the £600 millions owed to her by France.

Disputed debts were a symptom of much deeper divisions. Italy was immensely discontented with her share of the spoil, and in particular disliked the Mediterranean predominance of France, and the obstacles put in her Balkan path by France's allies, the little Entente. Buttressed by French support, Poland had tried to take all Silesia, and actually seized East Galicia, the Ukraine, and Vilna, all of which lay beyond the racial frontier and the 'Curzon line' which Britain recommended. Again, neither the United States nor the Dominions looked kindly on our alliance with Japan, which we therefore allowed to lapse and merged in the Washington agreements of 1922. These, though stabilizing naval strength as between Britain, America, and Japan, and guaranteeing peace in the Pacific, by preventing fortification of the Anglo-Saxon naval bases in those waters gave to Japan complete local supremacy. As for the defeated, Russia was bent on recapturing the influence she had lost, and territories of which, in her absence, she had been deprived; Turkey had forcibly overthrown the Allies' original settlement; Hungarian and German minorities were calling out for redress. In short, the peace treaties had hardly been signed before a clamour began for treaty revision.

Two chief objects of the peace were as yet unrealized. More than one clause in the treaty committed the Allies, morally, if not by their letter, to make the disarmament imposed on Germany a first step to disarmament all round, and for thirteen years, until the final break-down in 1933, commissions and conferences at Geneva explored every avenue. Practical difficulties of supervision, technical questions of naval tonnage, definition of armaments between aggressive or defensive types, all these were less insuperable than national jealousy and the method of measuring national needs. Italy and France could not agree on naval ' parity '; the United States would not accept British Admiralty estimates of cruiser requirements; France would not listen to our proposed abolition of submarines; Britain wanted to retain air-power to deal with frontier regions. Neither America nor Britain liked the French project of an international force; above all, France, the most heavily armed Power in Europe, would not disarm until satisfied on her security.

But the ' collective security ', for which the League Covenant stood, was merely on paper. America had never joined the League, Germany was not admitted until 1926, and Russia not until 1934; by which date both Germany and Japan had left it. More than one outrage on the treaties, by Poland and by Italy, was condoned. British opinion, equally set against isolation and revival of alliances, whole-heartedly approved collective security, yet it was made clear, in particular by the Dominions, that the British Empire would never bind itself to automatic commitments or underwrite every existing frontier. Having rejected, largely on account of this Dominion feeling, the Protocol supported by the French, which would have tightened up the machinery of sanctions, the Baldwin government in 1925 took the initiative in the treaties of Locarno. These made a regional pact, by which Britain and Italy guaranteed Germany, France and Belgium alike against aggression from one another. But from the language of our Foreign Secretary, Austen Chamberlain, it was plain that the security we thus undertook to honour in western Europe we should refuse to defend in the East.

For all that, and in great part by our mediation, by 1930 much had been done to restore an atmosphere of peace. Germany was admitted to the League and made a member of its Council; her reparations, already reduced by the Dawes scheme, in 1929 were once more scaled down by the Young plan. In 1930, five years ahead of the treaty requirement, the last foreign garrison left German soil, while by the London treaty of that year Britain, the United States, and Japan reached agreed figures for cruisers and light craft, as they had by the Washington treaty of 1922 for battleships.

Zeal to disarm was the special mark of British feeling during this armed peace. Government departments were instructed to act on the theory that no major war need be expected for ten years. Our Air Force, 187 squadrons strong in 1919, possessed only 31 in 1929. Our service estimates sank every year until 1934, we had disbanded 21 infantry battalions and 60 batteries, naval personnel had not been lower for forty years, and twice a Labour government suspended work on the naval dock at Singapore.

War and peace had also imposed on us heavy burdens of Empire, and here too much was achieved. For the ten years 1922–32, Cosgrave and those ready to operate the treaty controlled Ireland; agreement was reached on the Eire-Ulster boundaries and order restored by force. We had then to meet this new nationalism in much starker form in the East. Milner's mission of 1919 recommended a grant of independence to Egypt, over which the Coalition government differed and dallied; after more disorder, it was granted under Allenby's pressure in 1922. But the nationalist party founded by Zaghlul disputed the reservations we had attached, especially control of the Suez Canal and the Sudan, and an uneasy period set in of political murder, suspensions of the constitution, palace politics by the King, and intervention by the British high commissioner. Meanwhile, our obligations incurred in war involved us more dangerously in the Middle East. Between the hopes held out, especially through Colonel Lawrence, to the Arabs, and the French mandate over Syria, there was absolute conflict; between the Balfour pledge of 1917 for a Jewish ' national home ' in Palestine and the Arab majority, there was a contradiction even more dire. After some bloodshed Feisal, son of our ally King Hussein of the Hedjaz, was removed from Syria to become King in Iraq, which had been assigned to Britain under mandate; his brother Abdullah receiving the Transjordan territory under our protection. Strategical defence of the Persian Gulf, and vital oil supplies, prevented us from being indifferent to the fate of Iraq, yet both democratic feeling and the heavy cost prohibited military occupation, so the treaty with Feisal recognized his country's independence, leaving British controls to be lightly exerted through the Air Force, and in 1932 we supported the admission of Iraq to the League. Yet Arabian nationalism was still fiercely hostile to the French in Syria, and was further transformed after 1926 by the victories of Ibn Saud, the Wahabi Sultan of Nejd, over the house of Hussein and the holy places.

If we conceived that we had discharged our debt of honour, Palestine was always reminding us of our mistake. This half-barren country, the size of Wales, had for thirteen hundred years been Arab territory; our mandate bound us to safeguard Arab rights, but also to promote a Jewish national home. An influx of Jews, trebling their numbers by the early '30's, added industrial revolution to racial strife, for the Zionists were backed by British and American money, and belonged economically to a much stronger civilization. Savage rioting in 1929 began an unending spiral of repression and concession, enquiry, and contradictory solutions.

Farther east, nationalism had roused Persia and moved an incompetent Amir of Afghanistan to invade India in 1919, but our heaviest difficulty lay in India itself. There also the sacrifices of war stimulated nationality. Moslem indignation over the downfall of Turkey and Arab disappointment, and Congress's political theories, were blended by the Hindu Gandhi, a politician of supple craft, into unceasing demonstrations for which the Montagu-Chelmsford reforms proved inadequate, and in 1927 Baldwin appointed the Simon Commission to reopen the whole future. In 1929 it was announced that Dominion status was accepted for India, and conferences were pursued until the vast scheme of a federal self-governing India passed through Parliament in 1935.

Burdened with such responsibilities abroad, the Conservative government must wrestle to undo the ravages of war at home. Our party differences of the old sort were almost extinct. One dividing line vanished with the Irish treaty; another, older still, of Church against Dissent faded away with a decline of religious faith. A third, of free trade against protection, was in abeyance. For revenue and military reasons, some of the war measures, the McKenna duties and tariffs to safeguard key industries, were retained without much dispute. And though Baldwin had learned from his defeat in 1923 that systematic protection, or the full preferences asked by Dominions, could not be pursued without a mandate, the pure dogma of free trade held by the Labour Chancellor of the Exchequer, Philip Snowden, could hardly bind his party, which insisted on full employment at high wages.

Nor, again, was the democracy, which Peel had so dreaded and which Salisbury found so perilous in foreign affairs, any longer in question. The great extension of the franchise in 1918 was carried to its conclusion in 1928 by an Act giving women the vote at twenty-one, on the same terms as men, so adding 7 million electors and raising their total to 28 millions. Periodically, some small Conservative right wing would raise the question of damming the flood by strengthening the upper House. But in essence the controversy was no more about democracy, or even about Socialism : rather, over the degree to which Socialism could be wisely applied or economic democracy asserted. So with Conservative Cabinets, as with Labour, the power of the State continually advanced. A State-controlled electricity board was created in 1926, and yet another example of such an official, yet independent, public authority was given the same year in the British Broadcasting Corporation. The principle of contributory insurance for health and unemployment, greatly extended by Lloyd George, was carried much farther in 1925, Churchill's budget of that year creating such pensions for widows, orphans, and old age, in fulfilment of Neville Chamberlain's social policy. Yet, though using the same instruments, the Conservative and

Labour parties were far divided, because two rival philosophies were disputing the future.

The increased load left by war was in itself enormous. Gladstone's budget expenditure of £70 millions in 1881 had risen by 1913 to £197 millions; war had raised it to nearly £2700 millions, and it remained at £796 millions for 1924-5. Interest on the national debt alone was £350 millions, and direct taxation per head was nearly seven times the amount of 1914. It fell on a people whose rate of increase, as in all western Europe, was continuing to fall. From 1911 population rose by some 2 millions to 42,700,000 in 1921, and to over 44 millions in 1931; but in that year it was reckoned that only 81 marriageable women would replace each 100 of their predecessors, for the mid-Victorian birth-rate of 34 per 1000 had dropped to under 20, and though old people lived longer, many fewer children were being born. Of this dwindling, ageing race, 80 per cent now lived in urban areas and half of those in towns of 100,000 people or more, while 76 per cent were reckoned as wage-earners. Such was the last effect of industrial revolution on the 8 million people of 1801; then half-countrymen and almost self-supporting, but now dependent on imports for 60 per cent of their food.

On the nineteenth-century fabric of export, credit, and overseas investment, the war and its aftermath put an almost fatal strain. Inflation and deflation ran the same course as after 1815. As compared with the 1913 level, prices early in 1920 stood at 325 against 100, but by 1922 had tumbled again to 154. War also drove employment into engineering, shipbuilding, and mines, which the making of peace left overcrowded and redundant. During war, again, foreign States created industries of their own, which after peace they protected by high tariffs; on cotton, another overcrowded industry, fell the brunt of competition from Japan, so that cotton goods, which had once been half our exports, dropped to less than one-fifth. War, moreover, speeded up other changes which would test all our adaptability. In agriculture the landlord class were fast disappearing. In industry, larger units and amalgamations, from great commercial combines to co-operators, replaced individuals and small firms. More mechanism, inventions, and replacement of old processes, increased output but diminished employment: as the tractor replaced the ploughman, and as mechanical coal-cutting rose thirtyfold since the century began.

British prosperity of the rich previous age had been an international system; dependent on a free exchange of goods, at prices determined by the relation of each national currency to gold. This system, anchored in the experience and credit of London, assumed a free automatic movement of gold over the exchanges, which would correct disequilibrium of demand and supply; together with a free movement of capital, labour, and wages which would keep internal prices round about parity. But in the post-war years all these assumptions were falsified. Reparations confined the great German market to a one-way traffic. The United States, now the world's greatest producer and creditor, protected their industry by ever-rising tariffs, and demanded payment of balances in gold. Russia was almost eliminated from world trade. Sharp devaluations of currency in Germany, and then in France, unhinged the exchanges, while every device of tariff, quota, or subsidy was employed by many new suspicious States to beggar their neighbour.

This maldistribution of gold, nearly two-thirds of the world's supply being piled up in America and France, debts without assets, and wild migration of frightened money had wounded the old monetary system, which many political facts also threatened to destroy. The shifting of financial power to America exposed world trade to larger speculation and inadequate banking, while restrictions on immigration and political tariffs hardened the compartments between poverty and wealth. Within this country, fixed interest-charges on a huge debt and, still more, wage-rates which were kept rigid by trade unions and unemployment insurance prevented any easy readjustment of costs. In these conditions the wish of Britain to restore her pre-war stability was obstructed, and when in 1925 the Baldwin government returned to gold at the pre-war parity between the dollar and the pound, the external value of the pound was fixed higher than our internal prices warranted, and our export trade consequently suffered.

On the British State the effects of these post-war conditions were very various by 1929. The insured population in employment was larger than ever before; if our exports had declined in volume since 1913, those of manufactured goods were still the greatest in the world; real wages, measured by the cost of living, rose by 8 per cent between 1924–9 and, though lower than in the United States, were well above any in Europe; the hours of labour were 10 per cent less than before the war; and £100 millions in subsidies part-paid the rent of many working-class tenants.

Yet, though the real national income was much the same as before the war, our savings for reinvestment were almost halved, and after 1929 our emigration had in effect ceased; worst of all, the figures of the unemployed never fell below 1 million after 1922, and stood at 1,200,000 in 1929. The total payments to the unemployed in the eight years then ending might be put at £500 millions; one government after another was compelled to weaken the genuine insurance element in its assistance, — payment, that is, in relation to contributions, — and to extend benefit to many thousands who, for months or even for years, had been unable to contribute at all.

This unemployment differed from older poverty, in that it was almost restricted to a few industries and a few areas, and represented an historic catastrophe; that it gripped exactly those industries which had made the country economically supreme for a hundred years. The trades which suffered were in some cases, like cotton, ill-organized but they had been the heart of our exports, — textiles, shipbuilding, engineering, and coal. While, therefore, unemployment as a whole averaged about 12 per cent in this decade, in the Durham and south Wales coalfields it sometimes reached 40 or 60 per cent; employment steadily moved from the once powerful north to the midlands and the south and, while there were 600 unions under the poor law, 15 of them accounted for one-fifth of all poor-law relief.

Coal made the darkest spot. The industry was overcrowded, badly organized between 1400 separate undertakings, more penetrated than any other by class feeling, and more isolated in temper. After several strikes in the early 1920's, the miners' wage level left them in 1925 rather worse off than in 1914, and hence came about in 1926 the sympathetic or General Strike declared by the Trade Union Congress. To separate the miners' hard case from that constitutional question, of compulsion put upon Parliament by direct action, was almost impossible at the moment, though it would have to be done if Labour was to co-exist with parliamentary government. The immediate sequence of events was a great, if only partly conscious, national unanimity to defeat the strike, a drop in trade union membership from 8 millions to $4\frac{3}{4}$, a return of the miners to work at the same wage but with longer hours, and the passage of the trades disputes Act of 1927. This made a general strike illegal, allowed the trades unions' political levy to be taken only from members who expressly ' contracted in ', and forbade affiliation of civil servants to a political party.

These disputes were bound up with the future of the poor law, which had been much controverted since the royal commission of 1909 had issued majority and minority reports. As administered in East London, and in some distressed regions of Wales and the north, relief had been used to change the whole social standard, by scales of assistance which sometimes maintained one-fifth of the population on relief and certainly violated the existing law. Hence came about several measures, passed by Neville Chamberlain as Minister of Health, to curb the rise of rates and keep relief to its original principle, as against this programme of ' Poplarism ', — even by the supersession of the elected guardians.

In this sad picture of a permanent million unemployed, though its composition of course fluctuated and the hard core might be estimated as half a million, and in ' distressed areas ' from which hope and life and youth seemed to have fled, the post-war epoch expired and the Baldwin government went down. Its reforming measures had been substantial; a large increase of insurance to widows, orphans, and old age, and to some new classes; the derating of industry and agriculture, and the financial and administrative reforms of Chamberlain's local government Act of 1929. This abolished the guardians and transferred their functions to county councils and boroughs, centralized the control of roads and town planning in larger authorities, and provided whole-time medical officers of health. In lieu of the rates taken from them, local authorities would henceforth receive block Exchequer grants, having due regard to their unemployment. Most of all, its flexibility allowed them to use their own administrative schemes, which would, in effect, break down the partition between the poor law and other social services.

This, and Chamberlain's rating reform, were vital for future development, but would ask a long time for their full affect. At the moment, war and mass unemployment had forced to the front a conflict between the doctrines of the past century and those of the age to come. The Victorians had taught the virtues of self-help and saving; from the experience of the eighteenth century and Speenhamland, they derived a horror of outdoor relief and reliance on the State, and a conviction that the lot of the workless man ought to be less eligible than that of the man in work. New doctrines of ' the community ', reaching back to pre-Reformation principle, had always challenged these beliefs, found rein-forcement in the growth of political equality, and received confirmation in the spectacle of one million fellow-countrymen out of work, through no fault of their own. Having been given political power, democracy set out to translate it into economic fact, to put the responsibility on the community and not on the self-reliant citizen, and demanded ' work or maintenance ' as their right. Economists taught them that by monetary policy they could stabilize prices, secure full employment, transfer wealth by a peaceful revolution, and make a classless society.

How far such doctrines could proceed was as yet undecided. But, taken together with the distressed areas and the foundering of peace in Europe, it was enough to decide the elections of June 1929. Under our single-member constituency system the electorate, now swollen by 6 million new voters, returned 287 Labour members with 8,360,000 votes, 261 Conservatives with 8,664,000, and 59 Liberals with 5,300,000. This, though not a very clear-cut verdict, installed Ramsay MacDonald once more in power with a Labour government.

CHAPTER II

THE EMPIRE, 1919–1938

THE fruit had not yet dropped from the tree, as the wisest Victorians prophesied it would. During the great war ending in 1918 Canada raised 650,000 soldiers, Australia and New Zealand together much the same, South Africa and the non-Dominion Colonies each about 135,000, while from India came 1½ millions. Seamen, munitions, supply, labour corps, flowed in abundance from different races of every civilization and colour, remote islands and wide dependent kingdoms, massed into one instrument by British sea-power and British arts of government. Yet history notes another side to this broad shield. Over the question of compulsory military service Canada was torn between her two races, Australian Labour acutely divided, and Ireland in open rebellion; the declaration of war caused a rising in South Africa, and its strains led to upheaval in India.

How mighty, however, and potentially irresistible had become this Empire, planted so undeliberately by the Elizabethans and endowed so liberally, yet with such lack of interest, by Gladstone's generation ! As we leave it in the 1930's, it covered nearly a quarter of the world's surface. Its total population, mandated territories included, was roughly 520 millions, or a quarter of the human race; distributed through 46 millions in the British Isles, some 25 millions in self-governing Dominions (of whom 5 millions in South Africa were non-European), 62 millions in Colonies, protectorates, mandated territories, and 390 millions in India. The Empire provided a fifth of the world's trade, shipping in British registry, though far declined, still made over a quarter of the whole, while 40 per cent of British exports went to countries under her own flag.

Since 1880 Imperial distribution and structure had much changed. Through the Suez Canal, opening of Africa, the international scramble in the Pacific, discovery of oil as the motive of power, and the rapid increase of eastern populations when given hygiene and security, its strategic and economic centre had moved from the Atlantic to Suez and Capetown, Delhi and Singapore. Concurrently a developing democracy in its white races on one side, and on the other an addition of backward areas in every stage of progress, combined to make a sharpness of division which the older Empire had never known. As against five overseas units with Dominion status, — Southern Ireland, Canada,

Australia, New Zealand, and South Africa, — we must reckon three with some internal responsible government, in Southern Rhodesia, Malta, and Ceylon; a mass of Colonies proper, all controlled by a British Secretary of State, though widely differing in the extent of their liberty, ranging from ancient centres with elected councils, like Barbados, through others old and new (the Straits Settlements, the Gold Coast, or most of the West Indies) in effect ruled by official majorities, to those wholly directed by royal governors like Ashanti or St. Helena. Then came protectorates in various degrees of freedom; descending, for example, from Northern Rhodesia to Kenya and Bechuanaland; protected or part-protected States, Egypt, Malay States, Zanzibar or North Borneo; territories taken over by mandate from the League in 1919, Palestine, Tanganyika, the Cameroons, Togoland, Transjordania, with those mandated to various Dominions, South-west Africa, Samoa, or New Guinea; and last, a political world to itself, the Empire of India. From each group an administrative chain ended in its appropriate centre at Westminster, whether the Foreign Office or India Office or, after 1925, the two departments which formerly had been one, of Dominions and Colonies.

Within this Empire were contained most sources of wealth and sinews of war. From South Africa came nearly half of the world's gold; from Malaya and elsewhere, over half of its rubber and nearly one-third of its tin; from Canada, the great bulk of its nickel and a quarter of its wheat export; a quarter of its cocoa from the Gold Coast and Ashanti, and a quarter of its tea from Ceylon. Yet nothing was made more clear in the 1930's than the fact that this Empire, like others, was not self-sufficient, nor primarily cemented by economic interest. Hard strains of war and post-war economic trouble bore out what earlier history related, that each considerable British community lived under the shield of British sea-power and drew means of expansion from the London money market. Within that broad frame, however, each pushed to its full logic the self-government which they had received, in conditions changed only in degree since 1880; with the result that they enforced a wholly new conception of Empire.

Canada, the first-born, naturally took the lead, speeded on as well by another dominant fact in her history; that, besides making part of the British Empire, she was also part of an Anglo-Saxon continent. By American standards the growth of Canadian population has not been rapid, from the $3\frac{1}{2}$ millions at Confederation to $5\frac{3}{4}$ millions in 1901, and some 10 millions at the present day. The age of fastest increase was in the first years of this century, when in six years Canadian borrowings from London totalled £250 millions, and expansion flowed to the Middle West. Manitoba rose from 25,000 people at its making in 1871 to 425,000 in 1911; by which date two new provinces which had been carved out in 1905, Saskatchewan and Alberta, had risen to 492,000 and 374,000 respectively. Thence came the bulk of the grain harvests, the 400 million bushels of wheat exported. New trans-continental systems of railways, launched in optimistic extravagance, competed with the Canadian Pacific. Steamships opened up the far north and exploited oceanic connection with Hudson's Bay. Gold in the Yukon and immense nickel deposits in Ontario added minerals to the wealth of fisheries and prairies. Only Newfoundland, with her back to the Dominion and looking to sea, still remained outside the door.

The ratios, as they stood in 1935, for the Dominion House of Commons show the change of balance; as against Quebec's basic 65 members, Ontario now returned 82, the three prairie provinces had 55, the three Maritimes were reduced to 26. Time and the trend of immigration have lowered the British-derived population to a half of the whole, while ebb and flow over the thousand-mile open frontier with the United States, and a Radical democracy on new soil, have swept away second chambers, dissolved parties into economic interests, and borrowed in spirit as much from their southern neighbours as from the mother country.

Yet the special mark of the age following on Macdonald's death in 1891 was Canadian nationality, realized through a balance of many rival urgencies of sentiment or interest; a new western outlook, a continuing attraction towards reciprocal trade with America or conflict with American tariffs, the Monroe doctrine as against the British fleet, Imperialism or autonomy. The political leader of this generation was Wilfred Laurier, French Canadian, Catholic, and Gladstonian Liberal. From him, in particular, came the stand at Imperial conferences for independence rather than centralism, allied nations rather than an Empire, and Canadian control of Canadian affairs; as was shown, for instance, by separate negotiation of treaties with America and France, or the making in 1909 of the Canadian department of external affairs. By maintaining protection and pushing along the line of Imperial preference, he attempted to weld Macdonald's substantial legacy with the interests of his own Quebec, and the traditional Liberal defence of provincial rights.

If Canada is the natural mediator, Canada may also be the anvil for the two great masses of Britain and America, and disappointment with Imperial diplomacy, especially over the award on the Alaska frontier in 1903, sometimes alienated her from Empire. Furthermore, the furnace of two wars, in South Africa and then in 1914, lighted up the ancient factor of race. Quebec, fixed in the conservatism of its Catholic, prolific, peasant people, and finding historic material in disputes over mixed marriages or separate schools, hardened in its separatism, and Laurier's grasp withered with the rise of Bourassa, reincarnating the spirit of Papineau and 1839.

Yet Laurier's Conservative successor Borden, prime minister throughout the war period, carried farther and faster Laurier's claim for nationality, and the continuity of that claim, descending again to Laurier's Liberal inheritor, Mackenzie King, was the most potent force in transforming Empire. That a Canadian minister overseas and a Canadian commander should control a Canadian army in Europe, that Canada should sign the peace treaties and enter the League as a separate nation, that a Canadian minister at Washington should make a commercial treaty as the King's envoy, all these were signs of insistence on diversity as the condition of union. There was a second persisting continuance, however, in the relation of Canada to Britain, and of the Dominion to its provinces. Confederation having been in the nature of an alliance, its terms still turn on the Acts that made it; in which the intense spirit of Quebec finds its guarantee against an encroaching Dominion. Nothing but the Imperial Parliament could endorse a fundamental change in these terms of alliance; the Dominion's right to veto provincial laws, conflict over wide frontiers and far-stretching waterpower, or over rival religious stakes, still receive final interpretation in the Privy Council at Westminster.

This people of under 10 millions, having raised 600,000 men and spent £400 millions in one world war, was to enlarge that scale of sacrifice in a second; the potentialities of its future, still inestimable, match the riches, diversity, and grandeur which it has received from Nature and the character of its pioneers.

Belonging in everything but law to a different system, Australian nationality developed in conditions the very reverse to those of Canada. It was isolated, save for New Zealand a thousand miles away, from other British communities; its population was homogeneous, for 97 per cent in 1911 had been born in the Empire; its climate was tropical or north-African, and its political environment was Asiatic. By the mid-nineteenth century the British immigrants had come up against their economic frontier, beyond which no white men and arable crops — and hardly the nibbling sheep — could thrive, and though their population's increase was proportionately greater than any other Dominion's, it still remained a half-empty continent. It grew from 1,668,000 in 1871 to 3,824,000 in 1901, 5,000,000 in 1918, and now some 6,800,000. Forty per cent or more lived in six State capitals, and how concentrated remained the predominance of the original south-east may be judged from the representation in the Federal Lower House in 1928, when New South Wales and Victoria returned 48 members as against 27 for all the rest.

Their federation was accomplished, after many years' debate, in the Commonwealth Act of 1900, whose substance reflected not so much

American example as the separate history and distances of Australian States. To the Commonwealth were assigned some specified powers, — defence, customs and excise, foreign relations, inter-State commerce, and so forth; some powers, like direct taxation, are shared; but the State governments continued in their essence, their governors are not appointed (as in Canada) by the federation, but by the Crown, and with them remained the residue of powers. Alterations in the constitution require a majority of the electors in a majority of the States, and the Senate is composed in equal proportions from each of them. And if the choice of Canberra marks the power of New South Wales, it was also stipulated that the capital must be distant at least a hundred miles from Sydney.

As regards the mother country, a restriction on appeals to the Privy Council only defined more sharply the freedom Australia had long in fact enjoyed, and their later constitutional history has turned much more intensely on the relation of the States to the Commonwealth.

Three causes especially have filled up the scaffolding of 1900 with the substance of a Commonwealth. The States, in particular the smaller ones, must depend upon it for financial assistance. Again, from the needs of defence, against Bismarck's Germany and French New Cale-donia and Oriental immigration, the chief impetus towards federation had come and, as the Empire entered on the zone of war, the Imperial government encouraged Australia to speak and act as a single body. War itself, and then post-war economic strain, drew unity still closer in a unified command, greatly increased taxation, and common arrangements for immigration or British loans. Yet even more was done through the spread of industrialism across State frontiers, and the growing pre-dominance of Labour in politics. This federal power has been developed through the courts; by the High Court of Australia, to which appeals lie from the State courts, and the Court of Arbitration, which has pushed federal powers over industrial disputes and inter-State commerce to make national codes for livelihood and wage-standards.

Democracy demands uniformity, and in Australia — deriving from its earliest origins, the diggers, and contests against a land-owning aristocracy — it triumphed in the new century. Trade-unionism covered the shearers, as it had covered the miners; one in every seven Aus-tralians was a trade-unionist. Firm in the doctrine of a 'white Australia' and for closer land settlement, in alliance with the Imperialist Victorian, Alfred Deakin, Labour buttressed its own interest by high tariff duties, then stood out in its own strength, and by 1915 controlled both the Commonwealth and five State Parliaments. On the issue of conscription they broke with their own war leader, W. M. Hughes, whose coalition ministries carried the war period down to 1923.

These six million British people, so wasteful of old of their precious forests and water, so set upon the well-being of the average man, serried in political purpose and yet individually undisciplined, have in a hundred years made a nation. They sent 330,000 troops overseas in the first German war, and lost 60,000 of them. Their wool made a quarter of the world's supply; if gold production had fallen, wheat had prodigiously increased; their overseas trade doubled within thirty years and passed £200 millions in value in the 1930's. Many thousand miles of government railways linked up this scattered population, rivers have been turned back in their course to irrigate new settlements. Democracy is heedless of spending and Australia borrowed recklessly, £260 millions from Britain, for instance, within seven years. But when the depression of 1929-31 crushed primary producers all the world over, no country rationed itself so severely, or retrieved ruin with such resolution.

In the scales of world power New Zealand ranks low, for the 130,000 people of the '50's have even now hardly risen beyond 1½ millions, but no overseas community perhaps has seemed closer to the mother country, by the rich interest of its origins, a likeness in the climate both of nature and spirit, and experimentation in democracy. Nor can any match the service of New Zealand, except a few martial areas of north India, in sending one in every four of her people to serve in the war of 1914. This small Commonwealth was forced fast into unity soon after receiving responsible government in 1854, by Maori wars and chaos in land laws, borrowing and public works. Abandoning its first division of provinces and passing through the usual vicissitudes of new peoples in overspending and depression, in the age before 1914 it became a centralized Radical State, in the hands of MacKenzie, Pember Reeves, Seddon, and Joseph Ward.

Here the social solutions which Britain herself reached much later, of women's suffrage, labour exchanges, or old age pensions, were first worked out, and what has been deemed Socialism was manifested in its State banks, medical services, and insurance. Yet at its base it remained rather a co-operative community of small owners. Refrigeration multiplied exports from the soil, from which came two-thirds of the cheese and half the frozen mutton and lamb sold in Britain. Till a late date New Zealand's dependence on the British loan market was absolute, nor were there those threats of repudiating debt which have sometimes shaken the credit of Australian States.

Unconnected, unlike Canada, with any rival continental system and satisfied in fulfilling their Britishness by being left alone, the two Australasian Dominions have questioned less than Canada the fact and consequence of British allegiance. Yet, though moving in such different orbits and swayed by such varying motives, all three arrived at much the same fundamental relation to Empire. Very different, and very naturally so, has it been with the other Dominions, South Africa and Ireland, whose racial disputes and ancient history have shaped that relation on harsher lines.

South Africa's inner history has not departed from the conditions of the Union, or the light in which Union was seen by Botha and Smuts. The racialism which Hertzog championed, and caused Boer rebellion in 1914, has changed little in character if it has in degree. Power still turns on the two leading provinces, the Transvaal and the Cape, who together return over two-thirds of the Union Lower House; its exercise is governed by the same overruling facts, of overwhelming native numbers and dependence on British sea-power. Their loyalty to the British connection, as a sheer necessity of environment and very unlike the native sentiment of Australasia, was unlike it in still another way; that, in the hands of Smuts, it grew with and was dependent on the relation of the British Commonwealth to the League and its championship of small nations.

In 1936 the Union's European population was under 2 millions as against the combined numbers, three or four times as great, of African natives, Indian immigrants, and half-castes. The Indian question was largely confined to Natal and its semi-tropical industries, and more or less stabilized after much contest with Gandhi and the government of India, but that of the African natives involved the country's whole destiny. With it is bound up the existence of the gold mines, the maintenance of a white standard, and the attitude of white labour, the use of the soil, and a decision whether the Union can enlarge its borders. It contributed to the Southern Rhodesian vote in 1922 against joining the Union; it had equal responsibility for the Imperial Government's refusal to allow the Union to absorb the protectorates of Bechuanaland, Swaziland, and Basutoland.

Two strains thus run through the Union's political history since Botha died in 1919, worn out in keeping the peace. Smuts fought two elections on the issue of Imperial allegiance and the Union's right to secede; Afrikander racial feeling contributed to his overthrow and to instal Hertzog from 1924 to 1933; with which came a long symbolic dispute over the national flag, and strong assertion of nationhood at Imperial conferences. Yet Hertzog's victory was as much explained by social causes, striking to the deeper roots of colour, and tactically depended on white labour votes. The fruits of this alliance were seen in a triumph of Afrikander policy, a colour bar Act restricting natives in skilled industry, measures to segregate their settlement on the land and, most of all, Acts which in effect destroyed the Cape native vote and allowed them only minute representation on a separate roll.

That price was exacted again in the combination of Smuts with Hertzog in one government from 1933, which endured until the outbreak of the next war. It was born of the great depression, inter-provincial differences, this looming native question, and a revelation that large tracts of the population, both white and black, were miserably poor. And if in interpretation or inner hopes the two parties differed, there were hard facts on which they might compromise. Nine South Africans out of ten might agree on a native policy; they might agree, too, on finding their nationhood in an Imperial family of sister peoples. That process was marked by the separation of the offices of governor-general and high commissioner, and even more by the Status Act of 1934, which declared the Union a ' sovereign independent State ', with its own royal seal.

This declared separation in law, however inseparate might continue economic or even constitutional bonds, was simultaneously asserted in Ireland. In 1927 Cosgrave's lieutenant, O'Higgins, was murdered, and De Valera brought his republican party into politics, decided now to overthrow from within what they had failed to destroy by force. By 1932, when the electors returned him to power, his opportunities were much enhanced. World depression hit hard this small community, for the population of the twenty-six counties had fallen from over 5 millions to less than 3, and though 90 per cent of Irish exports went to Britain, nationalists aspired to make their country more self-sufficing ; moreover, the Statute of Westminster seemed to open a way for aggressive Irish legislation. President De Valera took that way, to abolish the oath of allegiance and appeals to the King in Council, to emasculate the office of governor - general, abolish the Senate, stop payment of the annuities which financed land purchase, and to declare an Irish citizenship distinct from the body of British law. The most liberal ' conventions ' controlling the relation of a Dominion to Britain were thus made rigid in terms of law, in virtue of a claim that an Irish nation, which was still partitioned by British force, could admit no right, whether springing from treaty or Imperial Act of Parliament, which conflicted with its complete sovereignty. Henceforward, at best, Irish-British relations must be reckoned as only international, meeting merely in the external use of the British Crown as a convenient agency to deal with foreign States. A tariff war, ruinous to Irish trade, rose out of the annuities dispute, while at the period's end De Valera was advancing to claim the naval ports, the use of which was stipulated for Britain by the treaty of 1921, and towards a doctrine of Irish neutrality in a British war.

These extensions of Dominion status make part of a long historical sequence, that logically followed in the operation of events since Durham's Report. Between the inner and outward sides of responsible government, which that Report distinguished, it was found that no dividing wall could be maintained. Control of their own lands could not be separated from control of native peoples, or the clergy reserves in Canada from the fate of the Maoris in New Zealand. Control of their own life also implied making their own tariffs, which led to treaties of commerce and foreign relations. Imperceptibly, the dual responsibility of the governor was whittled away. Colonial liberty might carry with it a freedom to go wrong, to corrupt, to dismiss civil servants, or pack second chambers, but by the end of the Victorian age the governor was no longer expected to intervene. Forms of legal dependence were still present in his veto or the power of disallowance, and more actually in the Colonial Laws Validity Act of 1865, which made invalid a Colonial law if ' repugnant ' to an Imperial Act affecting that Colony. But in substance they were obsolete ; more and more we perceive that, in so far as Imperial laws controlled these communities, that control was merely preserved, as by Canada and Australia, to serve their own internal purposes, as between federal and provincial, or State, rights.

With the new Imperialism of the '80's began a transformation of inter-Imperial relations, from one between a supreme and many subordinate members into a co-operative Commonwealth of equals. The history of their conferences before 1914 advances, in terminology as well as in fact, from the first Colonial conference of 1887 to that of 1907, when it was agreed to call ' Imperial ' conferences every fourth year, and to make them meetings between Prime Ministers ; until we reach that of 1911, at which South Africa joined this circle and to which Grey expounded the secrets of foreign policy. Historically, the capital decision of those conferences was a negative one ; their refusal, led by Canada first and foremost, then reinforced from South Africa, to adopt those means of closer union on which the minds of Chamberlain and Lyttleton and the Milner school of Imperialists were turning. Rejecting notions of a standing Imperial Council or a federal Imperial parliament, of an Imperial *Zollverein* or a unified Imperial navy, they limited their partnership to co-operation. Canada's example from 1897 in giving preference to British goods was followed by the others ; their individual naval squadrons were fitted into the British war plan, and they adopted Haldane's uniform principles for military training.

But co-operation is not union, nor mutual acceptance of sacrifice the same as joint responsibility. On this larger stage they were swept forward by the first German war, which demolished Asquith's Victorian view that direction of policy must rest solely with Britain. Lloyd George in 1917 invited the Dominion leaders to the Imperial War Cabinet, and together they made one Empire delegation at the Peace conference. Even so, led by the Canadian Borden, they insisted on signing separately as nations, and as separate nations entered the League ; both tests of war and strains of post-war conflict making it evident that co-operation might end in dissolution.

To this the new quasi-Dominion status of Ireland and India contributed, together with the isolation of Afrikanderdom and the more American isolationism of Canada. A common refusal to accept Lloyd George's diplomacy, a negative attitude towards commitments in Europe for the League, a standing aside from the peace of Locarno, were all symptoms of that nationalism. New examples followed some pre-war precedents, in an Irish appointment of envoys at foreign Courts, a separate commercial treaty between Canada and the United States of 1923, and South Africa's grant in 1928 of preferential duties to Germany. Prime Ministers now communicated direct with each other, not through the Dominions Office; High Commissioners diplomatically represented their interests at Westminster. A struggle of 1926 in Canada asserted that in the prerogative of dissolving Parliament a governor-general, neutral like his sovereign at home, must act on his ministers' advices and on that alone.

This new relationship was defined, so far as things so fluid and growing can be, at the Imperial conferences of 1926 and 1930, and implemented in the Statute of Westminster of 1931. ' Equal in status, in no way subordinate one to another ', though differing in ' function '; only united ' by a common allegiance to the Crown, and freely associated as members of the British Commonwealth '. Henceforth the governor-general of each Dominion would be appointed on the advice of its ministers, his other rôle of link with the Imperial government being taken by a British high commissioner. Disallowance, reservation, ' repugnance ', — all the checks on Dominion lawmaking disappeared, leaving them free to repeal, as the Irish promptly did repeal, such Imperial law as made up part of their own, and allowing the Imperial Parliament to legislate for a Dominion only at its own request.

Having thus, except for their own internal purposes, converted legal into moral bonds and made their inter-relationship international, Britain and the Dominions negotiated with each other the Ottawa preferential agreements of 1932 and acted in co-operation over the abdication of King Edward VIII in 1936. To this conclusion had led all that Burke's American speeches laid down nearly two centuries before, of the spirit of the English constitution which, ' infused through the mighty mass, pervades, feeds, unites, invigorates, vivifies, every part of the Empire '.

When we turn from these ' freely associated ' nations to the Colonies and dependencies, no uniform picture can be seen; nor is any one future predictable. The territories ' mandated ' in 1919 make a disappearing class. Iraq has become an independent ally; others cannot politically be severed from various Dominion systems, such as Southwest Africa and Tanganyika from the Union, or New Guinea from Australia. International, not Imperial, factors are decisive in the

Middle East. Jewish immigration, multiplying their numbers sevenfold since 1918, has made a revolution in Palestine, antagonizing the whole Arab and Moslem world, and insoluble by Britain acting alone. Geography, economic ties, and modern transportation have revolutionized the Colonial empire also, making its oldest limb, the West Indies, a member of the American system as much as of the British Commonwealth.

If that old Atlantic department was a survival, new considerations of strategic and economic power have made the pattern of Empire in Asia and Africa. With the possession of India came first the occupation, and then the defence, of strong points strung out along the two sea-routes, the Persian Gulf and Aden, Egypt and Malta, Mauritius and St. Helena and Simonstown. With India again, and then with Australia, came Singapore and Penang, Hong Kong, Fiji, and the clusters of Pacific isles. But vast spaces of sea and intervening foreign territory divide these settlements. Fourteen hundred miles separate Hong Kong from Singapore, over 2000 miles lie between Singapore and Port Darwin.

' Empire ' is a word covering many motives, which shift in weight as history proceeds, so that humanitarianism now claims a hold on territories which were first exploited by slave-ships, or taken as bases for war. Economically, our dependent Empire makes but a small part of our wealth, taking less than 10 per cent of the British export of manufactured goods. Much is desert, much undeveloped, and much very poor. Our whole trade with the West Indies is a bare £15 millions in value; in the Sudan and both Rhodesias there are less than ten inhabitants to the square mile. Our stake in the Far East is not one of direct trading but rather of investment and services, in shipping nearly half of Chinese commerce or that of Malaya, whose external trade is greater than all the rest of our Colonies put together.

What has been done for this dependent Empire in the enduring scale has been great, and much that we did amiss has been undone. Slave trade and slavery are both gone, the English cathedral at Zanzibar stands where in 1873 John Kirk had the great slave-market closed. It was only in the '90's that an end was made of Ashanti and blood-stained Benin; only in 1903 that Frederick Lugard entered Kano, from which horsemen in chain armour had ridden far for slaves. Wherever we have gone, an end has been made of torture, cannibalism, infanticide, and head-hunting. By early Stuart Churches in the West Indies down to modern missionary steamers on African lakes, and through many thousand dedicated individual lives, something better than the Roman sense has been given to ' Empire '.

In terms of politics we have been rewarded; in the 25,000 combatants from West Africa or the 15,000 from the West Indies in the war of 1914, in the £30 millions worth of Nigerian trade, or the sentiment which from Barbados to Basutoland has defied rival Powers and sharp peril. To many peoples and in many ages we have given their whole future; as our engineers' irrigation has revived Egypt, or as Ross, Manson, and the other pioneers of tropical medicine have attacked the scourges of Africa, or as our colleges on the Gold Coast have educated the African to teach, or to judge. A doctrine of trusteeship for the natives, insisted on by Burke and long ago applied both in India and Africa, has been publicly accepted as our first principle since the peace of 1919.

It is not a formula capable of instant application, nor one to be read apart from the inheritance of history, and everywhere we meet the clash of Europeans with primitive peoples. European economic expansion, which began with the slave trade, continued in the late nineteenth century with a forced stimulation of trade for export, of which South African gold is the greatest example; forced, not so much by compulsory labour, though sometimes that was known, as in the harnessing to Europe's industrial demand of rude native agricultural societies. In detail the process has varied indefinitely, according to historic or local circumstance. Sometimes a reckless reliance on a single means of wealth has brought ruin, as in the sugar of Jamaica. Sometimes, again, economic increase has inserted an entirely new racial factor, whether in the Indian coolies who were brought to British Guiana and Fiji, or in the Chinese who make up a quarter of Malaya's stock of labour. Sometimes a capitalist plantation system has held its own, as in Barbados and St. Vincent, but elsewhere a peasant farming has emerged, as in West Africa and Jamaica. Yet the all-important problems are everywhere much the same.

These problems are those of a humanity low in the scale, beaten down by the blows of Nature and man; drought and tornado and earthquake; great areas where the tsetse-fly kills cattle and beasts of burden; endemic malaria and hook-worm; peoples whose food brings leprosy, or peoples among whom syphilis is universal. Half a century ago the negroid sponge-fishermen of the Bahamas, in their lime-stone huts, had hardly advanced since their forefathers had been torn from Africa; in Africa peasant communities farmed, as Tacitus paints our own Teutonic ancestors, by moving their plots every few years, paid a bride-price for their wives in cattle, and by burning and over-pasturing eroded an arid soil. Poverty has hitherto restricted this Colonial Empire; enhanced by the increase of native numbers through the very peace which Europeans brought, and now exposed, as the depression of 1930 showed, to every change in European demand. Stinted in possibility of raising large revenues, British administration, which at home spends so many hundred millions on social services, cannot spare more than a few shillings a head for health and welfare in the Colonies. Meanwhile, the juxtaposition of two systems, of crops for export alongside crops for maintenance, and tribal clans alongside wage labourers, raise a hundred economic conflicts; questions of wage standards and the ' poor white ', of segregating the two peoples or the alternative of a large ' coloured ' population, of fixing native reserves, and limiting their supply of land.

Political means of government range, likewise, from the rigid racial policy of the Afrikanders to the native liberties that the Colonial Office upholds, in the light of which self-government for a European community, as in Kenya, must be conditioned by guarantees for native progress.   When the Crown in 1900 took Nigeria over from the Company and, amalgamating it with Lagos, made a State one-third the area of India and with 20 million people, Lugard and his successors introduced ' indirect rule ';   leaving native administration, sometimes through natural chieftains and sometimes through clan committees, ruling themselves and self-governing even in finance, and binding up native law with British legal principle through high-court decision and Order in Council.   This has since been extended to East Africa also. But what relation will this indirect system bear to the British goal of responsible government?   Many examples in the older West Indies in the last century, of a planter self-governing community being reduced to a Crown Colony, show the change in the Imperial attitude to a European minority rule;   strong interventions in West Africa and Kenya have asserted Imperial control over the vital question of the soil.   In these social foundations, rather than in the extent of a vote or the proportion of elected members of Council, are the great decisions that have to be made.

Of this heterogeneous dependent Empire the potentialities are great, incalculable, and still to be matured.   Strategically, its international future is uncertain.   After years of dispute since the grant of independence, Britain agreed in 1936 to withdraw her garrisons from Egypt to the Suez Canal zone;   communication with the Pacific rests on the outlook of several Dominions;   while the whole *raison d'être* of several communities might disappear with any revolutionary change in India.   Its sources of wealth, — gold, tin, and tungsten, cotton, copra, rubber, sugar, and oil — depend on the upward move of 60 million people;   ceaseless endeavour and experiment in health, soil betterment, forests and water supply, research in every human ill and every animal pest, and education, are attempting to overtake the past and to better an undecipherable future.

More great, more arduous, and more immeasurable still is India, the British occupation of which has directed the history of half the strong points in our Empire;   though in itself this occupation, not yet two hundred years old, makes only a pin-point in Indian history. Since the Mutiny the population of the sub-continent has increased by 100 millions, and now approaches some 390 million souls; divided in fundamentals as between two-thirds Hindu and one-third Moslem, speaking over 200 different dialects and some 15 principal languages, divided once more as to two-thirds in British India and the remainder in Native States. Torn to shreds by many ages of warfare and finally by the decay of Mogul supremacy, India was given such unity as it has by British rule in the nineteenth century. That uniformity was hastened when in 1858 the Crown took over control from the Company; in course of time the separate Presidency armies were suppressed, and with each decade centralized departments and government monopolies, of forests, irrigation, salt, or opium, massed together the instruments of power. Nearly 40,000 miles of government railways, pushed from the seaports up to remote mountain passes, telegraphs and military roads, move and control these many millions; while a vast machinery of relief against plague and famine crosses its internal frontiers.

The scale of Indian life is that of a continent. Fifteen hundred miles of an armed frontier guard the north-west. Since Dufferin's annexation of Burma in 1886, Indian armies must reach out to Siam and China; northwards, the veil must be pierced that shrouds Tibet and the high Pamirs; through mountain masses overhanging her from Afghanistan, the eyes of the Indian government must discern what is going on in the Oxus valley, and in Russian protectorates of Persia and the Gulf. The budget of the central government alone reaches £100 millions, and Indian trade £270 millions sterling a year; a million Indians served in the war of 1914.

Two separate, yet interlocked, problems govern British-Indian history since the Mutiny; the relation of British to Indians, and the relation of Indians between themselves. Curzon, the last Viceroy (1899-1906) of Queen Victoria's appointment, was also the last British autocrat; of a government which, through fewer than 3000 British administrators and some 50,000 British soldiers, passed down to this large section of all mankind. The speed and magnitude of his reforms, the publicity with which he reproached shortcomings, his zeal for Indian arts and antiquities, and arduous toil for the peasantry, left India more politically self-conscious. That political sense, however, had acquired a darker tinge of race. The gulf between rulers and subjects revealed by the Mutiny was deepened by every modern invention, while frequent leave home, a higher proportion of English women in India, and a centralization which kept the district officer more at head-quarters, all contributed to divide the two races, and diminish that intimacy which had marked British leaders from Warren Hastings to Henry Lawrence. Large events beyond India inflamed this feeling of nationality, such as the victories of Japan or the downfall of Turkey.

This consciousness, and the consequent British actions, work within a frame which history has never elsewhere seen. Other States have overcome differences of race, as deep as those which sever the primitive tribes of India from Aryan conquerors, or Afghan chieftains from Bengalis, and other empires have wrestled with religious hatreds, as fierce as those which play between Hindu and Moslem. What has distinguished modern India has been a stratification of cultures, the co-existence side by side of civilizations which are centuries apart.

Successive waves of conquest from the north, the rigidity of Hindu caste, and British paramountcy have one after another fixed these terraced levels. Fifty million depressed classes, ignored socially and religiously despised, underlie the Hindu priestly and educated castes, and a few hundred miles may take one from the philosophers and poets of Bengal to tribes which worship images daubed in ochre, make a religion of sexual animalism, or dedicate their daughters as temple prostitutes. Bhils and criminal castes, hill tribes whose women are beasts of burden, jungle-dwellers, make the other side of the account headed by the powerful Moslem gentry of Oudh, Rajputs whose feudal vassals still carry the sword, or the wealthy Parsi merchants of Bombay. These cleavages are the final force in a Continent which, not a century ago, was gripped in war and subject to brigands. The Indian army, upon which since Clive peace has depended, is a professional force recruited from martial classes and fighting areas. In the war of 1914 two-thirds of its combatants came from two such areas only, the Punjab and the United Provinces, as against one battalion from all Bengal; the fighting classes of Sikhs, Dogras, and Mahrattas among the Hindus are outnumbered by the Punjabi Mussalmen, Jats, and Pathans, with the Mohammedans of Oudh and Sind, and military strength is out of all relation to population or industry.

This society, whether crowded in the rich Ganges valley or thinly spread over unfertile hills, is predominantly one of illiterate peasants. Nearly 70 per cent of the people live on the land, in mud huts often far distant from rail or metal road, dependent on a favourable rain for their next year's livelihood, and on British-made law as against landlord and money-lender. While the British people make an annual income of £100 or more a head, a tenth of that sum is the maximum in India, and if two-thirds of the Indian budget is spent on defence, it is for one very good reason, that poverty forbids the raising of taxation. A bare 10 millions out of all these 390 millions can read and write a letter in their own language, while perhaps only between 2 and 3 millions are equally literate in English. For women the figures are very much lower, and nothing is more fundamental than the effects of almost universal child marriage among Hindus, or the *purdah* seclusion of women in northern India among both communities.

If the British roots have struck deeper than is commonly supposed, it hardly comes through their blood or religion. The community of mixed race, the Anglo-Indians, number not much above 100,000, and though there are above five million Indian Christians, a high proportion belong to the placid people of Madras, while numerically Christianity has hardly affected Hinduism or the fanatical Moslems. Indirectly, through every sort of example and human sympathy, Christian influence no doubt has been great and beneficial, inspired by their missionary leaders, but British intellectual and economic influence is much more measurable. Since the Whigs, Bentinck and Macaulay and Charles Wood, laid down the principle that education in the best that Britain could provide must be given to India, it has transformed the country; though here, too, in the form that Indian society dictates, descending from above and negligible below, resulting in a great mass of university graduates, but slow progress in primary schools. Economically, India has become one of the world's great Powers. Indian wheat outweighs that of all the Dominions combined, jute is her monopoly, in cotton production she is second only to the United States, while irrigation has brought water to an area as large as Britain. Indian foreign trade, whose value was only £14 millions in 1834, had risen to £340 millions in 1914, by which time she was Britain's largest customer.

Until about that time, British statesmen with one accord repudiated any intention of giving India responsible government. The Councils Act of 1861, Ripon's municipal reforms, Dufferin's Act of 1892, and the Morley-Minto reforms of 1909 went all ostensibly on the same principle; of final responsibility, firmly held through the Viceroy in Council, to the British Parliament, of a constitutional autocracy whose orders could be publicly debated with elected Indian representatives, but whose laws remained, for all that, orders from outside. But the legislators deceived themselves; free speech and association on the British parliamentary model worked out their own logic. The reforms of 1909 set up an elected majority in the provincial Councils, while even in the central legislature the right of discussing the budget accustomed elected members to the habit of a permanent opposition.

Meanwhile, educated in British literature and example, the intellectuals of Hinduism had in 1885 established Congress, which in 1906 was followed by the Moslem League. Irritated by Curzon's university reforms and his partition of Bengal (which was reversed in 1911), even Hindu moderates asked a faster advance, while their extremists engaged in conspiracy and murder. Pan-Moslem feeling, stirred in sympathy with events in Turkey, Persia, and Arabia, war-prices and heavy recruiting, and the ideal of self-determination for which the Allies fought, brought about in 1917 the Montagu-Chelmsford report and a long stride forward in the 1919 reform. Though the number of Indian members of the Viceroy's executive Council was increased and the legislative assembly would henceforward have an elected majority, the central government remained responsible to Parliament and amply provided with means, through the Viceroy's powers, of asserting its will. In the provinces, on the other hand, by the device which was christened ' dyarchy ', while the Governor in Council would control some important ' reserved ' functions, others — including education, health, and local government — would be transferred to Indian ministers fully responsible to the provincial Council.

Long before the ten years had elapsed, after which period the Act provided for re-examination, the new order had partly collapsed. A mass of reservations and special electorates for different communities, — landowners, depressed classes, Mohammedans, or Sikhs, — testified to the inherent difficulty of unifying political action even in a single province ; while the working of dyarchy either threw ministers into dependence on their officials, or tended to split the Governor's ' Cabinet '. Moreover, reform was launched in an atmosphere hot with recrimination, over measures of war defence, press and conspiracy laws, and excessive recruiting ; an advanced Hindu element, preaching ' Swaraj ' or Home Rule, declined to work the reforms at all. Famous already for his lead in championing the Indian colony in South Africa Gandhi, a lawyer from the Bombay presidency, now revealed his rare, elastic gifts ; sometimes upholding the depressed classes, at others allied with Moslems of the north, yet again to Bombay mill-owners, though on occasion invoking the spinning-wheel and the vision of an older India, rid of western industrialism. Though he professed that disobedience to law must be without violence, boycott and strikes led to bloodshed among mill-hands and peasants, superstitious in their faith and savage in their hatreds, and who could not read.

After some years the Swaraj party, changing their tactics, entered the provincial governments with the object of wrecking the reforms, in several instances forcing the governors to suspend the ' transferred functions ' and rule through executive power. Except perhaps in Madras, ' party ' in a British sense was never realized, tending rather to resolve itself into the fundamental feud of Hindu and Moslem, which self-government and separate electorates only seemed to harden. The central Legislative Assembly showed a growing responsibility, though a growing sense of nationalism. For India, though by no means a Dominion, had been represented as such in the making of peace and Imperial conferences ; it was admitted that she had a right to control her economic welfare, tariffs were built up to protect home industries,

and the excise duty on cotton, long enforced in the interest of Lancashire, was abolished. In 1927 a royal commission, named after its
chairman Sir John Simon, began investigation of the next step forward;
which was accelerated by the advent of a Labour government in Britain
in 1929, a concordat between Irwin the Viceroy and Gandhi, a declaration that India might expect Dominion status, and the urgent problem
of the Native States.

These were over five hundred in number, covering one-third of
India and about one-fifth of its people, ranging upwards from mere
feudal estates to a great State like Hyderabad with 14 million subjects,
to others of proved fighting tradition like Sikh Patiala or the Rajputs, or
to those, such as Baroda or Mysore, whose administration was as enlightened as a British province. Their rôle would be all-important, yet
their footing wholly differed from British India; their relation to Britain
had come by way of treaty with the Crown, their privileges had been
many times solemnly guaranteed, and though an advisory Chamber of
Princes had been set up in 1921, they stood in no direct connection with
the Imperial Parliament or the Indian legislature. It was not easy
to see them merging control of their internal affairs in a democratic
assembly.

This it was which decisively influenced the long conferences between
British and Indian leaders, which issued in the Act of 1935. It provided for a federal government at the centre, which should, however,
only come into force when the Native States returning half of the
princely representation should have given their consent. In effect, the
method of dyarchy, applied in 1919 to the provinces, was now to be
tried at the centre, for the Governor-general in Council retained large
powers over defence and foreign affairs, princes and minorities, credit
and tariffs. The major advance was to be made in the provinces, now
increased to eleven by new governments for Orissa and Sind, though
Burma was to be severed from India, and they were given responsible
government in all subjects, save for their governors' final powers in
emergency. Their electorates, increased to some 35 million voters
including some women, at the first election of 1937 returned predominantly Congress ministries. By this date about one-third of the administrative services were in Indian hands, an Indian naval force was in
existence, the King's commissions given to Indian officers after 1919 were
being extended, and Indianization applied to some entire regiments.

In the short space granted to the new scheme before the next outbreak of war, three major difficulties at least were instantly apparent.
Hindus and Moslems were in bitter conflict; the communal distribution
of seats was imposed, since they could not agree themselves, by the
Imperial government, and already the Moslems, dreading a Congress
majority, were calling out for a separate Moslem block of India, or

' Pakistan '. Nor did the princes give the assent on which federation depended, some of the most powerful deliberately holding aloof. Finally the new constitution, giving India appreciably less power of self-government than other Dominions had achieved, was repudiated by Congress, which now asked recognition of Indian independence. But whether either Dominion status within the Empire, or democratic self-government, is the destined future for India, or whether they can harmonize its deep divisions, are questions which will not easily be resolved.

They are, indeed, questions applicable to this Commonwealth as a whole, which is styled an ' Empire ' but is, in fact, a great number of communities, differing in policy, at every level of civilization, and connected with Britain by various bonds. Exhausted by war, and with all those communities who produce agricultural and raw material heavily hit by long depression, its conditions have altered much and may be judged more precarious since the end of the Victorian peace. The British no longer swarmed off overseas, for their migration to the Empire which took 223,000 souls in 1913 had dropped to 62,000 by 1929, and ten years later had begun a reverse flow homewards. Their relative power, or at least its old method, seemed to be declining. We had held 40 per cent and more of the world's shipping in 1914 but only 26 per cent in 1937, while our income from overseas investment had fallen heavily.

This Commonwealth, the events of the 1930's seem to prove, is not to be measured, or justified, primarily as an economic system. True, assisted in part by the tariff arrangements made in 1932 at Ottawa, the percentage of all British trade transacted with the Empire rose from the 25 per cent usual up to 1910 to above 37 per cent in 1935. Even so, there were plentiful signs of independence, as in India and Ireland, with their much reduced proportions of British imports ; agricultural revival in Britain was not easily reconcilable with Australasian producers, nor Canada's trade to the United States with a closed Imperial system. These last years, then, witnessed some retreat from the Ottawa tariffs, as was evident in the British-American treaty of 1938. There remains also one overruling fact, that this Empire is not economically self-sufficient. One-quarter of the British meat supply came from the Argentine, one-quarter of its coffee from Brazil, while only 5 per cent of the oil required could be obtained from British territory. No single country, however great, sends us much over 12 per cent of our imports ; our own market could not possibly absorb the native products of British Africa ; Australia discovered a mutual interest with the textile-makers of Japan. Once more, as Bolingbroke had said of a smaller relation to Europe, it was found that Britain's rôle was to be ' a good neighbour and a fair trader '.

Divided into three chief systems, — Dominions, Colonies, and India, — having astride its communications many new nations whom its own teaching has inspired, with no closed economic union, no single army or navy, the Commonwealth formally subsists in the powers of one royal prerogative and one Imperial Parliament. In truth, however, the sovereignty which gives this Commonwealth its community is that of a general will : the product of ages passed, of common aspirations for the future, and of services given, not for an Imperial but for a moral world order.

CHAPTER III

PERIL, 1929–1938

THE history of these years, not yet fully known or rightly to be judged, was distorted by two universal calamities : an economic depression which between 1929 and 1932 reduced world trade by two-thirds, and the seizure of power in Germany by Adolf Hitler's Nazi Party in 1933.

Only a very strong government could have survived the first, and Ramsay MacDonald's was not that, dependent as it was on an uneasy alliance with Liberal votes and deeply divided within itself. But the depression doomed it. The total of unemployed rose from the 1,200,000 of 1929 to 2 millions in 1930 and nearly 3 millions by Easter 1931, by which date the unemployment insurance fund was £100 millions in debt, growing without limit. With a budget deficit of over £30 millions, Snowden, Chancellor of the Exchequer, could not persuade his colleagues to his policy of economy, while in July an independent committee reported that one-third of the nation's income was being spent in taxes and rates, and predicted a deficit the next year of £120 millions.

This report made only the occasion for a grave decision, in which MacDonald and Lloyd George independently concurred, that this crisis was one too deadly for any one party to handle. Its deeper causes we have seen ; that British prosperity had been rooted in a world system, which economic and political chaos in the post-war world made unworkable. Our sober effort to restore the old system, which never succeeded in bringing back the trading figures of 1913, was annihilated late in 1929 in a huge speculative crash in America, an abrupt cessation of American lending to Germany, and sheer ruin in those countries, Australia included, which were producers of food and raw material. A hundred times more serious than in 1815, owing to the scale and velocity of modern finance, this may be deemed the first economic disaster, since American silver broke the sixteenth-century scheme, in which all the world shared. Wholesale prices fell by anything up to 20 per cent ; no lower price for wheat had been recorded for four hundred years ; our own black unemployment figures were much surpassed in Germany and the United States. Purchasing power dried up, millions locked up in short-term borrowings were frozen, and one State after another went off gold. A crash of the weak Austrian banks spread to Germany, and thence to the Bank of England, which lost £45 millions in gold in the one month of July 1931. Credits borrowed from France and America failed to stop the drain, the Bank officially reported that foreign credits could only be won by action that would prove a determination to pay our way; MacDonald and Snowden resolved to balance the Budget at all costs. That would involve not only higher taxation but less expenditure, which they proposed to achieve by cuts in every direction, including a 10 per cent reduction in unemployment benefit. Even so, Snowden argued that, with the lower cost of living, the unemployed would be better off than in 1924.

To these, however, neither the Trades Union Congress nor the Labour party would agree, nor a large section of the Cabinet, led by Henderson and Lansbury. In August, therefore, MacDonald called into council the Opposition leaders and offered his resignation to the King, with the suggested formation of a coalition. He took office at the head of a National government, followed from his own party by Snowden, Thomas, and Sankey the Lord Chancellor, and made alliance with Conservatives, headed by Baldwin and Neville Chamberlain, and a Liberal group led by Samuel. Their single mission was to save our finances and the value of the pound; what then should follow was left uncertain.

In these events, revolutionary in their effect both on party and policy, the principal architect in this country was Neville Chamberlain. Since their defeat in 1929 the Conservative party had been distracted; in part from loss of confidence in Baldwin as leader, in part because Churchill had broken with him, making opposition to the Indian reforms his opportunity, and again from a continued disagreement over tariffs. Having now become the second man in the party, Chamberlain believed that both national and party salvation were bound up with the cause of Empire trade. In social outlook a Victorian Radical, who reprobated Socialist finance as a policy of class bias and demoralization, he argued that there was no place for the continued existence of Liberalism, and still less need for an alliance with an opportunist like Lloyd George; indeed, a steady drift of former Liberal votes and Liberal ministers towards Conservatism confirmed his opinion. He had prepared and organized within his party machine the ingredients of a national policy, and was given his opening by the events of this autumn.

For though this emergency Cabinet balanced the budget, as to £75 millions by new taxation, £52 millions of which came from direct taxes, and as to another £70 millions by 'cuts' in salaries, the services, teachers, and unemployed, the foreign drain of gold continued and in September redoubled, when part of the North Sea fleet at Invergordon demonstrated against reduction of pay. On 21st September, by which date £200 millions had been withdrawn from London since mid-July, Great Britain went off gold.

One consequence was to hasten, what must soon in any case have come, the dissolution of the existing Parliament, in which the government had only a shaky majority, and which must seek a new mandate after these events. The powers which ministers asked for at the election of October were in general terms, to explore all means, tariffs included, for national recovery; the chief dread of the electors was inflation, and their verdict was overwhelming. By some $14\frac{1}{2}$ million votes as against $6\frac{1}{2}$ millions for Labour, they returned 558 supporters of the National government, of whom 471 were Conservatives, as against only 52 Labour members. Excepting Lansbury, virtually all the Labour ministers who had refused to follow MacDonald disappeared from Parliament.

Receiving power in these proportions, Chamberlain led the Conservatives to recover prosperity through the policy inherited from his father, and which he had himself developed. Our adverse trade balance was about £400 millions; our ' invisible ' exports of shipping and services had fallen by £200 millions, leaving us with a heavy debit balance; we had spent £700 millions on public works in the last seven years, with only an infinitesimal effect on unemployment. To correct the balance, to raise prices from depression, to get revenue, and to prevent a further decline of the pound, all these purposes, as all sections agreed, called for some restriction on imports.

When, however, they came to a permanent policy, in the Import duties Act of February 1932, a break-up of the government was only averted by a new formula, that this protection, like Catholic emancipation between 1812 and 1829, should be an ' open ' Cabinet question. The basis of the Act was a flat low-rate tariff, laying a 10 per cent duty on all goods, other than those given higher protection by an independent tariff board, or those remaining on the free list, which at present included wheat, meat, cotton, and wool.

Meantime British agriculture, arable farming especially, was in parlous depression, so too was production in the Dominions, while political and economic upheaval kept world trade in ruins. A conference at Lausanne in June, though at last promising to end the dreary futility of reparations from Germany, left final decision to depend on a settlement of the equally stiff question of Europe's debts to America. With that background, a strong delegation of British ministers set out to an Imperial Conference at Ottawa.

The Ottawa agreements of August were fundamental. Our government undertook to grant free entry to Empire products, and to give them a preference, which would involve, for example, laying duties on foreign wheat, butter, fruits, and timber. On the other hand, we should protect our own agriculture by restricting the volume of Dominion imports, and asked that Dominion duties on British goods should leave our traders on a fair competitive level. However these schedules and voluntary machinery might work out as between Britain and the Dominions, the Ottawa duties had the immediate effect of driving Snowden, Samuel, and Sinclair out of the Cabinet.

Henceforward this became an essentially Conservative government, little changed by Baldwin replacing MacDonald as Prime Minister at midsummer 1935. It had some faults as a Coalition, in that office was sometimes assigned in proportions of party rather than fitness, and the faults also of a government with too big a majority, which much over-represented its majority of votes. Its leadership was indecisive. Mac-Donald was an exhausted man, while Baldwin's gifts of judgment and sympathy were not equally accompanied by resolute action so that, altogether, not so much party advantage as an over-deference to persons and loyalties seemed to cumber this Coalition. Yet future history may perchance record that neither for national recovery nor social advance were the 1930's unimportant.

Their work must be done amid the debris of the economic system, and amid nothing less than a second industrial revolution. The first was signalized afresh by the total failure of the world economic conference of 1933, a default by Europe and then by Britain in their American debts, an immense devaluation of the dollar, and President Roosevelt's policy of raising internal prices as part of his ' new deal '. Meantime, with mechanization and chemistry and speed and science, the world's production of primary commodites, wheat, sugar, tin, or rubber, yearly accelerated, till it seemed that only restriction or destruction of goods could save men from the ruin their wealth would bring ; mass production in America and Germany, cartels and combines and rationalization, or more looms to every weaver, threatened to throw humanity out of employment, victims of their own machines.

Since the medium of gold and the mechanism of exchange had collapsed, and since each Continental State was obsessed by the vision of becoming self-sufficient, protecting its armed industry by every sort of monetary juggling, restriction, or tariff, the British Commonwealth painfully reconstructed its own economy. Our overseas trade henceforth hardly amounted to 60 per cent of its old figure, the volume of exports fell, the ratio of our income from overseas investment was halved. Yet at least the 3 millions unemployed of 1933 had fallen below 1½ millions by 1937, 11 million persons in insured occupation surpassed the 1929 total, and industrial output was up by 20 per cent. Real wages rose by about 4 per cent, middle-class and working-class savings had doubled since 1924, and 2½ million new houses had been built since the armistice of 1919. A substantial surplus marked the budgets of 1934-5, when the ' cuts ' made during the crisis were restored.

Chamberlain's administration at the Exchequer, taken with that of the Boards of Trade and Agriculture, rested on three principles : cheap money, a low tariff, and a planned economy, putting producers in an order of priority, — British, Dominion, and foreign. A bold conversion of debt in 1932 of £2000 millions of 5 per cent to a 3½ per cent basis was buttressed by a fund of £350 millions to iron out exchange fluctuations and enlarge our credit. If iron and steel bounded forward under a protective duty of 33 per cent, less than one-third of our imports were subject to duty exceeding 10 per cent, and the clear tendency of our agreements with other countries was to relieve trade from excessive tariffs. Though the proportion of our total imports which was taken from the Empire rose from the old average of 26 per cent to 37 per cent in 1937, our exports to the Empire increased much less, and various arrangements showed that, despite Ottawa, the chief countries in the Empire must depend on doing business with the world outside.

Nothing better showed the trends of this last age than British agriculture. The old tariff controversy, with its angry cries about the dear loaf, seemed to be dead. Applying a system designed to share markets between home, Dominion, and foreign producers, Chamberlain and his fellow-ministers discovered that this involved a detailed regulation of agriculture at home. Many different instruments were used ; not so much tariffs as restrictions agreed by separate treaties, quotas, subsidies, guaranteed prices, or controlled marketing ; which were applied in turn to arable crops, milk, eggs, and potatoes. By such means the acreage of wheat was increased by 40 per cent, British sugar-beet met nearly one-third of the demand, home-produced bacon was doubled.

It was then a Conservative administration, using all the means of nineteenth-century Socialism. In 1913-14 the budget had asked only £198 millions, in the middle 1930's it was always over £800 millions and took about 23 per cent of the national income. Something between £400 and £500 millions a year were spent on social services, — education, health, housing, pensions, — all of which the previous century had left almost entirely to self-help. This Conservative government spent many millions on enlarging roads, telephones, tramp shipping, and rail transport ; it was prepared to buy out two large entrenched property interests, tithe and coal royalties. Steadily this race, politically democratic for so long, realized a larger democracy in its society, as was seen again in the higher share taken by salaries as against the dwindling of profits and rents, in the inhabitants of the universities, or the savings and house-purchase of the working-class.

Yet keenly felt, and perhaps increasing, cleavages separated this Socialist-Conservatism from the Socialist party. As asserted in those years, they rose in part from the inheritance of the previous age, and not least from the urban slums; still more perhaps from that lost trade, possibly 20 per cent, which our ' recovery ' since the war had never overtaken, and which was felt most severely in exactly those basic industries, — coal, engineering, shipbuilding, and textiles, — by which Victorian England had become great. In those trades and those distressed areas was concentrated the hard core of unemployment, the claims for higher scales of relief, and the controversy over ' doles ', with a means-test for those receiving relief not covered by insurance. It was to put such controversies outside politics, and political auction, that Chamberlain brought about the creation of an independent Unemployment Assistance board.

But the controversy ranged deeper, in an old clash of rival doctrines. The principle of contributory insurance against all social misfortunes, by a triple partnership between the State, employers, and employed, could not satisfy those who would push their ideal of equality to its extreme, or believed that ' the community ', by controlling finance and the agents of production, could make democracy real through nationalization. At what price this could be achieved in an Imperial and industrial Commonwealth, at what sacrifice of old liberties, whether capitalism had failed or could be readjusted, whether the rival scheme meant a better society or merely the supremacy of another class, such were the questions underlying the elections of this decade.

One Victorian achievement, however, maintained unity of feeling in the nation, — that constitutional Crown to which, with a good many protests, Queen Victoria had finally come; a symbolic power now tested in adversity and vindicated by public service. It was seen in the silver Jubilee of the modest and sensible King George V in 1935 and, after his death the next year, in the strain brought by the determination of his son Edward VIII to make a marriage which caused the united opposition of the British and Dominion governments, and his consequent abdication. In that matter Baldwin faithfully represented the Commonwealth, and guarded the continuous character of the throne. But by that date his day was done, and the government he handed over to Chamberlain in May 1937 was weakened and beset by many dangers, in the handling of which neither MacDonald nor Baldwin, neither Labour nor Conservative, had succeeded.

We stand, even our sons will stand, too near in time to judge British foreign policy between the two wars, except to suggest a few stages and a few conclusions. If the peace of Versailles was not a bad peace, it was certainly a most precarious one, demanding union and time and clear-eyed resolution if it was to be made good. If measured in terms of the old diplomacy, it left great voids in the European system, for the German and Austrian Empires were destroyed, Russia was ignored and stripped of territory, Turkey was mutilated. Those empty spaces were filled up by thirteen petty States, unaccustomed for many centuries to power and now ruling dangerous racial minorities, as well as by new untried international arrangements in threatening areas, as in Danzig, Fiume, Syria, and Palestine.

This territorial settlement was linked to, and guaranteed by, a revolutionary international scheme, the Covenant of the League of Nations, which included one dangerous fallacy at least : that all nations, great and small, from France to Albania or from Germany to Afghanistan, had equal privileges and representation. It was linked also with an apparatus of financial reparations and war debts, which quickly proved unworkable. The general result, within a very few years, was to divide the world between ' satisfied ' States, such as France and Britain, and the ' dissatisfied ', whether the defeated or partitioned countries such as Germany and Turkey, or those like Italy, Russia, and Japan who judged their share was unjust, and would work for a change.

Broadly speaking, three trends may be found in British policy, in governments of either party, since 1919. There was an increasing acceptance of the view that the peace treaties must be revised, especially on their financial side ; historically in full accord with the old British instinct to mediate between extremes, and the prime British interest of international peace. There was, secondly, a loathing of war, a zeal for disarmament, an insistence on the League as the hope of the world. But there was also, in Britain and the Dominions alike, a refusal to commit ourselves in advance to fight, or automatically to defend the integrity of every existing State.

These may take us to the first dividing year of 1930. Before and in that year we meet, mostly by British pressure on France, a large scaling-down of reparations, the bringing of Germany into the League, withdrawal from Germany of foreign garrisons, and the beginning of the Disarmament conference ; with all the world, we accepted with acclamation the American-inspired Kellogg Pact of 1928, which outlawed war. But we meet, too, our refusal to accept the Protocol of 1923 which would have stiffened up sanctions against war, an intense unwillingness in the Dominions to be caught up again in the feuds of Europe and, by the peace of Locarno of 1925, a certain limitation of our commitments to areas which, like the Rhine frontier, were vital to our own existence.

We open the 1930's, therefore, with Britain engaged in an international scheme which had still to be proved or, indeed, still to be born. For the absence of the United States and Russia from the League half crippled it. Already it had been defied with impunity, in some forcible seizures of territory by Italy and Poland. Already, years of discussion over disarmament proved that no great European State was ready to disarm ; France least of all, unless she were given stronger guarantees for her security and that of her eastern allies, the Little Entente. And there were only three alternatives before us : isolation, which British opinion would condemn as immoral and impossible ; armed alliances which had caused the late war ; and ' collective security ' within the League. But though in words all British parties accepted the last, and any government which repudiated it would fly in the face of public opinion, no British party was prepared to carry out its full logic, which would entail keeping up a high level of armaments and a willingness to make war whenever, and wherever, peace was violated.

Three events, the financial collapse from 1929 onwards, the Japanese attack on China from 1931, the fall of the German Republic and Hitler's accession to power in 1933, proved the deadly flaws and inconsistencies in Europe. Economic nationalism, inflamed by the small States newly created and universal depression, added new fuel to racial hatred. ' Collective security ' was seen to be a phrase ; no State would make war except when its own interests were concerned ; no League without America and Russia, and far less any one State, 6000 miles away and with no adjoining military base, would begin a war against Japan. In 1933 Germany left both the Disarmament Conference and the League, and in 1934 France, declining to discuss disarmament further, turned instead to an alliance with Russia.

All this time, in the hands of MacDonald, Baldwin, and their Foreign Secretary Simon, the British government assiduously nourished every means of mediation or step towards disarmament ; each year our defence estimates were reduced, our Air Force had not reached even the level planned in 1923, while the Labour government of 1930 cut down our naval strength. By every conceivable test our public opinion showed the general desire for disarmament, so much so that the charge that the government were ' war-mongering ' was Labour's weapon at the election of 1935. For by that time our government were convinced that we must look to ourselves and begin the making of a new Air Force, second to none.

As we approach the fatal years of 1935–6, four all-important facts govern the scene. The last war had suggested, — new inventions and all our information confirmed, — the belief that future warfare would be in new dimensions, fought in the air, and on land with mechanized armies, and ' total ' war in the sense that the whole mechanical potential of an industrial State would be harnessed to victory. Politically, it was becoming clear also that France, our one unquestioned ally, was doubting, exhausted, and divided ; so torn by strife from 1934 that even civil war seemed in sight ; so hesitating, that its small allies in eastern Europe began to look elsewhere. More instant was the plain deter- mination of Nazi Germany to rearm, and to undo every remnant of the peace treaties ; even more formidable because Hitler imported into foreign affairs, with a strength never seen since 1789, a fixed and furious ideology. That warfare of ideas made faster, what internal revolution and the mistakes of the peace settlement had begun, a restoration of the might of Russia, which from 1934 sprang to the front not only in its ancient part of the Slav leader against the German, but as the armed apostle of extreme democracy.

Finally three successive crises in 1935-6 defied and destroyed the hopes and the fabric of 1919; the Italian invasion of Abyssinia, the German reoccupation of the Rhineland, and the outbreak of the Spanish civil war. Taken together, they revealed the cross-currents in British policy, and the isolation to which ' collective security ' had brought us, while they also involved a terrible disunity in public opinion on foreign affairs. Refusing to appeal to the electors for a mandate for rearmament, Baldwin like his opponents in the election of 1935 stood by the League and, as Italian aggression proceeded, Britain moved for economic sanctions. Rapidly it was proved that, while we spoke the language of the League and sincerely professed our faith in it, the world outside — and the British government with it — had returned to the maxims of the balance of power and armed diplomacy. Sanctions, it was believed, might mean war with Italy, and such a war France refused to contemplate, seeing in Italy a necessary part of her defence against Germany. But if we then were left to fight Italy alone, might not that war soon bring in Germany and Japan ? A war with three Powers at once, which our military advisers declared we were not equipped to meet. So, while the Hoare-Laval Pact, which gave Italy a practical supremacy over Abyssinia, represented a political device to escape this danger, the anger of the British people and the enforced resignation of Hoare in December 1935 represented a last glint of feeling for the League and all it stood for.

Yet when, seizing this golden hour of democratic confusion, in March 1936 the Germans entered the Rhineland, hardly a voice in Britain was heard which would approve a war to prevent the Germans retaking German soil; the original doubts as to the justice of the peace treaties thus dissolving our resolution to uphold peaceful means of change.

The League then, with America standing aside, was proved incapable of saving peace and, much against the grain, Britain hurried on the pace of rearmament. But from that time onwards a deadly contradiction crippled our policy. Still clinging to the ideal of the League, still so much detesting war that they would even resist rearmament, the Left wing of British politics saw a threat to their whole view of life in the Nazi and Fascist ideologies, and their brutal suppression of every freedom. In that fear they were confirmed by the savage war in Spain which they read as one of force put upon an elected Republican government by rebel soldiers, aided by German and Italian legions.

More and more — ignoring the Slav-Teuton feud, or the price which Russia would ask for assisting democracy—they looked towards Moscow.

On the other side stood the British government, under Baldwin until 1937 and thereafter under Chamberlain, bent on winning time to rearm, sceptical of any real support from the French, disillusioned as to the League, and in spirit going back to the method of Salisbury and Grey. If Germany and Italy had real grievances arising out of the peace treaties, they must be explored; ' appeasement ', the object declared in countless speeches by British politicians since 1931, must investigate whether, in their treatment of German minorities or Italy's Colonial claims, the treaties had been just or wise. They adhered to Canning's or Pitt's view that with the internal means of government in other countries, however tyrannical, Britain was not concerned. They were convinced that Great Britain, and even more the Dominions, ought not to be asked to fight again, unless interests vital to the Commonwealth's very life were at stake. Till that cause were proved up to the hilt, and until every marginal doubt in the treaties had been eliminated, they would continue to work for time, and husband our strength.

In that confusion of thought, in that dire peril, in these ill-requited, sincere, and high intentions, contemporary history must leave the Commonwealth. Since its humble beginnings, and its thin trickles of venturers and refugees from Europe, Providence had freighted it with many treasures, loaded it with fortunes, and conveyed it to the ends of the earth. Now ' the little body ', in which Canning had praised ' a mighty heart ', was extended through a world system.

BOOKS FOR FURTHER READING

THE present state of knowledge, with full bibliographies both for original sources and modern works, will be found represented in the Oxford Histories and the Cambridge Histories (Medieval, Modern, the Empire, and India); there are fuller lists in bibliographies for some special periods, such as Conyers Read's for the Tudors or C. L. Grose on *British History, 1660–1760*, as well as in some of the more recent books mentioned below.

The titles that follow make no attempt to detail the sources on which this book is based; and, except in the case of a few familiar classics, they do not include contemporary material. Though many naturally cover several sections, as a rule they are here mentioned once only.

PRELUDE

CHAPTER I. BRITAIN BEFORE THE ROMANS

Cyril Fox, *The Personality of Britain.*
Kendrick and Hawkes, *Archaeology in England and Wales, 1914–1931.*
Childe, *The Bronze Age.*
Crawford and Keiller, *Wessex from the Air.*
The County Archaeologies (Methuen).

CHAPTER II. ROMAN BRITAIN

Haverfield and Macdonald, *The Roman Occupation of Britain.*
Haverfield's articles in the Victoria County Histories.
Collingwood, *Roman Britain.*
Wheeler, *Prehistoric and Roman Wales.*
Roman London (Royal Commission on Historical Monuments).

BOOK I, 450–1066

CHAPTER I. THE COMING OF THE ENGLISH

Leeds, *The Archaeology of the Anglo-Saxon Settlements.*
Green, *The Making of England.*
Bury, *St. Patrick.*
Jolliffe, *Pre-Feudal England: the Jutes.*
Myres, *The English Settlements* (Oxford History).

CHAPTER II. THE LAND AND THE CONQUERORS

Chambers, *England Before the Conquest.*
Chadwick, *Origins of the English Nation.*

Stopford Brooke, *Early English Literature*.
Baldwin Brown, *The Arts in Early England*.
Publications of the English Place-Name Society.

CHAPTER III.   CONSOLIDATION OF THE CHURCH

Bede (ed. Plummer), *Opera Historica*.
Bede : His Life, Times, and Writings (ed. Hamilton Thompson)
Levison, *England and the Continent in the Eighth Century*.
Bright, *Early Church History*.
Deanesly, *History of the Medieval Church*.

CHAPTER IV.   ANARCHY, COLLAPSE, AND RECOVERY, 613-899

Stenton (Oxford History).
Hodgkin, *History of the Anglo-Saxons*.
Kendrick, *The Vikings*.
Asser, *Life of Alfred* (ed. Stevenson).

CHAPTER V.   THE HEIGHT AND FALL OF SAXON ENGLAND, 899-1017

Stenton, *The Danes in England*.
Maitland, *Domesday Book and Beyond*.
Armitage Robinson, *The Times of St. Dunstan*.
Robertson, *The Laws of the Kings of England, from Edmund to Henry I*.
Clapham, *English Romanesque Architecture*, vol. i.

CHAPTER VI.   DANISH RULE AND NORMAN CONQUEST, 1017-1066

Haskins, *Norman Institutions*.
Freeman, *The Norman Conquest*.
Stenton, *William the Conqueror*.
Vinogradoff, *English Society in the Eleventh Century*.
Corbett's chapter in *Cambridge Medieval History*, vol. iii.

BOOK II, 1066-1360

CHAPTER I.   THE TRANSFORMATION OF ENGLAND, 1066-1154

Pollock and Maitland, *History of English Law*, vol. i.
Stenton, *The First Century of English Feudalism*.
Knowles, *The Monastic Order in England*.
Brooke, *The English Church and the Papacy*.
Macdonald, *Lanfranc*.

CHAPTER II.   THE CROWN AND ITS RIVALS, 1066-1154

Davis, *England under the Normans and Angevins*.
Round, *Geoffrey de Mandeville*.
Lloyd, *History of Wales to the Edwardian Conquest*.
White, *The Making of the English Constitution*.
Bateson, *Medieval England*.

CHAPTER III. THE ANGEVINS, 1154-1213

Stubbs, *Historical Introductions to the Rolls Series.*
Norgate, *England under the Angevin Kings.*
Runciman, *History of the Crusades.*
E. Curtis, *History of Medieval Ireland.*
Powicke, *The Loss of Normandy.*

CHAPTER IV. PREPARATION FOR NATIONALI.

Stubbs, *Lectures on Medieval and Modern History.*
Haskins, *Renaissance of the Twelfth Century.*
Tait, *The Medieval Borough.*
Rashdall (new edition by Powicke and Emden), *The Universities of the Middle Ages.*
Page, *London: its Origin and Early Development.*
Little, *Studies in English Franciscan History.*
Chambers, *The Continuity of English Prose.*
Bond, *Gothic Architecture in England.*

CHAPTER V. REVOLUTION AND REFORM, 1213-1272

Cambridge Medieval History, vol. vi.
Powicke, *Stephen Langton* and *Henry III and the Lord Edward.*
McKechnie, *Magna Carta.*
Bémont (ed. Jacob), *Simon de Montfort.*
Treharne, *The Baronial Plan of Reform, 1258-63.*

CHAPTER VI. EDWARD I, 1272-1307

Cambridge Medieval History, vol. vii. (chapters by Johnstone, Terry, and McIlwain).
Lodge, *English Rule in Gascony.*
Cam, *The Hundred and the Hundred Rolls.*
Pasquet, *The Origin of the House of Commons.*
Maitland, *Memoranda de Parliamento* (Selden Society).

CHAPTER VII. THE CONQUEST OF WALES

Lloyd and Powicke, *Henry III* (as above).
Morris, *The Welsh Wars of Edward I.*
Rees, *South Wales and the March.*
Edwards, *Littere Walliae* (Introduction).

CHAPTER VIII. EDWARD II AND EDWARD III, 1307 TO 1360

Tout, *Political History, 1216-1377* (Longmans), and *Chapters in Administrative History,* vols. ii and iii.
Conway Davies, *The Baronial Movement under Edward II.*
Unwin (ed.), *Finance and Commerce under Edward III.*
Oman, *The Art of War in the Middle Ages.*
Mollat, *Les Papes d'Avignon.*

CHAPTER IX. ENGLAND AND SCOTLAND, TO 1369

Hume Brown, *History of Scotland*, vol. i.
Rait, *The Parliament of Scotland*.
Andrew Lang, *History of Scotland*.
Maxwell, *Robert the Bruce*.

CHAPTER X. GROWTH OF THE CONSTITUTION, 1215–1377

White and Tout, *Chapters* (as above).
Stubbs, *Constitutional History*, vol. ii.
Petit-Dutaillis *A Supplement to Stubbs' Constitutional History*.
Baldwin, *The King's Council*.
Pollard, *Evolution of Parliament*.
Clarke, *Fourteenth Century Studies*.
McIlwain, *The High Court of Parliament and its Supremacy*.
Lodge and Thornton, *Constitutional Documents, 1307–1485*.

BOOK III, 1360–1509

CHAPTER I. THE END OF THE MIDDLE AGES

Armitage Smith, *John of Gaunt*.
Lipson, *Economic History*, vol. i.
Davenport, *Economic Development of a Norfolk Manor*.
Bennett, *Life on the English Manor, 1150–1400*.
Unwin, *Gilds and Companies of London*.
Pirenne, *Histoire de Belgique*, vol. i.
Workman, *John Wyclif*.
Barraclough, *Papal Provisions*.
Ker, *English Literature, Medieval* (Home University Library).

CHAPTER II. REVOLUTION, 1376–1399

Tout, *Chapters*, vols. iii and iv.
Clarke (as above).
Perroy, *L'Angleterre et le Grand Schisme*.
Reville, *Le Soulèvement des travailleurs d'Angleterre en 1381*.
Owst, *Literature and Pulpit in Medieval England*.
Cambridge Medieval History, vol. vii (chapters by Manning and Power).
Steel, *Richard II*.
Gras, *Economic and Social History of an English Village*.

CHAPTER III. THE FIFTEENTH CENTURY

Power and Postan (eds.), *English Trade in the Fifteenth Century*.
Mrs. J. R. Green, *Town Life in the Fifteenth Century*.
Darby (ed.), *Historical Geography of England before 1800*.
Tawney, *The Agrarian Problem of the Sixteenth Century*.
Maynard Smith, *Pre-Reformation England*.
Robinson (ed.), *Chaucer's Works*.

Chambers, R. W., *Thomas More.*
Chambers, E. K., *The Medieval Stage.*
Graham, *English Ecclesiastical Studies.*

CHAPTER IV. LANCASTRIAN ENGLAND, 1399-1413

Stubbs, *Constitutional History*, vol. iii.
Fortescue (ed. Plummer), *Governance of England.*
Cambridge Medieval History, vol. viii (chapter by McFarlane).
Lloyd, *Owen Glendower.*

CHAPTER V. HENRY V, 1413-1422

Jacob, *Henry V.*
Wylie and Waugh, *Reign of Henry V.*
Pirenne, *Histoire de Belgique*, vol. ii.
Newhall, *The English Conquest of Normandy.*
Deanesley, *The Lollard Bible.*

CHAPTER VI. NATIONAL COLLAPSE, 1422-1485

Kingsford, *Promise and Prejudice in the Fifteenth Century.*
Vickers, *Humphrey Duke of Gloucester.*
Gairdner (ed.), *The Paston Letters.*
Schofield, *Life and Reign of Edward IV.*
Ramsay, *Lancaster and York.*

CHAPTER VII. HENRY VII

Pickthorn, *Early Tudor Government.*
Seebohm, *The Oxford Reformers.*
Allen, *The Age of Erasmus.*
Seton Watson (ed.), *Essays Presented to A. F. Pollard.*
Bridge, *History of France*, vols. i and ii.
Skeel, *The Council in the Marches of Wales.*

CHAPTER VIII. THE CONSTITUTION, 1400-1529

Stubbs, *Constitutional History*, vol. iii.
Chrimes, *Constitutional Ideas in the Fifteenth Century.*
Taswell Langmead (ed. Plucknett), *Constitutional History.*
Maitland, *English Law and the Renaissance.*
Gray, *The Influence of the Commons on Early Legislation.*
Leadam, *Select Pleas in the Court of Star Chamber.*

BOOK IV, 1509-1660

CHAPTER I. HENRY VIII, 1509-1529

Pollard, *Wolsey* and *Henry VIII.*
Brewer, *Reign of Henry VIII.*

Froude, *History of England*, vol. i.
More, *Utopia*.
Lindsay, *History of the Reformation*.

CHAPTER II. HENRY VIII, 1529–1547

Merriman, *Thomas Cromwell*.
Baskerville, *The English Monasteries*.
Dixon, *History of the Church of England*, vols. i and ii.
Reid, *The King's Council in the North*.
Tanner, *Tudor Constitutional Documents*.
Dodds, *The Pilgrimage of Grace*.

CHAPTER III. ANARCHY, 1547–1558

Gairdner, *The English Church in the Sixteenth Century*.
Muller, *Steven Gardiner*.
Pollard, *Cranmer*, and *Political History of England*, 1547–1603
Armstrong, *The Emperor Charles V*.
Rowse, *Tudor Cornwall*.

CHAPTER IV. THE REIGN OF ELIZABETH, 1558–1573

Neale, *Queen Elizabeth*.
Frere, *The Church under Elizabeth and James I*
Williamson, *The Age of Drake*.
Scott Pearson, *Thomas Cartwright*.

CHAPTER V. THE REIGN OF ELIZABETH, 1573–1603

Read, *Life of Walsingham*.
Corbett, *Drake and the Tudor Navy*.
Mariéjol, *Catharine de Medici*.
Cheyney, *History of England from the Defeat of the Armada*.
Usher, *Reconstruction of the English Church*.

CHAPTER VI. SCOTLAND, 1370–1603

Balfour Melville, *James I, King of Scots*.
Hume Brown, *History of Scotland*, vols. i. and ii.
Cambridge Modern History, vol. ii.
Tough, *Last Years of a Frontier*.
Henderson, *Mary Queen of Scots*.

CHAPTER VII. IRELAND : THE PROBLEM SET, 1460–1633

Conway, *Relations of Henry VII with Ireland and Scotland*.
Maxwell, *Irish History from Contemporary Sources, 1509–1610*.
Ronan, *The Reformation in Ireland under Elizabeth*.
Bagwell, *Ireland under the Tudors*.
Gardiner, *History of England, 1603–1642* (many chapters).
Burghclere, *Strafford*.

CHAPTER VIII. THE ELEVENTH HOUR, 1603–1629

Gardiner (as above).
Pearsall Smith, *Sir Henry Wotton.*
Notestein, *The Winning of the Initiative of the House of Commons.*
Usher, *The Court of High Commission.*
Holdsworth, *History of English Law*, vols. iv and v.
Scott, *History of Joint Stock Companies*, vol. i.
Everett Green, *Elizabeth Queen of Bohemia.*
Figgis, *The Divine Right of Kings.*

CHAPTER IX. THE DECISION, 1629–1642

Trevelyan, *England under the Stuarts.*
Trevor Roper, *Laud.*
Albion, *Charles I and the Court of Rome.*
Clarendon (ed. Macray), *History of the Great Rebellion*, vols. i and ii.
Lucy Hutchinson, *Life of Colonel Hutchinson.*
Izaak Walton, *Lives of Donne, Herbert, etc.*
Firth, *The House of Lords in the Civil War.*
Davies, *The Early Stuarts* (Oxford History).

CHAPTER X. THE CIVIL WAR, 1642–1646

Gardiner, *The Great Civil War.*
Firth, *Cromwell's Army.*
Buchan, *Montrose.*
Memoirs of the Verney Family.
Coate, *Cornwall in the Great Civil War.*
Bayley, *Civil War in Dorset.*
Broxap, *The Great Civil War in Lancashire.*
Lewis, *Lives from the Clarendon Gallery.*

CHAPTER XI. THE FALL OF THE MONARCHY, 1646–1649

Gardiner, *Commonwealth and Protectorate.*
Firth, *Cromwell.*
Woodhouse, *Puritanism and Liberty.*
Braithwaite, *The Beginnings of Quakerism.*
Ludlow (ed. Firth), *Memoirs.*

CHAPTER XII. DESTRUCTION AND RESTORATION, 1649–1660

Abbott, *Writings and Speeches of Oliver Cromwell.*
Carlyle (ed. Lomas), *Letters and Speeches of Oliver Cromwell.*
Firth, *Last Two Years of the Protectorate.*
Masson, *Life of Milton.*
Prestage, *Diplomatic Relations of Portugal with France, England, and Holland, 1640–68.*
Ranke, *History of England*, vol. iii.

CHAPTER XIII.   ENGLISH CIVILIZATION, 1540–1660

Lipson, *Economic History*, vols. ii and iii.
Unwin, *Industrial Organization in the 16th and 17th Centuries.*
Leonard, *Early History of Poor Relief.*
Cunningham, *History of English Industry and Commerce.*
Walter Raleigh (ed.), *Shakespeare's England.*
Chambers, *The Elizabethan Stage.*
Sidney Lee, *Life of Shakespeare.*
Willey, *The Seventeenth Century Background.*
Bush, *English Literature in the Earlier Seventeenth Century.*
Aubrey (ed. A. Clark), *Brief Lives.*

BOOK V, 1660–176c

CHAPTER I.   THE REIGN OF CHARLES II, 1660–1667

Ogg, *England in the Reign of Charles II.*
Bate, *The Declaration of Indulgence of 1672.*
Burnet (ed. Airy), *History of My Own Time.*
Marvell (ed. Margoliouth), *Poems and Letters.*
Airy, *Charles II.*
Bryant, *Samuel Pepys.*

CHAPTER II.   THE REIGN OF CHARLES II, 1667–1685

Barbour, *Arlington.*
Ady, *Madame.*
Christie, *Shaftesbury.*
Foxcroft, *Halifax.*
Feiling, *History of the Tory Party, 1640–1714.*
Pollock, *The Popish Plot.*

CHAPTER III.   JAMES II, 1685–1688

Clark, *The Later Stuarts* (Oxford History).
Macaulay, *History of England.*
Plumtree, *Life of Thomas Ken.*
Roger North, *Lives of the Norths.*
Winston Churchill, *Marlborough*, vol. i.
Trevelyan, *The English Revolution, 1688–9.*

CHAPTER IV.   WILLIAM III, 1689–1702

Hallam, *Constitutional History of England.*
Clark, *The Dutch Alliance and the War against French Trade.*
Lecky, *History of England*, vol. i.
Ward, *The Electress Sophia and the Succession of Hanover.*
Firth, *A Commentary on Macaulay's History of England.*
Clarke and Foxcroft, *Bishop Burnet.*

Chapter V. The Reign of Anne, 1702–1714

Atkinson, *Marlborough.*
Geikie and Montgomery, *The Dutch Barrier.*
Trevelyan, *England under Queen Anne.*
Wickham Legg, *Matthew Prior.*
Dicey and Rait, *Thoughts on the Scottish Union.*
Mathieson, *Scotland and the Union.*
Legrelle, *La diplomatie Française et la succession d'Espagne.*
Swift, *Journal to Stella,* and *Correspondence,* vol. ii (ed. Ball).

Chapter VI. The British Empire, to 1714

Williamson, *Short History of British Expansion.*
Cambridge History of the British Empire, vol. i.
Beer, *The Old Colonial System.*
Egerton, *Short History of British Colonial Policy.*
Andrews, *The Colonial Period of American History.*
Smith, *The Oxford History of India.*
Callendar, *The Naval Side of British History.*

Chapter VII. Hanoverian and Whig Supremacy, 1714–1724

Leadam, *Political History of England, 1702–1760.*
Michael (ed. Namier), *Beginnings of the Hanoverian Dynasty,* and *The Quadruple Alliance.*
Basil Williams, *Stanhope.*
Armstrong, *Elizabeth Farnese.*
Bolingbroke, *Letter to Sir William Wyndham.*
Hume Brown, *History of Scotland,* vol. iii.

Chapter VIII. Walpole and the Pelhams, 1724–1754

Namier, *Structure of Politics at the Accession of George III.*
Basil Williams, *The Whig Supremacy* (Oxford History).
Sykes, *Church and State in England in the Eighteenth Century.*
Yorke, *Life of Hardwicke.*
Vaucher, *Fleury et la politique de Walpole.*
Hervey (ed. Sedgwick), *Memoirs of the Reign of George II.*
Horace Walpole (ed. Mrs. Paget Toynbee), *Letters.*

Chapter IX. Pitt and the Seven Years' War, 1754–1763

Namier, *England in the Age of the American Revolution.*
Carlyle, *Frederick the Great.*
Basil Williams, *Chatham.*
Parkman, *Montcalm and Wolfe.*
Dodwell, *Dupleix and Clive.*
Lodge, *Great Britain and Prussia.*

BOOK VI, 1760–1852

CHAPTER I. FRAMEWORK OF A NEW AGE

Mantoux, *The Industrial Revolution*.
Fay, *Great Britain from Adam Smith to the Present Day*.
Turberville (ed.), *Johnson's England*.
Marshall, *The English Poor in the Eighteenth Century*.
Sidney and Beatrice Webb, *The Old Poor Law*.
Ernle, *English Farming, Past and Present*.
Wadsworth and Mann, *Cotton Trade and Industrial Lancashire*.
George, *London Life in the Eighteenth Century*.
Leslie Stephen, *History of English Thought in the Eighteenth Century*.
Southey, *Life of Wesley*.
Winstanley, *Unreformed Cambridge*.
Gibbon, *Letters* and *Autobiography*.

CHAPTER II. THE GOVERNMENT OF GEORGE III, 1763–1782

Sedgwick (ed.), *Letters of George III to Lord Bute*.
Fitzmaurice, *Life of Shelburne*.
Feiling, *The Second Tory Party*.
Grafton (ed. Anson), *Autobiography*.
Winstanley, *Lord Chatham and the Whig Opposition*.
Channing, *History of the United States*, vol. iii.
Van Tyne, *The American Revolution*.
Burke, *The Present Discontents*, and the American speeches.

CHAPTER III. RECONSTRUCTION, 1782–1792

Veitch, *Genesis of Parliamentary Reform*.
Holland Rose, *Life of William Pitt*.
Davis, *The Age of Grey and Peel*.
Halévy, *History of England in 1815*.
Weizmann, *Warren Hastings and Philip Francis*.
Feiling, *Warren Hastings*.
Lascelles, *Charles James Fox*.

CHAPTER IV. REVOLUTION AND WAR, 1792–1801

Brown, *The French Revolution in English History*.
Meikle, *Scotland and the French Revolution*.
Lewis, *Administrations of Great Britain, 1783–1830*.
Holland, *Memoirs of the Whig Party*.
Beer, *History of British Socialism*, vol. i.
Magnus, *Edmund Burke*.
Fortescue, *British Statesmen of the Great War*.

CHAPTER V. THE STRUGGLE FOR NATIONAL EXISTENCE. 1801–1815

Guedalla, *The Duke*.
Oman, *The Peninsular War*.

Coupland, *Wilberforce.*
Webster, *Castlereagh.*
Mahan, *Nelson.*
Marshall, *Rise of George Canning.*
Roberts, *The Whig Party, 1807–1812.*

CHAPTER VI. THE CONSTITUTION IN 1815

Halévy, *History of England in 1815.*
Dicey, *The Law of the Constitution.*
Keir and Lawson, *Cases in Constitutional Law.*
Evans, *The Principal Secretary of State.*
Holdsworth, *History of English Law.*

CHAPTER VII. CONDITION OF THE PEOPLE IN 1815

Clapham, *Economic History of Great Britain,* vol. i.
Hammond, *The Town Labourer.*
Johnson, *Decline of the Small Landowner.*
Smart, *Economic Annals of the Nineteenth Century.*
Barnes, *History of the Corn Laws.*

CHAPTER VIII. THE LIVERPOOL GOVERNMENT, 1815–1825

Temperley, *Foreign Policy of Canning.*
Aspinall, *Lord Brougham and the Whig Party.*
Cockburn, *Memorials of His Time.*
The Creevey Papers.
Wallas, *Francis Place.*

CHAPTER IX. CANNING, EMANCIPATION, AND REFORM, 1825–1832

Halévy, *History of the English People,* vols. ii and iii.
Trevelyan, *Lord Grey of the Reform Bill.*
New, *Lord Durham.*
Cambridge History of British Foreign Policy.
Butler, *The Passing of the Great Reform Bill.*
Bagot, *Canning and His Friends.*

CHAPTER X. WHIGS AND CHARTISTS, 1832–1841

Spencer Walpole, *Lord John Russell.*
Kitson Clark, *Peel and the Conservative Party.*
Hovell, *The Chartist Movement.*
Cole, *Chartist Portraits.*
The Croker Papers.
Hammond, *Lord Shaftesbury.*
Disraeli, *Coningsby* and *Sybil.*

Chapter XI. The Queen and Sir Robert Peel, 1837–1850

Young, *Portrait of an Age.*
Trevelyan, *Life and Letters of Macaulay.*
Morley, *Richard Cobden.*
Trevelyan, *John Bright.*
Letters of Queen Victoria.
Parker, *Sir Robert Peel.*
Disraeli, *Lord George Bentinck.*

Chapter XII. Britain and Europe, 1827–1852

Woodward, *The Age of Reform* (Oxford History).
Seton Watson, *Britain in Europe, 1789–1914.*
Algernon Cecil, *British Foreign Secretaries.*
Bell, *Life of Palmerston.*
Jones Parry, *The Spanish Marriages.*
Costin, *Great Britain and China.*
Malmesbury, *Memoirs of an ex-Minister.*

Chapter XIII. The New Empire, 1815–1852

Cambridge History of the British Empire, vol. ii.
Knaplund, *The British Empire, 1815–1939.*
Lucas, *Lord Durham's Report.*
Wrong, *Charles Buller and Responsible Government.*
Bell and Morrell, *Select Documents on British Colonial Policy.*
Morrell, *British Colonial Policy in the Age of Peel and Russell.*
Morison, *The Eighth Earl of Elgin.*
Walker, *History of South Africa.*
Scott, *Short History of Australia.*

Chapter XIV. Ireland, 1815–1848

Lecky, *Leaders of Public Opinion in Ireland.*
Gwynn, *History of Ireland.*
Gooch, *Later Correspondence of Lord John Russell.*
O'Brien, *Economic History of Ireland from the Union to the Famine.*
Memoirs of Sir Robert Peel.
McLennan, *Memoir of Thomas Drummond.*

Chapter XV. Thought and Religion, 1830–1860

Leslie Stephen, *The English Utilitarians.*
Mill, *Autobiography.*
Coleridge, *Biographia Literaria.*
Brillioth, *The Anglican Revival.*
Church, *The Oxford Movement.*
Wilfred Ward, *W. G. Ward and the Catholic Revival.*
Stanley, *Life of Arnold.*
Dicey, *Law and Public Opinion.*
Life and Letters of Charles Darwin.

BOOK VII, 1852–1918

CHAPTER I. CLIMAX OF THE VICTORIAN AGE

Clapham, *Economic History*, vol. ii.
John (Viscount) Morley, *Reminiscences*, vol. i.
Ponsonby, *Henry Ponsonby*.
Letters of Queen Victoria.
Walter Bagehot, *Biographical Studies*.
Hallam Tennyson, *Tennyson : a Memoir*.
Elton, *A Survey of English Literature, 1830–80*

CHAPTER II. COALITION, CRIMEA, AND THE TRIUMPH OF PALMERSTON

Temperley, *England and the Near East: the Crimea*.
Charles Greville, *Diary*.
Villiers, *A Vanished Victorian*.
Simpson, *Louis Napoleon and the Recovery of France*.
Lane Poole, *Life of Stratford Canning*.

CHAPTER III. INDIA : FROM WELLESLEY TO THE MUTINY

Cambridge History of India, vol. v.
Thompson and Garratt, *Rise and Fulfilment of British Rule in India*.
Alfred Lyall, *British Dominion in India*.
Ramsay Muir, *Making of British India*.
Morison, *Henry Lawrence*.
Curzon, *British Government in India*.
Roberts, *History of British India*.
Forrest, *The Indian Mutiny*.

CHAPTER IV. LIBERALISM, AT HOME AND ABROAD, 1859–1874

Morley, *Gladstone*.
Spencer Walpole, *History of Twenty-Five Years, 1856–1880*.
Monypenny and Buckle, *Life of Disraeli*.
Garvin, *Joseph Chamberlain*, vol. i.
Seymour, *Electoral Reform in England and Wales*.
Fitzmaurice, *Lord Granville*.
Bolton King, *History of United Italy*.

CHAPTER V. DISRAELI, 1874–1880

Monypenny and Buckle (as above).
Cecil, *Life of Lord Salisbury*, vol. i.
Newton, *Lord Lyons*.
Gathorne Hardy, *Life of Lord Cranbrook*.
Hardinge, *The Fourth Earl of Carnarvon*.
Seton Watson, *Disraeli, Gladstone, and the Eastern Question*.

CHAPTER VI. THE EMPIRE, 1850–1880

Knaplund and the Cambridge Histories of the several Dominions.
Trotter, *Canadian Federation*.
Grant (ed.), *Makers of Canada* series.
Chester Martin, *Empire and Commonwealth*.
De Kiewiet, *British Colonial Policy and the South African Republics 1848–1872*.
Macmillan, *Bantu, Boer,* and *Briton*.
Shann, *An Economic History of Australia*.
Pember Reeves, *The Long White Cloud*.
Adams, *Great Britain and the American Civil War*.
Keith, *Responsible Government in the Dominions*.
Johnston, *The Opening up of Africa*.
Coupland, *Exploitation of East Africa, 1856–1890*, and *Livingstone's Last Journey*.

CHAPTER VII. PERIL AND DECLINE, 1881–1914

Ensor, *Modern England, 1870–1914* (Oxford History).
Clapham, *Economic History*, vol. iii.
Bryce, *Studies in Contemporary Biography*.
Lord Acton's Letters to Mary Gladstone.
Charles Gore (ed.), *Lux Mundi*.
Wells, *Autobiography*.
Graham Wallas, *The Great Society*.

CHAPTER VIII. GLADSTONE AND THE IRISH QUESTION, 1880–1886

Hammond, *Gladstone and the Irish Nation*.
Garvin, *Chamberlain*, vol. ii.
Winston Churchill, *Lord Randolph Churchill*.
Barry O'Brien, *Life of C. S. Parnell*.

CHAPTER IX. SOUTH AFRICA, EGYPT, AND THE SUDAN

Walker, *South Africa*.
Cromer, *Modern Egypt*.
Allen, *Gordon and the Sudan*.
Milner, *England in Egypt*.
Basil Williams, *Cecil Rhodes*.
Holland, *The Eighth Duke of Devonshire*.
Theal, *History of South Africa*.

CHAPTER X. THE SALISBURY GOVERNMENT AND FOREIGN AFFAIRS, 1886–1892

Cecil's biography.
Gooch, *History of Modern Europe, 1878–1919*.
Grant and Temperley, *Europe in the Nineteenth and Twentieth Centuries*.
Spender, *Fifty Years of Europe*.
Brandenburg, *From Bismarck to the World War*.

Chapter XI. Home Politics and Parties, 1892–1905

Garvin, *Chamberlain*, vol. iii.
Haldane, *Autobiography*.
Spender and Asquith, *Life of Asquith*.
Gardiner, *Sir William Harcourt*.
Halévy, *Histoire du peuple Anglais; Épilogue*.
Hutchinson, *The Private Diaries of Sir Algernon West*.

Chapter XII. South Africa, 1884–1914

Walker, *De Villiers*.
Headlam, *The Milner Papers*.
Michell, *Cecil Rhodes*.
Cambridge History of the British Empire, vol. viii.

Chapter XIII. The Last of Liberalism, 1905–1914

Morley, *Reminiscences*, vol. ii.
Crewe, *Lord Rosebery*.
Lloyd George, *War Memoirs*, vol. i.
Austen Chamberlain, *Politics from Inside*.
Sidney and Beatrice Webb, *History of Trades Unionism*.
Cole, *Short History of the Labour Movement*.
Spender, *Great Britain, Empire and Commonwealth*.
Bell, *Randall Davidson*.

Chapter XIV. Foreign Affairs and the Steps towards War, 1895–1914

Newton, *Lord Lansdowne*.
Trevelyan, *Grey of Fallodon*.
Grey, *Twenty-Five Years*.
Fay, *The Origins of the World War*.
Gooch, *Before the War*.
Hendrick, *Life and Letters of Walter H. Page*.
Nicolson, *Lord Carnock*.

Chapter XV. The First World War

Cruttwell, *History of the Great War*.
Liddell Hart, *History of the Great War*.
Churchill, *The World Crisis*.
Duff Cooper, *Haig*.
Spears, *Liaison*.
Wavell, *Allenby*.
Lawrence, *Seven Pillars of Wisdom*.
Robertson, *Soldiers and Statesmen, 1914–18*.
Jellicoe, *The Grand Fleet, 1914–1916*.
Ian Hamilton, *A Gallipoli Diary*.

INDEX

NOTE.—Heavy type indicates years of reign or pontificate.

THE END